9669

Short Story Criticism

Guide to Gale Literary Criticism Series

For criticism on	Consult these Gale series
Authors now living or who died after December 31, 1959	*CONTEMPORARY LITERARY CRITICISM (CLC)*
Authors who died between 1900 and 1959	*TWENTIETH-CENTURY LITERARY CRITICISM (TCLC)*
Authors who died between 1800 and 1899	*NINETEENTH-CENTURY LITERATURE CRITICISM (NCLC)*
Authors who died between 1400 and 1799	*LITERATURE CRITICISM FROM 1400 TO 1800 (LC)* *SHAKESPEAREAN CRITICISM (SC)*
Authors who died before 1400	*CLASSICAL AND MEDIEVAL LITERATURE CRITICISM (CMLC)*
Black writers of the past two hundred years	*BLACK LITERATURE CRITICISM (BLC)*
Authors of books for children and young adults	*CHILDREN'S LITERATURE REVIEW (CLR)*
Dramatists	*DRAMA CRITICISM (DC)*
Hispanic writers of the late nineteenth and twentieth centuries	*HISPANIC LITERATURE CRITICISM (HLC)*
Poets	*POETRY CRITICISM (PC)*
Short story writers	*SHORT STORY CRITICISM (SSC)*
Major authors from the Renaissance to the present	*WORLD LITERATURE CRITICISM, 1500 TO THE PRESENT (WLC)*

ISSN 0740-2880

Volume 16

Short Story Criticism

Excerpts from Criticism of the Works of Short Fiction Writers

David Segal, Editor

Jeffery Chapman
Nancy Dziedzic
Jennifer Gariepy
Margaret Haerens
Marie Lazzari
Thomas Ligotti
Sean René Pollock
Associate Editors

Gale Research Inc.

An International Thomson Publishing Company

I⟨T⟩P

NEW YORK • LONDON • BONN • BOSTON • DETROIT • MADRID
MELBOURNE • MEXICO CITY • PARIS • SINGAPORE • TOKYO
TORONTO • WASHINGTON • ALBANY NY • BELMONT CA • CINCINNATI OH

STAFF

David Segal, *Editor*

Jeffery Chapman, Nancy Dziedzic, Jennifer Gariepy, Margaret Haerens, Marie Lazzari,
Thomas Ligotti, Sean René Pollock, *Associate Editors*

Pamela Willwerth Aue, Martha Bommarito, Ian A. Goodhall, *Assistant Editors*

Marlene H. Lasky, *Permissions Manager*
Margaret A. Chamberlain, Linda M. Pugliese, *Permissions Specialists*

Diane Cooper, Maria L. Franklin, Pamela A. Hayes, Arlene Johnson, Josephine M. Keene, Michele Lonoconus,
Maureen Puhl, Keith Reed, Shalice Shah, Kimberly F. Smilay, Barbara A. Wallace, *Permissions Associates*

Jennifer A. Arnold, Susan Brohman, Brandy C. Merritt, *Permissions Assistants*

Victoria B. Cariappa, *Research Manager*
Mary Beth McElmeel, Tamara C. Nott, Tracie A. Richardson, Norma Sawaya, *Research Associates*
Maria E. Bryson, Michele P. Pica, *Research Assistants*

Mary Beth Trimper, *Production Director*
Deborah Milliken, *Production Assistant*

Cynthia Baldwin, *Product Design Manager*
Barbara J. Yarrow, *Graphic Services Supervisor*
Sherrell Hobbs, *Macintosh Artist*
Willie F. Mathis, *Camera Operator*

Library of Congress Catalog Card Number 88-641014
ISBN 0-8103-8931-2
ISSN 0895-9439

Printed in the United States of America
Published simultaneously in the United Kingdom
by Gale Research International Limited
(An affiliated company of Gale Research Inc.)
10 9 8 7 6 5 4 3 2 1

I(T)P™   Gale Research Inc., an International Thomson Publishing Company.
ITP logo is a trademark under license.

Contents

Preface   vii

Acknowledgments   xi

Preface

A Comprehensive Information Source
on World Short Fiction

*S*hort Story Criticism (SSC) presents significant passages from criticism of the world's greatest short story writers and provides supplementary biographical and bibliographical materials to guide the interested reader to a greater understanding of the authors of short fiction. This series was developed in response to suggestions from librarians serving high school, college, and public library patrons, who had noted a considerable number of requests for critical material on short story writers. Although major short story writers are covered in such Gale series as *Contemporary Literary Criticism (CLC)*, *Twentieth-Century Literary Criticism (TCLC)*, *Nineteenth-Century Literature Criticism (NCLC)*, and *Literature Criticism from 1400 to 1800 (LC)*, librarians perceived the need for a series devoted solely to writers of the short story genre.

Coverage

SSC is designed to serve as an introduction to major short story writers of all eras and nationalities. Since these authors have inspired a great deal of relevant critical material, *SSC* is necessarily selective, and the editors have chosen the most important published criticism to aid readers and students in their research.

Approximately eight to ten authors are included in each volume, and each entry presents a historical survey of the critical response to that author's work. The length of an entry is intended to reflect the amount of critical attention the author has received from critics writing in English and from foreign critics in translation. Every attempt has been made to identify and include excerpts from the most significant essays on each author's work. In order to provide these important critical pieces, the editors sometimes reprint essays that have appeared elsewhere in Gale's Literary Criticism Series. Such duplication, however, never exceeds twenty percent of an *SSC* volume.

Organization

An *SSC* author entry consists of the following elements:

■   The **Author Heading** cites the name under which the author most commonly wrote, followed by birth and death dates. If the author wrote consistently under a pseudonym, the pseudonym will be listed in the author heading and the author's actual name given in parentheses on the first line of the biographical and critical introduction.

■   The **Biographical and Critical Introduction** contains background information designed to introduce a reader to the author and the critical debates surrounding his or her work.

■   A **Portrait of the Author** is included when available. Many entries also contain illustrations of materials pertinent to an author's career, including holographs of manuscript pages, title pages, dust jackets, letters, or representations of important people, places, and events in the author's life.

■   The list of **Principal Works** is chronological by date of first publication and lists the most important works by the author. The first section comprises short story collections, novellas, and novella collections. The second section gives information on other major works by the author. For foreign authors, the editors have provided original foreign-language publication information and have selected what are considered the best and most complete English-language editions of their works.

- **Criticism** is arranged chronologically in each author entry to provide a useful perspective on changes in critical evaluation over the years. All short story, novella, and collection titles by the author featured in the entry are printed in boldface type to enable a reader to ascertain without difficulty the works discussed. Also for purposes of easier identification, the critic's name and the publication date of the essay are given at the beginning of each piece of criticism. Unsigned criticism is preceded by the title of the journal in which it appeared.

- Critical essays are prefaced with **Explanatory Notes** as an additional aid to students and readers using *SSC*. The explanatory notes provide several types of useful information, including: the reputation of a critic, the importance of a work of criticism, and the specific type of criticism (biographical, psychoanalytic, structuralist, etc.).

- A complete **Bibliographical Citation,** designed to help the interested reader locate the original essay or book, follows each piece of criticism.

- The **Further Reading List** appearing at the end of each author entry suggests additional materials on the author. In some cases it includes essays for which the editors could not obtain reprint rights. Boxed material following the further reading list provides references to other biographical and critical sources on the author in series published by Gale.

Beginning with volume six, *SSC* contains two additional features designed to enhance the reader's understanding of short fiction writers and their works:

- Each *SSC* entry now includes, when available, **Comments by the Author** that illuminate his or her own works or the short story genre in general. These statements are set within boxes or bold rules to distinguish them from the criticism.

- A **Select Bibliography of General Sources on Short Fiction** is included as an appendix. This listing of materials for further research provides readers with a selection of the best available general studies of the short story genre.

Other Features

A **Cumulative Author Index** lists all the authors who have appeared in *SSC, CLC, TCLC, NCLC, LC,* and *Classical and Medieval Literature Criticism (CMLC),* as well as cross-references to other Gale series. Users will welcome this cumulated index as a useful tool for locating an author within the Literary Criticism Series.

A **Cumulative Nationality Index** lists all authors featured in *SSC* by nationality, followed by the number of the *SSC* volume in which their entry appears.

A **Cumulative Title Index** lists in alphabetical order all short story, novella, and collection titles contained in the *SSC* series. Titles of short story collections, separately published novellas, and novella collections are printed in italics, while titles of individual short stories are printed in roman type with quotation marks.

Each title is followed by the author's name and corresponding volume and page numbers where commentary on the work is located. English-language translations of original foreign-language titles are cross-referenced to the foreign titles so that all references to discussion of a work are combined in one listing.

Citing *Short Story Criticism*

When writing papers, students who quote directly from any volume in the Literary Criticism Series may use the following general forms to footnote reprinted criticism. The first example pertains to material drawn from periodicals, the second to material reprinted from books:

[1]Henry James, Jr., "Honoré de Balzac," *The Galaxy 20* (December 1875), 814-36; excerpted and reprinted in *Short Story Criticism,* Vol. 5, ed. Thomas Votteler (Detroit: Gale Research, 1990), pp. 8-11.

[2]F. R. Leavis, *D. H. Lawrence: Novelist* (Alfred A. Knopf, 1956); excerpted and reprinted in *Short Story Criticism,* Vol. 4, ed. Thomas Votteler (Detroit: Gale Research, 1990), pp. 202-06.

Comments

Readers who wish to suggest authors to appear in future volumes, or who have other suggestions, are invited to contact the editors by writing to Gale Research Inc., Literary Criticism Division, 835 Penobscot Building, Detroit, MI 48226-4094.

Acknowledgments

The editors wish to thank the copyright holders of the excerpted criticism included in this volume, the permissions managers of many book and magazine publishing companies for assisting us in securing reprint rights, and Anthony Bogucki for assistance with copyright research. We are also grateful to the staffs of the Detroit Public Library, the Library of Congress, the University of Detroit Mercy Library, Wayne State University Purdy/Kresge Library Complex, and the University of Michigan Libraries for making their resources available to us. Following is a list of the copyright holders who have granted us permission to reprint material in this volume of *SSC*. Every effort has been made to trace copyright, but if omissions have been made, please let us know.

COPYRIGHTED EXCERPTS IN *SSC,* VOLUME 16, WERE REPRINTED FROM THE FOLLOWING BOOKS:

permission of the author.—Schulz, Max F. From *Radical Sophistication: Studies in Contemporary Jewish-American Novelists.* Ohio University Press, 1969. Copyright © 1969 by Max F. Schulz. All rights reserved. Reprinted by permission of the author.—Sullivan, Jack. From *Elegant Nightmares: The English Ghost Story from Le Fanu to Blackwood.* Ohio University Press, 1978. Copyright © 1978 by Jack Sullivan. All rights reserved. Reprinted by permission of the publisher.—Warren, Austin. From *Connections.* The University of Michigan Press, 1970. Copyright © by The University of Michigan 1970. All rights reserved. Reprinted by permission of the publisher.—Zaccaria, Paola. From "'Fizzles' by Samuel Beckett: The Failure of the Dream of a Never-ending Verticality," in *Rethinking Beckett: A Collection of Critical Essays.* Edited by Lance St. John Butler and Robin J. Davis. Macmillan Press, Ltd., 1990. © The Macmillan Press Ltd. 1990. All rights reserved. Reprinted by permission of Macmillan, London and Basingstoke.

PHOTOGRAPHS AND ILLUSTRATIONS APPEARING IN *SSC*, VOLUME 16, WERE RECEIVED FROM THE FOLLOWING SOUCES:

Ardis Publishers: **p. 1;** Drawing by K. Rotov: **p. 10;** © Jerry Bauer: **p. 62;** © 1988 Pablo Campos: **p. 139;** Jacket of *Descent of Man*, by T. Coraghessan Boyle. Little, Brown and Company, 1979. Reprinted by permission of Little, Brown and Company: **p. 149;** © Thomas Victor 1986: **p. 159;** Jacket of *Da Vinci's Bicycle*, by Guy Davenport. The Johns Hopkins University Press, Baltimore/London, 1979. Reprinted by permission of The Johns Hopkins University Press: **p. 180;** © Meredith Waddell, courtesy of Stephen Dixon: **p. 202;** Reproduced by permission of Mansell Collection, London: **p. 220;** Reproduced by permission of Peter Haining: **pp. 229, 242;** Photograph by Robert Cerrito: **p. 260;** Illustration by Harry O. Morris, from *Songs of a Dead Dreamer*, Silver Scarab Press, 1985. Reprinted by permission of Harry O. Morris: **p. 278;** Photograph © 1981 by Thomas Victor: **p. 300;** Jacket of *Going Places*, by Leonard Michaels. Weidenfeld & Nicolson, 1970. Reprinted by permission of George Weidenfeld & Nicolson Ltd.: **p. 307;** Jacket of *Shuffle*, by Leonard Michaels. Farrar, Straus & Giroux, 1990. Reprinted by permission of Farrar, Straus & Giroux, Inc.: **p. 318;** © Thomas Victor: **p. 324;** Reproduced by permission of Jay Martin: **pp. 341, 373, 397;** Jacket of *A Cool Million: The Dismantling of Lemuel Pitkins*, by Nathanael West. Covici Friede, 1934. Copyright 1934 by Nathanael West. Reprinted by permission of Crown Publishers, Inc., a Division of Random House, Inc. Jacket of *The Day of the Locust*, by Nathanael West. Random House, 1939. Reprinted by permission of Random House, Inc.: **p. 360.**

Isaac Babel

1894-1941

(Also transliterated as Isaak, Izaak, and as Babel'; surname also cited as Emanuilovich; also wrote under pseudonym Kiril Liutov) Russian short story writer, playwright, scriptwriter, essayist, journalist, and autobiographer.

INTRODUCTION

Babel is considered Russia's most gifted short story writer of the post-revolutionary era. His concise, anecdotal fiction utilizes contrast and paradox to emphasize oppositions between violence and passivity, romanticism and primitivism, hero and antihero, and most importantly, between Jewish ethos in a non-Jewish environment. The war sketches of *Konarmiia* (*Red Cavalry*) and the picaresque stories of *Odesskie rasskazy* (*The Odessa Tales*) have consistently garnered praise for their emotional depth and poetic language and have earned him a prominent reputation as both a stylist and a sophisticated observer of human nature.

Biographical Information

Babel was born in the Jewish ghetto of Odessa into a middle-class merchant family. At an early age he undertook studies at a local business school as well as traditional Judaic studies in Hebrew, the Bible, and the Talmud. In his formative years Babel witnessed the pogroms of 1905, in which Cossack soldiers, acting under government authority, agitated riots that led to brutal assaults on Jewish citizens and the devastation of Jewish communities. These ruthless demonstrations fostered in Babel a concurrent horror of and fascination with Cossack existence that is reflected in his earliest published stories, "I soriya mori golubyatnei" ("The Story of My Dovecot") and "Pervaya lyubov" ("First Love"). In 1915, after graduating from Kiev Institute of Finance and Business Studies, Babel moved to Petrograd (formerly St. Petersburg, later Leningrad), hoping to publish the few stories he had written while in school. While in Petrograd he met Russian proletarian writer Maxim Gorky, resulting in the publication of two of his stories in Gorky's magazine *Letopis'*. Recognizing Babel's raw talent, Gorky advised him to gather more first-hand experiences to enhance his subsequent fiction. Babel agreed and enlisted in the Russian army, serving during World War I at the Romanian front until he contracted malaria. After military service, he claimed to have worked for a short time in Petrograd with the Cheka, a political police force designated to identify and eliminate counterrevolutionary or anticommunist groups that is often cited as a forerunner to the former Soviet Union's KGB. During this period Babel continued to write and publish, but his major literary development came in 1919 as a war correspondent with the Red Army. Under the

command of Semyon Budyonny, Babel rode with the Cossack cavalry against the Poles and White Czarist forces, and these experiences ironically became the inspiration for his most important stories. Although Babel received considerable literary recognition during the 1920s for the war stories of *Red Cavalry* and later, *The Odessa Tales,* his works were eventually censored by the Soviet regime for their erotic detail and lack of commitment to the communist cause. Thereafter Babel, who refused to write political propaganda, voluntarily restricted publication of his work. In 1934 he remarked on his self-censorship when he declared himself a "master of a new literary genre, the genre of silence." He was arrested in 1939 after subtly criticizing the Stalinist regime in a screenplay he was writing. He is believed to have died in prison in 1941.

Major Works of Short Fiction

The Cossack army, which had been the source of the destruction Babel witnessed in the ghettoes of Odessa during his youth, ironically became the source of inspiration in the impressionistic sketches recorded in his diary during his attachment to the Red Army. These pieces were later developed into the stories in *Red Cavalry,* now considered by most critics to be Babel's masterpiece. Diverse in subject matter, these sketches are linked by the first-person narrator Kiril Liutov, by the pathos of the Revolution, and by Babel's overriding concern with violence. Most critics observe that the major tension throughout *Red Cavalry* is the narrator's subliminal Jewish morality contrasted with the violent Cossack creed, and his desire to be no longer alienated from the Cossacks as a "four-eyed" intellectual. Thus, in the story "Moi pervy gus" ("My First Goose"), Liutov is morally unable to take a human life, and so wins the esteem of the Cossack regiment by ruthlessly murdering an old woman's goose. In the stories in his second major work, *The Odessa Tales,* Babel returns to the ghetto of his youth to create a legendary world of Jewish gangsters and racketeers. Benya Krik, the central character in several of these tales, is an elusive criminal who menaces wealthy Jews in the community. Throughout the *Odessa Tales,* Babel employed many of the themes and stylistic elements of *Red Cavalry,* but made greater use of his Jewish heritage and based the pieces on traditionally romantic and humorous situations. For these reasons they are generally considered to lack the depth of the more contemporary *Red Cavalry* stories.

Critical Reception

Babel's works were suppressed in the Soviet Union from the time of his arrest in 1939 to 1954, when the death of Joseph Stalin and Nikita Kruschev's rise to power initiated a brief, newfound freedom in literature and the arts. Babel and many other writers who had been incarcerated for slandering the "image" of Stalin were rehabilitated into Soviet culture. Thereafter Babel's stories and some of his previously unpublished works were collected and translated into English. Although Babel produced a relatively small body of work, his fiction has been widely praised by Western readers and critics, and today he is recognized as one of the masters of the Russian short story.

PRINCIPAL WORKS

SHORT FICTION

Konarmiia 1923
  [*Red Cavalry,* 1929]
Rasskazy 1925
Istoriia moei golubiatni 1926
Odesskie rasskazzy 1931
  [*The Odessa Tales* published in *The Collected Stories of Isaac Babel,* 1955]
Benya Krik, the Gangster, and Other Stories 1948
The Collected Stories of Isaac Babel 1955
Isaac Babel: The Lonely Years, 1925-1939 (short stories, letters, essays, and speeches) 1964
You Must Know Everything: Stories, 1915-1937 1969
The Forgotten Prose (short stories and diary excerpts) 1978

OTHER MAJOR WORKS

Zakat (drama) 1927
  [*Sunset* published in journal *Noonday,* 1960]
Mariia [first publication] (drama) 1935
I. Babel: Izbrannoe (short stories, dramas, autobiography, letters, and speeches) 1966

CRITICISM

S[emyon] Budyonny (letter date 1928)

SOURCE: A letter to Maxim Gorky, translated by Andrew R. MacAndrew, in *Isaac Babel: The Lonely Years, 1925-1939,* edited by Nathalie Babel, translated by Andrew R. MacAndrew and Max Hayward, Farrar, Straus and Giroux, 1964, pp. 384-87.

[*Budyonny was the commander of the First Cavalry Army to which Babel was assigned as a newspaper correspondent during the Russian Civil War in 1919, and around which he based his stories in* Red Cavalry. *When the stories were first published in newspapers in 1923-1924, Budyonny was outraged and in 1924 wrote a deprecating letter to the editors of* Krasnaya Nov' *expressing disapproval of Babel's work. In 1928, Maxim Gorky published an essay entitled "To Rural and War Correspondents—How I Learned to Write," in which he endorses Babel's portrayal of Budyonny and the Cossacks in* Red Cavalry. *The letter excerpted below, originally published in* Krasnaya Gazeta *on 26 October 1928, is Budyonny's public reply to Gorky's essay in which he explains his distaste for Babel's stories.*]

Dear Alexei Maximovich,

Our national dailies, *Pravda* and *Izvestia,* on September 30 carried an excerpt from your pamphlet "To Rural and War Correspondents—How I Learnt to Write."

In that piece, in discussing the main trends in literature—Romanticism and Realism—you state the following: . . .

> Comrade Budyonny has pounced upon Babel's *Red Cavalry* and I don't believe he should have, because Budyonny himself likes to embellish the outside not only of his men, but of his horses too. Babel, on the other hand, embellished his men on the inside, which, in my opinion, is better and more truthful than what Gogol did for his Zaporozhe Cossacks.
>
> Man is still a beast in many respects and, culturally, he is only an adolescent. It is always useful to embellish and to praise him.

Although it is very difficult for me to argue with you on literary matters, nevertheless, since *Red Cavalry* has come up as a subject of discussion once again, I must say that I cannot agree with you, Alexei Maximovich, despite all my respect for you, and I will try to explain why I criticized *Red Cavalry* and why I think I did so with good reason.

To start with, I believe [a writer] should know his source material and I dare say Babel was never and could never have been a genuine, active combat soldier in the First Cavalry. I know that he hung around with some unit deep in the rear, one of those units that, to our misfortune, were always a drag upon our fighting men. To be precise, Babel was in the backwaters of our First Cavalry.

What does Babel write about that gives him the right to use such a broad title as *Red Cavalry*?

Babel indulges in old women's gossip, digs into old women's garbage, and tells with horror about some Red Army man taking a loaf of bread and a chicken somewhere. He invents things that never happened, slings dirt at our best Communist commanders, lets his imagination run wild, simply lies . . .

The subject matter of Babel's stories is distorted by the impressions of an erotomanic author. His topics range from the ravings of a mad Jew to the looting of a Catholic church, to the thrashing the cavalrymen give to their own foot soldiers, to the portrayal of a syphilitic Red Army man and end with a display of the author's scientific curiosity, when he wishes to see what a Jewish woman raped by about ten Makhno men looks like. Just as he looks upon life as a sunny meadow in May with mares and stallions on it, so he also views the operations of the Red Cavalry and he sees them through the prism of eroticism.

I happen to know for certain that while Babel saw women's breasts and bare legs around the army's field kitchens, Pani Eliza's servants' quarters, in the middle of the forest, awake and asleep, in various combinations, there were a few other things the First Cavalry was doing that Babel did not see.

And that's quite natural and understandable. How could Babel possibly have seen from the deep rear the spots where the fate of the workers and peasants was being decided. He just couldn't have.

I believe that if Babel wanted to give a title which would correspond to his genre of writing, he should have called his book *In the Backwaters of the Red Cavalry*. That would have been more accurate.

Now I ask: did the author maintain even the most elementary truthfulness, the least respect for historical perspective that is a must for realistic art? He didn't and it is the more shocking in that he is dealing with men of whom some are still alive and with facts familiar to every Red Army man. Alas, Alexei Maximovich, there is not the least concern for truthfulness in it.

I believe, Alexei Maximovich, that you will agree with me that to describe the heroic class struggle, a struggle unprecedented in the history of mankind, it is necessary before anything else to grasp the nature of those classes, i.e., to at least be partly familiar with Marxist dialectics. And it so happens that Babel doesn't qualify by those standards. And that is why his attempt to depict the life and the traditions of the First Cavalry reads like a lampoon and is permeated by a petty-bourgeois outlook.

Of course, the heroic fighters of the First Cavalry are simple, plain, often almost illiterate, men, but "pieces of art" like this one, appearing at a moment when we are witnessing decisive battles between labor and capital, are not only unwelcome, but, I believe, outright harmful.

That is why I have criticized Babel's *Red Cavalry*. And I am not the only one to do so, for all the revolutionary masses with whom we are building socialism before your eyes are on my side.

How can one say, in view of all this, that Babel depicted his Red Cavalrymen better and more truthfully than Gogol did his Zaporozhe Cossacks? Is it possible that a sensitive person like you, Alexei Maximovich, has failed to feel that, even when he gave us his "beautiful untruth" about the Zaporozhe Cossacks, Gogol, being a great artist, avoided a sordid tone, while Babel, the alleged realist, has so embellished his fighting men from inside that, to this day, I keep receiving letters protesting against his crude, deliberate and arrogant slander of the First Red Cavalry.

For a long time, we have considered Babel's book as a lampoon, and I wouldn't have mentioned it again if it hadn't been mentioned by you, Alexei Maximovich, just when you were telling our new proletarian rural and war correspondents how to write.

I do not think that they should describe the inspiration of our days the way Babel did.

M[axim] Gorky   (letter date 1928)

SOURCE: A letter to Semyon Budyonny, translated by Andrew R. MacAndrew, in *Isaac Babel: The Lonely Years, 1925-1939*, edited by Nathalie Babel, translated by Andrew R. MacAndrew and Max Hayward, Farrar, Straus and Giroux, 1964, pp. 387-89.

[*A Russian novelist and critic, Gorky is recognized as one of the earliest and foremost exponents of socialist realism in literature. A Marxist theory, socialist realism demands of the arts an accurate, realistic representation of the evolution of the socialist state. Adhering to this aesthetic principle, Gorky's brutal yet romantic portraits of the working class broadly inspired the oppressed people of his native land. The letter from which the following excerpt is taken, originally published in* Pravda, *27 November 1928, is Gorky's reply to Semyon Budyonny's attack on Babel's works.*]

Dear Comrade Budyonny,

I cannot agree with your opinion of Babel's *Red Cavalry* and I firmly protest your evaluation of that talented writer.

You say that Babel "hung around with some unit deep in the rear." That cannot take anything away either from Babel or his book. In order to make soup the cook does not have to sit in the pot. The author of *War and Peace* never took part in the fighting against Napoleon, and Gogol was not a Zaporozhe Cossack.

You talk about Babel's erotomania. I have just re-read Babel's book and I found no symptoms of that disease in it, although, of course, I do not wish to deny the presence of certain erotic details in his stories. And this is as it should be. War always awakens an enraged eroticism.

And that is something you can learn from any war, from the behavior of the Germans in Belgium, as well as from the behavior of the Russians in East Prussia. I am inclined to consider it a natural although abnormal heightening of the instinct for the preservation of the species, an instinct common in people who are facing death.

I am a careful reader but I didn't find in Babel's book anything that suggests a "lampoon." On the contrary, his book awakened love and respect in me for the fighting men of the Red Cavalry by showing them to me as real heroes—they are fearless and they feel deeply the greatness of their cause. I cannot think of another such colorful, lively portrayal of individual fighting men, another such description of the psychology of the mass of the Red Army that would have helped me to understand the strength that enabled it to accomplish that extraordinary campaign; it has no parallel in Russian literature.

The attack of the French cavalry in Zola's *La Débâcle* shows only the mechanical movement of the mass of fighters and their mechanical clash.

Nor can I agree with you that our fighting men are "simple plain men." I wouldn't have thought they were even without Babel, who with such talent has supplemented my understanding of the heroism of an army which is the first in history to know what it is fighting for and what it is going to go on fighting for.

Allow me to tell you, Comrade Budyonny, that the abrupt and unjustified tone of your letter visits an undeserved insult on a young writer.

Our writers live in a moment of transition under the complex conditions of a country in which there are at least 20,000,000 individual owners and only 2,000,000 Marxists, of whom almost half mouth Marxist precepts about as intelligently as parrots repeat human words. It is impossible under these conditions to make very strict demands of ideological consistency upon these writers. Our life is contradictory and it is not at all as didactic as the past, which can easily teach us whom to love and whom to hate. A writer is a man who lives by the truth, using the color of imagination in order to generate in his reader a reaction of active love or active hatred. You must not forget that people have been brought up with religious views on ownership and that all the misfortunes, all the tragedies of life, all its nasty sides, are rooted in the proprietary instinct which from ancient times has been celebrated as the foundation of the state and the main source of private happiness.

It is impossible to re-educate in ten years people who have been brought up for thousands of years to worship gold and money. But we, in our own interest, must make allowances for and treat carefully every man who can help us in our struggle against the decaying but still strong props of the disgraceful past. Babel is a talented man. There are not so many of us that we can afford to spurn talented and useful men. You are not right, Comrade Budyonny! You are mistaken, and you have forgotten that scores of thousands of your fighting men heed your judgments. To be correct and useful a critic must be objective and considerate of our young literary forces.

Raymond Rosenthal (essay date 1947)

SOURCE: "The Fate of Isaak Babel: 'A Child of the Russian Emancipation'," in *Commentary*, Vol. 3, No. 2, February, 1947, pp. 126-31.

[*In the following excerpt, Rosenthal characterizes Babel as a writer whose works reflect both artistic detachment and an ingrained Jewish ethos.*]

In Babel's epic-like chronicle of the Civil War, *Red Cavalry*, nature, seen through the new eyes of a Jew, takes on the stylized perfection of a Byzantine mosaic: rivers, plains, and trees become the richly brocaded background for the crudest deeds of war. The coarse dialect of Budenny's Cossacks, newly encrusted with the jargon invented by the Revolution, and the liturgical eloquence of the Hasidic Jews, sound to him like the words of some ancient folk song. Certainly James Joyce's dictum that genius turns its very handicaps into "the portals of discovery" is wonderfully illustrated by Babel: he converted his very rootlessness into the organizing principle of a fresh perception of reality.

Red Cavalry is undoubtedly Babel's masterpiece. So far it is the only complete book of his to have been translated into English. The book purports to be a series of disconnected sketches, but actually it is a subtly counterpointed saga. When Sherwood Anderson said that he thought "the true history of life is but a history of moments," he was describing perfectly the aesthetic approach of Babel's concentrated *nouvelles,* which depend for their impact on the flash-like capture of a passionate moment. In one of his autobiographical stories, **"Maupassant,"** Babel also testifies to the profound influence that French writers, especially Flaubert and Maupassant, had on his sense of form. "A phrase," he says, "is born into the world both good and bad at the same time. The secret consists in a barely perceptible turn. The lever must be held and warmed in the hand, and must be turned once, and not twice."

Reason never speaks in Babel's work. Never is an attempt made at logical analysis or persuasion. Few writers have so completely depended on the immediate flow of sensible reality for their total effect. Overwhelmed by sensations, immersed in atmospheres, colors, voices, we are in contact with a universe that, grasped wholly by the senses, never requires the intervention of the reasoning intellect to explain it. Babel's mastery of the primitive and unthinkable joy of sensuous delight has secular affiliations with the Hasidic literature, but in him it is the ecstasy of experience as such, stripped of the religious logic of the Hasidim.

Equipped so bizarrely, Babel went out into the Civil War, in Heine's phrase, "like God's spy," and with great detachment recorded the brutal episodes of the Red Army's Polish campaign of 1921. At the center of his canvas stands the familiar figure of the alienated Jewish intellectual—the sceptical, ironic observer "with spectacles on his nose and autumn in his heart"—obviously Babel himself. He is in love with the Cossack's primitive directness of instinct, but he is also fascinated by the Hasidic Jew—the war is being fought on the traditional ground of the Jewish Pale—and holds him up as a counter-hero of the spirit to offset the Cossack's primitiveness. Babel identifies himself with a Cossack commander who, as he says, "looked on the world as a meadow in May—a meadow crossed by women and horses." But he is drawn to the Jews, too. Ghedali, the Jewish antique dealer, voices Babel's own discontent when he cries out: "Where is the joy-giving Revolution?" For moments, in certain of these stories, Babel's subtle shuttling back and forth between the two opposing groups of Cossacks and Jews seems designed to call up from all the disorder and bloodshed the image of a totally new man who would contain in himself the traits that attracted Babel in both Jew and Cossack. Not the natural savage of Rousseau, nor the Talmudic genius of ingrown religiosity, but the new and more rounded man that the social upheaval might produce, fills Babel with the longing that underlies his ***Red Cavalry*** stories.

The mood of elation that flares up so often in these stories reflects the dominant feeling of the Russian Jew immediately after the October insurrection. At one stroke he had been freed from the Czarist prison and had attained—so it appeared to him—the open arena of unlimited social possibility. From his own experience, the Jew knew the violent contrasts, the dizzying velocity of the transformation, more completely than anyone else in Russia. Compared with the 19th-century German emancipation, which had unfolded in organic fashion, permitting the Jews over a long period of years to infiltrate slowly into the bourgeois setup, the Russian liberation took place overnight. No wonder that it raised such intense hopes—above all in the Jew.

Soon after his success with ***Red Cavalry,*** Babel wrote the ***Odessa Tales,*** a group of exotic sketches about the ghetto of his youth. Here the hero is the fabulous Jewish gangster Benia Krik. Having found his true voice in the Civil War, Babel had returned to the streets and docks of Odessa to fashion a Jewish Cossack. These stories are based to a large extent on fact; Odessa provided fertile material, being more akin to Marseilles or Naples than to the ghetto towns of the Pale.

Odessa Tales was also the final symbolic action of Babel's creative life. His next stories are written in a pared, elegantly simple style that departs from his usual manner by going in for psychological investigation. They deal exclusively with reminiscences, not with contemporary events—as if Babel were impelled not only by a state censorship, but also by his own curiosity, to retrace the trajectory of his flight from the ghetto.

Although Babel's attitude towards art borrows dark overtones from romantic literature, it is still an intuitively keen analysis of the roots of his own alienation. For Babel was unquestionably an alienated artist. **"Maupassant"** is not simply a casual story, but contains a retrospective summing-up of his whole career, a kind of parable of what happened to his art. Yet to plaster the term alienation on Babel and imagine we have dealt deeply with him would be a grave mistake. For the artist is always a special case; it is in his very nature to be detached. He transforms his aloofness from life into a valid and functioning value, a movement of the nerves prior to any rupture occasioned by society.

Thinking of the process of alienation in this special sense, Henri Bergson regarded all artists as the fortunate products of a profound detachment. "Now and then," he declares in his book *The Creative Mind,* "by a lucky accident, men arise whose senses are less adherent to life. When they look at a thing, they see it for itself, not for themselves. They do not perceive simply with a view to action; they perceive in order to perceive—for nothing, for the pleasure of doing so. In regard to a certain aspect of their nature, whether it be their consciousness or one of their senses, they are born detached. . . ."

Surely Babel was such a "lucky accident." But to "perceive for nothing, for the pleasure of doing so"—precisely this had implications that eventually led to his opposition to traditional Jewish life. Even in the semi-cosmopolitan seaport of Odessa, the ghetto remained a village, with its strict ethical system, its own customs and rituals as a protection against the alien surrounding world. Any interest in the world, in sexual love for its own sake, in the uneconomic activity of art, in pleasure, was anathema to its code. At this point, when Babel was forced to break with Jewish life in order to become an artist, the process of alienation, a process already begun in his nerves, acquires a sociological meaning. Yet one can readily see that this is a peculiar alienation which has as its chief characteristic not sickly and introverted self-regard, but an outgoing and eager interest in the world. Isaak Babel was that rare figure in Jewish-nurtured literature, a Jew who found his purpose in enjoying the world.

Always ready for the "mystic" experience that the world might offer, Babel yet suffered from a flaw inside himself, an inherited sense of the ethical. In his most ecstatic passages, one can hear its harsh undertone. Like the Hasidic rabbis of modern times, he had learned all the prayers, but the miracle of complete possession which should have accompanied them never occurred. And only the "miracle" of revolutionary events brought his art to its highest achievement in ***Red Cavalry.*** But this was an external event, and the artist, in the long run, depends only on his own powers.

In the end, one recalls the final story in ***Red Cavalry,*** the one in which Babel presents the portrait of Ilya, "the last, cursed and unruly son" of the Hasidic prince, Rabbi Motaley Bratslavsky. Using a technique that reminds one of Eisenstein's montage effects, Babel compresses the whole history of Jewish participation in the revolutionary movement into one brief sketch.

Ilya has become a Bolshevik and a Red Army soldier, and now he lies on the dirty floor of the retreating troop train dying of typhus, surrounded by the lyrical disorder of this life. In elegiac tones Babel fondly enumerates the items, the images of Ilya's torn existence: " . . . the mandates of the propagandist and the memorandum books of the Jewish poet; the portraits of Lenin and Maimonides lay side by side; the knotted iron of Lenin's skull beside the dull silk of the portrait of Maimonides. A lock of woman's hair lay in a book, and the Resolutions of the Party's Sixth Congress, and the margins of Communist leaflets were crowded with the crooked lines of Hebrew verse. They fell in a mean and depressing rain—pages of the Song of Songs and those revolver cartridges . . . ”

And while Ilya, last prince of an aborted Hasidic destiny, waits for his death, “a monstrous and inconceivable Russia” tramps in bast shoes alongside the train. All the despair and confusion of military defeat sigh enormously over Ilya's dying body. “And I,” cries Babel, “who can scarce contain the tempests of my imagination within this primeval body of mine, was there beside my brother when he died.” Reading this story now, with Babel's real fate in mind, one thinks of him as he thought of Ilya—as the last of those joy-possessed Hasidic princes who rose out of the submerged but deeply spiritual ghetto world. And his lamentation for Ilya becomes his own lament for the loss of that hope of the marvelous, that perfection of joy which animated his entire life's search.

Steven Marcus   (essay date 1955)

SOURCE: “The Stories of Isaac Babel,” in *Partisan Review*, Vol. XXII, No. 3, Summer, 1955, pp. 400-11.

[*In the following excerpt, Marcus offers a balanced assessment of Babel's works, focusing on the role of violence in his short stories.*]

The publication of **The Collected Stories of Isaac Babel** should be welcome to everyone interested in the progress of literature. It brings before us the work of a unique and accomplished talent and revives the possibilities of a great but apparently senescent genre. In an admirable, informative introduction, Lionel Trilling has appraised Babel's achievement with compassion, educing from his life and writing the particular moral bias that informs them.

Babel's writing is most refreshing in its quality of directness—the style in which he addressed himself to experience and to his readers was calculated to be blunt in its effect of reality. Babel made only perfunctory gestures toward the contrivances of fiction; his stories are simply about himself—his experiences and his response to the experiences of others. Whenever he did write a conventional story the familiar, invented devices of the form plainly distracted him from exploiting his skill and intelligence. It was his great good fortune to discover at the outset of his career that his powers of observation accommodated all his other faculties to them; the brilliance of his registering eye made his use of any of the simpler literary means seem opaque, pallid and superimposed. Indeed, he was vexed by a self-consciousness of his superb aptitude as a witness, and he suffered Reb Arye-Leib's chastening without reply: “ ‘You have spectacles on your nose and autumn in your heart’ ”—not until his art reached an autumnal maturity could he bring himself to acknowledge with any satisfaction the handicaps of being an observer. His stories emanate a rare salubrity, the influence of a cultivated, self-possessed talent coming directly to holds with the trials of its experience. The canon of Babel's work is the story of his life, and because he could look at his life without being embarrassed by the very fact of his looking at it we are not embarrassed either, as we so often are by other contemporary writers who dissimulate their passions about themselves in the transparent formalities of “literature.”

In another way, however, Babel is one of the most indirect and elusive of writers—no recent writer, not even Joyce, has managed a more thorough impersonality. Babel rendered his impersonalness by means of a pervasive and extremely wrought irony. Irony, we all know, is an instrument of the intellect, and many of us seem to believe that it is virtually the intellect itself. That is probably because we do not often meet with an ironist so accomplished that he can deploy his irony against his intelligence. Babel's virtuosity in manipulating ironies was such that he frequently used it to fend off a warranted decisiveness, to blur a genuine distinction or to restrain himself from saying what he apparently had an impulse to say. For though he was a passionate man he severely mistrusted his passions, and in **Red Cavalry,** his most impressive and most flawed work, his irony served to neutralize their impact and to excuse him from moving in the direction of their prodding. He undercut himself consistently, finding, it would almost seem, a grim pleasure in self-contradiction, in the subversion of a story's design.

“Pan Apolek,” one of the **Red Cavalry** stories, is an example of this unfortunate habit. During one of the movements of the campaign of 1920 Babel finds himself in “the ruins of a town swiftly brought to confusion.” He billets in a church which possesses a set of remarkable frescoes and icons, the work of one Pan Apolek, an itinerant painter who, in the company of a blind accordion player, roams the countryside in “a state of blissful intoxication, with two white mice in his bosom and in his pocket a collection of the finest brushes”—the portrait naturally alludes to the culture and ideals of the Gospels. Apolek contracts to decorate a local church and becomes its rustic Michelangelo. “For five months Apolek, confined in his wooden seat, crept along the walls, around the dome and the choir.” At the unveiling of his work the people of the town recognize themselves in the characters of the sacred paintings. “The eminent citizens who had been invited by the priest recognized Yanek, the lame convert, in St. Paul, and in Mary Magdalene a Jewish girl named Elka, daughter of unknown parents and mother of numerous waifs and strays. The eminent citizens ordered the sacrilegious portraits to be covered up. The priest hurled threats upon the blasphemer.” But the common people of the town defend him even before the derision of their furious Vicar who insists that “ ‘He has surrounded you with the ineffable attributes of holiness, you who have thrice fallen into the sin of disobedience, distillers of brandy in secret, merciless usurers, makers of false weights, and dealers in your own daughters' innocence.’ ” Apolek, we are led to believe, is the genuine Christian of untroubled spirit and primitive faith. And then Babel pulls the rug out from under us by having Apolek relate his fantasy of the marriage of Jesus and Deborah, a maid betrothed to “a young Israelite who traded in elephants' tusks.” When Deborah's bridegroom approaches her “a hiccough distended her throat, and she vomited forth all she had eaten at the wedding feast.” Shame overcomes her and her family and she is mocked by her husband. Then Jesus, pitying her anguish and shame, “placed upon Himself the bridegroom's apparel and, full of compassion, was joined with Deborah, who lay in her vomit,” and Deborah bears his child. With this account, Babel has cleverly diverted the drift of his story.

Apolek suddenly appears as a disgusting clod, and his literalistic faith a grotesque vulgarity. Whatever may have provoked this twist—his anticlericalism, his dislike of the passive or submissive character—Babel abruptly suspends his original affection and respect for Apolek; that affection and respect are, presumably, to be remembered as subsidiary ironies in the newer, more "complex" pattern of the story. It is as if he were on the verge of an experience very much like that which Kafka describes in "In the Penal Colony," and then quickly turns and walks away. Like the explorer in Kafka's tale he is too discomposed by his revulsion to allow it to soften itself in disillusion, but unlike him, he cannot even allow his revulsion to act itself out. Nor should we mistake Babel's vulgarization of Christianity for the kind of naiveté of taste we find in *The Man Who Died*. The quality of **"Pan Apolek"** was deliberate and reasoned; it was a vulgarity itself, albeit an elegant one—and unwillingness to allow certain sentiments to suggest their own kind of justification.

Associated with this restricting, deflecting irony was Babel's reluctance to extend a story beyond the slightest possible duration; his finest effects are hit off with the shortest strokes. Like many first-rate short story writers he was possessed with the search for the single right word or phrase. "The secret lies in a slight, an almost invisible twist. The lever should rest in your hand, getting warm, and you can only turn it once, not twice." Only the unquestionable trenchancy of his insights justifies the brevity of his best work. "No iron can stab the heart with such force as a period put just at the right place," he wrote, alluding to that paragon of ironists, the writer of *Proverbs:* "Iron sharpeneth iron: so a man sharpeneth the countenance of his friend." And yet he frequently applied his ability to compress and foreshorten as he applied his ironic skill, to deflect and dissipate his passions. To the young Babel, literature sometimes seemed a deadly serious game which was played by hiding one's hand, by holding back secrets from one's audience and probably oneself. He negotiated this sophisticated coyness with the same facility with which he turned his irony, and his stories were damaged by it in the same way—it was a genuine embarrassment of riches.

Red Cavalry, in which all these faults are most obtrusive, is, nevertheless, a modern classic, quite in the category of excellence of *Dubliners* and *In Our Time.* In 1920 Babel served in the Polish campaigns of Budenny's Cavalry, troops of horse recruited principally from the Cossacks. Many of the sketches and stories of *Red Cavalry* were committed to writing in the midst of the campaign, Babel's powers of contemplation being so mercurial that he could sometimes transform experience into literature almost without a pause.

Red Cavalry is concerned with an appropriate response to the life of the times—this straightforward moral inquiry underrode all Babel's complexity of treatment. He found that the Cossacks' response was appropriate and because it was appropriate admired and cherished them. Babel conceived the times as substantially Hobbes' state of nature, where each man's hand was ready to be turned against his brother and where if one's life and death were

not gallant and glorious they would be poor, nasty, brutish and short. In **"A Letter,"** Babel records with tacit approval how a Cossack father and his sons, on opposite sides of the Revolution, methodically and remorselessly proceed to torture and kill each other, communicating his sense of the propriety that lay within the necessity of terror. The Cossacks had been made for this epoch of carnage, and they surmounted it with "the masterful indifference of a Tartar Khan." Like Tolstoy, he saw in the Cossacks a conjunction of beauty and fierceness, in which their athleticism gave grace to their aggressiveness. "And he swung his well-proportioned athlete's body skilfully out of the saddle. Straightening his perfect legs, caught at the knee with a small strap, he went with circus agility over to the moribund animal." This appears in **"The Remount Officer,"** where Dyakov has just had his horse collapse beneath him. The story continues:

> It fixed wide, deep eyes on Dyakov and licked from his ruddy palm a sort of imperceptible injunction. Immediately the exhausted beast felt a dexterous strength flowing from the bald and vigorous Romeo in the prime of life. Straightening its head and slithering on its staggering legs at the impatient and imperious flicking of the whip on its belly, the jade got up, slowly and warily.
>
> Then we saw a delicate wrist in a wide, flowing sleeve patting the dirty mane, and perceived how the whip cracked whining against the blood-stained flanks. Her whole body trembling, the jade stood on her legs, her doglike eyes, filled with love and fear, never for an instant leaving Dyakov's face.

This episode may call to mind similar ones in *Crime and Punishment, Hard Times* or *St. Mawr,* and it does not take much to discern in it a moral inclination at odds with them. Familiars of [William Faulkner's] "Spotted Horses," however, will at once notice a likeness of accent.

Babel and Faulkner resemble each other remarkably, especially in their understanding of that state in which men are possessed by a passion so huge and immolating that they are turned dispassionate in consummating it. In **"Prischepa's Vengeance"** Babel describes "a tireless ruffian who had been turned out of the Communist Party, a future rag-and-bone man, a carefree syphilitic, and a happy-go-lucky fraud," one of his characteristically gay destroyers. Prischepa's parents were killed by the Whites, and he returns to his village for revenge. "Prischepa went from neighbor to neighbor, leaving behind him the trail of his blood-stained footprints. In the huts where he found gear that had belonged to his mother, a pipe that had been his father's, he left old women stabbed through and through, dogs hung above the wells, icons defiled with excrement. . . . The young Cossacks were scattered over the steppe, keeping the score." After the massacre "he sent for vodka, and shutting himself up in the hut, he drank for two whole days and nights, singing, weeping, and hewing the furniture with his Circassian saber." For Babel as for Faulkner, violence was the great cathartic and revenge its sweetest and most corrupting form. But the butchery of Babel's Cossacks is not the despairing, forlorn and solitary mayhem of Faulkner's Southerners. They spread their carnage gayly, for they were born to this existence not driven to it. They are as much like Faulkner's Indians as they are like his Southerners—atavistic, immune to guilt, untrammelled in their celebration of the momentous circumstances of life. Writing of the burial of Squadron Commander Trunov, Babel wants us to recall the Homeric funeral games and to esteem the Cossacks as if they were Achaeans. "The whole squadron leaped into the saddle and fired a volley in the air, and our old three-incher champed forth a second time. Then we sent three Cossacks to fetch a wreath. They dashed off, firing, at full gallop, dropping out of their saddles and performing all sorts of Cossack tricks; and returned bringing whole armfuls of red flowers. Pugachov scattered them on the coffin and we began to move up to Trunov for the last kiss." Before Trunov died he had murdered a defenseless prisoner, an old man, cutting his throat with a sword and then riding away. "The sun came out of the clouds at that moment and impetuously surrounded Andie's horse, its lively pace, and the devil-may-care swing of its docked tail." Babel would like us to believe that the universe conspires with joy in the Cossacks' bright brutality. And here, in his exaltation of violence, Babel departs from Faulkner who is as concerned with it as Babel, but for different reasons. Faulkner's violence mourns the death of traditions and institutions which he loved. Babel's rejoices in the death of traditions and institutions which he had come to hate.

Precisely because the Cossacks were innocent of the traditional institutions of Russian society, Babel admired them. Having no piety toward the stations and duties of the old rotted society—existing, indeed, almost without any preconceptions about the virtue of society at all—they were delivered from any compunction about destroying it or whatever defended and represented it. For Babel they became the ironic embodiment of the Revolutionary ideal, the irresistible, anarchic simplicity that would execute the catastrophe of war and survive it as the first and finest fruits of the new society; for he had few expectations of industrial greatness or educated masses—the true revolution would create something like the Cossacks. He was more right than he knew.

In comparison with the Cossacks, however, Babel found himself miserably inadequate. As a Jew, an intellectual, a revolutionary, he was unable to meet the violent requirements of the revolution. When he is called upon to kill a wounded Cossack to prevent his falling into the hands of the Poles, he cannot. When he borrows a Cossack's horse he promptly afflicts the beast with saddle-sores. He wanders through a battle with an unloaded pistol, and convicts himself of lacking "the simplest of proficiencies—the ability to kill my fellow-men." The Cossacks, apprehending Babel's peculiar unfitness for his work, reproached him: " 'You're trying to live without enemies.' " Such, he confesses, is the fate of a man with spectacles on his nose.

But Babel did not castigate himself with any lasting bitterness for this failing. He realized that his time was unable to respond to him; it could not gratify his vagrant impulses of love. **"Gedali,"** one of his finest stories, expresses this dilemma beautifully. On a Sabbath eve Babel invokes his childhood. "In bygone days on these occasions my grandfather would stroke the volumes of Ibn Ezra with his yellow beard. His old woman in her lace cap would trace fortunes with her knotty fingers over the Sabbath candles, and sob softly to herself. On those evenings my child's heart was rocked like a little ship upon enchanted waves. O the rotted Talmuds of my childhood! O the dense melancholy of memories!" Roaming through the *shtetl* of a Polish town, longing to share his nostalgia, he finds an old Jew, Gedali, in his curiosity shop, presiding over the things boys love and remember, "buttons . . . and a dead butterfly . . . a labyrinth of globes, skulls, and dead flowers. . . ." But Gedali disdains to speak of the past, of the Sabbath eyes, and argues wistfully and uncomprehendingly about the Revolution—he too seeks an impossible communion, "an International of good people." In despair, Babel cries, " 'Gedali . . . today is Friday, and it's already evening. Where are Jewish biscuits to be got, and a Jewish glass of tea, and a little of that pensioned-off God in a glass of tea?' " Gedali simply answers, " 'Not to be had,' " and goes off to the synagogue to pray. It was not Babel's fault that he and Gedali could not meet each other, and the pathos of the story is in his knowledge of his innocence and helplessness.

Yet Babel could not treat the Polish Jews with similar justice. And here, I think, Mr. Trilling [in his introduction to Babel's **Collected Stories**] has been too generous with Babel, for he tends to acquit him of his excessive hatred for and spite against the Jews of the Polish villages. It is true that on certain occasions their suffering exists for him as "a spiritual fact of consummate value," but these occasions are special and few. The Polish Jews were constant objects of derision and ironic pity before his witnessing eye. "In the room I was given I discovered turned-out wardrobes, scraps of women's fur coats on the floor, human filth. . . . The two Jews rose from their places and, hopping on their felt soles, cleared the mess from the floor. They skipped about noiselessly, monkey-fashion, like Japs in a circus act, their necks swelling and twisting." In his sight, the sickly, anemic Jews of Poland, the Hasidic Jews, were of a species alien to his Jews of Odessa, "the stout and jovial Jews of the South, bubbling like cheap wine." "Hasidism kept that superstitious population of hawkers, brokers, and tavern-keepers in stifling captivity. . . . Human refuse and dung accumulate here for days. Depression and horror fill the catacombs with a corrosive stench and a tainted acidity." The torn trousers of a Rabbi's dead son reveal "the stunted, curly-covered virility of a wasted Semite." In contrast, "the captivating Savitsky," Division Commander in the Cossack Cavalry, lives with a Cossack woman "bearing her bosom on her high heels, a bosom that stirred like an animal in a bag," and lounges about with his revolver "lying against the bare skin of his stomach," the image of glamor and potency. Babel's denunciation of the Polish Jews was a great and cruel self-indulgence.

Just as the Cossacks implicitly stood for Babel's future society, the Jews came to represent the society he was engaged in pulling down. He felt that the hide-bound, tyrannical past of his country and his own life was concentrated in the culture of the decrepit Polish Jews—only the oblique brilliance of this insight could be equal to its calamitous untruth. In **"The Rabbi,"** companion-piece to **"Gedali,"** Babel sits with Rabbi Motale and his friends, the "possessed, liars and idlers," amid dingy and funereal surroundings, and the Rabbi, oblivious to the carnage and change about him, intones " 'Blessed is the Lord God of Israel Who hath chosen us from amongst all the nations of the earth.' " Revolted by the pathos of the Jews' insensibility Babel rises and goes to the railroad station where "in the propaganda train of the First Cavalry Army, there awaited me the flare of innumerable lights, the magical brilliance of the wireless station, the stubborn coursing of the printing presses, and my unfinished article for the *Red Trooper.*" No irony is intended here. In the crucifixion of the Polish Jews Babel sought the humiliation and subjugation of the past.

Babel respected the Jews only when they answered the violence done to them with violence of their own—a Polish woman cries out "with sudden and terrible violence" over the body of her murdered father, or the Jews of Volhynia and Galicia who "moved perkily, in an uncontrolled and uncouth way, but their capacity for suffering was full of a somber greatness, and their unvoiced contempt for the Polish gentry unbounded." Benya Krik, the hero of *Tales of Odessa,* was the kind of Jew Babel could admire unreservedly. "Gangster and kind of gangsters" in the Odessa ghetto, Benya "could spend the night with a Russian woman, and satisfy her," was able together with his brother Lyovka to cripple his father, received a proposal of marriage while he was in bed with a prostitute, and was a man whom nothing could dismay or deceive. He was, in other words, a kind of Cossack. These stories of Odessa seem to me unpalatable. Aside from their moral dubiousness, they affect a folksy amiability and relaxation which are not appropriate to their intense violence and chicanery. Unlike the stories of *Red Cavalry* they seem to have been "gotten up" into literature, but Babel's deliberation over them was unproductive of finer or more humane judgments.

The trouble lies, I think, in the fact that the young Babel made a too sizable investment in violence. Mr. Trilling vindicates this investment by emphasizing the qualities of native grace and address that may accompany violence, and in doing so discriminates against Babel's principal interest and fascination, its terrific actuality—its "brain-spattering, wind-pipe slitting" turbulence touched him more vitally than the delicacy and coolness of its commissioners. *Red Cavalry* is a discussion of the multifarious ways of destruction, and it is not even so much a discussion as it is an exposition, for, unfortunately, nearly all of Babel's reservations about violence were *merely* ironic. In **"Berestechko"** the Cossacks commit one of their senseless murders. "Kudrya of the machine gun section took hold of his head and tucked it under his arm. The Jew stopped screaming and straddled his legs. Kudrya drew out his dagger with his right hand and carefully, without splashing himself, cut the old man's throat." Later the Commissar makes a speech, " 'You are in power. Everything here is yours. . . . I now proceed to the election of the Revolutionary Committee. . . .' " In another story he writes, unforgivably, and without a shred of irony, "Then I stamped on my master Nikitinsky, trampled on him for

an hour or maybe more. And in that time I got to know life through and through. With shooting . . . you only get rid of a chap. Shooting's letting him off, and too damn easy for yourself. With shooting you'll never get at the soul. . . . But I don't spare myself, and I've more than once trampled an enemy for over an hour. You see, I want to get to know what life's like down our way." Here at its worst Babel's style was bloated with gore, "horribly stuff 'd with epithets of war."

Babel's overinvestment in violence led him into active personal brutality. **"My First Goose"** records how he gruesomely slaughtered a bird and upbraided a harmless old peasant woman in order to feel potent and mature and accepted by the Cossacks. Nor should we neglect the fact that Babel later became a member of the Cheka—though no information is available about what he did for it—and that he went along on the infamous grain-collecting expeditions of 1917-1918: on three separate occasions he was somehow associated with the dirtiest work of the Revolution. Mr. Trilling would persuade us that Babel entertained a dialectic which poised the spirituality of the Jews against the carnality, the bodily beauty, of the Cossacks, and in which one criticized and qualified the other. Again this seems to me an error of generosity. Babel's frequent and ingenious juxtapositions seem deliberate and contrived enough, I think, to warrant the supposition that he sensed his overcommitment to the way of violence; and so he called upon objects and sentiments which would have the appearance of compromising his rancor and destructiveness—he sought a dialectic, but this search was essentially strategic. The young Babel was inspired by the negating passions; his one powerful benign impulse was the will to record and understand and convey. This impulse fortified his sense of the need for a dialectic, but it could not alone supply him with one. I do not mean to imply that Babel had no strong affections—indeed he did; nor do I wish to maintain that his use of irony is altogether spurious. But what may appear to be a dialectic in this respect, is, I think, more accurately a duality, in which the spiritual and the fleshly find it politic to appear together in print—like two enemies compelled to associate in public. Actually, I find, Babel's ironies and contradictions often tend to destroy, rather than create, each other.

Babel's affinity for destruction and cruelty may be understood though not condoned through his early life. In two sketches of 1925, **"The Story of My Dovecot"** and **"First Love,"** he describes the most important day of his life—on October 20, 1905 there was a pogrom in Odessa. Babel's grandfather was killed, his father, "his soft red hair fluttering, his paper dickey askew and fastened to the wrong button," humiliated, and Babel himself crushed and terrified into a nervous disorder. He saw his father pleading on his knees before a Cossack officer who "rode as though through a mountain pass, where one can only look ahead." And he, young Isaac, who had just been allowed to buy some pigeons as a reward for his assiduous scholarship, saw his pigeons mangled in front of him. "I lay on the ground, and the guts of the crushed bird trickled down from my temple. They flowed down my cheek, winding this way and that, splashing, blinding me. The tender pigeon-guts slid down over my forehead, and I closed my

Caricature of Babel by K. Rotov. The inscription on the crumbling pediment is "Bourgeois Literature."

solitary unstopped-up eye so as not to see the world that spread out before me." In one day the male line of his family was disgraced and emasculated. Babel accommodated himself to these scarifying hours by coming to idealize the Cossacks and dislike the Jews. By living as a Cossack, immersing himself in brutality, he hoped to cleanse himself and his country of the filthy past. *Red Cavalry* is his great effort in that direction. Several of the stories reflect the effort literally—**"My First Goose,"** in which he tears apart a bird himself, is one. In another story he stands by while a Cossack shoots a Polish boy "and bits of brain dripped over my hands." And in a third he exacts retribution by urinating into the mouth of a Polish corpse: "It was pouring out of his mouth, bubbling between his teeth, gathered in his empty eye-sockets." In *Red Cavalry* he tried to rid himself of the past, and the final story ends in a hopeful self-deception. "Months passed, and my dream came true. The Cossacks stopped watching me and my horse."

As the years passed he continued to scrutinize his notions of the Revolution and of his Jewishness; he began to realize that he had deceived and indulged himself. Hesitantly, sorrowfully, he came to be critical of the unremitting violence of Soviet life, and as his trust in violence wavered he became increasingly involved in reminiscences of his childhood and lenient in his judgment of it. As his energy for carnage declined, he gradually ceased to disparage his Jewish endowments—curiosity, the love of irony, the love of ideas. He even asserted, once, that his savagery was an inherited gift too, a wistful and quickly abandoned illusion. And he perceived that the life of art had its own kind of violence, a self-inflicted sort, and reflecting upon Maupassant's final years his "heart contracted as the foreboding of some essential truth touched me with light fingers."

He was a wiser and a gentler man, but his art had faltered.

He picked at his Jewishness laboriously; it was not an immediate actuality but a sequence of memories and ideas upon which he ruminated and by which he tried to reveal himself anew. These later stories are the work of a fatigued and burdened talent—they took a long time to write, and Babel, unable to obey his own dictates about style, was forced to "turn the lever" more than once. Nor could he ever be at ease with the milder, retrospective sentiments; he tricked out his nostalgia in pseudo-ironic pathos, he recreated his memories and his Jewishness primarily in order to keep on writing about something. As he learned more about himself his subject-matter trickled away from him; his special talent did not thrive on the wisdom that comes with resignation. He had met life a ferocious young observer, and his best work was volatile, predatory and imperfect—with all its immoralities *Red Cavalry* is his enduring achievement. When his passion for "the state of nature" waned, his art, which in its way was a state of nature too, waned with it.

Before Babel silenced his own voice, however, he wrote one great story, **"Di Grasso,"** which along with **"Gedali"** is his finest work. It tells of an Italian troupe of players that stopped at Odessa one year; Di Grasso, the star performer in a rustic Sicilian melodrama, portrays a jealous shepherd who avenges himself on Giovanni, the city slicker that has stolen his love. "The shepherd . . . stood there lost in thought; then he gave a smile, soared into the air, sailed across the stage, plunged down on Giovanni's shoulders, and having bitten through the latter's throat, began, growling and squinting, to suck blood from the wound." This beautiful, savage leap has a profound effect on Babel, and on all the Odessans who witness it. Somehow it gets at the heart of Babel's greatest and truest appreciation of violence in a way that *Red Cavalry* never did. Perhaps the most significant reason for this is the fact that it takes place through the agency of art: it is art Babel is witnessing here, not life. And when he says of Di Grasso's performances that they confirm "with every word and gesture that there is more justice in outbursts of noble passion than in all the joyless rules that run the world," one wonders if he does not now have in mind the violence that only art can properly represent, and that only art, by its peculiar magic, can cause to vitalize our moral beings. One wonders also if he does not now have a deeper sense of what constitutes a noble passion, and a noble violence. Certainly it seems so to me, for his description of the humanizing influence of the performance upon even the "tricky customer" Nick Schwarz, to whom Babel had pawned his father's watch, and upon Nick's grenadier-like wife, is an indication that he senses where the real nobility and justice in violence lies: in its power to evoke the non-violent affections, to evoke love, even to evoke guilt, and always to evoke our moral humanity. After the play, Madame Schwarz says, "Now you see what love means," and with tears in her fishlike eyes she suddenly demands that her husband return Babel's watch to him—which he does, albeit with a "vicious pinch." Thus saved from his father's anger, Babel turns into Pushkin Street and "saw for the first time the things surrounding me as they really were: frozen in silence and ineffably beautiful." The violence of *Red Cavalry*—which was the violence of life itself—has passed. The violence of **"Di Grasso"**—which is the violence of art—has taken its place. And it is in the latter that we find the nobility and justice Babel sought. I think **"Di Grasso"** ought to be read after the stories of **Red Cavalry,** for then it would serve to instruct those of us who are so familiar with the literary modes of violence that we are inclined to forget what a monstrous actuality the thing in itself really is.

Ilya Ehrenburg on Babel, 11 November 1964: How did [Babel] mitigate the cruelty you can find in nearly all his stories? By love, by a conspiracy of compassion with his heroes and readers, by his enormous kindness of heart. He was a very kind man and a good man, not in the commonplace sense of the expression but in a very real sense, and what people say about his not having believed in the success of writers who were lukewarm in spirit sums up very well the whole nature of Isaac Emmanuelovich.

—Ilya Ehrenburg, in her Moscow Speech, reprinted in You Must Know Everything: Stories, 1915-1937 by Isaac Babel, 1966.

Irving Howe   (essay date 1955)

SOURCE: "The Right to Write Badly," in *The New Republic,* Vol. 133, No. 1, July 4, 1955, pp. 16-18.

[*A longtime editor of the leftist magazine* Dissent *and a regular contributor to* The New Republic, *Howe was a highly respected American critic and social historian whose criticism was informed by a liberal socialist viewpoint. In the following excerpt, he provides a favorable assessment of* The Collected Stories of Isaac Babel.]

The publication of [*The Collected Stories of Isaac Babel*], coming at a time when the dominant political and cultural trends are deeply hostile to his kind of imagination, is cause for happiness. Most of the stories have appeared in one or another English version, but now to have them in their proper order and thereby to receive their accumulative impact is to know that Babel is not merely, as Maxim Gorky claimed, the most gifted prose writer of post-revolutionary Russia, but one of the literary masters of our century.

This, in a way, is hardly news. Babel's work, when it first came out in the twenties, was quickly praised by the Russian and European critics: anyone with half an ear could recognize that he was, to put it bluntly, a genius. But we live in a culture so committed to opportunism that Babel's work, incompatible with the religiosity and obscurantism that have recently dominated the literary world, needs to be read as if it *were* new, a suddenly discovered gift from an earlier generation.

A few words about Babel's life may help illuminate the quality of his writing. Born in 1894, he was raised in a lower-middle-class Jewish family in Odessa, and during the pre-revolutionary period, when he lived and starved in Moscow as a literary bohemian, he became a protegé of Gorky. After five years of fighting in the revolution and civil war, Babel returned to his writing and won immediate fame as the author of **Red Cavalry,** a book of breathtaking stories that draw from his experiences with a Cossack unit in Budenny's army. But as the Stalin dictatorship hardened its grip, Babel wrote less and less (he was not, in any case, very productive) and after a time he lapsed into silence.

In 1934 Babel made one of his rare public appearances, at the first Russian Writers' Congress, partly to join in the ritual of pledging loyalty to the regime, partly to explain his failure to publish. His performance—it is vividly described in Mr. Trilling's introduction—was a remarkable political act. He practiced, said Babel, a new literary genre: he was "the master of the genre of silence." And in the midst of his praise for the regime and the party, he remarked, as if in passing, that they presumed to deprive writers of only one right, the right to write badly. "Comrades," he went on, "let us not fool ourselves: this is a very important right and to take it away from us is no small thing. . . . Let us give up this right, and may God help us. And if there is no God, let us help ourselves. . . ."

The right to write badly! —which is to say, to write from one's own feelings, even from one's own mistakes. It would be hard to imagine a more courageous, and a more saddening, gesture on the part of a writer whose every impulse was for the spontaneity, the freedom, the playfulness which his society denied. Babel, who was protected by Gorky and for whom, it is rumored, even Number One had a soft spot, suffered no immediate punishment, other than the continued silence he had imposed on himself. But in 1937 he was arrested and two or three years later he died in a concentration camp. Except for a memorial note on Gorky which appeared in 1938, Babel remained silent to the end, the master of his genre.

The stories in **Red Cavalry,** which form over half the present volume, impress one in endless ways, but their primary impact is shock. Hard, terse, violent, gorgeously colored, they come upon one like disciplined explosions. Primitive Cossack ways jar against Babel's sophisticated consciousness; the random brutality that is the inheritance of centuries of blackness suddenly lifts itself to a selfless red heroism, and in the very moment of doing so helplessly corrupts the heroism; extremes of behavior, weaving into one another as if to spite all moralists, bewilder Babel as narrator and the reader as onlooker.

The stories turn upon Babel's struggle with a problem that cannot be understood unless it is seen both in the immediate historical context (the Russian Revolution) and in the context of Babel's personal being and tradition as both intellectual and Jew. Though he was not, so far as we know, concerned with politics as ideological definition or power strategy, Babel understood with absolute sureness the problem that has obsessed all modern novelists who deal with politics: the problem of action in both its heroic necessity and its ugly self-contamination, the "tragic flaw" that is at the heart of an historical action which by virtue of being historical must to some extent be conceived in violence and therefore as a distortion and coarsening of its "self." But it must be stressed that Babel sees this problem not as a mere exercise in metaphysics: for him it is part of the very texture of action. And it is in this sense, despite the virtual absence of explicit politics, that the stories in *Red Cavalry* are profoundly revolutionary: under the red heat of Babel's passion, creation and contemplation melt into one.

The problem of historical action also absorbs Malraux and Silone in their best novels, and in Bert Brecht's great poem "To Posterity" it receives its most exalted and its most shameful expression, for here every word is bitterly true yet the poem itself is put to service as a rationale for Stalinism. For Babel, characteristically, the problem turns into one of personal assertion, his capacity to embrace and engage in, yet at some level of awareness to stand apart from, the most terrifying extremes of human conduct.

In his introduction, Mr. Trilling has raised, or perhaps I should say, abstracted, this problem into a kind of timeless moral dialectic. "In Babel's heart," he writes, "there was a kind of fighting—he was captivated by the vision of two ways of being, the way of violence and the way of peace, and he was torn between them." True as this is, I think it misses the center of Babel's concern, which was not so much the choice between "two ways of being" open to men in almost any circumstances and at almost any time, but rather the unbearable—unbearable because felt as entirely necessary—difficulties of being an artist committed to the fate of a desperate revolution. One very important side of Babel was a Bolshevik, or tried hard to be ("O regulations of the Russian Communist Party," begins one story, "You have laid headlong rails through the sour pastry of our Russian tales"), and precisely from this side of Babel came some of the energies and anxieties that give life to his work. Like it or not, we cannot blink this simple fact, nor the equally important fact that Babel, as a writer whose politics and esthetics meet in an appetite for extremes, does not lend himself very easily to those more reasonable modes of feeling which Mr. Trilling has designated as the Liberal Imagination. To deprive a writer of the immediacy, even the distracting immediacy, of his preoccupations is at times to lessen his capacity for disturbing and uprooting us.

Some of the most terrible stories in *Red Cavalry* are directed against Babel himself, against his inability to kill other men and his tragi-comic efforts to adapt himself to the ways of the Cossacks. The Jewish literary man, with spectacles on his nose and autumn in his heart, needs to prove to himself that, *given the historical necessity,* he can commit acts which for the Cossack are virtually second nature. But since he is also a human being and a writer of imaginative largesse, Babel in the course of "lending" himself to the Cossacks falls in love with their gracefulness of gesture and movement. (Mr. Trilling, linking Babel to Tolstoy, has some acute remarks on this.) Above all, Babel admires the Cossacks' sureness of manner, their unreflective absorption in inherited modes of life.

Yet he does not sentimentalize the Cossacks nor use them, as a modern literary man might, to sanction his own repressed aggressiveness. He remains in awed puzzlement before the ancient mysteries of their ways, and even when he achieves occasional rapport with them he does not pretend to understand them. But he grants them every possible human claim, and he trembles beneath the lash of their simple unqualified criticism.

In a magnificent five-page story called **"The Death of Dolgushov,"** a wounded Cossack, his entrails hanging over his knees, begs Babel to shoot him, but Babel, soft and scrupulous, funks it. A comrade of the wounded man does the job and then turns furiously upon Babel: "You guys in specs have about as much pity for chaps like us as a cat has for a mouse." In another five-page masterpiece, **"After the Battle,"** a Cossack curses Babel for having ridden into battle with an unloaded revolver ("You didn't put no cartridge in. . . . You worship God, you traitor!") and Babel goes off "imploring fate to grant me the simplest of proficiencies—the ability to kill my fellow-men." And at the end of *Red Cavalry* another Cossack pronounces his primitive sentence upon Babel: "You're trying to live without enemies. That's all you think about, not having enemies."

As counterforce to the Cossacks Babel turns to the Polish Jews, squatting in their villages while opposing armies trample back and forth, passive and impervious to the clamor for blood. Even as he fights in the Red Army, Babel listens, with the attentiveness of a child, to Gedali, the Hassid who believes that "the Revolution means joy" and who wants "an International of good people." "I would like every soul to be listed," says Gedali, "and given first-category rations. There, soul, please eat and enjoy life's pleasures. Pan comrade, you don't know what the International is eaten with. . . ." "It is eaten with gunpowder," answers Babel, "and spiced with best-quality blood."

The Jews of Poland, with their "long bony backs, their tragic yellow beards," pierce through the taut objectivity of Babel's narrative and stir in him a riot of memories ("O the rotted Talmuds of my childhood!"). He goes back and forth from the Cossacks, strange, cruel and beautiful, to the ghetto Jews, who "moved jerkily, in an uncontrolled and uncouth way, but [whose] capacity for suffering was full of a sombre greatness . . ." If *Red Cavalry* is a paean, ambiguous but ardent, to the force of revolution, it is also an elegy for the dying ghetto, for "the Sabbath peace [which] rested upon the crazy roofs of Zhitomer."

Even to mention Babel's style is to involve one's self in a tangle of contradictions and frustrations. Gestures of bare violence turn abruptly, without notice or preparation, into states of reflective quietness and repose. Objectivity seems the dominant mode, yet few modern prose writers would dare indulge in such lyrical apostrophes and such laments as fill Babel's pages. We have been taught to value terseness and understatement; but in Babel terseness has nothing whatever to do with understatement, since it is actually the consequence of the boldest political and metaphysical generalizations. Indeed, hardly another writer of our time has succeeded so well in making the generalization, even the political slogan, so organically a part of his imagery. One moves in these stories with a dizzying speed from conceptual abstraction to primitive notation: Babel never permits the reader to rest in any mold of style or upon any level of perception, he always drives one from surprise to surprise. In some of the stories there is a surrender to sadness as complete as the urge to motion and violence that accompanies it. In other stories the event itself has been removed from sight, and the surface of the prose is devoted to a few wry ripples of talk and a few startling images of place and weather.

The best observation on Babel's style has been made by John Berryman, who has noted certain similarities to the style of Stephen Crane. In both writers there is an obsessive concern with compression and explosion, a kinesthetic ferocity of control, a readiness to wrench language in order to gain nervous immediacy. Both use language as if to inflict a wound. But the differences are also important. Babel, as Berryman goes on to mention, is warm, while Crane is cold. And more important, I think, Babel has a wider range of effects; by comparison, Crane seems a little stiff-jointed.

The two main literary sources upon which Babel seems to have drawn, Russian and Yiddish, flourished most in the 50 or 75 years directly before he began to write; he was one of those writers who spring up at the end of such a creative period and absorb its energies as if they were still at their fullest. The Chekhov strain in Russian literature is strongly evident in Babel's miscellaneous stories (though not so much in *Red Cavalry* or his other group called *Tales of Odessa*); one quickly recognizes the pathos, the warm skepticism of the older writer. The Yiddish literary influence is less likely to be noticed by American critics (Mr. Trilling pays no attention to it). But surely no one who has read Sholom Aleichem can fail to see that in Babel's Odessa stories there is a remarkable parallel of effect: the comic grasp of social relationships, the sardonic arguing with God, the attraction to the undersides of history. Compare Babel's bitter wit with Sholom Aleichem's impudent reverence in writing about Jewish fate.

> [Babel]: "But wasn't it a mistake on God's part to settle the Jews in Russia, where they've had to suffer the tortures of Hell? Would it be bad if the Jews lived in Switzerland, where they'd be surrounded by first-class lakes, mountain air and nothing but Frenchmen? Everybody makes mistakes, even God."

> [Sholom Aleichem]: "Apparently if He wants it that way, that's the way it ought to be. Can't you see? If it should have been different it would have been. And yet, what would have been wrong to have it different?"

Sometimes the richness of emotion, and often the very phrasing of his idiom, is understandable only in terms of Babel's relationship to Yiddish literature. In a story called **"In the Basement"** the vulgar-loving rebuke of a grandfather to a boy who tries to commit suicide ("My grandson . . . I'm taking a dose of castor oil, so as to have something to place on your grave") is given its true value and inflection only if one knows that in the Jewish mores sui-

cide is taken to be not merely impious, but in a strictly human sense, shameful.

I shall have to stop in a moment, but before I do a word needs to be said about the underlying quality of Babel's work which gives it a special excitement for our time. Lost as he often is in melancholia and sadness, perplexed and perhaps even a little betrayed as he sometimes is by violence, Babel—through his simple readiness to accept his own desires—makes upon life the most radical of demands: the demand for happiness. In his work one finds a straining toward a union of passion and tenderness, those two elements of feeling which Freud says have become dissociated in the life of modern man and which, because they are dissociated, tend to decline into aggressiveness and impotence. I do not say that Babel often achieves this union, only that he will not let anything, not even "the regulations of the Communist Party," distract him from straining toward it. In his work everything becomes eroticized, everything becomes animated: love and energy come closer.

There is a lovely little story by Babel ["**Karl-Yankel**"] in which he describes how a baby named Karl-Yankel (half Marxist-half Jew) is being fought over by the two sets of believers. Babel, watching the comic struggle, ends the story by telling himself, "It's not possible . . . it's not possible that you won't be happy, Karl-Yankel. It's not possible that you won't be happier than I."

Stanley Edgar Hyman   (essay date 1956)

SOURCE: "Identities of Isaac Babel," *The Hudson Review,* Vol. VIII, No. 4, Winter, 1956, pp. 620-27.

[*As a longtime literary critic for the* New Yorker, *Hyman rose to a prominent position in American letters during the middle decades of the twentieth century. He is noted for his belief that much of modern literary criticism should depend on knowledge received from disciplines outside the field of literature; consequently, many of his best reviews and critical essays rely on his application of theories gleaned from such disciplines as cultural anthropology, psychology, and comparative religion. In the following review of Babel's* Collected Stories, *he examines the overall ambiguity of Babel's fiction.*]

Now that Frank O'Connor has been awarded "some claim to greatness" by Arthur Mizener, and Wyndham Lewis is celebrated as "the greatest prose master of style of my generation" by T. S. Eliot, perhaps it is time we heard more of Isaac Babel. In his lifetime this Soviet Jewish writer published three books of short stories: *Red Cavalry,* based on his experiences fighting in Poland in 1920, with Budenny's First Cavalry Army, in 1923; *Odessa Tales,* based on his boyhood, in 1924; and a collected volume with additional stories in 1932. Since 1938, when he published some reminiscences of Gorky, his name is said not to have appeared in a Soviet publication, and he is believed to have died in a penal camp in 1939 or 1940, with several conflicting accounts of his arrest and death available. *Red Cavalry* was brought out here by Knopf in 1929, in a graceless translation by Nadia Helstein, woefully bowdlerized and cut; and a small group of Babel's Jewish stories from all three books was published as ***Benya Krik, the Gangster and Other Stories*** by Schocken Books in 1948, beautifully translated by Avrahm Yarmolinsky; but out of their context in ***Red Cavalry*** and with their chronology reversed, the Jewish stories gave a distorted impression of Babel's work.

With the publication for the first time in any language of all of Babel's short stories [***The Collected Stories of Isaac Babel***], ably edited and translated by Walter Morison, with an introduction by Lionel Trilling, we finally have an adequate English text, and Criterion Books deserves fairly handsome congratulations. If Trilling's intelligent and sensitive introduction is not the last word, it is at least a good word, and his currently fashionable voice may succeed in introducing Babel to the thousands of readers the book deserves instead of the hundreds it might otherwise get. . . .

Reading the collected stories, one's first impression is apt to be that whereas any given story seems clear and sharp, as a group they become much more ambiguous and evasive. We are forced to come to terms very quickly with Babel's antinomies: he is a Soviet writer for whom the welcomed Revolution is mostly an image of the mindless animal brutality of Cossacks, a Jewish writer whose essence of Jewish life is "a violent smell of rotten herrings", a traditional Russian writer who identified so strongly with Maupassant (not with "the lion in the path", characteristically, but with the insane dying Maupassant regressively crawling on all fours and eating his own excrement) that for a while he tried to write in French.

Trilling describes one of Babel's major themes as "the test and the initiation", but I would prefer to characterize it more generally as changes of identity through rituals of rebirth. To my reading, there are not one but two narrators in ***Red Cavalry*** (besides the illiterate Cossacks who tell their stories in the first person), one a gentile intellectual addressed as "Lyutov", who refers to "the occult crockery the Jews use only once a year, at Eastertime", and sees the Polish Jews as living in filth and meaningless suffering, like animals; the other a Jewish intellectual, Babel himself, who gets away from the Red Army in Zhitomir on the eve of the Sabbath, "oppressed by the dense melancholy of memories", to search for "a Jewish glass of tea, and a little of that pensioned-off God in a glass of tea". One of the Odessa stories of Benya Krik, the Jewish gangster who "can spend the night with a Russian woman and satisfy her", is told, not by Babel, but *to* Babel by Reb Arye-Leib, an old man from the poorhouse, so that he can reproach Babel with being everything Benya is not, a coward "with spectacles on your nose and autumn in your heart". Arye-Leib says:

> What would you have done in Benya Krik's place? You would have done nothing. But he did something. That's why he's the King, while you thumb your nose in the privy.

Thus in ***Red Cavalry*** Babel is reborn as "Lyutov", without his Jewishness; still scorned as "you guys in specs" and "four-eyes", he is reborn again without his crippling intellectualism in the last story and accepted on terms of something like equality; that this *ersatz* Cossack is in turn an

inadequate *persona* only comes clear in the stories after ***Red Cavalry***, where it is succeeded by even more ambiguous personalities and culminates in the image of the little child Karl-Yankel, who is to receive the Soviet Kingdom. The physical horrors of ***Red Cavalry*** are a catharsis by violence, the agency of these rebirths. The narrators are never participants in the violence: "Lyutov" goes into action with no cartridges in his revolver, cannot bring himself to shoot a dying friend to keep him from Polish torture, and ironically implores fate "to grant me the simplest of proficiencies—the ability to kill my fellow-men". Out of the bloodshed and fury, as Babel saw it, would come the Revolutionary redemption he hoped for, but when Gedali, the Jewish proprietor of a junkshop in Zhitomir, tells him his dream of a Revolution of joy, an International of good people, Babel answers harshly that Gedali's impossible International "is eaten with gunpowder and spiced with best-quality blood".

The book's dichotomy is not simply between "the way of violence and the way of peace", as Trilling says, or between "the Cossack ethos" and "the Jewish ethos", as Raymond Rosenthal suggested in his seminal article, "The Fate of Isaak Babel", in *Commentary*, February 1947. "Violence" and "peace" are both ambivalent terms: going into action with an unloaded gun is neither, surely, but a kind of pacific violence; the narrator's refusal to shoot his friend Dolgushov, thus letting him die slowly, "entrails hung over his knees", or suffer torture by the Poles, seems a very violent peacefulness indeed. Within the image of the Cossack there is a similar duality: the aloof Cossack officer riding through Babel's childhood Odessa "as though through a mountain pass", his hands in lemon-colored chamois gloves, is not the subhuman Cossack trooper Babel knew in Poland, wearing bast shoes and a derby. The category "Jew" similarly includes the narrow-chested Polish Jews, "these long bony backs, these tragic yellow beards", as well as "the stout and jovial Jews of the south, bubbling like cheap wine". Babel writes in one of his autobiographical stories, "Like all Jews I was short, weakly, and had headaches from studying". However, he simultaneously knows of "that unexpected breed of Jews, the tough fighting men, raiders, and partisans", and in his own family there is Uncle Leo who died in a brothel in Los Angeles, his grandfather who lost his pulpit for blasphemy and forgery, and a considerable number of drunkards and seducers neither short, weakly, nor studious. If Elijah Bratslavsky's virility is wasted or spent, Benya Krik's is not, and even that least likely erotic image, Benya's sister Deborah, a forty-year-old goitrous virgin, concludes her wedding festivities

> urging her fainthearted husband toward the door of their nuptial chamber, glaring at him carnivorously. Like a cat she was, that holding a mouse in her jaws tests it gently with her teeth.

The true dichotomy in Babel's writing is between culture and nature, or art and the life of action, or freedom and necessity, or any philosophic phrasing of the Darwinian conflict between life in a moral order alienated from nature and natural law, and life in a natural order antecedent to morality. Babel's true quest is not to *be* a Cossack, but to form an organic unit, a horse-man, on a horse *like* a

Cossack, instead of covering the horse's back with festering sores. In the stories of Babel's boyhood this ambition was preceded by earlier passions for keeping pigeons and learning to swim, and here the Jewish tradition of a life outside nature is the enemy. "The hydrophobia of my ancestors—Spanish rabbis and Frankfurt money-changers—dragged me to the bottom," Babel writes, and the conflict of "rabbis versus Neptune" is only resolved when "the local water god", a gentile athlete, teaches him to swim and earns his love, "the love that only a lad suffering from hysteria and headaches can feel for a real man". This is a neat enough Christian baptism, but the story ends with the boy studying nature and the names of trees and birds with the same desperate monomania (culturally inherited from Spanish rabbis and Frankfurt money-changers) with which he had previously studied Talmud and Gemara.

In one of the finest comic stories in the book, **"In the Basement"**, the young Babel tries to drown out the sound of his eccentric relatives disgracing him before a respectable school friend by reciting Antony's speech over Caesar's corpse, louder and louder. This effort to use art to deny life is inevitably doomed when the art, as the rhetoric of filial loyalty and disloyalty, only brings him closer to his problem. At the end of the story, when the boy determines to end his ruined career by drowning himself in the household water barrel, his crazy grandfather (the defrocked rabbi, the blasphemer, the forger) pulls him out and has the last word on behalf of life. "Grandson," he says, "I am going to take a dose of castor oil, so as to have something to lay on your grave."

In this complicated conflict of nature and culture, the Jews represent the heirs of all the world's culture. Babel characteristically never puts this in terms of large statements about the Judeo-Christian tradition or the inheritance of Western humanism. Instead, Gedali's junkshop contains "gilt slippers, ship's cables, an ancient compass, a stuffed eagle, a Winchester with the date 1810 engraved upon it, a broken saucepan". To the beggars of Odessa at Jewish weddings come "fat-bellied jars of Jamaica rum, oily Madeira, cigars from the plantations of Pierpont Morgan, and oranges from the environs of Jerusalem". In a Jewish shop in Odessa are "olives that had come from Greece, olive oil from Marseille, coffee in beans, Malaga from Lisbon, 'Philippe and Canot' brand sardines, and Cayenne pepper". To the inn of Lyubka "the Cossack", a Jewish procuress and smuggler, come "cigars and fine silks, cocaine and files, unbonded tobacco from the state of Virginia, and dark wine from the Island of Chios". If the world's goods also include the sacred books of "that pensioned-off God" and Guy de Maupassant, the consequent disabilities start with the inability to swim or ride, and end with what the young Babel foresees in Maupassant's tragic end: "My heart contracted as the foreboding of some essential truth touched me with light fingers".

Much of Babel's imagery aims at the deliberate shock effect of surrealism: Christ's wounds are "oozing seed, a fragrant poison to intoxicate virgins"; in the Heavenly wings there is a "dismal electrician" with a "moon-extinguisher"; the great Rabbi Motale Bratslavsky greets the narrator piously, "surrounded by the liars and possessed" . . . ; fawning officers "fished for roast chicken in the Army Commander's smiles"; the Babel house is "impregnated with the smell of leeks and Jewish destiny". Very little of the terrestrial imagery is pictorial, with the consistent exception of the Moldavanka gangsters, who look as though they were in a child's painting: they wear raspberry waistcoats, russet jackets, and azure shoes; Benya himself wears a chocolate jacket, cream pants, and raspberry boots; they all dress like "birds of paradise" and drive "lacquered carriages".

If the touch occasionally falters, and the imagery turns cute ("An orange star which had slid to the very brim of the horizon gazed wide-eyed at them"), for the most part Babel's effects are meticulously successful. Presumably the narrator of **"Guy de Maupassant"** reflects the author's concept of craft when he writes: "A phrase is born into the world both good and bad at the same time. The secret lies in a slight, an almost invisible twist. The lever should rest in your hand, getting warm, and you can only turn it once, not twice. . . . No iron can stab the heart with such force as a period put just at the right place". The story that to my taste is Babel's finest, **"The Story of My Dovecot"**, is a triumph of delicate indirection and craft. It tells the narrator's experience during the 1905 pogroms without ever using the word "pogrom" until the very last sentence, summoning up all the violence and horror of the events with two "objective correlative" images: the boy's beloved pigeon crushed against his head, so that the warm guts trickle down his face, and his granduncle Shoyl, a fish peddler, lying murdered with a live pike perch still flapping in a rip in his trousers.

The progress of the stories is the traditional tragic or ritual one from Purpose through Passion to Perception. If the boy aspired to vengeance on Shoyl's murderers and eventual despoiling of the despoilers who looted his father's store during the pogrom, *Red Cavalry* is the purgation of those purposes. Both are "Cossack" ideals eloquently achieved in the book. Matthew Pavlichenko, slapped and insulted by his master, comes back with the Red Army and stamps the *barin* to death, "trampled on him for an hour or maybe more. And in that time I got to know life through and through." Prishchepa, whose parents have been killed by the Whites and their property seized by the neighbors, comes back when the Whites have been driven out and goes around the village collecting the family belongings: "In the huts where he found gear that had belonged to his mother, a pipe that had been his father's, he left old women stabbed through and through, dogs hung above the wells, icons defiled with excrement". But Pavlichenko has in reality got to know life no better, and Prishchepa has not really restored his despoiled home but only ravaged others, and now has nothing to do but put the furniture back in the empty house, set fire to it, kill all the farm animals, and ride wildly off.

When Babel returns to Odessa after the Revolution all impulse for revenge and recovery has been burned out of him, and he aspires only to recreate the image of the events in art, to win through to perception, and, "remembering those sorrowful years, I find in them the beginning of the ills that torment me, the cause of my early fading". The narrator of the story **"The Kiss"**, quartered in the home of a Polish schoolmaster during the fighting, and recognizing by the barricaded door and the trembling of his hosts that *he* has become the image of the persecutor, spends the night sleepless, "tormented and muddled". The next morning he says to the daughter of the family, "You must know that I have a law degree, and am reckoned a highbrow", desperately flaunting the personality he has been at such pains to suppress.

If the synthesis of Jew and Cossack (as Rosenthal first pointed out) is Benya Krik the Jewish "Cossack", his ultimate failure is that his fine comic play-acting, his masterful extortion-letters, have real consequences in the murder of an innocent Jew by one of his drunken gangsters; and Babel is with the victim's employer, shouting at Benya in fury, "A fine trick you've thought up, killing live people". Lyubka Shneiveis, "the Cossack", a maternal ogress who beats up peasants with her fists, fails as a synthesis similarly (as her mother's milk fails), and the old Turk lying in her courtyard on the way back from Mecca, refusing a doctor to die in sanctity, turns out in the story to be stronger in the integrity of his principles than she is in hers. If the boy's ambition was to be like Benya and have a "Cossack" father like Benya's father Mendel, the drunken and violent drayman, and a "Cossack" mother like Lyubka, the symbolic parents he finally achieves in **"Di Grasso"**, the last story in the book, are Jews as absurd, ineffectual, and ironically "good" as his own parents. They are the impresario Nick Schwarz, with whom Babel has pawned his father's gold watch, and his wife Madam Schwarz, who is so moved by the acting of an Italian company that she makes Nick give the watch back to the boy (accompanied by "a vicious pinch"), leaving young Babel suddenly able to see the living realities of Odessa around him "as they really were: frozen in silence and ineffably beautiful".

The last sentences of Babel's stories tend to carry a great amount of weight, as though eloquence could only burst through the taut style at the very last moment. Thus **"My First Goose"**, which recounts the narrator's only personal act of violence in *Red Cavalry,* his brutal killing of the landlady's goose to ingratiate himself with his fellow soldiers, ends: "But my heart, stained with bloodshed, grated and brimmed over". In **"The Rabbi's Son"**, the dead Elijah Bratslavsky is revealed to have been an ambiguous blending of Jew and Communist, and his spilled pack reveals

> mandates of the propagandist and notebooks of the Jewish poet, the portraits of Lenin and Maimonides lay side by side, the knotted iron of Lenin's skull beside the dull silk of the portraits of Maimonides. A lock of woman's hair lay in a book, the Resolutions of the Party's Sixth Congress, and the margins of Communist leaflets were crowded with crooked lines of ancient Hebrew verse.

The story concludes: "And I, who can scarce contain the tempests of my imagination within this age-old body of mine, I was there beside my brother when he breathed his last." **"Karl-Yankel"**, the comic story of an Odessa baby after the Revolution who is hotly contested by orthodox Jewry and Communist atheism (his grandmother is on trial for having him secretly circumcised in contempt of the Revolution) concludes:

> I had grown up on these streets, and now it was Karl-Yankel's turn. But they hadn't fought for me as now they were fighting for him: few were those to whom I had been of any concern.
>
> "It's not possible," I whispered to myself, "it's not possible that you won't be happy, Karl-Yankel. It's not possible that you won't be happier than I."

Ultimately, Babel's irony overwhelms everything, and Karl-Yankel is no more satisfactory a synthesis of warring opposites than Elijah the Rabbi's son, Benya and Lyubka the Jewish Cossacks no more adequate than Jew or Cossack alone. When old Rabbi Motale had asked the narrator "What is the Jew's occupation?" the answer was "I am putting into verse the adventures of Hersch of Ostropol", when his actual occupation at the moment was writing propaganda articles for *Red Trooper*. This identification with the Jewish folk hero Herschel Ostropolier, a trickster and jester who is never what he seems to be, manages to undercut both the Rabbi's values and *Red Trooper*'s. The sleepy old defense lawyer in **"Karl-Yankel"**, covered with tobacco ash, would be, we are assured, the head of the Sanhedrin, the Jewish high council, "if the Sanhedrin existed in our days". Is this a joke at Jewish tradition, Soviet jurisprudence, the modern world, or no joke at all?

In the last analysis, Babel evades all his categories, and our own. As Trilling writes, Babel's ambiguous art "was not a dialectic that his Russia could permit", and it seems clear that by the thirties Babel's fiction was unpublishable in the Soviet Union. Yet the signs of inner collapse and regression, the failure of any synthesis or resolution to sustain his vision, are so substantial that we need not look to external censorship to explain his silence. Ultimately Babel was neither so tough as Maupassant nor so shifty as Herschel Ostropolier. Not even his age-old body could contain the tempests of his imagination, let alone any combination of nature and culture, the Jewish community or the Soviet state. In the dozen first-rate stories he left us we have short fictions to rank with any in our time, and in his brief life and work we have perhaps the cautionary tale he saw in Maupassant's, the foreboding of some essential truth.

Renato Poggioli   (essay date 1957)

SOURCE: "Isaak Babel in Retrospect," in his *The Phoenix and the Spider: A Book of Essays about Some Russian Writers and Their View of the Self,* Cambridge, Mass.: Harvard University Press, 1957, pp. 229-38.

[*Poggioli was an Italian-born American critic and translator. Much of his critical writing is concerned with Russian literature, including* The Poets of Russia: 1890-1930 *(1960), which is considered one of the most important examinations of this literary era. In the essay below, he provides a biographical and critical overview of Babel's short fiction.*]

Now, when the American reader has at his disposal the whole body of Babel's narrative writings [in *The Collected Stories of Isaac Babel*], may be the time to reassess what is probably the best work of fiction that has ever appeared in Soviet Russia, one written partly within the framework of Soviet literature and partly outside of it. The best way to proceed is perhaps to relive first its author's *curriculum vitae,* which, in the light of the historical experience in which he was actor as well as victim, is both tragic and exemplary.

Isaak Emmanuilovich Babel was born in 1894, in Odessa, of a family of small Jewish merchants. He spent his childhood in Nikolaev, where, as his stories relate, he fully experienced what the life of a Jew under tsardom was really like. From his youth he must have asked himself the question which in **"The King"** he puts in the mouth of his hero, the gangster Benya Krik: "But wasn't it a mistake on the part of God to settle the Jews in Russia, for them to be tormented worse than in Hell?" In **"The Story of My Dovecot"** he re-evokes his own early struggle and toil to be admitted into a Russian school, inaccessible to all too few Jewish boys because of the *numerus clausus;* in the same tale and in **"First Love"** he recalls the murder of his granduncle Shoyl during the pogrom of 1905, as well as the humiliation of his father, whose kneeling down before a Cossack officer did not spare his shop from a looting mob, nor himself from ruin.

The work of Babel is often autobiographical, but never pathetic, and only indirectly does it reveal the most intimate secrets of the author's psychology and personality. Yet, from the reading of his tales, we easily discover that the writer was deeply affected by a sense of alienation from the world. That sense was rooted in the three curses of his life, which were race, poverty, and his calling as an artist. Perhaps the spectacles on his nose and the books under his arm estranged him from the world at large even more than his being a pauper and a Jew. Babel shared all his life that feeling of loneliness so characteristic of the prerevolutionary intelligentsia, with its unrequited and all too mystical love for the Russian masses. At the same time, as a denizen of the ghetto, or of the worst urban slums, he deeply felt as an added curse, for both the man and the artist within himself, his inability to commune with nature, to experience within his heart and mind all the lively and lovely things that organic life creates for the joy of man.

Babel's isolation is to be seen also in his attitude toward Jewish culture itself. When his family returned to Odessa, he failed to follow the trend dominating the Jewish cultural life of that prosperous and turbulent city. While Vilna was the capital of Yiddish writing, expressing the life of the "pale" in the vernacular language, with a prosaic realism, full of self-pity and irony, Odessa was the moral center of Zionism, and had generated a school of poets returning to the messianic and prophetic traditions of old, singing of the newly promised land in the sacred and symbolic accents of the ancient tongue. Thus his city really deserved the sad praise sung for it by one of the many rabbis we meet in Babel's masterpiece: "Odessa, a god-fearing town—the star of our exile, the involuntary well of our distress. . . ." But Babel refused both Yiddish and Hebrew, and chose instead Russian, the idiom of the goyim. He did so not merely to escape from the ghetto, but to turn, through Russia, to Europe and to the West.

In those years he had discovered his masters, who were not only Tolstoy, Chekhov, and Gorki, but also Rabelais, Flaubert, and Maupassant. It was the same urge, the urge to know a broader and nobler world, that led him to settle in Petersburg toward the end of the First World War. The city was then closed to Jews not settled there, and Babel lived in the capital illegally, without means of his own, and with great hardships, in order to start a literary career. His first stories appeared in print in 1917, under the aegis of Gorki, in the review the latter was then editing, *Letopis* (The Chronicle). They had a *succès de scandale,* and got the young writer an indictment for obscenity, but the trial never took place, because of the fall of the tsarist regime. In the meantime Babel had been drafted, and the February revolution caught him while he was fighting the Germans on the Rumanian front.

Babel saw in that great upheaval the first communal experience in which he could share, the first social and historical reality of which he could finally become an active and integral part. After October, although not a party member, he served enthusiastically the new communist order in varied missions and tasks, and was finally attached, first as a civilian, and later in uniform, to the "mounted army" led by Marshal (then General) Budenny in the Polish campaign and in the Civil War. He edited for that army *Krasny Kavalerist* (*The Red Trooper*), a propaganda sheet, and fought with it on the western and southern fronts. Then, after a few years of silence, he started writing again. "It was only in 1923," he stated later, "that I learned to express my ideas clearly and at not too great length." So he wrote down his impressions of those two campaigns in the form of sketches, which, as they were published, provoked the indignant protest of Budenny, who saw in them a libel against the troops under his command. In 1924 Babel collected about thirty of those sketches in the book known as *Red Cavalry* (or rather, "The Mounted Army," as the Russian title *Konarmiva* really means), which revealed to the Russian public that a new and gifted writer had been born.

Shortly afterwards he published the slim collection *Tales of Odessa,* which, however, passed almost unnoticed. In the meantime Russian social and political reality had been rapidly changing, and Babel did not feel any longer in tune with what was going on, on other fronts as well as the literary one. He was already considered a "fellow traveler," according to the sense which that term had been given by Trotski in his book *Literature and Revolution.* It was for writers like him that, after the introduction of the new literary orthodoxy represented by the dogma of "socialist realism," Gorki coined the formula of "revolutionary romanticism," so as to justify those mild heretics who still looked back with nostalgia to the tragic and epic years of the civil war, instead of looking forward and celebrating what the regime was now building on the ruins of the past. The changed atmosphere made it difficult for Babel to write anything important or new, although he tried his hand at a novel, and wrote a rather interesting play, *Sun-*

set, dealing with the same hero and the same milieu he had already treated in the *Tales of Odessa.*

Soon after this, Babel practically ceased to write, as he confessed, rather ambiguously, in a speech he gave at the 1934 Writers' Congress. At that time he was still free to travel abroad, and he went for a while to Paris, where, as he had already tried to do in his youth, he did some writing in French. Upon his return home, his creative vein dried out, and he published nothing but an augmented and revised one-volume collection of all his short stories, which appeared in 1934. Significantly enough, several political and historical allusions, dealing with the revolutionary role of Trotski, were expunged either by the author or the censor from this text. Babel's signature appeared in print for the last time in 1937; one year later he was arrested at the peak of the purges of Trotski's followers, supposedly for no other crime than an imprudent joke about Stalin, and he was sent to a concentration camp, where he died in 1939 or 1940. According to one version, he succumbed to disease or hardships; according to another, he was shot. In either case, what spelled his doom was that revolution in which he had so desperately willed to believe, and thus he died in the same alienation in which he had lived. Whatever happened to Babel the man, we know that the writer was officially condemned to death. After his disappearance, his works were proscribed, and his name was condemned to public oblivion.

Red Cavalry, which remains Babel's masterpiece, is a book hard to describe to those who are unacquainted with it. When we read its pages, we see all the western and southern marches of Russia: Volhynia, Podolia, and the Ukraine pass fleetingly by. We ride, in a cloud of powder and dust, amidst bursts of fire, and rattling of sabers, from the flat fields of Poland to the green slopes of the Caucasus. In the distance, among the felled trees and the burned huts, we watch, as they pass before us, the men and women, old and young, who are both the victims and the spectators of our endless raid. Jews in the cities and peasants in the villages look with unseeing eyes at the horsemen and their mounts, both of Cossack blood, that are trampling on their land and their lives. Sometimes, all of a sudden, a horse gallops by without his master, whom a Polish or "White" bullet has nailed forever to the wet mother earth. Some of the riders may turn their heads to salute the lost comrade, but the mounted army will never stop or slow down its relentless race toward war and death. And while riding along, we glimpse on the open skyline the giant shadow of the Russian masses on the move, and we wonder whether their march is an ordeal or a quest.

The reader will never forget the figures who appear fleetingly in the pages of this book. We shall mention a few of them. The mounted army's chief officer, the former tsarist "noncom," Semen Budenny, who smokes and smiles while threatening to shoot anyone who yields or turns back. The youthful giant Savitski, with his legs as handsome as a girl's in his shining boots. The red general Pavlichenko, still smelling of milk as he did when he was a herdsman, who could tame buffaloes and elephants as well as goats and sheep. Konkin, the former ventriloquist,

shooting prisoners as if they were clay pigeons. The young officer Kolesnikov, who knows how to do honor to his luck when the fortunes of war raise him to an exalted command. Dyakov, who was once a circus performer, and under whose will and skill a dying nag may still perform like a thoroughbred. And Afonka Bida, with his shrill feminine voice, who weeps over his dead horse and who raids the countryside for days and nights, in order to get himself a new mount as good as the old one.

On the other side there are all the meek and the weak, the poor and the humble, whom for their mischance we shall meet on our path: Apolek, the Polish wandering artist, a heretic and a mystic, portraying peasants, publicans, and country wenches in the saintly figures he paints on the walls of a Catholic church; his German friend Gottfried, the blind musician with white mice as pets; and numberless Jews, among whom there stands out the old Gedali, the Dickensian owner of a curio shop, who is unable to distinguish between counterrevolution and revolution, because he does not know where in the latter the good ends and the evil begins, and who dreams of another, impossible International, one made only of men of good will.

Unlike Gedali, Babel seems to know where the good ends and the evil begins. For him, the revolution is good, and the counterrevolution is bad. He may hope or believe that sooner or later we shall have another International, this time made only of decent people; but he thinks that in the meanwhile we must be satisfied with the Third, and pay for both the present and the future with sweat, tears, and blood. As his hero Benya Krik will later say in the *Tales of Odessa,* in the story entitled **"The King"**: "There are people already condemned to death, and there are people who have not yet begun to live." And many must die so that others may begin to live. By bowing to what one might call either historical necessity or revolutionary expediency, Babel ends by accepting as valid and just the ordeal of war: war taking victims from both enemies and friends, from the strong as well as from the weak. Thus one of the main antinomies of this book is the everlasting conflict between the army and the militia, between the volunteer and the professional soldier, between the man for whom war is an occupation or a calling and the man for whom war is an act of either freedom or necessity. A man with a faith like Babel's will fight out of a sense of ideological duty, and thus will treat any kind of military struggle as a civil war. But for the Cossacks of the unit to which he is attached, the enemy is always an alien or a stranger, and war itself is a job. Strangely enough, the realization of this contrast stirs within the soul of Babel what one might call an inferiority complex, and he feels his own unworthiness before all those martial murderers for whom killing is a natural habit, or a simple routine. Thus he defends the slaughter and the slaughterers from those who fear and condemn them: "She cannot do without shooting . . . ," he tells Gedali, "because she is the Revolution. . . ." Without being born a killer, he not only joins the killers, but wishes and tries to become one of them, "imploring fate to grant *him* the simplest of all proficiencies—the ability to kill *his* fellow men. . . ."

It is with a sense of great humility that he accepts as fully deserved the reproach of weakness leveled at him by those who are soiling their hands while "busy shelling and getting at the kernel for *him*." And he trembles in every vein when a Cossack sees through his chicken heart, all too full of worries, especially with the concern "to live without enemies," all too empty of bravery, even of the simple courage to cut short the torments of a comrade mortally wounded, with a violent and yet merciful death. Thus, in order to gain the friendship of the Cossacks, he beheads a poor goose, and propitiates them with his offering of the slaughtered animal for their evening meal: yet, at night, after the sacrifice, his heart feels stained by the blood he has shed. Despite this, the attitude of Babel toward the Cossacks remains that of an unrequited lover, while at the same time he turns his pity toward the victims of the slaughter, whoever they are, although in the main they are Jews like him. Often he even admires the moral strength of the meek and the weak, as when he says, speaking of the Jews of Galicia and Volhynia: "Their capacity for suffering was full of a somber greatness." The very man who accepts war as the apocalypse, and revolution as the palingenesis, of history, rejects the daily crimes and commonplace misdeeds they imply: "The chronicle of our workaday offenses oppresses me without respite like an ailing heart." Babel is thus of the devil's party, and knows it. His unavowed comradeship may go not to his war companions, but to their victims, and he certainly feels misplaced among the slaughterers whom he wishes to imitate, and cannot help but admire and love. Yet, although unable to fully identify himself with the murderers, he still remains with them, even if only as an outcast.

Mr. Trilling, who has written a penetrating essay about Babel, tries to explain his inner conflict in terms of the contrast between Jew and Cossack, claiming, however, that the writer has tried to reconcile that contrast within his mind and soul: "Babel's view of the Cossack was more consonant with that of Tolstoy than with the traditional view of his own people. For him the Cossack was indeed the noble savage, all too savage, not often noble, yet having in his savagery some quality that might raise strange questions in the Jewish mind." There is some truth in this, but not the whole truth. If the conflict could be reduced only to such terms as those, then its reconciliation would be a purely literary one. Mr. Trilling is undoubtedly right in mentioning Tolstoy in connection with this book. Yet the Tolstoy who has directly influenced *Red Cavalry* is not the youthful author of *The Cossacks,* but the old and classical master of *Hadji Murad,* as we could easily prove by examining Babel's style, and by listing all the reminiscences, especially in the form of images, that the reading of that late Tolstoyan tale has left embedded in the pages of this book. The difference between *The Cossacks* and *Hadji Murad* is not merely that in the latter the Cossacks are replaced by Caucasian Tartars, but that its characters are evoked in heroic rather than in sentimental terms. While in his earlier work Tolstoy looks at Luka and at his fellow Cossacks in the idealized light of a Rousseauistic vision, in his later one he represents Hadji Murad and his followers with objective simplicity, in an epic, not nostalgic, key. It seems to us both evident and significant that Babel's imagination had been influenced by *Hadji Murad* more than by *The Cossacks:* yet from another viewpoint,

the inspiration of *Red Cavalry* is rather mixed, and this makes it nearer to *The Cossacks* than to *Hadji Murad.*

What we mean is that both *Red Cavalry* and *The Cossacks* have been written out of a dual mood, out of their authors' double allegiance to opposite attitudes and values. In the case of Babel's book, one could say that the writer has made his own the antagonism between Jew and Cossack, or, as we prefer, between the killers and the killed. In brief, there are two main strains in this work, and neither of them dominates fully its atmosphere or its structure. The first strain is epic in quality, but, despite its power, acts within the book in a fragmentary and spasmodic way, or, in literary terms, as a rhapsody. Babel's epic breath is genuine, but, as in all moderns, rather short. Thus Babel fills the intervals between warlike episodes with a pathetic strain, which is antiheroic in character. Many critics have maintained that the book is based on a contrast between epic and lyrical values. We would say, rather, that the lyrical element appears in and results from only the juxtaposition of the heroic and pathetic ones. Mr. Trilling must have guessed this when he states [in his introduction to Babel's *Collected Stories*] that even when recording "violence of the extreme kind," Babel responds to the brutality so recorded "with a kind of lyric joy." In such moments, Babel reconciles within himself the man and the artist, in a reconciliation that is truly poetic, rather than merely literary.

The supreme manifestations of such a reconciliation are to be found in those crucial images through which Babel sums up an entire episode, or closes it. Think of the vision of the newly elected brigade commander, bowing his head under the burden of his responsibility, and yet standing out against the whole horizon while marching toward either glory or death: "And suddenly on the earth stretching away far into the distance, on the furrowed, yellow nakedness of the fields, we could see nothing but Kolesnikov's narrow back, his dangling arms, and sunken, gray-capped head." Think of the scene where the Cossacks ride calmly across the plain, with no other accompaniment but the tune and the words of an ancient ballad: "The song floated away like smoke." Think finally of the vengeance of Prishchepa, who first cruelly punishes all his fellow villagers who pillaged the property of his parents, executed by the Whites, and then ends by burning down his family hut: "The fire shone as bright as Sunday."

Babel submits to this kind of poetic transfiguration only what he has once seen with his own eyes, and feels still alive in his own soul. His imagination, which is strikingly original, prefers to operate at the level where mere invention can be dispensed with. Despite this, in *Red Cavalry* or elsewhere, he never writes autobiographical pieces in the narrow sense of the term. The character using the first person singular in his tales is more of a spectator than an actor; at any rate, he is never a central figure. That character is often identical with the writer himself, and yet he is not so much a person as a point of view. The vision conveyed through his perspective is often static; what the writer tries to recapture is the tension of being, when time seems to stand still, rather than the ever changing and daily drama of man's life. Many critics misjudged this quality, and this led them to accuse Babel of a lack of psychological depth or complexity. Perhaps they failed to realize that in his chosen medium, a short story as brief as a sketch and as tight as a prose poem, there is room for sudden epiphanies, but not for searching and slowly unfolding insights. We forget all too often that while the novel can be musical, the short story is plastic and visual in essence. And Babel works like a painter, representing on a flat surface and in a small space all the massive and colorful variety of reality. Like an old painter he yields to other figures the center of the scene, while tracing his own self-portrait in one of the corners of the canvas. The immediacy of his vision seems to suggest that he always writes under the shock or impact of the event; yet at second sight we realize that he represents the event itself as if it were detached in both mood and time. In his work rage is controlled by order, and the emotion is recollected in tranquillity. This is why these tales look at first as if they were only vignettes, but this impression is immediately corrected by the sense of their perfection, of their finicky polish and finish, which justifies up to a point the Soviet critic who defined them as miniatures. Yet, although many-colored and vivid, their moral contrast is as simple and elemental as the chromatic one between white and black, and this is why they remind us, more than of anything else, of Goya's engravings about the horrors, and even the splendors, of war.

Red Cavalry is not the whole of Babel's literary heritage. The *Tales of Odessa,* although inferior to *Red Cavalry,* as well as posterior to it, could perhaps serve as a better introduction to his work. While *Red Cavalry* is epic and lyric in character, the *Tales of Odessa* are picaresque and picturesque. They do not deal with the world at large, which is the world of history, but with a narrow and peculiar milieu, the Jewish quarter of Odessa, the so-called Moldavanka, of which the author gives us the glorified annals. The main characters of this book are rogues, mainly smugglers and racketeers, and its single hero is Benya Krik, "gangster and king of gangsters," but above all a passionate man, since "passion rules the universe." One could say that this little collection is a kind of *Beggar's Opera* in fictional form, with the difference that Benya Krik is a more human, and less cruel, MacHeath. This representation of Jewish popular life, with its allusions to Jewish folklore, with weddings, funerals, and feasts, goes against the grain of Yiddish writing, since, unlike the latter, Babel treats the denizens of the ghetto as romantic heroes and as plebeian caricatures at the same time. Here pathos merges into a kind of sympathetic grotesque, producing an art which reminds us of the engravings of Hogarth, or of the prints of Callot.

If **"The Story of My Dovecot"** lies halfway between the world of *Red Cavalry* and the *Tales of Odessa,* the piece entitled **"Guy de Maupassant"** occupies a place of its own within the canon of Babel's work. Inspired perhaps by Chekhov's "Mire," this simple narrative in the first person, certainly autobiographical in character, begins by re-evoking the author's illegal stay, and his bohemian way of life, in Petersburg. To make a little money, the protagonist accepts a position helping a rich Jewish lady with no literary abilities to translate into Russian the whole of Mau-

passant. The high point of the tale is the dramatic contrast between the plush vulgarity of her person, house, and milieu, and the noble and comic naïveté of her literary ambitions. This awkward situation is handled with great irony and pity, which redeem even the sexual climax of the story, when the two co-translators consummate an embrace in the propitiatory presence of Maupassant's ghost.

No story better testifies to the maturity of Babel's talent than this one. It is therefore only fitting that it contains the whole of his *ars poetica,* so to speak, in a nutshell. The author expresses his views about style, and his ideals of writing, in two statements, which are not merely personal asides, but observations naturally and directly related to the subject matter of the story, which is the translator's (or the writer's) task. Here is the first: "A phrase is born into the world good and bad at the same time. The secret lies in a slight, almost invisible twist. The lever should rest in your hand, getting warm, and you can turn it once, not twice." And here is the second, which is a development of the first: "I began to speak of style, of the army of words, of the army in which all kinds of weapons may come into play. No iron can stab the breast with such force as a period put at the right place." Babel's sympathy for Flaubert and his school justifies Lionel Trilling's claim that at least the first of these two passages has been dictated by an obsessive concern for *le mot juste.* Yet, if we look deeper, we shall find in both passages echoes of ideas that Tolstoy developed in *What is Art?* There is in that treatise an all too neglected page, where Tolstoy says that all art is merely a matter of a "wee bit" less or of a "wee bit" more: of avoiding or omitting here and there a little something insignificant in itself, but the absence or presence of which spells success or failure. What Babel has added to this theory is a series of dynamic and material images, mechanical and military in content. Yet they suffice to change into a skillful craft, or into a cunning strategy, what Tolstoy had conceived as an intuitive process or a tentative quest. In the same manner, Babel seems also to accept the Tolstoyan theory of artistic communication as a contagion of feeling, although even here he replaces the notion of contagion with a surgical, or even murderous, metaphor. And it matters very little that Babel seems to reduce the sorcery of words to the operation of a well-placed graphic symbol, of a mere sign of punctuation, which is, however, able to pierce our mind, as well as our soul. Perhaps the miracle of his art lies in this power to touch and wound, rather than to calm and soothe, through the magic of words. If this is true, then the best epigraph for the whole of his work was given by the author himself, in the very phrase by which he tried to define Maupassant's writings in this story named after him. We certainly can repeat for Babel's tales what he said of the stories of his French master: that they are "the magnificent grave of a human heart."

Frank O'Connor   (essay date 1963)

SOURCE: "The Romanticism of Violence," in his *The Lonely Voice: A Study of the Short Story,* The World Publishing Company, 1963, pp. 187-201.

[*O'Connor was an Irish short story writer and man of letters*

Babel on his publishing silence in the 1930s:

Some readers naively make a demand: "All right, describe me." And the writer thinks: "All right, I'll give him that description and make it true and honest." But that won't do. Into a description of Ivan Ivanovich there must be injected a philosophical view, some lofty ideas. For without ideas, there can be no literature.

Respect for the reader. I am suffering from a hypertrophy of that feeling. I respect the reader so much that it makes me numb and I fall silent. And so I keep silence. (Laughter) . . .

I am not happy about my silence. Indeed, it saddens me. But perhaps this is one more proof of the attitude toward the writer in this country.

I think that, as Gorky said yesterday, Sobolev's words, "We have everything" should be written on our flag. The Party and the government have given us everything, depriving us only of one privilege—that of writing badly.

It must be said frankly, without false modesty: it is a very important privilege that has been taken away from us and we took full advantage of it. And so, Comrades, we declare at this writers' congress: Let us renounce completely that old privilege.

Isaac Babel, "Our Great Enemy—Trite Vulgarity," in his Isaac Babel: The Lonely Years, 1925-1939, *1964.*

whose fiction is known for its realistic portrayal of small-town and city life in Ireland and its detached yet sympathetic humor regarding the human condition. In the following essay, he examines what he regards as Babel's romanticization of violence, particularly in Red Cavalry.]

The two most remarkable storytellers of the First World War were Ernest Hemingway and Isaac Babel. It may be a slight inaccuracy to link Babel with the European war when his connections were mainly with the Russian Civil War, but the two wars and the two men clearly belong together.

The two men have in common what I can only describe as a romanticism of violence. Hemingway's is clear enough. He never makes the mistake of celebrating "Mercy, Pity, Peace, and Love." The only virtue he exalts is physical courage. In reading Irish or Icelandic sagas we have to be prepared to exalt it too, for, like patience and industry, it is a necessary condition of existence, but our society has so conditioned us that we tend to relegate it to policemen and sailors, and even in wartime among the troops there is no particular enthusiasm for the fighting man who is superlatively brave. He is only too likely to get his comrades into trouble.

This is what I call romanticism and Babel shares it with Hemingway. One can only assume that the romanticism goes deeper than the mere accident of finding themselves either brave or timid in the conditions of modern warfare, and that it must be rooted in childish or adolescent experiences of suffering. One who in childhood has got himself the reputation of being a coward and in later life proves his own courage will naturally be inclined to attach more significance to it than the rest of us do.

What Hemingway's experience was we don't know, but it is easy enough to imagine that Babel's must be connected with the suffering and humiliation of a Jewish boy of genius in a half-barbarous society whose language gives us the word we use to describe anti-Jewish atrocities. Isaac Babel would have been a very queer Jewish boy—and indeed, a very queer boy—if he had not often imagined himself as the avenger with the gun.

And yet this fantasy contradicts something that goes very deep in the Jewish character—an instinctive apprehension that though money is excellent and power is good, books are in some way better; a conviction of the supremacy of mind over matter, of the word over the deed. That is why when a Jew turns vicious he turns very vicious indeed, because he acquires the dual character of a criminal and a renegade. Babel's romanticism of violence draws its intensity from the conflict in himself between the Jewish intellectual and the Soviet commissar. Only by romanticizing violence could he live with it.

Babel's most famous work is ***Red Cavalry*** (1926), a book of stories that influenced me very deeply when it appeared in English. It is not his most characteristic work, nor should I now say his best. There is more of the essential Babel in ***Odessa Tales*** which appeared in 1924, and still more in the occasional stories he wrote before he was murdered by the Stalinists on the outbreak of the Second World War.

The early stories already have something of the highly formalized manner of the later ones and which bears such a strong resemblance to Hemingway's manner. Since neither could have been influenced by the other we must trace the style of both to a common source, which is certainly Flaubert. Indeed, considering Flaubert's influence on the modern short story, it would not be too much to say that he should be considered among the storytellers. The extraordinary relationship he established between the object and the style is almost unmanageable in anything so long as a novel, but again and again in the short story we see how it serves to delimit the form, establishes the beginning and the end, and heightens the intensity that is so necessary in a story but so embarrassing in a novel, where everything has to have a sort of everyday quality.

In Babel's earlier stories we see much more clearly the personal need that gave rise to them, and with it, the slight element of falsity we have to correct, unless we are prepared to make the mistake that Lionel Trilling makes in his fine introduction to the stories. Having quoted Hazlitt's remark that "we are naturally drawn to the representation of what is strong and proud and feral," Mr. Trilling replies [in his introduction to Babel's ***Collected Stories***] that "we are, rather, drawn to the representation of what is real." Outside the sagas I am not very much attracted by what is strong and proud and feral, but if I were dependent for my idea of reality on the Odessa gangsters of Babel I should be in a bad plight indeed.

Babel's gangsters are much less real than Hemingway's Chicago gangsters, for these at least have been observed at third hand through the medium of films or *True Detective* magazines ("Cardazzo, the pale-faced, soft-voiced Brooklyn kid, who killed slowly, lovingly, with carefully-spaced thrusts of the knife"), but Babel's gangsters never existed at all outside the wild imagination of a delicate, scholarly Jewish boy, who had been hunted through the streets like an old dog, and whose mind was full of pirates in gorgeous colors.

Take, for instance, the marriage of the gangster's sister, described in the Flaubertian Technicolor of *Salammbô*.

> All that is noblest in our smuggled goods, everything for which the land is famed from end to end, did, on that starry, that deep-blue night, its entrancing and disruptive work. Wines from these parts warmed stomachs, made legs faint sweetly, bemused brains, evoked belches that rang out sonorous as trumpets summoning to battle. The Negro cook from the *Plutarch,* that had put in three days before from Port Said, bore unseen through the customs fat-bellied jars of Jamaica rum, oily Madeira, cigars from the plantations of Pierpont Morgan, and oranges from the environs of Jerusalem. . . . And now the friends of the King showed what blue blood meant, and the chivalry, not yet extinct, of the Moldavanka district. On the silver trays with ineffably nonchalant movements of the hand, they cast golden coins, rings and threaded coral.

Seriously, is this what Mr. Trilling calls "real"? "With ineffably nonchalant movements of the hand"? But these gangsters are straight out of *The Beggar's Opera!* Look how Benny Krik, the gangster, writes to the unfortunate man from whom he is demanding protection money: "Highly respected Ruvim, son of Joseph! Be kind enough to place, on Saturday, under the rain barrel, etc. If you refuse, as last time you refused, know that a great disappointment awaits you in your private life. Respects from the Bentzion Krik you know of." Does anyone believe that a serious magazine like *True Detective* would even print such stuff as "real"? But there is much better than that. When one of Benny's gangsters shoots an innocent Jewish clerk during a holdup, Benny not only buries the victim in Hollywood gangster style but with equal pomp buries the murderer beside him. Then he delivers a funeral address over the two graves.

> "There are people who know how to drink vodka, and there are people who don't know how to drink vodka but drink it all the same. And the first lot, you see, get satisfaction from joy and from sorrow, and the second lot suffer for all those who drink vodka without knowing how. And so, ladies and gentlemen and dames, after we have said a prayer for our poor Joseph I will ask you to accompany to his last resting place one unknown to you but already deceased, one Savely Butsis."

Now, anyone reading that passage might be excused for believing that the original author was Damon Runyon. But perhaps Damon Runyon was also a realist? I should describe it as Jewish humor at its dotty best and Ikie Babel

as a liar of colossal genius, but please, ladies and gentlemen and dames, do not let us get our terms mixed up! Whatever it is, it is not realism.

This, of course, is not all there is to the *Odessa Tales.* There are the stories of the pogrom of 1905, and though I feel sure that Babel, being the romantic he is, has dolled them up, they are too close to what all of us know of the reality of racialism not to move me.

What does concern me about these stories is something that is more important than the question of whether we call them romantic or realistic. It is the question of what the author's personality is really like. There are two personalities in them, that of the Jewish intellectual and that of the Soviet officer, and while one seems to say one thing the other often says the opposite. I am never quite certain which of them I am dealing with—Ike Babel or Comrade Babel. "The End of Saint Hypatius" is a typical post-revolutionary Russian story as is **"You Were Too Trusting, Captain"**; so, almost to the point of caricature is **"Line and Colour,"** a contrast between the vague idealist, Kerensky, and that master of the precise phrase and the revolver, Leon Trotsky. I am not quarreling with the idea—if it is an idea—nor with its expression; I am merely wondering what degree of importance I am supposed to attach to it. Is this the expression of an attitude to human life or merely a mood such as comes over us all at times? I am confused.

I am not confused but confounded by **"With Old Man Makhno."** In this a Jewish girl is raped by six Russian soldiers in succession. She would have been raped by a seventh except that the rape went by order of seniority, and Kikin, the seventh, realized that in the process she was being raped by another Communist hero reputed to be a syphilitic and, so as not to contract the disease, preferred to nurse a grievance which he expounds to the poor child who has been violated and infected by his comrades. At this point I really want to be vulgar, whip out my notebook and pencil, and ask, "Your point, Comrade Babel, your point? Are you implying that this is a small, inevitable tragic accident such as is bound to occur with Heroes of the Revolution, or do I detect a hint that hanging—as in certain capitalist armies—might best meet the case? Am I in fact speaking to Comrade Babel or Ike Babel?" But Babel, like Hemingway, is being so infernally tough that he leaves me in doubt about a perfectly simple question as to whether I should regard him as a real writer or as a dangerous lunatic.

Of course, there is the possibility that this is a mere failure in technique, but it occurs again and again. The person I regard as the Jew and genius writes **"Karl Yankel"** and **"In the Basement,"** but in **"The S.S. Cow-Wheat"** I am apparently expected to admire the conduct of Comrade Makeyev who reluctantly executes the drunken skipper of a boat that has been commissioned to bring urgently needed wheat to the Moscow region. This gives me the same sort of thrill I experienced when Comrade Shaw described enthusiastically how Comrade Lenin enforced punctuality on stationmasters by shooting them on the spot. Unlike Comrades Shaw and Lenin, I have suffered from stationmasters, and I think I know what can happen in wartime as a result of inferior transport, but I still feel that there are better ways of keeping trains on schedule than by shooting the stationmasters. In fact, unless Russian rail systems are far superior to European ones, shooting stationmasters would be just as ineffective as flogging witches, which is what one of Turgenev's characters did when his enormous carriage refused to start. It is not only wicked; it is silly.

What does emerge from these brilliant stories is an impression of an extraordinary attractive mixed-up Jewish kid. I am happiest with the later stories which are much more overtly Jewish, like the one that describes how the inhabitants of the Old People's Home by the cemetery make a comfortable living by hiring out a coffin which is seized by the Communists. But once more it is not of Chekhov or Maupassant but of Damon Runyon that I think when I read the address of Broidin, the overseer of the Jewish Cemetery, to the old people who have lost their only means of livelihood.

> "There are people who live worse than you, and there are thousands upon thousands of people who live worse than the people who live worse than you. You are sowing unpleasantness, Arye-Leib, and you will reap wind in the belly. You will be dead men, all of you, if I turn away from you. You will die if I go my way and you yours. You, Arye-Leib, will die; . . . and you, Meyer Endless. But before you die, tell me—I am interested in the answer—have we by any chance got Soviet power or haven't we? If we haven't, and I am mistaken, then take me along to Mr. Berzon on the corner of De Ribas and Yekaterininskaya, where I worked all the years of my life as a waistcoat-maker. . . ."

This is not "strong and proud and feral" or anything else of the kind; it is plain Jewish fun, and Babel is enjoying his own ability as a liar of genius. One must keep this in mind when approaching a book of stories like **Red Cavalry.** Mr. Trilling merely shrugs his shoulders at the protests of General Budenny who, rightly or wrongly, regarded it as a libel on his troops. I am not saying that atrocities don't occur (I have seen one or two), nor am I arguing that things were not infinitely worse in countries I have not seen, like Poland and Palestine. What I am saying is that when a Jew with an uproarious imagination describes scenes of violence one should ask oneself whether he is describing what he saw or what he thought he should have seen. Some of the things Babel describes I am quite certain he never saw. My own experience of Jesuits and Jews has been moderately pleasant, but as a reader of sensational fiction I realize that my experience is nothing to depend upon, for in sensational fiction all Jesuits are intriguers who have love affairs with sinister society women and all Jews people who drink the blood of Christian children. Babel is a new experience to me, for in him I get a description of Jesuits written by a Jew.

> Bone buttons sprang beneath our fingers, icons split down the middle and opened out, revealing subterranean passages and mildewed caverns. The temple was an ancient one and full of secrets. In its glossy walls lay hidden passages, niches, doors that moved noiselessly aside.

O foolish priest, to hang the bodices of your parishioners upon the nails in the Saviour's cross! In the Holy of Holies we found a trunk with gold coins, a morocco-leather bag with banknotes, Parisian jewellers' cases filled with emerald rings.

I wish some Jesuit would write like this about the synagogue. I know of one priest who puts up quite a good show in his regular monthly tirade, but he is not a Jesuit, and he hasn't the air of imbecilic rapture which Babel adopts. But is it even necessary to be satirical about this sort of thing? Can there be a reader so guileless as not to wonder whether Babel's Jesuit churches came out of Babel's experience or his imagination?

But if the reader and I agree on where the churches came from, what are we to say about the Russian family background as it seemed to an Odessa Jew? Dad, who has turned "traitor" and joined General Deniken's army, captures a Communist detachment which includes his two sons.

> And they took us all prisoners because of that reason and my brother Theodore came to Dad's notice. And Dad began cutting him about, saying "Brute, Red cur, son of a bitch!" and all sorts of other things, and went on cutting him about until it grew dark and Theodore passed away.

Now, we all know that in civil war father is often set against son and brother against brother, and no doubt from time to time they have killed one another. (In fact, when I was a prisoner I knew a father with a son among the guards, and when the father went for a walk the son walked beside him outside the wire and muttered, "Dad, Mother says how are you?" and the father replied sourly, "Go away, you son of a whore!") I have counted up in the pages of Maxim Gorky the number of wives kicked to death by their husbands, but I should still have said that this representation of paternal love was unique, even if it had not been improved by the picture of filial devotion that ensues, for Simon, Theodore's brother, in due course captures Father.

> But Simon got Dad all right and he began to whip Dad and lined up all the fighting men in the yard according to army custom. Then Simon dashed water over Dad's beard, and asked him:
>
> "You all right, Dad, in my hands?"
>
> "No," says Dad, "not all right."
>
> Then Simon said: "And Theo, was he all right in your hands when you killed him?"
>
> "No," says Dad. "Things went badly for Theo."
>
> Then Simon asked: "And did you think, Dad, that things would go badly for you?"
>
> "No," says Dad. "I didn't think things would go badly for me."
>
> Then Simon turned to us all and said: "And what I think is that if I got caught by his boys, there wouldn't be no quarter for me. —And now, Dad, we're going to finish you off."

I do not think we should blame General Budenny too much, if, lacking an artistic training, he did not regard this as a tribute to his troops. I know a lot of officers, Irish, English, and American, who would have felt just the same.

This is not quoted to exaggerate the element of falsity in Babel's stories. He probably saw things more searing to the imagination than most of us have seen, and, anyway, he was working out an emotional problem that cannot be judged by the literal standards of General Budenny and Mr. Trilling. We can appreciate that problem in the story of how the narrator irritated his comrades by riding into battle with an empty revolver to make sure that no man's blood would be on his head. We can appreciate it even better in a story like **"The Death of Dolgushov,"** in which the narrator during a retreat finds a mortally wounded man who begs to be dispatched before the enemy can torture him, shrinks away from the terrible responsibility, and as a result is himself almost murdered by his best friend, who having killed the wounded man, says to the narrator, "You four-eyed bastards have as much pity for your comrades as a cat for a mouse."

There, certainly, speaks the Jewish idealist. Nor are all the stories in which Babel celebrates physical violence false and strained. There is nothing faked in **"The Death of Dolgushov"** nor in another fine story called **"Prishchepcha's Vengeance,"** in which a young Cossack whose parents have been killed by the Whites goes from house to house, collecting the few family possessions that have been stolen by unfeeling neighbors and killing the possessors; and then, at the end of three days sets fire to his home and rides off. That might easily be an incident in an Irish or Icelandic saga and impresses us as the terrible incidents in these do, without taking from our feeling of the common humanity we share with their authors.

But I have no such feeling about the other story I have quoted. However attracted a young Jewish intellectual may be by violence, a Jewish father who had flogged his own son to death would not, shall I say, receive an enthusiastic welcome from the community, and a son who had flogged his father to death might even be treated with a certain reserve—at least in the communities I know. I feel the story is literary and faked in the same way as I feel that the description of the Odessa gangsters and the Jesuit church is literary and faked. In his enthusiasm for Cossack violence Babel has denied his ancestry.

For me Babel is always most moving when he remembers it and writes out of the conflict in himself, when he juxtaposes the two cultures—the barbaric culture of the Communists and the humane one of the Jews—and shows them to us in antithesis.

> His things were strewn about pell-mell, mandates of the propagandist and notebooks of the Jewish poet, the portraits of Lenin and Maimonides lay side by side, the knotted iron of Lenin's skull beside the dull silk of the portraits of Maimonides. A lock of woman's hair lay in a book, the Resolutions of the Party's Sixth Congress, and the margins of Communist leaflets were crowded with crooked lines of ancient Hebrew verse. They fell upon me in a mean and depress-

ing rain—pages of the Song of Songs and revolver cartridges.

One can study the conflict best in a fine story like **"Squadron Commander Trunov,"** where the formal construction is particularly revealing. Chronologically the story tells how Trunov was killing his prisoners and was rebuked by the Jewish narrator for not obeying orders. A squadron of American planes comes overhead, and Trunov and his buddy decide to try and fight them off while the squadron escapes. Trunov is killed and is given a hero's funeral with the fierce Cossack rites, while the narrator, as though seeking comfort for his own disturbed mind, drifts into the Jewish quarter only to find the Jews there quarreling about age-old points of doctrine.

> A section of them—the Orthodox Jews—were extolling the teachings of Adassia Rabbi of Belz. For this they were being attacked by the Hasidim of moderate doctrine, the disciples of Juda Rabbi of Gussyatin. The Jews were arguing about the Cabala, making mention in their discussions of the name of Elijah, Gaon of Vilna and scourge of the Hasidim.

Then in the place where a gypsy is shoeing horses one of a group of Cossacks attacks the Jew for having beaten up the hero Trunov that morning—a story we already know to be false, but the quarrel between the dead hero and the living Jew is becoming legendary.

It is a beautiful story that expresses allusively and movingly the tragedy of the idealistic Jewish lad who has abandoned his own people with their crazy religious squabbles in hope of a better future for humanity but will never be accepted by the wild Cossack throat-slitters whom he admires. It could have been told in direct narrative and chronological order as I have summarized it; it could have been told by a flashback from the wild funeral scene to the death of Trunov and then ended with the antithesis of the Jewish squabbling. Instead, because Babel decided to follow the line of his own troubled thought, it begins with the funeral, goes on to the argument among the Jewish sectarians, and ends with the quarrel over the murder of the prisoners and the heroic death of Trunov. Only in this audacious way could Babel have expressed without propagandist harangues his own final faith in Trunov and the heroic gesture.

There was, I suspect, a lot of Benny Krik in Babel, and he, too, for much of the time seems to have believed that "passion rules the universe." Accordingly, the stories in *Red Cavalry* contain more poetry than storytelling, which may be what I think is wrong with them. Passion can never rule the universe of the storyteller; it leaves too many things unexplained.

Nowadays, I prefer the later stories, like the enchanting Odessa story I have already quoted from, **"The End of the Old Folks' Home."** This, too, presents us with the antithesis between Communists and Jews, but a certain sly humor in it makes me wonder whether Babel himself had not begun to have doubts about the superiority of the Communists. They also left many things unexplained.

It is almost as though Babel had begun to realize that the

uneasy alliance between the Jewish intellectual who went into battle with an unloaded revolver and Comrade Babel who had steeled himself to describe massacre and rape was coming to an end, and that Comrade Stalin whose purposeful prose he had so dutifully admired would soon deal with him and his kind with revolvers that were not unloaded.

Victor Terras (essay date 1966)

SOURCE: "Line and Color: The Structure of I. Babel's Short Stories in *Red Cavalry*," in *Studies in Short Fiction*, Vol. III, No. 2, Winter, 1966, pp. 141-56.

[*Terras is a Russian-born American educator and critic who specializes in Slavic languages and literature. In the essay below, he identifies those stylistic traits which establish a particular story as an artistic creation separable from the whole of Babel's work and which "make for its peculiar beauty, harmony, and completeness."*]

The stories of Babel's *Red Cavalry* have been discussed often, almost invariably as a whole rather than as individual masterpieces. With good reason, for they *are* a whole in more ways than one. The homogeneity of setting and thematics is enhanced by the presence of a constant "I," presumably Babel himself, and by cyclic elements such as recurrent characters, events, and places. Certain conflicts recur so persistently critics have thought that the whole of *Red Cavalry* can be seen as a study in contrast and paradox. For instance: the *contrast* between Babel's "lyric joy" [Lionel Trilling, introduction to Babel's *Collected Stories*] and the horrors of war which he describes; the *paradox* of a bespectacled Jewish intellectual and pacifist appearing not only as a chronicler of the exploits of Budenny's Red Cossacks, but also as their friend and companion-at-arms. Certain recurring stylistic traits, such as the frequent use of *skaz* technique or the lyric pathos which is rekindled in almost every story, add to this impression of homogeneity.

I will not dwell on these unifying traits. They have been recognized and described exceedingly well by Poggioli, Struve and, best of all, by Lionel Trilling. I will, on the contrary, try to put in relief those traits which belong to a given story as such, which establish it as an artistic creation in its own right, which make for its peculiar beauty, harmony, and completeness. Such inquiry is, I think, justified on two counts: first, the *Red Cavalry* stories originally appeared one by one, in several journals, each attracting on its own merits the attention of the public and critics alike; and second, the heterogeneous, even discordant, features of these stories are just as important as are the common and the unifying. At least I believe so and will now try to demonstrate why.

If we use Emil Staiger's existential conception of the epic, dramatic, and lyric modes of poetic creation [*Grundbegriffe der Poetick,* 1961] the main themes of the stories in *Red Cavalry* must, I think, be distributed among all three genres.

There is, first of all, the epic theme of the ride to a strange place where adventure, passion, or even death are waiting: the ride to a rendezvous with destiny. Naturally, the

theme appears in "travesty" so to say [the critic defines "travesty" as "replacing (or distorting) the form of an original without, however, changing the content"], Parsifal disguised in the ungainly uniform of a soldier of the revolution, Amfortas wearing the rags of a poor Polish Jew. In the very first tale, **"Crossing into Poland,"** the "I" rides through the intoxicating beauty of a Ukrainian summer night, arriving at the ancient Volhynian town of Novograd past midnight. The poor Jewish home where he is billeted is turned into a haunted place by the grotesque nightmares that plague him when he finally falls asleep. In the end it reveals its solemn mystery. The old man at whose side the intruder has slept is not asleep but dead, murdered by the Poles the day before. His daughter's story then shows the old man to have died the glorious death of a martyr. The ride has taken our young adventurer to a sacred place, as well as to one of horrors.

The ride to a fateful encounter is a feature of several other stories. Pavlichenko, the avenger, returns to the estate of Nikitinsky, his former landlord, to get even with the old man for the wrong he has done him years ago, when the now Red general was herding Nikitinsky's cattle. The bizarre antics of the crazed lady of the manor turn the house into a "castle of horrors." The descent to the vaults of the mansion, where Nikitinsky, trembling for his life, shows Pavlichenko all his treasures, enhances this impression. The murder of the old man, a passionate yet purposeful act, is a fitting finale.

"Prishchepa's Vengeance" is thematically close to Matthew Pavlichenko's story. A young Cossack rides home to recover the property stolen by his neighbors after the Whites killed his parents. It culminates in a nightmarish orgy of revenge, destruction, and despair.

In **"The Story of A Horse,"** a tale in a somewhat lighter vein, Commander Khlebnikov rides a hundred versts in a stretch to the legendary Savicky's haunt, to claim the white stallion he loves. This time it is the intruder who is defeated. Khlebnikov returns without his white horse, a broken man.

In **"The Road to Brody,"** Babel gives the theme of the ride a lyric treatment. The nostalgic ride through the tall cornfields of the Ukraine, under "blazing, winged skies," stops short of the dented stones of the synagogues of the sacred city. It merges with the condemned Cossack's ride to Heaven in Afonka Bida's song. And the song itself joins the ride, "trailing along like smoke."

Some other stories are focused not in the ride, but entirely in the adventure at the end of the ride. In **"The Church at Novograd"** and in **"St. Valentine's Church"** the adventurer enters the "aromatically fierce," forbidden and fascinating world of a Catholic church; in **"The Rabbi"** it is the equally exotic world of a Hasidic synagogue; in **"Gedali"** it is the strange microcosm of an old curiosity shop.

Several stories are thematically close to the mode of the legend, featuring a saint or a hero. **"Sandy the Christ"** is a *vita sancti*—in travesty, of course—both explicitly and symbolically. Sandy, the simpleminded syphilitic and singer of songs is a saint. He feels it himself; the Cossacks who call him "the Christ" know it no less than their women, who seek solace and comfort from him. And isn't Sandy's stepfather a carpenter, and Sandy his helper? That he surrenders his mother to his stepfather to get permission to hire out as a shepherd, that he sleeps with women, that he is a soldier like the other Cossacks is the "travesty" part of it.

Another *vita sancti* is the story of Pan Apolek, [**"Pan Apolek"**], God's fool, drunkard, blasphemer, and artist of genius, who is in a way Babel's double. The solemn proem sets a tone which keeps ringing over the irony of the narrative and triumphs in the clausule:

> The wise and beautiful life of Pan Apolek went to my head like an old wine. In Novograd-Volynsk, a town crumpled in a hurry by the war, amidst twisted ruins, fate threw at my feet a gospel that had lain concealed from the world. Surrounded by the simplehearted radiance of nimbi, I then made a vow to follow Pan Apolek's example. And the sweetness of meditative spite, the bitter scorn for the curs and swine of mankind, the fire of taciturn and intoxicating revenge—all this I sacrificed to my new vow.

In the stories **"The Rabbi"** and **"The Rabbi's Son,"** Elijah Bratslavsky, last scion of a proud dynasty, is saint, hero, and prince all in one. The last words we hear from him are, "I got to Kovel . . . The kulaks opened the front to the enemy. I took command of a scratch regiment, but too late . . . I hadn't enough artillery. . . ."

The gentle poet, with the body of a boy and the wan face of a nun, was also a born leader of men. But the travesty is present even here: we meet the prince not only in defeat and despair, but also in shame and degradation. Babel shows some other heroes in more conventional epic situations of the human condition: victory or heroic death in battle. **"The Brigade Commander"** is a bright picture of ambition, strength, and triumph. The bowlegged peasant boy Kolesnikov is awkward and nervous before Budenny, but not so when he faces his brigade, much less the enemy. Budenny, the Cossacks, and the narrator himself, all watch the young man's first, victorious command performance with obvious pleasure. This is a Homeric episode—in travesty, for Kolesnikov, a fine soldier who fights "for glory," as befits the true hero, who after his victory displays "the masterful indifference of a Tartar Khan," is externally a drab and even a ridiculous figure!

Another Homeric episode in travesty can be found in **"Konkin's Prisoner."** The cocky Red hero, thrice Knight of the Order of the Red Banner, tells without boasting, "in his customary farcical manner," how eight well-armed Polish horsemen are easy game for two battleweary Cossacks, one of whom has been badly wounded earlier in the day. An elderly Polish general is cornered after putting up a brave fight. The old man's love of life gets the better of his honor and he is inclined to hand over his sword. Much as in similar Homeric scenes, the balance, after a good deal of suspense, tilts toward Hades: the general is done in by his captors after all.

"Chesniki" could have been called "Before the Battle," had not the following story been **"After the Battle."** We see at first Red cavalry getting ready for one of its headlong charges. The demigods Voroshilov and Budenny are personally directing operations. Then, much as it would in the Iliad, the scene shifts to an idyllic microcosm. Sasha, the Red amazon, is secretly getting her mare covered by the Commander's prize stallion. The beginning of the following story then brings one of the most stirring battle scenes in all Russian literature: the unforgettable cavalry charge of Chesniki.

In **"Squadron Commander Trunov"** the glory of a heroic death is only slightly dimmed by the usual travesty. The slaughter of the prisoners by the doomed Trunov acquires a mythic meaning if we perceive them as the sacrificial victims that accompany the epic hero in death. The very futility of Trunov's death has a certain grandeur about it. The American planes of Major Fauntleroy's air squadron, which kill swiftly, efficiently, and inexorably, are like intruders from another, superior world. Trunov challenges them, and dies like an epic hero who has challenged the gods. But the petty, squalid details of the setting disguise the main theme, enough for us to take the heroic epic poem for a naturalistic war sketch.

The elements of travesty are stronger in **"The Widow,"** the story of the death of Commander Sheveliov. He dies, to his last breath a hero and a leader, against a background of revolting animal life. Who would recognize the rivalry for the arms of the slain Achilles in the squabble for the dead hero's earthly belongings? But if we take an unprejudiced look at the theme of this story, and at those of the other "epic" stories in *Red Cavalry,* we see that they are in fact the common themes of the heroic epos of all times. It is most important to note that this is not merely a self-evident concomitant of the fact that Babel is writing about war and that his heroes are soldiers. The point is that the *sujets* of these stories reflect a vision of the human condition which is characteristic of a heroic worldview, of a heroic society.

A good many of the stories in *Red Cavalry* feature a dramatic rather than an epic theme, *e. g.,* a conflict based on social tensions. It is to this type of story that many of the interesting things said about Babel do particularly apply. It is mostly in these dramatic stories that Babel's ironies and ambiguities are in evidence: dramatic pathos thrives on such tensions, not epic ethos.

The easiest recognized of these tensions is that between the intellectual, usually represented by Babel's "I," and the Cossack. It may develop along many different vectors: the natural pacifist clashing with the man for whom killing, nay murder, is a business; the abjectness of the thinking man faced with a situation which calls for outright, courageous action—such as putting a bullet through a dying soldier's head to save him from being abused by the approaching enemy; the battle between the subtle irony of "specs," the commissar, and the unsuspecting good humor and exuberant physical vigor of the Cossacks and their handsome giant of commander, a battle which both parties win and lose: the bespectacled lawschool graduate cannot help becoming enamored of Savicky's imposing physique and reckless élan, also, for all his outward bravado, he knows all too well that he will always remain but a sorry killer—even of geese; the Cossacks couldn't ever, like their commissar, spy out the secret curve of Lenin's line, they naively see only what the learned man wants them to see as he reads the Leader's latest speech to them. And, the semiliterate Savicky, for all his manly charm, cuts a fairly ridiculous figure as a writer of military prose.

The most dramatic of all the stories in **Red Cavalry** is perhaps **"Argamak."** The world of **Red Cavalry** is a horseman's world in which the "I" must needs play the role of an intruder. In **"Argamak"** the intruder becomes doubly odious when given the Cossack Tikhomolov's mount Argamak. Also, while this is never made explicit, the man who is ruining Tikhomolov's glorious stallion is obviously a man of some authority, *viz.*, a political commissar. The tensions developing from this situation are many: Tikhomolov, the disgraced Cossack, fights to recover the horse that must be as dear to him as his life. He finally succeeds, by a feat of extraordinary bravery. The "I" struggles to gain the friendship of the Cossacks—in vain. He also struggles to conquer Argamak, who hates his involuntary tormentor no less than does Tikhomolov. There is also a conflict, hidden and subtle, between "line" and "color." Baulin, the squadron leader, is a genuine bolshevik: "The path of his life had been laid down, and he had no doubts as to the correctness of this path." Only the *line* matters to Baulin; passion, suffering, beauty are irrelevant. The pathetic story of Argamak is to him a routine disciplinary matter. The emotional, ethical, and aesthetical (yes, for isn't it a crime against beauty to give a great horse to a miserable horseman?) angles do not exist for him; they nearly kill the sensitive Babel.

The conflict between "line" and "color," which erupts openly and with great acerbity in such later stories as the one which actually bears the title **"Line and Color,"** or **"Froim Grach,"** can be recognized in some **Red Cavalry** stories as well. The story **"Evening"** shows it quite clearly. Galin, the walleyed communist fanatic, is absolutely confident of the victory of his party, whose line is likened to a pair of railroad tracks. It is Galin who utters the following prophetic words:

> You're a driveler, and we are fated to have to put
> up with you drivelers. We're busy shelling and
> getting at the kernel for you. Not long will pass
> and then you'll see that cleaned kernel, and take
> your fingers out of your nose and sing of the new
> life in no ordinary prose. In the meantime sit
> still, you driveler, and stop whimpering around
> us. . . .

Line will win over color. There is little consolation in the circumstance that Galin pays a price for his victory: he loses the contest for the graces of Irina, the laundress. Having sleepily listened to his tirades, she goes off to bed with Vasily, the cook.

Babel's dramatism depends on tensions between men, classes, nationalities, not on a man's inner conflicts. Dostoyevskian complexities or the isolation of the Chekhovian dramatic hero will not easily be found in **Red Cavalry.** Babel's drama is that of head-on clash. Hostility or loneliness, much rather than alienation or solipsism, trouble the Babelian hero.

Struve has pointed out, very shrewdly I think, that there

is something romantically conventional about most of Babel's characters [Gleb Struve, *Soviet Russian Literature,* 1951]. They do what we expect them to do. Almost invariably we meet them in moments of high crisis and so only see the highlights of their roles, so to speak. In other words, the Babelian character is devised to dramatize one of the tensions inherent in the world of **Red Cavalry.** We are shown the tension, not the whole man.

It is in its dramatic capacity that the Babelian short story takes on some traits of social satire. Such is the case in **"Salt,"** one of Babel's most famous stories, which dramatizes the unholy union between tough revolutionary phraseology and the self-righteous brutality of the semiliterate. Another such story is **"A Letter,"** with the eternal theme of father and sons fighting on different sides. The element of travesty is particularly strong in the latter story, so strong it almost turns it into a satirical allegory. The tragic pathos of fratricidal civil war is dragged through the mud of the narrator's low mentality and dulled by the brutish callousness of the principals of the drama. The heroic combat of Hildebrand and Hadubrand is replaced by two sadistic executions.

Several of the stories not mentioned so far display a strong affinity to a modern genre which for want of a better term I shall call "the nightmare": a piece the mode of perception and structure of which resemble an oppressive dream. **"Italian Sunshine"** is a good example. Its hero, Sidorov, obviously is an executioner of the Cheka who is on the verge of "cracking up" (or has he already crossed the threshold?). He dreams of being sent to Italy to organize the assassination of King Victor Emmanuel, but would, if worse came to worst, accept an assignment with the Odessa Cheka. The ravings of Sidorov, the "melancholy murderer," are set against a background of the "I's" own, almost somnambulant stream-of-consciousness.

"Zamoste" is another dreamlike piece, shreds from the stream-of-consciousness of a desperately tired man, alternating with dream scenes. The violent clashes in **"After the Battle"** are experienced as if in a trance: important details remain untold, the sequence of events is sharply discontinuous.

There are a few stories that are rather easily recognized as "poems in prose," thus belonging to the lyric genre. Such are **"The Cemetery at Kozin," "The Road to Brody,"** and **"The Song."** The lyric mode also prevails in **"Gedali"** and in **"Berestechko."** The remaining pieces can be classified as *feuilletons.* There are not too many of them: **"Discourse on the Tachanka," "The Remount Officer," "The Story of A Horse, Continued,"** and **"Treason."**

We see, then, that, while the setting and characters of **Red Cavalry** are quite uniform indeed, the structural-aesthetic thematics of these stories are extremely varied. The same Cossacks and Jews, soldiers and civilians, insensitive brutes and subtle dreamers appear in situations the aesthetic and emotive mode of which may be either epic or dramatic, heroic or satirical, sublime or comical, serious or frivolous. Such heterogeneity does not *per se* suggest that the stories of **Red Cavalry** do not follow the traditional canon of the classical *novella.* We know that it is in the structure rather than in the *sujet* that we find the distinctive traits of this well-defined genre. So let us ask: Do we find in Babel's stories the straight line of action, the limited but compact space, the dramatically coiled spring of time, all of which are characteristic of the *novella* from Boccaccio to Guy de Maupassant?

I believe that the stories written entirely, or almost entirely in *skaz* must be set aside as a separate structural type. Style is here the principal integrating factor. The author's determination to create a credible semblance of uneducated narrative is binding not only stylistically but also structurally. And so Kurdiukov's letter to his mother, Balmashev's letter to the editor of the *Red Trooper,* or the complaint of the three hospitalized Cossacks in **"Treason"** ramble along, mixing the relevant with the irrelevant, the serious with the comical, the touchingly sincere and poignantly true with the stupidly affected, brazenly phony rhetoric of the semiliterate.

The uneducated or semiliterate narrator finds it difficult to get to the point of his tale as he wades through a morass of irrelevant trivialities; and when he does get there finally, it is awkwardly off balance, and as if by accident. The murders in **"Salt"** and in **"A Letter"** seem just to happen, anticlimactically almost; and in **"Treason"** we discover, late in the story and among other things, that one of the three principals died four days after the incident described by his buddy. The entire narrative in these stories is characterized by what one might call "wrong accents"—stylistically, structurally, and emotionally.

While the stylized stories are among the best remembered, they do not, I believe, represent Babel's art at its loftiest. I think that Babel's claim to immortality rests entirely with those stories which reveal the stream-of-consciousness of a cultured, sophisticated, aesthetically and emotionally sensitive young man—young even though there may be "autumn in his heart."

Clearly, plot in the conventional sense (the Russian *fabula*) is not what gives unity to most of Babel's stories. In fact, the tales in which plot seems to play its customary role are mostly those written in *skaz* and, in my opinion, the least ambitious artistically. In many of the other stories we observe a curious phenomenon: what would have to be the plot of the story is condensed into a brief scene, or even into a single phrase, and made a distinct, concrete part of the narrative. Figuratively speaking, the plot is then a single figure on the face of a rug, not a pattern woven into the whole rug.

The martyr's death of the old Jew in **"Crossing into Poland"** is told in a few lines at the very end of the story. In **"The Rabbi's Son"** the story of Elijah's heroic stand and tragic failure appears as if in parenthesis. In **"The Rabbi"** the fascinating image of the last prince of the dynasty remains in the background and the story of his rebellion, glory and tragic end is only hinted at, even though Elijah is the hero of that tale also.

In **"The Church at Novograd"** the story of Pan Romuald's treason and death flashes by in a subordinate clause. In **"Italian Sunshine"** the mad, sordid career of Sidorov, the ex-anarchist and now Chekist, emerges from the chaos of

the second page of his letter; his roommate, who tells the story, dared not look for the beginning.

Some stories are veritable mosaics of intriguing, dynamic themes, each of which would be good for a fine short story. In the difficult-to-analyze story **"Berestechko,"** for instance, there are introduced, in order: an old Ukrainian with a bandore, singing of the ancient glory of the Cossacks; the murder of an old Jew, accused of spying; mad ninety-year-old Countess Raciborska, who would beat her son with a coachman's whip because he had given the dying line no heir; the echo of a story of love and separation in the fragment of a French letter, dated "Berestechko, 1820."

While Babel seems to be scornful of plot in the conventional sense, the clausule (Russian *kontsovka*) of the classical *novella* is very much in evidence throughout. However, much as with the plot, what looks like the "clausule" is sometimes a separate entity, independent of the rest of the story.

It may come in the form of an elegant conclusion of the plot, as for instance in **"Argamak," "Konkin's Prisoner,"** or **"Afonka Bida."** It may come as a lyric recapitulation of the subjective, emotional mood of the story, as in **"Gedali," "My First Goose,"** or **"After the Battle."** As a rhetorical peroration, as in **"The Rabbi's Son," "Berestechko,"** or **"The Cemetery at Kozin."** As a brief, poignant gnome, as in **"The Church of Novograd," "Story of A Horse,"** or **"The Life and Adventures of Matthew Pavlichenko."**

In many instances we see a definite rondo pattern (Russian *kol'tso*): the clausule returns to the proem, as for instance in **"Squadron Commander Trunov," "Evening," "Pan Apolek,"** or **"Gedali."**

Clearly, there couldn't be any greater variety. The same can be said of the exposition. A terse, matter-of-fact statement in the style of a military communiqué is the usual introduction ("Our division took Berestechko last night. . . ."). But this is deceptive. What follows is more often than not a colorful image—a landscape, a portrait, or a *nature morte*. Besides, Babel has many other ways to start a story: with a rhetorical proem (**"The Rabbi's Son," "Pan Apolek," "Evening"**), with a dialogue (**"The Rabbi"**), by taking the reader *in medias res* with a narrative passage (**"The Death of Dolgushov"**), or by raising the curtain with a description (**"My First Goose"**).

Really nowhere—with the exception of the *skaz*-type stories—do we have anything resembling conventional epic narrative. There are but few dialogues of any length. What we have is a kaleidoscopic sequence of descriptions of town and country; goyaesque scenes of violence and suffering; brief, racy dialogues (always "stylized"!); stream-of-consciousness-type passages; dreams and nightmares; rhetorical passages ringing with emotion; gnomes and *bons mots*; anecdotes, biographies, legends compressed into a single paragraph; scraps of "confessions"; a torrent of similes and metaphors which often enough are motives in their own right. Here, for example, is a breakdown into motives for **"Crossing into Poland"**:

An introductory line in the tone of a military communiqué. Then, as early as in the second sentence, "color" joins "line" in the form of first an adjective (the rearguard of the advancing army is called "clamorous"), then an adjective phrase which is a story all in itself (" . . . over the highroad from Brest to Warsaw built by Nicholas I upon the bones of peasants.") Half a page of elaborate landscape painting follows. Towards the end of this description the movements and noises of the army marching through the peaceful countryside take over. The connecting phrase "Far on in the night we reached Novograd" opens up a very different picture, the *intérieur* of a poor Jewish home, with its silent, puppet-like occupants.

At this point, the first dialogue line: "Clean this up," I said to the woman. "What a filthy way to live!" The Jews silently clean up and make the unwanted visitor's bed: a brief, but oppressive, nightmarish description.

After the connecting phrase "Silence overcame all," another lyric nature image (of the moon). Then another connecting phrase and a vivid, dramatic, grotesque nightmare dreamt by the "I." It is disrupted, finally, by the phrase " . . . and here I woke up, for the pregnant woman was groping over my face with her fingers."

Here then comes the first significant dialogue line which, flash-like, brings the woman to life: "Good sir," she said, "you're calling out in your sleep and you're tossing to and fro. I'll make you a bed in another corner, for you're pushing my father about." And now the ghastly revelation, in curt, dispassionate words, that the intruder had been pushing about a man whose throat "had been torn out and his face cleft in two."

Finally, the Jewess tells the story of her father's death. The narrator inserts an observation on the intonation of her voice. The woman's last words, which conclude the story, form a rhetorical question, uttered "with sudden and terrible violence": "I want to know where on earth you could find another father like my father?"

The story is quite typical of **Red Cavalry.** In longer stories we have, of course, even more different motives. The question arises: how are these many different motives, which are often quite heterogeneous in more than one respect, put together to form the marvelously integrated organism of the Babelian short story? This question is all the more legitimate as Babel himself is reported, by a reliable source [Paustovsky], to have seen his creations as assemblages of motives, integrated by painstaking craftsmanship:

> When I write down the first version of a story, the manuscript looks disgusting, simply horrible! It's an aggregate of more or less successful bits, joined together by the dreariest connecting links, so called "bridges," a kind of dirty ropes [. . .] This is where my work begins. I check sentence after sentence, and not once, but many times. First of all I throw out the superfluous words from each sentence [. . .] And so I go on, retyping the text each time, until I get to the point where, despite the most savage captiousness, I couldn't find a speck of dirt in the manuscript.

This gives us a valuable hint: we may view Babel's stories as compositions rather than as narrative prose in the conventional sense. As far as their genesis is concerned, they are closer to the lyric poem than to the epic narrative. A Babelian short story owes its completeness and unity to composition, more than to an inherent thematic or structural principle (such as plot, adherence to the established rules of a specific genre, or a dominating character).

Some recurring structural devices of Babel's stories resemble lyric more than epic or dramatic technique. The importance as well as the various specific types of the clausule are a trait which the *novella* shares with the lyric poem, and so is the rondo form found so often in Babel's stories. However, more often than not the proem, or the clausule, or both, are distinctly lyrical, particularly when they consist of an image or of a rhetorical ejaculation, which is often. It is also my impression that the frequent recurrence of a motive (usually an image) in the same story resembles a lyrical refrain as much as it does the "falcon" of the classical *novella.* I am thinking here of such items as the blood trickling through the bandage wrapped around Trunov's head, the shepherd-saint motive in **"Sandy the Christ,"** or the blinking of Galin's walleye.

Babel's is a static space, filled with vivid, sensuous images. Savicky's gigantic frame cleaves the hut "as a standard cleaves the sky." Afonka Bida comes galloping "framed in the nimbus of the sunset." Kolesnikov walks to glory "Bathed in the crimson haze of a sunset that seemed as unreal as oncoming death." A comparison of Babel's space to that in the paintings of the young Chagall has been rightly suggested. The space of both artists is color without a boundary, none even between heaven and earth. In this continuum of color there float images—some beautiful, some sordid; some delicately ethereal, some coarsely naturalistic; images of the peasants and Jews of Red Russia, their little towns, their huts, their horses and their cattle; and the moon in the most incredible, yet so real shades of color.

For the poet, "color" is of course a somewhat broader concept than for the painter, although in Babel's case the literal (rather than metaphoric) meaning of that word applies often enough. "Color" is the enchanting moonlit night into which are cast "dreams leaping about like kittens," "a satin-clad Romeo singing of love," Sidorov's mad letter under a flickering candle, a squabbling Jewish couple, a melancholy murderer's dream of Italian sunshine. "Color" is the fiery sunset over peaceful Ukrainian cornfields in **"Crossing into Poland," "The Death of Dolgushov," "The Brigade Commander,"** and **"The Road to Brody."** "Color" is the "burning brilliance of the skies" over "blue dust and Galician mournfulness" in **"Squadron Commander Trunov."** "Color" is the melancholy Sabbath eve atmosphere in **"Gedali"** and **"The Rabbi."**

The arrangement of images, shreds of dialogue, scraps of confession and stream-of-consciousness, rhetorical passages and aphorisms in this space of color likewise resembles the composition of Chagall's paintings. Time in **Red Cavalry** is not time as we know it from the classical *novella,* or even from the Chekhovian short story. It may be the leisurely change of evening to night, or of night to morning. It may be the unnoticed flow of the "I's" stream-of-consciousness, often quite timeless like a dream. Never is it the sharply felt time of anticipation or of regret. When there is action, time seems to be standing still. The cavalry charge of Chesniki is for us the static image of a "deathlike wall of black uniforms and pale faces" and Captain Yakovlev awaiting the charge with unsheathed saber, a gold tooth gleaming in his mouth and his black beard lying on his chest "like an icon on a dead man."

Not that the Babelian short story has not got line. What it hasn't got is a line typical of it, as the curve is of the Chekhovian short story. In *Red Cavalry* a good deal seems to depend on the theme of each story. In the more "epic" stories the initial bold sweep of the line that one sees in the opening paragraph of so many stories does not altogether dissolve into color, but continues, sometimes firm and clear, sometimes a mere hazy outline, straight to the climax of the story. Such are the stories featuring the epic ride to a rendezvous with destiny.

The stories of the life and death of a hero, or of a saint, tend to follow the rondo form. The substance of the "legend" is revealed in the solemn proem, the story itself then brings various vivid details, not necessarily in chronological order, and the conclusion is another encomium, echoing the mood, or even the image of the proem. Such is the pattern of **"Pan Apolek," "Squadron Commander Trunov,"** or **"Sandy the Christ."**

As to the dramatic tales, they all share the permanent un-

Caricature of Boris Efimov, based on Babel's story "My First Goose."

resolvedness of their conflicts. The tension between Cossack and bespectacled Commissar that is felt at the very beginning of **"My First Goose"** or **"After the Battle"** is only heightened by the several clashes that make up the plot of the story. The conclusion underscores, in each case, that the rift is irremediable. In this may lie the completeness of the story.

The ironies and ambiguities of Babel's art do not, I believe, create a "curve." The irony, if present, is constant and almost immediately obvious, so in the *skaz*-type stories, where the stylistic contrast between Babel's introductory words and the following skaz creates tension immediately. Neither does the mask of Babelian travesty deceive us: we soon recognize heroes and saints, leaders and martyrs, good men and murderers, in spite of their disguise.

A few times an ambiguity does seem to make for a structural break. In **"Gedali"** one has the feeling that the narrator is presenting to us a historical relic, a glimpse of the vanishing past, for which reason has but little regret, in spite of heart's nostalgia. Then suddenly this line: "She cannot do without shooting, Gedali, because she is the Revolution." This changes the mood of the story and introduces the ambiguity. With the brash young revolutionary having nothing better to offer to refute Gedali's simple philosophy, the old man's naiveté becomes wisdom.

In **"The Rabbi"** the atmosphere suddenly changes when, among the possessed, the liars, and the idlers, we perceive suddenly "a youth with the face of Spinoza, with Spinoza's powerful brow and the wan face of a nun." A little later the Rabbi chants: "Blessed is the Lord God of Israel Who hath chosen us from amongst all the nations of the earth." This would have been pure irony with Cossack horses neighing under the windows of the synagogue—but for the presence of the chosen youth, the prince. In **"The Rabbi's Son"** the break comes when we hear, to our intense gratification, that Elijah had proven himself a prince not only in spirit but in action as well. Yet this kind of structural break effected through the introduction of an ambiguity is not really typical of the stories of *Red Cavalry*.

So much, then, for "line." We know from Babel's diary that virtually every detail of *Red Cavalry* is based on actual observations. Babel said himself that he lacked "fantasy." The secret of his art, he said, lay in the way he reassembled the sundry scraps of a reality which was not in itself poetic. There are those who say it is essentially "style" that keeps Babel's stories together. This may be too simple an answer. I think that it is really composition, the details of which are different for every single story and practically for every single juncture.

I have already discussed "line." There are a few stories in which suspense is a factor. Will Ivan Akinifiev kill the Deacon, or won't he? Ironically, the story breaks off before the suspense is lifted. Will Konkin kill his prisoner? He does—as an afterthought, so to speak. But much more often suspense is momentary, a distinct, particulate entity—like images, gnomes, and rhetorical tirades. It comes and it goes, for instance, in **"The Death of Dolgushov"** or **"After the Battle,"** where for a moment Liutov's life hangs in the balance.

By and large Babel's stories are examples of ideological disinterestedness. But a few times it seems there is an epiphany which casts light upon the whole story. In **"Sandy the Christ,"** I think that the following passage is pivotal:

> "For the love of God, let me go, Tarakanych,"
> Sandy begged once more.
>
> "All the saints used to be shepherds."
>
> "Sandy the Saint!" guffawed the stepfather.
> "Caught syphilis from the Mother of God."

It is this brief dialogue that establishes Sandy as a saint in travesty. It is not difficult to detect allegory in this, and in a few other stories. But, I daresay that, once again, the allegory is a distinct motive rather than an element underlying the structure of the whole story.

There are a few lyric pieces in which lyric parallelism is the significant structural pattern (**"The Road to Brody,"** **"The Cemetery at Kozin"**), and one or two where contrast seems to act as the structural pivot. In **"The Song"** the squalor of poverty is set opposite the beauty of a song. In **"Berestechko"** the reeking Jewish ghetto stands opposite a genteel French letter, and a communist party meeting takes place at the foot of the castle of Count Raciborski.

Yet by and large, and surely in most of the stories in **Red Cavalry,** the composition must be accounted for motive by motive, transition by transition. Such great stories as **"Pan Apolek"** or **"The Rabbi's Son"** are original compositions which cannot be reduced to any particular pattern, or even to any particular genre.

The Babelian short story at its best seems to realize that poetic balance between thought and image, line and color, movement and structure in a way which is characteristic of great lyric poetry. The emphasis is on image, color, and structure, rather than on thought, line, and movement. Ehrenburg is quite right when he calls Babel a poet. Such non-lyrical ingredients as philosophical abstraction, plot, irony, and rhetoric are transformed by him into concrete verbal units, small and light enough to float about in Babel's space of color. Babel also displays a healthy dose of that Goethean "narrowness, enamored of reality," which is proper to the true lyric poet. In many respects Babel's art in **Red Cavalry** resembles that of the acmeist-imaginist school of lyric poetry, in particular that of the great acmeist poet Osip Mandelstamm.

Louis H. Leiter   (essay date 1966)

SOURCE: "A Reading of Isaac Babel's 'Crossing into Poland'," in *Studies in Short Fiction,* Vol. III, No. 2, Winter, 1966, pp. 199-206.

[*Leiter is an American educator and critic. In the essay below, he identifies Babel's technique in "Crossing into Poland" as based on language patterns that create dramatic effects.*]

Isaac Babel's **"Crossing into Poland"** is a tightly wrought story, somewhat non-committal on the surface, yet emotionally charged, startling in its use of metaphorical language, shocking in its violence, and puzzling in its apparent inconclusiveness. Of plot there is almost nothing: the narrator-soldier comments on his army's pursuit of the enemy into Poland, observes the buckwheat fields and the dark river that the soldiers must cross, arrives at a plundered house whose pathetic inhabitants he commands to clean up its filth, falls asleep, has a terrible dream, and is awakened by a pregnant woman who tells him that in his sleep he is kicking her father who has been brutally killed by the retreating enemy. Yet a close reading of this brief story, with particular attention to Babel's technique, will reveal a very conclusive structure: one built on language patterns manipulated with great care, and achieving effects as dramatic and significant as the plot is bare.

There are three of these patterns in all, and each one may be seen as an extension of the symbolic movement epitomized in the title—"crossing," or moving, into new country, a new world. In the first pattern, the words making up the connotative sequence dramatize the deepening defilement of the soldier as he pursues the enemy, as he moves further into the horror of war. The second pattern offers a contrast with the first: the narrator-soldier's unconscious but gradually urgent need for purification. Pattern three is a set of oblique references to a redemptive mythology that circumscribes, resolves, and transforms the other two patterns into a new awareness for the narrator and the reader. Together these word sequences—or patterns, or techniques—interact much as do thesis (symbolic movement toward defilement), antithesis (profound growth of an urgent desire for purification), and synthesis (transformation and illumination through traditional, though hidden, religious values). The interaction itself is thus part of the movement into Poland, as much a crossing as is the actual physical one performed by the army, the soldier, the war.

War is the immediate medium for the first pattern: it is war that drives the narrator and his army into a new country. With their progress into Poland, Babel delineates the very shape of defilement, and at the center of this shape stands the narrator, whose monologue reveals his progressive brutalization in an increasingly dirty war. Nor is defilement limited to the present. By having the narrator remember the advance of the "Noisy rearguard over the high-road from Brest to Warsaw built by Nicholas I upon the bones of peasants," Babel fuses present involvement with an awareness of past brutality and a suspension of humane concern. The present stamps itself upon the narrator's awareness—"Novgorod-Volynsk was taken at dawn today"—while the casual observations of external nature suggest a simultaneous emotional dislocation that is continuous, passing forward into the present like a stream: "The orange sun rolled down the sky like a lopped off head . . . the smell of yesterday's blood, of slaughtered horses" taints the evening and stains the narrator who gradually becomes a familiar of the defiling powers, until they erupt into violence in his dark nightmare.

Consonant with the symbolic movement of blackness encroaching on physical nature and deepening twilight spreading over the narrator's spirit (seen in the dislocation of the light of the sun, the spreading chaos of the coming night) is "the blackened Zbruch which roared, twisting it-self into foamy knots at the falls." Falling sun and water are caught up in the torrent which "gurgled among hundreds of horses' legs," looping man, animal, and organic nature into a tight knot of reciprocal involvement in the dark night of the army's progress. As though night were now a stain rushing over the light of day, the narrator watches the conquering darkness cover the face of the deep: "the river was dotted with square, black patches of the wagons, and was full of confused sounds. . . ." He sees the effects of these unholy times upon the men as "somebody sank [in the river], loudly defaming the Mother of God." The sacrilege flows almost indistinguishably into physical and human nature, joining dropping sun, falling water, and sinking man.

Billeted at night in the home of the plundered Jews, the narrator observes other forms of pollution and chaos: "turned-out wardrobes, scraps of woman's fur coats on the floor," and fragments of crockery. Although he was almost an automaton during the rush into Poland, he now rises in passion over the sight of the greater defilement of "human-filth," and a "disemboweled" mattress upon which he will lie down to sleep. Torn by war and gradually stained by the ubiquitous blackness of deepening chaos, the soldier turns on the inhabitants of the rifled house and forces the pregnant Jewess to clean the room, while his own contaminated mind transforms the Jews into "men skipping about noiselessly, monkey fashion, like Japs in a circus act, their necks swelling and twisting." The incongruity of the simile signals the narrator's own mental distortions, his own torn emotions so that he sees projected in the movements of the Jews his own grotesque involvement in the pursuit of the enemy into Poland.

His emotionally charged nightmare in the dark night on the disemboweled bed focuses the chaos of war, destruction, and movement toward human filth into a symbolic drama, which re-enacts the contamination of his spirit:

> And in my sleep the Commander of the VI Division appeared to me; he was pursuing the Brigade Commander on a heavy stallion, fired at him twice between the eyes. The bullets pierced the Brigade Commander's head, and both his eyes dropped to the ground. "Why did you turn back the brigade?" shouted Savitsky, the Divisional Commander, to the wounded man. . . .

The pursuit on the "heavy stallion" of the Divisional Commander embodies the rapid encroachment (again, *movement*) of violence and re-focuses the smell of slaughtered horses, the chaos of horses' legs in the black river into an animal form of the narrator's brutalized spirit. The animal's frantic galloping symbolizes the narrator's pursuit of the enemy into Poland, his involvement in the slaughter of human beings, and his earlier memory of the "bones of peasants" who died that the highroad might move forward. The stallion galloping through his mind releases his own numbed legs for further violence when the narrator lashes out at the sleeping Jew. The Divisional Commander himself assumes the form of those inexorable forces behind the order to cross over into Poland. His brutal shouts to his victim echo the tone of the narrator's commands to the Jews, and re-focuses his orders to the

pregnant woman into a new horror. The violence of Savitsky's shooting his own Brigade Commander in the head transforms the "lopped-off head of the setting sun" into a real drama of terror. The image of the Brigade Commander's eyes rolling out of his head transforms the narrator's observations of wardrobes plundered by the Poles into a spiritual wound, as though brutality against mankind had victimized him.

In this manner the narrator's violent nightmare catches up the movements of the preceding years, days, and hours and symbolically reproduces them in another shape as though in a drama of emotional pollution through involvement in the irrationalities of that war, the seal of a violent culture. The nightmare ends but consciousness reveals the same horror, for the split head and torn throat of the pregnant woman's father, whom the narrator has been kicking in his sleep, make nightmare and reality one.

This then is the thesis: a symbolic movement toward social and personal chaos, conveyed through images and descriptions that are both external and internal, natural and man-made, real and metaphoric. But simultaneously, though faintly at first, as shadowed forth in imagery antithetical to defilement, the essentially selfless human being seeks, however unconsciously, deliverance from blackening chaos.

Knotted intimately into the movement towards defilement is its antithesis, not a strong force at first, perhaps not a force at all, but rather a principle or a desire. Or perhaps only a mood—a kind of tranquility. Here external nature reflects internal emotional states. In spite of the war and the pursuits of a retreating army, the narrator sees that fields continue to blaze, if somewhat ominously, "crimson with poppies," and "a noontide breeze played in the yellowing rye." He observes that "virginal buckwheat rose like the wall of a distant monastery." His mind needs to register the purity of the buckwheat and to transform, in the face of chaos, unstable organic nature into permanent spiritual fact, just as it needs to record the "peaceful stream" which "wound weary arms through the wilderness of hops," or as it needed to solidify meaningless horror into a symbolic dream. His mind unconsciously tends to construct a spiritual architecture which cannot be destroyed by human defilement.

On the note of weariness, the narrator's emotions drop with the "lopped-off head of the setting sun," but rise faintly with hope when he observes the "mild light [that] glowed from the cloud gorges," and the "majestic moon" resting on the waves of the river. It is as though peace, rest, and dignity had risen from the waters of chaos, from the "blackened Zbruch," like the buckwheat monastery rising to counterbalance the violent pursuit and the memory of peasant bones.

After the narrator has arrived at Novograd, his need for withdrawal and release from pollution manifests itself in his orders to the pregnant woman to clean up the "human filth." He cries in disgust: "What a filthy way to live!" Before his anxious sleep, he observes the moon again and registers a profound but unspoken desire to resist defilement: "Silence overcame all . . . The moon, clasping in her blue hands her round, bright carefree face, wandered like a vagrant outside the window." Not the looseness and possible disintegration of "weary arms" and "serpentine trails" but stability in "clasping her blue hands"; not determined and deadly pursuit, but "wandering like a vagrant," carefree; not a "lopped-off head" but a "bright, carefree face"; not the "confused cries" and curses of the men in the black river, but "silence overcame all." Here the narrator achieves a vision of release from the contamination that seems to triumph in the subsequent dream of the day's violence and the age's horror.

The dream ends and he awakes: the pregnant woman is groping over his face with her fingers, as though he and she were reenacting and restating that image of the stabilizing moon that the narrator saw before sleep and the nightmare of the conquering defilement—the galloping stallion and the murderous Commander—erupted in his mind. Just as the violent Commander appeared to the narrator in his sleep, now the heavy bodied woman appears in his consciousness to erase the "heavy stallion." No longer are sleep and galloping animality the seal of a triumphant stain, for as the pregnant Jewess touches the narrator's face, she signals in him the rebirth of a force as resurgent and triumphant as that symbolized by the moon's "clasping in her blue hands her round, bright, carefree face. . . ." The conquering emotional darkness retreats. Thoughts of disembowelment and dreams of empty eye-sockets are replaced by the pregnant woman with the "rounded belly"; thoughts of the narrator's "numbed legs" are replaced by the actuality of the woman's rising on her own thin legs. His awareness of "rounded belly" fuses with his memory of the "round moon"; coming out of the darkness like the moon rising above the black river, the pregnant woman rises in answer to the narrator's cries in the night: "You're calling out in your sleep and you're tossing to and fro." It is as though she were waking a terrified child from a violent dream. By arousing him from that nightmare, she reproduces an action much like the narrator's seeing the moon on the waves immediately after the decapitation of the head of the sun, or his remembering the light shining from cloud gorges as darkness falls, or his seeing the buckwheat monastery after thinking of the road built on the bones of peasants. In the life-giving flesh of the pregnant woman is the vital force of purity that counteracts the gradual numbing of all the narrator's sensitive faculties.

At this point her "shaking up the feather bed" announces his return from the nightmare, from emotional fragmentation and exhaustion imaged in the "disemboweled" mattress on which he has been sleeping. In crossing into Poland, he has been unconsciously defiled by crossing into wanton, unprincipled chaos in which he has participated, as the woman's remarks serve to remind us: "I'll make you a bed in another corner, for you're pushing my father about. . . . The Poles cut his throat, and he begging them: 'Kill me in the yard so that my daughter shan't see me die.' But they did as suited them." In pushing the woman's father about, the narrator shares with the Poles and the Divisional Commander the possibilities of polluting, while himself being polluted, as his dream attests. But he is awakened to a new consciousness by the life-bearing Je-

wess who shows him the split head and torn throat of her father and cries, "I should wish to know where in the whole world you could find another father like my father?" The answer to her question has been implied in the narrator himself.

Shaken from his numbing sleep, the narrator awakens to an announcement, in the cry of the pregnant woman, of the possibility of preserving human dignity in the midst of absolute defilement. He awakens to the awareness of an act—even though the world has apparently moved into chaos—of pure and absolute selflessness on the part of the pregnant Jewess's father, an act that in itself answers his daughter's question: on earth as well as in heaven—wherever one found those aspects of character that mark a man with the selfless purity of the woman's father—there one would find the shape of the divine. From the violent and bloody image of the split head is born the new light of wisdom for the daughter and the narrator—it is like the light shining through the cloud gorges which he casually observed earlier. On this chaotic earth, caught in a defiling war, contaminated by one's own superiors in the urgency to triumph, one may find those men who refuse to be polluted, though they lose their lives by refusing. The tale ends here, suspended on the pregnant woman's question.

"Where on earth" forces the reader to re-focus his vision on Babel's story because the woman's cry points to the presence of spiritual overtones we may not have noticed before. And though these presences are not as obvious as the dark powers, nevertheless there are enough hints that the religious imagery, strengthened by the pattern of purification, will serve as a means of synthesizing conflicting themes.

The shape of divinity is reborn in the narrator's consciousness with the pregnant woman's last remark and majestic question. At the beginning of **"Crossing into Poland,"** the need for and the distance from that divinity were suggested by the narrator's observation of the "virginal buckwheat [that] rose like the wall of a distant monastery." It reappeared in the "majestic moon" that is traditionally associated with the pagan goddess of love and the Christian Mother of Love. It rests "majestically" on the blackened river and symbolizes the presence of the providential in the narrator and his world, in his twilight struck mind. The form of that divinity seemed to lie smashed on the floor of the pregnant woman's house with the "fragments of the occult crockery the Jews use only once a year, at Eastertime," when the incarnate Divinity, Himself born of a Jewish virgin, is smashed before descending into further darkness in order to lead man from Chaos. Divinity is then reconstructed in the image of the "carefree face" of the moon, as a vision of deliverance from the horror of crossing into chaos, the terror of descending into, and partaking of filth. Divinity finds its ultimate incarnation in the "round faced" moon and the "rounded belly" of the Jewess who previously labored to clean the house of "human filth" and now labors to waken the narrator from the nightmare in which he has been kicking her father, who, though his head has been split open, is absolutely alive in her memory.

The woman's feeling the narrator's face fuses the moon's rising (love and majesty) and the moon's clasping her face in her hands (stability; release from horror), while her act serves to transfer to the narrator's consciousness what she and the moon symbolize. He puts on the knowledge implied in her question. Nascent divinity takes the shape of a consciousness that although one has been defiled by war, dehumanized, brutalized, threatened with degrading death, one may still retain one's essential human dignity; like the father of the Jewess, one need not think only of one's self. The narrator learns from the pregnant woman that essential human selflessness is the incarnation of divinity in man.

The somewhat tenuous religious imagery serves to unite the symbolic action that points to defilement of the narrator's spirit and the pattern of images that suggest a counter-movement toward purification of his spirit. The religious imagery transforms both patterns into a higher spiritual synthesis by reshaping them in light of a transcendent ethic, which is then implied in the question of the grieving woman. The union is of course not as dramatic as the brutal action of the first pattern, nor as clear as the emotional tone of the second. *Tenuous* is the right word. Yet this tenuousness—a sort of shadow in the background, a vague sensation, like a memory or an apparition—is not at all detrimental to the synthesis the imagery performs. For in a world where roads are paved with human bones and fathers plead not to be murdered before their children's eyes, a transcendent ethic of sacrifice and selflessness is hardly a common concern. It does exist, as the request of the old Jew shows, and its power lingers, perhaps to reshape and flourish, as the question of the triumphant woman so beautifully implies.

Patricia Blake (essay date 1969)

SOURCE: A review of *You Must Know Everything: Stories, 1915-1937*, in *The New York Times Book Review*, July 13, 1969, p. 1, 42-3.

[*Blake is an American journalist, editor, and critic. In the following review, she examines Jewish themes in Babel's* You Must Know Everything.]

By nature, and by necessity, Isaac Babel was a secretive man. "His days," wrote his friend Ilya Ehrenburg, "were like the tunnelings of a mole." Indeed, much of his writing has been concealed for decades in these tunnelings, some of which were not of his making. At the time of his arrest in 1939, the Soviet secret police seized a trunkload of unpublished Babel manuscripts which rest somewhere in the labyrinths of the K.G.B. "archives," or have been destroyed. Since Babel's "posthumous rehabilitation" in 1954, all efforts to recover them have failed.

Fortunately, Babel had long been in the habit of secreting some of his stories in odd corners, among friends who harbored them during the 20-year-long night that descended upon Russian literature in the early thirties. The rescue, by Nathalie Babel, of 24 of these, and other hitherto unknown or obscure stories [in *You Must Know Everything: Stories, 1915-1937*] constitutes what Jews call a *mitsve*—a great and good deed—that will surely be counted, to the power of 24, in the heaven that is bound to be reserved for

the natives and friends of Odessa. Miss Babel has devotedly, and with great scholarly skill, collected, edited and annotated her father's work, and Max Hayward has translated it with a fidelity to the sense and style of the original that is very nearly miraculous.

Let no one think that this is one more collection of the fragments, variants, notes and other detritus that are ordinarily assembled after a great writer's death. At least six of the stories rank among his finest, and each of the others carries the singular and unmistakable resonance of Babel's genius.

The title story, **"You Must Know Everything,"** (1915) demonstrates that, at the age of 21, Babel was close to achieving the consummate laconicism of his later work. The writer describes the afternoon and evening of a Jewish boy, spent in the suffocating atmosphere of his grandmother's room. He does his homework, and endures a violin lesson under the fixed and terrible gaze of the old lady who is overwhelmed by reverence for his studies. In this airless chamber, in these eight pages, where not a single word is superfluous, is enclosed the whole world of the middle-class Jew growing up in Odessa, with its fierce ambitions, its futilities and forebodings.

"Study!" the old lady exhorts the child. "Study and you will have everything—wealth and fame! You must know *everything*. The whole world will fall at your feet and grovel before you. Everybody must envy you. Do not trust people. Do not have friends. Do not lend them money. Do not give them your heart!"

The somber, doom-struck quality of this early story suggests that Babel was still straining to escape the memory of grandmother's room. He writes, "There was silence . . . [after her outburst]. She was thinking about my future, and her stern commandments pressed down heavily—and forever—on my weak, untried shoulders. In the dark corner the iron stove glowed red hot and gave off a fierce heat. I was hot and stifled and I wanted to run outside into the fresh air and escape, but I hadn't even the strength to raise my head." Soon Babel was to find some release, and the somberness would give way to the ironic detachment with which he contrived to regard, in his art, the small and the great ferocities of this world.

Three stories in this collection illustrate the range Babel commanded in writing on wholly Jewish themes. **"Shabos Nahamu,"** another early story, is the folk-like tale of Hershele, the archetypal Jew from the *shtetl* (village in the Pale of Settlement), whose talent for inviting misfortune is matched only by his genius for telling stories. Hershele persuades a simple-minded housewife that the Shabos Nahamu (Sabbath of Comfort) she has been so eagerly awaiting is not a holiday, but a holy man descended from heaven, namely himself. He thus cons her into feeding him a sumptuous meal, and loading him down with presents for her relatives in the other world.

Babel's only completely good-natured story about Jews, **"Shabos Nahamu"** clearly derives from Sholom Aleichem, whose work Babel was admiringly translating into Russian during the late 1930's. (This translation, alas, has never been recovered.) Nonetheless, the whiff of mockery, even of cruelty, that rises from Hershele and his merry pranks is unmistakably Babel.

"Sunset" (1924-25) finds Babel at the height of his fascination for the prodigious and engaging Jewish thugs, gangsters, assassins, thieves and whores who peopled his imagination, and, to a lesser degree, the underworld of Odessa. He had completed his marvelous cycle, *The Odessa Stories,* and now, with **"Sunset,"** proceeded to surpass himself in this vein.

The scene is the front yard of the drayman, Mendel Krik, which serves as a ring for the bloody cockfights in which Mendel (nicknamed Mendel Pogrom) and his sons struggle to assert a kind of manhood undreamed of in the rooms on the other side of town where asthmatic little boys scratched away on their violins. A lunatic exuberance pervades the action as the sons hurl themselves at their father who "had the hide of the devil, and the stitches in it were made of cast iron."

Babel later turned **"Sunset"** into a play. But what director could be expected to render the story's images on stage: "Levka did something to his father's face that was like shuffling a new deck of cards"; "Stars—green stars on a dark blue background—were scattered in front of the window like soldiers relieving themselves"; "Women in starched clothes sat in the grass like white enamel teapots."

Of all the stories in this collection, **"The Jewess"** comes closest to the central theme of Babel's work, and especially of his masterpiece **"Red Cavalry"**; the Russian Jew's encounter with Bolshevism in its various aspects, its brutality and its heroics, its ruthlessness and its idealism. Lionel Trilling's brilliant essay of 15 years ago (introduction to Babel's *The Collected Stories,* translated by Walter Morison) continues to illuminate, even as more and more Babel is uncovered, the frightful anomaly of that encounter. He writes of Babel's fascination for what Trilling called "the savage glory" of the Jew-killing Cossacks in the Red Cavalry to which Babel was attached as a correspondent during the Civil War.

In **"The Jewess,"** written in the mid-thirties, Babel is concerned with a more modest but no less disquieting anomaly. Here a Soviet officer and political commissar is reunited with his widowed mother in his native *shtetl,* which has been reduced by revolution and Civil War to a rubble of human beings. The stench of poverty, disease and death seeps from the hovels of these aged waifs of Bolshevism.

The young officer, Boris Erlich, enters to embrace his keening mother: "Through her dress, through her loose and flaccid skin, he could feel the beating of her heart, and the beating of his own heart—they were one and the same. The smell of his mother's quivering flesh was so bitter and sad that he was overcome with unutterable pity for this heart, the heart of the Erlichs. The old woman wept, shaking on his breast decorated with the two orders of the Red Banner."

"The Jewess," published here for the first time in any language, is unfinished, evidently a first draft. Among Babel's notes on the manuscript are these: "More dialogue, less

pathetic narration? Strengthen the factual side—surnames, names, descriptions of the place?" Possibly Babel, in his passion for exfoliating his fiction, would ultimately have cut out the "quivering" and the "unutterable."

For those who have marveled at the hard, cool surface of Babel's prose, three other stories in this book offer an occasion to observe the writer in the actual practice of his art. In 1920 Babel adapted a portion of an account by a French Army captain, Gaston Vidal, of some grisly incidents he witnessed during World War I. We are much indebted to Miss Babel for having uncovered Vidal's obscure text, thus providing us with an illustration of Babel's method. She rightly notes that his adaptations are an exercise in compression.

Take the story **"The Deserter,"** where an officer shoots a 20-year-old who tries to desert to the Germans. In Vidal's text the officer is described in the purplest prose, "In battle he is a raging lion; at rest a brooding eagle. . . . He knows neither fear for himself nor pity for the enemy nor indulgence for his own men when they commit an error. . . . In civilian life, you will find him a kind and peaceful man, a perfect husband and a perfect father, as we say, friendly and helpful, overlooking the slight wrongs that might be done to him." Here is Babel: "Captain Gémier was a splendid fellow, and something of a philosopher as well. On the field of battle he would stop at nothing, but in private life he didn't take offense at small things."

Babel best expressed the intention behind his unremitting concern with form when he wrote that "no steel can pierce the human heart so chillingly as a period at the right moment." Trilling has observed Babel's affinity to Joyce in this, and other respects. I would submit—reaching far into another world of sensibility, culture and language—that Babel of Odessa is the blood-brother of Camus of Oran. Camus, I believe, did not know Babel's stories. But read the first page of *The Stranger* and find pure Babel. Both writers, equally absorbed by the spectacle of violence and death, succeeded, as no other modern writers, in investing the form itself with moral qualities.

There is another place where the two writers are joined: under the sun of their native lands. Men of the South, they invariably turned to the sun for the warmth and light that radiate beneath the surface of their work. In the sketch **"Odessa,"** Babel is amused by his own tropism. Why, he asks, is there no real, joyous description of the sun in Russian literature? Because "Russia is rotten and devious, because in Nizhny, Pskov and Kazan people are flabby, ponderous, unfathomable, pathetic and sometimes immeasurably and stupefyingly boring." Odessa, he says, will bring salvation: "There is a feeling that the blood must be refreshed. The atmosphere is stifling. The literary Messiah who has been awaited so long and so hopelessly will come from there—from the sunny steppes washed by the sea."

Among Camus's many celebrations of the sun, there is a passage I like to think speaks for Babel as well: "I am not a certain kind of optimist. I grew up to the drumbeat of the first World War, and since then our history has been murder, injustice and violence. But true pessimism, the kind that is common today, consists in exploiting all the cruelty and infamy of our time. I, for one, have never ceased to struggle against this degradation and I hate only the cruel. . . . There exist a few men at the center of whose work, however dark, burns an indomitable sun. I am far now from the country which first showed me the light, yet I am faithful still; its rays have found and nourished me even in the city of shadows, where fate holds me."

A reminiscence of Babel by Olga Andreyev Carlisle:

Babel and my father once undertook a motorcycle trip along the Seine, down to Rouen and Le Havre, to see the riverside landscapes described by Maupassant. At the end of their journey they spent long hours in bars in the port at Le Havre, sipping cider and listening to the conversations of seamen. Babel was delighted; he enjoyed watching simple people of any nationality. I remember the pleasure he got from a visit to a colony of Cossacks who had settled on a farm not far from Paris, where they managed to lead a primitive existence similar to the one they had known on the banks of the Dnieper. He told endless tales about those Cossacks, improvising new episodes as he went along. He was a marvelous, lyrical raconteur, but as a writer he was slow and rewrote his stories a great many times, striving for an absolute perfection. Babel's output was considered insufficient. Once, Ilya Ehrenburg had to speak for his friend at a Soviet Writers' Union meeting: "I am myself like a rabbit and can produce books by the litter," said Ehrenburg. "Babel works slowly—like an elephant he carries his baby for two years . . . the result is worth it."

Olga Andreyev Carlisle, in her Voices in the Snow: Encounters with Russian Writers, *1962.*

Patricia Carden   (essay date 1972)

SOURCE: *The Art of Isaac Babel,* Cornell, 1972, 223 p.

[*Carden is an American educator and critic who specializes in Slavic studies. In the following essay she examines the themes of childhood innocence and the emergence of adult perception in Babel's short stories.*]

Before *Red Cavalry* appeared as a book, Babel had embarked on a new project, a cycle to be called *The Story of My Dovecot.* Babel had intended to write a series of sketches or stories based on his childhood for a number of years, as is indicated by the story written during his student days, **"Childhood: At Grandmother's."** In 1925 he turned from work on *Red Cavalry* . . . (without completing his plan) to work on the new cycle.

It is customary to consider only four of Babel's stories as part of this cycle: **"The Story of My Dovecot," "First Love," "In the Basement,"** and **"Awakening."** I would also include **"Di Grasso," "Guy de Maupassant,"** and **"The Road."** These stories are united by their tone of presentation—a cool objective narration of his past by the older, wiser narrator—and by the theme of coming of age

through attaining to knowledge. Each returns to questions first raised in **"The Story of My Dovecot,"** and all may reasonably be included in the cycle, at least for critical purposes.

In this cycle, Babel adopts most directly the tone and form of autobiography. His model is the Turgenev of *First Love,* a debt he acknowledges in the title of one of the stories. Turgenev's narrator is a man of mature years looking back upon the events of his adolescence and recalling his initiation into the adult world through his first exposure to passion, violence, and death. The older narrator sees more now than he saw in his youth. He sees that he did not escape the effects of a too–early knowledge that has determined the course of his life. So too do Babel's stories reflect the youthful longing for knowledge and experience, while assessing the price paid for them.

It is difficult to know to what extent the stories are autobiographical in the usual sense of the word. Babel had this to say about them in a letter to his relatives abroad:

> Before my departure [from Moscow to the country] I asked Katia to send you and Zhenia each a copy of *Young Guard.* I make my debut there after several years of silence with a short excerpt from a book which will come out under the title *The Story of My Dovecot.* The subjects are taken from my childhood, but much is made up [*privrano*], of course, and much is changed. When this book is finished, it will be clear why I had to go through all that.

It seems safe to assert that these stories are not autobiographical in the sense of giving us the accurate details of Babel's experience (no more autobiographical are the *Red Cavalry* stories), but that, like Turgenev's *First Love,* they form a part of the author's spiritual biography. They reveal the formation of the attitudes toward life and experience that inform Babel's work.

The first of the stories to be written, the programmatic story for the cycle, is **"The Story of My Dovecot."** Here, Babel shows the pressure of history and social circumstance upon the individual life. It is an art he seems to have learned from Pushkin rather than Tolstoy: to "place" the individual in his historical context in a few lines and to show historical forces operating in the individual so that the reader's interest in his destiny is in no way diminished. The opening paragraphs of the story move outward from the center of the child's experience to the larger world, from the personal desire ("As a child I very much wanted to have a dovecot") to the historical placing ("That was in 1904"), from the past event to the narrator's present ("That province doesn't exist any longer. Our town was incorporated into the Odessa region").

Each of the first three paragraphs follows the same principle of development. The statement of the significant biographical fact ("I wanted a dovecot"; "I was only ten and I was afraid of examinations"; "I was good at learning") is followed by the drawing in of the surrounding circumstances that will determine the way the fact appears in the social context: that he wanted a dovecot in 1904 in Kherson province, that he was afraid of exams in a city where only two of forty Jewish aspirants would be admitted to the gymnasium, that he was gifted at learning in a situation where a man could buy his son's way into the gymnasium.

The story expands not only in the direction of the historical and social context but in the direction of the context of the family and the Jewish community. These tensions are encompassed in the boy's relationship with his father, centered in the father's generous promise to buy the longed-for doves, a promise hedged by his demands for outstanding performance in the admission examinations. This personal situation in the family extends to the situation in the Jewish community, for the child's admission to the school is a way of acquiring status for the family. When the grain dealer Khariton Efrussi buys his son's way into the gymnasium ahead of young Babel, who had earned the place, it is an indication of the father's failure, for had he succeeded in life he would have bought his son in.

The opening paragraphs of the story reveal the psychic violence inherent in the situation in the extremity of the boy's yearning and fear, in the harshness of the father's demands, in the extremity of the father's reaction to the thwarting of his desire. ("My father suffered a great deal then. The incident of the minus threw him into despair.") The situation threatens to erupt into physical violence: "He wanted to beat up Efrussi or to pay two longshoremen to beat him up, but mother dissuaded him."

The story turns outward at this point, from the insular world of the family and the Jewish community to the larger world, which for the boy is the world of school. The critical moments in the child's life are the times of exam-taking, for everything rides on his success for him and his father. The examinations are moments of delirium. Of the first examination he says: "I fell into an eternal waking dream, into a child's long dream of despair. I went to the examination in that dream and nevertheless did better than the rest." As the child undergoes the examination the following year (after having memorized the three text-books line for line), he falls again into the state of delirium: "The trustee's assistant asked me about Peter the Great. I experienced a feeling then of forgetfulness, a feeling of the nearness of the end, of the abyss, a dry abyss full of ecstasy and despair." Here as elsewhere in Babel's stories, the attempt at fuller definition as the story progresses leads to a paradox, the despair of the first examination becomes ecstasy and despair. The necessity for this paradox, which contains the essential wisdom of the story, will unfold before us as the story continues.

In the dreamlike atmosphere of the examination the child experiences his first moment of true knowledge and release:

> I knew about Peter the Great by heart from Putsykovich's history and from Pushkin's poems. I poured out these poems, the faces suddenly whirled around in my sight and became mixed up like cards from a new pack. They reshuffled themselves on the retina of my eyes, and in these moments, trembling, drawing myself up, hurrying, I shouted Pushkin's verses with all my might. I shouted them at length. No one in-

terrupted my insane mouthings. Through a crimson blindness, through the freedom that overcame me, I saw only the old, inclined face of Piatnitski with his silver-streaked beard.

The freedom the child experiences is the freedom of dream. He gives himself up totally to the imaginary world of his learning, and for the moment even the reality of the examination with its pressures slips away from him. The escape from reality into the world of the imagination is one of the poles of freedom. The first movement of the story, the "school" movement, reaches its climax here. The pattern is one of tension and release.

But before the movement ends, there are two preparatory developments of theme. The coercion by the father, the stress of the examinations, the freedom of performance have all been for the child flights from knowledge of his situation. He has lived in a special world. Now we are again reminded of the child's ambiguous relationship to the external world. As he waits outside the examining room for word of success or failure, he is stalked as prey by the Russian schoolboys. Sensing danger, he "wakes up" from his fatigue-induced reverie. He is saved by the kindly intervention of Piatnitski; thus his knowledge of the realities of the world in which he must live remains incomplete.

The other subject that remains to be introduced before we can turn to the story proper (we are still waiting for the story of the dovecot) is the family. It is introduced with the father's moment of success and release. Upon receiving the news of his son's success at the exams, he throws a peasant out of his shop and closes it down in celebration, then rushes off to buy a school cap for his son. Here emerge the differing views of the mother and father on how to cope with a hostile world. The father has sent out the child armed with the knowledge of three textbooks, and up to this point he has been proven right, for the child triumphs. But he triumphs in the special set of conditions that we call school, and it remains to be seen how his knowledge will serve him outside school. The father believes in aggressive action against the world, but he has little sense of its dangers: "All the men in our family were trusting toward people and quick to unthinking action." The Babel menfolk are an interesting breed, rebels, dreamers, madmen. They all have only a tenuous hold on reality, but their incipient madness leads them into lives of adventure like Uncle Lev (who kidnaped the daughter of a supply officer and fled with her to California, where he abandoned her and "died in a house of ill repute among Negroes and Malays") or into poetry like the inspired liar Shoyl.

Now the child is being educated into the Babel madness, and the symptoms of delirium are upon him. This leads to conflict with the mother, who takes a different view of the world. When the child returns with the news that he has passed the examinations, "my poor mother barely got me away from the insane fellow [the father]. Mother was pale in that moment. She was experiencing fate. By turns she petted me and thrust me away in disgust. . . . Mother was pale. She was experiencing fate through my eyes and she looked at me as upon a cripple with bitter compassion, for she alone knew how unfortunate our family was." The mother's clear-sighted view of the realities of their situation leads her to withdraw before the hostile world. She fears to buy a school cap too soon, for "God would punish us and people would laugh at us." She understands other aspects of their situation as well: "Like all Jews, I was short, thin and suffered from headaches from studying. My mother, who had never been blinded by her husband's pauper pride and his incomprehensible faith that our family would someday become the strongest and richest on earth, saw all this. She did not expect success for us." In spite of this truth, so clearly seen by the mother, the father persists in his imaginings, which reach their climax at the ball he gives to celebrate his son's "victory." The ball is a triumphant moment in the story, a celebration of the best features of the kind of Jewish community to which the family belongs. The family's friends are hearty commercial men, outgoing and gay. Among them is the learned Liberman, a pious man versed in the Torah. Nevertheless, the rejoicing, the boastful speeches, the whole "pauper's ball" are far out of proportion to the event that inspires them and are rendered by the author with light irony. The point is made that the Jews conceive of their situation as a battle and that they go into this battle eagerly so long as they have the choice of weapons: "Thus in ancient times David, the King of Judea, conquered Goliath and in like manner I had been victorious over Goliath. Thus our people would by the strength of the mind defeat our enemies who surround us and thirsted for our blood."

In the first half of the story, Babel sets in opposition Jew and Russian, desire and coercion, the historical and the private, knowledge from books and knowledge of life, reality and illusion. The characters are defined by the ways in which they fit into or react to these categories. But the process of definition of the categories becomes increasingly complicated as they cross into one another and blur. The Jew Efrussi is more the enemy of the Babel father and son than the Russian teacher Karavaev, who wishes the boy well. Karavaev's physical characteristics are emphasized, and it is a clear portrait of the enemy. His blond ruddiness links him with the peasant looters of the latter half of the story. Yet he is capable of feeling joy "for me and for Pushkin" when the child declaims Pushkin's verses on Peter the Great. There are categories in the story that transcend race, and the first of these is art and the community of art. Thus we see a pressure at work in the story toward a proper alignment of values, a pressure to find the true categories that "work" by supplying reliable information about the world.

The lines are drawn up and the author turns now to "the story of the dovecot." We have reached the moment when the boy and his family will cross the path of history. History appears, as it must always appear to the individual observer, as a series of ridiculous, meaningless incidents. But Babel here, as in the events of the Polish campaign, seeks to go deeper, to understand the meaning of history as it touches the child's life and the lives of his family in the form of incident. Thus once again at this key moment in the story the author reminds us of the date and of its significance: "The incident I am relating, that is my admission to the first class of the gymnasium, took place in the fall of 1905. Tsar Nicholas was then bestowing a constitu-

tion upon the Russian people. Orators in worn-out coats were clambering onto the high curbs next to the building of the City Duma and speaking to the people."

The Sunday of October 20, 1905, as Babel describes it, is filled with a series of startling and seemingly gratuitous events. The first of these seem high-spirited, even frivolous. "From early morning on October 20 the boys next door were flying a kite right across from the police station and our water carrier, pomaded and red-faced, had quit work and was walking about the streets. Then we saw the baker Kalistov's sons dragging a leather gym horse out into the street. They started to do gymnastics in the middle of the road."

In such frivolities is the experience of freedom expressed. Another ominous sign is the appearance of the local policeman in a fancy sash. "The policeman out of uniform frightened my mother more than anything." This is the mother's moment. Disaster is her milieu, as victory is the father's. Disaster confirms her sense of the nature of the world.

Disaster touches the Babel family in the form of the acts of violence that befall young Babel and Granduncle Shoyl. The two acts seem at first disparate in significance, for one leads to no physical injury while the other leads to death. Yet the boy learns the same lesson from both about the nature of reality and of his relationship to it. This lesson is nowhere explicitly stated, although it is suggested in a number of places. To understand it we must make explicit the links between the various acts of that Sunday, from baker Kalistov's vaulting sons to the mob's murder of Shoyl. Two threads are apparent in the events of the day: the continuing connection between man and things, and the expression of freedom through the release of desire.

Early in the story Babel alerts us to the special importance of a love of things: "No one in the world has a stronger feeling for new things than children. Children tremble from that smell like a dog on a rabbit's track and experience the madness which later, when we grow up, we call inspiration." The child and his mother are united in this love of new things, which draws them together in a special intimacy. The chief motive force in the story is the child's desire for the pigeons. This desire leads him through the series of acts that comprise his education, formal and informal. The Sunday of the story is presented as the occasion for the fulfillment of desire for the poor, who covet the things sold in the shops of the better-off (and Jewish) merchants. These desires might seem to us ignoble, but within the context of the story they cannot be so considered. The same inspiration felt by the mother and child burns in the face of the woman looter: "Along the street ran a woman with a flaming, beautiful face. She was holding a clutch of fezzes in one arm and a bolt of cloth in the other. In a happy, despairing voice she summoned her lost children." Her combination of joy and despair is the sign of that freedom which we have seen the child experiencing earlier in the story.

The second thread running through the events of the day is the desire to express desires, to engage in the free play of spirit, to be seen, to be taken cognizance of, to have one's day. The giving of a constitution means only one thing to the illiterate poor—freedom—and they interpret freedom in the light of their own necessities and desires. To them freedom is not political in content. It means doing what one wants to do, getting what one wants. Babel shows that liberation lies in this as much as in more "noble" forms of expression.

It remains to be shown what bearing these explanations have upon the central events of the day. Makarenko's brutal act in smashing the boy's pigeons against his face has tended to stun readers and to turn their attention away from the circumstances in which the act takes place. But in Babel's stories acts in themselves are opaque and can only be understood by reference to motivation. Thus one must look for motivation as well as examine the consequences of the act.

The explanation of Makarenko's act lies in the sequence of events that take place between the time the boy accosts him and the time he turns on the child. The child has overheard something at the bird market that he does not understand (a cryptic allusion to the death of Shoyl). He stops in the street to ask the crippled Makarenko, whom the children love and trust, about the news. But the old man is caught up in his own drama. He is absorbed in his wife's inventory of the goods they have picked up in the looting, and he experiences anguish at the thought of their inadequacy. ("He turned his whole body away from his wife as though knowing in advance that her answer would be unbearable.") His anguish is the opposite of that joyous freedom experienced by the successful looters, the anguish of a man deprived of his moment of freedom, of expression, of his place in the sun: " 'Bonnets,' shouted Makarenko. He choked and sounded as though he were crying. 'It's clear, Katherine, that God has picked on me, that I have to answer for everyone. People are carrying off whole bolts of cloth, people are getting everything that's coming to them, and we've got bonnets.' " The rationale of the looting as seen by its perpetrators is set forth clearly here. They are getting their just due, what God himself has allotted them.

But beyond this, Makarenko is victimized in a way more fundamental to Babel's code of justice: he is not seen, his desires are not taken cognizance of. First, he wheels his chair after the lady with the fezzes, shouting, "Where did you get that striped stuff?" She ignores him and runs on. Immediately after her a horse-drawn cart rumbles through the square, but the peasant boy inside it also ignores Makarenko's entreaties. The scene is stunning: the old cripple in his chair wheeling wildly about the vast square, crying out in entreaty and rage. He repeats the key line that "explains" his act: "God has picked on me. . . . But after all, I'm a human being, too." Only at this point does he turn to the child. Seeing the child's puffed-out blouse, he assumes that he has stolen something and in his desperation determines to have it. The final crushing disappointment is to discover nothing of value. " 'Pigeons,' Makarenko said and the wheels of his chair squeaked as he rode up to me. 'Pigeons,' he repeated and struck me on the cheek. He dealt me a stunning blow with the hand that was holding the pigeon . . . and I fell on the ground in

my new coat." The act seems horrendous—a man brutally striking a child. But even here there are two details that bring the two victims into more equitable relationship. The first of these is the sound of the wheelchair. The second is the new coat.

Chance has brought the child into the place where he becomes involved in the tragic denouement of another man's drama. Makarenko's drama ends with the blow he deals. It is the last act left to him, but the tragedy is that this act which would affirm his humanity exhausts it. The story turns away from him and to the child, for whom the blow is not an end but a beginning.

The blow is followed by a moment when the world severely contracts for the child. He lies on the ground:

> The world was tiny and awful. A little stone was lying in front of my eyes, a stone chipped off like the face of an old woman with a large jaw. A piece of string lay not far off and a bunch of feathers, still breathing. My world was tiny and awful. I closed my eyes so as not to see it and pressed myself to the ground that lay beneath me in soothing dumbness. This trampled earth in no way resembled our life, or waiting for exams in our life. Somewhere Woe rode across it on a great steed, but the noise of the hoofbeats grew weaker and died away, and silence, the bitter silence that sometimes overwhelms children in their grief, suddenly annihilated the boundary between my body and the earth that was moving nowhere.

The protecting illusion that the idea of school and study supplies the child is ironically called "our life." Now the boy's vision is focused on things in their barest essentials, and what he sees has no resemblance to that illusory "life."

But the moment when the world contracts is followed by the moment of expansion and release. The child, having broken through to reality for the first time, to the truth of his situation and to pain, now is freed by the truth and experiences joy:

> The earth smelled of the raw depths of the tomb, of flowers. I smelled it and began to cry without the least fear. I was walking along an unknown street set on either side with white boxes. I was walking in a getup of bloody feathers alone in the middle of sidewalks swept clean as on Sunday and I was crying bitterly, fully and happily as I have not cried again in my whole life.

Babel expresses here an attitude honored in Russian literature from Pushkin to Chekhov: the life-affirming power of recognizing necessity. What is the content of the knowledge that the child comes to, more as an awareness of the senses than as a clearly formulated idea?

The child hears of his race from an outsider for the first time at the examinations, when the trustee's assistant Piatnitski says, "What a people your Jews are. They've got a devil in them." The words are delicately ironic, for in the context they are complimentary, referring to the child's performance at the examinations, but in substance they echo the old reproach. The next time, he hears of his race from an outsider as he lies on the ground. Makarenko's wife, Katia, says, "We ought to wipe out their spawn. I can't stand their spawn or their smelly menfolk." (But compare this with the Babel mother's opinion: "She didn't like vodka and couldn't understand how anyone could like it. For that reason she considered all Russians insane and couldn't understand how women could live with Russian husbands.") The child can only be freed from the bonds of his Jewishness (his father's fantasies, his mother's anxieties) by having his Jewishness made explicit. At the moment when necessity intrudes most sharply, when the severe contraction of the world takes place, the spirit assents to freedom. In the careful tracing of the meaning behind the child's sensations we see most clearly the advantage of Babel's form of narration, which conveys to us the child's apprehension of the world, but informed by the adult's understanding.

As the child returns home he sees everywhere those incongruous episodes that are the substance of the day's history:

> In a side street a young peasant in a vest was breaking up the doorframe in Khariton Efrussi's house. He was breaking it up with a wooden mallet, throwing his whole body into it. Sighing, he smiled all around the kind smile of drunkenness, sweat and spiritual strength. The whole street was filled by the crunch, crack and song of the flying chips of wood. The peasant was hitting the frame only to bend double, to sweat and to shout unusual words in an unknown, un-Russian language. He shouted these words and sang, his blue eyes lacerating from within, until a religious procession appeared in the street coming from the Duma.

Thus, inadvertently, is justice done to Khariton Efrussi. But more important, thus is shown the full moment of exaltation and freedom, the moment of the "song." The scene has the intensity of a pagan rite; indeed, it is a pagan rite as witnessed by our anthropologist, the child, who has come among this strange tribe and whose eye wonderingly records its customs. The religious overtones of the scene are developed in the next scene, in which the procession is described.

The procession is another of Babel's bravura grotesque scenes. It might well have been painted by Pan Apolek: "Old men with dyed beards were carrying portraits of the neatly combed tsar. Banners with graveyard saints fluttered over the procession. Enflamed old women rushed forward." The crowd is described as a grotesque procession of unfortunates, and again we are reminded that this is the protest of the poor. But the incongruous elements are offset by the fierce energy of the forward movement. This mob is perhaps the very one that Shoyl challenged and that caused his death.

What was the meaning of Shoyl's death? Shoyl's stories, his inspired lies, were about the Polish insurrection of 1863 and how he saw the soldiers of Nicholas the First shoot Count Goldewskij and the other Polish insurgents. Shoyl lives in his fantasies, in a world of aristocratic heroism and self-sacrifice far removed from the realities of his fish market. He is the quintessential representative of the Babel male character, having stretched the span between reality and fantasy to the farthest points. Shoyl's death is the moment of realization of his fantasies, when he becomes fully himself by acting out his illusion of heroism.

The caretaker Kuzma instructs the child in the meaning of Shoyl's death. It is significant that at the end of the story the child returns neither to his father nor to his mother, but to Kuzma. Kuzma, like the mother, accepts things as they are, but his acceptance is casual and without fear. It is he who keeps vigil over dead Shoyl and prepares his body for burial. He has respect for the body, but no false shame before it. Kuzma approaches the body with homely simplicity. ("Kuzma fussed over the dead man's feet. He tied the jaws and kept glancing over the body to see what else he could do for the dead man. He fussed around as though over a new suit of clothes and settled down only after combing the dead man's beard.") In his actions he instructs the child in the proper attitude toward our physical, bodily weakness, toward our mortality.

One of the most striking things in the story is its treatment of the dead body of Shoyl. Babel does not spare the reader's sensibilities. He renders the scene in all its grotesqueness: "There were two perch stuck into grandfather: one in the fly of his pants, the other in his mouth, and although grandfather was dead, one of the perch was still alive and quivered." Kuzma mediates the gruesome reality of the dead man, making the link between the grotesque body and the heroic act: " 'He cursed them all,' he said, smiling and looked over the corpse with love. 'If the Tartars had come at him, he would have sent them packing, but it was the Russians with their women, Rooski women. It hurts Rooskies to forgive anyone. I know these Rooskies.' "

Kuzma admires Shoyl because Shoyl has taken a stand. As a simple man he appreciates the act of heroism without fully comprehending the intricate chain of associations that brought it about. He hints, too, at a complication in the view taken of the incident, for what had the Russian women to forgive in Shoyl? Was it not the offense he committed by standing in their way at their hour? In any case, having presented the child to the reality of his situation as victim, but also to the possibilities for heroism in that situation, Kuzma takes the child to his father. The child is now prepared to enter the world of Babel males, armed with a knowledge that they have not previously possessed. And having set forth the true and hidden meaning that he has discovered by his feat of understanding in writing the story, the narrator gives us, as his last word, the word he has withheld from us throughout the story: "Together with Kuzma I went to the house of the tax inspector where my parents were hid, having fled from the pogrom."

I have unfolded the implications of the story at length to show its depth and richness. Though we have returned to the southern regions of the Odessa stories, we have come a long way in our journey to understanding. The style of the new cycle of stories is austere in comparison with the old, in fulfillment of the desire that Babel expressed to a friend in the middle of the years he was at work on the stories: "It is more difficult for me to work than before. There are different demands upon me and the desire arises to transfer into another 'class'—the class of calm, clear, perceptive and meaningful writing."

The stories of childhood take their beauty from the intricate structure of understanding that unites their smallest details into a deeply resonant whole. The stories' sublime economy becomes a means of reaching out to encompass a larger area of human concern.

As he continues through the cycle, Babel applies the general hard-won understanding to one episode after another, showing how now this, now that incident is illuminated by the larger vision of human destiny, how experience is drawn together, given meaning, and made whole by the application of the new understanding. The understanding of desire that illuminates violence in **"The Story of My Dovecot"** is used to reveal the nature of passion in **"First Love,"** the nature of truth in **"In the Basement,"** the nature of art in **"Di Grasso."** In each story the other elements remain, for violence, passion, truth, and art are inextricably linked for Babel.

The story **"In the Basement"** deals more directly than any other story by Babel with the complicated relationships between truth and fiction. The opening sentences come straight to the point: "I was an untruthful little boy. That was because of reading." The story is centered in the child and in his growing awareness of the nature of truth, for, as he says, "What existed was more amazing than what I made up but at the age of twelve, I did not yet know how things were to be between me and truth in this world."

At first the child has no friends because he spends all his time reading; but when his classmates discover his remarkable imagination, he becomes popular. The head of the class, the rich boy Mark Borgman, takes him in hand and a new social life begins for the lonely child. This life leads him into the world and is the source of many fantasies, but in the long run it makes possible his turn from fiction to truth.

Among the people who surround him, the boy finds many instances of failure to distinguish truth from fiction. When he is invited to the rich Borgmans', his aunt Bobka takes this as the beginning of a brilliant career for her nephew. At the Borgmans' there is talk about Mark's father's becoming the Russian trade representative and taking the family to England. Not to be outdone, young Babel makes up suitably fantastic stories about his own relatives that cast a powerful spell over the earnest young Borgman.

The moment of truth arrives when young Borgman must be invited in his turn to the Babels'. The true nature of the Babel family is revealed in the drunken uncle Simon-Wolf and the half-mad grandfather. Aunt Bobka and the boy contrive to conceal the truth by sending the grandfather to the neighbors' and by giving Uncle Simon money for the tavern. As we suspect, the ruse does not work. Drunken Uncle Simon returns in the middle of Borgman's visit, bearing a great chest and antlers that he has been led into buying. A family fight ensues, he knocks Bobka down, and the mad grandfather comes dashing back to intervene. The wonderful mad scene is extremely funny, but Babel manages to preserve the note of pathos, to keep before us the boy's despair at Borgman's discovery of the truth.

After Borgman has fled, mumbling polite words of excuse, young Babel tries to drown himself in the water barrel in the basement. He is discovered and pulled out by his grandfather, who makes a succinct and unsentimental comment on the situation: "Grandson, I'm going to take castor oil so I'll have something to lay on your grave." The crisis resolves itself, as in **"First Love,"** in the boy's hysteria, which reflects his shock at coming face to face with truth but which will leave him prepared to live in the real world.

That reality has its compensations is kept before us throughout the story. When the boy manages to send Uncle Simon away before Mark's visit, he thinks: "The son of the bank director would never find out that my story about the goodness and strength of my uncle was false. Speaking in all conscience, if we consider the heart, this story was true and not a lie, but at first glance at the dirty and loud Simon-Wolf this incomprehensible truth was not apparent." Babel opposes the truth beneath the appearance of things to the fictions that we use to disguise the truth. The role of imagination is not to disguise the truth with fiction but to grasp the essential truth beneath the misleading disguise.

"Awakening" is among the most popular of Babel's stories. It shares with that other popular story, **"The Death of Dolgushov,"** a deceptive transparency that pleases the reader and gives him to understand that at last he knows what the story is about. In these stories Babel comes closest to the conventional surface of his subjects and presents them in their most palatable forms: killing as an act of mercy, repression as the rather comic and familiar story of the little boy who is forced to take violin lessons. To the extent that **"Awakening"** can be received as the conventional story it is unsatisfactory, for it conceals the anguished travail leading to understanding at the very time that it benefits from it for its point. In Babel's other stories, even in the other stories of the childhood cycle, the style preserves the tension of the creative act. We feel the cost involved not as clumsiness but as a peculiar brilliance and power that set the stories apart from other stories. In **"Awakening"** there is a relaxation of tension. No doubt this benign style comes from Babel's own sense of ease with the materials now that he has reached understanding through the writing of the earlier stories. Seen in the context of the cycle the story gains, for we see how we arrive at this tranquility and transcendence.

"Awakening" takes its place in the cycle by showing the boy's grasp of another facet of reality, the sensuous nature of the world. The story basks in the radiance of the Southern landscape, resurrected for the first time since the Odessa stories. As in **"In the Basement,"** the child's bookishness cuts him off from a direct, physical relationship to the world. The barrier that study creates between the boy and real life is symbolized in the hated violin lessons, another instrument of the father's ambitions. His father hopes that the son will be a prodigy, as so many other Odessa Jewish children have been, and thus bring glory to the family.

In his discussion of the story [introduction to *The Collected Stories*], Lionel Trilling calls attention to the ignorance of the natural world that was typical of the Jews of the eastern ghettos. It is touching to find Babel writing in his diary of the Polish campaign, "I am learning the names of plants." Babel displaces this fact back into childhood and makes a good Russian the "teacher" who reveals this knowledge to the boy. Old Nikitich, the true master who will educate the boy to his vocation of writing, is opposed to the false master, the violin teacher. Nikitich reads the boy's first literary effort, a tragedy, and advises him to acquire a greater knowledge of the natural world. "A man who doesn't live in nature like a stone or an animal won't write two lasting lines in his whole life."

The moment inevitably comes when the father discovers that the boy has been shirking his violin lessons. His rage is appropriate to a man who has had his life's dream torn from him. The boy locks himself in the toilet, where he hears his father outside the door recounting, in an insanely calm voice, a formula from his life of fantasy: " 'I am an officer,' my father said. 'I own an estate. I go hunting. The peasants pay me rent. I place my son in the cadet corps. I don't have to worry about my son.' " Aunt Bobka smuggles the boy out of the house to save him from his father's wrath. As the two fugitives advance along the street, the boy has an acute sense of the physical reality of the world. The story ends, "I thought of escape."

"Awakening" has a special significance in the cycle, for it reveals more clearly than any other story why the child "had to go through all that." The meaning of his ordeal lies in his future vocation. Babel gives here a portrait of the artist as a very young man. Each episode reveals the impact on the individual sensibility of a growing awareness of life's choices.

But the stories have a significance that extends beyond the illumination of the artist's destiny. The childhood cycle is the sternest test of the vision of the world to which Babel submits his materials. The child is by his very situation a natural victim, and when he is a Jew the possibilities for pathos seem limitless. Babel escapes the pathetic note by transforming the child's ordeal into a journey to understanding. Unlike *Red Cavalry,* where he presented the modes of the just life in dramatic juxtaposition, in the childhood stories we find a probing beneath the surface of each attitude to find what in it may be said to resemble its opposite. Thus the child and the father, though open enemies in their attempts to fulfill conflicting desires, are secret allies in their attitude toward the world. In the childhood stories Babel manages to see experience whole in a way that is wholly satisfying. The stories have the true note of understanding, and the interpretations do not seem provisional and imposed, as they often do in *Red Cavalry.* When he turns back upon his own experience the view of man invented in the Odessa stories and tested in the *Red Cavalry* stories, Babel finds the best and most convincing correspondence between incident and interpretation. These stories are the culmination of the search initiated with the invention of Benia Krik.

James E. Falen   (essay date 1974)

SOURCE: *Isaac Babel: Russian Master of the Short Story,* University of Tennessee Press, Knoxville, 1974, 238 p.

[*In the following essay, Falen explores Babel's use of language in* The Odessa Tales.]

Many of Babel's stories are based upon little more than a two-line anecdote. When shorn of their verbal adornment his plots seem too meager to support the weight of the finished tales. In a sense there is no plot skeleton to a Babel story; it exists almost totally in its verbal dimensions alone. Nothing else really explains how so many disparate components are so successfully united.

The highly original conception of form implied by such a structure is the subject of most of Babel's remarks about his art, and it is revealing to note that whenever he discusses his work he invariably turns to questions of craftsmanship. He speaks of language as a material to be forcibly shaped and manipulated through the agency of style, which he describes as an "army of words, an army in which all kinds of weapons may come into play." In a particularly memorable passage he describes a phrase as "born into the world both good and bad at the same time. The secret," he says "lies in a slight, an almost invisible twist. The lever should rest in your hand, getting warm, and you can only turn it once, not twice." With regard to timing and punctuation he informs us [in his story **"Guy de Maupassant"**] that "no iron can stab the heart with such force as a period put just at the right place." Elsewhere he speaks eloquently on the nature of the adjective and the shape of the metaphor, the subtleties of participles, and on the proper use of the paragraph. But never does he speak of controlling themes, motifs, or ideas in themselves; nowhere does he discuss construction in the broader sense—or, indeed, in any terms other than those of a man preoccupied with the problems of style.

For Babel, style itself is the basic ingredient of structure. He takes some ephemeral impression, some slight fragment of reality, and under his hands this simple kernel is shaped, cut, and faceted with words and then endlessly polished until it reveals the unsuspected beauty of its hidden depths. Babel himself is the severest analyst of his art, and the critic would do well to listen to what he says:

> . . . it's style that does it. I can write a short story about washing underwear and it will read like Julius Caesar's prose. It's all a matter of language and style. . . .

> What I do is to get hold of some trifle, some little anecdote, a piece of market gossip, and turn it into something I cannot tear myself away from. It's alive, it plays. It's round like a pebble on the seashore. It's held together by the fusion of separate parts, and this fusion is so strong that even lightning can't split it. And people will read the story. They'll remember it, they'll laugh, not because it's funny but because one always feels like laughing in the presence of human good fortune.

The first of *The Odessa Tales* ("The King") gives an excellent illustration of Babel's technique. The grain of sand around which this pearl of a story grows is a simple, mildly amusing anecdote; but through the agency of style it is transformed into an episode from some half-serious, half-comic saga, into a fairytale for grown-ups. The plot tells how Benja Krik and his men foil an intended police raid by burning down the precinct station. But a different "plot" is hidden in the verbal fabric of the story; to hear this tale one must heed the inner logic of the imagery and attend to motifs that are buried in word associations. This underlying plot of **"The King"** is a celebration of the rites of flesh: all of the apparently disconnected images coalesce around this theme like patches of color in an impressionist painting.

The story opens at the wedding of Benja's sister Dvoira. The very first words invoke the theme. First a brief nod toward the sanctification traditionally demanded by society before the enjoyment of conjugal bliss may begin— "The wedding ceremony ended, the Rabbi sank into an armchair"—then, with the religious ceremony over, the actual rites can begin. A description of the tables set up in the courtyard for the wedding feast sets the scene:

> There were so many of them that those at the end *thrust their tail* right out into Hospital Street. Velvet-spread, they *wound their way* down the yard *like so many serpents* with *variegated patches* on their bellies, and *they sang fullthroatedly,* those patches of *orange and red velvet* (italics added).

The italicized words all emphasize the voluptuousness of the central image, that of a serpent whose coiled entry into this garden of Eden (a garden blessed by the holy presence of the rabbi) is an insinuation of the presence of original sin. Even the apparently unmotivated reference to "Hospital Street" contributes to the underlying theme and helps to prepare for the direction of its subsequent development. The next paragraph begins with a short neutral sentence and then, in what might be called an invocation to the flesh, elaborates upon the implications of the initial image by introducing the motif of fire:

> The living quarters had been turned into kitchens. A sultry flame beat through the sootswathed doorways, a flame drunken and puffylipped. The faces of the old crones broiled in its smoky rays—old women's tremulous chins and beslobbered bosoms. Sweat with the pinkness of fresh blood, sweat as pink as the slaver of a mad dog, streamed this way and that over those mounds of exorbitant and sweetly pungent flesh.

It is startling to observe how virtually every word in this passage is concentrated upon a single effect. There is a sweet smell of decay about all of this sweating and abundant flesh (note the play on the words bosoms and mounds—Russian "grudi" and "grudy"), and the flames of this kitchen seem to suggest corruption and hell as much as they do the cooking of food. After this opening we are distracted by the arrival of an "unknown young man" who has news of the police for Benja. But this commencement of the outer plot does not detain us for long because the narrator almost immediately tells us he must digress to relate the interesting story of Sender Eichbaum. The supposed digression is actually a narrative ruse, a joke; it takes us right back to the original theme, for the "story of Sender Eichbaum" is a history of Benja Krik's own violent courtship.

We are told how Benja set about, through terror and extortion, to rob Sender Eichbaum of a goodly number of his cows. He threatens to kill all of Eichbaum's stock if rebuffed and gives point to his demands by putting his threat

into immediate action. Benja's final prize, however, is to win Eichbaum's daughter, and the slaughtering of the cows is really a kind of ritual preliminary to the ensuing nuptials:

> They came in the night, nine men bearing long poles in their hands. The poles were wrapped about with pitch-dipped tow. Nine flaming stars flared in Eichbaum's cattle yard. Benja beat the locks from the door of the cowshed and began to lead the cows out one by one. Each was received by a lad with a knife. He would overturn the cow with one blow of the fist and plunge his knife into her heart. On the blood-flooded ground the torches bloomed like roses of fire, and shots rang out.

The scene is etched against the night like a somber pagan ritual: nine priestlike ruffians officiate beneath nine flaming "stars." The torches, reflected in the sacrificial blood of the animals, bloom like roses of fire. Then the description is abruptly halted for a brief exchange of comic dialogue during which Eichbaum quietly accedes to Benja's demands. The raid has achieved its purpose, but the narrator explicitly tells us that "the wonder came later," that the real story is elsewhere and the climax not yet reached. The awesome ceremonies are invoked once more as the language again takes on its coloring of black magic:

> During the raid, on that dreadful night when cows bellowed as they were slaughtered and heifers slipped and slithered in the blood of their dams, when the torch-flames danced like darkvisaged maidens and the milkmaids lunged back in horror from the muzzles of amiable Brownings—on that dread night there ran out into the yard, wearing nought save her V-necked shift, Tsilya the daughter of old man Eichbaum.

The word associations here dispel all doubt as to the nature of the ceremony: the torches and maidens performing their dance in front of the revolvers, the heifers stained with their mothers' blood, and the reference to milkmaids all point to a ritual ceremony celebrating betrothal and the sacrifice of virginity.

Eichbaum is reluctant to relinquish his daughter, but Benja's powers of persuasion are sufficient and he attains his desires:

> And Benja Krik had his way, for he was passionate, and passion rules the universe. The newlyweds spent three months on the fat lands of Bessarabia, three months flooded with grapes, rich food, and the sweat of love's encounters.

There is a pun in the biblically resonant and expansive maxim about passion, for in context it contracts into a comically specific and literal meaning. Returning from a blissful three-month sojourn in Bessarabia (an occasion and setting slightly less legendary than a thousand and one Arabian nights, but with other advantages more attractive to the King of Odessa), Benja sets about the forcible marrying off of his forty-year-old virgin sister Dvoira, who suffers from goiter. Like Benja, Dvoira is to embark on her great adventure "amid the grape, rich food, and the sweat of love's encounters." The lingering description, which follows next, of the exotic wines and abundant foods at Dvoira's wedding feast has already been noted; only the third ingredient of this profane trinity, the sweat of love, remains to be fulfilled. The feast takes on a suitably fantastic air, half bacchanal, half courtly revel. Relatives, guests, and the shammashim from the synagogue all become drunk; the orchestra plays martial music as, in accordance with "ancient customs," the guests bestow gifts upon the newly wedded pair. The bandits, those "aristocrats of the Moldavanka," call upon the couple to kiss, chanting the traditional Russian cry of "bitter." The feeble little groom whom Eichbaum's money has purchased for Dvoira must find the word particularly appropriate as he glances at the forty-year-old bride sitting at his side, disfigured by disease, with swollen goiter and bulging eyes. Then, as the wedding celebration draws toward a close, there is a sudden moment of excitement. Something is burning:

> Over the courtyard there suddenly spread a faint smell of burning . . . the smoke cloud grew more and more venomous. Here and there the edges of the sky were turning pink, and now there shot up, narrow as a sword blade, a tongue of flame. The guests, half rising from their seats, began to snuffle the air, and the women-folk gave little squeaks of fear.

If the words of this climactic passage are compared with those of the story's opening, the cross-relationships of the two sections stand out in bold relief. The sultry flame and sweating bodies that began this tale of a wedding feast are reinvoked by the greater conflagration that serves as climax, but in a new light. The serpent, whose intimated presence at the initial celebration had contributed an ominous note of damnation, is exorcized and consumed by the devouring flames, and the "unknown young man" who had appeared earlier materializes once more to report with irrepressible delight on the fire—a further suggestion that the satanic serpent has given way to a rather merry, giggling Mephisto.

The fire is actually the burning police station that the bandits have set ablaze, but Benja's diversionary action in foiling the police is merely a corollary of the diversionary tactic of the narrative itself. The network of verbal associations and the pattern of images are what really dictate the fiery finale. Climaxing the theme of flesh and damnation, the fire unites this verbally conditioned understructure with the comic narrative surface that comprises the more obvious strand of the "plot."

The hidden tale is also essentially parodic in intention. The comic aspect of the conflagration dispels the notion of a blazing inferno of damnation, and the mockery of religious associations suggests that rather than flames of hell, these are flames of passion dedicated to carnal love and to the wedding night of Dvoira Krik.

The climax is not quite the end of the story. As is frequently the case in Babel's structural schemes the ending consists of a relatively short, sharp stroke that illuminates once more the general outlines of the tale. Here is the concluding paragraph in which the main dish of the wedding feast is at last served up:

> When Benja got back home the little lamps in

the courtyard were flickering out, and dawn was beginning to touch the sky. The guests had departed and the musicians were dozing, leaning their heads on their double basses. Dvoira alone was not thinking of sleep. With both hands she was urging her faint-hearted husband toward the door of their nuptial chamber, glaring at him carnivorously. Like a cat she was, that holding a mouse in her jaws tests it gently with her teeth.

"The King" was the first of the Odessa tales to be published and probably the first to be written. A veritable tour de force, it has the stamp of being the happy issue of a first inspiration and remains unique among *The Odessa Tales.* Although the same volatile ingredients are combined in the other stories of the cycle, it is not surprising that each of these tales exhibits some new and significant departures. The distinctions in narrative structure especially are interesting in themselves and illustrative of Babel's developing techniques. The second of the stories, **"How It Was Done in Odessa,"** stands apart from the others in a number of ways. It is the only one of the four that has a special narrator and perhaps for that reason the only one that achieves the totally oral effect of immediate narration. Much of the story is given over to dialogue; when the narrator is not reporting the talk of others he himself is a master monologist. Factual description is kept to a bare minimum, and when it does appear it is dominated by the declamatory and mythic tones in which it is phrased. In spite of the fact that this is the longest of the four stories and that its ostensible subject is the character of the hero Benja Krik, there are no involved psychological analyses or complications of the underlying anecdotal base. Almost everything contributes to the effect of speech.

What I do is to get hold of some trifle, some little anecdote, a piece of market gossip, and turn it into something I cannot tear myself away from. It's alive, it plays. It's round like a pebble on the seashore. It's held together by the fusion of separate parts, and this fusion is so strong that even lightning can't split it. And people will read the story. They'll remember it, they'll laugh, not because it's funny but because one always feels like laughing in the presence of human good fortune.

—Isaac Babel

"How It Was Done in Odessa" tells of Benja's rise to fame, of his raid on the merchant Tartakovsky, and of the funeral he arranged for one of his victims. Reb Arye-Leib, the garrulous old man who narrates the tale, speaks with the same Jewish rhythms as the other Odessa characters; an interrogative intonation is common and major remarks are almost always prefaced with a question. When asked, for example, why only Benja Krik of all the gangsters rose to unprecedented heights of power and glory, Arye-Leib's answer begins with a question: "Why he? Why not they, you wish to know?" There is a hint of biblical magnificence in the rhythm of this response as there is in the parablelike quality of the eventual answer itself, for Arye-Leib never takes the simple or direct path in his explanations; he chooses the more circuitous method of illustration through comparison. He is a "reb," a teacher, and the biblical mode of narration comes to him naturally:

> And now I will speak as the Lord God spoke on Mount Sinai from the Burning Bush. Put my words in your ears. All I saw, I saw with my own eyes, sitting here on the wall of the Second Cemetery next to Little Lisping Mose and Samson from the undertaker's. I, Arye-Leib, saw this—I, a proud Jew dwelling by the dead.

The "biblical" tone alternates, however, with a comic vulgarity:

> . . . [pretend that] your father is Mendel Krik the drayman. What does such a father think about? He thinks about drinking a good glass of vodka, of smashing somebody in the face, of his horses—and nothing more. You want to live, and he makes you die twenty times a day.

These examples from the narrative speech of Arye-Leib must be recognized as more than merely a means of characterizing the narrator linguistically. They indicate that oral devices permeate the entire compositional structure of the story and constitute its organizing principle. The sustained intonational rhythms, the digressions and bizarre detours, the pauses, the suggestions of gestures, the interpolated references to a listener, the bardic contrasting of a mundane present with an epic past, the repetition and word play—all point to the pronounced oral basis of the story, to its calculated effort to impose the illusion of improvised talk. So strong indeed are the effects of such oral devices that the story asks to be heard rather than read, or at least stimulates in the reader a desire to read it aloud.

As is usually the case in Babel's work, it is not the outer subject of the tale that provokes the most interest, but the manner of its presentation. It is style that reveals the inner clash of opposing visions and gives a tale its peculiar radiance—and in **"How It Was Done in Odessa"** style is what the story is all about. Since the narrator and narrative devices occupy center stage and constitute the structural frame for this story, it is they that require the reader's first and closest attention.

No other story of the four has such a distinct and recognizable personality as Arye-Leib built as a focus into the story itself. Standing close to the center of events, he has none of that "outsider" quality to his voice and none of that neutrality of tone that occasionally appear in the other three tales. He is deeply immersed in the milieu he describes and he even speaks, as we have noted, with some of the same intonations as do his heroes—or, rather, the characters of his narrative speak within the broad range of Arye-Leib's voice. Ultimately, almost all of the talk is his: it is his voice, with its comically twisted, almost palpable words, that makes Babel's fantastic fictional Moldavanka come alive.

Another unique feature of **"How It Was Done in Odessa"** is the listener, the "I" who appears at the very beginning of the story and to whom Arye-Leib tells his tale. The invention of this new figure, separate and distinct from the narrator, greatly complicates and enriches the narrative structure by providing a kind of distorting echo chamber for transmitting events to the reader. Furthermore, the lyrical strain now emerges in its own right, and this new focal point within the story allows Babel to explore some additional ironic and dramatic conflicts. By introducing the listener-romantic, Babel provides a contrasting sounding board for the narrator Arye-Leib, a foil against which the latter can exercise his wit and through which he can make his meanings sharper. Arye-Leib's language is by turns earthy and picturesque or solemn and biblical; it may even partake of the grand epic manner, but it is always consistent with the basic intonations of the Odessa jargon and Arye-Leib himself remains an integral part of the milieu he describes. The sympathetic listener, on the other hand, remains outside the tale's milieu: his language is literary and his discourse lyrical in intonation. It is the listening "I" who opens the story:

> It was I that began.
>
> "Reb Arye-Leib," I said to the old man, "let us talk of Benja Krik. Let us talk of his thunderclap beginning and his terrible end. Three black shadows block up the paths of my imagination. Here is the one-eyed Ephraim Rook. The russet steel of his actions, can it really not bear comparison with the strength of the King? Here is Nick Pakovsky. The simple-minded fury of that man held all that was necessary for him to wield power. And did not Haim Drong know how to distinguish the brilliance of the rising star? Why then did Benja Krik alone climb to the top of the rope ladder, while all the rest hung swaying on the lower rungs?"

The speaker's style gives us a sense of his personality. The heightened language, despite its sophistication, reveals a poetic dreamer, a naïve and romantic youth. The opening of the story is furthermore broadly suggestive of the Seder, the Hebrew religious ceremony during which a youth asks his elders profound questions and receives by way of answer stories from the history of the Jews. The next words spoken by the "I," with their biblically phrased adages, reinforce these religious associations:

> Reb Arye-Leib was silent, sitting on the cemetery wall. Before us stretched the green stillness of the graves. A man who thirsts for an answer must stock himself with patience. A man possessing knowledge is suited by dignity. For this reason Reb Arye-Leib was silent, sitting on the cemetery wall.

The silence of Arye-Leib lasts but briefly. Having introduced the story and himself, the "I" assumes his role of listener and retreats to the periphery of the narrative. The rest of the words belong to Arye-Leib.

These opening lines set the stage for the recital of legendary events. We are shown Benja Krik in the early days of his career, during the period when he first revealed himself as an exceptional man and at the crucial moment of his emergence as a king. In keeping with this revelatory aspect of the narrative, a triumphant, even solemn, tone is sounded again and again. We have noted already the generally biblical quality of the opening; here and there one may detect more concrete hints of a biblical grandeur: in the solemn invocation of Benja's awesome beginning and his terrible end; in the reference to a new and shining star; and in the image of Benja ascending a ladder. Arye-Leib, whose narrative style is full of biblical intonation, is quick to reinforce our impression; he tells his young companion to imagine himself for a moment in Benja's place: "If rings were fastened to heaven and earth, you would grasp them and draw heaven and earth together". Of course, given the specific context of the narrative, the effect of such a passage is mainly ironic and the tone one of mock rather than real solemnity. Benja's is an intentionally profane figure through which to suggest the uniting of the heavenly and the earthly, the spiritual and the physical.

Arye-Leib, in spite of the comic incongruity of epic treatment for a group of Odessa bandits, takes on the aspect of bardic singer. He treats events in a legendary manner, as if they had taken place long ago or far away. When he describes how Benja, early in his career, petitioned to join the illustrious band of Froim Grach, he speaks as of great and distant doings: "And the gangsters went into conference to consider the matter of Benja Krik. I wasn't at that conference, but they say that a conference was held."

The band's decision is to try Benja by sending him on a raid against Ruvim Tartakovsky, and the reader will not be wrong in seeing in the assignment the outlines of a mythic encounter. At first glance one is tempted to see a kind of comic parallel to the initiation trial of a knight-errant, with Benja a kind of sullied Galahad being sent in quest of a more than spiritual treasure. But there is another parallel, closer to home. The assignment given to Benja is a particularly difficult one: Tartakovsky has been afflicted by bandit raids nine times already; he has also had the distinction of a premature funeral service; and furthermore, though he is a rich man and has the soul of a murderer, he is one of them—an Odessa Jew. Indeed, Tartakovsky is a kind of legend himself, and although recognized as a merciless exploiter, he is given grudging respect by the community at large. Arye-Leib, with his comic rhetoric, makes it clear that he is a figure combining greed with power and that he is a worthy adversary for Benja:

> We used to call Tartakovsky "Jew-and-a-Half" . . . "Jew-and-a-Half" he was called because no single Jew could have had so much dash and so much cash as Tartakovsky. He was taller than the tallest cop in Odessa, and weighed more than the fattest of Jewesses.

Despite such constant intrusion of the comic into the conflict, Tartakovsky is a serious opponent. He is a rich and powerful oppressor of the poor and weak; half of Odessa, chained to his greed, labors endlessly in his shops. If Tartakovsky is really "Jew-and-a-Half," it is because he has sucked out the life of others, of slaves like his clerk Muginstein. In the story's symbolic and allegorical subtext, Tartakovsky even takes on a certain historical reso-

nance, and through the tale's network of religious imagery, Babel makes of him a Pharaonic symbol. It is a circumstance with intentional ironic effect: "Tartakovsky has the soul of a murderer, but he is one of us. He originated with us. He is our blood. He is our flesh, as though one momma had born us." It is his Jewishness that protects Tartakovsky from Jewish retribution. He is robbed, but his position is unassailed; he is buried, but only symbolically, so that he can rise from the grave to resume, like Pharaoh, his oppression of the people. In his answer to Benja's extortion note, Tartakovsky assumes the role of fellow Jew and sufferer, of one condemned to a life of endless convict labor. A different conclusion, however, may be inferred from Tartakovsky's specific list of woes and tribulations. "Ulcers, sores, troubles and insomnia" afflict him in the same way that the plagues of the Lord afflicted Pharaoh—and, like Pharaoh, Tartakovsky remains unmoved.

It therefore falls upon Benja, who in this context becomes as much deliverer as bandit, to visit upon Tartakovsky an unprecedented tenth raid, something the other bandits, for all their boldness, have steadfastly refrained from undertaking. In his note Benja warns Tartakovsky that if he once more refuses to comply with the demands made upon him a great disappointment awaits him in his "family life." The tenth and final affliction visited upon Pharaoh was, of course, the slaying of the firstborn, and the implication is unavoidable that Benja in his wrath is capable of being no less terrible than the vengeful Yahweh. It is this finally that sets Benja apart from all of the other "aristocrats" of the Moldavanka: he does not waver before the ultimate grim necessity, even when the enemy is unhappily within instead of without the tribe. The result of the raid is indeed a slaying, though not precisely of Tartakovsky's firstborn. Tartakovsky, we are told, raises a hue and cry through all Odessa, while Benja, who is not to be cowed, argues with unwitting irony that even God makes mistakes.

The story progresses, under Arye-Leib's direction, by fits and starts. He steps in and out of his tale as it suits him, sometimes to slow down the pace, sometimes to mystify and heighten suspense, sometimes to make an appropriate observation. Occasionally he employs the device of the mock parable, which parodies the usual presentation of moral truths. True to his intonational style he often proceeds as if unraveling a riddle, he himself supplying both question and answer:

> When Ephraim informed him accordingly, he said "O.K." and went out, banging the door. Why did he bang the door? You will learn this if you come where I shall lead you.

All of Arye-Leib's narrative devices are justified by structure or effectiveness. His digressions, intrusions, pauses, and repetitions are the very stuff of which his tale is made. After giving a detailed report of Benja's bargaining with Tartakovsky over how much the murdered clerk's mother is to be paid (a bargain in which each side overstates its case before coming to businesslike agreement with the other), he produces the following typical comment: "Then they used bad language at one another hammer and tongs,

Jew-and-a-Half and Benja. I wasn't present at this quarrel, but those who were remember it." Those present, of course, were only the principals to the argument, but this does not prevent Arye-Leib from knowing exactly how Benja was dressed for the occasion or from knowing precisely where he paused in his argument for rhetorical effect. He has the right details, and if he has them second-hand this only emphasizes that he is telling the stuff of legends, of mythic battles—though the battle here, like almost everything else in Arye-Leib's tale, is a thing of words.

But Arye-Leib's most effective rhetorical device, one which serves as an ironic refrain throughout the entire narrative structure and which gives the story its tension and conflict, is the sarcastic assault that he periodically makes upon his young listener. The lyrical "I," whose voice opened the tale, is silent throughout the rest of its pages, but never out of sight; Arye-Leib is able to conjure up his person whenever he wishes to instruct through negative precept. The bookish romanticist and lyric poet, as seen through the eyes of Arye-Leib (and behind him, through the controlling vision of the author), emerges as the direct antithesis of the hero Benja Krik. Arye-Leib's very first words challenge his youthful listener to imagine Benja by turning himself inside out:

> Forget for a while that you have spectacles on your nose and autumn in your heart. Cease playing the rowdy at your desk and stammering while others are about. Imagine for a moment that you play the rowdy in public places and stammer on paper. You are a tiger, you are a lion, you are a cat. You can spend the night with a Russian woman, and satisfy her.

He then asks the youth what he would have done if he had been cursed (or blessed) with a father like Benja's:

> What would you have done in Benja Krik's place? You would have done nothing. But he did something. That's why he's the King, while you thumb your nose in the privy.

Again, after telling how the guiltless Muginstein was murdered by a drunken member of Benja's gang, Arye-Leib asks the young listener:

> Now tell me, young master, you who snip coupons on other people's shares, how would you have acted in Benja Krik's place? You don't know how you would have acted. But he knew. That's why he's the King, while you and I are sitting on the wall of the Second Jewish Cemetery and keeping the sun off with our palms.

What Benja does, given the circumstances, is first to arrange for Muginstein's murderer to join him in the other world and then to organize for both the most sumptuous funeral Odessa had ever seen. Among the host of mourners are the employees of Ruvim Tartakovsky, dressed all in black and plodding along in shoes that "squeak like pigs in a poke." There are, says Arye-Leib, "a hundred of them, or two-hundred, or two thousand," but the actual figure is unimportant; they are a mass, not individuals, and the astonishing fertility imparted to them by Arye-Leib's rhetoric is a bitter and ironic comment on the

promise that the Lord's people should increase and multiply.

Arye-Leib's tale rises to a fantastic climax as he describes how Benja, in the midst of the funeral ceremonies, dramatically arrives to deliver the oration. He appears amid a cloud of fumes in a sparkling red automobile; its wheels cast thunderbolts and its horn plays an aria from the opera *Pagliacci*. The ludicrous improbability of this visitation does not quite conceal the biblical parallel as Benja steps up on a mound of earth and with out-stretched hands addresses the people. The speech itself is a pure piece of verbal legerdemain, eloquently demonstrative of Benja's style, and on the surface utterly devoid of logic. But Benja's apparently incongruous eulogy—to the effect that Joseph Muginstein had died on behalf of the working-class—contains an underlying seriousness and truth. "There are people already condemned to death, and there are people who have not yet begun to live," declares Benja, and his words suggest the misery of all those lives doomed to pass within the shadow of ghetto walls.

Benja, on the other hand, is outrageously capable of living. He is a man, as Arye-Leib informs us with pride, who can "spend the night with a Russian woman and satisfy her"; he is one of those, in his own words, who "know how to drink vodka," who can take the experience of life straight. Benja refuses to endure oppression of any kind, and his emergence from behind the walls of spiritual as well as physical ghettos is his challenge to the past, to the monotony and passivity of Jewish suffering—and it is his call, as a contemporary king of kings, to a new exodus for his people.

Having delivered his oration Benja descends from the mound and disappears amid the smoke, the thunderbolts, and the music of his red chariot. It is then that little lisping Mose, the quiet figure who has always occupied the best seat on the cemetery wall, first utters the word "King" in reference to Benja Krik. When we recall that Arye-Leib has prefaced this final climax of his story with words that sound the laconic splendor of the Bible ("And now I will speak as the Lord God spoke on Mount Sinai from the Burning Bush"), we may well conclude that throughout his tale he has played an eloquent Aaron indeed to the less articulate, lisping Moses, and we may well remember that the voice from the burning bush spoke to the Jewish people of an end to their bondage and of a land of milk and honey that would one day be theirs.

The story's final paragraphs strike an ironic note and at the same time give the narrative Babel's favorite circular form. Arye-Leib descends from the elevated style of his most impassioned rhetorical moment to inform his listener that on the very day of the funeral, on the same day that Benja was first called king, Tartakovsky closed up shop. In Arye-Leib's very last words he expresses a lingering doubt that the young man who has heard his tale will have truly understood it:

> "Now you know all. You know who first uttered the word 'King.' It was Little Mose. You know why he didn't give that name to One-Eyed Rook, or to Crazy Nick. You know all. But

> what's the use, if you still have spectacles on
> your nose and autumn in your heart?" .

The ironic repercussions of this closing are rich and complex. The lyrical dreamer whose words opened the story had been asked by Arye-Leib to imagine that he was someone else, someone like Benja Krik, for only a concerted effort of the imagination could make this tale of adventure and passion real for such a timid, untried, bookish youth. And yet, paradoxically, the young man possesses qualities that are indispensable to the perception and appreciation of the multicolored, exotic world Arye-Leib describes. The autumn in his heart is the romantic pathos that allows such fantasies a measure of reality, and the spectacles on his nose, though they may be of colored glass and though they suggest the image of an academic and reserved intellectual, nevertheless represent the means to vision for the otherwise sightless.

On the other hand, says Arye-Leib, the imagination is insufficient: you may know everything, but unless the knowledge you have is a part of the reality of your being you know nothing; you remain an outsider, an on-looker. Imagination may lead you part of the way, but it can also take you into the comfortable rut of hollow pieties and deceptive traditions. To understand fully why Benja alone among many bold and violent men was the "King" requires more than a mere recognition of the Hebrew monotheistic tradition; it demands as well recognition of Benja's fundamental iconoclasm, of his pure and primeval contempt for degenerate tradition and dogma. Benja's wrath, like that of Yahweh, may be hurled against the people he loves as well as against their enemies; if he does battle with those enemies who attack the Jewish people from outside its communal structure, he rejects no less the complacent assumption of moral superiority so jealously guarded by hypocrites within the ghetto walls. Pharaoh is everywhere, within as well as without, and the road from slavery to freedom, from subjugation to redemption, demands that Pharaoh be resisted wherever he may be. The Jewish houses will not be passed over in the necessary slaying of the firstborn, not if it is to be the true passage "from sorrow to joy, and from mourning to festive day, and from darkness to a great light" (from the Haggadah of Passover). Of course if Arye-Leib's rhetoric has enticed the reader into accepting his fantastic fairy-tale for a kind of reality, it is ultimately due to the subtle craft of the author, who, hidden behind all of his characters, peers at us enigmatically through his own thick lenses. Arye-Leib's mocking criticism of the dreamy literary youth has partly blinded us to the fact that he, too, is an incorrigible romantic, a dreamer sitting on the sidelines atop the cemetery wall and singing the incomparable lay of Benja the King.

The two remaining Odessa stories share with **"The King"** and **"How It Was Done in Odessa"** many stylistic and thematic characteristics, but at the same time Babel is attempting, not without difficulty, to expand and deepen the possibilities of his material. Both **"The Father"** and **"Ljubka the Cossack"** also celebrate antitraditionalism and vigorous physicality, but this time the central characters are women. In **"The Father,"** Benja Krik appears only toward the end; the dominant figure is Basja Grach, daughter of the one-eyed gangster Froim. Gigantic in her physique as well as her appetites, Basja, like Dvoira, is eager to find a mate. After casting about in the direction of an undersized grocery clerk (whose very name, Kaplun—Capon—is a mockery of her desires), she is matched with the King himself, the only character likely to survive the crush of her loving embrace. All of these women—Basja with her capon, Dvoira with her mouse-spouse, and the husbandless Ljubka—suffer from a lack of comparably vigorous male partners.

In the final story Benja does not appear at all, but the female protagonist, Ljubka, assumes a similar role. She is as rough and wild, as awesome in her way, as the King, and although the heroic, almost hagiographic, tone applied to Benja is absent here, the exaggerated, hyperbolic style is retained. Ljubka is presented as a figure larger than life and she partakes of a similar mythic-symbolic significance. The very nickname, "the Cossack," antithetical to "the Jew," suggests the same primitive attachment to physicality and force that characterized Benja and indicates that she has also rejected the cramped, segregated life of the ghetto. Ljubka's surname, in mocking contrast to her nickname, is Schneeweiss (Snow White). The two names, suggesting barbarous violence and gentle repose, reveal that typical fusion of incompatibilities that so often lies at the heart of Babel's vision. To be sure, there is an element of mockery; Snow White also evokes the image of Ljubka as a princess surrounded by dwarfs and freaks. But there is still another, less obvious relevance to the allusion: Ljubka is identified with Snow White the eternally pure, with the sleeping beauty who required the touch of a Prince Charming to bring the blush of life to her cheeks. Although Ljubka apparently has no husband, she would seem, since she does have a son, to have been visited by some kind of Prince Charming. His identity is problematical, but to judge from Ljubka's formidable personality no mere mortal could have been her match. The religious travesty becomes obvious when the dominant image of the story is seen to be that of madonna and child, and Ljubka is finally associated with the virgin mother of Christian tradition and her son with the Messiah. The inn over which Ljubka reigns is a stopping place for wayfarers and pilgrims, and among those who arrive bringing tribute are three sailors from distant parts: the engineer Mr. Trottyburn and his two companions, a Malayan and an English sailor. There are several indications that these travelers are to be identified with the biblical Magi, but the most compelling are the offerings they bring of tobacco, cocaine, and wine, and the orange star that gazes at them from the edge of the horizon.

Babel is once again in these allusions adjusting religious forms to modern secular usage, but what is strikingly new in this story is the admixture of specifically Christian motifs with the Hebraic elements used in the first two Odessa tales. If Benja had the aspect of an Old Testament Yahweh, Ljubka's son, who bears the royal name of David, suggests a sort of New Testament Messiah. He is admiringly described as "big as a Russian" and seems to be another of Babel's symbols for the emancipation from Jewish tradition. As in the biblical story, the young child and the hope he represents are threatened, but by the madonna-mother herself rather than by a Herod figure. Competing in the harsh world of smuggling, prostitution, and drink, Ljubka is more than a match for the roughest of her male customers, but she pays a price: she is unable, for all the amazon charms of her physique, to produce milk for her child. In performing an essentially male role she has lost a part of her femaleness, and it is a man, the wizened little Jew Tsudechkis (representing a transferred maternal figure much as Joseph in the Bible represents a transferred paternal figure), who weans the infant from breast to bottle. The weaning is typical of Babel, symbolic as well as actual, and suggests that the next generation will be the first to be truly emancipated, free not only of Egypt and the wilderness but of self-captivity as well. Little David remains, however, only a hope, tentative and unfulfilled, a promise rather than a revelation.

This story, like **"The Father,"** is interesting evidence of Babel's effort to go beyond the accomplishment of his first two Odessa tales. He did not completely succeed in his aim, and the problem appears to lie in his attitude toward his material. In the first of *The Odessa Tales,* **"The King,"** a controlling and sustaining feature is the author's sheer pleasure in the exuberance of his material; his captivating joy in the peculiarities of the Odessa speech contributes an essentially jocular spirit to the entire tale. Much the same can be said of the second story, **"How It Was Done in Odessa,"** in which Babel continues to exploit the natural potential of his material at the same time that he experiments with a deepening use of narrative and other stylistic devices. **"How It Was Done in Odessa"** is a sort of transitional story, more serious in its understructure than **"The King,"** and offers greater possibilities for creative development. The last two stories, however, attempt to use the same kind of material in a different way. The jocularity remains, but it no longer seems congenial to other demands that Babel makes of his characters. He gives his essentially comic Odessa in these stories a greater weight than it can naturally bear. Part of the problem is that Babel's women protagonists are unsympathetic. They exist on a single plane and embody his themes in a somewhat schematic and unappealing manner.

Still, the themes suggested by Babel's women are important ones. His juxtaposition of the powerful, voracious female and the faint-hearted, puny male is especially revealing. In such sexual encounters he sees a model for social reality, a way of portraying the conflict between aggressive and passive modes of behavior. In attempting to deny such basic, primitive facts, civilization itself in Babel's eyes becomes a source of turmoil and anguish. In the stories with women protagonists his inversion of the traditional male and female roles is thus an ironic statement that nature will somehow out, and the comedy of his mismatched couples contains more than a touch of bitterness and frustration. And yet, in their tragic contours, such portraits also reflect Babel's deep and ineradicable commitment to culture. Gentleness and aggression, the promptings of civilization and nature, are bound in unhappy union in the writer's heart.

With regard to solving this dilemma in his art Babel was one of those who, long before Andrej Sinjavsky, recognized that the spirit of the age demanded a fantastic, phan-

tasmagoric art, a vision of the grotesque. Profoundly cognizant of the discontents of civilization, he links the imagery of sexual rebellion with that of spiritual and political emancipation and creates a gallery of heroes who grope toward a new reality that is unclear even to themselves. *The Odessa Tales* is an optimistic work, one vesting the Revolution with hope. In his art Babel seeks in a sense to reconcile Freud and Marx, to redeem—not philosophically, but artistically—the harsh truths of the former with the noble hope of the latter. It is a sad commentary on the perspicacity of Soviet critics that they should find in Babel a writer whose talents were uncongenial to the epoch. The dilemma of Soviet life as well as Soviet art has always been that unfortunate contrast between the malingering present and the glowing future, and Babel, whose sin was an inability to nonchalantly confuse the two, doggedly insisted on locating his hopeful synthesis in the future.

Edward J. Brown on Soviet literary criticism:

Conventional Soviet criticism is no doubt right according to its own lights in finding that Babel's work is weighted with the details of brutality, and that he has missed "the rational principle in the Civil War, and the organizing role of the Communist Party." No doubt Babel himself could have constructed a final ironic anecdote featuring the Soviet literary critics who say such things. The great virtue of his stories is precisely their lack of political color, their apparently casual and fragmented structure. Not the least of Babel's ironies is the fact that the ideals of the socialist revolution, wrapped in facile phrases, have come into the possession of Russian peasant warriors incapable of understanding or realizing them.

Edward J. Brown, *"The Intellectuals, II,"* in his Russian Literature Since the Revolution, *revised edition, 1982.*

Carol Luplow   (essay date 1982)

SOURCE: *Isaac Babel's "Red Cavalry,"* Ardis, 1982, 122 p.

[*In the essay below, Luplow examines the function of Lyutov, the narrator of the stories in* Red Cavalry.]

Most of the stories in *Red Cavalry* are complete, coherent short stories. But certain of their structural features, such as a tendency toward plotlessness and a disjointed episodic structure, extreme brevity, the reintroduction of the characters, situations, and images of one story in subsequent ones, and the inclusion in the cycle of a few fragments which seem more like brief sketches than actual short stories, tend to give the stories a fragmented quality, to make them felt as segments of a larger whole. And in fact the stories form a unified, integrated cycle which has a broader and deeper significance than its individual parts.

From their inception Babel intended the *Red Cavalry* stories to be parts of a cycle. Many stories were subtitled

"From the book *Red Cavalry*" when they were first published in journals. There are several factors which unify the stories into a cyclical form. First, the cycle has a thematic unity. All the stories contribute to the development of basic themes and issues and to the creation of a particular vision of reality which is fully realized only in the cycle as a whole. Each of the stories, though it has its own thematic unity, both gains added dimensions of meaning in its relation to the other stories and adds further dimensions to the problems and vision of the cycle. Second, the cycle has a plot unity. It is organized as a chronological narrative of Budyonny's campaign against Poland, beginning with the army's entry into Poland and ending with the army in retreat. All the stories relate incidents which occur in the course of the expedition and involve characters who are either soldiers in the cavalry, civilians attached to the cavalry, or civilians met during the campaign. Furthermore, a number of characters, including Afonka Bida, Sashka the Christ, Grishchuk, Gedali, and Pavlichenko, appear in more than one story, and thus provide a sense of plot continuity. Third, the cycle gains a narrative unity through the use of a first person narrator, Lyutov, who is both unifying point of view and central character. He relates all but five stories (the *skaz* stories narrated by Cossack characters) and is himself either central protagonist or important participant in the majority of the stories [the critic states in a footnote that the term *skaz,* in his usage, denotes "a first person narration oriented toward oral speech with a narrator from a defined (usually lower) class who in his manner and style of narration . . . calls the reader's attention as much to himself and his character as to the events which he is relating"]. His observations, experiences, and dilemmas occupy the central position in the cycle. Finally, the stories are connected by a common set of narrative, compositional, and stylistic features, which are motivated by the use of the narrator, Lyutov, and are linked to his perception and vision of the world, but which are also found in the *skaz* stories and serve to connect them to the stories narrated by Lyutov.

Red Cavalry, then, is primarily the story of one man's experiences in Budyonny's cavalry campaign. It is he who poses, investigates, and grapples with the main historical, ethical, and philosophical issues of the cycle. It is he who experiences personally the basic dialectic of the cycle—the clash between radically different approaches to reality, ways of life, and value systems—and attempts to resolve the dilemmas created by the Revolution and by reality.

The stories in which Lyutov is not both narrator and major participant can be divided into three groups. In the first group—"The Remount Officer," "The Brigade Commander," "Chesniki," "Evening," "Pan Apolek," and "Two Ivans"—Lyutov is observer-narrator, but plays little or no role in the action. However, his presence is strongly felt as filtering consciousness. He depicts the experiences of others as they relate to his own interests and problems, so that they become significant as part of his own experience. As Patricia Carden points out [in *The Art of Isaac Babel,* 1972], these stories then tend to have two centers of gravity, a main character and the narrator, who,

as filtering consciousness, provides the point of view toward an interpretation of the characters and events.

In the second group of stories the central role of Lyutov as interpreter of reality is set in even greater relief. In this group, which includes "Prishchepa," "Sashka the Christ," and parts of "Pan Apolek," "The Widow," "Two Ivans," and "The Story of a Horse," Lyutov relates in detail stories or scenes which he himself did not observe, but which were told, or presumably told, to him. He then imaginatively fills in details, elaborating on scenes, working them into his own story telling mode and style, and presenting them from his point of view. For example, he did not witness the early scenes from the life of Pan Apolek, yet he describes them in detail, from the points of view of various characters. He did not observe the climactic scene between Khlebnikov and Savitsky in "The Story of a Horse," nor was the hysterical Khlebnikov in any state to relate the details to him. Neither did he witness the scene between the dying Shevelyov, Lyovka, and Sashka in "The Widow" or the first two days' events in "Two Ivans." In "Sashka the Christ" he relates Sashka's story in the form of a legend. And in "Prishchepa" he states that Prishchepa told him his story, but then tells the story not from Prischepa's point of view but from that of the townspeople who observe the episode from a distance. This first person narrative omniscience is carried still further when Lyutov briefly enters the mind of another character. In "The Remount Officer," for example, he describes the commander who stands listening to the complaining peasants as follows:

> His inflamed eyelids closed, he listened with apparent attentivenes to the peasants' complaints. But his attentiveness was merely a ruse. . . .
>
> To the soothing accompaniment of their disconnected and desperate clamor Z. attended peripherally to that mild crush in the brain which presages purity and energy of thought.

And in "Pan Apolek" Lyutov presumes to know why the innkeeper abandoned his pursuit of Apolek and Gottfried:

> But along the way Shmerel recalled Apolek's pink body, bathed in water, and the sunshine in his courtyard, and the peaceful pealing of the accordian. The innkeeper felt ashamed and, putting aside his stick, he returned home.

Lyutov makes no attempt to motivate his knowledge of some of these scenes or of characters' thoughts. The objective truth is not as important as the narrator's "truth," as his imaginative rendition of events and characters.

The third group of stories, the *skaz* stories, also develop and expand upon problems with which Lyutov is concerned. They illuminate issues from points of view alien to him and provide new points of view and fuller insights into the issues. These stories are not only closely connected to Lyutov's stories in theme, but are also narrated in a manner and style similar to Lyutov's narration. Only two of the *skaz* stories are specifically motivated to be included in a cycle "authored" by Lyutov. In "Konkin" Lyutov is in the audience when Konkin tells his story and in "The Letter" Kurdyukov dictates his letter to Lyutov.

But in **"The Life of Pavlichenko"** one must merely assume that Lyutov is in the audience which hears Pavlichenko's speech, an audience which is only implied by Pavlichenko's apostrophes. One can assume that Lyutov saw Balmashev's letter to the editor in **"Salt,"** since he worked for the newspaper. But Lyutov's access to the letter to the investigator in **"Treason"** is not motivated at all. These "inconsistencies," in which Lyutov oversteps his capacity to know as first person narrator, could show the hand of the author in the making of the cycle. But, as in the stories of the second group, the question of realistic motivation is not as important as the full rendering of Lyutov's experiences. The *skaz* stories expand upon the central dialectic and the moral and philosophical dilemmas experienced by Lyutov, and have a stylistic continuity with the other stories in the cycle.

It is essentially Lyutov's character, then, which determines the representation of reality and development of themes in **Red Cavalry.** Lyutov does not give us an objective view of reality, but rather his version of reality, reality filtered through his mind and imagination and transformed and interpreted by him. Furthermore, Lyutov is not merely a *persona* for the author, but must be distinguished from the separate and ultimately controlling authorial overview. In fact, Lyutov's view of reality is frequently ironically qualified by the author's overview.

Cover of Red Cavalry, *the first volume of Babel's* Collected Works *(1928).*

Lyutov is a Jewish intellectual steeped in the Jewish humanist tradition. With the values of this tradition and the intellectual's habits of thought and introspection, which make him primarily observer, recorder, and thinker, he enters the Cossack world of action, violence, and Revolution, a world whose values and way of life are radically opposed to his own.

Lyutov's character is perfectly suited to his role as observer and recorder in the cycle. He is insatiably curious. His attention is drawn to strikingly unusual phenomena. He has the sensitivity to perceive what is unusual and significant and the imagination to see reality in new ways, to draw new relationships between things. He is flexible and open to the experiencing of varied situations. He is a sophisticated, perceptive, imaginative person, and he can thus perceive and respond fully—emotionally, intellectually, and artistically—to the complex and ambiguous world of **Red Cavalry.**

But the reader cannot indiscriminately accept Lyutov's version of reality. His view of the world is shaped by a romantic, aesthetic sensibility which leads him to subjectively "distort" reality. This sensibility is succinctly and beautifully expressed in his metaphoric statement at the end of **"The Story of a Horse,"** in which he laments the departure of Khlebnikov, in whom he had found a kindred soul:

> We were both possessed by the same passions.
> We both looked on the world as a meadow in
> May, a meadow through which pass women and
> horses.

Central to Lyutov's romantic outlook is a vision of the paradoxical duality of reality. This vision strongly affects all other aspects of his romantic world view, which includes: a heightened aesthetic sensibility; a love for beauty and a tendency toward the detached contemplation of things for their own sake; a sense of the metaphorical relationships of things; a view of nature as a living, organic being; a belief in the important role which dream, imagination, and art play in reality; a general subjectivity of outlook; a penchant for exoticism, hyperbole, and the grotesque; and an attraction toward primitivism. Finally, Lyutov displays a heightened sensitivity to sense impressions and a love of the palpable, sensual phenomena of life.

Lyutov's sensitivity to and appreciation of beauty are reflected in his many descriptions of the beauty of landscapes, objects, and people. He often depicts them in a highly decorative style, rich in metaphorical elaborations which further aestheticize them.

> Fields of purple poppies flowered around us, the
> midday breeze played in the yellow rye. Virginal
> buckwheat rose on the horizon like the wall of
> a distant monastery. The quiet Volyn twisted
> about, the Volyn moved away from us into the
> pearly mist of birch groves; it crawled into vari-
> colored hillocks and its weakened arms got tan-
> gled in thickets of hop. The orange sun rolled
> across the sky like a lopped-off head; a tender
> light flared in the ravines of dark clouds; the
> standards of sunset fluttered over our heads.

["Crossing the Zbruch"]

Next to him lay the trappings of the dead horse, the intricate and fanciful attire of a Cossack stallion—breast-plates with black tassles, supple crupper straps studded with colored stones, and a bridle etched in silver.

["Afonka Bida"]

But Lyutov's vision of the paradoxical nature of reality, the co-existence of opposite qualities in reality, which is central to his romantic sensibility, leads him to see reality in terms of extremes, to exaggerate in order to bring polarities and contrasts into relief. Consequently, Lyutov's aesthetic sensibility encompasses a heightened apprehension both of what is beautiful, elevated, and splendid and of what is ugly, crude, or horrible. And he finds both poles equally worthy of artistic contemplation. Thus, at times he describes the ugly or horrible in stark relief.

Four feet with fat heels stuck out into the cool air, and we saw Irina's loving calves and Vasily's big toe with its crooked black nail.

["Evening"]

Her son lay snoring under the icon on a big bed strewn with rags. He was a dumb boy with a swollen, puffy white head and gigantic feet, like those of a grown man. His mother wiped his dirty nose and returned to the table.

["The Song"]

Lyutov not only draws a sharp distinction between the two aesthetic poles, but also paradoxically joins those poles. Usually, he aestheticizes or beautifies what is ordinarily perceived as low or ugly by decorating it with his elaborate style or by metaphorically connecting it with images of beauty. He thus creates a tension between the thing itself and the manner of its description, its stylistic transformation. (This device has specific functions in particular contexts, but as a whole serves to express the paradoxical vision of the cycle.) In **"Italian Sunshine,"** for example, Lyutov transforms the scene of a ruined city into a beautiful romantic image.

The burned out city—its broken columns and crooks of old women's evil little fingers dug into the earth—seemed to me to be raised into the air, comfortable and fantastic, like a dream. The naked radiance of the moon streamed onto it with inexhaustible strength. The damp mold of the ruins blossomed like the marble of an opera bench. And with anxious heart I awaited the appearance of Romeo from behind the dark clouds, a satin-clad Romeo singing of love . . .

["Italian Sunshine"]

Lyutov most frequently aestheticizes reality in this way in descriptions which would normally evoke a feeling of horror. At times this device serves to tone down the horror by aesthetically and emotionally distancing the object described.

Fixing its shining deep violet eyes on its master, the horse listened to Afonka's convulsive wheezing. In tender forgetfulness it traced its fallen muzzle along the ground, and streams of blood,

like two ruby breech bands, trickled down its breast, inlaid with white muscles.

["Afonka Bida"]

At other times the tension between the aesthetic surface and the underlying horror of the object throws the object into relief and thereby heightens the sense of horror.

. . . outside the window, in the garden under the black passion of the sky, flowed the iridescent avenue. Thirsting roses swayed in the darkness. Green flashes of lightning flared up in the cupolas. A naked corpse lay prostrate at the foot of the slope, and moonlight streamed over its dead legs, thrust wide apart.

["The Church at Novograd"]

On its [the horse's] spine ichor traced a lacework pattern between the strips of torn meat.

["Argamak"]

Sometimes the aesthetic poles are joined by the opposite device of deaestheticization. The inherent beauty of an object or scene is lessened, or a tension is created through a debasing metaphor or simile whose vehicle is something crude, ugly, or horrible. The image of the sun as a lopped off head in the nature description in **"Crossing the Zbruch"** serves this purpose, as does the following description of the pink sunset in **"Gedali":** "The sky was changing color. Tender blood flowed from an overturned bottle there above, and I was enveloped in a light odor of decay." And in **"Berestechko"** a brief description of a lovely sunset includes an image of the moon as a green lizard.

Lyutov's penchant for the exotic, for what is unusual, striking, or vivid, is closely related to his heightened sense of duality and paradox. He distorts reality through exaggeration and hyperbole, or colors it with a hyperbolic style and imagery, in order to reveal its most vivid, unusual aspect, to expose its polar oppositions. He not only exoticizes reality in descriptions, but also chooses exotic, flamboyant characters, scenes, situations, and themes. The stories often center on melodramatic incidents presented in a melodramatic manner, such as Pavlichenko's revenge in **"The Life of Pavlichenko,"** the fight between Lyutov and Akinfiev in **"After the Battle,"** and the confrontation between Savitsky and Khlebnikov in **"The Story of a Horse"** followed by Khlebnikov's theatrically hysterical outburst.

The stories in **Red Cavalry** are predominantly character studies which emphasize personality extremes and paradoxically contradictory traits within one personality. They depict characters who embody extremes of both cruelty and heroism, such as Trunov, who in **"Squadron Commander Trunov"** mercilessly kills his prisoners and then sacrifices himself in a grand battle with bombers in order to save his men, and Sashka the Christ, who in the story of that name combines within himself the qualities of both spiritual purity and physical impurity. **"Evening"** contrasts Galin's inner political and intellectual passion with his impotence in expressing his physical passion for Irina. And in **"The Rabbi's Son"** Lyutov describes a character, Ilya, who experiences strong conflicting loyalties both to the poetic and gentle Jewish tradition and to the pragmatic and harsh revolution of Lenin. In some stories Lyutov relates acts of a given character which seem to display totally contradictory personality traits. In **"The Death of Dolgushov,"** for example, Afonka Bida kills Dolgushov as an act of mercy but then turns on Lyutov and almost kills him out of rage. In **"The Remount Officer"** Dyakov forces a dying horse to stand up with a combination of tenderness and cruelty. And in **"Salt"** Balmashev first extends compassion and protection to a woman with a baby and then exacts merciless retribution from her when he finds he has been deceived. Lyutov also describes characters in whom external circumstances sharply belie the inner essence of the character. The Jewish family in **"Crossing the Zbruch"** seems steeped in poverty and degradation, but in the end the family displays true inner dignity and nobility. And Gedali in the story of that name seems to be an isolated old man steeped in a dying tradition, yet he reveals a great inner passion and strength which look to a vital new future.

Lyutov also focuses in many stories on sharp contrasts and clashes between opposite character types. In **"The Story of a Horse"** he contrasts the strong, hard Savitsky, who takes what he wants by force, with Khlebnikov, the aesthetic "lover of gray horses" and seeker of justice through law. In **"Evening"** the political fanatic Galin is juxtaposed to the cook Vasily, who looks upon humans as meat, and whose lack of sensibility and conviction frees his passions so that he easily possesses Irina. Lyutov himself is often contrasted to other characters, especially the Cossacks. In **"The Death of Dolgushov"** he, with his humanist values and sensibilities, is unable to perform a mercy-killing, while Afonka Bida's harsh nature allows him to pull the trigger. And in **"My First Goose"** the small bespectacled Lyutov is juxtaposed to the virile figure of Savitsky. But in **"Gedali"** Lyutov's harsh acceptance of the Revolution is juxtaposed to Gedali's rejection of it in the name of true compassion. In fact, Lyutov's ambiguous position in the dialectic between revolution and humanism, between violence and peace allows him to be an opposing voice in any given story, so that the tension between polarities is always maintained.

Paradox and polarity, always realized through individual characters and character contrasts, in fact dominate the thematics of the entire cycle, pitting humanism against revolution, peace against violence, reality against imagination, Jewish tradition against Cossack life, civilization against primitivism, past against present, the rational against the irrational, and the spiritual against the physical. But this duality also dominates more particular themes and issues, such as the opposite extremes of heroism and brutality in the war, and the themes of individual stories: for example, dream versus reality in **"Italian Sunshine,"** loyalty versus betrayal in **"The Widow,"** and the Church's distorted Christianity versus the "heretic" Apolek's true Christianity in **"Pan Apolek."**

Lyutov's aesthetic sensibility is also reflected in his sensuous apprehension of reality, his joy in the sensual richness of life. He expresses this most directly in his love and admiration for the richly textured and animated paintings of Apolek, which abound with vegetation, animals, chubby infants, and people, all moving, vibrant, colorful, and alive.

> These pictures were painted in oils on thin sheets of cypress. The priest saw on his table the burning purple of manteaus, shimmering emerald fields, and flowery counterpanes cast over the plains of Palestine.
>
> Pan Apolek's saints, that whole assembly of rejoicing and simple-minded old men, gray-bearded and red-faced, were crowded into floods of silk and glorious eventides.
>
> . . . . .
>
> Apolek worked diligently, and in only a month the new temple was filled with the bleating of herds, the dusty gold of sunsets, and pale yellow cows' udders. Bullocks with threadbare hides strained in harness, dogs with pink noses ran in front of flocks of sheep, and chubby infants rocked in cradles suspended from the straight trunks of palm trees. The brown rags of Franciscan monks surrounded a cradle. A crowd of Magi was interlaced with sparking bald spots and wrinkles bloody as wounds.
>
> **["Pan Apolek"]**

Lyutov's own nature descriptions equally depict this sensuous abundance and joy of life.

> Tarakanych and Sashka walked through the fields. The earth lay in April dampness. Emeralds glistened in black pits. Young green shoots embroidered the earth in intricate stitchwork. And the earth smelled acrid, like a soldier's wife at dawn. The first herds came thronging down from the burial mounds and colts gambolled about in the azure expanses of the horizon.
>
> **["Sashka the Christ"]**

Lyutov also reveals his heightened sensuality in his fascination with large-breasted females, who embody for him human animality and sexuality.

> And she [Savitsky's mistress] walked over to the commander, carrying her breasts high on her heels, breasts which stirred like an animal in a bag.
>
> **["The Story of a Horse"]**
>
> Sashka's body, blooming and stinking like the meat of a recently butchered cow, was exposed; her raised skirts revealed the legs of a squadron mistress, wrought-iron, well-formed legs, and Kurdyukov, a doltish fellow, sat astride Sashka and, shaking as if he were in the saddle, pretended to be overcome by passion.
>
> **["In St. Valentine's Church"]**

Early Soviet critics emphasized this sensual aspect of *Red Cavalry,* what they called Babel's "physiologism." In doing so they called attention to an important aspect of the world of *Red Cavalry* and of Lyutov's approach to it, although they tended to exaggerate it and thereby to distort the total vision of the stories. Novitsky, for example, insisted on Babel's obsession with "the primeval animal element of flesh," with the "primeval animal force of life," and with the dark, bestial, cruel, and primeval instinct of man [*I. E. Babel: stat'i i materialy,* 1928]. Voronsky, too, emphasized Babel's love of "flesh, meat, blood, muscle, . . . all that hotly and turbulently grows, breathes, smells, that is solidly rooted in the earth" [*Literaturnye tipy,* 1927].

Lyutov's sensuality, like his exoticism, is directly connected to his fascination with the primitive nature of man as embodied in the Cossacks' uninhibited sensuality, passion and unrestrained violence. And in fact Lyutov links sex and violence as naturally concomitant impulses. In **"My First Goose"** the Cossack "mystique" of rape directly links sex and violence, and the Cossack's suggestion that Lyutov prove his worth by raping a woman leads directly to the killing of the goose. Sex and death are similarly linked in **"Zamostye,"** where Lyutov's erotic dream shifts into a dream of his death, and in **"The Widow,"** in which the orderly Lyovka and Shevelyov's mistress Sashka make love in the grass beside the dying commander.

Lyutov's vision of paradox again leads him to contradictory attitudes towards the physiological, primitive side of man's nature. At times he idealizes and exoticizes it, especially in his images of the Cossacks and women, who embody natural, healthy life and sexuality. But this "naturalistic exoticism" is balanced by a crude naturalism in which Lyutov starkly details low natural functions *per se.* The sense of sex as mere bodily function is well illustrated in the scene in **"The Widow"** in which Lyutov describes Lyovka's acts of eating and sexual intercourse in identical terms. "Next to him sat Lyovka chewing his meat, smacking his lips and panting." And when Lyovka makes love to Sashka Lyutov writes: "Lyovka smacked his lips and panted in the bushes." Man's low physiological nature is depicted throughout **Red Cavalry** in images of urine and feces, vomit, blood, corpses, mutilated bodies, and sexual intercourse. Furthermore, it is revealed in what Novitsky calls the "primeval brute instinct for destruction" of the Cossacks.

Thus, Babel sees reality both in terms of luxurious splendor and exotic decorativeness and in terms of a destructive "struggle of elemental forces"; he colors reality, both its sordid and its elevated, beautiful side with his "romantic ornamentation and decoration" while at the same time he exposes in stark naturalistic detail its crude, drab, sordid side. And these opposite qualities may be paradoxically linked within the same person, scene, or image.

Lyutov in general has an acute awareness of the larger opposition in reality between the contrasting physical-sensual and spiritual-intellectual modes of life. This awareness, moreover, leads to an inner conflict within Lyutov himself. He suggests the possibility of reconciling these opposite modes in his presentation of some of the religious characters, but he does not develop the idea. This conflict between the two modes is Lyutov's central philosophical and moral dilemma in the cycle. . . .

Nature plays a significant role in **Red Cavalry,** and Lyutov perceives it, too, from his romantic-aesthetic viewpoint. He is highly aware and appreciative of the beauty of nature, as evidenced by his frequent descriptions of an exotic, vibrant nature. But more importantly, he feels nature to be a living being with a close relationship to man. He frequently depicts a personified nature, which mingles with and intrudes upon the world of man, as in the following scene from **"The Widow."**

> . . . [Lyovka] stretched his arms up toward the sky, surrounding himself with the night, as if with a nimbus. The tireless breeze, the pure night breeze, filled the air with its ringing and gently rocked the soul. The stars flared up in the darkness like wedding rings; they fell on Lyovka, got tangled in his hair, and died out in his shaggy head.

However, nature and man more often have a contrastive relationship. At the beginning of **"Crossing the Zbruch,"** for example, Lyutov's description of nature expresses its beauty, vitality, and purity. But in the second half of that description nature's positive qualities stand in stark contrast to the chaotic, destructive world of man.

> The odor of yesterday's blood and dead horses dripped into the cool of evening. The blackened Zbruch roared and twisted the foamy knots of its rapids. The bridges had been knocked out, so we forded the river. The stately moon lay on the waves. Horses entered the water up to their spines, sonorous currents oozed between the hundreds of horses' legs. Someone sank and loudly defamed the Mother of God. The river was strewn with the black squares of carts, it was full of howls, whistles, and songs resounding over moonlit snakes and glistening pits.

In **"The Song"** Lyutov draws a similarly sharp contrast between a peaceful, abundant hunting preserve he had once visited and the sordid actions of the soldiers, including himself, in the war. At times, as in **"The Song,"** nature stands aloof from man and symbolically recalls to him the ideals of beauty and purity. At other times nature comes as a soothing, "motherly" force to comfort man (Lyutov) in his solitude and anguish. In **"My First Goose,"** for example, after the resourceful Lyutov has carried out his sordid deed, nature comes to calm him.

> Evening wrapped me in the vivifying moisture of its twilight sheets, evening laid its motherly hands to my burning brow.

And in **"Evening"** nature soothes both Lyutov in his solitude and pain and Galin in his emotional anguish.

> Night consoled us in our sorrows, a light breeze fanned us like a mother's skirt, and the grass below glistened with freshness and moisture.

Lyutov sometimes perceives nature as a moral reflector of his, and man's guilt. After he kills the goose in **"My First Goose"** the moon appears to him as a "cheap earring," and his image of the setting sun as a chopped off head in **"Crossing the Zbruch"** comments upon the invading army.

Man, however, intrudes upon the world of nature only to destroy and defile it: in **"Crossing the Zbruch,"** as we have just seen, in **"The Road to Brody,"** where the Cossacks destroy the "sacred republics of the bees," and at the end of

"**After the Battle**," where the earth itself suffers from the wounds of war—"the countryside floated and swelled up, crimson clay oozed from its tedious wounds."

Lyutov's romantic-aesthetic outlook also gives rise to a sense that art, dream, and imagination play a major role in shaping our relationship to the "real" world, our perceptions of and reactions to reality. There are striking descriptions of various works of art and craftsmanship in many stories, such as the paintings and sculpture of Apolek in "**Pan Apolek**" and "**In St. Valentines's Church**," architecture in "**In St. Valentine's Church**" and "**Berestechko**," song in "**The Song**" and "**The Road to Brody**," the tombstone carvings in "**The Cemetery at Kozin**," the *tachanka* in "**Discourse on the *Tachanka*,**" and the oral tales in "**Pan Apolek**" and "**The Road to Brody**." At times Lyutov directly describes his strong emotional reaction to art and his wonder before it. But he expresses his awe before the beauty and power of art primarily through his detailed, lavish descriptions of the works, which are rich in both visual depiction and emotional connotation. He reveals his reaction in the use of such adjectives as "mighty" and "solemn," by descriptively illuminating the works with light, as if from a nimbus, and by stressing a natural setting which illuminates and heightens the effect of the work.

> I remember: between the straight, bright walls stood the spiderweb silence of a summer morning. The sun had laid its straight ray of light at the base of the picture. Glistening specks of dust swarmed in it. Straight out at me, out of the deep blue depths of the niche, descended the long figure of John. A black cloak hung solemnly on his implacable, repulsively emaciated body.
>
> ["**Pan Apolek**"]

> I was freed from work only about noon. I went over to the window and saw before me the cathedral of Berestechko—magnificent and white. It shone in the warm sun like a glazed earthenware tower. Midday flashes of lightning flared up in its lustrous sides. Their convex line began at the ancient green of the cupolas and race lightly downward.
>
> ["**In St. Valentine's Church**"]

The power of art derives not only from its beauty but from the truth which it reveals and from its ability to transform people's conception of reality and self. Apolek's greatest power as an artist is in the unique vision of reality which he expresses in his works. His paintings not only portray the bounteous vitality of life, but reveal the divinity of earthly life and ordinary people, and thus reveal to Lyutov a new view of life, a new truth.

Lyutov communicates a sense that art not only recreates and illuminates life but is itself an integral part of life. A fluid, not entirely distinguishable boundary exists between art, imagination, and reality, and the former two are as "real" as reality itself. Lyutov describes works of art as a felt reality, as living things, as in the following description of Apolek's status of Christ.

> . . . at an altar a velvet curtain began to sway, and tremblingly slid to the side. In the depths of the opened niche, on the background of a sky

furrowed with dark clouds, ran a bearded figure in an orange kaftan—barefoot, with a torn and bleeding mouth. . . . The man in the orange kaftan was pursued by hatred and overtaken in the chase. He thrust out his arm to ward off the raised blow; blood flowed from his arm in a purple stream.
>
> ["**In St. Valentine's Church**"]

The living quality of art even moves Lyutov and other characters to react to works of art as if they were real. Upon seeing the statue of Christ in "**In St. Valentine's Church**" one Cossack screams and runs away, and in "**Pan Apolek**" when Apolek tells the story of Deborah and states that she bore a son of her union with Christ Lyutov cries out: "Where is he?"

The power of art also stems from its ability to stimulate the imagination. At the end of "**Pan Apolek**," for example, Lyutov wanders around "warming in himself unrealizable dreams and discordant songs." In "**The Song**" he describes the intense physical response to the dreams which Sashka the Christ's songs stimulate in him.

> I listened to him, stretched out in the corner on a rotten mattress. Dream fractured my bones, dream shook the rotted hay under me, and through its scorching downpour I barely made out the old woman leaning her hand on her faded cheek.

And Lyutov himself possesses a wild, uncontained imagination which seems at times almost more than his body can endure. At the end of "**The Rabbi's Son**" he writes: "We buried him [Ilya] at a forgotten station. And I—barely able to contain within my ancient body the storms of my imagination,—I received the last breath of my brother." Lyutov further expresses the intensity and felt physical reality of imagination in his metaphoric description of his reaction to Sidorov's letter in "**Italian Sunshine**."

> I leaned over a sheet of paper, covered with writing, and with sinking heart, wringing my hands, I read his letter. Sidorov, that melancholy killer, tore to shreds the pink wadding of my imagination and dragged me into the corridors of his common-sense madness.

Some stories, however, set up a complex interplay between views of dream and imagination as visions of reality, as distortions of reality, as dreams of the future, and as escape from reality. In "**Gedali**" the old man is sustained in his sufferings by his dream of an International of good people. But Lyutov recognizes the impossibility of the dream and Gedali's alienation from contemporary reality. In "**Sashka the Christ**" Sashka envisions his longed-for sainthood in a daydream fantasy of himself as the Christ child in a cradle suspended from heaven. While this fantasy does embody Sashka's dream of sainthood, which is eventually realized, it is also a means of blotting out the crude reality of his parents' home, transformed in his fantasy into the child's stable. In "**The Song**," too, dream is a means of escape from an intolerable reality. Sashka's song stimulates dreams in Lyutov which blot out the smell of the rotting hay and the figure of the old woman with whom he has quarreled. And at the end of the story Lyutov says: " . . . I tried to fall asleep and started to day-dream so as to fall asleep with good thoughts." And in **"Argamak"** Lyutov states that he dreams constantly of being able to ride a horse like the Cossacks, adding: "My thirst for peace and happiness was not satisfied when I was awake, and so I dreamed."

"Italian Sunshine" treats dream and imagination in a particularly complex and ambiguous way, further expanding the vision of duality and paradox in the cycle. The story focuses on the juxtaposition and interplay of the various views of dream and imagination. In this story Lyutov's sense of the reality of dream and imagination and his belief in the important role which they play in life come into conflict with reality as the reader sees it. The story juxtaposes Lyutov's imaginative, romantic transformation of reality with the actual figure of Sidorov and with ordinary reality, and it ends with an ambiguous tension between a serious acceptance of Lyutov's imaginative vision and an ironic deflation of it. In walking out one moonlit night he imagines the ruins of a war-torn city as an opera stage on which Romeo steps out dressed in satin and singing about love. In his heightened mood he transfers this romantic image to his roommate Sidorov. Before this Sidorov had seemed to him to be a splenetic brawler, querulous misfit, and murderer, but now, after reading Sidorov's letter to his beloved, he suddenly sees him as a romantic dreamer and "real-life" Romeo. The facts related in Sidorov's letter, its colloquial language, and its ironic tone sharply contrast with Lyutov's fantasies and elaborate metaphoric language, and it is mostly Lyutov's interpretation that makes it seem romantic. The play with the theme of imagination and dream is further developed through the character and story of Sidorov, who seeks relief from the dreary monotony of army life in his impossible dreams of Italy, heroics, and his beloved Victoria. He is a would-be adventurer who can find no adventure, a would-be hero who can find no opportunity for heroics, a would-be lover hopelessly separated from his beloved, and a would-be anarchist fighting for the highly disciplined Bolsheviks with their "ready-made" plans for the future. Through the juxtaposition of dreams, imagination, and fantasy with prosaic reality, and further through the juxtaposition of elaborate poetic language with colloquial language, the story contrasts imagination and reality and suggests the possibility of momentarily transforming or transcending reality through the power of imagination. But within the imagery and the language there are also clues to an ironic interpretation, a deflation of both Sidorov's romanticizing of reality and Lyutov's romanticizing of Sidorov and of the reality surrounding them, so that they both come to seem exaggerated, escapist, and somewhat ludicrous.

Lyutov's intense, passionate, impressionable nature and his tendency to react strongly to whatever he sees and experiences also affect his narrative manner. It is marked especially by a frequently elevated emotional rhetoric, pathos of expression, and elaborate poetic language. Although this style often effectively heightens the emotional effect of Lyutov's narration, as in **"The Road to Brody,"** **"The Song,"** and **"The Rabbi's Son,"** at other times Lyutov over-reacts to and over-elaborates reality, so that an ironic disparity or tension is created between his pathos

or poetry of depiction and the object or situation itself, as for example, in **"The Church at Novograd,"** **"Italian Sunshine,"** and **"Evening."** Lyutov's love of heightened effects is countered, however, by his tendency to use the opposite extreme of expression—a dispassionate, laconic description of events which seem to call for a strong emotional reaction, such as his discovery of the dead man in **"Crossing the Zbruch,"** his description of the slitting of the old man's throat in **"Berestechko,"** and the torture of Aggev in **"Two Ivans."** This laconicism, too, can have a dual function. It often creates a tension between the horror of the scene and the laconicism of description, increasing the sense of horror by throwing the act into relief. It may also save a scene from the melodrama which could result from narrating an obviously horrible situation in an extremely emotional manner. But at other times the laconicism seems overdone, seems motivated by either an obvious attempt to maximally heighten tension or a perverse refusal to give the reader any emotional or value indicators to a situation or story. The latter plays a large role in creating the confusion in the cycle as to Lyutov's attitudes. In **"Two Ivans,"** for example, is Lyutov horrified by what he sees to the point of being unable to express a reaction, is he so steeped in his own sorrows and losses that he does not care, has he become so inured to violence that it no longer affects him, or does he feel that there is some justification for Akinfiev's revenge?

Lyutov's aesthetic-romantic outlook, then, with its emphasis on the paradoxical nature of reality, significantly colors and even distorts the view of the world which he presents to the reader and consequently greatly influences the development of the thematic issues of *Red Cavalry*. Furthermore, a tension exists throughout between Lyutov's romantic view and a more realistic view of reality which reveals itself behind his presentation. But the tension remains unresolved, for the romantic view of the world is never wholly deflated or rejected.

Lyutov has a moral as well as an aesthetic dimension; he is not only observer, recorder, and interpreter of reality, but is also a seeker. These roles are closely interrelated, as the moral dilemmas are colored by his aesthetic-romantic outlook and that outlook is qualified by his moral concerns. Moreover, his aesthetic-romantic and moral concerns sometimes clash, creating a tension in his subjective vision corresponding to the tension which the reader experiences between his romantic excesses and the actual nature of things.

The frequent images of travelling in *Red Cavalry* in part symbolize Lyutov's wanderings in quest of the answers to what he sees as the basic historical, philosophical, and ethical problems of his time. The radically new and different value system and way of life which Lyutov must face in the Revolution force him to question his own values. He confronts such basic questions as: is violence an acceptable and viable means to attain a worthy goal, or does it inevitably destroy all value and order; is there a viable alternative to violence as a means of effecting radical change; how can a person find a place in a world of totally different values, and particularly, how can a person free himself from deeply ingrained humanist values and reconcile himself to violence as a necessary means; how can an intellectual cast off his habits of thought, skepticism, and inertia in order to act as is needed in this new world; how is one to view in this context natural man, who is free, uninhibited, and decisive, but at the same time violent and crude? Thus, Lyutov confronts such basic issues as the respective values and defects of civilization versus the natural life, humanism versus revolution, the rational versus the irrational in man, and the physical, spiritual, and intellectual poles of man's nature.

While struggling with these issues Lyutov also tries to play a role as active participant in the Revolution. The stories in which he is central character generally relate his attempts to participate in the life around him, and here he is faced with a major psychological dilemma, a division in his own nature, as he tries to become a man of action and to immerse himself in direct experience.

In *Red Cavalry,* then, the reader sees the world through the eyes of an aesthetic, imaginative, romantic intellectual who is in search of a value system by which to come to terms with a violently changing world, who is trying to resolve his doubts and to find a place in or to mold himself to his time and to life. The complex interconnection between his roles as narrator-observer, seeker, and participant is central to the development of the themes of the cycle. The first person narrator thus not only unifies the cycle and gives it an organizing center, but also shapes and directs the ambiguities and complexities of vision in *Red Cavalry.*

As Wayne Booth states in *Rhetoric of Fiction* [1961], an author may for various reasons use a "confused" narrator (such as Lyutov) in order to confuse the reader. This tends to increase the reader's participation in the hero's drama so that he experiences personally the dilemmas which the hero faces. The reader is forced onto a level of alertness and heightened perception which makes him ready for more subtle effects, especially for the effects of irony, and makes him more capable of perceiving a complex view of reality. The heightened alertness and the breakdown of certainties about the truth which such confusion creates then make the reader, along with the narrator, "ready to receive *the* truth when it is offered him," if, that is, *the* truth exists and can be found. For it also leaves open the possibility of presenting a complex reality in which issues conclude in irresolution and ambiguity. As Booth states, "The effects of deliberate confusion require a nearly complete union of the narrator and the reader in a common endeavor [i. e. the search for the truth], with the author silent and invisible, but implicitly concurring, perhaps even sharing his narrator's plight."

In *Red Cavalry* the image of a complex reality in which issues are hopelessly entangled in ambiguities and paradoxes is further complicated by the inconsistent and not always clear relationship between narrative and authorial voices. Here, as in many of his stories, Babel places narrative voices between himself and the reader, voices which are not *personae* for the author, but which are yet not fully distinct from him. In this way the author keeps the reader in doubt as to his position; the reader is caught in a web of ironies and ambiguities, some of which are created by

the narrator and his complex character, some by the author's unclear overview, and some by a combination of both.

When there is no direct authorial voice, as in first person narration, there are, of course, means of indirectly deducing the author's position through the structure of the work: through the sequence of events, the decision to dramatize some episodes and relate others, the choice of characters, the personality of the narrator, the compositional scheme, and patterns of imagery. The manipulation of these devices, besides determining the reader's view of the narrator, characters, and events, provides the possibility for irony, especially the irony produced by the felt disparity between the events and characters as they are presented by the narrator and as they appear to the reader. An example of this in *Red Cavalry* is the disparity between Lyutov's romanticized depiction of reality and reality as the reader distinguishes it behind Lyutov's presentation. There may also be an obvious disparity between Lyutov's moral view and the author's as in **"My First Goose,"** in which Lyutov's acceptance of the need to commit a base act in order to be accepted by the Cossacks is implicitly criticized through irony. Babel also frequently uses imagery in order to make a submerged ironic commentary on events. For example, in **"My First Goose"** low erotic and fecal images and puns provide an ironic commentary on Lyutov's deed and on the Cossack values. Thus, just as Lyutov's aesthetic vision is sometimes "validated" by its consonance with the underlying authorial view and at other times is qualified or rejected by its disparity with the author's view, so his moral awareness may be consistent with or distinct from the authorial norms.

But despite the use of the above devices for revealing the author's position, the lack of a direct authorial voice, the use of a complex narrator, and the complexity of the issue of values in the work make it difficult, if not impossible, to fully distinguish at all times authorial and narrative positions. Thus, the final position of neither author nor narrator is fully definable. This ambiguity is one of the key devices in the establishment of the thematic irresolution of the cycle.

Lyutov's complexity is particularly important in this respect. First, he himself sometimes relates stories in a laconic, objective manner which makes it difficult to define his precise attitude. In such cases, because Lyutov is a sensitive, sophisticated person one cannot simply assume his unreliability or his non-recognition of the complexities and ironies of the stories. He is clearly aware of the complexity of the issues in the cycle. In some stories he is aware, or becomes aware, of the full meaning of events, so that his interpretation is identical with the author's (and reader's), as in **"In St. Valentine's Church," "Gedali," "Squadron Commander Trunov," "The Road to Brody," "Berestechko,"** and seemingly at the end of **"My First Goose."** But in other stories he seems unaware or confused, as in **"Italian Sunshine," "The Song," "Zamostye,"** and **"After the Battle,"** so that there is at least a partial disparity between Lyutov's perception and interpretation of events and the authorial overview. Although Lyutov is aesthetically sensitive, he is not always fully morally sensitive, especially with respect to his own behavior. His partial unreliability in moral and human judgment is established in the first story, **"Crossing the Zbruch,"** in which he misunderstands the plight of the Jewish family and consequently treats it contemptuously. In **"In St. Valentine's Church"** he initially underestimates the moral gravity of the desecration of the church. And in **"My First Goose," "The Song,"** and **"Zamostye"** he commits morally reprehensible acts against helpless old women. In the first story he feels remorse for his cruelty, but in neither of the other two stories does he overtly reveal any sense of wrongdoing.

Lyutov's reliability as narrator is questionable for several other reasons as well. His penchant for romanticizing reality on the one hand and exaggerating its meaner aspects on the other calls into question his very rendition of reality. Furthermore, Lyutov actually expresses inconsistent views in the course of the cycle as he searches for answers to his questions. In **"Gedali"** he speaks for the Revolution and its unrestrained violence, but in **"The Road to Brody"** he laments the destructiveness of the Revolution; in **"Pan Apolek"** he supports Apolek's values of compassion and love, even vowing to base his own life on them, while in **"After the Battle"** he prays for the ability to kill his fellow man. In some stories Lyutov expresses ambiguous feelings toward characters and events, as in **"Afonka Bida"** and **"Squadron Commander Trunov,"** where he is unable to make a final judgment on the main characters. In some stories Lyutov's concern for his own psychological dilemma seems to distract his attention from the more significant concerns of the story onto his own problems. In **"The Death of Dolgushov"** his concern over his inability to kill Dolgushov and, seemingly even more important to him, his concern over the loss of his friend obscure from him a recognition of the central problem of the story—the meaning of compassion in the context of the war. Because of Lyutov's inconsistencies and ambiguities in understanding and attitude, one can never be certain of his attitude when he refrains from directly expressing it, as in **"Two Ivans," "Chesniki"** and **"The Widow."** But the authorial view itself is similarly neither consistent nor fully identifiable, so that it resembles the vacillations and ambiguities of Lyutov. In **"Pan Apolek"** the values of compassion and love are affirmed, but in such stories as **"Squadron Commander Trunov," "Afonka Bida"** and **"The Death of Dolgushov"** violence is not totally rejected. Lyutov's refusal to judge Trunov, for example, is consonant with the final impossibility of judging him at all in the context of the whole story. Furthermore, the use of Cossack narrators who strongly and compellingly state their position further qualifies the humanist stand against violence, a qualification which is essentially the author's as well as Lyutov's.

The fact that in many respects the author and narrator bear a close resemblance further complicates their relationship. There is both external and internal evidence of this resemblance. **Red Cavalry,** first of all, has a clearly autobiographical origin. In many external characteristics Lyutov does seem to be a *persona* for Babel. Both are Jewish intellectuals who participated in Budyonny's campaign, and Babel himself used the name Lyutov on the campaign. The diary which Babel kept during part of the campaign reveals that many things which he saw, characters whom he knew, and events which he witnessed and experienced were put into the stories, sometimes with little change and sometimes totally transformed. The diary shows that he himself experienced many of the dilemmas which confront Lyutov. According to [I. A.] Smirin, who has had access to the diary, the "world" of **Red Cavalry** is similar to the world which Babel describes in his diary: exotic scenes and colorful characters; unusual people and events; a mixture of the exotic, the everyday, and the seamy side of life; the contrastive heroics and cruelty of the soldiers; the traces of history in the present; the Jewish settlements; and the various aspects of the Cossack character and way of life ["No puti K 'Konarmii,'" *Literaturnoe nasledstvo* LXXIV (1965)]. [L.] Livshits notes that certain basic questions, similar to basic issues in **Red Cavalry,** run through the diary: why do people wage war; what forces them to kill and endure the sufferings of war; since all war breeds cruelty, low passions, and inhumanity, will not this war lead to the degradation of the great aims of the Revolution; can the aim justify the horrors; can the Cossacks, professional soldiers, become new men, bearers of Communism? ["Maturialy K tvorcheskio biografii I. Babelia," *Voprosy Liersture,* No. 4 (1964)]. Babel expresses his dual attitude, especially toward the Cossacks, in several quotes from his diary, in some of which he expresses his admiration for their colorful and heroic qualities, in others his despair over their crudeness and cruelty, while in still others he simply remarks on the paradoxical combination of qualities.

> Ineradicable human cruelty . . . I hate war. What a terrible life!
>
> Why do I feel such unrelieved sadness? . . . Life is shattering to bits, I am at a big never-ending funeral.
>
> For whole days we ride from one brigade to another, we watch the battles, . . . Above us are the captivating heavens, a warm sun, around us breathe the pine trees, hundreds of steppe horses neigh, here one wants to live, but all our thoughts are directed toward killing. My words sound stupid, but war is truly sometimes beautiful, but in all circumstances harmful.
>
> I have spent two weeks in total despair here; this results from the ferocious cruelty which doesn't let up here for a single moment, and from the fact that I clearly realize how unsuited I am for destruction, how difficult it is for me to tear myself away from the old days . . . and from the fact that they are, perhaps, bad, but for me they breathed poetry like a beehive breathes honey, . . . well, what of it—others will make the Revolution, and I, I will sing of that which is to the side of it, that which goes deeper.
>
> The dirt, apathy, hopelessness of Russian life are insufferable; here the Revolution will accomplish something.
>
> I am riding with the division commander, a headquarters squadron; horses gallop; forests, paths, the red hat of the commander, his mighty

figure, trumpeters, beauty, new troops, and the commander and the squadron are as one body.

Budyonny's soldiers bring communism, a woman cries.

The remount officer Dyakov is an enchanting picture, red pants with silver stripes, a belt with an inlaid design, from Stavropol, the figure of an Apollo . . . incredible cursing . . . A dancer, accordian player, crafty, a liar, a most colorful figure.

What is our Cossack? . . . Layers: baseness, daring, professionalism, revolutionary spirit, bestial cruelty.

In his diary Babel grapples with the same issues, perceives the same paradoxes and tensions in the world, undergoes the same vacillations and ambiguities of attitude, and experiences similar personal crises regarding his own identity in relation to the Revolution and the Cossack community as does Lyutov in *Red Cavalry.* However, this does not prove a complete identity of author and narrator in the cycle. In fact, the author of the cycle often brings to bear upon Lyutov a distance, objectivity, and irony which separate him from Lyutov. But Lyutov also sometimes views himself ironically through an objective distancing as he looks in retrospect on his experiences.

A second external indication of the similarity between Babel and Lyutov is the fact that Lyutov's vision and the themes which he treats recur in Babel's work as a whole, especially in those written at about the same time as *Red Cavalry,* and seem to be basic to Babel's own artistic vision. In an interview with writers in 1937 Babel named Leo Tolstoy as one of his favorite writers. When asked how he reconciled this with his own writing he replied:

> In a letter from Goethe to Eckermann I read a definition of the *novella,* a very short story, that genre with which I feel more comfortable than with any other. His definition of the *novella* is very simple: it is a story about an unusual event. . . .

> Here's the point. Lev Nikolaevich Tolstoy had enough temperament to be able to describe all twenty four hours of the day, and besides that, he remembered everything that happened to him, but I, evidently, have only enough temperament to describe the most interesting five minutes which I have experienced. And that's how the genre of the *novella* was created. I have to think so.

This interest in a genre concerned with "unusual occurrences," with what is "most interesting," is evident in the exoticism which characterizes Babel's work at all stages of his career. It is most fully evident in his earlier work, including **"Odessa," "Line and Color,"** and the Odessa tales. Most of Babel's stories convey a sense of the vitality of life, of the physical, sensual, passionate essence of man. At the same time they reveal an obsession with violence, death, and sex, and their close interrelationship, as the most extreme and complete manifestations of man's physical being. These themes are central to **"The King," "The Kiss," "The Road," "The Story of My Dovecot," "First**

Love," "Di Grasso," "Guy de Maupassant," and **"Dante Street."** Moreover, in such stories as **"Guy de Maupassant," "DiGrasso," "Awakening,"** and **"In the Basement"** the treatment of art and imagination and their relationship to reality is similar to that in *Red Cavalry.* These works assert that there is far more of the unusual, unique, and significant in reality than anything one can dream or imagine, and that the value of imagination and art lies in their power of revelation, their ability to penetrate beyond the surface of things to their essence and to reveal the uniqueness and significance of reality. Furthermore, **"Di Grasso,"** like **"Pan Apolek,"** asserts the power of art to transform the perceiver's perception of the world and even to radically affect his behavior, to imbue him with a sense of justice and compassion toward his fellow man. Another feature of Babel's work as a whole is its romantic vision of reality. Many of the works treat the conflict between romantic vision and actual reality, but while in this conflict the distorting romantic *illusion* of reality is rejected or refuted by the authorial overview, the romantic *vision* is affirmed as it leads to a heightened awareness of the genuinely paradoxical, exotic and unusual nature of reality. In *Red Cavalry,* too, Lyutov's tendency to cloud reality with imaginative illusion and sentimentality is rejected, but the basic romantic vision is affirmed.

The problem of interpreting a decisive moral stand in *Red Cavalry* is complicated by the fact that the cycle profoundly questions traditional humanist values from various points of view: the basically coincident vacillating points of view of Lyutov and the author; the distinct and conflicting points of view of Lyutov and the author, as each represents various sides of the issues at various times; and the Cossack voices which present their one-side view of the issues. Moreover, all these voices are subsumed within one basic subjective narrative frame, that of Lyutov. The reader, who can be supposed to be educated to humanist values, is thus thrown off center and forced into the process of questioning and re-evaluating his own value system, for his normal frame of reference, like Lyutov's, is not adequate to judge the world of *Red Cavalry.* The cycle questions whether humanist values take cognizance of and cope with the realities of the world and human nature, yet also seriously questions the opposing values of the Cossack way. It suggests that there is more than one mode of existence; that different situations call for different values; that the value system of one mode cannot judge a different one; and that human nature consists of paradoxical qualities which one cannot moralize away, but which one must come to terms with. How can one judge Gedali and Pavlichenko, Apolek and Afonka Bida by the same standards?

Through Lyutov the cycle questions whether a person belonging to one way of life, to one system of values can understand or come to terms with another. The reader, like the narrator and author, is thrown into an open, fluid world with no single center and no single solution to the problem of values. If one is aware of all the complexities of reality he cannot come to a static, defined position in relation to it. Any answer or resolution can always be qualified and questioned. As Lionel Trilling writes [in his introduction to *The Collected Stories*], "Babel . . . was captivated by the vision of two ways of being, the way of violence and the way of peace, and he was torn between them. The conflict between the two ways of being was an essential element of his mode of thought." This conflict "implied that one might live in doubt, that one might live by means of a question. By its very form as a cycle of story fragments (irrespective of the organic nature of most of these "fragments") *Red Cavalry* points to the ambiguous and paradoxical nature of experience. The cycle consists of a series of experience fragments, filtered primarily through one man's consciousness, which may lead to temporary value judgments or conclusions, but which in their totality do not give decisive answers. One is left with moments of question, illumination, and resolution which may be contradicted by other moments of conflicting illumination and resolution. Furthermore, any given story may end with either a definite resolution, a qualified resolution, or no resolution at all, so that one can easily shift toward an acceptance of an opposing, contradictory revelation, which is in turn qualified as it is presented.

Red Cavalry, then, while concerned with specific questions and problems of value, ultimately reveals the paradoxical, dialectical nature of reality and the resulting impossibility of imposing one system of thought and value upon it. Reality consists of opposing, irreconcilable modes of existence with conflicting, incompatible value systems. And Lyutov, the author, and the reader are left in the end with the ambiguities and irresolution of such a paradoxical world.

FURTHER READING

Bibliography

Mihailovich, Vasa D. "Assessments of Isaac Babel." *Papers on Language and Literature* 9, No. 3 (Summer 1973): 323-42.
  Bibliographic survey of criticism on Babel's works.

Biography

Paustovsky, Konstantin. "Reminiscences of Babel." *Partisan Review* XXVIII, Nos. 3-4 (1961): 391-406.
  Recollections of Babel by a contemporary who was formerly the managing editor of the Odessa journal *Moryak,* which published many of Babel's early works.

Criticism

Alexandrova, Vera. "Isaac Babel (1894-1941)." In her *A History of Soviet Literature,* translated by Mirra Ginsburg, pp. 124-34.
  General biographical and critical introduction to Babel's life and major works.

Andrew, J. M. "Structure and Style in the Short Story: Babel's 'My First Goose'." *The Modern Language Review* 70, No. 2 (April 1975): 366-79.
  Detailed structural analysis of Babel's short story "My First Goose."

Bloom, Harold, ed. *Isaac Babel.* New York: Chelsea House Publishers, 1987, 277 p.
  Gathers together over fifty years of Babel criticism.

Brown, Edward J. "The Intellectuals, II." In his *Russian Literature Since the Revolution,* revised edition, pp. 87-104. Cambridge, Mass.: Harvard University Press, 1982.
  Discusses irony in *Red Cavalry,* which grimly suggests the failure of the Bolshevik Revolution.

Clyman, Toby W. "Babel as Colorist." *Slavic and East European Journal* 21, No. 3 (Fall 1977): 332-43.
  Focuses on Babel's use of color imagery, which to Clyman recalls Expressionist painting.

Davies, Norman. "Izaak Babel's *Konarmiya* Stories, and the Polish-Soviet War." *The Modern Language Review* 67, No. 4 (October 1972): 845-57.
  Discusses the historical inaccuracy of the stories in *Red Cavalry,* which he nevertheless regards as presenting an honest portrait of the dehumanizing effects of war.

Ehre, Milton. "Babel's *Red Cavalry:* Epic and Pathos, History and Culture." *Slavic Review* 40, No. 2 (Summer 1981): 228-40.
  Examines *Red Cavalry* as a study of stylistic contrasts between the "epic-heroic" and the "pathetic."

Freiden, Gregory. "Fat Tuesday in Odessa: Isaac Babel's 'Di Grasso' as Testament and Manifesto." *The Russian Review* 40, No. 2 (April 1981): 101-21.
  Argues that Babel's 1937 story "Di Grasso," written two years before Babel's arrest and disappearance, was his parting comment on the Stalin regime for its suppression of works that did not wholly serve its proletarian cause.

Gifford, Henry. "Isaac Babel." *Grand Street* 9, No. 1 (Autumn 1989): 212-27.
  Biographical and critical reassessment of Babel's literary importance.

Helstein, Nadia. "Translator's Note." In *Red Cavalry* by Isaac Babel, translated by Nadia Helstein, pp. v-viii. New York: Alfred A. Knopf, 1929.
  Declares that *Red Cavalry* is not concerned with the heroic deeds of an army at war, but rather with individual reactions to mundane aspects of war.

Howe, Irving. "Tone in the Short Story." *The Sewanee Review* LVII, No. 1 (Winter 1949): 141-52.
  Praises Babel as a genius of the picaresque tale who draws upon Russian and Yiddish culture to enhance his stories.

———. "The Genius of Isaac Babel." *The New York Review of Books* III, No. 1 (20 August 1964): 14-15.
  Laudatory critique of *Isaac Babel: The Lonely Years, 1925-1939.*

Iribarne, Louis. "Babel's *Red Cavalry* as a Baroque Novel." *Contemporary Literature* 14, No. 1 (Winter 1973): 58-77.
  Discusses Babel's use of stylistic devices and how *Red Cavalry* can be considered a baroque novel, suggesting that Babel originally conceived of *Red Cavalry* as a novel and that the story "Pan Apolek" serves as a unifying link between the collection's other stories.

Leviant, Curt. "The Jewish Stories of Isaac Babel." *The Jewish Quarterly* 13, No. 3 (Autumn 1965): 12-15.
  Examines the strain of Jewish skepticism in Babel's work.

Lowe, David A. "A Generic Approach to Babel's *Red Cavalry*." *Modern Fiction Studies* 28, No. 1 (Spring 1982): 69-78.

General discussion of *Red Cavalry* as "a cycle of stories."

Luplow, Carol. "Paradox and the Search for Value in Babel's *Red Cavalry*." *Slavic and East European Journal* 23, No. 2 (Summer 1979): 216-32.

Examines Babel's treatment of ethical, philosophical, and historical problems prompted by the Bolshevik Revolution.

Markish, Simon. "The Example of Isaac Babel." *Commentary* 64, No. 5 (November 1977): 36-45.

Survey of Babel's works in which the critic discusses *Red Cavalry* and *The Odessa Tales* as outstanding examples of Russian-Jewish literature during the Soviet Revolutionary period.

Mendelson, Danuta. *Metaphor in Babel's Short Stories*. Ann Arbor, Mich.: Ardis, 1982, 152 p.

Examines various aspects of metaphor in Babel's short fiction.

Murphy, A. B. "The Style of Isaak Babel'." *The Slavonic and East European Review* 44 (1965-66): 361-80.

Analyzes Babel's style in the original Russian.

Sicher, Efraim. "The Road to a Red Cavalry: Myth and Mythology in the Works of Isaak Babel' of the 1920s." *The Slavonic and East European Review* 60, No. 4 (October 1982): 528-46.

Examines the received myth of Babel's literary career.

Sinyavski, Andrey. "Isaac Babel." In *Major Soviet Writers: Essays in Criticism,* edited by Edward J. Brown, pp. 301-09. New York: Oxford University Press, 1973.

Discusses Babel's literary style in *Red Cavalry* and *The Odessa Tales.*

Stine, Peter. "Isaac Babel and Violence." *Modern Fiction Studies* 30, No. 2 (Summer 1984): 237-55.

Explores Babel's objective and distanced depiction of violence.

Stroud, Nicholas. "The Art of Mystification: The 'Prehistoric' Isaac Babel." *Russian Literature Tri-Quarterly* 13 (1975): 591-99.

Examines the commonly held image of Babel "as a mysterious, even mystifying human being."

————. Introduction to *The Forgotten Prose* by Isaac Babel, edited and translated by Nicholas Stroud, pp. 11-14. Ann Arbor, Mich.: Ardis, 1978.

Brief introduction to *The Forgotten Prose,* a collection of short stories suppressed in the former Soviet Union.

Struve, Gleb. "Prose and Poetry." In his *Russian Literature under Lenin and Stalin: 1917-1953*, pp. 39-75. Norman: University of Oklahoma Press, 1971.

Comments on Babel's use of contrast and paradox to create striking effects of pathos in his stories.

Trilling, Lionel. Introduction to *The Collected Stories*, by Isaac Babel, edited and translated by Walter Morison, pp. 9-37. New York: Criterion Books, 1955.

Perceptive analysis concerning Babel's cultural, moral, and personal involvement with the Cossack ethos as a Jewish soldier of a regiment and as a writer.

Williams, Gareth. "Two Leitmotifs in Babel's *Konarmija*." *Die Welt der Slaven* XVII, No. 2 (1972): 308-17.

Focuses on Babel's use of sun and moon motifs in *Red Cavalry.*

Young, Richard. "Theme in Fictional Literature: A Way into Complexity." *Language and Style* XIII, No. 3 (Fall 1980): 61-71.

Linguistic analysis of the theme of violence in "Crossing into Poland."

Additional coverage of Babel's life and career is contained in the following sources published by Gale Research: *Contemporary Authors,* Vol. 104; *Twentieth-Century Literary Criticism,* Vols. 2, 13.

Samuel Beckett

1906-1989

(Full name Samuel Barclay Beckett) Irish-born short story writer, playwright, novelist, scriptwriter, poet, essayist, and translator.

INTRODUCTION

One of the most celebrated writers in twentieth-century literature, Beckett is known for his significant impact on the development of the short story and novel forms as well as on contemporary drama. His works expound a philosophy of negation through characters who face a meaningless and absurd existence without the comforts of religion, myth, or philosophical absolutes. Often described as fragments rather than stories, his short fiction in particular evidences his use of sparse, economical language and stark images of alienation and absurdity to present truths that are free of rhetorical embellishment.

Biographical Information

Beckett was born and raised in Foxrock, near Dublin, Ireland. In 1927 he received his B. A. in French and Italian from Trinity College in Dublin. Beckett taught French for a short period in Belfast before receiving a fellowship to the Ecole Normale Supérieure in Paris. There he met James Joyce, who had a profound influence on Beckett's early writing. Beckett returned to Trinity College in 1930 for his M. A., after which he accepted a position as a French instructor at the college. In 1932 he resigned his post at Trinity to move back to Paris and concentrate on his writing. When World War II began, he worked for the French Resistance and was forced to flee Paris when the Nazis discovered his activities. After the war, Beckett began writing almost exclusively in French and translating his work into English, beginning his most prolific and, according to many commentators, his most artistically complex period. In 1969 Beckett received the Nobel Prize for literature. He died in Paris in 1989.

Major Works of Short Fiction

Beckett published *More Pricks than Kicks*, his first collection of short stories, in 1934. A series of related episodes describing the adventures of a fictional young Irishman named Belacqua Shuah, *More Pricks than Kicks* derived in part from Beckett's unpublished first novel *Dream of Fair to Middling Women*. In the collection, Beckett used an elaborate prose style and language in imitation of the style and language of Joyce. Most of Beckett's subsequent works of short fiction were originally written in French and translated into English by Beckett. *Nouvelles et textes pour rien* (*Stories and Texts for Nothing*) consists of three stories and thirteen prose fragments. The three stories feature protagonists whose lives are desolate and at the same

time highly comic. The prose fragments are rhetorically formalized vignettes with minimal narrative characterization. Beckett's style reached the extremes of minimalism in the 1960s and 1970s, when he abandoned both conventional plot and conventional syntax, stripping his language down to fragmented phrases and one-word expressions to mirror what he considered the difficulty, if not impossibility, of human communication. *Imagination Morte Imaginez* (*Imagination Dead Imagine*) takes place in an abstract rotunda, "all white in the whiteness," where two bodies reside in a state of minimal existence. *Bing* (*Ping*) uses depersonalized, machine-like language to describe a box containing a faceless and nameless figure. J. E. Dearlove has called *Ping* a "drama of the interaction between reader and form." In *Assez* (*Enough*) Beckett returned to a more traditional prose style. The first person monologue combines romantic and scientific language to describe a lost relationship. *Sans* (*Lessness*) is perhaps the most extreme example of Beckett's experimentation with language in his short fiction. Beckett wrote sixty sentences, placed each in one of six groups containing ten sentences, and drew sentences randomly to create a work of art ordered by chance. Set in a partially crushed cylinder containing an indefinite number of naked bodies, *Le dépeupleur* (*The Lost Ones*) examines the possibility that those who stop struggling against hopelessness will be the most content. *Companie (Company)* depicts the thoughts of an individual lying in bed alone in the dark.

Critical Reception

Initial response to *More Pricks than Kicks* was mixed. While the book received positive reviews outside of Ireland, Irish commentators found its ornate style distasteful. Beckett's later short works fared better with critics as the critical schools of Post-structuralism and Deconstruction complemented his linguistic experimentation. While generally not as highly regarded as his novels—particularly the trilogy *Molloy, Malone meurt (Malone Dies)*, and *L'Innommable (The Unnameable)*, considered his masterpiece—Beckett's short fiction is acclaimed for its verbal experimentation and artistic formalism.

PRINCIPAL WORKS

SHORT FICTION

More Pricks than Kicks   1934
Nouvelles et textes pour rien   1955
   [*Stories and Texts for Nothing*, 1967]
Imagination morte imaginez   1965
   [*Imagination Dead Imagine*, 1965]
Assez   1966
Bing   1966
   [*Ping*, 1966]
No's Knife: Collected Shorter Prose 1945-1966   1967
Sans   1969
   [*Lessness*, 1970]
Le dépeupleur   1970
   [*The Lost Ones*, 1972]
Premier amour   1970
   [*First Love*, 1973]
First Love and Other Shorts   1974
Foirade   1976
   [*Fizzles*, 1976]
Six Residua   1978
Companie   1979
   [*Company*, 1980]
Mal vu mal dit   1981
   [*Ill Seen Ill Said*, 1982]
Worstward Ho   1983
Collected Shorter Prose 1945-1980   1984

OTHER MAJOR WORKS

Murphy   (novel)   1938
Molloy   (novel)   1951
   [*Molloy*, 1955]
Malone meurt   (novel)   1951
   [*Malone Dies*, 1956]
En attendant Godot   (drama)   1952
   [*Waiting for Godot*, 1954]
L'Innommable   (novel)   1953
   [*The Unnamable*, 1958]

Watt   (novel)   1953
Fin de partie, suivi de Acte sans paroles   (drama)   1957
   [*Endgame, Followed by Act without Words*, 1958]
All That Fall   (radio drama)   1957
From an Abandoned Work   (drama)   1958
Comment c'est   (novel)   1961
   [*How It Is*, 1964]
Happy Days   (drama)   1961
Poems in English   (poetry)   1961
Come and Go   (drama)   1967
Mercier et Camier   (novel)   1970
   [*Mercier and Camier*, 1974]
Not I   (drama)   1971
Breath and Other Shorts   (drama)   1972
Footfalls   (drama)   1976
That Time   (drama)   1976
Ends and Odds   (drama)   1976
Rockabye   (drama)   1981
Ohio Impromptu   (drama)   1984

CRITICISM

Raymond Federman   (essay date 1965)

SOURCE: "Belacqua and the Inferno of Society," in his *Journey to Chaos: Samuel Beckett's Early Fiction*, University of California Press, 1965, pp. 31-55.

[*Federman is a French-born American critic and educator whose works include* Samuel Beckett: His Works and His Critics *(1970) and* Samuel Beckett: Cahier de L'Herne *(1976). In the following excerpt from his book* Journey to Chaos: Samuel Beckett's Early Fiction, *Federman offers a character analysis of Belacqua Shuah, the protagonist of the stories in* More Pricks Than Kicks.]

As represented in Beckett's early English fiction, social reality corresponds to a traditional and realistic setting in which conventional characters remain helplessly caught in "the muck" of life's routine. The fictitious heroes Belacqua Shuah, Murphy, and Watt seek to forsake this environment not only through mental alienation, but by aspiring to an existence no longer controlled by rational and logical conditions, an existence situated in a fictional surrounding appropriate to their eccentric temperament. Recognizing that "the nature of outer reality remains obscure" (*Murphy*), deceptive, and incomprehensible, unable to reconcile themselves to the unavoidable dualism of matter and mind, they try to negate all notions of reality, thereby rejecting the mediocrity of social life. To succeed in this ascetic quest, to reach this apparently blissful condition, these protagonists must learn to exist beyond their own physical and emotional needs, indifferent to the human body, exiled from the society of man. None of Beckett's early heroes is capable of such complete moral and physical detachment. Therefore, they find themselves constantly oscillating between the world of man (social reality) and the make-believe world of the mind (fictional absurdity). In their struggle to free themselves from worldly concerns they endure a succession of embarrassing failures which confines them to social reality and forces them into acts of self-destruction.

The three major figures of Beckett's English fiction, Belacqua, Murphy, and Watt, share one obsession, one desire— to find a refuge away from the sociorealistic "fiasco," somewhere beyond the restrictions of organized society, and ultimately beyond the boundaries of traditional fiction. In other words, subconsciously they aspire to the absurd condition Beckett later grants his French creations. Too lethargic to participate in the social game, doubting the validity of external reality, neglecting the natural demands of the human body, these protagonists attempt to escape the common world to enjoy the fancies of their imagination. They seek as their ideal an institution (or fictional setting) where they can vegetate, uncommitted to the tedious activities of everyday life, an insane asylum where lunatics indulge in their "own pernicious little private dungheap" (*Murphy*), and where mental chaos is equated with creative freedom. Thus, while physical needs are cared for, the mind can perform its extravagances, unconcerned with bodily functions, relieved of doubtful notions and memories.

The better-known novels of Samuel Beckett, *Molloy, Malone meurt, L'Innommable,* and the recent *Comment c'est,* are, as Martin Esslin states, "*sui generis,* unclassifiable, disturbing, funny, cruel, and inspiring"; they defy all attempts at interpretation, and are not even easily accessible ["Samuel Beckett," in *The Novelist as Philosopher,* ed. John Cruickshank, 1962]. To gain insight into the structure and meaning of these complex, unrealistic works, one must investigate Beckett's early English fiction, which contains, in a more traditional form, the essential elements of his later achievements. For though they rely on linguistic dexterity and intellectual exhibitionism, Beckett's early works can be apprehended on the level of conventional realism. Such is the case with Beckett's first extensive work of fiction, the now rare collector's item, *More Pricks Than Kicks,* a work ignored by Beckett's critics.

Published in 1934, the book consists of a collection of ten short stories loosely related through a common protagonist, Belacqua Shuah, whose eccentric actions and amorous adventures are described comically in a picaresque manner, from his days as a student until his death and burial as a thrice-married man. Although these stories lack consistent overall structure, unifying plot, and recurrent motifs, they acquire thematic unity through the hero's personality; in spite of the ambiguous changes he undergoes from one story to the next, he remains faithful to his indolence, his extravagance, his antisocial attitude, and above all his sensual desires. Thus *More Pricks Than Kicks* can easily pass for a novel rather than a series of disconnected episodes. In fact, an unfinished, unpublished first version of this book exists in novel form. Entitled *Dream of Fair to Middling Women,* a good portion of its material was used in *More Pricks Than Kicks,* though a careful examination of the two texts reveals the extent to which Beckett reworks his manuscripts. The hero of the first draft was also named Belacqua.

As the firstborn of Beckett's family of outcasts, Belacqua stands as the prototype for all his successors. His actions,

obsessions, and idiosyncrasies prepare the personalities of the later eccentrics. Compared, however, with Beckett's French derelicts, most of whom spend their absurd existence vegetating in some nameless, moribund landscape, Belacqua is a normal and traditional hero. Primarily concerned with the physical self, he functions as a social man who has to cope with all the trivialities of life in society. If Beckett's more recent creatures dwell in a timeless and spaceless region no longer limited by realistic norms, Belacqua's fortunes evolve in a pattern controlled by chronological events. His environment remains identifiable and realistic. Moreover, he has a past, an ancestry, an education, and rational beliefs that determine his behavior. He has basic emotional and sexual relationships with numerous ladies and enjoys "many a delightful recollection of their commerce." He succeeds in marrying three of them. These are worldly pleasures of which Beckett's senile French heroes are deprived; for them marriage, love, sex, and the remembrance of such activities are reduced to grotesque gestures or obscene thoughts. However, being thus cornered by social, physical, and marital impositions, Belacqua assumes a lethargic, sardonic, and particularly a cowardly posture in all his actions. He is, as Beckett describes him, "an indolent bourgeois poltroon, very talented up to a point, but not fitted for private life in the best and brightest sense. . . ."

Belacqua, like his creator, is a Dubliner, descendant of "the grand old Huguenot guts," a Trinity man, a poet, student of Dante, and somewhat of a dilettante. He, too, has traveled abroad, and likes to brag about it to the point that one of his early conquests complains, "You make great play with your short stay abroad." Indeed, Belacqua is very much inclined toward self-exhibitionism, and, as Beckett himself tends to do in his early works, he abuses the knowledge, the erudition, the foreign languages with which he is familiar. His speech is punctuated by Latin, German, Italian, and French expressions, so much so that the author feels obliged to apologize for his hero: "Pardon these French expressions, but the creature dreams in French." However, the comparison between author and protagonist ends here.

Throughout the book, Belacqua appears as a neurotic pedant who cannot reconcile himself to having been born, and to having to adjust to social conventions. He prefers to enjoy prenatal memories in a state of idleness, to entertain romantic notions as a rejected artist, and to indulge in self-pity. Consequently, he shows very little respect for the Dublin institutions, his fellow citizens, and his family. In the opening story, **"Dante and the Lobster,"** he refers to one of his relatives as that "lousy old bitch of an aunt," and throughout the stories shows a particular distaste for the people with whom he comes in contact, even his lady friends.

Belacqua refuses to play the social game, but out of cowardice submits to its rules. His only defense and self-justification is indolence; when forced to act, his behavior is marked by irresponsibility and eccentricity. He rents flashy cars which he can hardly drive; he cannot bear to sit on a person's right side; he is very particular about his food, and meticulous about the preparation of his meals;

he loves burnt toast and "a good green stenching rotten lump of Gorgonzola cheese," and, were it not for his cowardice, he would go so far as to assault the grocer who tries to cheat him of his pleasure:

> He looked sceptically at the cut of cheese. He turned it over on its back to see was the other side any better. The other side was worse. They had laid it better side up, they had practised that little deception. . . . Belacqua was furious. The impudent dogsbody, for two pins he would assault him.
>
> 'It won't do' he cried, 'do you hear me, it won't do at all. I won't have it.' He ground his teeth.

Such obsessions hardly ingratiate Belacqua to the reader; in this he is unlike most later Beckett heroes who, despite their deformity, depravity, vulgarity, and cruelty, beg for compassion. Belacqua is detestable, and as a result his own creator constantly ridicules him. Worst of all, he drinks heavily and evades all commitments "by pleading that he had been drunk at the time, or that he was an incoherent person and content to remain so, and so on." His overindulgence in gin and tonic often places him in bizarre situations. Under the influence of alcohol, he does not hesitate to undress in the street to enjoy the trickling of rain on his bare chest. In another instance, while walking, drunk, down the street "his feet pained him so much that he took off his perfectly good boots and threw them away." When intoxicated Belacqua is quite unpredictable; once he buys four seats in heaven from a woman peddler in a pub who tells him, "For yer frien', yer da, yer ma an' yer motte," but does not offer one to Belacqua who hardly deserves paradise. Whereas Beckett's later heroes may consider themselves in purgatory, Belacqua finds himself hopelessly caught in the inferno of society.

Belacqua Shuah may not be a typical Beckett hero, but one can detect in his physical defects and mental deficiency many attributes of Beckett's later creations. He is afflicted with all sorts of minor torments: his face is broken out with impetigo; he has spavined gait and ruined feet, from which he suffers continuously, and eventually he undergoes a toe and neck operation; his temperament is marked by anxiety and morbidity, he suffers fits of depression, has suicidal inclinations, and shows a flagrant aspiration to lunacy. His eccentricity and moral irresponsibility become prominent traits of his successors.

If Belacqua seeks to escape the "real" world of men, but repeatedly finds himself thrown back into the grips of reality, by contrast Beckett's later derelicts no longer need to forsake a social or human environment. They exist outside society, outside reality, and struggle merely to reconcile themselves to the condition imposed upon them by their creator. There may be little glory in being reduced to such an inhuman status, but in the middle of their illusory condition Beckett's French characters suffer *heroically*.

Belacqua never achieves a heroic state because he insists on acting too humanly. To become a true Beckettian hero, he would have to renounce all ties with society, all affinities with the human condition, and be willing to accept the consequences of social alienation. This requires a courage of which Belacqua is not capable. Therefore, his erratic ac-

tions, his social antagonism, his cynicism, his faculty for acting with insufficient motivation, and "his gratuity of conduct" may show a potential aspiration toward genuine fictional existence, but too often it is marked by cowardliness. When caught, he meekly surrenders to the laws and regulations of society, and presents a hypocritical and submissive front. His eccentricity may be a gesture of revolt, or simply a means to escape his environment, yet it is never carried far enough, or conducted with enough conviction, to be effective.

Throughout the book, whenever he is faced with the embarrassing outcomes of his irresponsible actions, Belacqua quickly retreats into a humble and apologetic attitude. In the story **"A Wet Night,"** while on his way to a Christmas Eve party, already quite drunk and disorderly, Belacqua comes face to face with a policeman. The comic encounter exemplifies his submissive behavior:

> Subduing a great desire to visit the pavement he catted, with undemonstrative abundance, all over the boots and trouser-ends of the Guard, in return for which incontinence he received such a dunch on the breast that he fell hip and thigh into the outskirts of his own offal. . . .

Sprawled on the sidewalk, Belacqua clumsily collects his thoughts:

> He bore no animosity towards the Guard, although now he began to hear what he was saying. He knelt before him in the filth, he heard all the odious words he was saying in the recreation of his duty, and bore him not the slightest ill-will. . . . It distressed him to learn that for two pins the Guard would frog-march him to the Station, but he appreciated the officer's dilemma.

Undoubtedly, Belacqua would gladly redeem himself:

> 'Wipe them boots' said the Guard.
>
> Belacqua was only too happy, it was the least he could do. Contriving two loose swabs of the Twilight Herald he stooped and cleaned the boots and trouser-ends in the best of his ability. . . .
>
> 'I trust, Sergeant,' said Belacqua, in a murmur pitched to melt the hardest heart, 'that you can see your way to overlooking my misdemeanour.'

The policeman orders him to move on, and, as he walks away clutching the crumpled newspaper with which he cleaned the boots, Belacqua curses the officer under his breath, but waits until he is safely around the corner and out of sight before dropping the litter to the pavement.

Unlike the hero of ***More Pricks Than Kicks,*** most Beckett characters show little respect for the numerous policemen who abound in Beckett's fiction. Instead they mock and play tricks on them, insult them openly, and in one instance two of Beckett's bums (Mercier and Camier) go so far as to attack and eventually kill a policeman. Belacqua would never dare indulge in such acts of rebellion. Like many protagonists of contemporary novels, he is one of these "crackpots thumbing their noses at society from the safety of some sordid room" [K. W. Gransden, "The Dustman Cometh," *Encounter,* July, 1958], or the safety of their own solipsism. Yet, though he brags of having furnished his mind that he may live there in peace, Belacqua finds that his bodily functions, his physical needs, and his relationships with the outside world prevent him from enjoying mental privacy. Therefore, he expresses his desire for escape by three unfulfilled wishes: to return to a prenatal condition (which is impossible), to commit suicide (which he attempts but fails to conclude successfully), and to be confined to an insane asylum (which is denied him because he remains too rational). Unable to realize his hopes, constantly frustrated, and "being by nature however sinfully indolent, bogged in indolence," Belacqua is caught in the trap of his own weaknesses, in the limbo of his incapacity. He never achieves fictional freedom (the freedom of controlling his mind and actions) and finds himself totally subjected to the rules of social reality.

It is in the fourth canto of Dante's *Purgatorio* that Beckett encountered the prototype for the hero of *More Pricks Than Kicks.* Dante's Florentine friend, the slothful Belacqua, not only shares his name with Beckett's protagonist, but "colui che mostra sè più negligente / che se tigrizia fosse sua serocchia." ["He who shows himself more indolent / than if sloth were his sister"], also offers his indolence and symbolic fetal position as a recurrent attitude and posture for Belacqua Shuah, who in turn becomes a model for later figures in Beckett's universe.

Belacqua, hiding in the shadow of a rock on the steep slope of the mountain that Dante and his guide painfully ascend, is described in the following way: "E un di lor, che mi sembiava lasso / sedeva e abbracciava le ginocchia, / tenendo il viso giù tra esse basso" ["And one of them, who seemed to me weary sat clasping his knees / and holding his face low down between them"]. Dante's Belacqua, who has failed to repent, assumes a lethargic fetal position in order to review his former terrestrial life before he is allowed to enter paradise. In moments of drunkenness or depression, the hero of *More Pricks Than Kicks* also adopts "the knee-and-elbow" position of the indolent souls in purgatory—not, however, to recapture fleeting memories or to evaluate his life, but to obliterate reality. All Beckett's creatures are described or describe themselves in that position at one time or another. The protagonists of Beckett's two English novels, Murphy and Watt, in their inability to cope with reality, long to return to the womb, and often unconsciously assume the appropriate pose. The anonymous narrator of **"L'Expulsé,"** one of Beckett's early French stories, after having been kicked into the gutter from the comfort of his paternal home, explains: "Under these circumstances, nothing compelled me to get up immediately. I rested my elbow on the sidewalk, funny the things you remember, settled my ear in the cup of my hand and began to reflect on my situation, notwithstanding its familiarity." Condemned to wander aimlessly, he repeatedly regrets having been expelled not only from his home but from the womb.

The wandering Molloy also compares himself with Dante's Belacqua: "I was perched higher than the road's highest point and flattened what is more against a rock the same colour as myself, that is grey . . . crouched like Belacqua, or Sordello, I forget." Sordello, one recalls, is

also in the circle of the indolent souls in purgatory. But, although Dante ascribes to Belacqua the characteristic Florentine shrewdness, of Sordello he says, "Come ti stavi altera e disdegnosa / e nel mover delli occhi onesta e tarda!" ["How lofty and disdainful was thy bearing / and what dignity in the slow moving of thine eyes"]. Thus, if Molloy confuses Belacqua and Sordello, it is because Beckett's heroes share attributes of both these Dantesque figures; they retain a mixture of wit, indolence, pride, scorn, and dignity. However, while the protagonists of Beckett's early English fiction aspire to the "Belacqua bliss," as Murphy calls it, and hope for salvation or for an end to their misery, the undying heroes of Beckett's French works seem to have evolved beyond that hope. Caught in a zone where memories of happier days are failing them, and where the hope of possible salvation is negated, they resign themselves to their futile and static plight: "Their path begins and ends at Belacqua's rock; their movement is, like Zeno's arrow, a state of rest" [Walter A. Strauss, "Dante's Belacqua and Beckett's Tramps," *Comparative Literature,* Summer, 1959]. In Beckett's last novel, *Comment c'est,* once more the pitiful narrator-hero compares himself with Dante's Belacqua, but this time his grotesque posture mocks the literary reference:

> endormi je me vois endormi sur le flanc ou sur le ventre c'est l'un ou l'autre sur le flanc lequel le droit c'est mieux le sac sous la tête ou serré contre le ventre serré contre le ventre les genoux remontés le dos en cerceau la tête minuscule près des genoux enroulé autour du sac Belacqua basculé sur le côté las d'attendre oublié des coeurs où vit la grâce endormi
>
> asleep I see myself asleep on the side or on the belly the one or the other on the side which one the right side it's better the bag under my head or tight against the belly tight against the belly knees folded the back arched the head minuscule near the knees coiled around the bag *Belacqua toppled over on his side tired of waiting forgotten by hearts where Grace still exists asleep* (Italics mine.)

In *More Pricks Than Kicks,* Belacqua's wish to return to the womb implies a conscious but feeble revolt against the physical world. His animosity is directed against the conditions of the social and material environment in which he exists, and which dictate a pattern of behavior. Because man has a body he must act to satisfy the needs of that body. Belacqua craves to exist in total mental alienation, or to be back "in the caul," in the dark forever; but since life (or matter, in the form of a body) is inflicted upon man at birth, Belacqua cannot escape physical existence, nor can he avoid his social fate. Consequently, he resigns himself to his condition, curses the day he was born, and, like Dante's slothful friend in purgatory, chooses to spend the duration of his lifetime in the least demanding manner. All Beckett's creatures share this penchant for conscious inaction and idleness. They refuse to allow the body its most natural functions, either for its sake or for the sake of belonging to an organized system. But when Molloy, Malone, The Unnamable, or the narrator-hero of *Comment c'est* take on the fetal posture, it is no longer, as with Belacqua Shuah, a gesture of revolt against the material world, but a resigned expression of metaphysical anguish. They are lonely beings curling like worms in a desolate plot of earth.

In the *Divine Comedy,* Belacqua's fate is to remain in purgatory, or, more precisely, antepurgatory, since he has committed the sin of having delayed repentance, for a period equal to the duration of his prior earthly lifetime. Accordingly, his purgation is also delayed, and the Florentine is not permitted to ascend the mountain to paradise until the heavenly bodies have circulated around him as often as they did during his physical existence. It is, no doubt, to emphasize the indolence of Belacqua that Dante insists on the steepness and length of the ascent. Dante's former friend conceals his resignation and lack of motivation in a state of complete lethargy. Yet when asked why he sits there in idleness, his answer contains no anguish, for he knows that his present condition is limited.

Such a predicament appears ideal for those Beckett heroes who, like Dante's Belacqua, seek to spend the duration of their lifetimes (from womb to tomb) oblivious to reality, unconcerned with the world, satisfied merely to indulge in the whims of their imaginative and somewhat irrational minds. For Belacqua Shuah, the prospect is even more desirable since he firmly believes in the possibility of escaping his present condition, either to be locked in a mental institution or to enjoy the eternal bliss of an afterlife. Thus, if he can compare his existence to that of Dante's friend, it is because it progresses toward a definite end: lunacy or death. In fact, he and Murphy, who shares the same naïve belief, are the only two Beckett protagonists to encounter death; the later heroes vegetate endlessly and hopelessly in absurd immortality.

In Beckett's French novels and plays the line of demarcation between present and future, between life and death, has been abolished. The heroes exist in a region that extends beyond the limits of birth and death. It is an existence that can never end, since it really never began, an existence that allows no progress, no change. Caught in this static condition, these undying creatures convince themselves that their clumsy motions will lead them out of their present state, yet they are aware that these movements are mere illusions—illusions of progress created from despair and fictional necessity. These derelicts are deprived of any choice. They exist outside physical, social, and psychological restrictions, but they are also exempt from death. For them fictional life is death in progress. Therefore, if their actions seem more absurd than those of Belacqua, it is because they have neither motive nor purpose, or, as Maurice Blanchot puts it:

> Il n'y a rien d'admirable dans une épreuve à laquelle on ne peut se soustraire, rien qui appelle l'admiration dans le fait d'être enfermé et de tourner en rond dans un espace d'où l'on ne peut sortir même par la mort, car, pour y tomber, il a fallu précisément déjà tomber hors de la vie. [*Le Livre à venir,* 1959].

Belacqua Shuah, on the contrary, is convinced that his feeble actions and motions will undoubtedly bring an end to his physical misery. Because his life is finite he is able to toy with the notion of physical reality, and he boasts of

having achieved mental freedom. In this respect he is *de mauvaise foi* in his claims, and his anguish remains strictly intellectual, for he can always end his discontent—either by resuming a normal life among his fellowmen, or by committing suicide. His distress is self-imposed even though unjustifiable; his attitude is hypocritical because he can choose an alternative to his condition. He exists within a system that provides him with safety margins: the reality of physical life on the one hand, and that of death on the other. The essential difference then between his predicament and that of Beckett's ageless bums rests on a temporal basis. Belacqua's condition, like that of Dante's souls in purgatory, is limited, and contains the hope of redemption, whereas the waiting and the suffering of Beckett's more recent and tragic heroes are infinite in their absurdity. The heroes no longer hope for a quick death and a blissful afterlife, nor do they return to social reality.

Whether or not the hero of **More Pricks Than Kicks** succeeds in escaping the social inferno to enjoy what he imagines to be a delightful mental purgatory is totally inconsequential since his existence is abruptly curtailed by a death that cures him of the naïve hope he had for an afterlife. Belacqua's immediate successor, Murphy, suffers from a similar delusion. He, too, aspires to the "lee of Belacqua's rock and his embryonal repose" (*Murphy*), and, moreover, claims that he is able to penetrate the ideal zones of his mind. Like Belacqua Shuah, he equates mental existence with a purgatorial state, and neither of them is willing to recognize the infinite anguish that inner life or afterlife can produce. In fact, Murphy thinks "so highly of his postmortem situation, its advantages were present in such detail in his mind, that he actually hoped he might live to be old" in order to enjoy as restful a state as that of Dante's friend. Beckett refers to Murphy's systematized hope as "his Belacqua fantasy," and adds that "it belonged to those that lay just beyond the frontier of suffering, it was the first landscape of freedom." For the heroes of Beckett's early English fiction this desired condition lies either within the mind, beyond the restrictions of the human body, or in some endless afterlife, beyond the limits of earthly existence.

Neither Murphy nor Belacqua achieves mental freedom or immortality in some paradisiac region. Murphy's body and mind are disintegrated in a gas explosion, and his ashes swept away on the floor of a London pub. As for Belacqua Shuah, he, who had often looked forward naïvely to meeting all his girl friends in some peaceful heaven ("What a hope!"), must endure a final sarcastic derision even as he lies marble cold on his deathbed: while his widow flirts with his best friend, the author comments, "Death had already cured him of that naïveté."

Though he declines to participate in the social and physical effort of existence, Belacqua is conditioned by the demands of external reality. While seeking mental isolation, he curses the moment of his birth, and longs for physical annihilation. He expresses this longing not only by his desire to return to the womb, but also through repeated suicidal wishes. For Belacqua death remains an alternative that can end both physical and mental distress. His anxiety and his obsession with self-destruction constitute "a breakdown in the self-sufficiency which he never wearied of arrogating to himself, a sorry collapse of my little internus homo, and alone sufficient to give him away as inept ape of his own shadow." His suicide attempts stem from his inability to cope with life either socially or intellectually. Even before Albert Camus' 1942 essay, *Le Mythe de Sisyphe,* Beckett expressed intuitively the relationship between absurdity and suicide. All Beckett's exiled heroes consider suicide at one time or another as a means of ending their absurd existence, but, aside from Belacqua and Murphy, no Beckett hero succeeds in dying. Instead, Beckett's French derelicts remain suspended in a state of endless expectancy, and often devise means of parodying self-destruction.

In the story **"Love and Lethe"** the sexual act is presented as an ironic substitute for suicide. Belacqua has managed to convince his girl friend, Ruby Tough, that she should commit the act of *felo de se* with him. Together they proceed to a deserted spot at the top of a mountain. Belacqua carries, in a bag, a revolver and bullets, some veronal, a bottle of whisky with glasses, and the suicide note which he describes "as the notice . . . that we are fled." In spite of its implied seriousness the situation quickly turns to grotesque comedy. When they reach the chosen place, Ruby, who has removed her skirt in order to "storm the summit" with more ease, succeeds in pouring half the bottle of whisky down Belacqua's throat, and she herself swallows the other half. The hero is then incapable of carrying out his suicide scheme, fires the gun "in terram," and together they find a justification for their failure by indulging in the act of love. Beckett, with his usual irony, cannot prevent himself from peeping at the lovers and from interjecting a lyrical but sarcastic comment:

> So that they came together in inevitable nuptial. With the utmost reverence at our command, moving away on tiptoe from where they lie in the ling, we mention this in a low voice.

> It will quite possibly be his boast in years to come, when Ruby is dead and he an old optimist, that at least on this occasion, if never before nor since, he achieved what he set out to do; *Car,* in the words of one competent to sing of the matter, *L'Amour et la Mort*—caesura—*n'est qu'une mesme chose.*

> May their night be full of music at all events.

Belacqua's suicide having failed, only one other alternative remains: "A mental home was the place for him." It is the author who makes this suggestion, but Belacqua himself is quite aware of his mental deficiency. Suitably enough the two-word suicide note which he proudly displays for Ruby's inspection reflects his awareness. Painted in large letters on an old license plate, it reads: "TEMPORARILY SANE."

Insanity, or a similar condition that does not require rational commitments, is the state most desired by Beckett's people. "We are all born mad. Some remain so," proclaims Estragon in *Waiting for Godot,* as though madness were the preferred condition for man's passage through life. Beckett's creatures mistrust the vague notions they have of the past; they strive for a mental posture that can

free them from rationality and whatever doubtful memories they preserve. These rootless beings alienate themselves from society through a conscious denial of their memory's validity. They repeatedly question the time and place that should determine their present condition: "You're sure it was here!" —"What?" —"That we were to wait." —"He said by the tree." Yes, but is it the right tree, and what kind of tree is it? And is it the right day? "You're sure it was this evening?" —"What?" —"That we were to wait." —"He said Saturday . . . I think." —"But what Saturday? And is it Saturday? Is it not rather Sunday? Or Monday? Or Friday?" In their state of anguished expectancy, Beckett's heroes stand as witnesses for the failure of logic, reason, or whatever mental process man utilizes for the discovery and understanding of the external world. Thus, by pretending insanity, or merely aspiring to such a state, they reject all notions of reality and the sum of human knowledge. This self-imposed alienation produces ignorance, meaninglessness, and mental chaos.

Most Beckett protagonists would willingly relinquish future and past, or even the hope of eventual redemption, to enjoy the privileges of lunacy. These are perhaps best defined in *Malone Dies* when Macmann, a creation of Malone's delirious mind, arrives in an asylum and the anonymous keepers explain:

> You are now in the House of Saint John of God, with the number one hundred and sixty-six. Fear nothing, you are among friends. Friends! Well well. Take no thought for anything, it is we shall think and act for you, from now forward. We like it. Do not thank us therefore. In addition to the nourishment carefully calculated to keep you alive, and even well, you will receive, every Saturday, in honour of our patron, an imperial half-pint of porter and a plug of tobacco.

If Macmann is allowed to enter a mental institution, it is because he has reached such a state of physical and mental deterioration that there is no question as to his admittance into the world of lunacy.

Life in an insane asylum provides a certain physical irresponsibility, a certain mental freedom that few humans ever enjoy. For not only are lunatics given the daily care necessary for the human body, but they are left free to indulge in their private fancies. In Beckett's universe, the madman's existence is not only comparable to ascetic isolation, but also to that of the secluded artist locked in his ivory tower. It is not accidental then if several of Beckett's heroes think of themselves as writers (Molloy, Moran, Malone) and present their mental delirium as artistic creation.

In *More Pricks Than Kicks,* all Belacqua's actions and reflections are intended to negate what others consider rational or logical. His refusal to submit to the concepts that govern knowledge, his claim to a lack of memory and understanding, his extravagance, his fear of the conventional, and his distaste for material life are all aspirations toward mental alienation, toward lunacy. But Belacqua is far from being totally deranged, and though he contemplates life in an insane asylum as the most ideal type of existence, his physical and social obsessions prevent him from entering "the spacious annexe of mental alienation."

Belacqua cannot forsake the "big world," therefore he is not permitted to enter the Portrane Lunatic Asylum and must continue to play the fool in a world that appears to him even more foolish than he is. Though "a mental home" is recommended for him, he fails to be admitted to such an institution. He remains outside the tall wall surrounding the Portrane Lunatic Asylum and resigns himself to contemplating the "big red building" from a nearby hill. He says to one of his conquests, Winnie, as they observe the lunatics playing gently below in the courtyard: "My heart's right there." Winnie remarks that the lunatics seem very "sane and well-behaved," and her companion agrees whole-heartedly.

Since neither suicide nor insanity can save Belacqua from his social fate, and since he depends too much on his past, his memories, and his acquired knowledge of which he is very proud, when confronted with the absurdity of life he suffers moments of anxiety and fits of depression. In spite of his eccentricity he functions too rationally to be granted mental or even fictional freedom. To reach such a state, he would have to learn to practice the kind of asceticism mastered by Beckett's later heroes, which consists of freeing oneself from the physical by withdrawing into the mental world. Surrounded by "aesthetes" and "impotents," as he calls his fellowmen, involved in the petty activities of daily life, submitting to the regulations of society, cornered by his own habits, and, cowardly, obeying the orders of lawmakers and law enforcers, Belacqua leads a schizophrenic existence that denies both physical and mental escape. Neither lethargy, drunkenness, suicide, nor madness can save him from habitual and conventional impositions. Therefore, faced with this dilemma which appears to be a conspiracy of what he calls "the Furies," he suffers moments of utter panic.

The major cause of Belacqua's anxiety, perhaps his most stubborn enemy, is time. In Beckett's universe, time, clocks, and those elements of nature that mark the passing of time with obsessive recurrence, are closely associated with the characters' notions of reality. If the heroes of Beckett's more recent works are able to toy with temporality, to distort or negate time's dimensions and eventually escape its empire, it is because they exist outside the material world. Belacqua, however, must submit to its tyranny. He may feel a particular revulsion toward clocks, yet he cannot avoid their stubborn presence.

Belacqua endures one of his most dreadful moments when, in the story **"What a Misfortune,"** his second-wife-to-be, Thelma bboggs, announces that his wedding gift has arrived:

> 'The first thing I did was to set it.' [She said.]
>
> The hideous truth dawned on his mind. 'Not a clock' he implored, 'don't say a grandfather clock.'
>
> 'The grandfather and mother' she did say 'of a period clock.'
>
> He turned his face to the wall. He who of late

years . . . would not tolerate a chronometer of any kind in the house, for whom the local publication of the hours was six of the best on the brain every hour, and even the sun's shadow a torment, now to have this time-fuse deafen the rest of his days. It was enough to make him break off the engagement.

Belacqua's only solution to avoid "the hideous truth" is to think that "he could always spike the monster's escapement and turn its death's-head to the wall." But this would be too simple and would bring only temporary relief. Throughout the stories, Beckett hardly gives a moment's respite to his hero. Numerous parenthetical remarks remind both the reader and Belacqua of time's impositions: "Now the sun, that creature of habits, shone in through the window," or elsewhere, "let us call it winter, that dusk may fall now and a moon rise." An even more poignant allusion to clocks is interjected when, in the early hours of morning, upon leaving Alba Perdue's apartment, Belacqua strikes a match to look at his watch: "It had stopped. *Patience, a public clock would oblige*" (italics mine).

Beckett inserts these parenthetical statements within the narration not only to reinforce the irony of his social satire, but to emphasize particularly the inevitable passing of time and its importance on Belacqua's actions:

> Anxious that those who read this incredible adventure shall not pooh-pooh it as unintelligible we avail ourselves now of this lull, what time Belacqua is on his way, Mrs. Tough broods in the kitchen and Ruby dreams over her gloria, to enlarge a little on the latter lady.

This ironic aside not only ridicules human activities, but makes jest of the narrative technique itself. By subjecting his characters and their actions to linear temporality, Beckett emphasizes the absurd need man has for "passing the time."

Man's slavery to time is a primary affliction which Belacqua must endure as a member of society, and accordingly he must also submit to habit. Time and habit are two of his darkest bêtes noires. In his 1931 essay on Proust, Beckett explained that "habit is a compromise effected between the individual and his environment, or between the individual and his own organic eccentricities, the lightning-conductor of his existence. Habit is the ballast that chains the dog to his vomit." Belacqua is often subjected to all sort of cruelty, although his inability to accept the habitual results primarily from his failure to effect the "compromise" between himself and his "environment," between himself and "his own organic eccentricities."

In the story **"Dante and the Lobster,"** after having reduced all human relationships to their most trivial aspects, Belacqua is deeply troubled when he learns that lobsters are boiled alive—a fact quite unbearable to the human mind until grasped and accepted as a mere convention beyond all rational reflection. Belacqua's life may be governed by habits, but because his mind refuses to accept human actions at face value and proceeds to intellectualize these actions pedantically, he suffers strokes of mental confusion. This contributes to what Beckett calls the "sorry collapse" of his "little internus homo." Yet Belacqua must submit to the shocking discovery that lobsters are always boiled alive:

> 'Have sense' she said sharply, 'lobsters are always boiled alive. They must be.' She caught up the lobster and laid it on its back. It trembled. 'They feel nothing' she said.
>
> In the depths of the sea it had crept into the cruel pot. For hours, in the midst of its enemies, it had breathed secretly. . . . Now it was going alive into scalding water. It had to. Take into the air my quiet breath.
>
> Belacqua looked at the old parchment of her face, grey in the dim kitchen.
>
> 'You make a fuss' she said angrily 'an upset me and then lash into it for your dinner.'
>
> She lifted the lobster clear of the table. It had about thirty seconds to live.
>
> Well, thought Belacqua, it's a quick death, God help us all.
>
> It is not.

"It is not" a quick death! This objection, no doubt formulated by the author as an answer to the hero's resigned statement, echoes throughout Beckett's work as the perpetual lament of all the crippled, blind, mute, infirm, deformed beings who stubbornly resist total disintegration, and are never permitted to die completely. Belacqua seems to recognize the doomed lobster as a paradigm for man. His horrified reaction when his aunt tells him that lobsters are boiled alive and "feel nothing" is more a gesture of fear than one of revolt or compassion.

The ordeal of the lobster that "crept into the cruel pot," and whose strange death startles Belacqua, forecasts the ordeal of the many Beckett creatures who, in subsequent works, are also helplessly placed in pots, garbage cans, or urns. Though Belacqua does not end in a pot, but in a coffin, his death is just as disconcerting as that of the lobster. While in a hospital room waiting for a neck and toe operation he suffers anguish and disgust at the thought of knowing that "at twelve sharp he would be sliced open—zeep! —with a bistoury." As he observes the busy nurses, doctors, cleaning women, and elevator boys performing their duties with solemnity, going in and out of his room to feed him, remove his tray, bandage his sores, take away his chamber pot, prepare for his operation, all done as a ritual, a series of habitual gestures, Belacqua reflects on the uselessness of their motions, their routine, the absurd game they are playing in the process of preserving life. He sees himself caught in this too-well-organized system, and yet is incapable of reacting violently. He surrenders to the situation by "closing his eyes"—a most feeble (lobsterlike) effort. His only consolation, he muses, is that his "sufferings under the anesthetic will be exquisite" but unfortunately he will "not remember them." Faced with the absurdity of the moment, he ponders a little question: should he assume the attitude of Heraclitus weeping, or that of Democritus laughing?

It is true that he did not care for these black and white alternatives as a rule. Indeed he even went so far as to hazard a little paradox of his own account, to the effect that between contraries no alternation was possible. But was it the moment for a man to be nice? Belacqua snatched eagerly at the issue. Was it to be laughter or tears? It came to the same thing in the end, but which was it to be now?

He chooses laughter, for it comes to the same thing, since laughter and tears negate each other in the end. His course is clear. He arms his mind with laughter; but, as the title of the story (**"Yellow"**) implies, it can be only a cowardly laughter, *un rire jaune,* that overcomes the frightened Belacqua.

Though everything is meticulously prepared for Belacqua's operation, yet, "By Christ! he did die" of the anesthesia—"They had clean forgotten to auscultate him." The irony of the situation is stretched beyond Belacqua's accidental death and is carried to the scene of his funeral and burial. Thus, even as a corpse Belacqua remains a target for Beckett's sarcasm.

Throughout the book Belacqua receives a most unsympathetic treatment from his creator. Yet his complete disregard for personal property, neglect of the human body and its natural functions, passion for bicycles, aversion to clocks, fear of policemen, his physical ailments, extreme indolence, recurrent wishes for death or a return to the womb, and leanings toward mental instability identify him as a true member of Beckett's family. However, Belacqua's pedantry, arrogance, egocentrism, and morbidity reject the compassion aroused by Beckett's later heroes. No doubt few readers will grant human status to these irresponsible, irrational, obscene, smelly-mouthed, smelly-footed, half-paralyzed creatures, and yet in the middle of their misery these derelicts preserve enough wit and humanity to evoke pity, whereas Belacqua Shuah appears totally repulsive.

Though Beckett introduces himself as a personal friend of his hero ("We were Pylade and Orestes, for a period, flattened down to something very genteel"), eventually he rejects Belacqua: "He was an impossible person in the end. I gave him up in the end because he was not serious." One may wonder if Belacqua Shuah was "not serious" enough as a person or as an artistic creation to deserve such a judgment. In any event, Belacqua is the only protagonist who fails to reappear in subsequent Beckett fiction. The two burlesque heroes of the jettisoned novel *Mercier et Camier* receive a derogatory mention in *The Unnamable,* but not Belacqua: "To tell the truth I believe they are all here, at least from Murphy on, I believe we are all here," even the "pseudocouple Mercier-Camier."

If Beckett gave up Belacqua in the end "because he was not serious," nevertheless it would be a mistake to ignore this hero completely. He deserves to be remembered because through him are focused the essential themes of the works to come. *More Pricks Than Kicks* is not technically as accomplished as other Beckett achievements. It is overburdened with clever and obscure allusions, abuses foreign expressions and wordplays, relies heavily on linguistic pedantry, and may be categorized in part as intellectual exhibitionism—the work of a young but talented writer who had yet to find himself. The book fails to express clearly the later Beckett concerns, hardly exploits the various literary and philosophic references it borrows, lapses too much into subtle craftsmanship—but should one agree with Hugh Kenner, who states that "none of this needs to be revived, though it is enlightening to know it exists" [*Samuel Beckett: A Critical Study,* 1961], and simply reject this revealing and unusual beginning of Beckett's literary career? One finds in *More Pricks Than Kicks* more than "the detritus of the mind of an academic bohemian preoccupied with its own cleverness and inclined toward macaronic effects. . . ." This harsh judgment, again formulated by Hugh Kenner, extends to all Beckett's early efforts in prose and poetry prior to the publication of *Murphy* in 1938, yet of all these early experiments, *More Pricks Than Kicks* most truly deserves rediscovery. This work contains in essence much of the eccentric humor and strangely striking absurdity that was to be subsumed under a more effective and original class of comedy in those later works that established Beckett's reputation. Belacqua is a remarkable creation in his own right; his problems of adjusting to his environment are no less interesting because he does not arrive at the same solution as do his progeny and heirs in Beckett's French fiction.

An excerpt from *Texts for Nothing:*

Only the words break the silence, all other sounds have ceased. If I were silent I'd hear nothing. But if I were silent the other sounds would start again, those to which the words have made me deaf, or which have really ceased. But I am silent, it sometimes happens, no, never, not one second. I weep too without interruption. It's an unbroken flow of words and tears. With no pause for reflection. But I speak softer, every year a little softer. Perhaps. Slower too, every year a little slower. Perhaps. It is hard for me to judge. If so the pauses would be longer, between the words, the sentences, the syllables, the tears, I confuse them, words and tears, my words are my tears, my eyes my mouth. And I should hear, at every little pause, if it's the silence I say when I say that only the words break it. But nothing of the kind, that's not how it is, it's for ever the same murmur, flowing unbroken, like a single endless word and therefore meaningless, for it's the end gives the meaning to words.

Samuel Beckett, in his Texts for Nothing, *in* Stories
and Texts for Nothing, *Grove Press, 1967.*

Brian Finney   (essay date 1975)

SOURCE: "*Assumption* to *Lessness:* Beckett's Shorter Fiction," in *Beckett the Shape Changer,* edited by Katharine Worth, Routledge & Kegan Paul, 1975, pp. 61-83.

[*In the essay below, Finney surveys Beckett's short fiction.*]

The reader of Beckett's writing finds himself in a similar position to Gulliver in the land of the Houyhnhnms. Confronted with a series of Yahoo-like tramps, his instinctual

reaction is to deny any resemblances between himself and these repulsive creatures. Like Gulliver, however, he cannot remain aloof for long. Beckett's derelicts are no fools; they have thought a great deal more about their seemingly meaningless predicament than has the average reader. Any certainties he may have entertained about his superiority to them are quickly undermined by these professional sceptics, to whom man's reasoning powers are a subject of particular ridicule. 'We may reason on to our heart's content', as the protagonist of **'The Expelled'** observes, 'the fog won't lift.' Man only uses his reason to deceive himself into thinking that life will yield some kind of sense and purpose. But the uncertainties of death and beyond annul the rational certainties of life and leave everything in a terrifying state of confusion. 'The confusion is not my invention,' Beckett protested to Tom Driver. 'It is all around us and our only chance is to let it in' ['Beckett by the Madeleine', *Columbia University Forum,* Summer, 1961].

Beckett lets into his art both the confusion and man's even more confusing flight from it. The inhabitants of his world fluctuate between rational illusion and the despairing cries of the living damned. Tragi-comedy is his natural mode. The laughable effects of man's attempts to create a semblance of order (Belacqua's lunch ritual, Watt's endless lists, Winnie's stocktaking, the searchers' elaborate rules of conduct in ***The Lost Ones***) alternate with terrifying glimpses of man's suffering in the face of unending uncertainty ('But whom can I have offended so grievously,' asks the voice in ***Texts for Nothing,*** 'to be punished in this inexplicable way'). The greatest uncertainty of all arises from the subjective bias of our method of perceiving both others and ourselves. The final insult for Beckett is man's inability to know even himself, especially as, like so many writers of this century, he sees the artist's function as 'excavatory, immersive', an exploration of the self. Because the self is unknowable, he told John Gruen in 1970, 'when man faces himself, he is looking into the abyss' ['Samuel Beckett talks about Beckett', *Vogue* (London), February, 1970].

Beckett's world has remained remarkably consistent. His first published work in 1929 ('Dante . . . Bruno, Vico . . . Joyce') already talks of 'this earth that is Purgatory'. His most recent work to date, *Not I,* makes a similar identification. There is no better commentary on a work or Beckett's than the rest of his writings. Each successive piece of writing amplifies, comments on, progresses from, and negates, its predecessor. Belacqua sought refuge in motion, Murphy in stasis. Watt acknowledges his prior existence as Murphy and so on through to the last of the first-person narrators, 'Bom', who is still Belacqua crouched up in the familiar foetal position, but 'fallen over on his side tired of waiting forgotten of the hearts where grace abides asleep'.

The fiction that has appeared since 1961 is what Beckett calls 'residua', what remains, as he explained to me, both from larger original wholes and from the whole body of his previous work. As such it is connected with the earlier fiction in precisely the same fashion, pursuing problems of self-perception while demolishing previous models ('All that goes before forget', ***Enough*** begins) or exploring their antitheses (like 'the unthinkable end' in section 15 of *The Lost Ones*).

Beckett's shorter fiction has inevitably received less attention than the longer works owing to its early inferiority and its later difficulty. Yet it has its own distinctive contribution to make to our knowledge of his world. It is a form uniquely suited to Beckett's stark and deliberately simplified vision of man's predicament. For over a decade now it has constituted his only fictional output. Even where it fails artistically, it can throw fascinating light on subsequent works. All the uncollected shorter fiction up to *More Pricks Than Kicks* comes into this category. There are the two early stories **'Assumption'** (1929) and **'A Case in a Thousand'** (1934), besides two self-contained extracts from his suppressed first novel *Dream of Fair to Middling Women* published as 'Sedendo et Quiescendo' and 'Text' in 1932. Despite their obscurity in both language and meaning they contain nuggets Beckett was to mine later.

In **'Assumption'** the male protagonist is locked in an unnatural 'humanity of silence'. Contact with a woman leads to nightly crucifixion ('each night he died and was God') from which he longs to be released into 'the light of eternity'. Finally love breaks down his dam of silence and with 'a great storm of sound' he dies. Beckett still had to discover the imprisoning effects of time-bound speech on those desiring dissolution into a timeless void. But the story is potent with themes that continue to obsess him. The collapse of a lifetime's silence that leaves the suffering victim 'fused with the cosmic discord' is a situation he has recently reverted to with great effect in *Not I*. The concept of man as a suffering God, crucified by the world and sexuality in particular, anticipates numerous parallels between successive heroes and Christ: the stoning of the hero of **'The End'**; Molloy making his entry to his Jerusalem on a bicycle; Macmann and 'Bom' stretched out on the ground in the attitude of the cross: the list is endless.

In particular the association Beckett makes between women and death in **'Assumption'** is developed more fully in his subsequent fiction. In **'Assumption'** the woman contemplates the hero's 'face that she had overlaid with death'. In the chapter **'Love and Lethe'** from *More Pricks Than Kicks* Belacqua sets out on a suicide pact with his latest girl, Ruby, only to end up making love instead. Beckett claims sardonically that 'at least on this occasion, if never before nor since, he achieved what he set out to do'. Love means exile from the self; for Beckett this is a little death in a less playful sense than that punned on by his Elizabethan predecessors. It constantly distracts Belacqua in both *Dream of Fair to Middling Women* and *More Pricks Than Kicks* from seeking refuge in his mind, which both he and Murphy saw 'as the last ditch when all was said and done'. Murphy goes one better than Belacqua in managing to turn his back on Celia, the first of many prostitutes that feature as the heroines of his subsequent fiction.

Behind Beckett's paradoxical attitude to love and sexuality lies his vision of man's suffering condition. The illusory joys of sex lead to the all-too-real suffering of a new life. His opening remark to John Gruen in 1970 was: 'The major sin is the sin of being born'. He went on to claim

that he has a clear memory of his own foetal existence, one of agony and darkness. This could well explain the enigma inherent in Beckett's other early short story, **'A Case in a Thousand',** where Dr Nye, the protagonist, refuses to accept man's universal sadness as anything but a personal disorder. Only after his nurse has related to him 'a matter connected with his earliest years' too trivial to 'be enlarged on here' can one make any sense of his earlier proposition: 'Myself I cannot save'. He has already undergone the trauma of birth, but can at least avoid bequeathing it to a further generation. To Beckett midwife and gravedigger are indistinguishable.

Dr Nye anticipates Belacqua's wish 'to be back in the caul, on (his) back in the dark for ever', which would at least avoid the 'night-sweats' of his sexuality. *More Pricks Than Kicks* (1934) has been given more attention than Beckett would have liked (to judge from the blurb on the Calder & Boyars reissue of 1970), primarily because Belacqua stands first in his long line of fictional derelicts. He shares with them many of the distinctive features which instantly set Beckett's protagonists apart from so-called normal experience. His physical disabilities and his associated love for bicycles, his sloth, his abhorrence of clocks and other reminders of his temporal condition, his distinction between mind and body, his 'faculty for acting with insufficient motivation', and his penchant for lunatic asylums all find parallels in the heroes of the subsequent novels.

What is distinctive about this first book of short stories is its concentration on Belacqua's sexual misadventures. During the course of the book Belacqua is paired off in turn with Winnie Coates, Alba Perdue, Ruby Tough, Lucy, Thelma *née* bboggs, and the Smeraldina. In each relationship Belacqua's conduct reverses the norms of gallantry. A moment of tenderness for him on Winnie's part strikes Belacqua as 'a drink of water to drink in a dungeon'. Love at the least is an imprisonment—with minor privileges for good conduct. Belacqua appears to be seeking a wife or mistress who is so uninterested in him sexually that he is freed of his bodily compulsions, able to seek slothful peace in an extended 'Beethoven pause' of the mind. Only that bluestocking, the Alba, seems capable of such selflessness; yet their platonic night together ends with the comment in German 'Not possible . . .'. Ruby lets him down badly, depriving him of his 'temporarily sane' determination to commit suicide with the 'ignis fatuus' of her sex appeal. Much to his disappointment Lucy stubbornly refuses 'to establish their married life on [the] solid basis of a cuckoldry'. Belacqua's idea of marital happiness is only achieved when she has been 'crippled for life and her beauty dreadfully marred'.

Belacqua seeks to escape from the bondage of his sexuality by playing the peeping Tom. It is an inadequate solution to a problem which is solved in more solipsist style by his successors in the *Nouvelles* and the trilogy (*Molloy, Malone Dies,* and *The Unnamable*), who resort to onanism. But at least it detaches him one remove from the evil of procreation, besides saving him the physical effort in the spirit of Dante's original, 'sloth's own brother'. Lucy does not survive her accident long, and only after his own death is Belacqua finally able to enjoy the prospect of his third wife, the Smeraldina, taking Hairy as her cicisbeo because 'this is what darling Bel would wish'. Simultaneous detachment from, and satisfaction in, the sexual act is only permissible to the dead. The living are already in Purgatory. Belacqua's lifelong endeavour to attain a god-like omniscience from sex ('I am what I am' he claims, like St Paul, to whom the title also refers) is doomed to failure in a godless world. There are more pricks than kicks to life in every sense.

Belacqua's fictional successors learn faster the bitter connection between their sexuality and the curse of their own conception. Molloy even admits to sometimes confusing his mother's image with that of his old lover, Ruth, an experience that he finds 'unendurable, like being crucified'. Rather than inflict the pain of existence on another generation, the French heroes set out to reverse the pattern of growth, to return to the tomb of the womb, to spend their last days, like Mahood, in their mother's entrails. Their efforts to effect the impossible are comic, their failure tragic. Conception is irreversible and these heroes are constantly being ejected from their womb-like refuges and thrown back violently on to the stage of life, like the Player in *Act Without Words.*

This image of repeated expulsion first surfaces as a dominant motif in the four *Nouvelles* ("Premier amour," 'L'Expulsé', 'La Fin', and 'Le Calmant' respectively translated as **"First Love,"** '**The Expelled'**, '**The End'**, and '**The Calmative'**), Beckett's earliest French fiction, written in 1945 before both *Mercier and Camier* and the trilogy. In all but one story (**'The Calmative'**) the hero makes his fictional entrée on being expelled from a womb-like room, which in the case of **"First Love"** has been bequeathed him by his father. In all three stories the exiled anti-hero spends his time wandering in search of a substitute refuge, which when found proves hopelessly inadequate. In the initial room the hero, like the foetus, was at least fed and evacuated regularly. But the coffin-shaped cab of **'The Expelled'** (the title speaks for itself), the sitting room emptied of its furniture in **"First Love,"** the hut in **'The Calmative'**, and the basement room, cave and shed in **'The End'** all fail to reproduce even the substitute convenience of the initial room. In **'The End'**, for example, the hero is only saved from starvation by the chance arrival of a cow; and where previously he had had his chamber pot emptied daily, in his shed he dirties his own nest. As he sardonically says of his tragi-comic predicament: 'To contrive a little kingdom, in the midst of the universal muck, then shit on it, ah that was me all over.' Interestingly, there is less comic detachment in the earlier version of this story which reads in place of the last phrase 'ah the pity of it'.

Far the most interesting of the *Nouvelles* in this context is **"Premier amour"** (**"First Love"**), which Beckett withheld from publication until 1970 and which only appeared in English translation in 1973. Beckett wrote to me saying he withheld **"Premier amour"** because he found it 'even less satisfactory than the others', and now regrets having released it for publication. I must confess that I still find it the most fascinating of the four *Nouvelles.* From the beginning the first-person narrator links marriage with

death, his own marriage to Anna with the death of his father. Marriage can only bring mortality to the child born from it into sorrow. Considering that the narrator remembers the trauma of his own birth, the date of which lies graven in his memory 'in figures that life will not easily erase', it is surprising—even to him—that he should so quickly be involved in inflicting the same agony on another. What emerges from his account of his first love affair is that yet again he is only seeking in this woman a return to the womb. Expelled from the room in his father's house, his clothes dumped outside it like an afterbirth, he recreates the image of his initial room in the house of Anna, the prostitute he meets and goes to live with. Although she undertakes all the maternal functions of feeding him and emptying his pot, he is driven to desert her by the birth-cries of what she alleges is his child, cries which continue to haunt his memory for the rest of his life.

Crudely summarised in this way, the story sounds like the neurotic outpourings of a sick mind. What above all saves it from this charge is Beckett's comic detachment. As Nell says in *Endgame,* 'nothing is funnier than unhappiness'. The narrator is life's victim, doing his best to avoid the gross errors of his fellow creatures, but finally and hilariously proving just as vulnerable. Fleeing from Anna, his first love, he takes refuge in an abandoned cow-shed. There

> for the first time in my life, and I would not hesitate to say the last if I had not to husband my cyanide, I had to contend with a feeling which gradually assumed, to my dismay, the dread name of love.

Above all what convinces him that he must be in love is finding himself tracing the word 'Anna' on 'time's forgotten cowplats'. By this Augustinian juxtaposition of love and excrement, as of sublime language and banal action, Beckett induces us to laugh at the essential tragedy of existence. For existence is not all suffering. As the narrator has come to realise: 'Catch-cony life! To be nothing but pain, how that would simplify matters! Omnidolent! Impious dream!' Such temporary wisdom and detachment fails to prevent him being ricocheted between the extremes of love's tortures and relative happiness. He even finds himself pulling up nettles under the evil influence of love, instead of manuring them as was his usual custom, Beckett informs us, tongue in cheek, with all malevolent weeds. Weeds remind him of the reality of things which is only concealed by the ephemeral beauty of flowers. Repeatedly the hero of the *Nouvelles* obtains hyacinths or crocuses as *memento mori* over whose decay and promise of oblivion he perversely rejoices.

Apart from the unforgivable association between love and birth, the narrator also finds love a distraction from what he sees as his only hope in life, 'supineness in the mind, the dulling of the self and of that residue of execrable frippery known as the non-self and even the world, for short'. This search for the oblivion of womb or grave that obsesses the heroes of all his subsequent fiction can only be conducted by being oneself: 'For when one is [oneself] one knows what to do to be less so', he claims, little appreciating the epistemological complications awaiting his fictional successors pursuing this programme. Whereas love on the other hand means exile from the self, 'and it is painful to be no longer oneself, even more painful if possible than when one is'. Paradoxically true as this may be, the narrator of **"First Love"** is unable to use this theoretical insight to extricate himself from Anna. His expulsion from her refuge is ironically forced on him by the unforgivable reproduction of life, in which he may have played an unwilling part.

"First Love" contains so many of the major themes of the French fiction in embryonic form that it deserves greater attention than it has received to date. The narrator experiences all the problems of perception that are to torture his successors. The outside world, other people, even his own memory are not to be trusted, since, as Beckett said in *Proust,* 'the individual is a succession of individuals, the world being a projection of the individual's consciousness'. Words like 'love' and 'beauty' remain enigmas to this lover, qualities he has read about but is liable to apply to the wrong situations, owing to the subjective nature of his perception. Despite her age and permanent squint, Anna could well be beautiful, he claims, if he had some data on beauty—which none of us has, Beckett implies. Constantly the certainties of daily living are being undermined by the narrator's painfully honest scepticism. For example, he returns to the bench for the fourth or fifth time, 'at roughly the same hour, I mean roughly the same sky, no, I don't mean that either, for it's always the same sky and never the same sky, what words are there for that, none I know, period'. The incomprehensible nothingness of reality can only be approximated to by the writer's use of such mutually annihilating antitheses.

In fact the entire story is constructed in this manner. The narrator loves death and hates love, that death of the self. He seeks out the self to escape it. He tells his story so as to reach 'là où le verbe s'arrête', as Beckett wrote in the French version but omitted from his English translation ('the point where speech ceases'). For, like the heroes of the other *Nouvelles* and the trilogy, he is a writer whose writings 'are no sooner dry than they revolt me'. As a writer he is particularly aware of the vulnerability of language: 'I heard the word fibrome, or brone, I don't know which, never knew, never knew what it meant and never had the curiosity to find out. The things one recalls! And records!' Words are as arbitrary as life and as meaningless. How can one person ever be sure that the meaning of what he says is not understood wholly differently by the recipient? How can we ever get outside our own heads? If we can't, then all life becomes a fiction, and, like the narrator of **"First Love,"** we can decide to alter someone else's name from Lulu to Anna without more than our usual inconsistency.

Like his contemporaries, Nabokov and Barth, Beckett never lets his reader forget the deceptive nature of the form he is using. He plays linguistic games throughout the *Nouvelles.* The narrator of **'The Expelled'** ends up unable to explain why he told this story rather than another: 'Perhaps some other time I'll be able to tell another. Living souls, you will see how alike they are'—alike because they emanate from the same brain. In all the *Nouvelles,* as the narrator of **'The Calmative'** explains, 'we are needless to

say in a skull'. Like his successors in the trilogy he tells himself 'this story which aspires to be the last' to calm himself in the terrifying face of death. Repeatedly Beckett reminds us that life is a fiction of our own invention: 'So much for that description' he will make his hero exclaim with satisfaction, or 'No reason for this to end or go on. Then let it end.' In parodying fictional conventions he is mocking the artificiality of the life we have invented for ourselves: aesthetic and metaphysical considerations become indistinguishable in his work.

The remaining three *Nouvelles* anticipate the structure and major themes of the trilogy quite closely at times. Both sets of works present the same protagonist, exiled from the oblivion of the womb in a world of his own invention, seeking to end his suffering existence by coming to know his unknowable self. Like Belacqua, Murphy and Watt before him, and Molloy, Moran, Macmann and Mahood after him, the hero of **'The Expelled'** finds his body a very imperfect instrument of locomotion. Whenever he attempts mentally to correct the clumsiness of his gait he 'managed a few steps of creditable execution and then fell'. Mind and body are related to each other too precariously to withstand any conscious interference by mind alone. It is appropriate that the dualist philosopher Geulincx's *Ethics* should be mentioned by name in the same story. The hero of the *Nouvelles,* like those of the trilogy, wears his father's hat and greatcoat, suffers from similar sores of the scalp, and tramps across the same landscape with its fortified town, hills, bogs and coastline.

The links between the two trilogies of stories and novels are of two kinds: similarities in situation, and references in the novels to events in the stories. There are a number of striking parallels between **'The Expelled'** and *Molloy,* **'The End'** and *Malone Dies,* and **'The Calmative'** and *The Unnamable.* In the first pair both heroes begin their wanderings in the prime of life, have a contretemps with policemen, knock down old women or their dogs and confess to being the author of their own stories. In the second pair both heroes seek to create their own fictional death; both seek out rooms in which their food is fetched and their pot emptied regularly, only to lose these conveniences; both slowly degenerate into tramps, now sitting on the bench by the river first introduced in **"First Love,"** now exposed to the elements; both end drifting out to the open sea in a boat to meet their imagined end. The final pair, **'The Calmative'** and *The Unnamable,* both imagine the continuation of mind and voice after the body has died. Both heroes are tortured by fictional assassins or tyrants of their own invention in a place of terror that both identify with the inside of their distant skulls. Both attempt to escape into the silence of their true self by telling their own story rather than one about a fictional counterpart, and both in effect conclude: 'All I say cancels out, I'll have said nothing'—and go on.

If these parallels suggest repetition, the way in which each subsequent work demolishes its predecessors suggests progression of a kind. Not only does each of the four *Nouvelles* trace the roughly chronological career of the same protagonist (twenty-five years old in **"First Love,"** ninety years old when he died according to **'The Calmative'**) but all three novels that follow draw on the *Nouvelles* for incidents in their characters' past history. Molloy remembers his past incarnation as the hero of **'The End'** who put out to sea in a boat and wonders if he ever returned from that journey. This memory of his is promptly undermined by speculating whether any relationship is possible between past and present selves, the one setting out and the one returning. Likewise Malone has a photograph of the ass by the shore that carried him to his cave in **'The End',** a cave that Malone now remembers with pleasure, where in the earlier story he had felt compelled to abandon it. Once again memory is playing tricks on its victim. Even the Unnamable acknowledges his past origins in the *Nouvelles* by quoting the opening sentence of **'The End',** 'They clothed me and gave me money.' He sees all his predecessors from Belacqua to Malone in orbit around him and disowns them all as fabrications of a self that still remains inaccessible, because unnamable. Each protagonist acknowledges his fictional predecessors in order to demolish them, another example of Beckett's use of mutually destructive antitheses.

Beckett's gallery of moribunds extends beyond the *Trilogy* to *Textes pour rien* (1955), translated as *Texts for Nothing* and *Comment c'est* (1961), translated as *How It Is.* In both cases previous incarnations are evoked only to be dismissed as illusions seen from the perspective of the present. In *Texts for Nothing* the voice tries to free itself of its author by treating him 'like a vulgar Molloy, a common Malone, those mere mortals'. In *How It Is* Bom recalls an image from his past life in **'The End'** where he was growing a crocus in a basement area, only to dismiss this and other memories as 'rags of life in the light', too concrete to be of relevance to his present more realistic state of darkness and confusion. In both **'The Calmative'** and *Texts for Nothing* the voice recollects the story of Breen or Breem that his father told him as a child. With its happy ending it had acted on him as a calmative in his youth and he still hopes to repeat its soothing effect on him in the *Nouvelles.* But by *Texts for Nothing* he has learnt to see it as 'a comedy, for children' that he could never believe, partly because of its impossibly happy ending, partly because in his memory he had usurped his father's function, having told and listened to his own story, trapped in the solipsistic prison of his own head.

Beckett's *Texts for Nothing* cannot properly be labelled either shorter fiction or a novel. Other commentators have already pointed out that it is modelled on a musical form. Beckett himself calls the last section, XIII, a coda. Viewed in a wider context the whole work is a coda to the trilogy. The voice in *Texts for Nothing* is the same voice as in *The Unnamable.* But instead of the Unnamable's gradual breakdown in punctuation before a growing torrent of words, each of the Texts represents an 'evening's' worth of fiction. The voice now finds it harder to find subjects for self-narration and anticipates the far more frequent pauses for breath that subdivide *How It Is* into its numerous short phrases and paragraphs.

Texts for Nothing represent Beckett's penultimate attempt in fiction to explore his own existence in the first person in a world 'where to be is to be guilty'. Because life is for him a fiction, the writer shares his predicament with the rest of mankind. All the texts are almost wholly occupied with the writer and his creations. His principal creation in *Texts for Nothing* is the voice that is forced to assume responsibility for actions in the writer's past, but which the writer has foisted off on to an invented character because of the fictitious nature of his own memory. Just as Pim is to be tortured into speech by Bom, so the victimised voice (I) is given a pseudo-existence independent of its author (he): 'If at least he would dignify me with the third person, like his other figments, not he, he'll be satisfied with nothing less than me, for his me.' The protagonists from Belacqua to Watt were overtly paraded as fictions in the third person. From the *Nouvelles* through to *How It Is* Beckett deliberately exploits the use of the first person to demonstrate the more forcefully his complete inability to reach any satisfactory understanding of himself.

'It is impossible for me to talk about my writing,' he told John Gruen. 'It is impossible because I am constantly working in the dark. It would be like an insect leaving his cocoon'. Instead Beckett has enlarged the dimensions of his interior life to let us glimpse into the abyss, however obliquely. The difference between *The Unnamable* and *Texts for Nothing* is formal, not thematic. Both voices share a similar predicament, 'knowing none, known of none'. But the futility of their effort is shaped differently. If each quest for the self is doomed to failure then the shape of the fiction must be made to reflect the antithetical forces that constantly dispatch new search parties and as constantly thwart them from reaching their goal.

Beckett applies the principles of progression and circularity that were present as themes in his earlier work to the form of *Texts for Nothing.* There is an appearance of progression from text to text that frequently surfaces in the opening sentences. New questions are asked that offer the illusory possibility of a final solution ('Where would I go . . . ?' or 'How are the intervals filled . . . ?' or 'Did I try everything . . . ?'). Or the previous section is curtly dismissed ('Leave, I was going to say leave all that' or 'Give up'). Yet many of the texts prove circular by the conclusion, the final lines mockingly echoing the opening lines as in Text IX or XIII. Or the question asked in the opening sentence is negated by the answer in the final sentence as in Text IV.

Equally within each text Beckett elaborately constructs a whole series of grammatical equations whose answer is nought, as in Text XI which starts 'When I think no that won't work', or as at the end of Text XIII which imagines a time when it will be 'all said, it says, it murmurs'. Often these circular sentences are imbued with all the beauty of the transient world from which the author through his invented voice is seeking to escape:

> Ah, says I, punctually, if only I could say,
> There's a way out there, there's a way out some-
> where, then all would be said, it would be the
> first step on the long travelable road, destination
> tomb, to be trod without a word, tramp tramp,
> little irrevocable steps, down the long tunnels at
> first, then under the mortal skies, through days
> and nights, faster and faster, no, slower and
> slower, for obvious reasons, and at the same time

faster and faster, for other obvious reasons, or the same, obvious in a different way, or in the same way, but at a different moment of time, a moment earlier, a moment later, or at the same moment, there is no such thing, there would be no such thing, I recapitulate, impossible.

The illusion of progression in the first half of this sentence is quickly dispelled in the second half in a maze of self-negating phrases: faster . . . slower, different way . . . same way, earlier . . . later—they all reduce themselves to the same nothingness by the end. Progression in time becomes stasis (or unending progression) in a context of timelessness, which is why recapitulation is impossible. The voice is at the mercy of an author who 'protests he doesn't reason and does nothing but reason'. The structure of the thirteen texts is an elaborate demonstration of this flaw in man's search for a meaning to life.

This self-annihilating quest for certainty by a first-person narrator ends with *How It Is,* a novel whose tripartite form parallels this theme of apparent progression and actual circularity with immense skill. Bom's journey through space and time turns out to be both circular and infinitely repeatable, and the concluding pages ruthlessly demolish the whole fragile, illusionistic fable. Since 1961 Beckett has only written shorter fiction or what he calls 'capita mortua': *Imagination morte imaginez,* translated as *Imagination Dead Imagine, Assez,* translated as *Enough, Le Dépeupleur,* translated as *The Lost Ones, Bing,* translated as *Ping,* and *Sans,* translated as *Lessness* (in that order of composition, except for the final section of *Le Dépeupleur* which was written immediately prior to its first publication in 1970). Apart from *Enough,* the first person gives way to the third person in all of these pieces and the voice telling itself stories from its past life is now reduced to a murmur, the 'murmur of memory and dream' as the voice calls it in *Texts for Nothing.* John Fletcher was told by Beckett that *Enough* 'is out of place in the series'. Beckett added, 'I don't know what came over me' [*The Novels of Samuel Beckett,* 1970]. It must represent a throw-back to his previous phase of writing, not just because it uses the first person, but because, as I shall show, it concentrates on the delusive dream, where the other works strive (vainly) for an image of unpalatable reality.

It is as if Beckett as narrator has abandoned his earlier pretensions of discovering the self when he paraded his own involvement in his fiction with the first person singular. Instead he offers us a series of narrative ideograms in the familiar convention of the third person. In all of them man is close to unconsciousness, inanimate but for breathing and blinking in *Imagination Dead Imagine,* 'entering night' in *Enough,* 'languishing . . . imperceptibly' in *The Lost Ones,* 'a nature only just' in *Ping,* 'face to endlessness' in *Lessness.*

With the exception of *Enough,* these works are more closely interrelated than might be realised. *Imagination Dead Imagine* shares with *The Lost Ones* a similar fluctuation of heat and light, to the confusion of the bodies suffering between these extremes. *Bing,* as Beckett informed me, 'is a separate work written after and in reaction to *Le Dépeupleur* abandoned because of its complexity getting beyond

control'. If one examines the earlier drafts of *Bing* published in Federman and Fletcher's bibliography, the first text shows similar atmospheric variations, and the little body rests his hands on a ladder leaning against a niche in the wall, features identical to those in *The Lost Ones.* By the tenth and final draft of *Bing* light and heat have become static, ladder and niches have disappeared, and the body is left in its coffin-like box in silence and stasis. *Lessness* is written in direct reaction to *Ping*'s image of 'ruins true refuge'. Within the first paragraph the body is deprived of its latest shelter to confront the reality of infinitude: 'Blacked out fallen open four walls over backwards true refuge issueless.' *Lessness* is to date the last in a series that began with *Imagination Dead Imagine,* just as *How It Is* can be traced back to *More Pricks Than Kicks.* The later series constitutes the residual distillation of the earlier line of fiction. The little body that faces endlessness in *Lessness* confronts Beckett's first hero Belacqua with the predicament he sought to evade so resourcefully, but without success.

What Beckett calls 'the art and craft' in *Enough* assumes major importance in these last works. Both form and language are bent to his purposes in increasingly radical ways between *Imagination Dead Imagine* and *Lessness. Imagination Dead Imagine* begins with the predicament in which many of the heroes of the French novels found themselves: 'No trace anywhere of life, you say.' With immense confidence the unseen narrator dismisses their solipsistic defeatism with: 'pah, no difficulty there, imagination not dead.' Once again there is the expectation of making real progress, of winning so much ground from infinity. All that is needed, claims the narrator, is a more rigorous form of imagination, one that can construct its image of human existence in the head with the exactitude of a mathematician. Embryonic man and woman are plotted geometrically, their dimensions are measured, phenomena are timed to the second, variations in temperature are calculated and scientific tests executed. To buttress further the solidity of his image Beckett borrows the language of science and technology: diameters, right angles, semicircles, numbers and letters proliferate.

And yet from the start another language, that of the supposedly dead subjective imagination, disconcertingly intrudes amidst the pseudo-scientific jargon. So between the rise and fall of light and heat there may intervene 'pauses of varying length, from the fraction of a second to what would have seemed, in other times, other places, an eternity'. Measured time falters before experienced time. The certainties of mathematics are used to construct the impossible, a 'world still proof against enduring tumult'. The yearning poetic language betrays the hopelessly subjective bias underlying the sham knowledge. As doubt grows, Beckett places his use of scientific method and terminology in ever more absurd contexts: 'Neither fat nor thin, big nor small, the bodies seem whole and in fairly good condition, to judge by the surfaces exposed to view'. What starts out as an objective statement ends up as self-parody.

The theory of relativity is not so new to philosophy as to science. All perception is relative to the perceiver. It is this form of relativity which begins to interfere with the image of the rotunda as time passes. The fluctuations in light and heat (those manifestations of eternity and infinity) begin to affect the perceiver. Inspection is no longer easy as memory begins to distort his reactions. The contrast between stasis and movement becomes 'striking, in the beginning, for one who still remembers having been struck by the contrary'. Habit, our 'guarantee of a dull inviolability', erases the past. Finally the image of suffering humanity proves too much for the observer. The rotunda and its occupants that at first seemed so solid vanish in the last sentence in language of haunting but transient beauty. Poetry has replaced logic and doubt has dispelled scientific certainty. The perceiver has vetoed his perception of reality and fallen victim to his own shortcomings. The promise of progress so confidently predicted in the opening lines has proved circular once again. Like its title it returns to its beginnings.

Illusion proves too attractive to be resisted not just in *Imagination Dead Imagine* but in *The Lost Ones* and *Enough.* Even the end of *Ping* is no end seen from the perspective of *Lessness.* Rather than face the intolerable reality of his condition man prefers to go on believing in the possibility of a way out in *The Lost Ones* or deliberately falsifies and idealises his past life in *Enough.* In *The Lost Ones* an impersonal narrator, like Gulliver, observes Lilliputian man closing his eyes to the inferno which he inhabits. In *Enough* the last of the many 'I's' eliminates his remaining memories of unpleasantness in order to imagine himself in a paradise of flowers. Dante continues to hold Beckett's imagination. If the *Purgatorio* is Belacqua's natural habitat, *The Lost Ones* owes more to the *Inferno* and *Enough* to the *Paradiso.*

Dante is the only proper name to figure in *The Lost Ones.* But even without his appearance in person the connotations are unmistakable: 'What first impresses in this gloom is the sensation of yellow it imparts not to say of sulphur in view of the associations.' The black humour suggests that man's life on earth is hell, a fact he would recognise if only he could be granted the omniscient viewpoint of the narrator. But he is himself suspect with his eternal 'ifs' and 'would be's'. If where we are is hell, then the narrator is no exception and can only achieve his Mephistophelian clarity of vision by postulating a probability ('if this notion is maintained' he keeps saying) that remains outside the scope of proof. As *Ping* shows, man is liable to lapse into the illusion that the search may reach an end. Even *The Lost Ones* has an apocalyptic vision of, not the end, but 'the unthinkable end'.

Rather than face the pointlessness of their search, Beckett's little population of bodies prefers to construct rules governing the conduct of their search so labyrinthine that no one is able to foresee the complete inaccessibility of their goal. Not even the vanquished searchers manage to discover 'the all of nothing'. The passion to search has simply died in them—or rather, almost died, as they are still liable to recommence their search in accordance with the laws of relativity governing this microcosmic world. As in *Imagination Dead Imagine* and the earlier drafts of *Bing,* conditions are such that no certainty is possible. The regular variations in light and heat are subject to random

interruptions when 'the questing eyes . . . fix their stare on the void' to their intense discomfort. Far better to search than suffer such agony, even if the search leads to growing blindness and defeat. Man prefers to fill the void of existence with an assumed purposiveness which he pursues with rationally devised codes for his better deception.

Life on earth, divided as it is into days and nights, summers and winters, birth and death, marvellously disguises from man its real timelessness. Far from enlightening him, the repetition of days, weeks, months and years only serves to blind him with the illusion of finitude and an end to his suffering existence. Even the rules he constructs for himself are skilfully devised to give the monotony of a meaningless existence a semblance of variety and purpose. As the voice in *Texts for Nothing* exclaims in sardonic wonder: 'What agitation and at the same time what calm, what vicissitudes within what changelessness.' It is the same malignant 'harmony that reigns in the cylinder between order and licence'. Man can only look for an escape to 'the unthinkable end' of Section XV. Like 'the unthinkable past' the end is a chimera of the rational mind of the narrator. The reality is the unending search for an end. In giving *The Lost Ones* an ostensibly fictitious end, Beckett is mocking those Aristotelian norms of art (and life, itself a fiction), the beginning, the middle and the end. It is all middle. Any termination is unthinkable.

Enough is closer to *The Lost Ones* than might appear at first. Beckett is again concentrating on man's unwillingness to face the horror of his meaningless existence. But the viewpoint is different; in place of an omniscient narrator conducting a pseudo-socio-historical survey we enter the mind of a first-person narrator. Like his predecessors in the novels he is an artist seeking a 'way out'. His solution is to tell himself more and more congenial stories about his past life. He revels in his memory's natural deficiencies and seeks to escape from himself into a world of dream and fantasy. The narrator has already parted company with his earlier, older self (in the sense that the child is father to the man). His youthful self had some remaining links with the world around him: 'Of the wind that was no more. Of the storms he had ridden out'. But even these vestigial reminders of life's unpleasantness are excluded from the self's latest fiction, a pastoral world in which 'the very flowers were stemless', 'as if the earth had come to rest in spring'.

To convert a hell of suffering into a dream of heaven, the self has been driven to extremes of inventiveness, finally erasing everything from his memory but the flowers through which he had dragged with his youthful counterpart. Expelled from paradise into the hell of life on earth, he seeks to reverse his fate and return to an Eden of his own creation. *Enough* begins and ends with an ostentatious display of the 'art and craft' used by the narrator to reconstruct his past life in a fiction that fulfils his fondest wishes. Even the earlier self suffered from the natural distortions of perception (he only viewed the sky in a mirror); the present self adds to these the distortions of memory. The fiction he invents is based on falsity. His idyll has all the beauty and transience of a mirage, but the 'stony ground' of the desert of existence can only be denied for the duration of the story he tells himself.

The language in *Enough* is reminiscent of those poetic passages in *Imagination Dead Imagine* in which the old illusory imagination of 'islands, waters, azure, verdure' reasserts itself. Beckett consciously summons language of haunting beauty to convey his narrator's wish-fulfilment: 'Night. As long as day in this endless equinox. It falls and we go on. Before dawn we are gone.' In all his mature work lyricism of this kind is invariably associated with self-deception, with what 'Bom' calls 'last little scenes' of 'life in the light'. The problem for a writer like Beckett, who is constantly trying to penetrate deceptive appearances so as to see into the heart of things, is that language itself is subjective and reflects the deceptions practised by its users. Like Mrs Rooney, we are all struggling with a dead language. Beckett's reaction, as he told John Gruen in 1970, has been to turn 'toward an abstract language', one which approximates to the purity of mathematics. As Watt discovered, even logic and arithmetic are incapable of defining nothingness, but they can better indicate its inescapability than the emotionally charged language of the very early works like 'Text' or 'Sedendo et Quiescendo': 'I won't kiss your playful hand, dass heisst spielen, my dolorific nymphae and a tic douleureux in my imperforate hymen, what's the Deutsch for randy, my dirty little hungry bony vulture of a whorehen. . . .'

Both *Ping* and *Lessness* make frontal attacks on what might be termed the Joycean linguistic tradition. In both works 'sentences' embrace a series of linked images. Syntax is minimal, all the verbs being reduced to participles in *Ping,* all the definite and indefinite articles being omitted in both works except for the incursions of past memories and dreams. *Ping* presents the image of a body on the point of reaching unconsciousness by a process of becoming all-conscious. Total knowledge and whiteness are identified with each other, and reality is represented as 'Bare white body fixed white on white invisible'. However, vestigial traces of the old life of imperfect knowledge and perception (which intrude with a 'Ping') still prevent the body from becoming merged with the 'white infinite'. These traces bear the linguistic hallmarks of the old dead language of illusion. 'Only the eyes only just light blue' or 'Ping of old only just perhaps a meaning a nature' contain those give-away definite and indefinite articles that remind the reader of what *Lessness* calls 'the days and nights made of dreams of other nights better days'.

The language of endlessness must be devoid of colour, sound, emotion, and meaning itself. *Ping* claimed to attain this desired end by a process of knowing all. *Lessness* rejects this solution as another fiction. All is unknowable. Infinity cannot be grasped by a finite process. But it can be indicated allusively. In *Lessness* the body is removed from its protective white box of knowledge to confront the endlessness of true existence. But simultaneously it is made to perform the impossible: 'One step in the ruins in the sand on his back in the endlessness he will make it'. Beckett repeatedly uses paradox to reflect the paradoxical nature of man's predicament. Faced with endlessness, how ridiculous to make one step more. But we all do it. In at-

tempting to know all, the body in *Ping* was doing just that. But the white walls screened off the changelessness all around. Outside the white chamber, as Clov reported, all is 'light black', like the 'grey air' of *Lessness.* Night and day, black and white, are perceptual illusions from the vantage point of eternity. Speed up the camera of man's eye and universal greyness covers all: 'Never but this changelessness dream the passing hour.'

In *Lessness* Beckett has devised a form that perfectly reflects the relativity of man's perspective. Order and disorder, symmetry and chaos are reflected in the construction of its 120 sentences. Man's obsessive need for order is given formal expression in the fact that each sentence in the first half is repeated in the last half, and that, as Martin Esslin was told by Beckett, the sixty sentences belong to six groups of images, ten sentences in each. (The Calder & Boyars cover lists these as ruin, exposure, wilderness, mindlessness, and past and future (1) denied and (2) affirmed.) But the random order of endlessness is suggested by the random reappearance of each sentence in the second half, the random sequence of the six images, and the random length of the paragraphs. Unlike *Ping*'s false sense of an ending, *Lessness* could continue to oscillate between these poles to infinity.

Beckett has travelled a great distance from the verbal exuberance of his early short fiction. Linguistic acrobatics have given way to the conscious dislocation of language. The puns and scholarly wit of *More Pricks Than Kicks* have no place in his latest work, where a sparse vocabulary is ranged against itself in a series of mutually annihilating paradoxes. Thwarted by the relativity of perception, Beckett has concentrated, increasingly as time has passed, on inventing literary forms that can overcome the subjective limitations of traditional fiction, obsessed as it is with 'figments' like love, beauty, time and memory. In the last phase of his writing he has sought literary structures that admit the chaos of man's meaningless existence while not excluding man's hopeless search for an order and a meaning to life. The result has been a series of prose texts whose difficulty is matched by their originality. The little population of lost ones, the pastoral idyll of *Enough,* and the body face to endlessness join their predecessors in a gallery of unique and compelling images that reflect Beckett's lifelong search for that impossible shape that will capture in its own destruction life's ultimate shapelessness.

J. E. Dearlove   (essay date 1977)

SOURCE: " 'Last Images': Samuel Beckett's Residual Fiction," in *Journal of Modern Literature,* Vol. 6, No. 1, February 1977, pp. 104-26.

[*In the following essay, Dearlove explicates* Imagination Dead Imagine, *"Ping," and* Lessness.]

Although upon first acquaintance Samuel Beckett's recent fictions might strike the reader as utterly alien and incomprehensible residues, the pieces are in fact logical extensions of the essential Beckettian literary experience. The artist and his need to create confront the fact that there is nothing to create, nothing with which nor from which to create, no power and no desire to create. The world of

Beckett's fiction remains a world without certainty, absolutes, or reliable material reality. In such a world the problem for the artist remains how to create a work of art without belying either the artwork or the chaos; how to avoid mere substitution of one artificial structure for another; how to reconcile a form that is negating itself with a content that is dissolving into non-meanings and almost-epiphanies. In his early fictions Beckett seeks to solve these problems by parodying and satirizing the traditional forms he adopts. Uncomfortable with conventions because they are based on assumptions he rejects, Beckett has these conventions break down into self-conscious, unwieldly, and illogical constructions. Unable to reconcile form and content, Beckett mocks and destroys the very forms he employs. In his middle works Beckett seeks to corroborate the chaos with the "narrator/narrated." The narrator's words and silences become the only reality. Existence and continuation are inseparable from the present act of speaking. The only possible conclusion lies not in death or in sleep, but in the cessation of the voice. It is this voice and its words which constitute our experience of how it is. In his latest pieces however, Beckett rejects both the narrating "self" and the fluid forms. In their place he creates a rigid structure that mathematically and scientifically describes fantastic objects, people, and images. No longer content to suggest the chaos through "imitative form," Beckett develops deceptively objective analyses of highly articulated forms. Paradoxically, the very artifice of these carefully constructed forms points toward their real formal meaninglessness, while the arbitrariness beneath their order gestures toward a more fundamental absence of order. The pieces are images of the abyss, structures enclosing the void. Although Beckett's works have always demanded the reader be engaged in the interrelationship of form and content, in the latest pieces the burden of interpretation is placed increasingly upon the reader. It is he and not the artist who attributes meaning to the inexplicable; he and not the artist who manipulates form in order to understand content.

If an art is honestly to accommodate an impersonal, orderless, meaningless "mess," then that art must increasingly eliminate even the implicitly personal, ordered, and meaningful. If the narrator of the middle period does not actually invite our identification, nonetheless he does postulate a "self," a being separate from the chaos, a "figure" imposing order on Neary's "ground." The speaker returns to the works the connotations, associations, and correspondences which had been stripped from plot and character. The impersonal is thus made personal and the orderless, ordered. The latest pieces, on the other hand, strive for a more objective pose. The self begins to dissolve into the impersonal, "omniscient" voices of *Imagination Dead Imagine, Ping,* and *Lessness.* The pieces analytically deal with the admittedly imaginative. Despite their starkness, the images of Beckett's previous fictions are still connected to a conventional world. Although the tins and openers of *How It Is* may be only verbal postulates, nevertheless they correspond to real, material objects. Conversely, the most recent images are fantastical; the white figures and cylindrical worlds are imaginative constructions. While the nature of language prevents Beckett from totally escaping an external structure, the fantasies free him from pre-established implications and innuendoes. Like the second zone of Murphy's mind, the images are of forms without parallel in another mode. Though art cannot attain the formlessness of the dark zone, it can at least avoid the mimetic parallels of the light. The resulting works of the half-light compose a new type of intellectual novel. The burden of meaning is thrust upon the reader. *Lessness* presents a random collection of words, images, and sentences which the reader must organize. It is the reader who must order Beckett's structures in order to glimpse the ineffable lying beyond art.

The objective pose evokes a simple, declarative prose. Instead of the scintillating and amazingly long sentences of the early works, we are given brief and elliptical ones. Instead of the fluid phrasing of the middle period in which one idea imperceptibly flows into the next, we are presented with choppy, almost unrelated sentences. The absence of transitions emphasizes the fragmentary nature of the world described. The words themselves are precise, unencumbered by unintentional connotations. The prose admits no more than its surface statements allow. Fluidity pointing to chaos is replaced by rigidity enclosing a void. The pieces are exceptionally brief in order to limit their worlds. The fantasy must not become too real or too familiar lest a new "reality" and order be substituted for the old, lest the structures which are meant to point beyond themselves are mistaken for the whole. A new attitude toward art is suggested. Obscurity and confusion come not from omission as in the middle period, nor from excessive addition as in the early period, but from the inability of the mind to retain an objective image, "no question now of ever finding again that white speck lost in whiteness" (*Imagination Dead Imagine*). Protestations of impotence or mastery disappear as the persona analytically states, as best he can, what he can. It is for the reader to notice the absences those observations entail. Cumulative "symbols" and mantic meanings are replaced by an ordering device similar to that in music. Repetition and refrain supplant conventional manners of meaning. Words, like notes, are arranged mathematically and affects us subliminally. Moreover, like notes, not chords, each word strives to strike only one meaning, strives to be "pure" not connotative, scientific not emotional. But the words, and the images, break down. Without reneging on his own postulations and rules, Beckett's latest pieces accomplish what the earlier pieces unsuccessfully attempted: they offer a form that is self-disintegrating. The printed texts provide the scenario for the reader's efforts to create meaning. Ultimately, however, the reader is forced to return to the text, to the residual structure which provocatively refuses to mean. The pieces are, as Beckett titled them, Residua.

The self-destruction of the analytic prose of *Imagination Dead Imagine* (*Imagination Morte Imaginez,* 1966) offers a glimpse into the realms beyond analysis, beyond the residue. As the title implies, the piece is based on a paradox: imagination is necessary to envision a state in which imagination is dead. The essential situation is thus briefly and simply described, yet that situation is itself paradoxical if not impossible, ambivalent if not unclear. The imperative mood in both title and work demands involvement, but we do not know from whom. The second person remains unspecified and could refer equally well to us, to the persona, or to some unidentified other, "No trace anywhere of life, you say, pah, no difficulty there, imagination not dead yet, yes, dead, good, imagination dead imagine." Unlike the assuring interventions of the eighteenth century which carefully lead us from one scene to the next while explaining how each came about, the persona's injunctions, "go in," "Go back out," add to our confusion. Who is to go? Go in where? How? Go back out to what? Explanatory transitions are deliberately omitted. The rotunda is treated simultaneously as an object to be entered and as a mental fabric woven from imagination. Perception of the piece as an imaginary fabric undercuts the need for scientific precision. When all is fantasy, the narrating "self," like the verifying witness, is irrelevant. Instead of a speaker with whom we might identify, we have a voice moving through his descriptions like a camera, zooming in for a close up of the unblinking eye, panning the rotunda's floor, dropping back for a panoramic shot of the "plain rotunda, all white in the whiteness." Issues of identity are supplanted by the impersonal and objective. Indeed the piece evokes diagrams and tabulations.

But the scientific, objective pose increasingly breaks down. Like the elaborate time structure in *Murphy,* the mathematical precision of **Imagination Dead Imagine** is only an overlay. As we read we realize that the rational numbers are only crude estimates made under adverse conditions:

> Wait *more or less* long. . . . *More or less long,* for there may intervene . . . pauses of *varying* length. . . . the sighting of the little fabric quite as much a *matter of chance.* . . . left eyes which at *incalculable intervals.* . . . *In this agitated light,* its great white calm now so rare and brief, *inspection is not easy* [here and elsewhere all italics in passages from **Imagination Dead Imagine** are mine].

Metaphoric terms and colored words seep into the analytic language:

> . . . solid throughout, a ring *as in the imagination* the ring of bone. *Piercing pale blue the effect is striking.*

The voice's objectivity merges with subjectivity as fact and observation yield to assumption and opinion:

> . . . the bodies *seem* whole and in fairly good condition, *to judge by the surfaces exposed to view.* The two faces too, *assuming* the two sides of a piece, *seem* to want nothing essential.

Apparent contradictions are not explained, "No way in, go in . . ." Although the rotunda's dimensions make it too small to hold three bodies, and although the whole is described as solid, we "go in" to view the two figures lying on the floor. Indeed, much of our information about the rotunda is based on our experience of it. The experience itself is made problematic by man's tendency to adapt to all situations. Habituation deadens our powers of observation, turning "such variations of rise and fall" into "countless rhythms." Things which initially strike us as strange may soon pass unnoticed. Even language seems to be vitiated by experience. Notice, for example, how the following sentence runs down and trails off into prepositional phrases and the passive voice after its initial, direct observation:

> Between their absolute stillness and the convulsive light the contrast is striking, in the beginning, for one who still remembers having been struck by the contrary.

Experience, moreover, makes everything, even eternity, relative. Our analytic prose is itself coming apart. The failure of the diagrammatic and precise intimates the underlying, nebulous flux. Not the image but its dissolution, not the object but its breakdown, contains whatever "meaning" there is.

Just as we may become too habituated to the rotunda to be struck by the contrary, so too we are in danger of becoming too accustomed to Beckett's images. The pieces can only briefly gesture to an instant of dissolution before the concrete structures of language erect new systems of order. To postpone the influx of meaning, the voice uses negative propositions to describe the rotunda. We learn not what it is, but what it is not: "Islands, waters, azure, verdure, one glimpse and vanished, endlessly, omit. Till all white in the whiteness of the rotunda," not what we can say happens, but what we cannot say happens:

> Leave them there, sweating and icy, there is better elsewhere. No, life ends and no, there is nothing elsewhere, and no question now of ever finding again that white speck lost in whiteness, to see if they still lie still in the stress of that storm, or of a worse storm, or in the black dark for good, or the great whiteness unchanging, and if not what they are doing.

Similarly, the voice suggests meanings without directly postulating them. The fetal positions of the figures imply, but never assert, a womb-like structure. While the rotunda may have when rapped a tomb-like ring, "as in the imagination the ring of bone," the figures' misting of a mirror belies any sepulchral readings. Although the presence of both a male and a female figure does suggest an androgynous nature for the rotunda, although those figures do assume, as H. Porter Abbott has noted [in *The Fiction of Samuel Beckett: Form and Effect*], a reversed yin and yang position, nonetheless the figures remain distinct and reversed. They have not yet become the sketchy, sexless, and single figure in **Ping.** The variations of life are reduced to rhythmic repetition. Not only are there fewer sets to be permuted than in previous works, but those sets are reduced from powers of action (Murphy's biscuits) and methods of arrangement (Molloy's sucking stones) to mere presence or absence of heat and light. Beckett's image of life is coming closer to the cyclic rhythm of respiration dramatized in *Breath* (1966). Imagination is gone, but traces of life remain in unblinking eyes, slightly sweating bodies, and a misted mirror. Language too strives to be minimal. Although no one word is rejected as too strong, the whole is told from a discredited viewpoint, "Rediscovered *miraculously* after what absence in perfect voids it [the rotunda] is *no longer quite the same, from this point of view, but there is no other.*" Concrete meanings are avoided as sentences are made fragmentary and disjointed:

> Only murmur ah, no more, in this silence, and

at the same instant for the eye of the prey the infinitesimal shudder instantaneously suppressed.

The resulting ambiguous syntax admits diverse interpretations. For Brian Finney the "ah" of the above passage is murmured, almost experimentally, by the reader to break the silence the couple seeks [*Since* How It Is: *A Study of Samuel Beckett's Later Fiction,* 1972], while for Ruby Cohn the "ah" is a sign of life performed by the figures and noted by whomever the "eye of prey" represents [*But to Beckett,* 1973]. The burden of interpretation rests on the reader because a deceptively analytic prose refuses to mean, because a highly articulated from is made to imply a more fundamental formlessness.

Ping (*Bing,* 1966) continues Beckett's rigid reductions. The recondite, allusive, and foreign language of Beckett's earliest pieces is replaced by a few simple and common words repeated and rearranged. Complex, interrelated sentences and self-conscious structures yield to simple and even fragmentary phrases dealing with imaginary worlds. The "narrator/narrated" disappears as an impersonal voice dispassionately pronounces phrases. Not only "I" but also "he" and "she" are gone. Even the personal observations, opinions, assumptions, and occasional poetic phrases of *Imagination Dead Imagine* have been eliminated. The depersonalized, computer-like voice of *Ping* focuses attention on its words, not on itself. Moreover, the words are themselves less emphatic, less concrete. The image can no longer be objectively analyzed and measured. The diagrammatic language of *Imagination Dead Imagine* is restricted to a box, "white one yard by two" containing a fixed and featureless figure. Instead of entering a cylinder almost at will and observing its inhabitants, we are confined to a box in which everything keeps fading and disappearing in the shining "white on white invisible." But in spite of its reductions in language, character, plot, and narrator *Ping* remains a surprisingly dramatic piece. *Ping* is the drama of the interaction between reader and form.

Though apparently simpler than preceding works, *Ping* is one of Beckett's more difficult works to read. The common words, arranged and rearranged into recurring phrases, compel the reader to become what Ruby Cohn has described as a "fellow-writer, rearranging the words on paper in order to see the significance of repetition, permutation, combination, or singularity." In this verbless work it is the reader who performs the action. *Ping* invites tabulations and computation. In her own efforts to "see the significance" Professor Cohn reveals that the English text contains 1,030 words—of which 120 are permuted—gathered into seventy sentences, punctuated only by periods, and printed as an unbroken block on the page. In this unbroken block "white" appears some ninety times while "ping" occurs thirty-four times—nine times followed by "elsewhere," seven times by "murmur(s)," four times by "silence," twice by "a nature," twice by "not alone," once by "image," once by "a meaning." The simple words describe a simple, minimal world of "only just almost never." No longer does Beckett need to call any word too strong, for he has created phrases that take away more than they give. When we read "that much memory almost never" our dominant impression is of memory's absence,

not of its feeble persistence. In a similar fashion the negation of "over"—"white colour alone unover"—emphasizes not continuation, but termination. Being over becomes the positive state, and definition is through negative proposition, through reference to what no longer exists. *Ping* deals not with what is enough, but with ephemeral and fading velleities. Measurements are replaced by qualifying phrases and fleeting moments: "perhaps a nature," "brief murmurs," "one second." Like the image of "blue and white in the wind," like the figure, indeed like the box itself, all of which disappear into whiteness almost before they have been glimpsed, *Ping* fades and dissolves almost before we can read it. The reader is left with a form that gestures toward formlessness and with phrases that suggest but never mean.

The verbless, unbroken block of words that constitute *Ping* is given movement and shape by the intermittent and enigmatic "ping"s which begin and interrupt sentences. The word "ping" itself is meaningless: it is a nonsense word, a short, quick ringing sound like that of a rifle bullet, a sound so instantaneous as to be almost as if it never were. Indeed, Beckett's revisions show a movement toward briefer, more ephemeral sounds from "paf" to "hop" to "bing." In the English text Beckett alters even the voiced "b" of "bing" to the voiceless, and hence even slighter, "p" of "ping." The sound, like the light in *Play,* seems to control the flow of words, to mark the movement of thoughts. It indicates the points where the mind skips or changes focus: Beckett has magnified the stream of consciousness until he can actually show the infinitesimally brief moments in which the mind, as it were, blinks. However, the precise nature of the "ping" remains ambivalent. We never know, for instance, whether an external interruption or an internal hesitation causes the jumps. Although they may alter our focus slightly, the "ping"s never take us outside the box. The most we know is that the figure is within a box and that there is a soundless but unknowable elsewhere. Like stage directions or time signatures, the "ping"s control the meter and rhythm of the piece, separating the phrases into longer and shorter groups. Whereas many of Beckett's other works emphasize time as unending cycle or an eternal present of waiting, *Ping* reduces time to the fleeting "one second perhaps" and to memories so dissipated and remote as to be almost nonexistent. The passage of time itself is dramatized as the increasing frequency of the "ping"s parallels the increasing fragmentation at the end of the piece.

While "ping" remains an individual and distinct sound, most words in the piece are grouped in phrases. We read in blocks of words: adjective plus noun, adverb plus verb form, "Light heat / white floor / one square yard / never seen" (my divisions). Unlike the early works in which the word was the unit of meaning, meaning in *Ping* resides in the phrase and its permutations, in variations within repetitions. If the words may be likened to notes and the phrases to chords, then the phrases themselves are grouped into themes. Descriptions of the body are counterpointed by those of the box. Occasionally a new motif may appear such as the scarred and torn flesh, but for the most part the piece recombines elements elaborating its initial chords, "All known all white." Even other colors are accompanied by the pervasive whiteness—"light grey almost white." In such a work meaning becomes rhythmical, cumulative, associational.

The movement and drama of the piece comes from the reader's involvement with the musical motifs of the permuted phrases. Gradually descriptions of setting and figure make the initial propositions intelligible. Everything is known; everything is white. Within that known white everything of a one yard by two, rectangular white box of some light and heat is fixed a bare, elemental body, itself unable to perceive the box, mistaking shining white walls for a shining white infinite, "Planes meeting invisible one only shining white infinite but that known not." We have lost not only the dual figures of *Imagination Dead Imagine,* but also the precision with which they were described. Our new figure is shapeless and sexless. Like a ragdoll its legs, toes, and seam-like mouth appear "joined like sewn." Slowly the figure becomes, if not more lifelike, at least more distinct. Repeated occurrence draws the basic outline of a "bare white body fixed" with "hands hanging," "palms front," "head haught," "white feet," "heels together right angle." A single mention sketches in other details, "mouth white," "heart breath," "nose ears," "nails fallen white," "long hair fallen white." No longer is life revealed in a slightly sweating body or a misted mirror. Indeed, even "heart breath" seems to be negated by its following phrase, "no sound." If not already over, the circulatory and respiratory systems are so reduced as to be imperceptible and soundless. The body's life signs are restricted to barely tinged flesh, "given rose only just," and fading eyes, "Eyes alone unover given blue light blue almost white." These pale blue eyes in fact provide the major contrast to the overwhelming whiteness. They are the only objects not yet over:

> Bare white body fixed only the eyes only just.
>
> Only the eyes only just light blue almost white.
>
> Eyes alone unover given blue light blue almost white.
>
> Only the eyes only just light blue almost white fixed front.
>
> Eyes holes light blue alone unover given blue light blue almost white only colour fixed front.
>
> Only the eyes given blue light blue almost white fixed front only colour alone unover.
>
> Only the eyes given blue fixed front light blue almost white only colour alone unover.

Notice in the above examples how a slight alteration in the order of the phrases, along with the introduction of phrases previously associated with another part of the text (that is, the movement from the "bare white body fixed" to the eyes "fixed front"), slowly increase our understanding and enable the voice to present longer, more complicated sentences. The incremental effect allows the voice to present its fullest, most sustained depiction of the figure:

> Bare white one yard fixed ping fixed elsewhere no sound legs joined like sewn heels together right angle hands hanging palms front. Head

haught eye holes light blue almost white fixed front silence within.

Ironically, it is after this summary in which the figure is most clearly described that the whiteness begins to take over completely. The expanded portrait is abruptly pulled apart and contracted, while the blue of the eyes is suddenly removed from the familiar phrases:

> . . . eye holes light blue almost white last colour ping white over. Ping fixed last elsewhere legs joined like sewn heels together right angle hands hanging palms front head haught eyes white invisible fixed front over.

The work, beginning in stark whiteness, gradually teases life and variety into its world only to deny those possibilities and thus heighten its barrenness.

The movement toward sterility is reflected in the treatment of image and sound. The "ping"s guide us through a world whose silence is broken neither by sounds from within the box ("silence within") nor by external noises ("elsewhere no sound"). Yet, just as a fading blue somehow persists in a world of whiteness, so too brief and almost imperceptible murmurs exist in a world of stillness: "Brief murmur only just almost never all known." More minimal than even the "ah" of *Imagination Dead Imagine,* the murmurs are too indistinct to be quoted directly, too fleeting to be recorded—"murmur only just almost never one second perhaps." The low, infrequent murmurs, like the rapid, glancing "ping"s, underscore rather than interrupt the overwhelming silence. Like setting and figure, the murmurs are "always the same all known." Yet it is precisely these murmurs, the least tangible elements in an already ephemeral world, that offer the most vibrant passages in *Ping.* They both relieve and emphasize the starkness by suggesting and recalling what no longer is present. In a world that increasingly approaches absolute zero, vitality persists in the murmurs and their postulations of what is not. Imagination is not yet dead; life still adheres to our reduced figure; "perhaps [there is] a way out," "perhaps a nature," "perhaps a meaning," "perhaps [the figure is] not alone." Although the figure does not experience escape, externality, order, or even an "other," he never discounts them. Indeed his murmured memories imply that a meaning, a more colorful nature, and even another figure were once available to him. Just enough memory remains to recall dimly a different order; just enough is left from that "afar flash of time" to highlight the present stillness: "Ping murmur only just almost never one second perhaps a meaning that much memory almost never." The images that can be recalled are drastically reduced from those scenes that lightened Pim's world. The "fine image fine I mean in movement and colour blue and white of clouds in the wind" (*How It Is*) becomes the sporadic and shrinking, "Ping perhaps a nature one second with image same time a little less blue and white in the wind." Moreover, with each recurrence the image dwindles as rearrangement of the phrases shifts emphasis from the image itself ("blue and white in the wind") to its unchanging character ("with image always the same time a little less"), to its transitory nature ("Ping image only just almost never one second light time blue and white in the wind"). Indeed, by the last mention of the image the blue and white have disappeared altogether: "Ping perhaps not alone one second with image same time a little less dim eye black and white half closed long lashes imploring that much memory almost never."

Significantly, the image "blue and white in the wind" disappears when the provocative black and white eye is first clearly discerned. This second eye is thus implicitly linked to the images, memories, and murmurs. It is part of the imaginary world with which the figure decorated his encompassing white box. Yet the description of the eye remains apart from the other murmurings. Although its appearance is anticipated by two sentences postulating "black" ("Traces alone unover given black light grey almost white on white"), this eye does not really evolve from permuted phrases. Similarly, though dim, unlustrous, and half-closed, this black and white eye does not really belong in a world of fading pastels and overwhelming whiteness. While our figure is at best roughly outlined, the black and white eye is presented in fine detail. Instead of reducing the eye to "eye holes light blue almost white fixed front," we are given a close-up of the eye "half closed long lashes imploring." "Imploring" stands out from the impersonal, unemotional prose in which *Ping* is written. Like the eyes which haunt Krapp (*Krapp's Last Tape*) and Croak (*Words and Music*), the imploring eye suggests other worlds of emotion, character, and plot. Suddenly the figure's rather wistful murmur "perhaps not alone" becomes desperately significant. Was he alone in that past he can hardly remember? Is he alone now? Are those "grey blurs" and "traces alone unover" the shadowy and fading outlines of another figure? The questions go unanswered. While our figure feels there might be a meaning, *Ping* refuses to dictate one. Murmurs, memories, and blurring traces alike offer "signs [with] no meaning." It is the reader, cursed as in *Enough* by "the art of combining," who attempts to order the phrases and trace a meaning.

Although the reader may try to find a meaning, may try to read "White scars invisible same white as flesh torn of old given rose only just" as a symbol for suffering and sacrificed mankind, *Ping* is too slight and elusive to bear even an emblematic meaning. Like the "ping"s and the murmurs which disappear into silence almost before they have been heard, like the image and the box which fade into whiteness almost before they have been glimpsed, *Ping* dissolves into formlessness almost before it has been read. The reader's manipulation of Beckett's phrases yields not a discourse about that fleeting instant when absolute zero is finally achieved, but a dramatization of that moment. Minimal life of "only just almost never" is used to gesture toward the void of "henceforth never" lying just beyond life and art. Not only must we slowly and painstakingly come to an understanding of the little we have been given, but, more devastatingly, we are forced to see the rapid dissolution of even that little. We are thrust into the end by the abbreviation of phrases and body, by the fragmentation of time, by the increase in white. *Ping* is the drama not of the "fixed elsewhere," nor even of the "white infinite," but of the "one second perhaps": it is a drama of the end in which everything is presented to heighten our perception of that end. *Ping* becomes a catalogue of what is

finally over. Consistent with Beckett's other works, the last element in this catalogue to be alone unover is not the "heart breath" nor even the blue eyes, but the murmur. Just as in *How It Is,* where the important vision comes not from the blue eyes but the others at the back of the head, so too here life is associated with the murmured, with the imagined, with the "never seen," "invisible," "no trace." Moreover, it is not simply a murmur, but the murmur of perhaps another that is the last thought to evaporate before all is over:

> Head haught eyes white fixed front old ping last murmur one second perhaps not alone eye unlustrous black and white half closed long lashes imploring ping silence ping over.

When even the murmur has ended and the last "ping" faded away, the piece is over. Like the box which keeps disappearing into the "shining white infinite but that known not," *Ping* creates an image of that which is imageless.

By thrusting on us the burden of creating order and meaning, the Residua demand a new critical response. Not only are conventional analyses inadequate to explain the pieces, but even traditional literary terms seem inappropriate. Instead of comparing the works to novels and short stories, we are forced to find parallels in music and drama, or, as H. Porter Abbott does, in a new species of poetry. Beckett is dealing not simply in words and sounds, but in words and sounds whose real impact is subliminal or preconscious. He is striving to create, through the medium and limitations of language, an art that can use those limitations to suggest that which lies beyond language. Whereas *music, drama,* and *poetry* all suggest an art that is ordered and coherent, an art that yields an encompassing and unified vision, the Residua increasingly insist upon being taken apart and analyzed. In order to come to terms with the pieces, we must read them not as a whole, nor even as paragraphs or sentences, but rather as permuted phrases and repeated words. They deal not with order, but with the arbitrariness of order; not with fiction, but with assumptions masked by fiction. *Lessness* (*Sans,* 1969) takes the anti-literary tendency of the Residua even farther. In order to read the work at all the reader must reverse Beckett's creative process and break the piece back down into groups of sentences and into permuted phrases within those groups. No longer content with satirizing, negating, or dissipating his own forms, Beckett creates a work that insists upon being unmade.

Beckett's method of composition in *Lessness* is, at best, disconcerting. He wrote sixty sentences, each belonging to one of six groups, each group consisting of ten sentences. Next he randomly drew the individual sentences from a container to yield the order of the first half of the piece. By mixing the sentences and again drawing them randomly, Beckett established the order for the last half of the piece in which each of the sixty sentences is repeated. To determine the paragraphing, Beckett wrote, as Cohn explains,

> . . . the number 3 on four separate pieces of paper, the number 4 on six pieces of paper, the number 5 on four pieces, the number 6 on six

pieces, and the number 7 on four pieces of paper. Again drawing randomly, he ordered the sentences into paragraphs according to the number drawn. . . .

The very idea of an art work ordered by chance is unsettling. Even after classical conceptions of perfection, harmony, and balance had made way to admit arts of imperfection, discord, and imbalance, the artist's purpose and control were still jealously guarded. Beckett, on the other hand, yields a portion of his control to the laws of probability and permutation. Art is implicitly consigned to the mathematician and computer programer. Indeed, J. M. Coetzee resorts to a Univac 1106 to deal with *Lessness* ["Samuel Beckett's *Lessness*: An Exercise in Decomposition," *Computers and the Humanities,* 1973]. His results verify mathematically what the reader suspects: no significant ordering principle governs the arrangement of phrases, sentences, or paragraphs. In fact the paragraph is not even a different kind of structural element from the sentence. Component parts are "interdependent and connected," arranged and rearranged according to mathematical rules.

Although disturbing, the "rule-governedness" of *Lessness* is purposeful and deliberate. Like all literary works, *Lessness* is based on assumptions, but its assumptions are mathematical. Instead of pretending that some inherent ordering process—be it thematic, chronological, associative, or symbolic—controls the displacement of words, *Lessness* is openly the product of chance. Meaning is dependent on the random arrangements of a finite set. The piece could have continued until all possible permutations of the sixty sentences had been presented, but nothing would have been changed or added. A single repetition is sufficient to suggest that all of the millions of possible reorderings are equally authoritative, equally meaningless. Just as mathematics is a mental construction which is completely knowable because it is completely imagined, so too the concept of order is an arbitrary abstraction which originates and exists only in man's mind. By structuring *Lessness* upon the admittedly arbitrary rules of combinational mathematics, Beckett reminds us of the equally arbitrary rules of all systems and languages. Moreover, if man is, as we have come to think of him since Descartes, a solipsistic animal, then the most valid systems are the admittedly imaginative. Ordering devices which depend on external authority are problematic. By pretending to a reality they don't have, such systems, like the box in *Ping,* enclose our minds so deceptively that we are unaware they are enclosed. The rule-governed, random order of *Lessness* frees us from the encircling assumptions inherent in language and literature—frees us, like the little body in a world of ruins fallen open, to face the endless, issueless, true refuge of non-order.

In spite of its random arrangement, *Lessness* is provocatively resonant. We are tempted to find purpose in the dispositon of sentences as, for example, the initial paragraphs establish setting and situation before introducing either the "little body" or a past or a future. Similarly, the last paragraph seems to conclude the whole work appropriately. It is hard not to feel that the final sentence is a deliberate and conscious climax. Indeed, even critics who are aware of Beckett's method of composition are enticed into interpretation by the powerful ending. The impact of *Lessness* resides somewhere between mathematics and art. Though organized randomly, the piece suggests meanings beyond the rules of probability. Even J. M. Coetzee's computer analysis concludes not with the statistical, but with the interpretive:

> The residue of the fiction is then *not* final disposition of the fragments but the motions of the consciousness that disposes them according to the rules we have traced, and no doubt to others we have failed to trace.

Lessness is random, but significance still adheres to it.

Since the order is random and since no new arrangements will change the work significantly, the reader must look to the sentences for any vestiges of meaning. The sentences, like those in *Ping,* are composed of repeated and permuted phrases dealing predominantly with a setting and a body but also postulating an imaginative realm of dreams and future possibilities. Instead of interrupting "ping"s, pauses are indicated by white space and paragraphs. But along with the "ping"s the sense of movement and dramatization has disappeared from the prose. Although *Lessness* has greater variety than *Ping*—more nouns, more directional adverbs, more images—and although it frees the body from a container and reinstates verbs, *Lessness* is a more static work. It deals with the unending rather than the dwindling, with the unchanging rather than the dissipating. Unlike the fragmented sentences in *Ping* which combine phrases of setting and body with those of murmur and memory, each sentence in *Lessness* is homogeneous. In fact, the sentences can be divided thematically into groups of families. Although the themes may be elusive, the divisions seem fairly clear. For example, Ruby Cohn and Martin Esslin find different significances and hence different labels for similar groups:

Ruby Cohn

1) the ruins as "true refuge"

2) the endless gray of earth and sky

3) the little body

4) the space "all gone from mind"

5) past tenses combined with "never"

6) future tenses of active verbs and the figment sentence, "Figment dawn dispeller of figments and the other called dusk."

Martin Esslin

1) the ruins

2) the vastness of earth and sky

3) the little body

4) the fact that the enclosed space is now forgotten—"all gone from mind"

5) a denial of past and future

6) an affirmation of past and future.

The first four families elicit fairly consistent titles. However the last two groups give rise to discrepancies not simply because they lack identifying refrains such as "the little body" or "all gone from mind," but more importantly because their essential character remains ambivalent. To Cohn the distinction between the two groups is one of tense, whereas to Esslin the difference is one of assertion. The lack of agreement is significant for it emphasizes the qualitative differences between sentences of the first four groups and those of the last two. The first groups describe setting and body—the known or observable aspects of the present situation. They present the rules and limitations under which *Lessness* must operate. The last groups, on the other hand, are less clear, less precise, and more enigmatic because they deal not with given data, but with the imaginative and mental, with daydreams and figments. Like the murmurs in *Ping* they contain much of the mystery and vitality of the work. Indeed, the tensions in *Lessness* are reflections of the tensions between these two types of groups, between the imaginative and the given.

"Ruins true refuge long last towards which so many false time out of mind." The initial sentence of *Lessness* introduces the first group of sentences, those characterized by the appearance of the phrase "true refuge." This group describes the situation of *Lessness* without any mention of the little body. The four walls of a container, such as the one in *Ping,* have fallen open into scattered ruins, thus revealing at long last an ash grey, soundless, and issueless true refuge. All of the sentences in the group repeat and rearrange the same small set of ideas and phrases. Moreover, many of these ideas and phrases—such as the greyness, the soundlessness, and the "fallen open" endlessness—are picked up and repeated in other groups until the dominant impression is of a world so blank and so minimal as to be an image of nothingness, of nonbeing. The fluctuations of light and dark in *Imagination Dead Imagine* and even *Ping*'s shining white infinite are reduced to a pervasive and passive grey. However, Beckett introduces into this nondescript grey a tenuous sense of affirmation. The four walls have fallen not "over" into destruction, but "open" into rebirth and freedom. The ruins are "issueless." The description captures our attention not simply because "issueless" appears independently rather than in a phrase, but also because "issueless" remains ambivalent. It suggests simultaneously that the ruins are without progeny, without egress, and without points of question, dispute, or decision. The issueless true refuge offers no means of escape, yet it also offers no matters for contention. A refuge that is "true" exists when man stops to escape formlessness through artificial containers and accepts the grey endlessness, when man ceases to tell himself stories to pass the time until there is an end to passing time and accepts the unchanging and eternal present as the only possible endlessness.

"All sides endlessness earth sky as one no sound no stir." The second sentence of *Lessness* introduces the second group of sentences. This group expands our understanding of the situation by describing the setting in more detail. Although there is no refrain appearing in all of the sentences, each sentence mentions either the greyness or the endlessness or both. Thus this group continues the image of nothingness begun in the "true refuge" section. The sentences are developed not so much by repeated phrases as by similar phrasing. Grey is applied to every aspect of setting: "Same grey all sides earth sky body ruins," "Earth sand same grey as the air sky ruins body fine ash grey sand." The grey endlessness is brought into perspective by the introduction of the "little body only upright." But this body is presented here only as an aspect of setting. Like the earth and the sky it too is grey, it too is without sound or stir: "no sound not a breath," "no stir not a breath." Indeed, the body's sole significance seems to be that it is the only thing upright in the "flatness endless."

It is in the third group that the body takes on what minimal shape it has. In contrast to the ragdoll figure of *Ping* with its mouth, legs, and toes "joined like sewn," the little body of *Lessness* is rigid and blocklike: "Little body ash grey locked rigid," "Legs a single block arms fast to sides." The body becomes the only untoppled column in the midst of ruins. Its contours have been eroded and "overrun." Its features, like those of a weather-worn statue, are barely defined: ". . . grey face features slit and little holes two pale blue," ". . . grey smooth no relief a few holes," ". . . grey face features overrun two pale blue." Although the slit-like holes are too indistinct to be called eyes, their pale blue persists. In fact, were it not for this pale blue and the "heart breath," we would mistake our immobile figure for part of the ruins. Though diminutive in size and significance, nonetheless the "little" body is still there, still alive, and still the "only upright."

While the third group describes the appearance of the "little body," the next family of sentences defines the body's intellectual capacities through negative proposition. The sentences increase the stillness by offering a litany of what is now "all gone from mind." The body has lost the powers of reasoning—"calm eye light of reason all gone from mind"—and of observation and sensual perception—"Face to calm eye touch close all calm all white all gone from mind." Images from Beckett's other works, particularly *Ping* are rejected. The "mighty light," the "sheer white," the "four square" walls, and the "blank planes" are all gone. The true refuge is not in a circumscribed "little void," but in the vast unending. Contrasts rather than repetitions link this group of sentences to the other groups. The phrases speak of what no longer exists, of "white" not "grey," of "blank planes" not "fallen open four walls over backwards," of "calm eye" not "little holes," and of "little void" not "all sides endlessness." *Ping* offered an infinitesimal world on the verge of nonexistence: *Lessness* rejects even that world. Now "all [is] gone from mind."

Whereas the fourth group describes what no longer exists even in the mind, the fifth group postulates the things that are not except in the mind, except in dreams and figments: "Never but this changelessness dream the passing hour." This group is the richest of the six sections. Although some repetition and some phrases from other groups are incorporated, these links from "reality" are always set in opposition to the figments and dreams. Emphasis is not upon the "silences" and the "grey air timeless," but rather upon the imagined laughter, cries, and passing light which fail to mask the silent vastness:

> Never but silences such that in imagination this wild laughter these cries.

> Never was but grey air timeless no sound figment the passing light.

The mind divides endlessness into dreams of "the passing hour" and of "the days and nights made of dreams of other nights better days." In imagination the eternal present can be momentarily ignored by the "happy" illusion that there can be an end, that there is "only one time to serve." However, these illusions of a passing time are consistently labelled as illusions, dreams, and figments. In the timeless "true refuge" of nonbeing, human time is one of the broken containers, one of the scattered ruins which have fallen over backwards. The mere mention of these scattered ruins—of passing time, of days and nights, of light, of wild laughter and cries—enriches both this group and the entire work by relieving the grey endlessness. Similarly, the ambiguous syntax and unusual word choice of the section add to its elusive charm. The sentences seem to mean more than they say. For example, the negation "never but" elicits at least two responses. As implied by Cohn's description of this group—"past tenses combined with never"—the figments of passing time never were anything other than dreams. The figment light never existed outside the imagination. On the other hand, Esslin's description—"a denial of past and future"—suggests that the phrase not only negates the reality of the figments in the past, but also denies any present or future possibilities. The present contains nothing except one "changeless dream." Even murmurs and other imaginings are excluded. Ambivalences are compounded as a negating phrase appears in only nine of the ten sentences. An almost imperceptible hope adheres to that tenth sentence, the sentence which so tantalizingly and provocatively concludes *Lessness*: "Figment dawn dispeller of figments and the other called dusk." The sentence is lovely, moving, and enigmatic. A similarly striking but elusive image occurs in the sentence, "Never but imagined the blue in the wild imagining the blue celeste of poesy." The archaic and obsolete words draw attention to themselves, making the "blue celeste of poesy" more vibrantly present than other dreams, than even the given grey endlessness. The heavenly power of imagination persists even amid the scattered ruins; its images and sounds, its dreams and figments, add an inexplicable, perhaps subliminal, layer of meaning to the world of *Lessness.*

The final group of sentences, like the dream and figment section, is rich in possibilities and variations. It contains no identifying phrase and few repetitions. Instead, the section deals with future possibilities, with the return of a diverse world in which man can act and speak. This future man is distinct from his present counterpart. Unlike the "little body" that blends into the ruins, future man is made strangely personal by Beckett's return to the pronoun "he" and by his ability to distinguish himself from his environment through motion. It is the hypothetical figure of the future—not the present figure with "legs a single block"—who will take a step in the sand, who will "live

again the space of a step." Whereas the "little body" has become so petrified that it no longer murmurs "ah," the future man's power of motion returns to him traces of plot and suggestions of heroic action. In spite of everything he will move "one step more," "he will make it":

> In the sand no hold one step more in the endlessness he will make it.

> One step more in the ruins in the sand on his back in the endlessness he will make it.

> One step more one alone all alone in the sand no hold he will make it.

Like Job, he will be able to "curse God again as in the blessed days." The future is a return to past possibilities. When viewed from the scattered ruins, the limitations endured by the characters of Beckett's middle period suddenly become hoped for blessings. To be able to walk, crawl, live again, and turn one's face to "the open sky the passing deluge" become affirmative actions. Emphasis is on what can again be done "as in the blessed days." Man can stir again, his heart will beat again, the privilege of being rained on will return again. Even the return of unhappiness is a blessed relief, "Old love new love as in the blessed days unhappiness will reign again." The days and nights only dreamt of in the fifth section will come to pass, "He will live again the space of a step it will be day and night again over him the endlessness." Man will be returned to the image that haunts Beckett's works "of blue the passing cloud." But in this subtly cyclic work, the return again to diversity and action is also an implicit return to the false refuge of imagined days and mental containers. The future possibilities are undercut by the recurring image of man with something over him again:

> It will be day and night again over him. . . .
> He will go on his back face to the sky open again over him the ruins the sand the endlessness.

Passing days and passing light will again enclose man. He will be on his back, face to the sky, underneath the passing deluge, below the passing cloud. The return to order and action is a return to false containers. By presenting the impossible future Beckett forces us to see what does not and cannot be in the "true refuge."

By thus breaking *Lessness* down into sentences and phrases, by regrouping the components, and by analyzing the resulting families of sentences, the reader is able to envision the "true refuge." Meaning and interpretation depend on the reader's involvement, depend on his manipulation of the moving yet enigmatic sentences. Just as *Lessness* deals with the tensions between being and nonbeing, between temporal and eternal, between imagined orders and the given endlessness, so too the piece exists between composition and decomposition, between form and formlessness. Beckett encloses his perception of order fallen open into the true refuge of nonorder, in an order which is itself so arbitrary that it begins to unravel. Instead of creating new containers, Beckett creates in *Lessness* an art that seeks to be unmade, an art that pushes the assumptions of language and literature over backward to admit the chaos "long last towards which so many false time out of mind."

In his latest works Beckett successfully accomplishes what his earliest pieces failed to do: he creates forms that disintegrate without belying their own assumptions. He develops an art that accommodates the mess without turning it into another kind of order. Although Beckett never rejects imagination nor totally discards the body, he moves away from the Joycean kind of art which can do, can know, art which reflects in its carefully controlled and inter-connected images an external world. Instead of a scintillating, print-oriented, and traditional art, Beckett offers, first, the spoken narration of an impotent narrator struggling with language and then impersonal and abstract images expressed in simple yet elliptic words and phrases. Characters and narrators are replaced by the objective, analytic prose of a mind in dialogue with itself. External references yield to arbitrary and fantastical images which dissolve almost before we have finished reading. The pieces are difficult not because too much has been included, nor because too much has been omitted but rather because they present images of an underlying void. We can glimpse nothingness only momentarily before we inevitably begin fabricating our own orders to cover the void. The Residua create from fiction, poetry, drama, music, and mathematics a new genre which demands the reader's intellectual involvement, yet also relies on subliminal responses, on sound and pattern, to effect meaning. Paradoxically the pieces use deceptively objective analyses of highly articulated forms to enclose a more basic formlessness and a more fundamental absence of order. Beckett uses the limitations of language and literature to capture the essence of the void by implication and exclusion: he expresses the chaos by avoiding it. He evolves in his short works a style that adheres ever more rigidly to the need to create in the face of nothingness. His pieces move from parodic stories to serious though fleeting glimpses into the true refuge of endlessness. The study of Samuel Beckett's residual fiction is the study of a journey to the self-dissipating image: " . . . soon there will be nothing where there was never anything, last images."

An excerpt from *Enough*:

He was not given to talk. An average of a hundred words per day and night. Spaced out. A bare million in all. Numerous repeats. Ejaculations. Too few for even a cursory survey. What do I know of man's destiny? I could tell you more about radishes. For them he had a fondness. If I saw one I would name it without hesitation.

We lived on flowers. So much for sustenance. He halted and without having to stoop caught up a handful of petals. Then moved munching on. They had on the whole a calming action. We were on the whole calm. More and more. All was. This notion of calm comes from him. Without him I would not have had it. Now I'll wipe out everything but the flowers. No more rain. No more mounds. Nothing but the two of us dragging through the flowers. Enough my old breasts feel his old hand.

Samuel Beckett, in his "Enough," in Six Residua, *John Calder, 1978.*

Laura Barge   (essay date 1977)

SOURCE: "Life and Death in Beckett's Four Stories," in *South Atlantic Quarterly,* Vol. 76, No. 3, Summer, 1977, pp. 332-47.

[*In the following essay, Barge considers the nature and relationship of life and death as represented in four stories by Beckett.*]

Samuel Beckett has said in an interview with Israel Shenker that all of his best work was written between 1946 and 1950 ["Moody Man of Letters," *New York Times,* 6 May 1956]. During 1945 he had returned to France from a brief visit to Ireland to see his mother and brother, had served with the Irish Red Cross in a field hospital located at Saint-Lô, and by winter had settled into his Paris apartment and begun a period of profuse creative productivity. The work he produced from this time until 1950 includes some poems and art criticism, the two plays *Waiting for Godot* and *Endgame,* the trilogy and one other novel, *Mercier and Camier,* the thirteen *Texts for Nothing,* and four short stories—three of which are published in English as *Stories* and in French as *Nouvelles.* The fourth story in this group, **"First Love" ("Premier amour")**, was withheld from publication until 1970, with the English version appearing in 1974.

The inclusion by Beckett of these stories (titles of the other three are **"The Expelled" ["L'Expulse"], "The Calmative" ["Le Calmant"],** and **"The End" ["La Fin"]**) in the group of what he considers his most significant work is not the only reason for their importance. Stylistically and thematically, they mark what is probably the most distinct transition in the entire canon. Shifting from the English third person (of *More Pricks Than Kicks, Murphy,* and *Watt*) to the French first person, Beckett creates a fictional hero and environment so uniquely and consistently characteristic that they are recognizable (although often changed in certain particulars) throughout the remainder of his published prose. The hero is no longer undecided, as the earlier heroes Belacqua, Murphy, and Watt are, between life in the macrocosm of the outer world or in the microcosm of the mind—his choice is the microcosm, a descent inward toward the core of the self ("I whose soul writhed from morning to night, in the mere quest of itself"). This descent becomes a quest which, fully defined in the trilogy and developed ever more intensively in the subsequent fiction, undergirds all of Beckett's work as a dominant theme, the quest for whatever constitutes metaphysical reality, for the essence of human experience. That this reality can finally be described only as nothing, as a Plenum-Void that never yields any substance but continually recedes into infinity, does not negate the centrality of this quest in Beckett's oeuvre. The failure of the quest does, however, negate anything that might be called development of character. Neither in these stories nor in the fiction that follows does a protagonist show real gain or make progress beyond his initial state. Thus the hero is frozen into a definite shape that is little changed beyond this point. He is in exile but longs for a home ("I longed to be under cover again, in an empty place, close and warm" ["The End"]), and is abused by nearly all the elements that make up his world. Consequently, his responses become those of abuse or loathing, although he is haunted by a yearning for companionship. Like Watt, he is hindered by a failure to understand or to communicate, but unlike Watt, he feels no real compulsion to do either. Instead he is content to relate countless fictional episodes, to use words only because words are all that he has been given to fill space and time. He regards these fictional episodes with the contempt he feels they deserve. As for his body, it is rotting away and loathsome with sores and disease (also with disability in the later fiction). Detached from this body, his mind is likewise deteriorating—even to a state of uncertainty as to whether it exists in a condition of life or death.

Although a sequence of events takes place in each story (and a general sequence, with much repetition, in the four stories as a whole), these happenings can hardly be labeled as plot because they are parts of a futile circle, a rigmarole, ending where it begins. Thus Beckett has abandoned even the sardonic plots of his earlier novels (Watt may not have accomplished anything, but he does learn something—even if the something he learns is that he can learn nothing) and is anticipating the circular endlessness of the trilogy. Setting becomes neither Dublin, London, nor the unnamed countryside of *Watt,* but a landscape that is everywhere and yet nowhere, a soulscape that is portrayed in later fiction in forms that vary from the closed room of *Malone Dies* to the slimy and Dantean hell of *How It Is* to the collapsed world of grey and empty ruins in **Lessness.**

It is also in these stories that the ill-defined "they" make their appearance. Resembling some malignant god or Kafkan high official who delights in tormenting his creatures without known reason, these obscure and mysterious personages (or personage), although never explicitly said to exist, are sensed by Beckett's heroes as being those ultimately in charge of the miserable and absurd affair known as life on the planet Earth. Depicted as whoever evicts the hero of the stories from his initial shelter, this power is given the proper name of Youdi in the second section of *Molloy* and is designated as a witness called Kram and Kram's scribe, Krim, in *How It Is.* The inhabitants of the cylinder in **The Lost Ones** are strictly controlled by specific laws formulated by someone or something that is responsible for their existence.

If the first-person narrator of the stories can be said to retain his personhood (after Belacqua, Murphy, and Watt, Beckett almost ceases to create persons; each hero becomes Everyman), he is nevertheless in the process of becoming only a voice, still bodied at the beginning of the trilogy but disembodied by its end, who is an indistinct blend of protagonist, narrator, and author. This blending of roles results in another change in the stories—a subtle difference in Beckett's use of irony. Through *Watt* Beckett remains reasonably close to the conventional use of literary irony. In such use, two levels of ironic awareness are in operation—the narrator's description of the ironic

scene or object and the reader's awareness that this description is ironic, that is, that the material that the narrator is presenting is deliberately falsified from what he actually intends the reader to perceive. But a third level of ironic awareness appears in the stories and reappears throughout the remaining fiction. Because there is a blending of the consciousness of the narrator and the protagonist (who is playing the role of narrator by relating the tale), the protagonist often becomes aware, in a subtle, undercover way, of the ironic implications of what he is relating about himself with a straight face. He becomes cognizant of the falsity of his own statements or actions. This third level at times seems to disappear, and the ironic awareness is thereby once again restricted to the narrator and the reader. When Watt expresses his confident hopes that his visit to Mr. Knott's estate will end his confusion about life, he is truly hopeful that the quest will be successful. Only we, as readers, share with the narrator the knowledge of the futility of any such expectation. But when the protagonist of **"The End,"** in an apparent effort to find direction for his quest, raises his eyes toward the heavens, he seems subtly aware that the whole business is nothing but a joke and ridicules his own action. This spilling over of ironic awareness from the protagonist as narrator onto the protagonist as character never blunts the edge of Beckett's irony, but instead increases its effectiveness in the succeeding fiction.

Of all the specifics indicating these stories as a point of transition, none is more significant than the permeation of the tales with the concept of mortality. Not that Beckett has not been obsessed with mortality before: both Belacqua and Murphy are fascinated by death as a possible state of "embryonal repose" in which they can possibly escape the frustrations of life in the macrocosm. But oddly enough, the fact that they do die (a release Beckett never again gives any hero) and find death to be nothing other than annihilation robs these early works of the existential anguish, the *Angst,* associated with mortality in the subsequent fiction. Watt does not die, but following the failure of his epistemological quest, his existence becomes a continuing crucifixion. It is not some character's death, then, but the fact of death that begins overtly to overshadow Beckett's fiction in the conclusion of *Watt* and in the stories. Agreeing with the writer of Ecclesiastes that "all is vanity. All go unto one place: all are of the dust, and all turn to dust again," Beckett conceives of mortality as the abnegation of all value in life and begins to define life itself as an event of death. As the eloquent Pozzo explains, "one day we were born, one day we shall die, the same day, the same second. . . . They give birth astride of a grave, the light gleams an instant, then it's night once more" (*Waiting for Godot*).

Breaking his usual pattern of reticence in offering comment on his work, Beckett has said that the experiences of the protagonists of these stories can be taken as three phases of one existence—"prime, death, and limbo." We cannot, however, be certain which phase designates which story. Since the protagonist of **"The Expelled"** describes himself as being in "the prime of life" and **"First Love"** has to do with something that is first or early, we can assume that both of these pieces should be included in the "prime" phase. Because **"The End"** relates an experience that ends with death, it might be matched with death, but **"The Calmative,"** in its puzzling opening comments, also reveals a preoccupation with death. The protagonist does not know when he died but is now in a state of rotting. The possibility that the story he decides to tell may be of a coming back to life after death is highly improbable; it would be most unlike him to make such a return. But if **"The Calmative"** takes place in a postmortem state, such a state has familiar landmarks—a "sky, sea, plain and mountain" of this earth.

This difficulty of trying to separate the stories into states of life or death is a small part of the larger dilemma encountered in attempting to define the word symbols *life* and *death* as used by Beckett, not only in the stories, but also in all the fiction that follows. Because Beckett conceives of physical life as an experience of dying and because he suspects that human consciousness or being does not end with physical death, the meanings of the words merge—life becomes death, and death is a continuation of life. In an interview with Tom Driver, Beckett discusses the relationship of what Driver calls the "life-death question" with the disordered meaninglessness of existence that Beckett terms as "chaos." The equating by Beckett of life with light and salvation, and of death with darkness and damnation is strongly reminiscent of the defining of life by the Apostle John, although presumably Beckett's equations have no theological implications. Beckett explains that it is because man is faced with the dual existence of both light (life) and darkness (death) that the human "situation becomes inexplicable." That is, innately aware of the desirability of qualities such as truth, love, justice, beauty, and happiness, man confronts a universe in which the realization of such qualities is simply not possible. Pointing out in the interview that modern man cannot accept either a Jansenist (that man, created good, became morally evil and therefore deserves such a universe) or a Greek (that man must encounter darkness in order to be finally "illuminated") explanation for this duality, Beckett finds "clarity" about the human condition impossible. Thus he has no choice but to "write always about distress," a distress resulting from the "inscrutability" of being ["Beckett by the Madeleine," *Columbia University Forum,* Summer, 1961]. It is this distressful perception of an absurd universe that the Beckettian hero associates with the idea of death.

Certain remarks that Beckett made to the actor Martin Held during a German production of *Krapp's Last Tape* in the Schiller Theater of Berlin are of interest in exploring Beckett's concept of death. What Krapp senses apprehensively in the darkened areas away from the lighted table (into which he makes brief excursions throughout the drama) is death. Beckett told Held that Krapp perceives that "Old Nick's there. Death is standing behind him and unconsciously he's looking for it" [Ronald Hayman, *Samuel Beckett*]. Undoubtedly, physical death is stalking the sixty-nine-year-old Krapp, and any release from an existence compounded now of bananas and sexual fantasies would not be unwelcomed. But physical death is not all that is lurking in the darkness, either within the context of Beckett's statement to Held or in the play itself. As we

have noted from Beckett's remarks in the interview with Driver, the symbolizing of death by darkness rests on the association of death with something that is inexplicable (or absurd) or that causes distress. It is dying without ever having lived that is associated with the idea of death here. Krapp's life has amounted to nothing—companionship, love, and ambition have turned out to be only "The sour cud and the iron stool." This nothingness is capsuled in Krapp's taped recollection of his mother's death. Sitting on a bench outside the house where his mother is dying, Krapp is almost alone ("Hardly a soul") and unable to communicate with any person who still happens to be around (the eyes of the nursemaid are like "chrysolite"). Wishing the ordeal of his mother's dying were over, he nevertheless suffers acutely from his personal encounter with mortality ("Her moments" are "my moments"), an experience that becomes nothing more nor less than a window blind being suddenly lowered and a small black ball Krapp has been playing with relinquished forever to a dog:

> . . . the blind went down, one of those dirty brown roller affairs, throwing a ball for a little white dog, as chance would have it. I happened to look up and there it was. All over and done with, at last. . . . A small, old, black, hard, solid rubber ball. (*Pause.*) I shall feel it in my hand, until my dying day. (*Pause.*) I might have kept it. (*Pause.*) But I gave it to the dog.

The quintessential anguish of death is that death (and, by implication, life) consists of nothing more than two such events. Twice during the play Krapp absentmindedly sings a few lines from the Christian hymn of fulfillment and rest,

> Now the day is over,
> Night is drawing nigh,
> Shadows of the evening
> Steal across the sky,

as a travesty and, in some of his final lines, pronounces the earth to be an "old muckball."

Although Beckett's comments in *Proust* are primarily about Proust and should not be uncritically applied to Beckett's own work, certain observations in this criticism are relevant at this point. The anguish associated with death is not directly related to a fear or dread of death per se. Because of the numbing effect of what Proust calls Habit, unless death is made concrete by being forecast at some particular point in the future, it has no meaning in the present because its "possibility" remains "indistinct and abstract." Instead, the anguish derives from the impermanence of any given moment before the onslaught of time. The "reluctance to die" is a "long and desperate and daily resistance before the perpetual exfoliation of personality." The terrible realization of the narrator, Marcel, that his grandmother is "dead" occurs not at her actual death but when, in the abeyance of Habit, he sees her suddenly as "a stranger whom he has never seen." The real villain of Proust and of Beckett is not death (although the perception of Beckett's hero is not numbed by Habit, rather than fearing the occurrence of death, he often seems to relish the event as possibly offering some release from the burden of consciousness) but time—"that double-headed monster of damnation and salvation" that makes each passing day a "calamitous day" by continually destroying and recreating for further destruction its "victims and prisoners." Having reached such a conclusion, we can make the further statement that, beginning with the stories, physical death becomes for Beckett a metaphor for the existential anguish of sensing infinity in a finite world, of longing for selfhood in a universe of continual change that denies the possibility of being.

In spite of his sick humor (which nevertheless succeeds in being funny) and detached irrationality (he has either five or six feet, none of which function properly), the protagonist of the stories suffers acutely from a dislocation with his universe defined in terms of exile. When the hero of **"The Expelled"** is thrown out of his childhood home, he is *expelled*—either from some undefined state before birth or from some Paradise that exists only as an intuitive consciousness of a world that should be. However the haven is defined, the hero is evicted, and all subsequent events become what the earlier protagonist Murphy has called "a wandering to find home"—a search for an ending of exile, for a place of belonging, a sanctuary for the human spirit.

This dislocation or exile can be defined in existentialist terminology (although with obvious distinctions and a rejection on Beckett's part of any existentialist solutions) as estrangement. Beckett's hero is Heidegger's man being "thrown" and left in a world not of his own making. He is man without a resting place for his heart in Nietzsche's nihilistic universe, and Sartre's man, forlorn and orphaned in an alien environment where he can never be at home. Or, in a more limited sense, Beckett's tramp is Camus' Meursault, a stranger so imprisoned within himself that whether he is actually behind prison walls is of little significance in determining his alienation. More definitively, the tramp's exile can be likened to the estrangement of the prodigal son of Luke's gospel, who is separated both from his father and from his father's house. Although, unlike man as described by Nietzsche and Sartre, Beckett's hero is not consciously aware of any need for a missing God, and although, unlike the prodigal son, he has made no choice that has caused his homelessness, the hero is nonetheless existentially estranged. Reincarnated in the Unnamable, this hero speaks with false bravado of a place "made for me, and I for it" (*Three Novels*). But he has no valid grounds for such a hope: he is "Going nowhere, coming from nowhere," and the place that he inhabits is only a "black void."

It is precisely this suffering of dislocation that is expressed as a metaphorical undercurrent in the stories by images or events of death. In the first three stories, death appears either as an inconsequential mentioning of some object, as a chance remark or thought of the narrator, as the meaning of some symbol, or as an integral part of the episode that is being related. Making up a disjunctive collection, the death references in these stories are parallel in form to the loosely structured narratives of the stories themselves. The references to death in the fourth story, **"First Love,"** exhibit a pattern corresponding to the tighter structure of

this story—the references occur at specific points in what might ironically be called the cycle of life or of love.

Following his eviction, and after he is confusedly told by a policeman (or perhaps two separate policemen; he is not certain) to stay off both the sidewalk and the street, the now homeless tramp of **"The Expelled"** is passed by a funeral. Although this funeral is only mentioned (it has no discernible connection with the tale itself), the tramp proceeds immediately to enter a cab, which he describes as a "big black box" with a "musty" smell. Dozing off, he is perturbed by the cabman's question as to where he wants to go, because he wants to remain where he is. His only interest in the cab is as a shelter of sorts (perhaps death is the same), and later, when the cabman offers the friendly suggestion that he and the tramp ride together on the outside seat, the tramp refuses: "for sometime already I had been dreaming of the inside of the cab and I got back inside." Also, the cabman cannot be hired for the entire day because he has been engaged for a funeral that afternoon. Another inconsequential mention of death is found in **"The End."** Having secured temporary shelter in the basement room of the Greek (or Turkish?) woman, the tramp plants a crocus bulb, which sprouts but, in spite of his care, becomes "a wilting stem and a few chlorotic leaves," finally dying. Similar plants are introduced into **"First Love"** and into the later novel *How It Is*. Also functioning as an image of death in this later work, the crocus is probably the same as that of the tramp of **"The End."** The plant is "in an area in a basement," and a hand manipulates an attached string to swing it into the light (*How It Is*).

When the tramp of **"The Expelled"** is evicted from his original haven, he recollects, apparently by chance, that this dwelling is the one in which he has expected to die, that the only exit he has envisioned is one in which the door opens and his body is brought out feet first. Twice more, before the actual event, this protagonist entertains chance thoughts of his death—the tale he contemplates relating in **"The Calmative"** will probably be one of his "old body" vanishing in a multiple shattering of its images, and, in the same story, during the visit to the cathedral, he imagines being found "stretched out in the rigor of death" and subsequently being "put . . . in the evening papers." Offhandedly, the tramp remarks in **"The End"** that his former tutor (who had given him the *Ethics* of Geulincx) had been found dead, not in a cathedral but in a water closet.

Death appears symbolically in references throughout the first three stories to the sea. Leaving the cabman's stable (he has had enough of the horse's company), the tramp of **"The Expelled"** comments on his habit of following the rising sun and states that in the evenings he continues to pursue the sun's path below the horizon of the sea until he is "down among the dead." Irresistibly drawn toward the sea, the protagonist of **"The Calmative"** nevertheless fears it as a "dead haven. . . . the black swell was most perilous, and all about me storm and wreck. I'll never come back here." Leaving the shore and hastening toward the town, he is careful not to retrace his steps in the direction of the sea, "where I had sworn never to return." But the resolute hero does return: **"The End"** records his death, drifting with "the currents and the tides," in a boat from the bottom of which he has pulled the plug, assuring himself of a watery grave.

Repeating the theme of exile, **"First Love"** defines love as a banishment ("What goes by the name of love is banishment") and the cycle of human life as a cycle of death. Thus, as in the first three stories, death becomes a metaphor for the suffering of existence, which is by definition an exile. As such a metaphor, death presents itself in some form at each significant point in the life cycle of the hero. His comments concerning the place of his birth center upon his father's death and the cemetery where his father is buried. The hero enjoys this spot of earth because he does "not find unpleasant"—in fact he finds "infinitely preferable to what the living emit"—the "smell of corpses, distinctly perceptible under those of grass and humus." The bench in the park where he meets his partner in love, Lulu, is "backed by a mound of solid earth and garbage," and is enclosed by "a pair of venerable trees, more than venerable, dead, at either end of the bench." While living in the cowshed and longing for the absent Lulu, the hero inscribes her name (as he lies on his face in the moonlight) on "an old heifer pat"—dead animal matter. A more obvious image of death is the hyacinth (already mentioned in connection with the crocus in **"The End"**) that Lulu places in the room of the hero after they come to live together. The hyacinth looks as if it might live but instead dies and begins to smell "foul." He refuses to allow it to be removed from the room, and the day Lulu announces the impending birth of their child (possibly the child is theirs; Lulu is a practicing prostitute while married to the hero) one of her eyes (she is cross-eyed) seems riveted on the remains of the hyacinth.

When the birth cries of the child banish the protagonist from the house of his marriage ("they pursued me down the stairs and out into the street"), the "leaves were falling already," and he remarks that he dreads the winter. Thus nature, which traditionally joins love with life in spring, joins it instead with death in winter, and Beckett's tale becomes not a life cycle but a cycle of death. The cries of the new-born infant pursue the hero relentlessly to the grave, apparently never to cease, and thereby are defined as the cries of death: "but what does it matter, faint or loud cry is cry, all that matters is that it should cease. For years I thought they would cease. Now I don't think so any more."

If life becomes an event of death, then it is possible to conceive of death as simply a continuation of this death-in-life. What Beckett is doing is to distort John Donne's triumphant assertion that death shall die into the terrifying possibility that life shall live—a mystery that in Beckett's world is reason enough for despair. For Beckett, the play or story can never be finished, and a significant aspect of the hell that his protagonists endure is that existence goes on and on. The reason his heroes cannot experience the release of death is because they have never achieved being in life. As the Unnamable laments, "I'll be born and born, births for nothing, and come to night without having been" (*Three Novels*). This inability of matters to end fi-

nally, of everything to come to a close, is introduced into the Beckettian canon in the stories. Life and death become so merged in a cycle of continual flux that neither can be defined as a beginning or as an end. The protagonist of **"The Expelled"** notes that the events that befall him are simply a conglomeration of many "cradles" and "graves," and the disillusioned lover of **"First Love"** adds that the earth has "many graves in her giving, for the living." This latter hero is a writer, but the only piece he has produced that meets with his approval is his epitaph, a bit of jargon that succeeds only in bewildering us as readers until we sense its purposely confused blending of life with death and of death with life. Quoted with my words or phrases supplied to indicate this blending, the epitaph reads as follows:

> Hereunder [in death] lies the above [one who has
>   lived] who up [in life] below [in death]
> So hourly died [experienced death in life] that
> he survived til now [experiences life in death]

As is so often the case with Beckett's ironic witticisms the agony lies just below the surface of the words.

A more profound portrayal of life and death as parts of the endless and tormenting cycle of being can be seen in a comparison of the final pages of **"The End"** with the opening paragraph of **"The Calmative."** As already stated, the protagonist of **"The End"** dies (whatever this verb means) by getting in a boat, removing the boat's plug, and drifting out to sea. His death is described as a dramatic explosion into the nothingness of space: "The sea, the sky, the mountains and the islands closed in and crushed me in a mighty systole, then scattered to the uttermost confines of space." But this death by explosion fails to give any release from the burden of life. The hero remains damned with consciousness ("without the courage to end or the strength to go on") and a compulsion to continue, to tell another story, one he "might have told, a story in the likeness of my life."

John Fletcher notes [in *The Novels of Samuel Beckett*] that if this dramatic explosion is only a vision, and if in actuality this protagonist "merely dwindles away," then the "shadowy state" in which he finds himself is that of his counterpart in **"The Calmative."** The relationship of this story with **"The End,"** however, is much more explicit than this observation. Although the hero does die of the explosion, the first paragraph of **"The Calmative"** begins exactly where the last paragraph of **"The End"** stops. The protagonist of **"The Calmative"** is "alone in my icy bed [the boat]" and is "older than the day, the night, when the sky with all its lights fell upon me." The paragraph from **"The End"** mentions "the lights of the buoys" which "the sea seemed full of" and the "distant fires, on sea, on land and in the sky." He decides to tell himself "another story" and is aware that his present state is after his death. We know that Beckett wrote **"The Calmative"** as the last story in this series, and that **"The End"** was written first. Obviously he is making an endless cycle of the stories as he does of Molloy's and Moran's narratives in *Molloy*. The state termed as death is defined by the hero of *Malone Dies,* Malone, who is fearful that, although he is dead, "all continues more or less as when I was not" (*Three Novels*). Beckett's heroes are damned with the curse Swift places on his Struldbruggs—the curse of an endless life that is essentially the same as the present one. Hence neither in life nor in death is there an ending of exile, a finding of some haven which will be what the Christian God was for Augustine—a sanctuary for man in which he is able to find rest for his spirit.

Alec Reid   (essay date 1979)

SOURCE: "Test Flight: Beckett's 'More Pricks than Kicks'," in *The Irish Short Story,* edited by Patrick Rafroidi and Terence Brown, Humanities Press, Inc., 1979, pp. 227-35.

[*In the essay below, Reid evaluates the stories in* More Pricks Than Kicks *in light of Beckett's subsequent works.*]

Much of *More Pricks than Kicks* is material originally destined for a novel *A Dream of Fair to Middling Women* on which Beckett had worked for two or three years before jettisoning it. The ten stories are all concerned with one character, Belacqua Shuah, whose adventures, if we may so dignify them, and whose love life we follow from the university to the cemetery. Although each of the episodes is self-contained there are numerous cross-references within the stories.

Of the ten stories, one **"Dante and the Lobster"** deserves inclusion in any anthology of Irish short stories; two others, **"A Wet Night"** and **"What a Misfortune"** are fine pieces of localised satire. The other seven all have their good things but do not merit much detailed examination.

In his study of Beckett, *The Long Sonata of the Dead,* Michael Robinson remarks that in their present form the short stories are uneven in quality and are evidently the work of a young man intent on exploring the possibilities of his learning and early impressions. Since Mr. Robinson himself was well under thirty when he passed this judgement it is tempting to dismiss it as an example of shallow calling unto shallow, but there is too much truth in the comment for that. *More Pricks than Kicks* is undeniably *juvenilia* with all the exhibitionism, the arrogance and the shallowness of a very clever, very erudite young man. But there is more to it than that. Maturity apart, in the lives of some artists there seems to be a watershed separating irrevocably the 'prentice work from the masterpieces. Just as few could have foreseen that "Mister John Keats", rightly trounced by *Blackwoods* for the Cockney vulgarities of his early poetry would leave behind him the *Poems* of 1820, so the Beckett of *More Pricks than Kicks* gives little hint of the future Nobel prize-winner. Beckett, the man, has changed from the promising young academic of the thirties to one who, to quote George Devine, "seems to have lived and suffered so that I might see and he was generous enough to pass it on to me". Beckett as artist is no longer a cosmopolitan aesthete but a writer utterly committed to discovering the inner world of the self. The Dublin of Belacqua Shuah, hero of *More Pricks than Kicks,* is redolent of what now seems Edwardian euphoria. The gulf between *More Pricks than Kicks* and say

Molloy or *Waiting for Godot* is no less than that which separates *Stephen Hero* from *Finnegans Wake*.

Of all the *genres* at which Beckett has tried his hand, the short story is probably the one which interests him least, certainly in the sense used by Sean O'Faolain when he described it as a piece of prose in which the tension is sustained. Tension is rarely found in Beckett's work, and where it does occur it is generated not by the content, the sequence of events, but by the writing itself in its constant attempt to say the unsayable, transcend the limitations of traditional form.

In examinations of the Irish short story certain ideas tend to come up again and again—What is the author's feeling for Ireland and the realities of Irish life? Does he accept them or does he reject them? Does Ireland become a character? What are the author's feelings for the people he has created? What are his relations with the reader? The author of *More Pricks than Kicks* seems concerned only with the last two of these. Of Belacqua he has a good deal to say: "We were Pylades and Orestes for a period, flattened down to something very genteel, but the relation abode and was highly confidential while it lasted". By nature, according to the narrator, Belacqua was "sinfully indolent, bogged in indolence" while his mental and moral position, an attempt to separate himself as far as possible from the world around him, was equally pathetic and ignoble.

> In his anxiety to explain himself, he was liable to come to grief. Nay, this anxiety in itself, or so at least it seemed to me, constituted a breakdown in the self-sufficiency which he never wearied of arrogating to himself, a sorry collapse of my little internus homo, and alone sufficient to give him away as inept ape of his own shadow. But he wriggled out of everything by pleading that he had been drunk at the time, or that he was an incoherent person and content to remain so, and so on. He was an impossible person in the end. I gave him up in the end because he was not serious.

Even Miss Alba Perdue, the most sympathetic of Belacqua's lady-loves, was scarcely bowled over by him. Looking at him as he arrives at a party, bedraggled and slightly the worse for drink, she reflects that "she had never seen anybody, man or woman, look such a sovereign booby. Seeking to be God, she thought, in the slavish arrogance of a piffling evil".

As for the reader, Beckett addresses him often enough in an almost conspiratorial tone, or as one needing enlightenment on detail:

> "And the rosiner" said Mrs Tough, "will you have that in the lav too?"
>
> Reader, a rosiner is a drop of the hard.
>
> Ruby rose and took a gulp of coffee to make room.
>
> "I'll have a gloria" she said.
>
> Reader, a gloria is coffee laced with brandy.

Even with such aids the book is not unfairly described by Katherine Worth as "one to defy translation".

In feats of gallantry Belacqua is by preference a *voyeur* and only reluctantly a practitioner. Similarly Beckett seems more interested in the act of authorship in *More Pricks than Kicks* than in involvement with it. The very title was chosen, one cannot help suspecting, to stimulate the attention of the Irish Censorship of Publications Board, a body much in the minds of other avant-garde spirits of the time. If so, it succeeded.

Given Belacqua and his creator we should be content to look for amusement only. But this we find in plenty. Once we become attuned to a sardonic, detached point of view and to a very gifted writer light-heartedly trying his wings, we find there is a good deal of fun to be had. There is Belacqua in **"Ding Dong"** unassumingly seeking *Nirvana* in his favourite sombre hostelry only to be accosted by a beshawled female with "a white voice" who sells him two seats in heaven for tuppence each and bilks him of his small-change.

In **"Love and Lethe"** Belacqua and his "current one and only", a lady suffering from an incurable disease and finding the opportunities for gallantry decreasing as her desire for them sharpens, decide to end it all together. In the event, despite Belacqua's provision of a revolver, poison and a notice saying "temporarily sane" they make a botch of the business, ending up in each other's arms.

Then there is much satire of Dublin's provincial intelligentsia such as gathered at the party thrown by Miss Caleken Frica:

> Two banned novelists, a bibliomaniac and his mistress, a paleographer, a violist d'amore with his instrument in a bag, a popular parodist with his sister and six daughters, a still more popular Professor of Bullscrit and Comparative Ovoidology, the saprophile the better for drink, a communist painter and decorator fresh back from the Moscow reserves, a merchant prince, two grave Jews, a rising strumpet, three more poets with Lauras to match, a disaffected cicisbeo, a chorus of playwrights, the inevitable envoy of the Fourth Estate, a phalanx of Grafton Street Stürmers and Jemmy Higgins. . . .

Another delight in the book, for those who find such things pleasurable, are the frequent erudite in-jokes, the tones of exact recondite scholarship in surroundings of seedy disarray. Thus when Belacqua in **"Fingal"** takes Miss Winifred Coates who was "pretty hot and witty in that order" to the Hill of the Wolves looking down on Malahide Castle in North County Dublin, it is not long before he finds himself a very sad animal and we recall Galen and his *tristis post coitus*. In **"A Wet Night"** the sister of the hostess unveils the refreshments.

> "Cup! Squash! Cocoa! Force! Julienne! Pan Kail! Cock-a-Leekie! Hulluah! Apfelmus! Isinglass! Ching-Ching!"

> A terrible silence fell on the assembly.

> "Great cry" said Chas "and little wool".

And the cognoscenti preen themselves as they recognise the headline from the copy books used in the National Schools, the works devised by Vere Foster.

Again there is the delight of parody. Only those with a good knowledge of James Joyce's "The Dead" will appreciate the Frica's party to the full but few readers will fail to enjoy the witty parody of the famous conclusion to that work. Beckett's arrogant self-confidence is astonishing:

> But the wind had dropped, as it so often does in Dublin when all the respectable men and women whom it delights to annoy have gone to bed, and the rain fell in a uniform untroubled manner. It fell upon the bay, the littoral, the mountains and the plains, and notably upon the Central Bog it fell with a rather desolate uniformity.

Closely associated with this zest for parody is the young man's exuberant enjoyment of his own linguistic powers. Later Beckett was to achieve a style of chastened, chilly economy. In **More Pricks than Kicks** he luxuriates in verbal excess, delighting for example in sustained passages of the mock-heroic, exulting in his verbal energy. And at moments, almost against the grain we find an imagination and an intellect at work:

> The groundsman stood deep in thought. What with the company of headstones sighing and gleaming like bones, the moon on the job, the sea tossing in her dreams and panting, and the hills observing their Attic vigil in the background, he was at a loss to determine off-hand whether the scene was of the kind that it termed romantic or whether it should not with more justice be deemed classical. Both elements were present, that was indisputable. Perhaps classico-romantic would be the fairest estimate. A classico-romantic scene.

Despite such moments, the stories as a whole do not have the stamp of authentic genius. On their showing, Beckett could fit snugly enough into an Irish tradition of verbal brilliance with little behind it, another fashionable Dublin literary wit. Once only in **More Pricks than Kicks** a deep, more lasting note is sounded, strangely enough in the first story, **"Dante and the Lobster"**. Here we meet Belacqua for the first time as he wrestles with an obscure passage from Dante's Purgatory. When the Angelus rings, he closes his book and turns to "the three great obligations of the day, lunch, lobster and his lesson". The first of these inspires a mock heroic account of how Belacqua prepares and organises his meal, two rounds of thoroughly toasted bread smeared with mustard and then taken to the grocer's for their filling, a piece of gorgonzola, thence to a rather low pub where Belacqua can enjoy them in peace. Lunch is a ritual which can be easily violated but on this day it goes well. From the pub, Belacqua makes his way to a fishmonger's to collect a lobster, already wrapped up, which he and his aunt will eat that evening. The fishmonger assures him that it is "leppin fresh". Then comes the Italian lesson with Signorina Ottolenghi, "a lady of a certain age who had found being beautiful and young and pure more of a bore than anything else". While he is with her the lobster, left on a hall table, is almost snatched away by a cat belonging to Mlle Glain, a French teacher in the same institute. Eventually without hurt it reaches the kitchen of Belacqua's aunt where Belacqua discovers to his horror that when the fishmonger had described it as "lepping fresh" he was speaking no more than the truth. Even now it is still alive.

"What are you going to do?" he cried.

"Boil the beast" she said, "what else?"

"But it's not dead" protested Belacqua "you can't boil it like that".

She looked at him in astonishment. Had he taken leave of his senses?

"Have sense" she said sharply, "lobsters are always boiled alive. They must be". She caught up the lobster and laid it on its back. It trembled. "They feel nothing" she said.

In the depths of the sea it had crept into the cruel pot. For hours in the midst of its enemies, it had breathed secretly. It had survived the French-woman's cat and his witless clutch. Now it was going alive into scalding water. It had to. Take into the air my quiet breath.

Belacqua looked at the old parchment of her face, grey in the dim kitchen.

"You make a fuss" she said angrily "and upset me and then lash into it for your dinner".

She lifted the lobster clear of the table. It had about thirty seconds to live.

Well, thought Belacqua, it's a quick death, God help us all. It is not.

The last short sentence is a master stroke, breaking in like the trump of doom to scatter our facile, self-induced indifference to the diabolical actions afoot. Here is Beckett speaking in his authentic, unmistakable voice, austere, insistent, unrelenting. It is hard to know if he is addressing the reader, or any audience at all, or whether this is not the voice which we shall hear in all the later work, a voice speaking for man into a universal darkness simply because it cannot stay silent. Here are the originality, the compassion, the sheer mastery which, as the Nobel prize jury said, have enabled Beckett to elevate human wretchedness to the level of art.

But this lies far ahead. In 1934, Beckett was still a young man though, as Joyce said of him, of undoubted talent. The war was to come with two years' work in the French Resistance in Paris and three in hiding for his very life. There will be a switch from stories to novels, from English to French, and a change of style from the early highly polished pedantic elegance and excess to an earthy violent incoherence, a demotic economy, somehow saying far more. Amazingly *More Kicks* will lead to *Lessness.*

More Pricks than Kicks is only a start, light-hearted, clever, amusing, notice served that here is a writer of wit, ready to laugh, in a slightly condescending way perhaps, at the world around him, but above all, at his own learning and at himself.

> **An excerpt from *The Lost Ones:***
>
> Abode where lost bodies roam each searching for its lost one. Vast enough for search to be in vain. Narrow enough for flight to be in vain. Inside a flattened cylinder fifty metres round and sixteen high for the sake of harmony. The light. Its dimness. Its yellowness. Its omnipresence as though every separate square centimetre were agleam of the some twelve million of total surface. Its restlessness at long intervals suddenly stilled like panting at the last. Then all go dead still. It is perhaps the end of their abode. A few seconds and all begins again. Consequences of this light for the searching eye. Consequences for the eye which having ceased to search is fastened to the ground or raised to the distant ceiling where none can be. The temperature. It oscillates with more measured beat between hot and cold. It passes from one extreme to the other in about four seconds. It too has its moments of stillness more or less hot or cold. They coincide with those of the light. Then all go dead still. It is perhaps the end of all. A few seconds and all begins again. Consequences of this climate for the skin. It shrivels. The bodies brush together with a rustle of dry leaves. The mucous membrane itself is affected. A kiss makes an indescribable sound. Those with stomach still to copulate strive in vain. But they will not give in. Floor and wall are of solid rubber or suchlike. Dash against them foot or fist or head and the sound is scarcely heard. Imagine then the silence of the steps. The only sounds worthy of the name result from the manipulation of the ladders or the thud of bodies striking against one another or of one against itself as when in sudden fury it beats its breast. Thus flesh and bone subsist.
>
> *Samuel Beckett, in his* The Lost Ones, *in* Six Residua, *John Calder, 1978.*

Enoch Brater   (essay date 1980)

SOURCE: "Why Beckett's *Enough* Is More or Less Enough," in *Contemporary Literature,* Vol. 21, No. 2, Spring, 1980, pp. 252-66.

[*An American critic and educator, Brater is the author of* Beckett at Eighty/Beckett in Context *(1986) and* Beyond Minimalism: Beckett's Late Style in the Theater *(1987). In the essay below, he contrasts* Enough *with other works of short fiction by Beckett.*]

"Reduce, reduce, reduce!" wrote Marcel Duchamp, proclaiming a new credo for artistic composition. Beckett has taken the manifesto at its word, for in his short prose pieces to construct means quite literally to reduce. Ideas collapse into words, contemplation backslides into sensation, and stories revert to color, texture, sensibility, and sensuality. Definitively incomplete, Beckett's formal condensation undermines the elusive and sometimes suspicious relations between his minimalist prose and all other things: "Objects give us everything," Duchamp continued, "but their representation no longer gives us anything." Disengaged from representational imagery and therefore not emblematic, Beckett's work makes us discover in residual prose the literary potential of compressed and frequently abstract patterns, their human overtones, their fleshy colors, and, above all, their pervasive texture of "mucous membrane."

As early as *Imagination Dead Imagine* Beckett offers us a story without the intrusion of any proper subject: "No trace anywhere of life, you say, pah, no difficulty there, imagination not dead yet, yes, dead, good, imagination dead imagine. Islands, waters, azure, verdure, one glimpse and vanished, endlessly, omit." Beckett asks his reader to imagine a totally white world in which imagination itself has finally died. Given such an impossible situation, anything so baroque as a landscape should be logically impossible for any reader to imagine or any writer to organize on paper. But logic is always false. Patterns, shapes, and forms soon appear to revitalize the empty space. The mind's eye quickly visualizes what the mind itself cannot see, two human forms in a fetal embrace halfway between organic bodilessness and mechanical functioning. The determined confusion of this transitory realm is, moreover, geometrically and visually unmistakable. Had the narration failed to mention that the dome's two inhabitants are lying on their right sides, there would have been two possible spatial configurations for the ABCD coordinates:

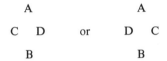

But within this rotunda the picture is singular and, so far as the coordinates are concerned, unambiguous. Only the second configuration accurately plots the particulars of this "arsyversy" visual horizon:

> Still on the ground, bent in three, the head against the wall at B, the arse against the wall at A, the knees against the wall between B and C, the feet against the wall between C and A, merging in the white ground were it not for the long hair of strangely imperfect whiteness, the white body of a woman finally. Similarly inscribed in the other semicircle, against the wall his head at A, his arse at B, his knees between A and D, his feet between D and B, the partner. On their right sides therefore both and back to back head to arse.

Concentrating on images drawn, abstracted, and metamorphosed from nature, *Imagination Dead Imagine* celebrates an imaginative vision that is concrete and sensual and anything but dead. Creating through reduction a white world existing in some fourth dimension of non-Euclidean geometry, *Imagination Dead Imagine* confronts us with its own uneasy presentness. As readers we become obsessed with the materialization of this precise illusion, its menace and its progressive validation. Beckett transforms imaginative vulnerability into imaginative power. Though his language here has no range of application and meaning authorizing us to make a subtext from the text we read, it makes a shocking immediacy out of incompleteness and instability. Central to the composition is consistency, not symbolism. The story is concerned solely with linking its own absolute qualities, its own inner vitality and definiteness, within the limits of its small boundaries. The evocative force of *Imagination Dead Imagine* makes no appeal to any reality outside itself; it is, instead, a combination of its own visual and verbal certainties:

> Leave them there, sweating and icy, there is better elsewhere. No, life ends and no, there is nothing elsewhere, and no question now of ever finding again that white speck lost in whiteness, to see if they still lie still in the stress of that storm, or of a worse storm, or in the black dark for good, or the great whiteness unchanging, and if not what they are doing.

Enough, however, situates reduction in a far more elaborate verbal environment. In this work Beckett makes us trace the shape of an emotion, not the shape of any steady object. The problem for the reader is to understand the terms of a human relationship, not in its existence:

> One day he told me to leave him. It's the verb he used. He must have been on his last legs. I don't know if by that he meant me to leave him for good or only to step aside a moment. I never asked myself the question. I never asked myself any questions but his. Whatever it was he meant I made off without looking back. Gone from reach of his voice I was gone from his life. Perhaps it was that he desired. There are questions you see and don't ask yourself.

Beckett evokes a note of real tragedy, something elegiac, an emotion of deep melancholy. Shaping into words a sense of loss, textuality here is "bereft, rid if you prefer, of occasion in every shape and form, ideal as well as material."

Enough is Beckett's *A la recherche du temps perdu* in miniature. Proust's multivolume canvas is, in effect, reinvented to conform to the reduced scale it occupies within the limits of Beckett's small planet. As Marcel remembers images before recalling the density and specificity of significant detail, *Enough* gives us "all that goes before forget." Referential images are alternately arithmetic or romantic, evoking the old antinomy between reason and imagination. Tempting us to do some "literary book-keeping" outside Beckett's text, this piece recalls Keatsian "flowers at my feet" from "Ode to a Nightingale," Shelley's lyre from "Ode to the West Wind," and Yeats's mythic bird from "Leda and the Swan." The couple in *Enough* has ambitions as sidereal as those of any romantic. In this "endless equinox" the younger member of the pair has "Aquarius hands," and the two are die-hard stargazers: "In order from time to time to enjoy the sky he resorted to a little round mirror. Having misted it with his calf he looked in it for the constellations. I have it! he exclaimed referring to the Lyre or the Swan. And often he added that the sky seemed much the same." As steadfast as Keats's "bright star," Beckett's seedy pathfinders choose to gaze at constellations sharing a fate as mysteriously linked as their own. Lyra and Cygnus float in space next to one another and appear in April as a dual "mansion above."

A work which on first reading may seem to refer to nothing outside of itself, *Enough* slowly begins to operate on more than one level of meaning and in more than one dimension of form. Such an assumption leads us to unexpected discoveries, warning us not to look at this work superficially, for it contains more than first meets the eye. In making consistent use of inherited stellar imagery, Beckett constructs the language of *Enough* from the ruins of the romantic past. But made of remembrances rather than events, this astrological swan's way is also a variation on a theme by Proust. Unlike *Imagination Dead Imagine, Enough* is, then, a monster of allusion.

When we discover that there is both a surface and a depth to this small piece, we try to focus on one or the other. When we deliberately focus on the surface, the depth becomes apparent and gets in the way. When we try to focus on the depth, the surface distracts us. Although this brings dynamic vitality to the text and seems to offer us important options in our response, it raises more problems than it solves. *Enough* will not put itself to rest. Though a pattern of romantic allusion hovers beneath the surface, we are not quite sure of its function when we uncover it. Tragedy? Irony? Humor? All three? Certitude proves to be not very much to the point, for it is the possible plurality of intention which engages our imagination and makes us read the piece further—or again—in the hope of finding additional clarification.

Mathematics merely heightens the determined confusion of all specificity. Though their talk is seldom of "geodesy" (the pun on *odyssey* indicating that branch of applied mathematics which attempts to learn about the earth's surface by looking at the sky), Beckett's odd couple takes flight, nonetheless, in more literary numerical strategies: "we must have covered several times the equivalent of the terrestrial equator. At an average speed of roughly three miles per day and night. . . . What mental calculations bent double hand in hand! Whole ternary numbers we raised in this way to the third power sometimes in downpours of rain. Graving themselves in his memory as best they could the ensuing cubes accumulated." As we quickly see, the number three exercises an especially mantic power in *Enough.* Though he spends his days "wedged together bent in three," the narrator speculates that given "three or four lives I might have accomplished something." The personal testimony features a continuing preoccupation with multiples of three as well: (3X2) "I cannot have been more than six when he took me by the hand"; (3X3) "Nine times out of ten [his murmurs] did not concern me"; (3X100) "The fact remains we often came upon this sort of mound some three hundred feet in height." "The art of combining," asserts the same narrator, "is not my fault. It's a curse from above." Probability and statistics, a special damnation for the Beckett hero, fall into similar numerical trios. There are, naturally enough, nine varieties of "communication" and "redeparture" offered in the text. The negating statement, "I never asked myself the question," appears three times, and the narrator even refers to his "disgrace" on three separate occasions.

The significance of the number three, though it brings unity to the composition of *Enough* and makes us search for the kind of symbolic texture we have already said we

were not going to look for, seems to be as arbitrary as it is consistent. It is, however, a formal contrivance asking us to draw a metaphysical implication from a trinity whose only certainty is stylistic virtuosity. It points nowhere but back to itself. For in *Enough* the numbers that recur, the allusive content, and the emotional effect by no means coincide or even mutually support each other. "I am concerned with a thing's not being what it was," Beckett's collaborator Jasper Johns observed, "with its becoming something other than what it is, with any moment in which one identifies a thing precisely, and with the slipping away of that moment."

Certainty continues to elude our fingertips in *Enough,* for its numerology is not nearly so tightly encased as the pervasive trinitarian regularity might lead us to assume. In Beckett's world not everything works out. Let us look for a moment at some of the disturbing reports cited in the text:

> (1) . . . we must have covered several times the equivalent of the terrestrial equator. At an average speed of roughly three miles per day and night.

> (2) . . . the end of this long journey was my life . . . the last seven thousand.

> (3) It is then I shall have lived . . . ten years at the very least.

> (4) If I arrive at ten years it is thanks to our pedometer.

> (5) I am speaking of our last decade comprised between the two events described. It veils those that went before and must have resembled it like blades of grass.

> (6) He was not given to talk. An average of a hundred words per day and night. Spaced out. A bare million in all.

If the narrator is to be trusted, he traveled with his companion a little over 10,000 miles or an average of approximately 1,000 miles during each of the years "between the two events described." Statistically, however, this estimation is off by almost 100 miles. The couple actually covers an average of closer to 1,100 miles per year:

$$365.25 \times 3 = 1,095.75 \text{ miles per year}$$

Thus begins a whole series of numerical irregularities and uncertainties. Though the text makes it clear that the narrator has been accompanying his partner since childhood, it never tells us anything definite about the duration of this experience. Several decades seem to be involved. Besides the crucial ten years "between the two events described," the "latter" decade mentioned in the text implies a minimum of twenty years and "our last decade" indicates a minimum of thirty. This leads us to another problem. Though the couple has apparently done this "several" times, how long does it take them to traverse a distance equal to the terrestrial equator? If we assume that we are dealing with our own planet (the earth's equator = 24,902.45 miles), a matter by no means specified in Beckett's story, the problem works out something like this:

$$24,902.45 \div 1,095.75 = 22.725 \text{ years}$$

If it takes approximately 23 years to travel this distance, three outings, a total of approximately 69 years, might be a likely figure. Unfortunately for those of us with a passion for precision, this solution fails to coincide with that of the next problem we address. If the narrator's companion spoke "an average of a hundred words per day and night," we come up with slightly more than 23 years:

$$1,000,000 \div 100 = 10,000 \text{ days}$$

$$10,000 \div 365.25 = 27.38 \text{ years}$$

Despite all our "mental thuggee," the figures cannot be correlated with anything resembling exactitude. Everything remains only "more or less, more or less." In this way Beckett's numbers, both the neat triplets and the Dada mathematics, assume their actuality in potentiality. Integers are disturbingly alive, glistening with possibility, demanding that we look at them as well as the words signifying them with a new responsiveness. The "preoccupation with the significance of numbers" simultaneously parodies and re-energizes the poetic use of figures in Dante and their symbolic use in Joyce. But we must seek no mediation, no correlation, and no final reconciliation, for numbers, like everything else in this story, are simply and dynamically present. Like metaphors, they are expressive and evocative rather than scientific or informative.

In its reliance on familiar romantic images and in its curious transformation of elementary number concepts, *Enough,* unlike *Imagination Dead Imagine,* is by no means the tight little island unto itself that it initially appears to be. This short piece is rife with the broken fragments of recognizable Beckett iconography. Its first paragraph notes the "art and craft" of a writing implement as heroic as the inspired collaborator previously memorialized in *Malone Dies;* the title resurrects Grehan's "ample" Spenserian ending in the poem "To Nelly" which Mr. Hackett recites to the Nixons in *Watt:* "Enough—." Even the "flowers" fall into line within Beckett's "stiff interexclusiveness." As stemless as Monet's "water lilies" (though they can be eaten, "no brightening our buttonhole with these"), they are mysteriously sunken into earth as is Winnie herself. We have seen such self-reference before in Beckett's work. But fragments come in different shapes and sizes; those in *Enough* carry just enough weight to keep the technique from disappearing completely.

Sex in *Enough* is similarly self-referential. For though Beckett's narrator realizes Molly Bloom's fantasy ("When he told me to lick his penis I hastened to do so"), femininity is nowhere suggested until the conclusion, when "breasts" startles us as the only mention of gender identification—an ambiguous one at that. In the interim the couple has turned "over as one man," the same strange writhing Molloy has asked us to consider:

> Louise was a woman of an extraordinary flatness, physically speaking of course, to such a point that I am still wondering, in the comparative silence of my last abode, if she was not a man rather or at least an androgyne. She had a somewhat hairy face, or am I imagining it, in the interests of the narrative? . . . Could a woman

have stopped me as I swept towards mother? Probably. Better still, was such an encounter possible, I mean between me and a woman? Now men, I have rubbed up against a few men in my time, but women? Oh well, I may as well confess it now, yes, I once rubbed up against one. . . . She went by the peaceful name of Ruth I think. . . . Perhaps after all she put me in her rectum. A matter of complete indifference to me, I needn't tell you. But is it true love, in the rectum? That's what bothers me sometimes. Have I never known true love, after all? She too was an eminently flat woman. . . . Perhaps she too was a man, yet another of them. But in that case surely our testicles would have collided, while we writhed. Perhaps she held hers tight in her hand, on purpose to avoid it.

Enough features encounters more elliptical, but no less pornographic:

> I bowed right down. He halted and waited for me to get into position. As soon as out of the corner of his eye he glimpsed my head alongside his the murmurs came. Nine times out of ten they did not concern me. But he wished everything to be heard including the ejaculations and broken paternosters that he poured out to the flowers at his feet.
>
> He did not like to feel against his skin the skin of another. Mucous membrane is a different matter.
>
> We turn over as one man when he manifests the desire. I can feel him at night pressed against me with all his twisted length. . . . With his upper hand he held and touched me where he wished. Up to a certain point. The other was twined in my hair. He murmured of things that for him were no more and for me could not have been.
>
> Ejaculations. Too few for even a cursory survey.

Like Molloy and Malone, like Hamm and Clov, like the murmurers in the mud in *How It Is,* the "he" in *Enough* is on his "last legs." One is literally overwhelmed by such an amazing variety of "funambulistic" staggers. But no Sucky Moll postscripts "oyster kisses" here. In their place Beckett offers words, each leading in a different direction, for condensation and reduction means that there is more than one source of images clamoring for the attention of the conscious mind. "Ejaculations" are, then, simultaneously phallic and verbal, each alternative competing for the reader's attention. Surface and depth, foreground and background, are perpetually set in verbal motion.

Though *Enough* displays a speaker who is as much an Astrophel as his kinsman Murphy or the narrator searching for the Wains at the end of **"First Love,"** in terms of tone and imagery this piece most closely parallels the spirit of *Mercier and Camier.* "Fraught with more events than could fit in a fat tome," the novel could be read as the genuine article for which *Enough* might be a possible abstract. That strange, possibly homosexual pair, whose rites of passage we study in miniature in *Enough,* are the literary descendants of the novel's two heroes. Sharing a sack, an umbrella, a handkerchief, a raincoat, and a pencil, Mercier and Camier experience similar intrigues "as one man":

> This brought them to the end of the alley where, as one man, they turned back again.
>
> Soon falls back began to enter into play, now Camier accompanying Mercier (in his fall), now the reverse, and now the two collapsing simultaneously, as one man, without preconcertation and in perfect interindependency.

Unhappily married to Toffana, a very tough Anna Livia Plurabelle that we never see, Mercier is curiously without desires: "Were I not without desires, said Mercier, I would buy me one of those hats, to wear on my head." The passive partner in his travels with detective Camier, Mercier follows the leader as willingly as the unnamed "I" in *Enough* says he/she follows his/hers:

> I did all he desired. I desired it too. For him. Whenever he desired something so did I. He only had to say what thing. When he didn't desire anything neither did I. In this way I didn't live without desires. If he had desired something for me I would have desired it too. Happiness for example or fame. I only had the desires he manifested. But he must have manifested them all. . . . We must have had the same satisfactions. The same needs and the same satisfactions.

Each story, though one is realistic and the other abstract in comparison, outlines the break-up of what seems to have been a beautiful but impossible relationship. In place of how-it-is, we learn the-way-it-was. In *Mercier and Camier* the narrator is "with them all the time" and records the density of incident and experience. *Enough* traces only that very little bit "that goes before forget." Reduction cancels everything but the flowers.

Though *Mercier and Camier* foreshadows Gogo and Didi's delightful "little canters," the mathematical computations of Molloy, the time schedules of *Watt,* the inventories, agendas, and lists of *Malone Dies,* Zeno's millet grains from *Endgame,* the "quincunxes" of *The Lost Ones,* and the "arsy-versy" of *All That Fall* and *Imagination Dead Imagine,* it brings to *Enough* the salient features of flowers, mucous membrane, and absurd gymnastics necessary to insure adequate star-gazing:

> I see our sister-convict Venus, said Camier, foundering in the skywrack. I hope it's not for that you dragged me here.
>
> Further, further, said Mercier.
>
> Camier screened his eyes with his hand.
>
> Further north, said Mercier. North, I said, not south.
>
> Wait, said Camier.
>
> A little more, a little less.
>
> Is that your flowers? said Camier.
>
> Did you see? said Mercier.
>
> I saw a few gleams, said Camier.

> You need to have the knack, said Mercier.
>
> I'd do better with my knuckles in my eyes, said Camier.
>
> The ancients' Blessed Isles, said Mercier.
>
> They weren't hard to please, said Camier.
>
> You wait, said Mercier, you only barely saw, but you'll never forget, you'll be back.
>
> What is that grim pile? said Camier.
>
> A hospital, said Mercier. Diseases of the skin.
>
> The very thing for me, said Camier.
>
> And mucous membrane, said Mercier.

As the "stink of artifice" in *Mercier and Camier* is reduced to the miniaturized "art and craft" of *Enough,* the "moreness" of Beckett's early work prepares us for the "lessness" of his late style.

Mercier and Camier are on a journey to nowhere in particular. "What does it matter," cries Mercier, "where we are going? We are going, that's enough." They set off to leave town only to discuss whether or not they should return. It is the journey and not the arrival that matters, for this is another Beckett work-in-process, not progress. No incident of plot is elaborated and no psychological motivation is probed. The journey in fact consists only of words.

But *Mercier and Camier* are hardly the same abstracted ejaculators we encounter in *Enough.* ("If there's one thing I abominate, said Mercier, it's talking walking"). The novel places the pair in a fictionalized Ireland, in the area immediately surrounding Dublin with its canals. Saints Patrick and Teresa work in a barroom owned by Mr. Gast and managed by Mr. Gall, the latter making a return engagement after his role as piano-tuner in *Watt.* Francis Xavier Camier, a Soul-of-Discretion detective like Jacques Moran, has a rendezvous with a Mr. Conaire, listed as an "hors d'oeuvre" in the French. No matter how far the pair roams, they are never far from the fair Helen's Kidderminster carpet, on which strange murmurings take place on damp forenoons. When we first meet Mercier and Camier, they are "old young." But time, that "old fornicator," makes their weariness physical as well as spiritual:

> Looking back on it, said Camier, we heard ourselves speaking of everything but ourselves.
>
> We didn't bring it off, said Mercier, I grant you that. He took thought a moment, then uttered this fragment, Perhaps we might—.
>
> What a deathtrap, said Camier, wasn't it here we lost the sack?
>
> Not far from here, said Mercier. . . .
>
> All . . . more or less nowadays? said Mercier.
>
> Pardon? said Camier.
>
> I ask if all is, you know, more or less, with you, nowadays.
>
> No, said Camier.

A few minutes later tears welled up into his eyes. Old men weep quite readily, contrary to what one might have expected.

And you? said Camier.

Nor, said Mercier.

Enough gives us a similar sense of loss, but without the realistic events to frame the sentiment. The result is an emotion not so much absent as abstracted, reduced to the eloquent dimensions of a fragment. In *Mercier and Camier* there are abrupt transitions from chapter to chapter and from paragraph to paragraph; in *Enough* they are from sentence to sentence and from word to word. Whereas *Mercier and Camier* provides us with summaries at the end of every two chapters, resembling the Addenda to *Watt, Enough* offers us no such tidy aids to reflection. There is only just "enough" plot to keep the emotion going. And though the thread of plot is distinct, the impression of the whole is one of mistiness and melancholy. What remains is pure atmosphere. We are no longer in the realm of fiction, but in that of mood and mystery.

In Beckett's late style a little language is a dangerous thing. Words, appearing in new compositions and relationships, are in a constant state of becoming, condensing in their wake not only traditional concepts of time, but also of space on the page. In *Enough* memory is Beckett's principal subject and he makes it the measure of time by embracing several decades in a succession of briefly recorded moments. In this work, despite all our mathematical calculations, there is, in fact, no real time. Images evoke events which make their own conjunctions. Only images remain in "all that goes before forget," for the nature of rational thought is illusory. Despite its rich allusive flavor, *Enough* therefore defies the reader to construe the piece as an imitation of anything but a raw emotion recollected in its own miniaturized tranquility.

Within the dimensions of its own small boundaries, *Enough* is, therefore "a whole." Beckett sets "enough" in a variety of verbal situations: "One pair of gloves was enough," "That was enough for him," "And as if that was not enough, I kept telling myself he was on his last legs," and finally, "Enough my old breasts feel his old hands." "Enough" is even present in its Latin equivalent, *satis:* "We must have had the same satisfactions. The same needs and the same satisfactions." Within the work "enough" achieves special power when it is frequently contrasted with the opposing qualities of excessiveness and deficiency: "Too much at a time is too much," "Too much silence is too much," "Or it's my voice too weak at times," "Mine was naturally too loose for years," and "Too few for even a cursory survey." The narrator claims to have not enough knowledge ("when brought up short by all I know") and not enough time ("Given three or four lives I might have accomplished something"). Against the measurements of enough (enough what?), too little, and too much, Beckett has his narrator tease us with the hint of some unspecified something that is more than enough: "All I know comes from him," "I won't repeat this apropos all my bits of knowledge," "To those engulfed years it seems reasonable to impute my education for I don't remember having learnt anything in those I remember," and

"It is with this reasoning that I calm myself when brought up short by all I know." Recycling Didi's calm from *Godot* ("The English say cawm"), this narrator never tells us calmly or otherwise what he knows and what he does not know. "After such knowledge," we wonder along with Eliot, "what forgiveness?" "What do I know of a man's destiny?" speculates the Beckett hero; "I could tell you more about radishes." Out of this dilemma, however, Beckett weaves his ironic whole, punning all the way: "One day . . . he explained to me that anatomy is a whole," "They had on the whole a calming action," "We were on the whole calm." Offering us an encounter with integration out of fragmentation, the restricted verbal landscape of *Enough* therefore retains its individual concrete identity.

All density is in language itself. There is no need to introduce anything foreign to the actuality of this text: its words have already accumulated in their singular compactness an enormous quantity of intentions and suggestions. *Enough* is, therefore, gigantic, for it attempts to show through the ebb and flow of its own words the possibilities and relativities inherent in existence. The "eve of my disgrace" is both a moment in the narrator's personal history and a deliberate pun on the memorable Fall of Man. In this density of word texture meanings overlap rather than exist side by side. There are none of those vacant spaces another composition might be tempted to fill in with elaboration. "A hundredth of a second for an insect that lives for some minutes," wrote Marcel Brion in the pages of *Our Exag,* "will be loaded with as many experiences as a year for a long-living animal." Since there is a danger at any moment of rising up into rhetoric or, worst of all, symbolism, Beckett manipulates language the way T. S. Eliot said it was necessary to treat English: with animosity. Conventional language is the medium of "cunning literary artificers," worn-out and threadbare. Beckett, like Joyce before him, desophisticates language. Indexification is refined out of existence, an unnecessary intrusion. Objects, motivations, explanations, the paraphernalia of fiction, have been subjected to a rigorous cleansing process of cancellation and omission. Like Cézanne capturing light and shadows falling on rooftops by painting them as geometric shapes, Beckett in *Enough* is no longer interested in any occasion on which to situate his story. The language is tonal and linear, for the attempt is to make a word vibrate with the resonance and richness of an image.

Enough is, therefore, quite enough: its narrow boundaries frame, ironically, an enormous range of potentiality. No two encounters with this text can ever be exactly alike, for the simultaneity and multiplicity of readings forever compete for our attention. Here brevity is not only the soul of Beckett's wit, but the mark as well of that unique transfiguration he has worked in just enough prose to make the adventure of reading this work a continuous temptation. A combination of completion and continuity, *Enough* upsets our rational expectation of form and content in favor of free extension in a world of possibility. Reduction becomes a "form to accommodate the mess" because within the dimensions of extreme brevity Beckett imposes beginnings, middles, and endings which serve as tottering structures, but structures all the same. A world of "more or less," "thereabouts," "enough," and "imagination dead imagine" coalesces with the concreteness and clarity of the most classical of all virtues, spartan simplicity. "The forms are many," writes Beckett in *Malone Dies,* "in which the unchanging seeks relief from its formlessness."

Parrish Dice Henry   (essay date 1982)

SOURCE: "Got It At Last, My Legend: Homage to Samuel Beckett," in *The Georgia Review,* Vol. XXXVI, No. 2, Summer, 1982, pp. 429-34.

[*In the essay below, Henry focuses on the allusions in* Company *to Beckett's earlier works.*]

Company's fifty-seven pages make it rather an extended utterance from the master of compression whose appearances of the recent past have carried titles like *Lessness, Ends and Odds,* and *Fizzles.* What's more, it is a strikingly intimate book, arriving as something almost in the nature of a backstage pass, an invitation to the studio, and thus offering unique pleasures for admirers of Beckett's work. But this is a tale for careful telling, of necessity oblique.

Samuel Beckett's career as a noted author began, of course, with the astonishing success of *Waiting for Godot,* first published in France in 1952. That same year saw the release in the United States of *Limelight,* a film that is arguably Charlie Chaplin's most personal effort. *Limelight* is set in London in 1914, the place and very nearly the time of Chaplin's own stage beginnings with the Fred Karno Pantomime Troupe. Charlie plays Calvero, a once famous music-hall comedian now grown old and troubled by self-doubt and alcohol. The film has all the marks of finale, of nostalgia, of chastened age's return to the scene of youth's love and triumph. Chaplin includes his family—like a painter doing a *Last Supper* for his own final canvas and putting his relatives at the table in period costume. Even his children have roles, and Edna Purviance (who had appeared as Chaplin's leading lady in some thirty-five films between 1915 and 1923) also returns as an extra in a ballet scene.

And Buster Keaton—it's he who jogs the Chaplin-Beckett connection, after all. Buster Keaton's there too. *Limelight* pairs the two supreme artists of silent-film comedy (for the only time) in roles as music-hall comedians presenting a concert recital. Chaplin plays the violin while a nearsighted Keaton attempts a piano accompaniment. It's all you'd dream, an impossible minuet of disasters, exquisite skills determined upon the portrayal of incompetence. (So Samuel Beckett, in 1949: "to be an artist is to fail, as no other dare fail.")

All this history and homage, this allegedly necessary roundabout, is nurtured by the shared qualities prominent in both works. *Company,* like *Limelight,* is insistently retrospective and openly autobiographical, and both pieces, in their hint of conscious finale, suggest more than a little of *The Tempest.* But it is Keaton, surely, who highlights the relationship. If Beckett, in all his work, has paid the artist's highest praise to silent-film comedy in general—by making its world one with the somber fabric of his own—he has singled out Keaton for his particular hero. There

are little allusive nods to film comedy throughout the stories and plays—the "hardy laurel" of *Watt,* for example—but of course it is *Film,* the twenty-four minute short of 1964 (Beckett's only venture in cinema), that brings Keaton most forcibly to mind. He is its star, very nearly its only character, and the film derives much of its strange power from the viewer's knowledge that the face so determinedly averted until the final tableau is Keaton's famous deadpan.

Film is only one among *Company*'s many retrospections, but the allusion is sharply explicit—in this latest work's reference to "the eye. Filling the whole field. The hood slowly down. Or up if down to begin." This is how *Film* opens, and the eye is Buster Keaton's. Published accounts of the Beckett-Keaton collaboration are few and brief, but they make for lovely reading. Tom Dardis' fine biography of Keaton (*Keaton: The Man Who Wouldn't Lie Down*) mentions the restaurant conversations where Keaton regaled the company with stories from the great days in the twenties—the days of *The General* and *Go West* and *The Navigator.* "Beckett would listen intently to Buster's stories, a small smile of pure delight on his face."

The same "small smile" is available in *Company* to Beckett's own reader/listener, the one who has seen *Godot* and *Happy Days,* has read *Malone Dies,* just as the Beckett who listened to Keaton had seen and loved his films. Beckett even gives this smile a name in one out-of-the-way spot (a 1936 review)—it's "the profound *risolino* that does not destroy"—and *Company* nourishes it throughout. It's a smile, as Beckett puts it in the early story **"Walking Out,"** which is "proof against all adversity" and which is of a piece with the author's encompassing compassion, the sorrowing love for all creatures evident in all of his work. Molloy, for example, meets a shepherd with his sheep and asks if they are bound to the fields or to the shambles. Receiving no answer, he finds himself thereafter troubled by "persisting doubts, as to the destination of those sheep, among which there were lambs."

Company presents its own instances of such compassion—as, for example, when the introduction of a fly is considered: "Let there be a fly. For him to brush away." A moment, however, is sufficient for reconsideration: "But no. He would not brush away a fly." (Files, too, have buzzed before in Beckett's pages, and recur here as yet another instance of *Company*'s retrospections. In "Serena I," a poem published in 1935, a "common housefly" is addressed as "my brother the fly.")

Beckett, then, has come to his readers as an unclamorous Ahab, a bowed affirmer, master of those who don't know, chronicler of the "little murmur of unconsenting man" (this from *The Unnamable*). Reading his stories, watching his plays, one learns to be attentive to small gestures, to the tiny victories which appear as patches in a fabric of loss: Vladimir gives his coat to the sleeping Estragon in *Godot,* and then walks about swinging his arms to keep warm. Negg, in *Endgame,* saves part of his biscuit for Nell, and Holloway, in *Embers,* comes alone at night through the snow at Bolton's call. Such gestures may seem trival, a matter for no great rejoicing, but they are completed in a world where gestures of any kind are accomplished only at great cost. And they are appreciated, too, by their beneficiaries, who do not ask lightly. When one asks something of another, Beckett tells us, one is, "Begging. Of the poor" (this from *Embers*). Winnie, in *Happy Days,* muses at some length on this matter:

> One does not appear to be asking a great deal, indeed at times it would hardly seem possible— to ask less—of a fellow creature—to put it mildly—whereas actually—when you think about it—look into your heart—see the other—what he needs—peace—to be left in peace—then perhaps the moon—all this time-asking for the moon.

Winnie, like the Keaton of *Film,* is also brought on in *Company,* though her appearance is a subtle one—as easily missed as the appearance of Chaplin's young children in *Limelight.* It causes no interruption, but it brings up the small smile, the *risolino,* when it's noticed. "What a mercy to have that to turn to," says *Company* at one point. This immediately suggests Winnie, since she's the most determined optimist in all of Beckett's "gallery of moribunds" (this from *Molloy*), the one who speaks continually, from her scorched mound, of the "many mercies" and "great mercies" that console her.

But Winnie, in addition to her optimism, is also a thoroughgoing Miltonist, numbering among the tatters of her "classics" several tags from *Paradise Lost.* The *risolino* thus deepens when the reader, put in mind of Winnie by *Company*'s reference to "mercy," finds the phrase "darkness visible" in the same paragraph. These are recondite matters, certainly, an insider's pleasures, and they may have the taint of self-gratulation upon them as well, but the pleasure is nonetheless a fine one, attendant on the shared experience which makes such obliquities possible. At any rate, *Company,* as it unfolds these intimacies, is surely the closest thing to *apologia,* portrait of the old man as an artist, likely to appear from this supremely reticent master.

Company opens with multiple perspectives immediately deployed. "A voice comes to one in the dark. Imagine." A story is thus set in motion, two "characters" moved to interaction, a first (voice) brought to a second (one). There is, additionally, a third, shortly to be named (provisionally) "another devising," to whom the terse imperative, "Imagine," may be addressed.

The story that is *Company,* then, apparently devised by Samuel Beckett, dawns upon the initiation of another story, the product of "another devising." A series is broached, the process of fabulation introduced as theme. This comes as no surprise—characters in stories who are themselves storytellers abound in Beckett's universe. Hamm, for example, in *Endgame,* tells Clov with some pride that he's "got on with my story."

What is new in *Company* is the explicitness of motive— what purposes impel the telling of these stories, the devising of these "characters"? —and the tenacity with which the series of tellers is pursued to its source. Suggestion of motive comes early, in the same phrase which names the narrator: "another devising it all for company." The title itself directs attention to this phrase, here appearing in the

text for the first time. It's for company the deviser devises, imagines stories, creates characters and moves them, like Malone, "down the long familiar galleries, with my little suns and moons that I hang aloft." It's for company he puts himself to such exertion, imagining "figments to temper his nothingness" much as Vladimir and Estragon temper their own with all the distractions, every "little canter" they can muster.

In telling his story the deviser of *Company*—"a head abandoned to its ancient solitary resources," as *The Unnamable* styles him—bases his narrative decisions upon such criteria. Which alternative, each time alternative inspirations present themselves, will provide, being chosen, "the better company"—this is the question of moment. Given, for example, a problem of lighting, a choice between two possible shades or types of darkness: "The test is company. Which of the two darks is the better company."

This is the heart of the enterprise, then, the company itself, the fellow creature of our own devising who preserves us, however briefly, from the horror of solitude. The passage from *Godot,* deservedly famous, where Vladimir and Estragon discuss hanging themselves, centers on precisely this horror. A lengthy dispute over precedence—each wishes the other to hang himself first—is resolved at last by Estragon, in his most sustained logical effort of the play. "Gogo light—bough not break—Gogo dead. Didi heavy—bough break—Didi alone. Whereas—"

"Didi alone"—that's to be avoided, so long as it's possible, so long as company can be devised. This is the true motive, the heart's real cry, the need that moves drooling idiots to sleep with dolls in asylums. Malone's explanation is direct: "Yes, a little creature, I shall try and make a little creature, to hold in my arms, a little creature in my image, no matter what I say." And if each effort ends in failure—if *Company* closes with "you as you always were.// Alone." —what matters in the interim is the impulse toward creation, the need for "a little creature in my image" which links the whole series, devisers and devised.

What *Company* does, persistently, is to trace this chain of narrated narrators to its origin, the unsaid, unsayable sayer, the nothing source of all. "And whose voice asking this?" begins the central passage, as searching as anything Beckett has written:

> Who asks, Whose voice asking this? And answers, His soever who devises it all. In the same dark as his creature or in another. For company. Who asks in the end, Who asks? And in the end answers as above? And adds long after to himself, Unless another still. Nowhere to be found. Nowhere to be sought. The unthinkable last of all. Unnamable. Last person. I.

We knew it all the time, of course, that "in the end" it was "I"—Samuel Beckett himself, the ultimate homunculus, tiny within all the others, last generation, first person. Didn't we? But wait—the whole force of such musings operates to call into question such apparent integrities and identifications. This "I" stands revealed, in the light of such analytics, as no less "creature" and "figment" than any other finally unnamable character. Such probings have long been standard in the Beckett repertoire. In

Proust, for example, published in 1931, one reads that the "aspirations of yesterday were valid for yesterday's ego, not for to-day's," and this because "we are other, no longer what we were before the calamity of yesterday."

Having thus undermined conventions basic to the craft it practices, **Company** goes on to fly in the teeth of its own knowing. Its ubiquitous retrospections and its passages of unabashed autobiography present themselves in a relationship of open paradox to the suggested impossibility of an enduring self. This too will not surprise Beckett's readers—things admitted impossible but nonetheless asserted are recurrent in his art. "I can't go on, I'll go on," concludes *The Unnamable*. **Imagination Dead Imagine** is a prose piece published in English in 1966, and among the figures of **The Lost Ones** are some seen "making unmakable love."

Prominent among **Company**'s retrospections is "the old lutanist" described as "now perhaps singing praises with some section of the blest at last." This is none other than the Belacqua (newly arrived in purgatory when Dante passed through nearly seven hundred years ago) who gave his name to one of Beckett's earliest antiheroes—the doomed philanderer, *Paradiso* fan, and spavined Gorgonzola eater: Belacqua Shuah (from **More Pricks Than Kicks,** published in 1934). Appropriately enough, since much has been made here of the "profound risolino," it is Belacqua who brings this same smile to the sober face of Dante. The lazy actions and laconic speech of the unzealous penitent move him to "smile a little" ("poco a riso").

Everybody's smiling, it seems—surely Beckett's reader does—to see again old Belacqua, back like Edna Purviance in *Limelight,* returned for a last curtain call. That's what **Company** is, at bottom: a family reunion, a curtain call for Belacqua, for Winnie, for all the greatcoat wearers from Watt to the "you" of **Company,** for Woburn from *Cascando*—for all the "gallery of moribunds" who brought company to their creator and to his readers. The autobiographical sections—the climb to "near the top of a great fir" and the subsequent jump so that the "great boughs break your fall" is one example—serve at last to summon the author too, to make him one with his company.

With **Company** Samuel Beckett tells us again, at seventy-five, that "Now does my project gather to a head./ My charms crack not, my spirits obey." With Malone he can say, again, with justice, "Got it at last, my legend."

Here they are, assembled on the stage, bowing gravely in the limelight, from their wheelchairs, urns, and garbage cans. Standing by their bicycles, crutches shipped across the handlebars, rocking in their chairs, immured in their greatcoats, tethered to their masters, their kites at their sides. What a fine company they are! How firmly they have established a home in our minds and our hearts! We can do our part, we who are his readers, his critics, his reviewers, his audience—we can do what Mann had the good sense to do for Kafka when he wrote an introduction for *The Castle.* He labeled it "Homage." We can give the help of our good hands to this Prospero. We can say thank you.

An excerpt from *Company*:

A voice comes to one in the dark. Imagine.

To one on his back in the dark. This he can tell by the pressure on his hind parts and by how the dark changes when he shuts his eyes and again when he opens them again. Only a small part of what is said can be verified. As for example when he hears, You are on your back in the dark. Then he must acknowledge the truth of what is said. But by far the greater part of what is said cannot be verified. As for example when he hears, You first saw the light on such and such a day. Sometimes the two are combined as for example, You first saw the light on such and such a day and now you are on your back in the dark. A device perhaps from the incontrovertibility of the one to win credence for the other. That then is the proposition. To one on his back in the dark a voice tells of a past. With occasional allusion to a present and more rarely to a future as for example, You will end as you now are. And in another dark or in the same another devising it all for company. Quick leave him.

Samuel Beckett, in his Company, *Grove Press, 1980.*

Antoni Libera   (essay date 1983)

SOURCE: *"The Lost Ones:* A Myth of Human History and Destiny," in *Samuel Beckett: Humanistic Perspectives,* edited by Morris Beja, S. E. Gontarski, and Pierre Astier, Ohio State University Press, 1983, pp. 145-56.

[*In the following essay, Libera views* The Lost Ones *as a mythic narrative that portrays the evolution of the human species.*]

The Lost Ones, like other works by Samuel Beckett, reflects two separate but parallel realities, one objective and one subjective, but the latter is only another way of perceiving the former. In other words, while the narration of **The Lost Ones** is a description and a source of information, apparently objective, it is at the same time an interpretation and a commentary. Someone—whom we shall call the observer—finds himself in an unrealistic, seemingly underground universe ruled by its own internal time so that we cannot determine how long he has been there. His observations enable him to establish a synthetic image of this strange world. After explaining to himself the life and laws of this universe, he reports them on the basis of his own inferences. The text of **The Lost Ones** is the result, and it resembles a report or a treatise. It is at once an account and a speculation. Analyzing it, one has to distinguish information from interpretation, fact from hypothesis, and to bring to the fore those questions that the observer avoids.

The universe is described as a cylinder some sixteen meters in diameter (fifty meters circumference) and sixteen high, made of an unknown, rubber-like substance, which produces no sound when hit and which somehow emits light and heat. In the upper half of the wall, all the way round, there are twenty niches, disposed in four irregular quincunxes. Many of them are connected by tunnels hollowed in the wall, but some are blind. The niches and tunnels are something of a mystery. We never know whether they were made by the inhabitants of the cylinder or are natural features. Their irregular patterns as well as the fact that some are blind make the observer believe that they were probably drilled or dug by the cylinder dwellers: some "completed" by meeting other tunnels, one simply abandoned, "as though at a certain stage discouragement had prevailed." The observer, however, never speculates about the discouragement. In fact, he avoids a series of significant questions. He does tell us that the wall is so hard that even scratching a mark into it seems impossible and that the only tools available to the cylinder's inhabitants are their hands and the rungs of the ladders. But he doesn't speculate about how the niches might have been dug or what happened to the excavated substance? These are the sorts of questions the observer should be asking himself. He does, for example, explain a similar phenomenon, the missing rungs, which "are in the hands of a happy few. . . ." But how could the bodies arrange the niches so harmoniously, since, we learn, they plant their ladders randomly, without looking at the walls? Moreover, according to the observer, no one in the cylinder can appreciate this harmony. The origin of the niches and tunnels finally remains a mystery.

But there are aspects of the cylinder that we know with some certainty. It contains fifteen ladders that are part of the environment. The interior of the cylinder fluctuates with light and heat, which oscillate origin-less but regularly from wall, floor, ceiling, and even tunnels. The light increases and decreases four times per second, and the temperature changes from five to twenty-five degrees and back in eight seconds. From time to time suddenly and unexpectedly, both vibrations cease. This period never lasts more than ten seconds, in which time all activity in the cylinder stands still.

The cylinder is the abode of two hundred and five naked bodies of either sex and all ages. They differ in their motion and in the types of activities they perform and are divided into four groups: those who are in motion, those who pause sometimes, those who lead a sedentary life, and those who remain perfectly still. We learn that the first group contains twice as many members as the second, the second three times as many as the third, the third four times as many as the fourth, and the fourth group consists of 5 members. Thus one can easily calculate that 20 of the cylinder dwellers sit (4×5), 60 pause (3×20), and 120 are in motion (2×60). Four of the five still bodies ("the vanquished," as the observer calls them) sit with their backs against the wall in the position that "wrung from Dante one of his rare wan smiles." It is the position of Belacqua (a version of whom we saw in Beckett's early short stories) in Dante's Purgatory. Seeing him, Dante smiled and described his posture as follows: "one of them, who seemed to me weary, was sitting and clasping his knees, holding his face low down between them." Beckett echoes the image with the description of "the first among the vanquished": "She squats against the wall with her head between her knees and her legs in her arms. The left

hand clasps the right shinbone and the right the left forearm. . . . The left foot is crossed on the right."

The bodies in motion either circle around the arena, wait their turn to climb the ladders, look for an appropriate queue or an appropriate place to plant the ladder, stand in line or on the ladder, climb it, sit in the niches, or crawl in the tunnels. All these activities, and the order of performing them, are subject to certain rules, which the observer attempts to reconstruct. However, he is only partly successful. The helpless questions he asks prove that certain things remain unexplained.

All activities seem to have one purpose: finding a way out of the cylinder. But is there evidence that this is indeed the motive pushing the bodies to act? The various movements and actions may be merely a disorderly bustle. One has to admit finally that in the description of the life in the cylinder there is no proof that the action is purposive. Besides, a purely behavioristic description cannot in itself constitute a proof, since behaviorism does not explain intentions. All that we know about these motives comes from the observer.

He says, "From time immemorial rumour has it or better still the notion is abroad that there exists a way out." Those words are followed by a characterization of two fundamental beliefs shared by the inhabitants of the cylinder concerning the type and location of the exit: "One school swears by a secret passage branching from one of the tunnels and leading in the words of the poet to nature's sanctuaries. The other dreams of a trapdoor hidden in the hub of the ceiling, giving access to a flue at the end of which the sun and other stars would still be shining." But how does the observer know about all this? We assume he does know because he gives the information so categorically. Whenever he does *not* know or only suspects something, he never fails to make that clear. He states repeatedly that there are things he does not know—what is beyond the cylinder, for instance ("nothing but mystery")—and he does not find the ultimate explanation to many phenomena. There are no grounds, therefore, to believe that in this case his abilities are out of the ordinary. His intelligence and cognitive possibilities seem to be average. So how can he know the content of their beliefs? Granting that he does not possess supernatural powers, the only source of information is speech or writing, but the bodies in the cylinder do not use language (this is why the phrase "rumour has it" has been replaced by "the notion is abroad").

In such circumstances the observer's knowledge comes from introspection. We shall discuss shortly how this knowledge is possible, what it means, and what results from it. It is worth noticing now, however, that it casts a new light on the observer. It means that in a way he belongs to the cylindrical universe and that he is neither an outsider nor a stranger. Moreover, he seems to be connected or even tied to it. "The fact remains," he notes, ". . . that of these two persuasions the former is declining in favor of the latter but in a manner so desultory and slow and of course with so little effect on the comportment of either sect that to perceive it one must be in the secret of the gods." And earlier, ". . . Here all should die but with so gradual and . . . so fluctuant a death as to escape the notice even of a visitor." The observer is then not a visitor, but is in a privileged position, "in the secret of the gods."

The description of these beliefs, however, does not explain why the bodies look for the exit. It is not clear whether they want to leave their abode in order to find out what lies beyond its limits or simply to learn whether or not there is an exit. The members of the first group want only to satisfy their curiosity, since they believe that the mythical trapdoor in the ceiling would lead to a long chimney that itself would be impossible to climb. The others are closer to having the desire to leave the cylinder. However, considering the ambiguity of the expression "nature's sanctuaries," one does not know what they really expect on leaving their abode. It seems, however, that both beliefs indicate a longing for a world of nature as we understand it. For the first group, it is symbolized by the phrase "the sun and other stars," for the second by the abstract notion of "a sanctuary."

Let us now return to the observer's hypothesis. He believes that the process he discerns is the principle of life in the cylinder. The fact that the bodies are divided according to motion and that the immobile ones formerly moved like the others leads him to conclude that the quest is not perpetual and invariable, but is diminishing and one day will cease completely. This deduction, "the notion" as he calls it, enables him to create a general theory of life in the cylinder. In the very beginning, all the inhabitants were in motion: "all roamed without respite"; but finally, after a long period of constant bustle, the first body ("the woman vanquished") gave up. What was the reason? Was it due to the lack of force or rather to a lack of belief in the existence of the exit? We have no direct answer. However, the fact that the observer names the still bodies "the vanquished ones" and their attitude "abandonment" suggests that it was the second case, a failure of belief. He also stresses that the perfectly still cannot be considered as blind, that is, as people unable to continue to search. Significantly he attributes such a mistake to a "thinking being coldly intent on all these data and evidences," who seems to ignore the cylinder's fundamental secrets. These observations are further proof that the observer is not a mysterious stranger but a native.

After "the woman vanquished" came others, and the slow process—in which the bodies, one by one, grew motionless—was begun. The process suggests deterioration; the body begins to stop; then it assumes the sedentary position, and finally stops moving altogether. Sometimes the transition is more violent. In most cases, however, the change from one stage to another is neither abrupt nor irreversible. The body that assumed a sedentary position can continue its search just as before, until finally, having exhausted this need, it becomes immobile. Before it becomes perfectly still, however, it resumes the sedentary position and tries to search with its eyes. In order to describe the pace of this evolution, the observer uses the following simile: "Even so a great heap of sand sheltered from the wind lessened by three grains every second year and every following year increased by two. . . ." But no one comes back to the state of perpetual motion. Those

who paused will never circle incessantly again. This is perhaps the grain by which the metaphorical heap diminishes every second year.

The gradual abandonment of the quest leads inevitably to complete cessation. Considering that each body requires a different amount of time to go through the whole cycle, the body that will remain will be the one that requires most. The observer suspects that after waking from lethargy the most persistent body will begin its last search. By this time, the others will have renounced it long ago. After performing some movements (it is difficult to predict which), it will finally approach "the woman vanquished" and look into her eyes, where it will see nothing but "calm wastes." Then it will leave her and squat somewhere, becoming immobile forever. At the same time, the light will fade and the temperature will drop to zero. The supposition is astonishing, since it assumes that the light and heat depend somehow on the bodies and their quest. But according to the laws of the cylinder, the relationship should be reversed; motion should depend on energy fluctuation. But the future is finally beyond the observer, except for a creative (fictional) possibility: "Then light and climate will be changed in a way impossible to foretell. But the former may be imagined extinguished as purposeless and the latter fixed not far from freezing point." It is also worth noticing the observer's attitude to the notion of the exit. His description of life in the cylinder and his vision of the end make us believe that there are two possibilities: he is convinced either that there is no exit or that there is no possibility of finding it, at least in the time allowed to the most persistent body. However, we never learn the observer's direct opinion on this question. Whether an exit exists or not, and, if it does, where it is located, are questions never settled. He says only that the abode is "vast enough for flight to be in vain." The force of this statement is pragmatic. It neither explains the reason for this futility nor provides information. It only shows the observer's ignorance on this matter. We can assume that if he did have something in mind, he would put it forward. Once more we are led to believe that he belongs to the world of the cylinder.

Now that we have characterized the life in the cylinder and learned how it is seen and understood by the observer, we may try to determine the meaning of this world. What do the cylinder and its inhabitants represent? Who is the observer? And finally, how are we to understand the interpretation that he calls "the notion"? We have already suggested that the observer belongs to the world of the cylinder and, at the same time, uses human language and is familiar with Western culture (he knows Dante, for example). He symbolizes, therefore, a form of humanity in its weird abode, and the cylinder may be interpreted as the human world, or more precisely, its allegorical image. The two hundred naked bodies inhabiting the cylinder would be the humans living on earth, and their situation and behavior would represent the human condition and activity. Life in the cylinder is a model of human history. The anonymous observer, who is not one of the bodies, but knows at least as much about the cylinder as its inhabitants do and, moreover, can draw conclusions and speculate, is the personification of the human mind, which, in spite of being tied down to the earth, can, nonetheless, grasp it and learn the truth about it. He is the spirit of humanity—its power of self-analysis, its self-knowledge—which, though restricted by the boundaries within which man is confined, goes far beyond the individual consciousness. It is the sum of human experience and therefore a common property. This is why the result of its speculation, the observer's report (the text of *The Lost Ones*), is not written in the first person. His attempt, which we are shown, to gain both descriptive and interpretative knowledge constitutes not an individual observation but a myth, the myth of the history and destiny of humanity. His "notion" is a theory of history, and the final vision, an apocalyptic prophecy.

But what then is the significance of the myth? How does it help us interpret man and his life on earth? The gradually ceasing search for the exit, which is the essence of the bodies' lives, has a double meaning. It shows that the inhabitants of the cylinder long for a world different from the one they know. The need to leave their abode indicates that they are not "comfortable" there (there is not enough space, and it is at the same time too hot and too cold). This feeling is not, however, eternal and after some time dies down. Hence adaptation to these conditions *is* possible. The abandonment of the search means that the bodies have grown accustomed to the situation and no longer seek change. Adaptation, however, means closing one's eyes and ceasing to see, that is, not accepting the surrounding reality. This total renunciation leads to a final disappearance of the whole environment. After the last body becomes motionless, everything will turn into darkness, which in a way will annihilate the cylindrical world. It seems that the cylinder is not a cage into which the bodies were crammed but a lighted space created by the bodies themselves. The cylinder is just a glow that assumes an illusory shape in the middle of the neutral and boundless darkness. The cylinder is not, therefore, a necessary condition of the existence of the bodies but rather their function, or, still better, merely their way of being. The fact that this way of life restricts and compels the inhabitants of the cylinder and provokes them to run away, or alter their situation, means that its foundation—that is, the essence of being—is corrupt, false, and unfulfilling. Since the source of the erroneousness is the mere fact of existence, the only way of eliminating it is complete annihilation. This will not be attained immediately, but slowly, due to the gradually growing, albeit at first absent, awareness of the dependence. It is a process of purging, and this is the essence of the bodies' life.

What will happen when this process reaches its end? Or rather, putting aside the destruction of a given form of being, what is this end? The answer is to be found in the position the bodies finally assume, the position of the vanquished ones. At this point, let us notice that this very position is assumed by the two bodies in the white rotunda in *Imagination Dead Imagine*; there it suggests the fetal stage of life. Hence one can view the liberation from one form of life as a return to the starting point or to an even earlier phase. The two bodies in the white rotunda, however, and the two hundred bodies in the dark cylinder are something completely different. So the liberation is not

quite a return to the original starting point, but rather the approach to the beginning of a new one. It is like a return to a point situated in the same place but on a different circle of a spiral.

Beckett gives us no hint of the future. What is going to happen next? One can only guess. If we assume that in Beckett's late prose the human body symbolizes the potentiality inherent in the world of being something like man, and the eyes, by opening, the means by which that potentiality is realized, then the general vision of existence suggested by Beckett would be as follows: the world as substance wants to find a form for itself. It does this by lighting up its darkness with the light it can produce. However, the world as substance does not know what this form should be. In other words, it does not know how to go about illuminating itself, and by what light. This is why the comportment of the world resembles a persistent process of experimentation.

Originally it assumed the form of a rotunda, as in *Imagination Dead Imagine.* But the form was not satisfactory. The memorable words, "there is better elsewhere," express this. "Elsewhere" means here "differently," a different way of self-illumination. So the world "opens" itself anew and becomes the reality of the cylinder. But this again proves unacceptable. From this perspective it longs for a "natural" reality, with the sun and other stars. But there is no possibility of passing from the cylinder to that reality. There can only be a new "opening," a new self-illumination. This is why, the moment the world assumed the form of the cylinder, the light began to fade, which in practice meant a gradual abandonment of the quest. When the light disappears completely, the world comes back to the starting point and everything may begin again. What will be the result of the new attempt? What reality will the eyes see when they open once more in another way? Perhaps they will see that much-desired reality with the sun and other stars. Thus instead of the cylinder there will be the boundless firmament and the bodies will find themselves on the earth as true human beings. Will this be a successful and final attempt? *Is* it a successful and final attempt? *Is* the world satisfied with this world? To judge from our experience as human beings, it is not. If it were, the work entitled *The Lost Ones* could never have been created.

The dialectic of the world manifests itself not only in the ontological sphere but also on lower levels of cognition. The fluctuating substance of life that during millions of years appeared in various shapes, only to be subsequently rejected, assumed finally the human shape. Each of those forms—a protozoon, an alga, a Neanderthal man—was concentrated only on itself. Everything it did was meant to prolong the life of the species, to ensure its survival. In fact, however, this always resulted in the abandonment of that form and its attributes, and the passage to a different stage. Such was also the case with our predecessor, the Neanderthal man. He, gathering all the force he could muster, fought to withstand nature, to struggle for existence, to propagate his own kind, such as it was—hairy, a little stooped, and seemed with the very breath of his being intent on preserving his species, his Neanderthal world. And yet so intent, he destroys it with every step, with every act of propagation; so intent, he removes himself from it, razes it, thrusts it into oblivion. Instead of preserving his essence, he dissipates, annihilates it; instead of remaining himself, he becomes man.

Man's behavior is similar. He gradually exhausts all the possibilities of his existence. He becomes, for instance, the man of antiquity: he creates religions and laws that he retains for some time and then rejects in order to become a Christian. He is successively the man of the Middle Ages, the man of the Renaissance, the man of the Enlightenment. Each of these stages or forms of humanity is different, each has a different foundation, each represents a different kind of quest; each gives a different cognitive perspective and reveals a different vision of the world. For some this is a progression. For Beckett it is a regression. It is the elimination of various paths leading back to some starting point. The history of the world is in fact the history of "depopulation." It is the history of man's freeing himself from himself. Such a conviction is expressed in the very first sentence of *The Lost Ones*: "Abode where lost bodies roam each searching for its lost one" in the French version, "son dépeupleur." The entire text seems to support this thesis. The mysterious word *dépeupleur,* which appears only in the sentence quoted above, may finally refer to the way of getting out of oneself, a search for a radical way of enabling one to stop being oneself. The bodies search for an exit, but in fact each searches for its lost one. They want to leave their abode, but in fact they relinquish the search, which is the essence of their life. People build and expand man's kingdom on earth, but in fact they are leading to the exhaustion of their possibilities and attributes. They want to be more human and leave behind the world of animals, but in fact they begin to turn into a species that has nothing in common with man.

Does this myth utter a truth? There can be no final answer to this question. However, as opposed to other myths created by man, it does not pretend to be ultimate and unshaken, nor does it require blind faith. On the contrary, it seems to stress its own relativity. The constant refrain-like repetition, "if this notion is maintained," suggests the observer's skepticism toward his own ideas, which is quite understandable; for if he maintains the inconstancy and relativity of everything, he cannot exclude himself from this rule, and must question his own "notions."

Finally, it is also worth considering that the vision of man's history presented in *The Lost Ones* has much in common with the conceptions of Giambattista Vico. It might even be said that *The Lost Ones* is a poetic representation of his famous argument that all human actions lead to goals different from the original motivating force of those actions, namely, to the realization of the goals of divine Providence. And in this case, divine Providence is the will to change from one form of existence to another.

Rubin Rabinovitz   (essay date 1984)

SOURCE: "Learning to Live with Death: 'Echo's Bones'," in his *The Development of Samuel Beckett's Fiction,* University of Illinois Press, 1984, pp. 55-63.

[*Rabinovitz is an American critic and educator. In the following excerpt from his book* The Development of Samuel Beckett's Fiction, *he discusses "Echo's Bones," a story deleted from* More Pricks than Kicks.]

In its original version *More Pricks than Kicks* had not ten but eleven stories. However, an editor at Chatto and Windus (the firm that was about to publish Beckett's novel) decided that the last story, **"Echo's Bones,"** should be dropped. **"Echo's Bones"** has never appeared in print: the shortened version was used for all subsequent editions of the novel. It is easy to imagine why Beckett's editor—no doubt motivated by the best intentions—found the story objectionable. The setting is unrealistic, the plot improbable, the characters bizarre. The narrator's urbane conceits give way to thighslappers of a lower order (like a joke about an ostrich named Strauss who simply waltzes along). Even the costumes are outlandish: a cemetery groundsman, clad only in truss and boots, has a tattoo with the motto "Stultum Propter Christum" on his stomach.

At the beginning of the story Belacqua—dead, buried, and in most quarters forgotten—makes a return appearance. He may have given up the ghost, but he retains many bad habits—picking his nose in the presence of ladies, for example. He has acquired a taste for cigars, and a stock of them. Death has deprived him of his shadow, and he can no longer see his reflection in a mirror. But he is still a self-centered snob with a love for abstruse conversation.

The narrator presents three episodes as representative examples of Belacqua's postmortem activities. The first one begins with Belacqua sitting on a fence, deep in meditation. Suddenly Zaborovna Privet, an alluring woman with a taste for "sublime delinquencies," emerges from a nearby hedge (Privet from hedge: another thighslapper). Zaborovna introduces herself to Belacqua and, after a long exchange of erudite banter, invites him home. The prospect of collaborating in her sublime delinquencies leaves him cold, but when Zaborovna offers him fried garlic and Cuban rum, he lets himself be persuaded. (Death, so inhibitory to other pleasures, has left Belacqua with an enhanced appreciation of olfactory sensations.) The garlic is prepared, consumed, washed down with rum, but when Zaborovna tries to embrace Belacqua, he vanishes. She is left alone with nothing but "the dream of the shadow of the smoke of a rotten cigar."

The next episode begins with a pensive Belacqua again sitting on a fence. His meditations are interrupted when he feels a sharp pain in his back—Belacqua has been hit by a golf ball. Its owner approaches, putter in hand. He is Lord Gall of Wormwood: landowner, connoisseur, raconteur, inventor; a man of gigantic proportions, distinguished lineage, and unparalleled athletic skill. One tragic circumstance makes Lord Gall as bitter as his name suggests. Because he is childless and impotent, his estate will eventually revert to the Baron Extravas, his archenemy. Not only is the baron degenerate, evil-hearted, reptilian, and a bounder, but the syphilitic condition of Moll, Lord Gall's wife, can be attributed to him.

Lord Gall, his paternal instincts aroused, asks to be permitted to call his new acquaintance Adeodatus (after St. Augustine's illegitimate son). He then takes Belacqua to his aerie, a crow's nest on a great tree, and after a long exchange of recondite discourse proposes that Belacqua father a child on his behalf. The mercurial Belacqua, so recently a fugitive from Zaborovna's embraces, agrees. Unworried about hygienic complications ensuing from Moll's unfortunate illness, he joins Lord Gall on his mount (Strauss, the ostrich) and they gallop off. Belacqua meets Moll, whom he finds boring and repulsive, spends the night with her nevertheless; and proves to be remarkably virile, for a dead man. The episode, until now a blend of fairy tale, dream, and myth, ends as a shaggy-dog story. Moll becomes pregnant, but—alas for Lord Gall and his hopes for an heir—she gives birth to a girl.

Belacqua is again seated at the beginning of the last episode, not on a fence this time but on his own headstone. He encounters a character from "Draff," the cemetery groundsman who introduced the fable of the roses and the gardener. Now the groundsman is given a name, Doyle, as well as the striking truss-and-boots costume mentioned earlier. Doyle carries with him a considerable assortment of tools; as he explains, he plans to steal Belacqua's corpse. Belacqua assures him that such an endeavor would be pointless: he himself is the body. Doyle, however, ignores this as so much hocus-pocus. It may be that he is conversing with the spiritual remnant of Belacqua, but he nevertheless has every expectation of finding the corporal residue in the grave. Belacqua proposes that they bet on the question. After a long, arcane conversation Doyle accepts the bet and they dig down to the coffin and open it. Inside they find a handful of stones.

This incident (as the title, **"Echo's Bones,"** hints) refers to one Ovid describes in the *Metamorphoses:* when Echo is spurned by Narcissus, she wastes away until her bones turn into stone. Nothing remains but her voice; because her chatter once distracted Juno, she is condemned to repeat the last thing she hears. Echo, like many of the figures in the *Metamorphoses,* must endure a form of retribution appropriate to her misdeeds. Belacqua's punishment is based on a similar idea. His conversation has annoyed others; now he cannot remain silent. Once he urged his fiancée to take a lover; in the afterlife he becomes the lover of another man's wife. The narcissistic Belacqua can no longer see his face in a mirror; this, he says, is more agonizing "than all the other pains and aches of the reversion." His expiation, says the narrator, will improve Belacqua: he will become "a trifle better, dryer, less of a natural snob." The drying process leaves Belacqua desiccated, and finally his physical remains, like Echo's, turn into stone.

Dante also describes forms of expiation that correspond to the sinners' vices. In the *Purgatorio* Dante's Belacqua assumes a hunched-over position that symbolizes his moral lassitude. The fence-sitting of Beckett's protagonist is similarly a literal description of a figurative state. Dante's Belacqua must languish in purgatory for as many years as he lived on earth; Beckett's hero must also endure his purgatorial existence for a lifetime. In **"Echo's Bones"** Beckett's hero yearns for the bliss of nonbeing, but he is forced to return to life because he made such a mess of it

the first time around. His resumption of existence is an "atonement for the wet impudence of an earthly state." However, like his counterpart in the *Purgatorio,* he is given a chance to redeem himself. He looks forward to the time when his heart, "drained and dried in this racking guttatim, should qualify at last as a plenum of fire for bliss immovable. . . ."

Beckett, like Dante, uses a description of the afterlife to examine moral and psychological aspects of life on earth. Belacqua's expiation in **"Echo's Bones"** is a form of guilt fantasy, an inner act of contrition that brings relief from the torments of conscience. The purgatory in **"Echo's Bones"** resembles the inner world in *Dream of Fair to Middling Women* and it also is called a "womb-tomb."

This type of setting reappears in some of Beckett's later works. **"Echo's Bones"** describes Belacqua's fears that he will never achieve nonbeing, that the "old would of his life had no intention of healing." He therefore tries to bring an end to consciousness by thinking of his "exuviae as preserved in an urn or other receptacle in some kind person's sanctum. . . ." A similar situation occurs in *The Unnamable,* where the pain of a consciousness that persists after death is an important theme; Mahood, whose remains are kept in an urn, longs for oblivion but fears it will never come. When Belacqua is unable to imagine himself in an urn, the narrator speculates about whether his "imagination had perished" when he died. A similar question becomes a central theme in **Imagination Dead Imagine.** The narrator of **"Echo's Bones"** describes the world Belacqua inhabits after his death as a place with "shafts and manholes back into the muck" (that is, leading back into physical existence); these anticipate the tunnels and trapdoors in **The Lost Ones.** Though Beckett was forced to jettison **"Echo's Bones"** he clearly never lost interest in the themes he had introduced there.

Beckett though of **"Echo's Bones"** as the "recessional story" of his novel, and wanted it to serve as the culmination of the action. The Zaborovna episode is related to the earlier stories dealing with Belacqua's love affairs. Zaborovna (like some of the earlier heroines, her name ends in "a") is kind to him. But he finds her sexuality threatening—at one point she takes on the appearance of a Gorgon—and he makes his getaway. This epitomizes his dealings with many of the women in the book: he enjoys their companionship, takes advantages of their generosity, but vanishes when the relationship becomes sexual.

One reason for this characteristic behavior emerges in the Lord Gall episode. A passing reference to Belacqua's mother calls attention to the fact that his parents are seldom mentioned in the earlier stories. Lord Gall, however, in many ways suggests a mythic father: he towers over Belacqua, takes him by the hand, even puts him on his shoulders. When Belacqua agrees to sleep with Lord Gall's wife, the incest theme becomes obvious. This suggests an underlying reason for Belacqua's behavior with women: he may seem blasé, but he is torn by an inner conflict related to his incestuous feelings.

Belacqua becomes more human in other ways. As the narrator says, he is less of a snob. He is never condescending toward Doyle, a clownish working-class figure. In the earlier stories he seemed incapable of accepting criticism; he missed the point of his Italian teacher's remark about the passages where Dante shows compassion, for example. But in **"Echo's Bones"** Belacqua pays attention when Doyle and Lord Gall complain about the eccentricities of his conversational style.

Another hidden side of Belacqua's personality emerges when it is revealed that his bones have turned into stone. Belacqua's public side is represented by Narcissus, but inwardly he is more like Echo. Belacqua suffers because he cannot give up the narcissistic side of his personality. This situation resembles Ovid's description of Echo wasting away because she cannot give up her love for Narcissus:

> But still her love clings to her and increases
> And grows on suffering; she cannot sleep,
> She frets and pines, becomes all gaunt and
>   haggard,
> Her body dries and shrivels till voice only
> And bones remain, and then she is voice only
> For the bones are turned to stone.

Belacqua also is haggard and unable to sleep, his body dries and shrivels, and even after death he keeps up his mindless chatter.

In the *Metamorphoses* Echo suffers because she has been spurned; Narcissus, because he cannot embrace his reflected image. Belacqua's unhappiness is related to both dilemmas: Echo represents his need to love another, and Narcissus stands for his inability to give of himself. Love is demanding; narcissism is unrewarding; Belacqua shuttles between these extremes and is left emotionally drained. By the end of the story he is more like Echo than like Narcissus, so parched and shriveled that he is little more than a voice and some stones.

In *Dream of Fair to Middling Women* Beckett used a similar technique—again involving figures from Ovid—to illustrate Belacqua's inner conflicts. There, three aspects of Belacqua's personality are described: "Centripetal, centrifugal and . . . not. Phoebus chasing Daphne. Narcissus fleeing from Echo and . . . neither." Phoebus Apollo represents Belacqua's unfulfilled need for love (Apollo, like Echo, has been rejected). Narcissus again represents the self-involvement that prevents Belacqua from giving of himself. A third category ("neither") negates the first two, and indicates that Belacqua's psychological state is too complex to be defined by a simple antithesis.

In **"Echo's Bones"** there is no third category; instead, the recurring details are used to enhance the complexity of the narrator's characterization of Belacqua. The most obvious of the recurring elements is a reiterated passage of over one hundred words that appears first in **"Draff"** and then in **"Echo's Bones."** The length of the passage (a description of the view from the cemetery where Belacqua is buried) indicates that the inclusion of recurring elements in the novel is not careless but intentional.

Beckett's technique resembles one Ovid uses in the *Metamorphoses*. Though Echo is forced to repeat the last thing she hears, her remarks are not nonsensical. The speeches of Narcissus end with phrases that, when Echo utters them, express her own feelings. The following passage is an example:

> "Keep your hands off," he cried, "and do not
>   touch me!
> I would die before I give you a chance at me."
> "I give you a chance at me," and that was all
> She ever said thereafter. . . .

Beckett's echo device is based on a similar principle: the repeated phrases take on a new meaning in a different context. When Belacqua tells Winnie he wants to go off by himself for "sursum corda," the excuse seems plausible; when he later gives Lucy the same excuse, his sincerity is called into question. Other repeated passages emphasize inconsistencies that reveal Belacqua's contradictory impulses: his desire to become involved in a relationship, and his desire to run away.

Ostensibly the narrator identifies only with the narcissistic side of Belacqua: he condones Belacqua's behavior and conceals his faults. But like Belacqua (who is in a sense his alter ego), the narrator has a trait that makes him comparable to Echo: he keeps repeating things. The narrator may pretend that Belacqua is no more than an insensitive egotist, but the recurring passages illuminate the more vulnerable side of Belacqua's personality. The Narcissus theme is emphasized in the content, and depicts Belacqua's mask; the Echo theme is hinted at by the formal devices that suggest what lies behind the mask. In this way Beckett ingeniously preserves a union of form and content.

Clearly, **"Echo's Bones"** must be considered an integral part of *More Pricks than Kicks*. Beckett wrote to a friend that the deletion of the story, "into which I had put all I knew and plenty that I was still better aware of, discouraged me profoundly." Beckett's complaint is certainly justified: without **"Echo's Bones,"** an essential part of the novel's complex structure is lost. Even editors with the best intentions might think twice before forcing unwanted revisions on unknown authors. *More Pricks than Kicks* is subtle, intricate, brilliant work; the removal of **"Echo's Bones"** has made it needlessly obscure.

Dougald McMillan   (essay date 1984)

SOURCE: "Worstward Ho," in *On Beckett: Essays and Criticism*, edited by S. E. Gontarski, Grove Press, Inc., 1986, pp. 207-09.

[*In the essay below, originally published in the* Irish Literary Supplement *in 1984, McMillan examines various points of style and theme in* Worstward Ho.]

Samuel Beckett's new piece of short fiction is both familiar ground and, as its title suggests, a progression into new territory. Beginning with Belacqua Shua in *More Pricks than Kicks,* a series of overlapping Beckett protagonists have been struggling "on" toward unattainable relief from compulsion. They are either compelled from without to push "on" in a physical journey in quest, flight from pursuers, or movement in some abstract pattern. Or else they are compelled from within to "say on" until some story is completed or there are no more words to use up.

Each new Beckett character in a new situation is also another stage in an apparently endless progression. Like one of these characters, Beckett seems compelled to present all of the possible situations. Together, the succession of protagonists is his attempt to exhaust his own mind. ***Worstward Ho*** is thus, as the narrator informs us, the "latest state" in the process of "all gnawing to be naught. Never to be naught."

An unidentified speaker ruminates to himself. Slowly out of the verbiage a vision emerges of narrator represented by a skull "oozing" words out of one black hole. He is observing an old man and a child who plod hand in hand toward a final scene at a graveyard, where they observe the bowed back of an old woman. In its starkest outlines Beckett presents the essentials of a life cycle: love (presumably), birth, paternity, death, loss, and return in memory.

The multiple puns of the title point out and define the movement "on" through space, time, and the Beckettian dimension of words. (In Beckett's world characters are located not only in space and time, but on a verbal continuum, their position defined by how much they have said and still have to say.) The movement is toward "the worst"—but significantly only *toward* that point. The real worst is that the speaker is not yet able to arrive at the worst. Finality is unattainable.

Worstward Ho is in the most apparent sense "Westward Ho!" through space. The comparison of the plodding of the man and the boy toward the graveyard with the pioneers' arduous trek across the American plains suits well to portray the experience here. It points out first of all the ironic contrast of expectations. (Notably, Beckett's "Ho" lacks an exclamation point.) It also suggests a landscape devoid of many individual marks of the humanity that traverses it and yet not the ultimate abstraction which a desert might represent. Similarly, there are only enough details of specific depiction of the man and the boy in this landscape to convey the impression of an individual experience. This experience, although highly abstract, is not yet the ultimate universal abstraction we might imagine as possible. As usual with Beckett, we are in a quintessentially penultimate world.

The graveyard, which is the destination of the westward trek, represents the "worst" presumably because it is where the mind must confront the memory of the dead—the "shades" as the narrator calls them.

This spatial movement is also "worstward" because while it leads toward a distant point on the horizon, it does not confer any distance from the observing narrator. In visual paradox, the man and the boy plod "unreceding on."

Throughout Beckett's work, movement toward the west retains the conventional association of passage through time. The movement here is both forward and backward

in time. There is progression toward the final, most recent scene in a life cycle; but that is a moment of memory and so, as the speaker says, "back is on." Like the movement through space, the movement through time confers no distance or respite from painful events and is therefore toward the worst.

More than "Westward Ho!" through space and time, the title points to a journey through dubious linguistic terrain: Worst*word* Ho. The process is so exhaustive that it leads through "worsening words." and it requires the ungrammatical form "worser" to express the state beyond bad and worse but not yet the worst.

It is one of the tricks of the mind to track consciousness back across any verbal matter it may have encountered, however trivial or tawdry. Beckett, the sophisticated Irishman who left English for the distilled formality of French, is now faced with a mind that insists upon pressing forward even through clichéd American colloquialisms.

At the end of this process there is the word *nohow*. The text begins, "Somehow on. Till nohow on," and ends "nohow on." Even for linguistically democratic American westerners, *nohow* is a markedly aberrant usage, almost as much a part of the clichéd portrayal of rustic Americans as *begorra* for Irishmen or *wee* for Scots. It is usually a double negative used where *anyway* would be the accepted form. Beckett's mind has taken him not only in the direction of the low level of discourse of American western colloquialism, but to a superlatively bad specific example of it. *Nohow* is also the worst word because as the final destination of this linguistic trek, it is a disastrous confirmation of the impossibility of ever reaching an end: There is not any "knowhow," expertise, or any other known means of progression to a final state. It also suggests the time when even the search for the impossible means will have been abandoned—the time when *nohow on* will replace *on anyhow*. Finally, and most importantly, *Nohow* presents Beckett's most recent summation of the balanced alternatives of his persistent dilemma. On the one hand, *No!* —the negative acknowledgement and shrinking away from the impossibility of it all. On the other hand, *How?* —the commitment, albeit questioning, to find a way to continue.

Worstward Ho is deceptively unprepossessing at first—traversing a landscape which Beckett himself acknowledges as "mere-most minimum" and undesirable. But as his most recent attempt to exhaust the possibilities of language and of his own mind, it reveals upon closer examination Beckett's characteristic linguistic control and brilliance. It is all the more impressive, moving, and enjoyable because of his willingness to go on in the face of the dubious medium imposed upon him by his own mind.

Kateryna Arthur   (essay date 1987)

SOURCE: "Texts for *Company,*" in *Beckett's Later Fiction and Drama: Texts for Company,* edited by James Acheson and Kateryna Arthur, Macmillan Press, 1987, pp. 136-44.

[In the essay below, Arthur examines the structure and themes of Company.*]*

Beckett's novella *Company* exhibits more strikingly than any other of his later works a double impulse—towards order and coherence on the one hand and towards chaos and indeterminacy on the other. Associated with these poles are other antithetical positions between which the work moves. Whereas *Texts for Nothing,* written two and a half decades earlier and exploring many of the same problems as *Company,* could be said to have adopted confusion as its governing principle, *Company* is governed by division and rupture.

Although doubleness and multiplicity have been features of Beckett's work from the beginning, *Company* is unusual in the explicitness with which the opposing or contradictory drives are presented in its structure as well as in its themes. The suppression of the subjective 'I' which is everywhere implied in *Company,* its dispersal into the second- and third-person narratives, is the most immediately visible structural evidence of the deeply and variously divided nature of this work. The 'company' that the work speaks of is the accumulation of self-generated constructions in the form of inventions and memories which inhabit the world of the imagination and which, for a writer, provide the material (the Yeatsian 'rag and bone') for the world of his works. But what companionship can these fragments offer and what relationship do they bear to the writer? Is he their creator or do they create him? These are some of the questions that *Company* asks. Avoiding simple answers and single positions, *Company* takes up various attitudes provisionally and experimentally and, unlike many other of Beckett's works that explore problems of the speaking subject and of writing generally (notably *The Unnamable* and *Texts for Nothing*), *Company* does not generate a sense of despair or futility. Although it is schismatic to the point of schizophrenia, it is creatively and constructively so.

The term 'schizophrenia', used in a nonempirical way and without any clinical implications, is peculiarly appropriate for *Company.* It is adopted as the basis of a theory of analysis and interpretation by Gilles Deleuze and Felix Guattari in their book *Anti-Oedipus.* Their theory, which I can only briefly outline here, provides a useful interpretative framework for the reading of *Company* and also, more generally, for reading Beckett. There is much in the Deleuze/Guattari approach that is in harmony with Beckett. While Beckett is quoted as having said 'I'm working with impotence, ignorance. I don't think impotence has been exploited in the past', Deleuze and Guattari in a similar spirit claim: 'We are still too competent. We would like to speak in the name of absolute incompetence.' The theorists and Beckett both align themselves against closure, smoothness of form and unification of meaning.

They give primacy to *process* rather than to completed events and they recognise process (in this context the process by which language yields interpretations) as chaotic and broken. 'For literature', write Deleuze and Guattari, 'is like schizophrenia; a process and not a goal, a production and not an expression', and they argue for an understanding of language as 'no longer defined by what it says,

even less by what makes it a signifying thing, but by what causes it to move, to flow and to explode—desire.' *Company,* a work which is driven by clusters of conflicting desires, is, in their terms, a schizophrenic text. It exemplifies and illuminates their theory.

The anti-Freudian approach that Deleuze and Guattari advocate has its roots in an anti-fascist vision. In proposing 'schizoanalysis' to replace Freudian analysis, they offer the freewheeling schizophrenic consciousness as a model for a politics and an interpretative approach that are goal-free and undirectional. As Michel Foucault explains in his preface to their book, Deleuze and Guattari's politics is

> a radical politics of desire freed from all beliefs. Such a politics dissolves the mystifications of power through the kindling, on all levels, of anti-Oedipal forces . . . that escape coding, scramble the codes and flee in all directions: orphans (no daddy-mommy-me), atheists (no beliefs) and nomads (no habits, no territories).

It is striking how well this description of schizoanalysis accommodates Beckett's writing practice in general and also how closely the metaphors used for the anti-Oedipal forces describe his typical characters.

Company, by virtue of its explicitly schismatic construction, is a special case of schizophrenic writing or of what might be called 'scripsophrenia'. It is unusual (though by no means unique in Beckett's oeuvre) in that it sets up a very orderly and well-defined structure from which to present a vision of unstructuredness and indeterminacy. The earlier work to which *Company* is related in many ways—*Texts for Nothing*—adopts a much looser structure. The comparison allows us to see how the incongruence between form and content in *Company* brings to the foreground its contradictory and fractured nature, so strengthening the barriers against interpretative procedures that might seek to unify or homogenise it.

At the centre of Deleuze and Guattari's theory is the idea that the will to unification or totalisation, whether in analysis or in writing, tends towards unproductive closure and needs to be resisted. Hence their concept of disruptive driving impulses called 'desiring machines' which work not by linear movement towards a known goal but in fits and starts, taking no predetermined course:

> In describing machines everything functions at the same time, but amid hiatuses and ruptures, break-downs and failures, stallings and short-circuits, distances and fragmentations within a sum that never succeeds in bringing its various parts together so as to form a whole. That is because the breaks in the process are productive. . . . Desiring production is pure multiplicity, that is to say, an affirmation that is irreducible to any sort of unity.

In their individual ways *Company* and *Texts for Nothing* both correspond closely to the terms of this description. Putting aside the question of affirmation for the moment, *Texts* appears to offer the closer correspondence. Here, for example, is a piece from Text XI:

> [W]hen comes the hour of those who knew me,
> it's as though I were among them . . . watching
> me approach, then watching me recede, shaking
> my head and saying, Is it really he, can it possi-
> bly be he, then moving on in their company
> along a road that is not mine and with every step
> takes me further from that other not mine either,
> or remaining alone where I am, between two
> parting dreams . . .

The inability clearly to define and locate the speaking subject, the fragmentation of self, the sense of separation from
self and others and the general confusion about place and
identity are all recognisably schizoid features of the narrative as are, in other parts of *Texts,* the sudden shifts in
point of view, grammatical dislocations, disruptions of
time and space. But, in a less overt way, *Company* is at
least schizophrenic. Beginning with the clear statement,
'A voice comes to one in the dark', the narrator explains
and elaborates: 'That then is the proposition. To one on
his back in the dark a voice tells of a past'. The narrator
describes, with painstaking care, not only the relationship
between the supine figure and the voice, but also the grammatical patterning of the work with its explicit prohibition
of the first-person pronoun:

> Use of the second person marks the voice. That
> of the third that cankerous other. Could he
> speak to and of whom the voice speaks there
> would be a first. But he cannot. He shall not.
> You cannot. You shall not.

The precise scene-setting appears, at least superficially, to
be the antithesis of the scene-dissolving that occurs in the
extract from Text XI, but far from establishing certainty,
it wittily generates confusion about the relationship of the
'you' and the 'he' to the reader, the narrator, the author
and to the third (infinitely multipliable) possible 'other' to
whom the narrative periodically alludes: 'May not there
be another with him in the dark to and of whom the voice
is speaking?'

The narrative, with fluctuating degrees of irony and self-
parody, generates indeterminacy at the same time as it appears to fix its fictional participants into a rigid frame, and
while adopting the tones and postures of omniscience, it
comically questions the convention of the omniscient narrator. Further, by carrying to extremes the judicious 'objectivity' of its reporting, it mocks the task that it is engaged in and, once again, questions the convention.

It can be argued, then, that *Company* is a more subversive-
ly schizophrenic text than *Texts for Nothing* or *The Unnamable,* which consistently admit to and dramatise their
confusion, ignorance and failure. *Company,* by contrast,
adopts voices and structures that suggest order and clarity
without ever actually providing them. There are two main
ways in which structural order and clarity of communication are undermined in *Company.* One is by direct and
carefully reasoned questioning of its own logic, of the kind
that occurs early in the work when doubt is cast on the
number of listeners there might be:

> If the voice is not speaking to him it must be
> speaking to another. So with what reason re-
> mains he reasons. To another of that other. Or

of him. Or of another still. To another of that
other or of him or of another still. To one on his
back in the dark in any case. Of one on his back
in the dark whether the same or another.

The effect of this kind of 'reason-ridden' speculation is to
draw attention to the general literary question of *whom*
texts address. Readers as well as the multitudes of supine
listeners conjured by the writing are drawn into the wide
circle of speculation. In the process of being infinitely mul-
tiplied, the 'one on his back' loses any tenuous identity he
may have been gathering. The reader is forbidden identification of any kind as the 'one' loses its unitariness and the
single focus of traditional third-person narrative on a specific 'he' or 'she' is splintered. The effect of this is to keep
the reader's attention wary and mobile, forcing it away
from any central focus, enabling it to move freely from the
worlds of the work to the worlds of reading and writing.

The second way in which the text subverts its own coherence is by the strategy of splitting the narrative into the
apparently orderly arrangement of alternating segments of
third-person commentary directed at the reader and second-person description directed at the listener (with some
minor further shifts within these segments).

While this gives to *Company* a much more neatly symmetrical shape than that of *Texts,* which appear to have been
organised more by chain of association and the panic of
the moment than by a predetermined formula, the ultimate effect of the dividing of the narrative in this self-
conscious way is to reveal the splits, chasms and lacunae
that exist *everywhere* in narrative. Manipulation of point
of view becomes a subject of the writing as well as being
an element of its own practice. In *Texts* the voice is continuously compelling. However much it speaks of fractured
identity and dissolution of purpose, the voice induces the
reader to follow it along its tortuous ways. In *Company*
the double narrative prevents that kind of following by
forcing attention repeatedly upon the divisions themselves
and so upon the process of narration, especially upon the
arbitrariness of its organisation. The elaborate explanations of how the individuals and speech segments are organised lead the reader to ask why this should be so and thus
to engage with the writing's strategies as much as with the
voices and figures that it shapes—its company of figments.
Because of the high degree of metafictional foregrounding
of narrative processes this company is repeatedly dispersed and dissolved while it is being made: 'Need for
company not continuous. . . . Regret then at having
brought them about the problem how dispel them'.

The writing allows no resting place for the reader, not
with the initially comfortable notion of company which is
progressively eroded nor with the carefully prepared narrative structure which is itself a disorientating and alienating device. There are frequently moments in the third-
person commentary when speculation leads the voice into
the sphere of the second-person narrative or even towards
the forbidden first as, for example, in this extract: 'To confess, Yes I remember. Perhaps even to have a voice. To
murmur, Yes I remember. What an addition to company
that would be! A voice in the first person singular'.

Here and elsewhere the writing constructs and simultaneously deconstructs the concept of company, developing it as a reassuring possibility with all its human connotations of community, communication and friendship, while also parodying it by presenting it as merely an aspect of narrative, a textual device or a conjuring trick invented by the writer-deviser who is himself 'devised': 'Devised deviser devising it all for company'. Beckett's elusive deviser is an example of Deleuze and Guattari's 'vagabond, nomad subject', and his oscillating narrative answers to their description of disjunctive writing that ceaselessly 'composes and decomposes the chains [of meaning] into signs that have nothing that impels them to become signifying'.

However, not all of *Company* is as resistant to interpretation and reader identification. While the third-person commentary tends to be mobile and disruptive, the second-person narrative is frequently devoted to the telling of stories whose mode is autobiographical in spite of the second-person construction they adopt. Some of these stories are more movingly evocative of highly significant personal experiences in childhood and youth than anything else Beckett has written. How do these pieces of undisguised autobiography fit in with the metafictional scripsophrenia of the rest of the text? And how can Beckett justify including highly expressive stretches of romantic evocation in a work that elsewhere questions, as Beckett's work has consistently done over the years, the possibility of expression? The 'contradiction' can again be explained by invoking the Deleuze/Guattari model which, as the authors explain, allows us 'to think about fragments whose sole relationship is sheer difference'. The memory fragments are each coherent, unified and highly expressive. But by virtue of their difference from the third-person sections they deepen the text's disjunctiveness and make their own metafictional contribution by throwing as much light on rhetorical processes as they do on remembered events. They also bring into focus the *act* of remembering with its internal rifts and fissures. *Company* is very much concerned with the puzzles and paradoxes inherent in the closely related processes of remembering, imagining and writing.

'The important thing for the remembering author is not what he experienced', writes Walter Benjamin, 'but the weaving of his memory' ['The Image of Proust', *Illuminations, 1968*]. This tells us that the remembering writer is at least twice removed from the experiences he recalls—once by the act of recollection (which is an act of the imagination) and once again by the act of writing. Both acts demand that experiences are sifted and sorted in ways that require as much forgetting as they do remembering—'Penelope work', as Benjamin calls it, of weaving and unravelling. A memory is never complete or finite. It is open to endless revision as Beckett well knows. *Company* demonstrates the extent to which remembering is not simply recuperative. It involves processes of cutting and editing. To remember is also to dismember. And so memory, in its contradictoriness, contributes to *Company*'s dividedness, to its scripsophrenia. For to remember is both to come close to one's experience and to distance oneself from it sufficiently to observe it. It is simultaneously a journey back to lived events and an artificial construction of a new thing which itself alters the one who remembers. When

Beckett offers variations on the formula, 'Deviser of the voice and of its hearer and of himself. Deviser of himself for company', he is giving recognition to this paradox.

Beckett's choice of the second-person narrative for the memory segments throws into prominence the way in which a person is constructed by memory (and by the imagination more generally), made 'other' by it, and even, in the process of 'conjuring something out of nothing', *invented* by it: 'He speaks of himself as of another. He says, speaking of himself, he speaks of himself as of another'. And this other joins the ranks of all the fictional creations—in Beckett's case a long lineup, many of them alluded to in *Company*— of the imagination. Far from being simply a matter of recovering something lost, memory, understood in these terms, allows a dizzy glimpse into the abyss of infinite change and motion.

In *Company* Beckett is like Deleuze and Guattari in his ability to view endless change and difference 'without having recourse either to any sort of original totality (not even one that has been lost), or to a subsequent totality that may not yet have come about', and to recognise this vision as being creative and liberating. *Company* demonstrates that writing is, as another writer has put it, *inaugural*— 'the writer is himself a new idiom, constructing itself' [Jacques Derrida, *Writing and Difference*]. The work's highly schismatic nature with its multiple breaks and interruptions underlines for the reader the fact that all writing is like this, however much it might appear otherwise, and so it gives the reader a lesson in reading. All texts are what Roland Barthes calls 'broken texts', requiring plural readings or commentaries. 'The work of commentary', writes Barthes [in *S/Z*], 'once it is separated from any ideology of totality, consists precisely in *manhandling* the text, *interrupting* it.' In *Company* Beckett has already done much of this work for the reader and made it all the more visible by doing it within a symmetrical structure. *Company* is a *reading* as much as a writing of the bits and pieces that can be gathered to shape identities, memories and dreams.

While in *Texts for Nothing* the gaps and chasms that the narrative faces moment by moment are presented, however comically, as disabling, *Company* exploits them, making them a part of its orderly structure and so bringing them under control. *Company* has a double vision of writing, of memory and of self. For all its recognition of writing as conjuring, of the world as phantasm and of the self as infinitely dispersed, *Company* affirms writing's power to create worlds that are substantial and significant and that can momentarily hold at bay the chaos of endless multiplicity while at the same time fully acknowledging it. Although the work ends with the observation that the listener is 'as you always were. Alone', that aloneness, like the 'nothingness' that is also confronted, *is* to the same extent tempered by the narrative's 'fabling'. While this work can be described as schizophrenic because it generates contradictory visions, it is also schizoanalytic in that it allows the reader to see that all texts are caught in the same tangle of unresolvable contradiction and that this can be a source of power.

Susan D. Brienza (essay date 1987)

SOURCE: *"Texts for Nothing:* 'Going On' through Stylistic Devices," in her *Samuel Beckett's New Worlds: Style in Metafiction,* University of Oklahoma Press, 1987, pp. 20-47.

[*In the essay that follows, Brienza observes that the stylistic devices Beckett employs in* Texts for Nothing *serve to compensate for the lack of conventional characterization and incident in these works.*]

After *The Unnamable,* Samuel Beckett realized that he faced a problem of how to go on artistically and linguistically. By the last novel in the trilogy, character, setting, and plot had all disintegrated, the paragraph had disappeared, and even the sentence had stretched out of shape. What is left is a babble of words, yet the next Beckett storyteller, the narrator of *Texts for Nothing,* describes his predicament with surprising good humor: "No, no souls, or bodies, or birth, or life, or death, you've got to go on without any of that junk, that's all dead with words, with excess of words . . . they'll find some other nonsense, no matter what, and I'll be able to go on. . . ." At least words themselves continue in *Texts for Nothing,* "texts" meaning by one definition simply the wording of something written. The Unnamable ends his monologue paradoxically, "I can't go on, I'll go on," and the narrator of the texts continues this sense of a linguistic impasse: "Suddenly, no, at last, long last, I couldn't any more, I couldn't go on." Yet he does go on with nothing but style, "text" by another definition having "the Latin sense of literary tissue or style" [Ruby Cohn, *Samuel Beckett: The Comic Gamut*]. Where words are not cohesive units of grammatical sentences and paragraphs, and where these in turn do not compose the traditional elements of a novel or short story, how does a fiction writer manage to string words together and still have them mean something, or—more difficult still—have them convey "nothing" at all?

By employing a noncharacter as a narrator, Beckett opens up a world of possible content, the creation of a protagonist. Also, by attempting to produce a main character, Beckett links the thirteen texts and thus provides a kind of dramatic unity, despite the lack of plot and of coherent sentences. Acting on the premise that the modern writer has nothing to express and yet the urge to express, Beckett uses several tricks of language which enable him to multiply the number and variety of words and phrases without having them add up to a narrative expression. This allows his fiction to "go on," and thus by about 1950, stylistic devices emerge as Beckett's most important means of continuing his fictional voices' murmurings. As with the Unnamable (who reasons, "If only I were alive inside one might look forward to heart-failure . . ."), the goal of the narrator throughout the text is to create himself so that he can then cease to exist—to be truly born so that he can unequivocally die. As he labors to be delivered, he calls up or invents memories of things and beings, and all these provide material for his murmurs. The invention of more than one voice makes possible a dialogue with the self—and again other words: "My den, I'll describe it, no, I can't. It's simple, I can do nothing any more, that's what you think." Already, in Text 1, both a first-and a second-

person pronoun exist, reflecting the Cartesian mind/body dichotomy that has intrigued Beckett since *Murphy.* Soon we will hear a "he" and a "they" as the split self becomes a multi-persona, as in *Molloy,* an inner and outer voice at the very least, and often a voice in three parts: "Ah yes, we seem to be more than one, all deaf, not even, gathered together for life. Another said, or the same, or the first, they all have the same voice, the same ideas." Echoing the layered voices in *The Unnamable,* the murmurs in **Texts** bounce back yet more rapidly and with even more fragmentary structure and uncertain tone.

Since in French the title phrase **Textes pour rien** suggests "mesure pour rien," a musical silence, a bar's rest, it is not surprising that at times the different selves seem to be orchestral parts singing in a kind of harmony—"I can follow them well, all the voices, all the parts"—and that the voices sing as a "duo" or "trio," seeking a coda of silence. As the texts regress, however, the "we" breaks down increasingly into an "I" and a "he," or an "I" and a "they," who try to trick each other. A Cartesian universe includes potential deception by an evil demon (occurring in Beckett's work since the French stories) who strives to confuse man about his own physical existence and the physical reality of the world. Beckett invokes this deceptive spirit subtly by changing a verb in an earlier version from "taken in" to "deceived"; and later he actually brings the demon out into the open: "if there was a way out, if I said there was a way out, make me say it, demons, no, I'll ask for nothing." As Beckett himself searches for a "way out" of his artistic predicament, a fictional retrenchment becomes attractive.

Whereas, in a traditional story, action usually develops through conflict between two main characters, in these texts Beckett derives all the conflict he requires (to keep the dialogue and the words in general going) within one noncharacter. As the antagonism between the different parts of the self reaches a crescendo, disharmony shatters the silence and plays itself out through a clashing of pronouns: " . . . what's to be said of this latest other, with his babble of homeless mes and untenanted hims, this other without number or person whose abandoned being we haunt, nothing." Here Beckett self-consciously employs the grammatical classifications "person" and "number" to depict this pronoun with no noun to back it up. Use of a pronoun implies a noun referent, but our narrator is never given a name (not even "Unnamable") so that all his pronouns falsely refer to a nothing, analogous to two-dimensional cardboard figures that are facades only, that have nothing behind them. Different parts of the "I" serve as both subjects and objects, both speakers and addressees; and fictional personas created by the narrator also populate the text, beings who nearly become other characters he can interact with or merge into. The narrator hypothesizes that one way to "get born" is to tell a story and then to infuse himself into a character. Like the Unnamable, though, his pensum is to relate the *correct* story, the "right aggregate" of words. At first he tries calling up memories, but people from his past do not provide inspiration because in these recollections he is limited to the past tense, while true stories must be told in the present in order to earn the character an existence in time. Thus he experiments with different verb tenses as well as with various pronouns in order to compose a proper story in which he can embody himself. (By tracing the series of manuscripts and type-scripts leading to *Texts,* one can observe Beckett himself trying out different tenses and temporal signals, even inserting the word "tenses" into a phrase about time.)

In Text 3 the voice tries to imagine events in the future tense: "I know how I'll do it, I'll be a man, there's nothing else for it, a kind of man, a kind of old tot, I'll have a nanny, I'll be her sweet pet, she'll give me her hand, to cross over, she'll let me loose in the Green, I'll be good, I'll sit quiet as a mouse. . . ." But the narrator soon realizes that all the contracted "will's" in the world cannot will him into being—especially if he is trapped in limbo between childhood and old age. His wistful "if only it could be like that" refers not only to the impossibility of being a child with a nanny, but also the impossibility of creating a self-defining story with this device. "I know it's not me," he admits. Later in this text he again laments that he has no current existence, and this directs him once more into the future tense, but a future that implies a past. In a wonderfully comic passage, the speaker invents an old army buddy—because, after all, every man must have old war stories on tap:

> No no, I'll speak now of the future, I'll speak in the future, as when I used to say, in the night, to myself, Tomorrow I'll put on my dark blue tie . . . I'll have a crony, my own vintage, my own bog, a fellow warrior, we'll relive our campaigns and compare our scratches. Quick, quick. He'll have served in the navy, perhaps under Jellicoe, while I was potting at the invader from behind a barrel of Guinness, with my arquebuse. We have not long, that's the spirit, in the present, not long to live, it's our positively last winter, halleluiah.

After starting in the future tense, moving through the future perfect construction "he'll have served," and arriving at the present tense, the narrator concludes this section with the conditional verb "would," the verbal mood for speculation, for imagination: "He'd nourish me . . . he'd ram the ghost back down my gullet . . . he'd prevent discouragement . . . I'd say to him, come on, gunner, leave all that. . . . We *were,* there we are past and gone again. . . ." The "I" continues for a while in the past tense, but then, rejects it with "no, that's all memories, last shifts older than the flood." Only in a present-tense chronicle can he create a current, living self: ". . . I'd join them [black dancers] with a will if it could be here and now, how is it nothing is ever here and now?"

His next attempt to situate himself, though, falls back on the conditional and the subjunctive: "And what if all this time I had not stirred hand or foot from the third class waiting-room of the South-Eastern Railway Terminus . . . and were still there waiting to leave. . . ." A return to the past tense, a reversion to mere memories, produces self-condemnation; to pretend he is alive and therefore capable of the peace of death, of silence, he must try again to tell a self-creating story. But this narrative incarnation fails because neither the present tense nor the

third person pronoun can be maintained: the man he imagines disintegrates into an amorphous mass of flesh and bones, an impersonal "it."

Making a detour in Text 8, the narrator—instead of attempting to relate a story—tries to fabricate a character (himself) by dramatizing place, time, costume, and props. "But what is this I see, and how, a white stick and an ear-trumpet, where, Place de la République, at pernod time, let me look closer at this, it's perhaps me at last." Bowler hat and brown boots "advance in concert, as though connected by the traditional human excipient," but the "I" rejects the temptation of infusing himself into the body of this other vagrant because "I would know it was not me, I would know I was here." As this bum begs for money, the narrator acknowledges that he himself is begging for the greater alm "of being or of ceasing"; and this disparity between the physical, practical beggar and the metaphysical, figurative quester is too wide—even for the lies and self-deceptions of this persona.

For his last try at self-creation in Text 12, the narrator evokes a setting with a combination of present, future, past, and present participle verbs: "It's a winter night, where I was, where I'm going, remembered, imagined, no matter, believing in me, believing it's me, no, no need. . . ." The introduction of a third-person "he" who is viewing his own body delineates a character, a shell the narrator then tries to enter. But the timing of the he/I merger is tricky here (as reflected in the various verb tenses juggled), and some outside force ("the others"?) must finesse it: "Will they succeed in slipping me into him, the memory and dream of me, into him still living, amn't I there already, wasn't I always there . . . and from now till he dies my last chance to have been. . . ." This last gamble must have failed; in Text 13 the "I" admits that he is an "unmakable being." Nonetheless in all the futile attempts to make a being, Beckett has gone on with sixty-five pages of words, words that depict imagination, invention, and creativity even if they never create a character or define a self.

Thus it is possible to construct a formal text without any traditional elements of narrative, elements that are mocked by the narrator of *Texts for Nothing.* After "I" starts to depict a realistic setting and the religious atmosphere of a Sunday for the Mr. Joly episode, he catches himself with "Here at least none of that, no talk of a creator and nothing very definite in the way of a creation." While he concedes that a narrator usually requires characters, he rejects the typical romantic themes of adventure novels in one of the most humorous passages of the work:

> there has to be a man, or a woman, feel between your legs, no need of beauty, nor of vigour, a week's a short stretch, no one's going to love you, don't be alarmed. No, not like that, too sudden, I gave myself a start. And to start with stop palpitating, no one's going to kill you, no one's going to love you and no one's going to kill you. . . .

Although the "I" here debunks both romances and murder mysteries, he feels that something must happen in his narrative. By Text 6 he is still promising to tell "a little story, with living creatures coming and going on a habitable earth crammed with the dead," almost a *T.V. Guide* summary of a later Beckett fiction, *The Lost Ones.* Finally, by Text 13, the possibility of a narrative, and even the word "story," has been abandoned; now the "I" would be content with merely a "trace" of its existence. All traces, all murmurings vanish because "to speak of instants, to speak of once, is to speak of nothing." As for the voice, "it breathes in vain, nothing is made," but this nothing is still conveyed in words, and these words are arranged in an intricate shape.

Beckett advertizes not nothing, but *texts* for nothing. In this piece, more than in earlier Beckett fiction, the process takes precedence over the endproduct, and the creative process forms the only plot. Alternating with a search for the self-defining story is the theme of "giving up" the search for self, and this vacillation between hope and despair, this cancellation of yes by no, determines that in each of the thirteen texts the "I" must start again; there is no cumulative solution. For the artist struggling with words, each piece, each sentence, is a continual rebeginning: an oscillation between the yes of creation and the no of revision. *Texts'* form mirrors the configuration of the narrator's artistic journey: every text starts with the illusion of progress but ends in a thwarted circle. In the larger structure of the whole, the "I" finally decides that the time has come for him to begin at the conclusion of Text 7, about the midpoint of the work. As in *Endgame,* the literary process consists not in a building up but in a winding down. The "I" starts with a body, a head, a heart, and several selves, and ends with a voice. He begins with a setting, memories, and stories, and ends with only lies and murmurs. He commences with plans and hopes for being, and concludes by despairing of existence itself.

In Text 1 the narrator is the closest he will ever be to a conventional character of fiction; all he needs is to collect himself—literally. Beckett lends him a mother, a father, and a home he can see in the distance, all realistic touches; but surrealism supercedes when the narrator cannot locate himself precisely in space and time. Moreover, any story line dwindles when he is paralyzed in determining whether to remain or to go on; thus "I can't" becomes the refrain for the first text. His inability to decide or to act produces a desire to rest: thoughts about the close of day and memories of bedtime stories lead to sleep—and thus to perfect poetic closure.

Text 2 elaborates on the idea that the "I" is in some sort of dead world and that above, in the light, are the living. Still concerned with time and location, he differentiates himself, down below, with, "Here you are under a different glass. . . ." When he considers going above again (the same phrase occurs repeatedly in *How It Is,* "above in the light"), he contemplates a return to conventional fiction, since the term "above" recalls realistic scenery from Text 1: the sea, valleys, cliffs, and forests. This possibility calls up memories of people from above: Mother Calvet, Mr. Joly, and (apparently) Piers Plowman. Ironically, though, the "I" repudiates memory, wishing, "If only it could be wiped from knowledge." Throughout this text, it is his present, not his past, that he wants to understand; but time

has expanded and become indivisible, "one enormous second." Wherever he is, he knows he must continue to utter words until he is at home, and "home" now means silence.

The beginning of Text 3 thrusts aside the ending of Text 2—"Leave, I was going to say leave all that"—and yet undercuts this very rejection. An earlier desire to know what happens, to reconstruct history, becomes now a need to tell a story; the narrator must fabricate his own past as life yields to art. Stories and departures, the two motifs of Text 3, are logically linked because either narrating a self-defining story or moving in time will create the "I." He fails at both and, even worse, cannot will himself a head or a body through either method. (We have regressed from Text 1, where a body was implied, and from Text 2, where the "I" was inside a head.) Both present and future appear dismal and uncertain for this non-being: "Here, nothing will happen here, no one will be here for many a long day." Like the Unnamable, whose first sentence is "Where now?" and whose last sentence begins "The place," this "I" strives to locate himself in space and time, to be "here and now."

Text 4 begins with already familiar queries: Where will I go? and, Who am I anyway? The new addition here is a split between the "I" and a "he," maintained (with a few denials) throughout the text. Either the "I" is making his figments talk, or "he" has created "I" as one of *his* figments, or there is only one "I" who tells lies, or. . . . (Similar nested layers of speakers and listeners determine the style and substance in the more recent Beckett fiction, *Company*, displaying a near-infinite regression of pronouns and voices.) The advantage of doubling an "I" and a "he" is that they can argue about who is at fault for the story's failure, and thus a dialogue of sorts can fill the void. Recriminations and accusations preface the courtroom scene of Text 5, but there the "I" ultimately escapes blame by denying the necessity of a story; simply his life will do. The split selves in Text 4 prepare us for the separation of the "I" into defendant and scribe in Text 5, and another foreshadowing occurs in the term "accusative"—"It's the same old stranger as ever for whom alone accusative I exist"—with its grammatical and legal connotations. (This word was added to the English version in the middle of the translation process; there is no equivalent in the French.) In this imaginary courtroom, both being and nonbeing are punishable: "to be is to be guilty." On the witness stand of existence "nothing appears, all is silent, one is frightened to be born, no, one wishes one were, so as to begin to die." Although death's silence is the goal, the silent void is continually filled with phrases—one of the many transgressions of this linguistic criminal. The "I" still wonders where he is, wonders if he should go, yet ends up staying; as his degrees of freedom are more constricted, analogously his artistic choices become constrained.

Besides serving as both speaker and recorder at court, the "I" digresses on such literary topics as nature, setting, atmosphere, and the hero: "the sky and earth, I've heard great accounts of them . . . I've noted, I must have noted many a story with them as setting, they create the atmosphere. Between them where the hero stands a great gulf is fixed, while all about they flow together more and more, till they meet, so that he finds himself as it were under glass. . . ." This is exactly where the protagonist found himself earlier. Like a guilty defendant psychologically unable to pronounce a victim's name, he is reluctant to utter the disturbing words "nearness" and "life": "Out of the corner of my eye I observe the writing hand, all dimmed and blurred by the—by the reverse of farness"; "they want to create me, they want to make me, like the bird the birdikin, with larvae she fetches from afar, at the peril—I nearly said at the peril of her life!" Frequently insisting that he is "far" (from those above?), his birth is never complete, and thus genuine death is impossible. Text 1 ended with sleep after toil and play; Text 5 ends with fatigue after toil only. Regression continues.

The apparitions which begin Text 6 may derive from Text 5's court scene or from resident phantoms, but the "keepers" surely refer to prison wardens. Here the "I" seems imprisoned in his own body, a fate also suffered by the Unnamable:

> . . . I'm in something, I'm shut up, the silence is outside, outside, inside . . . nothing but this voice and the silence all round, no need of walls, yes, we must have walls, I need walls, good and thick, I need a prison, I was right, for me alone, I'll go there now, I'll put me in it . . . [*The Unnamable*].

Worse than that, the "I" of Text 6 has metaphorically become an insect imprisoned in a display case—hence the repeated description of him as "under glass." Feeling self-conscious and vaguely guilty, he shares J. Alfred Prufrock's fear of observation and condemnation as when "formulated, sprawling on a pin." Like a butterfly, he was "quick dead," becoming merely "a little dust in a little nook, stirred faintly this way and that by breath straying from the lost without. Yes, I'm here for ever, with the spinners and the dead flies, dancing to the tremor of their meshed wings. . . ." In translating from the French to the English *Texts,* Beckett enhances the butterfly imagery: *flottant* becomes "flaunting and fluttering," and *perspectives,* that is, "openings," are rendered as "glades." As butterfly, the narrator possesses first an ephemeral life and in death a kind of permanence: "What can have become then of the tissues I was, I can see them no more. . . . The eyes, yes, if these memories are mine, I must have believed in them an instant, believed it was me I saw there dimly in the depths of their glades. I can see me still with those of now, sealed this long time, staring with those of then, I must have been twelve, because of the glass. . . ." Here, in a linguistic shift, the glass over insects becomes a "round shaving-glass" which the mother and father of the narrator (suddenly a real little boy) share. In French the equivalent word *glace* means both "mirror" and "ice," and this double sense may have prompted Beckett to slide surrealistically from earthly life to an afterlife. Besides having lived for a time on earth, the "I" insists that he also inhabited purgatory and hell. Instantly he is one of Dante's damned—buried in ice up to his nose, and crying frozen tears. Between the weeping and the speaking he will, like a tormented sinner, be compelled to confess his

errors, to recount somehow the required painful story; he, ironically, gives us his "word."

But in Text 7 he considers abandoning the search for identity because, clearly, he is not talking of himself; *he* is a creature who can just barely remember what it was like to move, yet a real being requires locomotion. Rather, he is discussing, and has been discussing, "X, that paradigm of human kind, moving at will, complete with joys and sorrows, perhaps even a wife and brats, forbears most certainly, a carcass in God's image and a contemporary skull, but above all endowed with movement. . . ." Meanwhile, the narrator may actually be sitting motionless in a railway terminal. Nothing is certain, and Beckett ironically uses legal, logical language recalling the courtroom scene to underline this scepticism: "In that case. . . . Whence it should follow, but does not . . . that this lump is no longer me and that search should be made elsewhere. . . . That is why one must not hasten to conclude, the risk of error is too great." His linguistic maneuver is to narrate a third person story and then to translate it into the first person, to glide from "he" to "I"; but often these personal pronouns give way to the vague "one." Finally, the notion of night as a starting point, which has recurred, especially in the conclusions, ends this text as the "I" decides (near the midpoint of the book) that it is "time too for me to begin."

Text 8 recapitulates many of the themes we have already heard: the flow of words as tears, the location of the self, the possiblity of nonexistence, the light above, the hope of a story, the feeling of living inside a head, the inability to know anything, the guilt of being, and the search for the right words in order to find rest. Much of Text 8 is a lament for an ending: "But it will end, a desinence will come," where "desinence" means a termination or a final line of verse, and also—in linguistic contexts—an inflection or a suffix. Lov*ed* differs from lov*ing* by the terminal letters only, yet "loved" is over while "loving" continues; in words, in sentences, in stories, and in lives, the ending determines the interpretation of the whole: " . . . it's for ever the same murmur, flowing unbroken, like a single endless word and therefore meaningless, for it's the end gives the meaning to words." The new note introduced into Text 8 is the motif of begging, ultimately a seeking for the end of time. As he begs, the narrator shies away from any selfhood with his inability to utter the possessive "mine": "And the hand old in vain would drop the mite and the old feet shuffle on, towards an even vainer death than no matter whose." Even grammatically, he will not grant himself being.

Both the style and the substance in Text 9 seem more disjointed and confusing than those of the others, so a hint from the narrator is welcome: "What am I doing now, I'm trying to see where I am, so as to be able to go elsewhere. . . ." Specifically, he wants to ascertain if he ever had a physical body, if he ever died, and if there is a "way out" now, where "way out" may represent an escape from life or from mimetic fiction. However, he ultimately becomes drowned in a meaningless drift of words—or, as he puts it, buried in an "avalanche" of "word-shit"—and temporarily abandons his former pursuit of a story. The prison motif continues from Text 6, and a comparison with the French original confirms that the narrator's crime is still that of existence: "par lequel malgré eux les gens vous accusent" becomes "with which the fellow-creature unwillingly betrays your presence." Guiltily questioning his origins, the "I" decides that he is lost somewhere between womb and tomb, and he recalls a time when he was slinking "to and fro before the graveyard" asking to be killed. The phrase "gates of the graveyard" cumulatively gains the force of a chant as, spinning in a frenzy, the "I" cannot recall whether he is "here" or "there, coming and going before the graveyard." Caught between the "here" of potential reality and the "there" of the imagination, he becomes so distraught that he confuses the recurring motif of the previous texts, "it's not me," with the refrain of Text 9, "There's a way out there"; and now the "way out" fervently desired is a departure from all these words. He concludes, with circularity, "The graveyard, yes, it's there I'd return, this evening it's there, borne by my words, if I could get out of here, that is to say if I could say, There's a way out there . . . ," as if the sentence itself would effect an escape. With even greater force than in *Malone Dies,* the saying makes it so; assertions forge reality. If the "I" plays God the creator, if he has only to say "Let there be X" for there to be X, then with the correct solution to the variable he can speak himself into existence.

"Give up" begins Text 10, but since the narrator has already capitulated in Text 7, he wryly concedes "it's nothing new." Taking a personal inventory, the "I" tries to assess what he has lost: a head, a hand, a heart (all present in Text 1); and the senses as well are failing. Later the "I" asserts that he must go on without body or soul. Any more content than this, however, evaporates because Text 10 is composed almost entirely of devices of language which permit words to continue without allowing any narrative to creep in. At the barest minimum, the narrator will "have gone on giving up," yet even this minimal effort requires more words.

By Text 11 the narrator's self-consciousness and confusion prevent him from merely beginning the text. His mind (and his syntax) wanders, and he is literally at a loss for words. The new refrain here becomes, "I don't know, I shouldn't have begun," as every term raises some doubt about its very legitimacy. The only words that hold the others in the text together, "when come those who know me," were carefully chosen: as a subordinate, dependent clause it cannot complete its thought until followed by an independent clause. Beckett refuses to finish the sentence until the end of the text, keeping the first clause in suspension and thus unifying the passage. When the "I's" thought finally is completed, though, it reveals itself as a false solution to his problem of self-creation: "when comes the hour of those who knew me, it's as though I were among them, that is what I had to say, among them watching me approach, then watching me recede, shaking my head and saying, Is it really he, can it possibly be he. . . ." The "I" temporarily achieves being through the Berkeleyian/Beckettian method of being perceived, but the perceiver, who should be the Other, is "I" also; and thus we circle back to the predicament of split selves. Al-

though realizing that he moves nowhere with his ramble of words, that he is no closer to an answer now than when he started, the narrator almost deludes himself that conditions have improved; "it's not true, but I say it just the same. . . ." If the utterance itself would make it so, if words indeed had ritualistic, magical powers, then the artist could succeed. Perhaps, then, all he lacks is *fewer* words.

Trying to remove all but the essential terms for his formula of self-creation, the narrator cancels out (with the phrase "no, no need") the unnecessary inventions: belief that the creature "going" is himself, belief in the presence of "others," and in the power to move somehow. (A similar revision-in-process occurs in a later fiction, **"All Strange Away,"** with the title phrase used to delete unwanted details.) What remains is simply a winter's night with a light emanating from neither stars nor moon, but needed—light necessary so that the being, created with the mere mention of a "he," can see his own body. The "I" will capture the body and voice of this other, and haunt him in a kind of ghostly possession. When this fails, the protagonist reverts to the notion that creating his existence requires only the presence of others, now not as possible bodies to inhabit but as possible eyes to witness him. In despair, however, the "I" (like Watt) follows an infinite regression and realizes that a god, an unwitnessed witness, would also be necessary. He consoles himself with the thought that, unlike in Text 11, here fortunately he did not even begin anything: ". . . what a blessing it's all down the drain, nothing ever as much as begun, nothing ever but nothing and never, nothing ever but lifeless words." Ironically though, these words pulsate with linguistic life—with parallel structure, prose rhythm, and even internal rhyme (ever/Never). Paradoxically, a lamentation that nothing has begun re-begins the begetting of words.

After twelve texts, we have rich textures but still no hope of a story, or any other means to the narrator's embodiment. At the conclusion even the voice "that tried in vain to make me" is dying down. Text 13 provides excellent closure of **Texts for Nothing,** suggesting that despite their circularity the texts could not go on indefinitely: "there it dies, it can't go on, it's been its death, speaking of me. . . ." Gradually, the "I" has lost his spirit, body, heart, head, and hand, but the voice becomes totally disembodied only in Text 13. Stressing the death of the voice in the English **Texts,** Beckett translates "elle se fait lointaine . . . ou elle baisse" as "Dying away . . . or dying down." Grammatically the narrator has diminished from an "I" to an "it." Many other physical and emotional regressions reach their zero points in Text 13. Although one critic prefers to speak of "progression" rather than "regression," "counterpoint" rather than "contradiction," and "reintegration" rather than "fragmentation" [J. E. Dearlove, *Accommodating the Chaos: Samuel Beckett's Nonrelational Art*], it is difficult to discern any positive conclusion in **Texts**—unless it exists solely in the reader's mind. In Text 6 the "I" described himself as dust blown by breath; in 13 he finds stasis in the still air that hardly disturbs the still dust. A weary voice now describes its first goal in the past: "that was the only chance, get out of here and go elsewhere. . . ." This last text, like others, is punctuated with a refrain; but here, instead of driving a frenzied pace and a frantic tone, the repetition of "it says" creates a sense of distance and non-urgency. The "I" no longer pursues himself by spilling out torrents of words in order to find the answer to the riddle of existence. Now the "it" almost calmly "wonders what has become of the wish to know, it is gone, the heart is gone, the head is gone, no one feels anything, asks anything, seeks anything, says anything, hears anything, there is only silence." Yet the compulsive rhythmic reiteration of "[verb] anything," the enumeration of nothing, produces strings of something; and the last words, "it says, it murmurs," still disturbs the silence. The truth of "Weaker still the weak old voice," the start of Text 13, is illustrated by its final clause, in which "murmurs" has a much weaker volume and connotation than the verb "says." Ultimately, the "going on" of this voice produces the circularity of the piece, while its softening produces the overall structure of decline.

Texts for Nothing, if graphed, might appear as a curve from some negative number to some minuscule negative fraction approaching zero, but its structure is obviously circular as well. A return to one's starting point accomplishes "nothing," and Beckett has stylistically managed to "go on" and to go nowhere simultaneously. Most of the individual texts turn back on themselves so that a model of *Texts for Nothing* would consist of thirteen small overlapping circles within one large zero. There is a marvelous irony in that Beckett's picture of the void is intricate indeed, that nothing is filled with such linguistic brilliance.

In *Texts for Nothing,* when Beckett has reduced the novel to a murmuring narrator, and has further restricted the protagonist to a voice talking "for nothing," each word bears the horrible and paradoxical responsibility of meaning as little as possible. The circular imitative form of the work as a whole is reinforced by an imitative style in which the narrator's struggle with language, with finding the right words, takes place at the phrase level. Porter Abbott sees this reduction to strings of words in both *The Unnamable* and *Texts for Nothing:* "Without story, without people, without things, without space and time, the books become their words and syntax. It is here that we get the direct attempt to imitate in form the experience the speaker is going through" [*The Fiction of Samuel Beckett: Form and Effect*]. Of course, one difference between the two works is the tight formal structure of the *Texts*—just the opposite of *The Unnamable*'s rambling and amorphous flow. The thirteen divisions, rebeginnings, repeated narrative attempts become the only story within a style that embodies its own futility. It is possible to classify four elements of this imitative style: absurd hypothesis, cancellation, the analysis of words, and the incomplete sentence. Other characteristics, including authorial comment, literalism, and self-contradiction, have been analyzed as comic devices. These and more subtle verbal maneuverings, when used in concert, compose an orchestrated opus of silence.

One method of approaching but never reaching a linguistic deadend, as Beckett's Watt knew very well, is the sheer repetition of words and phrases, compounding the confusion with permutation of words in a phrase and of phrases

in a sentence, until all words lose all sense. Analyzing repetition in *Watt,* Bruce Kawin differentiates three variations of the permutation strategy: (1) "Listing every relevant fact or object in an attempt to fence in the phenomenon . . ."; (2) "Listing the logical permutations in an attempt at problem solving . . ."; and (3) "Carrying logical permutation to the language itself . . ." [*Telling It Again and Again: Repetition in Literature and Film*], as in Watt's inversion of letters. In *Texts,* words sometimes are simply transposed within phrases: "I am alone, I alone am." Whole clauses can be essentially repeated, for instance when Beckett uses parallel construction (repetition in syntax) substituting different adjectives or predicate nominatives: ". . . I won't be any more, it won't be worth it any more, it won't be necessary any more, it won't be possible any more, but it's not worth it now, it's not necessary now, it's not possible now. . . ." The shift of the verb "be" from intransitive to transitive doubles its function, and negation of these resulting variations then multiplies the possible phrases by two. When this device is combined with paradox and extended by self-conscious remarks on style, then the (humorous) result is a string of self-propelling phrases, each one set into motion by the grammatical patterns of its predecessor:

> What variety and at the same time what monotony, how varied it is and at the same time how, what's the word, how monotonous. What agitation and at the same time what calm. What vicissitudes within what changelessness. Moments of hesitation not so much rare as frequent, if one had to choose, and soon overcome in favour of the old crux, on which at first all depends, then much, then little, then nothing.

At first the "I" simply echoes the same ideas using a slightly different clausal structure so that the nouns are in a sense "repeated" as adjectives. At the phrase level Beckett uses repetition to urge the narrator onward by extracting a segment from an earlier sentence to begin some later sentence in the same text. For example, in Text 7 part of the first sentence ("Did I try everything, ferret in every hold, secretly, silently, patiently, listening?") launches the third sentence: "In every hold, I mean all those places where there was a chance of my being. . . ."

In other passages, before a clause can be restated, or even fully stated, half its terms are challenged, and this very fussiness over semantics consumes more words. A quibble about meaning can evade a question instead of answering it: "How long have I been here, what a question, I've often wondered. And often I could answer, An hour, a month, a year, a century, depending on what I meant by here, and me, and being, and there I never went looking for extravagant meanings, there I never much varied, only the here would sometimes seem to vary." A semantic twist or an eccentric redefinition also names words while not allowing a sentence to finish: "Another thing, I call that another thing, the old thing I keep on not saying till I'm sick and tired, revelling in the flying instants, I call that revelling, now's my chance and I talk of revelling . . . ." Also, this narrator shares stylistic quirks with the narrators of the trilogy, the reversal or distortion of a cliché or proverb which pulls the reader up short. He maintains that he is "dead and kicking above," and promises that he will learn to keep quiet "if nothing foreseen crops up."

Conversely, the "I" often insists on the literal meaning of a word, thus providing a gratuitous pun: "The day had not been fruitful, as was only natural, considering the season, that of the very last leeks." A pun initially appears to produce a doubling of meaning, taking us far from the ideal of narrative emptiness; but by insisting upon two or more definitions simultaneously, a pun produces a paralysis of interpretation. For Beckett's characters "the only supremely satisfying form of language is the *pun*—the absurdity of words turned in upon themselves, where meanings cancel each other out and leave yet another Néant, a sudden reverberating silence within the 'big blooming buzzing confusion' of sound and significance . . ." [Richard Coe, "God and Samuel Beckett," in *Twentieth-Century Interpretations of "Molloy," "Malone Dies," "The Unnameable,"* ed. J. D. O' Hara]. At least once in the English version Beckett adds a play on words not present in the French original: "you may even believe yourself dead on condition you make no bones about it." Even the "end sheets" in Text 13 can refer to sheets of paper as well as to death. One of the narrator's favorite phrases, "in a manner of speaking," repeatedly plays over the surface; this aside "takes on an ironic smile when the whole work is concerned with the manner of artistic speaking . . ." [Francis Michael Doherty, *Samuel Beckett*]. At times Beckett exploits the literal meaning of a figurative expression to absurd limits of signifiers and signifieds: "And I'm in good hands again, they hold my head from behind, intriguing detail, as at the hairdressers. . . ."

With the phrase "intriguing detail," the narrator critiques his own verbal handiwork, and throughout *Texts for Nothing* self-reflexive judgments about language inflate his narrative. More so than Beckett's trilogy narrators, he is ludicrously self-conscious about his style as well as about his story: "Never had the sea so thundered from afar, the sea beneath the snow, though superlatives have lost most of their charm." In Text 5 the narrator/scribe remarks on his punctuation and dictation with "full stop, got all that." Moreover, in some stylistically self-defeating passages the narrator's critical evaluations consume as much space as the original statement:

> And it is possible, just, for I must not be too affirmative at this stage, it would not be in my interest, that other fingers, quite a different gang, other tentacles, that's more like it, other charitable suckers, waste no more time trying to get it right, will take down my declarations, so that at the close of the interminable delirium, should it ever resume, I may not be reproached with having faltered. This is awful, awful, at least there's that to be thankful for.

Of course a pedantic search for the perfect word obsessed Molloy and Malone too, but the difference in *Texts* is that linguistic journeys subsume physical ones and obviate any plot whatsoever. In the passage above self-references impede the progress of the sentence, while in many utterances they kill the sentence outright: "When I think, no, that won't work, when come those who knew me, perhaps even know me still, by sight of course, or by smell, it's as

though, it's as if, come on, I don't know, I shouldn't have begun." For encouragement and impetus, the narrator provides positive as well as negative criticism: he counsels himself on what to utter (using the imperative mood) and plans how he will proceed (using the future tense): "somehow somewhere calm, what calm here, ah that's an idea, say how calm it is here, and how fine I feel, and how silent I am, I'll start right away. I'll say what calm and silence . . . yes, I'll say all that tomorrow. . . ." By playing with verbs and commenting on comments (and by humorously contradicting himself) the voice goes on manufacturing words without finally making a statement.

Following the fine example of Molloy, the narrator poses countless queries to ascertain his nature, his location in time and space, his task, and his future. In the tradition of the tramps in *Godot*, he also cross-examines himself simply to pass the time. The movement of Text 1 proceeds through several problems: "Who are these people anyway? Did they follow me up here, go before me, come with me? . . . Do they see me, what can they see of me? . . . How long have I been here, what a question . . . And that other question I know so well too, What possessed you to come?" But by Text 13 there is only one question mark to be seen, because the "I" has lost the desire for knowledge. He decries the "old questions, last questions" despairingly: "Unfortunately it is not a question of elsewhere, but of here, ah there are the words out at last. . . . " In the interim, the interrogative quality of the texts serves its purpose—getting on with the words—for replies provide numerous opportunities for lists, for "ors," for "ifs," and for "perhapses." The narrator poses questions quite consciously because he hopes that someday the answer will be the correct one and thus be the road to silence. In the courtroom scene of Text 5 the narrator becomes increasingly self-conscious about his sentence forms and their punctuation: "And now birds, the first birds, what's this new trouble now, don't forget the question-mark." But Beckett does "forget" the question mark, especially when queries are one clause long and embedded in lengthy sentences. For a confused voice questions are often the only possible statements.

In seeking solutions to his problem of nonbeing, the "I" pursues rhetorical questions to lend validity to a newly posited self. In fact, queries about a hypothetical existence almost create being: "Is it there I came to a stop, is that me still waiting there, sitting up stiff and straight on the edge of the seat, knowing the dangers of laissez-aller, hands on thighs, ticket between finger and thumb . . . it's there, it's me." No, it can't be he—at least not for very long—because the narrator is not located in time, but rather in a timeless state of pre-birth reflected in the jumbled verb tenses of "at first I only had been here, now I'm here still, soon I won't be here yet. . . ." And, no, the "I" cannot be "me" because the "I" drowns in the profusions of pronouns in Text 13.

Many times the response to a question will be both yes and no—a double answer which is in reality a null answer. Contradiction, exploited by Beckett so effectively in the trilogy, becomes both a stylistic device and a thematic issue in *Texts for Nothing.* In Text 13 the "I" reviews previous testimony and concludes that there were "so many lies, so many times the same lie lyingly denied." Vacillations and cancellations reach a climax in this last text, as style and substance both sum to zero: "It's not true, yes, it's true, it's true and it's not true, there is silence and there is not silence, there is no one and there is someone, nothing prevents anything." Here even the word "prevent" balances conflicting meanings: its archaic meaning of to come before, to prepare, or to anticipate, and its modern one of to keep from happening or existing. In *Texts for Nothing* the striving for nothingness anticipates the something of its structure, and yet this nothing reduces the probability for creation. Often, the "I" contradicts itself to deny its own existence: "That's so that I'll never stir again, dribble on here till time is done. . . . It's not me, it's not true, it's not me, I'm far." Contradiction alone succeeds in forcing the narrator backwards, and used in conjunction with questioning, repeating, and quibbling over semantics, it results in near nothingness: "How many hours to go, before the next silence, they are not hours, it will not be silence, how many hours still, before the next silence?" Like many of the texts, this sentence moves in a circle and describes a void; yet this denial of language's meaning paradoxically requires the reassertion of language.

A child would link a flow of words with the simple conjunction "and," but a mature, reasoning voice like the narrator of *Texts* speaks in logical options joined with "or"'s: "What possessed you to come?, unanswerable, so that I answered, To change, or, It's not me, or, Chance, or again, To see, or again, years of great sun. . . ." Many sentences begin with "or" because a new clause is less a new proposition in *Texts for Nothing* than a further possibility. The "I" wonders about the fate of dead bodies and souls in Text 10: "Or has it knelled here at last for our committal to flesh, as the dead are committed to the ground . . . or for our reassignment, souls of the stillborn, or dead before the body, or still young in the midst of ruins, or never come to life through incapacity or for some other reason, or the immortal type, there must be a few of them too. . . ." As this passage shows, the use of alternatives within alternatives deflects the speaker further away from the initial issue, and therefore closer to a diffused nothingness. . . .

Other times proliferating "or's" produce comic effects, a kind of linguistic burlesque: "I stay here, sitting, if I'm sitting, often I feel sitting, sometimes standing, it's one or the other, or lying down, there's another possibility, often I feel lying down, it's one of the three, or kneeling."

Reasoning about events occurring in various atmospheres necessitates frequent use of the conditional mood; and "perhaps" with other related locutions allows the voice to multiply his word output without committing himself to a statement of narrative fact. In Text 10 the voice proceeds rationally from "I'm nothing new" to "Ah so there was something once, I had something once. It may be thought there was." In Text 9 the narrator uses the phrase "what if" to consider past events, but more often the little word "if" enables Beckett's voice to take two steps forward and then three steps back. Specifically, the clause "if it's me"

repeatedly undermines character incarnation, and permits the "I" to spin one false story after another. In the courtroom scene the narrator tires of playing scribe, defendant, and judge simultaneously: " . . . I'd be tried of it, if I were me. It's a game, it's getting to be a game, I'm going to rise and go, if it's not me it will be someone, a phantom. . . ." Here the conditional mood slides into the future tense as a stylistic device to avoid a present existence.

Most of these stylistic techniques produce an accumulation of sentences with a dissolution of meaning. Taking the beginning as a high point, Mary Ann Caws traces a "line of reductions and diminutions" in the *Texts*: "definite statement is reduced to qualified determination, . . . the easiest clichés of natural speech to linguistic fumblings. . . . [and] [t]he most frantic cries diminish in tone to a helplessly polite monotony . . ." ["A Rereading of the Traces," *L'Esprit Créateur*, Fall, 1971]. Other critics, however, praise the lyrical richness of *Texts for Nothing*. When rearranged, the opening of Text 4, albeit full of conditionals, shows "duple rhythm, caesural pauses, even rhyme" [Marilyn Gaddis Rose, "The Lyrical Structure of Beckett's *Texts for Nothing*," *Novel*, Spring, 1971]:

> Where would I go, if I could go,
> Who would I be, if I could be,
> What would I say, if I had a voice,
> Who says this, saying it's me?

It is almost as if rhythm replaces plot; the lyric supplants the narrative. But although the narrator of *Texts* is capable of imagistic poetry, he never manages a simple first-person story.

Instead, in these thirteen pseudostories, experiments of all kinds with verb forms of all sorts occur so often that the voice itself despairs of ever maintaining the authorial present. In trying to create a fictional origin, the narrator shifts from the conditional mood to an even more remote past conditional: "I'd have a mother, I'd have had a mother." Besides failing to situate his stories in the present, he cannot locate himself chronologically: "It's me all right, and ceasing to be what is more, then quickening my step, so as to arrive before the next onslaught, as though it were on time I trod. . . ." Beckett's concern with time and its grammatical markers is revealed in his numerous revisions of verb tenses and in other changes that highlight this same obsession in the narrator: "all mingles, times mingle" becomes in a revised typescript "all mingles, times and tenses." By Text 13 the "I" still has no time frame, as it speaks of past events with present participles and infinitives ("of being past, passing and to be"), and murmurs of endings in the present tense ("we're ended who never were"). Readers had been warned of this confusion as early as Text 3, where the narrator, then playing Shakespearean actor, advises, "let us be dupes, dupes of every time and tense, until it's done. . . ." The rapid switching of tenses expands the text because it permits repetition of similar clauses with different verb phrases, thus obviating continuity of plot or story line. The chronologically fragmented anecdotes and memories represent the temporally fragmented narrator, able to create only a minimal narrative about the struggle to invent a character. With changing tenses Beckett ensures that the "I" will never arrive at any continuous existence—one criterion for being. In these ways Beckett works against his own narrator, allowing him neither to stop nor to succeed.

Besides exploiting tricks with verbs, Beckett also manipulates pronoun changes to prevent the narrator from achieving being. The Unnamable has a similar problem: language cannot bring him into existence and "it's the fault of the pronouns, there is no name for me, no pronoun for me, all the trouble comes from that . . ." (*The Unnamable*). In Text 11 the "I" almost succeeds in fabricating a body through a fantasy memory racing from infancy to schoolboy days to old age. Here words truly invent, as the fiction forces itself to become reality with "sobs made mucus, hawked up from the heart, now I have a heart. . . ." But undermining construction of being is destruction of the "I" through a modulation of pronouns. One phrase recurs in the story, but with significant variation: "having terminated my humanities," "having terminated his humanities," and "having terminated their humanities." This shift from "my" to "his" to "their" distances the fiction's events further from the "I," so that the attempt to forge a self degenerates into the old question, "who is this clot . . . who takes himself for me."

A possible answer to the question "who?" is the impersonal pronoun "one," a pronoun also exploited by Virginia Woolf in her short fictions about the imagination, particularly in passages about mirror reflections (a common metaphor for identity). With this pronoun Beckett can have his "I" speak of himself under false pretenses and evade the harsher realities of his nonexistence. In Text 5, when the voice learns that to be is to be guilty, he muses, "That is why nothing appears, all is silent, one is frightened to be born, no, one wishes one were, so as to begin to die. One, meaning me, it's not the same thing. . . ." Thus the narrator seems aware of his linguistic ploy, as he attempts yet another method of evasion—denying responsibility and culpability in the courtroom scene by relying on the passive voice so that the action's agent need not be specified: "it's noted"—but by whom? This grammatical passivity continues, with the help of null pronouns, to the end of Text 5, until, "Yes, one begins to be very tired, very tired of one's toil, very tired of one's quill, it falls, it's noted." By the end of all the texts, the "I" masks his identity in multiple pronouns—"it and me, it and him, him and me, and all our train, and all theirs"—until he is buried far below the impossible affirmation of being, "I am."

These devices to keep empty language going on are quite effective solo, but arranged in counterpoint they sing of nothingness with an immense variety. Speaking of a way out in Text 9, the voice seems hypnotized by its own repetition, contradiction, permutation, and alternation: "down the long tunnels at first, then under the mortal skies, through the days and nights, faster and faster, no, slower and slower, for obvious reasons, and at the same time faster and faster, for other obvious reasons, or the same, obvious in a different way, or in the same way, but at a different moment of time; a moment earlier, a moment later, or at the same moment, there is no such thing, there would be no such thing. . . ." The "way out" has been lost forever after this wordplay, and other texts similarly combine

questions, authorial comments, changes in tenses, and shifts in pronouns to go on producing words for nothing, "in vain." The following proposition begins with some preconditions for the "I" and ends by dismissing the "I" altogether:

> If I were here, if it could have made me, how I would pity it, for having spoken so long in vain, no, that won't do, it wouldn't have spoken in vain, if I were here, and I wouldn't pity it if it had made me, I'd curse it, or bless it, it would be in my mouth, cursing, blessing, whom, what, it wouldn't be able to say, in my mouth it wouldn't have much to say, that had so much to say in vain.

In this sentence, like many others in *Texts for Nothing,* syntax is so disjointed that, as the narrator puts it, "the subject dies before the verb." In this case the consequent, what should be the independent clause, is stated but then contradicted, and reasons for the contradiction are exhaustively pursued. Thus, "I would pity it" eventually becomes "I would bless it"; however, before the sentence can end, the "it" is analyzed out of existence. These sleights of language produce very long "sentences" with no direct line between subject and predicate, that is, no relationship between the actor and his action, or between a cause and an effect. This is one given of the texts: absence of standard characters and genuine action. So Beckett has created an appropriate imitative style for *Texts for Nothing,* a work in which there is "no talk of a creator and nothing very definite in the way of a creation."

Each linguistic device helps to make style and content reflect each other endlessly as in a fun house mirror. Since the voice is searching for the correct utterance, it is only natural that he should employ repetition and permutation, that he should try all possible word strings. He shuffles different phrases hoping to find some formulation that is stable; "that's why I say it, patiently, variously, trying to vary, for you never know, it's perhaps all a question of hitting on the right aggregate. So as to be here no more at last. . . ." Because the "I" can be certain of nothing, he resorts to questions, contradictions, and conditionals: his very existence is one big "if." In a world of polar opposites like life and death, being and non-being, and speech and silence, the only sincere means of expression reduces to contradiction and paradox. And if the "I" must define himself through the texts, then using semantics to compose a self becomes logical: "With a cluther of limbs and organs, all that is needed to live again, to hold out a little time, I'll *call* that living, I'll *say* it's me . . ." (my italics).

Separate voices never really harmonize, contradictions are never resolved, questions are never answered; and words merely cancel out each other to form texts for nothing: "Blot, words can be blotted and the mad thought they invent . . . wipe it out, all you have to do is say you said nothing and so say nothing again." The narrator's analysis of his writing style in *Texts* recalls Celia's analysis of Murphy's speaking style: "She felt, as she felt so often with Murphy, spattered with words that went dead as soon as they sounded; each word obliterated, before it had time to make sense, by the word that came next; so that in the end she did not know what had been said. It was like difficult music heard for the first time." Through carefully chosen stylistic devices Beckett can go on writing without characters or plots. Using circular structure and a style that freezes his content near zero he can continue—as he demonstrates in *How It Is* and the more recent prose fragments—as long as there are words.

Texts for Nothing has gotten mixed reviews (some critics arguing that it merely provides a sequel to *The Unnamable,* for example), but it did extricate Beckett from an artistic impasse through experiments with short, discrete, and structured sections. Beyond this it anticipates several of the subsequent fictions; in particular, its images provide points of departure for many a later fragment. The narrator's situation at the start of *Texts for Nothing* resembles that of the speaker in *From an Abandoned Work*: "Quag, health up to the knees, faint sheep-tracks, troughs scooped deep by the rains. It was far down in one of these I was lying, out of the wind" (*Texts*). The bracken and larch of Text 1 reappear as the thicket of *Abandoned Work*. Both narrators are obsessed with butterflies, fluttering things in general, and clocks, but primarily with wombs and tombs. *From an Abandoned Work* can be imagined as an expansion into story form of one sentence from Text 8: "Yes, my past has thrown me out, its gates have slammed behind me, or I burrowed my way out along, to linger a moment free in a dream of days and nights, dreaming of me moving, season after season, towards the last, like the living, till suddenly I was here, all memory gone."

Another *Texts* location consists of hills and valleys, and such terrain, of course, provides the setting for *Enough*. The narrators of *Texts* and of *Enough* both deny any independent knowledge (all information comes from "them" or from "him"), and both plead "not guilty" to an unnamed crime. Just as the "I" at the beginning of *Enough* watches a disembodied hand write the words of a disembodied voice, the "I" of *Texts* divides into a scribe and a speaker: "Yes, I see the scene, I see the hand, it comes creeping out of shadow, the shadow of my head, then scurries back, no connexion with me." At the end of *Enough* the narrator wipes out all but the flowers, thus cancelling out most of its fiction; similarly, as we have seen, the "I" of Text 13 "blots" and "wipes out" segments of his nonstory. If the narrator of *Enough* is taken to be male and an older version of its former self, then one passage from Text 1 condenses the substance of the later fiction:

> Yes, I was my father and I was my son, I asked myself questions and answered as best I could, I had it told to me evening after evening, the same old story I knew by heart and couldn't believe, or we walked together, hand in hand, silent, sunk in our worlds, each in his worlds, the hands forgotten in each other. That's how I've held out till now. And this evening again it seems to be working, I'm in my arms, I'm holding myself in my arms, without much tenderness, but faithfully, faithfully. Sleep now, as under that ancient lamp, all twined together, tired out with so much talking, so much listening, so much toil and play.

Similarly, we leave the couple in *Enough* faithfully "wedged together bent in three" after much talk.

The struggling, panting creature of *Texts for Nothing* is also related to Pim in *How It Is*. Resonances between these two works—short, staccato phrases; and the theme of expiation for past sins—suggest that some of *How It Is* grew out of the courtroom scene in Text 5. Verbal echoes are numerous: "I say it as I hear it," "it's noted," "above in the light," and "bits and scraps." And the same motifs—the split self, the need to be witnessed, and the curtain and drama images—permeate both works. A long series of attackers and victims in the third section of *How It Is,* depending on each other for existence, is foreshadowed in Text 12: "That's the accountants' chorus, opining like a single man, and there are more to come, all the peoples of the earth would not suffice, at the end of the billions you'd need a god, unwitnessed witness of witnesses. . . ." The narrator of *Texts* predicts of its imaginary artistic creation "perhaps it will end on a castrato scream," which is exactly how *How It Is* does end. More important is their similar phrasal structure. In *Texts for Nothing,* Beckett's style develops from the very long, unbroken linguistic strings of *The Unnamable* to sentences of reasonable length composed of repeated short phrases and clauses separated by commas. Sentences like these, when written as individual jagged, condensed segments, form the paragraphlike passages of *How It Is,* while *Text*'s phrases and clauses become short spurts of syntax that are now minus all commas, most connectives, and most verbs, to form the tortured language, the "midget grammar," of Pim and friend.

Beckett's conception for *Ping* also may have derived from a metaphor in *Texts,* but its style marks a new departure from the comparatively traditional style of *Texts.* The "ragdoll rotting" in Text 2 is transformed into the puppet-like white body of *Ping.* In Text 5, eyes—so prevalent in Beckett's later fictions—are mentioned explicitly: "It's an image, in my helpless head, . . . or before my eyes, they see the scene, the lids flicker and it's in. An instant and then they close again, to look inside the head, to try and see inside, to look for me there, to look for someone there. . . ." The repeated phrase "fixed ping fixed elsewhere," which could refer to the blinking motion of eyes, may be *Ping*'s condensed version of clauses like those in Text 7: "an evening shadow you follow with your eyes, thinking of something else, yes, that's it, the mind elsewhere, and the eyes too, if the truth were known, the eyes elsewhere too." Also, "ping" suggests the ticks or bells of a clock, and analogously, in Text 11 the narrator remarks that "time devours on. . . . Or it's in the head, like a minute time switch, a second time switch. . . ." Repetitions of "one second" mark time in *Ping* and may measure the duration of eye movements or of memories. The narrator decides in Text 13 that the only requisite for a story is "something somewhere that can leave a trace," and the minimal action of *Ping* reduces to "traces blurs signs."

The white vault of *Imagination Dead Imagine* had its blueprints drawn in *Texts for Nothing* as well, where "perhaps we're in a head, it's as dark as in a head before worms get at it, ivory dungeon." An alternating hot and cold environment in *Imagination*'s white rotunda is elucidated by passages in *Texts*: "It's mechanical, like the great colds, the great heats, the long days, the long nights, of the moon. . . ." While the narrator of *Imagination* tries to invent some sort of story despite imagination's death and all traces of life vanished, the "I" of Text 6 has a similar but more feasible goal: "I have high hopes, a little story, with living creatures coming and going on a habitable earth crammed with the dead, a brief story, with night and day coming and going above . . . ." Two static creatures in *Imagination*'s vault may wait for a small society in another tale, in a different storm.

The small society of *The Lost Ones* comes and goes within the same alternation of cold darkness and hot light hinted at in *Texts* and appearing in *Imagination*; finally the brief story of "creatures coming and going" gets told. The "I" of *Texts* wonders if he will find the "way out"—"Shall I never see the sky again"—just as the lost ones wonder if they will ever return to the sky and stars, which they believe to be outside their cylinder. Twisting tunnels are searched for a "way out," but all journeys end in death, just as the narrator of Text 9 had predicted: "if only I could say, There's a way out there, there's a way out somewhere, then all would be said, it would be the first step on the long travelable road, destination tomb, to be trod without a word, tramp tramp, little heavy irrevocable steps, down the long tunnels at first, then under the mortal skies. . . ." The lost creatures never escape from the long tunnels out into the skies, but with *Lessness* the "refuge" has fallen open and the later Beckett traveller is exposed to the void.

Thus a similar stylistic journey is reduced to the one step the creature in *Lessness* is vainly trying to make. The narrator of the *Texts* posits the sine qua non of a narrative: "Start by stirring, there must be a body, as of old . . . ," and later imagines a story of "faint stirs day and night, as if to grow less could help, ever less and less and never quite be gone." This lesser movement prepares the way for the "little body" of *Lessness*. Or its aborted being could reincarnate one of the phantoms of Text 5, "those of the living and [those] . . . who are not born." Also, the "issueless" body in the ruins of *Lessness* recalls the souls contemplated by the "I" in Text 10, "souls of the stillborn, or dead before the body, or still young in the midst of the ruins, or never come to life through incapacity . . . among the unborn hordes, the true sepulchral body. . . ." Figments, blessings, curses, and screams that are discussed in Text 13 materialize in *Lessness*. In *Texts* day is a "disperser of phantoms," and in *Lessness* dawn is a "dispeller of figments." But while many of the motifs of *Lessness* come from *Texts for Nothing*, its form is innovative, in fact startling.

New forms, new arrangements of words, are the somethings Beckett has left after *Texts for Nothing*. These thirteen texts offer stark yet rich images which serve as catalysts for the minimalist stories to come; but more important, the texts provide testing grounds for the stylistic experimentation of the later fictions. Many critics, and the author himself, judged *Texts for Nothing* to be a failure, although, if it redeemed Beckett's language and gave birth to the stylistic varieties of the later prose, it was a fortunate fall indeed. Writing *about* the impasse itself provides a "way out" of the impasse, as Beckett chronicles his struggle to go on despite and through linguistic challenges by creating self-reflexive fictions.

Paola Zaccaria   (essay date 1990)

SOURCE: "*Fizzles* by Samuel Beckett: The Failure of the Dream of a Never-ending Verticality," in *Rethinking Beckett: A Collection of Critical Essays,* edited by Lance St. John Butler and Robin J. Davis, Macmillan Press, 1990, pp. 105-123.

[*In the essay below, Zaccaria presents an analysis of the stories collected in* Fizzles.]

It is very difficult to give an account of the genesis and chronology of the short stories collected in the volume *Fizzles* (Fr. *Foirades*). The five *Fizzles,* written between 1950 and 1960, were published in the French magazine *Minuit* in 1973; in 1976 four editions in volume of the *Fizzles* were published: *Pour finir encore et Autres Foirades, For to end yet again and Other Fizzles,* and two American editions by Grove Press and Petersburg Press respectively. Each of the four editions arranged the stories in a different order, with the result that there can be countless readings of the text.

In this paper, I will discuss the short stories following the order of the Grove Press edition, namely:

  1 'He is barehead'

  2 'Horn came'

  3 'Afar a bird'

  4 'I gave up'

  5 'Closed space'

  6 'Old earth'

  7 'Still'

  8 'For to end yet again'.

In the Petersburg Press edition, which collected only the original five *Fizzles/Foirades,* the text, published both in French and in the English versions, are enriched with thirty-three etchings by Jasper Johns. The back cover gives some information about the collaboration between the two artists:

> The French texts first appeared in 1972; the English texts were written by Samuel Beckett in 1974 for this collaboration. The etchings were made by Jasper Johns and proofed and printed at the Atelier Grommelynck in Paris in 1975 and 1976. . . . Each book is signed by the author and the artist: two hundred and fifty numbered 1 to 250 . . . French text Editions de Minuit 1976. English text Samuel Beckett 1976.

Foirades/Fizzles, Beckett/Johns, text/engravure, text/etching: this bilingual, bi-textual, bi-medial edition redoubles the frustration effect experienced by anyone who wants to trace *a* meaning in Beckett's work. The fact that he does not opt for *one* language tells us about his refusal of a language which he, like Joyce, seems to feel as a nationalistic net, as a limit; the inclusion of another form of art, etching, in his own text, tells us about his refusal of separation, his will to elide bounds, to mix the verbal with other signs: here with painting, in the theatrical works he very often erases the verbal sign to substitute it with *the* sign—the gesture, which can also be non-gesture, absolute stillness.

The interwoven play of double texts, double readings, double textures and double writings of signs discloses both Beckett's and Johns' intention of emitting multiple and contradictory signals.

Fizzles/Foirades is considered by Beckett himself as being a work with a modular structure since each story can be arranged in different, endless orders. As a work which can be discomposed and recomposed, in the Petersburg Press edition *Fizzles* widens its possibility of arrangement because the reader can place a story in English near one in French and then look at one of the etchings; or the English version of the French text can be read after a different French text and a different etching, and so on.

Contradiction and permutation, typical features of the Beckett microtext (stories), are also at the basis of his macrotext (*Fizzles*): linguistic permutation (French/English), artistic permutation (stories/etchings in the Petersburg Press edition), intratextual permutation (different arrangement of texts), extratextual permutation (segments of previous texts are inserted in the stories). Permutation as a way out of repetition, as novelty but also as underlining of the repetition itself. Permutation also as a denouncing of the void in which contemporary art operates: no longer a microstructure which has a logical relation to the macrostructure, but fragments to be arranged in endless possible ways by the author himself, by the editor, by the reader.

A text without binding, or with innumerable bindings, *Fizzles* puzzles the reader because of its appearance of an unfinished work. Each section or single story can be interchangeable, the 'character(s)' of each story can be exchanged: they, or rather the 'unnamed'—actually pronouns—are, deep down, endless reflections of the first pronominal entity described in the first story of the Grove Press edition, **'He is barehead'**:

> He is barehead, barefoot, clothed in a singlet and tight trousers too short for him, his hands have told him so, again and again, and his feet, feeling each other and rubbing against the legs, up and down calves and shins. To this vaguely prison garb none of his memories answer, so far, but all are of heaviness, in this connexion, of fullness, of thickness.

His sememe is lack: nameless, ageless, sightless, 'barehead' and 'barefoot', without memories (he finds difficulty in reconstructing the past, with the exception of the remembrance of the narrowest sideways and the noisiest falls), this creature is the most complete portrait Beckett sketches in *Fizzles.* This essential sketch-wandering-in-a-labyrinth has the same fragmented body as the entities inhabiting the other stories, the same blindness ('Do his eyes, after such long exposure to the gloom, begin to pierce it? No, and this is one of the reasons why he shuts them

more and more'). Blind, he cannot see other people/himself/*in*-self, though he always hopes that

> some day he'll see himself, his whole front, from the chest down, and the arms, and finally the hands, first rigid at arm's length, then close up, trembling, to his eyes.

Unable to see himself, he needs someone who, from without, *seeing him, describes him:* the narrator who, most of the time, in this story, observes 'he' from a distance and describes his movements, using the camera from a short distance, sometimes the seeing eye offering unmerciful close-ups, sometimes offering the camera to the reader thus making use of the phatic function, while acting as a directorial narrator.

By offering the reader an interlocutory function as regards the object of the discourse (*he*), the narrator reduces *he* to a thing which can only be portrayed, to the victim of a pitiless, indifferent, ironic eye/I.

If we take into account the text *Fizzles* according to the arrangement of the Grove Press edition, we witness a 'progressive sliding' of the narrator-role, a continuous readjustment of the narrator-object-of-the-narration relationship.

In Fizzle 2 (**'Horn came'**), there is the introduction of the narrating *I* who, at night, receives Horn-*he*, listens to him speaking in the dark after having consulted his notes by the light of an electric torch: 'Then he switched it off and spoke in the dark. Light silence, dark speech'. But since in the dark the narrator/*I* cannot see Horn, one night he begs him to 'light his face', thus marking the shifting from being a detached narrator, one who can see his character even in the dark (**'He is barehead'**), to the intradiegetic narrator who, besides being able to see 'the other', loses his characteristics of 'pure' narrator, outside narration, to become one of its subjects. As a matter of fact, his difficulty in seeing the other man both hides and is associated with the greater difficulty of seeing himself and of allowing himself to be seen:

> It was five or six years since anyone had seen me, to begin with myself. I mean the face I had pored over so, all down the years. Now I would resume this inspection, that it may be a lesson to me, in my mirrors and looking glasses so long put away. I'll let myself be seen before I'm done.

He has hidden himself from other people and from himself, but now he decides to re-enter the hall of mirrors, specular writing, the *I* who narrates. In this way, Horn, by offering the vision of 'a waning face disclosing, more and more clearly the more it entered the shadow, the one I remembered', functions as a Narciss-us-effect. By the light of a torch, surrounded by mirrors and looking-glasses, interrupting Horn's words, though he 'did not like anyone to interrupt him', *I* sees *he*, his like, his peer. When he raises his eyes from the place of signs and sheds light on the darkness from which the words come and, in so doing, silences the words, *I* sees himself in the other, the narrator in the character, he recognises him(self): 'No doubt about it, it is he'.

There is a sudden equation between the narrator and the

narrated, the eye and the I. Although *I* says that these images organise themselves in the outer space and that if he interposes his hand between the outside and his eyes, if he closes his eyes and takes off his glasses, he cannot see these images any longer, or they become blurred, he has to admit that this is 'a help, but not a real protection, as we shall see'. From which images does *I* want to protect himself? The image of himself? Of the other? *I* as it once was? *I* as it is today? Maybe he wants to protect himself from the re-inscription in the text, from seeing himself on the page at a time when *I* believed he was at last outside of it for ever:

> I thought I had made my last journey, the one I must try now try once more to elucidate, that it may be a lesson to me, the one from which it were better I had never returned. But the feeling gains on me that I must undertake another.

To close one's eyes, to take off one's glasses, is not enough to protect oneself from mirrors. To be tired and confined to bed is not enough to protect oneself from the necessity of the journey (a mental journey, as the verb *elucidate* reveals), from the desire to see clearly. Either one goes to the place of no return—death, silence—or invalidity will not protect one from the compulsion to hold in one's hand the stick for the journey/the pen/the mirror.

> —*Dark word, light silence, mirror vision*/CLICK 1/

> —*To turn on the light, interrupt the word and in the silence, seeing (oneself)*/CLICK 2/

> —*To turn off the light, interrupt the vision and regain the word*/CLICK 3/

since neither darkness nor glasses protect one from the images of the 'other' space. When an image has been fully exhausted and a new failure has been experienced, one starts again on the journey, plays again the same tune.

CLICK 1—CLICK 2—CLICK 3: (*Fizzle 3*)

CLICK 1—CLICK 2—CLICK 3: (*Fizzle 4*).

Other journeys, other intermissions, other maskings-unmaskings of textual subjects and objects. Pro/nominal division (*I/he*) instead of pro-nominal (*I*-Horn). The pronominal assimilation shortens distances, smooths the differences that *I* insists on proclaiming. The vehemence with which the *I* proclaims the differences denounces the interior caesura which cuts *I*. His exaggerated need to deny his existence betrays his disconnection with the self, his blockage of identification, his fear of existing as a body: I, the narrating being, diacritic subjectivity and, as such, bodiless, never born (it is impossible to trace back the birth of the first story), never dead (as long as there is man, there will be stories). The urgency to deny one's existence is so strong that it needs to be reaffirmed in two repetitive short stories (**'Afar a bird'** and **'I gave up'**). Endless repetition of the denial which unmasks the feeling of uncertainty of the one who denies (himself). Repetition as regression and stillness—the repetitive syntagmas derive from the compulsion to repeat, from the beating and rebeating of the death pulse. Horizontal repetition (of words) and vertical

repetition (as an attempt to reach the core of the words) with the body (*he*) forcing the mind (*I*) into production.

The strenuous fight between *I/He* of Fizzles 3 and 4 has been lethal for both fighters or, at least, has been so exhausting that both agents of narrative have, for the time being, been confined to silence and rest. The two opposing forces of the short stories—contradiction and repetition—have produced the destruction of the narrative tissue. Beckett, by means of such devices as opposition, denial, contradiction, has enacted the neurosis of dialectics. At the end there is the discovery that one cannot pose questions or wait for answers, one can only think with an a-categorical thought: weariness, stillness, labour and dumbness are the other side of thought. The philosopher/artist, says Michel Foucault, must let himself be absorbed by '*la bêtise*', the boundless monotony of an ever-returning present ['Theatricum Philosophicum', in b. Deleuze, *Différence et répétition*].

Repetition destroys, but it can also free the subject: as in the psychoanalytical process, the cure is a journey towards the depths whence the impulse to repetition comes. Sometimes the traveller feels the need to remove the mirrors orientated toward himself, to turn them from the self elsewhere, from within to without. Fizzle 4 ended with the assertion, 'there is nothing left in his head, I'll feed it all it needs'. Since there is nothing left to take from *he*'s head, since *I* has completely dispossessed *he*, *I* allows him(self) the possibility of a truce; he also retires as the narrating voice residing *within* which, like a parasite, feeds on the other's body. He transforms himself into an impersonal entity which is completely absent from the text which, at this point, deals with external closed space:

> Place consisting of an arena and a little ditch. Between the two skirting the latter a track. Closed space. Beyond the ditch there is nothing.

In the arena live millions of people, 'Never seeing, never hearing one another. Never touching'. In the ditch, which is almost black, whereas in the beginning 'it was all bright', there are millions of bodies. The track, which goes around the circumference,

> is made of dead leaves. A reminder of bedlam nature. Dead but not rotting. Crumbling into dust rather. Just wide enough for one. On it no two ever meet.

It is a concentric space consisting of three circles: the outer ditch, the track and the arena. Raising his eyes from the closed space of the written text—the hall of mirrors, a body with a mirror *inside*—the writer turns to rest them upon the closed space of life— the arena, a world enclosed by track and ditch. Movement from the asphyxia of personal existence to the asphyxia of public life where, as happens between *I* and *he*, there is no danger of sickness by contagion ('never touching'); on the contrary, people live fearing any contact whatever, they can only run along the track which is only wide enough for one. This narrow, circular track reminds the reader of the labyrinth of the little man in the first Fizzle: it is asphyctic, skirts the ditch and is in-between arena and ditch. The dead leaves, a 'reminder of beldam nature', stress the idea that it shares both of death and of life. The man in the labyrinth was threatened by falling masses, the man running along the track is threatened by its contiguity to the ditch. The former risked being crushed, the latter risked crushing himself. The greater freedom of the man on the track—he is *outside,* in the open air, and is not menaced by dangers coming from above—is only apparent. His place is closed, nonetheless: he runs, alone, towards death with no chance of meeting another body, another eye/I.

Moreover, as in **'He is barehead'**, movement is possible only in a vertical direction: one can climb */up/* the track, or go */down/* the arena, or fall */down/* in the ditch. In the first Fizzle, *he* went zigzagging */up/* for the climbing or */down/* the slope. Even the noises were produced by *vertical* falls. Man falls */down/* in life and then falls */down/* in death. Sometimes it seems possible to go uphill—the uphill sideways—but ultimately these chances reveal their deceptive, tricky nature of *fizzles,* because track and climbing are on the edge of the ditch.

Labyrinths, walls, tracks, arenas, ditches: prisons, borders, 'closed spaces'. And also: home, placenta, tomb. Actually, one is never really born in the sense of coming out in the air. From up, down: fall, descent, precipice, even in birth, even in death. From inside, outside (birth), or from outside, inside (death), always on account of a vertical expulsion. The horizontal space is so narrow that nothing can move from right to left, or vice versa. The law of gravity requires masses to fall */down/,* human bodies to fall */down/.* The compact falls and produces fragments and splinters (as far as masses are concerned), death and disintegration (as far as bodies), fragmentation of the discourse (as for narration), dust and rotting (as for the word).

Even bodily sensations are felt along the vertical line: *he* in Fizzle 1 touches, sees, or will see himself, vertically. He does not embrace himself (horizontal movement), the walls do not allow him to touch himself, to touch *in*-self—the *I* which is within him; the walls prevent him from reaching himself, from reuniting his selves. It is a prohibited pleasure for the little man in a singlet, as well as for the writer who has lost his self in the writing labyrinth (he has abandoned the insecure, no-way-out sideways) to reconcile *he* with *I,* body and psyche, the narration and the narrator. But if the writer abandons the labyrinth metaphor and the crushing theme, he falls into the 'closed space' metaphor. This text, which in French is entitled 'Se voir', does not actually tell of any being who sees himself. Dead bodies and living bodies are mentioned, and even if the detailed description of the place presupposes an eye which sees other people and, by ontological transition, himself, nobody assumes the paternity of the voice, nobody says *I.* Pretensions to a-personal narration which the following short story, **'Old earth'**, immediately belies. Here, the eyes which see are attributed to an *I:*

> Old earth, no more lies. I've seen you, it was me, with my other's ravening eyes, too late. You'll be on me, it will be you, it will be me, it will be us, it was never us.

The self-vision of **'Closed space'** was the vision of '(my) other's ravening eyes'; he who sees the earth is an *I* who has borrowed his eyes. That is, most probably, why he

could not, in **'Closed space'**, say whose eyes were the seeing eyes: though they were his, placed in his skull, they also belonged to the 'other'. They were the depersonalised eyes of the ontological vision of the world—they could be anybody's eyes.

Now, *I* has finally seen the earth, though 'too late', when the earth is on the point of re-covering him, of initiating him to the osmotic process of corpse-earth which will finally cancel the otherness ('it will be you, it will be us'), and dust will return to dust. The old game of affirmation-negation is played once again. Once again, but without antithetical asperities, as if the narration were going tiringly on, as if *I* were not aware of the uselessness of opposing himself, of placing himself upright (*I*) with respect to the earth, the old enemy which is awaiting *I* to shift from the vertical posture to the horizontal one. When, tired at last, *I* will lie on it, the earth will swallow the body, slowly, gradually assimilating it to herself.

Oppositions, contrasts, denials, bars, pens belong to the vertical order, to put an end to the *I/he* opposition means to succumb to the horizontal—to death. Actually, the *I* of **'Old earth'** has just the first symptoms of sinking, he still postpones the end (of the story and of life) as the image of himself 'still, *standing* before the window' (the italics are mine), contemplating the sky, suggests. Though he is violently shaken by 'gasps and spasms', *I* succeeds in *standing,* in placing himself against the earth, in continuing to look at the sky, ('a childhood sea, other skies, another body'). He looks upwards, to something which reminds him of childhood, the beginning, and not downwards, towards the earth which means the end.

This lyrical short story, with a quotation from Dante, *'Tristi fummo nell' aere dolce',* deals with memories which are more consistent and emotional than in the other *Fizzles*:

> For an instant I see the sky, the different skies, then they turn their faces, agonies, loves, the different loves, happiness too, yes, there was that too, unhappily. Moments of life, of mine too, among others, no denying, all said and done. Happiness, what happiness, but what deaths, what loves, I knew at the time; it was too late then.

Though the passage speaks of happiness, deaths, loves, the emphatic and overcharged tone makes the reader suspicious of some sort of irony.

The lyrical, airy flights of **'Old earth'** are briskly interrupted by the beginning of the following Fizzle, **'Still'**. As we have seen, the little bareheaded man of Fizzle 1 has transformed himself into the narrating *I* at the mirror (**'Horn came'**), has narrated the impossible fight between he who writes and he who is written down (**'Afar a bird'** and **'I gave up'**), has then completely disappeared in **'Closed space'** where a bodiless voice speaks of the three circles of existence and, finally, has moaned for the pains and joys of life (**'Old earth'**). After all this, he sits now in a wicker chair, at the window, and becomes again a camera, an eye (though not an *I*): he resumes distance from his self again. The fall into sentimentalism of **'Old earth'** has left him shameful and with the urge to put an end to his personal life. The idea of end opens the story **'Still'**:

> Bright at last close of a dark day the sun shines
> out at last and then goes down. Sitting quite still
> at the valley window normally turn head now
> and see it. . . .

Eyes see, arms move, legs go to the window and then back to the chair, a trunk shifts from one position to another, although everything would convey the idea of stillness:

> though actually close inspection not still at all
> but trembling all over. Close inspection namely
> detail by detail all over to add up finally to this
> whole not still at all but trembling all over. But
> casually in this failing light impression dead still
> even the hands clearly trembling and the breast
> faint rise and fall.

The text entitled **'Still'** speaks of mobility and tremors, of a being identified only by fragments of body (eyes, arms, wrist, hands, legs, head, trunk), of an entity which is not even a pronoun: there is no *he*, all reference is made impersonally, in the infinitive—perhaps he speaks of himself in the third person or is using the imperative tense. It is the extreme journey toward the killing of any corporeity (of voice) that has been so far accomplished in *Fizzles*; all the movements of the (un)still being are described in detail, but there is no trace of thought. At last out of labyrinths, underground spaces, the creature—though fearing movement—experiments with short syncopated movements and does what he vaguely remembered in **'He is barehead'**: he touches a part of the body—the head—with his hand; at last he can rest the burden of his head in his hands. Nonetheless, the erasure of the two diegetic entities—the subject who narrates and the narrates subject—seems doubtful because of the repetition of the time complement: *now, this hour.* Now when? And where? In the room with the wicker chair? And who says 'now'? The still man or he who portrays him? Now in the writing-room? Now in the reading-room? Here, now, at this hour, there is just a fragmented body, apparently still, actually shaken with tremors, who can at last rest his head in his hands: he makes the head—the place of thoughts, memories, where writing was born—touch the hand, the agent of writing. The two parts reach for each other and 'the still' must surrender to the hand's will ('head to rescue as if hand's need the greater'). And it is not by chance that the fingers which hold the head are the ones used in writing: thumb, forefinger and middle finger.

The impersonal character of the prose of **'Still'** is contradicted by the tremors which make the head shake before the hand comes to rescue it. Is, perhaps, the (un)still trying to check (himself), to still (himself), to master (himself and) his need of writing? Could the mental and physical stillness be only an attempt to stop the hand from writing and the head from thinking? Anyway, the attempt is useless: the head, which wants to stand upright, which does not like to depend on the hand, falls towards this latter, 'as if hand's need the greater'. Night falls: night is a dark word, 'in the dark . . . even more than ever necessary . . . the further shelter of the hand'.

To hold one's head in order to think, but also to sustain

the head's words with the hand's transcription: this solution is in fact chosen in the end, when it is decided that instead of leaving 'it so all quite still', there will be an attempt at 'listening to the sounds all quite still head in hand listening for a sound'. In the dark, listening to sounds: all seems to suggest that the sounds do not come from outside, but from the inside; Beckett himself, speaking of his search to find the voice of his 'lost self' says that one must sit in all tranquillity and 'get below the surface, concentrating, *listening, getting your ear down so you can hear the infinitesimal murmur'*: just what 'the still' man is going to do.

The *in*finite, circular writing presents in a dramatic way the image of the still man in Act viii of *Fizzles,* **'For to end yet again'**:

> For to end yet again skull alone in a dark place
> pent bowed on a board to begin.

End—skull alone in the dark; closed space—forehead on a board; to begin: the reader re-encounters in this beginning the topoi common to the previous seven acts, whereas the internal opposition 'to end/to begin' tells of the interchangeability of the two acts: to end a text means also to begin another and, inevitably, the beginning of a text already implies its ending.

Interchangeable contradiction which, being double-faced, undoes itself; of course, it means to go back to short story 1,2,3, . . . *n*th, 'and yet' means also to go on; some steps back 'and yet' one goes onwards: the acquisition of a new small element justifies the *n*th story and, on the other hand, it contributes to stretch the story towards its ending, to bring the writer toward the word 'end', man toward his end, although the end is never actually reached because, maybe, both man and narration do not so much want to come to an end as to escape the condition of stillness or, as J. Hansford says, nothing can end 'because nothing can be said to have begun' ['*Imagination Dead Imagine*: The Imagination and Its Context', *Journal of Beckett Studies,* Spring, 1987]. The illusion of progression is defeated: 'Progression in time becomes stasis (or unending progression) in a context of timelessness'. This sensation of 'end' is stressed by the language which speaks of death, though the Beckettian *persona* does not die: he tiringly moves from chair to window, switches on his thoughts drawing signs which speak of an impersonal presence/absence, of human remains.

The true failure of *Fizzles* lies, most probably, in the impossibility of writing the end, in the impossibility of (writing the story of) death. Hence, *Fizzles* are stories where the living are unborn (**'He is barehead'**) and the dead do not die; the narrator fails to narrate death and succeeds in representing the degenerative process of physical and epistemological ageing in a lifeless, deathless and timeless universe.

The language itself is entirely built around funeral vocabulary whose task is to call for death (quoting only from the first eight lines: 'skull . . . , dark place . . . , board . . . , skull in the dark . . . , void . . . , no neck no face . . . , the box . . . , last place . . . , dark . . . , void . . . , place of remains . . . , dark . . . , a remain . . . , remains. . . . '), though there are hints that, even surrounded by remains, dust, still air, the 'skull' is not yet without pulp—it still belongs to a living, though agonising creature. It takes but a little—the vision of two 'white dwarfs' against the grey—to set the camers to work again, to lengthen the scriptorial tape, to give movement to the scene, matter to thought.

The scene takes place in the skull, cemetery of ruins, remains, falls. But, surprisingly, instead of 'going out of work', this skull goes on again:

> (i) Thus the skull makes to glimmer again in lieu of going out;

> (ii) Thus then the skull last place of all makes to glimmer again in lieu of going out.

In the skull is also set the time(lessness) of the happening: in it 'a leaden dawn' first rises then grows 'less dark till final grey'. This *grey* immediately colours the landscape, the time, the living being, the story. From the initial black with a few patches of white (the dwarfs, the sheets of the barrow), to grey. The last/first short story is varnished with colour's non-colours, with grey predominating over black and white. *Grey:* the intermediate, the indeterminate, neither black nor white, the *un*-colour which colours also the in(side), the *I*. Grey sky, grey sand, grey body of the living creature who is called 'the expelled'. And then dust everywhere, dust coming from the disintegration of the fallen fragments and which, in its turn, produces other ruins, other destruction. 'Strak erect amidst his ruins the expelled' sees all that greyness, but perhaps cannot see the white barrow carried by the white dwarfs:

> Yet to imagine if he can see it the last expelled amidst his ruins if he can ever see it and seeing believe his eyes.

This confirms that the scene is set in the (grey) skull of the writing being: he has created a grey place, a grey time, a grey body, and has wrapped everything in dust; then, for a change, he has made a fragment fall ('first change of all in the end a fragment comes away and falls'), has introduced on to the scene the dwarfs, Swiftian freaks, circus memories, who push a wheelbarrow left and right for 'dung litter of laughable memory'. But, at this point, something does not work in the skull—too much grey, perhaps—if it repeats 'first change of all a fragment comes away from mother ruin and with slow fall . . . ' . The third change (the first was the fall of fragments; the second, the vision of the dwarfs) is again first change not simply because it repeats the first, but because the skull seems to have forgotten he has already seen it. This skull tiringly works with worn-out material, and it confuses what he has already seen/written with the new material. The very forgetfulness betrays the fact that consciousness removes experience and that the imagination shapes the present after the past. The similarity to a film-script is almost openly declared towards the last third of the short story:

> Then on so soft the eye does not see them go driftless. . . . Long lifted to the horizontal faces closer and closer strain as it will the eye achieves no more than two tiny oval blanks.

The skull-with-eyes, at the end, records the last dramatic change:

> Last change of all in the end the expelled falls headlong down and lies back to the sky full little stretch amid his ruins.

This is the true happening of all the stories: the shift from the vertical position of the various 'living failures' inhabiting all the stories, to the horizontal, oddly human posture of the last expelled who falls 'headlong down and lies back to the sky'. The humanity of the last one to be expelled lies in his 'lapislazuli eyes' (a hint of blue, again), stubbornly open, even after his body looks marble-like. At this point the reader suspects, once again, that the skull with open eyes of the fallen body belongs to the spectator-writer of the scene because, all of a sudden, the relationship between the seeing eye and the dying expelled becomes very close, as denounced by the unexpected intrusion of a dialogical relation between the writing skull and the fallen body: 'fall fall never fear no fear of your rising again'. The phonetic and lexical redundancy (*fall fall, never fear no fear*) which betrays emotivity, besides the 'you' that the writing eye gives to the fallen body, suggests a relational closeness between the two which nothing said before had suggested. The antithesis without any chance of synthesis of similar situations in other stories disappears here, as if the fallen body, almost dead, had put an end to the old antagonism between *I* and *he,* as if piety had at last touched that skull which persisted in surrounding himself with grey, in stiffening movement, in blocking emotivity, as the rigid, upright position of the living-dying man suggested.

To yield to the horizontal, to erase the antithesis (*I/he*), to lie down, means to lose one's control, to become flabby, impotent. The vertical posture held by the various living beings of the previous stories was the only possible weapon in opposing impotence, scriptural sterility and death.

Once the erection has subsided, once the vertical barriers have fallen, the so far pitiless eye of the cameraman perceives the fallen being as too similar to himself and addresses him with 'you', the pronoun which presupposes a familiar relationship, and discreetly switches off the scene which has been taking place in the skull:

> Sepulchral skull is this then its last state all set for always litter and dwarfs ruins and little body.

The skull-vision room-sepulchre closes on a panoramic image of all the elements of the film/short story which in this way remains stiffened: the vision, when fixed in writing, clots, becomes rigid. The oneiric-diegetic character of the vision is openly stated in the end: it has only been a

> dream of a way in a space neither here nor there where all the footsteps ever fell can never fare nearer to anywhere nor from anywhere further away. No for in the end for to end yet again . . . dark falls there again . . . Through it who knows yet another end beneath a cloudless sky same dark . . .

And the word 'end', which the narrator had never approached so closely in the previous *Fizzles,* though resounding in the final one, is no longer called for: an end there will be, if there absolutely has to be one. In the meantime, the switch is turned off: dark again. The fact that **'For to end yet again'** is the last story in the American edition and the first in the French and English editions, speaks worlds about beginnings and endings of stories and of life: the last story yet, again, a story of a failure of a dream. Last act or first act, what does it matter? From the dark other voices (other's words) will come (dark word; light silence) to end . . . ? To begin . . . ? Again . . . ?

Charles Krance   (essay date 1990)

SOURCE: *"Worstward Ho* and *On-*words: Writing to(-wards) the Point," in *Rethinking Beckett: A Collection of Critical Essays,* edited by Lance St. John Butler and Robin J. Davis, Macmillan Press, 1990, pp. 124-40.

[*In the essay that follows, Krance analyzes Beckett's use of language in* Worstward Ho.]

'Words', observes Eugene Kaelin in *The Unhappy Consciousness: The Poetic Plight of Samuel Beckett,* 'suggest meanings in the images they create.' In Beckett's recent microtrilogy—**Company, Ill Seen Ill Said,** and **Worstward Ho**—words persistently suggest meanings in the images they cut short of being created.

The first of these texts, **Company** (1980) is centred about the point of contact, or possibly the hypothetical lack thereof, between the Word transmitted by the voice and the Flesh of its intended receiver. The opening fragment—'A voice comes to one in the dark. Imagine'—introduces the narrative as an extended metaphor of the word-bearing process, 'imagined' from the vantage point of reader as surrogate recipient. What oozes forth from the creative coupling of the 'one in the dark' with the reader, however, bears only a tangential and often antithetical relationship to what may have been originally intended: 'Only a small part of what is said can be verified. As for example when he hears, You are on your back in the dark. . . . But by far the greater part of what is said cannot be verified. As for example when he hears, You first saw the light on such and such a day' (Fragment 2). Such, of course, is the company that we all keep whenever we put pen to paper: however immediate the conception may appear to be at the moment that the word emerges into meaning, by the time the metaphorical ink dries, the word is often little more than the distanced representation of a gleam gone awry in our conceptual eye.

It is in Fragments 7 and 8, however, that we first receive the full impact of what it means to have meaning and image cut each other off:

> A small boy you come out of Connolly's Stores holding your mother by the hand. . . . You make ground in silence hand in hand . . . and after some hundred paces the sun appears above the crest of the rise. Looking up at the blue sky and then at your mother's face you break the silence asking her if it is not in reality much more distant than it appears. The sky that is. The blue sky. Receiving no answer you mentally reframe your question and some hundred paces later look up at her face again and ask her if it does not appear much less distant than in reality it is.

> For some reason you could never fathom this question must have angered her exceedingly. For she shook off your little hand and made you a cutting retort you have never forgotten. (Frag. 7)

This painful (though certainly not unhumorous) reconstruction of suppressed verbal intercourse with the mother is singularly instrumental in the voice's 'homeward' bound attempts to unsay all that was, and will have been said (to be) - before as well as after this 'ground(ing) in silence'. For his unrepressed response to the tropistic influence of the rising sun, the son is rewarded with the very act the (subconscious) fear of which had led him, in the first place, to stick his neck out from behind the folds of his own censored phallocentricity. This initiatory venture into the discourse of the father leaves him castrated, good and proper, by the mother—at least figuratively. Literally, is another mat(t)er. For what specifically constitutes his infraction is the co-incidence in time of his breaking the silence, or *speaking,* and his looking at the mother's face, or *seeing.* He is in a word, and in a single one at that, guilty of having tried to take *it* all in at a glance, 'asking her if it is not in reality much more distant than it appears'. This breaking of the silence while grounded in the mother's grip creates an unbridgeable gap, cutting him loose and leaving him forever suspended between the literal and the figurative. For the *it,* whose distance, 'in reality', from its 'appearance' is in question, here is at one and the same time the sky, the mother's face, the silence . . . and the sun, whose appearance 'above the crest of the rise' was enough to set the son off on his self-alienating projection into the waywardness of language. Once it (the word) is out, he is left to contemplate the hologram of the unforgotten, and unforgiven, figure of *it all,* turning away in its wholeness from the groundless pattern of its own absent projection.

The very next fragment (8) reopens the hypothesis that 'If the voice is not speaking to him it must be speaking to another. . . . To another of that Other. Or of him. Or of another still', and so on. Much of the tension involved in keeping **Company** from 'lapp(ing) as it were in its meaninglessness,' is hinged on this particular junction in the text. For in the face of the taciturn mother who held her ground firmly against the son's ill-conceived attempts to engage her in discourse, Beckett puts into question our most deeply-rooted (and commonly repressed) conceptions of linguistic acquisition; namely, the place and status of the word in our psychogenetic world. For it is not dialogue, but the absence thereof that functions as the alienating experience, or mirror stage, of **Company**'s auditor-cum-narratee. The mother's 'cutting retort' is thus both a literal act and a symbolic, verbal gesture, linked forever in his affective memory, and repeated each time another voice is heard from within the matrix of his consciousness. Concomitantly, each time it resurfaces as the voiced presence of a hypothetical (m)other, it reframes the mirrored opposition of self to other in a context of a never-to-be-fulfilled desire. Rather than provide the means of self-inscription within the folds of the (m)Other, the Word in Beckett's late discourse constitutes instead 'a potent tool for repressing knowledge of that gap, the face in the mirror', in a word, 'the Other' [Caryl Emerson, 'The Outer Word and Inner Speech', in *Bakhtin,* ed. Gary Saul Morson, 1986]. Beckett's auditor is thus left hanging, hungering for that lost locus where there might be constituted the hypothetical 'him' to whom language is spoken as well as the equally hypothetical 'he' who has it speak.

'Headed toward death', writes Foucault, 'language turns back upon itself; it encounters something like a mirror; and to stop this death which would stop it, it possesses but a single power: that of giving birth to its own image in a play of mirrors that has no limits.' This epigraph to Vincent Pecora's recent essay on Joyce's ' "The Dead" and the Generosity of the Word' (*PMLA,* 101, no. 2, March 1986) connects nicely with the second panel of Beckett's triptych, *Ill Seen Ill Said* (1981). This fragmented text attempts to tell the story of an old spectral figure who, spellbound by the image of her own star rising in the heavens, and unable fully to absorb the spectacle of it all, prepares her exit from 'the inexistent centre' (Frag. 2) of her own mirrored absence:

> Absence supreme good and yet. Illumination then go again and on return no more trace. On earth's face. Of what was never. And if by mishap some left then go again. For good again. So on. Till no more trace. On earth's face. Instead of always the same place. Slaving away forever in the same place. At this and that trace. And what if the eye could not? No more tear itself away from the remains of trace. Of what was never. Quick say it suddenly can and farewell say say farewell. If only to the face. Of her tenacious trace.

Her fate, like that of her appendage, the 'drivelling scribe' who from the beginning of the text spurs her 'on', is to remain in a state of perpetual suspension between the spell of the ill-seen image and its achievement in an equally ill-fated representation: 'Such equal liars both'.

'From where she lies she sees Venus rise', as the very first line of the text informs us. (The name of Venus, here, can refer simultaneously to the planet named after the goddess of love and beauty, and to the double-pointed pencil stub with which Beckett's narrator has been inscribing the record of his own demise, ever since *Malone Dies.*) It is *she,* who, as bearer of language for her scribe, is 'headed toward death', encountering 'something like a mirror' as she goes on. What that 'something' is, or rather what form the encounter with that something may take, constitutes the speculative and backsliding progression of the microtrilogy, as it spills over into the third slender volume, *Worstward Ho* (1983).

'Somehow again on back to the bowed back alone. Nothing to show a woman's and yet a woman's. Oozed from softening soft the word woman's'. In a textual universe as hellbent on achieving impossible extinction as *Worstward Ho*'s is, it is perhaps not a mere accident that it is precisely in this fragment that the word 'word' appears, or rather oozes—for the first and last time—in its singular singularity. The word 'woman's', which also makes its initial appearance in this fragment, is of course what the word 'word' is meant to designate. But, in the process, the word

'word' is also cut off from its own signified—appended, as it were, to nothing, with 'Nothing to show' for it. The word 'woman's', in all its possessiveness, has thus reduced (indeed emasculated) the signifier to the role of pointless pointer: the oozing by means of which the word 'woman's' finds its way into the text appropriates—by its engulfing absorption with itself—the very sign of the pointer whose only reason for being is to give it body and thereby bring it into focus. We have here an instance of that precise point around which the Beckettian enterprise is structured. The singular Word, having been oozed out, or literally ex-pressed from Nothing ('Nothing to show a woman's and yet a woman's') can only be seen as the result of a deliberately repressed attempt to reinscribe the hypothetical locus of lost speech (abandoned, left hanging by the (m)other, but never quite forgotten) with an internalised phallocentric Verb. The word 'word', in all its unspoken potential, illustrates precisely what Caryl Emerson designates as the 'potent tool' for repressing knowledge not only of the Other, but also of 'the gap between inner and outer speech'. With the word out, on the other hand, we 'Ooze on back not to unsay but say again the vasts apart'.

Worstward Ho thus constitutes an attempted project whereby the signifier, left to its abandoned resources, strikes out to charter a new passage through—and, indeed, on the other side of—language. Eugene Kaeline observes, with regard to *Texts for Nothing,* that 'writing as an experience becomes the discovery of finding a way out' of the relationship that binds creator to creature. This notion presents a rather involved problematic: for whatever else enters the relation out of which writing, as an experience, can hypothetically discover a way, accommodation must be made for the act of writing itself. *Worstward Ho* offers us just such a picture of writing, searching for a way to write itself out. The initial difficulty that the reader experiences in the negative progression of this quest is due to 'Beckett's constant concern for getting it right, for making the direct point indirectly, to *show* and not merely to tell' [Anna-Teresa Tymienecka, in her introduction to *The Unhappy Consciousness*]. Which is another way of saying that intrinsic to *Worstward Ho*'s project is its commitment to get it all wrong . . . *it* being the ideal reintegration, from within the writing act itself, of the abandoned signifier with its signified gone awry—an unveiling, as it were, of the very matrix of the *oeuvre's* mystery.

Fragment 35 makes this direct point indirectly as well—or as ill—as another:

> Whose words? Ask in vain. Or not in vain if say no knowing. No saying. No words for him whose words. Him? One. No words for one whose words. One? It. No words for it whose words. Better worse so.

The underlying strategy of such writing can be traced back to Beckett's famous dictum of 1949: 'There are many ways in which the thing I am trying in vain to say may be tried in vain to be said', at the heart of which lies Beckett's pronounced 'fidelity to failure', whose principle he recognised in the works of Bram van Velde: 'to be an artist is to fail, as no other dare fail'. Failure, as a measure of the success that the writing process may or may not achieve, can only be recognised at the expense of its own project. The reason for this paradoxical quagmire is that writing, as an act, is not only predicated on the occasion that gives it rise— even if that occasion is the commitment to failure itself— but in addition secretes its own endless chain of cause and effect. Beckett's choice of words to express van Velde's heroic stance in the face of the proliferation of the feasible is in itself revealing: 'I suggest that van Velde is the first whose painting is bereft, rid if you prefer, of occasion in every shape and form, ideal as well as material'. To emulate van Velde's heroic standoff, for the writer, is tantamount to submitting to the ineffable appeal of the principle of failure as occasion—hence, as prime mover in the relation between creator and creature (or 'representer and representee'). It is of course this relation itself that Beckett consistently seeks the means of subverting:

> I know that all that is required now, in order to bring even this horrible matter to an acceptable conclusion, is to make of this submission, this admission, this fidelity to failure, a new occasion, a new term of relation, and of the act which, unable to act, obliged to act, he makes, an expressive act, even if only of itself, of its impossibility, of its obligation.

Thus, 'what Beckett must have seen' in van Velde's pictures, according to a later interpreter, is 'a visible demonstration of forms laboring to achieve formlessness . . . for here creation seems to disarticulate itself into conflict, catastrophe'. And in Beckett's own words, also from 1949, this excerpted description of van Velde's painterly process: 'An endless unveiling, veil behind veil, . . . towards the unveilable, the nothing, the thing again.' The closer such writing comes to the unveiling of its own matrix—as is clearly the point with fragment 45: 'Next the so-said seat and germ of all. . . . skull and stare alone'—the nearer it gets to that 'place of impenetrable nearness', the 'burial in the unique' which Beckett long since sensed was behind the impossible task that the painter Bram van Velde had set for himself. Fragment 35 thus represents just one of many moments in the Beckett *oeuvre* which openly skirt the issue of zeroing in on the source of it all; for once the final nail is struck, what need remains of the hammer (unless, of course, other 'devisers devising' conjure up additional lids to nail down).

However, unlike countless other attempts before it to get it all said so as to have unsaid it all, *Worstward Ho* commits the initial error of predicating (i. e. grounding) its entire strategy of undoing itself on the projection into beinglessness of nothing less than Being itself. Thus, from its very inception, the opening vocable, *On,* or *being* in Greek, engages the ensuing enterprise upon an endlessly predatory 'gnawing' away at the meaning of being— 'Preying since first said on foresaid remains' 'Gnawing to be gone'.

As Eugene Kaelin notes, with regard to 'Beckett's fundamental aesthetic project', 'The expressiveness of the aesthetic context results from the saturation of the linguistic symbols, and is felt as the tense opposition between the negative and the positive held necessarily together as they are forged into synthesis by the author's opening and clos-

ing words'. The opening *and* closing words of *Worstward Ho,* however, are already firmly embodied in the opening fragment, thus foreclosing the 'expressiveness' of the 'aesthetic project' by preempting the saturation point of those selfsame 'linguistic symbols' whose 'tense opposition' is already projected as having been resolved: 'On. Say on. Be said on. Somehow on. Till nohow on. Said nohow on.' 'On' already embodies the entire project within the preempted space of its own projectability. It *appears in* the text as *being* itself, while at the same time—and in the same space—foreclosing the need to go on. Whence the negative—the presence of which is essential for the expressiveness to be felt as tension—in such an opener, which avowedly foreshadows its having succeeded to fail? Could the pointlessness of the whole project lie in the very unnegativibility of negation itself? If such is the case, then the writing which endows the project with its dynamism must on the one hand be directed towards the point of pointlessness, while on the other hand it must relentlessly avoid, circle, and skirt the point towards which it is directed. The writing of *Worstward Ho,* in other words, must derive its tension from the incapacity of its words to contain *and* express, in the same breath, the worstwardness of its negative progression.

On is the very word of Being, the sign of which is its utter needlessness of language. Therein, perhaps, lies the greatest impossibility to date that Beckett has (playfully?) set out for himself to undo in the writing of *Worstward Ho:* for the *isness* of *Being* can only be shown *to be* by the needlessness of linguistic utterance, while the latter, in turn, can only demonstrate, or ex/press *its* needlessness by *describing* itself out of 'the house of Being', namely 'Language' itself (Butler, *Samuel Beckett and the Meaning of Being).* The 'negativisation' of discourse in this text of Beckett enters a sphere of writing (or literary space) that is not unlike that of Maurice Blanchot. Writing, for both Beckett and Blanchot, is a way out of—or at worst away from—the point of contact between sign and signified. For the one as for the other, writing is 'a kind of clustering of tentative entries into the narrative' [Gilbert Sorrentino, 'Language—Lying and Treacherous', *New York Times Book Review,* 25 May 1986], while at the same time it traces a process of endless evasion from its own foreclosure, which is always already there, in the thereness of its own, articulated inscription. In a work like *Worstward Ho,* not only is syntax *grounded* on a 'grammar for being elsewhere', its writing project itself, and the *désoeuvrement* which it embodies, constitute a quest for a more fruitful field of failure in which to be inscribed.

Indeed, the entire course that a text like *Worstward Ho* charts out, in its self-proclaimed quest for the place of ultimate failure, seems (as we've already suggested) to encircle the point of its own pointlessness. What's more, its writing makes this point most pointedly, as it reiterates itself to(wards) the point of near-nothingness. The project of this kind of writing, as Blanchot describes it, points in a direction which is diametrically opposed to the premise of its own perfectability. It is a writing away from its own writeability, an inscription begging out of its inscribableness. The kind of true writing to which Beckett and Blanchot have dedicated their lives begins at the threshold of its own undoing; its point of departure lies within its own impetus to write itself out . . . and, in the process, to (re)inscribe itself with the very outwardness of its self-annihilating projection, as it seeks that point where nothing remains to be revealed, short of the point of intimate contact where *here*ness and *nothing*ness meet.

'Whenever art happens' (Heidegger writes) 'i. e. whenever there is a beginning—a thrust enters history, history begins either for the first time or over again' ['The Origin of the Work of Art', in *Philosophies of Art and Beauty*, ed. Albert Hofstadter and Richard Kuhns, 1964]. With the thrust onward of 'On', however, it would seem instead that what happens thereafter is simultaneously breaking new ground *as* it begins all over again: 'All of old. Nothing else ever. Ever tried. Ever failed. No matter. Try again. Fail again. Fail better' (Fragment 4). 'A genuine beginning' (Heidegger goes on) 'is, as a leap, always a leap forward, in which everything to come is already leaped over, even if as something disguised. The beginning [thus] already conceals within itself the end'. *Worstward Ho,* on the other hand, rather than conceal its end within its beginning, openly displays it, as the opening fragment preempts the possibility of its own thrust's inclusiveness within the area of the fiction to come (Heidegger's 'everything to come as something disguised'). Or, to put it another way, the groundlessness of the fiction to come is already grounded—indeed embodied—in Being, whose *On*(e)-ness, once iterated, leaves little room for any activity other than its own reiteration.

The entire project of *Worstward Ho* constitutes a quest for what little remains remain for the creative activity to embark upon as it sees itself being closed in by the embodiment of its own previous ventures towards nothingness. Picking up where *Ill Seen Ill Said* left off, in the self-consuming search for 'the wrong word' with which 'to end yet again', Beckett has perhaps at last lighted upon the right 'wrong word'. *One* right wrong word. *On.* On: the embodiment of Being whose pre-emptive presence casts all else in the shades of Nothingness, a beginninglessness opening on to an endless disclosure of its own beginninglessness. The figure and ground, rolled into one, of hereness and nothingness in endlessly repeated juxtaposition. *On*—'the so-said seat and germ of all'—is always already there, projecting itself into being through the reiteration of everything the presence of which (and of whom) it preempts. *On* thus provides the hologrammatic outline of absence, which simultaneously besets and is beset by presence: 'On. Say on. Be said on. . . . Till nohow on.' —A more laborious articulation of the loss of the writer's love's labour is indeed hard to imagine. Yet this is precisely what these demanding texts require. Let us not abandon ship, therefore, but instead take another look at the obsessiveness of these reiterations.

'On', the opening vocable in *Worstward Ho,* is a reiteration of the second statement of its predecessor, *Ill Seen Ill Said,* in which it clearly functions as prod: 'From where she lies she sees Venus rise. On. From where she lies when the skies are clear she sees Venus rise followed by the sun. Then she rails at the source of all life. On.' The 'On' which sets the old woman in *Ill Seen Ill Said* off from the outset

derives from Beckett's translation of 'Encore' (in *Mal vu mal dit*). As if it were not enough for her to personify figuratively ageless imagination labouring on, in the French text Beckett has her bearing witness, *reflexively,* to her own star rising, and, in the process, to the reiteration of her own embodiment, *in absentia* (as it were), 'At the inexistent centre of a formless place' (*Ill Seen*, Frag. 2): '*Da sa couche elle voit se lever Vénus. Encore. . . . Elle en veut alors au principe de toute vie. Encore.*' It is the reiteration of *Encore* that gives rise to her embodiment, *en corps,* against whose life-source she rails in vain—a fact made explicitly clear (for once) by the time we light upon the beginning fragments of *Worstward Ho,* when from the opening 'On. Say on' we fall under the labouring spell of *Ill Seen,* Frag. 2 ('Quick then still under the spell of Venus . . .'), and follow through, in Fragment 3 of *Worstward Ho*, with 'Say a body. Where none.'

Two beginnings, (col)lapsing towards worstwardness: 'First the body. No. First the place. No. First both' and 'So on . . . Still worse again' (*W. Ho*, Frag. 5). The problem with beginning lies in its very un-iterability; the attainment of an end is therefore always in serious question, held in abeyance, postponed indefinitely, or at least till end and beginning—'Now the one. Now the twain' (Frag. 14)—join hands. In his introductory comments to his *Dialogues avec Heidegger* (1973) Jean Beaufret makes the distinction between *commencer* (to enter into question) and *débuter* (to depart from), and adds that it is within the purview of *début* to keep in its shadows the enigma of commencement. Seeking the resolution of the enigma in Greek thought, he concludes with the observation that as concerns the point of departure of all beginning, 'the Greek word, on this point, remains enigmatic' ('*La parole grecque, sur ce point demeure enigmatique*'). We are thus thrown right back to *On:* the embodiment of the place of beginning, 'the so-said seat and germ of all', whose function as *début* is displayed in proportion as what it departs from is kept in the shadows. Its thrust heads nowhere but towards its own goallessness, as it casts the ensuing project in a process of *désoeuvrement* whereby the *but,* or goal, of its foregrounded point of departure as embodied *début,* is persistently and systematically forestalled, put off, held in abeyance, left (forever) gaping towards the projected image of its (endlessly) reiterated irresolution.

A quarter of a century ago, Beckett had already almost worked the problematics of beginning to death (his entire *oeuvre,* for that matter, like Blanchot's, is an ongoing *désoeuvrement* of the 'death sentence', or *Arrêt de mort,* with which it is inscribed). For, coming on the heels of 'I can't go on, I'll go on' with which he closed his macrotrilogy, he followed suit, and reopened old wounds, beginning, it would seem, all over again. I am referring, of course, to *Comment c'est* and its re-entry into question of *How It Is* (. . . to begin). Rather than reopen that can of worms here, however, let us return, momentarily, to Heidegger's dictum regarding what happens 'whenever art happens'.

What happens in Heidegger's equation of happening and beginning, quite simply stated, is that it states itself into being in and of itself: it *shows* its *being* by *saying* how *it is.* Let us begin to quote him again, with no interruption save his own: 'Whenever art happens—i. e. whenever there is a beginning' (etc.). The triggering mechanism here—explicited to the point of its being 'leaped over, as something disguised, thus concealing within itself the end'—is the 'i. e.', *id est,* the *is*ness of Being displayed in its utterly unadorned, genderless, neuter presence. *Whenever art happens* (in other words), *it is.* Or, to continue through with the chain, 'Whenever art happens . . . is whenever there is a beginning.' Beginning is thus predicated on happening, with *is*ness left alone (i. e. eclipsed?) to bask in the radiance of Being. Being, however, as we know it, and for it to be known, requires the presence of consciousness for it to be *there,* i. e. constituted in the *there*-ness of there is. The (impossible) task that Beckett seems to have set his writing to achieve, in *Worstward Ho,* can now be summarised thus: as writing, its communicative function must be strictly confined within the sphere of its initial happening (the seat and germ of all to which Being is eternally open); at the same time, however, the stakes that it places on its very communicability, even (and especially) if so restricted, are such that its projection, from the initial point onward, cannot allow itself to eclipse that point itself—knowing, all the while, that the consciousness of the Being of the work, the requisite for *its being there,* is precisely that which, though engendered *by* the writing, undermines it. It is a writing, 'pointed at both ends' (*Three Novels*), whose reason for being is the reason for Being. No more. No less. *Worstward Ho* shows us more clearly than ever what being Beckett means.

What *being,* on the other hand, *does* Beckett mean? That, of course, is the question which provides the grounds for the ongoing quest of the writing and the saying in *Worstward Ho.* As Derrida writes in *Writing and Difference,* 'Meaning must await being said or written in order to inhabit itself, and in order to become, by differing from itself, what it is: meaning.' We should not lose sight—for the writing of *Worstward Ho* certainly does not—of the word for Being with which the text happens to be: the *On,* which goes thereupon (*there*-up-*on*) begging for recognition, differing from itself through its manifestly repeated reincarnations (Encore/en corps—On/Being—No[how] On . . . ?), and deferring the disclosure of the meaning with which it is inhabited until the instance of its having been (said), in order to become what it is (. . . and know happiness to boot?).

—'On. Say on. Be said on. Somehow on. Till nohow on. Said nohow on.'

—'Such thinking, which recalls . . . Being itself . . . tills the ground and plows the soil. . . . But what still appears as ground . . . is presumably something else, once it is experienced in its own terms—something as yet unsaid [. . .]. Such thinking [is said to be] "on its way" ' [Heidegger, 'The Way Back']. Such thinking—*in deed*—such writing provides the very fabric of *Worstward Ho*'s regressive progression, 'projected' on its way to(wards) meaning as it 'points the way back' to the ground of Being, repeatedly landing (us), along the way, in pitfalls of 'utter [t]error': 'Something not wrong with one. Meaning—meaning! —meaning the kneeling one' (*W. Ho,* Frag. 36).

'How did it come about,' Heidegger queries, toward the

end of 'The Way Back into the Ground of Metaphysics', 'that with Being It really is nothing and that Nothing really is not?' This question, voiced from authorial ground, is heard again and again throughout *Worstward Ho,* as it is experienced, from within the groundlessness of its own figurative projection into the questionable ground of fictional musing (one hardly dare call this 'fiction'). Or, as Lance Butler writes, Beckett's work is indeed 'an attempt to find an objective correlative for being—a parable that will somehow manage to "say" the ontological nature of the world' (*Samuel Beckett and the Meaning of Being*). Fragment 35 (which we've already touched upon) provides a clear instance of this parabolic attempt:

> Whose words? Ask in vain. Or not in vain if say no knowing. No saying. No words for him whose words. Him? One. No words for one whose words. One? It. No words for it whose words. Better worse so.

If such an instance as this illustrates the attempt to find a fitting parable (an attempt whose failure we are primed to accept), it is precisely by virtue of its showing, as well as its saying, what this parable consists of: a placing beside, a juxtaposition of potential objective correlatives—Him? One. One? It—which, if ever singled out would of course bring the whole process to a screeching halt. For (among other things) *One,* as an objective correlative, is a fictional aberration of Being: it barely disguises its likeness to *On,* which, to the bilingual author, beckons the French word for one (*on*), they, people in general—i. e. the Heideggerian '*Das Man*', the configuration of inauthenticity itself, the faceless herd, which Butler describes as 'the indefinite, collective neuter. Something like an impersonal goad, in fact' (*Beckett and the Meaning of Being*). Hence the instantaneous (or so it seems) leap on from *One* to *It:* 'One? It. No words for it whose words. Better worse so.'

What might appear to be a mere exchange of one neuter goad for another is in reality an attempt to avoid, or skirt, the pitfall of communicable utterance (engendering *other*ance), whose very communicability would project the consciousness of Being into the community, and out of its immediate sphere of inarticulable presence. The onwardness (in other words) of the text's reiterations must not allow itself to be disposed of as a representation of its own otherness: this is why, as a parable of ongoing failure, it *must* fail—which also provides the reason for its unprecedented urgency to succeed.

> If I were obliged to name the class of things to which [poetry] belongs, I should call it a secretion. (A. E. Housman, *The Name and Nature of Poetry*)

The centre toward which *Worstward Ho* is drawn, in its fragmentary 'voyage outward and return home to self, existing alone and anguished to know how and why' (Kaelin, *The Unhappy Consciousness*), like that of Blanchot's, is both movable and fixed. It is to be found (concealed) everywhere that the closure of signification beckons words in their onward search for a way out of their vain attempts to get it all said. It is already always *there.* It is its thereness that makes it unattainable while at the same time drawing all activity towards it. It is Being with no knowledge (nor need thereof) of Nothing. It stands for want of Nothing.

It was in Fragment 6 that we saw the first clear sign of what questionable ground this circuitous search for a way out of representation is grounded in: 'It stands. What? Yes. Say it stands. . . . Say ground. No ground but say ground'. From there on in (or is it out?), everything seems to point toward the It and the question which it goads (both of which here make their initial appearance in tandem) as the point around which the book (and the whole Beckettian *oeuvre* in tow) is centred, and away from which the writing—as it proceeds onwards to write itself out—must be directed. It is the Being-there of It—which stands in place of Being—that determines the itinerary of the journey worstward, towards the pointlessness of its reiterations. In Blanchot's *Literary Space* the point toward which the work avowedly seems to direct itself is the gaze of Orpheus. In *Worstward Ho*, the focal point towards which the double-pointed Venus pencil traces its regressive progression is Fragment 58:

> Enough still not to know. Not to know what they say. Not to know what it is the words it says say. Says? Secretes. Say better worse secretes. What it is the words it secretes say. What the so-said void. The so-said dim. The so-said shades. The so-said seat and germ of all. Enough to know no knowing. No knowing what it is the words it secretes say. No saying. No saying what it all is they somehow say.

It is here that the *it* re-*ite*rates itself to the point of utter confusion: secreted words uttered forth unknown, oozing back unknowable, into the all-inclusive secret—'the so-said seat and germ'—of *it all*. Textual here-say based on Nothing to be known. A *per*formative playing to the recesses of consciousness. . . . A *pre*formative plying of remanded memory. A dumbfounded journey through 'shades of void'. An ill-founded attempt to get it all said, expressed, oozed out—while through the back door, other voices creep in, rearranging the movable fixtures as they see fit.

> Not another word. Home at last. Gently gently.
> (*Ill Seen Ill Said*)

'In [Borges's] preferred story', writes Anthony Kerrigan in his Preface to *Ficciones*, 'a man must pick up a knife . . . and go out into the brainless night. . . . Why? He does not know. All our knowledge has led us exactly to this point, just where we started, endless ages ago. We have only been playing a game, an immortal game all along.' I have tried in this essay to make a few pointed remarks concerning the game being played out in *Worstward Ho*: an anything-but-childish game, whose impetus (perhaps) lies in 'the never forgotten' 'cutting retort' with which the mother 'shook off [the] little hand' in *Company* . . . for no apparent reason other than to have raised a pointed question. With all its desperate playfulness, *Worstward Ho* has still not found a way to dislodge 'No's knife' from 'Yes's wound'.

Lawrence Graver (essay date 1990)

SOURCE: "Homage to the Dark Lady: *Ill Seen Ill Said,*" in *Women in Beckett: Performance and Critical Perspectives,* edited by Linda Ben-Zvi, University of Illinois Press, 1990, pp. 142-49.

[*Graver is an American critic and educator. In the essay below, he analyzes the protagonist of* Ill Seen Ill Said *as an instance of Beckett's representation of women.*]

Most readers looking for the main source of the drama and the interest of *Ill Seen Ill Said* are likely to locate it where it is customarily found in Beckett's fiction since *The Trilogy:* in the scene of the writing; in the narrator's fevered, indeflectable effort to flesh out a figment, to embody in language the ghostly figure of a dead old woman who haunts him. The action as usual takes place in the speaker's skull (that "ivory dungeon") where his different perceptual faculties are engaged in a psychic civil war—eye and mind unable to distinguish between what is remembered and what imagined, and language as always the most suspect, persistently indicted of expressive instruments. In what the speaking voice calls this "farrago of eye and mind," each faculty and instrument is continually accused of betraying itself and others: "The mind betrays the treacherous eyes and the treacherous word their treacheries." The result is a narrative of almost unendurable (and yet miraculously endured) pressure. The miracle, as we've come to expect from late Beckett, is in the astral beauty of the language—a prose as compacted, luminous, and densely resonant as any he has ever written.

But what makes *Ill Seen Ill Said* unique in the Beckett canon is less the drama at the scene of the writing, or the narrator's travail, but rather the subject embodied in that astonishing poetic prose—the old woman who is a most singular figure among Beckett's creations. . . . [Nearly] all the women in Beckett's fiction are satiric targets or long-suffering victims (and often both). Those seen from a distance (in the early fiction, for example) are usually mocked through irony as frisky, libidinous, threatening figures who create and/or sustain life and won't let the beleaguered male protagonist cultivate his solipsism or get on with his dying. In *The Trilogy* the mockery (though still comic) becomes more corrosive and grim, approaching at times a kind of Swiftian ferocity. For Molloy all women become "one and the same old hag, flattened and crazed by life. And God forgive me, to tell you the horrible truth, my mother's image sometimes mingles with theirs." And by the time we hear the Unnamable, there are only "two cunts into the bargain, the one for ever accursed that ejected me into this world and the other, infundibuliform [funnel-shaped], in which, pumping my likes, I tried to take my revenge." Even Malone's Moll, despite her amiable lubricity and blasphemous dental work, is also seen through the lens of a grotesque, if comic, disgust.

No matter how they are perceived, though, the women of the novels are nearly all ancillary figures; the women of the plays (especially after the opening of *Happy Days* in 1961) are more important. Those seen or heard close-up (Maddy Rooney, Winnie, the wife and mistress in *Play,* Mouth, May, and the Woman in *Rockaby*) are—for all their splendid differences—long-suffering, sometimes self-deluded, always self-divided, often extravagantly resilient but ultimately unfulfilled and incomplete; indeed, in the famous, repeated image, not properly born; or, as in the case of the spectral May of *Footfalls,* not even there. Obvious exceptions exist: the affectionately drawn, prominent Celia in *Murphy* is the most notable; and if you read the narrator of *Enough* as a woman, so is she; but on the whole these broad generalizations hold up.

What makes the old woman in *Ill Seen Ill Said* unique is that she is entirely exempt from irony—neither mocked nor exposed—and she is given a dignity matched by very few, if any, figures (male or female) in Beckett's work. The main source of her dignity is that she both embodies in her physical being and enacts in her behavior values that for Beckett—despite his unremitting skepticism—have always been positive. And, in several mysterious ways, she seems also to be one of the most significant of the elusive others that his narrators have for more than half-a-century been trying to track down.

The woman's ancient frame, frail yet rigid and erect, everywhere reflects what Beckett once described in a tribute to his friend, Avigdor Arikha, as indelible "marks of what it is to be and be in the face of." She appears to have endured the immemorial afflictions of her species and registers them in a way that generates a shivery respect and even wonder. "The long white hair stares in a fan. Above and about the impassive face. Stares as if shocked still by some ancient horror. Or by its continuance. Or by another. That leaves the face stonecold. Silence at the eye of the scream." Long white hair is perhaps the most familiar feature of the late Beckett protagonist, and the old woman of *Ill Seen Ill Said* shares it with May of *Footfalls,* the male figures in *That Time, A Piece of Monologue,* and *Ohio Impromptu,* and the shadowy inhabitants enclosed in Beckett's hermetic *Residua.* But her most unforgettable and expressive signature is the faintly bluish white face that impassively yet all at once registers the shocks of past, present, and future adversity.

The old woman is never heard to speak; she no longer even talks to herself. Yet if in her silence we are prompted to imagine the chilling "eye of the scream," we perceive other very different things as well. Despite her great age and the marks of suffering, she is described as moving with a stately purposefulness that makes her seem monumental. When the hovering eye closes in on her eating her slops in the dark, he sees how, "at last in a twin movement full of grace she slowly raises the bowl toward her lips while at the same time with equal slowness bowing her head to join it."

The beauty of this depends in large measure on the sense that the grace has been hard won through countless, unimaginable vicissitudes, the suffering a kind of refining fire. At another point the woman's face is compared to "a calm slab worn and polished by agelong comings and goings. . . . How serene it seems this ancient mask. Worthy those worn by certain newly dead." Indeed, throughout the narrative, the woman is perceived as substantial *and* spectral, as being in time and yet in ways beyond it— beyond surprise and human need—which has always been

something of a hallowed state in the Beckett universe, a state that partakes at once of the mysteries of presence and absence.

The powerful, eerie sense of the woman being at the same time here and elsewhere is reinforced throughout the text by the repeated emphasis on her paradoxical monumentality and wraith-like delicacy. Indeed, just after the image of her face as a serene and ancient mask, the narrating eye startling reminds us of those jet black lashes that are the remains of the brunette she once was, "perhaps once was. When yet a lass." Or even more startling is this scene of the woman at her husband's tomb:

> Seated on the stones she is seen from behind. From the waist up. Trunk black rectangle. Nape under frill of black lace. White half halo of hair. Face to the north. . . . Voidlike calm as always. Evening and night. Suffice to watch the grass. How motionless it droops. Till under the relentless eye it shivers. With faintest shiver from its innermost. Equally the hair. Rigidly horrent it shivers at last for the eye about to abandon. And the old body itself. When it seems of stone. Is it not in fact ashiver from head to foot? Let her but go and stand still by the other stone. It white from afar in the pastures. And the eye go from one to the other. Back and forth. What calm then. And what storm. Beneath the weeds' mock calm.

In addition to catching so memorably the strength and vulnerability of the "old so dying woman," this passage illustrates the provocative kinship between the perceiver and his subject. As David Read has helpfully observed [in "Beckett's Search for Unseeable and Unmakeable: *Company* and *Ill Seen Ill Said*," *Modern Fiction Studies,* 1983], the description incorporates a characteristic Beckettian ambiguity into the eye's relationship to external (even if imagined) reality. "Is it the eye's apparent flux that causes the object to shiver—the observed infected with the mobility of the observer—or is it only the eye's perseverance that enables it finally to perceive a shiver that was always present in the object—the observer infected with the mobility of the observed?" But the ambiguity is less an invitation to resolution than a reminder that whether the shiver is caused by the eye or inherent in the object, one effect of so intensely sustained an act of perception is to enlarge and in this instance to ennoble the thing perceived.

Equally important in the process of expansion is the fact that the shadowy old woman is both votary and protestant. Morning and evening she worships Venus, standing rapt before the sky, marveling; and many of her days are spent on bone-wearying journeys from her cabin back and forth across the zone of stones, carrying a cross or wreath to the tomb of someone she venerates—a tomb formed of a stone very much like her in shape and size. It seems natural enough to think of the tomb as her husband's—as many readers have done—but its identity is never confirmed. Similarly, she herself seems to be the object of ritual attendance by a ring of obscure figures called the Twelve—a typically Beckettian piece of provocation—for that highly charged number suggests not only the Apostles and the festival of the Epiphany but also (as Marjorie

Perloff has remarked [in "Between Verse and Prose: Beckett and The New Poetry," *Critical Inquiry,* 1982-83]) the signs of the Zodiac; but it too is never made explicit and is finally as elusive as the stone tomb itself.

Like any Beckett character in good standing, the old woman will sometimes protest against her existence, railing against the sun and savoring Venus's revenge when it rises as the sun sets. But for most of the narrative her fury remains bottled, and she is increasingly seen as a paradoxically frail yet commanding, almost mythological, figure in touch with lambs and birds, and someone for whom natural processes bend and stop. Once, when she visits the stone tomb, the sun stands still, and when she heads for home, "Time slows all this while. Suits its speed to hers." Indeed, it is not far-fetched to be reminded of Wordsworth's Lucy rolling "round in earth's diurnal course, / With rocks, and stones, and trees"; even if Beckett's old woman can hardly be described as "a thing that could not feel / The touch of earthly years."

Many of the objects associated with her seem in provocative ways sanctified or preternatural. Her tarnished silver pisciform buttonhook hangs from a nail and trembles faintly without cease, as do her house key (trembling and shimmering in the light of the moon) and the greatcoat hanging as a curtain in the cabin. "Same infinitesimal quaver as the buttonhook and passim." At the end, when she is approaching death, another one of her nails is described as "set to serve again. Like unto its glorious ancestors. At the place of the skull. One April afternoon. Deposition done."

This allusion to the crucifixion is part of the old woman's own deathbed scene and is one of only half-a-dozen overt allusions in *Ill Seen Ill Said.* But the most notable of these allusions also work to magnify the frail old woman by linking her to real or legendary figures who are associated with passion, suffering, and acts of great magnitude. King Lear and Gloucester are evoked when the old woman's eye is called "vile jelly"; and Job's question, "Hast thou eyes of flesh, / Or seest thou as man seeth?" is echoed in her "eyes of flesh." The stone tomb has a rough-hewn air, as if it were the product of some human hand forced to desist, "as Michelangelo's from the regicide's bust," a reference to the great unfinished bust of Brutus in the Bargello—that incarnation of fortitude, resolution, and inner torment. And finally, at the close of the passage quoted earlier describing the old woman lifting the bowl of slops, she strikes "the rigid Memnon pose," a reference to the great statue at Thebes, which was famed for making a musical sound at day break when Memnon greeted his mother, Eos, the goddess of the dawn.

That all these are masculine figures associated with passion and power (and that there are no women at all alluded to in the narrative) tells us something vital about Beckett's views of magnitude and indomitability. Although figures like Maddy Rooney in *All That Fall* and Winnie in *Happy Days* are gritty and flamboyant survivors, they are continually seen as comic in their rhetorical extravagance. Women like Mouth in *Not I* or May in *Footfalls* are not viewed comically, but they are perceived as integrally defective, incomplete. In *Ill Seen Ill Said* it is the men associ-

ated with uttermost striving, ultimacy (and rarely with laughter)—Lear, Job, Michelangelo—who provide the touchstone for measuring Beckett's conception of the protagonist's hardihood.

Nowhere is this seen more vividly than in the description of the old woman's last moments, a chillingly graphic and yet lyrically fulfilling sequence in which microscopic delineations of bodily collapse exist along with gleams of hope and sweet foretastes "of the joy at journey's end." As the narrator's steely yet still-ill-seeing eye closes in on death, a constant yet merciful process of denudation begins. All that is left to his distilling gaze is the woman's inscrutable, unyielding face ("Of the rest beneath its covering no trace.") Painstakingly, he moves past the "slumberous collapsion" of the cabin to record the sensory details of her dying moments: unexplained sounds and "sigh upon sigh till all sighed quite away. . . . Last sighs of relief." Conflating past, present, and future, he examines the sclerosis-inflicted eyes of the old woman. And then suddenly "farewell say say farewell. If only to the face. Of her tenacious trace." The phrase "tenacious trace" is in this context an honorific term for Beckett, because it captures just about the most of what (in his world) one can hope to remain—a vestige, a barely discernible indication of some quality, characteristic, or expression—and yet (if lucky) tenacious, stubbornly, persistently held.

And then, unexpectedly, in the astonishing close, comes not a victory of the residual, of the barely remaining, but a triumph of voracious desire and perhaps the closest thing to fulfillment any Beckett character has ever achieved.

> Farewell to farewell. Then in that perfect dark foreknell darling sound pip for end begun. First last moment. Grant only enough remain to devour all. Moment by glutton moment. Sky earth the whole kit and boodle. Not another crumb of carrion left. Lick chops and basta. No. One moment more. One last. Grace to breathe that void. Know happiness.

Much of the power here comes from the surprising exuberance—what might even be called the gusto—of Beckett's threnody. Death is described not in terms of deprivation but of heartily satisfied appetite: to devour the world, breathe the void, and die—this surely is the consummation devoutly to be wished by so many of Beckett's desiring questors.

In *Ill Seen Ill Said,* then, the achievement of ultimacy is given to a woman, as it is nowhere else in Beckett's work. But if the "old so dying woman" and the ritual conduct of her last solitary days are exempt from irony, some aspects of the narrator's responses to her are not. Although the woman achieves fulfillment in dying, she is a product of the narrator's insatiable need; indeed, she exists only through his fiercely focused efforts to imagine her accurately. Thus she remains in more ways than one the inquiring narrator's subject. His struggle to embody her mirrors her gallant journey across the zone of stones, her vigil at the tomb, at the window, and elsewhere. Her enterprise and his are correlative; and even his insistence on her being unseeable and unmakeable is a tribute not only to her mystery but to his own minimalist mastery. As Christopher Ricks has observed: "How much dignity of mystery remains unviolated even after the most imaginative exploration. When all is said and done" ["The Hermit of Art," *Sunday Times* (London), 12 September 1982]. So for all her grace, vigilance, and nobility, it is the narrator's achievements at the scene of the writing—his ability to respect her unfathomability and to give her the death she desires and deserves—that the majority of readers are most likely to celebrate. "Imagination at wits end" *has* spread "its sad wings."

And there are, too, some important questions that someone looking at *Ill Seen Ill Said* from feminist and/or psychoanalytical perspectives might ask: what, for instance, is the significance of the fact that the narrator's struggle to express depends on bringing a dead woman back to life, on obsessively charting the last days of her suffering, and reproducing her death? Given the ardor with which the old woman is described and the dignity she is granted, she is clearly an idealized form whose reincarnation in language is a necessary stage in the narrator's search for the other. And the other is powerfully associated with idealized forms of both the mother and of death.

As Susan Rubin Suleiman observes in a recent essay, "Writing and Motherhood," psychoanalytic theory often views artistic creation (like motherhood) as the child's drama. "In both cases," she says, "the mother is the essential but silent Other, the mirror in whom the child searches for his own reflection, the body he seeks to appropriate, the thing he loses or destroys again and again, and seeks to recreate" [*The (M)other Tongue,* eds. Shirley Nelson Garnet, et al.]. And one recalls, too, Melanie Klein's theory of artistic creation, in which the writer is impelled by the "desire to rediscover the mother of the early days, whom [he] has lost actually or in [his] feelings" ["Love, Guilt, and Reparation," in her *Love, Guilt, and Reparation and Other Works, 1921-1945,* 1977]. The work of art itself suggests the mother's body, restored or "repaired" in the act of creation. Klein's image, incidentally, appears often in recent criticism, most vividly perhaps in *The Pleasure of the Text,* where Roland Barthes (speaking of language and "the mother tongue") describes the writer as "someone who plays with his mother's body . . . in order to glorify it, to embellish it, or in order to dismember it, to take it to the limit of what can be known about the body."

It is well known that Beckett—in his seventies—wrote a sequence of works (*Footfalls, Rockaby,* **Company,** and **Ill Seen Ill Said**) that drew on memories of the elusive figure of his mother and that these texts remind nearly all who read them of May Beckett, or of their mothers or of some archetypal image of *the* mother. Speculation about the biographical significance of this cannot go very far until scholarly studies tell us a good deal more than we now know about the fiery relationship of May Beckett and her son. But at this point it is worth observing how extraordinary it is that the mother-haunted **Ill Seen Ill Said** should be—for all its provisionality and anguish—arguably the most conclusive and serene of the old master's works.

FURTHER READING

Abbott, H. Porter. *The Fiction of Samuel Beckett: Form and Effect*. Berkeley: University of California Press, 1973, 167 p.
    Contains chapters on Beckett's early short fiction and the relationship between his stories and novels.

Astro, Alan. *Understanding Samuel Beckett*. Columbia: University of South Carolina Press, 1967, 222 p.
    Contains discussion of both the early and later short fiction.

Brienza, Susan D. *Samuel Beckett's New Worlds: Style in Metafiction*. Norman: University of Oklahoma Press, 1987, 290 p.
    Contains chapters on most of Beckett's short fiction in an examination of the metafictional qualities of his work.

——————. "*The Lost Ones*: The Reader as Searcher." *Journal of Modern Literature* 6, No. 1 (February 1977): 148-68.
    Argues that the form and style of *The Lost Ones* echoes the theme in forcing the reader to search for meaning and a "way out."

Catanzaro, Mary. "Enough or Too Little? Voicings of Desire and Discontent in Beckett's *Enough*." In *The World of Samuel Beckett*, edited by Joseph H. Smith, pp. 16-29. Baltimore: Johns Hopkins University Press, 1991.
    Analyzes *Enough* in terms of Beckett's use of the themes of coupling and partnership.

Farrow, Anthony. *Early Beckett: Art and Allusion in* More Pricks Than Kicks *and* Murphy. Troy, N.Y.: Whitston, 1991, 187 p.
    Attempts "to relate the discrete narratives of *More Pricks than Kicks* and *Murphy* to Beckett's notions about art and fiction."

Kenner, Hugh. "Queer Little Pieces: *Enough, Imagination Dead Imagine, Ping, The Lost Ones, Lessness*." In his *A Reader's Guide to Samuel Beckett*, pp. 176-82. New York: Farrar, Straus, and Giroux, 1973.
    Examines Beckett's writings in the 1960s as examples of his growing tendency toward "ultra-compression."

Knowlson, James, and Pilling, John. "Ends and Odds in Prose." In their *Frescoes of the Skull: The Later Prose and Drama of Samuel Beckett*, pp. 132-91. London: John Calder, 1979.
    Analyzes Beckett's short work from *Fizzles* to *For to End Yet Again*.

Levy, Eric P. *Beckett and the Voice of Species: A Study of the Prose Fiction*. Dublin: Gill and Macmillan, 1980, 145 p.
    Contains chapters discussing *More Pricks than Kicks, Texts for Nothing, The Lost Ones*, and *Fizzles*.

Locatelli, Carla. "*Worstward Ho*: The Persistence of Missaying Against the Limits of Representation." In her *Unwording the World: Samuel Beckett's Prose Works After the Nobel Prize*, pp. 225-70. Philadelphia: University of Pennsylvania Press, 1990.
    Asserts that in *Worstward Ho*, Beckett "achieves a powerful apotheosis of subtraction as an epistemological instrument, as a procedure for the critical investigation of representation and of the 'essence' of language itself."

Nagem, Monique. "Know Happiness: Irony in *Ill Seen Ill Said*." In *"Make Sense Who May": Essays on Samuel Beckett's Later Works*, edited by Robin J. Davis and Lance St. John Butler, pp. 77-90. Buckinghamshire, England: Colin Smythe Limited, 1988.

> Argues that *Ill Seen Ill Said* "is a complex, ironic narrative whose textual features reflect a strategy meant to excoriate the labour of the writer."

Pilling, John. "Shards of Ends and Odds in Prose: From *Fizzles* to *The Lost Ones*." In *On Beckett: Essays and Criticism*, pp. 169-90. New York: Grove Press, 1986.

> Contends that the pieces in *Fizzles* are "transitional works" because they contain allusions to motifs that Beckett had already used, as well as prefiguring motifs he would employ in his later short fiction.

Rabinovitz, Rubin. "*Fizzles* and Beckett's Earlier Fiction." In his *Innovation in Samuel Beckett's Fiction*, pp. 137-57. Chicago: University of Illinois Press, 1992.

Discusses Beckett's allusions in *Fizzles* to his other works.

Rose, Marilyn Gaddis. "The Lyrical Structure of Beckett's *Texts for Nothing*." *Novel* 4, No. 3 (Spring 1971): 223-30.

> Contends that Beckett's narrative voice in *Texts for Nothing* is "a lyrical utterance of the most intimate epistemological dilemma: the integrity of the articulating mind."

Zurbrugg, Nicholas. "*Ill Seen Ill Said* and the Sense of an Ending." In *Beckett's Later Fiction and Drama: Texts for Company*, edited by James Acheson and Kateryna Arthur, pp. 145-59. London: Macmillan Press, 1987.

> Asserts that "*Ill Seen Ill Said* is not so much a story, as a poetic evocation of those rituals by which the living and the dead within Beckett's fiction endlessly, and quite ineffectively, strive to attain a definitive 'sense of an ending.'"

Additional coverage of Beckett's life and works is contained in the following sources published by Gale Research: *Contemporary Authors*, Vol. 5-8, rev. ed.; *Contemporary Authors New Revision Series*, Vols. 33, 130; *Concise Dictionary of British Literary Biography, 1945-1960*; *Contemporary Literary Criticism*, Vols. 1, 2, 3, 4, 6, 9, 10, 11, 14, 18, 29, 57, 59, 83; *DISCovering Authors*; *Dictionary of Literary Biography*, Vols. 13, 15; *Dictionary of Literary Biography Yearbook: 1990*; *Major 20th-Century Writers*; **and** *World Literature Criticism*.

T. Coraghessan Boyle

1948-

(Full name Thomas Coraghessan Boyle) American short story writer and novelist.

INTRODUCTION

An author of irreverent comic fiction replete with satiric and ironic twists, Boyle is often linked with such absurdist and experimental writers as John Barth, Donald Barthelme, and Thomas Pynchon for his use of black humor and stylistic blend of formal language and modern argot. Described as anarchic, bawdy, and lyrical, Boyle's short stories often focus on the banality and bestiality of contemporary life and cover a wide range of topics. Michael Adams has argued that "for all Boyle's similarities to other artists, no Americans in the 1980s write about the diverse subjects he does in the way he does."

Biographical Information

Born in Peekskill, New York, Boyle grew up in a working-class, Catholic family. After graduating from college, he taught high school English in order, he has said, "to stay out of Vietnam." After teaching for four years and having a story published in the *North American Review*, he entered the Iowa Writers' Workshop in 1972 and graduated from the University of Iowa with a PhD. in 1977. He also served as a fiction editor for the *Iowa Review* and in 1977 received a Creative Writing Fellowship from the National Endowment for the Arts. In 1979 Boyle published his first volume of short fiction, *Descent of Man, and Other Stories*. He currently teaches English and creative writing at the University of Southern California, Los Angeles.

Major Works of Short Fiction

Boyle's short fiction ranges widely from amusing satire to somber stories depicting human frailty and emotional development. In his humorous and satirical works, he frequently examines American culture and the anxieties of modern society. "The Big Garage" concerns a man's slavish attachment to his automobile and the ordeal of taking it to be serviced. "Peace of Mind," in which a suburbanite purchases a home security system to guard against rampant crime, and "Bloodfall," in which a group of people numbed by drugs and television find a persistent rain of blood merely annoying and possibly damaging to their material possessions, comment on paranoia and materialism. The fear of sexual intimacy is explored in "Modern Love," in which a woman requires her lover to wear a full-body condom. In "The Hector Quesadilla Story," which depicts an aging player's last chances at glory, Boyle treats

baseball as a metaphor for art and life. Boyle also frequently examines relationships between animals and humans. In "Heart of a Champion," for instance, Lassie, the dog from the popular television series, abandons her master Timmy for a sexually attractive coyote. "Descent of Man " concerns a scientific researcher who leaves her boyfriend for a brilliant chimpanzee who is translating works by Charles Darwin and Friedrich Nietzsche into Yerkish. Bizarre and irrational behavior is also a common topic, as in "Sinking House," in which a grief-stricken woman floods her house by turning on all the water faucets. Boyle has written numerous parodies as well. "The Devil and Irv Cherniske" is a retelling of Washington Irving's "The Devil and Tom Walker"; "Me Cago en la Leche (Robert Jordan in Nicaragua)" draws on Ernest Hemingway's *For Whom the Bell Tolls*; while "Rupert Beersley and the Beggar Master of Sivani-Hoota" parodies the Sherlock Holmes detective story. Among Boyle's somber works are "Greasy Lake," a coming-of-age story about a young man's confrontation with death and violence; "If the River Was Whiskey," a poignant portrayal of the relationship between a well-meaning alcoholic and his son; and "Thawing Out," a love story in which a man overcomes his fear of commitment.

Critical Reception

Commentators on Boyle's short fiction have praised him as a gifted storyteller whose strengths lie in his highly imaginative plots, word choice, and the comic effects he achieves through the use of hyperbole and unusual metaphors and similes. Although some critics dismissed much of Boyle's early work for lacking depth, many contend that his later work in such collections as *Greasy Lake, & Other Stories* (1985) and *If the River Was Whiskey* (1989) displays a greater range of emotion and an increasing ability to go beyond the comic premise of a story to genuine social criticism. Commenting on Boyle's oeuvre, Larry McCaffery wrote "that beneath its surface play, erudition, and sheer storytelling power, [Boyle's] fiction . . . presents a disturbing and convincing critique of an American society so jaded with sensationalized images and plasticized excess that nothing stirs its spirit anymore."

PRINCIPAL WORKS

SHORT FICTION

Descent of Man, and Other Stories 1979
Greasy Lake, & Other Stories 1985
If the River Was Whiskey 1989
The Collected Stories 1993
Without a Hero, and Other Stories 1994

OTHER MAJOR WORKS

Water Music (novel) 1981
Budding Prospects: A Pastoral (novel) 1984
World's End (novel) 1987
East Is East (novel) 1990
The Road to Wellville (novel) 1993

CRITICISM

David Emblidge (essay date 1979)

SOURCE: A review of *Descent of Man*, in *Saturday Review*, New York, Vol. 6, No. 7, March 31, 1979, p. 53.

[*In the review below, Emblidge praises the stories in* Descent of Man *as humorous and provocative.*]

Several stories in this impressive first collection [*Descent of Man*] recall a familiar aesthetic point: Beautiful words in artful combinations make even the hideous, obscene, and terrifying a mysteriously beautiful experience for the imagination. In **"Drowning,"** Boyle shows us a vulgar, fat, young male misfit who rapes a tanned, sleeping nude girl on a beach. Boyle's tenderness in recognizing the fully human emotions of both rapist and victim, plus his verbal acuity, make us love even this seemingly repulsive story.

The book's dominant mood, however, is outrageous humor. The title story [**"Descent of Man"**] satirizes a researcher who gives up her human lover and loses herself to her subject, a genius chimpanzee. In **"Heart of a Champion,"** Lassie, the TV dog, is only superficially loyal to Timmy, her little-boy master. She drops Timmy as soon as a horny coyote comes her way.

Boyle parodies Muhammad Ali (and Pavlovian behaviorists) in **"The Champ,"** concerning a world-title eating bout reminiscent of John Belushi's face-stuffing in *Animal House*. Even the high moral drama of *Alive!* (a true account of a plane crash in the Andes), which examines the dilemma of cannibalism versus survival, is lampooned in **"Green Hell."**

There are surreal, darkly serious stories as well. A man's insistent yearning to learn the mysteries of womanhood by becoming one (first psychologically, then surgically) is the theme of **"A Women's Restaurant."** Best of all is the absurdist black humor, with loud echoes of Kafka, Pynchon, Sartre, and Ionesco, of **"The Big Garage."** In this story the protagonist's car breaks down and is towed to a repair shop, which becomes a prison-labyrinth, run by sadistic mechanic-guards. His total dependence on his automobile makes him a slavish extension of his broken machine.

The few dead moments in the book are minor lapses in an otherwise uproariously comic, discomfortingly provocative collection. T. Coraghessan Boyle is a writer to savor and to watch.

Max Apple (essay date 1979)

SOURCE: "Characters in Search of a Difference," in *The New York Times Book Review*, April 1, 1979, pp. 14, 39.

[*An American educator, novelist, short story writer, and critic, Apple is best known for* The Oranging of America, and Other Stories *(1976). In the review below, he offers a favorable assessment of* Descent of Man.]

A volume of stories, bereft of continuity in plot and character, is often unified only by the writer's obsessiveness. A certain restlessness, a temporary energy takes over, a singing in the brain that is too intense to live with for the duration of a novel. That energy roams the lines of the story looking for a way out. James Joyce called that way out an epiphany, but in our time it is more like the quick release of passion than the stately illumination of the intellect.

Descent of Man is loaded with energetic language. On the dedication page, T. Coraghessan Boyle offers us Tarzan's "Ungowa," and with that half-comic, half-desperate signal we launch into this first collection. Tarzan is an appropriate voice of introduction: The jungle is as dominant in Mr. Boyle's imagination as the parlor is in Jane Austen's. Rot and overgrowth are among Mr. Boyle's favorite subjects, but his style is as crisp as if it has been quick-frozen.

The title story [**"Descent of Man"**] begins with the narrator's lament: "I was living with a woman who suddenly began to stink." This is not just the petty vindictiveness of the scorned lover; this man's Jane really does stink, since her new lover is Konrad, a brilliant chimpanzee who is translating into Yerkish Darwin's *Descent of Man,* Chomsky's *Language and Mind* and Nietzsche's *Beyond Good and Evil.*

The story is characteristic of Mr. Boyle's obsession with the origin of the species. It is this comic-imaginative quest that makes the collection seem so unified. Characters are in search of the differences between man and beast, man and woman, plunderer and hero, art and silliness.

Though the stories are sometimes merely clever, Mr. Boyle is capable of the sublime. In **"A Women's Restaurant"** his narrator is obsessed by a restaurant that admits only women. His imagination runs wild because he is excluded. This underground man wants to enter society, but in our time he finds that he is barred by femininity rather than by the old standbys, wealth and culture:

> There are times, at home, fish poached, pots scrubbed, my mind gone blank, when suddenly it begins to rise in my consciousness, a sunken log heaving to the surface. A women's restaurant. The injustice of it, the snobbery, the savory dark mothering mystery: what do they *do* in there?

Mr. Boyle likes to imagine his characters "in extremis"; the melodramatic is where he begins. In **"Heart of a Champion"** he gives us Lassie and Tommy in the midst of their never-ending crises:

> The boy's eyes startle and then there's a blur, a smart snout clutching his pantleg, the thunderblast of the trunk, the dust and spinning leaves. "Golly, Lassie . . . I didn't even see it," says the boy sitting safe in a mound of moss. The collie looks up at him (the svelte snout, the deep gold logician's eyes), and laps at his face.

This Lassie momentarily gives herself to a coyote, blurring the distinction between man's friend and enemy, but she will see her boy through his predictable emergencies. She hasn't much choice, it's built into the genre.

"Descent of Man" is characteristic of Mr. Boyle's obsession with the origin of the species. It is this comic-imaginative quest that makes *Descent of Man* seem so unified. Characters are in search of the differences between man and beast, man and woman, plunderer and hero, art and silliness.

—*Max Apple*

In **"Green Hell"** Mr. Boyle has a wonderful time with an even more melodramatic circumstance—a plane crash and its survivors. They crash in the jungle, of course, bury "twelve rugby players" and try to establish their little society in the wilderness. "The pilot talked of the spirit of democracy, the social contract, the state of nature, the myth

of the noble savage, and the mythopoeic significance of Uncle Sam."

But Mr. Boyle does not use melodrama, rot and decay exclusively as parody. In **"Bloodfall"** it rains blood. In a number of the stories Mr. Boyle is fascinated with describing blood and clots of gore. In this story he gives his descriptive power free rein. The brutal irony of the story is lodged in how the bored rich communards watch the blood fall and listen to their "thirty-six-inch Fisher speaker in the corner," knowing that it might be "Judgment Day." They smoke and eat and watch in this charged but calm atmosphere still another "descent of man."

The circumstances in these stories are always surprising. An astronaut comes home from the moon to a house that has rotted away; an old Norse bard laments the bad days a plunderer sometimes has to endure. In **"Dada,"** Idi Amin comes to New York as the guest of honor at a Dada festival. He heads for Harlem, where he reserves "the fourth floor of the Hotel Theresa" and offers wifehood to his hostess, who answers Big Daddy's "Why you laugh?" with, "I was thinking of Bergson."

There is no lack of cleverness in *Descent of Man,* but sometimes the cleverness is all, or it is only a partial cleverness, as in **"The Big Garage"** or **"The Champ."** But the failures are the honest failures of an energetic writer who is willing to try anything. That "Ungowa" on the dedication page is a joyful announcement: An adventurous new bird, T. Coraghessan Boyle, has come to roost in the literary jungle.

Steven Crist   (essay date 1979)

SOURCE: A review of *Descent of Man,* in *The Christian Science Monitor,* June 29, 1979, p. 19.

[*Crist is an American journalist, nonfiction writer, and critic. In the following review, he offers a mixed evaluation of* Descent of Man.]

If "bizarre," "unsettling" and "odd" describe your cup of short story, then T. Coraghessan Boyle's first collection [*Descent of Man*] may be for you. He is an enthusiastically peculiar writer, one who seizes on popular culture and literary genres, puts them under glass for jaundiced inspection, and usually squashes them into engaging, if not always successful permutations.

An episode of "Lassie" is transformed into a staggeringly unpleasant tale of pain and blood, Idi Amin presides over an international Dada festival; a man turns transvestite in an attempt to penetrate an all-women's restaurant. In these and 14 other pieces. Boyle depicts our world through his funhouse mirror.

As might be expected, some of these efforts hit the mark dead on while others seem contrived and tasteless at best. There seems an inverse ratio between Boyle's attempts to shock us and his success: those pieces where he abandons the role of the spaced-out critic are the most successful. It is unfortunate that he underestimates his ability to tell a story, for he is a remarkably good storyteller. **"Green Hell,"** the story of a plane crash in the Amazon, and **"The**

An excerpt from "Greasy Lake":

I don't know how long I lay there, the bad breath of decay all around me, my jacket heavy as a bear, the primordial ooze subtly reconstituting itself to accommodate my upper thighs and testicles. My jaws ached, my knee throbbed, my coccyx was on fire. I contemplated suicide, wondered if I'd need bridgework, scraped the recesses of my brain for some sort of excuse to give my parents—a tree had fallen on the car, I was blindsided by a bread truck, hit and run, vandals had got to it while we were playing chess at Digby's. Then I thought of the dead man. He was probably the only person on the planet worse off than I was. I thought about him, fog on the lake, insects chirring eerily, and felt the tug of fear, felt the darkness opening up inside me like a set of jaws. Who was he, I wondered, this victim of time and circumstance bobbing sorrowfully in the lake at my back. The owner of the chopper, no doubt, a bad older character come to this. Shot during a murky drug deal, drowned while drunkenly frolicking in the lake. Another headline. My car was wrecked; he was dead.

When the eastern half of the sky went from black to cobalt and the trees began to separate themselves from the shadows, I pushed myself up from the mud and stepped out into the open. By now the birds had begun to take over for the crickets, and dew lay slick on the leaves. There was a smell in the air, raw and sweet at the same time, the smell of the sun firing buds and opening blossoms. I contemplated the car. It lay there like a wreck along the highway, like a steel sculpture left over from a vanished civilization. Everything was still. This was nature.

I was circling the car, as dazed and bedraggled as the sole survivor of an air blitz, when Digby and Jeff emerged from the trees behind me. Digby's face was crosshatched with smears of dirt; Jeff's jacket was gone and his shirt was torn across the shoulder. They slouched across the lot, looking sheepish, and silently came up beside me to gape at the ravaged automobile. No one said a word. After a while Jeff swung open the driver's door and began to scoop the broken glass and garbage off the seat. I looked at Digby. He shrugged. "At least they didn't slash the tires," he said.

It was true: the tires were intact. There was no windshield, the headlights were staved in, and the body looked as if it had been sledge-hammered for a quarter a shot at the county fair, but the tires were inflated to regulation pressure. The car was drivable. In silence, all three of us bent to scrape the mud and shattered glass from the interior. I said nothing about the biker. When we were finished, I reached in my pocket for the keys, experienced a nasty stab of recollection, cursed myself, and turned to search the grass. I spotted them almost immediately, no more than five feet from the open door, glinting like jewels in the first tapering shaft of sunlight. There was no reason to get philosophical about it: I eased into the seat and turned the engine over.

T. Coraghessan Boyle, in his Greasy Lake, & Other
Stories, *Viking, 1985.*

Big Garage," a wonderful fantasy about getting a car repaired, stand above the rest of the entries because there is so little self-conscious manipulation of the reader; they are delicious tales, briskly and smartly told.

The specific genre parodies are only partially successful. **"We Are Norsemen"** is stunning as imitation of Old Norse barddom but tiresome once one catches on. **"Heart of a Champion,"** the story of an eating contest, is a thoroughly unnecessary (and uncomfortably similar) rendition of Damon Runyon's "A Piece of Pie." One wonders why Boyle bothered to do his own version of this story.

Boyle's writing is so perpetually reminiscent of two masters of the short story that he can aptly be called a cross between the two—in this case, Roald Dahl and Donald Barthelme. At his best, he effectively combines the wonderfully perverse twists of Dahl's plots with Barthelme's disjointed use of language. But too often, he merely ends up being unpleasantly odd.

Imperfect a volume as this is, it is exciting to be in the presence of such a playful sensibility. Even more exciting, Boyle is a legitimate, major talent who can be forgiven his excesses for the clear promise of better things yet to come.

Louis Burnard (essay date 1980)

SOURCE: "Camp Conflicts," in *The Times Literary Supplement,* No. 4030, June 20, 1980, p. 718.

[*In the following review, Burnard presents a mixed assessment of* Descent of Man.]

There is a facile nastiness about many stories in this small collection [*Descent of Man*] which can be intended only hypothetically to outrage. In truth, of course, we are all far too urbane to be moved by such hackneyed situations as the anthropologist's wife having it away with an ape, the skies raining first blood and then shit on a houseful of happy hippies, an astronaut first farting and then masturbating in zero gravity, to say nothing of the various spiders ("as big as a two egg omelette") which turn up with surprising regularity within these pages. Faced with the high (low?) camp of an eating contest described in a sickening amalgam of American menu-ese and Harry Carpenter at his most poetic, the correct reaction is all too predictable: Mr Boyle is, indeed, a "master of black humour" and "genially disillusioned about the human condition"—it says so, right here on the blurb. (Even for a blurb writer, even in these godless days, that juxtaposition of disillusionment and geniality might perhaps have given some occasion for hesitation—but let it pass).

What oppositions, then, are mediated by these tales? Well, of course, we have those good old bogies of modern American writing—dirt, blood, vomit, etc, versus plastic forks deodorants, etc (**"Descent of Man", "Bloodfall", "Green Hell", "Earth Moon"**); we have Women—curse them for their intractable otherness—versus Us Chaps (**"A Women's Restaurant", "John Barleycorn Lives", "Drowning"**); we have The Media versus Reality—a very one-sided affair with Reality hardly getting a look in ("**Heart of a Champion**", "**Dada**", "**De Rerum Natura**", "**Second Swimming**"); In this last category particularly, mock-bathos (deflation) slides with ironic frequency into the genuine article (sinking), so that the response is a genuine groan. The juxtaposition of General Idi Amin Dada, for example, with the posturing of contemporary New York dadaists might have been funny as a passing thought, but I do not think anyone now finds General Amin amusing. Equally, "**The Second Swimming**" might have been bearable as a Monty Python one-liner; as it is, a Chairman Mao who plans to have "wieners with Grey Poupon mustard for breakfast" and exhorts his barber to "buff the pate" is merely silly. The same sub-Perelman smartness mars an otherwise exemplary evocation of comic book Norsemen; when their leader sums up the newly-discovered Newfoundland with the crisp and novel aphorism "That place'll never amount to a hill of beans", this reader at least is not as convulsed as might have been desired.

Stylistically Mr Boyle belongs to the Creative Writing school of modern prose masters. His text coruscates equally with verbless sentences, flat similes and brand names, set in a timeless continuum of present indicatives. Two stories deserve exception from this blanket condemnation however—both (I think) at least partially intended to parody greater masters of the form. "**Quetzalcoatl Lite**" (though marred by the same sort of silliness as "**Norsemen**") recalls Borges or Nabokov in its gallant attempt at conveying the inner workings of an obsessive collector, while "**John Barleycorn Lives**" is oddly reminiscent of the later Kipling in its hearty celebration of the great practical joke. By and large, however, the closest Mr Boyle comes to expressing an opinion is in the pseudo-Vonnegutese of the "extinction tales". "What's a species here, a species there? This is where extinction? becomes sublime." Sublime extinction? What is the world coming to?

Larry McCaffery   (essay date 1985)

SOURCE: "Lusty Dreamers in the Suburban Jungle," in *The New York Times Book Review*, June 9, 1985, pp. 15-16.

[*McCaffery is an American educator and critic. In the following review of* Greasy Lake, & Other Stories, *he praises Boyle's "vibrant sensibility" and perceptive commentary on contemporary America.*]

For the assorted politicians, teen-age toughs, baseball players, whale lovers, blues singers and ordinary suburbanites who speak to us in T. Coraghessan Boyle's brilliant new collection, *Greasy Lake,* life in contemporary America is pretty much a roller coaster ride, filled with peaks of exhilaration and excitement but also fraught with hidden dangers and potential embarrassments. One moment they're clutching a bottle of stolen bourbon, up higher than they ever thought possible. From up there the vista is enormous, gorgeous; the adrenalin is pumping; escape velocity from all that weighs them down is nearly achieved. But just a second later the inevitable descent has begun, and something has gone terribly wrong, the seat belt has disengaged, they're hurtling to a crash landing amid laughter, sawdust, plastic cups, stale generic beer.

Mr. Boyle used variations of this tragicomic trajectory to wonderful effect in an earlier story collection, ***Descent of Man,*** and two novels, *Water Music* and *Budding Prospects,* all widely (and justly) praised for their manic wit, lush, baroque language and narrative invention. What hasn't been sufficiently emphasized, however, is that beneath its surface play, erudition and sheer storytelling power, his fiction also presents a disturbing and convincing critique of an American society so jaded with sensationalized images and plasticized excess that nothing stirs its spirit anymore. As a Presidential candidate in one of Mr. Boyle's new stories puts it, "The great, the giving, the earnest, energetic, and righteous American people had thrown in the towel. Rape, murder, cannibalism, political upheaval in the Third World, rock and roll, unemployment, puppies, mothers, Jackie, Michael, Liza: nothing moved them." It is into this world that Mr. Boyle projects his heroes, who are typically lusty, exuberant dreamers whose wildly inflated ambitions lead them into a series of hilarious, often disastrous adventures.

The story "**Greasy Lake**," whose title and epigraph are borrowed from Bruce Springsteen, shows off his irreverence, his gifts for social satire and slapstick humor, and most of all his razzle-dazzle verbal energy. It's a warm June night, and three male spirits are driving around looking for the heart of Saturday night. Bored, drunk, clad in torn-up leather jackets ("We were bad"), these suburban teen-agers are anxious to stir up some action. But what's a fella to do when Thunder Road leads only to more housing developments and shopping malls? They wind up out at Greasy Lake, a mythic spot once known by the Indians for its clear waters but now littered with broken glass, beer cans and contraceptives. "This," the narrator explains, "was nature."

And it's here that all the really "bad" kids come, hoping "to snuff the rich scent of possibility on the breeze, watch a girl take off her clothes and plunge into the festering murk, drink beer, smoke pot, howl at the stars, savor the incongruous full-throated roar of rock and roll against the primeval susurrus of frogs and crickets." On this particular night, however, the rich scent of possibility turns sour in a hurry—a vicious thug is mistaken for a buddy, car keys are lost, a fight ensues, a tire iron emerges, skulls are rattled, and soon the narrator retreats into the primal ooze of Greasy Lake itself. There, covered with slime and utterly humiliated, he has a grisly encounter with the corpse of a dead biker and is forced to endure the whom-whomp sounds of his family station wagon being demolished.

The problem of these youths, frustrated in their efforts to find a suitable outlet for their passions and energies in America's shiny new suburban jungles, is echoed in a number of the other stories, but Mr. Boyle's control of a wide range of narrative styles and voices insures that nothing ever really seems predictable here. These styles include literary pastiche in "**The Overcoat II**" (an updated, Soviet version of Gogol's surreal classic) and "**Rupert Beersley and the Beggar Master of Sivani-Hoota**" (a clever spoof of the detective yarn), as well as myth and fantasy in "**The**

New Moon Party" (where a Presidential candidate is swept into office by promising to replace our old, pockmarked moon with a glittering manmade replacement) and **"The Hector Quesadilla Story"** (an aging Mexican ballplayer is inserted into a baseball game that apparently will go on forever).

Even the most realistic stories seem bizarre, partly because of Mr. Boyle's emphasis on quirky narrators and unusual personal relationships. In **"Caviar,"** for example, a childless couple, under the guidance of an unscrupulous doctor, bring a surrogate mother into their home to bear a child for them with disconcerting results. In **"All Shook Up,"** a lonely abandoned husband gets involved in a doomed affair with the young wife of an aspiring Elvis Presley imitator. And in **"Not a Leg to Stand On"** (one of the collection's real triumphs), a senile old man, still full of spirit despite his confusion and the loss of a leg, takes up residence in an utterly depraved household of drunks and thieves.

Interestingly enough, what may be the collection's most powerful piece—**"Stones in My Passway, Hellhound on My Trail"**—is one of the few whose effect is not comic. It describes the last engagement of Robert Johnson, the blues singer and guitarist of the Great Depression, destined to die at 24. The story concludes with a passage of extraordinary beauty that illustrates Mr. Boyle's feel for human passions and sensuous, evocative prose:

> His bowels are on fire. He stands, clutches his abdomen, drops to hands and knees. "Boy's had too much of that Mexican," someone says. He looks up, a sword run through him, panting, the shock waves pounding through his frame, looks up at the pine plank, the barrels, the cold, hard features of the girl with the silver necklace in her hand. Looks up, and snarls.

Mr. Boyle's literary sensibility, like that of Robert Coover and Stanley Elkin, thrives on excess, profusion, pushing past the limits of good taste to comic extremes. He is a master of rendering the grotesque details of the rot, decay and sleaze of a society up to its ears in K Mart oil cans, Kitty Litter and the rusted skeletons of abandoned cars and refrigerators. But if such fiction often makes us squirm, it also impresses us with its use of a broad variety of cultural, historical and literary erudition to illuminate and focus specific moments. Mr. Boyle is a writer who alludes to a Verdi opera in one breath and to Devo's "Satisfaction" or the Flying Lizards' version of "Money" in the next—or who might cite Shakespeare, Screamin' Jay Hawkins and George Romero's *Night of the Living Dead* in a paragraph.

This rapid-fire modulation between high and low culture is sure to put off some readers (and it has led to the inevitable comparisons to Thomas Pynchon and Tom Robbins). But more important is the fact that Mr. Boyle's perception of what is happening in contemporary America seems remarkably sure and accurate. He is probably at his best in his novels, where his exuberant imagination has more room to roam. But despite some unevenness in execution, the stories in *Greasy Lake* display a vibrant sensibility fully engaged with American society—and with the won-

der and joy that defiantly remain a part of our culture as well.

Dennis Drabelle   (essay date 1985)

SOURCE: "The Wild World of T. Coraghessan Boyle," in *Book World—The Washington Post,* June 23, 1985, p. 11.

[*In the review below, Drabelle remarks favorably on* Greasy Lake, & Other Stories.]

T. Coraghessan Boyle is the sort of writer who inspires even poker-faced reviewers to grin and start dusting off their superlatives. He has written two much-praised novels, and some of his early stories, collected in *Descent of Man,* were virtuosic show-stoppers. I recall particularly **"Heart of a Champion,"** in which Lassie is exposed as a secret canine slut, and **"Bloodfall,"** in which a bout of bad weather segues into a rain of blood. There was something breathtaking about the way Boyle could posit such jolting premises and then guide them into esthetically satisfying channels.

Greasy Lake, & Other Stories contains a few entries built on brazen foundations: **"Ike and Nina"** celebrates an imaginary love-affair between the golfing president and the cherubic wife of Premier Khrushchev; **"The New Moon Party"** features a politician elected president on the strength of his promise to replace the tarnished natural moon with a shiny new artificial one. The author elaborates such donnés with his customary flair, but it happens that these stories are among the least impressive in the new batch.

Boyle has evidently reached the point—and it is a lofty one—where he can put aside his sorcerer's wand and dazzle the reader merely by telling prosaic tales extraordinarily well. The title piece [**"Greasy Lake"**] is an example. It's a coming-of-age story in which a prank played by some suburban youths goes amok. It begins with a sure-footed prelude that accounts for Greasy Lake's tribal appeal.

> We went up to the lake because every one went there, because we wanted to snuff the rich scent of possibility on the breeze, watch a girl take off her clothes and plunge into the festering murk, drink beer, smoke pot, howl at the stars, savor the incongruous full-throated roar of rock and roll against the primeval susurrus of frogs and crickets. This was nature.

Then comes the prank—a shivaree that targets the wrong couple. The baited male swings into action. The narrator lays him out with a wrench. Redneck reinforcements arrive. The narrator plunges into the lake, where he makes a hideous discovery. Recovered, the main redneck goes on a rampage. "Tire iron flailing, the greasy bad character was laying into the side of my mother's Bel Air like an avenging demon, his shadow riding up the trunks of the trees." Eventually the rednecks leave, the shaken suburbanites regroup. As they drive away from the lake, their battered car shakes off "pellets of glass like an old dog shedding water after a bath."

Greasy Lake, & Other Stories displays a range and catholic empathy missing from Boyle's earlier, showier work.

—*Dennis Drabelle*

This is all told so straightforwardly that there seems to be nothing to it. Nothing that is but subjects like sex, violence, death, and remorse, all developed with flawless pacing and word-choice that seems the verbal equivalent of perfect pitch.

In **"All Shook Up"** Boyle grabs a hold of a trendier subject, Elvis impersonation, but not with the surreal grip that a fan of his earlier work might expect. (One can imagine such outlandish possibilities as the dead Elvis rising vengefully from the grave to pull down the proscenium pillars on a stage full of these parasitical illusionists.) This pseudo-King is so pathetically awful that he drives his Kewpie-doll wife into the arms of their neighbor, who accepts her for fling purposes only to realize that she and her squalling infant mean to stay.

It's another plain tale, told with marvelous economy and spiked with telling observations, like the response Elvis tended to evoke in those too young to catch him in his prime.

> By the time I gave up pellet guns and minibikes and began listening to rock and roll, it was the Doors, Stones, and Hendrix, and Elvis was already degenerating into a caricature of himself. I remembered him as a bloated old has-been in a white jumpsuit, crooning corny ballads and slobbering on middle-aged women.

"Overcoat II" updates Gogol's classic fable to the consumer hell of contemporary Moscow. **"Not a Leg to Stand On"** takes the reader deep into the life of an aged pensioner, wheelchair-bound, who reconciles himself to boarding with a family of ever-stoned petty burglars because the alternative of a nursing home is even less attractive. These and other stories display a range and catholic empathy missing from Boyle's earlier, showier work.

Boyle will always be able to pull off a consciousness-razing extravaganza when he wants to, but in this collection he demonstrates that he doesn't need lurid devices like blood-sleets and dog-sluts to make a profound impact. T. Coraghessan Boyle is one of the most gifted writers of his generation (he is still in his thirties), and in *Greasy Lake, & Other Stories* he has moved beyond a prodigy's audacity to something that packs even more of a wallop: mature artistry.

Jonathan Dee   (essay date 1985)

SOURCE: "Serious Fun," in *The Village Voice,* Vol. XXX, No. 31, July 30, 1985, pp. 49-50.

[*In the review below, Dee comments on the humor and tragedy of the stories in* Greasy Lake, & Other Stories.]

The scarcity of literary humor sometimes gives rise to a subtle critical prejudice—when an author's comic imagination is cited, it's cited to the exclusion of all else. Such praise, much like being tagged a "writer's writer," cuts you off from as large an audience as it wins you. It's no simple matter, then, to discuss *Greasy Lake*, T. Coraghessan Boyle's short-story collection, since humor is only one among an array of skills at this writer's disposal.

Boyle evokes compassion for the broadest, most degenerate of targets—Elvis imitators, over-the-hill athletes, survivalist yahoos, swastika-painting white trash. Yet his protagonists reserve their harshest judgments for themselves; a sympathetic act from which these stories draw their strength. **"Ike and Nina,"** a howlingly funny tale, reveals the details of the torrid, secret romance between then-President Eisenhower and the wife of Nikita Khrushchev. There are a few barbs at the expense of these ancient icons ("Ike was sixty-five, in his prime, the erect warrior, the canny leader, a man who could shake off a stroke as if it were a head cold"), but the humanization of the star-crossed pair, the sense of private tragedy commonly forbidden to public figures, gives this fantasy its lingering charm. "I think of the Cold War," the narrator concludes, "of nuclear proliferation, of Hungary, Korea, and the U-2 incident, and it all finally pales beside this: he loved her, and she loved him."

In a handful of the stories, Boyle toys with genre fiction. **"Rupert Beersley and the Beggar Master of Sivani-Hoota"** starts off as a pleasingly familiar suspense story in the Sherlock Holmes mode, told by a bewildered and reverential Watson. Beersley and sidekick are summoned to colonial India to solve the mystery of the local nawab's rapidly disappearing children. But instead of discovering the culprit, Beersley discovers opium; utterly unhinged, he is dragged away from a drawing room full of assembled suspects, screaming accusations which are self-righteous, logical, and completely wrong. The wonderful **"Hector Quesadilla Story"** similarly undermines conventions when a fat, achy baseball player who should have retired years ago finds his moment of glory not in winning the big game but in prolonging it. Hector is a worthy stand-in for his creator, who resuscitates the genre through sheer love of it—the difference being that Boyle's best days are clearly ahead of him.

The humor is darker and more momentary in the best of these stories. It is, as the narrator of **"Two Ships"** says, "a quick cover for alarm and bewilderment." When that cover is blown, Boyle's ill-prepared characters are left to circumstance; the stories complete a fateful trajectory into fear and sometimes tragedy. The title story [**"Greasy Lake"**]—best in the collection—begins as a light, slightly wistful reminiscence of the narrator's naughty teenage nights: "I drove. Digby pounded the dashboard and shouted along with Toots & the Maytals while Jeff hung his head out the window and streaked the side of my mother's Bel Air with vomit." By dawn, though, when two separate encounters with death have left the boys terrified, nothing seems funny anymore. The story is haunting in a way more somber fiction could never be.

If there is a vision uniting these disparate stories, it's an old one, of men and women adrift in a natural world which will always be foreign to them. Sometimes they're aggressors, sometimes victims, but they are forever at odds with their habitat. In **"Rara Avis,"** a child awed by the beauty of a bird roosting on a roof sees that it is wounded and turns on it; in **"The New Moon Party"** a presidential candidate rallies the country around the proposed construction and launching of a man-made moon ("Jupiter had twelve moons, Saturn ten, Uranus five. What were we?"), with disastrous results. In the moving **"Whales Weep,"** a man's discovery of nature's primal beauty leads him to an imitative act which sets off a chain of all too human misfortunes; Nature resides in man as well, according to Boyle, and even there is tampered with only at great peril.

Among his contemporaries, Boyle reminds me most of Tom McGuane. Both yoke a swift, masterful style to a hip sensibility that guards with humor what it holds most dear. Boyle is the more forthrightly comic of the two, but *Greasy Lake* suggests that he may move away from the genre stories—which he can take only so far, before descending into parody—and refine the darker vision of his novels, *Water Music* and *Budding Prospects*. If that happens, a more apt comparison might be to Evelyn Waugh—heady territory for any writer.

Elizabeth Benedict   (essay date 1989)

SOURCE: "Having a Good Time with Our Worst Fears," in *The New York Times Book Review,* May 14, 1989, pp. 1, 33.

[*Benedict is an American novelist, short story writer, and critic. In the following review of* If the River Was Whiskey, *she praises Boyle's humorous, satiric treatment of contemporary society as entertaining but finds his somber stories more rewarding.*]

Half a dozen shysters, a talking three-foot-tall statue of the Virgin Mary, a mendacious adoption counselor, a Los Angeles public-relations man hired to "upgrade" Ayatollah Ruhollah Khomeini's image, a woman who makes her lover wear a "full-body condom" when he goes to bed with her—even the Devil himself—make appearances in T. Coraghessan Boyle's daring, irreverent and sometimes deeply moving new collection of stories, *If the River Was Whiskey.*

With the linguistic acrobatics and hip, erudite audacity we've come to expect from his two other story collections and three novels, Mr. Boyle here lampoons our most terrible fears—that our homes are not safe and our lovers are riddled with communicable diseases—and ridicules our cupidity, racism and cultural insensitivity. In his universe, those who live by the deal—the Ivan Boeskys, the snake-oil salesmen—always get their comeuppance. But before the marshals arrive, the nice guys among us, saps and all, have been snookered out of our life savings. Only in the title story [**"If the River Was Whiskey"**] and **"Thawing

Out"** does Mr. Boyle completely drop his comic persona and insistent cynicism and tell straightforward stories about human frailty, love and loss.

"Humor resides in exaggeration, and humor is a quick cover for alarm and bewilderment," a character says in **"Two Ships,"** a story in Mr. Boyle's second collection, *Greasy Lake.* The sentiment still holds. In his choice here of conceits, characters and figures of speech, Mr. Boyle remains a four-star general of hyperbole. A woman gives a man "a look that would have corroded metal." An explosives expert "waited till the flame was gone from his throat and the familiar glow lit his insides so that they felt radioactive." A character's wife "clung to his arm like some inescapable force of nature, like the tar in the La Brea pits or the undertow at Rockaway Beach." Mr. Boyle's plot lines are no less outrageous. A crazed Hungarian daredevil rides the axle of a truck from Maine to Los Angeles. A stock trader meets up with the Devil in his backyard.

Many of Mr. Boyle's characters, in their immensity and their colorful, inflated gestures, loom like Mighty Mouse in the Macy's Thanksgiving Day Parade. He's so huge that we have to pay attention, even marvel at how he was put together—and how he stays up there—but for all the space he takes up and the impression he makes, he doesn't leave us much in the way of depth to remember him by.

Sometimes Mr. Boyle's parade is fun, sometimes it's hilariously funny, and often his imaginative leaps and midair somersaults are breathtaking. He is fluent in any number of slick American dialects: the hip patois of the vanishing 1960's counterculture, the sleazy patter of Hollywood agents and P.R. men and the lingua franca of those who speak *haute nouvelle cuisine.* And though he sneers at an inordinate number of his characters, putting them down with easy shots—corrupt businessmen who wear gold chains have become Mr. Boyle's Jewish-mother joke—he clearly feels a playful affection for others. He's fond of them not because they're lifelike—often they're not—but because they represent impulses more akin to his own than bilking people, and fears closer to his heart than, say, the threat of nuclear attack, which he exploited brilliantly in **"On for the Long Haul"** in *Greasy Lake.*

Call them impulses and fears writers can relate to. Albert, the chef in **"Sorry Fugu,"** believes himself to be "potentially one of the great culinary artists of his time." When he's visited by the hard-nosed food writer Willa Frank, he's determined to win her over, to get a great review from the toughest critic out there. He distracts her lunkish boyfriend with burned steak and boiled peas—"shanty Irish" food, the chef calls it, like the fellow's mother used to make—and lures Willa into his kitchen for a supreme culinary seduction. She tumbles to his taglierini alla pizzaiola and admits that her negative reviews reflect her boyfriend's tastes. Why not her own? "To like something," she says, "to really like it and come out and say so, is taking a terrible risk. I mean, what if I'm wrong? What if it's really no good?"

Zoltan Mindszenty (a. k. a. the Human Fly) couldn't care less about critical acclaim. Wearing tights, a cape, swimming goggles and a red bathing cap, be marches into the closet-size office of a Hollywood agent and announces, "I want to be famous." In a series of wacky, death-defying stunts—including an attempt to ride on the wing of a jet—the Human Fly gets his wish. And his agent, who now and then feels ambivalent about watching "a man die for ten percent of the action," gets his: a bigger office.

In **"Thawing Out"** and the title story, Mr. Boyle reveals the naked "alarm and bewilderment" he usually cloaks in humor. **"Thawing Out"** is a somber, eloquent love story about the redemptive powers of water, and of love. A cocky young man abandons his girlfriend, Naina, and then returns. Naina and her mother belong to the Polar Bear Club; in the dead of winter, they swim the Hudson River. They are made, he comes to realize, of tougher stuff than he is.

I know of no other story by Mr. Boyle that is nearly as powerful or poignant as **"If the River Was Whiskey."** It's the last story in the collection, and so different from the others in texture and tone that it is startling to come upon. A young boy, Tiller, spends a summer month at a lakeside cabin with his parents, fishing and trying to become closer to his troubled alcoholic father, who has recently lost his job. After two weeks in the cabin, Tiller's father still hasn't "done one damn thing" with him. "You haven't even been down to the lake," scolds his wife. "What kind of father are you?"

As the story unfolds in vivid, tightly written vignettes told in alternating points of view—Tiller's and his father's—it becomes clear that the answer is "not much of one." His attempts at being a better parent are occasions for heartbreak. After his wife's scolding, he vows not to drink and goes fishing with Tiller, who, with "the novelty of his father rowing, pale arms and a dead cigarette clenched between his teeth, the boat rocking, and the birds whispering . . . closed his eyes a minute, just to keep from going dizzy with the joy of it." Mr. Boyle evokes their shared pain with a sure hand.

I have no way of knowing whether the story is autobiographical, but it has the ring of something deeply felt. Its placement at the end of the book was a shrewd move, for if we wonder, as we read nearly all of the previous 15 stories, what makes Mr. Boyle run, what psychic forces drive his hyperactive prose, what childhood losses have inspired his cynicism, we can look on the title story as an analyst's gold mine. If we choose not to read it as autobiography, but simply as a departure onto the rocky terrain of emotional candor, we nevertheless come to the last page feeling a more profound respect for Mr. Boyle than many of his satiric stories inspire.

Humor and exaggeration have served Mr. Boyle well. He is a consummate entertainer, a verbal showman, an explosively gifted satirist. If he uses humor to provide "quick cover" for his "alarm and bewilderment," and for other more powerful feelings, it's refreshing now and then—it's almost a relief—when he ditches his cover, as he does in the last story, and allows us a peek at his heart.

An excerpt from "Sorry Fugu":

The next day was the blackest of Albert's life. There were two strikes against him, and the third was coming down the pike. He didn't know what to do. His dreams had been feverish, a nightmare of mincing truffles and re-animated pigs' feet, and he awoke with the wildest combinations on his lips—chopped pickles and shad roe, an onion-cinnamon mousse, black-eyed peas vinaigrette. He even, half-seriously, drew up a fantasy menu, a list of dishes no one had ever tasted, not sheiks or presidents. La Cuisine des Espèces en Danger, he would call it. Breast of California condor aux chanterelles; snail darter à la meunière; medallions of panda alla campagnola. Marie laughed out loud when he presented her with the menu that afternoon—"I've invented a new cuisine!" he shouted—and for a moment, the pall lifted.

But just as quickly, it descended again. He knew what he had to do. He had to speak to her, his severest critic, through the medium of his food. He had to translate for her, awaken her with a kiss. But how? How could he even begin to rouse her from her slumber when that clod stood between them like a watchdog?

As it turned out, the answer was closer at hand than he could have imagined.

It was late the next afternoon—Thursday, the day before Willa Frank's next hatchet job was due to appear in the paper—and Albert sat at a table in the back of the darkened restaurant, brooding over his menu. He was almost certain she'd be in for her final visit that night, and yet he still hadn't a clue as to how he was going to redeem himself. For a long while he sat there in his misery, absently watching Torrey as she probed beneath the front tables with the wand of her vacuum. Behind him, in the kitchen, sauces were simmering, a veal loin roasting; Marie was baking bread and Fulgencio stacking wood. He must have watched Torrey for a full five minutes before he called out to her. "Torrey!" he shouted over the roar of the vacuum. "Torrey, shut that thing off a minute, will you?"

The roar died to a wheeze, then silence. Torrey looked up.

"This guy, what's his name, Jock—what do you know about him?" He glanced down at the scrawled-over menu and then up again. "I mean, you don't know what he likes to eat, by any chance, do you?"

Torrey shambled across the floor, scratching the stubble of her head. She was wearing a torn flannel shirt three sizes too big for her. There was a smear of grease under her left eye. It took her a moment, tongue caught in the corner of her mouth, her brow furrowed in deliberation. "Plain stuff, I guess," she said finally, with a shrug of her shoulders. "Burned steak, potatoes with the skins on, boiled peas, and that—the kind of stuff his mother used to make. You know, like shanty Irish?"

T. Coraghessan Boyle, in his If the River Was Whiskey, *Viking, 1989.*

Tom LeClair   (essay date 1989)

SOURCE: A review of *If the River Was Whiskey,* in *The New Republic,* Vol. 200, No. 24, June 12, 1989, pp. 40-1.

[*LeClair is an American educator and critic. Below, he offers a mixed review of* If the River Was Whiskey, *lamenting that the stories lack "exploratory risk."*]

T. Coraghessan Boyle has published six books in the last ten years, and they haven't been 3/8-inch volumes. *Water Music* and last year's PEN/Faulkner award-winning *World's End* are thick, expansive, and inventive novels that required historical research for, respectively, their 19th-century African picaresque and colonial New York family chronicles. *Budding Prospects,* though smaller in size and subject, has in its comic account of a year-long marijuana growing project in Northern California the verbal vigor and caressed details of Boyle's longer novels. The 17 stories in *Descent of Man,* his first book, and the 15 in *Greasy Lake* are heterogeneous in situation, jagged in form and style. While the decade's minimalists were describing trailer-park lives and psoriasis of the soul, Boyle was building a considerable reputation telling tales about Mao swimming, an endless baseball game, and the beggar master of Sivani-Horta.

Like his other collections, *If the River Was Whiskey* ranges beyond the American ordinary: two stories are set in Latin America, one in Ireland, another in Iran. Characters include the famous (the Devil and the Virgin Mary, Hemingway's Robert Jordan, a woman who lives with apes) and the eccentric (a Hungarian daredevil, members of a Polar Bear club, several deranged homeowners). Most are third-person narrations, but Boyle lets several of his people have their say: a Chilean student of Derrida reports an import-export scheme, a Woody Allen talent agent recalls the daredevil.

All of the stories first appeared in our best general magazines (the *Atlantic, Harper's*), in leading literary quarterlies (*Antaeus,* the *Paris Review, Granta*), and in reputable glossies (*Playboy, Gentlemen's Quarterly*). This range of publication could signify Boyle's talent and accomplishment: stories so powerful and artful that editors who wouldn't lunch together want to publish them. But I don't think so, because I can't tell the stories apart, can't distinguish the *Granta* story from those in *Playboy.* What the array signifies, instead, is the collapse of the high (or relatively high) literary into the popular in periodical publishing. Boyle is no fool. Beneath the variety of *If the River Was Whiskey* is a consistency of method that identifies and places the stories but limits them, pulls them toward the occasional, the journalistic.

Three-fourths of the stories here are what I'll call "feature fictions," sometimes imaginative, often witty, and once in a while sophomoric developments of newspaper material, daily life. The Ayatollah's "lizard eyes" inspire a parodic narrative by a p. r. man called in to soften the old demon's image. AIDS anxiety leads to a story about a woman who invents the full-body condom. Brokers' greed generates a rewrite of the Faust compact with securities replacing

knowledge. Nicaragua is a good place to send a punk version of Robert Jordan.

Boyle also reads the back pages, where oddities, desires, and fears flourish. **"The Miracle at Ballinspittle"** seems inspired by recent reports of a weeping religious statue in Chicago. Even Dear Abby would have difficulty advising Boyle's women victimized by a hellish adopted child in **"King Bee"** and a violent adopted ape in **"The Ape Lady in Retirement,"** an update of **"Descent of Man."** The real estate and home-security boom in Southern California gives Boyle a setting for drama in **"The Sinking House"** and **"Peace of Mind,"** stories in which yuppie safety is violently penetrated by the elderly and poor.

The newspaper restaurant review even provides Boyle the source for the artistic parable, **"Sorry Fugu,"** that introduces *If the River Was Whiskey.* When chef Albert D'Angelo opens a new restaurant, he says he wants the tougher of the paper's two critics to rate his food. He gets his wish, but the WASP reviewer, Willa Frank, seems disappointed during her first two visits. After Albert manages to distract her thick-palated companion, who likes only steak and potatoes, Willa visits the kitchen, samples the variety of Albert's food, and then confesses to having enjoyed fugu at another restaurant: she likes the way the Japanese fish numbs her mouth, because she has been unsure of her taste and afraid to praise the kind of rich and lovingly cooked food that Albert serves.

I have an appetite for just the kind of story that **"Sorry Fugu"** implies Boyle is purveying this collection. But unlike Albert's dishes, Boyle's stories are not always made from scratch or painstakingly prepared. Beginning with media material, Boyle sometimes simply inverts it for broad comic effect, as in **"The Little Chill,"** which describes a reunion of lumpish high-school classmates. Or Boyle predictably plays out an initial absurdity, as in **"Modern Love,"** where a prospective lover is dismissed by his disease-conscious girlfriend because of a minute health risk in his family.

Most of the stories are about menace—disruptions of the ordinary by the animal or the holy, by the crazed old or crazed young—and they are peopled by persuaders: agents, sellers, teachers, a seducer, a minister, a screenwriter. Boyle's devil is a "born closer." Fast-talking characters give the fictions richness, but too often Boyle borrows their hyperbolic expression to microwave a story's events 'or significance. It's Boyle, not some submerged narrator, who says a set of triplets is "twice as destructive as Hitler's Panzer Corps." Given this kind of stylistic exaggeration, one understands why Boyle's favorite trope for menace is the horror movie, the fugu of popular culture.

Several of the stories based on more direct observation of human exchange seem to have demanded more care from Boyle, an understanding and development not filtered through the media. Though less exotic than the Feature Fictions, **"Thawing Out,"** about a floating young man who fears the weight of his Ukrainian girlfriend, and the title story [**"If the River Was Whiskey"**], about a young boy

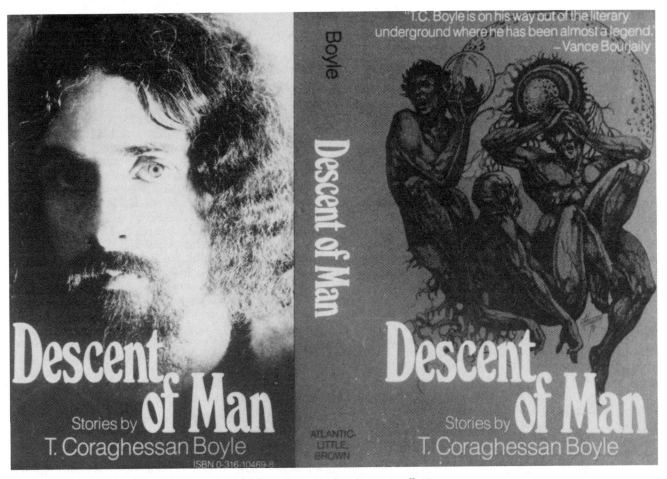

Dust jacket for Boyle's first short story collection.

and his burned-out guitarist father, have off-center characters, the menace of emotional engagement feared or exhausted, and a language that does not overheat the situations they present.

In **"Sorry Fugu,"** Boyle suggested that he welcomed the demanding critic. The icy Willa was seduced by the courtly Albert, but I'm less charmed, maybe more hard-boiled. Boyle is best in his novels, where he has to burrow into the material he makes up and where his exuberant language and the book's mass balance each other. If Boyle's stories are not as ingenious as Donald Barthelme's or as suspicious of popular culture as Robert Coover's, Boyle is smarter and funnier than Max Apple—of the writers with whom Boyle is compared. In *If the River Was Whiskey,* though, Boyle seems content with productive self-replication. Editors are happy to have these stories. After all, they validate the media as source and inspiration. What I miss at this stage of Boyle's successful career—at least in his stories—is exploratory risk: the experimental extravagance in *Descent of Man* or the elaboration of life that gives *World's End* its weight.

T. Coraghessan Boyle with David L. Ulin   (interview date 1989)

SOURCE: An interview in *The Bloomsbury Review,* Vol. 9, No. 6, November-December, 1989, pp. 4-5, 16.

[*In the following excerpt from an interview conducted in May 1989, Boyle discusses his aims as a writer, the writing process, his literary influences, and his background.*]

[Ulin]: *To what extent does the form [of a work] dictate the content?*

[Boyle]: With a novel, you have a longer idea. It's more complex and you want to say several things. With a story, you probably want to say one thing. These sixteen stories in particular—the *If the River Was Whiskey* stories—are more topical, percentage-wise, than either of my other two collections. I think the reason is that all these stories—with the exception of **"The Hat,"** which is slightly older—were written immediately after *World's End.* And three years of *World's End* had the storing up of a lot of material: Everything that happened every day in society, everything that happened to me, all the ideas I had to put on hold. It came out in a spate when I finished the novel. . . .

What about prior to **Descent of Man***?*

149

I was a student in school. At the point when **Descent of Man** came out, I had written maybe fifty stories and published maybe forty, and I collected seventeen. But that's my juvenilia, period.

Any plans for this body of uncollected stories?

I don't want to collect them. There are a lot of them, and some are pretty good. But I see the collections as books that I have chosen, and I want them to stand in this way and to be arranged in this way, and I don't want to deal with the other stories at all. J.D. Salinger, obviously, feels the same way.

When you arrange the stories into books, what kind of logic do you use?

I asked John Cheever this when I was a student and he said, "You put the real strong ones first, then in the middle you put the ones that aren't quite as strong, and then you end with a real bang!" That makes sense. But you also arrange them so they play off of each other. In the case of this collection, I had thought of arranging them in groups, because there are sort of groups of stories in here. But then I thought, "No." I mean, one of the things that has attracted an audience to me is the variety of the stories, so why not play to that? I don't *write* them in groups. I might write a story like **"If the River Was Whiskey"**—a non-comic and, I hope, rather moving story—and the next day I might write **"Hard Sell,"** which is a laugher. It's just what I feel like doing at the moment.

How long does it generally take you to write a story?

About a month.

And do you work on more than one at a time?

No. I only work on one thing at a time.

How many drafts do you do?

Probably three finished drafts. But I rewrite each line and paragraph over and over again, so any given part of that could have been written twenty times.

Other work habits?

I have an old typewriter my mother gave me when I went away to college, an old manual typewriter. There's a certain amount of voodoo invested in it. I have a large tin pail under my desk and I bleed a chicken into it each morning; I put my bare feet in it while writing. I find this has been very helpful for me.

You live in Los Angeles, a city that's often considered to be outside the literary mainstream.

Most definitely. And I like that because I'm a rare bird in L.A., whereas in Manhattan everyone is a writer, you know? Everyone in L.A. is a *screen*writer. I don't particularly like to hang around and schmooze with other writers. My friends are artists, musicians, non-specialized degenerates and maniacs; I don't have that many writer friends. I've met a lot of writers, but I don't necessarily hang out with them or have any need to feel part of the literary community. I do my work on my own regardless of what happens; whether the reviews are good or bad or I make money or don't. This is my life, this is what I do.

Who do you see as your ideal audience? Besides everybody . . .

The answer *is* everybody, you know? I'd like to have all bookshops in America devoted exclusively to my books, sort of in the way that Mao had a pretty good sale of the *Little Red Book* over there in China.

I think I am fortunate to have the literate audience of this country already, and have had a real cult following for years now. But I was pleased to see a lot of high school students at a reading I just gave—all diehard fans. That's great. You know, they talk about how nobody reads anymore; I think maybe they do. My ambition has been to go beyond the book people, and reach a wider audience. The people who don't normally read good literature or maybe any literature at all. That's one reason I like to give performances. I love to walk into a hall, and maybe there's a guy, he's a freshman in college and he hasn't read a book in twelve years and his girlfriend dragged him—or the boyfriend dragged the girl, whatever—and I come in. I've got my tiger-striped jacket on, and they kind of give me a funny look, and then I blow them away. Just blow them away. And maybe they go and buy a book and read it, my book or somebody else's book. That's the audience I want to reach. The people who are marginal, who might have had an experience of reading when they were younger and drifted out of it—like all people in this moronic society—and just watched the tube twenty-four hours a day.

For a lot of people, school kills reading.

Yes. School kills reading, and I want to demonstrate when I read at schools and colleges that some writers are still alive, you know? And it's OK! It's even cool, it's hip! It's hip to read! It's groovy, you know? It's great!

How old were you when you started writing?

I probably walked into a class as a junior in college. I would have been about nineteen, twenty.

You didn't write as a child at all?

No.

Were you a tale teller?

Not really, but looking back on it, I think my close friends and I have always valued stories and told each other stories, just in the way that everybody in the world tells each other stories. "What happened?" "Well yesterday, man, you should have seen what happened to me." We have to have stories.

Now for the ubiquitous "Who are your influences?" question . . .

Well, I am a fan, a diehard fan, and anything that I think is good I'm happy to read and be influenced by. I had very little background in literature as a kid or in undergraduate school, so when I first began to write, the current writers who most interested me were the ones who formed my way of looking at things and my style. People like Robert Coover and Donald Barthelme, John Barth, Thomas Pynchon, Gabriel Garcia Marquez; a little earlier, Flannery O'Connor. The absurdist playwrights like Samuel Beckett, Ionesco, Genet, also had a way of looking at things that was very appealing to me. It was just the same way that I looked at the world.

> **My ambition has been to go beyond the book people, and reach a wider audience. The people who don't normally read good literature or maybe any literature at all.**
>
> **—*T. Coraghessan Boyle***

Some of your stories seem to be directly connected with your influences: homage stories, if you will. For instance, there's **"Me Cago En La Leche (Robert Jordan In Nicaragua),"** *which you've called the sequel to* For Whom the Bell Tolls. *Or* **"The Overcoat II."**

Sure, sure, and I make no bones about it. For me anything that exists in any place is a potential story. Sometimes I'll do homage to a given piece: **"The Devil and Irv Cherniske"** is a rewriting of "The Devil and Tom Walker" by Washington Irving. I do stories like that every once in a while. I set stories in places I've never been, just to try to jam it up, just to see what it might be like. Why not? Why limit yourself?

Stories such as **"Miracle at Ballinspittle"** *and* **"Bloodfall"** *are built around religious imagery and events. How important is religion as a part of your life and of your background?*

Obviously, I couldn't have written **"Miracle at Ballinspittle"** if I hadn't had some Catholic training as a boy. My parents were not overly religious; maybe every Sunday to church was about as far as it went. I didn't go to Catholic schools or anything as the character in that story did. And as soon as I took Earth Science, that was it for religion as far as I was concerned. I would, I suppose, really be happy to believe . . . and maybe I will someday. I think everybody has to be superstitious in some way, because there is no reason for our existence, and we want reasons. We need reasons.

Many of your stories—like **"Ike and Nina"** *or* **"The Hector Quesadilla Story"**—*are wild, bizarre, new, interesting, and fun. Where do they come from?*

They're part of my twisted mentality, I guess, part of the gift, and my particular view of the world. That's what makes the stories unique. I don't think anybody else would have written a story like **"Ike and Nina,"** for instance, revealing a secret and passionate love affair between Ike—Dwight Eisenhower—and Nina Khrushchev. Or **"The Hector Quesadilla Story,"** for that matter. Or *East Is East;* I don't think anyone is going to beat me to that idea, you know? It's just: If you're a good artist, I think you do something that no one else can do, exactly.

Let's talk about your background. You grew up in Peekskill, New York . . .

Yup, got tall.

What did your parents do?

My parents were both working class. My father was a bus driver, my mother a secretary. My father went to the eighth grade, my mother graduated from high school as the salutatorian of her class. It was during the depression and there were no scholarships for college, and she never went, and always regretted that. Both my parents, though they were working class and very poor, always made me feel the equal of anyone and let me know that I was capable of anything, and encouraged me to be scholarly and go to school and whatnot. And of course, I went full-cycle in one generation and rejected all that, like everyone else, and was just a wild hooligan and vandal. But the values they instilled in me early, I think, emerged a little later on, when I discovered what my work was in life and began to do it.

You graduated from college, then went back home to teach.

I taught high school in the Peekskill area because I was going to be drafted for Vietnam and, to say the least, I didn't believe in the war. I was very violently opposed to it, and didn't want to go. There were many options that I had, and I suppose about the easiest was to teach high school in the area in which I grew up. It was considered vital to the national security because, with the baby boom, there were so many kids at school that there weren't enough teachers. I hadn't taken any teaching courses. In fact, I had never laid eyes on a kid, but I went in and did the job.

What did you teach?

I taught English. It was very hard because it was a pretty wild school and it was a tough schedule, and so on and so on. But it was good for me. It put me before an audience, and I realized that I really enjoyed teaching.

How long before you went to graduate school?

Four years. I worked four years.

What made you decide to go?

I always wanted to go back to school and learn all the things I should have learned as an undergraduate when I was steadfastly cutting classes and being drunk, stoned, and irresponsible. And after a while, I had the opportunity. The opportunity was given me by the Iowa Writer's Workshop—the only one I'd ever heard of. I got a story published in the *North American Review,* and then I began to think, "Well, gee, maybe I could get into one of these programs."

"We Are Norsemen"?

No, that was in *Harper's,* a little later. This was a story called **"The O.D. and Hepatitis Railroad or Bust."** It was about shooting heroin, and it was a way for me to convince myself to not do it anymore. So I applied to Iowa, where they accept you solely on the basis of your work. I sent that story and two others—another one that had been accepted for the *North American Review* and **"Drowning,"** which was the only old story in my first collection. And they accepted me. The first day I got there, instead of just taking the workshop classes, I began to take the Ph. D.

classes. I hadn't taken any GRE's, and had like a 2.1 average, and I wouldn't have gotten in if I hadn't been in the Writer's Workshop. But I wanted to know things. You might say you're going to read the complete works of John Milton next week, but you never will. If it's your job, though, and you're in class, you do it. And I was a perfect student. Sat in the front row, took notes, loved it. Did great, you know? I had grown up, and decided what I wanted to do.

"Miracle at Ballinspittle" pokes fun at some of the more credulous believers. I see it as a tall tale, sort of the tall tale genre of exaggeration, like **"The Champ,"** for instance. That kind of story has always appealed to me. Coming out of the Mark Twain tradition, you know?

I think if Mark Twain were publishing today, nobody would like him. The reviewers would hate him, because they don't seem to recognize just joy in storytelling. Or humor, or fun. It's got to be heavy and weighty and ponderous and dull, and nothing happens and nobody dies: minor revelations and no movement. I've always felt the opposite. Especially at a time when we've got so many media distractions, stories should grab you, should be entertaining—wild, bizarre, new, interesting, fun. As well as deep, thought-provoking, etc., etc., etc. You can't divorce the two, otherwise literature loses its audience.

How much of your work is autobiographical?

Any story has autobiographical elements, but only the author would know what they are. Some of my stories are a little closer to autobiography than others. But I've never been one to write strictly autobiographical work or even largely autobiographical work. There are elements in certain characters or certain situations in stories that are very true to my own experience. **"Greasy Lake"** would be very close to my own experience, probably. **"If the River Was Whiskey,"** perhaps. I know Walter Van Brunt and his attitude towards things would be very similar to mine at the same age.

In the end, it's not really relevant, is it? What's relevant is, does the story work and does it move you, does it interest you, does it make you laugh? Does it touch you in some way? Have you been there? Have you been to **"Greasy Lake"**? Everybody has, and that's why that story has been so popular.

You're not a particularly overt political writer, but World's End *is a political book, and, because they are topical, many of your stories have a certain political or social stance.*

Very much so. I think that the satire is meant to have a moral correlative, you know? I mean, Woody Allen is one of my favorite artists—he gets right out on the street in Manhattan and tells you who's good, and who's bad.

Do you write, then, from a sense of rage or responsibility?

When I won the PEN/Faulkner Award, Russell Banks was one of the judges. In his citation, he said that what he had liked about the book [*World's End*] was that it *was* about class, and sex, and racism, and that there was a lot of range in the writing. I liked that. I think that's probably true. Obviously, you can read my stories and know what

I stand for and what I stand against—although I don't think my primary purpose is political; it's aesthetic. I think an integrated work of art, though, can have many dimensions, and should. I don't mind a story like **"The Champ,"** for instance, which *can* have political connotations—I *am* always obsessed with our eating up the world and our consumption—but beyond that it's simply a tall tale kind of story. There's nothing wrong with that, but I think the best stories have a lot of ramifications, and they can operate at many levels and say many things.

You mention an obsession with eating. Is this tongue in cheek, or do you really feel that you're obsessed?

Everything I say is tongue in cheek, but I really think you could make a good case for some kind of obsession. I mean: **"The Champ,"** the "Fatima" chapter of *Water Music* (where Fatima's father forces her to eat so she'll become *enormous* and beautiful). There's an eating thing even in *East Is East, World's End*. There's been a lot of it. I'm not exactly sure why, but when I'm asked the question, I begin to think about it, and I begin to realize that it's probably because I am very upset about our conspicuous consumption and our gnawing up all the world's resources, and the vast difference there is between just what we have in any given household here, and what they have south of the border, for instance, in Guatemala, where I've been, where I know people. It's a terrible thing.

Joe David Bellamy (essay date 1989)

SOURCE: "Dazzling Excesses," in *The North American Review*, Vol. 274, No. 14, December, 1989, pp. 59-61.

[*Bellamy is an American educator, editor, novelist, poet, and critic. In the following review of* If the River Was Whiskey, *he praises Boyle's imagination and skill as a storyteller.*]

At the 50th anniversary celebration of the Iowa Writers' Workshop in 1986, Raymond Carver and T. Coraghessan Boyle were members of a panel called "Renaissance of the Short Story." Carver stood up and explained why he thought realism was the dominant mode in the short story, always had been and always would be. Coming from the man who had helped to turn the American story back toward realism, it was quite a plausible and convincing statement, presented very much in the manner of a Carver story—direct, spare, authoritative.

Boyle stood up to respond. He was wearing red Converse All-Stars, a black t-shirt, and a boiled linen jacket. He was as loose-jointed as a spider monkey, and his electric hair would have made an inviting roosting place for several species of birds. In short, he resembled a character from a story by T. Coraghessan Boyle. Boyle said, essentially, "Ray is absolutely right about his kind of fiction, but that's only half the story. Some of us can't write that way and shouldn't have to, and there ought to be a place for us in the world of literature too; and in fact, there is."

Perhaps the best argument for the accuracy of Boyle's statement that day in Iowa City is the success of his own work. Over the last decade, he has given us six books:

three novels (his most recent, *World's End,* a winner of the PEN-Faulkner Award) and three collections of stories.

In his latest story collection, *If the River Was Whiskey,* we are faced once more with a sensibility keen about comedy, playfulness, protean horror, madcap imaginative leaps, and the dazzling excesses that have become Boyle's trademarks.

Boyle has, in fact, become the most credible inheritor of the mantle of those postmodernist writers of the sixties and early seventies—Barth, Donald Barthelme, Coover, Hawkes, Pynchon, Vonnegut—whose excesses, subterfuges, formidable cerebral indulgences, and rampant experimentalism sometimes seem to have driven a generation of American writers back toward realism, if only to locate a different venue (but most probably for several other reasons as well).

But unlike some of the most demanding of the postmodernists (or superfictionists), Boyle is a writer who never forgets his audience. He is less an experimentalist than his immediate brilliant postmodern predecessors, and more of a showman. Boyle's main connection to the superfictionists is in his baroque imagination. Most of the time, Boyle is simply not interested in prosaic reality, but in the magical, the visionary, the unexpected, the horrific, and the comically bizarre.

And yet there is good evidence in his latest work that Boyle does not wish to become simply the Gary Larson of our literature. *If the River Was Whiskey* shows a wider range than his previous collections, *Descent of Man* and *Greasy Lake.* The funny stories are as funny or funnier, but often more probing than some of the earlier work, braced with a more mature satirical intention that goes beyond the joke to something very much like social criticism.

As a satirist, Boyle is sometimes light-hearted, but he is often crueler and angrier than mellow Vonnegut, though less political and practical (less realistic) than John Irving or Tom Wolfe. Yet Boyle is certainly as capable of writing for the mass audience (while still pleasing the élite or intellectual audiences) as any of these big three.

In *If the River Was Whiskey,* Boyle seems more interested, in general, in taking a look (and in taking potshots) at suburban Americana, rather than dealing exclusively in exotic locales, as was often the case in his previous stories—though even in suburbia Boyle finds traces of the primitive, the jungle, or hell itself.

In **"The Devil and Irv Cherniske,"** for example:

> Just outside the sleepy little commuter village of Irvington, New York, there stands a subdivision of half-million-dollar homes, each riding its own sculpted acre like a ship at sea and separated from its neighbors by patches of scrub and the forlorn-looking beeches that lend a certain pricy and vestigial air to the place.

Irv Cherniske is a cynical stock trader who resides in this Eden, but one evening when an errant chip shot takes him deeper than usual into the woodsy gloom near his backyard, he meets a dark stranger (a very persuasive guy), and

the reader gets a comic but harrowing contemporary rendition of what it might mean to sell one's soul to the Devil. This is magical realism, where the Devil actually enters the fiction as a credible character, though with real devilish (i. e., supernatural) powers. But the vision seems based as heavily on a contempt for materialistic values, that is, on a satirical intention, as on any desire simply to tell a whimsical or magical tale.

In **"Sinking House,"** an elderly woman whose husband had just died has an unusual response to death and loneliness—she turns on all the water faucets in her house. Next door are the Terwilligers, a nice conventional couple: Meg, who spends her life doing stretching exercises, listening to CDs, and running errands, and her husband Sonny, who "was shocked anew each time the crisply surveyed, neatly kept world he so cherished rose up to confront him with all its essential sloppiness, irrationality, and bad business sense." When the widow's water begins to inundate the Terwilliger's house and yard, what is there to do but call the police and eventually have the old woman carted off to the looney bin? But a smidgin of the old woman's anguish seems to take root, before the end, with consciousness-raising potential, in the mind of Meg, the young matron; and no one, including Boyle, is exactly laughing at the implicit heartlessness of these featureless suburban landscapes, where people are far more worried about the appearance of their yards than the catastrophes in their neighbors' lives.

> **Boyle is simply not interested in prosaic reality, but in the magical, the visionary, the unexpected, the horrific, and the comically bizarre.**
>
> **—Joe David Bellamy**

"Peace of Mind" is another story about the insanity and paranoia of modern suburban life, where even the reputed tranquility of safe streets and shops is no longer dependable. The protagonist is a yuppie alarm-systems saleswoman who goes around telling true-to-life horror stories of rape, murder, and senseless torture to the nice families who are her potential customers, causing one worried hubby to brood:

> "He'd been a fool, he saw that now. How could he have thought, even for a minute, that they'd be safe out here in the suburbs? The world was violent, rotten, corrupt, seething with hatred and perversion, and there was no escaping it. Everything you worked for, everything you loved, had to be locked up as if you were in a castle under siege."

All this is a preliminary to his laying out $5000 + for a security system. But, ironically, because of the "Armed Response" signs in his front yard, a maniac picks out his house for special treatment and murders the man and his family with uncommon viciousness.

Even the more comical and magical stories often feature at least a dollop of moral ire or provide a platform for outraged rectitude. In **"The Miracle at Ballinspittle,"** Boyle dispenses with the Laws of Nature as we know them to poke some irreverent fun at Catholicism and at human vanity and sin. A forty-year-old Irish-American named Davey McGahee, on a pilgrimage to Ireland to visit a "snotgreen likeness of the Virgin," has the time of his life: a celestial visitation. All of his sins are enumerated and dramatized before the crowd of petitioners: huge kegs of liquor fall from the sky, bales of marijuana. The Virgin screams "Gluttony!" and McGahee is "surrounded by forlornly mooing herds of cattle, sad-eyed pigs and sheep, funereal geese and clucking ducks, . . . even the odd dog or two he'd inadvertently wolfed down in Tijuana burritos and Cantonese stir-fry."

McGahee's "Sins of the Flesh" include visions not only of every woman he has ever made love to, starting in the twelfth grade, but every one he has ever lusted after, including Linda Lovelace, Lot's wife, and the "outrageous little shaven-haired vixen from Domino's Pizza. . . . The mist lifts and there they are, in teddies and negligées, in garter belts and sweat socks, naked and wet and kneading their breasts like dough." McGahee is even accused in the "False Idols" category, of having an autographed picture of Mickey Mantle.

Of course Boyle seems to be kidding when he goes into one of these fire and brimstone tirades, and he is, but not entirely. It is easy enough to laugh at Davey McGahee's anguish, but Boyle's ending to **"The Miracle at Ballinspittle"** brings the onus of sin back into the reader's own living room:

> For who hasn't lusted after woman or man or drunk his booze and laid to rest whole herds to feed his greedy gullet? . . . Ask not for whom the bell tolls—unless perhaps you take the flight to Cork City, and the bus or rented Nissan out to Ballinspittle by the Sea.

In **"The Human Fly,"** a down-at-the-heels Hollywood agent receives a strange visitor, a weirdo who wants to be famous. First the new client, on his own initiative, hangs in a bag from a skyscraper for two weeks and creates a sensation. Then he goes on to greater fame and glory by dangling from the wing of a DC-10 in flight and, later, from the axle of a Peterbilt truck from Maine to Pasadena. The story is a comical and satirical meditation on the American ideal of success and how it can drive people to destruction—and how there are always those ready to capitalize, commercialize, and mythologize such behavior.

In a few of the stories collected here, we also see a new, more mournful Boyle, capable of depths of feeling, regret, pathos, a writer willing to pass up the temptation for an easy joke in order to try [**"If the River Was Whiskey"**] is the most impressive instance of this sort of departure. It is a sensitive realistic piece of work, an initiation story which poignantly describes the relationship between a young man and his well-meaning alcoholic father.

Whether this story represents a new phase for Boyle or is simply his way of proving that he can "do" realism too,

if he really wants to—he can—is yet to be seen. Updike wished to prove, at one point, that he could write like Donald Barthelme, and, sure enough, he could. But the effort didn't seem to do any permanent damage to either writer.

There are also several charming love stories here to be relished. In **"Modern Love,"** a comic fable about the trials of contemporary courtship, the narrator is in love with a beautiful girl who places a high premium on sanitation. The story begins: "There was no exchange of body fluids on the first date," a line that epitomizes an age and an attitude. His love smells, romantically, of Noxzema and pHisoHex. But when the involvement leads inevitably to passion, she asks him to wear a full-body condom.

In **"Thawing Out,"** a young teacher overcomes his fear of commitment and the glib advice of a friend—"Before you know it you got six slobbering kids, a little pink house, and you're married to her mother"—to finally claim his lovely Naina. But not before he nearly loses everything he most wants and needs.

Also highly recommended: **"The Hat"** examines jealousy and mating rituals at a lodge in the Sierras over the Christmas/New Year's holidays—with a bear hunt thrown in for good measure. In **"The Ape Lady in Retirement,"** Boyle shows his skill at point-of-view narration by returning to the ape-and-human interaction that he mocked so hilariously in the title story of his first collection, **Descent of Man.**

Throughout this collection, Boyle's strengths are in plot, in dramatic instinct, in sheer imaginative vitality, in his knack for spotting cultural shibboleths in need of a pasting. He is a master of the pregnant transition, the loopy departure, and the infallible punchline. The average Boyle story can skewer as many pretensions as a shish kebab and turn from the fantastic to the vulgar, from the sweet to the almost unthinkable, within a page. If there is a renaissance in the American short story, then Boyle is certainly a part of it—riding onward, carrying his own peculiar kind of banner—and American fiction is the richer for his outlandish contributions.

Greg Johnson (essay date 1990)

SOURCE: "Jokers Are Wild," in *The Georgia Review*, Vol. XLIV, No. 4, Winter, 1990, pp. 713-22.

[*Johnson is an American educator, novelist, poet, short story writer, and critic. In the following excerpt, he praises Boyle's humor and the links Boyle creates between contemporary society and the Western literary tradition in the stories from* If the River Was Whiskey.]

In *If the River Was Whiskey,* Boyle's third collection, the comedy derives from bizarre situations and characters, but above all from the author's corrosive wit and inventive use of language, virtues which are notable throughout these zany, energetic stories. What if a man in pursuit of fame were to transform himself into a human fly? What if a young woman were to follow the concept of "safe sex" to a grotesque extreme? What if a public-relations man were assigned to improve the "image" of the Ayatollah

Khomeini? Boyle pursues such questions with a near-manic intensity even as he exerts careful control over his narrative structures, many of which are reminiscent of Twain in their combination of boisterous humor and a piercing commentary on contemporary experience.

Boyle combines a wealth of detail about 1980's America with a keen awareness of literary tradition: his stories are furnished with compact discs, cellular phones, home security systems, and specific details about our food and drink, clothing, and entertainment; yet they also allude to fairy tales and the Faust legend, to Hemingway and Joyce and Kafka. Like many of the so-called minimalist writers, he has a fondness (at times excessive) for mentioning brand names, but his obsessive documentation of contemporary reality does establish a connection—as most minimalists either fail or refuse to do—between that reality and the spectrum of Western literary tradition, as if to place contemporary America within the ongoing progression of human folly.

Many of Boyle's characters are enmeshed in a comically desperate strife with a fearsome Other. In **"Sorry Fugu,"** a male restaurateur labors to please a female restaurant critic whose standards seem impossibly high. The effort assumes almost metaphysical proportions: "He had to speak to her, his severest critic, through the medium of his food. He had to translate for her, awaken her with a kiss." The sudden allusion to Sleeping Beauty, in the midst of a tale set in the present-day world of trendy restaurants and sexual *angst,* is entirely characteristic. In **"Modern Love,"** for instance, Boyle updates the simplest of boy-meets-girl plots by focusing on his female character's fear of AIDS. She insists upon making love in a full-body condom ("her skin had suddenly turned to Saran Wrap," the narrator says mournfully), and she enjoys obsessive discussions of the most recently discovered infectious diseases. What makes **"Modern Love"** so painfully effective is our awareness that Boyle's plot, in this instance, is only slightly exaggerated: it expresses through humor the very real fear of sexual intimacy that has developed in recent years. **"Peace of Mind,"** whose main character sells home security systems to suburbanites terrified of rampant crime, also treats a particular anxiety of the 1980's—as does **"King Bee,"** a hilarious and appalling story of an emotionally disturbed adolescent. In the latter tale, the protagonist and his wife have begun getting death threats from their runaway adoptive son (*"I eat the royal jelly. I sting and you die. Bzzzzzzzz. Pat too, the bitch"*); the story ends with an apiarian nightmare that recalls Hitchcock's *The Birds,* rendering this family's dissolution in a scene of surrealistic horror.

The volume's best story, **"Sinking House,"** also employs black comedy, in this case to convey a woman's grief over the death of her husband. In what seems a ritual act of both purification and self-destruction, the widow turns on the water throughout her house: "It trickled and trilled, burbling from either side of the house and driving down the terrible silence that crouched in the bedroom over the lifeless form of her husband." When the seepage gets the neighbors' attention, the story broadens to suggest that such "irrational" grief is simply part of the human condi-

tion. As in the work of Kafka (clearly one of Boyle's masters), the bizarre lies just beneath the surface of the mundane, waiting to be unleashed.

At times, Boyle's cleverness seems to exist for its own sake: **"The Little Chill"** attempts to send up the popular film *The Big Chill,* but it's a one-joke story that quickly gets stale. Likewise, **"The Miracle at Ballinspittle,"** which deals with an appearance of the Virgin Mary in Ireland and traffics in over-familiar stereotypes of the bibulous Irish, is both awkward and heavy-handed. Even some of the better stories, such as **"Sorry Fugu," "Modern Love,"** and **"Peace of Mind,"** are gratuitously harsh in their treatment of women, who are by turns presented as vicious, demented, and dishonest. In others they are either sexually rapacious (Regina in **"The Hat"**) or a bit light between the ears (Meg in **"Sinking House"**). Though these sexist characterizations mar Boyle's writing, it's hard to imagine any reader not responding to the comic resourcefulness he displays in this book, or to the vibrant energy of his prose.

Malcolm Bull   (essay date 1994)

SOURCE: "Corn," in *London Review of Books,* Vol. 16, No. 1, January 6, 1994, pp. 19-20.

[*In the excerpt below, Bull comments on Boyle's* The Collected Stories, *noting the opposition between body and reason and the prominence of such motifs as water and alcohol.*]

If Haile Selassie, whom some remember as a bit of a biker from his days of exile in the West of England, had been stretched to 6'3" and given a part in *Easy Rider,* he would have looked rather like Tom Coraghessan Boyle as he appears on the front of the **Collected Stories**—an improbable confection of soulful eyes, hollow cheeks, frizzy facial hair and black leather. But although the impression that Boyle is a low-life lion of the interstates is strenuously maintained by his publishers—who report that he was a child of the Sixties, 'a maniacal crazy-driver' who ate anything he could lay his hands on, bought heroin for £5 a bag and listened to music with Linda Lovelace—his writing suggests an altogether less exotic and more wholesome milieu. Boyle studied at the Iowa Writers' Workshop and teaches at the University of Southern California, and his fiction often relies on the kind of farmboy irony that may come naturally to Ross Perot, but which appears to have been institutionalised in some American creative writing programmes. In such stories, the setting is the affluent suburbs: the Mercedes is in the garage, the *National Geographic* is on the table, and the jokes are about newfangled technologies that don't work or have unexpected consequences—security alarms, genetic engineering, research on primate intelligence. The implication is always that back on the farm, no one would have been fooled in the first place. . . .

[If] government causes political problems, psychiatrists madness, and doctors illness, how do the people live? How is it possible to survive in a society where being part of the solution automatically makes you part of the problem?

One answer to this question is given in a story called **'Modern Love'**. Having eaten a . . . meal of 'cold cream-of-tofu-carrot soup and little lentil-paste sandwiches for an appetiser and a garlic soufflé with biologically controlled vegetables for an entrée', two lovers watch *The Boy in the Bubble,* a film about the germ-free adolescence of a child without an immune system, and then put on full-body condoms for sex. But their promising, if intactile, relationship ends when, for wholly trivial reasons, the man fails an exhaustive medical examination taken at the insistence of the hypochondriacal woman. . . . [It] is the doctor who invents the diseases that keep the sexes apart; the suggestion is that anyone who conforms to the divisive morality of public health will eventually find themselves sealed into a private bubble and deprived of the reassuring intimacy of human contact.

The contrast between the isolated world of modernity and the tactile 'way of the centuries' is, in part, the usual comic juxtaposition of the body against reason, common sense against professional expertise, the familiar past against the uncertain present. But in Boyle's writing, these dichotomies are given an almost obscurantist degree of polarisation, with the result that the proffered alternative to the isolation created by dysfunctional expert systems is not rational communication, but primitive communion. As the abstract of his PhD (a collection of short stories, not, as the publishers claim, a study of Victorian literature) puts it: there is an 'opposition between the primitive (irrational) and the civilised (rational) poles of man's nature', and in 'a universe in which certainly is both essential and impossible, superstition is no less viable than rationality.'

This is a philosophy with a long history. In the 20th century it might almost be called the unofficial social theory of the novel. But Boyle's version is particularly unsatisfactory because he gives little evidence of being able to imagine what the superstitious intimacy of human relationships might actually be like. He appears to have no feeling for the primitive values he espouses. On the contrary, the characters he realises most successfully are self-absorbed egomaniacs. . . .

When Boyle's characters do manage to connect, interaction is usually lubricated by water or alcohol. In **'Greasy Lake'**, one of his best stories, three teenagers have to drive to the shores of the lake in order to find the drunken excitement for which they have been searching unsuccessfully all evening. . . . This parallel between water and alcohol (and the dangers inherent in both) is made explicit in **'If the River Was Whiskey'**, the story of a family splitting up as the result of the man's alcoholism. Father and son talk only when sharing a beer or fishing on the lake, but when the father dreams of being separated from his son, he sees him drowning.

There are many such drownings in Boyle's fiction; . . . his lakes are littered with floating corpses, in case we forget that water and alcohol can dissolve individuality as well as lubricate sociability. The starkest of these stories is **'Drowning'**, in which a girl sunbathing at the edge of the water is repeatedly raped while, five hundred yards along the beach, the one person who might have saved her swims out to sea and drowns unobserved. It is a chilling but un-satisfactory tale, and it raises the question of whether the author could have written a convincing story in which the victim and her potential saviour were not just well-greased monads moving in synchronisation, but individuals able to intervene in one another's lives. No doctor sealed the bathers into separate bubbles, but Boyle gives them no more chance of meeting than the lovers in **'Modern Love'**.

John Mort   (essay date 1994)

SOURCE: A review of *Without a Hero,* in *Booklist,* Vol. 90, No. 12, February 15, 1994, p. 1035.

[*In the following excerpt, Mort comments favorably on* Without a Hero, and Other Stories.]

If he wants to, Boyle can summon the angst for your standard realistic novel. In this collection's title story [**"Without a Hero"**], for example, he tells of a newly divorced fellow who inadvertently becomes the host of a young Russian woman who is awestruck by the bounty of America; our distinctly unheroic narrator won't marry her and thus forces her into prostitution. Boyle draws from this premise an indictment of capitalism as well as two engaging character studies. His mockery is at the center of things elsewhere, however, in stories that are less psychological studies than satirical conceits, such as **"Big Game."** Set on a hunting preserve near Bakersfield, it's a send-up of *Green Hills of Africa,* complete with Boyle's deadpan gun lore and a decrepit but still deadly charging elephant. **"Hopes Rise"** features two frazzled, precious, altogether contemporary characters, or caricatures. The story seems to lament the universal death of frogs and impending ecological disaster but, in the end, comments instead on the separation from nature that urban lifestyles entail. Perhaps Boyle's most arch effort is the slight **"Filthy with Things,"** about people so inundated with possessions they must enter a recovery program. Boyle's fabulist tendencies are much restrained here; not every story is remarkable, but at his best he reminds you of Evelyn Waugh.

Publishers Weekly   (essay date 1994)

SOURCE: A review of *Without a Hero,* in *Publishers Weekly,* Vol. 241, No. 11, March 14, 1994, p. 68.

[*Below, the critic presents a favorable review of* Without a Hero, and Other Stories.]

Most effective of the 16 technically ingenious and rudely funny, satirical stories in Boyle's fourth collection [**Without a Hero**] are the sketches of disaffected individuals who take refuge in hermetic surroundings, self-help programs, political causes and conspicuous consumption to hold at bay the banal world of convention and compromise. In **"Big Game,"** Bernard Puff, impresario of Puff's African Game Ranch in Bakersfield, Calif., peddles a simulacrum of the African bush. His carefully nurtured fantasy world is punctured by the arrival of a cynical young real estate mogul who detects "every crack in the plaster," and whose rapacious hunting leads to a grisly twist of fate when the animals revolt on the veldt. In **"Filthy with Things,"** a pathological couple whose home is sinking under the weight of their "collectibles" enlists the services of an evangelical professional organizer who banishes them to a "nonacquisitive environment" while she takes inventory of their astounding clutter ("three hundred and nine bookends, forty-seven rocking chairs [and] over two thousands plates, cups and saucers"). Other poignant tales tell of an ephemeral romance between a Russian and an American, the introduction of anti-drug rhetoric in a suburban grade school and the experience of growing up in postwar suburbia, a world Boyle regards with anxiety, nostalgia and a properly grim sense of humor.

Lorrie Moore (essay date 1994)

SOURCE: "No One's Willing to Die for Love," in *The New York Times Book Review,* May 8, 1994, p. 9.

[*Moore is an American short story writer, novelist, educator, and critic. In the review below, she remarks favorably on the stories in* Without a Hero *but laments Boyle's inability to go beyond sarcasm.*]

Readers of T. Coraghessan Boyle's amazing stories are probably most familiar with the salacious Lassie in **"Heart of a Champion,"** the Bruce Springsteen song run amok in **"Greasy Lake"** or the updated Gogol of **"Overcoat II."** Mr. Boyle situates his fictional ideas at the center of an available culture and then bursts forth with strange, engaging narratives that neither deconstruct nor reconstruct but perhaps, skeptically and inventively, *dis*construct. His dreamed-up reconfigurations seem nocturnal, pouched, alternatively formed and conceived—like animal life in Australia or a half-mad cousin from Dubuque.

In *Without a Hero,* Mr. Boyle's fourth collection of stories, once more there is nothing casual or tired; the literary performances here retain Mr. Boyle's astonishing and characteristic verve, his unaverted gaze, his fascination with everything lunatic and queasy. His stories are artifacts of psychic aberrance, lampoons fashioned in shadow and void, and they fill a reader (as they are intended to do) with the giddy nausea of our cultural and theological confusions.

In **"Big Game,"** a Hemingwayesque story impossibly reset in Bakersfield, Calif., a man runs a "safari" hunting range filled with decrepit elephants and lions from downsized zoos and circuses. For large sums, he allows rich people to shoot the poor beasts, though, in a rare pang of conscience, he still regrets "the time he'd let the kid from the heavy-metal band pot one of the giraffes." Nonetheless, he reminisces, "he'd taken a cool twelve thousand dollars to the bank on that one."

In **"Filthy With Things"** the protagonist—a man who wants to "go up to the mountains and let the meteor showers wash him clean, but he can't"—hires a "professional organizer" to help him make neatness and sense of his myriad possessions. The organizer, a chic, black-garbed woman (dressed much like the figure of Death in Jean

Cocteau's film *Orpheus*), treats her clients as addicts and their spouses as co-dependents. She catalogues and removes the man's belongings. He may have one thing back each day for 60 days, but he has to ask for them specifically, one by one.

"You'd be surprised how many couples never recall a thing," she says, "not a single item." Stripped of his material clutter, he is left with nothing of substance to take its place—except, perhaps, litigation. "When he shuts his eyes he sees only the sterile deeps of space, the remotest regions beyond even the reach of light. And he knows this: it is cold out there, inhospitable, alien. There's nothing there, nothing contained in nothing. Nothing at all."

In **"Hopes Rise"** a young man, after a lecture by an eminent biologist, becomes obsessed with the dying frogs of the world. But when at last, searching for some, the young man finds a pond full of them, they function merely as an aphrodisiac for him and his increasingly exasperated girlfriend. In their attempt to outwit the bad news of the world, the couple enact and express what seems to be even more bad news: a false rapture, a road-show holiness.

In the title story [**"Without a Hero"**], one of the book's best, a divorced man tells the story of his "passionate Russian experience" with a Soviet émigré lover named Irina: "Slovenly, indolent, nearly inert, she was the end product of three generations of the workers' paradise, that vast dark crumbling empire in which ambition and initiative counted for nothing. Do I sound bitter? I am bitter." Irina consumes large quantities of sushi and Grand Marnier; she quizzes her lover about mutual funds. She bemoans a world in which no one is willing to die for love. "I am the one who can die for love," she says finally to the narrator.

"Then die for it," he says, and the reader feels the intended violence of the moment so purely, strongly and sadly that it is a surprise: such moments are rare in the brash, wacky world of Mr. Boyle's fiction.

The reason, of course, is that Mr. Boyle is not typically that kind of writer. He is not psychological. He's all demography and *Zeitgeist,* a nerdy wizard of literary what-ifs (given the what-ares). He is fairly bored, it seems, with the nuances of the ordinary human heart; he does not linger there for long, or without tap shoes and sparklers.

Indeed, it is hard to think of writers to compare him with. In his sheer energy and mercilessness, his exuberantly jaundiced view, he resembles perhaps a middlebrow Donald Barthelme, or Don DeLillo crossed with Dr. Seuss, or Flannery O'Connor with a television and no church. The emotional complexity that could secure his characters at a safe distance from caricature confines him, slows him down. In his few stabs at poignancy or earnestness, as in one story here, **"Acts of God,"** he cannot shake the mean and theatrical habits of irony, the repudiating hiccup of sarcasm: "The house was gone, but he'd lost houses before—mainly to wives, which were a sort of natural disaster anyway; that he could live with—and he'd lost wives, too, but never like this. It hit him then, a wave of grief that started in his hips and crested in his throat: Muriel."

Part P. T. Barnum, part F. Lee Bailey, Mr. Boyle here is the dying Mercutio, unable convincingly to leave the stage. He is the biologist from his own tale, pulling dead frogs from his pockets and crying, "We're doomed, can't you see that?" while "the audience sat riveted in their seats." There are writers who intend to satirize a thing but then forget. They tip their hands. They reveal too much affection for and participation in the very object of their satire and their literary performance falters. Mr. Boyle is the opposite of such a writer. His prolific pen is, perhaps, in satirical overdrive. He may try to smile warmly, wisely, sadly, but his Cheshire grin won't go away.

One of the most successful exceptions here is the story **"The Fog Man,"** an evocative first-person narrative of one suburban boy's brief foray into racism. It is a beautifully narrated story of the misty demarcations in a child's knowledge and innocence, in a neighborhood's poison and magic, and the telling seems almost to overflow the form. It seems to want, as novels do, to re-create exhaustingly a time and world within our own, rather than make quick reference to the one we already inhabit—a necessary aspect of stories. One can imagine a whole novel spilling forth from this tale; it constitutes a strange and lovely fusion, a collision with another book entirely, and it is evidence of the author's true range. Elsewhere in this collection, Mr. Boyle's impulses—his penchant for the sardonic, for the put-on, for the manic unanswerable question—are perfectly suited to and accommodated by the short story's brevity and force.

God knows, Mr. Boyle can write like an angel, if at times a caustic, gum-chewing one. And in this strong, varied collection maybe we have what we'd hope to find in heaven itself (by the time we begged our way there): no lessen-ing of brilliance, plus a couple of laughs to mitigate all that high and distant sighing over what goes on below.

FURTHER READING

Criticism

Kakutani, Michiko. "Books of the Times." *The New York Times* (22 May 1985): C24.
> Praises Boyle's prose and limitless imagination in *Greasy Lake, & Other Stories* but finds his characters lacking in depth.

Kearns, Katherine. Review of *Descent of Man*, by T. Coraghessan Boyle. *Carolina Quarterly*. XXXI, No. 3 (Fall 1979): 103-07.
> Praises Boyle's adept use of language but faults some of the stories as clichéd.

Ulin, David L. "Lost in the Funhouse." *The Bloomsbury Review*. Vol. 9, No. 6 (November-December 1989): 5.
> Positive review of *If the River Was Whiskey*.

Wilson, Robley, Jr. Review of *Descent of Man*, by T. Coraghessan Boyle. *Fiction International* 12 (1980): 273-74.
> Favorable review.

Interview

Adams, Elizabeth. "An Interview with T. Coraghessan Boyle." *Chicago Review* 37, Nos. 2-3 (1991): 51-63.
> Interview in which Boyle discusses his background, writing habits, and influences.

Additional coverage of Boyle's life and career is contained in the following sources published by Gale Research: *Contemporary Authors,* Vol. 120; *Contemporary Literary Criticism,* Vols. 36, 55; and *Dictionary of Literary Biography Yearbook: 1986.*

Guy Davenport

1927-

(Full name Guy Mattison Davenport, Jr.) American short story writer, essayist, poet, editor, illustrator, translator, educator, and critic.

INTRODUCTION

Davenport is a scholar and translator of classical literature whose fiction, poetry, and criticism are influenced by the Modernist Movement, particularly the works of Ezra Pound. Like Pound, Davenport infuses his writings with historical, literary, and mythic allusions, seeking to reveal the perpetuity of human history by relating the archaic and the modern within the context of new literary forms. Davenport refers to his method of composition as "foraging" and he relies heavily on techniques associated with collage, particularly parataxis, to rearrange and correlate ideas and events and to broaden their implications. Davenport's six collections of short fiction display his extraordinarily broad erudition that enables him to create highly stylized and complex stories that he calls "assemblages of history and necessary fictions."

Biographical Information

Davenport was raised in Anderson, South Carolina. He excelled in academics and attended Merton College, Oxford as a Rhodes Scholar from 1948 until 1950. After serving in the U.S. Army Airborne Corps from 1950 until 1951, Davenport took a teaching position at Washington University in St. Louis. He earned his PhD from Harvard University in 1961, and wrote his doctoral dissertation on Ezra Pound's *Cantos*. Davenport was a professor at the University of Kentucky in Louisville from 1963 until his retirement in 1991, and has commented that his writing is an extension of his teaching. Gathering entries from several notebooks in which he writes daily, Davenport began composing the stories included in his first collection of short fiction, *Tatlin!*, when he was forty-three. In addition to teaching and writing fiction and essays, Davenport has been a frequent reviewer of books for a variety of popular journals.

Major Works of Short Fiction

Davenport's first two collections, *Tatlin!* and *Da Vinci's Bicycle*, have received critical acclaim for their inventive use of literary allusions and his idiosyncratic language. The montage style that Davenport achieves in his short fiction is often created by "writing over" texts of other authors. In *Tatlin!*, for example, Davenport manipulates two

accounts of a 1909 air show written by Franz Kafka and Kafka's biographer Max Brod to create the story "The Aeroplanes at Brescia." Critics have noted that this story exemplifies Davenport's interest in conveying historical perceptions rather than simply incorporating historical facts. In the piece, Davenport reorganizes the perspectives of Kafka and Brod and offers his own ideas of what they, and such other notable personages as English philosopher Ludwig Wittgenstein and Italian composer Giacomo Puccini, may have observed at the air show. "The Dawn in Erewhon" is another example of Davenport's interest in reshaping the works of other authors to enlarge or redirect fictive perspective. In this story, an updating of the influential nineteenth-century novel *Erewhon* by Samuel Butler, Davenport examines utopian ideals from the perspective of fictional Dutch philosopher Adriaan von Hovendaal. In *Da Vinci's Bicycle* the central characters are mainly historical figures whose accomplishments were often neglected by their contemporaries, including Ezra Pound, Franz Kafka, and photographer Jacques-Henri Lartigue. "Au tombeau de Charles Fourier" is considered by many critics to be the most significant piece in the collection. In this elaborately constructed story, Davenport weaves together references to the cosmology of the Dogon tribe of

West Africa, the linguistic innovations of Gertrude Stein, and French social theorist Charles Fourier's prescriptions for creating a utopian society through sexual liberation. Fourier's philosophy also pervades Davenport's trilogy, which consists of the stories in *Apples and Pears, The Jules Verne Steam Balloon,* and the novella "Wo es war, soll ich werden" in *The Drummer of the Eleventh North Devonshire Fusiliers.* The stories in these volumes convey Davenport's concern with resuscitating an Edenic innocence by creating settings in which his characters can uninhibitedly display affection.

Critical Reception

Davenport's earliest collections, *Tatlin!* and *Da Vinci's Bicycle,* are generally considered his finest works of fiction. Some critics have commented negatively on Davenport's treatment of homoerotic themes in his later short fiction, but most reviewers agree that he achieves stylistic virtuosity in these stories through his ideogrammatic language. Davenport has been widely praised for his innovative mythopoeic techniques and his ability to manipulate archaic allusions in his fiction. However, commentators have also noted that Davenport's complex narrative methods and his use of arcane literary and historical sources can result in exaggeratedly symbolic characterizations. Nonetheless, critics commend Davenport as a writer who is extraordinarily adept at synthesizing antiquated ideas and modern narrative techniques to create a holistic view of history and humanity.

PRINCIPAL WORKS

SHORT FICTION

Tatlin! 1974
Da Vinci's Bicycle 1979
Eclogues: Eight Stories 1981
Apples and Pears, and Other Stories 1984
The Jules Verne Steam Balloon: Nine Stories 1987
The Drummer of the Eleventh North Devonshire Fusiliers 1990

OTHER MAJOR WORKS

The Intelligence of Louis Agassiz: A Specimen Book of Scientific Writings (editor) 1963
Carmina Archilochi: The Fragments of Archilochos (translations) 1964
Sappho: Poems and Fragments (translations) 1965
Flowers and Leaves: Poema vel Sonata, Carmina Autumni Primaeque Veris Transformationum (poetry) 1966
Herakleitos and Diogenes (translations) 1980
The Geography of the Imagination: Forty Essays 1981
Thasos and Ohio: Poems and Translations, 1950-1980 1985
Every Force Evolves a Form: Twenty Essays 1987

CRITICISM

Richard Wertime (essay date 1975)

SOURCE: A review of *Tatlin!,* in *The Georgia Review,* Vol. XXIX, No. 4, Winter 1975, pp. 948-57.

[*In the essay below, Wertime praises the thematic depth and complexity of the stories in* Tatlin!, *but notes that Davenport's esoteric language often becomes overbearing.*]

Some writers move slowly toward fulfillment, over decades; others, no less laudable, appear to reach out casually and fetch successful products in with so impressive a gift of ease that we are led to wonder, sometimes, why it isn't that easy for everyone. John Updike is such a writer; his talent bloomed early and has proved at least to my mind to be of tough, durable stock. His career, moreover, illustrates the truth that the early starter is positioned advantageously in the literary marketplace in significant respects.

But there are countervailing advantages to getting started late—or, to put it more accurately, making one's appearance late—and they are illustrated handsomely in Guy Davenport's *Tatlin!* These six stories have a maturity, a philosophic depth, and a richness of effect beyond the reach of the younger writer, even one like Thomas Pynchon, whose artistic ambitions and temperament are not so different from Davenport's. What distinguishes these two, mainly, is a difference in orientation: Davenport is an erstwhile friend and devoted student of Ezra Pound's; and in its intense, eclectic and well-nigh overbearing erudition, *Tatlin!* is offered to us as a fit companion to, if not a worthy competitor of, *The Cantos, Ulysses, Finnegans Wake,* and Eliot's major works. This is no small self-assertion; but then, Davenport's fiction asks to be weighed on such scales. And if I have reservations, they pertain to the problems of esoteric fiction in general, and are couched within an admiration that I hope will become self-evident.

Guy Davenport is currently a scholar and teacher at the University of Kentucky. In addition to writing fiction, he is a poet, does translations, reviews and illustrates books— in short, is a genuine man of letters, a living rebuke to the many members of academe who believe that disciplinary narrowness is the only "responsible" way to conduct one's intellectual life and who think that bulk and speed of production are accurate indices of talent. He refutes, as well, those who think that a serious scholar and writer cannot inhabit the same skin. He has allowed himself an apprenticeship well-suited to his aims: a leisurely yet arduous one, one that has enabled him to know with utter certainty the nature of his abilities, the drift of his instincts. This is, exactly, the advantage of getting the late start. The writer who appears before his talent is fully settled lives with pressures from the public—which he often internalizes— that may interfere finally with the utilization of that talent, and so, in the end, subvert it.

Tatlin! is, to begin with, more than an aggregate of stories. As much as Welty's *Golden Apples,* or Anderson's *Winesburg, Ohio,* or Selby's *Last Exit to Brooklyn*—all so very different—it is a cohesive, total work. Two longer pieces, both novella-like in their scope, frame four shorter tales. In subject and effect these middle pieces are lighter than the two flanking stories. As other reviewers have pointed out, this is not "short fiction" in the customary sense. These are tales full of essaying, imaginative renditions of historical facts, revolving meditations on the philosophic problems that have most vexed our century. Davenport has virtually contrived a new genre to house the breadth of his interests. Happily, to my mind, his work is still fictive in essence. In fact, its most striking attribute is not the intelligent commentary on the human condition—and there is plenty of that—nor yet the dazzle of its language, about which I shall have a good deal more to say later; it is, rather, the keenness of the eye which observes. It is a funny, often hilarious book, one packed with the drama of the mundane, the minor. It also jolts us by rehumanizing historical figures who have grown remote and unreal with the passage of time. Franz Kafka appears implausibly as a tourist off in Italy, and Edgar Allan Poe appears in a parallel tale, in St. Petersburg. We watch the philosopher Herakleitos take his morning exercises with slave, student, and servant-girl. Like the humor, such characterization is didactic in its intent: we are forced to be sceptical of overly lofty notions and encouraged to see the unity in the diversity of the world. Davenport's Herakleitos says that "the most beautiful order of the world is still a random gathering of things insignificant in themselves." This "in themselves" is tricky. For the artist both does and does not "give" his subjects beauty. As another character says, in rather more impacted language, "It is elective affinities that knit the discrete particulars of the world into that artificial fabric whose essence we perceive as beauty." Kierkegaard provides the means of reconciling these statements in his definition of admiration as happy self-surrender. *Tatlin!* is a work informed, indeed, suffused with admiration.

The first story, **"Tatlin!"**, is an epic of sorts in miniature—though I suspect that such a description of it will strike some readers as odd. It concerns one Vladimir Tatlin, versatile Russian of this century, who (as the dust jacket informs us) was a victim of the Soviets' brutal and stifling ideology. What the story does, essentially, is to weave together pieces of this man's personal life with pastiche glimpses of the restless Western world during the years that Communist Russia was promoting, then reneging on, its political promise. The final effect is panoramic: art, aviation (both enduring themes in all these stories), engineering, modern philosophy, world travel, childhood dabblings; all of these collect to express the "spirit of the age," which, though less grim for Davenport than it was for Joyce and Pound, is nevertheless bewildering and awesome in its complexity. The drawings, done by the author, help to drive the point home: a hopeful young man (Tatlin? Russia? this century?) cedes his pictorial space first to Lenin and then to Stalin; between these two tyrants, whose severe and arrogant figures move oppressively closer to us as the story moves forward, we are shown, as in antithesis, a spate of cubist drawings. We see Lenin and Stalin not just once, but three times apiece; the repetition of appearances suggests the monotony of despotism. As Tatlin ruminates near the end of the story, "A genius has no interest in controlling people with anything so

crude as power. The artist has true power. The intellectual may hunger for power as his ideas prove to be weak, but he is for the most part content to live in his mind."

Tatlin! is, to begin with, more than an aggregate of stories. This is not "short fiction" in the customary sense. These are tales full of essaying, imaginative renditions of historical facts, revolving meditations on the philosophic problems that have most vexed our century. Davenport has virtually contrived a new genre to house the breadth of his interests.

—*Richard Wertime*

This story acts as an induction to the rest of the book in both its presentation of character and its technical brilliance. The utilization of counterpoint; the sprinkling of aphorisms; the energizing use of names of everything imaginable; the *entrelacement* lifted, perhaps, from medieval narrative; the devotion to quaint tidbits that light up suddenly—these typify, like the character of Tatlin himself, much of what follows. Tatlin is, first, an essentially guileless human being (I suspect that guile is the first of the Seven Deadly Sins for Davenport). He enjoys, like Picasso, another hero of this work, a child's holistic wonder at, and immersion in, the natural world. In lyric shots of Tatlin as a small child playing, we see how free of clutter the native scientific spirit is—how logically it extends the mythic fantasies of youth (the individual's, the culture's) into substances on the one hand and abstract postulates on the other. Technology and philosophy are joined at the root, just as man is—or can be—equally childlike and dignified regardless of age. Like most of the other characters, Tatlin is basically a loner at heart. He grows, travels, paints, invents, and gains esteem; then, at an exhibition where he is showing his proposal for a monument to the greatness of the Soviet cause, Lenin appears and evaporates the plan and Tatlin's stature with a wordless glance. His fate, though less gruesome than the poet Mandelstam's, is hardly less wasteful. He is dismissed into obscurity, graphically depicted as the far side of the moon, one of whose desolate craters bears the name of *his* hero, the brilliant Tsiolkovsky, inventor and visionary, whose fate parallels Tatlin's and a galaxy of others.

In **"The Aeroplanes at Brescia,"** the second story in the collection, we find Franz Kafka off in Italy with friends, a reminder of the fact that Kafka is not, indeed, a character in a fiction by Kafka. The story is set at an aerial show; the stars are Curtiss and Blériot, two of the early heroes of mechanical flight and competitors of the Wright brothers. Kafka is awed by it all (again the childlike wonder) and makes, as Poe does later in **"1830,"** a series of brilliant observations; his about the effect of light in Italy and Prague, Poe's about the American inability to "keep things up." Wittgenstein is there too, unrecognized and wild of mien; so is Pinocchio, oddly, who appears in phantom snatches like a resident *djinn.* At the end of the story, while the show is winding up, Kafka's eyes mist over suddenly with an undefinable emotion. Does he feel the odd joy of watching a new era open? Or are there darker intimations, a vague prophetic sense of what this new era will bring?

The next story, **"Robot,"** extends the theme of ambiguity as well as the kindly, whimsical tone. It chronicles the discovery of the Lascaux cave-paintings by a dog and a group of boys out playing in the woods. It is during the early days of World War II when the *Résistance* is taking shape. Robot is the dog (pronounced *robo*); he is spontaneous, youthful, and quite unmechanical—like the boys and the ancient lithic art they accidentally stumble upon. The distinguished scholar Abbé Breuil, aging but still youthful, comes to examine the paintings, and as we listen to him speak, the millennia of darkness separating us from the prehistoric men who executed these splendid works evanesces, almost magically. Picasso, we are told, is essentially one of these painters:

> The *Guernica* with its wounded horse, its hieratic bull, its placing of images over images, is a prehistoric painting. It honors and grieves and stands in awe. I have copied hundreds and hundreds of these beasts until they file through my dreams. God will take me to them when I die, to the saucy Shetland tarpans whose jet manes run the length of their backs, to the long red ox and woolly rhinoceros. But perhaps the *Guernica* I see is not the one everybody sees. The painting I see is as old as Lascaux.

Random accident, here, shades over into serendipity, into epiphany, and the implication is that the same is true of most of man's great discoveries.

The next story in the book, **"Herakleitos,"** is about celebration, and is itself a celebration. A young man, Knaps, has come from his rocky Arkadian homeland to listen to the wisdom of Herakleitos. The story spoofs beautifully the life of a college teacher; of all the characters assembled between the covers of *Tatlin!*, Herakleitos is most conspicuously a *persona* for Guy Davenport. Knaps is comically typical as the eager undergraduate; he argues, takes notes which diminish the master's sayings woefully, but he also listens. And so he learns in the best way: his life is made to change, improve; and as he grows to be a part of the Herakleitian household, as he begins to discover the power of music and dance, he begins, truly, to comprehend the odd, poetical words which the old man speaks. At the story's conclusion, Herakleitos and his "family" make their offerings in the temple of an unnamed female deity, who is probably Artemis, Mother of Lions; and the book Herakleitos lays at her black basalt feet, in announced fulfillment of his promise, is also this one, *Tatlin!*, Davenport's own.

Tatlin! may be properly said to crest with **"Herakleitos."** The two stories following it, the one very short and the other very long, are, if not darker, at least more complicated and troubled by perplexity. But the figure of Herakleitos persists; and he has emerged by the work's end as one

of the two presiding geniuses of the author's philosophy. The other is Pythagoras, inventor of abstract order, lover of pure numerical harmony. These two exist in absolute complementarity and paradoxical otherness; together they unite the worlds of mind and random matter. Blake figures heavily in this synthesis too; and the author's debt to him is made explicit later on.

I must scant the penultimate story (the one about Poe in Russia) in order to get to **"The Dawn in Erewhon,"** which occupies fully half the collection under consideration, and which is the story that best exemplifies the peculiar strengths and limitations of Davenport's writing. The reader of *Tatlin!* will know, almost as soon as he opens the book, that it is a man of staggering erudition whose company he is sharing. And he will be impressed rightly. This is a writer, in addition, who knows the risks which he has taken, and who feels up to whatever quarrel he may have with our sensibilities. Authentic mastery and madness are the only two things which lend a writer this sort of confidence. And Davenport—one scarcely need say—isn't mad. Consider this passage, for example, with its elegant incisiveness:

> Account for it as you will, it is America that is old. . . . The land itself is old, you see, and the first Americans, like the Muscovites and Finns, built in wood. These early buildings are brothers of the ark. We did not bring with us that talent for keeping things up, so that a village in the Carolinas looks a thousand years older than a French village which in fact was built in the time of Montaigne.

Or this, for its wit:

> And a Persian colonial official stopped his litter to watch. He remembered the day the Ephesians reorganized their assembly before the Satrapeia. This man Herakleitos had been called as one of the local magicians or wise men or grammarians. He had come to the rostrum with a cup into which he poured wine from a skin. He then broke in herbs, stirred the mixture, and drank it. Smacking his lips with satisfaction, he scanned the faces of the assembly and stepped down.
>
> —What did *that* mean? the Satrap had whispered to his secretary.
>
> There had been broad smiles among the Ephesians, all of whom protested that they had no idea what the philosopher could have meant by so enigmatic a gesture. He speaks in riddles, when, of course, he speaks at all. A taciturn Greek!

There are also many passages of a clear, pure lyricism, such as those describing the paintings in the cave at Lascaux. But the verbal diet, already rich in the first five stories, becomes in **"The Dawn in Erewhon"** so heavily virtuosic as to be, at times, cloying. One begins to wonder if Davenport isn't waging war against *Finnegans Wake,* isn't out to capture the record for the number of different vocables used. This is, let me emphasize, a first and not, possibly, a lasting impression; I would demean the author wrongly if I portrayed him here as having trundled out his knowledge for the paltry purpose of leaving his readers stunned. After all, difficult language has a number of varied ways of justifying itself amply—as Pound, Joyce, Eliot and Hart Crane were instrumental in showing us. And one of these ways—indeed, I think the principal among them—is to "layer" one's language, to endow it with such deep resonance that it constantly calls the reader back. When Proust talked of metaphor as giving to words in literature their *éternité,* he was thinking along lines like these.

And Davenport is a "layerer." Yet hearty banqueting has its limits; and these are limits that will fix themselves, like a kind of floating boundary, between the tolerance of the reader and the economy, the utility, of the author's style. *Tatlin!* enters a world not overly tolerant of opulence, especially verbal opulence of the traditional and allusive sort. In prose, as in poetry, the contemporary writer fears the charge of dandyism a great deal more than that of flatness. And this is, in many ways, unfortunate.

But I must still take up the quarrel. And to do so, I will have to turn to plot and structure. What actually happens in **"The Dawn in Erewhon"**? Although the story doesn't lend itself to easy summarizing, it does have distinct narrative strands which interweave. The most conventional and accessible of these concerns Adriaan Floris van Hovendaal, a contemporary Dutch philosopher. Adriaan teaches at a university and writes on odd subjects, like the psychodynamics of small enclosures—desk-drawers, rooms, gardens—as well as on Erewhon, Butler, Fourier. He also, and this is of equal importance, is building his own private kingdom of freedom whose principal liberty is sex. In a sense, **"The Dawn in Erewhon"** is "Herakleitos" much extended; and if Herakleitos looks like a *persona* for Guy Davenport, Adriaan might well be his chosen alter ego. Adriaan is working as a gardener one summer in order to close the gap between himself and the natural world. The decision is a good one: it leads him into a relationship with a girl named Kaatje, a girl of natural decency and potent sexuality. After a bit of hesitation, she discovers a lack of shame in herself as wholesomely prelapsarian as that of the tanned adamic Adriaan (whose name is, I take it, meaningfully androgynous to the English ear). They make love prodigiously, take sun in the buff almost as often, and blend their rapt sensuality with a daily fare of study and thought. The resultant philosophizing comprises a good chunk of the narrative. Bruno, a friend of Adriaan's and younger than he, is brought into the circle, and a *ménage à trois* is then established.

As one can see from this much, there is a pleasantly unworldly quality to the plot's erotic aspect. And Davenport chooses to play it good-naturedly. While this strand of action works its way toward its conclusion, a conclusion not very surprising but nonetheless a little disquieting, the other strands—so different, it seems—are gradually revealing their relation to, their oneness with, the more evident doings. Out of antithesis comes synthesis. The moon is used to symbolize this synthesizing motion. Near the beginning of **"Dawn in Erewhon"** we are presented, in syncopation with the more mundane actions, harsh, granitic descriptions of the lunar light and shadow:

The shadow of the earth moves across the moon.

Its precise edge flowing over the rand of Clavius climbs red monadnocks as a tide of soot flecked golden green with dying earthshine and rises like silver rust on sulphur scree, blackening gorges of shale and umber bergs.

High cliffs in Fra Mauro, stone fjords, griked gneiss dykes of gangue flash with the iceblink of the earth's ocean mirror before the curved shadow of the Pacific's horizon sinks them in absolute night.

These passages are eerie, even more so in context, and convey like nothing else I've read the alien desolation of the moon's mineraled surface. The interwoven passages, from Wittgenstein in German, amplify this distant, harsh, dislocating effect. Yet by the final page of *Tatlin!* the staggering distance separating moon and earth is closed both geographically and psychically. As Neil Armstrong takes man's first step into extraterrestrial dust, we are made to see, if we haven't already, that that familiar slogan, "whole earth," means by an implication startling in its necessary simplicity "whole cosmos" as well. With his good looks and blue eyes, Armstrong is the new Adam awakening to the new Eden, the Eden of space. **"Dawn in Erewhon,"** then, is an aubade, a hymn; the nowhere of Erewhon is the plenum of infinity, through whose magical lens one may glimpse the back of one's head, if one has vision heroic enough.

This motif of travel as the means of achieving closure informs the other important elements of the plot. As befits the universality of paradox and contradiction, **"The Dawn in Erewhon"** is a sort of *ave atque vale,* an intricate satire a la Swift as well as a hymn to the new age. A traveller, Gulliverian in his uncritical receptivity, arrives in a fantastic utopian kingdom that is the land of the Houyhnhnms upgraded—and ornamented with diverse bits of other, now-dead civilizations. Its inhabitants, the Erewhonians, are committed to an antimechanistic, naturalist worldview, the governing principle of which is "Physique is character." This motto sounds almost plausible at first, but it proves, in the end, as much a *reductio ad absurdum* as the Erewhonians' banishment of all contrivances but the windmill. Not that the indictments of our present age of the automobile don't have point. Utopian simplicity reveals, through its exaggerations, actual social faults. In scenes that ring with echoes of *Gulliver's Travels* and Wyndham Lewis's *Human Age,* we are shown how our ambitions—and our simple lack of imagination—can undo our common sense. (Kafka: "Did men know anything? Man was man's teacher. Anyone could see the circle in that.") Those who like Pirsig's *Zen and the Art of Motorcycle Maintenance* would do well to go on to *Tatlin!* next.

What do I find to criticize, then, in such an intelligent effort? The problem is one of achieving that proper blend of language and action, of securing for each an interest which will justify its density as well as carry the reader forward. In his book, *The Characters of Love,* the English critic John Bayley makes a point about Joyce's later work that might prove helpful. Joyce, Bayley says, ends by creating a verbal mesh which imprisons the reader—as opposed, say, to Shakespeare, whose verbal elegance finally creates an illuminating transparency, a transparency through which the reader (or spectator at a play) may seem to glimpse life, direct, undivided, entire. And also unannotated. Now I know it's unfair to ask of fiction what only drama can give; and I am equally aware that Bayley's stance is prejudicial: Bayley favors realism as both a mode of execution and as a philosophy of narration. But by tempering his conservatism we might apply his observation to *Tatlin!* Not only does Davenport push too far in his searching out of fancy words for inessential purposes, but there is a corresponding thinness in the actual human doings which exacerbates the matter. Again, I am speaking only of **"The Dawn in Erewhon."** Comical prolixity ceases to be funny if overextended; and even idyllic hedonism has, for onlookers anyhow, decided limitations. The voluptuous Kaatje is a case in point: how little, really, we know of her beyond her bedding habits. There is ardor and trust and kindliness in all these characters, but not much warmth and curiosity. Or should I say, perhaps, attentiveness—attention to all the things which lie between the riot of copulation and the antipodal calm found in philosophic thought.

This "middle zone," as it were, is where the most important action in our literature occurs. Earlier I said that most of the characters in *Tatlin!* lead disjunctive lives, lives alleviated by periods of happy conjunction. **"Erewhon"** appears to be an exception to this rule, but in fact it is not. Probably our lives *are* for the most part lived disjunctively; and I admire Guy Davenport for expressing his impatience with the usual sorts of relationships on which our fiction gluts itself. But the fact still stands that his particular sort of realism, of conjunction-in-disjunction, inverts the essential condition of intimacy as most of us know it, and as the Western novel has known it for a couple of hundred years. The tension in most fiction, both good and bad, results from a revelation to someone—someone "close" to someone else—that the conjunctive state by which they have been habitually defining themselves has become, or is becoming, a fraud, a mask, a mere formality. It is then that the painful fragility of human relationships opens up into something which can only be rendered fully by means of a visible social act. It is only then, for instance, that tragedy—a word used often in the pages of *Tatlin!* to describe the intellectual quandaries that modern man has fallen into—can possibly occur. The point at which the lovers have arrived at the conclusion of **"Erewhon"** is pregnant with suggestions of just such complex human developments. But it is as if the story's form has conspired with authorial reticence to keep them from maturing.

It had occurred to me, along the way, to cite Hawkes's *The Blood Oranges* as a piece of fiction whose merits and problems are parallel to those of **"Erewhon."** But *Tatlin!* even **"Erewhon"** alone, dwarfs John Hawkes's novel. It dwarfs many another novel to have appeared in recent years as well; it is, for all the complaints which I have marshalled here, a brave and magnificent undertaking—arrogant, individual to a nearly perverse degree, endlessly rewarding in its bestowal of special benefits. *Tatlin!* is not likely to attract a wide following—such works never do, at least not quickly—and it is not very likely to encourage imitation. This would suit Guy Davenport. *Tatlin!* is a *summa,*

in design a cosmic comedy; it is tragical-comical-historical-pastoral; scene individable and poem unlimited. One could do worse.

Richard Pevear   (essay date 1975)

SOURCE: *"Tatlin!,* or the Limits of Fiction," in *The Hudson Review,* Vol. XXVIII, No. 1, Spring 1975, pp. 141-46.

[*In the following excerpt, Pevear comments on Davenport's innovative narrative techniques in the stories of* Tatlin! *and argues that the "ruling spirit of* Tatlin! *is not constructivism, it is the spirit of reverie."*]

A storyteller is not a fictionist. But we are so used to fiction, because we live within fiction, in a way, and see it from the inside, that we are not sure what the difference is. Storytelling declined as fiction writing increased. But it is not a question of written forms driving out oral forms. The books of Apuleius, Malory, Rabelais are not fiction either, and *Don Quixote* is not fiction, though it is often called the first novel. Fiction became clear to itself when it saw that it must be absolute, that it must displace the reader's existence with its romance of reality. The key to the nature of fiction is that under its spell both the author and the reader disappear. Verisimilitude is of less importance than the spell, the unique consistency of the performance. Evgeny Zamyatin, the Russian modernist, experimented with the fantastic, the stylized, the most abstract constructions in his fiction, yet the spell remains intact. In an essay on "Theme and Plot" (originally a lecture to students of the writer's craft) Zamyatin gives the following advice against authorial intrusions and lyrical digressions:

> These were often employed by Gogol, as in his "Troyka." Among the new writers, we find such digressions in Remizov and Bely, both of whom derive from Gogol. This device, however, although it achieves its end, giving the reader a rest and diverting him from the flow of the plot, has a serious drawback: it permits the reader to awaken for a time, it cools him and weakens the spell of the work. *It is as though an actor were to remove his makeup in the middle of the play, say a few words in his own voice, and then go on.*

I have underlined this last sentence to make clear how precisely Zamyatin has defined, in principle, what Brecht would have called an alienation-effect. Brecht conceived of the use of alienation-effects as a way of playing thought against illusion in his theater, a way of breaking the spell of the performance and re-establishing its humanity. It is this that Zamyatin indirectly counsels against.

Brecht's was an art of interruption, quotation, dialectic; Zamyatin's an art of continuity, coherence, persuasion. There are ways in which both principles are at work in *Tatlin!* But to the extent that they can be compared with other work, the stories in *Tatlin!* recall Zamyatin's stories in that, although they contain a wealth of narrative invention, the invention does not go outside the limits of fiction. There is reason to think that it might have done so, and even that that is what Davenport intended. But what is really at stake here? . . .

Brecht understood, despite his play with ideology, that the art of storytelling was free and that it was the opposite of the fiction writer's demonic performance. In the situation of storytelling, the teller and the listener cannot forget each other's presence; the story is spun out between them, and its images are interwoven with their reality without obscuring it. Storytelling was the first form of theater; it was also, in a way, the first art of assemblage. Stories handed down to us in books, which we can read as fiction, are only scripts left over from a dramatic event that took place once, and repeatedly, in the telling. The situation of storytelling abounds in alienation-effects; belief in the story is freely offered and is always provisional; it is not enforced by illusionary techniques, the rule of consistency, the double disappearance of author and reader. Plato preserved the situation of storytelling in his dialogues, and it is clear that what he prized was the non-obligatory nature of the story and the shared freedom of hearing and speaking. The principle of dialogue is interruption, as the principle of storytelling is interweaving. By contrast, the principle of fiction is non-interruption, the unbroken flow of the writing, which is like the flow of dreams. And we are present to fiction as we are present to our dreams, in suspension.

The storyteller and his listener are equals; at any moment they may change places. But an author, Chaucer's *auctor,* is an authority, who decants truth into his readers, as Mandelstam said, by virtue of the physical law of unequal levels. The pedagogical model is a recurrent motif in *Tatlin!*, a thread that ties the stories together: Tatlin, in the title story ["Tatlin!"] is shown teaching at the Ceramics Institute, the Abbé Breuil at Lascaux, Herakleitos at Ephesus, Adriaan van Hovendaal at the university and in private with his disciple Bruno. The law of unequal levels applies in each case. The master speaks, the pupils admire and take notes. No questions are asked, there is no dialogue. Knowledge is an attribute of personality. This pedagogical model is the averted face of fiction.

The cult of authors, and by extension the cult of all eminent authorities, is a natural outgrowth of fiction. It is perpetuated subjectively in the reader's preference for one fictional world over another, objectively in biographical and historical criticism, or in aesthetic connoisseurship, which are ways of avoiding the work while dealing with it. The cult of authors takes the place of a free participation in the truth of the work. We understand art better than anyone ever has, but we no longer know what to do with it.

The highly developed critical sensibility of the modern era is a product of fiction. The *Tatlin!* stories are, in part, essays in a criticism by mimesis. The most difficult thing for an article to convey about the writing in *Tatlin!* is its subtle use of known voices and styles of prose. The first chapter of the title story captures, by an act of imaginary eavesdropping, the exact tone of someone present at an exhibition of Tatlin's constructivist works in the Moscow of 1932, the eggshell walk we know from memoirs of that period. The opening sentences of **"The Aeroplanes at Brescia"** are at once a description of Kafka, who is the central character of the story, and a condensed rendering of Kafka's vision and voice: "Kafka stood on the seawall at

Riva under the early September sky. But for his high-button shoes and flaring coat, his easy stance had an athletic clarity. He walked with the limberness of a racing cyclist." It is Kafka not as he saw himself but done in his own style. And the story **"1830,"** which is about Poe, has the tonality of nineteenth-century prose, though if you look for direct imitations of that rhetoric you won't find them. The book is, simply, superbly written, and I know of no one in our language who can equal its accomplishment.

In method the stories are comparative, analogical; they develop through parallels and oppositions, through contrasts built around the same motif—for instance, the motif of the flying machine, which Tatlin attempts to humanize in his glider or "air bicycle," which appears in the Kafka story as an awkward bit of flying junk, but reappears in **"Robot"** as the Messerschmidt, and in **"The Dawn in Erewhon"** finally as the craft that takes Neil Armstrong to the moon. It is a historical-critical method, aware of evolutions, affinities, echoes, recurrences; a method that will join together the German planes flying reconnaissance over southern France with the discovery of Aurignacian paintings at Lascaux.

But it is above all a fictional method. The stories are described in the book as "assemblages of history and necessary fiction." In a note attached to the original magazine publication of **"Robot"** Davenport says, "My story is an *assemblage* of facts insofar as they can be known." But the stories function least as assemblages, more as essays in criticism, most as fictions. The story **"Tatlin!"** includes a number of drawings by the author, meticulously finished; heads of Lenin appear serially in the opening pages, heads of Stalin in the closing pages; in between there are drawings of Tatlin's constructivist works, which are assemblages of discrete materials mounted on panels. These drawings strike me as strange. They are portraits of art-works in which the medium of the portrait negates the medium of the art-work. If Ingres had made drawings of Monet's water-lily paintings, the effect would be similar, but here the negation is still more absolute because the art-works are assemblages. The stories are like these drawings. They are assemblages to the extent that they are composed of materials taken from various sources. But they have been reduced to the uniform consistency of fiction. If they had been allowed to stand as assemblages, the book would be very different.

The ruling spirit of *Tatlin!* is not constructivism, it is the spirit of reverie. And it seems to me that the origin of the stories must have been more in reverie than in thought: dreams of an educated mind, the sort of thing that comes into your head as you sit among the books and objects in your study (Dürer's St. Jerome) and invoke the name "Wittgenstein" or "Herakleitos," or think the words "Picasso" and "Cro-Magnon" together, or "glider" and "Daedalus." The words "Kafka" and "Brescia" bring together certain local sensations: de Chirico perspectives, a furtive Pinocchio, the image of a ruined castle (Brunnenburg in Merano, where Pound lived; there is a photo of it in Kenner's *Pound Era*), recollections of the peculiar force of Kafka's parables, in the midst of modern excitement an inexplicable sadness. And it is possible to imagine that Kafka might have rubbed elbows with Wittgenstein at the air show at Brescia without knowing who he was but as if sensing that he would in time become "Wittgenstein." The word "designer" also has certain overtones, at once archaic and modern, which can be used to characterize Tatlin as a primal artist. Such elusive material makes up the separate continuum of art-romance.

Reverie attaches to ideas as well. **"The Dawn in Erewhon"** is a tissue of ideas that are elegantly formed, savored for their resonance, made fragrant with strong coffee and the honey and tar of tobacco, and never really thought. They are ideas as beautiful objects, ideas as tokens of an ingenious mind; what counts is not the ideas themselves but the feeling of having them. In the story **"Herakleitos"** a young Arcadian named Knaps comes to learn from the master. Toward the end the narrator says, "Knaps had heard beautiful sentences since he came. *Character is fate. How can you hide from what never sets? Defend the law as you would the city wall.*" Etc. Beautiful sentences. It is impossible for us to approach the world of Herakleitos; what little of it appears in his fragments is, however, nothing like the simple dream Davenport records in this story. The thesis, expressed elsewhere in the book, that modern thought is a resurgence of Herakleitean thought, is embodied here in the person of a little professor on sabbatical in the Greek islands, a friendly and eccentric man with good taste in music and a collector's eye for antiques, who punctuates his talk with quotations from Herakleitos. He is not unlike the Abbé Breuil in **"Robot,"** though Breuil is a more successful portrait because he was, in a way, what Davenport imagines Herakleitos to have been, part priest and part connoisseur.

Dreams of the wise man are an important part of **Tatlin!** These figures are represented as having wisdom, though what they think remains unthought in the stories. Fiction is a medium for reverie, for the romance of reality, for synthetic portraiture; it is not a medium for thought. But the preponderance of thematic ideas in these stories seems to call for thought. Ideas are not presented as traits of character; on the contrary, characters are chosen because they represent ideas. But the repetition of the same cluster of ideas throughout the book makes one feel, after a while, that the characters are trapped in them and limited by them, that they are tired of speaking these incantations that have frozen them into attitudes. The end of **"Tatlin!"** and the end of **"The Dawn in Erewhon"** have the same melancholy; it is like a sudden aging. Fiction encourages us to see the characters in **Tatlin!** as living human beings, but the author's hand pushes them toward abstraction and caricature. Yet the author is forbidden by the techniques of fiction to let his hand show.

"1830," perhaps the most perfect fiction in the book, is also in part a parable of fiction itself, one law of which is the disappearance of the author. The narrator of the story is Poe, though that name is never mentioned. But he is really Proteus. He appears in the story as Edgar A. Perry, discoursing on astronomy and the Greek war of independence with a Russian prince and his sister, in a language permeated with Greek architectural orders. It is discov-

ered, however, that this strange American poet is registered at his hotel under another name, Henri de Rennet. When the sister demands to know who he really is, he becomes flustered, denies any mystery, and leaves. But on his way out he imagines saying to the prince, "I am André Marie de Chénier. I was **guillotined** thirty-six years ago, *le septième Thermidor, l'an 1.* I am a ghost." All of this is Poe's recollection, if not his dream. But in fact he is not Poe either, he is no-man, because the story itself is apocryphal.

No-man is of course the author of **Tatlin!** He has not quite disappeared. He portrays himself, and does not portray himself, in the final story which is half the length of the book, in the equivocal character-caricature of Adriaan van Hovendaal, a Dutch professor and writer, who is our contemporary. The story, which draws together the other five and at the same time reflects back on them, is itself polymorphous; it maintains the spell of fiction, yet is also a fantasia on the writing of fictions; its ideas, particularly its Utopian theme, are presented seriously in one place but travestied in another; its ideal man, both thinker and gymnast, rebirth of the archaic in the modern, is shown at the same time to be narcissistic, epicurean, vague, pretentious, and ill-at-ease. Why is it all so curiously two-sided? I think that is the right question to ask of the story, provided it is asked inquiringly. Reverie and critical intelligence mingle in various ways in **Tatlin!**; here they are in complex opposition. If the story were resolved either into consistent fiction or into satire, it would lose its peculiar rightness.

The puzzle of Adriaan van Hovendaal holds the materials of the story together. He is presented rather simply, as a light-hearted visual thinker, an orderly sensualist, a dreamer of worlds. Of all the pairs of opposites that are the forms of his reverie, one pair is missing, the one pair that most fundamentally shapes human existence: the opposition of necessity and will. Labor reveals the bond between necessity and will: men labor out of necessity, but it is against necessity that they set their will and articulate it. No one works in the stories in **Tatlin!**, and in that sense existence is unrecognizable in them. But the absence of work, and of any notion of work, is conspicuous in **"The Dawn in Erewhon."** Adriaan van Hovendaal is a man of leisure. He thinks analogically, brilliantly, easily; he has an appetite for thinking. But his thought meets no opposition, and therefore it has no conception of necessity and is devoid of will. In this contradictory condition there is a real and disturbing truth, a truth of character that is also a truth of history. It seems almost to have taken the story by surprise.

Pathless on all paths: something of this realization comes over Adriaan van Hovendaal in the next to last chapter of the story, though its tragic poetry is colored by epicurean melancholy and a stoic resolution. His pathlessness is the impasse of fiction, the inner condition of our time, and if it has been recognized critically before, it has rarely been given such familiar likeness. It is a portrait relieved of gravity but not of seriousness, at once a self-confession and a self-satire, a study in the problematics of the modern neo-pagan, city-dwelling intellect.

Much of Adriaan van Hovendaal's thought is involved

with an Orphic myth-making. He toys with myths as if searching for some motive in his floating life. But the game is dangerous. Myths and their demonic power are the model for all fiction. Kafka understood this, and he understood that the true storyteller is a myth-breaker. To say that he foresaw the totalitarian state in *The Trial* is not enough. He put a revealing **sent**ence into the mouth of the ape in "Report to an Academy": "I imitated people because I needed a way out, and for no other reason." Since the story is not really about a talking ape, it is also not a question of a real cage.

Guy Davenport with Barry Alpert   (interview date 1976)

SOURCE: An interview in *Vort,* Vol. 3, No. 3, 1976, pp. 3-17.

[*In the interview below, Davenport comments extensively on the major influences and interests that shape his short fiction.*]

[Alpert]: *Do you live in any scheduled way; that is, do you set aside a certain time for writing or drawing or painting?*

[Davenport]: I don't think so. I write when I feel like writing, I draw when I feel like drawing. I frequently move from one to the other. Sometimes I can best express myself doing a painting . . . or an essay. **"The Aeroplanes at Brescia"**, in *Tatlin!,* started out as a research essay on Kafka. The story **"Tatlin!"** itself was originally, I think, a kind of plan for a history-of-art book, once I found some of the elements there about the beginnings of modern art in Russia. **"Tatlin!"** began as an oil portrait of Tatlin from an old photograph which is upstairs. Frequently I will abandon a piece of writing and draw it, or abandon a drawing and write it, or do both. This painting up here, which is called "The Contention of Erewhon", must be the first note of the *assemblage* that became **"The Dawn in Erewhon"**, the last story in *Tatlin!* I tend to live with a set of ideas—over years I think—and they eventually will find where they want to go. So it's really, I suppose, a whole process . . . If you're a teacher, you're constantly working with diverse materials. You may get up in the morning and you've got Keats' *Odes* to take some sophomores through, and you've got a chapter of *Ulysses* for your graduate students, and the mind gets in the habit of finding cross-references among subjects. This is the best way in the world to make my *assemblages,* as I call them. I don't think I've ever written a story. If Henry James wrote stories, if Dostoevski wrote stories, I don't write stories.

Even though you categorize them as "stories" in your bibliography?

I didn't know what else to call them. It looks pretentious to call them *assemblages,* which is a French word and taken from art history.

Do you ever rank, in terms of personal priorities, your activity as scholar, literary critic, essayist, reviewer, story-teller, translator, poet, draughtsman, painter . . . ? Or do you prefer to think of these honed faculties as making possible most of the public occasions that arise?

I've never been lucky enough to have the leisure to find out; I don't know. On a desert island with materials to write and to draw, I would probably become an oceanographer and live in the surf.

Might you elaborate on your view of the imagination? The descriptive detail you've used in the past seems to approach the language of Agassiz.

Okay, my theory of the imagination is this: that in the evolution of man this was the moment in which we became what we call human. That is, it's an amazing ability to see something with your eyes closed. Which is what imagination is. We must have lived for millions of years with only a dim notion that we could remember faces. Or, that we could somehow manipulate things in our memory: that you can remember a face and you can remember it as a yellow face, once you've learned to do arbitrary color with your imagination. Surely this is where art comes from and what art is serving, is it not? The ability for you to make me see what you can imagine is a power of communication so high that I can't think of humanity doing any better. We can't do it electronically: there's no electronic device whereby your vision of Paris in the springtime, which you can convey to me in a poem or in a passage in a novel, can be conveyed to me by any kind of mechanical device, right? It's still an immensely human . . .

That seems to approach [Stan] Brakhage's conception of hypnagogic vision: what you can see with your eyes closed.

His experimentation with the seen, the visual form, is I think an immense break-through. He is as different from what we call the movies as Joyce from Dickens. He has found ways of getting at elements in the imagination and in the consciousness and the subconscious. Have you seen his new films? They get more and more beautiful.

The most recent one I've seen is The Act of Seeing with One's Own Eyes, *which was an overwhelming experience.*

I gave that film its title. He called up when he was filming it and asked me what the word *autopsy* meant. I said it's a Greek word and it means seeing with one's own eyes. And he said thanks. He must have written it right down on a piece of paper.

What have you been working on this summer? Do you think in terms of projects?

Yeah. There's a box in the next room full of projects, each labelled. I've just finished the introduction, finally, to Ronald Johnson's RADI OS. I've written an article on Charles Olson. I have another one to write on Whitman. I'm writing, in effect, a short book on Eudora Welty, who I think is the greatest living prose stylist. In America, let's say. Okay, Sam Beckett and Eudora Welty are the two prose masters who are alive today. I find her work immensely meaningful. She has been neglected. I think I can demonstrate that her kinship with the very highest art of the century is very close. With Joyce for instance, and she isn't talked about this way at all. She is regarded as a Mississippi regionalist. Critical clichés are very difficult to kill.

Is most of your critical writing stimulated by editorial requests?

I have never written a critical article that wasn't asked for. It's all by assignment; I think this is perfectly legitimate.

That's how I like to work.

Well, it works out fine. I can remember way back in one's green youth that I felt perhaps being a literary man might be a life of perfect charm and ease, sitting in a large oak-panelled library and writing what came to mind. That has never ever happened. The only things I have ever made up on my own are my poems and my stories.

Have you worked on any stories this summer?

Well I worked very hard on a story with a deadline for the *Georgia Review,* and I missed the deadline because the story would not hold together. That happens. It's not happened with a story before because I have never had a story with a deadline. This is, no one had ever asked for a story. I've had several requests now mainly from very small magazines. The first time I had one was from the *Hawaii Review* and my response was, "I'm the author of a book of short stories; I do not write for undergraduate magazines." And then I was instantly filled with shame and said, "Good God!" And wrote them a story which was **"The Richard Nixon Freischütz Rag"**, which got into the O. Henry. And they were very pleased and I was very pleased, but I almost didn't write it, out of stinking pride.

Are you working on another collection of stories comparable to **Tatlin!***?*

Well, I don't want to try to repeat it. It's a group of stories, the first of which is about Robert Walser, the unknown Swiss writer who . . .

Yes, you talk about him in your criticism. Christopher Middleton translated his work?

Yeah. Chris Middleton is an old friend of mine. We were at Oxford together, we bummed about Europe on foot, and have remained friends. Though I haven't seen much of him in the last few years—our academic worlds are so far apart. I remember the very first Walser I ever saw was in Chris' unpublished translation way back 25 years ago. He is of course one of the leading Walser scholars. It wasn't anything of his, though, but a book by George Avery called *Inquiry and Testament,* a rather thorough and painstaking Ph. D. thesis on Walser that gave me all the elements I needed for writing. **"Tatlin!"** is about a genius who was prevented from fulfilling himself because of a repressive political context. Walser is exactly the opposite. He gave up writing because he didn't think there was anybody anymore to be an audience for writing. This fascinates me because I think any writer in his worst moments feels this: that there's a bunch of uneducated dumb bunnies out there. This is a horrible thing to feel and if it can stop a single writer from writing, it's tragic. And it stopped Walser from writing.

That would be the title story for the volume?

I don't know. These things have to be worked out. ***Tatlin!*** was originally ten stories. I had a good editor at Scribners who chose the best six and took out the four dull ones, which were then taken to pieces. My writing unit is such that I start literally with scraps of paper and pages from

notebooks. Every sentence is written by itself; there are very few consecutive sentences in my work. This has been commented on. People feel the non-sequence.

Like Wittgenstein's Zettel?

Something like. I have eight or nine notebooks that I always write in as soon as I get up in the morning. The day begins with a cup of coffee and working in the notebook, and the day ends with working in the notebook. If it's a Saturday or it's summertime, I've been known to write in the notebook in the middle of the day. Especially on trips—they're always taken on trips. It's marvelous to write while waiting for buses, trains, and planes.

Single sentences?

Single sentences, which are revised eight or nine times. And I find a place for them, so that the actual writing of any of the stories in **Tatlin!** was a matter of turning back and forth in a notebook and finding what I wanted.

*I was going to ask you to describe the process of composition of a post-***Tatlin!** *story, "Au Tombeau de Charles Fourier".*

Okay, that I think can be explained. First of all, we start with the fact that I wanted somehow to get into English the information in Marcel Griaule's *Le Renard pâle,* as it says in the note at the end. So those sections having to do with Ogo and the Dogon are my condensation and translation of a five-hundred page French book which I found fascinating. I didn't know what to do with this. It was first written out just so and called "The Man in the Phrygian Cap" since Ogotemmêli wore a Phrygian cap. And he narrated the story. So I had to recast the entire thing out of his narration into a third-person perspective. Not knowing what to do with this, I chopped it up and decided that I would take an idea out of it. Namely, that man is a kind of forager in an unknown universe. I became interested in the whole idea of foraging, which is a very American thing. The whole pioneer experience. I think we still do it: why else do we ride around idly in automobiles—what are we looking for? It's foraging. Well, nature's great forager is the bee or the wasp. I just happen to like wasps; I let them in the house. There's a wasp nest in the studio, you may have noticed. I like to watch them. So I purchased a book about wasps and wrote passages about wasps, still not knowing how these were to fit in. Then I decided that the people who began the century. . . . That is one of my themes, I think. I like beginnings, the archaic facts. So I decided Gertrude Stein riding around Paris in her T-model Ford was something like a wasp out foraging. She is a writer out for a new kind of experience. She's the first American writer to go up in an airplane, by the way. Then her friend Picasso is a kind of forager, a kind of wasp as it were. And then I'd been reading a book on the Wright brothers and realized that what the Wright brothers had done was make a mechanical wasp, or bee. It's an insect— it's not a bird. It doesn't flap its wings. So, all the elements in the story are examples of foraging. Ogo the desert fox, which the Dogon feel is the very essence of the universe. And then there's the figure 8 to hold things together: everybody moves in a figure 8 the way a wasp flies. That's how it got written. I put them together without any hope that anybody would see this, or see how it fits together, but that's a true *assemblage*.

When did the drawings enter into the compositional process?

The drawings were asked for by John Irwin. And I said, "John, do you mind if the drawings have nothing to do with the story?" And he said, "I think that's marvellous." They do. The Gertrude Stein is a sentence (in her car—the drawing at the first). And the mask of Dionysus at the end is the final statement, because that is the earliest known example of the actor's mask. That is the thing through which you speak lines that don't belong to you, and you pretend to be somebody else, which seems to me to be the essence of what you're doing when you're writing this kind of thing. The other drawings were drawn simply because they were images that I found congenial. One of them generated part of the story: there was no part of the story about Lartigue. But the drawing of Lartigue, once it was done, then had to have a piece of writing somehow to justify it. That's the only time . . .

Do the titles of your stories register focus, priority, or . . . ? For example, the stress on the Fourier material implied by the title "Au Tombeau de Charles Fourier".

I think Fourier is the greatest mind of the nineteenth century, and that one of the tragedies of modern times is that he was not paid attention to. As an American, I feel very much the idealism of the spirit of Fourier in Transcendentalism and in the American Fourieriste communities. It seems to me to be part of our present mess that we didn't allow some of these to mature. I don't think they could have happened in Europe. Europe is too old, too congested, and their kind of idealism is far too wise. It needed foolish people, gloriously foolish people like the early Americans. Something like Shakers and Quakers and Owenites and so on. So the entire piece is an elegy. I did go to the tomb of Fourier in Paris after I had written **"The Dawn in Erewhon"**, to photograph it and somehow to feel that I was that close to the bones of the man. In order to pull the story together, I took what I understand to be the master forager: a man could have started civilization on the . . .

I see. Let me turn to another story. I wanted to know, how deliberately researched is your piece "C. Musonius Rufus"? His name appears occasionally in your critical writing but I wondered if your initial interest began as early as your visits to Pound at St. Elizabeth's?

Oh sure. It began with the line in the *Pisan Cantos*, "Honor to the tough guy, Musonius". I didn't know who Musonius was. I looked him up to discover that only six authentic sayings of his survive, and I was in business, because I like things that almost don't exist.

What were your intentions in inserting your recreation of the Pound/Mussolini meeting?

Pound identified with Musonius. Pound survived those awful thirteen years by emulation. His first book was called *Personae*—masks. He wore masks. You remember when he was released and the newspaper reporters asked him to make a statement he said, "Ovid had it a lot

worse." Musonius had it a lot worse than Ovid. Ovid was only exiled; Musonius was sentenced to a chain gang by Nero. I saw Pound in Musonius, and I saw the whole problem of authority and the artist, a theme that's always fascinated me, the greatest statement of which is Hermann Broch's *The Death of Virgil*: Virgil and Caesar. The whole point of that story is to understand the agony of a stoic, and I'm not certain I like stoics. But they fascinate me— they're like early Christians. I couldn't be an early Christian. Nor could I be a stoic. But I admire their courage and I admire their absolute way of dealing with things that can't be dealt with, such as pain, fatigue, total despair. So Musonius and his emperor . . . Then I turned around and I took an emperor who had the shortest reign in all of Roman history, Balbinus. And I tried to show that an emperor really is human and I could only do this by putting him in his afterlife. All that's Swedenborgian, by the way. Swedenborg says that the soul that didn't realize what it wanted in this life will wander about as a kind of ghost. And Balbinus is a man whose life was totally eaten up by authority and who died because of it. So I give him back in all its childlike innocence a life in amongst leaves and rabbits and a mouse and those councillors of the dead which are angels out of Swedenborg. So we have three vectors—I was about to say three-ply but it's not three-plies, it's three vectors—and they all cross somewhere in what seems to me that tragic encounter between Pound and Mussolini where I'm certain Mussolini had no notion who Pound was, and made his statement that Pound honored so much, "Ma quest' è divertente!" —"But how amusing!" It's the kind of compliment no artist deserves. Because men in authority don't know what art is. Charles de Gaulle used to write notes to novelists to say he'd read their novels and that he liked them or he didn't like them. That's about as close as I know of. So: intimacy between authority and the freedom of artists.

Why the footnotes concluding "The Invention of Photography in Toledo"? For me, they push the "story" towards "criticism". Do you hope to widen the literary conception of what "kinds" of activity and material can occur within established formats, or is that just a minor consideration when you decide to write something?

The editor, John Bernard Myers, asked me to put them there.

Oh, it's as simple as that. Let me then ask, "Does the descriptive activity in your stories benefit and ultimately derive from your Poundian study of Louis Agassiz?"

I hope so.

*In what order did you write the stories composing **Tatlin!**? How much deliberate connection was there among the stories, other than the fact that they may have been consciously written during one period of time? Did you leave out any stories you may have had around? Why or why not? You already mentioned that the editor cut, but how rigorous was your conception and realization? I gather that commercial houses have difficulty selling collections of short stories and that they prefer those which approach the seeming coherence of a novel.*

Well, the thesis that's been written on the book by John

Wilson of the University of California argues that it is a coherent seamless piece of writing. It would seem cruel to disabuse him. What order there is, is more intuitive than planned. The first of the stories was **"The Aeroplanes at Brescia"**, which is the first creative writing, so called, I have done since an undergraduate, 1948.

That was the first one. I see.

The very first. I sent it to the *Hudson Review* and they accepted it. I was amazed. Then I wrote a story called **"The Antiquities of Elis"**, which was put into *Tatlin!* and then removed as being too repetitious: it was about philosophers and ancient Greece. That was a kind of invention, because it's a translation of so many pages of Pausanias chosen at random. I decided any five pages of Pausanias were interesting. And I translated them and then I put in the onions and the dust . . . Pausanias never mentions these things, so I had to imagine them. The third story of all was **"Robot"**, which grew out of (I think) various reviews I'd written of books about pre-history.

I wondered how much relationship there was between the two activities for you.

Oh, reviewing is marvellous. It gave Eliot practically all of his ideas.

Your review of Mowrer's autobiography began with a passage rather like the opening of "The Aeroplanes at Brescia".

Oh, yeah!

Was the story written not too long after the review? Two years?

More like five years. A thing like that sticks in the mind. **"The Aeroplanes at Brescia"**, of course, was written on top of a story. There is a story called "The Aeroplanes at Brescia" by Kafka. And it's the first thing he ever published.

I thought that was a piece of journalism, though.

It is. It is.

And not a story.

Oh no. But once you know Kafka wrote it, you can read it as a Kafka story.

There was a source, then.

Yeah.

Was Kafka's piece open on your desk, or at least convenient, while you were writing "The Aeroplanes at Brescia"?

Oh yes. I used every sentence of Kafka, one way or another, and Max Brod's account of the same event. It's copied. If anybody's interested, they'll have lots of fun finding. . . . Everything I've written is something authentic and had to be found. I don't know that I could ever recover these at all. I used Primola's contemporary photographs for what one place and people looked like. I read a history of aviation—several, as a matter of fact. The likelihood of Wittgenstein's being there is simply a guess. These is no biography of Wittgenstein, but he was at the

Glossop air-station working on the torque of a propeller. It stands to reason that in September of 1909 he would have been at either the Berlin air-show where the Wright brothers flew, or at Brescia. And I don't know which he was at. I mean this is a guess. And I don't know what it means that he was or was not there. One of the reviewers of the book said that he was at the 1909 air-show and that neither Wittgenstein nor Kafka was there, as if he could have known. (Laughter) You asked the order of the stories in *Tatlin!* We've gotten three—we have three to go. **"1830"** was written directly onto the typewriter without any drafts, though I gathered up phrases from notebooks as I went through. I had just been reading about meteorites in Alexander von Humboldt's *Kosmos* and remembered that von Humboldt was a great hero of Edgar Allan Poe. That story was put in because (as no one has noticed) that room where the Prince of Tavris was talking with Poe, who does not identify himself because he had no identity at that time, is the room where Lenin met the first Communist Congress after the Revolution. So it's actually a little flip-flop; it belongs with the **"Tatlin!"** story.

Did Poe actually visit that prince?

We don't know. The biographies say that in 1830 Poe said that he went to Saint Petersburg to enlist with some Russians to go and fight for Greek independence. All the biographies assume he was telling a whopping lie. I simply take him at face value.

Would you ever write a critical essay about Poe, or does "1830" serve the function for you?

I would love to write a critical essay about Poe—no one's asked me.

I was surprised at how Poe and Herakleitos "rhymed", as it were: how deliberately were you making the parallel— first by placing "1830" immediately after "Herakleitos" in the collection and secondly by phrasing each figure's speech in language which often seems nearly interchangeable. Here are two quotations: "It always has been, it is, and always shall be: an everlasting fire, dying and flaring up again." & "Flare and die, flare and die is the pulse of the world."

The first is a fairly exact translation of Herakleitos. The second is a paraphrase from Edgar Allan Poe's first poem, "Al Aaraaf." I didn't make the conjunction—they made the conjunction.

Did Poe pay much attention to Herakleitos or did they just rhyme?

Poe was fascinated in "Al Aaraaf" by images of fire. The subject of the poem (his most difficult and unknown poem) is about the supernova that Tycho Brahe saw and described. It flared up in 1572 and died out. Poe takes this as a symbol of youth, beauty, all the things that perish. He would have known one or two dicta of Herakleitos in his education. He wouldn't have known a great deal. Herakleitos is a modern writer for all practical purposes.

*In **"The Dawn in Erewhon"**, Bruno "remembered the day Adriaan had come in his lecture to C. Musonius*

Rufus . . ." What's the connection between the writing of the story "C. Musonius Rufus" and the other story?

None.

Do you ever lecture about C. Musonius Rufus?

No.

How long have you been familiar with the work of Adriaan van Hovendaal?

There is no such person.

Then what's the function of the note where you indicate that you translate from two of his works?

All right. That story, if it is a story, is about Samuel Butler's *Erewhon*. In a sense I'm updating Butler's *Erewhon*. It seems to me to be the most prophetic book of the nineteenth century. A very witty and charming book. And one of those books where I think that Butler said far more than he wanted to say. That's not the way to say that. Butler said more than he knew he was saying. It's an immensely suggestive book in its contradictions, as well as a very modern book. Since there is no Erewhon, I then decided to do everything in a tricky kind of negative. The story is set in Holland, because Holland is the nether land. Adriaan van Hovendaal is Ludwig Wittgenstein opened up. We know very little about Wittgenstein's sex life, but it seems to have been agonized and horrendous. And that he suffered a great deal because he could not absorb it. So I imagine a modern Dutchman who does express himself with his body as well as with his mind and seems to me (or at least I want to suggest this) that he lands in an Erewhon. That is, there's no such human behavior ever going to be generally permissable. What Fourier asked for. So we make him a student of both Fourier and of Sam Butler. He's a kind of latter-day disciple of Epicurus. Van Hovendaal means "the gardener". I make him a literal gardener. He keeps trying to construct an Erewhon and of course I could have looked at it another way and the story would be quite tragic and terrifying. But I chose to look at it through his own eyes. That if he can have a moment of sensual pleasure, in his furtiveness, then I can zone away the world for awhile. Symbolically I meant him to be an Orpheus, descending into a new underworld (another reason for the Netherlands), trying to find something like the natural archaic spirit of man, which I gather is what all philosophers and religious thinkers are trying to find. Now Orpheus is a tragic figure: he found his Eurydice but he looked at her as he was not supposed to and he lost her forever. This myth is a very modern story. Holland, you know, has no laws whatsoever for sexual conduct. So his Eurydice is both sexes. I wanted this ambiguity there because it seemed to me to be a very modern ambiguity and part of van Hovendaal's renaissance of a primal spirit, as I tried to suggest with entirely too many symbols. Does that answer that question?

Yeah. Is the diction deliberately arcane, even parodically so? I think Paul Metcalf offered up that suggestion.

He says it's a joke. It's meant to be comic. I call it International Davenport Erewhonian. Part of my problem was that we have no words for sensuality. We have no public

diction for talking about making love. We have some jazzy terms, we have some indecent terms, and I had to face the problem of finding words. So that I made up the diction; it is wholly artificial.

Why so much Dutch? Is that a language you're at ease with?

I don't know a word of Dutch. All those phrases are out of a Dutch phrase-book. I can give you the exact title if you wish to recover them. They're there the way Hemingway put in the occasional Spanish phrase to indicate that we're among Spaniards. I like Dutch; it seems to be a kind of elfin language. Someone once said that if German is a noble horse Dutch is a donkey. It looks like English; it's easily guessed at.

I enjoyed guessing, actually. Is there any particular significance to the forty numbered sections and the indication within the story that van Hovendaal is forty years of age? There's no numerology; forty is just accidental?

I think so.

What's been your reaction to the critical response to **Tatlin!***?*

I've been amazed. You see I didn't think anyone would ever publish the book, so it was written without a sense that it would ever see the light of day. There have been some sixty reviews, several critical essays . . . I'm very pleased that several of them have been by ex-students of mine, like Alan Williamson and Richard Wertime. And the thesis that was written on it was a marvellous surprise. I did not know the thesis was being written; John Wilson did not pester me, as it were. Out of the blue I got a xerox copy of it and read it with perfect disbelief.

Does it interest you to look back at your early stories, or is there really no connection with the work you've been doing more recently?

There are no early stories. You mean back in undergraduate days.

Yes.

Those as far as I know don't exist. They must have been awful.

The same goes for the early poems?

Flowers & Leaves was fifteen years in the writing, so it's both.. .

When did you begin it, then?

I made a decision somewhere that if I were to try to write poetry, it's just as sensible to keep everything under one hat, as it were. So I kept a kind of notebook with a vague sense that it was going to be a longish Wallace Stevensy kind of philosophical poem called *Flowers & Leaves*. One time the manuscript was lost in the Negev Desert—I had to start over from scratch. I never thought that would be published either. No, that's not right. *Tatlin!* is the only thing, except for three stories, that I have ever sent off without an invitation. And I really didn't send *Tatlin!* off cold; Scribners had written me saying that they had read *Sappho* and would I write a book about sensuality and sex, or something like. And I said, "No, but I have some short stories I've been collecting up and I will send you those.". . .

Why did you end your connection with National Review?

Because I faced up to the fact that I was by that time working for eight publications regularly: *New York Times Book Review, Life, National Review, Hudson Review, Poetry,* the *Los Angeles-New York Times Book Review Service, Book Week,* and the *Louisville Courier-Journal.* I began to panic that I would never write anything of my own. I didn't consciously have any notion that I wanted to write whatever these things are—short stories or *assemblages.* But it wasn't until I faced up to the fact that I simply had to quit reviewing . . . It literally filled all your time. If you're a full-time teacher . . . These things came out of the blue, you never knew when: *New York Times* used telegrams, *Life* used the phone, *National Review* used the phone, *Hudson Review* a letter on good stationary, and so on. But as soon as you got working on one review, here was an order for another. I think I wrote my share of book reviews in those eleven years. I could have become a professional book reviewer, but I didn't want to.

In 1970 within a review of five books about Ezra Pound you note, "Now that we have entered the post-modernist age, we are at last free to make certain observations the rightness of which was hitherto in doubt. One is that the giants of the period were of two sorts: those who invented themselves, apparently out of nothing; and those who performed the most painstaking study of their craft known to the history of art, and thus evolved by infinite experimentation perplexing and radically new forms." Might you name some giants of the first sort and comment on why you've given them considerably less attention than those of the second sort?

I wrote that sentence to say that Wyndham Lewis belonged to the first category; he invented himself. This I think is illusion. We simply are not familiar with Lewis' sources. Lewis' prose style is highly idiosyncratic, to use the right word. I suspect it has demonstrable sources. Lewis is one of the most original people in the century. Another one you want to put in that category is Gertrude Stein. And again this is, I think, illusion. It's just we aren't that familiar.

What about Marcel Duchamp, for example? You pay very little attention to him, yet he seems to me a giant of the first sort.

He probably is.

But you're simply not very interested in him?

Yes I am, very much so. It's just that Duchamp, I think, was a man who was *completely* locked up in himself. There are no lines of communications out. Now all right, people have stolen from him. He is a seminal figure. I think that as time goes on, though, we will see that the real master of what Duchamp was up to was Max Ernst. He is the man with the substance that Duchamp did not have. Duchamp—well the big thing about him was that he was an artist who eventually did not make any art. This seems to me to be where the snake has with metaphysical impossi-

bility swallowed itself, starting with the tail and there's nothing there.

But within your memorial of Ezra Pound printed in Arion *you note: "His generation had assumed that a life was a work of art. . . ." I can grant Duchamp the same donnè I used to reserve for Pound and Olson, without at the same time being overburdened with "writing".*

Duchamp was an hermeticist. This kind of artist comes along from time to time and there's nothing really you can do with the hermetic artist. His symbols cannot ever be deciphered—they can only be guessed at. Gertrude Stein has an hermetic body of work which probably can all be explained as . . . Well, to be blunt about it—as love poems about her and Alice, which she did not feel free to write out and also didn't feel was anybody's damn business, but yet she could still write the poems. No, Duchamp is a man who is his own significance. He's a trail blazer. I like the great painting of the bride stripped nude by her bachelors, that's smashed and then pasted back together, showing that he really wanted the work to exist. But it is practically an Egyptian magic papyrus for me. Scholarship can say something about it but it can't ever penetrate the work and the work will not give back a resonance of meaning the way, say, Joyce's *Ulysses* or Pound's *Cantos* or any meaningful art does. I don't know that what Duchamp was doing really can be called art. I don't mean that in any philistine way. It was kind of private activity. Compare him to Joseph Cornell. Cornell was just as hermetic, but Cornell wanted people to understand his boxes. And though no one has done it yet, I think you can start putting all the hotel names and the parrots and the movie stars and the Medici quotations and the wine glasses and the marbles and the bits and pieces of maps together. That this will render up as much sense as say Marianne Moore, or another artist who worked with found objects of this sort. But Cornell is an open, accessible figure. Duchamp is closed. He was a misanthrope. He hated people. He hated art. From what I gather, he became simply a bitter recluse for the last three quarters of his life. He may have been a man who had one or two ideas and was terrified that if he used them up he wouldn't have any more. So he got the same effect by not using them.

Or prolonging them.

He didn't have the faith that I think anyone who makes things has: that you must use up *everything* on the work table everytime you do something. Hugh Kenner, when he writes a book, seems to me to put everything he happens to know at that moment in the book. *Everything.* That is, he sweeps the table clean. Every scrap, and it's all worked beautifully into a coherence. And then of course he can start over again. I think if ever there were a Hugh Kenner who was stingy with his perceptions and his ideas, and said he was going to save back most of them so that he won't run out and get to be an old man and not have anything to say—he would dry up. So there's this wonderful paradox of the more you make, the more you can make.

That's interesting, You also don't seem to pay too much attention to two movements (one could name figures within them): Dadaism and Surrealism. I was wondering what was at the root of your disinterest. You talk about Picabia occasionally, but do those two manifestation's simply interest you less than Imagism and Vorticism, for example?

No, not at all. The house is full of books about Surrealism and Dadism. I know an awful lot about both, I think. If I had to make a criticism, I would say that Surrealism is all too easy to do and invited an awful lot of fakes into the business. Dali for instance, I think, is a man who systematically exploited and ruined himself, and really didn't have anything to say to begin with. That's just personality—the man did not have a deep and a rich mind. *The* Surrealist of all is Max Ernst, I think, and secondly I would place Delvaux, who is one of the greatest painters of the century. The fact that Picasso did only a few Surrealist works says an awful lot about Surrealism. Because it's damned difficult to think of something that couldn't interest Picasso; he was interested in everything and he wasn't really interested in Surrealism. Surrealism is after all simply dream. The six stories after *Tatlin!* are all surrealistic, are they not? **"The Richard Nixon Freischütz Rag"** has Dadaist strategies; **"The Haile Selassie Funeral Train"** is a dream: it is intended to be surrealistic.

One of your dreams that you reworked?

It's a real dream. I put down as much of it as I could literally.

And that was the story?

That is the story. And I did it because I was reading a biography of Max Ernst and Max Ernst said that Freud is a lot of crap, though dreams are one of the most interesting things that we have. To interpret them is to look at a dream from its most uninteresting perspective. That what's *really* interesting about a dream is the fact that it is a dream. Nevermind whether you're in love with your mother or you're jealous of your wife or you have an inferiority complex or you're turning into King Oedipus of Thebes. Look at the dream in all of its charm. Ernst all his life said that what saved him was noting that dream content can be thought of without any reference to Freud whatsoever. This is why he could use such powerful images; he simply said there is no Freud. Now look at Dali who never did anything without his Freud open. You look at a Dali painting and you say well, you know, he's decided that he's going to do *the* phallic image. So he's got the dream so obvious that nothing happens at all.

Jerome Klinkowitz   (essay date 1979)

SOURCE: "Cycling through History," in *Book World— The Washington Post,* July 15, 1979, p. H3.

[*Klinkowitz is an American critic and short story writer who has written several books on contemporary innovative fiction. In the essay below, he offers a positive review of* Da Vinci's Bicycle *and compliments Davenport's innovative "rearrangements of history" in the collection.*]

"History is a dream that strays into innocent sleep," we are told in this remarkable collection of short fiction. Leonardo Da Vinci invents a bicycle and imagines ranks of soldiers riding it into battle, "a phalanx of these *due rote*

bearing lancers at full tilt." The history of photography is recounted, from the days when any movement simply erased the image from the artist's plate. A Greek reporter, contemporary of Marcus Aurelius, looks about and remarks, "How old the world!"

The world, Guy Davenport instructs us, is all a matter of perception. **Da Vinci's Bicycle** is a set of imaginative exercises on characters who do not match up with our memory of the past. Leonardo inventing a bicycle in 1493 certainly qualifies, but look at Davenport's other choices: Gertrude Stein reading the comics to Picasso, Greek philosophers inventing a mechanical pigeon, Richard Nixon bombing the DMZ to impress his host, Chairman Mao. Our very nature is formed by how we see history, Davenport's technique suggests. Or, as one of his figures insists, "The Mind is what it knows! It is nothing else at all, at all."

Davenport's fiction is appealing and attractive, then, because deep down it reflects the way our imaginations create a world. A better correspondence between the act of reading and the act of writing would be hard to find, and so it's fitting that the Johns Hopkins University Press, publisher of those heady structuralist and deconstructionist tracts by René Girard and Jacques Derrida, should begin its fiction program with a book like **Da Vinci's Bicycle.**

But Davenport does not stop with mere method. Each of his stories is embellished with scores of quirky little touches, things a reader will remember long after the plot has been forgotten. Ezra Pound's anecdote of how the body of William Butler Yeats was lost at sea by a drunken navy crew, Nietzsche signing the guest book at a Rapallo inn with the admonition, "Beware the beefsteak"—these are the incidental clothes in which Davenport dresses his methodological fictions. And as with any good fiction, they are the deft touches of the master which tell us all.

Therefore the history of photography, summarized in one of these cautionary tales, shows how this most modern of aesthetic media catches the spirit of our consciousness for history. "A photograph of Lenin reading *Iskra* at a Zurich cafe accidentally includes over to the left James and Nora Joyce haggling with a taxi driver about the fare," we read, and are delighted as only someone of our own times and manners could be. "A Philadelphia photographer made several plates of paleolithic horse fossils at the Museum of Natural History," we read on. "In one of the pictures two gentlemen stand in the background, spectators at the museum. One wears a top hat and looks with neurotic intelligence at the camera. He is Edgar Allan Poe. The other gentleman is cross-eyed and wears a beret. God knows who he is."

The point, which Davenport's fiction has made clear in its process, is that "for the first time in the history of art the accidental became the controlling iconography of a representation of the world."

The camera, by its very rigidity, rattles our perception and makes us see things we never noticed were there. Fiction should do the same thing, but after years of dominance by one style it takes an innovator like Guy Davenport to

Davenport's fiction is appealing and attractive because deep down it reflects the way our imaginations create a world. A better correspondence between the act of reading and the act of writing would be hard to find. . . .

—*Jerome Klinkowitz*

shake matters up and make stories in a slightly different way. Even within his tales he reminds us that all is provisional and comparative. Several actions take place at once, and the reader is asked to consider the Paris of the moderns with the rites of primitive ritual—a technique Picasso used in these same days, and which Davenport reinvents for fiction. Sometimes it's done by metaphor, as in the reduced circumstances of a once mighty man: "O Lady Mouse, I breathe, your well wisher here who has come to visit, the round of nothing before you in this fine grass, was the emperor of Rome." Fine writing and fresh perceptions are the mutually shared joys of Guy Davenport's fiction. Reading it is a life experience.

Da Vinci's Bicycle complements Davenport's first collection of stories, *Tatlin!,* published in 1974. His concern there was to show the modern age at the edge of history—Kafka and Max Brod attending an air show and by chance meeting Wittgenstein; Picasso, still a realist, admiring the cave paintings at Altamira; Cézanne and Lenin struggling to shape the modern revolutionary mind.

This new volume encompasses a broader range of experience, proving that Davenport's talent is well grounded and that his rearrangements of history have more to offer than mere novelty. His fiction itself is like "a dream that strays into innocent sleep." The dreamer's work, with the writer's, is necessary to know one's self. "Everything," these stories tell us, "is an incongruity if you study it well."

William F. Van Wert   (essay date 1980)

SOURCE: "Some Manhattan in New England, Some Enchantment in Ohio," in *The Georgia Review,* Vol. XXXIV, No. 2, Summer, 1980, pp. 441-48.

[*In the following review of* Da Vinci's Bicycle, *Van Wert compliments Davenport's experimentation with language and manipulation of historical perspective.*]

["Experiment"] can be a consummate kind of thing, producing sometimes the kind of dream-state fiction that nobody but the author ever dreamed of, and in such unlikely places as The Johns Hopkins University Press and the Ohio Historical Society. If Guy Davenport's *Da Vinci's Bicycle* is any indication of what John T. Irwin will bring out in the future at Johns Hopkins, then that press will likely become as well known as Illinois, Missouri, Iowa,

and L.S.U. as an outlet for good, serious short fiction outside of New York.

Davenport's "experiment" in *Da Vinci's Bicycle* is a high-risk, no-holds-barred, committed literature. His love for the "foragers" of history is apparent in every sentence. He inserts languages as freely as James Joyce did and perhaps to equal purpose. Davenport's precision is that of an archeologist on the dig of a lifetime, but his personal appropriation of "history" is as bizarre and freeing as that of any Surrealist. And perhaps there is synecdoche of a new sort in his making everybody in history contemporary, in his magnifying the lunatic fringe to Everyman status. In my favorite selections—**"The Richard Nixon Freischütz Rag," "The Haile Selassie Funeral Train"** (in which Joyce appears), **"The Invention of Photography in Toledo,"** and **"A Field of Snow on a Slope of the Rosenberg"**—Davenport moves from the dry memorial to a short Oriental-feeling poetry that shocks, from witty and laconic dialogue that would do justice to Barthelme in "The New Music" to a poetic resonance that's hard to hang on to because it "promotes the octopus" and moves in all directions at once. In **"The Richard Nixon Freischütz Rag,"** for example, Davenport mixes Nixon's visit with Chairman Mao with Da Vinci at work on the bicycle with Gertrude Stein with . . . etc. The marvel of such fiction is that Davenport respects history, and so his arranged meeting of the umbrella and sewing machine upon a dissection table in both words and images (his elaborate drawings) does what most people credit [E.L.] Doctorow with doing in *Ragtime.* Only Davenport does it better.

George Kearns   (essay date 1980)

SOURCE: "Guy Davenport in Harmony," in *The Hudson Review,* Vol. XXXIII, No. 3, Autumn, 1980, pp. 449-52, 454.

[*In the following essay, Kearns praises Davenport's strategy of foraging through history to establish affinities between historical figures and concepts and create a holistic and potentially harmonious universe in the stories of* Tatlin! *and* Da Vinci's Bicycle.]

Stories, Guy Davenport calls them, so they are stories. Yet none of our usual senses for "story" suggests the combination of audacious invention, sentence-by-sentence surprise, playfulness and archaic wonder of the world Davenport began mapping out in *Tatlin!* and continues to explore in *Da Vinci's Bicycle.* We may take story, says the OED [*Oxford English Dictionary*], as an aphetic of history, and then recall that before history became social science, or even a "continuous methodical record," it was a "knowing by inquiry, an account of one's inquiries." Davenport inquires widely, among familiar things seen or positioned freshly: Nixon in China; Stein in Paris; Mussolini's posturing rhetoric; the prehistoric paintings at Lascaux and Altamira; Picasso's *Guernica*; and among things half-forgotten or likely to lie outside our field of vision: Balbinus, poet and briefest of emperors, speaking to us from a jug; the liberated and liberating imagination of Charles Fourier; Robert Walser, Swiss writer who spent twenty-seven years of self-imposed exile in mental hospitals; the anthropologist Marcel Griaule listening to the harmonies of Dogon cosmology; or Joseph Nicéphore Niepce making, in 1816, the earliest known photographic plate ("Geese walking back and forth across the barnyard erased themselves during the long exposure."). The results of his investigations invite us to participate in plotting connections among points on a multi-dimensional mapping, while Davenport fashions them into a stylish world of pleasure, offering nothing less than the possibility of paradise regained. It is not often, now that I am grown up, that I take such primitive delight in stories.

We may begin arbitrarily at any point on this map, this unpredictable Möbius strip, this time-warp where Herakleitos intersects with Niels Bohr and reminds us (*Tatlin!*) that *the same road goes both up and down* and *the beginning of a circle is also its end.* Begin with a minor "character," the photographer Jacques Henri Lartigue, who pops up (**"Au Tombeau de Charles Fourier"**) surrounded by Dogon myths, but not too far from Wilbur Wright, Gertrude Stein, Beckett talking to Guy Davenport in a Paris café, Henry James observing Blériot descend from the first cross-channel flight (although what James saw "he did not bother to say")—and Da Vinci's bicycle. With luck, Lartigue has appeared before Davenport's foraging attention, and finds a place in his universe. In the frontispiece to a collection of his photographs, preface by Ezra Bowen, we find Lartigue himself, in 1903, a small boy in high button shoes, clutching a huge box camera, staring at us with a delighted, omnivorous grin. His image, abstracted from the Bois de Boulogne and attendant female relatives, Davenport has meticulously reproduced in a drawing, which in turn forms an enigmatic ideogram with a horned totemic animal and a blond American ephebe in a jockstrap. If we are seeing things as Davenport invites us to see them, we understand at once his attraction to a six-year-old boy who wrote in his diary, having just been given his first camera: "Now I will be able to make portraits of everything . . . *everything*. I know very well that many, many things are going to ask me to have their pictures taken." A mind that hears *things* speak, and for which, as Bowen comments, "anything was fair game—so long as it was pretty, exciting or fun."

Lartigue's pictures, images from and for a terrestrial paradise, include many of what he called the "magic adventure" of flying: kites, gliders, primitive flying machines—as well as bicycles. The Wright brothers came from a bicycle shop, making the imaginative leap that Leonardo missed, intent as he was on birds, and we are now in several worlds at once, returning to that first bicycle of 1493, crudely sketched by the master's ten-year-old protégé and buried from sight until our own time. Lines reach out, suggesting complex codes beyond chronology, structures that shift and glimmer, get charmed by passing gods ("Persephone stood at all the angles of time"), making us wonder at times if we have seen what we think we have seen. Lartigue went on taking pictures over a long lifetime, but did not show them publicly until 1963, a solitary persistence of vision unconcerned with the rewards and demands of civilization (in Fourier's damning sense of the word). That persistence, too, would appeal to Davenport,

whose characters, he says, are "pioneers of the spirit" and have the "instinct to forage."

Davenport himself is prime forager among them, crafting glorious *bricolage* out of their provisions for the life of the spirit, communicating, with the help of dizzying parataxis and continuous subversion of our expectations, the sheer verve of his and their pragmatic intelligence. Almost twenty years ago he compiled examples of *The Intelligence of Louis Agassiz,* the Swiss-American naturalist who scorned, in brilliant and loving detail, the materialistic science of his time, then marching hand in hand with Fourier's civilization. For Agassiz, "the connection of all the known features of nature into one system exhibits thought, the most comprehensive thought, in limits transcending the highest wonted powers of man." Davenport's foragers have all intuited at least a portion of a holistic universe to which familiar categories—mind/matter, myth/history, fact/fiction, sanity/madness—are no longer a helpful guide, a universe whose irreducible particularity forms a complexity forever resistant to system and generalization. (As Wittgenstein came to see: he appears in *Tatlin!*, watching airplanes, an "engineer," not yet a "philosopher," in 1909; later, as a presiding spirit for the Dutch philosopher Adriaan van Hovendaal, a Doppelgänger of Davenport.) The foragers are shaped into a phalanx against all who believe that "the gods are indifferent to gravity. . . . Those who go to the inhuman to place their hopes upon its alien rhythms, its bitter familiarity with nothing, its constant retreat from all that we can love," making them "hostages to vastation" (Balbinus in **"C. Musonius Rufus"**). Through his or her own *techne* each shares a Pythagorean vision in which, as the Dogon say, "a thing is an example of a plan"; they search out "the harmonies, the affinities, the kinship of the orders of nature"; they know that "all of nature is a series and pivot, like Pythagoras' numbers"—this is Fourier, for whom the Greek philosopher was *un prélat révéré*—"like the transmutation of light. Give me a sparrow, he said, a leaf, a wasp, an ox, and I will show you the harmony of its place in its chord, the phrase, the movement. . . ." They see with the eyes of a Leonardo, who has already forgotten his bicycle, and no wonder:

> He turned to the basket of flowering grasses, reaching for his silver pencil. Bracts and umbrels fine as a spider's legs! And in the thin green veins ran hairs of water, and down the hairs of water ran light, down into the dark, into the root. Light from the farthest stars flowed through these long leaves . . .
>
> —Maestro, Salai said, when will the chain [for the bicycle] be ready?
>
> —Chain? Leonardo asked. What chain?
>
> He drew with his left hand a silver eddy of grass. It was grace that he drew, perfection, frail leaves through which moved the whole power of God, and when a May fly lights on a green arc of grass the splendor of that conjunction is no less than San Gabriele touching down upon the great Dome at Byzantium, closing the crushed silver and spun glass of his four wings around the golden shaft of his height.

From which we pass in rapid juxtaposition back to civilization, Nixon and Kissinger bombing Laos and Cambodia.

But vertiginous vision is not an end in itself; it clears the ground of civilization's narrow sight, making way for edenic possibilities. Fourier, in whom discourse was never *happier*, saw Eden as "a thousand documents and traditions attesting to the existence of a happiness vanished and lost, but which may stimulate *les modernes* to seek/rediscover (*rechercher*) another social order" (*Théorie de l'unité universelle*). Davenport's characters—modern or ancient, they are all contemporaries—holding fragments of these documents and traditions, meet in unexpected combinations within his paragraphs and sentences: "Butler is an intellectual cousin of Fourier. . . . Reason uncorrected by instinct is as bad as instinct uncorrected by reason. . . . Butler like Agassiz returns intelligence to nature, envisioning like Fourier a life that would cooperate with the instincts rather than deplore them." Within these stories, we need not wait for the new social order, a new discovery, or some distant system to be perfected. "Nature loves to hide," says Herakleitos in *Tatlin!* "The most beautiful order in the world is still a random gathering of things insignificant in themselves." On the first page of *Da Vinci's Bicycle* a Chinese official, fearful that Richard Nixon may be too enraptured with the Great Wall and the tombs of the Ming emperors, tells him that Chairman Mao has declared that the past is past. Nixon, having a hard time keeping up with the conversation, asks, "All over?" The stories that follow demonstrate that it is not all over, that the past is available for us to use now, soon. The direct reply to Mao comes on the next-to-the-last page of the book, in the mind of Robert Walser: "The past, I have known for years, is the future. All that has mattered is a few moments, uncongenial while they happened, that turned to gold in the waves of time."

Fourier called the evil Civilization, erected on bayonets and famine, false industry, the world *à rebours,* a hell of suppressed desires, almost lifeless: "The parades of the civilized are insipid with monotony. In Harmony they are infinitely varied." Writing with an assurance that Harmony will arrive, he oscillates in impatience and immediate imagination between the future and present tenses. Davenport is less sure that Harmony will come with time, although the escape hatch of language seems always within reach. Civilization's tragic rumblings are in the background. Nero's Rome, which shackles the philosopher C. Musonius Rufus to a chain gang. British justice, which executes one John Charles Tapner, whose grave is honored by Victor Hugo, himself in exile from the civilization of Louis Napoleon. Stalinism, crushing the false Soviet dawn in the mind of the artist-engineer Tatlin, crushing it so well that you will not find Tatlin's name in the index of the Great Soviet Encyclopedia, although in an article explaining the errors of Constructivism he is remembered as the designer of practical uniforms for workers. Mussolini, about to invade Ethiopia ("LA GUERRA SARA ASPRA E DURÀ"). Nazi planes above the Lascaux caves, whose painting were produced "before Europe began to think in any way that we can understand." Banks, pitilessly remembered by Walser in his asylum. German hunters who shoot the last quagga, that animal Fourier had so counted upon. Civilization explains itself through the assassin of the visionary writer and politician, Rathenau: "*He was the finest man of our age, combining all that is most valuable of thought, honor, and spirit, and I couldn't bear it.*" Kafka weeps at the end of **"The Aeroplanes at Brescia,"** not knowing why; but we know why: man's newly realized dream of flight is about to be co-opted by Civilization.

Central among Davenport's stories, his masterpiece I suppose, is the astonishing and erotic novella, **"The Dawn in Erewhon"** (*Tatlin!*), where his themes and many of his characters converge, as Adriaan van Hovendaal and companions of both sexes achieve a miniature up-to-date phalanstery of "amorous innovations" in the midst of the twentieth century. While Davenport's stories may be read separately, they offer their fullest pleasures when allowed to modify each other, as within a single field. Our pleasure is to watch characters appear, find themselves transformed and developed, take on different meanings as different minds pass through them. He will find, if he is lucky, a critic-anthropologist as sensitive as a Lévi-Strauss, but inevitably there will be duller explainers, term papers, panel discussions, dissertations. I imagine letters arriving in Lexington. Who is the tourist who observes the beginning of the twilight of the gods in the lovely **"The Antiquities of Elis"**? Answer: Pausanias. My library has nothing by Adriaan van Hovendaal, whose works, says the dust jacket of *Tatlin!*, are "some of the strangest of modern times." Where can I find them? Answer: Try the Erewhon University Press. In 1909, Wittgenstein was studying engineering in England; how could he have been present with Kafka and Puccini at Brescia? Answer: Does it matter? What religious assent must we give these stories? Answer: As Fourier said, the true tone of our relations with God should be friendship, and not belief.

Now is the time to read Davenport, before we are obliged to restore from criticism the innocence of his *ordre dispersé* (Fourier's cherished method of composition); now, for (Gertrude Stein on painting) "when everybody knows it is good the adventure is over." Adventures these stories are, in which the trinity of *delectet, moveat,* and *docet* move together in harmony. "But let us desist," as Robert Walser says, about to meet his fate on **"A Field of Snow on a Slope of the Rosenberg,"** "lest quite by accident we be so unlucky as to put these things in order."

Robert A. Morace (essay date 1981)

SOURCE: "Invention in Guy Davenport's *Da Vinci's Bicycle*," in *Critique: Studies in Modern Fiction,* Vol. XXII, No. 3, March 1981, pp. 71-87.

[*In the following essay, Morace discusses the stories in* Da Vinci's Bicycle *and contends that "imaginative redemption" is the thematic focus of the collection.*]

In his recent and generally disapproving study of contemporary American fiction, John Gardner names just four writers whose work possibly "will outlast the century": Bernard Malamud, Joyce Carol Oates, Eudora Welty, and Guy Davenport. Readers of *On Moral Fiction* may find Davenport a rather odd, even arcane choice. Perhaps better known (when known at all) as a scholar and translator than a fiction-writer (he is also a poet, illustrator, librettist, and professor of English at the University of Kentucky), the mid-fifty year-old Davenport has published only two collections of stories: **Tatlin!** (1974) and **Da Vinci's Bicycle** (1979). For those familiar with his fiction, there is another matter. As one reviewer complained, "Davenport mixes chronologies, tones, voices, languages, and chunks of other learned books to create dizzying collages that are often impressive in their cleverness and intricacy, but sometimes wearying in their self-conscious erudition" [*Saturday Review,* 7 July 1979]. The stories—or "*assemblages* of history and necessary fiction," as Davenport terms them—do seem at first glance to be not the "moral fiction" Gardner espouses but the "linguistic sculpture" (illustrated, in Davenport's case) that he denigrates. Although Davenport's stylistic complexity will awe most readers and frighten away more than a few, the "sheer precision and uncompromising artistry" Gardner finds in his work does repay the considerable attention and effort it requires. His essentially modernist aesthetic results in a richly allusive, intricately structured prose in which the chief delight is the author's keen sense of narrative voice. What is more important, Davenport, following the modernist assumption that a life is "a work of art," creates a fiction that is very clearly, in Gardner's sense of the word, "moral": it takes both as its method and as its subject that "process"—the voyage in search of (or in the creation of) affirmative human values—which characterizes "moral fiction."

In the ten stories comprising **Da Vinci's Bicycle,** this search is made explicit by means of a travel metaphor. **"The Richard Nixon Freischutz Rag,"** which opens the collection, uses the China trip of 1972 as its base and depicts Nixon as a type of modern tourist, a man so devoid of imagination that travel is for him an entirely unaffecting experience. His deadness of spirit is made apparent through a series of contrasts, the first involving the exoticism of the setting and the rhythm of the prose on the one hand and the flatness of Nixon's responses on the other:

> On the Great Ten Thousand Li Wall, begun in the wars of the Spring and Autumn to keep the Mongols who had been camping nearer and nearer the Yan border from riding in hordes on their przhevalskis into the cobbled streets and ginger gardens of the Middle Flower Kingdom, Richard Nixon said:
>
> —I think you would have to conclude that this is a great wall.

A contrast is also made between the politician Nixon and the poet-Chairman Mao, who is linked, in some degree, with da Vinci (at the time he was inventing the bicycle and Columbus was discovering America) and Gertrude Stein (touring Italy) whose awesome yet graceful imaginations are recorded in brief sketches embedded in Nixon's Freischutz Rag. While Leonardo

> drew with his left hand a silver eddy of grass. It was grace that he drew, perfection, frail leaves through which moved the whole power of God, and when a May fly lights on a green arc of grass

the splendor of that conjunction is no less than San Gabriele touching down upon the great Dome of Byzantium, closing the crushed silver and spun glass of his four wings around the golden shaft of his height,

Nixon, inspired by Henry Kissinger, orders the destruction of Cambodia by B-52's; that, Kissinger had told him, "would impress Chairman Mao." Mao's prophecy, "Imperialist reactionary make trouble and fail until own destruction," turns out to be true—not politically but in terms of imaginative vision. Nixon's view of the "world" is limited to the narrowly mimetic form of television: to what can be televised and to who is watching what is being televised.

Davenport's heroes differ from the Richard Nixons in that they are concerned less (if at all) with their public selves and historical facts than with mystery and personal exploration. The title character in **"C. Musonius Rufus"** is trying to discover who he is. For Musonius, the problem of self-definition is difficult because he must resist the false, or incomplete, identities others have imposed on him. "I am the emperor Balbinus kept in a jug" does nothing to define his true character. Musonius, a Stoic, finds the way to the virtuous life both perilous and unending. He can be humorously vulgar—"the slut Aphrodite"—and full of pity for his bewhiskered wife who, in their separation, must also suffer his frequent imprisonments. What chiefly characterizes Musonius is not his philosophy, his suffering, or his sense of injustice, but rather, his searching vision and his vast and hopeful imagination: "The first arrest and sentence, from which I came back. *I came back.* That is the reason I endure this shit." Condemned that first time to an island without any drinking water (the penal island Gyaros is left unnamed in the story), "I looked for water and found C. Musonius Rufus." For Musonius, "damned to sanity and to hope," "Discovery is always more than what you meant to find." The reader might very well draw the same conclusion, for this Musonius is both the "jugged" prisoner and a voice within a jug, a voice which transcends time but which, like Musonius's Consilarii, might also admit, "Our sources are confused. We are only messengers."

The true hero of **Da Vinci's Bicycle** is the imagination—or, invention, as the metaphor in the title implies. Historical fact is always a point of departure in these stories, never a thing in itself worth verifying: "The world is out there, independent of your will," Musonius says; but "out there" is, in his timeless story, alternately the Roman Empire in the first century A.D. and Fascist Italy under Mussolini. Similarly, Davenport, for whom "The idea that time cannot be reversed is mere Enlightenment dogma, Liberal twaddle," dispenses with historical chronology and assembles his own **"The Haile Selassie Funeral Train,"** the corpse in one car (despite the fact that Selassie did not die until 1975) and James Joyce, Guillaume Apollinaire, and the narrator in another. (Whether they are in front of or behind the Emperor's car, the narrator, appropriately, does not know.) Another story, **"Au Tombeau de Charles Fourier"** (the title recalls Mallarme's "Tombeau d'Edgar Poe"), is comprised of various narrative lines, including a visit to the grave of the visionary socialist, Fourier; early aviation history; Gertrude Stein driving a car and chatting; the creation myth of the African Dogons. Whether all his readers will bear with Davenport as he intricately weaves these often seemingly disparate lines into a single fiction is unlikely. What is likely is that more readers will know *how* to read this complicated story thanks to **"The Wooden Dove of Archytas,"** which is similarly but more simply constructed. Half of this short work is narrated by Aristopolites, "one of a wheen of tanlings" taught by the Pythagorean, Archytas of Tarentum. Over dinner, the boy reports his mentor's latest invention, a wooden dove that flies; his father is skeptical, and "Mama said I was neglecting my squash." The boy has greater faith and imagination. The story's other half is a Faulknerian account of three Indians, the black cook Hannah, a white woman named Miss Fanny, and the funeral of Dovey, the Indians' ringdove which has been crushed to death by a wind-shut door. When Miss Fanny says of Dovey's death, "I hate it that it had to happen," the Indian Anne Breadcrust is "shocked at the Presbyterian phrase but dismissed it as so much ignorance." The funeral ends, as Davenport's reader knows it will, with the defeat of Miss Fanny's predestined universe; for the Indians this means the resurrection of Dovey and, for the reader, the triumph of the imagination: "—We kick the door, Dovey! Anne cried. We kick the door! —She gone, Jack Frost said." Immediately, the reader finds himself back in Italy:

> There was a whomp and hiss in the air, and Pappas lifted me up so that I could see the dove leaking winter breaths of steam slide up the ramp, unfold its wings, and shoot upward. It whistled up like an arrow from a bow, fluttered with the stagger of a bat, and banking into a long high wheel, soared over the chronometer tower, the fane of Asklepios, the armory, the hills. We all cried with delight.

Instead of polarizing primitive myth and scientific discovery, Davenport makes clear, as Whitman and Pound did, that they derive from the same wellspring: man's searching and redemptive imagination. His chief characters never subscribe to any hard-and-fast theory of election and damnation; rather, they are believers in process: "So many beginnings all her life made Gertrude Stein Gertrude Stein." In contrast are those who prefer stasis to purposeful flux, the "we" of the following: "In Professor James the nineteenth century had its great whoopee, saw all as the lyric prospect of a curve which we were about to take at full speed, but mistaking the wild synclitic headlong for propinquity to an ideal, we let the fire die in the engine." According to Dogon myth, "Amma is the inside of everything. The world is God's twin. Amma and his world are twins. Or will be, when there is a stop to the mischief of Ogo." Ogo is the imp of the perverse, the element of chance in an *otherwise* orderly world. Thanks to Ogo the first creation, an acacia tree, was botched: "Amma began a second time to make the world. For the new world he invented people but he decided to keep the acacia too." What is the lesson in this to be learned by man and, specifically, by the artist? Probably to follow the course taken by the hapless Amma, who "tried to do what he could with the things Ogo created, so that they would fit togeth-

er somehow, someway"; and too, like Ogo's sign, the acacia, to search "in sunlight the completion of its being," to "search forever, never finding, like Ogo." The endlessness of the search is certainly not cause for despair, as it is in Beckett, for it represents the imagination's boundless possibilities. Thus, Davenport's adaptation of the epic catalog: ending some paragraphs with a sentence that seems to be a complete list—"The trees are the baobab and tamarind"—and then continuing the list at the beginning of the next paragraph—"The trees are kahya, flame-tree, butternut, *sa,* jujube, and acacia." Besides, Ogo's perversity is "all for fun, all for fun," and one need not be a myth-minded semanticist to see that "ogo" is at the heart of "Dogon." As Musonius learns from his Consilarii, "Accident . . . is design." Or, as the teacher makes even clearer, the signs Ogo "marks with his paws are the signs we must live by that day. For it is Ogo's gift that he built accident into the world's structure." Because "We are born into Ogo's world, . . . our work is . . . to organize." Davenport's characters find themselves in a world of randomness and set themselves the task of finding order— that is, of inventing it, discovering it, imagining it. One search leads to Fourier's tombstone and the words, "The series distributes the harmonies," which leads the narrator to imagine an order in the search for order: Linnaeus died when Fourier "was six, Buffon when he was sixteen, Cuvier was his contemporary. Swedenborg died the week before he was born. All searched out the harmonies, the affinities, the kinship of the orders of nature." The bewildering abundance of **"Au Tombeau de Charles Fourier"** is neatly packaged in thirty numbered sections; twenty-eight are comprised of nine subsections or paragraphs each, while the tenth, cryptically summing up Davenport's view, reads simply and musically: "What works in the angle succeeds in the arc and holds in the chord."

Davenport's interest in the arbitrariness of order (including history) naturally suggests an affinity with the innovative post-modern and post-contemporary American writers, whom he has praised "for returning to literature that awe and wonderment which no amount of pessimism or scientific certainty can ever remove from the fact that we are, that we exist, and that we exist in a damned strange way utterly divorced from what reason argues or passion claims, and that we don't know why." There are other similarities, too. The narrator of **"Ithaka"** is, though unnamed, very much the Pound-scholar Guy Davenport. Indeed, at times the stories have a self-reflexive element: "What the hell comes before Cnossos if this sentence is to be a long one?" asks a speaker who is not clearly identified as Gertrude Stein until the next paragraph of **"Au Tombeau de Charles Fourier."** **"The Antiquities of Elis"** is a story about writing a guidebook (*The Description of Greece* by Pausanias, the story's unnamed narrator), a story which becomes that guidebook: the innkeeper's wife had heard that "I was . . . writing the picture of Elis for the Romaioi. . . . Would I mention the inn, its moderate prices, its desire to accommodate the better sort of traveler? I do. It is the Xenodokheion Hermes on the Hodos Marathonos. The straw is clean, the wine salubrious, the bread excellent." Like John Barth, who has said reality is a nice place to visit but he would not want to live there, one of Davenport's narrators laments, "But real life is all that photography has." Davenport has much more; he has fantasy on his side. Of a Spanish photographer he writes, "His wife Lucinda came to the edge of Scotland and shouted over the wall that he was to come home immediately to Madrid." Like Donald Barthelme, he has a keen eye for the incongruous and an uncanny ability to shake us out of our accustomed patterns of thought and out of our passive, virtually drugged acceptance of the world around us:

> A small town safe in its whereabouts, Titus Livy said of Toledo. It sits on a promontory at a convergence of rivers.
>
> Has not a silver cornet band strutted down its streets in shakos and scarlet sashes, playing with brio and a kind of melancholy elation *Santa Ana's Retreat from Buena Vista*? Swan Creek flows through its downtown into the blue Maumee, which flows into Lake Erie. It bore the name of Port Lawrence until Marcus Fulvius Nobilor erected the *fasces* and eagles of the SPQR in 193. Originally a part of Michigan until Andrew Jackson gave his nod to Ohio's claim, the fierce violet of its stormy skies inspired El Greco to paint his famous view of the city. It was in Toledo that the Visigoths joined the church and made Spain Catholic. And in 1897 Samuel L. (Golden Rule) Jones was elected mayor on the Independent ticket. Its incredible sunsets began to appear in late Roman eclogues.

So much for "a small town safe in its whereabouts." As this story, **"The Invention of Photography in Toledo,"** suggests, all the attempts at pinning down reality to a single word ("Toledo") or to a photographic representation are doomed to failure. In a photography by Joseph Nicephore Niepce—one of the *two* possible fathers of photography, "Geese walking back and forth across the barnyard erased themselves during the long exposure." Photographs of the Russian revolution have been doctored by the Soviets, who have erased Trotsky and substituted Stalin, "even when he was a hundred miles away eating borshch." And as the narrator speculates, "A photograph of Socrates and his circle would simply look like an ugly old man with bushy eyebrows and the lips of a frog." Photography not only misrepresents the world, charges Davenport, but also weakens man's imagination. While its invention, the narrator says, was itself valuable in that it exposed the "accidental" base upon which all reality rests, photography has become further evidence that in the Twentieth Century we have indeed "let the fire die in the engine." Since the invention of photography, mystery has given way to fact, dreams are no longer dreamed in color, and no one seems able to believe in (that is, imagine or invent) the possibility of a harmony beyond "the accidental." Fortunately, Guy Davenport can, as the story's two final and perfectly balanced paragraphs—or imaginative photographs—attest:

> On a spring day in 1913 the monster, *Nessiteras rhom bopteryx*, a plesiosaurus with lots of teeth, saw Betun as clearly as his Jurassic vision allowed, an insect with five feet, black wings, and one large eye that caught the sun with a fierce flash. As a detail of the Out There, Betun held

little interest, and until he came into the Here he would not eat him.

> Betun's photograph shows a long wet nose and lifted lip, an expressionless reptilian eye, and a gleaming flipper. It was published in *La Prensa* upside down and in the London *Times* with a transposed caption identifying it as the Archduke Franz Ferdinand arriving in Sarajevo for a visit of state.

Davenport, however, does not turn his back on reality and merrily lose himself in fiction's funhouse. His purpose is to reinvest reality with meaning and mystery. In his guidebook story, for example, factual descriptions are never rendered in the style of Karl Baedeker but instead are heightened, almost mythified, by the rhythms of the author's prose. As Davenport well knows, reality can be overwhelming, as in **"Ithaka,"** the collection's shortest, only previously unpublished story and its most autobiographical and conventionally realistic story. Tracing a day Davenport spent with Ezra Pound and Olga Rudge, the story develops a remarkable portrait of Pound's stubbornness and pettiness and also his courage and tragic defeat. Not Odysseus come home to Ithaca to save his queen and claim his rightful place, Pound is presented as a diminished figure, at times almost a boy being admonished by his maternal Penelope to take his pill, not to swim out too far into the bay at Rapallo. As the day and the story end together, Davenport writes, "*Addio!* he used to say. Now, anguish in his eyes, he said nothing at all." What makes **"Ithaka"** seem so odd is its being the only work in the collection in which the imagination fails to redeem the world or a character in it. Perhaps understanding the kind of work **"Ithaka"** is will help explain this anomaly. Since it closely follows Davenport's essay of 1973 on Pound, one can plausibly argue that the story is less fictional and, conversely, more historically factual than the other nine pieces which comprise *Da Vinci's Bicycle.* Translated into the terms developed here, **"Ithaka"** presents little chance of any imaginative redemption because it contains so little imaginative reconstruction of historical reality; historical reality is reflected, not remade. Still, **"Ithaka"** cannot be wholly reduced to this formula, for despite its similarity to the form of the factual essay, it shows clear signs of the imagination's reworking of the basic historical/biographical details. The most significant sign is in the way the story begins and ends. While it concludes with the melancholy fact of Pound's self-imposed silence, it begins with these lines of quite different import:

> There was, as Ezra remarked, a mouse in the tree. We sat under the *pergola di trattoria* above San Pantaleone in Sant' Ambrogio di Rapallo. His panama on the table, his stick across his lap, Pound leaned back in his chair. In the congenial mat of vine and fig above him there was, as he said, a mouse.
>
> —So there is, Miss Rudge said. What eyes you have, Ezra.

In his review of *The Life of Ezra Pound*, Davenport points out that biographer Noel Stock's Pound has a voice (his political views) but "no eyes" (sense of beauty). What Davenport does in **"Ithaka"** is to rescue Pound "the powerful inventor and renovator" from Stock's narrow view of the poet as "the victim of genius." If Pound's tragedy is one indisputable fact in the story, his strikingly undiminished power of perception is another.

A second story which makes use, more or less, of the conventions of realism is **"John Charles Tapner."** Its narrator is John Martin, the Queen's provost on Guernsey, who meets Victor Hugo during the latter's exile on the island in the 1850's. Before his arrival, Hugo had tried unsuccessfully to save a Guernsey man, Tapner, from the gallows. Unwittingly, he fares better with Martin who, although he quickly perceives Hugo's shortcomings—his pride and his bluffing, is fascinated by the writer's immense imagination and is, thus, saved from the narrow-mindedness which afflicts his neighbors. In a sense, Tapner is saved—from obscurity by imagination—by Martin's story. Similarly, C. Musonius Rufus worries about his obscurity: "Has anything of mine survived? I signed my name over and over. I was never politician enough to kill my enemies, they are great sources of fame. My name must be in a list somewhere. Some schoolmaster will say my name to little boys on their benches." Musonius had good reason to worry: the *Encyclopaedia Britannica* gives him only the briefest of paragraphs. Davenport, who heard about Musonius from Pound during the latter's con-

Dust jacket for Davenport's 1979 collection of short fiction, in which many of the characters are historical figures whose accomplishments were unappreciated by their contemporaries.

finement at St. Elizabeth's Hospital for the Criminally Insane, gives him his own twenty-eight page story and an immortal voice. Just as "Da Vinci's Bicycle" is the perfect title for a book which celebrates man's inventiveness, da Vinci's daydream in which a troop of lancers goes into battle astride bicycles (which occurs in Twain's *A Connecticut Yankee in King Arthur's Court*) is its perfect metaphor: Guy Davenport is astride his own invention, *Da Vinci's Bicycle,* battling history and historical realism and rescuing history's hostages: Musonius, Tapner, Pound, Imagination.

Davenport's most comic and complex Quixote is Robert Walser, the narrator of **"A Field of Snow on a Slope of the Rosenberg"**:

> I was born on Leonardo da Vinci's birthday the year the bicycle suddenly became popular all over the world, the seventh of eight. My father ran a toy shop in which you could also buy hair oil, boot blacking, and china eggs. My mother died when I was sixteen, after two years of believing that she was a porcupine that had been crowned the queen of Bulgaria, the first sign that I was to end up here.

"Here" is the insane asylum where Walser is a patient, along with Waslaw Nijinsky, and from that snowy slope he tells his curious and curiously told tale. For the most part, the story is drawn from the biography and literary works of Robert Walser (1878-1956), a Swiss writer who is probably best known—if at all—for his influence on Kafka and who was rescued from obscurity in 1957 by Christopher Middleton. Davenport, too, rescues Walser but in a different way, for his Walser is not the historical figure but the fictional character whose homeless wandering, paranoia, tragicomic suffering, and fragmented vision make him fully as much the archetypal twentieth-century protagonist as J. Alfred Prufrock, whom he resembles in many ways. What makes Walser an especially curious character and his sanity even more suspect is precisely Davenport's usual method of narration: a total disregard for narrative consistency and chronological order (Walser freely wanders back and forth over the seventy years of his life), voice (some passages are read from books), and even language (he frequently slips into his native German).

In the very first sentence of the story, Walser suggests both his own implausibleness and the major problem he and his reader must face:

> For a man who had seen a candle serenely burning inside a beaker filled with water, a fine spawn of bubbles streaming upward from its flame, who had been present in Zurich when Lenin with closed eyes and his thumbs hooked in the armholes of his waistcoat listened to the baritone Gusev singing on his knees Dargomyzhsky's *In Church We Were Not Wed,* who had conversed one melancholy afternoon with Manet's Olympia speaking from a cheap print I'd thumbtacked to the wall between a depraved adolescent girl by Egon Schiele and an oval mezzotint of Novalis, and who, as I had, Robert Walser of Biel in the canton of Bern, seen Professor William James talk so long with his necktie in his soup that it functioned as a wick to soak his collar red

and caused a woman at the next table to press her knuckles into her cheeks and scream, a voyage in a hot-air balloon at the mercy of the winds from the lignite-rich hills of Saxony Anhalt to the desolate sands of the Baltic could precipitate no new shiver from my paraphenomenal and kithless epistemology except the vastation of brooding on the sweep of inconcinnity displayed below me like a map and perhaps acrophobia.

The conscious artistry of this remarkable sentence—its rhythmic flow, which recalls the opening section of Whitman's "Out of the Cradle Endlessly Rocking," and its anti-climax—works to distract the reader from "the sweep of inconcinnity" about which Walser complains and to suggest Davenport's solution to the problem of epistemology and aesthetics Walser faces. Walser sees the disharmony of the world (his companion likens the view from their balloon to the view from Brueghel's Tower of Babel); the reader, on the other hand, understanding "inconcinnity" both in the sense Walser explicitly uses it and in its aesthetic meaning, sees (and sees through) the apparent disharmony of Walser's story.

As his narrative proceeds, it tends to become more and more chaotic; sections become shorter and more diffuse, the changes between them more abrupt. Consequently, the reader may have need of his own "map" if he is to succeed where, temporarily at least, Walser has failed: "After Nietzsche, as the wag said, there *had* to be Walser", (italics added). If the modern map which shows "inconcinnity" and the map of antiquity which Walser kept in his room are both useless, what way out of the chaos is there? Perhaps Walser's fellow balloonist, the German neo-Kantian Ernst Cassirer, offers the most plausible solution: "The animal man," he says, "is a chiasmus of complementary and contradictory functions." He combines "the hysteria of the monkey" and "the level intellect of an English explorer," "irrational faith" and "faithless reason." In *An Essay on Man* (1944), Cassirer claims that in his symbols "Man discovers and proves a new power—the power to build up a world of his own, an ideal world"; he goes on to say, what man calls reality is actually a matter of those mental images he himself creates. As he tells Walser, their "Ballonfahrt" is the modern version of the epic journey, symbol of the collective unconscious; but "heroes in our day must take to the ice wastes of the poles, the depths of the sea, the air" because the hero's role and the very nature of heroism are no longer certain. Walser is especially uncertain about the nature of his own role: "All my rooms have been like this," he explains, "cramped cells for saint or criminal. Or patient." A similar ambivalence motivates the assassin of Walser's friend, Walther Rathenau (an industrialist and German cabinet minister who was killed in 1922): "*He was the finest man of our age, combining all that is most valuable of thought, honor, and spirit, and I couldn't bear it.*" Aloft in the balloon, Cassirer's voice fills "the emptiness of the wind" but unfortunately can be heard only in snatches. Cassirer propounds a philosophy which explains his and Walser's voyaging and which reconciles opposites; Walser, on the other hand, seems to succumb to the multiplicity of the world, to become a victim of randomness and of what Marshall McLuhan calls "information overload": "We are an animal that has been

told too much, we could have done with far less," Walser says.

Walser's rage against the explainers, especially his psychiatrists—"all my ideas are symptoms for you to diagnose. Your science is suspicion dressed in a tacky dignity"—is matched by his rage against the commercial spirit of the Twentieth Century. Walser's criticism of "this terrible age," his "silence," his confinement to an insane asylum (where he is visited by younger writers), and his fondness for Chinese poetry all suggest a likeness to Ezra Pound: both the Pound who once told Davenport, "Usury, I wish I had never heard the word," and the skilled craftsman who wrote to shore the fragments against our ruin, against the encroachment of the money-minded world. In this light, Walser takes on added stature, but of course Walser is *not* Pound. Walser once wrote a story which began, "Once upon a time, in a Swiss valley, there was born to an honest couple a baby that had a jack-o'-lantern for a head," a story he claims Kafka stole and rewrote as "The Metamorphosis"; he admits that Kafka "improved upon it." (Another of Walser's plagiarists is Thomas Mann, whose *The Magic Mountain* is an obvious source for Davenport's story.) Moreover, although the "paraphenomenalist" Walser can agree with the phenomenalist Ernst Mach that "the mind is what it knows! It is nothing else at all, at all" and with Heraklit's image of the river defining itself "by its flow," Walser's own mind remains extraordinarily troubled: all flow without any of the shaping coherence which characterizes Davenport's fiction. At least so it seems. However, whether Robert Walser is actually as powerless to order his life and the story of his life as he seems is not entirely certain.

"A Field of Snow on a Slope of the Rosenberg" may be construed as Davenport's parodic bow to Walser *or* as Walser's (perhaps mad) telling of his autobiography *or* as another of Walser's own fantastic and autobiographic fictions. Although he claims to have given up writing "because I had nothing at all, any more, to say," he nonetheless does address a reader directly on one occasion—"O Leser"—and does at times prove himself a quite self-conscious artist: "O Claribel, Claribel. No memory of her can elude for long our first *contretemps*. That is too bookish a word. Our wreck." Walser's comic sensibility further attests to his conscious artistry. He transforms a recollection from his student days at Herr Benjamenta's Institute for Butlers (the setting of Walser's novel, *Jakob von Gunten*) into an artfully controlled piece of slapstick and turns the illustration of "the waywardness of accidents" into an exemplum on the power of art to transcend such "waywardness." Walser also delights in puns: "The past . . . is the future. All that has mattered is a few moments, uncongenial while they happened, that turned to gold in the waves of time." For a man who rails against the money-worshipping world, the choice of "gold" here surely is no accident. The "silence" Walser speaks of refers literally to the quiet of his hospital setting; it also calls to mind Walser's literary silence, his Prufrock-like separation from his society, and too the general alienation of modern man from a natural world which he, unlike the Dogons, considers inanimate. Walser makes a more elaborate pun in his expression of the inevitable and comic rhythm of modern life: "One came to pieces. One used the very words. You had to pull yourself together again." In that he has suffered some sort of psychological breakdown (the actual Walser was diagnosed as schizoid), Walser can be said to have gone "to pieces." These pieces, however, also refer both to those fragments one ultimately "comes to" in the incoherent world of the Twentieth Century and to those autobiographical and literary fragments which comprise the substance of Walser's story: recollections from his life, episodes culled from his own writings and recalled as if they are autobiographically true, and even a fragment of an Egyptian poem (like Pound's "Papyrus"). Words are, in a sense, fragments, too—fragments to be "used" in order to make sentences (sense) and, further, to reconstitute one's world and one's self harmoniously. When early in the story Walser says, "This way. The bracken is very fine a little farther on. Trajectory is all," he literally seems to be addressing some unnamed visitor (perhaps the Swiss writer Carl Seelig, often a companion during Walser's twenty-three years at the Herisau sanitarium) whom he is leading along the "slope of the Rosenberg" where it is his custom to walk. Figuratively, however, Walser may be again addressing his "Leser," guiding his reader as best he can through his dense and convoluted tale to something "very fine a little farther on."

Walser knows where he wishes his "walk" to take him. "And of life," he points out, "we can ask but continuity. That, as I explain to my doctors, is my neurosis. I have been, I am, I shall be, for awhile, but off and on, like a firefly." Musonius makes a similar complaint: "I exist without continuity." Certainly, the reader may well say the same thing, overcome by Walser's confused ramblings. No matter how confusing the story may become, it remains a comic rendering of its disparate parts. We do not question here whether the randomness will add up to "caries or cabals," as in Pynchon's *V.,* nor worry whether Walser will metamorphose, like Gregor Samsa, into some monstrous vermin or, like Prufrock, into an insect "pinned and wriggling on the wall." Walser is a "firefly," fitfully illuminating his darkened world. Although he has lost track of time (he is unsure if the day is Christmas, the day the real-life Walser died), he has seen the tracks of a rabbit, a traditional symbol of rebirth. The rabbit is superior to man, Walser says, because it can think and live at the same time, thus achieving a balance which modern man does not have. In a sense, the difference between rabbit and man is the difference between the poetic and the prosaic, as Walser's choice of verbs implies: "He lasts, we wear. He leaps, we endure."

In his review of Richard Brautigan's *Trout Fishing in America,* Davenport makes a point of particular relevance to our understanding of Walser's character: "Mr. Brautigan locates his writing on the barricade which the sane mind maintains against the spiel and bilge, and here he cavorts with divine idiocy, thumbing his nose. But he makes it clear that at his immediate disposal is a fund of common sense he does not hesitate to bring into play." Whether Walser also possesses "a fund of common sense" is open to question; clearly, however, his creator, Guy Davenport, does. The fragmented structure of his stories and his translations of the literary fragments of Sappho and Ar-

chilochus should not in any way suggest his acceptance of the view held by one of Barthelme's narrators that "Fragments are the only forms I trust." As he has explained more than once:

> Fragments, when they are but motes (the unfinished works of a Spenser or a Michelangelo are a different matter), touch us as the baby glove of the pharoah that moved William Carlos Williams to tears, or the lock of Lucrezia Borgia's hair that drew Byron back day after day to gaze (and to steal one strand for Landor); they "brave time" with a mite's grasp, missing by a rotten piece of linen or a grammarian's inadvertent immortality the empty fame of the sirens' song.

Those fragments which make up **"A Field of Snow on a Slope of the Rosenberg"** are not, of course, the fragments of some now-lost poem. Rather, they are the shards which mirror the modern world's incoherence—fragments of a now-lost harmony which Robert Walser stubbornly and wisely continues to search out, first from his balloon and later from his slope. His balloon is, like da Vinci's bicycle, an appropriate metaphor for the imaginative spirit. Like an hourglass, it leaks sand and time; it rises, humorously enough, by virtue of its own hot air; it enables the writer Walser and the poetic philosopher Cassirer to see the "inconcinnity" of the world and at the same time to transcend that disorder, both literally and figuratively.

At one extreme of the American imaginative spirit, Davenport says, we have Walt Whitman with his vision of a coherent society and at the other "our anti-Whitman," Charles Olson—"a prophet crying bad weather ahead, and has the instruments to prove it." Davenport accepts Olson's pessimism but not to the point of allowing it to overwhelm his fiction. Rather, starting from Olson's distinction between history and "the dream of history; fact and interpreted fact, or fable," Davenport, writing his "*assemblages* of history and necessary fiction," sets himself the imposing task of re-imagining Whitman's vision—of remembering and filling in what history leaves out (thus the *necessary* fiction) and of using the imagination to counter and defeat the "constant and numbing dullness" of contemporary life. The same emphasis on the redemptive powers of the imagination Davenport also finds in the writings of Fourier:

> Charles Fourier, who thought civilization a mistake, said that man's first duty is to keep the Sacred Flame, which he understood to be both our kinship to God and those livelinesses of spirit man himself had invented—the dance, poetry, music, mathematics, communal genius like French cuisine, Cretan stubbornness, Scotch scepticism, Dutch housekeeping.

About Whitman's poetic use of Fourier's ideas and his attempt to close "the widening distance between poet and audience," Davenport has written approvingly. Elsewhere, however, he has remarked less than approvingly on the democratizing of literature and has shown that his own literary preferences generally run to such writers as Pound, Eliot, Stein, and Louis Zukofsky, the writer he has called "a poet's poet's poet" and to whom *Da Vinci's Bicycle* is dedicated. What attracts Davenport to Zukofsky is not simply his being "the most Apollonian of our writers" but that "his Apollo cavorts with Pan and Priapus." This same balance of playfulness and high craftsmanship characterizes Davenport's second book of fiction. In the earlier collection, *Tatlin!,* which also concerns the twin subjects of the aliveness of the past and the imaginative spirit, these two qualities are less fully realized. Its playfulness is outweighed by the author's skepticism about the uses to which man's imagination and inventions are put. Although the collection's six stories are all "*assemblages* of history and necessary fiction," in at least four the assembling itself seems to be the primary object. Compared to **"A Field of Snow on a Slope of the Rosenberg,"** the Poe-parody **"1830"** reads like a literary exercise; and in the long and repetitive **"The Dawn in Erewhon"** the language is occasionally lush to the point of bathos. Despite the mastery displayed in the title piece and the author's separately published explanation of the intricate ways in which he constructed each story and the collection as a whole, *Tatlin!* remains a less satisfying work than *Da Vinci's Bicycle* precisely because the playfulness and craftsmanship in the latter are more consistently developed in relation to the author's thematic purpose: imaginative redemption. The two qualities are as much the property of the stories' heroes as they are the stylistic characteristics of the book's author. They make plain that what heroes and author want is not some final absolute order (and certainly not disorder either): what they want is the chance to go on searching, imagining, inventing new forms ("*assemblages* of history and necessary fiction," for one), and rediscovering what has been forgotten (Walser, Musonius). Appropriately, we have this conclusion: at the end of the story that is at the end of the book, Robert Walser (the old) speaking from his sanitarium and Guy Davenport (the new) writing at his desk, merge into a single narrative voice: "But let us desist, lest quite by accident we be so unlucky as to put these things in order." Davenport's kind of intellectual play will never appeal to a wide audience, but it does establish his place among those modern writers he has called "foragers in the world of ideas, custodians of disciplines in thought and writing that have proved themselves vital to the best minds of the century."

Bruce Bawer (essay date 1984)

SOURCE: "Guy Davenport: Fiction à la Fourier," in his *Diminishing Fictions: Essays on the Modern American Novel and Its Critics,* Graywolf Press, 1988, pp. 234-45.

[*In the following essay, which was originally published in December 1984, Bawer discusses the influence of French social theorist Charles Fourier and American poet Ezra Pound on the inventive philosophy, language, and form of the stories in* Apples and Pears.]

It's hard, these days, not to be suspicious of experimental writing. So much of it seems to be produced by ego-happy no-talents whose main reasons for writing in an unorthodox manner are that (a) they are incapable of writing in the usual way, and (b) they know that it is a great deal easier to attract attention in some critical quarters by being different than by being good. So familiar is this phenomenon in the land of letters that when a genuinely gifted writer, having a very clear idea of what he is doing and why,

attempts to reach us by an unfamiliar route, we are often, understandably, less than willing to pack up our gear and meet him half-way. Guy Davenport is such a writer. *Apples and Pears* is his fourth volume of stories (the first three were *Tatlin!, Da Vinci's Bicycle,* and *Eclogues*), and he has yet to give us anything that an average contemporary reader would recognize as a conventional short story. Not for him the isolated incident, the limited setting and time frame, that have been the earmarks of the form since Edgar Allan Poe; not for him the deadeningly spare prose, the commonplace characters, and the no-ideas-but-in-things approach of the Bobbie Ann Masons and the Raymond Carvers. To Davenport—whose wide range of tastes and talents has been amply demonstrated by his poetry (*Flowers and Leaves*), classical translations (*Archilochos, Sappho, Alkman*), scholarly editions (*The Intelligence of Louis Agassiz*), and critical essays in literature, art, history, and philosophy (*The Geography of the Imagination*)—life is a banquet and most short-story readers are starving to death.

The typical Davenport story, then, is a smorgasbord of colorful people, intriguing ideas, and rich, resonant language (plus, quite often, striking illustrations by the author, who is, on top of everything else, a very gifted artist). In **"Tatlin!"**, Vladimir Yevgrafovich Tatlin, the Russian Constructivist artist, engineer, and theoretician, zips through the world of Nicholas II, the Revolution, Lenin, Stalin, *Kulturbolschewismus, la vie tzigane,* Chagall, Picasso (who tells him, "Plan nothing: make"), Diaghilev, Nijinsky, Jacques Lipchitz, Moholy-Nagy, and Juan Gris, making buildings and airplanes, painting with a "wild boldness [that] was a childhood, a drunkenness of style," and philosophizing ("Art must die and be reborn in everything"; "A house is a vocabulary. A city is a language"; "Cézanne + Lenin ⅔ Konstruktivizm"). In another story from *Tatlin!,* **"The Airplanes at Brescia,"** Kafka and Max and Otto Brod go to Brescia for an air show put on by Blériot and Curtiss, walk in the footsteps of Da Vinci, cross the paths of Puccini and a strange man who turns out to be Wittgenstein, and observe that modern ideas and inventions have made the world new again: "This new thought was naked and innocent; the world would wound it in time. . . . Did men know anything at all? Man was man's teacher. Anyone could see the circle in that." In **"The Haile Selassie Funeral Train,"** from *Da Vinci's Bicycle,* James Joyce (d. 1941) and Guillaume Apollinaire (d. 1918) ride the funeral train of the Ethiopian emperor (d. 1975); while the train takes them "down the boulevard Montparnasse, which was in Barcelona," they talk about man, war, art, God, energy, Ibsen, and Orpheus.

It should be clear by now that Davenport has tended to pluck his protagonists from the most rarefied purlieus of twentieth-century intellectual and cultural history. He is, needless to say, a foursquare modernist; more than that, he's a devout Poundian, whose first three volumes of stories—with their profusion of philosophical tidbits, cross-cultural references, dropped names, and foreign words—inevitably recall the *Cantos*. Davenport even embodies the same paradoxes as Ezra Pound. His obsession with ideas goes hand-in-hand with a profound suspicion of them

("The mind is a washout," says a Davenport character who seems to speak for her creator. "Only the soul counts. Only feeling"). And his flat-out antipathy for the twentieth century is more than balanced by an overweening enthusiasm for the thinkers and artists who have helped to define it.

Apples and Pears is, essentially, more of the same. It's a Poundian's paradise from the word go, borrowing its epigraph from Ezraphile Louis Zukofsky and the title of the first of its four stories, **"The Bowmen of Shu,"** from a poem by Pound ("The Song of the Bowmen of Shu" appears in *Cathay*). Perhaps no Davenport story is as purely Poundian as this one. It takes as its subject the life of the sculptor Henri Gaudier-Brzeska, Pound's friend and fellow Vorticist, who died in the First World War at the age of twenty-three and whose first biographer was *il miglior fabbro* himself. As Pound makes clear in *Gaudier-Brzeska*, he valued the young sculptor because he was an artist "as independent as the savage" who, like the Paleolithic cave painters, put instinct over reason every time. **"The Bowmen of the Shu"** reflects this view. Its form also owes a great deal to Pound's book, which is a grab bag of straight biography, anecdotal memoir, reprints of Gaudier-Brzeska's theoretical writings on art, the texts of his letters from the front, and photographs of his major works. **"The Bowmen of Shu"** is a disciple's distillation of all this—a *Canto*-like mosaic in words, illustrated by two Gaudier-Brzeska drawings and a dozen or so drawings by Davenport of Gaudier-Brzeska sculptures. It's as if Davenport has tried to put together the sort of thing Pound would have manufactured himself, had he chosen to memorialize his friend in a prose poem (which is what **"The Bowmen of Shu"** really is) rather than a book. Davenport aims, all at once, to convey the horror of the war in which Gaudier-Brzeska died, to persuade us of the astuteness of the man's artistic theories, and to give us a sense of the disparity between his humble origins and the glorious artistic and literary circles he ended up in. The result is a *tour de force* of compression. Davenport gives us forty-two paragraphs—none of which is connected by either time, setting, perspective, or logic to its neighbors, and many of which are only a line long—and in that confined space managers to carve a vivid word sculpture of his subject. In one paragraph, he has Gaudier-Brzeska describe the trenches ("white smoke and drizzle of sparks blowing across barbed wire in coils, the stink of cordite"); in another, he adumbrates the sculptor's relationship with Sophie Brzeska ("SOPHIE / All night by her bed, imploring her. It is revolting, unspiritual, she said"). Davenport drops every name remotely worth dropping (among them Flint, Hulme, Tancred, Mansfield, Jacob Epstein, Modigliani, and Lewis) and quotes every theoretical statement worth quoting—as, for example, these first few sentences of Gaudier-Brzeska's "Vortex" (originally published in *Blast*):

SCULPTURAL ENERGY IS THE MOUNTAIN

Sculptural feeling is the appreciation of masses in relation. Sculptural ability is the defining of these masses by planes. The Paleolithic Vortex resulted in the decoration of the Dordogne cav-

erns. Early stone-age man disputed the earth with animals.

The idea of the modern age as a return to the primitive—to the "Paleolithic Vortex"—is as central to Davenport's philosophy, and to **"The Bowmen of Shu,"** as it was to the art of Gaudier-Brzeska. Davenport's story is, in fact, perhaps best understood as presenting what is to its author an archetypal and profoundly ironic modern tragedy: namely, that Gaudier-Brzeska, an artist whose imagination has been liberated from convention by a Paleolithic Renaissance, is destroyed by a civilization that has, at the same time, abandoned its Victorian self-control and reverted to the instinctive savagery of primitive man. (As anthropologist Robert De Launay says to Gaudier-Brzeska in the trenches: "we are learning the Paleolithic in a way that was closed to us as *savant* and *sculpteur.*") When the penultimate paragraph of **"The Bowmen of Shu"** records Gaudier-Brzeska's death ("CORPORAL HENRI GAUDIER/Mort pour la Patrie. 4 Octobre 1891 - 5 Juin 1915"), the lesson we are supposed to take away with us is, manifestly, that life in this century is as ugly as its art is beautiful. If *Apples and Pears* is, in a sense, a one-man symposium on the problems and promise of the twentieth century, **"The Bowmen of the Shu"** is a clever and concise keynote address.

The forty-two views of Gaudier-Brzeska are succeeded by **"Fifty-seven Views of Fujiyama,"** whose title recalls Wallace Stevens's "Fourteen Ways of Looking at a Blackbird." Like Stevens's poem, Davenport's story—composed of fifty-seven long, unlinked paragraphs—is something of an exercise in perspective. The odd-numbered paragraphs constitute the first-person account of a journey to the north of Japan by the late-seventeenth-century poet Matsuo Bashō, and are based on Bashō's own writings. During the course of his travels, Bashō observes, communes with, and writes poems about nature—sometimes in the company of the fellow poets whom he meets along the way:

> In Obanazawa I visited the merchant poet Seifu, who had often stopped on business trips to see me in Edo. He was full of sympathy for our hard way across the mountains, and made up for it with splendid hospitality. Sora was entranced by the silk worm nurseries, and wrote: *Come out, toad, and let me see you: I hear your got-a-duck got-a-duck under the silkworm house.* And: *The silkworm workers are dressed like ancient gods.* We climbed to the quiet temple of Ryushakuji, famous for being in so remote and peaceful a site. The late afternoon sun was still on it, and on the great rocks around it, when we arrived, and shone golden in the oaks and pines that have stood there for hundreds of years. The very ground seemed to be eternity, a velvet of moss. I felt the holiness of the place in my bones; my spirit partook of it with each bow that I made to the shrine in the silent rocks. *Silence as whole as time. The only sound is crickets.*

Remote, peaceful, silent, holy: this is the world of Bashō as described in the odd-numbered paragraphs of **"Fifty-seven Views of Fujiyama."**

The even-numbered paragraphs are a more complicated proposition. Some of them form the first-person account of a contemporary American male who goes hiking in the Vermont woods with a seventeen-year-old girl, "with no purpose but to be in the wilderness, to be in its silence, to be together deep among its trees and valleys and heights." But things don't go well. He sees a mill that turns out not to be there; they lose the trail, stray into a swamp, get cold, hurt, and upset; and when they skinny-dip in the shallows of a brackish lake, they are intruded upon by a Boy Scout leader with "a Biblical air." Some of the even-numbered paragraphs describe what appear to be the same man's encounters with various noteworthy survivors of the modernist period, notably Ezra Pound (an extremely similar account appears in "Ithaka," a story in *Da Vinci's Bicycle*); some paragraphs describe his trip (in the company of a number of bourgeois tourists) to historic sights in Greece; and a couple of paragraphs constitute cut-and-dried textbook descriptions of the provenance of various species of plants:

> *Sequoia Langsdorfii* is found in the Cretaceous of both British Columbia and Greenland, and *Gingko polymorpha* in the former of these localities. *Cinnamomum Scheuchzeri* occurs in the Dakota group of Western Kansas as well as Fort Ellis. . . . *Cinnamomum Sezannense,* of the Paleocene of Sezanne and Gelinden, was found by Heer, not only in the upper Cretaceous of Patoot, but in the Cenomanian of Atane, in Greenland. . . .

The point of this inventive (though surprisingly unanimated) fugue seems to be that whereas Bashō, in his time and place, could perfectly and harmoniously integrate the roles of historian, wayfarer, poet, and naturalist, contemporary Western man suffers from a dissociated sensibility; the way our society is structured, and the way we have been taught to think and behave, make it impossible for us to bring the disparate elements of our lives into a happy conjunction, and to experience the natural world, in all its manifestations, as fully as possible. This is, as I say, what Davenport *wants* us to get out of the story. The actual effect of "Fifty-seven Views of Fujiyama" is something else again. The Bashō sections, which at first seem to possess a luminous and fragile beauty, soon begin to sound mechanical and monotonous, and eventually evoke a picture of medieval Japanese life and poetry that is, alas, so numbingly dull that, at the end of the exercise, one is almost inclined to fall to one's knees and thank God for being born in the Atomic Age. This is, one can be sure, not quite what Davenport had in mind.

"The Chair" is the shortest and slightest story in *Apples and Pears,* and the only one in which the paragraphs cohere throughout in the manner most of us are used to. It describes an encounter at Marienbad between Franz Kafka and the Rebbe from Belz, and seems to have been written so that Davenport could ask, "Who will write the history of affection?" (answer: *he* will, in the following story), and so that Kafka, at the end, could offer up a prayer to God, acknowledging that it is "absurd . . . for one insignificant creature to cry that it is alive, and does not want to be hurled into the dark along with the lost.

It is the life in me that speaks, not me, though I speak with it, selfishly, in its ridiculous longing to stay alive, and partake of the presumptuous joy in being." Modern literature as a cry of life, an assertion of the joy in being: this is the perfect note for Davenport to strike at this point in *Apples and Pears.*

For the next (and last) item in the book is the novel-length "Apples and Pears," which is by far Davenport's longest work of fiction and arguably his most ambitious and adventurous exploration ever of life, art, thought, and affection in the twentieth century. To a large extent, the purpose of the three stories that precede "Apples and Pears," is simply to prepare us for it. If "The Bowmen of Shu" means to remind us what this cruel, primitive century is capable of doing to brilliant, primitive modern artists, "Apples and Pears," set in 1981, presents us with a young artist named Alexander Floris who is as primitive and modern as Gaudier-Brzeska but who, unlike that painter who died "pour la Patrie" in World War I, rejects the world and its alarms entirely and finds thereby a happy, fulfilling life. If "Fifty-seven Views of Fujiyama" implies that the contemporary Western sensibility is a shattered one, "Apples and Pears" purports to depict some contemporary Western Europeans who recover for themselves the simple, natural harmony that Bashō knew. And if "The Chair" describes the desperate desire of Franz Kafka, that prototype of the tortured modern mind, to "partake of the presumptuous joy in being," "Apples and Pears" seeks to show a group of modern types partaking, *Angst*-free, of all that life has to offer.

The subtitle of "Apples and Pears" is "Het Erewhonisch Schetsboek, Messidor-Vendémiaire 1981." According to a copyright notice in the front of *Tatlin!*, *Het Erewhonisch Schetsboek* is the title of a book by one Adriaan van Hovendaal from which parts of Davenport's story "The Dawn in Erewhon" (published in *Tatlin!*) are derived. Some of the characters of that story, set in the 1950s, reappear in "Apples and Pears," and there's no indication whether, and to what degree, the characters and situations described in "Apples and Pears" are actually taken from the works of van Hovendaal. At any rate, the story does, as the subtitle suggests, take the form of the diary-*cum*-notebook of van Hovendaal, a middle-aged Dutch philosopher, who describes therein his "complex friendship" with the aforementioned Alexander Floris, a nineteen-year-old Dutch painter whose serenity, sensitivity, sensuality, and lack of inhibition are all equally remarkable, and whom Adriaan has apparently helped, over the past couple of years, to educate and civilize. Like Gaudier-Brzeska, Sander (as the young painter is called) is a born savage who puts instinct over reason ("All I'm doing, Adriaan, is what I know how to do. I don't know what it means"). He and his sister Grietje are lovers, and Adriaan makes love to both of them, sometimes one at a time, sometimes *à trois.* After a brief ramble through Paris and an interval on an idyllic island, the three of them move into a cheerful, unpretentious little house in Amsterdam that they name Florishaus, and there they live a simple, natural life full of affection, creation, and contemplation. And that's about it. What action there is in the 240-page story consists largely of the comings and goings of the various members of the supporting cast, which includes: (a) two pubescent boys, Hans (Adriaan's nephew) and Jan, who are in love with each other and who (when they are not modeling nude for Sander) couple endlessly; (b) Joris Oudveld, a bashful eighteen-year-old German Lenin groupie (he kisses his bust of Vladimir Ilyich when he leaves his room) who thinks of his "hankering to hug gossoons" (i. e., young boys) as a form of Marxist rebellion; (c) Olaf, also eighteen, a Danish gymnast who runs a YMCA-like "wolfden" in Copenhagen where pubescent lads make love to each other (and to him); (d) Godfried Strodekker, "chairman of the Nederlands Student en Arbeiterverbond voor Pedofilie," who gives closely argued lectures on pederasty; (e) Sweetbriar, an English philosopher; and (f) Wolfgang, a little street orphan whom Adriaan takes into Florishaus as Sander's assistant and (eventually) lovemate.

Depraved? Well, yes. But Davenport doesn't mean it to come off that way. On the contrary, he wants us to be enchanted—and, to a remarkable degree, he succeeds. Though a synopsis may make **"Apples and Pears"** sound like a low-budget pornographic movie, the story is actually quite reminiscent of pastoral poetry. Like the shepherds in Theocritus and Virgil, Davenport's characters are impossibly good, happy, and affectionate, and they live (for the most part) in a world that is impossibly lovely, tranquil, and timeless. For them, there are no taboos—they feel affection for one another, and sex (whether with man or woman, child or sibling) is their way of expressing it. Might such indiscriminate carrying-on be wrong? The question arises only fleetingly. "Why must we try to figure out why we're hugging anybody . . . ?" asks Grietje. "Love is love." "Human affinities," says Olaf, "come from any direction. My *slubberter* here are after affection one way or another, and are also heroically generous in giving it. Their puppy longing to hug and lie close is as God intended." Simple as that.

In **"Apples and Pears,"** nobody feels hurt or jealous or guilty; nobody's being abused or psychologically damaged, nobody's in danger of contracting a social disease; there's no real conflict, no significant threat at any point to anybody, no substantial changes from day to day, no money worries, no authorities from the child protection bureau knocking at the door (though Grietje does mention this possibility at one point). Even Hans's and Jan's parents, liberal-minded folk that they are, are amenable to the exceptional goings-on at Florishaus. None of it, of course, is believable; but we believe. Davenport, magician that he is, *makes* us believe in (and even cherish) this bucolic never-never-land where everyone is innately good, no one does anyone harm, and love conquers all.

"Apples and Pears," then, is about the human race not as we know it, but as Davenport would like it to be. His vision derives largely from the work of a man whom he has called "the only philosopher of happiness," the French philosopher François Marie Charles Fourier (1772-1837), to whom *Apples and Pears* is dedicated and whose presence in it is even stronger than that of Ezra Pound. Indeed, after lurking in the background of Davenport's previous books of fiction, Fourier, with *Apples and Pears,* takes

center stage in Davenport's fiction. This is not to say that Davenport takes Fourier's philosophy seriously *qua* philosophy. Like his character Sander, he thinks of Fourier as "a sweet idiot," and considers his sincere proposals for the alteration of human society to be utterly impracticable, but "is nevertheless taken with the vision." The vision in question (which Fourier spent most of his life constructing) was of a utopia called Harmonium, where man's natural virtue (as posited by Rousseau, and believed in devoutly by Fourier) would, through the elimination of the tensions that destroy human society, be permitted to prevail, and where, as a result, everyone would live in peace, happiness, and harmony. And how would those destructive tensions be eliminated? Sex. Fourier felt, you see, that if we took the fetters off our various passions—sexual attraction being the primary one—and indulged them fully, all those tensions would vanish and life would be a dream. In short, as Davenport observes in **"The Dawn in Erewhon,"** Fourier felt the answer to mankind's problem was "a life that would cooperate with the instincts rather than deplore them." To this end, Fourier urged the establishment of "phalansteries," communities that would constitute a sort of proving ground for Harmonium. And this, more or less, is the idea in **"Apples and Pears."** Though nobody in the story ever quite says so, Florishaus (whose residents aim for "society as poetry rather than the newspaper prose of history") is to all intents and purposes a Fourieristic phalanstery.

But Fourier is not the only utopian in the picture. The names of Samuel Butler and his novel *Erewhon* crop up frequently in **"Apples and Pears,"** and with good reason; for like the Erewhonians, Davenport's people detest machines, which more than anything else have made the twentieth century what it is. "Butler's insight," notes Adriaan, "was that the machine enslaved us, changing all work to drudgery. All work became pandering to the reproduction of the machines." He reflects

> that no phalanstery anything like Fourier's is possible without an Erewhonian revolution, canceling machines. To return movement to walking, horseback riding, and the true dance. To return music to the instrument and occasion. To return love to passion as it arises. To return work to communal duty, to the sense of usefulness. To have the beginning and end of everything kept in sight and in the discourse of the whole phalanstery. To take happiness from money and restore it to the harmony of work and its reward, ambition and its achievement. To put mind and hand in concert. To reorganize society after its disastrous dispersal by train, automobile, airplane. . . .

There's another thing the characters in **"Apples and Pears"** share with the Erewhonians: they're extremely attractive and well-bred, and have a nearly Nazistic regard for youth, strength, and beauty. This regard, as it happens, is as much Fourieristic as it is Erewhonian. "Physique is character," which might well have been a Hitler Youth slogan, is a Fourieristic principle quoted in **"Apples and Pears."**

As should be clear by now, **"Apples and Pears"** is only

partly narrative. Though constructed chronologically, it is formally similar to **"The Bowmen of Shu,"** with its mosaic of disconnected paragraphs that jump from narration to reflection to recondite quotation. Within a single diary entry, Adriaan is likely not only to tell us what he and Sander did, discussed, and ate today, but to quote passages (from a variety of poets, biologists, philosophers, and the like) that apparently strike him as affirming some tenet or other of Fourierist doctrine, and to recite chunks of grand-sounding gibberish (for example, about a parade of *chérubins et chérubines* and *séraphins et séraphines*) that don't even begin to make sense unless one is familiar with Fourier's complicated and bizarre blueprints for Harmonium. There is the usual Davenport-manteau of dropped names (e. g., Poussin, Picasso, Proust, Stravinsky, Satie, Schiele), but there are some unfamiliar names too. As if to emphasize that his story does not take place in the real world (as well as to acknowledge the story's indebtedness to a philosopher who lived during the Napoleonic new order), Davenport has Adriaan give dates according to the Napoleonic calendar; thus **"Apples and Pears,"** set in summer and autumn, takes us through the months of Messidor, Thermidor, Fructidor, and Vendémiaire. Davenport's elegant, accomplished illustrations—which capture the story's exuberant and innocent sensuality in styles based variously on the Greek *kouroi,* Athenian vase paintings, and the works of Mondrian, Picasso, Braque, and other modern artists—similarly underscore the otherworldliness of the story's "elemental, clear joy." And Davenport's offbeat diction serves much the same purpose; when he is not using strange English words (such as *snurf, snurp, nicker, fritz, thrip, quiddit,* and *tallywhacker*), he is using Dutch words—most of them, fortunately, cognates (*erotisch, kameraad, puberteit*)—or dipping into French, German, Danish, Latin, or Greek. Often these deviations in diction occur when the subject is sex. Hence, Davenport describes Jan and Hans as "wucking and snuffling," and has one boy entice the other to disrobe by saying, "Come on, *vriendje . . . poedelnaakt* like me."

Which brings us to the major problem with **"Apples and Pears"**: namely, that every so often it stops being a lyrical portrait of an otherworldly world ruled by affection and becomes—well, something else.

Sometimes, for instance, affection steals away into the background, leaving behind nothing but sex, sex, sex. At such moments, Davenport—as in some of his earlier stories—is likely to break into detailed descriptions of the male sex organ (for which he has more names, in English *and* Dutch, than the Eskimos have for snow) or of the extremely skimpy briefs and swim trunks that are the subjects of many of his illustrations (boxer shorts, like machines, seem to be *défendu* in Davenportland). At other times, more disturbingly, Davenport injects politics into his pastoral, apparently taking seriously his characters' beliefs that a universal "faith in good will" can be substituted "for the Capitalist assumption that all exchanges are of something for money"; that it is possible "to breed meanness out of human nature" simply by taking the world economy "from the greed of merchants and the vicious manipulation of the stock market and put[ting it] into the care of children on ponies"; and that Western so-

ciety's refusal to allow children "erotic affection and a fully sensual life is an injustice too long imposed by puritanical prejudices, ignorance, and the narrowness of bourgeois propriety." Such silly rhetoric is hardly new to Davenport's fiction; like Pound, he has always tended to blame certain failings of human nature on Western democracy.

And that's a shame. But, as with Pound, the perverseness of Davenport's politics in no way negates the value of his work or the significance of his contribution to American literature. And make no mistake about it, that contribution is considerable. At a time in history when the prime criterion of excellence in American short fiction seems to be a sort of mindless, impersonal monotonousness, Guy Davenport's inimitable adventures in the realms of philosophy, language, and literary form are to be treasured. Davenport at his best reminds us how exciting and valuable literary innovation can be. And he does something else that is even more important: he reminds us of our humanity, and (however bizarrely) of the importance of affection. Dostoevsky, it is said, found Fourier's social program ridiculous, but praised him nonetheless for his obvious "love of humanity." He might well, one thinks, have done the same for Davenport.

Alain Arias-Mission   (essay date 1986)

SOURCE: "Erotic Ear, Amoral Eye," in *Chicago Review,* Vol. 35, No. 3, Spring, 1986, pp. 66-71.

[*In the following essay, Arias-Misson discusses the stories of* Apples and Pears, *noting that Davenport fails to maintain a mythical purity in the eroticism of the title story because "the weight of its utopian didactics bursts the elasticity of its fiction."*]

Erotic Ear

The eleventh century *jongleur* Raimbaut d'Orange said of his song, "I pensively interlace rare, sombre and colored words," (poets, jugglers and acrobats were close cousins in those richly inventive days)—all of which might be said of Guy Davenport. The question one asks is: will he be able to keep this miraculous juggling act up in the air?

Guy Davenport's reputation as inventor of a dazzling and disconcerting "philosophical" story-form and as wielder of the wickedest chisel in American prose, uncannily able to whorl anything—apple or pear or human gesture—out of midair has been made in his previous collections, *Eclogues, Da Vinci's Bicycle* and *Tatlin!* This poetic gift and the intellectual ozone in which his world swims blur the edges of story with essay and poem (for example when we eavesdrop on Ernst Mach telling a whimsical anecdote of Henry James, or watch with delight, through Stanley Spencer's modelling eye, the airy carnival of the Henley Regatta in *Eclogues*), and similarly his sparkling essays in *The Geography of the Imagination* exchange fire—its light, not heat—with the imagination of fiction.

In *Apples and Pears* the stories are put together out of visually detached paragraph blocks, except for the telegraphically brief **"The Chair"**—a marvel of economy and wit worthy of Kafka's letter to Max Brod, which it retraces; more accurately which it tracks as tightly as a bloodhound's nose to a warm trail, as most of the letter is absorbed into his story. Kafka described his outing with the Rebbe of Belz, an eccentric and charming "wise man" of his day, and Davenport has "illuminated" this encounter with deft verbal strokes of Dufyesque color and characterizations of a fluid line comparable to the marginal *drôleries* of mediaeval manuscripts. While he has added light and flesh to this epistolary skeleton of Kafka, the latter has no doubt molded Davenport's usual paragraph-assemblages into his own irresistible structure. A tour de force—hats off!

In **"The Bowmen of Shu"** the plasticity of its paragraphic blocks marks a more characteristic style: a life of Gaudier-Brzeska, sculptor and admired friend of Ezra Pound, is cut, chipped, picked out of (what is the most vigorous verb? Gaudier-Brzeska muses at one point—"The chisel does not cut the stone . . . It bites.") the blocks—his letters from the French front 1914-15, the primitive dynamics of his sculpture, a passionately "spiritual" marriage to an erratic runaway Polish spinster twice his age, camaraderie with "Ezra cutting his wicked eye at me from his Villon face . . . with the godlike poet Brooke and the catatonically serious Middleton Murry," his school-days wrapped in the drawings of birds and insects, finally death at age 23 in a courageous assault on the German "Labyrinth" near Souchez—in an order of neither logic nor time but the spatial. "Planes, the surfaces of mass, meet at lines each tilted at a different angle to light. The mass is energy. The harmony of its surfaces the emotion ever contained, ever released" we read of his "Font de Gaumes." This story is a sculptured self-portrait of Gaudier-Brzeska, illuminated as the paragraphs meet and tilt like the planes of his own sculpture, because the language has depth, mass: Davenport's textual images are so honed, so whistle-clean, ultra-vivid that they seem scooped out of three-dimensional space; it's as if he wears his eyeballs on his fingertips. The quasi-visionary intensity of the language owes its hypersensitive tactility, glow, to the plumbline he has dropped into the primary medium of language: sound. To the flattening cinematic eye of most contemporary fiction and its resultant evanescence, instability, of the word, he opposes an "ear of the imagination," a language of unheard-of phonetic densities.

"Fifty-seven Views of Fujiyama" braids half a dozen narrative sequences or miniature stories out of its 57 paragraphs: the central braid is a poetic journey recounted by Basho and, strung along it like pearls his haiku; an arduous camping trip by a man and his younger girl-companion along the Vermont Trail, close to the ground, damp with vegetation and love-making; technical meditations on botany which chime unaccountably like poems; a waggish voyage down the Adriatic on the deck of the Kriti with "two Parisian typists of witty comeliness; two German cyclists blond, brown and obsequious; a trio of English consisting of a psychiatrist and her two lovers, one an Oxford undergraduate, the other the Liberal Member from Bath; and a seasoned traveler from Alton, Illinois, a Mrs. Brown," since all the cabins have been taken by the Mexican Rotary and their wives, etc. . . . These self-contained sequences alternate, shift and whirl by one another in some dervish logic about the mysterious Totum

of a never-glimpsed Fujiyama. Unlike a similar braiding technique of Cortázar, whose story-telling spell-binds one narrative sequence with the other until at some unobservable moment of magic, hand quicker than eye, the one is merged into the other. Davenport shuns any narcosis of the irrational, preserves the separateness of each event in pellucid arrested flight, holds them up before the eye as objects for intellectual delight, aesthetic contemplation. Davenport might be said to be an analogical, Cortázar a metaphorical writer. The reader is caught in, seduced by, the latter's fiction, a victim like his characters; with the former the reader must become active collaborator, an intellectual energy is needed to correlate these juxtaposed objects, to tie the knots of their contiguities.

Objecthood, this substantiality of Davenport's writing, is everywhere apparent, a fiction of *nouns,* while most contemporary writing is all verb, event as verb not noun, collecting no moss of existence, pure transiency. The molecule of his writing is the string of nouns one often encounters: "Tulip, drum, camel, ladybug, glass-blowing, genial arrogance, Rubens, purple, eroticism as gourmandise, zamindari, the Caliphate of the Ummayads, Haroun al-Raschid," taken at random. The DNA of his entire book, its genetic braiding, may be glimpsed here: an energy of images produced by their bright collisions and disjunctions, their subtle progression signalled by the phonetic transformations, from the posed, quiet beat of "tulip, drum, camel" through the slowly accumulating gutturals and nasals to the grand flourish of "Haroun al-Raschid," with all the inevitability of a miniature Ravellian bolero crescendo; a *semantic* music of course as the sound of words is inextricably meshed with the image.

If the fourth and title-story, **"Apples and Pears,"** were the whole book instead of four-fifths of it, *Apples and Pears* might well be the most controversial of the season; or is that an overestimate of the contemporary moral sensibility? Not because it is a bad boy book nose-thumbed at the *epaté* bourgeois—ever since supermarkets began carrying housewives' glandular gothic compared with which *Ulysses* pales, the scandal tactic won't work; but precisely because in the light of its contents it is read as a book of the good and wise children: sunlit terraces of the platonic mind, serene landscape touched with prophetic aura.

Adriaan, a very hip Dutch philosopher (from whom nothing will elicit more than an amused eyebrow), narrates largely through his journal notes (labelled Messidor, Thermidor, Fructidor, the fruitful months of the French Revolution) on the tiny, windswept, butlerian island of Erewhon, settled with his now 19-year-old protégé Sander; Sander's sister and lover, Grietje; assorted friends; and abandoned children—a settling unsettling in some ways described in Davenport's previous [collection], *Eclogues,* as well as in journal notes labelled there in the seeding and sprouting months (appropriately, as a lot of both went on). Having done a Doolittle on and civilized Sander (former street urchin, wildly debauched, now domesticated-debauched), Adriaan discovers his artistic talents, orients him toward a vocation, and organizes the erotically enthusiastic band into a microscopic Fourierist society, putting the 18th century philosopher's principles into pandemonic practice. Scenes of painterly sittings (huggings, coucheries, 69 *quoi*!) are stitched in with others of giddy domestic alarum, and philosophical musings on almost everything from Picasso to pears and paedophilia alternate with sexual embraces of the minutest detail. Through it all a thread is drawn out of Fourier's utopian wet-dream swarming with his childish hordes, which invade the serenity of these pages mounted on their quaggas (I didn't know either) and organized in phalanxes of love, dream-episodes which are the most fictive-electric of the book. If the three adults, Adriaan, Sander and Grietje are the ostensible principals, the real actors are the children: Hansje and Jantje (charter members of the Greater Amsterdam Erewhonian Society), Saartje, Jenny, Jaap, Wolfje, Edvard, Jens, Peter, Ulrik etc., endless little boys mostly, entwined in bunches like 19th century puffy-cheeked plaster-of-paris cherubim—only here in the viscous entanglements of a 20th century paradise gone mad: encouraged in libidinous relations by the avuncular philosopher and progressive paedophilic "wolfden" leaders, the kiddies are lovingly observed, fondled and masturbated but not abused (?) by the adult men.

"**Apples and Pears**" is erotic but not puffed up by the pornographer's detached retina which produces a manipulated object "out there"; Davenport sees—with an erotic ear; the eye is sucked into the fleshy resonance of the word. He assembles the sonorous equivalent of erotic acts: delicate consonantal muscle ripples out with the milk of English vowels; Dutch words liberally sprinkled throughout the text exhibit a guttural, fricative, hairy sex: the words' sound adheres elastically to the contour of the thing. Paradoxically just as this vigorous and connubial language evokes the flesh, in the next moment it deflects the prurient attention back to its own phonetic weight, bounce and juiciness—a *jouissance* of language which substitutes for the erotic object. Paragraphs cataloguing the local, exotic, savory names of pears, for example, yield . . . an orgasm of pears.

Amoral Eye

As hyperreal reading of a purely possible—hence unreal—world, what is morally unacceptable becomes a dream beating against the limits of reality. "In our time we long not for a lost past but a lost future," writes Adriaan. But this future and that past revolve in mythic time: time made present, circularity made its shape, periodicity and repetition its unceasing tides. The temporal axis of "**Apples and Pears**" is, we have seen, a mythical calendar (seeding and germination in *Eclogues*)—fruition and harvest: "apple" and "pear" are a literalized myth of sacred time.

As Davenport determines a physicality like that of painting and sculpture—what is "**Apples and Pears**" if not a gallery of (erotic) still lifes? —for his fiction, so he reclaims a myth-making role in the visionary presence of his world. More intimately: against the demythification of the language of contemporary fiction, the void in which its words spin, the game it plays in the arbitrary emptiness between signifier and signified, Davenport appears to have recovered a third dimension of the word in the thickness of its phonetic material: *la Parole retrouvée.* He has invented a (story-) telling (all telling, no story): this telling is the con-

dition of myth, told face to face; the sauce in which "**Apples and Pears**" is cooked is *de la Parole.* Why (story)? Because myth is not fiction; when myth becomes a good story it is no longer myth.

Now myth—*pace* John Gardner—is not moralist; the descriptive and the normative are blurred: hierophany. Only remember the soap-opera treacheries of the Greek gods versus the moral depths of an *Antigone,* torn apart by the contradictions of the *polis.* The ecstatic sexuality of "**Apples and Pears**" never rubs against the real world. Its hypertensity is in the manner of the sacred: eroticism of little boys and temple prostitution; child sexuality emblematic of a prelapsarian (or superpostlapsarian!) innocence. One suspects the sensualist and rationalist ("Romanticism must die or day-dreaming will drown us all in a great muck") Adriaan of a touch of *Schwärmerei*; apple is incarnation and pear resurrection for instance, biblical references not infrequent: in the volcanic eruptions of Holy Ghost freedom in the third century AD (the Adamites, their cult of nakedness, and a return to innocence) and often thereafter one also catches a whiff of debauchery mingled with the odour of sanctity. Has the Socratic ratio of *Eclogues* tipped here into a gnosis beyond good and evil? "See, understand, enjoy," says the initiate.

Above, the erotic embrace of a tactile language with the world and the flesh was seen to reverse into a copulation of word with word. The iconicity of the word—that is, the exact shape and fit of signifier with signified—is so exacerbated that *Parole* collapses or is inverted in on itself. "The romping in bed is all symbol," says the philosopher Adriaan, "sex is a sublimation, not things of sex." For this to be true, sex must finally be language. Now we see the whole "Harmonium," the future-myth of "**Apples and Pears**," float up into the metonym of the "story" (metonym as "no order except in this reduced aesthetic object"); "**Apples and Pears**" becomes the sole locus of the myth; a small explosion, and dematerialization ensues as thorough as any "self-referential" novel.

If Davenport had been able to maintain the mythical purity of Erewhon and the New Harmony he might have succeeded in an impossible juggling act. But the "future" holds a utopia which after all yields a programmatic pressure which cracks the cloudless aesthetic microcosm. It is not true that his world never rubs against the other, real one. Once, an oblique glancing blow is struck: the leader of a Danish paedophilic society declares with moral outrage that in the repressive United States a man can be punished with 30 years for "loving a boy," and only six for killing him by drunken driving; his public (mostly children) murmurs in sympathetic outrage. For an instant, a wound is opened in reality—one million children a year exploited by pornography, tens of thousands abused, raped and murdered. When the progressive Dokter Groenvink speaks of "security, reciprocity, moral awareness, giving and taking, erotic sophistication" regarding paedophilia, the polysyllabics ring hollow, and the erudite solicitude of kindly Dutch, Danish and German progressives for the little boys who live "in a moral concentration camp," not "free to love or be loved," specious. It is this programmatic bias of the novella which thins out the fictive atmosphere; the miraculous equilibrium of philosophy and fiction, poetry and prose, comes tumbling through in a scintillation of words. The vision fails, not because the supramundane, luminous language is inadequate, but because the (a)moral weight of its utopian didactics bursts the elasticity of its fiction. Intromission of the adult eye shatters the truly mythical crystal-world of childish sexuality. Still, a sort of innocence hovers about these Danish professors and Dutch philosophers. One recalls the wistful (and frustrated) photographic caress of Lewis Carroll's little girls and of that philosopher's impossible voyage through their looking-glass.

Lance Olsen   (essay date 1986)

SOURCE: "A Guydebook to the Last Modernist: Davenport on Davenport and *Da Vinci's Bicycle*," in *The Journal of Narrative Technique,* Vol. 16, No. 2, Spring, 1986, pp. 148-61.

[*In the following essay, Olsen asserts that the stories in* Da Vinci's Bicycle *adhere to the definition of modernist fiction that Davenport puts forth in his essay collection* The Geography of the Imagination.]

For Guy Davenport—whom he told me John Barth once called the last modernist—modernism is "a renaissance of the archaic." In other words, it is the ancient fertility myths underlying *The Waste Land,* T. E. Hulme's imagist insistence on "classical" hard, clear, precise poetry, Picasso's use of the cave paintings at Altamira. It is also Gertrude Stein's cutting "her hair short to look like a Roman emperor and to be modern" (*Da Vinci's Bicycle*), Joyce's basing *Ulysses* on Homeric structures and exploring the origin of Indo-European languages in *Finnegans Wake,* Olson's use of the epsilon on the omphalos stone at Delphi in "The Kingfishers." It is even the echo of Democritus in Niels Bohr and Heraclitus in Ludwig Wittgenstein.

Modernism, again according to Davenport [in *The Geography of the Imagination*], was a renaissance that began around 1910 and which was over by 1916 because of World War I which had "blighted" a cultural rebirth "as brilliant as any in history." Except for those who were at that time already modernists moving toward full maturity (Joyce, Pound, Eliot, and so on), the twentieth century ended before its second decade was done. By implication, what has come to be called postmodernism is the failure of the renaissance in our century. And for Davenport *postmodernism* is a particularly apt term since it refers to a between-times, a lack of clear purpose, perhaps even a return to a kind of barbarity: "Olson's *Maximus* and Zukofsky's 'A' are too symbolically and verbally complex, respectively, to command large audiences especially in an age when a college degree is becoming a certificate of illiteracy." Like Yeats, Davenport believes "we do not. . . . live in an epoch; we live between epochs." We have "let the fire die in the engine" (*Da Vinci's Bicycle*). He would probably agree, then, with George Steiner, who argues [in *Language and Silence: Essays on Language Literature and the Inhuman*] that with postmodernism

> the house of classic humanism, the dream of reason which animated Western society, have largely broken down. Ideas of cultural development, of inherent rationality held since ancient Greece and still intensely valid in the utopian historicism of Marx and the stoic authoritarianism of Freud (both of them late outriders of Greco-Roman civilization) can no longer be asserted with much confidence.

Another way of discussing this distinction between the modern and the postmodern is to employ Jean-François Lyotard's definitions [in *The Postmodern Condition: A Report on Knowledge*]. For him the former is that which "legitimates itself with reference to a metadiscourse . . . making an explicit appeal to some grand narrative, such as the dialectics of Spirit, the hermeneutics of meaning, the emancipation of the rational or working subject, or the creation of wealth." The latter, on the other hand, harbors an "incredulity toward metanarratives. . . . The narrative function is losing its functors, its great hero, its great dangers, its great voyages, its great goal." That is, the modern appeals to a metanarrative that binds the universe together, a metatext that tells the story about knowledge and culture. The postmodern, however, does not appeal to such a metanarrative. Here the metatext can no longer serve as a unifying force. Rather, with postmodernism the universe has become one of micronarratives, plurisignification, intertextuality striving against unification. The modern mind believes in what I shall call the transcendental signified—some ultimate realm of truth, some eventual coherence, some *over there* that in the end helps define, articulate, unify and make intelligible the *here*. For example, the surrealist mind (Breton, Dali, Aragon) strives toward a transcendent area that is somehow deeper and richer, more in tune with our fundamental principles, than this one. Joyce believes in the omnipotence of language to order existence, Stevens in the Supreme Fiction, Hemingway in his Code, Eliot in the Great Tradition, Yeats in Byzantium. Opposed to this is the postmodern mind (Beckett, Pynchon, Robbe-Grillet) which seeks to deconstruct the transcendental signified. Here is the first mode of consciousness that appears to be for and against everything and nothing

With this in mind, John Barth's claim begins to make sense. Davenport—fiction writer, essayist, poet, editor, illustrator, librettist, translator of classical Greek, scholar, but "primarily a teacher" who argues that "all my writings [are] extensions of the classroom," who wrote his first fiction since his undergraduate days when he was forty-three, back in 1970—is the last modernist to the extent that he is one of the last of a generation to have been influenced more profoundly by creators such as Pound, Picasso, and Joyce, than by those such as Ashbery, Warhol, and Barthelme. He is, along with Marx and Freud, one of the late outriders of classical humanism. Along with them he dreams the dream of cultural development and inherent rationality that once animated Western society. His fictions share the modernist belief in a transcendental signified of fragments shored against the ruins, in the omnipotence of language, in the archaic. And, like his creation C. Musonius Rufus, those fictions are "damned to sanity and hope."

That there are *ten* stories in his second collection, *Da*

Vinci's Bicycle (1979), is then significant because ten is the perfect number, one which holds the other nine within itself—*three* for the soul, *four* for the body, *seven* for the complete man. St. Augustine argues that divine law is indicated by the number ten. Ten is the basis of our number system. Though we speak in many languages and write in a tangle of scripts, for all scientific work there is only one system, and it consists of ten symbols, and all other numbers can be expressed by means of these two handfuls of signs. Ten is also the sacred number for the Pythagoreans, a number which was symbolized by the dotted triangle (*tetractys*), the source and root of all nature. In other words, *ten* is the signal of reason, culture, the possibility of coherence. It is the announcement of the transcendental signified.

In his essay "Narrative Form and Tone," Davenport paraphrases Russian formalist critic Boris M. Ejxenbaum (and Davenport often returns to the formalists in his writing), saying that "short stories tend to accumulate along thematic lines," and the overarching theme of *Da Vinci's Bicycle* is suggested by another observation by Davenport, this time about his youth: "I spent my childhood drawing, building things, writing, reading, playing, dreaming out loud, without the least comment from anybody. I learned later that I was thought not quite bright, for the patterns I discovered for myself were not things with nearby models." As with Davenport the child, all the characters in *Da Vinci's Bicycle* (and the title itself indicates a dedication to the imagination, as well as a biographical fact, that Davenport does not drive a car)—all the characters from history, many from Western civilization's childhood—spend their time drawing, building things, writing, reading, playing, dreaming out loud, without the least comment from anybody. That is, they are all pioneers somehow out of step with their contemporaries, ignored, bullied, or misunderstood, invariably thought not quite bright, even silly, for the patterns they discover in the world are not the patterns that their contemporaries discover.

The alpha fiction, **"The Richard Nixon Freischütz Rag,"** is about the geography of three imaginations. All are, as the title hints, freeshooters who enjoy jazzy solo performances. And all are explorers, inventors, detectives (and detectives of ontology and epistemology abound in this work) searching out various harmonies. Richard Nixon reverses the path from east to west that Western civilization took and flies to China in 1972 to meet with Chairman Mao in order to reunify east and west. He is the politician, a figure who will turn up frequently in the following fictions (Nero, Mussolini, Napoleon), usually in the form of a megalomaniac, usually dangerous, here with an astoundingly prosaic imagination. When shown the Great Ten Thousand Li Wall, all he can comment is, "I think you would have to conclude this a great wall." When read a poem by the artist Mao, all he can comment is, "That's got to be a good poem." When speaking with the Chinese leader he metamorphoses into an absurd gremlin-like tourist who "sank too far into his chair, his elbows as high as his ears." But below the silly prosaism pulses a destructive imagination as well, one that, before flying to China, orders a hundred and twenty-five squadrons of B-52s to

bomb the DMZ in Vietnam because it knows "Chairman Mao would be impressed by such power."

Such a twentieth-century mind is juxtaposed to the poetic and creative mind of the fifteenth century when in the second appears Leonardo thinking about Paola Toscanelli, an astronomer, physician, and geographer who saw Halley's comet in 1456 and apparently encouraged Columbus to strike out into the Atlantic. Nixon's flat, hard, tough mind gives way to a mind that thinks of the earth "round as a melon, plump and green," and believes "the world was knit by prophecy, by light":

> Meadow grass from Fiesole, icosahedra, cogs, gears, plaster, maps, lutes, brushes, an adze, magic squares, pigments, a Roman head Brunelleschi and Donatello brought him from their excavations, the skeleton of a bird: how beautifully the Tuscan light gave him his things again every morning, even if the kite had been in his sleep.

Leonardo who, ironically, delighted in imagining the machines of war—in 1482 he sent a letter to the regent of Milan with plans for armored tanks, cannon, catapults, and various traps—who left his most famous work (*The Last Supper, The Mona Lisa*) unfinished, and who invented a gadget for cutting threads into screws, an adjustable monkey wrench, designs for a steam engine and airplane, here works with his young assistant (and perhaps lover) on a "two-wheeled balancing machine." This is what Hugh Kenner calls the Cartesian Centaur [in *Samuel Beckett: A Critical Study,*], a bicycle a man will ride, a machine in harmony with the human, a mechanical body that allows the Cartesian mind to balance atop it. Indeed, Leonardo searches everywhere for a binding force, something that will pull the microcosm and macrocosm into accord. He looks at a blade of grass and sees the universe: "And in the thin green veins ran hairs of water, and down the hairs of water ran light, down into the dark, into the root. Light from the farthest stars flowed through these long leaves."

Leonardo and what appears to be his boy-lover parallel the other set of homosexual lovers in this short fiction, Gertrude Stein and Alice B. Toklas. Their section, like many in this collection, proceeds by indirection. Stein is never named, and Toklas is referred to only as Alice. In his essay on Max Ernst, Davenport mentions that Russian formalist critic Victor Shklovski "felt that art served a purpose by 'making the familiar strange,' a process of regeneration (of attention, of curiosity, of intelligence) the opposite of narcosis." He could as well have been describing this section, or Stein's fetish for cubist painting that tries to make one see without conventions—as Davenport will shortly do in **"Au Tombeau de Charles Fourier."** That the Stein section is the only one in this first fiction told in the first person is fitting. It suggests itself as a new way of seeing, a subjectivity of perception, a twentieth-century pattern without nearby models.

"C. Musonius Rufus" drops us back even farther in time. When Nero's spies in 65 A.D. brought him word of a widespread conspiracy to overthrow him, he put Seneca, Lucan, Petronius and others to death. At the same time he exiled Musonius, who was one of the most sincere and consistent of the Stoic philosophers in first-century Rome. The Roman Stoics scorned metaphysics and turned instead to a philosophy of conduct whose essence was self-control. Through the subordination of passion to reason, they felt they could attain human decency, family unity, and social order. Musonius perhaps more than any other Stoic took this philosophy of conduct seriously. He taught equality for women. He taught that women should be educated. He spoke against gladiatorial games at the Circus and insinuated that by attending them the Emperor was as bestial as the fighters he witnessed. He spoke—like Pound (and Davenport in a letter to me dated 8 July, 1985, writes that "The Musonius story is about Ezra Pound")—against taxes (Davenport's *bete noire*), war, slavery of any kind, and even premarital sex. For his trouble he was, as Pound told Davenport, first sent to a waterless Aegean island, then to a chain gang. And according to this second fiction he was then taken into a forest and murdered. Musonius tells his story, like Beckett's *Unnamable,* from beyond the grave. His remains are kept in a jug, and he is literally in search of a self. He discovers death is a spinning, that "to turn is to exist" in this new dimension. The world, in other words, has gone topsy-turvy for him in death just as it did in life. He remembers, like a good Stoic, "with perfect unconcern" about his exile; about how he was forced to slave on a canal connecting Corinth and the Saronicus, from dawn to dusk; about the hurt he caused his wife when he became a philosopher; about his time on the island; about his murder. Now, exiled even from his own body, he feels himself become some kind of orb. Like Leonardo, he equates light with binding power: "Spirit must be a substance very like light. Old polarity of head and butt no longer maintains." He both leaves and does not leave his jug, having somehow become able to diffuse into the world, to become a part of everything. Even in death, then, he is an explorer. He merges with a tree, hurls into the clouds, chats with donkeys, whirls into the core of the earth, darts into a sunflower. And what he finds is that all is off balance, out of proportion: "I see lizards the size of elephants clumping through ferns as big as oaks." And sometimes, hard as he might try to the contrary, the world evaporates and there are "days when I can hear nothing, see nothing, feel nothing. I am loneliest then, and fearful. I have learned to search the white for a yellow dot, which grows if I stare at it, until a gnat-swarm of bilious specks gathers around it and becomes a detail: a horse's eye, a jug of olive oil, a whetstone," and, through an act of imagination, he can pull the universe into being again, a good Cartesian. Elsewhere Davenport says that "southerners take a certain amount of unhinged reality for granted," and in Musonius' mind there is no doubt that reality has become unhinged, that "the world is mad," and that it is maddest in its politics. Rome has for Musonius fallen apart, and the city—"the unit of civilization"—"is a shapeless bundle of shitten pissburnt sweatscalded bubonic rotten rags held together with a bronze wire of discipline." Western culture has exiled its philosophers, its creative minds, and has gone rotten in the teeth.

It is no wonder when suddenly this second fiction zigzags from the first into the twentieth century with the intrusion of Mussolini, the modern-day Nero, since for the Stoics things do not happen in time. Time for them is a dimen-

sion of things, and the eternal course of the universe is cyclical, not progressive or regressive. The decay at the heart of the world in the first century is an analogue for the decay at the heart of the world in the twentieth. Things have not progressed or regressed, the structure of the fiction argues. They have spun in a circle. For to turn is to exist.

"The Wooden Dove of Archytas" spins us back another four centuries to Archytas the Pythagorean, dictator of Tars. Archytas believed in a communist aristocracy. He was the man at whom Plato became angry because Archytas was carrying on experiments in mechanics that corrupted the pure realm of geometry. Archytas developed the mathematics of music, wrote various tracts on philosophy, doubled the cube, scribed the first treatise on mechanics. He invented the pulley, the screw, and the baby rattle. As a Pythagorean he believed that philosophy was a mode of conduct that would lead to the salvation of the soul. At the center of that philosophy was the belief that for salvation man must be in harmony with other forms of life and with the cosmos. That is, Archytas' imagination and that of Aristopolites, the boy who narrates this fiction, parallel those of Leonardo, Stein, and Musonius. In an essay called "Finding," Davenport writes that "childhood is spent without introspection, in unreflective innocence. Adolescence turns its back on childhood in contempt and sometimes shame. We find out childhood later, and what we find in it is full of astounding surprises." This romantic myth informs **"The Wooden Dove of Archytas,"** a fiction about child-like imaginations who find the world "full of astounding surprises." Archytas invents a wooden dove—some strange echo, perhaps, of Yeats' bird in Byzantium, a wonderwork of art—that runs by steam. He puts it together, sets it up, and, in a moment both scientific and mystical, "it whistled up like an arrow from a bow, fluttered with the stagger of a bat, and banking into a long high wheel, soared over the chronometer tower, the fane of Asklepios, the armory, the hills."

This narrative is intersected by another, one set in the backwoods of the south in the nineteenth century, a Faulknerian tale where an Indian visits some blacks and asks for a matchbox to use as a coffin for her ringdove that died when it ran into a door. After receiving the box, she journeys back with the others for the burial where the dove's soul ascends. As Robert A. Morace notes, "instead of polarizing primitive myth and scientific discovery, Davenport makes clear, as Whitman and Pound did, that they derive from the same wellspring: man's searching and redemptive imagination." Both subnarratives are tales about the force of the imagination, both are about magic and ascension. And there is at least a hint that there is some Pythagorean transmigration of souls here ("The idea that time cannot be reversed is mere Enlightenment dogma, liberal twaddle," says Borgesian Davenport in one of his essays in *Geography of the Imagination*.) But here it is a whimsically backwards one, from a once-living dove to a mechanical one. As with Leonardo's bicycle, the living and the artificial fuse to form a new harmony between the animate and inanimate. Another binding in the cosmos takes place, another glimpse of the transcendental signified.

"John Charles Tapner" is the first fiction here that does not wheel through time. The reader moves from ancient Greece and the southern United States in the last story to an island off the coast of France in the 1850s in this one. At the fiction's center is another exile, Victor Hugo, who has fled from Louis Napoleon, going first from Belgium to Jersey, and then from Jersey to Guernsey, because he has failed to acknowledge that Napoleon the Third is the Emperor of France. He travels to Guernsey to visit the grave of John Charles Tapner, an unknown man on whose behalf he wrote a letter to the Queen of England asking that Tapner not be hanged for allegedly cutting the throat of his mistress, Miss Saujon. Hugo argued against capital punishment "on the lines . . . that two wrongs don't make a right. Says it makes a murderer of society." His visit to where Tapner was hanged and buried on February 10, 1854, makes him into a kind of detective, a searcher, like the reader himself, who is not informed of Hugo's name until the story is half over. Davenport says he learned early in life that "the search was the thing," not the finding, and at the core of this mystery are several murders that are never solved. Though the reader is never sure beyond a reasonable doubt that Tapner committed the crime he was accused of, the people of Guernsey, who, like Richard Nixon in the first fiction, possess prosaic and destructive imaginations, are quick in their conclusions: Tapner and Miss Saujon "were seeing each other in a sinful way. Moral degeneracy in one respect leads to any other." Why society would murder a murderer is also a mystery here. Hugo's exploration of this makes him, like Tapner before him, an outcast. At one point the narrator's wife Polly comments: "Your Frenchman, I've been told, has a wife for show and another woman for the sin of it. . . . What's more, they're all Papists, and not a moral among them." The narrator, Martin, the Queen's Provost, does not argue with her. In the imaginations of the prosaic, the idealist is an aberration.

Often Davenport generates textual density by creating gaps—mysteries—on the page that the reader must fill. In addition, he writes in his essay [in *Geography of the Imagination*] on his first story collection, *Tatlin!* (1974), there are three other ways to create textual density: 1) "through a knitting of sound patterns"; 2) "through a knitting of imagery"; 3) "by invoking names of people and things." Davenport employs all these ways in **"Au Tombeau de Charles Fourier."** The result is by far the most difficult fiction in *Da Vinci's Bicycle.* With this fiction in mind, Davenport could have been talking about himself when he called Louis Zukofsky "not so much a poet's poet as a poet's poet's poet." This is also the kind of fiction that has prompted Jack Sullivan to argue that Davenport's "dizzying collages" are "often impressive in their cleverness and intricacy, but sometimes wearying in their self-conscious erudition," and Robert A. Morace to point out that "Davenport's kind of intellectual play will never appeal to a wide audience." More than a fiction, **"Au Tombeau"** is what Davenport calls an *assemblage,* a blend of history, voices, languages, drawings, times, places, chronologies, and so on, all of which serve to produce an "architectonic form" that "absorbs and displaces narrative" so that "the meaning shapes into a web, or globe, rather than along a line." The outcome moves narrative from a horizontal plane of traditional plot to the vertical plane of lyricality, thereby deconstructing the nineteenth-century version of story-telling. The realist work transforms into the cubist, where the whole becomes "a hieroglyph, a coherent symbol, an ideogram."

The impetus to construct such a narrative goes back, again, to Davenport's childhood in South Carolina:

> There were summer drives for finding hog plums, wild peaches, and blackberries on the most abandoned of back dirt roads, autumn drives in search of muscadines and scuppernongs, the finding of which, gnarled high in trees like lianas, wanted as sharp an eye as an arrowhead. We were a foraging family, completely unaware of our passion for getting at things hard to find. I collected stamps, buttons, the cards that came with chewing gum, the other detritus, but these were private affairs with nothing of the authority of looking for Indian arrowheads.

Hugh Kenner once called Davenport's projects "self-portraits" and, in a special way, they are. **"Au Tombeau,"** for instance, is a translation of the childhood need to forage into the adult world.

At its center are the Dogon, a primitive people of West Africa, who are trying to find God's complete plan of the universe and who "must search forever, never finding." And like Linnaeus, Picasso, Leonardo and the others in this assemblage—including the reader, who finds himself metamorphosed into a detective attempting to solve a mystery through the logical assembling and interpretation of palpable evidence—"all searched out the harmonies, the affinities, the kinship of the orders of nature," some self-created mythology that unifies microforces into a macroforce, some overarching transcendental signified. As Davenport tells us [in *Geography of the Imagination*], **"Au Tombeau"** "proceeds like an Ernst collage" and focuses for the most part on seven kinds of foragers, while the sixteen drawings that are interspersed throughout the story "are meant to be integral with the prose of this story (one hears a lot of the *logos* with one's eyes)" and "turn the text into a *graph* ('to write' and 'to draw' being the same Greek verb)."

The first foragers are Gertrude Stein and the cubists, who search for "a primitive and intelligent way of looking," a "tilting of vision," a "ceasing to pretend that we see with our heads in a clamp." Next are the wasps who are "out to forage," "memorizing with complex eye and simple brain the map of colors and fragrances." Third come the Dogon and their god of foraging, Ogo, who like the Pythagoreans—and like all the other foragers here and elsewhere in this collection—seek to understand "the system and the harmonies." Fourth comes Charles Fourier, a utopian socialist who believed that because men had been created by a benevolent god and yet allowed themselves to wallow in their misery they had failed to carry out the divine plan, according to which happiness would replace misery, unity would replace division, and harmony would replace civilization. To accomplish this, Fourier argued, humanity would have to be reorganized into phalanxes (like wasps) of eighteen hundred men, women and children, where every person would find a use for his or her special talent, and where all would live and work communally and contentedly. Fourier's life became an extended search to develop a single trial phalanx, and along the way he denounced the exploitation and lies inherent in the family, church, society and state—and in commerce most of all. The next foragers are the flying machines of Bleriot and the Wrights, who again attempt like Archytas and Leonardo to join the animate and inanimate into some larger whole. Sixth is the photographer—and the idea of photography will be picked up in the eighth story of this collection—Lartigue who quests after a way to see the world differently, to make us see the universe in a new light, a man trying, like Wittgenstein, "to get us to wake up in the midst of dreaming." Last is Guy Davenport himself, both as a character in the assemblage who recounts his visits with Samuel Beckett and his trip to Fourier's tomb, and as the overarching imagination outside the assemblage conceiving all the other imaginations—the ultimate forager, that "single intelligence" William James discusses that "permeates [the assemblage's as well as the world's] every part, from the waves of the ocean to the still hardness of coal and diamond deep down in the inmost dark."

"The Haile Selassie Funeral Train," a fiction like the last four where death pulses at the heart, proves what Davenport will have Robert Walser say in the collection's final story: "everything is an incongruity if you study it well." Though it soon turns into a web of contradictions that catches and destroys the facile logic of the detective-reader, it appears to begin easily enough. A nameless narrator situated in the present recounts to art critic James Johnson Sweeney a journey that took place in 1936—the trek of Ras Taffari's funeral train on which a number of important figures (including James Joyce and Guillaume Apollinaire) are but never meet. To this extent, it is a story about what does not happen, about narrative indirection. But almost immediately it transforms into a story about what cannot happen, about the presence of absence, when certain inconsistencies start cropping up.

In *Geography of the Imagination* (which is dedicated to Hugh Kenner) Davenport admires Kenner, Beckett and Pound because they are writers who "condense, pare down, and proceed by daring synapses," and **"Funeral Train"** is a short tight work filled with deliberate gaps. For instance, Ras Taffari, who at his coronation as the Lion of Judah took the name of Haile Selassie, which translates as "The Power of Eternity," died in 1975, not 1936. He was the last emperor of a three-thousand-year-old monarchy in Ethiopia, the end of a culture, and hence a fitting image for Davenport to choose, but one which neither Joyce nor Apollinaire knew. Davenport told me that the narrator was no one, just a disembodied voice, but there is also at least a suggestion (the narrator recalls Richmond, Virginia, with nostalgia; he remembers the Blue Ridge Mountains) that another transmigration has taken place, here of Poe's spirit forward in time, or perhaps Davenport's backwards. By the end of the story, when the reader realizes that the train's trip has been a big circle from Deauville to Deauville, the reader comes to realize he has been on some celestial railroad in a Stoic universe

where the power of eternity is cyclical. By implication, the reader finds himself at the end of Western civilization's monarchy, and at the beginning of some new, some Yeatsian second dispensation, but in this between-times as Apollinaire announces "we have no shepherds," and the barbarians are on the way: "What in the name of God could humanity be if man is an example of it?". Through a certain optic, then, this is another fiction about foraging, about the creative imagination (the narrator's, Davenport's) slicing across space and time and reunifying in a startling, metalogical way.

Compared to most of the pieces in **Da Vinci's Bicycle**, **"Ithaka"** is a particularly accessible fiction. In many ways it borders on being an essay which simply recounts, in the first person, a visit Davenport paid to Pound in Italy. Narrator Davenport arrives in time to help Ezra move into Olga Rudge's—his companion's—house in an olive grove above Rapallo where she had lived before the Second World War. Afterward they all go swimming—Pound plunging too far out—and then to lunch, where Pound makes a game of staying wordless, all the while filled with "stubbornness," "glaring and silent." In earlier days, at St. Elizabeth's Hospital for the Criminally Insane in Washington he used to talk, but now he can go through a whole day with only a word or two. The title of this fiction suggests the legendary home of Odysseus, the island in the Ionian Sea, where the hero returned after his quests and battles. But this modern Odysseus, this "immensely old man . . . , old as Titian . . . , standing in gondolas in Venice like some ineffably old Chinese court poet in exile," has been hurt by the prosaic world into pain and silence, while his Penelope looks on, hopeful and helpless. The use of the archaic here both connects Pound to what was once most familiar to us as a culture, and reminds us of what we have lost. As Davenport writes in his essay "The Symbol of the Archaic": "behind all this passion for the archaic . . . is a longing . . . for energies, values, and certainties unwisely abandoned by the industrial age."

"The Invention of Photography in Toledo" is also less fiction than some kind of strange ratiocinative Borgesian essay. Though the piece is full of esoterica about the 1826 discovery of photography by two men in two Toledos (by Joseph Nicéphore Niepce in the one in Spain, by Friedrich Wilhelm Herschel in the one in Ohio), and descriptions of actual photographs (Lenin in a Zürich café with James and Nora Joyce in the background; the only one of Van Gogh, which captured only the back of his head; the Soviet ones where Trotsky's image has been erased) and imagined ones ("A photograph of Socrates and his circle would simply look like an ugly old man with bushy eyebrows and the lips of a frog"), what it focuses on is an historian of photography, Foco Betún y Espliego, the chronicler rather than the chronicle. In 1912 Foco Betún y Espliego abandoned his history of photography to devote his life to getting a shot of the Loch Ness Monster. To do so, he becomes an exile, a man who "suffered awful loneliness in his vigil on the gray shores of Loch Ness. The bagpipes ruined his kidneys, the porridge his stomach." What he has done is abandon prosaic photography, the gravity of the mimetic, which emasculates the imagination, and all its universe implies (names, dates, scholarship), in favor of poetic photography, the buoyancy of the creative, which liberates the imagination, and all its universe implies (magic, timelessness, swimming dragons). And this pioneer succeeds in giving the lie to the claim that "real life is all that photography has." On a spring day in 1913 Betún traps the image of a plesiosaurus on film. It "shows a long wet nose and lifted lip, an expressionless reptilian gaze, and a gleaming flipper." He has recorded a moment of revelation, a glimpse of the transcendental signified, through what everyone thought was an "objective" medium. But the poetry of Betún is read only as so much prose by the world. The photo "was published in *La Prensa* upside down and in the London *Times* with a transposed caption identifying it as the Archduke Ferdinand arriving in Sarajevo for a visit of state."

"The Antiquities of Elis" purports to be a travel guide written in the second century A.D., and more than most fictions in *Da Vinci's Bicycle* is composed out of style that registers, as Davenport comments about *Tatlin!*, a "Flaubertian detachment," a style "controlled by artifice." Elsewhere Davenport notes that "writing in the twentieth century has for its greatest distinction the discovery of the specific: " 'Things,' Proust said, 'are gods.' " And this fiction is a first-person list of things in Elis, the area in the western Peloponesus founded by Aeolus, where Olympia was, and hence where the Olympic Games were held for centuries. Pisa was also there until Pelops, who was exiled there in 1238 B.C., made it independent. It is an area famed for its horses. It is an area famed for its shrine of Hera that goes back to 1000 B.C., a shrine whose ruins—fragments of thirty-six columns and twenty doric capitals still survive—are the oldest temple remains in Greece, a symbol of the archaic, an echo of Western culture's beginnings: "there is a mortality even in children which we cannot discern in old temples, which, in surviving generation after generation, have taken on that grace by which their sacredness shall probably survive Greece and Rome. Earthquake and impiety cannot destroy them all." Pythagoras visited Elis, as did Thales and Anaxagoras. It is the home of another Sophist, Hippias, who lived in the fifth century B.C., and taught math and astronomy and protested against artificiality in city life. And it is the home of skeptic Pyrrhon—"the philosopher . . . who would admit nothing"—who through his student Timon of Philus taught that certainty is unattainable and that since all theories are false one might as well accept the myths and conventions of one's own time and place. All this is recorded by Pausanias, a sightseer, traveller, and topographer, an explorer who wandered through Greece roughly in 160 A.D. and described it in his *Periegesis* (translated as *Tour*), the first guidebook—and one that consists of ten books, just as this collection consists of ten stories. Davenport wrote me that " **'The Antiquities of Elis'** (though translated from Pausanias, with onions and dust added) is my way of recording a trip across Greece with a young friend in 1960. It is full of private jokes and allusions, and the elder character is my tomcat Max, personified." But it is also about how, even in the second century A.D., Pausanias senses the loss of the archaic, the decay of our culture, the disappearance of our heritage, our slide toward ignorance. And so his mission becomes an analogue for Davenport's in his fictions and essays—to shore up fragments of culture against the ruins, to record the past, fasten down a civilization, collect and freeze in art what is left of our heritage.

"A Field of Snow on a Slope of the Rosenberg" is an omega of madness that returns us to the twentieth century between the two world wars, just after the failure of the modern renaissance. Paul Cassierer (director of the Neue Sezession art gallery, where Walser worked for a time as a secretary) and Robert Walser take a hot air balloon flight from Bitterfeld to the Baltic one windy February. While on their modern epic journey, Walser, the Swiss novelist, who was born on Leonardo's birthday (April 15th), 1888, and who died in 1956, having spent the last thirty years of his life crazy, drifts into memories about how he conversed one afternoon with Manet's Olympia who spoke to him from a print; how he saw William James accidently dip his tie into a bowl of soup and keep it there so long it began working as a wick; about his time as a servant at Count Rufzeichen's Schloss Dambrau, where he realized that "freedom is a choice of prisons"; about an old man's comical heart attack (Walser himself died that way on Christmas Day, while out for a walk); about a Scot who levitates himself and flies out a window; about his work as a bank clerk ("We do not make chairs, we make money. We do not make shoes, we make money"), a soldier ("Our cities are vanishing from the face of the earth. Big chunks of nothing are taking up the space once occupied by houses and palaces"), as author of his masterpiece *Jakob von Gunten,* which came out in 1908 ("Mann stole it, and Kafka stole it, and Hesse stole it, and were talked about. I have been invisible all my life").

At one point he tells what he calls "my own parable" about the professor at the Sorbonne who electrocuted himself so badly in class that he shot across the lecture hall. When he opened his eyes again he saw his feet, one on each windowsill of the room. His torso had gone into orbit. His left arm was in the cloak room. His right arm was on a table. What Walser realizes is that the professor "came to pieces. One used the very words." What he imagines, in other words, is the literal fragmentation of modern man. It is a nightmare vision of the twentieth century where modernity becomes "a dream in which confusion has seeped into reality." Back in the balloon "you could not tell whether you sailed past the clouds or the clouds past you." All is a "flip-flop of reality," a pure relativity. And no sane man can stand pure relativity for long.

For Walser in his balloon the world has become, as Stein said it would earlier in this collection, a cubist painting. The world has become an assemblage just like *Da Vinci's Bicycle.* And, like Pound in **"Ithaka,"** Walser has been hurt into madness by such a recognition. The center has let go. He cannot locate the harmonies any more. The idea of culture spins away from him. And there is Robert Walser, a forager, an exile, drifting above it all, one of the last modernists, webbing a world in his mind, writing, playing, dreaming out loud, without the least comment from anybody, crazy by everyone else's standards, and, by everyone else's standards, an imp of chaos. "But let us desist," he concludes, tongue in cheek, "lest quite by accident we be so unlucky as to put these things in order."

Nancy Blake   (essay date 1986)

SOURCE: " 'An Exact Precession': Leonardo, Gertrude, and Guy Davenport's *Da Vinci's Bicycle,*" in *Critical Angles: European Views of Contemporary American Literature,* edited by Marc Chénetier, Southern Illinois University Press, 1986, pp. 145-52.

[*In the following essay, Blake discusses Davenport's use of quotation and reference to manipulate time and perspective in the stories in* Da Vinci's Bicycle.]

For some of us at least, it is true that space and time are not opposites; nor are they absolutes, but rather they are arbitrary definitions of a multidimensional reality, what we call metaphors. Since Einstein's demonstration in 1905, most of us recognize what some of us knew all along, that between what is named "future" and "past" there exists an interval whose extension in time depends on the distance in space between an event and its observer. The present is not limited to a moment in time. To gain time, increase space. The farsighted have every advantage.

Guy Davenport's collection **Da Vinci's Bicycle** persistently displaces the realms of space and time so that the words recur with an effect of *Unheimlichkeit.* What he is saying is at once excessively familiar and excessively strange. It is familiar because his writing depends on writing—other people's, what we call quotation, or reference. Gertrude Stein, one of Davenport's favorite voices, liked to say that there is no such thing as repetition. For Davenport, there is no such thing as quotation. Even the illustrations accompanying the texts in **Da Vinci's Bicycle** are "derived" and "acknowledged." They are taken from other drawings or, often, from photographs; they are copies of copies—the same and different.

Guy Davenport's text follows the trail marked by other texts, by human thought. Texts always following the same curves in the landscape may eventually wear a path. Perhaps. Davenport's project may then seem to be to render homage to the spirits of his predecessors and so to renew their vital force, and ours. This is Gertrude Stein speaking through Davenport: "He [Apollinaire] could see the modern because he loved all that had lasted from before. You see Cézanne by loving Poussin and you see Poussin by loving Pompeii and you see Pompeii by loving Cnossos. What the hell comes before Cnossos if this sentence is to be a long one?" Yet this supposition, like all those one can make, in the context of Davenport's book is only as true as it is false. For, rather than tell, the text demonstrates that the loss of a reference is not of any real importance. All that counts is the loss of balance, the upsetting of equilibrium that allows one to take another step, the loss of equilibrium that means life.

This is Leonardo Da Vinci speaking without any help from Davenport:

> Contemplate this flame and ponder its beauty,
> close your eyes, then look: what you saw of it

> was not; what it was
> is no more . . .

> What is it that regenerates that which unceasingly dies of engendering?

"I think, therefore I was," yet am. The same and different. The world is a metaphor for the world and Davenport's text is fittingly able to turn itself "leisurely inside out and back again, like candlesmoke in a still room."

At this point it may be useful to note that what Stein called, in a voluntarily unoriginal way, "the question of identity," is traditionally, at least since Heraclites, mixed up with the notion (which is arbitrary, but nonetheless bothersome) of time. Yesterday's identity invalidates today's being. The *Unheimlich* is perhaps nothing more than the feeling of inauthenticity one has when faced with a past self. On the other hand, if one postulates an identity in time, this identity can only exist on some sort of general level roughly equivalent to the similarity between one individual and another. The narrator of **"The Antiquities of Elis"** is interested in rhythms. Time becomes timing: "It was Herakleitos who said that some things are too slow to see, such as the growth of grass, and some too fast, like the arrow's flight. All things, I have often thought, are dancing to their own music. A Lydian song is soon over, but the music to which the zodiac is turning requires twelve times three thousand years to close its harmony, if we may follow the calculations of Pythagoras, and the rhythms of time for a child are so much slower than for a man that we have lived for centuries before our beards arrive."

One of the leitmotifs of Stein's *Geographical History of America* is the phrase "these are simple ideas." It is a fact, however, that nothing is less simple for the mind to grasp than the idea of simplicity. Our thinking always comes up against the improbable character of any identity, i. e., the improbability of reality.

One simple aphorism governs all of Leonardo's thought: "*Col tempo ogni cosa va variando*" (With time, everything changes). Thanks to a perspicacity worthy of Stein, Leonardo leads us to the brink of the unthinkable. In his apparent cliché is expressed the experience of the inconceivable: the same body is not always the same. And space itself is not a trustworthy container for being. Vehicles for time, space, and the objects seen in it are always in movement, always the momentarily possible result of an infinite series of relationships. From Brunelleschi to Piero della Francesca, a world *certo ed abitabile,* based upon linear perspective, had excluded the dimension of time.

The faces painted by Leonardo, like his blades of grass, are crossroads for transient forces. The nature of these forces is a mystery, the velocity with which they travel, stupendous. As you blink, the world is transformed: "Contemplate this flame and ponder its beauty, close your eyes, then look." The mystery of the Mona Lisa is in the illusive quality of the air at dusk, humid and dulled by a vapor through which the daylight can no longer penetrate. This atmosphere erases the outlines of the face while it accentuates the relief, as if a portrait were a landscape. So the Mona Lisa is not the painting of a woman, but rather that of a certain quality in the air, a certain harmony in the universe, represented by means of a human figure. Leonardo's lesson is interwoven through all the pages of Davenport's book: "You must understand, Beckett said, that Joyce came to see that the fall of a leaf is as grievous as the fall of man."

The artist is a spider in the midst of the intricate web of temporality. It is only if time is understood as "being-there" (*dasein*), Heidegger pointed out, that the traditional phrase concerning time can be meaningful: time is the principle of individuation. Leonardo said the same thing differently:

> The water of the rivers that you touch:
> last of the waters that were,
> first of the waters that will be:
> present tense.

In his *Philosophy of Experience,* William James, who has several walk-on parts in **Da Vinci's Bicycle,** evokes the "essentially provisional and therefore unreal character of everything that is empirical and finite." Present experience is insufficient and therefore unreal, not only because it is present, but by definition. It is no use trying to add up all past and future existences, in a Proustian effort to transcend time; the whole is never equal to the sum of its parts. The real is something like "a unilateral being whose mirror reflection does not exist," according to Ernst Mach. Davenport quotes the Dogon myth that explains creation, not as the perfect reflection of God, but rather as the mischief of Ogo who was searching for a twin. "The real," says Clement Rosset, "is that which has no double." "Space and time were still the same thing, unsorted. So before God extended time or space from his mind, Ogo began to create the world. His steps became time, his steps measured off space. You can see the road he took in the rainbow: *To see creation!*"

All thought is an endless wandering between tautology and deviation. Therefore: "A rose is a rose is a rose is a rose." In Stein's succinct theory of reality and of writing, the notion of the referential is irrelevant. What can you say about the real? If we follow Stein's logic, once we have named it we have gone about as far as we are likely to go, which is, in fact, quite a distance.

What is being? Philosophy asks the question that myth articulates: "In the beginning, he said, there existed God and nothing. God, Amma, was rolled up in himself like an egg. He was *amma talu gunnu,* a tight knot of being, Nothing else was. Only Amma. He was a collarbone made of four collarbones and he was round." The question of being is not one to respond to binary logic. Leonardo dealt with it in terms of power and unbalance: "Force is what I call a spiritual power—unbodily and invisible, which comes into being like a brief life in bodies, every time that accidental violence brings them outside of their natural rest and being." All that counts is the upsetting of equilibrium that allows the body to take another step forward, the lack of balance that is being.

What Leonardo, Stein, Picasso, and Wilbur Wright have in common, besides their "genius," is, of course, that they

I write when I feel like writing, I draw when I feel like drawing. I frequently move from one to the other. Sometimes I can best express myself doing a painting . . . or an essay. **"The Aeroplanes at Brescia",** in *Tatlin!,* started out as a research essay on Kafka. The story **"Tatlin!"** itself was originally, I think, a kind of plan for a history-of-art book, once I found some of the elements there about the beginnings of modern art in Russia. **"Tatlin!"** began as an oil portrait of Tatlin from an old photograph which is upstairs. Frequently I will abandon a piece of writing and draw it, or abandon a drawing and write it, or do both. This painting up here, which is called "The Contention in Erewhon", must be the first note of the *assemblage* that became **"The Dawn in Erewhon",** the last story in *Tatlin!* I tend to live with a set of ideas— over years I think—and they eventually will find where they want to go. So it's really, I suppose, a whole process . . . If you're a teacher, you're constantly working with diverse materials. You may get up in the morning and you've got Keats' *Odes* to take some sophomores through, and you've got a chapter of *Ulysses* for your graduate students, and the mind gets in the habit of finding cross-references among subjects. This is the best way in the world to make my *assemblages,* as I call them. I don't think I've ever written a story. If Henry James wrote stories, if Dostoevski wrote stories, I don't write stories.

Guy Davenport, in an interview with Barry Alpert in Vort, *Vol. 3, No. 3, 1976.*

were all, whether they knew it or not, Pythagoreans, materialists. Davenport's text celebrates force and light as the matter they so unbelievably are: "Bitumen of Judea dissolves in oil of lavender in greater or lesser densities of saturation according to its exposure to light, and thus Joseph Nicéphore Niepce in the year of Thomas Jefferson's death photographed his barnyard at Châlon-sur-Saône. Hours of light streaming through a pinhole onto pewter soaked asphalt into lavender in mechanical imitation of light focused on a retina by the lens of an eye." The universe in which we live and write is an infinity of relationships. The light enabling us to apprehend the real changes what we see as we see it. A problem for contemporary physics: how to measure the effect of a photon emitted in order to enable the observer to see his experiment. An element for a future text by Guy Davenport: the correspondence between Albert Einstein and Niels Bohr. Einstein: "When a mouse looks at the world, the world does not change." Bohr: "Yes it does, a little."

Existence is literally a movement out of the self. Writing, the act of writing, carries on a necessary relationship with the absence of being. It is, no doubt, an imaginary mirror for the temptation we all feel to reconstruct the image of a fictive identity. But also, and more importantly, writing is a response to an absence closely related to the *Unheimlich* that threatens all perception, all thought: "It says in the pages of Mach that the mind is nothing but a continuity of consciousness. It is not itself a thing, it is its contents, like an eye and what it sees, a hand and what it holds. Mach's continuity, like Heraklit's river, defines itself by its flow."

When Gertrude Stein wondered what was the use of being born a little boy if you were going to grow up to be a man, she was not questioning causality, not really. She was simply saying that when we look at our own life, we might as well be schizophrenic, because we are looking at the history of another. This is the refrain of the whole of *Da Vinci's Bicycle.* Yet the most disturbing piece is perhaps the final one, **"A Field of Snow on a Slope of the Rosenberg,"** which reveals the fact that the act of writing is not as safe as it has seemed to be. At times the distance necessary to appreciate metaphor collapses. Then Nijinsky is not like a horse, he is one.

All the other texts in the collection used a collage of voices to illustrate the web of relationships that link perceptions. This one unveils the genius of psychosis: the power and anguish of coming face to face with the real. "I wander out every afternoon, the same way, and have my walk. Every day now for twenty-seven years. Could I once have written books? Once drifted across Europe in a balloon? Once been a butler in Silesia? Was I once a boy?"

Guy Davenport's art is a grammar for languages with declensions: Toledo, Ohio is a form of Toledo, Spain; time is an aspect of space, being of nothingness, force of light. "And of life we can ask but continuity. That, as I explain to my doctors, is my neurosis, I have been, I am, I shall be, for awhile, but off and on, like a firefly." Order and chance are not opposites certainly; perhaps they are absolutes, but only if the word absolute is sidetracked by a literal translator so that it read "without solution." Heraclites, for whom the opposition of contraries is harmony not suppression or reduction of difference, but rather infinite coaction, irreducible contrast, would be an ideal reader for *Da Vinci's Bicycle.*

The unbelievable juxtapositions of Davenport's texts and collages may indeed seem to deserve Wallace Stevens' term of "necessary fictions." But more than this, as works of art, their message is one that tells us all we know and all we need to know about reality itself. For what is the only universal characteristic of reality? —its singular unexpectedness.

Douglas Messerli   (essay date 1987)

SOURCE: "Writers from the Diaspora of Truth," in *Los Angeles Times Book Review,* December 6, 1987, p. 8.

[*Messerli offers a positive review of the stories in* The Jules Verne Steam Balloon.]

Over the last 2½ decades, Guy Davenport . . . [has] come to be recognized as [one] of the leading postmodern fiction writers, that is as [a] fiction [writer] working against the normative patterns of psychological realism es-

tablished by authors of the 1940s and 1950s such as Robert Penn Warren, Saul Bellow, Norman Mailer and John Cheever. Of course, fiction—even 20th-Century fiction—has always included far more than the psychological novel allowed, as Davenport . . . [is] aware. In this sense, perhaps, it is a disservice to confuse these writers with something standing entirely apart from the modern tradition. For Davenport's interconnected stories, *The Jules Verne Steam Balloon* owes more to the high modernist collage-fictions of Max Ernst and to the pre-modern philosophical treatise-fictions of Soren Kierkegaard than to the self-referential modes of much of contemporary writing . . .

Indeed, Davenport's story-series might be best illuminated in the context of a modern masterwork of interrelated tales such as Eudora Welty's *The Golden Apples.* True, where Welty and writers like her use myth and history as symbols to reveal the psychological complexities of the lives of ordinary characters, Davenport employs outlandish figures who inhabit a world in which myth and history are demeaned, forgotten, or down-right dangerous. In **"Pyrrhon of Elis"** the Skeptic philosopher Pyrrhon levels all meaning—in an ironic reversal of Descartes—by doubting the existence of everything around him, including himself: "I may not be, I think." In **"We Often Think of Lenin in the Clothespin Factory,"** the characters speak nostalgically of art and artists from Pushkin, Canaletto, Rilke, and Robert Walser to the Aleksandr Deineka, "Workers' Summer Vacation Pool" and "Lenin Taking a Walk in His Car" as if all were equal. And in **"Bronze Leaves and Red,"** Davenport approaches the unforgivable in writing a tale in which our century's monster, Adolf Hitler, is represented as living in an idyllic world of social calls to Wagner's widow, chess games, music, macaroons and metaphysical discussions. These stories present, in short, exactly that world which Welty and so many other great modern writers feared for us.

But these are purposeful intrusions of possible evil in a world that otherwise is as idyllic as Welty's King/Zeus figure, Davenport's Hugo Trevmunding romps in a world alive with sexual excitement and desire. Through his interleaving of botanical descriptions and the actions of his various Scandinavian pan-sexual lovers, Davenport's Sweden literally throbs with an almost adolescent agitation of its sexual parts. Brother and sister, brother and brother, sister's lover and brother, brother and sister's lover's students—everyone gets into the act in Davenport's panegyric to free sex. And indeed, living as we do in an AIDS-conscious culture, Davenport's liberated 1960s Sweden becomes as mythic, as magical and desirable as the Greek myth embedded in Welty's 1940s small Southern town.

And as in Welty's world, the worst dangers to the boys of Hugo's NFS Grundtvig lie not in the past—in outmoded laws or in parental displeasure—but in a loss of the present made meaningful by dreams of the future and understood through the past. The villains of *The Jules Verne Steam Balloon* are those levelers of meaning as exemplified by Hugo's mysterious bicycle rider, a young man he encounters, falls vaguely in love with, and attempts to teach. But the bicycle rider, lost in neural hallucinations of LSD, marijuana, cocaine and the promises of a fradulent Transcendental Meditation Group, will not be taught. In that throbbing world of the living, the bicycle rider experiences nothing but the phantoms of his own non-acts. It is Hugh, like Welty's Virgie Rainey, who can see clearly the signs of the heavens, who has the vision to transform his acts into meaning in life. For Virgie, the vision is represented in the image of Perseus severing the head of Medusa; for Hugo, it is a wonderful contraption of the 19th Century, the steam balloon, inhabited by creatures of some science fiction future: Here the present truly meets the future in its past.

One wonders how these "stories" read apart from each other; together they make perfect sense.

John Ash   (essay date 1988)

SOURCE: "Guy Davenport's Mind of Many Colors," in *Book World—The Washington Post,* January 31, 1988, p. 9.

[*Ash is an English critic and a respected poet of experimental verse. In the following review, he finds Davenport's treatment of the sexual relationships of adolescents in* The Jules Verne Steam Balloon *"unbearably coy," but praises the shorter pieces in the collection, specifically "The Pyrrhon of Elis."*]

The Jules Verne Steam Balloon is . . . problematic. Most of it is taken up by a linked sequence of long stories concerning the sexual awakenings of a group of adolescents in Denmark. Since the vast majority of the characters are male the stories tend to devolve into prolonged idylls of mutual masturbation. Tedium soon threatens but it is worth persevering, and, once again, it helps to regard these stories as Alexandrian. What could be more Hellenistic than romantic friendship between handsome ephebes? The problem lies in the fact that we no longer live in the age of Theocritus, and in our time it is difficult to present these couplings (and triplings) as natural, guiltless celebrations of Eros. Davenport's idyll lapses into sentimentality and his sexual vocabulary can be unbearably coy.

This coyness also invades what we might call the second, mythological plane on which these stories work. This is the plane of the Jules Verne steam balloon and its pilots Quark, Buckeye and Tumble. This trio of tiresome amoretti take the form of 10-year-old boys and turn out to be immortals sent by some vague, higher authority to watch over and advise favored mortals.

The chief focus of their attentions is Hugo Tvemunding, assistant classics master, gym-instructor and mentor to Kim, Andres, Franklin and all the other "golden lads" so busily playing with their erector sets (to allude to Nabokov). Hugo is writing a thesis on the survival of pagan elements in the gospels, particularly the concept of the *daimon.* Since it is only to Hugo that our three immortals manifest themselves we are obviously meant to conclude that they are the *daimons* he is writing about. In the most compelling scene in all four stories he expounds his thesis while Quark and Tumble gambol about the room, invisible to everyone but Hugo: "The whole crunch of theology . . . is to what extent do people imagine that creatures of another realm, higher or lower, or invisibly within ours, interact with our lives?" This, I take it, is also "the whole crunch" of this sequence of stories, but it is still unclear to me why immortals should be so interested in a tender-hearted gym-instructor and some randy teen-age boys.

If these stories remain puzzling there can be no doubt about the value of the shorter pieces in this volume, especially **"Pyrrhon of Elis,"** a masterly account of the life and beliefs of a skeptic philosopher whose "great teaching was that we should resist reality with all our might." So, we are informed in a magnificent final sentence lasting nearly a page, Pyrrhon lives most of his life in the charming town of Elis surrounded by all the color and diversity of the late Greek world, surrounded in short by "a fine round world of people and things, seasons and years and rumors of other worlds as far away as the Indus or the Nile, the Thames forever hidden by fog and the Danube said to be as blue as a Doric eye; but was honestly uncertain that he did, and would never admit to any of it."

At his best Davenport is one of the true poets of prose. **"Pyrrhon of Elis"** is also a reminder that his fictions should be read together with his essays. A question raised in an essay on Joyce: "What is the relationship between figure and ground?" has its echo in **"Pyrrhon"**: "Everything is known as a figure in a ground or not at all." So Joyce turns out to have concerns in common with a philosopher who was a near contemporary of Alexander the Great, and though the axiom "Every force evolves a form" may sound like Heraclitus it was invented by Mother Ann Lee, the founder of the Shakers.

Michael Harris   (essay date 1990)

SOURCE: A review of *The Drummer of the Eleventh North Devonshire Fusiliers,* in *Los Angeles Times Book Review,* November 11, 1990, p. 6.

[*Harris offers a positive review of* The Drummer of the Eleventh North Devonshire Fusiliers, *noting that the homosexual relationships in the stories take place in settings that allow characters to "explore not only their sexuality but the nature of affection itself."*]

Guy Davenport has a problem. Few people read serious fiction. Even fewer read serious fiction that is frankly gay. Fewer still read serious, frankly gay fiction that demands so much from its audience—stylistically rich, philosophically speculative, structurally adventurous. Yet Davenport has been blessed, or cursed, with the ability to write the stuff, and must feel that he has no choice.

Davenport acknowledges as much. "My few readers," he says wryly, "will recognize that **'Wo es war, soll ich werden'** [the novella that accompanies four short stories in *The Drummer of the Eleventh North Devonshire Fusiliers*], completes a trilogy begun with *Apples and Pears* and *The Jules Verne Steam Balloon.*"

This collection has internal links, too. The stories—about students playing blind-man's buff, Roman soldiers soiled by battle feigning purity to carry the captured statue of a goddess, a boy in Depression-era Appalachia who wears dresses, another boy in Scandinavia who, to mask his fear as he seeks his first homosexual encounter in a park, sees everything through the eyes of an imaginary dog—all hint at the existence of magic spaces, mini-Edens where young people can explore not only their sexuality but the nature of affection itself: friendship, intimacy, love.

The novella, set in a boys' prep school in Denmark, expands on this theme. Its title, translated to **"Where It Was, There I Must Begin to Be,"** comes from Freud; it refers to the human organism's ability to reconstruct itself around a healing wound, like a pearl around a grain of sand. Variously wounded, a young professor, a dormitory prefect, a jock and a 12-year-old prodigy help one another learn and grow in an atmosphere of extraordinary civility, spiced by some delightful girls. Such a school, academically rigorous but sexually laissez-faire, could not exist—certainly not in America—but Davenport's vision of it shames our diminished ideas of education, our stunted selves.

Michael Heyward   (essay date 1991)

SOURCE: "Images of Desire," in *Book World—The Washington Post,* January 27, 1991, p. 9.

[*In the following review, Heyward comments on the style and themes of the stories in* The Drummer of the Eleventh North Devonshire Fusiliers.]

In *The Geography of the Imagination,* the collection of essays he published in the early '80s, Guy Davenport wrote: "The imagination is like the drunk man who lost his watch, and must get drunk again to find it." Davenport's fiction, freely borrowing from the techniques and themes of his essays until it is not always readily distinguishable from them, is consonant with this intuition: a highly deliberated attempt to locate in euphoria what soberly one thought beyond reach.

Davenport is a gifted reader: his fiction and his essays emerge from his reading in a way that is at once insouciant and hyper-concentrated, a learned, high-octane mix of invention and description. What connects the two forms is a brilliant capacity to recombine detail—often oblique, recondite detail picked out by a connoisseur's eye. All his work is in this sense collage, and this is why he cares so much about the formal finish of his writing, each sentence polished until it glitters like cut glass in sunlight. He has the aesthete's conviction that in the perfection of the style lies the truth of the insight.

The "stories" in Davenport's new collection, *The Drummer of the Eleventh North Devonshire Fusiliers,* are, like some of those in his previous collections *Apples and Pears* and the *The Jules Verne Steam Balloon,* sustained images of desire. They conjure into being an ideal imaginary world, richly colored and wilfully exact, depicted with a hallucinatory vividness of detail inseparable from the construction of a narrative that obeys many of the conventions of realist fiction while in fact resembling no world but the one constructed on the page. "You have to know what you want to look like," one of the characters muses in **"Wo es war, soll ich werden"** the novella-length story in this collection. "Nature complies." In Davenport's fiction nature hankers for the condition of art, even the condition of desire itself.

Several of the stories in *The Drummer of the Eleventh North Devonshire Fusiliers* are set in Scandinavia, "seamed with frost and blue with hindered green." This is the geography of Davenport's imagination. His location of his characters in these remote, and relentlessly beautiful boreal landscapes is an attempt to make actual a landscape empty of shame, from which guilt has been banished. His northern arcadia is peopled by boys aware for the first time of sex in an environment that allows them to exist to their fullest potential, intellectually and physically. Davenport explicitly celebrates the sexuality of adolescent boys: its urgency, its manifestation in groups, its tendency for experiment that is definitionally innocent. In the first story a gang plays a game of "Colin Maillard" or Blind Man's Buff, where the object of the game is for those blindfolded to catch a boy dressed as a girl. In **"Wo es war, soll ich werden"** Pascal, a 12-year-old, produces a learned paper "comparing the geology of the Galapagos and Iceland," which is accepted for publication by a scholarly journal. "At twelve," says a boy called Allen in another story, "you understand everything. Afterward you have to give it up and specialize."

If this is a sensuous world, where hands are always diving into briefs, where bodies share sleeping bags while the rain drums on the tent roof, and where boys kiss and hug as they discuss Klee's *Notebooks* or D'Arcy Thompson's *Growth and Form,* it is also one wrought by an art of maximum refinement like that evoked in Yeats' "Sailing to Byzantium," "a form as Grecian goldsmiths make / Of hammered gold and gold enamelling." Davenport's dialogue, for instance, crucial to the development of the stories, is very sharp, pared to the bone, but sometimes not true to actual speech with its false starts and spare fat.

Davenport began publishing stories comparatively late. His modern masters are Pound and Joyce: from Pound he learned the principle of eclectic reading and maximal formal restraint; from Joyce how to manage an over-ripe language that subverts the naturalism it seems to aspire to. But one also intuits behind his work the example of the ancient Greeks, the amatory and intellectual passion evident in the poems of Sappho (which Davenport has translated) or Plato's dialogues. And with its unapologetic commitment to high artifice, extolling the charms of boyish love, his work brings to mind Virgil's *Eclogues*—a title Davenport himself stole for a previous collection of stories. There is also a whiff of Shakespeare's love comedies, *A Midsummer Night's Dream* or *As You Like It,* in his delineation of a zest for life that is at once silly and wise, irresistibly attractive, though the reader need not share the vision informing it.

The Drummer of the Eleventh North Devonshire Fusiliers
is finally a lament for the world it celebrates, that art cannot in the end make real what it so vividly imagines, that
in our own history the kind of love for which Davenport's
fictions are an apologia has been stifled and punished. Two
boys, we learn in **"Wo es war, soll ich werden."** Ensign
James Hepburn, and Tom White, the drummer of the
Eleventh North Devonshire Fusiliers, were hanged on
March 7, 1811 for the crime of fondling each other "in a
room above a public house on Vere Street." Ultimately,
though, what Davenport is intent on defending is the
imagination itself, its capacity to make something from
nothing. His writing is a search, as one of his characters
says, for "new kinfolks . . . people who can make their
inside outside." Thus his manufacture of a world without
guile or self-consciousness, so good-natured and unbuttoned, where "The great thing is affability, not the kinship
but the kindness of one thing to another."

FURTHER READING

Criticism

Burgin, Richard. "Dying for Love." *The New York Times
Book Review* (21 October 1990): 24.
　　Brief, positive review of *The Drummer of the Eleventh
　　North Devonshire Fusiliers.*

Coale, Howard. Review of *The Jules Verne Steam Balloon*,
by Guy Davenport. *The New York Times Book Review* (22
November 1987): 32.
　　Criticizes the exaggeratedly symbolic nature of the col-
　　lection's characters, but praises Davenport's poetic and
　　sensual language.

Horvath, Brooke K. Review of *The Drummer of the Eleventh*

North Devonshire Fusiliers, by Guy Davenport. *The Review
of Contemporary Fiction* XI, No. 1 (Spring 1991): 313.
　　Notes the "robust wholesomeness" that pervades Dav-
　　enport's treatment of homoerotic themes in *The Drum-
　　mer of the Eleventh North Devonshire Fusiliers.*

Kenner, Hugh. "Assemblages." *National Review* XXXI, No.
39 (28 September 1979): 1238-41.
　　Commentary on Davenport's modern linguistic devices
　　in *Da Vinci's Bicycle.*

Kramer, Hilton. "After the Archaic." *The New York Times
Book Review* (6 September 1981): 7, 21.
　　Offers a negative assessment of *Eclogues*, noting that
　　Davenport's arcane allusions and idiosyncratic language
　　often make the stories in the collection difficult to follow.

Oldham, Gerda. Review of *The Drummer of the Eleventh
North Devonshire Fusiliers*, by Guy Davenport. *The Antioch
Review* 49, No. 1 (Winter 1991): 150-51.
　　Brief review of the novella "Wo es war, soll ich werden"
　　in *The Drummer of the Eleventh North Devonshire Fusil-
　　iers.*

Schöpp, Joseph C. " 'Perfect Landscape with Pastoral Fig-
ures': Guy Davenport's Danish Eclogue à la Fourier." In
*Facing Texts: Encounters between Contemporary Writers and
Critics*, edited by Heide Ziegler, pp. 128-39. Durham, N.C.:
Duke University Press, 1988.
　　Examination of "The Jules Verne Steam Balloon" in the
　　context of Davenport's "critical and poetic oeuvre."

Steiner, George. "Rare Bird." *The New Yorker* LVII, No. 41
(30 November 1981): 196, 199-202, 204.
　　Discusses the complexity of the literary allusions and in-
　　ventive vocabulary in Davenport's short stories. Steiner
　　places Davenport in the tradition of what Samuel Taylor
　　Coleridge referred to as "library cormorants" and notes
　　the influence of Ezra Pound on Davenport's narrative
　　perspective.

Additional coverage of Davenport's life and career is contained in the following sources
published by Gale Research: *Contemporary Authors*, Vols. 33-36 rev. ed.; *Contemporary
Authors New Revision Series*, Vol. 23; *Contemporary Literary Criticism*, Vols. 6, 14, 38;
and *Dictionary of Literary Biography*, Vol. 130.

Stephen Dixon

1936-

(Born Stephen Ditchik) American short story writer, novelist, and editor.

INTRODUCTION

A prolific experimental writer, Dixon combines disjointed prose and extended passages of dialogue to examine the lives of individuals who are overwhelmed by the frantic pace of civilization. By focusing on sensitive young male characters involved in problematic romances, Dixon explores such themes as the difficulties of friendship and communication, the clash between mundane and aberrant elements of human existence, and the significance of consequence, coincidence, and chance in life and art. Commenting on the antiheroic nature of Dixon's protagonists, Peter Bricklebank has stated: "[The] repetition of error, failure to learn from experience, [makes for] much humor and humanity in Dixon's characters. Compounded with the tragedy that it inevitably brings, it screws the lens through which we look at the world into a disquieting blur, giving disproportion a clarity all its own."

Biographical Information

Born in Brooklyn, Dixon is the son of a dentist and an interior decorator. After earning a bachelor's degree in international relations from the City College of New York in 1958, Dixon began working as a radio news reporter in Washington, D.C. During the next few years he worked as a news editor for CBS and as an editor for two detective fiction magazines. Beginning in 1964 Dixon spent a year studying creative writing at Stanford University on a fellowship, and his short stories began appearing in such publications as *Paris Review* and *Atlantic Monthly.* His first collection of short stories, *No Relief,* was published in 1976. Since 1980 Dixon has taught creative writing at Johns Hopkins University in Baltimore, Maryland, where he is a professor and the chairman of the university's Writing Seminars program.

Major Works of Short Fiction

Dixon's short stories are often set in urban surroundings and feature fast-paced narratives, satire, wordplay, and lengthy portions of dialogue. In his initial collection, *No Relief,* Dixon uses first-person narration to probe disparate facets of failed love and the role of fate in daily life. *Quite Contrary: The Mary and Newt Story* (1979), a volume comprising eleven interrelated short pieces, focuses on the three-year courtship of a young couple whose frequent breakups become their primary bond. Dixon's use of self-reflexive techniques and fragmented structures has prompted Jerome Klinkowitz to describe this work as "a perfectly natural reinforcement of form and content." *14*

Stories (1980), collects short fiction from throughout Dixon's career, including the often discussed title piece, which documents a series of events that results from a man's suicide, and "Love Has Its Own Action," in which the narrator seeks his ideal woman through a rapid succession of affairs and marriages. In the stories contained in *Movies* (1983), Dixon implements realistic dialogue, elaborate digressions, and surreal effects to explore the realms of fantasy and reality. The second half of *Time to Go* (1984), parts of *Love and Will* (1989), and the collection *Friends: More Will and Magna Stories* (1990), are often considered as part of a narrative cycle focusing on Will Taub, a mild-mannered teacher and writer and his wife Magna. Throughout the Will-and-Magna cycle, Dixon examines various dimensions of death, loss, and family relationships. Critics have also commented on the cyclic nature of *Frog* (1991), which comprises a collection of short stories, two novellas, and a novel focusing on the relationship between Howard "Frog" Tetch, his wife Denise, and their two daughters.

Critical Reception

Dixon has garnered many prominent awards and honors

for his short fiction, including a National Endowment for the Arts grant, a Guggenheim fellowship, and two O. Henry Awards. While some reviewers feel that Dixon's highly prolific nature as a published writer of more than four hundred short stories has detracted from the quality of his work, others consider Dixon one of the most important and innovative short fiction writers in American literature. Jerome Klinkowitz has observed that "Dixon manages to take the most familiar and even overexploited conventions and reinvest them with a sense of novelty unknown within contemporary realism."

PRINCIPAL WORKS

SHORT FICTION

No Relief 1976
Quite Contrary: The Mary and Newt Story 1979
14 Stories 1980
Movies 1983
Time to Go 1984
The Play, and Other Stories 1988
Love and Will 1989
All Gone 1990
Friends: More Will and Magna Stories 1990
Frog (short stories, novellas, and novel) 1991
Moon 1993

OTHER MAJOR WORKS

Work (novel) 1977
Too Late (novel) 1978
Fall and Rise (novel) 1985
Garbage (novel) 1988

CRITICISM

Frederick H. Guidry (essay date 1977)

SOURCE: "Catching the Sound of a Suitor," in *The Christian Science Monitor*, January 10, 1977, p. 22.

[*In the following review, Guidry praises the humor and narrative viewpoint of the stories collected in* No Relief.]

The five stories in [*No Relief*] show a fine talent for getting at the sound of a particular voice—that of a sensitive young man with a romantic problem. (Maybe these protagonists are not all that young; but their thought and speech patterns have the ring of early adulthood—never mind the age.)

The settings are all New York, but the particulars of streets and neighborhoods do not get in the way of a reader's recognizing them as everyday urban. The truly universalizing element, however, is the sense of helpless grappling with boy-girl relationships, of friendships crumbling despite frantic efforts to keep things going, of communica-tion taking place but failing to do the job it was hoped to do.

There is wry humor in all of these tales, which counteracts the potentially tiresome viewing of life always from the single standpoint of a goodwilled, aggressive-diffident narrator. To be sure, this discerning and fairminded person faithfully records conversations involving him, and even surmises the judgments others make concerning him. But the voice stays the same.

If you happen to recognize the voice as remarkably like your own, this book will warm your heart. Even if you have outgrown the viewpoint but have an affectionate regard for the post-adolescent stage of life, it will still have a certain nostalgic appeal.

"Mac in Love" typifies the collection, with its account of an absolutely irrepressible young suitor, who genially ignores the firmest farewells of his ex-girl friend. Shut out of her apartment, he attempts conversation from the street, and when that fails, he tries to involve neighbors with shouted entreaties. He is annoying and likable; his plight, the author seems to be saying, is just one of those things.

Indeed, the stories as a group stick to a formula, fashioning a pleasant, questing hero and generating sympathy for his hesitant approach to life, while populating his world with individuals on deliberately different wavelengths, for the reliable, mild pathos this creates. And the modest undertaking succeeds.

Julia O'Faolain (essay date 1977)

SOURCE: "Small Goods in Small Packages," in *The New York Times Book Review*, July 31, 1977, p. 15.

[*O'Faolain is an English-born Irish novelist, short story writer, translator, and editor whose works of short fiction include* We Might See Sights! *(1968),* Man in the Cellar *(1974), and* Daughters of Passion *(1982). In the following review, she censures the "bad taste" of the stories in* No Relief.]

Stephen Dixon's publishers describe him as "one of the decade's most widely published fictioneers," and Webster defines fictioneer as "a prolific writer of mediocre fiction." . . . His lead story [in *No Relief*], **"Mac in Love,"** might be a parable about unloved wordmen. Mac, repulsed by Jane, keeps yelling wistful nonsense at her balcony until she calls the police. He promises to stop. They let him go. He yells again. They come back, and so on *da capo*. All the stories in the book—Dixon's first—are about matings and mismatings.

Bad taste is probably so deliberate it is naive of me to mention it. It is most blatant in **"Last May,"** a story in which Bud and Marlene keep vigil in hospital, he by the bedside of his dying dad, she of her dying mother. Need I say that as life ebbs from the progenitors the young engage in the life-making activity? The dying die and so does passion. Bud ditches Marlene. To quote another Dixon story: "It was probably better in the end for us both and other rationales and I left, walked, took a bus, went to a movie, couldn't stay, cafeteria, couple of bars, got home." If you read this fast, it has the pulse of life. If you keep reading, it may affect your syntax.

Allen Wier   (essay date 1981)

SOURCE: "Glimpses into the Heart," in *Book World—The Washington Post,* February 22, 1981, p. 10.

[*Wier is an American short story writer, critic, and educator. In the following review, he praises Dixon's style but finds many of the pieces in* 14 Stories *superficial.*]

Most of the stories in Stephen Dixon's collection [*14 Stories*] are shaggy-dog stories. There are few resolutions. The book presents a Rube Goldberg fiction in which elaborate diagrams become the ends rather than the means. Sometimes there is great pleasure in watching Dixon invent, juxtapose, make connections; sometimes I wish there were more beneath the surface.

There are 13 stories in the book. The title story ["**14 Stories**"] refers to the 14th story of a hotel in which a man named Eugene Randall commits suicide, and the title suggests the many other stories we glimpse because of this one story, the many lives touched: the hotel maid who hears the shot, the lovers who find a suicide note that blew out of the window, the boy on the roof of a nearby building where the spent slug falls, the boy's neighbor who calls the police, the boy's mother who meets the neighbor who asks her out, the hotel operator who relays calls about the suicide, etc. The point of this and other stories in *14 Stories* seems to be the odd cause and effect relationships connecting so many things in the universe—simultaneity, coincidence, chance.

Dixon is aware of the possibilities of language; his prose is flat, clean, wry. At times he overdoes jokes, at times he extends word play until it becomes predictable, as it is in **"Milk is Very Good for You"** and **"Names."** A good deal that could have been comic in *14 Stories* strikes me as too obvious, too heavy-handed. The stories that do work, especially **"Love Has Its Own Action," "Cut,"** and **"The Security Guard,"** do so because their deeper implications are subtler and resonate longer.

Lee Abbott   (essay date 1981)

SOURCE: A review of *Too Late, Quite Contrary* and *14 Stories,* in *The South Carolina Review,* Vol. 13, No. 1, Fall, 1981, pp. 133-34.

[*In the following review, Abbott discusses Dixon's treatment of city life in his fiction, generally finding his short stories more successful than his novels.*]

In *Work,* his first novel, and *No Relief,* an early collection of stories, Dixon proved himself a comic but careful chronicler of mania in megalopolis, bringing us cabbie and cop, bozo and bureaucrat in prose quick and fine enough to be the best of works, art. His strengths, like city-living itself were many and apparent: energy, variety, and invention. His weaknesses, equally apparent to the country mouse in any critic, were few: surface mistaken for substance, eccentricity for character, and material for matter. The good news now is that Mr. Dixon remains the ever-watchful writer-baron of the asphalt jungle; the bad news is that, well, life in the city can be boring.

Too Late, a 1978 novel, is a dash, dizzying of pace, provoking of yawn—a dash through the mean streets attended by those good 20th-century villains Nightmare, Paranoia and Malaise. At the movies one evening, Art A. Aliman learns from his girlfriend Donna that the film is too violent. She's going home, alone. She'll meet him later. She doesn't, of course, and what follows is a horror-show of high-jinks, Chaplin-like slapstick and heavy-duty cruelty as our hero-narrator-victim takes to the streets and the phone to find a woman who, even at book's end, remains beyond the beck of kith and ken; she's vanished into a Pandemonium of murder and mayhem, of wist and woe. At his best, Dixon uses his plot to fix Art's place among and relationship to, as Mr. Rogers says, "the people in the neighborhood"—from junky to jerk to street-corner Jesus. At his worst, Dixon wastes his considerable skills and eye for detail showing us what we've seen before: *Mondo Cane* cavalcade of lunacy and loss. For all its verve and comedy, *Too Late* is more atlas than novel, a sore misreading of Mr. James's notion that "landscape is character."

Quite Contrary, a 1979 collection of connected stories, on the other hand, is tuneful testimony to Dixon's ability to exploit Gotham's hugger-mugger to the lasting advantage of his people. Caught on what's billed as "the cutting edge of NYC," Mary LeBroom and Newt Leeb suffer each other as only lovers dare—through break-up and reconciliation, through abortion and infidelity, through want and wealth—in a chronicle, told from end to beginning (a sweet way of having your ache and eating it too!), that works from the glory and gut of a character. In this 11-story volume, Mr. Dixon, with the care and patience that seriousness brings, thrusts us into a relationship run at full tilt, a relationship fueled by need and hope and dread—the right stuff that's real *and* realized.

More recent is *14 Stories* (actually 13, but that's a story itself), part of the Johns Hopkins series of poetry and fiction. His clunkers aside, of which there are a handful, Dixon's finer efforts (**"The Security Guard," "The Intruder"** and the title story [**"14 Stories"**]) recall the virtues of Michaels (Leonard), Barthelme (Donald), and Marx (Groucho)—namely, passion, daring and elan. Especially noteworthy is **"Love Has Its Own Action,"** in which love, the peril and promise of it, hustles the narrator at breakneck speed through a series of affairs and marriages, searching for a woman who had "intelligence, understanding, and a good nature and sense of humor and was thoroughly feminine, seemingly talented and self-sufficient and she very much appealed to my groin." High-order Action, indeed. In this collection, Dixon has turned his interest from city to citizen, his stories swift with the sense of folks, modern and therefore crazed, busy with the business of living and, uh, loving—in the Village, in the Streets, and in hotels without a 13th storey.

Lastly, what remains notable about even Dixon's less accomplished work is style: pure Nighttown, a Broadway-Bowery of zip, pop and snap-crackly. When he presses, when he's setting you up, when his reach exceeds his etcetera, he's cute, self-indulgent, lazy: "Maybe me because so far it's so far from what's what I believe." When he's right, he's as true as fine science: "Donna has very small breasts, way below average. She was either ultra-high newspaper and magazine fashion, shampoo or bubbly soap on tv or gloves or stockings or shoes with the top of her body removed." Ah, such is meet and choice, writing to remember and to celebrate—even outside the city limits.

Walter Cummins   (essay date 1982)

SOURCE: "Story Worlds," in *The Literary Review,* Fairleigh Dickinson University, Vol. 25, No. 3, Spring, 1982, pp. 462-72.

[*In the following excerpt from a review, Cummins discusses the style and characterization of the pieces in* 14 Stories.]

[The pieces collected in Stephen Dixon's *14 Stories*] have their source in a comic imagination. Yet they manage to be more troubling than funny. Laughter dissolves because we cannot remain detached from his worlds. The reader would have to stay only an observer to enjoy the comic effects. But Dixon pulls us inside his environments to experience the dislocation and dissociation, the lack of certainty and control, the rule of accident. Although they are not realistic, Dixon's stories serve as paradigms of contemporary urban America, especially of existence in New York.

Rhythm is the main quality of his work, the fundamental fact behind his story worlds. This rhythm is reminiscent of early silent films in that everything, all the objects, are recognizable; but the pace and stylization of delivery makes the reality unique.

Dixon deliberately seems to allow rhythm to dominate. He keeps the prose swift and direct, with many assertions of fact, one after the other. He uses few figures, a bare minimum of qualification and descriptive elaboration. Characterization is also minimized. His people, isolated from environment and from each other, have no power over their lives. They are swept up in a rush of events like swimmers struggling for direction against an overwhelming current.

The opening paragraph of **"Streets"** goes on for a page and one-half of simple declarative sentences that read like notes for the choreography of an action:

> Two people stand on a street corner. Or rather she stands on the corner. He's gone into a corner store. She looks up. A jet plane passes. She waves at the plane and laughs. She looks at the cars passing on the avenue. A bus. She waves at the people in the bus. A young boy in the bus waves back. She sees me waiting at a bus stop. She smiles. I smile. The man comes out of the store. He holds a package he didn't seem to have when he went into the store. She takes the package and puts it in her pocketbook and runs. He walks after her. She sees him walking after her and runs faster. He starts jogging after her. She sees him and begins to run as fast as she can. At least it seems like that. . . .

The entire story is an escalation of movement, action, violence, and confusion. The narrator becomes involved in the physical activity of the other two, "as if I'm part of a threesome." The man who bought the package hits the woman, who is stunned unconscious for a few seconds. Then the narrator's view is blocked by a crowd. Somehow a bystander who tries to help the woman ends up with a knife in his chest, and the woman lies on the sidewalk again, this time with her head in a circle of blood. But the narrator is not sure what happened to cause these injuries, and no one will tell him.

The story then becomes tangled in the convolutions of producing an explanation and getting help. Every detail of the sequence turns out an ordeal—finding a dime to call for help, arguing about tourniquets, wondering whether the little girl who went to call got distracted, watching an ambulance rush past, seeking a public phone. By the end of the story, the narrator, who has tried to call the police from a hardware store, is beaten over the head with a wrench by the store owner and lies as one of six gravely injured people waiting for aid that may never arrive.

No one in this story is named. People are called "the man," "the woman," "the girl," "a man," "someone." Although the streets and stores are not described either, Dixon conveys a complex world, one we can feel more than we see, a world of menace and violence in which the most casual encounter can turn into disaster. Yet human concern is lacking. After twelve pages we understand the logic of this world: things go from bad to worse; all attempts to help result in greater chaos and pain.

Dixon's feat is impressive. In one sense he is a minimalist, that is, in eschewing details of characterization, place, setting, and objects. He works mainly with the barest reports of actions. And yet he creates a realm of disturbing intensity because his people are swept up in the rhythm of a process that usually becomes an obsession.

Peter Bricklebank   (essay date 1984)

SOURCE: A review of *Movies,* in *Carolina Quarterly,* Vol. XXXVI, No. 3, Spring, 1984, pp. 85-7.

[*In the following review of* Movies, *Bricklebank praises the humor, insight, and originality of Dixon's dialogue and narrative style.*]

Movies contains all that is characteristic Stephen Dixon. . . . Not only is he again holding his slightly distorted mirror up to life, but his tape recorder is running apace. The dialogue is uncannily accurate but yet constantly surprising. Shuffling through contradiction and digression, hesitation and inversion, each step of a character and twist of a tale is gloriously funny—and often a wrong step, and often a tragic twist. But in addition to previous collections such as *14 Stories* and *Quite Contrary,* these pieces seem less convoluted and more straightforward in narrative line. In **"The Frame,"** a customer wishes to hang a photocopy and returns to a store he's not visited for many years. There he is struck by the likeness of the assistant to his dead sister; and past is 'framed' in present. This more obviously 'literary' quality provides counterpoint to Dixon's lusher linguistic jungles.

I was reminded in these stories of T. S. Eliot's magic lantern which threw "nerves in patterns on a screen." In the title piece [**"Movies"**], a couple's polarized reactions to a new rave flick casts their relationship into the grotesque. The movie is incomprehensibly surreal—giant lips amidst a nauseating array of cinematography—and the man retreats to a peep show and television. These are at least understandable escapes, if ineffectual ones. But as often in Dixon, mis- and multi-interpretation is always possible, always a problem. Variations on telling a story—**"The Barbecue"**—or telling the truth—**"Small Bear"**—are open ended yet limited. What is the man to do when the surreal slips from screen into real life and his wife announces that she wishes to separate? Deal with it, perhaps; it's an everyday occurrence. But when she adds she'll move in with the woman who took the seat next to her when he left? And this because of one movie? In a marvelous speech as off-the-wall as that movie, the wife attempts to put everything in focus. The movie showed, she explains (and summarizes this collection), " '. . . the sometime absurdity of living together as couples and the possibility of undiscovered courage . . . the voices we hear. . . .' " There is a direct link then between the fantasy world of the cinema screen and the man in the street. Finding and understanding the borderline of the irrational that separates the two leads to much questioning throughout these 17 tales. . . . But there is no escape from the inevitably useless answer, or the super-realism associated with the screen but more accurately of the sidewalk.

Even with this heightened 'realism,' it is not much of a comparison, as has been made, to see Dixon's work as "Kafka-esque." There are no unusual events here, no symbols or secondary levels of meaning. These are stories of cops and robbers, lovers, the un-streetwise, all that is first slapstick and then tragic. Characters are rarely described in any detail. Unless, like the misunderstood 'hero' of **"Cy,"** they are hit by grenade, car and bicycle beyond redemption of that ultimate of make-up artists, the plastic surgeon. They are extras in their own B-movie horror; superfluous to their employers, hardly the heart-throbs of their lovers. If they come remotely close to becoming pin-ups, it's only because they're Wanted—or have socially skewered themselves—perhaps on the boom mike—and are still trying to talk their way out of it.

These are ordinary people surprised by the fickleness of mundanity: sometimes life unprovokedly bites. As those rendered goofy by "Candid Camera" or voluble by a news lens, they perform accordingly. They stare or say the wrong thing. They get what they think is a joke when there isn't one. They cherish their mother (who's awaiting them with an axe). They arrive blithely on the scene of a construed crime oblivious that they are stepping into the spotlight of interrogation as prime suspect.

Often their predicaments are self generated by the most humane of errors and motives. They mistakenly give a pocket watch instead of a coin to a panhandler on the spur of the moment (**"The Watch"**), or they are embroiled in their conscience and debate over borrowing a wheelchair to visit their sick baby (**"Not Charles"**). Often they fight back at a world too grossly unfair with a kind of celluloid courage spliced with true concern, but they are harshly treated. After great emotional and financial loss, they find themselves howling "You bum, you bum" after the panhandler or find, having finally secured the wheelchair, they're too late, their baby is dead, their hopes and journey in vain. There is a hopelessness about many of the characters' predicaments. In the 1982 O'Henry Prize story, **"Layaways,"** the all too familiar events of a store robbery occurs. When one young man tries to fight back, he manages to get his mother killed, only to repeat his mistake later with his best friend. He proves only that screen heroism has no place in our murky urban badlands. This repetition of error, failure to learn from experience, is one that makes for so much humor and humanity in Dixon's characters. Compounded with the tragedy that it inevitably brings, it screws the lens through which we look at the world into a disquieting blur, giving disproportion a clarity all its own.

The tattered social fabric through which these individuals rush pell mell is uncomfortably recognizable. Throughout **"The Hole"** bombings occur in civic places with spiralling frequency and death tolls, in the same heartlessly casual way as those in the news of recent months. But these are the background to the (in)human story of a teacher who refuses to let his trapped class escape until all, including himself, can be saved. When his son is beaten to death, so too is the possibility of any happy endings, leaving a disquiet verging on paranoia that suffuses not only these tales, but very possibly the street or bookstore (remember the bag check?) where you bought this review. . . .

Dixon's narratives run and jump through hoops of possibilities, taking on, as always, lives of their own. Ringing true of the rhythms of life—the spoken word, the unspoken thought—these tales are 'documentaries.' They are also farce; Dixon makes us laugh, cry, and feel the world of the little man or woman, inescapably the one we're in. It is only by seeing the minutiae of life, its hassles, its waiting in lines *outside* cinemas, that we can come to terms with that inside. The small people here wonder whether it will be worth it as they wait in line. They check that they have the increased price of admission and yearn alternatives. Of these—as many characters here—reading is one. Certainly *Movies* would be a fine investment. Not only does it repay attention with humor, insight and originality, but it shows us just how hectically absurd our world really is.

Tom LeClair (essay date 1984)

SOURCE: "Overheard Stories," in *Book World—The Washington Post,* August 5, 1984, pp. 8-9.

[*LeClair is an American educator and critic who regularly contributes book reviews to such publications as* The New York Times Book Review, New Republic, *and* Saturday Review. *In the following review of* Time to Go, *he criticizes the repetitive qualities of Dixon's stories.*]

Stephen Dixon's *Time to Go* . . . suffers from sameness: all the stories are about loss—taking leave of parents, children, lovers, friends, students, places—and are composed in a militantly banal style, as if Samuel Beckett were recording the telephone conversations of middle-class Baltimoreans. Several are wonderful, arresting in their simplicity: **"The Bench,"** about a handyman who tries to learn from gossip and speculation where a loving father and infant daughter he used to watch have gone, and the title story [**"Time to Go"**], in which a grown son can't get rid of his father's voice, advising, cajoling, criticizing, loving. But too many are either sterile completions of Dixon's "going" pattern or lack any imaginative lift, a quality of perception or style that raises a trivial subject to attention. Particularly weak are the stories about the writer Will, whose problem is lack of subjects.

Mike Moyle   (essay date 1984)

SOURCE: A review of *Movies* and *Time to Go,* in *The South Carolina Review,* Vol. 17, No. 1, Fall 1984, pp. 113-15.

[*In the excerpt below, Moyle discusses what he views as the uneven quality of Dixon's short stories.*]

Unfortunately, and as is often the case in the work of writers who are prolific, Dixon's short fiction . . . has been a bit uneven, some of his more than two hundred published stories if technically proficient, downright bad; on occasion he wastes his time, and he shouldn't always trust his belief: I'll even go as far as to say that Dixon has written *too* much, that he seems unable at times to pass over what's better left alone. *14 Stories,* generally an impressive 1980 collection . . . , offers a few examples. **"The Sub,"** for the most part an interior monologue about a substitute teacher's fantasies and their relationship to reality, is skillfully sustained but, I'm afraid, dull; and **"Signatures,"** the story of a man who for a living collects the John Hancocks of the famous, the near-famous, and the potentially-famous and who has an unmemorable encounter with a playwright, is mercifully brief but insipid. . . . When we read Dixon, we sometimes feel that production is all he's interested in.

Though in the end they shine quite brightly, *Movies* and *Time to Go,* Dixon's newest collections and the ones under consideration here, provide more of the same. In the former, **"Stop"** contains vintage Dixon material—a man is being chased by the police through the streets and across the rooftops of a New York waterfront neighborhood—but is curiously lifeless; and **"Joke,"** despite Dixon's limiting himself to three incredibly fast-paced pages, is tedious in its recounting of what could be but isn't a prank played on the narrator by a woman with whom he's sexually involved. In *Time to Go,* **"Self-Portrait,"** a monologue from a writer-teacher who goes on ad nauseam about how he'd like to draw himself, rather than get down to his real business for the day, is well written but self-indulgent: the story ostensibly concerns one Will Taub (as do all the stories in this second section of the book), but we feel as if we're reading a Dixon warm-up exercise. **"The Beginning of Something,"** which *is* in part about Taub's limbering up for a few hours bout with his typewriter, made me plain angry—it is a lamentable piece of metafiction that caused

me momentarily to forget how good Dixon can be. Finally, in **"Magna Takes the Calls,"** during the course of which Taub receives the news of the passing of his uncle and the murder of a friend's wife, Dixon takes what Yeats considered one of the two great subjects, death, and makes us yawn.

Fortunately, these kinds of clunkers clearly constitute a rarity, not a rule. By and large the two volumes contain stories that range from the recommendable to the just-can't-be-missed. At his absolute best, and he's there surprisingly often, Dixon is both gut-wrenching and funny. For instance, the *Movies* tale **"Darling"** touches us with its depiction of the plight of the ne'er-do-well narrator, whose wife has kicked him out of their home and who has found a job a thousand miles away taking care of a bedridden invalid, at the same time that it makes us giggle over some of the torments the narrator inflicts upon his charge because he can't take the pathos and frustrations of their combined situations any longer and wants her to fire him—doing everything except what she asks of him and intentionally spilling water on her. Similarly, *Time to Go's* **"Goodbye to Goodbye,"** an account of another narrator-loser's efforts to come to grips with his wife's abandoning him, stabs our emotions as it teases our brains: trying to bid adieu to bidding adieu, the man gives us five versions of his predicament, four uproariously outrageous (and each in its turn acknowledged as a lie), one presumably—and sadly—true. In addition, the title story [**"Time to Go"**] and **"Don"** work on us in similar ways. The latter is brilliant, a seemingly random outpouring of paragraphs that jump around in time and tense to form a full portrait of the titular character, a portrait that many lesser writers would have stretched into a novel. . . .

Only a little less pleasing is Dixon's ability to be purely serious, or nearly so, in fashion that makes us feel the practically unutterable pain of some of his characters while it assiduously avoids sentimentality. In **"The Frame,"** the final story in *Movies,* for example, the male narrator goes into a small shop to buy a picture frame and is aided by a deformed woman; she poignantly reminds him of his dead sister, who hobbled through a significant portion of her twenty-five-year life with a similar ailment. **"The Package Store,"** the last piece in the first section of *Time to Go,* presents the quiet tragedy of a small-business owner and his wife trying to eke out a living in a Baltimore neighborhood consisting of more robbers, it nearly seems, than customers. And **"Cy,"** a standout among even the best stories in *Movies,* is reminiscent of *The Elephant Man,* though perhaps more heart-rending; here's the terribly disfigured, purblind, but in his own way savvy title character-narrator telling us of his reunion with his mother, who's been under the impression that he's dead, after he has been virtually chased by unbelievably cruel neighbors out of the apartment he has called refuge: "I don't dare kiss her cheek yet. I kiss the air instead. I've forgotten what it's like to hold another human being. The feeling can't be physically or mentally reproduced. How often I've hugged my pillow. Myself, if only to embrace some person's flesh . . . Not even a dog have I kissed the nose of or hugged in ten years." Moving stuff, that.

Last are the stories, slightly less satisfactory because ultimately more ephemeral than those which are humorously tragic or simply devastating, that I can classify only as knee-slappers and wild fun. In *Movies* we have **"The Hole,"** hilarious mania about a rash of bombing in the "City" and the off-duty policeman who gets involved in the rib-tickling rescue of some of the victims, one unreasonably reasonable schoolteacher in particular. And in *Time to Go* there's **"Eating the Placenta,"** a romp about Will Taub's frantic attempt to escape the verbal clutches of a pestering student and run home to his pregnant, almost let's-get-to-the-hospital-I-think-it's-time wife—only to be harried by the persistent undergraduate over the phone when he reaches his destination, though Taub's final triumph is sweeter than aspartame.

I would enjoy going on at greater length showering praise on gems like **"Layaways"** and **"Not Charles"** in *Movies* and **"Wheels"** and **"Reversal"** in *Time to Go,* but the limitation of allotted space prohibits me. So since I've written rather specifically of Stephen Dixon, purposely treating him as someone with whom you're likely familiar if you're a regular reader of these pages, let me end more generally. These two books aren't as unified as their publishers make them out to be, and once in a while Dixon doesn't dazzle. But as an unidentified reviewer says on the dust jacket of *Movies,* Dixon is "always professional," and his most pedestrian efforts usually bristle and pulse with life.

John Domini   (essay date 1984)

SOURCE: "Day-to-Dayness," in *The New York Times Book Review,* October 14, 1984, p. 34.

[*In the following review of* Time to Go, *Domini offers an unfavorable assessment of Dixon's short fiction.*]

Mr. Dixon's imagination [in *Time to Go*] sticks close to home. His principal subject is the clash of the mundane and the aberrant, those unsettling run-ins with wackos or former lovers all too familiar to anyone who's ever lived in a city. Here that city is nearly always New York, where Mr. Dixon has spent most of his life, and most of the time the protagonist is an unmarried male writer in early middle age. On top of that, more than half the stories are about the same writer, Will Taub, who teaches in a university very much like Johns Hopkins University, where Mr. Dixon teaches.

Time to Go does have touches of exotica. The title story ["Time to Go"] features a running conversation between Taub and his dead father (the ghost proves one of the liveliest talkers in the book), while other stories disrupt chronology or, Barth-like, reflect on the story in process. But only one story genuinely breaks away from the metropolitan settings and writerly circumstances. And that one, the surreal **"Come on a Coming,"** is grounded in such obvious symbolism and is so patly predictable as to suggest Mr. Dixon is better off with his more down-to-earth urban encounters.

In these stories, everyone arrives eventually at the same conclusion—that the day-to-day is preferable to the outlandish—and their logic provides the best moments. Mr.

Dixon allows every character his or her moment of enjoyably lunatic self-defense. There is a prolonged analysis, for instance, of how best to catch the eye of a woman you once lived with. Such bits are entirely familiar but rich with cranky charm nonetheless.

Outside of such moments, however, *Time to Go* is awfully underdone. The opening story, **"The Bench,"** concerns some subdued and pointless gossip about an unnamed father and his baby girl, and the last story, **"Reversal,"** offers nothing more than the depressing thoughts of a character diapering his child.

When some excitement does occur—even the robbery of a wedding ring—it too is handled with a stick-figure soullessness. . . .

All Mr. Dixon's encounters lack any but the most general physicality. And the quieter moments, which a writer interested in day-to-dayness would be expected to savor, are handled with the same abstraction. The changing of diapers in **"Reversal"** is presented as it might be in a how-to manual:

> He raises her bottom by holding her feet up in one hand, slips the double diapers out from under her, sets her down, keeps one hand on her chest so she won't roll off the changing board to the floor, drops the wet diapers into the diaper pail and closes it.

The repression of rhetoric and an emphasis on the trivial are hallmarks of many contemporary short stories. But Mr. Dixon is so unrelenting in both regards that he ends up compounding a lack of imagination with a near absence of passion. His characters' theorizing all starts to sound the same after a while, and his endings, deprived of even the least bubble of poetic effect, suffocate. Despite its sensitivity to its characters' bad moments and its pleasing attention to structure, *Time to Go* amounts to less than Mr. Dixon's *14 Stories.* Its failures point up the dangers in the fashion for the understated.

Jerome Klinkowitz   (essay date 1984)

SOURCE: "The Self-Apparent Word," in his *The Self-Apparent Word: Fiction as Language / Language as Fiction,* Southern Illinois University Press, 1984, pp. 86-121.

[*A professor of English at the University of Northern Iowa, Klinkowitz is the author of such critical studies as* Literary Disruptions *(1975; revised, 1980) and* The Life of Fiction *(1977) as well as several books on the noted American novelist and short story writer Kurt Vonnegut. In the following excerpt from a chapter in* The Self-Apparent Word, *Klinkowitz discusses the style and themes of Dixon's short fiction.*]

Dixon manages to take the most familiar and even overexploited conventions and reinvest them with a sense of novelty unknown within contemporary realism. His own sense of playfulness expresses itself in titles and structures, as in his volume *14 Stories* which contains only thirteen pieces but whose first, **"14 Stories,"** takes place on the thirteenth story of a hotel—which is, in common superstitious practice, designated as the fourteenth floor. Dixon's sense of artful whimsy helps structure the story, which begins where a conventional tale might end. "Eugene Randall held the gun in front of his mouth and fired. The bullet smashed his upper front teeth, left his head through the back of his jaw, pierced an ear lobe and broke a window that overlooked much of the midtown area." Already the reader has been told more about the shell's trajectory, by which the story's line of action will proceed, than about poor Eugene; but the tacky signs and symbols of his worldly life have been worked to death by realistic fiction, while the path of that utterly improbable bullet opens the way to genuinely interesting material.

The gun's sound has penetrated several floors of the hotel, alerting a maid; one of his suicide notes has drifted out the broken window; and the bullet itself lands a block away on a brownstone roof, startling a boy and setting off a complicated episode, the effects of which reach far into the future. The maid must clean up Randall's gory mess, a young couple argue over what to do about the recovered note, and on and on through a series of consequences no less real because they don't touch Eugene Randall's fading life in the cozily humanistic way conventional realists teach readers to expect. Instead of answering questions, Dixon's story generates new fictions, as when the boy claims someone has tried to shoot him. "Now what kind of story is that?" a neighbor asks, as this new thread of narrative spins itself out, among many others, from Eugene Randall's terminal act.

"14 Stories" is a good example of how Dixon avoids the facile signaling of conventional realism in favor of the richer possibilities of signs at play. Makes of autos, tastes in music, styles and qualities of clothing—all these are bits and pieces of the real world which realists use to signal a certain type of character or development of plot. They locate the reader in an identifiable world and serve as a shorthand notation of attitudes and values the author wishes employed. There is always the danger that fiction might become sociology when these signals take over and become the work itself; in any event, they allow the writer to escape working with his or her fiction, falling back instead on the catalogue of social mores the reader already knows.

Dixon's talent is to stick it out with his materials, to write fiction with them rather than to signal predetermined attitudes, and so he never lets his signifiers rush off into the world in search of the things they represent. Eugene Randall's suicide in a shabby hotel room could easily start a movie running in our heads, but then Dixon's story would be out of control, happening somewhere off the page. Thus the reader is given no more than one line of it before the chambermaid downstairs is seen worrying about the sound, and no more than a moment of that before an equally interesting narrative begins about the kid up the block who has been nearly nicked by the shot. With such rapid shifts there is no time to lose oneself in the illusion of story, for another one is ready to begin; soon the play of signs becomes a self-conscious act in itself. From sentence to sentence there is a great deal of writing to be done before anyone can sit back and say they know it all.

Unlike the conventional realists who pretend the world is an easy place to have and hold, Dixon knows that things go on. At least six distinct actions take place in the title story, more if every new involvement is counted. Moreover, with each little tale there is an endless regression of fact. For example, the boy's neighbor never should have touched the bullet before calling the police. "If I'd been smart I should have let him pass when he came flying downstairs," the man admits. "I never should have left my flat for cigarettes—never should have been smoking, in fact. Cancer I'll get, and also a jail sentence. In fact, I never should have taken my first puff when I was young and everyone said don't take your first puff, Willy, because it will lead to bad things. Little did they know. Do you smoke, Warren?" he asks the boy, and we are back to the first level of narration, ready for more. There is no end to it, as the true genius of signs knows: the world goes on and on, and to section off any part of it is an act of artistic fraudulence.

So many simultaneous interests might be a strategy prompted by the short attention spans and precipitous boredom of contemporary audiences, but this habit of stretching things to their full extent and beyond runs through all of Stephen Dixon's work and serves a deeper purpose. In **"Mac in Love"** from his first collection, *No Relief,* the narrator's girlfriend is breaking off their affair (a perennial Dixon theme), and under these conditions nothing is simple, as the story's techniques show. A nice day? Yes, blue sky, but there is pollution which the eye cannot see "because of something to do with particles and refraction" and on and on while the relationship, tenuous even in its better days, is sustained now only by language. Even on his way out the door there are conversations which by virtue of words and syntax can be stretched to infinity, just as the repercussions from Eugene Randall's bullet generated any number of succeeding texts. Consider this final variation on a sentence which has grown through the preceding paragraphs: "Will you please thank Ruth for telling Mrs. Roy to tell Ruth to tell you to tell Mrs. Roy to tell Ruth to tell you your watering can's on the window ledge?" Robbe-Grillet's phenomenological realism is capable of laborious description, but never with such comedy behind it—and never with language's own action, rather than the object's, as its substance.

In Dixon's work a five-hundred word sentence is not unusual, though its variety of combinational techniques rarely makes it boring to read. What begins as an attempt to capture it all, as in the seemingly realistic sketch of a narrator's comatose father dying in a hospital, ends as a virtual recreation of the old man's helpless state. Simple instructions for communication—blink once if you hear me, twice if you don't—soon extend themselves to the ridiculous even as they try harder and harder, through qualification after qualification, to succeed. The hallmark of this behavior, and of this style, is persistence. Both Dixon's narrators and his sentences go on and on, until credibility turns incredible and then back into the believable again. Mac keeps saying goodbye until the police warn him, and then again as they carry him off. Another narrator annoys a woman in a cafeteria through all manner of brush-offs, rejections, threats, physical violence, and mayhem. In Stephen Dixon's work there is no simple end to anything, as if the conventions of realism are a Pandora's box which, once opened, must be faithfully and persistently explored. . . .

The question which occupies the center of Dixon's work—the fragility of human relationships, compounded by the danger of reality running off into infinite digressions and qualifications as stability collapses—is answered by the book which synthesizes his talents as a short fictionist and novelist: the integrated collection, *Quite Contrary: The Mary and Newt Story.* These eleven fictions treat the three-year, off-and-on affair of a couple the likes of which run through nearly all of Dixon's writing. Such involvements, he says, include endless complications; love begets much more than love in return. Their first meeting and the start of their relationship, for example, are based on parting:

> "I don't know. I don't like the roles. You asking. Why couldn't I have asked you? Because again, I don't want to. Why not whatever we might do only when and if we feel like it? Let's start by leaving here. Do you want to?"
>
> "Yes I do."
>
> "Me too. Then if out front we still want to walk together, okay. And if not, or even going downstairs we want to part, then we do. If we don't want to part on the stairs or in front of the building, and a block away, let's say, we still want to be together, then we will. And on and on like that till either of us doesn't want to be with the other person or both of us don't want to stop. Well, sometimes in the future one of us will want to stop, but not until that person says so, okay?"

Dixon's couples are a fated mismatch: he is "too demanding," she has just departed one marriage and doesn't want to be tied down again too soon. Their tendency to break up is in fact the cement of their relationship. If Newt tries to tell a friend that he and Mary are "this time really through," he faces the reply: "Nah, you two are never really through. You're a pair: Tom and Jerry, Biff and Bang. You just tell yourselves you're through to make your sex better and your lives more mythic and poetic and to repeatedly renew those first two beatific weeks you went through."

Like the parting scene in **"Mac in Love,"** these particular qualities of the Mary and Newt story lend themselves to articulation—endless articulation—and what otherwise in a relationship might not even be noticed is here endlessly explained. Self-effacing realism would miss these elements, since they are the stuff of language rather than of event. Conversely, a less linguistically self-apparent affair might be over and done with before much fiction could be made from it; it is unlikely a conventional realist would ever tell the couple's story, since so much of it depends upon their self-apparent words which Dixon's techniques profile. Mary and Newt's experience is sustained by language and therefore kept before our imaginative attention.

The story-collection form of *Quite Contrary* lets Dixon use form as well as content to accomplish his narration, and here we see how his views of human relationship and the quality of reality which self-apparent fiction catches are one and the same. Mary and Newt's rocky affair provides material for storytelling, but also hints for different ways to structure their tale. Indeed, the telling is the story. **"Man of Letters"** prints sixteen drafts of a single break-up letter which concludes with the decision not to split up at all—a choice encouraged by the textuality of the narrator's own writing, an example of how technique can become its own substance and sustenance. **"The Meeting"** tries to explain the odd circumstances of a relationship which began with a sustained parting. Under the gun of explaining such odd behavior the narrator finds he cannot tell a straight story and so pleads: "Let me start again, though keeping my confusion in. I don't know why, but right now that seems important to me." If his writing effaces itself, the special point of the relationship will be lost, and so instead he opts for self-apparency, "To involve the reader in the actual writing act." This self-questioning continues throughout the story and makes its own point, which the puzzling content alone might have obscured. **"Em"** and **"Mary's Piece"** are the two narrators' attempts to make sense of one another, and *making sense* is defined as a writing problem (they even discuss submitting these very stories to magazines). **"The Franklin Stove"** begins with the narrator off at a writers' colony, composing a Mary and Newt break-up story; it ends back in his apartment with Mary herself seducing him away from his typewriter—and away from his apparent intention to leave. When the affair does reach its finish (as finally as possible, for the book itself is coming to a close, with only ten pages left) the writer presents an aptly named "Prolog" in which his grief is so massive and disruptive that it can no longer be screamed, spoken, or even typed, "so I type goodnight."

From *No Relief* and *Quite Contrary* Dixon has proceeded with collections which cohere without any formal theme except the exercise of technique, which in itself proves to be as interesting as the illusion of story. The true synthesis for any self-apparent writer is finally on the level of form. Among the pieces collected in *14 Stories,* an old man dying in a hospital (**"Cut"**) is the focus of a dozen different actions, including those of relatives, visitors, doctors, nurses, orderlies, and so on, not to mention his own concerns. Shifting point of view from paragraph to paragraph thus tells the same story and many different stories all at once; the most common of realistic techniques is here used self-apparently to show how many different realities compete around this pitifully wasted man who cannot exert his own dominance. Speech and dialogue, two more simple parts of realism, yield marvelously transformative effects simply by having their consonants juggled, as in the otherwise pornographic story **"Milk Is Very Good For You"** which becomes a slapstick farce: "We were in red, Jane heated on top of me, my sock deep in her funt and linger up her masspole . . ."; the normal turn of events is further thrown off center by having the characters express insatiable desires for milk. A simple event, such as a whirl-wind romance and just as sudden breakup, is told again and again with the winds of love and disaffection whirling faster each time (**"Love Has Its Own Action"**); writing this way soon changes reality into absurd improbability, though each step has been small enough so that one never knows just where common sense turns crazy.

How stories need reshaping (for truthfulness of effect) is demonstrated by Dixon's fourth collection, *Movies.* The title piece shows how the substance of a popular film has less effect than its interpretation, and that all interpretations are different, to the point of human relationships foundering in their wake. **"The Watch"** combines several Dixon techniques to create a situation in which the narrator gives a panhandler his pocket watch by mistake, and must then argue with the bum, a gathering crowd, and the police as he tries to clarify the situation. In **"The Barbecue"** a party guest tries to tell the company a story, but only their promptings for changes and embellishments allows him to finally get it "right." When a bear wanders across a cottage site in Maine, a man and wife have great trouble reporting the incident to each other, let alone to the game warden and other authorities, and when a newspaper story appears the next day, the facts are changed once again (**"Small Bear"**). The most amusing story of this group is **"The Moviemaker,"** in which a writer publishes his novel about his breaking up with an old lover only to have her phone him with demands that she adapt it for the movies. Her script will contain numerous revisions, with persons, places, and things altered to fit the image she had tried to project in their relationship. As before with real life, the narrator now resists her tampering with his story. She counters with the taunt that he will probably concoct a salable short story from her present phone call—as he obviously has to judge from the piece of fiction being read. These techniques are not reflexive or metafictional, for something "real" is taking place in each. Yet those elements of reality are conventionally self-apparent, for the reader is urged to take part in the compositional nature of each event, no part of which may be taken for granted. The affairs of life are dangerously unstable, and reporting them is even more volatile a business than trying to live them, as Dixon's besieged lover/narrators learn at every turn.

The other self-apparent principle *Movies* demonstrates is how fictions are generated. In earlier stories by Dixon whimsy was often the structural basis for affairs, romantic or bureaucratic, which went on and on according to their own ludic possibilities. In this collection **"The Shirt"** recalls the playful style: the narrator is given an ill-fitting, uncomfortable shirt by a well-meaning neighbor, and for page after page endures an ever-complicating series of events (involving inputs of everyone else's trouble) as he tries to give the shirt away. New for Dixon are stories which accommodate this structure to less comic circumstances. In **"Cy"** a disfigured narrator undergoes an unending series of humiliations and inflictions of cruelty, each more unspeakable and inhumane than the last, as if to test both the writer's genius and the reader's patience at enduring such unpleasantness. **"Darling"** begins with the polite, courteous, and loving exchanges between a bedridden invalid and the narrator who is hired to care for her. But within this gentle rhythm Dixon soon inserts incidents of wanton cruelty, which escalate until the narrator is unleashing virtual mayhem upon his helpless victim (he finally burns the house down). The collection's most deft

use of the generating principle, however, is in the concluding piece, **"The Frame."** Here the narrator is visiting a shop to have a picture framed. The clerk is a handicapped woman whose affliction reminds him of his late sister's disability. What begins as a casual conversation on this subject—interspersed, of course, with the typical Dixon busyness with the fuss and bother of getting the right frame ordered—soon surrenders its focus to a second story of the sister herself dying in a hospital, attended by the narrator and other family members. For a time the two stories alternate, but at the crucial concluding moment they merge, with the narrator glancing at another customer as he leaves the store and suddenly seeing the elevator door open and his mother arrive outside his dead sister's room.

Love and Will returns Dixon to his more familiarly humorous appraisals of life, only here the humor extends from content to structure. In **"The Rehearsal,"** for example, the narrator courts an opera singer from afar as she rehearses an open-air concert in the Central Park band shell. They meet and arrange a date, but only on the last of twenty pages, the nineteen previous having been devoted to his preparation for their meeting. **"Heat"** helps explain Dixon's fascination with the internal gears of bureaucracy which are a perfect model for the generating principles of short stories (which also have only their own existence to justify their reason for being). For the story's length the narrator fights with his landlord and the city to get some heat to his freezing apartment building; but at the story's end, with the heat finally restored, his quizzing of the building inspector as to how he and the other tenants can avoid such problems in the future is answered by the inspector's own question as to where the next address on his complaint sheet may be found—ultimate solutions to such problems cannot be found if the system is to be maintained.

Such an appreciation of what the stuff of life is gives *Love and Will* its sense of vital humanity. From its repetitious heartbeat, life goes on by virtue of its routine, but that very routine can generate the conflicts which tear people apart, as in the story **"The Argument,"** which has begun with one partner leaving a room because the other has entered it.

> Now we're still discussing things in a relatively unquarrelsome manner. But you want to know why we're about to get into another bad argument? Because you insist on doing something you know is impossible for me to allow you to do without our getting into another bad argument, which is the main reason we got into the last bad argument that led up to all this. Now please, for both of us, turn around and go into one of the other rooms or outside or anyplace else, but leave me alone in this room.

"Tails" suggests how this seemingly organic nature to quarrel and debate is built into the structure of human relationships, thanks to the nature of language, which as Wittgenstein pointed out is at the root of all philosophical problems.

> "I'm cold. You must be cold. Let me feel your lips. Usually your lips are cold if it's cold out. Your lips are cold. Very cold. So it must be cold

out. Very cold. I like cold. I'm going out." She goes out.

Life is problematic, Dixon shows, in both its experience and depiction, because both are functions of language. And language, despite its reluctance for self-apparency, is the commerce of fiction. The type of honesty both life and fiction demand creates a realism one can never take for granted. Knowing the world—and all that can happen in it—is an epistemological adventure, and it is Stephen Dixon's achievement that familiar techniques can be used for such a unique process of reading. There are no "conventions" in his stories, for everything is happening quite literally for the very first time. The stories of *Time to Go* bear out this sense of reality's novelty. **"The Bench"** begins with an affectionate portrait of a new father bouncing his baby on his knee for all to observe in a public park. But after several weeks both he and the baby disappear, and everyone who has seen them has a different story to account for their absence. And once the man himself reappears, minus baby, he is ready to disavow ever being there in the first place. But a half dozen stories have been generated by the experience, which justifies the production of Dixon's text. In **"Meeting Aline"** the narrator finds his own experience segmented into three distinct levels: dreaming of an encounter with an old lover, meeting her by chance in a public square, and preparing himself for the inevitable reintroduction. **"Don,"** one of Dixon's longest stories (8,000 words as compared to his customary 2,500), is a cubist narrative of disjunctive paragraphs, each giving a single incident in the protagonist's life linked by only the most superficial of associations; again, the difference in levels of experience produces a distortion when thrown so closely into line.

The title story of this most recent collection shows Dixon at his fullest as a self-apparent master of technique. **"Time to Go"** takes the familiar circumstance of a father's lingering influence over his son and, through the convention of dialogue, projects it as a real object in itself, despite the fact that it is plausibly impossible. What would otherwise be two narrative tracks, the realistic and the fantastic, are here melded, as the long-dead father accompanies his son to buy an engagement gift for a young woman of whom the old man disapproves. Next time out it is to buy wedding bands, and as the young couple are fitted the father's presence makes itself felt, not as reminiscence or superstition but as an integral part of the story's narrative.

> "Something very simple," I say.
>
> He holds up his ring finger. "Nothing more simple and comfortable than this one. I've been wearing it without taking it off once for forty-five years."
>
> "That's amazing," Magna says. "Not once?"
>
> "I can't. I've gained sixty pounds since I got married and my finger's grown around it. Maybe he'll have better luck with his weight. He's so slim now, he probably will."
>
> "More patter," my father says. "Then when you're off-guard they knock you over the head with the price. But remember: this is the Dia-

mond Center. The bargaining's built into the price. Here they think it's almost a crime not to, so this time whatever price he quotes, cut him in half."

> "Single or double-ring ceremony?" Nat asks.
>
> "Double," Magna says, "and identical rings."
>
> "Better yet," my father says. "For two rings you have even greater bargaining power. Cut him more than half."

When the son resists, his father chides; when Magna adopts his line of reasoning, he cheers her on. The fact that he never speaks to her nor takes part in their conversations is hardly noticed, so dominant is his presence within his son's memory—and it is that memory, and not external credibility of action, which establishes the textual plane of the story. When at last the son adopts his father's standards of value and begins exercising them, the father fades into the background, confident that the story's form will do the job. At the end, celebrating his son's wedding, he is embraced . . . and disappears.

Greg Boyd   (essay date 1986)

SOURCE: "The Story's Stories: A Letter to Stephen Dixon," in his *Balzac's Dolls, and Other Essays, Studies, and Literary Sketches,* Légèreté Press, 1987, pp. 131-38.

[*In the following essay written in the form of a letter to Dixon, Boyd discusses the themes and narrative techniques of Dixon's short fiction.*]

August 16, 1986

Dear Stephen,

This is the sixth—no, the seventh—opening I've tried to write to this letter, which is really to be an essay of sorts on your fiction. The other six attempts are on the floor under the table, where they crash landed after I pulled them forcefully from the typewriter and threw them into the air all in one fluid motion. Each of these openings is quite different from the others. One begins, "It's a beautiful day here today, hot but not too smoggy. . ." Maybe if I picked these pieces of paper up and retyped each, one after the other, adding only some transitions, this new collective introduction would illustrate some point about what I want to say about your writing, about your narrative voice, style, and self-generating constructions more specifically. Or I suppose I could just keep typing what seemed to be the first thing that came into my mind, not really seeming to you like I'm writing criticism or a letter at all, but rather like I'm just typing to try to find my rhythm, on and on until something clicks for you and it all starts to make sense, brilliant sense, even the beginning which had seemed at first so amateurish and wasteful. Now I'm pressing my luck to make a point; still, there are probably quite a few other letters hiding within this letter, just as there are many possible stories within any one story. But I'll get to that soon enough. First things first.

The first thing a reader must notice about your fiction that sets it apart from other work is the conversational intimacy of the first person narration. Whether you're writing dialogue or narration, it's always a speaking rather than a writing voice that the reader hears. Thus the rhythms are most often the familiar rhythms of unpremeditated thought. While these narratives are seldom internalized monologues, the conversation seems almost always to be self-consciously directed (hence the characters say too much, seem to babble spontaneously, and constantly confuse themselves, each other, and the reader) rather than directed out toward the conventional expectations of a fiction-reading audience. And although your highly personal, almost confessional first person narrators appear to be verbalizing or setting down what composition theorists would term "writer-based" rather than "reader-based" prose, the effect is, as Michael Stephens notes in his *Dramaturgy of Style,* both poetic and dramaturgical.

The excessive verbalization so characteristic of many of your works has a kind of comic or at least deeply ironic effect in even the most serious stories. These stories have the dramatic dynamics of silent films, in which broad gestures are substituted for dialogue. But paradoxically, in your work the exaggerated gestures are distinctly verbal. **"Mac In Love"** from your first collection, *No Relief,* illustrates just how broad these gestures can be. In fact, the whole story hinges on the verbal insistence of the narrator, whose locutions are his last hope of sustaining, even from moment to moment, a tie to his broken relationship. When, after building a maze of verbalization, Mac finally yells to his lover from the street, "Will you please thank Ruth for telling Mrs. Roy to tell Ruth to tell you to tell Mrs. Roy to tell Ruth to tell you your watering can's on the window ledge?" I can almost see the character pressing both his hands to either side of his brow or pulling his hair in exaggerated anguish.

Out of this verbal style and narrative spontaneity seems naturally to stem the idea that, just as language can be disruptively manipulated far beyond the surface conventions of conversation and the narrative thought process extend the limits of fiction, so can the conventions of plot be disrupted within the confines of a given story. Since you've liberated your first person narrators and created the illusion that they think and talk and change their minds as participants within the story, why not also allow them to change their minds about the story itself and how it should be told? Then what's to stop the narrator from saying what's really on his mind, even if he's in the process of coming to terms with it himself and changes the beginning, the ending, or even the middle several times in the course of his narrative?

Is this a kind of heightened realism?

Jerome Klinkowitz seems to think so. In his book *The Self-Apparent Word,* he writes that your techniques "are not reflexive or metafictional, for something 'real' is taking place in each. Yet those elements of reality are conventionally self-apparent, for the reader is urged to take part in the compositional nature of each event, no part of which may be taken for granted." He goes on to discuss a sense of "reality's novelty" which he finds in your work. That's a nice phrase, I think, and it really suggests something essential about how your fiction affects the reading process.

In many of your best stories (and certainly in *Fall and Rise* as well) sub-texts, or really co-texts, are generated one after the other. These texts interlock and interrelate. They co-mingle and cohabitate within a given narrative. And because they change so rapidly, they force the reader to stay within the instant. Reading your fiction I always have the feeling that what I'm reading is just now happening. By building stories with such thin walls you make the reader an eavesdropper and sometimes a true participant.

For example, in **"Meeting Aline,"** a story from *Time to Go,* the narrator sets his pleasant dream about a former lover against his hazy memory of their breakup. On that level we have the text of the dream, which is in the present, co-existing with the text of the narrator's memories, which, because they are his *present* memories, are both ironic and deeply rooted to the instant. Later the same day, when the narrator sees this woman eating her lunch with a friend in the park, he thinks to himself how he will approach her, what he will say to her, and how she might respond to him. As he watches her eat her lunch, in his own mind he plays out a number of possible scenarios. He even wonders what he would do if she asked him to go back to her apartment to make love. Then he thinks of telling her about the dream he had earlier, in which they did make love. Again text and sub-texts co-mingle, as the narrator overlays his fresh memories of the dream onto his projected future meeting: "If she wanted to know what she said in the dream and what her sex was like, I'd mention her wanting to take my clothes off and that her last words in the dream after our lovemaking was over were 'That was very good for me, I'm sure it was for you.' That's what she said. I remember it now." Finally, the narrator does go over to speak to Aline. But her reaction triggers a new sub-text, one in which the narrator is forced to more honestly reconsider their breakup of three years prior. Because he had hit her before leaving, Aline now refuses to talk to him, places her hands over her eyes to avoid seeing him, and urges her friend to guide her quickly away. Dream-like and bizarre, this scene fuses all the previous texts. Later that same evening, the narrator thinks of calling her to apologize but doesn't. That night he dreams of her again. When he tries to analyze the meaning of the two dreams, he comments on the nature of his own conscious/unconscious reality, for like dreams his own feelings and memories are open to different mutable interpretations: "Dreams are dreams. They mean one thing, they mean another, they mean many things."

Another story from *Time to Go,* **"The Bench,"** illustrates how "realistic" the fictional impulse is. In this story the narrator notices a man and his baby come to sit for several hours on a bench in a neighborhood park over a period of several weeks. One day the man and his child stop coming to the park. When the narrator asks what happened to the man, everyone in the neighborhood tells him a different story about the fate of the man and his family. Months later, when the narrator sees the same person alone in the park, the man denies having a child or ever having been to the park before. Here the sub-texts, each generated by the simple presence then absence of a stranger with a child, are more interesting and important than the actual event, which remains to the end a mystery. Yet the story seems as natural and unforced as the question, "What happened . . . ?"

In **"14 Stories"** (which Klinkowitz thoroughly analyzes in *The Self–Apparent Word*) and a number of stories in *Movies,* problems of interpretation also help generate the narrative. The title story **"Movies,"** for example, explores the reactions of a married couple to a popular film. As a result of their different sex, background, and personality, each person sees the same images in a completely different manner, the husband as a tedious artistic exercise and the wife as an artistic experience that is both profound and full of personal significance. When neither one can accept the other's interpretation, they realize that their marriage is doomed and decide to separate.

It seems to me that such exaggerated consequences are common in your work. Along with their exaggerated verbal gestures (always the difficulty of language, subjective reality, communication) your characters play for high stakes. So it seems natural that there are lots of breakups in your work—marriages that fail, relationships that come apart. And along with the failures of interpersonal relationships, come serious breakdowns of social order: the absurdity of one man's problems in society, the violence, crime and cruelty of city life. As the story unwinds, so does the fabric of life. And everything's coming apart.

This destructive attitude would be depressing were it not for two saving features. First, out of the debris of the demolished-life situations rise new stories full of possibility. Thus, even the worst experiences are infused with a renewing creative force, or at least the chance that things will be better this time around. When Newt and Mary in *Quite Contrary* break up over and over, their endings provide them with a series of new beginnings. Even in the grisly tale of **"The Intruder"** in *14 Stories,* the reader experiences the moment-to-moment hope and chance that the narrator might use the table leg against his tormentor. As in **"Not Charles,"** the reader never quite loses hope until the experience is over.

Humor, even if it is an uncomfortable, deeply ironic humor, also helps keep the world view you present from appearing hopeless. Your novel *Too Late* does inspire a kind of Kafkaesque fear of the world suddenly making no sense, a fear of losing control over the surrounding environment. Yet though the novel concerns the disappearance of a loved one (ironically, after she has decided to leave the narrator at a movie theater where he is watching a film she thinks is "too violent") and the narrator's ensuing confusion, despair, and eventual decline, parts of the book are very funny. The scene where the narrator bargains with a burglar who has just stolen his watch and his television set and who is trapped in the dumbwaiter, is wonderful slapstick comedy.

Out of the many forms of exaggeration you use comes a comedy of limits pushed to their extreme. In **"Love Has Its Own Action"** (*14 Stories*) you parody one of your most familiar themes—the breakup of a couple. The narrator in this story moves from love affair to love with increasing rapidity, first suffering through a jilted marriage, then meeting a girl the next week while on a camping trip. A

short time later he falls in love with a married teaching colleague, then falls for the maternity nurse as the teacher gives birth to their child. After running off with the nurse to live in Canada, the narrator meets a woman on the train, and the two of them pull the stop cord and jump off the train together. When these two stop at a diner, the narrator leaves with the waitress. Finally, he leaves the waitress on the highway outside the diner after thumbing a ride from a man with whom he falls in love on sight when he opens the car door.

In **"Milk Is Very Good For You"** (*14 Stories*) the exaggeration takes the form of sexual excess, which is highlighted by switching around the consonants in vocabulary associated with parts of the body and sexual practices, and which is further contrasted with the participants' equally wild craving for milk. Such symbolism and pseudo-gibberish hilariously and almost surrealistically documents the fantasy of unrepressed sexuality.

Still another kind of exaggeration you use for comic effect—and the stories in which you employ this technique are among my own favorites—is the self-generating story about writing a story. **"The Beginning of Something"** in *Time to Go* seems to be a story about the process of writing a story. The narrator tells the reader he's a writer who has been on vacation and has not written anything in weeks, and that what he is writing is his attempt to begin a story. At first the narrative seems to go nowhere, as the narrator gets sidetracked by his personal problems—an argument he's had with his wife—and can't seem to get off to a satisfactory start. After ten pages of rambling text, the writer decides to make peace with his wife, who, when he tells her that he's been writing about his problem with her, then wants to read his unfinished story. As they talk it suddenly becomes clear that the story is really about their relationship. Yet, after several pages of dialogue between husband and wife, the narrator tells the reader that he "went upstairs and recorded or tried to record as close as I could what went on since the end of the last paragraph, or rather, since I went downstairs to try to work things out with Magna." Pure fiction.

Similar in general construction is **"The Franklin Stove,"** in *Quite Contrary.* The story begins: "My story's burning. As I write this." The narrator, a writer working on stories at an artist's colony, burns the first draft of a story, only to regret having done so. Consequently, he begins the story again, pieced together from his memory. What results is a ridiculous narrative (that might well be a parody of Bukowski's fiction) about a man named Hank who returns home after twenty years. His mother at first doesn't recognize him. Then after she does, she spits in both his eyes. He learns that his father's dead and decides to take a nap. When his bastard son arrives and threatens to kill him, he punches him in the nose and drags him downstairs to put out by the trash. Finally, he mouths off to a cop he had known in high school and is arrested. As he writes this narrative, the writer changes the details and makes many new versions, only to admit halfway through that there was no original story to burn and no Franklin stove to burn it in. Then the narrative takes a turn as the narrator details his relationship with Newt, a writer friend who inspired him to begin the story he's writing. The relationship between Newt, Stritin, and his wife unwinds, almost as strange as the story of Hank. In the end the reader learns that the narrator is not really Stritin, but rather Newt after all. The story ends with Mary making love to the narrator as he tries to type: " 'Mary, Mary, Mary,' I say, her two hands on my shoulders as she goes up and down on me, 'which do you like best: "Mary comes into the room" or "Mary comes in the room" or "Mary came into the room" or "She came in" or "comes in" or "comes into the room," which?' "

So much for humor. It's all part of the package—the narrative voice, the imprecision of language, the multiple perspectives of the story's stories.

I should say something now about the books themselves, how they hold together as collections, or how they work as novels, but I'm getting tired and should go to bed because I have to baby-sit tomorrow, which I just can't cope with well without some sleep the night before. Others have mentioned that your first two novels, *Work* and *Too Late*, read like your short stories extended in scope and length, but sacrifice the focus and intensity of the shorter pieces. This may be true, though *Too Late* is still a fine novel by any standard. As for your most recent novel *Fall & Rise*, I think splitting the narration between the two main characters, while still providing the kinds of multiple perspectives typical of your work in both narrators, deepens the novelistic frame of reference and helps make it your most successful novel to date. Still, your most obvious achievement is as a writer of short stories, the connected collections or inter-collections in particular. In *The Dramaturgy of Style,* Michael Stephens calls you "the best ongoing practitioner of short fiction in our country today." Good, better, best, it hardly matters: your short stories are wonderful.

Of the three unrelated collections, *No Relief,* *14 Stories,* and *Movies,* only the latter has any kind of unifying device beyond the unique narrative voice and recurring themes that characterize all your books. The stories in *Movies* fit roughly into the conventions of film: there are domestic comedies, adventure tales, crime movies, slapstick comedies, personal dramas, and Hollywood insider films all cleverly disguised as short stories.

More unified still are the two inter-collections *Quite Contrary* and the second part of *Time to Go.* Both these collections contain stories about the lives of a pair of characters, Newt and Mary in the former book, and Will and Magna in the latter. *Quite Contrary* documents the on-again, off-again relationship of its two central figures. Because the events of the characters' meetings and various breakups and make-ups are related roughly in reverse chronological order, the collection reads like a novel, though certain chapters—in particular **"The Franklin Stove"** and **"Man of Letters"**—tend to discourage such a classification. If *Quite Contrary* is a book about unsettled people in a relationship based on the excitement occasioned by a lack of commitment, the Will and Magna stories in *Time to Go* are studies of a man mature enough to explore his own childhood in **"Will As A Boy,"** to try to locate himself in space in **"Self-Portrait,"** and to dare to compare his mem-

ory of his wheelchair-bound invalid father to his feelings for his baby daughter in her stroller in **"Wheels."** In the title story, the narrator is haunted by his dead father as he prepares for his wedding day. It's a brilliant story that revitalizes a familiar convention through its original treatment. If I had to pick my favorite among your books, I'd probably choose *Time to Go.*

Which reminds me.

It's a beautiful day here today, hot but not too smoggy and with just enough of a breeze to keep me from sweating too much at the typewriter. No, that won't work. Usually letters that get published or that are written with an eye toward future publication either as an introduction or postscript to a literary work start with some kind of chatty general observation which the author then skillfully, almost seamlessly, uses as a point of departure for a much more specialized exploration. It's a rhetorical curve that allows the train-hopping reader to jump into the slow-moving boxcar of the subject and find a comfortable spot alongside the king-of-the-road himself, which in this case is you.

That was one of the other six openings I mentioned at the beginning of this letter, the one closest to my right foot, so naturally the one I happened to reach for first. The point is there are lots of letters I might have written about your work. But since I don't have a Franklin stove in my office I'll just end here.

Regards,

Greg

Jenifer Levin   (essay date 1989)

SOURCE: "Too Sad to Tie His Shoes," in *The New York Times Book Review,* June 4, 1989, p. 19.

[*Levin is an American novelist and short story writer. In the following review of* The Play, and Other Stories, *Levin expresses her admiration for Dixon's work.*]

Over the past dozen years, Stephen Dixon has produced five short-story collections and four novels, becoming a master of the short-story form. His latest collection, *The Play and Other Stories,* shows his talents at their peak. Here craft and technique are fully refined, and so is the message they convey. Mr. Dixon is a highly distinctive writer, one whose work has grown deeper and richer over time.

He writes about a particular sort of person: the disaffected, no longer young, anything-but-successful urban American male. These characters have only one weapon left in their arsenals, intellect, a weapon aimed invariably at themselves. They are playwrights who cannot write, thinkers driven mad by their own thoughts, former homeowners staggering homeless through the rain, lovers banished from a beloved's presence, fathers incapable of protecting cherished children, impoverished men dreaming, in vain, of seeking spiritually fulfilling employment. Caught up in the impersonal movements of a godless universe, they feel unrecognized, impotent, beyond rescue.

"He can't be helped," Mr. Dixon says of the protagonist in **"The Bridge,"** a man so isolated and filled with a sense of defeat at his life of failed jobs and failed relationships that even the everyday details of a six-block walk, tying his shoes, thinking his thoughts, become so overwhelming that he is driven into counseling. "Life," he tells himself, "takes you one way, takes you another. You have no control over it. Just when you think you have something, you don't. Just when you think you've caught on to something and can hold it, it's gone."

Mr. Dixon's men are half-seen presences stalking city streets, dwelling in a limbo of socially imposed (and self-imposed) defeat. Yet—as proof of some irrepressible life force that flows through them—they can never quite resist the impulse to lift up a shade, peek around a corner, open a forbidden letter, ask a fatal question, continue in the throes of a hapless, hopeless love. Even if the world they inhabit is godless, they will appeal as a last resort to the gods; and, at least in their dreams, there is sometimes a reply. "The restorative potion you asked for will work," they tell the narrator of **"The Last Resort"** as he prays desperately for a miracle to save his much-loved, fatally ill wife. "The gods have been . . . more receptive to your request than they have to almost any other mortal's over the years, maybe because no one beseeches them anymore. . . . These days we're not exactly overworked."

If the characters' timid hearts are more often than not betrayed, crushed by seeming failure, they are still clearly impelled—to the bitter end—by love. This is the poignancy of Mr. Dixon's message. It is why the reader can forgive him when he sometimes becomes unnecessarily embroiled in a show of style at the expense of substance.

The technical choices Mr. Dixon makes render his characters more or less devoid of distinct personality. They are, rather, mere vehicles, pure expressions of his own thematic concerns—with the temporary, illusory nature of material possessions and human relationships; with the fragility of the boundaries between fantasy and reality, life and death, desire and aversion, passivity and violence. Mr. Dixon is particularly concerned with the dissolution of the boundary that separates *enough* from *too little.* Thus his protagonists function as representations of tiny ideas that implode and explode. In his fiction, apartment dwellers are easily dispossessed, lovers casually betrayed or abandoned, suicide readily contemplated. Offers of help turn quickly to deceit, danger and trouble. Thoughts wind down tortured roads ending in futility.

This is relentless, nerve-racking art that occasionally becomes grating and tiresome. More frequently, though, it rises to a level of simple beauty. In **"The Rescuer,"** the finest story in this collection, the protagonist witnesses a young child falling to his death from an apartment window, tries (but fails) to break the fall and ultimately goes mad with anxiety and guilt. Here Mr. Dixon lets his descriptive emotional powers off the leash, achieving a hallucinatory intensity that resounds in the reader's memory:

> It starts to rain, and he sees tiny children falling from the sky and running down his face. He suddenly screams when a child lands a few feet from him in the street and disappears into the hole its

fall made. He looks down the hole. It goes so deep he can't see the end of it. Then he sees liquid rising in the hole. It's blood, he smells. . . . He dives into the hole to pull the child out. He finds himself diving off the bridge that connects this city with the one across the river. He closes his eyes and waits for this image to change into another one, but it doesn't. He tries to imagine himself being caught in his son's arms.

This author's world view will not be everyone's cup of tea. It is not always mine. But one is nevertheless moved to admire his work. At its best, it is understated poetry: witty, heartbreaking, eye-opening. Stephen Dixon's genius (or compulsion) is to observe, then to speak; not because he chooses to, perhaps—but because, as with all compulsion, he simply cannot stop himself.

Eric Larsen (essay date 1989)

SOURCE: "Filler and Foam, Nonstop," in *Los Angeles Times Book Review,* December 3, 1989, pp. 2, 9.

[*Larsen is an American novelist, short story writer, and critic. In the following review of* Love and Will, *he unfavorably compares Dixon's short stories with the work of Samuel Beckett.*]

Reading these 20 irritating, unstoppable, sometimes amusing and on rare occasion touching stories [in *Love and Will*] by Stephen Dixon puts one in mind of Samuel Beckett, and of the words Beckett once put in the mouth of his character Molloy, in the famous novel of that name: "Not to want to say, not to know what you want to say, not to be able to say what you think you want to say, and never to stop saying, or hardly ever, that is the thing to keep in mind, even in the heat of composition."

The prolific Dixon's gift, indeed, seems to lie precisely in this ability "never to stop saying," to keep spinning out words no matter what, to fill up the page against the horror of—of what? In Beckett's case, it was done in an admittedly doomed attempt to fight against the horror of the existential abyss of nothingness. In Dixon's, it seems, it's done for another reason: to fight against the horror of—well, against the horror of not writing another story. Surely, one thinks, the aims must be higher than that, the themes deeper and the purpose grander. Perhaps so. But both in subject and manner, the pieces here often strain such a hope.

These are stories that come to the reader always at a fast-forward, breakneck, cartoon-like pace, as if time were about to end and the writer had better hurry. Take **"Arrangements,"** for example, chronicling in seven pages an entire marriage, from meeting to death: "She comes into my room. I hold her hand, She kisses my lips. We undress one another and go to bed. Later, she dresses and leaves. I sleep for a little while and dress and go outside. I see her talking to a man on the street. I say, 'Hey, how are you?' " And at the end: "She nods, closes her eyes, dies. I go off, but it's never the same with anyone after that."

Maybe that really is Dixon's theme, one thinks: time itself, that we're running out of it. In **"Said,"** indeed, Dixon manages to tell a story in a satirically bright ultra-shorthand that thrives on the omission of all that's conventional and thus unnecessary ("He said, she said. She left the room, he followed her. He said, she said. She locked herself in the bathroom, he slammed the door with his fists. He said. She said nothing . . ."). And he tries to do the same also in **"Grace Called,"** about a man (one of many here) whose life appears at first as sadly/hilariously empty as any Beckett clown's: "Grace calls. I drink a glass of beer. I hang the mop over the bathtub. I cut my hair. Grace calls. I run in place. I eat a celery stick. . . ."

The rub comes when, time and again, Dixon lets such initially skillful, incisive, and suggestive stories wander off into the very conventions one supposes him to be taking courageous flight from: the quick-fix explanations of the standardized psychological-maudlin, for example (the man in **"Grace Calls"** ends up being traumatized by the death of a pet in his childhood), or the gratuitous tropes of having "something happen" (the fighting couple in **"Said"** end up in a taxi wreck).

Dixon's austerely promising philosophical wit, in other words, shows all the signs of being ephemeral, brief, and, above all, easily lost sight of by its possessor, and the stories here—in its thunderous absence—remain often curiously trivial, sluggishly flat, and banal. In **"Buddy,"** a man walks through his neighborhood meeting people he knows; in **"A Friend's Death,"** another pallid and lonely man gets a terminal disease, then dies; in **"In Time,"** a man is imprisoned for eight years by two old ladies, then is let go; in **"The Postcard,"** a man tells his wife about his eccentric and unsavory relatives; in the gag-and-shtick-filled **"Dog Days,"** two men get bitten by a transvestite's dog, which then can't be located for a rabies check.

The growing and disheartening suspicion that Dixon is in fact writing about nearly nothing intensifies with those stories that are about the writer writing. **"A Sloppy Story"** is the animated-cartoon-paced tale of a writer selling a story idea ("This guy comes in and says to me and I say to him and he says . . .") to a producer whose company then goes bankrupt. The ambiguity of Dixon's title (the sale takes place on a rainy day) comes to seem an attempt to head of anticipated criticism (that it's a "slapdash story") through a disclaimer of the come-on-this-is-just-a-bauble-so-don't-take-it-so-seriously variety. Which is fair enough, except that Dixon plays the same card—lightheartedly admitting his own deficiencies—too often for it to keep working as an anodyne or charming sop to the less-than-infinitely-patient reader-critic.

"I stopped writing that last sentence because it was getting confusing," says the writer in **"Magna . . . Reading."** (Then go back and rewrite it, says the critic.) The self-appointed task of this nameless character is to finish writing another story (He's already got "two-fifty to three hundred of them") before Magna, who is reading downstairs, "finishes the other four." So: "Fill up this page, go right on to another. How many pages more will it take to make a story, go right on to another, have one ready for her. . . ."

And is Dixon, too, writing just to write? Writing just to fill pages? In **"The Last,"** a writer talks about his "biggest manuscript" and says: "Been working at this so long I forget what I do, why I do it, when I did it." What can an increasingly bored and by now slightly infuriated reader say to such a shameless, narcissistic, logorrheic wearing of the writerly heart on the writerly sleeve? Yet on goes the heedless and unstoppable Dixon. In the title story, a high school teacher, who loses his girl, says of himself: "I often say . . . things simply because I think they might or do sound metaphysically comical or epistemologically profound or just plain bright or yuk yuk funny and she'll enjoy my company more for my having said them than if I hadn't or some such stuff."

Beckett's sea of words was an ocean of crafted and conscious drowning; Dixon's is mainly filler and foam.

Joyce Reiser Kornblatt (essay date 1989)

SOURCE: " 'Listen to This,' I Say," in *The New York Times Book Review,* December 17, 1989, p. 23.

[*Kornblatt is an American novelist, short story writer, and educator. In the following review of* Love and Will, *Kornblatt suggests that Dixon should more often develop the spiritual aspects of his characters.*]

Although Stephen Dixon has a reputation for being what we call an experimental writer, his new collection of stories, *Love and Will,* suggests that, at least for Mr. Dixon, the results of the literary experiment are already in. In urban America, he has concluded, we have wound up talking to ourselves. Nervous monologues, dialogues between strangers, the dead-end scripts of lovers too exhausted to argue or too exhausted to stop—in this crass and noisy world, narrative goes nowhere and the ancient impulse to tell stories makes less and less sense. Mr. Dixon's latest book is nearly an elegy for itself; a writer this honest runs the risk of convincing his readers that the sharing of tales is a worn-out ritual, no longer worth our effort.

Consider the narrator of **"A Sloppy Story"**: " 'Listen to this,' I say. 'This guy comes in and says to me and I say to him and he says and I say and the next thing I know he does this to me and I do that to him and he this and I that . . .' "

In **"The Village,"** a man witnesses another man falling (or jumping) out a second-story window, but his witnessing serves no purpose to the other people who are at the scene: "I wanted to say something to correct their information or interpretation of the situation and even of this neighborhood, but didn't." And the speaker in **"Guests,"** after spending so much energy trying to make his potential listener comfortable, wonders: "Anyway, what was it again I had to talk to you about? Suddenly I forgot."

When making (or not making) a story is not the central activity in a Stephen Dixon tale, it is some other form of communication that fails his characters. Phone calls, postcards, newspapers, memory: none of these can be counted on to help make the connections that narrative requires if it is to be a source of coherence in our lives. By reaching for humor, however dark, and a jazzy staccato prose style that entertains even as it embodies anxiety, Mr. Dixon manages to avoid the gloom his vision inspires.

A few of his characters, however dire their situations, even show a moving sort of courage. In the story called **"In Time,"** a man named Charles rebuilds his life after being kidnapped and imprisoned by two wacky sisters. And in the final story, **"Takes,"** a woman screams threats out her window at a man who's attacking another tenant; the next day, "she goes to church, kneels, prays for the girl's life and that the man is caught and that the whole city becomes more peaceful again, at least as peaceful as it was about twenty years ago, but if only one prayer's answered then that the girl lives."

That Stephen Dixon chooses to end his collection with a tale of violence and a prayer for redemption suggests a spiritual yearning that his characters seldom articulate and his work rarely probes. Perhaps, after so many years of refining his chronicles of noisy manic despair, he might slow his own pace—this is his 11th book—and attend, patiently and fully, to that shrewd believer who, though on her knees, knows that when it comes to mercy God is a miser. Ask for the world, but be willing to compromise: "that the girl lives," she'll settle for that. "She sits," Mr. Dixon writes, "covers her eyes with her hands, just let things come into her. It's quiet in here, she thinks. For now, this is the only place."

It's a place Stephen Dixon hasn't explored much. But what might he create if he joined her there, in that quiet, and just let things come into him? With his formidable skills, he might find his way toward a narrative in which the soul refuses to abandon meaning, however crazed the world might be. We could use a story like that, while we still remember how to read it.

Irving Malin (essay date 1990)

SOURCE: A review of *Love and Will*, in *The Review of Contemporary Fiction*, Vol. X, No. 1, Spring, 1990, p. 305.

[*Malin is an American educator, critic, and editor. In the following review of* Love and Will, *he discusses the message of Dixon's short fiction.*]

Although Stephen Dixon has written more than two hundred stories, he has received little critical attention. His works appear to be easy, "natural" monologues which rush past us; they never stand still. Dixon's strategy is deceptive; he gives us profound philosophical fictions disguised as "sloppy," urban vignettes.

Here is a representative beginning of a Dixon story: "Stop, go, don't write anymore. She's downstairs reading my work. Stop, go, don't write anything anymore. Reading what I've written the last two months. Stop, go, go for more, get another quick one in while she's reading my work, anything to relieve the, divert the, take my mind off the anxious feelings I have about her reading my work. Because she is reading my work. I hear a page turning." It is clear that the narrator worries; he moves in compulsive circles; he cannot control his running thoughts. The casual reader—or "listener"—cannot "stand" the chatter, *that* "*voice*"!

And it is that very voice which is at the heart of the matter. The narrator "stops" and "goes," "stops" and "goes." He wants to understand "her" reactions; he wants, if you will, to master the world so that we can finally relax. But he cannot look objectively at pell-mell reactions, events, thoughts.

The Dixon story never underlines its message(s); it does suggest, however, that the "mind" and "word" and "world" are at odds. They cannot come together in any meaningful(!) way; they are enemies—constantly. And it is this very battle which shakes us. If we cannot "connect" *forces* within and without us, we cannot gain the fullness of being. And yet we recognize (if only briefly) that our "human nature"—a sloppy phrase—is precisely this mysterious "gift" of plus and minus, stop and go, arrangement and derangement. We are, whether we like it or not, in time's cruel motion. Dixon's stories [in *Love and Will*] oddly offer some solace. They proclaim that we want "something," "anything." Unfortunately, we are "nothing." But these "things" are illusions, mere words. And words? They are marks, traces, trials (trails).

Steve Erickson (essay date 1990)

SOURCE: "Innocents Undone," in *The New York Times Book Review*, July 1, 1990, p. 18.

[*Erickson is an American novelist, editor, and journalist. In the following review, he discusses the theme of the unfairness of life in the stories collected in* All Gone.]

Here [in *All Gone*] are 18 short stories to make you crazy. Some do it by design, and some do it by irritating you like a nervous tic.

A student, moonlighting as a cabdriver, is held at gunpoint one night by a passenger. Compelled to drive senselessly through the neighborhood in circles, break various laws and generally provoke every policeman in sight, he's finally "rescued" by the police, only to have his passenger convince them that in fact it was he who was hijacked by the student. The student goes to jail, his girlfriend abandons him, his dreams are aborted. He finally gets out of jail and becomes a waiter in a coffee shop, where night after night he serves dinner to the passenger, a college professor who doesn't appear to remember him or the incident in the least.

A woman has a theater date with her lover, but the lover disappears. He doesn't answer his telephone or call her, he never shows up at his apartment or the theater, no one has seen or heard anything of him. After days have passed, it turns out that the lover had been pushed in front of a subway train and killed. The woman spends large stretches of the following months sitting in the station trying futilely to find his murderers.

A man is offered a job as a rental agent. Interviewing for the position, he learns that the landlord does not want to rent any of the apartments to blacks. When the man tries to back out of the job, he's threatened with physical retribution by the landlord's goons, with familial estrangement by the relative who first got him the interview, with scorn and moral exile by his friends, who want him to report the landlord's practices to the authorities.

Stephen Dixon's eighth volume of stories is an almanac of incidents in which life's semblance of fairness goes haywire. These incidents can last a moment (a man throwing a flowerpot from a window to get a lover's attention) or an hour (a man having a drink in a bar with a prostitute) or an afternoon (a biker's brief affair with a countergirl at a doughnut shop) or a lifetime (a marriage in which the husband can't get anyone to believe that his wife is beating him). When such incidents don't utterly consume a life, they divide that life in half, leaving it irrevocably altered.

Mr. Dixon's writing is direct and guileless, usually in the voice of whatever particular fool fate has chosen to sabotage. Almost never does one of these voices betray bitterness or cynicism at the disastrous turn of events, which makes the turn that much more heartbreaking. Sometimes, though, the stories are so cruel that they leave the reader no choice but to laugh. Because all his victims have an innocence about life, Mr. Dixon's book can properly be called an act of literary terrorism, since it chooses its targets not despite their innocence but because of it.

Toward the end, **All Gone** risks becoming tedious. But it's difficult to be certain whether this tedium comes from the same effect being attempted over and over, or whether it's because the later stories just aren't as successful. Some of Mr. Dixon's experiments with form seem to exist for their own sake; for example, in **"Heads,"** a story about a woman who spots a couple of human heads lying in the park, the narrative shifts through a succession of voices even though the voices themselves don't change much and the shifts don't really illuminate anything. And the dead-pan flatness of the writing can become ostentatious ("Glasses, I should repair my glasses. Get them repaired I mean"), until one suspects that the effect in style is in fact an affectation of vision.

Nevertheless, the best of these pieces are so skillful that when every one of them reaches its moment of surreal implausibility, we assume that Mr. Dixon has placed the moment there on purpose, to test the irresistibility of the nightmare logic that's at work. Nightmare logic wins. Its victories ring in the ears as the stuttered blurts of a paranoia too well earned and too well served.

FURTHER READING

Criticism

Klinkowitz, Jerome. *Structuring the Void: The Struggle for Subject in Contemporary American Fiction.* Durham, N.C.: Duke University Press, 1992, 182 p.

> Includes scattered discussions of Dixon's short fiction and novels.

Martin, Richard. "The Critic as Entertainer: Ten Digressions and a Diversion on Stereotypes and Innovation." *Amerika Studien—American Studies* 30, No. 3 (1985): 425-27.

> Includes commentary on situational and ideological stereotypes in Dixon's "Goodbye to Goodbye" from *Time to Go.*

Additional coverage of Dixon's life and career is contained in the following sources published by Gale Research: *Contemporary Authors New Revision Series,* Vol. 17; *Contemporary Literary Criticism,* Vol. 52; and *Dictionary of Literary Biography,* Vol. 130.

M. R. James

1862-1936

(Full name Montague Rhodes James) English short story writer.

INTRODUCTION

James is considered the creator and foremost craftsman of the modern ghost story. Writing in the tradition of Joseph Sheridan Le Fanu, whom he thought "stood in the first rank as a writer of ghost stories," James avoided the atmospheric Gothicism of his predecessor's work and instead employed a simple narrative style designed to heighten the terrifying effect of his tales. In the works of Le Fanu and other Gothic writers, terror arises from both psychological and supernatural sources; but in James the agent of fear is entirely an objective phenomenon outside character psychology. As critics have pointed out, his characters are pursued to their unpleasant doom for no apparent reason aside from their being in the wrong place at the wrong time.

Biographical Information

James was raised an Evangelical Christian. His father was rector of the Suffolk village of Livermere, and James maintained his childhood faith with complete orthodoxy throughout his life. An intensely studious child, he grew up to devote himself to studying apocryphal documents connected with the Old and New Testaments and cataloguing medieval manuscripts, on which he was a world-renowned authority. His academic offices included fellow, provost, and vice-chancellor at King's College, Cambridge, and provost of Eton. His first ghost stories were read at meetings of the Chitchat Society, a Cambridge literary club organized "for the promotion of rational conversation." Urged by club members to produce more stories, he did so and eventually published *Ghost Stories of an Antiquary*. Collections of James's ghost stories were immensely popular, and his candlelight readings at Cambridge became a Christmas Eve tradition. James died in 1936.

Major Works of Short Fiction

James published four volumes of original tales between 1904 and 1925; these were republished in 1931 as *Collected Ghost Stories*. Though not a professional or even frequent writer of fiction—he wrote his stories strictly to amuse himself and friends—James was a self-conscious artist who followed specific literary guidelines in his tales of terror. "Canon Alberic's Scrapbook," first read to friends in 1893, then published in the *National Review* in 1895, set the pattern for his later stories, which generally begin in familiar, realistic settings with characters involved in ordinary pursuits, often of an academic nature.

The inevitable intrusion of malevolent supernatural forces does not detract from—and indeed seems to intensify—the aura of believability established from the start. Rather than mobilizing the familiar wispy apparition, James's ghost stories commonly feature such substantial horrors as the hairy-handed thing in "Canon Alberic's Scrapbook," the demonic cat in "The Stalls of Barchester Cathedral," and the tentacled companion in "Count Magnus."

Critical Reception

While critics generally consider James a master of the ghost story, citing as evidence his realistic settings and plausible plots, S. T. Joshi suggests that his restrained prose limits, rather than explores, the supernatural possibilities introduced in his tales. For James himself, critical acceptance was a less valid measure of his success than was a story's ability to make his reader "feel pleasantly uncomfortable when walking along a solitary road at nightfall, or sitting over a dying fire in the small hours."

PRINCIPAL WORKS

SHORT FICTION

Ghost Stories of an Antiquary　1904
More Ghost Stories of an Antiquary　1911
A Thin Ghost and Others　1919
A Warning to the Curious, and Other Ghost Stories　1925
Collected Ghost Stories　1931

OTHER MAJOR WORKS

Guide to the Windows of King's College Chapel, Cambridge (nonfiction) 1899
Old Testament Legends, Being Stories Out of Some of the Less-Known Apocryphal Books (nonfiction) 1913
The Wanderings and Homes of Manuscripts (nonfiction) 1919
The Lost Apocrypha of the Old Testament (translation) 1920
The Five Jars (juvenilia) 1922
The Apocryphal New Testament (translation) 1924
The Apocalypse in Art (nonfiction) 1931
Forty Stories, by Hans Christian Andersen (translation) 1930; also published as *Forty-two Stories* [enlarged edition], 1953

CRITICISM

Mary Butts　(essay date 1933-1934)

SOURCE: "The Art of Montagu James," in *The London Mercury,* Vol. XXIX, November, 1933–April, 1934, pp. 306-17.

[*In the following excerpt, Butts asserts that James's critical reputation as a classic short story writer is undeservedly compromised by his choice of subject matter.*]

It is the writer's belief that is Doctor James had chosen to write stories about any other subject under the sun, he would be considered the greatest classic short story writer of our time. Yet, in his case, it is more than usually silly—so completely fused with one another are his style and his subject—to suggest such a thing. It is impossible to think of him as writing about anything else than what is rather foolishly called "The Unseen." Idiotically, in his case. "Unseen," indeed! When the essence of his art is a sudden, appalling shock of visibility. The intangible become more than tangible, unspeakably real, solid, *present.* He is not a writer—say like Mr. Algernon Blackwood—who relies on suggestion, a strengthening atmosphere in which very little ever happens; or rather one is not sure whether it has happened or not. It is what his people *see* that Doctor James is busy with; not how it affects them. After it has happened they either die, or leave home or go to bed; or, years after, tell it to him, with permission to make a story out of it. It sounds simple. It is not. It is matter-of-fact. A very different thing. Yet in its unpretentiousness, in its absence of worked-up atmosphere, its lack of hints, it carries the driest, clearest kind of conviction. If his stories

were about anything else (which heaven forbid) Doctor James would be praised for something of the same qualities for which we praise Horace and Catullus and Villon, for something terse and poignant and durable, and looked at with both eyes wide open. While, in our day at least, writing on the 'Occult'—another inadequate, loosely-used word—is felt to be a bastard of the Muses; a kind of entertainment, a kind of trick. Not quite respectable. The implication being that our emotions are stirred by situations which are essentially impossible: by a lie. That, as letters are more than a game, it is not quite fair.

The attitude is not quite consistent. Poets are allowed the full use of this material. The subjects of *Sister Helen* or *Rose Mary* do not make these poems faintly disreputable. There is *The Listeners,* one of our most popular anthology numbers. Think of the Ballads. Though there the attitude of 'it was all a long time ago, and we'll hope it didn't happen,' and, 'poor devils, they knew no better' doubtless enters in.

It is strange: to try and separate Doctor James' precise, elegant, detached style, where never a word is wasted, from his matter; to wish, even to imagine, it employed in any other direction, is to dislocate one's imagination, one's sense of what is conceivably possible, so perfectly is the instrument adapted to its end.

His matter. It is taken from his own surroundings and experience, in the University town, the library, the cathedral, the country inn and the country house. His people are the people who live and work in such places; the country gentleman, the student, the don. They are going about their business. Then, as a man might turn a corner or the page of a book, they meet the Unspeakable. Are brought up sharp against the dead who are not dead; who are out and about on hellish business; who, if they have long remained quiescent, are stirred by some trivial accident into hideous activity.

Or these tranquil ordinary men of learning come suddenly upon creatures, tangible as men, but of a different order; intelligences 'less than that of a man, more than that of a beast'; and of the malignancy of hell. Sometimes they escape. Not always. While neither Doctor James' Dead nor his Demons appear in any of the categories or conventions which other writers, using tradition, or maybe their own experience, have accustomed us. His ghosts, demons, 'elementals' are utterly original. New minted. And owing nothing (while at the same time everything) to the vast corpus of tradition—and whatever truth lies behind it—on the existence of such things. . . .

Passing tactfully by the real effect on their nerves and on their sense of truth by the matter of Doctor James, the critics often reserve their praise for his incomparable evocation of the past. "Here," they say, "is imaginative scholarship. How he uses his research to take us back three centuries, or two, or one."

They are quite right. Though there are not many such stories, seven in all; out of which two could be called "Early Victorian." While there is one only as early as James I. One in the time of James II; and the rest somewhere in the

> It is strange: to try and separate Doctor James' precise, elegant, detached style, where never a word is wasted, from his matter; to wish, even to imagine, it employed in any other direction, is to dislocate one's imagination, one's sense of what is conceivably possible, so perfectly is the instrument adapted to its end.
>
> —*Mary Butts*

Eighteenth Century; and one in two parts, over the space of a hundred years, from the middle of the Eighteenth to the middle of the Nineteenth. These settings, each one an earlier version of the milieu he uses to-day, are more than a historic reconstruction, however skilfully done. There is something distilled about them. It is not as if one were in a picture gallery, a spectator, but inside. How does he do it? Doctor James has waved his wand, but what is the spell? Again, it is by a kind of simplicity, a directness of attack. People are confused about this. If the attack comes from an unexpected quarter, they will call the work obscure; not told in the right way. This is not what they mean. The point is that the essential meaning of a tale—from whatever quarter—must "come at" the reader, undeflected, at its proper pace; which, in works of Doctor James' kind, is usually swift; so that *everything,* however brilliant or diverting, must be omitted that interferes with "telling the tale."

The economy is the same in his display of character. His presentation owes something to Dickens, but all are observed, not without sympathy, but with complete ironic detachment. The marvel is that, when he tells us so little, without, for instance, a hint of physical description, that we know so much. It is true he has no time to make us acquainted at length. He has to get on at once to his point, to the appalling experience that is in store. Many writers would have been content with lay figures; yet, on learning what sort of an inheritance was Mr. Humphreys', one finds out what sort of a man he was. As unlike Dennistoun or Mr. Poynter, Dr. Haynes or Squire Richards in nature, as he resembles them in representing a class of our society. While in dealing with their servants, Doctor James may be said to let himself go. They are as full of 'humours' as an Eighteenth Century play; more tenderly handled, but as little sentimentalised. He has no objection to driving in the obvious nail, that the better educated you are, the more you are likely—if not to experience—to observe, to be affected, to understand, to be curious about what is happening to you. . . .

Doctor James has been asked if he believes in ghosts. Here he will not commit himself—at least in print. I think we are in the presence of a mystery. By sheer art, which is in itself 'a magic,' perhaps the greatest of the magics, he has given us profound aesthetic pleasure; by a subject considered to-day to have no relation to reality, and by means of a technique as realistic as de Maupassant's.

Again it is curious. If Doctor James were to get up and say that he believes every word he has written, that he has evidence for the essential truth of each one of his stories, he would be believed, in the same way that a scientist is believed. He is the sort of man whose word is taken. While he is a great scholar, and the scholar is elder brother to the scientist.

In one form or another, his subject has haunted man's imagination since the beginning. The Un-Dead Dead, and the potencies, good and evil, but more noticeably evil, which have been thought to crowd about between the threshold of his life and any other forms of life that there may be. The evidence for their existence is, from many angles, as strong as the evidence for their non-existence. But—it is harder to follow; commonsense or even learned incredulity is essentially easier and simpler. Also more *à la mode.* For such beliefs are mixed up, almost inextricably, with superstition, wish-fulfillments, exaggerations, axes to grind, scores to pay off—with every variety of human inaccuracy and imbecility. Above all, to-day, for good and bad reasons, those that do credit to humanity and those which do not, such beliefs are unfashionable. (Though less unfashionable than they were in our fathers' day, engaged as they were, by the light of Science, in a great spring-cleaning of the human mind). . . .

Perhaps the doubt felt about Doctor James' subject is not only shallow scepticism, but sound, self-protective sense. Better not—certainly for the majority—better not enquire too closely; ask too many questions as to the existence of such things. Everyone who has lived much out of doors *feels* something of what he tells. Not by association with tradition, but by a direct kind of awareness, an impact on the senses—and something more than the senses. It can be a recurrent, almost an overwhelming, experience. Much ancient bogey-lore was a rationalisation of it. To-day we talk of suggestion, exorcise with the magic word "unscientific." But I doubt if our ignorant scepticism is any nearer truth than our ancestors' ignorant credulity.

It is certainly safer as it is, safer to have Dr. James give us the experience at second hand. Work his magic; imprison such things safely for us inside the covers of a book, an enduring book. And remember that, thanks to him, we have undergone an adventure which might have been deadly, with more than safety, with delight.

Peter Penzoldt (essay date 1952)

SOURCE: "Dr. M. R. James (1862-1936)," in *The Supernatural in Fiction,* P. Nevill, 1952, pp. 191-202.

[*In the following excerpt, Penzoldt examines what he terms the "calculated" structure and style of James's ghost stories.*]

Dr. Montague Rhodes James, provost of Eton College since 1918, is perhaps the most successful ghost-story writer of this century. Eight of his tales first published in 1910 under the title of *Ghost-stories of an Antiquary* were reprinted eleven times before 1938. Two editions of his collected ghost stories were brought out in 1931 and these were republished in 1934, 1939 and 1942. In 1935 the Albatross Press published ***Thirteen Ghost-stories by Mr. James.*** There is hardly a single recent anthology that does not contain one or two of his tales.

There are many reasons for James' extraordinary success. One is certainly that he is the most orthodox ghost-story writer among his contemporaries. His stories are straightforward tales of terror and the supernatural, utterly devoid of any deeper meaning. They are what the orally-told ghost stories originally were: tales that are meant to frighten and nothing more. They contain no study of human nature as do those by W. F. Harvey, Walter de la Mare, Robert Hichens, Conrad Aiken and others of his contemporaries, and no moral lesson as do Dickens' and Stevenson's tales. They have none of Kipling's poetry. In this respect James can only be compared with F. M. Crawford, though the two authors differ fundamentally in taste, style, technique and the atmosphere of their stories. It can therefore be said with truth that James is at once an orthodox and original writer. Orthodox, because he chose for his tales a form that is older than fiction itself; original, because he alone in the 20th century still believed that the simple ghost story could be thrilling if only it were well enough told.

It seems that his ideas were as much in favour with many readers as they were out of favour with most of his colleagues. A great part of the public still wanted simply emotion and terror. They did not want their ghosts analysed or explained. They desired something lighter than those psychological ghost stories that have to be read with a hand-book on psychiatry close by, which they found afforded them little relaxation and sometimes came just a little too close to reality to be really entertaining.

Naturally, such tales as James chose to write demand a far more elaborate form than most types of ghost story. A horror with a natural explanation, e. g. an illusion caused by mental disease, appears to the reader as being at least possible. Such a story can be presented in a very direct fashion. But when a manifestation of the supernatural forms the climax of the story, and no natural explanation is vouchsafed, the tale becomes far less acceptable to the reader, who because he does not, as he once did, believe in the supernatural, has to be approached with care and brought gradually into a state in which his disbelief is suspended. James' success proves both that he has perfected the technique of 'make believe' and that a large public prefers his kind of story to those with a natural explanation.

I will attempt to analyse the constituents of this 'technique'. James himself gives us little information on the general principles underlying his treatment of the ghost story. In his introduction to *Ghosts and Marvels* he writes:

> Often have I been asked to formulate my views about ghost stories and tales of the marvelous, the mysterious, the supernatural. Never have I been able to find out whether I had any views that could be formulated. The truth is, I suspect, that the genre is too small and special to bear the imposition of far-reaching principles . . . The ghost story is, at its best, only a particular sort of short story, and is subject to the same broad rules as the whole mass of them.

Maurice Richardson, who quotes this paragraph in his excellent introduction to W. F. Harvey's *Midnight Tales,* adds: 'Not, I think you will agree, enormously illuminating. In fact, all he tells us is that a ghost story is a ghost story'. I hope, however, that this study will have proved clearly that James was mistaken when he thought that the ghost story obeys the same rules as the other types of short stories.

The introduction to *Ghosts and Marvels* contains, if no general principles, at least some details concerning the technique of the ghost story. James writes:

> Some such qualities I have noted, and while I cannot undertake to write about broad principles, something more concrete is capable of being recorded. Well, then: two ingredients most valuable in the concocting of a ghost story are, to me, the atmosphere and the nicely managed crescendo.

'Atmosphere' is rather a vague term, but 'nicely managed crescendo' gives us a direct clue to one of James' outstanding characteristics as a writer: his sense of rigorous construction. A little later in the same paragraph he tells us how this crescendo is managed:

> Let us, then, be introduced to the actors in a placid way; let us see them going about their ordinary business, undisturbed by forebodings, pleased with their surroundings; and into this calm environment let the ominous thing put out its head, unobtrusively at first, and then more insistently, until it holds the stage.

James' stories all begin in the most casual manner. . . . The supernatural is then gradually introduced. It usually only reveals itself fully towards the end of the story.

A good example is **'The Diary of Mr. Poynter'**, though almost any other of James' tales would do as well. A gentleman has just built a new house somewhere in Warwick. Wishing to know more about the history of the country, he buys four volumes of a diary which he hopes will contain some material of local historical interest. The first two pages of James' story contain nothing but a detailed description of an important London library. They could introduce any short story on any subject. Coming home, the gentleman finds to his dismay that he has forgotten to purchase the curtains for his new house. His aunt, who lives with him, is thoroughly annoyed. Carelessly, she takes up one of the volumes, drops it, and out of it there falls a sample of what they consider to be the most delightful pattern of curtains ever imagined:

> 'It is a most charming pattern', she said, 'and remarkable too. Look, James, how delightfully the lines ripple. It reminds me of hair, very much, doesn't it? And then these knots of ribbon at intervals. They give just the relief of colour that is wanted. I wonder . . .' 'I was going to say', said James with deference, 'I wonder if it would cost much to have it copied for our curtains.' 'Copied? How could you have it copied, James?' 'Well, I don't know the details, but I suppose that is a printed pattern, and that you could have a block cut from it in wood or metal.' 'Now, really, that is a capital idea, James. I am almost

inclined to be glad that you were so—that you forgot the chintzes on Wednesday.'

This paragraph is about five pages from the beginning. These five pages are purely introductory, and nothing at all out of the ordinary is presented in them. The paragraph quoted contains the first indirect allusion to the climax. To be more precise it is the sentence: 'It reminds one of hair, very much, doesn't it?', that gives the reader the feeling that there is something unpleasant waiting for him. However, if he does not expect a ghost story, which is indeed unlikely, he may remain entirely unimpressed.

The next allusion to the climax comes two pages later. It is more explicit and naturally longer. As yet there is no direct allusion to the supernatural, but the sense of foreboding is increased. The following paragraph reproduces a conversation between the gentleman whom we met in the introduction, and the manager of the printing firm which is to copy the pattern for the new curtains.

> 'Do you think it would be popular if it were generally obtainable'? asked Mr. Denton.
>
> 'I 'ardly think it, sir', said Cattell, pensively clasping his beard. 'I 'ardly think it. Not popular; it wasn't popular with the man that cut the block, was it, Mr.' Iggins'?
>
> 'Did he find it a difficult job?'
>
> 'He'd no call to do so, sir; but the fact is that the artistic temperament—and our men are artists sir, every one of them—true artists as much as many that the world styles by that term—it's apt to take some strange 'ardly accountable likes or dislikes, and here was an example. The twice or thrice that I went to inspect his progress: language I could understand, for that's 'abitual to him, but reel distaste for what I should call a dainty enough thing, I did not, nor am I now able to fathom. It seemed', said Mr. Cattell, looking narrowly upon Mr. Denton, 'as if the man scented something almost Hevil in the design'.

The third allusion to the climax follows after one more page:

> At breakfast next morning he was induced to qualify his satisfaction to some extent—but very slightly. 'There is one thing I rather regret', he said, 'that we allowed them to join up the vertical bands of the pattern at the top. I think it would have been better to leave that alone'.
>
> 'Oh?' said his aunt interrogatively.
>
> 'Yes: as I was reading in bed last night they kept catching my eye rather. That is, I found myself looking across at them every now and then. There was an effect as if someone kept peeping out between the curtains in one place or another, where there was no edge, and I think that was due to the joining up of the bands at the top. The only other thing that troubled me was the wind'.
>
> 'Why, I thought it was a perfectly still night'.
>
> 'Perhaps it was only on my side of the house, but

there was enough to sway my curtains and rustle them more than I wanted'.

After this, none can doubt that there is a supernatural agency at work. Only the actors in the tragedy remain unaware, as is often the case in ghost stories, but the reader knows that the climax will follow as soon as the principal actor (or victim) enters the chamber with the haunted curtains. . . .

Something must be said of James' style. Introducing two of his tales in their anthology, *Great Tales of Terror and the Supernatural,* Herbert A. Wise and Phyllis Fraser speak of James' 'subtle reticence in choice of detail, enhanced by the academic preciseness of his style'. This is about the best general statement one could make, but I should like to give a closer analysis of the particular way in which he writes the exposition and presents the climax.

To take first the style used for the exposition: my analysis of **'The Diary of Mr. Poynter'** as well as James' own words quoted from the Introduction to *Ghosts and Marvels* show that he prefers an everyday scene for his introduction. He apparently thought that an apparition becomes more terrifying when met with in a place where nobody expects it. The reader is not, of course, in the least interested in this scenery, but it must be described and must take definite shape in the reader's brain, if the contrast with the supernatural climax is to be effective. James employs a number of tricks to make his exposition as short and as impressive as possible. These tricks are, of course, far from being his own invention, but his use of them is rather original. He opens his stories with a leisurely description of some place or character. This beginning is usually written very much like the opening of a novel. The author seems to have all the time he needs and refuses to hurry towards the action as do most short-story writers. Then suddenly the rhythm changes. As soon as James thinks that the reader has been sufficiently introduced to the scenery and the actors, he deliberately cuts short his description in a single sentence. This sentence clearly proclaims its function; the author makes no mystery of his intention. For instance: . . . 'It is no part of my plan to repeat the whole conversation that ensued between the two'. . . . ; or 'Lake expressed his concurrence with Worby's views of restoration, but owns to a fear about this point lest the story proper should never be reached. . . .', or something of that kind. From this point on everything that does not directly concern the action is, as a rule, merely sketched. Conversations, for example, give the impression of being overheard telephone calls: The answers of one partner are simply omitted. James is not even afraid to use an 'etc., etc.', to get on faster, for example: ' . . . You'll excuse me mentioning it, only I thought it a very nice evening for a ride. Yes, sir, very seasonable weather for haymakers: let me see, I have your bike ticket. Thank you, sir; much obliged: you can't miss your road, etc., etc.' New actors that appear on the stage are no longer introduced with a description but simply reveal their characters in speech and action. In this respect, of course, James does not differ greatly from most modern short-story writers. Sometimes he goes a little too far in stressing the picturesque. There are too many frightened maids and butlers, who deliver speeches in cockney or dialect, and too many characters who always repeat the same proverb. Such devices are amusing once, but when they appear again and again they become rather tiresome. They are, however, excusable, if we remember that the author is chiefly interested in the supernatural part of his story, and if he describes reality it is chiefly for the contrast with the apparition. James' masterly imitation of the legal and ecclesiastical cant of past centuries adds much more to the atmosphere of his stories than do his modern cockney speeches. Being a student of ancient and medieval lore, he also had a general interest in history and was extremely well read. The exact language of the century in which he places his stories, or from which he 'quotes documents', gives his stories an air of authenticity which is missing from the work of most ghost-story writers who take their themes from the past.

It is in the direct presentation of the supernatural, that is to say in the climax, that James' style is most remarkable. He uses short, impressive sentences and simple words. All that is glimpsed of the apparition is described with great directness and precision. Of course, James is careful to ensure that not too much is seen, and what he reveals of the ghost always leaves plenty of room for the reader to imagine additional horrors.

> And now we are in his bedroom, with the light out and the Squire in bed. The room is over the kitchen, and the night outside still and warm, so the window stands open.
>
> There is very little light about the bedstead, but there is a strange movement there; it seems as if Sir Richard were moving his head rapidly to and fro with only the slightest possible sound. And now you would guess, so deceptive is the half-darkness, that he had several heads, round and brownish, which move back and forward, even as low as his chest. It is a horrible illusion. Is it nothing more? There! something drops off the bed with a soft plump, like a kitten, and is out of the window in a flash; another—four—and after that there is quiet again.
>
> 'Thou shalt seek me in the morning, and I shall not be'.

The sentence 'Thou shalt seek me in the morning, and I shall not be' brings us to one of the most interesting aspects of James' technique. It is a quotation from the Bible and the pretext for introducing it into the story (together with three similar sentences: 'Cut it down', 'It shall never be inhabited' and 'Her young ones also suck up blood') is a 'sors Biblica'. According to superstition the Bible can, in certain circumstances, be used as an oracle. The reader can obtain guidance by opening the book with his eyes closed and pointing to a certain passage. A brief sketch of the outline of the plot will make clearer the importance of these sentences.

In a little English community of the 17th century a witch is executed. She is convicted mainly upon the evidence of the Squire of Castringham, and dies full of hatred against him. Some time later the Squire sees a mysterious animal with 'more than four legs' running up and down the ashtree near his bedroom window. The next night he dies by

poisoning, according to the verdict given later. A friend then draws the 'sortes' to find some explanation for his mysterious death and the Bible yields the three answers I have quoted above. The second Squire never returns to the chamber where his father died, and is only disturbed by unaccountable losses among his cattle. But the third Squire is less prudent and dies under the same circumstances as his grandfather (climax). The day before his death he again draws the 'sortes', in jest, and this time the answer is: 'Thou shalt seek me in the morning and I shall not be'.

The story has a double climax. The explanatory part of the double climax begins when the ashtree is burned and a number of huge spiders together with the skeleton of the witch are discovered in a hollow beneath. As the story proceeds, the different meanings of the four sentences gradually dawn on the reader. 'Cut it down' refers to the ashtree, 'It will never be inhabited' to the grave of the witch that was found empty. 'Her young ones also suck up blood' and 'Thou shalt seek me in the morning, and I shall not be' refer to the witch and the spiders, although the second 'sors' can also be interpreted as an allusion to the third Squire's death.

There is no doubt that these mysterious quotations add immensely to the general atmosphere of the tale especially as James is skilful in repeating them in the right places, as for example in the climax. I believe that there are two main reasons for the strong impression they make.

Firstly, the quotations are fraught with unpleasant suggestion. They hint not only at what may be going to happen but also at the true explanation of the first Squire's death, the horrifying circumstances of which have not yet been revealed. Thus they fulfil a double function. They set the reader's imagination to work on the part of the story he has already read, so that he helps to heighten his own terror, and becomes more receptive to suggestions from the writer, and, by leading him to expect a grisly climax, they further increase the suspense.

Secondly, they give the story an air of authenticity. We are always suspicious of the author. Deception is his trade; we know that he wants to make us believe things that are in flagrant contradiction with our own experience of reality. We are ready to doubt every word he says. Throughout, his skill and our scepticism wage furious war. Of course, in this battle we wish the author to win, but will not give up without a struggle. If the author can incorporate extracts from some respected 'authority' in his tale, we feel less sceptical. Though we know that such extracts give them no real support, it is impressive to find the author's statements apparently confirmed from such a reliable source. Quotations from the Bible are therefore particularly effective.

Such quotations as those in **'The Ashtree'** are extremely frequent in James' work. They are mostly in Latin, but are not always chosen from the Bible. Often James invents them, as for example, the text with which **'The Treasure of Abbot Thomas'** opens. Other good examples are such stories as **'Oh Whistle and I'll come to you my Lad'**, in which the ghost is whistled for, and the whistle bears the inscription 'Quis est iste qui venit'. Often James places his quotations (true or invented) in the explanatory part of the double climax. They are just as effective there as in any other part of the story. In **'An Episode of Cathedral History'** an anonymous altar-tomb is haunted. The climax is the opening of the tomb out of which jumps a monster that disappears too quickly for the bystanders to recognise it. Only much later, on a photograph of the destroyed tomb, the 'author' of the story deciphers the words 'Ibi cubavit Lamia' (Vulgate of Isaiah). . . .

It is hard to analyse in a few pages the work of an author whom many consider one of the greatest, if not the greatest, ghost-story writer England has ever produced. Curiously enough James was a sceptic and a scholar. Why should a scholar compose better thrillers than many professional writers? Why should a scientific and sceptical mind invent such frightful supernatural horrors and never offer a natural explanation? These are questions which I shall not attempt to answer here, but the Introduction may offer a partial explanation. I can only say that Dr. James' scientific mind was certainly of great help to him in his writing. His stories are as carefully constructed as an experiment. Every sentence tells and the author has so calculated the effect that it is seldom that the reader finds himself out of the clutches of the tale. The rigid rules of composition followed by James, and his undeniable success as a ghost-story writer, are, despite his own views on the subject, proof of the theory that the structure of the weird tale follows rules of its own. The casual opening, that makes no reference to the climax, the sudden build-up of the tension, and the use of the double climax are all peculiar to the ghost story. This type of construction is, as I hope to have shown, the foundation of the success of James' stories.

Austin Warren   (essay date 1970)

SOURCE: "The Marvels of M. R. James, Antiquary," in *Connections,* University of Michigan Press, 1970, pp. 86-107.

[*Warren was an American educator and critic whose critical writings usually focus on writers whose works evince a strong religious or philosophical interest. In the following excerpt, he provides a thematic overview of James's ghost stories.*]

James was a scholar, not a philosopher, theorist, or even concerned justifier and rationalizer of his own professional work. A friend tells a characteristic anecdote: once asked why he was interested in some particular piece of research, his spontaneous answer was, "Why is any one interested in anything?" The implication is that no interest can be very deeply rationalized; that interests are their own justification to the interested—a view inimical to any attempt at constructing a hierarchy of values among intellectual activities. His was the view of the specialist, who makes no effort to see his work in relation to that of others; who says, "I work at what fascinates me; let others do the same."

When he was not doing 'research,' James read novels, the latest, or old favorites like those of Dickens and Le Fanu.

And, during the years when he was dean and later provost of King's and at the height of his activities as Apocryphal scholar and cataloguer of manuscripts in college and cathedral libraries, he was writing stories, scholarly and horrific stories, of the occult, the first volume of which, *Ghost Stories of an Antiquary,* appeared in 1904. The two-fold nature of his publications was wittily recognized by the Public Orator of Oxford. Presenting James for an honorary doctorate in 1927, he characterized the honored as a scholar who, "ex omni scrinio, armaria, fenestra, pariete, cryptoporticu litterarum atque miracula, ne dicam lamiarum monstra et terricula in lucem protulit."

The two activities were ostensibly, and something more than ostensibly, linked together by the fact that the tales were such as an antiquary might tell. Not that they are literally by-products of his scholarly researches—as Andrew Lang's Blue and Red Fairy Tale books might be said of Lang's, or the Grimm brothers' *Märchen* of theirs: James makes it clear that almost all of the "ostensible erudition" in his tales is "pure invention." But it takes a scholar to invent such plausibly ostensible erudition as James's.

The question with what relative seriousness James took his modes of utterance is engaging to a critic, but of no concern to James. He was shy and taciturn when it came to speaking in his own person; was voluble and eloquent, his friends say, only when he was impersonating someone else, when he was speaking through a mask. Thus, his one really disappointing performance is *Eton and Kings,* a sizable book written at a publisher's request; for despite a few factual statements about his own activities the book is less autobiography than a collection of reminiscences of tutors and classmates, school and college jokes, anecdotes reduced to allusion, flat and pointless to any outside the family circle and when deprived of the impersonating voice. The scholar in him is bound to a kind of literal accuracy. He is not, as he would be in a fiction, free to indulge in plausibilities and imagined possibilities. What he thought of narrative fiction, the art of plausible invention, can only be conjectured. Did he think of it as mere entertainment, diversion from research, or as having some form of truth and seriousness peculiar to itself? Or (*dulce et utile*) as combining both, in a mode not, by a gentleman, to be pressed for definition? Presumably this last.

Just how James came to be a writer of tales is unclear, except that it began with oral storytelling. He told stories to the choirboys of King's College on Christmas eve, as later he read many of his tales, often completed just in time, to his friends, also on Christmas eve.

The Christmas season was, in England, the appropriate time for ghost stories. One thinks of Dickens' annual Christmas books. And Henry James's *Turn of the Screw* was supplied for similar use: when, he writes in a preface, "I was asked for something seasonable by the promoters of a periodical dealing with the time-honored Christmas-tide toy, I bethought myself at once of the vividest little note for sinister romance that I had ever jotted down." Curious that Christmas eve should be the occasion for tellers of ghost stories; but we read in *Hamlet* that, "some say," at the hallowed season the cock sings all night.

And then, they say, no spirit dare stir
    abroad . . .
No fairy takes, nor witch bath power to
    charm . . .

Perhaps, by forgotten tradition, the telling of ghost stories is then not only safe but even a form both of defiance and thanksgiving.

James's ghost stories were written between 1894 and 1927; were published in four volumes, beginning with *Ghost Stories of an Antiquary* (1904); and the four volumes were assembled in 1931 as *Collected Ghost Stories.* In his chary Preface, their author refused to explain "how I came to write them," avowing that, as they were said to have "given pleasure of a certain sort" to readers, he had attained his "whole object in writing them"—a statement unlikely to be the whole truth about any author. There are other motives for writing than doing so for money (according to Dr. Johnson, the only reason why a sensible man would thus exert himself), or for fame, or to entertain readers; and James presumably derived a certain sort of pleasure from writing his tales, and expressing an otherwise unexpressible part of himself.

He did write an Introduction to *Ghosts and Marvels* (1924), a collection of 'uncanny' tales issued by the Oxford Press in its 'World's Classics' series. The choice of writers and tales, which ranges from Defoe through George Eliot to Algernon Blackwood, and includes his own **"Casting of the Runes,"** was, for some reason, not left to James, who felt therefore the more free to comment. "Schalken the Painter" is singled out both as "one of the best of Le Fanu's good things" and as conforming to James's "own ideals" for the ghost story better than some of the others.

And Sheridan Le Fanu was, indeed, James's especial favorite among his predecessors. He spent considerable time tracking down the writings of Le Fanu in the periodicals—usually the *Dublin University Magazine,* in which most of them, many of them anonymously, appeared. In 1923 he published a selection from them, *Madam Crowl's Ghost and Other Tales of Mystery,* writing in his Preface: Le Fanu "stands absolutely in the first rank as a writer of ghost stories. That is my deliberate verdict, after reading all the supernatural tales I have been able to get hold of. Nobody sets the scene better than he, nobody touches in the effective detail more deftly."

It is customary to describe Dr. James's tales as in the tradition of Le Fanu, the founder of the British succession, as Poe is of the American; the resemblance is not, however, close. Le Fanu had a wider range of themes and styles; and he wrote a few really powerful pieces—notably "Carmilla," his vampire story, and "Schalken" for another, probably "Mr. Justice Harbottle," and possibly "Green Tea." He was an educated gentleman with a sense of history; but, by comparison with James, he lacks method (possibly the reason why he is less readily appreciable by an American reader). He lacked James's sense of humor, his gift at vernacular dialogue, and his distinction of narrative style. But, as any anthology will show, there is scarcely a British author who has not at some time or other written a story of the occult; and to read through the collection, *Ghosts and Marvels,* or Summers' *A Supernatural Omni-*

bus, is to see how Le Fanu emerges as the first specialist or professional. Certain it is that James's admiration for him has been shared by other subsequent British specialists like Summers and Dorothy Sayers, who undertook a biography of Le Fanu, left unfinished.

The only two Americans in the collection are Poe and Hawthorne. James makes it clear that "Ligeia," "which in many people's judgment . . . ranks as a classic," does not in his; and "Young Goodman Brown," assuredly a masterpiece, he passes by without comment. The American tradition of the supernatural, the American Gothic, lies outside of his sympathy, almost certainly as too 'psychological'—as placing the emphasis not upon intruding, objectively existing spirits, but upon the ghost-seers, the hauntable, upon those who see their shadows, their repressed or otherwise other selves, who project their guilt and their terror.

It is the distinction of "The House of Usher," among Poe's tales, that in it the narrator, with whom normal readers may relatively identify, enters the doomed house from without, and, at its end, gets back over the drawbridge into a mundane reality, the reader escaping with him. But in Poe's tales generally, whether told in the first person ("Men call me mad," says Aegeus) or in the third, the chief person is highly neurotic if not completely mad; and the incestuous stories involve twin *personae*—the mad Ligeia is seen by the mad narrator. Others (like "The Black Cat") are told by the hallucinatorily persecuted. And Hawthorne's "Young Goodman Brown" more than admits it must be said, of a purely psychological interpretation.

The 'ghostly stories,' as Edel calls them, of Henry James (an author not included in *Ghosts and Marvels,* and never mentioned by the other James) have as their chief character—even if we chose to reject the widely current interpretation of *The Turn of the Screw*—someone hauntable. The horror, real and powerful as it is in "The Jolly Corner," is subjectively horrible; only the particular person who returns to his old home can see the maimed, aggressive self he sees. And consider "The Friend of the Friends" and "Maud-Evelyn."

Montague James's ghosts are those of people who in their lives were set apart—witches, wizards, unjust judges, specialists, and traffickers in the occult. But those to whom they, or their effects, appear are themselves ordinary sensible people—"patients," to use his own word—with whom the reader can identify: indeed, only for a here and now normal reader can there be a real supernatural.

This is James's special note and method; and, in a few paragraphs of his introduction to *Ghosts and Marvels,* he is uncommonly and delightfully explicit about how properly to handle the "small and special" *genre.* As for time, he writes: "The detective story cannot be too much up-to-date: the motor, the telephone, the aeroplane, the newest slang, are all in place there. For the ghost story, a slight haze of distance is desirable. 'Thirty years ago,' 'Not long before the war,' are very proper openings. . . . On the whole, I think that a setting so modern that the ordinary reader can judge of its naturalness for himself is preferable to anything antique. For some degree of actuality is the charm of the best ghost stories; not a very insistent actuality but one strong enough to allow the reader to identify himself with the patient. . . ."

As for the "atmosphere," he remarks, "Let us, then, be introduced to the actors in a placid way; let us see them going about their ordinary business undisturbed by forebodings, pleased with their surroundings; and into this calm environment let the ominous thing put out its head, unobtrusively at first, and then more insistently, until it holds the stage"—an admirable account of his own method. He adds that sometimes a loophole may be left for a natural explanation of the horrendous, "but, I would say, let the loophole be so narrow as not to be quite practicable." Here, however, he is being reluctantly permissive of the practice of others; for it is impossible to think of any James story in which finally, and after preliminary possible ambiguities, there is any naturalistic interpretation, including the psychological, which is left available.

How far the Antiquary himself believed in ghosts is a matter of conjecture. Asked the question, he replied, "I am prepared to consider evidence and accept it if it satisfies me." It may be surmised that he was neither a dogmatic believer like the Reverend Montague Summers, that prolific and credulous author of books on all manner of uncanny things, witches, werewolves and vampires, nor yet a "Sadducee," a dogmatic disbeliever, like the positivist Professor of Ontography in **"Whistle and I'll Come to You My Lad."**

In his intermediate position, involving at least the temporary suspension of disbelief, he found, as a narrativist, help by invoking 'tradition,' that hallowed intermediary between fact and fiction, or history and theology. He had tried, he half-jocosely observes, to make his ghosts act in "ways not inconsistent with the rules of folklore." What are these alleged rules? Let us construct some out of memory. There are no happy *revenants*. Ghosts are unquiet spirits, keeping their fantasmic life because they have either suffered some evil which must be revenged or perpetrated some evil for which they must suffer, or because they are earthbound by obsessive concern with their earthly interest—classically (as in the **"Abbot Thomas"** story) their buried treasure. They haunt the place where once they lived (a limitation James sometimes violates); they appear between midnight and cockcrow, either in the white of the burial shroud or in the garb habitually worn in the flesh. How are they to be dispelled? Sometimes, having had their revenge, they are satiated. Sometimes they tire of their watch; appear less and less frequently, till they fade away. Sometimes they can be confined, driven into a cupboard, a barrel, or a bottle—a procedure to be undertaken by the clergy, with their books of Latin and their exorcisms—though of course the clergy, if scholars, are also peculiarly liable to *libido sciendi* and the use of magic. Ghosts can sometimes be kept from wandering by driving a stake through their bodies, a precaution taken with the bodies of suicides, or by burning the body.

Local legends of supernatural happenings James does not use; but the sense of locality is highly significant in his stories. The British annexation of India made accessible to English authors the possibility of introducing the occult as at a plausible distance; but James's tales (unless laid, as a few are, in nearby France, Sweden, or Denmark) are English in setting.

It is places, not persons, which are hauntable; and rather the country than the city. Places are haunted by their own past, their own history. Britain is haunted by its successive invasions, successive stratifications of cultures: the Celts, the Anglo-Saxons, the Romans, the Normans; by its successive religions—Druidic, Celtic Christian, Roman Christian, and, in alternations, Catholic, Anglican, Puritan, Catholic, Anglican. The vanquished peoples and religions are never completely extirpated. The overturned and overthrown and outmoded lie beneath the surface or at the periphery, waiting. The latest culture temporarily tops its predecessors, as excavation—literal or imaginative, historical or psychological—unearths layer after layer. Fragments of past grandeur, Druidic circles and Roman baths and temples survive to mock modern hopes of being the last as well as the latest.

Such a strain dimly echoes Browne's *Urn Burial,* doubtless the greatest poem an antiquary ever wrote—at least an English antiquary. But the sense of the past is, with every antiquary, bound up with things, places, local attachments.

The stories are all meticulously and lovingly framed in time as well as localized in setting. For time in his tales, James has at sensitive command the centuries from the Middle Ages (and their medieval Latin) on; he empathizes their concerns, their view of the world. Our antiquary can veraciously imitate their literary styles, whether of letter writing or journals, or, in more and dignified urbanity, of sermons and contributions to the *Gentleman's Magazine.*

The antiquary and the mimic combine in the delight, and the skill, with which James varies the time of his stories. The time is often double: the traditional device of the discovery and reading *now* of some document written in the remote or more recent past.

Thus **"The Stalls of Barchester Cathedral"** opens with an obituary notice which a recent cataloguer of manuscripts for a college library reads in the obituary section of the *Gentleman's Magazine* for 1818, in which Archdeacon Haynes is elegantly characterized: "His sermons, ever conformable to the principles of the religion and Church which he adorned, displayed in no ordinary degree, without the least trace of enthusiasm, the refinement of the scholar united with the graces of the Christian." The antiquary then discovers in the library of the college to which Haynes belonged a tin box of the Haynes papers, bequeathed by his sister; and from the mysteriously deceased archdeacon's letters and diary extracts are quoted. The explanation of the strange death belongs to the narrating antiquary.

"Count Magnus" purports to be written on the basis of papers which came into the narrator's hands, he will not tell how—papers collected for the composition of a travel book, "such a volume as was a common product of the [eighteen] forties and fifties. Horace Marryat's *Journal of a Resident in Jutland and the Danish Isles* [a fictitious

M. R. James shortly after the publication of Ghost Stories of an Antiquary.

book by a fictitious author] is a fair specimen of the class to which I allude." **"The Treasure of the Abbot Thomas"** concerns an antiquary of the mid-nineteenth century who is started on his quest by reading, in an eighteenth-century Latin history of a German abbey dissolved after the French Revolution, the life of an abbot who dies early in the sixteenth century. **"The Diary of Mr. Poynter"** recounts the twentieth-century discovery at a London book auction of a 1710 diary, the author a fictive member of the circle of Oxford antiquaries centered on Thomas Hearne; and in the diary, under the date of 1707, Poynter has written:

> Old Mr. Casbury, of Acrington, told me this day much of young Sir Everard Charlett. . . . This Charlett was a personable young gent., but a loose atheistical companion, and a great Lifter, as they then call'd the hard drinkers. . . . He was a very beautiful person, and constantly wore his own Hair, which was very abundant, from which, and his loose way of living, the cant name for him was Absalom, and he was accustom'd to say that indeed he believ'd he had shortened old David's days, meaning his father, Sir Job Charlett, an old worthy cavalier.

James has confessed that some of his stories were suggested by specific places, in France, Denmark, and England. In pre-Reformation stained glass, wall-painting, sculpture, organs and organ cases, and choir screens, he had especial expertness; like his friend A. C. Benson, he had a

fondness for Jacobean and Restoration fittings as well as for medieval. In **"The Stalls of Barchester Cathedral"** and again in **"An Episode of Cathedral History,"** he expresses, once in his own person, his distaste for the work of the Gothic Revival. "When you enter the choir of Barchester Cathedral now, you pass through a screen of metal and colored marbles, designed by Sir Gilbert Scott, and find yourself in what I must call a very bare and odiously furnished place." "There was a lot of lovely stuff went then, sir," says the verger of the destruction and purification which preceded the choir's restoration to its former hypothetical state. "Crool it was . . . all that beautiful wainscot oak, as good as the day it was put up, and garlands-like of foliage and fruit, and lovely old gilding work on the coats of arms and the organ pipes." Then there are the elaborate descriptions, in **"Count Magnus,"** of the seventeenth-century Swedish church with adjoining mausoleum and in **"An Uncommon Prayer-Book,"** the seventeenth-century private Royalist chapel.

For his domestic architecture, there may be cited the opening of **"The Ash Tree"**:

> Everyone who has travelled over Eastern England knows the smaller country-houses with which it is studded—the rather dank little buildings, usually in the Italian style, surrounded with parks of some eighty to a hundred acres. For me they have always had a very strong attraction: with the grey paling of split oak, the noble trees, the meres with their reed-beds, and the line of distant woods. Then I like the pillared portico—perhaps stuck on to a red-brick Queen Anne house which has been faced with stucco to bring it into line with the 'Grecian' taste of the end of the eighteenth century. . . .

There is another and differently constituted framing of the *Ghost Stories,* one which no single story completely exemplifies but which is the pervasive pattern. This framing is partly a matter of social classes. The outermost framework is that of the educated and socially well-placed—which is either the world in which James lived, the world of scholars, of professors and fellows and the cathedral clergy, or the world he well knew—that of the landed gentry—good, cultivated, sensible gentlefolk. These, persons not easily hauntable, are the "patients" of his tales. They are such persons as Dr. and Mrs. Ashton of Whitminster or the Anstruthers of Westfield Hall, Essex, in **"The Rose Garden,"** with their golf, their gardenings, and their sketching, or antiquarians like Dennistoun of Cambridge.

Then there is the world of the various lower classes, carefully distinguished: butlers and managers of estates, housekeepers, innkeepers, clerks, vergers, and other guides, peasants. The characters in this repertory are all, one may suppose, variants of Johnson and Barker, the butcher and the grocer of 'Monty's' boyhood and boyish dialogue with his brother; but, with his masterly mimicry, James discriminates many characteristic kinds of speech. He took most pleasure, it would seem, in that of the half-educated—those who, by their habitual association as aids to scholars and gentlefolk, collect scraps of Latin and polysyllabic words and other misplaced adornments. These delightful people, though (like Miss Bates, in

Emma, whom James mentions) they are copious of utterance, are hard to extricate from the stories in which they flourish; but one of the choicest, certainly, is Mr. Cooper, the bailiff of **"Mr. Humphreys and His Inheritance"**—Mr. Cooper, who describes the heir's uncle as "a complete, through valentudinarian" and describes himself as of a summer sleeping *"in status quo."*

Lower down, and farther away, and rather indicated than directly presented are 'peasants,' rustics, country folk. They constitute a kind of chorus; and their function is to keep alive the traditions of supernatural visitations which, remembered by at least the oldest inhabitant of a village, they are reluctant to confess, lest they be laughed at by the city modernists. 'Yet there is always,' it is a kind of motto for the ***Ghost Stories,*** 'something in what country people say'—something at peril disregarded.

Thus, gradually, by the pleasurably winding road which leads into the stories—the time, the place, the normal and living, we reach their eruptive center—the horror, about the nature of which something explicit must be said.

There are verses in the thirty-fourth chapter of Isaiah (one of them James cites in a tale) which picture the horror of desolation—the wasted land inhabited by cormorants and bitterns and owls and dragons. "The wild beasts of the desert shall also meet with the wild beasts of the field, and the satyr shall cry to his fellow: the screech owl also shall rest there . . . then shall the vultures also be gathered, every one with her mate."

Except for the *satyr,* a mysterious word which means either a compound of man and ape, or the *lamia,* that famous monster in half human shape which sucks the blood of children, these are all traditional *natural* objects of human aversion, beasts and birds of ill omen associated with death and the devouring of dead bodies. In James's stories, owls, bats, and rats and spiders, the traditionally ominous creatures of the night are frequent. But more terrifying than the literal creatures are their properties, operating of themselves: multiple tentacles, for example, which reach out and entwine themselves stranglingly about the human intruder.

Hair is invoked in double signification: often the creatures are described as having their arms or what pass for their bodies covered with gray or grisly hair; a hairy man is a primitive like the Ainus of Japan; he recalls our anthropoid ancestry. But then there is another, opposite but equally repellent, signification of hair: the effeminate long hair of Sir Everard Charlett, the long hair of Absalom, the King's son, who was caught by his hair as he rode horseback through the forest, who was hanged by his own hair. The wallpaper made from a stuff pattern of Sir Everard's hair, the rippling lines, the almost curling waves of tresses, have their serpentine terror, their menace of entanglement. These are the rival fears of the primitive and the decadent.

More characteristic of James's terrors is the terror of the amorphous. In **"Whistle and I'll Come to You, My Lad,"** the only tale which incorporates one of James's own dreams, the presumed figure of a Knight Templar, perhaps of the fourteenth century, materializes itself out of

"the bed-clothes of which it had made itself a body": the living spectator's face; and, as he looks, he sees the face of the other, "an intensely horrible face of *crumpled linen.*" So, analogously, comes, at the end of **"The Uncommon Prayer-Book,"** a roll of white flannel, four or five feet high, with a kind of face in the upper end of it, the face earth-covered, the eyes, "much as if there were two big spiders' bodies in the holes." It falls from a safe where the venomous prayer book has been stored; and, falling, it inflicts a serpent-like bite which kills the dealer who had stolen it from a seventeenth-century chapel dedicated to a Royalist's sole object of passion—the hatred of Oliver Cromwell.

Ghosts, as commonly conceived of—white, visual images—rarely appear, and then at some distance. More frequently they are heard in cries, moans, or (more disturbing yet) whispers and murmurs; or their presence in a room, or a landscape, is felt. When, however, the evil dead are menaced, they come close and grow heavy. James rarely uses the word 'nightmare,' and then not with technical accuracy, yet his chiefest horror is some version of the incubus—something partly human, partly animal, partly *thing* which presses down, grasps and grips, threatens to strangle or suffocate, a heavy weight of palpable materiality—not 'psychic' but sensually gross—a recall not of shroud but of corpse, of a living dead or death.

Thus, the Abbot Thomas, at the bottom of the well, guarding his treasure bags, is an *it* as well as a *he.* "It hung for an instant on the edge of the hole, then slipped forward on to my chest, and *put its arms around my neck.* . . . I was conscious of a most horrible smell of mold, and of a cold kind of face pressed against my own, and moving slowly over it, and of several—I don't know how many—legs or arms or tentacles or something clinging to my body." That night, the creature of darkness—its sounds and its odor—pervaded the narrator's hotel; and it was relief indeed when daybreak came and he and his servant were able to put the slab of stone back over the well and what inhabited it.

The tales of Dr. James are a continuing delight. Indeed, they are so rich in detail, and told with such seemingly artless art, that it is only upon repeated readings that they are properly cherished—so far are they from being mere shockers the pleasure of which is exhausted after the first blunt impact is spent. They have, indeed, to be read closely, for they are to be read for their surface as well as their structure—so far as these two can be disengaged.

James is the author of much more than a few anthology pieces. The two commonly included, **"Casting the Runes"** and **"Whistle and I'll Come to You, My Lad,"** are both excellent stories and excellent James stories; but the level is extraordinarily high. Of the thirty included in ***Collected Ghost Stories,*** there are, say, eighteen others as good, some of them better. A list of the best should include **"Lost Hearts," "The Ash Tree," "No. 13," "Count Magnus," "The Rose Garden," "The Stalls of Barchester Cathedral," "Mr. Humphreys and His Inheritance," "The Residence at Whitminster," "The Diary of Mr. Poynter," "An Episode of Cathedral History," "A Disappearance and an Appearance," "The Haunted Dolls' House," "The**

Uncommon Prayer-Book," "A View from a Hill," and "An Evening's Entertainment." Even this narrowing down has required sacrifices; for it must be said that in every story of James there are touches, 'passage-work,' phrasings not to be missed. And, for his reader who has the tastes of a scholar, there **is the** recreative research of tracking down his allusions, **which**, according to his scholarly fancy, are sometimes genuine and sometimes feigned—to discover whether there was a minor Greek author called Polyaenus or a seventeenth-century English organ builder named Dallas, or even to learn what Dr. Blimber really said in Chapter XII of *Dombey and Son.*

This last item (***Collected Stories***) is one of Dr. James's own extranarratorial touches, discoverable upon close examination of the stories. He does not hesitate to appear in his own person, either in stories told in the third person or by a feigned narrator. Strictness of 'point of view' is no fetish of his. Yet such are his lowness of pitch and ease of manner (both despite the *horrendum* which awaits us) that no desirable illusion is shattered. He is a born storyteller with no sense of shame at being one—no sense of 'stories' as undignified or even untrue because they are not 'history.' Born storytellers are oral storytellers, and the sound of the storyteller's voice as well as of the many mimicked voices is heard in all James's writing; it not only abounds in dialogue but is itself speech pleased with the resources of speech.

Within the limits of their genre, James's stories have very considerable range and variety, both of theme and treatment, scarcely to be conveyed by defining in a phrase given to each what they are 'about.' There are several stories about the wicked Judge Jeffreys, the 'hanging judge' who was lord chancellor under James II and died in the Tower of London, with phrases and images drawn from the State Trials, which were of Hawthorne's reading as well as James's: at the end of one, the parsons of the neighborhood are summoned to drive a stake to imprison the wandering guilty spirit of the judge. There is a story of a hung witch, whose vengeance follows her judge and his heirs till the ash tree in which she lived as a spider is burned down; and one about a *lamia* which escapes from its tomb in a cathedral, and another about a cathedral prebendary and archdeacon who contrived the death of his predecessor and who was in turn killed by the ghosts of the predecessor, aided by a tomcat, one of the grotesque sculptures on his cathedral stall which had been carved of wood from the Hanging Oak and come to life. One is about a Royalist lady who had issued an illicit Prayer Book with provision for celebrating Cromwell's birthday by prayer for his death, and another about a grasping lady landowner who removes the ancient landmark in order to extend her own estate. There is a story ("**A View from a Hill**") about a pair of field glasses "filled and sealed" with a distillation of dead men's bones through which one can see a Priory town and a gallows which existed only in the past. There is in the story about Count Magnus, a vampire Swedish nobleman who made the black Pilgrimage and who, escaping from his tomb, pursues to England and kills the traveler who let his spirit loose; and there is another story about a Danish hotel room 13, which vanishes except by night, when it is then haunted by a magician who has sold his

soul to Satan. And, finally, there are tales concerning pre-Christian and pagan mysteries—Mithraism and the Druids—and the Templars, and the Italianate Englishman, who, with the aid of an Italian, builds the maze and Satanic sundial which are Mr. Humphreys' "**Inheritance.**"

Such an enumeration not only inadequately conveys what the stories are about; it also gives a misleading impression of the ***Ghost Stories*** as a museum of "Gothic" horrors, which it is not. It does, however, properly demonstrate the use to Dr. James's subtle fictions of something crude and violent as their matrix. There must be some gross, refractory matter to withstand the counterforce of refinement, of carving and polishing.

The ghost stories of Montague James have their rightful place in the final chapter of recent books on the tradition of the Gothic Romance. Even such parts of its 'machinery' as the gloomy old press with its secrets, James can use, with the affectionate, half-parodic bow of an antiquarian. But he is the master of a new and probably inimitable mode in his special combination of erudition, dry, precise, rather donnish style, realistic dialogue, humor, and treatment of the supernatural—a supernatural never explained away but variously interpreted by characters dramatically differentiated. He has common sense, and uncommon, too.

Julia Briggs   (essay date 1977)

SOURCE: "No Mere Antiquary: M. R. James," in *Night Visitors: The Rise and Fall of the English Ghost Story,* Faber & Faber Limited, 1977, pp. 124-41.

[*Briggs is an English critic. In the following excerpt, she analyzes style and theme in James's ghost stories.*]

Montague Rhodes James set out his rules for the ghost story, such as they were, in the various brief prefaces to his collections of tales. Unlike Vernon Lee, he believed it important to establish a setting that was

> fairly familiar and the majority of the characters and their talk such as you may meet or hear any day. A ghost story of which the scene is laid in the twelfth or thirteenth century may succeed in being romantic or poetical: it will never put the reader into the position of saying to himself, 'If I'm not very careful, something of this kind may happen to me!'
> (Preface to *More Ghost Stories of an Antiquary,* 1911)

He also attempted to answer some of the more obvious questions his readers put to him, explaining why he wrote his tales: '[if] they have given pleasure . . . my whole object in writing them has been attained'; when he wrote them—they were 'read to patient friends, usually at the season of Christmas', and whether he believed in ghosts, to which he replied that he was 'prepared to consider the evidence and accept it if it satisfies me'.

As an author, James maintained an attitude of critical detachment which seems to have been the exception rather than the rule. He did not share the concern shown by other writers (Blackwood or Le Fanu, for instance) with the significance of spirits, the state of mind in which ghosts are seen, or the condition of a universe that permits the maleficent returning dead. His stories assert a total acceptance of the supernatural that his scepticism apparently denies. It is as if the implications of what he wrote never disturbed him, and he enjoyed writing them primarily as a literary exercise, governed only by certain rules he had evolved. A classicist both by temperament and profession, James had read a great many ghost stories and worked out from them his own methods, employing traditional themes in highly original settings.

His scepticism about ghosts did not derive from a general agnosticism. The son of a clergyman, M. R. James was a committed Christian and theologian who spent many years collating the Apocryphal Gospels, perhaps in the hope that they might provide some independent evidence of Jesus's supernatural powers with which to refute the 'Higher Criticism'. His ghost stories seem almost to parody his scholarly investigations into Holy Writ, for they frequently adduce biblical or literary references to prove the existence of spiritual forces, yet these appear to be introduced in the spirit of an academic joke, to show that anything can be proved by the citation of learned texts. Such allusions also function as an effective device for convincing the reader, by giving a spurious air of academic authenticity.

That suspension of the laws of nature which makes many of these stories so irrationally alarming results partly from his detached attitude and partly from the minor rôle that his fiction played in his life. It was simply a bagatelle for an idle hour, the construction of a delicate edifice of suspense with which to entertain the young people whose company he so much enjoyed. He saw his main career as one of dedicated scholarship, as a theologian, bibliographer and iconographer, a Fellow of King's College, Cambridge, and subsequently Provost of Eton. It is one of time's ironies that he is now remembered for his ghost stories long after his contributions to scholarship have been bypassed or superseded. A story by James is almost *de rigueur* in any ghostly anthology, and he is the only writer whose **Collected Ghost Stories** have remained continuously in print.

Like Henry James and Vernon Lee, M. R. James admitted to finding places 'prolific in suggestion', and his earliest stories were inspired by visits to France (**'Canon Alberic's Scrapbook'** is set in St Bertrand de Comminges, near Toulouse) and Scandinavia (Viborg, in Denmark, is the scene of **'Number 13'**, and **'Count Magnus'** takes place in Sweden). **'Lost Hearts'**, apparently the second story he wrote, is set at Aswarby Hall, a tall, red-brick house, built in the reign of Queen Anne. Similar houses are Wilsthorpe, Mr Humphreys' inheritance, and Castringham, of **'The Ash-Tree'**, although the latter has a stuccoed façade, and a pillared portico added later in the eighteenth century. Commonly these country house are set in East Anglia, his home for nearly fifty years. His father was Rector of Livermere, near Bury St Edmunds, until his death in 1909 and, being based here and at Cambridge, James had explored a great deal of the area on foot or bicycle. The east-coast resorts of Felixstowe and Aldeburgh are lightly disguised

as Burnstow and Seaburgh, in **" 'Oh, Whistle, and I'll come to you, My Lad' "** and **'A Warning to the Curious'**.

James describes scenery and domestic architecture with knowledge and affection, but when he comes to ecclesiastical architecture, he is in his element. Barchester and Southminster ('blends of Canterbury, Salisbury and Hereford', he explains) are described in detail, and with the warmest enthusiasm for their baroque interiors, before Sir Gilbert Scott and the Gothic Revival destroyed them forever. **'The Stalls of Barchester Cathedral'** set in 1810, takes a paragraph to depict the classical pediments and gilt cherubs then in evidence. The events of **'An Episode of Cathedral History'** actually occur during the Gothic renovations, and the old verger, Worby, laments the beautiful carvings being wantonly destroyed. The chapel at Brockstone Court, in **'The Uncommon Prayer-Book'**, is, however, a perfect example of seventeenth-century decoration, and after Mr Davidson has gloated over 'the completeness and richness of the interior', the author pulls himself up with the remark that 'this is not an archaeological review'. Detailed accounts of screens, organs and stalls may not always have an essential bearing on the story but scholarly enthusiasm of this kind lends an air of conviction to the narrative.

Accurate and vivid description becomes of primary importance when particular objects play key rôles in the story, as they so often do: **'Canon Alberic's Scrap-Book'**, **'The Mezzotint'**, the Anglo-Saxon whistle in **" 'Oh, Whistle' "**, the stained glass window with its odd juxtaposition of Job, John and Zechariah in **'The Treasure of Abbot Thomas'**, **'The Tractate Middoth'**, **'The Stalls of Barchester Cathedral'**, and **'The Uncommon Prayer-Book'**. In each case, the style and period of the object is carefully established. The contents of the renaissance scrapbook are described in great detail, and James informs us that, minus the satanic illustration, it is now 'in the Wentworth Collection in Cambridge'. It is somehow fitting that the 'unprincipled Canon. . . who had doubtless plundered the Chapter library' of its manuscript treasures, should have entered into further negotiations with the powers of darkness for more conventional wealth. In describing objects such as the scrapbook, James not only conveys their physical appearance, he also provides them with inscriptions, often in Latin, in the correct style for the period. In fact there is a great deal of literary pastiche throughout his work. Nineteenth-century diaries and letters are imitated in **'The Stalls of Barchester Cathedral'**, **'The Residence at Whitminster'** and **'The Story of a Disappearance and an Appearance'**. **'Mr Humphreys and his Inheritance'** includes an ornate passage from an imaginary seventeenth-century sermon, and **'The Diary of Mr Poynter'** itself also dates, supposedly, from the same period. **'Martin's Close'** is the most sustained of his inventions for it takes the form of a verbatim account of a trial before Judge Jeffreys. His peculiar ability to imitate the different styles and tricks of different periods, in both English and Latin, was probably linked with his powers of mimicry, which he first demonstrated at prep school. S. G. Lubbock has described how Monty and his brother Herbert used to adopt the personae of two quarrelsome Suffolk tradesmen, Barker and Johnson. 'Barker' continued to be a favourite impersonation of

James's all his life, and may be the original of some of his humorous minor characters. Gwendolyn McBryde referred to James as 'a born actor', adding that he 'would sometimes personate some countryman or cockney'.

Yet despite his ability to re-create the past in lucid pictorial detail, James gives several of his most fearful spirits, quite ordinary, even prosaic locations. He understood the importance of a 'fairly familiar' setting, and some of his worst moments take place in modern hotel bedrooms, or even in one case, on an electric tram. Recent inventions are utilized: a special pair of field-glasses which make the past visible ('looking through dead men's eyes') is the subject of **'A View from a Hill'**, and a magic lantern show is used to create panic at a children's party by the maleficent Karswell, in **'Casting the Runes'**. This story is an exercise in what the other James termed 'the strange and sinister embroidered on the very type of the normal and easy'. The fatal runes are planted on the victim in the British Museum Reading Room, and returned in a railway carriage. An advertisement in a tram window becomes a portent of death, and the victim, putting his hand under his pillow to find a match, discovers—well, something very unpleasant. The idea of an invasion of one's bed, of a horror lurking beneath the pillow (the very place where one expects to feel secure) is deeply disturbing. If we are not safe in our beds, then the last sanctuary has gone. The peculiar sense of violation that arises at the thought of one's bedroom being invaded is effectively exploited in **" 'Oh, Whistle' "**, where the bedclothes on an empty bed are possessed by an evil spirit. Many sensitive readers have subsequently experienced a certain reluctance to sleep in a room containing an unoccupied bed. And if hiding under the bedclothes is one traditional resort better avoided, so is pulling the curtains to shut out the dark, for the curtains themselves may be harbouring a restless ghost, as they do in **'The Diary of Mr Poynter'**. James has shown us fear in a handful of dust, in a Punch and Judy show, and a fragment of wet cloth sticking out of a cupboard.

Fear of the supernatural is essentially circular, for what we fear most is the sensation of being afraid, which endows the most familiar objects with frightful possibilities. The source of terror in a ghost story may be totally irrational, and even incapable of inflicting anything but the experience of fear itself, as in **" 'Oh, Whistle' "**, perhaps the most terrifying of all. Here the 'intensely horrible face *of crumpled linen*' seems to possess this power alone: 'The Colonel . . . was of the opinion that if Parkins had closed with it, it could really have done very little, and that its one power was that of frightening.' Yet this is a far more effective piece than the otherwise similar story, **'A Warning to the Curious'**, where the phantom actually murders the victim. By placing too great a strain on the reader's credulity, the effect of terror is here diminished, rather than increased.

When it comes to describing the source of fear, the ghost story writer must tread delicately. A certain vagueness, an element of mystery is essential. Too much power over the material world, such as the ability to commit a murder, can reduce the creature's potential effect. Henry James laid down that the writer must make his reader '*think the

evil . . . and you are released from weak specifications'*. M. R. James had none of Henry James's subtle powers of suggestion, but he too recognized that a vague description might be far more disturbing than a precise one. Often the witness is, in any case, too distraught to describe what he has seen with any accuracy, so that he only provides hints on which the reader's imagination may build:

> I was conscious of a most horrible smell of mould, and of a cold kind of face pressed against my own, and moving slowly over it, and of several—I don't know how many—legs or arms or tentacles or something clinging to my body.
>
> **('The Treasure of Abbot Thomas')**

> I don't know,' he said, 'but I can tell you one thing—he was beastly thin: and he looked as if he was wet all over: and . . . I'm not at all sure that he was alive.
>
> **('A School Story')**

> What he chiefly remembers about it is a horrible, an intensely horrible, face of crumpled linen.
>
> **(" 'Oh, Whistle, and I'll come to you, My Lad' ")**

Sometimes there are allusions to incidents that are never actually related, for example, at the end of **'Casting the Runes'**, 'Harrington repeated to Dunning something of what he had heard his brother say in his sleep: but it was not long before Dunning stopped him.' Such vague allusions help to prod the imagination into action. They are also part of a more general use of understatement that characterizes James's style. Implicit in the restrained, gentlemanly, even scholarly tone is the suggestion that it would be distasteful to dwell on unpleasant details, and this consistent 'meiosis' serves to increase our apprehension. Recognition that the story teller is deliberately understating his case serves to increase its effectiveness. James may have learnt the use of a deadpan narrative technique from such French exponents of *Grand Guignol* as Mérimée, Maupassant and the Erckmann-Chatrian collaborators, but it was quite evidently a tone that came perfectly naturally to him, perhaps because it is also a characteristically English one.

Although James relies largely on the traditional character of his spirits to make them fearful, he often likes to touch up the standard shapes with a few details of his own. The sheeted ghost becomes 'a horrible hopping creature in white' which makes away with a child in Karswell's sinister magic lantern show, or the summoned spirit in the bedclothes in **" 'Oh, Whistle' "** which, having no eyes, 'seemed to feel about it with its muffled arms in a groping and random fashion'. It does not finally discover Parkins until he lets out an uncontrollable cry of disgust. Since skeletons have become the familiar property of art and medical students, James resorts instead to the resuscitated corpse, an unclean thing of decaying flesh whose appearance is hinted at in **'Lost Hearts'**: ' . . . what he saw reminds me of what I once beheld myself in the famous vaults of St Michan's Church in Dublin, which posses the horrid property of preserving corpses from decay for centuries.'

Sensations of normal physical repulsion are also used to reinforce supernatural terrors. Flies (by association with the Lord of them) haunt the sites of satanic pacts in **'An Evening's Entertainment'** and **'The Residence at Whitminster'**. The guardian of **'The Treasure of Abbot Thomas'** which slips its horrid arms round Somerton's neck was 'perhaps more like a toad than anything else', and there is a truly nightmarish sequence in **'Mr Humphreys and his Inheritance'** where the effect derives from an unpleasantly familiar analogy: 'It took shape as a face—a human face—a *burnt* human face: and with the odious writhings of a wasp creeping out of a rotten apple there clambered out the appearance of a form.'

Perhaps the commonest of James's domestic terrors is the spider, used either to provide a point of comparison, as the spinner of gloomy cobwebs, or, in **'The Ash-Tree'**, as the agent of evil itself. The hairy and horribly emaciated demon of **'Canon Alberic's Scrapbook'**, the prototype of a number of such creatures in James's work, may well have been inspired by a similar figure crouching in Brueghel's painting of the Archangel Michael. When first encountered in the scrapbook illustration, it resembles 'one of the awful bird-catching spiders of South America translated into human form'. At the climax Dennistoun, alone in his room, first notices 'A penwiper? No, no such thing in the house. A rat? No, too black. A large spider? I trust to goodness not—no. Good God! a hand like the hand in that picture!'

Draped cobwebs are a source of horror in **'The Tractate Middoth'**. The form that the unfortunate librarian, Garrett, encounters in the Cambridge University Library has its face covered from eyebrows to cheekbones with them. At the end of the story, the only living things present at the scene of Eldred's death are large spiders, running in and out of a mass of cobwebs. Both the apparition in the library, and the apparently harmless spiders of the ending seem to be connected with the unpleasant old man who left his will in the Tractate, and demanded to be buried in the bricked-up room beneath the spot where Eldred died so mysteriously. In **'The Ash-Tree'** spiders act as the agents of the witch's maleficence, apparently springing from her buried bones, and feeding, like vampires, on the blood of her enemies. **'The Ash-Tree'** is a most carefully constructed piece, each episode building towards a final climax where the familiar is brought into a grotesque juxtaposition with the surreal in the account of Sir Richard's death. The reader does not yet know the exact form that the inhabitants of the ash-tree take:

> . . . it seems as if Sir Richard were moving his head rapidly to and fro . . . And now you would guess, so deceptive is the half-darkness, that he had several heads, round and brownish, which move back and forwards, even as low as his chest. It is a horrible illusion. Is it nothing more? There! something drops off the bed with a soft plump, like a kitten, and is out of the window in a flash.

The sense of discomfort here results from the different interpretations offered. They alternate alarmingly from normality (a man moving his head) to total abnormality (a man with several heads, sharply realized by the adjectives

'round and brownish'). The final comparison to a kitten, an animal connected primarily with the pleasures of touch, appalls, particularly on a second reading, when the reader will mentally contrast the attractive feel of the kitten with the repulsion of the spider. All through the passage runs the suggestion of the spider's characteristic movement, rapid, silent (except when it falls to the floor) and intimately linked with the fear it arouses.

The spiders of **'The Ash-Tree'** will work on our sense of physical repulsion if we share with its author 'a horror of spiders, especially large ones and of the lone spider which will turn up unaccountably in the bath'. The theme of the story, witchcraft, relies on more intellectual responses. Most readers know something of the seventeenth-century witch hunts, and have some idea of the supposed practices of witches, if only from *Macbeth*. The 'slips of yew' there presented as a standard cauldron ingredient can be paralleled by the springs of ash collected by the malevolent Mrs Mothersole, particularly when it is remembered that the ash is often associated with black magic, the witch's besom being traditionally made of ash. In case some of this esoteric lore is unfamiliar, the Bishop of Kilmore reminds Sir Richard in the course of the story that his Irish peasants consider 'it brings the worst of luck to sleep near an ash-tree'. The spiders, then, provide a fresh elaboration on the traditional theme of the witch's *maleficium*. The familiar characteristics of her behaviour help to authenticate the tale.

M. R. James adapted a variety of time-hallowed themes from folklore and legend, myth and ballad, and his stories are largely constructed from such traditional elements. Recognizing this process, he wrote: 'I have tried to make my ghosts act in a way not inconsistent with the rules of folklore.' His ability to manipulate familiar material is everywhere in evidence; so too is his scholarly interest in it. In 1914 he edited that strange hotchpotch of legend and learning, Walter Map's *De Nugis Curialium*, which contains several stories of the returning dead, and he published a group of medieval ghost stories he had unearthed in the *English Historical Review* in 1922. He had also read many nineteenth-century ghost stories, both fictional and veridical, his favourite author being Joseph Sheridan Le Fanu, whose imaginative treatment of Irish folklore he greatly admired. He found in the ballad a useful source of supernatural episodes, and was particularly interested in the Danish and Breton versions. It is worthwhile, in the light of his interest in the ballad, to consider how far his own narrative technique was influenced by it. The prosaic, matter-of-fact tone with which natural and supernatural events alike are presented, the buildup of suspense by steps, the overall importance of the action and the subordination of characterization to it, the stiff and conventional nature of the character-drawing, and perhaps above all, the sense of a background of shared traditional beliefs conveying further implications to the audience—all these qualities are present in James's work. We need to know something of the hats o' the birk and the red cock to understand the events of **'The Wife of Usher's Well'**, just as we need to know something of the associations of witches and ash-trees for **'The Ash-Tree'** to work on us as its author intends. It may be that the self-effacing story-teller, the impersonal narrative technique and the extensive use of understatement were characteristics that James took over from the ballad, the supreme form for a tale of terror, as the Romantic poets had realized.

Much of the effect of his stories depends on our recognizing certain archetypal patterns of temptation and vengeance as typifying the workings of the supernatural world. The different allusions in a single story do not derive from any one origin, however, but from a compound of sources both in literature and folklore. It is often difficult to distinguish these elements completely, since ancient beliefs survive in a variety of contexts. In " 'Oh, Whistle, and I'll come to you, My Lad' " the malevolent spirit that appears in response to Parkins' blowing the whistle may be connected with the sailors' superstition about whistling on deck, the prototype of which is at least as old as Homer, and Odysseus' *contretemps* with the bag of winds. Witches, too, traditionally had power over the winds, as Shakespeare showed in *Macbeth*. As late as 1814 wise women sold winds to sailors, for in that year Walter Scott recorded buying one from a certain Bessie Miller of Stromness, Orkney. In the course of the story, the Colonel points out that Northern Europeans still believe that a sudden wind has been whistled for, adding 'there's generally something at the bottom of what these country-folk hold to'. Thus the very antiquity of a superstition is put forward as some sort of evidence of its validity. The horrible thing that responds to the summons is bodiless, as traditionally spirits often were, so it has to assume the body of bedlinen.

It first appears on the beach as Parkins returns from the Templars' Church, having found, but not yet blown, the whistle: 'an indistinct personage who seemed to be making great efforts to catch up with him, but made little, if any progress.' The sight of this figure throws up a completely new and quite different literary allusion, this time to Bunyan's Apollyon, which Parkins involuntarily associates with the distant pursuer, wondering what he would do

> . . . if I looked back and caught sight of a black figure sharply defined against the yellow sky, and saw that it had horns and wings? I wonder whether I should stand or run for it. Luckily that gentleman behind is not of that kind, and seems to be about as far off now as when I saw him first.

The spirit's identity becomes clearer in Parkins' subsequent dream of flight along the beach. Its failure to catch up with him on that first afternoon had been due to the fact that he had not yet actually blown the whistle, thus placing himself, both literally and metaphorically, within its reach. Another significant literary reference lies in the title, taken from a song of Burns, the refrain of which has a distinctly sinister ring:

> Though father and mother and brother go mad,
> Oh, whistle and I'll come to ye, my lad.

This elaborate network of allusion helps to provide a focus for our fears, which are themselves the more alarming for being vaguely familiar. The superstitions and quotations exploited here seem to lend an air of almost historical verification to the evil spirit that comes, just as the Sortes

Biblicae in **'The Ash-Tree'**, or the quotations from Ecclesiasticus and Isaiah at the end of **'Canon Alberic's Scrapbook'** convince by apparently supplying evidence from the Book of Truth itself.

Because the ghosts and demons in these tales act in accordance with certain traditional rules, they acquire an alarming predictability, which James exploited to increase his reader's anticipation. When whisperings are first heard in the cellar or the rose garden, a man feels that he is being followed or has a vivid and curious dream, the reader's attention is alerted, and certain vague apprehensions take shape, based on our existing knowledge of similar manifestations—witches, ghouls, demons or whatever. The protagonist of the story, however, frequently does not share this response, and fails to impute significance to the events, so that the reader is in the position of the child at the pantomime, wanting to warn the actor of what stands behind him. This gives an extra degree of involvement, which is part of the secret of James's success. He stated his own rules for this gradual opening, which so often puts the reader one step ahead of the protagonist, in his introduction to *Ghosts and Marvels*. The majority of his tales adhere to them rigorously:

> Let us, then, be introduced to the actors in a placid way; let us see them going about their ordinary business, undisturbed by forebodings, pleased with their surroundings; and into this calm environment let the ominous thing put out its head, unobtrusively at first, and then more insistently, until it holds the stage.

The hero's insensitivity to forebodings, his cheerful frame of mind, which may even cause him to dismiss the first 'unobtrusive' appearances of the thing, whatever it is, are among the means by which we are involved in his situation.

For James, the plot was of paramount importance, and characterization is accordingly reduced to a minimum. In this respect his practice contrasts strikingly with that of Henry James, who felt 'the thickness in the human consciousness' to be essential to the ghost story since it is 'the only thickness we do get'. M. R. James keeps his characters thin to the point of transparency. They are quite deliberately washed free of all subtlety or complexity which might cloud or impede the all-important progress of the plot. In the delineation of character James employed no tricks; there were no new developments, no sudden revelations to catch the audience unprepared, for all the devices of surprise are limited to that element of the story which concerned him most, the plot. Psychology is totally and defiantly excluded from his writings.

James's characters are types or what E. M. Forster calls 'flats', and he often uses the same device for creating 'flats' as, Forster points out, Dickens does (perhaps not surprisingly for he admired Dickens intensely and knew extensive passages by heart): this device is the reiterated phrase or speech trick. So Catell, in **'The Diary of Mr Poynter'**, has a Shakespearian quotation, delivered in broad cockney, to meet every situation. 'The last', James adds, with a wry admission of the inevitable, 'began with the words "There are more things".' Dialect, either country or cockney, usually denotes simplicity and honesty, often a reliable witness, for example Mrs Bunch, the kind housekeeper of **'Lost Hearts'**, or Patten, the old retainer in **'A Neighbour's Landmark'**. Many similar characters remain unnamed and unidentified, except in so far as their speech shows them to be 'locals'. They often play important rôles in the build-up of suspense. The frightened lad in **" 'Oh, Whistle' "**, who wails 'Ow, I seen it wive at me out of the winder . . . and I don't like it', is one example; the old man who starts Paxton on his disastrous quest, in **'A Warning to the Curious'**, is another.

Apart from the use of dialect and speech tricks to 'place' them, James's characters qualify as flats because of their total predictability. A single line usually suffices to describe them, and they never deviate from this first account of them, whether pleasant—'Professor Parkins, one of whose principal characteristics was pluck . . .', or 'Mr Garrett was a cheerful and pleasant-looking young man . . .' —or sinister, in which case they are usually identified by an *absence* of information: 'Very little was known of Mr Abney's pursuits or temper . . .', or ' . . . just at present Mr Karswell is a very angry man. But I don't know much about him otherwise . . .' Secrecy is itself suspicious and these early intimations are confirmed when Abney and Karswell turn out to be dabblers in the black arts, and even murderers.

What has been said of James's minor characters also applies to the central figure, the hero who dominates the situation and acts as the focus of the supernatural events. These characters have a transparent simplicity, transparent, because we are required to look *through* them at the unfolding plot, where the emphasis is placed. The reader sees not merely what *is* happening, but also what is going to happen, anticipating, if only vaguely, the disaster that is on the point of overtaking the hero, and is filled with a corresponding sympathy and alarm on his behalf. These transparent, anonymous heroes, often distinctively twentieth-century in their practical, sceptical approach to life, are frequently academics of some kind, if their professions are referred to at all. They have a selfless enthusiasm for knowledge (or perhaps a fatal curiosity) which ironically leads them on 'where angels fear to tread', as old Cooper warns Mr Humphreys. From one angle the hero is thus a reflection of his sceptical and detached creator; from another he is the clear window through which the reader perceives the plot unfolding, unfolding far faster than the hero himself realizes. For this hero unknowingly inhabits an animistic world where anything might happen, a world into which only the minor characters are given intuitive glimpses so that they may warn the protagonist of what impends. But the hero's materialism, his doubt, prevents him from giving due weight to the warnings he receives.

Such a warning is usually provided in the early stages of the tale, partly in order to increase the sense of suspense and imminent danger, but also to provide an element of dramatic justice. In everyday terms, the hero is mildly culpable in that he wilfully rejects, because of his scepticism perhaps, the advice of wiser or older men. In metaphysical terms, his refusal to be warned is symptomatic of a wider rejection of unproven forces and inexplicable powers, and hence is duly revenged by these powers, whether they are conceived as emerging from an outer darkness or an inner id. Nearly all of the stories provide this warning element in some form or another: in **'Canon Alberic's Scrapbook'**, there is not only the excessive anxiety of the sacristan and his daughter, but even the sight of the fearful drawing itself; in **'The Ash-Tree'**, the Bishop of Kilmore warns Sir Richard with his allusion to Irish peasant beliefs. The Colonel fulfils this function in **" 'Oh, Whistle' "**. **'The Treasure of Abbot Thomas'** provides a caveat at the end of the coded message, 'Gare à qui la touche'. Thus the hero has to some extent wilfully placed himself 'on the edge'. In the rare cases where visitations fall on the totally innocent, as in **'Casting the Runes'**, the victim is provided with helpful friends, as Dunning is with Henry Harrington, whose advice he is only too eager to adopt.

The warnings constitute dramatic justice only, however, and there is inevitably a degree of disproportion in their working. Yet there is nearly always a distinct moment when the hero commits some error, perhaps a form of hubris, by taking a wrong decision, or by choosing against advice to prosecute some scheme or investigation on hand. What impels him to press on at this juncture in the plot may be one of a variety of emotions; it may involve avarice or covetousness, but equally it may be simply a desire to carry through a projected plan perfectly innocent in itself, such as having curtains made up in an eighteenth-century design, opening up an old maze, or building a rose garden. There is no apparent folly in such undertakings and the act of hubris then lies in not heeding warnings or signs. But perhaps the emotion that most frequently lures the unwitting hero on is curiosity, sometimes quite justifiable, and at other times, strange, even perverse. Curiosity is always marginally present, often accompanying avarice, or the desire to complete a projected plan, but in several tales it provides the primary motivation, as in the purest example of this motif, the tale of Bluebeard. Sometimes an investigation is carried out in the spirit of scientific enquiry, as when Parkins blows the whistle, or Anderson investigates room 13. Sometimes there is a motive of historical discovery, as there is for Dennistoun with the scrapbook, or for Paxton with the Anglo-Saxon crown, but behind every rationalization lies the dreadful itch of pure curiosity, morbid, perverse and inexplicable. It drives the wretched Wraxall, to his own apparent astonishment, to repeat three times, 'Ah . . . Count Magnus, there you are. I should dearly like to see you.' Each time he utters this, one of the three padlocks falls from the Count's massive tomb.

The story that resembles the prototype, Bluebeard, most closely is a short piece called **'Rats'**, in which one Thomson, 'in a mood of quite indefensible curiosity' unlocks the door of a room in his lodgings and discovers a horribly animated corpse. Before finally leaving the house, he feels compelled to visit it again, and this time his intrusion arouses it. The tale is inconclusive: Thomson has received a lasting fright, and the landlord is left to observe grimly 'what he may do now there ain't no sayin'. . . .' Curiosity has its academic and obsessive aspects; perhaps James's experience of the former gave him some insight into the latter. Both are dramatized in the large group of stories that conform to this pattern, in which the central character, whether deliberately or accidentally, fails to heed a vital warning. To a certain extent, all authors who write of the supernatural are expressing their feelings of curiosity about it, however publicly they may declare their scepticism and lack of interest in psychic research. Yet for the majority such curiosity stops short of direct investigation, and their ghost stories embody a form of speculation which may be safely indulged from the sidelines.

A more sinister and reprehensible curiosity is the subject of James's stories of black magic, and its disastrous consequences for those who practise it. Here the model is no longer the innocent curiosity of Bluebeard's wife, but the legend of Faust's hunger for forbidden knowledge, which ultimately proved fatal. In the tales based on this theme, a necromancer ventures too far in his dark enquiries, loses control of the spirits he has summoned up, or perhaps tries to evade the final reckoning, and is destroyed by the spirits he has attempted to exploit, or otherwise carried off. James first used this motif in an early tale, **'Lost Hearts'**, but it occurs more frequently in his later work, for example in **'The Residence at Whitminster'**, **'An Evening's Entertainment'** and **'A View from a Hill'**. These three pieces are elaborately and amusingly presented, but their denouements are marred by the excessive violence which often weakens his handling of this theme. Two of the tales described in a late essay, **'Stories I Have Tried to Write'**, deal with the same subject: in the first, an evil Roman priest is destroyed by the familiar he has called up to destroy another, while the second tells of a sixteenth-century Cambridge witch, carried off by a mysterious company. Both these stories would have employed a historical setting which, for James, frequently accompanied this plot.

The last group of James's stories, considered thematically, is perhaps the most classical and traditional: these are stories of revenge spirits, familiar from Shakespeare and his contemporaries, as well as from the great Victorians such as Dickens, Wilkie Collins and Le Fanu. As in *Richard III* or *Macbeth* the ghosts of the murdered appear to haunt the murderer and hasten his final downfall. These spirits seem to derive their power from the guilt caused by a forbidden action, such as murder, particularly of the helpless or weak. This classic pattern is used in **'Martin's Close'**, **'The Stalls of Barchester'** (where further spirits come to effect the punishment of the guilty) and **'A Disappearance and an Appearance'**, each time with ingenious elaborations on the basic pattern of murder revenged.

All James's ghost stories resolve themselves into one of these three basic patterns, 'Bluebeard', 'Faust' or the spirits of revenge—even those stories which he did not finally complete, and this is hardly surprising in view of his enormous respect and feeling for classical structures. Nevertheless, one cannot help noticing that many of his most successful stories occur in the first two collections, and that the two later volumes are largely made up of variations on earlier designs: **'The Haunted Dolls' House'** is, quite openly, a replay of the dazzlingly simple idea of **'The Mezzotint'**, while **'A Warning to the Curious'** recombines many of the elements of **" 'Oh, Whistle' "**, less successfully. Probably this sort of repetition is inevitable. It is certainly common to a number of other ghost story writers,

including the admired Le Fanu, and may well be a measure of the form's limited possibilities, as James himself once suggested. His avowed motive in writing was to tell a good story, and having discovered from his wide reading certain well-established structural patterns, he adopted them and made them the bases on to which he grafted a variety of settings, incidents and characters. Throughout his work, he was strictly regulated by his particular notions as to how the suspense and climax should be achieved, and his practice reveals a close adherence to a limited number of techniques that he had evolved for himself, through his acquaintance with so many examples of the genre. He was perhaps the only writer who deliberately studied the ghost story in order to write it himself, and the resulting pieces exhibit a unique degree of critical control and an exceptional grasp of the force of traditional elements. Without being in any sense experimental or exploratory, his stories demonstrate the power that the classically well-made tale may still exert over a modern reader.

Jack Sullivan (essay date 1978)

SOURCE: "The Antiquarian Ghost Story: Montague Rhodes James," in his *Elegant Nightmares: The English Ghost Story from Le Fanu to Blackwood,* Ohio University Press, 1978, pp. 69-90.

[*Sullivan is an American educator and critic whose writings focus on English supernatural fiction, particularly the development and major authors of ghost stories of the late Victorian and Edwardian period. In the following exerpt, he examines technique and style in James's restrained approach to writing ghost stories, comparing his works with those of J. S. Le Fanu.*]

"Count Magnus," from M. R. James's *Ghost Stories of an Antiquary,* is haunted not only by its own ghosts, but by the ghost of Sheridan Le Fanu. Mr. Wraxall, the hero of the tale, dooms himself by peering at a terrifying sarcophagus engraving which should have remained unseen and opening an obscure alchemy volume which should have remained closed. By doing these things, he inadvertently summons the author of the alchemy treatise, the dreaded Count Magnus, from the sarcophagus. To make matters worse, he also summons the count's hooded, tentacled companion. Anyone who has read Le Fanu's "Green Tea" knows that such creatures are easier summoned than eluded. Mr. Wraxall flees across the Continent, but his pursuers are always close behind. They arrive at his remote country house in England before he does and wait for him there. Not surprisingly, he is found dead. At the inquest, seven jurors faint at the sight of the body. The verdict is "visitation of God," but the reader knows that he has been visited by something else.

In both incident and vision, **"Count Magnus"** is darkened by the shadow of Le Fanu. The basic dynamic of the story, the hunt, is symbolized by the sarcophagus engraving:

> Among trees, was a man running at full speed,
> with flying hair and outstretched hands. After
> him followed a strange form; it would be hard
> to say whether the artist had intended it for a
> man, and was unable to give the requisite simili-

tude, or whether it was intentionally made as monstrous as it looked. In view of the skill with which the rest of the drawing was done, Mr. Wraxall felt inclined to adopt the latter idea.

Upon reading this insidiously understated passage, the reader who is familiar with Le Fanu immediately knows two things: that the fleeing figure will soon be Mr. Wraxall himself and that the outcome of the pursuit will be fatal for him. Such a reader will not be surprised by the mysterious illogic of the plot, the absence of any moral connection between the hunter and the hunted. Mr. Wraxall is no Gothic villain or Fatal Man; he is a singularly unremarkable, almost anonymous character. He resembles several Le Fanu characters (especially in "Green Tea" and "Schalken the Painter") in that he is a pure victim, having done nothing amiss other than reading the wrong book and looking at the wrong picture. We are told in an ironic passage that "his besetting fault was clearly that of over-inquisitiveness, possibly a good fault in a traveler, certainly a fault for which this traveler paid dearly in the end." We are not told why he is any more overly inquisitive than James's other antiquaries, many of whom are never pursued. The narrator sums up the problem near the end of the story: "He is expecting a visit from his pursuers—how or when he knows not—and his constant cry is 'What has he done?' and 'Is there no hope?' Doctors, he knows, would call him mad, policemen would laugh at him. The parson is away. What can he do but lock his door and cry to God?" This fragmented summary of Mr. Wraxall's final entries in his journal suggests that the horror of the situation is in the chasm between action and consequence. In the fictional world of Le Fanu and James, one does not have to be a Faust, a Melmoth, or even a Huckleberry Finn to be damned. The strategy of both writers is the same: to make the reader glance nervously around the room and say, "If this could happen to him, it could happen to him, it could happen to me."

The style also owes much to Le Fanu. In an odd sense, **"Count Magnus"** is more in the Le Fanu manner than Le Fanu. James's use of innuendo and indirection is so rigorous that it hides more than it reveals. Le Fanu creates a balance between uneasy vagueness and grisly clarity. But James tilts the balance in favor of the unseen. Tiny, unsettling flashes of clarity emerge from the obscurity, but usually in an indirect context. We are allowed to see the protruding tentacle of one of the robed pursuers, for example—but only in the engraving, not in the actual pursuit. In the most literal sense, these are nameless horrors.

James also follows Le Fanu's example in his use of narrative distance, again transcending his model. Le Fanu separates himself from his material through the use of elaborate, sometimes awkward prologues and epilogues which filter the stories through a series of editors and narrators. Sometimes, as in **"Mr. Justice Harbottle,"** the network of tales within tales results in a narrative fabric of considerable complexity. In **"Count Magnus,"** the narrator is an anonymous editor who has access to the papers Mr. Wraxall was compiling for a travelogue. The story consists of paraphrases and direct quotations from these papers, a device which gives the narrative a strong aura of authenticity. The transitions from one document to the other, occur-

ring organically within the text, are smooth and unobtrusive. They are also strangely impersonal, as if the teller in no way wishes to commit himself to his tale.

James's reticence probably relates as much personal temperament as to the aesthetic problem of how to write a proper ghost story. It is commonly accepted, largely because of the work of James and Le Fanu, that indirection, ambiguity, and narrative distance are appropriate techniques for ghostly fiction. (Material horror tales, such as Wells's "The Cone" and Alexander Woollcott's "Moonlight Sonata," are another matter.) Supernatural horror is usually more convincing when suggested or evoked than when explicitly documented. But James's understated subtlety is so obsessive, so paradoxically unrestrained that it feels like an inversion of the hyperbole of Poe or Maturin. I find his late work increasingly ambiguous and puzzling, sometimes to the point of almost total mystification. It is as if James is increasingly unwilling to deal with the implications of his stories. What begins as a way of making supernatural horror more potent becomes a way of repressing or avoiding it. Often he appears to be doing both at once, creating a unique chill and tension.

Although he claimed to be merely a follower of Le Fanu, his work has a different feel, despite the obvious similarities in vision and style. Indeed, he unwittingly created his own "school," a surprisingly large accumulation of tales for which James serves as a paradigm. At least two of his more talented admirers, E. G. Swain and R. H. Malden, are far closer to James than James imagined himself to Le Fanu.

James published four volumes of ghost stories during his lifetime (1862-1936): *Ghost Stories of an Antiquary* (1940), *More Ghost Stories* (1911), *A Thin Ghost and Others* (1919), and *A Warning to the Curious* (1925). He was originally a teller, rather than a writer, of ghost stories. His first two stories, **"Lost Hearts"** and **"Canon Alberic's Scrapbook,"** were written down to be read aloud at an 1897 meeting of the Chitchat Society, a literary gathering which met for "the promotion of rational conversation." The readings were intended to enliven what had become a listless, apathetic (if "rational") group. They must not have been entirely successful, for although the readings continued, the group dissolved in 1897; as James put it, in his typical phraseology, the society "expired of inanition." Nevertheless, the meeting marked the beginning of a yearly ritual in which James would deliver 11 p.m. Christmas readings to friends, first at King's and later at Cambridge. At some of these meetings, James read Le Fanu (with "great relish," according to one of his friends), thus beginning the Le Fanu revival which culminated in James's edition of rare Le Fanu ghost stories. Some of the listeners, like A. C. and E. F. Benson, were connoisseurs of the weird and became ghost story writers themselves. Partly because of their prodding, and partly because James's friend James MacBryde agreed to be his illustrator, James published his first and most famous collection, *Ghost Stories of an Antiquary.* As the prodding continued, so did the other collections, even though MacBryde (who, according to James, was the main reason he decided to publish anything at all), died suddenly before completing the illustrations for *Ghost Stories.* The climax of this curiously reluctant career was the publication of the *Collected Ghost Stories* in 1931. By then, in its review of the collected stories, the *Spectator Literary Supplement* was able to refer to James as "long" having "been an acknowledged master of his craft."

Other than a lifetime fondness for oldness, James's life demonstrates little direct connection to his fiction. His reputation rests not on his fiction, still relatively unknown, but on his contribution to medieval scholarship (though this situation is rapidly changing). James prepared an estimated fifteen to twenty thousand bibliographic descriptions of medieval manuscripts, as well as the *Apocryphal New Testaments.* Unlike Le Fanu, he did not steep himself in Swedenborg or any other esoteric doctrines, but remained, according to the obituary notice of the British Academy, "a devoted son of the Church of England." Nevertheless, his prodigious scholarly activities provided him with the learned tone and much of the content of his stories. Though largely fabricated, the names of churches, manuscripts, villages, and allusive scholarly minutiae in his stories always sound unerringly authentic. In all outward respects, his life was conservative, the perfect embodiment of a successful post-Victorian man of letters: he was a Fellow of King's College, Provost and Vice-Chancellor at Cambridge, Director of the Fitzwilliam Museum, and finally Provost of Eton. Although Protestant, "he liked a grave and dignified ceremonial." In politics, he was "uninterested but faintly conservative."

James once described the ghost story as an inherently "old-fashioned" form. Yet in the context of his life, the writing of ghost stories seemed eccentric and unorthodox, almost a blemish on an otherwise spotless career. Sir Stephen Gaselee refers with embarrassment to the "pile of 'shockers' in his room." (The "shockers" included, among others, Conan Doyle, Blackwood and, of course, Le Fanu.) Gaselee doesn't like James's "or any other ghost stories," but adds condescendingly that "experts tell me they are among the best of their kind." James's biographer and lifelong friend, S. G. Lubbock, devotes only a single page to the ghost stories.

But the most stubbornly unhelpful commentator on James's fiction is James himself. In his odd preface to his *Collected Ghost Stories,* James states that the only reason he is yielding any commentary at all is that "a preface is demanded by my publishers." Given the demand, the preface "may as well be devoted to answering questions which I have been asked." The answers, to put it mildly, are brief: "First, whether the stories are based on my own experience? To this, the answer is No. . . . Or again, whether they are versions of other people's experiences? No. . . . Other questioners ask if I have any theories as to the writing of ghost stories. None that are worthy of the name or need be repeated here: some thoughts on the subject are in a preface to *Ghosts and Marvels.* . . . Supplementary questions are: Do I believe in ghosts? To which I am prepared to consider evidence and accept it if it satisfies me." This delightful evasiveness represents a consistent effort on James's part to dissociate himself from the clichés which usually dominate discussions of ghost sto-

ries. But it also represents an oblique refusal to comment on the craft of ghost story writing (a subject which Edith Wharton, L. P. Hartley, Robert Aickman, and others have always been eager to discuss). The reference to James's supernatural fiction anthology, *Ghosts and Marvels,* is as sneaky and underhanded as any of James's apparitions. If, as James suggests, we search out that rare volume for enlightenment, we find this statement: "Often I have been asked to formulate my views about ghost stories. . . . Never have I been able to find out whether I had any views that could be formulated."

This is more than simple modesty. James's aggressively deflationary attitude toward himself and his material is part of the mystique of his fiction. The stories use every available verbal resources to avoid calling attention to themselves, as if the otherworldly phenomena are creepy enough on their own not to require a loud voice for their exposition.

Moreover, the stories fit thematically into this context, for they often imply a kind of emptiness and restlessness on the part of the characters. It is not "overinquisitiveness" that gets Mr. Wraxall into trouble so much as ennui. James's stories assume a radical breakdown of the work ethic in which the forces of evil take advantage of idleness. Mr. Wraxall is like most of James's heroes in that he is a roving antiquary, a bachelor who is wealthy and cultivated but seems to have no fixed place in society: "He had, it seemed, no settled abode in England, but was a denizen of hotels and boarding houses. It is probable that he entertained the idea of settling down at some future time which never came." Though James does not make much of the idea, the supernatural in his stories has a way of materializing out of a void in people's lives. In **"The Uncommon Prayer Book"** (one of his happiest titles), Mr. Davidson spends a week researching the tombs of Leventhrop House because "his nearest relations were enjoying winter sports abroad and the friends who had been kindly anxious to replace them had an infectious complaint in the house." Even those who have a "settled abode" are curiously unsettled.

There is thus an implicit "Waste Land" ambiance to these stories. The characters are antiquaries, not merely because the past enthralls them, but because the present is a near vacuum. They surround themselves with rarefied paraphernalia from the past—engravings, rare books, altars, tombs, coins, and even such things as doll's houses and ancient whistles—seemingly because they cannot connect with anything in the present. The endless process of collecting and arranging gives the characters an illusory sense of order and stability, illusory because it is precisely this process which evokes the demon or the vampire. With the single exception of Mr. Abney in **"Lost Hearts,"** James's men of leisure are not villainous, merely bored. Their adventures represent a sophisticated version of the old warning that idleness is the devil's workshop.

This is a crucial difference between James and Le Fanu. In Le Fanu, supernatural horror is peculiarly militant—it can emerge anytime it pleases. In James's antiquarian tales, horror is ever-present, but it is not actually threatening or lethal until inadvertently invoked. For Le Fanu's characters, reality is inherently dark and deadly; for James's antiquaries, darkness must be sought out through research and discovery.

It is true that the final discovery is always accidental: James's stories are distinctly different from the more visionary stories of Blackwood and Machen, stories with characters who are not bored, but stifled, and who consciously seek out weirdness and horror. Nevertheless, there is a half-conscious sense in which the antiquary knows he may be heading for trouble but persists in what he is doing. An example is Mr. Parkins in the (again) wonderfully titled **"Oh, Whistle and I'll Come to You, My Lad,"** a man whose bed clothes become possessed. Parkins brings this singularly unpleasant fate on himself by digging up a dreadful whistle and having the poor sense to blow it. He doesn't *have* to blow it. He is given ample warning—certainly more than any of Le Fanu's victims ever get—from a Latin inscription on the whistle: "Quis est iste qui venit?" ("Who is this who is coming?") "Well," says Parkins with a nice simplicity, "The best way to find out is evidently to whistle for him."

Another aspect of James which separates him from Le Fanu is the radical economy of his style. Although he hides more than Le Fanu, he etches what he chooses to reveal in brief but telling detail. An example is the apparition (of a man burned at the stake) in **"The Rose Garden"**:

> It was not a mask. It was a face—large, smooth, and pink. She remembers the minute drops of perspiration which were starting from its forehead: she remembers how the jaws were clean-shaven and the eyes shut. She remembers also, and with an accuracy which makes the thought intolerable to her, how the mouth was open and a single tooth appeared below the upper lip. As she looked the face receded into the darkness of the bush. The shelter of the house was gained and the door shut before she collapsed.

Another, more colloquially rendered, is the library apparition in **"The Tractate Middoth"**:

> This time, if you please—ten o'clock in the morning, remember, and as much light as ever you get in those classes, and there was my parson again, back to me, looking at the books on the shelf I wanted. His hat was on the table, and he had a bald head. I waited a second or two looking at him rather particularly. I tell you, he had a very nasty bald head. It looked to me dry, and it looked dusty, and the streaks of hair across it were much less like hair than cobwebs. Well, I made a bit of noise on purpose, coughed and moved my feet. He turned round and let me see his face—which I hadn't seen before. I tell you again, I'm not mistaken. Though, for one reason or another I didn't take in the lower part of his face, I did see the upper part; and it was perfectly dry, and the eyes were very deep-sunk; and over them, from the eyebrows to the cheek-bone, there were *cobwebs*—thick. Now that closed me up, as they say, and I can't tell you anything more.

Le Fanu would not have cut either scene off as quickly, nor would he have been as prosaic. Compared to the state-

liness of Le Fanu's prose, James's seems spare and unadorned. Terse and controlled, his stories give the sense of a ruthless paring down of incidents and characters, a constant editing out of anything which might clutter up the supernatural experience or the antiquarian setting. But the scheme is not rigid enough to exclude a frequent light touch, as the **"Tractate Middoth"** scene amply demonstrates. Indeed, the editing itself is often accomplished with droll humor: "Tea was taken to the accompaniment of a discussion which golfing persons can imagine for themselves, but which the conscientious writer has no right to inflict upon any non-golfing persons" (**"The Mezzotint"**). There is also a frequent impatience with the inevitable stereotypical horror scene: "Next day Sir Matthew Fell was not downstairs at six in the morning, as was his custom, nor at seven, nor yet at eight. Hereupon, the servants went and knocked at his chamber door. I need not prolong the description of their anxious listenings and renewed batterings on the panels. The door was opened at last from the outside, and they found their master dead and black. So much you have guessed" (**"The Ash Tree"**). Assuming the reader knows the basics, James is ever-anxious to move ahead toward his own variations.

This implicit understanding between writer and reader is a phenomenon common to much post-Le Fanu ghostly fiction. We know basically what is going to happen, and (if the writer is reasonably sophisticated) the writer knows that we know: the interest lies in how he is going to bring it off, in whether he can play a spooky enough variation on the basic theme to make us turn up the lights. Thus the concern with technique in Le Fanu becomes almost an obsession in James, who makes a programmatic, somewhat artificial use of understatement, innuendo, and precisely orchestrated crescendo.

But it would be a mistake to think that James is concerned solely with performance. The premises themselves are frequently startling and imaginative. His contribution is to demonstrate that the old forms of supernatural evil are still respectable, still viable, if seen through different glasses. It is as if the reader were looking through the haunted binoculars in **"A View from a Hill,"** watching a familiar landscape transform itself in sinister, ever-changing ways. Vampires, for example, are familiar enough by the twentieth century, but in **"An Episode of Cathedral History"** James creates a vampire posing as a saintly relic in a fifteenth-century cathedral altar-tomb. The church renovators, surprised at finding a full-length coffin in the altar, are more than surprised when the red-eyed inhabitant of the coffin, annoyed at being disturbed, leaps out in their faces. Witches are also commonplace in fiction, but James's witch (who inhabits **"The Ash Tree"**) has some uniquely unsavory traits, among them the ability to breed gigantic spiders. In all cases, James moves from the traditional concept to his own variation with such swiftness and conciseness that the reader almost forgets he is reading a reworked version of old, sometimes trite material.

On rare occasions, James makes manifesto-like statements about the need for linguistic economy. The Ezra Pound of ghost story writers, James once criticized Poe for his "vagueness"; for his lack of toughness and specific detail;

for the "unreal" quality of his prose. The charge is similar to Pound's denigration of Yeats's early poems. Actually, Poe and James were attempting very different things. Poe's tales are not ghostly but surreal. They immerse themselves in the irrational, whereas James's tales only flirt with it. The power of James lies in his ability to set up a barrier between the empirical and the supernatural and then gradually knock it down—to move subtly from the real to the unreal and sometimes back again. The distinction between the two is much more solid than in Poe, where nightmare and reality constantly melt into one another. James's stories assume a strong grounding in empirical reality. In this context, his refusal to accept the existence of ghosts until he encounters "conclusive evidence" is consistent with the attitude of his stories. The stories are consciously addressed to skeptical readers, readers with a twentieth (or eighteenth) century frame of reference. In making us momentarily accept what we instinctively disbelieve, the burden falls heavily on the language. The way to reach such a reader, James implies, is through clarity and restraint: the hyperbole and verbal effusiveness of the Gothic writers are to be strictly avoided, as are the "trivial and melodramatic" natural explanations of Lord Lytton and the neo-Gothic Victorians. To James, both overwriting and natural explanations in ghost stories are related forms of cheating. Although James usually avoids issuing these anti-Gothic manifestoes, he indirectly pans the Gothic tradition in the introduction to the *Collected Ghost Stories* by refusing to acknowledge any literary debt to it.

To James, only Le Fanu is worth imitating: "He stands absolutely in the first rank as a writer of ghost stories. This is my deliberate verdict, after reading all the supernatural tales I have been able to get hold of. Nobody sets the scene better than he, nobody touches in the effective detail more deftly." Interestingly, James's use of detail is far more selective, small-scaled, and particular than Le Fanu's. For all his "deliberateness" and "leisureliness," Le Fanu's vision frequently opens out onto a large canvas which depicts nameless energies sweeping across the cosmos. The gigantic blob-like entity which hurtles through the trees in "Ultor de Lacy" could not inhabit the cramped world of a James story: there would be no room for it. Instead, such creatures invade the more accommodating outdoor stories of [Algernon] Blackwood and [H. P.] Lovecraft.

In James, even the visionary scenes seem almost prosaic—yet strangely effective for being so. When Parkins, for example, blows his ill-omened whistle, he has the most compact of visions:

> He blew tentatively and stopped suddenly, startled and yet pleased by the note he had elicited. It had a quality of infinite distance in it, and, soft as it was, he somehow felt it must be audible for miles round. It was a sound, too, that seemed to have the power (which many scents possess) of forming pictures in the brain. He saw quite clearly for a moment a vision of a wide, dark expanse at night, with a fresh wind blowing, and in the midst a lonely figure—how employed, he could not tell. Perhaps he would have seen more had not the picture been broken by the sudden surge of a gust of wind against his casement, so

sudden that it made him look up, just in time to see the white glint of a seabird's wing somewhere outside the dark panes.

If Blackwood had written this passage, he would have used the "quality of infinite distance" as the tenor for a series of elaborate visual metaphors, converting sound into several layers of perception. But James opts for direct images, indeed a single "picture" seen "quite clearly for a moment." The combination of momentariness and clarity make for a kind of ghostly epiphany. Yet though the outlines of the vision are sharply drawn, the center is obscure. Lonely, anonymous, and mysteriously threatening, the central figure remains an enigma throughout the story. We never know who he is (or what he was)—or why he is so fond of Parkins's whistle.

One exception to James's habitual terseness can be found in the descriptions of some of his settings. If the present is lacking, the past is always alive. Whenever James describes the antiquarian lore which provides the settings for all of his stories, his prose instantly becomes crowded with historical or scholarly detail. The opening paragraphs in **"Lost Hearts"** and **"The Ash Tree"** are learned, graceful little essays on styles of architecture in the early and late eighteenth centuries as they relate to the houses in the stories. They provide no "atmosphere," at least not in the Gothic sense which James so despised, and no ominous forebodings (which come later). Indeed the narrator of **"The Ash Tree"** admits that the entire opening section is a "digression." These stories are saturated with nostalgia, yet never in a propagandistic context. In contrast to the stories of Machen and Blackwood, there are no Yeatsian spokesmen for the glories of the past. The emptiness of the present and richness of the past are implied by the distinct absence of the one and overwhelming presence of the other, but James never forces his fetish for the old down the reader's throat.

The paradox in James is that this very oldness is invariably a deadly trap. If antiquarian pursuits provide the only contact with life, they also provide an immediate contact with death. Even in tales where there is no dramatic coffin-opening scene, there is always an implicit analogy between digging up an art object and digging up a corpse. In the antiquarian tale, evil is something old, something which should have died. Old books are especially dangerous as talismanic summoners of this evil. The danger is trickier in James than in similar evil-book tales by James's contemporaries in that neither the nature nor titles of the books necessarily betrays their lethal potential. Chambers's *The King in Yellow,* Yeats's *Alchemical Rose,* and Lovecraft's *Necronomicon* (all imaginary books) are works with spectacularly demonic histories which the collector in a given story opens at his own risk. But James's collectors are liable to get in trouble by opening almost anything. In **"The Uncommon Prayer Book,"** a remarkable rag-like monstrosity is summoned by a psalm (admittedly a "very savage psalm") in an eighteenth-century prayerbook. For James's antiquaries, even the Holy Scriptures can become a demonic text. Undermining the very thing they celebrate, the plots seem to symbolize, perhaps unconsciously, the futility of the entire antiquarian enterprise.

Illustration of "Canon Alberic's Scrapbook," by James McBryde, published in Ghost Stories of an Antiquary.

In a curious way, the style reinforces this contradiction. The most striking aspect of this style, even more striking than its ascetic brevity and clarity, is the gap between tone and story. This gap is especially telling in the more gruesome tales. In **"Wailing Well,"** a small boy is tackled and brought down, much as in a football game, by an entire field of vampires. He is found hanging from a tree with the blood drained from his body, but he later becomes a vampire himself, hiding out with his new friends in a haunted well. (James wrote this cheerful tale for the Eton College troop of Boy Scouts.) More gruesome yet is **"Lost Hearts,"** which tells of an antiquary who, in following an ancient prescription, seeks an "enlightenment of the spiritual faculties" through eating the hearts of young children while they are kept alive. (James is as unsparing of children as Le Fanu.) In the end, the children rise from the grave to wreak a bloody, predictably poetic justice. In both stories, the style is distinguished by a detachment, an urbanity, and a certain amount of Edwardian stuffiness which are entirely at odds with the nastiness of the plots. The narrators seem determined to maintain good manners, even when presenting material they know to be in irredeemably bad taste. Alternating between casualness and stiffness, chattiness and pedantry, James's narrators maintain an almost pathological distance from the horrors they

recount. This contradiction between scholarly reticence and fiendish perversity becomes the authenticating mark of the antiquarian ghost story. For James's narrators, sophisticated literary techniques are a form of exorcism in a world filled with hidden menace. To stare the menace in the face is unthinkable; to convert it into a pleasant ghost story is to momentarily banish it. The reader, however, experiences an inversion of this process: the very unwillingness of the narrators to face up to implied horrors makes the stories all the more chilling and convincing.

James disguises unpleasantness in several ingenious ways. Narrative coolness is one disguise, but he sometimes builds others directly into the plot. There is a whole class of stories in which the dark center is enclosed, and occasionally buried, by several layers of supernatural apparatus. These stories move toward a gradual uncovering of the layers, but the anticipated climax, the final revelation, is less compelling than the means of arriving at it. The disguises do not appear in the form of occult mystification, as in the *Mythologies* of Yeats—James almost never uses elaborate occult material; nor do they appear in the form of complex visionary mechanisms, as in the Georgian fantasies of Dunsany and de la Mare. Like everything in

James, the device is disarmingly straightforward rather than metaphysical. It involves the re-evoking, not of an actual supernatural being, as in **"Count Magnus,"** but of a supernatural melodrama from the past. The twist in these stories is that the art object acts not as a mere catalyst, but as the substance of the experience. Although the scene itself is invariably grotesque and horrifying, the interest lies in the eccentricity of the mode of perception. Moreover, the antiquary is not physically threatened: he is a mortified, though by no means unwilling, spectator.

James first tried this method in **"The Mezzotint"** (1904), a story which became a paradigm not only of several later James stories, but of several efforts by R. H. Malden and E. G. Swain. **"The Mezzotint"** is James's most original creation. In many of his stories, such as **"Canon Alberic's Scrapbook"** and **"Count Magnus,"** old engravings serve as the prelude to an apparition. Meticulously described, they seem almost to come alive, and they are sometimes more frightening than the spectres they prefigure. In **"The Mezzotint,"** James gives us a picture which really does come alive: the picture itself is the apparition. Initially only a mediocre topographical engraving of a house, it undergoes a series of transformations which are all the more startling for their inexplicability. The collector, Mr. Williams, observes a skeletal, shroudlike figure who mysteriously materializes on the lawn in the mezzotint, crawls into the house and emerges later with a baby in its arms. The final view of the picture is James at his best:

> There was the house, as before, under the waning moon and the drifting clouds. The window that had been open was shut, and the figure was once more on the lawn: but not this time crawling cautiously on hands and knees. Now it was erect and stepping swiftly, with long strides, towards the front of the picture. The moon was behind it, and the black drapery hung down over its face so that only hints of that could be seen, and what was visible made the spectators profoundly thankful that they could see no more than a white dome-like forehead and a few straggling hairs. The head was bent down, and the arms were tightly clasped over an object which could be dimly seen and identified as a child, whether dead or living it was not possible to say. The legs of the appearance alone could be plainly discerned, and they were horribly thin.

The passage is an ideal example of James's art. What we see, we see clearly, as in an etching: what we don't see, we are "profoundly thankful" for not seeing.

There are two layers of supernatural storytelling here: the transformation of the picture and the scene it recreates, itself a supernatural tale. The former is far more mysterious than the latter. The ghost at least has a reason for coming back to life: Williams discovers that the house belonged to an extinct family, the last heir of which "disappeared mysteriously in infancy" shortly after the father had a man hanged for poaching. But the picture has no such reason. Only James could have written a tale at once so sophisticated and so lacking in metaphysical, symbolic, or even causal connections. His weird pictures are utterly unlike those of his predecessors: the picture of Chief Justice Harbottle in Le Fanu's "An Account of Some Strange Disturbances in Aungier Street" is chilling because it reminds us of the evil Harbottle; that of Hawthorne's Edward Randolph in "Edward Randolph's Portrait" because of its symbolic associations. But James's mezzotint is intrinsically spooky. There is no reason for it to change—it simply does. And to make matters stranger, it never changes again.

We take it for granted in James that art objects are inherently demonic—or at least have the potential for being so. Here we must assume that more mechanical phenomena can be haunted as well. As lean and as calculated as James seems as a writer, he nevertheless possesses the romantic impulse, investing even chemical processes with spiritual powers. Gadgetry and machinery can be as talismanic as art.

Yet James is a closet romantic at best. If we decide that the ghostly power of mezzotints is the theme of the story, we are left with curiously little to say, for James is not interested in expounding romantic or occult theories. The wry, typically understated conclusion discourages the reader from using the story as a brief for any demonic precept:

> The facts were communicated by Williams to Dennistoun, and by him to a mixed company, of which I was one, and the Sadducean Professor of Ophiology another. I am sorry to say that the latter, when asked what he thought of it, only remarked: "Oh, those Bridgeford people will say anything"—a sentiment which met with the reception it deserved.

> I have only to add that the picture is now in the Ashleian Museum; that it has been treated with a view to discovering whether sympathetic ink has been used in it, but without effect; that Mr. Britnell knew nothing of it save that he was sure it was uncommon; and that, though carefully watched, it has never been known to change again.

The brisk parallelism of the syntax in the final paragraph moves us out of the story before we have a chance to speculate on metaphysical ramifications. James's fiction is self-enclosed in that it rarely refers to any system of ideas or values outside the confines of the plot. Mystery writer Gerald Heard's statement that "the good ghost story must have for its base some clear premise as to the character of human existence—some theological assumption," can refer only to a class of stories (Kipling's are a good example) to which James's are opposed. If there is any theological "premise" in James, it is never developed—and is certainly not "clear." James himself, in the preface to *Ghost Stories of an Antiquary,* is careful to deflate any "exalted" notions of ghost story writing: "The stories themselves do not make any very exalted claim. If any of them succeed in causing their readers to feel pleasantly uncomfortable when walking along a solitary road at nightfall, or sitting over a dying fire in the small hours, my purpose in writing them will have been attained." What is attractive about James's stories is precisely that they succeed in maintaining this weird balance between the pleasant and the uncomfortable.

Other "Mezzotint" stories include **"The Rose Garden,"** **"A View From a Hill,"** and (the most fanciful variation) **"The Haunted Doll's House,"** all of which involve visions within visions which tie themselves into mysterious knots while seeming to unravel. These are the most radically distanced of James's works. In **"The Mezzotint,"** the narrative is a third-hand account of a story which itself concerns something never directly experienced. And the character with whom the story is ultimately concerned—the occupant of the house in the mezzotint—is entirely invisible.

Another device James uses to disguise or distance his horrors is humor. Humor and horror, as we have seen in Le Fanu's case, are often two sides of the same coin. Eliot's famous reference to "the alliance of levity and seriousness (by which the seriousness is intensified)" is useful, for James's humor does not defuse horror so much as intensify it by making it manageable and accessible. Without James's deadpan wit, these stories might seem unreal and "Gothic" to a sophisticated reader.

James's use of humor is more conscious, sophisticated, and programmatic than Le Fanu's, whose humor seems more spontaneous (and occasionally unintentional). Often, James will concoct a situation which is inherently funny. An example is Mr. Somerton's encounter with a toad-like creature in **"The Treasure of Abbot Thomas"**:

> Well, I felt to the right, and my fingers touched something curved, that felt—yes—more or less like a heavy, full thing. There was nothing, I must say, to alarm one. I grew bolder, and putting both hands in as well as I could, I pulled it to me, and it came. It was heavy, but moved more easily than I had expected. As I pulled it towards the entrance, my left elbow knocked over and extinguished the candle. I got the thing fairly in front of the mouth and began drawing it out. Just then Brown gave a sharp ejaculation and ran quickly up the steps with the lantern. He will tell you why in a moment. Startled as I was, I looked round after him, and saw him stand for a minute at the top and then walk away a few yards. Then I heard him call softly, 'All right, sir,' and went on pulling out the great bag, in complete darkness. It hung for an instant on the edge of the hold, then slipped forward on my chest, and *put its arms round my neck*.

The jolt we experience on reaching the italics springs as much from the absurdity of the situation as from the horror: it scarcely matters whether we shudder or laugh. Ideally, we should do both.

James frequently entrusts major scenes to colloquial, clownish narrators—usually cockney servants. The servant's account of Mr. Potwitch's death in **"The Uncommon Prayerbook"** is both ghoulish and comic:

> And then, sir, I see what looked to be like a great roll of old shabby white flannel, about four to five feet high, fall for-ards out of the inside of the safe right against Mr. Potwitch's shoulder as he was stopping over; and Mr. Potwitch, he raised himself up as it were, resting on his hands on the package, and gave a exclamation. And I can't hardly expect you should take what I says, but

> as true as I stand here I see this roll had a kind of a face in the upper end of it, sir. You can't be more surprised than what I was, I can assure you, and I've seen a lot in me time. Yes, I can describe it if you wish it, sir; it was very much the same as this wall here in colour (the wall had an earth-coloured distemper) and it had a bit of a band tied round underneath. And the eyes, well they was dry-like, and much as if there was two big spiders' bodies in the holes. Hair? no, I don't know as there was much hair to be seen; the flannel-stuff was over the top of the 'ead. I'm sure it warn't what it should have been. No, I only see it in a flash, but I took it in like a photograft—wish I hadn't. Yes, sir, it fell right over on to Mr. Potwitch's shoulder, and this face hid in his neck—yes, sir, about where the injury was, —more like a ferret going for a rabbit than anything else.

Though James's rendering of dialect is skillful and idiomatic, he tends to overuse these servant recapitulations of horror scenes. After a while, the cockney narrators—in **"A View from a Hill,"** and **"An Episode of Cathedral History,"** among others—become an annoying mannerism.

In some stories, James's use of humor has little to do with the basic premise, but seems an end in itself. This deliciously sardonic digression in **"Wailing Well"** could almost have been written by Evelyn Waugh or Roald Dahl:

> The practice, as you know, was to throw a selected lower boy, of suitable dimensions, fully dressed, with his hands and feet tied together, into the deepest part of Cuckoo Weir, and to time the Scout whose turn it was to rescue him. On every occasion when he was entered for this competition, Stanley Judkins was seized, at the critical moment, with a severe fit of cramp, which caused him to roll on the ground and utter alarming cries. This naturally distracted the attention of those present from the boy in the water, and had it not been for the presence of Arthur Wilcox the death-toll would have been a heavy one. As it was, the Lower Master found it necessary to take a firm line and say that the competition must be discontinued. It was in vain that Mr. Beasley Robinson represented to him that in five competitions only four lower boys had actually succumbed. The Lower Master said that he would be the last to interfere in any way with the work of the Scouts; but that three of these boys had been valued members of his choir, and both he and Dr. Ley felt that the inconvenience caused by the losses outweighed the advantages of the competitions. Besides, the correspondence with the parents of these boys had become annoying, and even distressing: they were no longer satisfied with the printed form which he was in the habit of sending out, and more than one of them had actually visited Eton and taken up much of his valuable time with complaints. So the life-saving competition is now a thing of the past.

Although the passage is irrelevant to the plot, it is highly relevant to the relationship of the narrator to his materials. The understated savagery of the humor establishes a context which trivializes the value of life and death, removing the narrator from the suffering and cruelty he is about to recount by allowing him to treat it all as a grim joke.

A more underhanded means that James uses to create distance is deliberate obscurity. Occasionally he moves so far in the direction of mystification that he runs the risk of leaving us completely behind. This device, James's ultimate disguise, occurs with increasing frequency in the later stories. **"The Story of a Disappearance and an Appearance," "Two Doctors," "Mr. Humphreys and His Inheritance"** and **"Rats"** read more like dark enigmas than finished works of fiction. The narrators often seem aware of the problematic nature of this material, even to the point of sometimes warning the reader in the opening paragraph. The narrator of **"Two Doctors,"** for example, describes his tale as an incomplete dossier, "a riddle in which the supernatural appears to play a part. You must see what you can make of it." James ungraciously provides only the outline of a gruesome tale in which one doctor uses an unexplained supernatural device to do in another. The tale is densely packed with fascinating hints: a rifled mausoleum; a reference to Milton ("Millions of spiritual creatures walk the earth/Unseen both when we wake and when we sleep."); a haunted pillow which enfolds the head of the sleeping victim like a strange cloud; a recurring dream of a gigantic moth chrysalis disclosing "a head covered with a smooth pink skin, which breaking as the creature stirred, showed him his own face in a state of death." Since there are so many ways to piece together the information, the tale becomes more ominous with each reading. The initial reading is curiously empty and frustrating, almost as if James demands that we try again.

Furthermore, he takes it for granted that we know his earlier stories which, for all their nonrational connections, are easier to fathom. The structure of **"Two Doctors"**—a sketchy presentation of lawyers' documents—is so fragmented that whatever piecing together we do must be based, at least in part, on patterns from *Ghost Stories of an Antiquary*. "Death By the Visitation of God," the surgeon's verdict, makes little sense unless we see it as a reference to the same verdict in the earlier **"Count Magnus,"** a story which has its own stubborn mysteries, but which is clearly a tale of demonic pursuit. Once this connection is made, **"Two Doctors"** becomes thematically related to a whole class of Le Fanuesque pursuit tales by James: **"Count Magnus," "Lost Hearts," "A School Story," "The Tractate Middoth," "Casting the Runes," "The Stalls of Barchester Cathedral,"** and **"The Uncommon Prayer Book."** But seen in isolation, the ending of **"Two Doctors"** makes almost no sense.

These sly cross references are another indication of the self-referential character of James's fictional world. His narrative posture, at least in the late tales, assumes an audience of connoisseurs, an elect readership which can extrapolate a plot from a sentence. The demands James makes on his readers are somewhat at odds with his determination to present himself as an aggressively "popular" writer whose sole function is to entertain and amuse in as undemanding a way as possible. This is minor fiction to be sure, but fiction which nevertheless succeeds in creating

a universe of its own which can be apprehended only through careful, thoughtful reading. Like so much quality ghostly fiction from this period, James's stories fall into the uniquely alienated category of being too controlled and sophisticated for "horror" fans, yet too lightweight for academics. In his relation to twentieth-century culture, James is very much a ghost himself, or very much like his own Mr. Humphreys in **"Mr. Humphreys and His Inheritance,"** a man lost in a haunted maze.

If James is not a major writer, he nevertheless deserves a larger audience than he currently enjoys. His fictional palate is admittedly restricted, even in comparison with other writers of ghostly tales. His stories have considerable power, but only muffled reverberation. He exhibits little of Henry James's psychological probity, none of Poe's Gothic extravagance, none of Yeats's passion—but he delivers a higher percentage of mystery and terror than any of these. If he is merely a sophisticated "popular" writer, content with manipulating surfaces, those very surfaces are potent and suggestive.

James is far more innovative than he pretends to be. In R. H. Malden's preface to *Nine Ghosts,* he reminds us that James "always regarded" Le Fanu as "The Master." Yet Malden also speaks of a distinct James "tradition," implying that James refined, modified, and transgressed Le Fanu's precepts in ways profound enough to set James apart as an original. He brought to the ghost story not only a new antiquarian paradigm of setting and incident, but also a new urbanity, suaveness, and economy. To a contemporary audience, conditioned by the monotonous brutality of so many occult novels and films, James's use of subtlety to evoke ghostly horror is likely to seem as radical and puzzling as ever. Both academics and popular readers tend to associate supernatural horror in fiction with hyperbole, capitals, promiscuous exclamation marks, and bloated adjectives. Yet the field is crowded with undeservedly obscure writers—L. T. C. Rolt, E. G. Swain, R. H. Malden, Ramsey Campbell, H. R. Wakefield, Russell Kirk, Arthur Gray, Elizabeth Bowen, and Robert Aickman, among many others—who follow James's example.

James also gave the ghost story a new theme. His ghosts materialize not so much from inner darkness or outer conspiracies as from a kind of antiquarian malaise. Remaining modestly within the confines of popular entertainment, his fiction nevertheless shows how nostalgia has a habit of turning into horror. This is a distinct departure from Poe, where antiquarian pursuits are tied to sensationally deranged psyches such as Roderick Usher's. In James, the antiquaries are stolidly normal, and their ghosts are real. Above all, James's collectors clearly enjoy what they are doing: those who survive these stories would not dream of giving up their arcane pursuits simply because they were almost swallowed up by unearthly presences.

But the real enjoyment is ours. As readers, we can immerse ourselves in the process of discovery without taking any risks. We can even indulge in expecting the worst. Alfred Hitchcock has often said that terror and suspense grow not out of shock and surprise, but out of thickening inevitability. James, who had already learned this lesson from Le Fanu, is careful to keep us one step ahead of the character so that the dreams and premonitions are as eerie as the apparitions they announce. This is the delightful paradox of James's ghost stories: the more of his stories we read and reread, the more we know what to expect, but that very reservoir of expectations infuses each reading with added menace. The sheer pleasure of these gentlemanly horror tales continually rejuvenates itself.

Michael A. Mason   (essay date 1982)

SOURCE: "On Not Letting Them Lie: Moral Significance in the Ghost Stories of M. R. James," in *Studies in Short Fiction*, Vol. 19, No. 3, Summer 1982, pp. 253-260.

[*In the following essay, Mason discusses James's depiction of realistic settings, supernatural forces, and intelligent characters motivated by universal moral dilemmas.*]

In her study of stories about the uncanny, a study entitled *Night Visitors: The Rise and Fall of the English Ghost Story*, Julia Briggs has reminded us that the ghost stories of M. R. James have never fallen out of public favor. They have remained in print ever since he first published them. The apparent moral purpose of his doing so may be worth investigating, although the moral force of these stories is unlikely to be the main reason for their popularity.

By 1894, when James began to publish the ghost stories which were to bring him a far wider fame than all his scholarly researches, educated readers could feel perfectly safe in dismissing his apparitions as entirely without objective existence. Anyone could experience ghosts if he deliberately cultivated the state that Tennyson had got himself into by re-reading Hallam's letters to him; just as, two or three generations into the twentieth century, anyone who stares at the sky for long enough can discover flying objects, whether or not he can identify them. From time to time, the sanity of people who described their own strange experiences might be in question; but otherwise freak weather conditions or indigestion could provide a sufficient explanation for an age as far above the vulgar errors of its ancestors as electric power could raise it. However, since this new unbelief did not seem to make the world more tolerable, perhaps tales of the uncanny might, in a limited way, minister to psychological necessities inherited by modern man from his ignorant forefathers. Besides, there is a peculiar pleasure in being terrified vicariously.

Montague Rhodes James wrote his ghost stories over a period of some forty years. "I never cared," he tells us in an epilogue to his **Collected Ghost Stories,** "to try any other kind." Researchers into mediaeval and other documents helped to inspire in his imagination a host of demons that might irrupt into the human dimension. His difficulty, of course, is to persuade us that they could; to give them a reason, or at least an excuse, for doing so; and to make them behave interestingly when they arrive. The first of these he achieves by the use of time, tradition, and a sense of reality.

James believes in setting a discreet barrier of time between the event and the reader. "The detective story," he says with authority, for he had read a great many of these,

cannot be too much up-to-date. . . . For the ghost story a slight haze of distance is desirable. 'Thirty years ago,' 'Not long before the war,' are very proper openings. If a really remote date be chosen, there is more than one way of bringing the reader in contact with it. The finding of documents about it can be made plausible; or you may begin with your apparition and go back over the years to tell the cause of it; or . . . you may set the scene directly in the desired epoch, which I think is hardest to do with success. On the whole . . . I think that a setting so modern that the ordinary reader can judge of its naturalness for himself is preferable to anything antique. For some degree of actuality is the charm of the best ghost stories; not a very insistent actuality, but one strong enough to allow the reader to identify himself with the patient; while it is almost inevitable that the reader of an antique story should fall into the position of the mere spectator.

By "actuality" James means sense of present time fully as much as realism. Some of his own settings are quite remote, but he counters an effect of too much distance by precision in dating. Two periods far apart, neither of them contemporary, may be exactly given, and both events clearly described: in **"The Residence at Whitminster"** these are 1730 and 1823-4. That the present time is the viewpoint is scarcely hinted. If there is a midway period, the latest time being the present, the remotest period may be shadowy and the origin of ghosts. **"An Episode of Cathedral History"** is one of the best examples of this telescopic technique. It has a very obscure foundation in the fifteenth century, when considerable trouble since lost to history must have been experienced. When, however, the satyr escaped from its tomb in the summer of 1840, a number of people were able to guess at the nature of what had happened before. That summer of 1840 is the story's narrative area, told to "a learned gentleman" by the elderly Head Verger, who remembers in 1890 that particular adventure of his boyhood. More than twenty years later, the learned gentleman hands the story to our narrator; and now, beyond his time, the modern reader adds yet another perspective to what already had so much of the mysterious haze of distance.

A true impression of historical distance can be achieved only by a writer with a real sense of historical time, including an idea of the kind of English spoken for instance in the criminal courts in which Judge Jeffreys distorted justice in the 1680s. James's reading of the *State Trials* helped him here. So did the immense scholarship of his work as an antiquary and manuscript editor, for this kind of learning gave him an authentic fictional context for the discovery by some of his characters of those manuscripts and inscriptions which left them wiser and far more wary—if they survived—than they had been before. His use of Latin, usually translated at some point, is a particular feature of James's stories. If the teacher of Latin wants to ensure that his students remember the genitive case after *memini,* or the construction of a conditional sentence with a future consequence, he cannot do better than read them **"A School Story."** *Si tu non veneris ad me, ego veniam ad te* comes through with sinister force. A ghost of a feeling persists that Latin, the legal, political, religious, and linguistic root of so much of western history, is the proper tongue in which to conjure and dismiss apparitions, and there is about it a certain solidity and conciseness that gives authority to the stories about them.

The sense of reality resides in James's power to create the ordinary, normal rhythm of life. His adventurers are intelligent people and, for most purposes, sensible. They are not complex characters, and are therefore, in their outlined form, all the easier for the reader or listener to identify with. A number resemble James himself in being university dons with enough freedom—in terms of seventy or eighty years ago—to go on short-range expeditions out of England as far as to Southern France or Scandinavia. Within their reach are the resources of local wisdom or of level-headed friends whose advice they would have done better to follow. It is safer, at times, to be humble and ignorant. Indeed, this is the happy state of all those people who pass on oral tradition about bygone people and places and comment occasionally on what is happening in the cathedral, the distant woods, or the quiet country mansion. Through the normality of these people—innkeepers and housekeepers, gardeners and butlers, cathedral vergers, retired colonels, and so forth—the reader keeps in touch with the everyday world at the same time as he follows his intrepid hero into a confrontation with the uncanny. The general public of the countryside accordingly act as guarantors of the reality of the supernatural, in which they can believe without any difficulty.

When we come to consider the reasons for the intrusion of the supernatural into ordinary life, we find that they can be summed up in one word: disturbance. Some kind of sensitive environment has been violated by an act of thoughtlessness, often in defiance of good advice as well as good sense; and it is then that the question of provocation arises. Provocation on the part of the disturber makes him vulnerable to some act of malice roughly classifiable as revenge.

At this point we should note that, in certain professions, encounters with the supernatural are occupational hazards. The clergy are particularly vulnerable; professors and scholars may also find themselves in strange company, as may travellers, amateur archaeologists, experimenters of many kinds, and even medical men. The reasons for vulnerability often amount to the single trouble of ambition. "That last infirmity of noble mind" it may well be, but its range—in James's stories, at least—encompasses a very wide spectrum from the simplest unnecessary curiosity to overweening vanity and uncompromising arrogance. This kind of motivation will lead a man to investigate a locked room at the inn where he is staying; or to hasten into the next world some elderly relative or superior who seems to be reluctant to remove himself from the surface of this one; or to improve his own status by deliberately seeking what certain powers of the unseen world can do for him, in return—presumably—for access through him to the physical universe. Through this channel there then passes an illicit two-way traffic, which has, however, its penalties.

We therefore often find ourselves observing a living person who has awakened trouble for himself by his temerity or even by his criminal actions. In the latter event, the kind of retribution he suffers may be no more than his just, if unmerciful, punishment. More often, what occurs is a kind of wild justice visiting any offence with death, or at least with the fear of it. The predicament of the victim is naturally the one with which the reader identifies; it is, in mundane terms, an insoluble one. It cannot be avoided. It must, like a typhoon at sea, be encountered head on and, if possible, survived. As for identification with the avenger itself, this is—by its very nature—impossible.

Although the reader feels more at ease, if this expression may be allowable in such a context, with the spirits of dead people rather than with spiritual entities of which he can have no understanding, the dead have often been those who have isolated themselves so effectually in life as to have alienated the sympathy of other people even then. James bestows upon the dead the fate of haunting their old homes for some evil action committed in life. It seems as if his earthbound spirits have chosen to keep for themselves a treasure or power of some kind in their earthly existence, and have thus bound themselves, or some part of themselves, whether voluntarily or not, to the safeguarding of it. No fruitful contact with them seems to be possible. In fact, it is essential, for James's narrative purposes, that no contact of either a prolonged or an intelligent kind ever be established. The ghost is to have all the disconcerting advantages of appearance and disappearance—rather like the ghost of Banquo—but without the chance of presenting its case for reprieve, if it has one. Prolonged contact would weaken the unfamiliarity and therefore the mystery of the supernatural, and—if intelligent as well—could easily bring the story down to the colloquial level of Scrooge and Marley in *A Christmas Carol*: with Marley—it will be recalled—presenting his former business partner with a whole battery of unpaid professional consultants for Scrooge's eternal benefit. James's tales are as cautionary as Marley's advice to Scrooge, but his ghosts are all inimical. His advice can therefore take only one course: leave them alone by not tempting them out. They are powerful forces rather than individual personalities, and probably cannot do anything but whatever they are programmed, robot-like, to do. One might as well try to argue with Grendel.

Unfortunately, by the time this has become evident to the victim of such an entity's attentions, and to his friends, it may be too late for any action but a final conflict. If the enemy itself is of such a nature as to have forfeited forgiveness for sins committed, it cannot be expected to forgive any offence against itself. It is also solid enough to inflict considerable damage; James seems to prefer the tangible Scandinavian entities to be met with in saga and folklore. In his preface to the collected edition he claims to "have tried to make my ghosts act in ways not inconsistent with the rules of folklore." He edited the Latin texts of "Twelve Medieval Ghost-Stories" for the *English Historical Review* in July, 1922, and found these to be "redolent of Denmark." They were local to Yorkshire and included ghosts with those powers of attacking and grappling with humans that he introduces into his own stories.

The motivation of his own spirits is, however, James's personal invention. We have noted the vanity or self-seeking of some potential victims, as well as the greed or avarice which has condemned people of former times to undergo whatever eternal trouble they are now in. Still alive or long dead, such human principals in the stories have been tainted by pride and must endure the penalty for selfish independence. No satisfying exorcism, as in Kingsley Amis's *The Green Man,* no outright defeat of supernatural evil by straightforward human means, will occur in James's stories; for it does not seem to be his purpose to offer remedies, but rather to point out the risks.

However, in James's mysterious world there are many variations. It may be possible to divert the intending attacker of Mr. Goodman on to another target. If so, what target more suitable than the Mr. Badman who has been directing his supernatural agent against Mr. Goodman? One of James's better-known tales is called **"Casting the Runes."** Mr. Badman is an authority on the occult and resents an unfavourable review that someone has written about a book of his. Authorities may, of course, be of different kinds, just as a winegrower and an alcoholic may both claim with some authority to be experts about the same product. Mr. Karswell, the Mr. Badman in this affair, has taken some kind of apprenticeship in order to become an authority. It is not scholarly authority in the usual sense that he has, but practical experience of the occult. Regrettably, Mr. Karswell also desires to be recognised as a scholar, which he is not; and he takes such great personal offence against a certain adverse critic of his scholarship as to ensure that one of his own unusual friends shall make away with the critic. To repeat this success, which he ultimately designs to do with another offender, he chooses, reasonably enough, to employ the same technique: one of its vital preliminaries being the delivery to the victim of a slip of writing which he must freely accept, though he will not be able to comprehend the writing. The slip is duly given to the second victim; but, before Mr. Badman's familiar can operate, the brother of the first victim is contacted for advice and assistance. Second victim and brother of first victim then co-operate in returning the slip of writing to Mr. Badman; and he, having freely accepted it as part of a larger package, becomes in turn the victim and is deservedly eliminated.

I have referred to the non-human entities as powerful forces rather than personalities. James's emphasis on their impact deprives their behavior of subtlety, and requires that they call attention to themselves by sheer unpleasantness. In James's first published story, **"Canon Alberic's Scrapbook,"** written in 1894, the intrusive demon is described as having "intelligence beyond that of a beast, below that of a man." This artistic precision is less admirable than a little more artistic restraint would have been, and James would not again venture a comment of this kind on a supernatural character's IQ. A concentration of evil might indeed have some such disastrous effect on a former human being, whose behavior might in consequence become interestingly bizarre. In **"Number 13,"** written in 1899, a human being has apparently become a demon. At any rate, Mr. Anderson, a Church historian visiting Denmark to examine archives of the sixteenth century, finds that the inn at which he has Room Number 12 also has a Room Number 13, but only at night. This interesting discovery coincides with his reading of archival correspondence about the alleged activities of a certain Magister Nicolas Francken in the time of the last Bishop to hold the see under the Church of Rome. What Magister Nicolas Francken had done had not been set down in any surviving detail, but could be summed up in the expression "secret and wicked arts" which appeared in the accusations against him. The matter was apparently never brought to trial, as the Bishop referred to the defendant's having been "suddenly removed from among us," and this ended the documentation.

Mr. Anderson abruptly found himself able to continue it, after a fashion, when the occupant of the neighbouring room began that same night to dance and sing. The dancing, though surprisingly vigorous—as revealed by the antics of his shadow against the blank street-wall opposite his room—was silent. His singing was not, besides being of such a disturbing quality as to bring to his door a reluctant deputation armed with crowbars and a desperate determination to discover what manner of thing this was. It is at this moment of truth that the test of the writer also comes. James cannot allow a meeting, so he compromises. While the weapons are being fetched, the occupants of Rooms 12 and 14 are on guard outside the door of Room 13. While the nearer man has his head turned from it in order to address his companion, "the door opened, and an arm came out and clawed at his shoulder." If James takes the event that far, he must go a little further. "It was clad in ragged, yellowish linen, and the bare skin, where it could be seen, had long grey hair upon it." This is as far as James will go. Anderson pulls Jensen out of the way, the door shuts again, "and a low laugh was heard." This incident is enough to alarm the witnesses; to demoralise the reinforcements who hear of it when they arrive soon afterwards; to impel Mr. Anderson to encourage and organise them for the attack; and, in fact, to allow a sufficiently plausible time to elapse between the incident and the eventual attack on the door: so that, as the attack is delivered, the moment of dawn arrives and Number 13 disappears. Before the next sunset, the discovery of relics under the floorboards removes the chance of its reappearance.

The living characters in the story of **"Number 13"** are merely witnesses of what had apparently been happening for some time: the Faustian figure of Nicolas Francken had been translated into something extremely unpleasant, and certainly much less human than he had been in life. It is, however, when we come to consider the behavior of a demon without human origin, that we appreciate all the more the wisdom of letting them lie. **"An Episode of Cathedral History"** describes the architectural ambitions of a reforming Dean of the Cathedral of Southminster in the summer of 1840. James takes the opportunity to show that some architectural reforms can amount to desecration. However, the demolition revealed "many interesting features of older work," as James's narrator expresses it. The most interesting feature of all was an altar-tomb of the fifteenth century, quite plain, but with a defect in the form of a slight gap between two slabs on the north side.

The cathedral renovations most unfortunately coincide with a wave of ill health among the local residents. Unpleasant dreams disturb them and sickness actually carries some of them off. The boy who, as an elderly man, tells the story to James's narrator remembers especially the nocturnal phenomenon known as "the crying"—as this was the time when he and his dog would, by mutual agreement, share his bed until it had stopped for that night, as the dog would know. The reader's identification with a boy and his dog is, of course, strong—and almost as strong with the boy and his friend who, being members of the choir, had easy access to the cathedral and to the attempts being made to plug up the hole in the altar-tomb. After listening to an argument between foreman and plasterer about a failure to do this, the boys are alone by the tomb. One of them has looked into the gap, and seen something. "I says to Evans, 'Did you really see anything in there?' 'Yes,' he says, 'I did indeed.' So then I says, 'Let's shove something in and stir it up.'" So they roll up a music sheet and shove it in, and then, when nothing happens, Worby—our informant—whistles. Inside, something moves; the roll of music, shoved in again, is held fast and has to be torn free; and the boys, having certainly stirred up something, take fright and run. A night or two later the crying is worse than ever before, and the day after that the cathedral authorities, duly armed with crowbars, assemble in force and watch while a bar is used upon the gap in the north side of the altar-tomb. The demon emerges, though only Worby's father seems to have been favored with a view of it, and it escapes by the north door, never to be seen again. At the end of such a sickly season as that had proved to be to the residents of Southminster, it is unfortunate to have to report that the reforming Dean was none the wiser for the trouble he had initiated, and none the worse either, except for having been bowled over by the emerging demon—and even that he had managed to identify as the Canon in residence.

For ghosts as gothic as these are, as normal a setting as possible is very suitable. Everyday normality does not negate the likelihood of other dimensions. The folk wisdom of those people in James's stories who are consulted on local history seems to confirm this. In **"The Rose Garden"** an old man is remembered who had advised a lady's father many years before against the removal of certain garden furniture, or perhaps particularly a single post: "he's fast enough in there without no one don't take and let him out." But oral tradition is not always passed on to newcomers, and the point of this advice is not understood until the removal of the post makes it clear. We may, if we wish, discover in James's stories of such phenomena forces that exist within the human heart rather than in the universe outside us, and we can believe in them easily enough when we survey the realities of terror and horror that human beings daily inflict upon one another. Of the consequences of such actions upon the evildoers themselves as well as upon their victims we also see something. If—to keep to literary examples—Banquo's trust in Macbeth as his host leads to Banquo's murder, that murder itself has its retribution in the despair and eventual killing of Macbeth, lured to his fate by the evil forces on the health.

But the evil forces themselves as objective existences are

harder for us to accept. In James's stories they may to some extent even be useful, performing upon human evildoers the work of sharks or scavengers. Persuading us to believe that there are superhuman powers of evil may be James's oblique way of convincing us also of the strength of their opposites, though these seem to rely on human agents alone to battle against the enemy. If the healing touch is less evident in these stories than is the touch that withers, let us recall that James, for many years Provost of Eton School, must have found that the cautionary tale worked very well upon creatures of wild nature such as boys. If a class in school were told the story of **"There Was a Man Dwelt by a Churchyard,"** and the chief masculine genius in obstreperousness were fixed on in good time as the target, it might be possible to position oneself in readiness for the climax, and then to drop on him with the most gratifying effect. This, however, may be found merely to illustrate how easy the temptation can be to imitate the punitive forces in James's stories rather than those of toleration and understanding.

Michael Cox   (essay date 1987)

SOURCE: An introduction to *Casting the Runes, and Other Ghost Stories* by M. R. James, Oxford University Press, Oxford, 1987, pp. xi-xxx.

[*In the following excerpt, Cox surveys the major themes and techniques of James's short fiction, asserting that the most important element of the tales is their "implausible plausibility."*]

'Do I believe in ghosts? I am prepared to consider evidence and accept it if it satisfies me.'

There [in the preface to his *Collected Ghost Stories* (1931)], with typical reticence, spoke Dr. M. R. James, O.M., Provost of Eton, and world authority on the manuscripts of Western Christendom, whose reputation as a scholar had been achieved by an enormous capacity for industry and a rare skill in making sense of disparate fragments of information. Though the careful consideration of evidence was thus second nature to him he was never prepared to discuss publicly what exactly constituted evidence for the supernatural, or on what side of the argument for the existence of ghosts he felt the balance of probability tipped. Natural caution, together with a desire not to compromise his public position, encouraged an evasion of the obvious questions about his stories.

But there was a private side to the scholar who was only prepared to consider the evidence for ghosts impartially. The voice of this man—of the much loved Monty James, who enjoyed pantomimes and writing Dodgsonian letters to young female friends (and receiving replies addressed to 'Dear Dr Apple Pie'), who devoured detective fiction, relished P. G. Wodehouse, and mimicked friends and colleagues uncannily to the life—can be caught at many points in the ghost stories. This side of him almost certainly felt the truth of Hamlet's celebrated admonition to Horatio (alluded to at the end of **'The Diary of Mr Poynter'**): 'There are more things in heaven and earth . . . / Than are dreamt of in your philosophy.' In the context of his Christian faith he was unshakable in his belief that human relationships are not irrevocably sundered by death. Writing to his friend James McBryde, whose father had recently died, he spoke of his 'strong belief that instead of being cut off and separated from you by an immeasurable distance, he has as living an interest in you and your doings as ever'. Though he had no interest at all in either psychical research or Spiritualism (how glad he was that J. S. Le Fanu, his favourite writer of ghost stories, had been a 'decided foe' to 'spirit rapping') he had firm views on the question of the survival of bodily death, which he discussed with his sceptical friend Arthur Benson in 1905: '[James] showed a petulant and childish mind,' Benson tartly recorded in his compulsively kept diary, 'confusing a scientific certainty with an inherited prejudice. He showed himself to be of the school . . . who when they say that they *believe* that a thing will happen only mean that they will be much annoyed if it does not.'

But were there other ways in which the living and the dead could interact, apart from the 'living interest' James had spoken of to McBryde? At Eton in 1881 he had publicly maintained that something like 10 per cent of ghost stories had a basis of truth in them, but were dismissed simply because people did not like the idea of such things happening. As for himself, in private he was far more inclined to believe in supernatural possibilities than his few public pronouncements suggested. Commenting to his parents in 1891, when he was a young Fellow of King's, on a tale attaching to a wood near Livermere, he admitted that 'These things always give me *an impression of truth*. I should be very unwilling to spend a night there, and heaven send I may not have to walk that way at six o'clock in November.' (My emphasis.) M. R. James, it seems, could never quite *dis*believe in the supernatural. Late in life he wrote to McBryde's widow Gwendolen—half playfully, but also surely half seriously: 'Just now as I re-entered my room what should I see but a toad hopping across the floor . . . It has retired behind the curtain near the door. Will it clasp my leg as I go out? and what does it portend?' This same receptive core is uncovered in a story recounted by Nathaniel Wedd, who for some years had rooms below James in King's. Every night Wedd would knock out his pipe on the mantelpiece before going to bed: 'Monty told me how often and often when in bed he heard the tap, tap, tap he used to lie shivering with horror. He couldn't believe it wasn't a ghost in his outer room, though he knew all the time exactly how the sounds were produced.' We may distrust that 'shivering with horror' and yet agree with Wedd that James possessed the 'Celtic sense of the unseen', exemplified in 1917 when, at two o'clock in the morning, James heard taps at his window, 'which may well have been the magnolia outside—and then for several seconds an appearance of a curtain being pulled aside from the window again and again. I lighted up at once and watched, but there was no one: I could make nothing of it.' Even the great considerer of evidence could occasionally drop his guard slightly, as when he recorded reading 'with horrified interest De Lancre's *Tableau de l'Inconstance des Mauvais Anges,* 1612—chiefly confessions of witches, very carefully recorded, and I quite think with a good deal of fact at the back of them'.

James's object in writing ghost stories was to give 'plea-

sure of a certain sort'—what the American writer Edith Wharton called 'the fun of the shudder'. He had always enjoyed frightening others—and himself. As a boy at Eton he reported being 'engaged for a "dark seance", i. e. a telling of ghost stories, in which capacity I am rather popular just now.' The social context of his stories was to remain an essential catalyst. Their scholarly trappings—the footnotes, Latin phrases, and bibliographical references—are more than technical devices, innovative though they were for the English ghost story, to suspend the reader's disbelief: they also present a faintly ironical, at times almost self-mocking, image of himself as a scholar and antiquary that was more apparent to his first audience of *listeners* than to later readers. (The dedication of **Ghost Stories of an Antiquary** was, appropriately, 'To all those who at various times have listened to them.') More than this, the stories reflect the enclosed and privileged world in which James—and many of his friends—lived, a world bounded in his case by Cambridge and Eton, country houses and cathedral closes, museums and libraries, and by the holiday points of call—East Anglian inns, comfortable continental hotels, country railway stations—that this bachelor don regularly encountered during the palmy quarter century before the First World War.

The first of his ghost stories to be published, **'Canon Alberic's Scrap-book',** was written some time after April 1892, when James visited S. Bertrand de Comminges (where the story is set), and before October 1893, when it was read at the 601st meeting of the Chitchat Society, a select and convivial weekly gathering at Cambridge which James had joined as an undergraduate in 1883 and to which he gave several papers. Early in 1894 James sent the story, then called 'A Curious Book', to his friend Leo Maxse, owner and editor of the *National Review,* who eventually published it in March 1895. **'Lost Hearts',** first published in the *Pall Mall Magazine* in December that year, was written at about the same time as **'Canon Alberic',** with which it was read to the Chitchat in October 1893.

The Chitchat readings coincided with the arrival in King's of James McBryde, who came up from Shrewsbury in the autumn of 1893. Despite his non-Etonian background McBryde soon found a place in Monty James's rather exclusive inner circle and for eleven years, until his early death in 1904, provided Monty with what was perhaps the most significant friendship of his life. McBryde accompanied him on several continental holidays, including the Scandinavian trips that inspired **'Number 13', 'Count Magnus',** and McBryde's own illustrated comic fantasy, *The Story of a Trollhunt.* By the turn of the century the ghost stories had become part of a yearly ritual enjoyed by a gathering of James's close friends at King's over Christmas. The party varied from year to year, but amongst the regulars were McBryde, [H. E. Luxmoore, James's tutor at Eton and a lifelong friend], Walter Morley Fletcher, E. G. Swain (Chaplain of King's and himself the author of Jamesian ghost stories), Arthur Benson, Owen Hugh Smith (who purchased several of the manuscripts of the ghost stories after James's death), and S. G. Lubbock, author of the 1939 *Memoir* of James. The story was often composed at 'fever heat'; as one listener recalled:

'Monty emerged from the bedroom, manuscript in hand, at last, and blew out all the candles but one, by which he seated himself. He then began to read, with more confidence than anyone else could have mustered, his wellnigh illegible script in the dim light' [Oliffe Richmond in unpublished reminiscences (King's College)].

Early in 1904 McBryde, then studying art at the Slade, was laid up in bed with appendicitis and to pass the time he suggested to James that he should illustrate some of his stories, with a view to publication. James responded enthusiastically and sent a list of six stories he considered suitable: **'Canon Alberic', 'The Mezzotint', 'The Ash-tree', 'Number 13', 'Count Magnus',** and **" 'Oh, Whistle, and I'll Come to You, My Lad' "**. By the beginning of May McBryde had made good progress with several drawings; but in June, following an operation, he died, leaving only four pictures completed (two each for **'Canon Alberic'** and **" 'Oh, Whistle' "**), two unfinished illustrations for **'Count Magnus'** (the interior of the De la Gardie mausoleum, and Mr Wraxall's meeting with his pursuers at the cross-roads), and a preliminary sketch for **'Number 13'**. A drawing had also been planned for **'The Ashtree'** based on a real tree at Ingmanthorpe Hall in Yorkshire, the family home of McBryde's wife Gwendolen.

Ghost Stories of an Antiquary, published by Edward Arnold in November 1904, was seen by James principally as a memorial to McBryde. To fill up the volume he decided to include **'Lost Hearts'** (which he said he didn't care for) and wrote a new story, **'The Treasure of Abbot Thomas'**, suggested by some stained glass he had examined that summer at Ashridge Park, Hertfordshire. The book was neither widely nor particularly enthusiastically reviewed, but in due course Arnold asked James for more stories and was confident enough to offer improved terms. ***More Ghost Stories of an Antiquary,*** containing seven tales, duly appeared in 1911, followed by *A Thin Ghost and Others* (five stories) in 1919, and *A Warning to the Curious* (six stories) in 1925. All twenty-six stories were gathered together in 1931 as the *Collected Ghost Stories of M. R. James,* together with **'There Was a Man Dwelt by a Churchyard', 'Rats', 'After Dark in the Playing Fields',** and **'Wailing Well'**. The latter, written for the Eton Boy Scouts and read to them at Worbarrow-Bay in Dorset by James himself in the summer of 1927, was published in a limited edition of 157 copies (seven signed by the author) by Robert Gathorne-Hardy and Kyrle Leng at the Mill House Press in 1928. The *Collected Ghost Stories* concluded with 'Stories I Have tried to Write' (first published in 1929), in which James briefly described ideas that had failed to ripen. Three stories are missing from the collected edition: **'The Experiment'** (1931), **'The Malice of Inanimate Objects'** (1933), and **'A Vignette'** (posthumously published in 1936). All three are reprinted herein.

Enthusiastic early readers of James's stories included Arthur Machen, S. M. Ellis (who with James was responsible for establishing the canon of J. S. Le Fanu's ghost stories), Montague Summers, Theodore Roosevelt, A. E. Housman, and Thomas Hardy. In 1913 Housman sent Hardy *Ghost Stories of an Antiquary* and *More Ghost Stories,* recommending in particular **" 'Oh, Whistle' "** and **'Count Magnus'**. In his letter of thanks Hardy wrote that 'Two or three of them have been read aloud in this house [i. e. Max Gate, Dorchester], and I was agreeably sensible of their eeriness, even though the precaution was taken of keeping them at a safe distance from bed-time. There is much invention shown in their construction, especially in those you mention.' The inventiveness of the stories is indeed one of their chief delights and emphasizes James's freshness of approach to a literary form which by 1904 was well worked. Already in the first collection James's characteristic narrative method is highly developed and confidently applied. In **'Canon Alberic',** for instance, the cardinal points of Dennistoun's character are quickly established with a few deft strokes—such as the passing indication of his well-bred pretence of not noticing the sacristan's fervent supplications to the painting of St Bernard (which Dennistoun—no familiarizing Christian name is given—loftily dismisses as a 'daub'): for him it is clearly bad form both to give way to emotion and to notice such failure in others. Though he himself comes to feel the intensest terror, the fundamentals of his 'North British character' remain unviolated: ' "I had no notion they came so dear" ', he remarks when arranging a Mass to be said for the soul of the unprincipled Canon Alberic.

In the same way it is easy for the reader, who as always in James's best stories quickly becomes engrossed in the atmosphere and the working out of the plot, to overlook the subtle shifts of perspective in the narrative. The narrator/author—for there is little practical distinction between the two—is both distanced from the action and part of it: it is he who shows the drawing of the demon to a **'Lecturer in Morphology',** and the description of the drawing is the narrator's own, not Dennistoun's in report. But when the climax is reached a brief paragraph sets the reader for a moment in Dennistoun's place; past tense changes to present as we see through his eyes when he becomes aware of the menacing object lying at his left elbow. The viewpoint then reverts to the narrator's: 'The lower jaw was thin—what can I call it?—shallow, like a beast's . . .' . Though James always implicitly denied that his stories were anything more than the products of idle moments, such control of narrative dynamics indicates an instinctive artistry.

'Canon Alberic' is in many ways the quintessential M. R. James ghost story. Here, as elsewhere, James dramatizes with great skill—and with touches of characteristic humour—the unlooked-for revelation of an alien order of things, of a wholly malevolent Beyond, linked to our world by a perplexing and dangerous logic: a chance word, an unthinking action, curiosity, or simply being in the wrong place at the right time, can all spring the trap. This thematic continuity is matched by a consistent, almost formulaic technical approach:

> Let us, then, be introduced to the actors in a placid way; let us see them going about their ordinary business, undisturbed by forebodings, pleased with their surroundings; and into this calm environment let the ominous thing put out its head, unobtrusively at first, and then more insistently, until it holds the stage.

In **'Canon Alberic'** James also puts his scholarly expertise to effective use, creating convincing background details that anchor the seemingly impossible to apparent fact and establishing an instantly recognizable style. Though the use of documentation and antiquarian detail had been used to some extent before, James may be said to have originated a new narrative mode for the English ghost story. It was for him a natural reflex: even as an Eton schoolboy he had put his specialist knowledge to mildly deceptive purposes (he once forged 'sixteenth-century' instructions for finding buried gold which, he claimed, had deceived both his tutor and the Master in College), whilst his mimetic gift showed itself in contributions to the *Eton College Chronicle,* including extracts purporting to come from a fifteenth-century Etonian's diary.

Dennistoun himself defines the typical protagonist of an M. R. James story, a bachelor scholar of independent means whose 'ordinary business' involves quiet delvings into history and antiquities. Such is Mr Williams in 'The Mezzotint' who is engaged in enlarging the Ashleian Museum's collection of topographical drawings; yet 'even a department so homely and familiar as this may have its dark corners, and to one of these Mr Williams was unexpectedly introduced.' Mr Williams is only a passive observer of a supernatural event and survives the experience. Mr Wraxall in 'Count Magnus' is less fortunate. Wraxall is intelligent and cultivated, a Fellow of Brasenose, Oxford, whose only fault—pardonable in a traveller, as the narrator remarks—is over-inquisitiveness. His fate is sealed by articulating the seemingly trivial desire to see the long-dead Count Magnus. Once expressed, the wish is fulfilled. On the other hand, scepticism, not scholarly curiosity, is Professor Parkins's flaw in " 'Oh, Whistle, and I'll Come to You, My Lad' ". Parkins is a keen golfer (not something James means us to admire), precise of speech, humourless, a modern Sadducee dismissive of 'antiquarian pursuits'. Like Mr Williams he survives his experience, though he has to come face to face—literally—with one of James's most celebrated agents of vengeance.

The final story in the first collection, 'The Treasure of Abbot Thomas', which begins audaciously with a whole page of Latin, introduces elements of the Holmesian detective story in the ingenious unravelling by the clerical antiquary Mr Somerton of the clues that lead him to the gold hidden by the unscrupulous Abbot Thomas in the sixteenth century. Like Parkins, he disregards a warning ('*Gare à qui la touche*') and by this point in the collection we expect the worst. What awaits Mr Somerton in the well at Steinfeld is a truly nightmarish encounter with something that cannot strictly be called a ghost (the same is true of several other Jamesian entities) but whose very lack of definition intensifies the shock and revulsion Somerton experiences: " 'I was conscious of a most horrible smell of mould, and of a cold kind of face pressed against my own, and moving slowly over it . . .' " The post-Freudian reader may speculate that this repulsive moment of intimacy perhaps exteriorizes a fear of sexual contact in James himself; at any rate it is one of the most disturbing moments in his fiction, matched only by the violation of Mr Dunning's bed—the one place where he ought to feel safe—in 'Casting the Runes'.

In the world of M. R. James's antiquaries, passions are aroused not by human contact, or even money or power, but by intellectual endeavour and discovery. Dennistoun again is typical: 'All at once Dennistoun's cherished dreams of finding priceless manuscripts in untrodden corners of France flashed up . . .'. The same cerebral pleasure is shared by Mr Somerton, by Mr Anderson in 'Number 13', by Paxton in 'A Warning to the Curious'; even the amateur Mr Humphreys, in 'Mr Humphreys and his Inheritance', anticipates the drawing up of a *catalogue raisonné* as being 'a delicious occupation for winter'. Women figure rarely in James's stories, for this is a world where sex is not. The sacristan's daughter in 'Canon Alberic' is merely 'a handsome girl enough', whilst the married state as depicted in 'The Rose Garden' is one of petty domestic tyranny on the part of Mrs Anstruther and a perpetual pining for the golf links on the part of her husband. Garrett in 'The Tractate Middoth' does feel the pull of sexual attraction; but it hardly impinges on the story. Only the tragic mock-wooing of Ann Clark in 'Martin's Close' (*More Ghost Stories,* 1911)—one of a handful of stories with historical settings, this one drawing on the State Trials of the late seventeenth century—has sexual overtones; and here, unusually for James, the female ghost is as much a victim as her imagined lover and murderer George Martin, sentenced to hang by the implacable Judge Jefferies. James linked sex with needless physical horror as things to be avoided by the ghost story writer: 'Reticence may be an elderly doctrine to preach,' he wrote, 'yet from the artistic point of view I am sure it is a sound one . . . sex is tiresome enough in the novels; in a ghost story, or as the backbone of a ghost story, I have no patience with it.'

The sexlessness of James's fiction reflects a social structure that faces neither disruption nor tension. His characters move in an unthreatened world—until, that is, 'the ominous thing' puts out its head. Order and custom prevail, with social distinctions, expressed through standard and non-standard language, quietly taken for granted. Though James's treatment of his minor characters—the servants, housekeepers, gardeners, tradesmen, bus conductors, and various factotums—may now seem occasionally patronizing, his delight in the vigour of vernacular idiom was genuine and is evident, for instance, in the loquacious Mr Cooper in 'Mr Humphreys and his Inheritance', or in the narrative of the admirable Mr Worby in 'An Episode of Cathedral History'.

It is not people, however, but places and landscapes that sharpen the focus of James's prose. (Places, he once said, had been 'prolific in suggestion'.) It is landscape that draws forth a rare passage of carefully modulated lyricism in 'Canon Alberic':

> It was time to ring the *Angelus*: a few pulls at the reluctant rope, and the great bell *Bertrande* high in the tower began to speak, and swung her voice up among the pines and down to the valleys loud with mountain-streams, calling the dwellers on those lonely hills to remember and repeat the Salutation of the angel to her whom he called Blessed among women.

Landscape, again, turns description into meditation in 'A Neighbour's Landmark':

The sun was down behind the hill, and the light was off the fields, and when the clock bell in the Church tower struck seven, I thought no longer of kind mellow evening hours of rest, and scents of flowers and woods on evening air . . . but instead images came to me of dusty beams and creeping spiders and savage owls up in the tower, and forgotten graves and their ugly contents below, and of flying Time and all it had taken out of my life.

Set in the landscapes of James's stories are the small country houses (often East Anglian) he loved so much. It is M. R. James in *propria persona* who writes in the opening paragraph of **'The Ash-tree'** (1904) of the

grey paling of split oak, the noble trees, the meres with their reed beds, and the line of distant woods. Then, I like the pillared portico . . . the hall inside . . . I like the library, too, where you may find anything from a Psalter of the thirteenth century to a Shakespeare quarto . . . I wish to have one of these houses, and enough money to keep it together and entertain my friends in it modestly.

James's sensitivity to place and to the living presence of the past gives his stories a resonance and edge that more than compensate for the occasional flatness or stereotypicality of his characters. For the kind of ghost story James wrote, atmosphere and incident are more important than subtle character delineation, for we need to feel that there is nothing peculiar to the protagonists that singles them out for supernatural violation. As Mr Somerton remarks plaintively in **'The Treasure of Abbot Thomas'**: " 'Well, what would any human being have been tempted to do . . . in my place?' " In James's fictional world we are meant to feel the capriciousness of supernatural malevolence and realize that rules exist of which we have no knowledge—as indicated by a stone or a prayer-book that must not be removed, a whistle that ought not to be blown, a wish that should not be spoken a crown that must not be dug up. Though we are shown wrongdoers who receive their just deserts, such as Karswell or John Eldred, many of James's characters are baffled victims, the most baffled of all being Mr Wraxall: 'His constant cry is "What has he done?" . . . What can he do but lock his door and cry to God?'

The 'ghosts' themselves are various in form but united in their malevolence and palpability. They are all fearfully present to the physical senses. James is especially adept at conveying tactile horror:

He put his hand into the well-known nook under the pillow: only, it did not get so far. What he touched was . . . a mouth, with teeth, and with hair about it, and, he declares, not the mouth of a human being.

                    (**'Casting the Runes'**)

I was resting my hand on one of the carved figures . . . the wood seemed to become chilly and soft as if made of wet linen.

          (**'The Stalls of Barchester Cathedral'**)

James's facility for tapping natural sources of revulsion can be seen in the brilliantly executed climax of **'Mr Hum-**

phreys and his Inheritance'. Combined with this is an unerring eye for the telling detail that makes his ghosts so unsettling:

It was not a mask. It was a face—large, smooth, and pink. She remembers the minute drops of perspiration which were starting from its forehead: she remembers how the jaws were cleanshaven and the eyes shut. She remembers also, and with an accuracy which makes the thought intolerable to her, how the mouth was open and a single tooth appeared below the upper lip.

                    (**'The Rose Garden'**)

Though few of James's executors of unappeasable malice have a specific *literary* lineage, he was contributing to a form that by 1895, when the first of his stories were published, was well established. We encounter ghosts in Homer, Chaucer, the ballads; in Shakespeare and Jacobean tragedy; and in the melodramatic spooks of Gothic romance. But it is not until the 1820s that the short literary ghost story began to mature into genuine art, with Sir Walter Scott's 'Wandering Willie's Tale' (from *Redgauntlet*, 1824) and 'The Tapestried Chamber' (from *The Keepsake*, 1829). A decade later the first ghost stories of Joseph Sheridan Le Fanu (1814-73) began to appear in the *Dublin University Magazine*. In James's estimation (and his opinion carries weight) the best ghost stories in English were all by Le Fanu, who succeeded in inspiring 'a mysterious terror' better than any other writer. James observed in Le Fanu the necessity to pace a ghost story: 'The gradual removal of one safeguard after another, the victim's dim forebodings of what is to happen gradually growing clearer; these are the processes which generally increase the strain of excitement.' He took note too of the effect of 'unexplained hints': 'The reader is never allowed to know the full theory which underlies any of [Le Fanu's] ghost stories, but this Le Fanu has in common with many inferior artists. Only you feel that he has a complete explanation to give if he would only vouchsafe it.' The most complete of Le Fanu's 'unexplained hints' occurs in 'The Familiar' (first published as 'The Watcher', 1851), a story James rated highly. Captain Barton, like Professor Parkins in **" 'Oh, Whistle' "**, starts out by being 'an utter disbeliever in what are usually termed preternatural agencies'; but he becomes convinced by his experiences that

there does exist beyond this a spiritual world—a system whose workings are generally in mercy hidden from us—a system which may be, and which is sometimes, partially and terribly revealed. I am sure—I know . . . that there is a God—a dreadful God—and that retribution, follows guilt, in ways the most mysterious and stupendous—by agencies the most inexplicable and terrible . . .

We might perhaps deduce some such 'system' at work in James's stories, but none of his victims ever experiences Captain Barton's epiphanic certitude. The narrator's comment on the aftermath of Parkins's adventure at the Globe Inn is merely that 'the Professor's views on certain points are less clear cut than they used to be'. Even more than Le Fanu, the power of omission (a feature, too, of many traditional ballads with a supernatural theme) is apparent throughout James's work, so that the gulf between action and reaction is never satisfactorily bridged. 'The reading of many ghost stories', he concluded, 'has shown me that the greatest successes have been scored by the authors who can make us envisage a definite time and place, and give us plenty of clearcut detail, but who, when the climax is reached, allow us to be just a little in the dark as to the workings of their machinery.'

Though James's stories owe much to his keen enjoyment of Le Fanu over many years (he had, he said, lost count of how many times he had read *The House by the Churchyard*) they are far from being blatantly Le Fanuesque in either theme or treatment. Superficially more controlled than Le Fanu's, James's stories are actually more anarchic in their implications. Their cumulative effect is to suggest an ineradicable perplexity in the mind of their creator which pulls against the humour, against the consoling anchorage of historical detail, and against the pose of narrational detachment. According to James, in the 1931 Preface to the collected edition, only one incident in his tales derived from his own experience (in " 'Oh, Whistle' "); but did his last ghost story, **'A Vignette',** set at Livermere and narrated, unusually for James, in the first person, perhaps refer to another—an inexplicable childhood incident that (as the story puts it) 'had some formidable power of clinging through many years to my imagination', making adult scepticism about the supernatural (whatever he maintained publicly) impossible? An experience, to borrow words from **'A Neighbour's Landmark',** which he could neither explain away nor fit into the scheme of his life? Though **'A Vignette'** must not be read as unadorned autobiography its tone is quite unlike any of James's other stories and suggests a strong personal element—not just in the actuality of the setting, but more particularly in the confessional mood of the piece (appropriate at this point in his life). The narrator remarks: 'That I was upset by something I had seen must have been pretty clear, but I am very sure that I fought off all attempts to describe it.' Such reticence is wholly in keeping with James's disinclination to place his obvious fascination with the supernatural in a personal context. It also has the ring of psychological truth, for as another of James's narrators (in **'Rats'**) noted: 'I have not had other experiences of the kind which are called super-natural, or -normal, or -physical, but, though I knew very well I must speak of this one before long, I was not at all anxious to do so; and I think I have read that this is a common case.' On the other hand, **'A Vignette'** may be nothing more than an embellishment of what James identified as the definite source of his interest in ghosts: a cardboard Ghost in a toy Punch and Judy set—'a tall figure habited in white with an unnaturally long and narrow head . . . and a dismal visage. Upon this my conceptions of a ghost were based, and for years it permeated my dreams.'

When all is said and done, though, we do not read the ghost stories of M. R. James—or indeed any ghost story worthy of the name—for biographical revelations or enlightenment on the mysteries of life and death but for the supplying of that 'pleasure of a certain sort' to which he himself referred. Even if we are not frightened by the stories (and some people are not) there remains much to ad-

mire and enjoy: their inventiveness and quiet humour; the controlling presence of a learned and humane intelligence; the allusive texts; the evocation of place and time. James's method of creating a convincing reality into which the supernatural can be intruded has its own fascination and inspired others to write antiquarian ghost stories, beginning with his colleague at King's Edmund Gill Swain, whose *Stoneground Ghost Tales* (dedicated to James) appeared in 1912. By 1919 Arthur Gray, Master of Jesus College, Cambridge, had taken the deadpan antiquarian approach to its limits in *Tedious Brief Tales of Granta and Gramarye,* and the 1940s saw two accomplished collections (both associated with King's) that continued the Jamesian style: R. H. Malden's *Nine Ghosts* (1943, though the earliest story first appeared in 1912) and A. N. L. Munby's *The Alabaster Hand* (1949), with its Latin dedication to James. But these form only the tip of a considerable iceberg, and it is probable that M. R. James has generated more imitators than any other English ghost story writer.

The English ghost story is a vigorous and varied form and deserves more critical attention than it currently enjoys. Happily, it has never lacked enthusiastic readers, for whom the tales of M. R. James remain as entertaining, and as implausibly plausible, as ever. The secret of their success is at once obvious and impenetrable; but perhaps a quatrain by W. F. Harvey, himself a respected writer of ghost stories, comes as close to definition as we need:

> I will tell you what always has frightened me most
>
> In reading or writing the tale of a ghost:
> Not details, however grotesque or uncouth,
> But the lurking belief that the story's the truth.

M. R. James on the setting of a ghost story:

The ghost story must have a setting that is fairly familiar and the majority of the characters and their talk such as you meet or hear any day. A ghost story of which the scene is laid in the twelfth or thirteenth century may succeed in being romantic or poetical; it will never put the reader into the position of saying to himself, "If I'm not very careful, something of this kind may happen to me!"

M. R. James in his More Ghost Stories of an Antiquary, *1911.*

S. T. Joshi   (essay date 1990)

SOURCE: "M. R. James: The Limitations of the Ghost Story," in *The Weird Tale; Arthur Machen, Lord Dunsany, Algernon Blackwood, M. R. James, Ambrose Bierce, H. P. Lovecraft,* University of Texas Press, 1990, pp. 133-42.

[*Joshi is an American editor and critic whose writings focus on the study of horror and fantasy fiction, particularly the works of H. P. Lovecraft. In the following essay, he offers a negative appraisal of James's ghost stories, characterizing them as "thin and insubstantial."]*

Montague Rhodes James was born on August 1, 1862, in Goodnestone, Suffolk, the son of an Anglican priest. He showed precocious antiquarian interests while at Temple Grove preparatory school at Eton, immersing himself in the study of medieval manuscripts and biblical apocrypha. He entered King's College, Cambridge, in 1882, and after graduating stayed on to become a fellow in 1887. In his distinguished career he rose to be provost of King's from 1905 to 1918 and vice-chancellor of the university from 1913 to 1915, but took greater pride in his function as director of the Fitzwilliam Museum from 1893 to 1908 and in his service on the University Press and Library syndicates. Although he never married, he played a leading role in Cambridge literary and convivial societies, and on vacations enjoyed cycling tours with friends in Britain and France.

In 1918 James was appointed provost of Eton and in later years served on several royal commissions and was appointed a trustee of the British Museum. He was made a commander of the Order of Leopold for his aid to Belgian refugees in World War I and received the Order of Merit in 1930.

James's scholarly work gained him great respect, especially in the fields of codicology, Christian art, and biblical research. He catalogued many manuscript collections, including those of the Fitzwilliam Museum, most of the Cambridge colleges, and Canterbury, and was well known particularly for his edition of *The Apocryphal New Testament* (1924). He reached a wider audience as a master of the ghost story in the volumes **Ghost-Stories of an Antiquary** (1904), **More Ghost Stories of an Antiquary** (1911), **A Thin Ghost** (1919), and **A Warning to the Curious** (1925). His **Collected Ghost Stories** appeared in 1931, and his memoirs, *Eton and King's,* in 1926. James continued as provost of Eton until his death on June 12, 1936.

M. R. James is the subject of universal respect: Lovecraft, Clark Ashton Smith, and other *fantaisistes* have paid homage to him; modern critics like Julia Briggs, Jack Sullivan, and others have discussed his work almost reverently—and acutely; James has inspired a miniature school of disciples, among them A. N. L. Munby, E. G. Swain, and perhaps Russell Kirk. The provost of Eton College, a recognized scholar on medieval manuscripts, was of such a genial temperament as to have inspired hallowed treatment in the accounts of such of his friends and associates as Stephen Gaselee and Shane Leslie. It seems difficult to say anything bad about James: he perfected the ghost story; his polished, understated, erudite style is as different as possible from either the perfumed prose-poetry of Dunsany or the dense texture of Machen or Lovecraft. Only James could successfully set a ghost story almost entirely in a library (**"The Tractate Middoth"**); only he would open a story with a stunning and flawless imitation of a late medieval Latin treatise, a 150-word passage in Latin followed by the narrator's tiredly casual remark, "I suppose I shall have to translate this" (**"The Treasure of Abbot Thomas"**). If I take a dimmer view of James's work than many of his devotees, it is because I am frustrated

that James knowingly limited his talents to a very restricted field and was profoundly out of sympathy with related branches of the weird tale. Lovecraft could enjoy both James and Dunsany, although he realized that they were at "opposite pole[s] of genius"; for James, his contemporaries Machen, Blackwood, and Lovecraft (whom he may have read) all wrote in vain, while he pays only the most frigid respect to Poe.

My first concern with James is to examine the nature of his "ghost." Curiously, it seems remarkably material, and there are actually relatively few tales in which it retains the nebulosity of the traditional specter. Many commentators have noted the *hairiness* of the James ghost; perhaps Lovecraft expressed it best when he said that "the average James ghost is lean, dwarfish, and hairy—a sluggish, hellish night-abomination midway betwixt beast and man—and usually *touched* before it is *seen*." This is true enough, and the prototype is the figure in **"Canon Alberic's Scrap-Book"**:

> At first you saw only a mass of coarse, matted black hair; presently it was seen that this covered a body of fearful thinness, almost a skeleton, but with the muscles standing out like wires. The hands were of a dusky pallor, covered, like the body, with long, coarse hairs, and hideously taloned. The eyes, touched in with a burning yellow, had intensely black pupils, and were fixed upon the throned King with a look of beast-like hate. Imagine one of the awful bird-catching spiders of South America translated into human form, and endowed with intelligence just less than human, and you will have some faint conception of the terror inspired by this appalling effigy.

What such a ghost symbolizes for James—the scholar and academician—is the routing of intelligence. The Jamesian ghost embodies all those traits of primitive human beings that are most frightening to the civilized and rational: not merely ignorance but aggressively violent ignorance. The effect is achieved in remarkably subtle ways: hairiness is frequently used as a symbol for barbarity, but note the simple description of a figure "crawling on all fours" in the peculiar mezzotint in **"The Mezzotint"** or the dog motif that crops up in **"The Residence at Whitminster," "The Diary of Mr. Poynter,"** and **"An Episode of Cathedral History."** The dog, too, one supposes, is representative of primitive savagery.

The taint of primitivism affects even the human characters in the tale. Of the evil scholar in **"Lost Hearts"** it is said that he wished to reenact "certain processes, which to us moderns have something of a barbaric complexion"; needless to say, the victims of the "processes" return to exact ghostly revenge. Analogously, the central character in **"The Treasure of Abbot Thomas"** "screams like a beast" when the monster embraces him in the well. The rational mind cannot endure contact with the supernormal and itself descends to barbarism. There is, in fact, only a single story—**"Casting the Runes"**—in which a character even attempts (here successfully) to counteract the effects of the supernatural agency; in all other instances the Jamesian figure is singularly passive and resigned.

The "eccentric composition" of some Jamesian ghosts is remarked on by Lovecraft; he in particular found effective the "face *of crumpled linen*," italicized in pseudo-Lovecraftian fashion, in " 'Oh, Whistle, and I'll Come to You, My Lad.' " I wonder, however, whether Lovecraft or others have perceived that this tale—or, rather, the ghost at the center of it—may actually be a *parody* of the old-time ghost story with its sheeted figure mistily floating down some centuried corridor. Here the figure materializes itself in a prosaic seaside inn where a professor is vacationing; but I think we are to regard the jarring juxtaposition of unconventional setting and pseudoconventional ghost—here literally manifesting itself in a bedsheet—as a bit of fun on James's part. This is by no means to deny the unquestioned power and even originality of the conception, for the ghost is of course not the bedsheet itself but some invisible monster who can be seen only when embodied behind some material substance like a bedsheet.

The loathsome creature in **"The Treasure of Abbot Thomas"** is initially described as "some rounded light-coloured objects . . . which might be bags"—a hideously colloquial description. But later the monster, more clearly seen, is said to be a "horrid, grotesque shape—perhaps more like a toad than anything else." Similarly, in **"The Haunted Dolls' House"** we encounter "a frog—the size of a man." I can trace no especial symbolism behind this amphibian motif, save in its repulsiveness. The Abbot Thomas ghost not merely appears, however, but "*put its arms around my neck*" (those charming italics again)—a grotesque parody of affection. It is a theme similar to that of Robert Hichens's famous story "How Love Came to Professor Guildea" (1900), where, I think, it is handled even better.

James reveals a virtual obsession with the mechanics of narrating the ghost story. In many of his tales the narrator or central figure (very often they are not the same) pieces together various documents and presents them in artfully edited form. This method serves at least two purposes. First, it emphasizes the fundamental rationality of the character, as it does in Machen's "Novel of the Black Seal" and Lovecraft's "Call of Cthulhu," otherwise tales as profoundly different from James's as can be imagined; second, it distances the narrative, frequently by several stages. This idea of distancing was very important to James. In his introduction to *Ghosts and Marvels* he notes: "For the ghost story a slight haze of distance is desirable." Here he refers, of course, to chronological distance, and this accounts for another curious phenomenon in James: the setting of many of his stories in the eighteenth or early nineteenth century. James's method appears to require a modern setting, since he remarks in an essay on the need for the "setting and personages [to be] those of the writer's own day." This statement appears to contradict the "haze of distance" idea, but only superficially: for a scholar like James, accustomed to dealing with the ancient and medieval world, the eighteenth or nineteenth century would have appeared—as they did to a similar antiquarian, Lovecraft—a "fairly recent yesterday." Hence **"Two Doctors"** is set in 1718; **"The Residence at Whitminster"** begins in 1730, then advances another century or so; **"Lost Hearts"** is set in 1811–1812; **"A School Story"** is set around 1870.

There is, however, a problem with even this pseudoremoteness. The specificity of dates used by James compels the reader to envision a precise historical period, and the sense of familiarity with the characters and settings is, if not destroyed, at least muted. James warns against this by saying: "It is almost inevitable that the reader of an antique story should fall into the position of the mere spectator." This certainly argues a very elastic conception of history—and, perhaps, more elastic a one than James could rightfully assume in his readers. He would have been better off, I think, being a little vaguer in the dating of events. In only one tale, the very late **"Rats,"** does he skillfully solve the problem: "I cannot put a date to the story, but I was young when I heard it, and the teller was old." In an entirely different way, **"Martin's Close"** is a tour de force in its attempt to reproduce the actual diction of a late seventeenth-century court case, presided over by (as we all know from Macaulay) the redoubtable Judge Jeffreys. This is merely an extension of a principle running through James's work: the inclusion of pseudodocuments in his tales. We have already noted the lengthy Latin passage that opens **"The Treasure of Abbot Thomas,"** but we can also marvel at the perfect replication of the platitudinous eighteenth-century obituary (reputedly from *The Gentleman's Magazine*) in **"The Stalls of Barchester Cathedral"** or the paraphrasing of various eighteenth-century documents in what might be James's most powerful story, **"The Ash-Tree."**

This finally brings us back to the role of the narrator or central figure, who acts as "editor" of this documentary material. The degree to which the narrator wishes to dissociate himself from the actual events is frequently remarkable: in **"Count Magnus"** the narrator paraphrases the victim Wraxall's paraphrase of documents he has discovered. Perhaps the greatest indirection occurs in **"A Warning to the Curious,"** in which at one point we have the principal (unnamed) narrator paraphrasing the account of a subsidiary (unnamed) narrator who meets a traveler, Paxton, who has heard a curious legend from a rector—and the rector himself has heard this legend from the "old people" of the community. This is certainly narrative distance with a vengeance! In fact, the principal narrator never returns after he has yielded to the subsidiary narrator; just as well, one supposes, as by the end we have forgotten about his existence.

James can carry this indirection too far. In **"The Rose Garden"** the tale is so obliquely told that it is difficult to ascertain what exactly happened; in **"The Residence at Whitminster"** the many layers of narration ill conceal the tale's pointlessness and prolixity. James's narrator can also be quite disingenuous: in **"The Stalls of Barchester Cathedral"** he remarks at one point, "I digress to put in a document which, *rightly or wrongly* [my italics], I believe to have a bearing on the thread of the story." This false ignorance fools no one.

James also has a peculiar inclination to obtrude himself in the narrative at odd moments. **"Canon Alberic's Scrap-Book"** begins with a third-person narration about the character Dennistoun, but all of a sudden we encounter this passage: " 'Once,' Dennistoun said to me, 'I could have sworn I heard a thin metallic voice laughing high up in the tower. . . .' " It is significant that this is the first intimation of the supernatural in the story, but the very abrupt distancing is clumsy. In **"The Mezzotint"** we have this strange interruption: "He lighted the candles, for it was now dark, made the tea, and supplied the friend with whom he had been playing golf (for I believe the authorities of the University I write of indulge in that pursuit by way of relaxation);. . . ." This will, no doubt, be cited by James's supporters as an example of his dry wit; dry it certainly is.

In later stories James is fond of placing the central narrative—or, at least, the portion of the narrative that definitely involves the supernatural—into the mouth of a half-educated person who tells the tale in a roundabout and colloquial fashion. Two goals are met by this method: narrative distance is achieved, and the corrupting influence of the ghostly phenomena on those closest to them is suggested. Even James, however, never—thankfully—carried this practice to the grotesque lengths that we find in the subnarrative of Zadok Allen in Lovecraft's "The Shadow over Innsmouth."

James frequently goes out of his way to avoid any suggestions of sensationalism as his climax approaches. The italics to which he succumbed in **" 'Oh, Whistle' "** and **"The Treasure of Abbot Thomas"** are rare exceptions; in other stories the purported climax is handled with absolutely no fanfare. This is doubly peculiar in that James speaks of the need of a "nicely managed crescendo" at the end of a tale. To be quite honest, I find no such crescendos in James; in fact, often the reverse is—quite consciously—the case. The "climax" of **"The Stalls of Barchester Cathedral,"** the death of Archdeacon Haynes, is conveyed by a euphemistic eighteenth-century obituary; similar is the death of Eldred in **"The Tractate Middoth."** The curious result of this and other of James's elaborately self-conscious narrative methods is to draw attention away from the events and to focus it on the narration itself. There may also be a partial contradiction of James's principles of ghost-story writing. In speaking (presumably with Algernon Blackwood in mind) derisively of the intrusion of "psychical" theory, James writes: "I feel that the technical terms of 'occultism,' if they are not very carefully handled, tend to put the mere ghost story . . . upon a quasi-scientific plane, and to call into play faculties quite other than the imaginative." While James does not indulge in occultism, this "quasi-scientific" atmosphere is exactly what we find in much of his work. I am not referring to all the pseudoscholarship (imagined medieval texts, bogus footnotes, and the like) that abounds in his writing; rather, it is more like what Lovecraft experienced when reading some of H. G. Wells's stories: "I *can't* derive a really *supernatural* thrill from matter which keeps my *mental* wheels turning so briskly; and yet when I think of some of his things *in retrospect,* supplying my own filter of imaginative colour, I am reduced to doubt again." Analogously, in James the reader must frequently expend so much energy simply following the obliquely narrated plot that there is no room for the "imaginative" faculty to come into play. It is as if writing a ghost story has become an intellectual game for James.

James has profounder limitations than this, and the principal one is simply that all his tales resolve, morally, into a naive tit-for-tat vengeance motif. James is certainly right to emphasize the "malevolent or odious" nature of the ghost; but in almost every one of his stories the malevolence is directed at someone who has committed some obvious moral outrage. This is a limitation, evidently, of the traditional ghost story in general and gives to James's tales a curious repetitiveness and one-dimensionality; it is simply not possible to ring many—nay, any—changes upon this one theme. In some stories, of course, we are faced with apparently hapless characters who are destroyed by what seems to be the random vindictiveness of the ghost; but what conclusion we are to draw from this is not clear. Jack Sullivan writes: "The characters are antiquaries, not merely because the past enthralls them, but because the present is a near vacuum. They surround themselves with rarefied paraphernalia from the past—engravings, rare books, altars, tombs, coins, and even such things as dolls' houses and ancient whistles—seemingly because they cannot connect with anything in the present." This sounds very pretty, but there is no textual evidence to support it. James's antiquarians are either professionals or amateurs: they pursue the past merely because it is their job or because it amuses them; the metaphysical angst implied in what Sullivan calls the " 'Waste Land' ambiance" of the stories is just not there. Occasionally we have dim indications that these characters have brought doom upon themselves: there is, in **"Canon Alberic's Scrap-Book,"** a hint of Dennistoun's irreligiousness when he scoffs at wearing a crucifix to protect himself ("Well, really, Dennistoun hadn't much use for these things"), while, in **" 'Oh Whistle,' "** Parkins's radical disbelief in ghosts itself amounts to a religious dogma:

> "Well," Parkins said, "as you have mentioned the matter, I freely own that I do *not* like careless talk about what you call ghosts. A man in my position," he went on, raising his voice a little, "cannot, I find, be too careful about appearing to sanction the current beliefs on such subjects. . . . I hold that any semblance, any appearance of concession to the view that such things might exist is equivalent to a renunciation of all that I hold most sacred."

But these hints are vague and, in the end, harmlessly jocular.

The fact is that it is simply not possible . . . to derive a general philosophy out of James's stories. They are simply stories; they never add up to a world view. The tales are all technique, a coldly intellectual exercise in which James purposely avoids drawing broader implications. It is not even especially fruitful to trace themes through his work, for both the vengeance motif and the ghost-as-savage theme remain virtually unchanged throughout his corpus. The vengeance motif is, moreover, not merely monotonous but ultimately unconvincing: this moral accounting for supernatural phenomena will simply not work for modern readers. Some sort of pseudoscientific approach must now be used—either the quasi-scientific method of Lovecraft or, indeed, the very occultist rationalizations so scorned by James in the work of Blackwood: whatever we may feel about occultism, supernatural phenomena "explained" by it at least become subsumed into a viable *Weltanschauung*.

It is also quite obvious that James's inspiration began to flag very early on. If we concede that the eight tales in **Ghost-Stories of an Antiquary** (1904) are nearly perfect examples of the form, we must also add that the rest of James's work does little but ring increasingly feeble changes upon those tales. James's first collection is all that anyone need read of his work. It is particularly unfortunate to see James spin such an incredibly tedious tale as **"Mr. Humphreys and His Inheritance"** (avowedly written to "fill up" his second volume); all the later tales are dogged by hints of this sort of prolixity.

As it is, perhaps James is rather more interesting as a critic and theorist of the form. We are now concerned with three documents: the preface to **More Ghost Stories of an Antiquary** (1911), the introduction to *Ghosts and Marvels* (1924), and the lengthy essay "Some Remarks on Ghost Stories" (1929). The first two are principally theoretical, and impeccable as far as they go; they prove that James had clear principles for ghost-story writing (Sullivan makes much too much of James's apparent coyness and indefiniteness in this regard) and that he followed them closely enough, with the exceptions noted above. The final essay is a fascinating history of the ghost story— fascinating precisely because it is so bizarre. Admittedly, James seems to be narrowly restricting himself to the avowed "ghost story" so that perhaps it is understandable that such figures as Machen or Dunsany have no place in his account. But James's highly ambiguous stance toward Poe is of interest. The editor of *Ghosts and Marvels* had selected Poe's "Ligeia" for inclusion, and James was forced to comment upon it. His cautious remark, "Evidently in many people's judgments it ranks as a classic," scarcely conceals his distaste. "Some Remarks on Ghost Stories" is more ambivalent, as he speaks of "some Americans" (i. e., the pulp writers) who fancy that they "tread . . . in the steps of Edgar Allan Poe and Ambrose Bierce (himself sometimes unpardonable)," but the hint of disapproval is strong. What offended James so much? Clearly it was the concentration on what he felt was the merely physically gruesome, as can be inferred in his slap at Bierce and also in his comment on E. F. Benson: "He sins occasionally by stepping over the line of legitimate horridness." Certainly he has nothing good to say about the American pulp writers: "The[y] are merely nauseating, and it is very easy to be nauseating." This is really an unprovoked attack, since the pulp writers never considered themselves "ghost-story writers" and should therefore not even have been mentioned in James's essay. I think James's squeamishness prevented him from appreciating the fact that there is a lot more to the work of Poe, Bierce, Machen, and Lovecraft than merely loathsome physical horror; James's idol LeFanu can be just as revolting, but evidently his indirection appealed to James.

I have studied James here not because I have much enthusiasm for him—this much is obvious from my discussion—and not even because I think him an especially good writer overall. I sincerely believe he is much inferior to the other writers I am studying here [Machen, Dunsany, Blackwood, Bierce, and Lovecraft], largely because his work is ultimately thin and insubstantial. James showed little development over his career; if anything, there is a decline in power and originality and a corresponding preoccupation—bordering upon obsession—with technique. I discuss him here because he is clearly the perfecter of one popular and representative form of the weird tale; but in his very perfection of that form he showed its severe limitations in scope. I have nothing to say about his disciples; only Russell Kirk—if we are even to consider him a "disciple" of James—has escaped these limitations to write work that is vital and significant. The ghost story as such does not allow very much room for expansion or originality; when some writers attempt to do so, they either fail (James's followers) or, in succeeding, produce tales that can no longer be called ghost stories (Oliver Onions). It is quite possible that James came to realize this and that this is the reason for the very peculiar, self-reflexive nature of his later work: with **Ghost-Stories of an Antiquary** James had already exhausted the form and could do nothing but move his limited number of components into various permutations to create an illusory sense of newness. But it didn't work, and few of his readers—even his valiant supporters, if they would only admit it—were taken in.

FURTHER READING

Biography

Cox, Michael. *M. R. James: An Informal Portrait.* Oxford: Oxford University Press, 1983, 268 p.

> Anecdotal description of James's life that includes a brief critical overview of his ghost story collections.

Criticism

James, Montague R. "Some Remarks on Ghost Stories." *The Bookman* LXXVII, No. 459 (December 1929): 169-72.

> James's assessment of ghost stories—the only article he wrote specifically to address the critical evaluation of the genre.

Haining, Peter, ed. *M. R. James: The Book of Ghost Stories.* New York: Stein and Day, 1982, 128 p.

Collection of writings by and about James; includes five previously uncollected short stories and articles, photographs of James and his contemporaries, and drawings which accompanied the original editions of his ghost stories.

Additional coverage of James's life and career is contained in the following sources published by Gale Research: *Contemporary Authors,* Vol. 104 and *Twentieth-Century Literary Criticism,* Vol. 6.

Thomas Ligotti

1953-

(Full name Thomas Robert Ligotti) American short story writer and essayist.

INTRODUCTION

Ligotti writes short fiction in a literary tradition which began with the eighteenth-century Gothic novel and later comprised the works of Edgar Allan Poe, Arthur Machen, M. R. James, and H. P. Lovecraft. Eschewing graphic, visceral description, Ligotti employs a dense, elaborate narrative style which suggests rather than depicts unspeakable horrors.

Biographical Information

Ligotti was born in Detroit, Michigan, in 1953 and educated at Macomb County Community College and Wayne State University. His first published story, "The Chymist," appeared in the horror magazine *Nyctalops,* edited by Harry O. Morris, in 1981. He has since published fiction and essays in numerous small press and professional magazines. Morris's Silver Scarab Press brought out his first collection of stories, *Songs of a Dead Dreamer,* in 1985. Two subsequent short story collections have appeared: *Grimscribe: His Lives and Works* (1991) and *Noctuary* (1994). Ligotti resides near Detroit.

Major Works of Short Fiction

The major themes of Ligotti's fiction include fate, the essential unreality and randomness of everyday life, and an all-pervading existential terror. In such stories as "Dr. Locrian's Asylum" and "The Greater Festival of Masks," Ligotti proffers a view of the universe as a disordered nightmare, presenting sequences of seemingly random, terrifying events that nonetheless adhere to what critics Stefan Dziemianowicz and Michael A. Morrison term their own "strange rhythms and obscure logic." In the novella-length "Last Feast of Harlequin," dedicated to the memory of Lovecraft, Ligotti employs a more traditional narrative to tell the story of an academic investigating a small town's mysterious midwinter festival. He has articulated his philosophy of horror fiction in several essays, including "The Consolations of Horror," "Some Notes on the Writing of Horror," and "In the Night, In the Dark: A Note on the Appreciation of Weird Fiction."

Critical Reception

Ligotti is much admired by writers and critics of horror fiction but little known outside the circle of genre enthusiasts. Horror critics praise his unique narrative voice, commending in particular his avoidance of explicitly portrayed horrors in favor of subtly suggestive prose that has

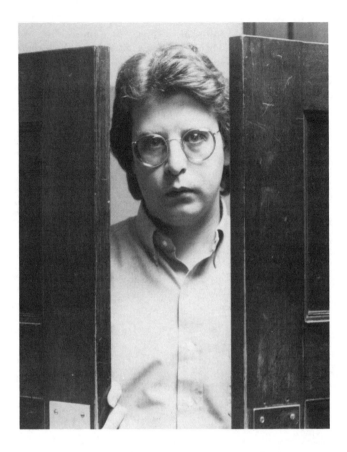

been described as hallucinatory, elegant, and complex. Mainstream reviewers have been more conservative in their assessments of Ligotti's fiction, citing his stories for occasional weaknesses in plot and characterization, overly ornate prose, and general obscurity. Most commentators on Ligotti's fiction, however, concur that his works successfully fulfill the dictates outlined in the essay "In the Night, In the Dark" on the function of weird fiction: "to recover some of the amazement we sometimes feel, and should probably feel more often, at existence in its essential aspect."

PRINCIPAL WORKS

SHORT FICTION

Songs of a Dead Dreamer   1985, rev. ed., 1989
Grimscribe: His Lives and Works   1991
Noctuary   1994

CRITICISM

Ramsey Campbell   (essay date 1985)

SOURCE: An introduction to *Songs of a Dead Dreamer* by Thomas Ligotti, Silver Scarab Press, 1986, pp. 5-6.

[*Campbell is an English novelist, short story writer, essayist, and critic specializing in supernatural and horror literature. In the following excerpt, he praises Ligotti's subtlety, wit, and originality.*]

I don't know when I have enjoyed a collection of an author's horror stories more than [*Songs of a Dead Dreamer*]. I'll go further: it has to be one of the most important horror books of the decade. . . . Ligotti is one of the few consistently original voices in contemporary horror fiction, one of the few whose work is instantly recognizable.

He belongs to the most honourable tradition in the field, that of subtlety and awesomeness rather than the relentlessly graphic. At times he suggests terrors as vast as Lovecraft's, though the terrors are quite other than Lovecraft's. He's capable of writing tales as dismayingly horrifying as any of his contemporaries—**"The Frolic"**, for example—yet even there one finds a hint of more than horror, an extra dimension of awe. Others of his tales—**"The Troubles of Dr. Thoss"**, **"The Greater Festival of Masks"**, **"Dr. Voke and Mr. Veech"**—read like dreams prompted by memories of M. R. James, dreams stranger than anything the good doctor ever wrote: perhaps the dreams of the consciousness glimpsed behind one of Ligotti's most elaborate stories, **"Dream of a Mannikin"**. Despite faint echoes of writers he admires, however, Ligotti's vision is wholly personal. Few other writers could conceive a horror story in the form of notes on the writing of the genre, and I can't think of any other writer who could have brought it off.

In **"The Consolations of Horror"** (a companion piece, published in *Dark Horizons* 27, to **"Professor Nobody's Little Lectures"**), Ligotti defines the consolations of the genre thus: "simply that someone shares some of your own feelings and has made of these a work of art which you have the insight, sensitivity and—like it or not—peculiar set of experiences to appreciate." In his case the consolations also include an elegant and witty style, an inimitable imagination, a willingness to expand the genre, and a timelessness which ought to mean that his fiction will be read with as much pleasure a hundred years from now. May this book bring him the acclaim which he certainly deserves.

Stefan R. Dziemianowicz   (essay date 1988)

SOURCE: " 'Nothing Is What It Seems to Be': Thomas Ligotti's Assault on Certainty," in *Dagon*, Nos. 22-23, September-December, 1988, pp. 17-26.

[*Dziemianowicz is an American critic whose writings focus on the works of contemporary horror and supernatural fic-*

tion writers. In the following essay, he examines the role that the element of doubt plays in Ligotti's fiction.]

In his tongue-in-cheek essay **"Professor Nobody's Little Lectures on Supernatural Horror"**, Thomas Ligotti singles out the important role the element of doubt plays in supernatural horror:

> Just a little doubt slipped into the mind, a trickle of suspicion in the bloodstream and all those eyes, one by one, will open to the world, will see its horror as it has never been seen before. Then: no belief or body of laws will guard you; no friend, no counselor, no appointed personage will save you; no crowded schoolroom, no locked bedroom, no bright kitchen will protect you.

Doubt, as readers of supernatural horror fiction know, is essential to the willing suspension of disbelief, the means by which the writer induces the reader to accept the unacceptable. The writer gets the reader to accept something inconsistent with what the reader knows to be true—usually by creating a fictional world that is consistent with the reader's world, except that the supernatural is *not* inconsistent with the characters, situations and events of that world.

In supernatural horror fiction, then, the element of doubt is most often a means to an end, a device the writer uses to neutralize the reader's defenses against unreality just long enough for the spectre, the monster or the supernatural creature to slip through. Where Thomas Ligotti departs from most of his contemporaries is in his use of doubt as an end in itself. Rather than depict a world in which the natural and supernatural co-exist side by side, distinct from one another, Ligotti so discomposes the certainty of the "real" world of his stories that characters are forced to redefine what they consider "real" and "unreal", "natural" and "supernatural". Although Ligotti's stories abound with eccentric characters, nightmarish landscapes, even the occasional inhuman creature, it's the overpowering force of uncertainty running through them that presents the greatest threat: it has as tangible a presence as any supernatural monster, and it sends the vulnerable fleeing in terror from it.

Although Ligotti is best known for his dreamy, metaphysical stories, his most traditional tale, **"The Frolic"** offers a good example of the subtle ways in which he brings the certainty of a familiar world into question. The story opens with a homely domestic scene: Dr. David Munck, a new psychologist at a state penitentiary, is having cocktails with his wife Leslie one evening, while their daughter sleeps upstairs. On the surface, all appears to be well—but it isn't. Munck was disturbed that day by a counseling session with a nameless prisoner referred to only as John Doe. Doe has been imprisoned for "frolicking" with children, an act which is never described but that, from hints of the appearance of bodies found afterward, Munck assumes is a euphemism for a perverse act.

Doe has told Munck that he wanted to be captured, that he can leave the penitentiary anytime he wishes but stays because he finds his incarceration stimulating, also that "he made the evidence look that way as a deliberate afterthought, that what he really means by 'frolicking' is a type of activity far beyond the crime for which he was convicted". In this standard madman/sane man confrontation there's no way that Munck can disprove anything that Doe says. Yet there's no doubt in Munck's mind that Doe is a typical psychopath. He bases his diagnosis on the "blasphemous fairyland" in which Doe says he lives and "frolics". Munck tells his wife that Doe:

> . . . talked about a place that sounded like the back alleys of some cosmic slum, an inner dimensional dead end. Which might be an indication of a ghetto upbringing in Doe's past. And if so, his insanity has transformed these ghetto memories into a realm that cross-breeds a banal streetcorner reality with a psychopath's paradise. This is where he does his "frolicking" with what he calls his "awe-struck company", the place possibly being an abandoned building of some kind or even an accommodating sewer somewhere. I say this based on his repeated mentioning of the "jolly river of refuse" and "the jowled heaps of shadows", which are certainly imaginative transmutations of the local dump. Less fathomable are his memories of a moonlight corridor where mirrors scream and laugh, dark peaks of some kind that won't remain still, a stairway that's "broken" in a very strange way, though this last one fits in with the background of a dilapidated slum.

> But despite all these dreamy backdrops in Doe's imagination, the mundane evidence of his frolics still points to a crime of very familiar down-to-earth horrors. A run of the mill atrocity.

Trained psychologist that he is, Munck assumes that Doe's world is no more than the product of a "ramshackle ruin of a decaying mind" distorting the images of the normal world. It's impossible for him to concede that because not *everything* Doe describes has a clinical analogue, perhaps Doe isn't raving, that there may actually be something uncanny about him. This in spite of the fact that Doe appears to know something of Munck he shouldn't: during their dialogue, Doe asked whether Munck had a child of his own, and asked in such a way as to suggest that he knew of Munck's daughter by name. Munck looks in on his own daughter early in the story, sees her sleeping contentedly with her arms wrapped around a stuffed animal, and with that innocent image in his mind comes downstairs to deliver "the wonderfully routine message that Norleen was peacefully asleep". At the end of the story, though, when he discovers that the stuffed animal was not purchased by Leslie, Munck returns to his daughter's room, feeling "as if I know something and don't know it at the same time", and finds her gone, the animal disemboweled on the bed and a note from John Doe attached to it saying that he and Norleen have gone frolicking.

What is it that Munck knows but doesn't know? Quite possibly that he has overestimated the certainty of what he believes to be true. Consciously, Munck has made an effort to fit things he is certain he knows about Doe into what he calls a "pattern of coherency" (i. e., a conventional diagnostic profile), in the hope that, ultimately, the things he is uncertain about will also fall into place. Sub-

consciously, though, Munck is aware that his encounter with Doe has left him questioning certainties in his own life.

In response to Leslie's question about how he is after his day at the office, Munck replies:

> "Severely doubting, that's how I am". He said this with a kind of reflectiveness.

> "Anything particularly doubtful, Dr. Munck?"

> "Only everything", he answered.

This laconic, seemingly harmless smalltalk between husband and wife takes on an ominous meaning as the story progresses, for Munck realizes that he has indeed begun to doubt things he once took for granted. As Munck prepares to tell Leslie about his unsettling day, he:

> . . . felt his own words lingering atmospherically in the room, tainting the serenity of the house. Until then, their home had been an insular haven beyond the contamination of the prison, an imposing structure outside the town limits. Now its psychic imposition transcended the limits of physical distance. Inner distance constricted, and David sensed the massive prison walls shadowing the cozy neighborhood outside.

As Munck senses that a refuge he once thought secure is now threatened, the secure borders of the physical world seem to dissolve. In his mind, the real and the imagined have become intermingled.

Woven more deeply into the fabric of the story are ethical and moral ambiguities that come to light in the course of the evening. Leslie, it turns out, has bought a sculpture at the prison workshop to cheer David up. "It was the head of a young boy described in gray formless clay and glossily glazed in blue. The work radiated an extraordinary and intense beauty, the subject's face expressing a kind of ecstatic serenity, the labyrinthine simplicity of a visionary". David recognizes the sculpture, because he "even forced a grudging compliment for the craftsmanship of the thing. It's obviously remarkable". Nevertheless, he shocks Leslie when he tells her that the artist is Doe and that the subject of the artwork is "his last—and according to him his most memorable—frolic". Leslie "thought it would be a help to support those prisoners who are doing something creative instead of . . . destructive things", but David points out to her a dichotomy she didn't even consider: "Creativity isn't always an index of niceness".

Yet David can understand how Leslie, not knowing the background of the sculpture and thus perfectly objective in her appreciation of it, could be attracted to it, for he experienced something of the same detachment, only on a more conscious level, in his conversation with Doe:

> The conversation we had could even be called stimulating in a clinical sort of way. He described his "frolicking" in a kind of unreal and highly imaginative manner that wasn't always hideous to listen to. The strange beauty of this thing in the box here—disturbing as it is— somewhat parallels the language he used when talking about those poor kids. At times I

couldn't help being fascinated, though maybe I was shielding my feelings with a psychologist's detachment. Sometimes you have to distance yourself, even if it means becoming a little less human.

Just as there is more than one side to the artwork of John Doe (who, not uncoincidentally, is described as having a multiple personality), so does David reveal a personal duality that's a consequence of his work as a psychologist: it's possible for him to be intrigued professionally by what disgusts him personally.

As these ambiguities accumulate, Ligotti heightens their effect through a playful, almost devious, use of puns and double entendres—not the least of which is the real meaning of the word "frolic"—as if to show that even language has a natural inconsistency. It gradually becomes clear to the reader (if not David and Leslie) that the reliability and certainty of many commonplace things are qualified by circumstance of the moment: there's no assurance that they won't acquire a different, perhaps completely opposite, meaning when viewed in a different context. In the world as it's presented in **"The Frolic"**, it's difficult to determine anything with *absolute* certainty. Thus, by the end of the story, David—who assured Leslie earlier that "Prisoners like [Doe] don't escape in the normal course of things. They just bounce off the walls but not over them"—admits to uneasiness over the safety of Norleen and the family because "Much of the time I talked to him I had the feeling he was beyond me in some way, I don't know exactly how. I'm sure it was just the customary behaviour of the psychopath—trying to shock the doctor. It gives them a sense of power". At this point, though, on the verge of going up to check on Norleen for the last time, David knows he's contradicting himself. He's not sure about his family's safety any more than he's sure about anything else he's discussed that evening. At every point where he has sought reinforcement for what he thinks, he has found only contradictions or alternative possibilities. By the end of the story, he must confront the fact that his self-assurance has blinded him to many uncertainties, and that in a world where nothing is absolutely certain, the reality of what John Doe says can be doubted, but it can't be ruled out conclusively.

"The Frolic" ends with the characters realizing they've greatly overestimated the autonomy of what they consider to be real in their own world. In this respect, it's probably the most merciful of Ligotti's tales, which typically end with characters doubting everything they once thought true about their world because they've been swept into some other, incomprehensible, but more terrifyingly persistent "reality". It should be noted, though, that in Ligotti's fiction, any given reality is revealed to be a matter of perception. Characters may eventually come to think of the un-reality in which they become trapped as "more real", but ultimately unknowable.

Many of Ligotti's stories evolve out of the relationship perceived between some aspect of the normal world and its opposite. With the slightest inconsistency in the normal world or the least eccentricity on the part of people living in it, the borders between the normal and the abnormal

break down, and characters begin to doubt not only the certainty of what they know to be real, but even their own objective existence. The relationship between life and art is at the centre of **"The Troubles of Dr. Thoss"** and **"Alice's Last Adventure"**. The first story tells of Alb Indys, an insomniac artist with no imagination, who appropriates other artists' images and mixes them together in a completely alien context. After reading the legend of Dr. Thoss, who was thought to have gone mad but continued to practice medicine (much to the misfortune of his patients), Indys falls asleep. When he wakes up, he finds himself in an altered world in which it appears that Dr. Thoss is pursuing him. His grisly death at the end suggests that he himself may have been a little more than an image appropriated by someone else and mixed into a scenario containing the legendary Dr. Thoss. In **"Alice's Last Adventure"**, the woman telling the story is a writer of children's books who was named for the Alice of Lewis Carroll's stories. Recalling the scene where Alice peers into the looking glass and sees a room "not as 'tidy' " as her own, the author likens it to her own untidy life, which has been pockmarked by "nervous breakdown, divorce, remarriage, alcoholism, widowhood, stoic tolerance of a second-rate reality". Her account of several inexplicable experiences in the past year interspersed between the usual disorganized moments of her life leave the reader sensing that her life may just be a less tidy reflection of some more ordered existence being lived elsewhere.

Subjective and objective perceptions of reality are the basis of **"The Mystics of Muelenburg"** which opens with the narrator offering the following argument:

> If things are not what they seem—and we are forever reminded that this is the case—then it must also be observed that enough of us ignore this truth to keep the world from collapsing. Though never exact, always shifting somewhat, the *proportion* is crucial.

The narrator, we learn, has been told of a medieval town where, coincidentally, every person's mind "wandered in the shadows" at the same time, so that the unendurable truths underlying their perceptions of reality were revealed. This plants doubts about the real world in the narrator's mind, yet he must remain forever in doubt, for there is no way that he, as an individual, can test the validity of the argument.

All of Ligotti's stories have a psychological focus, especially the paranoia characters feel once they sense that reality is being manipulated by forces beyond them. Since many of his stories are told in the first person, the reader never knows how much to trust the sanity of the narrator. In stories like **"Alice's Last Adventure"**, **"The Mystics of Muelenburg"** and **"Dream of a Mannikin, or the Third Person"**, one might almost say the reader is *encouraged* to suspect the narrator's sanity, helping to establish yet another point of view on what is happening in the story. Ligotti explores the point at which the boundaries between sanity and insanity become blurred in **"Vastarien"**. This story tells of Victor Keirion, who seeks access to the world of dreams through a book a mysterious man buys for him. Keirion kills the man when he discovers the book was bought for him only so that the man could steal from Keirion the dreams he himself can't have. At the end of the story, which we have been seeing through Keirion's eyes, it's revealed that Keirion is imprisoned in an insane asylum for having committed the murder. Was the man, as Keirion claims, "using him in a horrible way, a way impossible to explain or to make credible?" Or is Keirion just a madman who killed someone and then fabricated an elaborate rationale for doing so? Either possibility is reasonable.

The opposite reality of which Ligotti seems to be fondest is the world of dreams. The relationship between reality and dream in his stories is summed up in a passage from **"Vastarien"**, in which Victor Keirion compares the town he sees in waking life to the dreamworld of the title:

> Victor Keirion belonged among those possessed by the conviction that the only value of this world lay in its power—at certain times—to suggest another world. Nevertheless, the place he now surveyed through the high window could never be anything but the most gauzy phantom of that other place, nothing save a shadowy mimic of the anatomy of that great dream. And although there were indeed times when one might be deceived, isolated moments when a gift for disguise triumphs, the impersonation could never be perfect or lasting. No true challenge to the rich unreality of Vastarien, where every shape suggested a thousand others and every sound disseminated everlasting echoes, every word founded a world. No horror, no joy was the equal of the abysmally vibrant sensations known in this place that was elsewhere, a place where all experiences were interwoven to compose fantastic textures of feeling, a fine and dark tracery of limitless patterns. For everything in the unreal points to the infinite, and everything in Vastarien was unreal, unbounded by the tangible lie of existing.

In Ligotti's dream stories, it's the very surreality of dreams—their capacity to make the smallest detail seem representative of something larger than life, something that transcends mundane existence—that makes them seem more real than waking life. However, it must be said that characters who encounter the dreamworld are grossly unequipped to deal with this immensity, and find that their experiences leave them bereft of any sense of a familiar, ordered reality. **"The Sect of the Idiot"** opens with its narrator arriving in his idealized conception of a small town, which he refers to, ironically, as "a land of dreams". He derives "a sense of serene enclosure" from the town's overhanging roofs and balconies. "Even the infinite nights above the great roofs of the town seemed merely the uppermost level of an earthbound estate, at most a musty old attic in which the stars were useless heirlooms and the moon a dusty trunk of dream". At the same time that it's a "clausrophobe's nightmare", "the town also conveyed a sense of endlessness". For the narrator, "this paradox was precisely the source of the town's enchantment".

That evening, the narrator has an unusual dream that opens him up to a sense of the vastness beyond his idealized perception.

> I felt that unseen things were taking place in obscure corners of this scene, none of them having any kind of reality to them, all of them vague and carried out in a state of sluggish inertia . . . I seemed to be an unseen speck lost in a convoluted festival of strange schemes. And it was this very remoteness from the designs of my dream universe, this feeling of fantastic homelessness amid a vast alien pattern, that was the source of unnameable and possibly limitless terrors.

Indeed, the narrator feels so alienated within his dream that he's almost displaced out of it: "nothing supported my existence, which I felt at any moment might be horribly altered or simply . . . ended. In the profoundest meaning of the expression, my life was of no matter".

In this dream, the narrator is drawn to a room that he sense runs on a different time stream, yet is "no different from any of the old rooms, the high and lonely rooms I had known in waking life, even if this room seemed to border on the voids of space and time and its windows opened onto the infinite outside". Inside this room the narrator is appalled to find a group of hooded, tentacled creatures who inspire in him a vision:

> This revelation—in keeping with the style of certain dreams—was complicated and exact, allowing no ambiguities or confusions to comfort the dreamer. And what was imparted to my witnessing mind was the vision of a world in a trance; a hypnotized parade of beings sleepwalking to the odious manipulations of their whispering masters, those hooded freaks *who were themselves among the hypnotized.* For there was a power superseding theirs, a power which they served and from which they emanated, something which was beyond the universal hypnosis by virtue of its very mindlessness, its awesome idiocy. These cloaked masters, in turn, partook in some measure of godhead, passively presiding as enlightened zombies over the multitudes of the entranced, that frenetic domain of the human sphere.

Upon awakening, the narrator finds himself looking at the world from an entirely new perspective. "The streets that I looked upon that motionless morning were filled with new secrets and seemed to lead into the very essence of the extraordinary . . . And somehow this undercurrent of deception, of corruption in disguise, served to intensify the town's most attractive aspects". But then he comes upon the room he saw in his dreams, and finds that it looks unnervingly the same. There are no hooded figures, but there is a little man whom he encountered at another place the day before. The man now appears "to be no more than a malignant puppet of madness", and he tells the narrator that he belongs to the hooded ones. The narrator flees, but upon arriving home discovers that one of his hands has turned into a tentacled appendage like those of the hooded ones, and that the transformation is slowly taking over his entire body.

As usual with Ligotti's fiction, the interpretation of this story is left open. The narrator's conclusion that "I have been lured away by dreams; all is nonsense now" suggests that he believes his dreams have lead him into madness.

Yet, his lament that "to suffer a solitary madness seems the joy of paradise when compared to the extraordinary condition in which one's own madness is merely an echo from the world outside" implies that he senses an even more profound dilemma: if he is not really mad, if his perceptions are actually an echo from the outside world, then that world is utterly intolerable. For what the narrator has come to understand is that the world and the people in it, including himself, may be no more than characters in the dreams of the hooded ones (who may themselves be figments of something else's dream). This realization is supported amply, though not conclusively, by what he felt during his dream: his personal sense of insignificance and the familiarity of the room of the hooded ones. It's as though in his dream, he was awakened to a reality to which he was oblivious, but in which he had been participating all of his life. This could account for the different appearance of the town upon his awakening and especially for his perception of another human being, who is not similarly enlightened, as "a puppet of madness". The end of the story leaves him trapped in a self-awareness that at the same time he is apart from this world, he is a part of it.

The sudden self-consciousness of characters that they're only passive figures not in control of their world is crystallized in the image of the puppet or mannikin, a recurrent motif in stories like **"The Sect of the Idiot", "Dr. Voke and Mr. Veech"** and especially in **"Dream of a Mannikin, or the Third Person"**, possibly Ligotti's most chilling deconstruction of reality. In this story, a psychoanalyst writes to a psychoanalyst friend with occult interests about Amy Locher, a patient the friend referred to him. Miss Locher, who says she is a secretary in her waking life, tells the analyst of a dream she had in which her job consisted of dressing mannikins in a store window. As the mannikin dresser, she has a dream in which she finds herself in a hallway that is supposed to be her bedroom, but is full of "people dressed as dolls . . . some of them have actually become dolls . . . others are at various intermediate stages between humanness and dollhood". To her horror, she realizes that she is posed in exactly the same way as the dolls. When a menacing presence grabs her from behind and speaks to her in the same type of voices she uses when dressing mannikins in her "waking" life, she awakens directly back into her life as Amy Locher—but upon looking behind her, she sees a mannikin face jutting through the headboard that only gradually withdraws back into the wall.

The psychoanalyst raises the possibility of Miss Locher's nightmare being like the solipsistic dream of Chuang Tzu—who awoke one morning from dreaming that he was a butterfly and could not be sure that he wasn't a butterfly dreaming he was a man—only to dismiss it. One would know when one was dreaming, says the doctor, since "the horrific feeling of unreality is much more prevalent (to certain people) in what we call human 'reality' than in human dreams, where everything is absolutely real", what Ligotti describes in "Vastarien" as "nightmare made normal". The psychoanalyst offers another explanation for the dreams of Chuang Tzu, which it turns out is also a pet theory of the occultist friend: "that which you call 'divine masochism', or the dotting of a Bigger Self terrorizing its

little splinter selves, precisely that Something Else Altogether scarifying the man-butterfly with uncanny suspicions that there's a game going on over its collective head".

The psychoanalyst has reason to suspect that his occultist friend either planted this notion in Amy Locher through post-hypnotic suggestion, or that Miss Locher and the friend are conspiring to upset him. For when Miss Locher failed to come to her second appointment and he went to search out the address she gave to him, he found it to be for a clothing store, with a mannikin in the window that looks exactly like her. When the physician confirms from a nearby phone booth that the phone number Amy Locher gave him is indeed the number to that store (one at which he discovers his friend buys clothes), he notes how "It seemed you might have accomplices anywhere, and to tell you the truth I was beginning to feel a bit paranoid standing in that phone booth". Driving home, he thinks he sees something in his backseat, but upon turning around finds nothing. "But the point is I had to check in order to relieve my moment of anxiety", he admits. "You had succeeded, my love, in getting me to experience a moment of self-terror, and in that moment I too became your accomplice against myself". The psychoanalyst also begins having dreams like Amy Locher's, in which he finds himself in an attic room full of "people dressed as dolls, or else dolls made up to look like people dressed as dolls", who invite him to " 'Become as we are . . . Die into us' ".

The story ends with the physician saying:

> Consciously, of course, I still uphold the criticism I've already expressed about the basic silliness of your work. Unconsciously, however, you seem to have awakened me to a stratum (*zone*, you would say) of uncanny terror in my mind-soul. I will at least admit that your ideas form a powerful psychic metaphor, though no more than that . . . Suppose I admit that she somehow was just a dream . . . Suppose I even admit that Miss Locher was not a girl, but actually a multi-selved *thing*—part Man, part mannikin—and with your assistance, reproduced itself for a time into existence, reproduced itself in human form just as we reproduce ourselves with an infinite variety of images and shapes, including mannikins. You would like to have me think of things like this. You would like to have me think of all the mysterious connections between different things.

The one suspicion that the physician doesn't voice, the one on which the story ends, is the one he is obviously laboring to rationalize away: that he is a smaller self who has suddenly become aware that he is being terrorized by a larger self "splintering and scaring itself to relieve its cosmic ennui"—in other words, that he and his entire world are merely a fictional diversion created by some incomprehensible Other.

Ligotti has written one tale which is not told from the victim's point of view. It would be unique for this reason alone, but Ligotti also explores what might be termed the ultimate breakdown between reality and unreality. **"Drink to Me Only with Labyrinthine Eyes"** is the account of a mesmerist hired to provide entertainment for "fancy persons at a fancy house". The mesmerist is not fooled by all of his audience's pomp and decoration: he observes that, "despite all the wealth, prestige and honors mingling in this rather baroque room tonight, I think they know how basically ordinary they all are". The mesmerist comes to this conclusion after the show he has just presented. He has put his assistant Seraphita, a somnambule, through the usual paces, having her perform contortions that seem only possible under the power of hypnosis. As a finale, he attempts to transform his assistant before the audience's eyes, into an angelic image of "celestiality discarnate". The image lasts but a moment and when the audience responds with only perfunctory applause, the mesmerist reasons, "They don't understand. They actually like all the mock-death and bogus-pain stuff better. These are what fascinates them".

This echoes an observation Ligotti makes in his incarnation as Professor Nobody, that we have a natural fascination with horror as a consequence of being "both victims and witnesses to this gruesome circus of living tissue". As the only creatures on earth who are self-conscious of their own morbidity and mortality, humans have an ambivalent relationship with supernatural horror. In one sense, part of us finds in it "a simple and necessary justification of the inevitable". Yet another part of us wants to "keep us from being absolute victims, striving to avoid our doom". It's in our failure to admit that "a sense of beauty and order, compassion for human hurt, offering others the benefit rather than the disadvantage of our doubts, nurturing a rich respect for the phenomena of decency and nobility—all of our best attributes are also our most troublesome and serve to bolster, not assuage horror" that we indulge "a penchant for self-torment, or mania to preserve a demented innocence in the face of gruesome facts".

This is what the mesmerist finds so "ordinary" about his audience: their fascination with "the mock-death and bogus-pain stuff" only reveals them to be obsessed with the underlying reality of their own mortality, no matter how much their extravagant lifestyles seem to deny it. So he intends to fulfill their unspoken wish. Seraphita, it turns out, is not the hypnotic subject—rather, she's a corpse whom the mesmerist has everyone believing is beautiful. Musing on mortality, the mesmerist notes how, "It is said that death is a great awakening, an emergence from the trance of life. Ha, I have to laugh. Death is the consummation of mortality and—to let out a big secret—only heightens mortal susceptibilities". Seen in this light, Seraphita is not the opposite of the living partygoers, but a more intensified expression of them. By the illusion of her beauty that he sustains, the mesmerist is all but saying that life itself is nothing more than a dream momentarily covering over the reality of death.

The scene with which the story ends is unsettling to say the least: as he has done at many other parties before, the mesmerist has left a posthypnotic suggestion for the partygoers that they will awaken at the sound of a chime. We leave the mesmerist outside on the front porch of the house, his fingers poised over the doorbell, and thinking, "We showed them what you could be, O Seraphita, now let's show them what you really are". There is perhaps no better image than this to sum up Thomas Ligotti's approach to supernatural horror. For one can see in the mesmerist's desire to cater to his audience's tastes—morbid as they may be—a resemblance to Ligotti the author. And one can't miss the suggestion here, as in the rest of his fiction, that he considers what we call reality to be little more than a dream from which we are about to be rudely awakened.

Thomas Ligotti with Carl T. Ford   (interview date 1988)

SOURCE: An interview in *Dagon,* Nos. 22-23, September-December, 1988, pp. 30-5.

[*Ford is an English critic who edited the award-winning horror fanzine* Dagon. *In the following excerpt from an interview, Ligotti discusses his beginnings as a horror writer, principal influences, and literary style.*]

[Ford]: *Your early fiction published in such journals as* Fantasy Macabre, Fantasy Tales *and* Nyctalops *seemed to project a maturity rarely glimpsed in a writer's first published efforts. Does this mean you have been writing fiction for quite a while before you sought publication?*

[Ligotti]: Not exactly. Aside from assignments in creative writing classes, I had written almost nothing until I stumbled upon the world of small press horror magazines around 1977. What I did write—and this can be traced back to my elementary school days—was always twisted and bizarre in some way, which seemed to be my natural manner. A strong literary urge was developed only after I entered college, but it was entirely without focus or direction. Consequently, I dreamed about writing a great deal and in a very abstract way, while having no clear idea what to write. Although I was a devoted reader of Lovecraft from the early 1970s, I believed that, with the exception of popular books and movies like *Rosemary's Baby,* the pursuit of supernatural horror in art died in a hospital room in Providence. It never occurred to me, having lived a somewhat sheltered existence as far as literary matters were concerned, that a cult of supernatural horror had survived into my lifetime. Then I came across a book entitled *Lovecraft at Last,* which listed in its bibliography the addresses of *Nyctalops* and *Whispers.* I wrote to *Whispers* and eventually received the most recent issue, number nine, and all available back issues. Enclosed with these magazines was the latest catalogue from Robert Weinberg, which fortunately listed several issues of *Nyctalops,* as well as a wealth of other small press publications. It was these magazines which made me realize that people were still writing horror stories and that—eureka! —this was exactly what I wanted to do. After working at it for a few years, some of those dream-inspiring magazines began accepting my stories, beginning with Harry Morris's publication of **"The Chymist"** in *Nyctalops.*

Cliché question, I'm afraid: Why do you prefer to write horror tales? What attracted you to the genre in the first place? And which writers would you say have influenced your work to the greatest extent?

It's not really a question of *preference,* since I've never been tempted to write anything that was not essentially nightmarish. The traditions and conventions of supernatural horror offer everything I need and answer all the sensations and attitudes that are important to me. What attracted me to horror? A cliché answer. Like many addicts of the genre, my introduction to supernatural horror came in the form of movies. I tortured myself indiscriminately and often with late-nite shockers on television and weekend matinees at the local theatres. And I still have nightmares in which I am watching something on a television or movie screen that, given the dream's power of suggestion and confusion, is literally *too horrible for description.* My introduction to horror fiction came much later and quite accidentally. When I was eighteen, I happened to be assisting at a garage sale held by my aunt, and among the items on display was a box of popular novels which included Shirley Jackson's *The Haunting of Hill House.* I vividly remembered a film called *The Haunting* and, after reading the first few paragraphs of the novel, I realized that this great film had been based on Jackson's book. You can see how ignorant I was. After finishing the novel, I felt a definite hunger for more horror stories, but not necessarily those of the Jacksonian type. As a kid, I always preferred the more clichéd Gothic horror movies set in the Victorian era over the ones with modern characters, and this was the kind of horror fiction I was seeking, the progeny of Poe's tales. But where was I to find it? Until reading Jackson's horror novel, I had read only a few works of literature in my entire life and almost all of those were reluctantly scanned under the duress of assignments in school. Having been something of a burn-out in the late 1960s, I never really learned my way around a library and the concept of bookstores was wholly alien to me, though I had at one time purchased a few occult books and underground comics in "head" shops. In any event, the first place I looked in my quest for horror literature was the local drugstore, of all places. What strange luck that contained in its racks was a paperback entitled *Tales of Horror and the Supernatural* by Arthur Machen. And I soon discovered that this was *exactly* what I had been looking for. The next book I bought, from that same drugstore, was the Ballantine edition of *Tales of the Cthulhu Mythos,* Volume 1. I found other paperback editions of Lovecraft's works in the book sections of department stores. Later I bought two selections of Algernon Blackwood's stories in a K-Mart store. Eventually I found out about bookstores, and my infancy as a reader, though not as a devotee of supernatural horror, was over.

Obviously, this thumbnail history doesn't really disclose what formed the basis of my attraction to the world of artistic horror, terror, nightmare, uncanny tales, weird tales, and all the other various terms that define nuances of what is essentially the same phenomenon. And the answer to *that* question, for me, would be no different from what it is for anyone else who has ever known the strange, terrible, and depressing experience of being alive. Who hasn't discerned the spectral quality of things, including ourselves? Or perceived that every avenue of our lives is finally lost in shadows? All it takes is a little disruption in our daily routine and the unknown opens up to us with all its charms and its horrors. Naturally we are attracted, in va-

rying degrees, to sympathetic recreations of this universal and all-important experience. I tend to emphasize this experience in my reading and writing because I've been very susceptible to it throughout my life, especially since my late teens. Recurring seizures of intense panic are just the thing to make you aware that you are living in the same universe that Poe and Lovecraft described.

As far as influences go, horror writers whom I have most slavishly taken as models are pretty obvious, primarily Poe and later H. P. Lovecraft, with a little Machen, James, and Blackwood creeping in along the way.

Some of your earlier stories contained touches of Lovecraftian lore, and you have recently incorporated Mythos themes in such tales as "Vastarien", "The Mystics of Muelenburg" and "The Sect of the Idiot". . . . What fascination do Lovecraft's cosmic tales hold for you?

I'm afraid the question involves too many ideas and emotions to give a thorough response. I can only answer in general terms that, in my eyes, Lovecraft dreamed the great dream of supernatural literature—to convey with the greatest possible intensity a vision of the universe as a kind of enchanting nightmare. While his materialistic brain would not allow him the solutions offered by supernaturalism, his deepest feelings demanded an answer or outlet in transcendent terms. No existing doctrines of the supernatural were acceptable to him, and so he could not avail himself of their core of mysticism, which he required to explain his sensations about the world. Hence, he had to invent a supermundane order of existence *that he could be sure was fallacious,* paradoxically allowing himself the freedom to vent, in completely good faith, his overwhelming sense that things are not what they seem. And thus he endeavored to symbolize those fascinating and intolerable "truths" that captivated him since early childhood. Such was his dream, as he incessantly delineated it in his critical writings and in his letters. Is it any wonder that he had so much difficulty in establishing this dream in prose fiction and so often fell short of this ideal? But whatever its flaws, his work is always true to the spirit of supernatural horror and is among the few achievements in literature to effectively express the most elusive and critical feelings of the race.

In a recent survey of amateur fiction in Crypt of Cthulhu, *Stefan Dziemianowicz outlined the similarities between "The Mystics of Muelenburg" and Lovecraft's "The Call of Cthulhu", in terms of plot structure and outcome. Was this a conscious development on your part?*

No, but I see Mr. Dziemianowicz's point. The opening of that story definitely does reflect my affection for those essay-like introductions that Poe and Lovecraft often used. The ending in which the narrator states: "And I, of course, am not to be believed"—I thought of as ironic, because the story is sort of melodramatic and unrealistic from the outset and isn't very scrupulously devoted to proving that there's any literal truth to the narrative.

Your prose often avoids excessive graphic imagery in favour of a subtle blend of psychological terror and cosmic awareness which keeps the horror off the printed page. Have you ever felt inclined to perhaps linger on graphic detail involv-

ing your terrors? Or do you feel that underscribed horror is far more potent when allowed to fester in the mind of the reader?

I have to admit that I have no aversion to violence in the arts. Quite the opposite, in fact: I can't think of a single film that I've ever admired that wasn't based on violence or the threat of violence. The only problem with violence in films is that so often it is not sufficiently grotesque and intense to be effective. As a reader of fiction, however, I tend not to respond to violent scenes transmitted through the medium of words printed in neat little lines on a page, such lines as: "And then the creature bit off the man's head". On the other hand, I greatly admired *Alien*. Given this peculiar viewpoint on violence, I don't often find myself tempted to make use of it in fiction, except in that oblique manner that seems to me the best way to commit fictional mayhem. . . .

[Your] tales often focus on society's "misfits" who find themselves seeking that escape away from the "real world" to the grey zones wherein reality is transformed and matter is grossly distorted. Often these characters discover this secondary world by undergoing a change, either mentally or physically. Why do you prefer to set your tales in these dreamlike/nightmarish zones? And why are your characters most often misfits of society?

The following may sound strange but hear me out. I discovered some time ago that I am not necessarily interested in fictional confrontations between the so-called everyday world and the world of the supernatural. If I am affected by a writer's vision, it is never because he has caused me to believe during the course of reading that there is truth to a given supernatural motif. If this were the case, I would long ago have gone mad following my first reading of "The Call of Cthulhu". And, in fact, I find Lovecraft's fastidious attempts at creating a documentary style "reality" an obstacle to appreciating his work. A related technique in supernatural fiction is to emphasize ambiguity regarding whether or not some extraordinary phenomenon actually occurred or was simply imagined by a character in the story. I don't find this to be the most profitable approach to writing supernatural fiction. What seems important to me is not whether the spectre is within or outside of a character—and the dictionary accepts both definitions, which should tell us something—but the power of the language and images of a story and the ultimate vision that they help to convey. For all that, everything that happens in every story ever written is merely an event in someone's imagination—exactly as are dreams, which take place on their own little plane of unreality, a realm of nowhere in which outside and inside are of equivalent ontological status, where within is without and both are phantasmal in essence. Lovecraft's Cthulhu aided his expression of certain sensations that were profoundly important to him. The pure *idea* of such a creation—not if it exists or doesn't—is the only thing of consequence. That idea may be rendered poorly or with great power, and beyond that—nothing matters. To me, reading a horror story should be very much like dreaming and the more dreamlike a story is, the more it affects me. I'm not the first to say that the nightmare, *not* the morning newspaper is the

ideal model for horror fiction. Even the supernatural element of a story is expendable. Nonetheless, what remains crucial is the *sensé* of the supernatural, the feeling of something dreadful and marvellous beyond all analysis, a feeling that may very well be inspired by something usually considered to be "natural" such as insanity or death. (Poe does this with incredible effect, especially in "The Tell-Tale Heart", where a merely gruesome vignette is used to evoke all the potential strangeness, mystery, and spiritual horror of death and madness). And the sense of the supernatural is something that arises from the confrontation of a reader with a story, not something that is dependent upon a division *within* the story between the real and the unreal. Of course, levels of fictional reality are fine and useful, but they are not necessarily a source of horror. Once you're trapped in a nightmare—I mean a really *good* nightmare—nobody has to ask you to suspend disbelief in the horror that is about to overwhelm you. Lovecraft considered the violation of natural law the most terrible conception of the human mind, but in a supernatural story this violation could just as easily deliver one from terror, depending on who is doing the violating and to what purpose. (I submit the benign wonders of Machen's "The Bowmen"). Lovecraft himself resented the bondage of time and dreamed of being liberated from it, yet the possibilities of this liberation are no sweet dream in his own "The Shadow out of Time". The meaning of an event depends upon the emotional colouration it takes from participants or spectators, how that event is experienced or portrayed. There are many examples in literature wherein a supernatural "intrusion" into ordinary reality is treated in a matter-of-fact manner and is not disturbing in the least. It all depends on how the material is presented by a writer and perceived by a reader. The feeling of horror derives from the dual nature of a phenomenon that is at once extraordinary and threatening in some very particular way. Thus the wide variety of forms that horror takes on in fiction—from the malefic midgets of Machen to the gargantuan gods of HPL. It's all extremely subjective. Point of view, whether in fiction or life, is everything. Universal chaos might be one hell of a good time, given the right perspective. And there are, after all, people who maintain a vivid belief in the supernatural without becoming conspicuous lunatics. So: Horror is not a matter of metaphysics but of emotion. This is why atmosphere is so important—it is the signal and generator of meaning; it can quicken an objectively neutral event with emotion.

Have any of your tales ever had an autobiographical basis?

No, not really, except in a strictly interior sense. Many of the stories reflect what I was reading at the time, the most obvious instance of this being "Alice's Last Adventure", written after my first reading of Lewis Carroll. And a number of stories, especially the early ones, were more or less imitations of the self-consciously histrionic romanticism of Poe and Nabokov. Diluted shadows of Gogol are in there too, as well as Beckett, Stanley Elkin, the Metaphysical Poets, and a whole pack of others. Recently I've consciously worked to give my tales a Lovecraftian cast, although more in the way of HPL's early stories such as "The Music of Erich Zann" and "The Festival" rather than the long scientific extravaganzas.

Many of your tales conjure up memories of those European horror movies of the early 20th century. Themes and motifs echo scenes from such classics as Murnau's Nosferatu, *Wiene's* The Cabinet of Dr. Caligari *and Carl Dreyer's* Vampyr. *Are you a big fan of these movies and has any of your fiction been written with these films in mind?*

Yes, I admire many of the images in those films, but that is about all I admire about them. I would even say that I prefer to look at stills rather than the films themselves, which to me appear crude and childish in their scenarios, acting, etc. The signature images of *Nosferatu, Caligari,* and *Vampyr* were familiar to me long before I actually saw them as films, and I imagined these works as far more strange than they turned out to be. However, it's the early misconception that I seem to recall when I think about the films and consequently much of their mystique remains in my imagination. No doubt I borrowed from *Caligari* the somnambulist act in **"Drink to Me only with Labyrinthine Eyes"**.

Kirkus Reviews   (essay date 1990)

SOURCE: A review of *Songs of a Dead Dreamer* in *Kirkus Reviews,* April 15, 1990, p. 524.

[*In the following review of* Songs of a Dead Dreamer, *the critic suggests that Ligotti's evocative, suggestive style is often effective but occasionally obscure.*]

First book—a collection of 20 stories—by a much-hailed stylist in the horror field.

All of Ligotti's pieces—written and published in small magazines over a span of seven years—show a growing mastery of poetic language, often at the expense of story. Despite the occasional vampire, there is no horror here, although H. P. Lovecraft breezes about Ligotti's imagination. Among the standouts are two "nonfiction" pieces that slip into fiction and parody: **"Notes on the Writing of Horror"** and **"Professor Nobody's Little Lectures on Supernatural Horror."** Essentially, Ligotti suggests rather than shows. This can lead to artistic triumphs, but too often here the occult event being suggested has to fight its way through a gummy luminescence. Recent stories are more effective for being less wordy. **"Vastarien,"** one of the winners, tells of the buying of an occult book that is not about something but is the thing it's supposedly about—in this case the shadowy empire of Vastarien, which is stolen from the book-buyer's mind every time he goes to sleep and dreams of Vastarien: he at last dreams his mind away. The best tale is **"The Lost Art of Twilight,"** about a young man, son of a dead human father and ripped from the womb of a just-killed vampiress, who finds himself changing over a long period from a half-human being into a full-blooded vampire: his once-beloved evening twilight is now the radiant dawn of night and hunger. This story has several fresh vampire effects too lively to be revealed here. The opening stories—**"The Frolic"** and **"Les Fleurs"**—are among Ligotti's weaker tales.

Now for the first novel? It could be an original, though one hopes for more richly human characters.

Michael Swanwick   (essay date 1990)

SOURCE: "Retribution and Redemption," in *Book World—The Washington Post,* September 30, 1990, p. 10.

[*Swanwick is an American science fiction and fantasy writer and critic. In the following review of* Songs of a Dead Dreamer, *he commends Ligotti's elaborate narrative style.*]

Midway through Thomas Ligotti's **Songs of a Dead Dreamer** is a story that comes close to summarizing his art. A hypnotist with impossible, "labyrinthine" eyes entertains a houseful of partygoers with illusions of surpassing beauty and strangeness. All they want, he knows, are cheap tricks, patently fraudulent death and make-believe pain. Determined to enlighten them, the hypnotist sets the revelers to dancing and flirting with his seemingly beauteous assistant, a woman only he can see is actually a resurrected and rotting corpse. The story ends at the instant he breaks the illusion and the unity of the dreadful and the sublime stands revealed.

Songs of a Dead Dreamer is full of such inexplicable and alarming delights. Nothing is rationalized. More often than not the horrors are only suggested. Everything is subordinate to the main task of evoking a wondering sense of supernatural dread. It is as if each individual work were but one facet of a single darkly transcendent vision of the world.

Rubbed free of the specifics of time and place, Ligotti's creations seem to float within their own private universe. The feel and language of **"Masquerade of a Dead Sword,"** in which a Renaissance bravo is persecuted by the dark soul of the world, are not greatly different from those of **"Dr. Locrian's Asylum,"** wherein a town must live with the legacy of authority abused. Even when Ligotti takes on the gleefully mad person of **"The Chymist,"** the voice is unmistakably and uniquely his own.

The unique, occasionally purple prose carries a heavy load of artifice—narrative frames, stories within stories, diary entries and quotes from imaginary works. At one point in **"Eye of the Lynx"** experience is rendered as pages in a nonexistent book. Given this self-conscious focus, it is no surprise that several works have a writer for protagonist. **"Notes on the Writing of Horror: A Story"** is a bravura example of this, a horror story disguising itself (at first) as an essay on the craft of writing. It's a star turn, and one that ought not to work, but in Ligotti's hands it does, gracefully and effortlessly.

These stories appeared first in small press magazines with names like *Nyctalops* and *Crypt of Cthulhu,* and as a result Ligotti's strange talent has grown and blossomed far from public view. He comes before us fully developed and in peak form, the most startling and unexpected literary discovery since Clive Barker.

If there is a justification of genre, it lies here. For this book is the pure quill, corestuff, a shot straight from the heart of horror. It is difficult to imagine someone who doesn't love the genre properly enjoying **Songs of a Dead Dreamer.** Put this volume on the shelf right between H. P. Lovecraft and Edgar Allan Poe. Where it belongs.

Darrell Schweitzer   (essay date 1990)

SOURCE: A review of *Songs of a Dead Dreamer*, in *Aboriginal Science Fiction*, November-December 1990, p. 29.

[*Schweitzer is an American fantasy and horror writer, editor, and critic. In the following review, he briefly surveys Ligotti's career through 1990 and commends the dreamlike imagery of his fiction.*]

So far, Thomas Ligotti has had an extraordinary career. Virtually all his short stories—there have been no novels—have been published in the little magazines—*Nyctalops, Crypt of Cthulhu, Dagon, Dark Horizons,* etc. Of the nineteen items in the [1990 edition of *Songs of a Dead Dreamer*], only one is reprinted from a professional source (Jessica Salmonson's *Heroic Visions II*). Even **"Alice's Last Adventure,"** acknowledged from Douglas Winter's *Prime Evil,* had its origins in the non-professional press. (Which is itself extraordinary. *Prime Evil* featured *new* work from Stephen King, Peter Straub, Clive Barker, and other heavies, but only Ligotti was allowed in with a reprint.) Normally this strategy would be the route to complete obscurity, but before long Ligotti was a kind of a legend, a latter-day H. P. Lovecraft who completely ignored the commercial markets in order to write his own, very unique fiction, which he would then toss away, with gentlemanly-amateurish naïveté, to any small-time editor who asked.

Sounds like the self-justification of a failed writer, right? Not in this case. It so happened that Ligotti *was* good and he *was* unique, and before long he was being praised by top writers and editors. The present collection is an expanded, revised edition of Ligotti's first book, also entitled **Songs of a Dead Dreamer,** published by Silver Scarab Press in 1986 in an edition of 300 copies and already one of the great rarities of our day. (It's been called "the *Outsider* of the '80s," referring to the seminal, and very collectable, Lovecraft omnibus of 1939.) Despite everything, Ligotti's reputation continued to grow. It works out like this once in a generation, if that often.

Now that the general public can actually read Ligotti's tales, they'll find a decidedly *odd* writer, very different from the typical straightforward and visceral horror novelist. Ligotti is closer to Robert Aickman or Walter de la Mare than to Clive Barker, and *weirder* than either. His stories are best described as J. K. Potter photo collages come to life. There is relatively little in the way of ordinary plot or sympathetic, reader-identifiable characters. The prose is straightforward enough—very precise, with a normal vocabulary—but Ligotti will be for most a difficult writer, simply because it's so hard to touch down to our own experience in his stories.

But his fiction has the flavor of disturbing dreams. The images are fresh and startling. Consider, for instance, the character who takes a prostitute (literally) to heart. No explanation. These things just happen in Ligotti stories:

> . . . But watch out for escapees. Actually she made only a single attempt. It wasn't serious, though. A drunk I passed on the sidewalk saw an arm shoot out at him from underneath my shirt, projecting chest-high at a perfect right

angle from the rest of me. He staggered over, shook the hand with jolly vigor, then proceeded on his way. And I proceeded on mine, once I'd got her safely back inside her fabulous prison, a happy captive of my heart.

("Eye of the Lynx")

Some characteristics of Ligotti's fiction:

One of Ligotti's dark charms is that his fictive voice does not fit into any neat marketing niche of esthetic pigeonhole. This narrative he writes is not splatterpunk or dark fantasy or Brit-style nasties. It's hardly an original comparison, but his two most obvious shelfmates might be Poe and Lovecraft. His tone suggests Poe as that worthy might have developed had he been accelerated into the 20th century; and Lovecraft, if H.P. had learned more adroit use of a modifier-filter.

Ligotti's prose is brooding, highly textured but precise, evocative. It's literate and unafraid to use vocabulary beyond the high school level when it has to. While Ligotti generally depends on atmosphere and suggestion for galvanizing shock, he also knows when and where to insert the steel needle of more literal terror. The effect is usually sparing, but it goes right to the raw nerve.

Most typically, Ligotti stitches together dark velvet crazy-quilts from the ragbag of nightmares. Dream imagery abounds. Probably no one currently in horror uses it better.

Edward Bryant, in a review of Grimscribe: His Lives and Works, Locus, *February, 1992.*

Michael Harris   (essay date 1990)

SOURCE: A review of *Songs of a Dead Dreamer,* by Thomas Ligotti, *Los Angeles Times Book Review,* December 23, 1990, p. 6.

[*In the following review, Harris praises Ligotti's ability to portray "a world of 'ultimate insanity' where the terror of the human condition can and must be faced."*]

In the last of [the stories in **Songs of a Dead Dreamer**], Thomas Ligotti describes its anti-hero this way: "Victor Keirion belonged to that wretched sect of souls who believe that the only value of this world lies in its power—at certain times—to suggest another world."

This is an idea that whispers or bellows throughout **Songs of Dead Dreamer.** A Renaissance swordsman, an American vampire, a children's author, a serial child killer, a lecturing "Dr. Nobody," members of secret societies, outcasts in lonely rooms and surreal cityscapes, the administrator of an asylum who tries not to cure the mentally ill but to drive them even crazier—all are drawn, willingly or unwillingly, to a world of "ultimate insanity" where the terror of the human condition can and must be faced.

Mystics tell us that the other world is a paradise.

Ligotti, . . . is an anti-mystic who tells us that the other world is merely true: "The only real thing is horror." Images of dolls and puppets recur; malign forces pull people's strings. Deluded by art and culture (symbolized by the hypnotist with "labyrinthine eyes" who narrates one story), we dance with a rotting corpse while embracing what we call "reality"—the fiction that it is a beautiful woman.

Fans of the genre will find Ligotti's stories closer to Poe's than to Stephen King's. Few of his characters are the kind we would care to identify with; most of his atrocities are suggested rather than explicit. He tests our patience with long blocks of exposition and the hermetic monologues of lunatics. Everything depends, then, on his wit and style, the quality of his inventiveness, the hypnotic, prophetic authority of his voice. And here Ligotti, darkly, shines.

Thomas Ligotti with Stefan Dziemianowicz and Michael A. Morrison   (essay date 1990)

SOURCE: An interview in *Science Fiction & Fantasy Book Review Annual, 1991*, pp. 109-18.

[*In the following excerpt from an interview that was conducted in 1990, Dziemianowicz and Morrison note the nightmarish imagery and symbolism of Ligotti's fiction and query the author regarding his inspirations and influences.*]

Since 1981, Thomas Ligotti has labored to transcribe nightmares into fiction. Of course, metaphorically speaking, this is what all horror writers strive to do—but Ligotti's preoccupation with the dark side of dreamland is literal. Like the phantoms of troubled sleep, his characters are grotesques who wear the idiot grin of the harlequin or the mask of tragedy and move with the jerky awkwardness of marionettes. The murky, claustrophic settings they inhabit resemble dreamscapes littered with images and symbols whose full meanings lie just out of reach. And Ligotti's horrors overtake them with the momentum of a nightmare rushing inexorably toward some inscrutable goal.

The "bad dream" is hardly a new motif in supernatural horror fiction; authors have exploited it for centuries, either as an intrusion of the irrational into the rationally-ordered world or as an elaboration of the fantastic in their fictions. But Ligotti departs from his predecessors in his use of the geography of dreams to render (in his words) "the sense of the supernatural, the feeling of something marvelous and dreadful beyond all analysis." Though his worlds are not unrealistic, he skews reality to generate moments of disorienting surreality in **"The Voice in the Bones"** and **"The Greater Festival of Masks,"** a sense of oppressive paranoia in **"The Troubles of Dr. Thoss"** and **"The Christmas Eves of Aunt Elise,"** baroque images of corruption in **"Drink to Me Only with Labyrinthine Eyes"** and **"The Chymist,"** and new perspectives on the distinction between the ostensibly real and the unreal in **"Dream of a Mannikin"** and **"The Strange Design of Master Rignolo."** That these effects seem perfectly natural, given the settings of the stories, in no way diminishes the sense of supernatural dread they evoke.

Although they radiate intimate knowledge of the tradition of supernatural horror, Ligotti's stories are respectful, rather than derivative: Poe's imprint glistens in the rich, thickly textured prose that creates their almost suffocating atmosphere; the influence of Lovecraft is evident in their metaphysical foundation, the sense of a malignant universe springing horrors randomly upon hapless victims; and, like M.R. James' ghosts, Ligotti's horrors compel a shudder by suggesting that there is more to them than meets the eye. At the same time, one sees traces in Ligotti's tales of his familiarity with writers whose fiction is *sui generis:* the wicked word play of Nabokov, the philosophical rumination of Borges, the interplay of humor and horror in Gogol. Ligotti synthesizes these and other influences through his vivid imagination into a vocabulary that combines controlled description and skillful juxtaposition of images to render his eerie visions with disturbing clarity.

Thus, Ligotti's fiction forces us to discard the yardsticks by which we measure most modern horror stories. We become engrossed less in his plots than in his arrangement of events, their strange rhythms and obscure logic. We rarely sympathize with his characters, for their lives seem funhouse mirror distortions of our own. Above all, we cannot gauge the impact of his horrors by their veracity for Ligotti strives to loosen the bonds between the reader's world and the world of his fiction. Ultimately, we share with the denizens of those worlds only the terrifying discovery that the masters of our fate are incomprehensible and anything but benign.

To date, Ligotti's artistry has earned him the admiration of a small group of devoted readers but scant notice from the literary mainstream. To some extent, his neglect by horror fans is understandable, for the contents and contexts of his stories deviate sharply from those found in most modern horror fiction. One can read **"Alice's Last Adventures," "The Frolic"** and **"Conversations in a Dead Language"** as life studies from the darker corners of our own world, but most of Ligotti's work lacks the realistic concerns that predominate in the genre: the familiar trademarks (name brand products, contemporary social and political issues), locales (the isolated New England cottage, the urban street scene, the mundane suburban neighborhood), characters (the nuclear family, the angst-ridden teenager, the magically-endowed child) and situations (alienation on the job, financial hardship, divorce). Rather than create a semblance of reality into which horror obtrudes, he evokes a world where horror is the norm. Small wonder that, with the exception of the vampire who instructs the reader in **"The Lost Art of Twilight,"** his stories are virtually devoid of traditional agents of the supernatural, monsters in the conventional sense of the word.

Not surprisingly, Ligotti's fiction resists categorization: it steers clear of the graphic excesses of splatterpunk, but its intensity exceeds that of dark fantasy. Furthermore, although working in a genre which market forces have increasingly driven towards novels, Ligotti writes short fiction—he even has expressed reservations about the suitability of the novel length for works of supernatural horror. Indeed, his essays **"The Consolations of Horror"** and **"Notes on the Writing of Horror,"** reveal him as one of the few writers working today with a clearly articulated philosophy of horror. As a result, his work has been all but banished to the small press ghetto, in magazines like *Eldritch Tales, Grue, Crypt of Cthulhu, Dagon, Fantasy Macabre, Nyctalops, Nocturne* and *Deathrealm*.

[Dziemianowicz]: *In your 1988 interview with Carl Ford in* Dagon, *you mentioned that your first real reading experience in supernatural horror fiction was Shirley Jackson's* The Haunting of Hill House. *Yet you went from Jackson's work to less-modern authors like Machen, Blackwood and Lovecraft. What did you find lacking in Jackson that made you want to pursue these author's works further?*

[Ligotti]: To a large extent, the appeal of Jackson's book was a carry-over from the film, *The Haunting,* which I found had been a scrupulous adaptation. Aside from their obvious spectral highpoints, I admired the way that both the novel and the movie were so single-mindedly focused on conveying the sense of something gone rancid in the supernatural order. There's almost a complete absence of distractions from this aim, very little intrusion of ordinary life which can break the spell of a horror story. But in Jackson's novel, like all novels written in the objective manner, there's practically no feeling of the author's presence. And this is very much the feeling you get when reading Lovecraft, Machen, Poe, and a few others—the sense that here is someone who's really haunted by the nightmares he's writing about.

So the personality of these authors as reflected in their fiction particularly interested you. What did you, a writer for the Eighties, find so attractive in turn-of-the-century writers, what stimulated you to write in the tradition they had created?

In the case of Lovecraft, yeah, I was immediately inspired to, as you put it, "explore the tradition." My first ambition as a horror writer, as I recall, was to contribute a single Cthulhu Mythos story to the raggedy canon. That was my earliest infantile memory. The appeal of the older authors was not necessarily the same in every case and not necessarily related to the period in which they wrote. With Lovecraft it was much more thorough at every level than it was with Machen. Machen's Catholicism is an obstacle for me, whereas for Lovecraft there are very few matters of philosophy or personal temperament that I can't relate to my own experience. But every one of the authors who appeal to me are considered rather eccentric in many aspects of both their lives and their works. "Naturally fouled up," as the poet Philip Larkin put it.

I believe that in the Carl Ford interview you also said that your introduction to Lovecraft was through volume one of the Ballantine Books edition of Tales of the Cthulhu Mythos. *I find it interesting that you got turned on to Lovecraft through that book, because while it included "The Call of Cthulhu," some of the other contributions were among the worst Mythos stories ever written. One might just as easily have been put off from the Mythos, thinking, "Well, maybe one person could write this stuff, but no one else can." Do you think you would have reacted as strongly to Lovecraft if, instead of "The Call of Cthulhu," the first of his stories*

you read had been a Poesque one, like "The Outsider" or "The Rats in the Walls"?

I think about the only stories I might not have reacted to would have been the Dunsany imitations. I think whatever I read by Lovecraft, I would have reacted pretty much the same way that I reacted to "Call." There's a lot in his work that says: Here is somebody who has swept everything in the world aside. All daily life, society, everything that makes up almost all of fiction, almost all of literature, really. Lovecraft's work is focused on one very narrow experience, and that is the experience of the knowledge of something terrible.

I feel that the Cthulhu Mythos was something I wanted to emulate as an expression of some ultimate view of things. Just the idea of a forbidden knowledge, and its transcription, or attempted expression; something too terrible to live with, and at the same time captivating as a strange transcendent evil.

You're getting at something that I enjoy about Lovecraft and yet have problems with. In a way, his stories trivialize the very idea of writing a story in order to describe what is going on. I guess that's a problem in all horror fiction. The enormity of the concept the writer is dealing with sort of overwhelms the idea of trying to transcribe it into words. I haven't been able to decide if Lovecraft was trying to create an "out" for himself, so he could say "I can't describe it, because there are no human words to do so," or if that was indeed part of the intended effect of his work, that he would leave you saying, "Well of course you can't describe it, but it was a nice try."

A lot of times, with any horror writer, you feel, "this person is faking it." No matter how profound and intense the motive for writing this story and the vision behind the story, you still have somebody writing words on paper, and the sentences follow one another, and all the characters are moving in and out of rooms . . . that whole artifice. So yes, there's an innate hypocrisy in probably all of literature, but it becomes really evident in horror fiction, which intends to tell of some extreme experience. Whereas if you have somebody writing about their trip to the drug store, you wouldn't accuse them of faking it.

This broadens the whole idea of willing suspension of disbelief—

I hate that term! The idea that a reader deigns to accept fantastic incidents in a work of literature is itself utterly bizarre. My interest in a story diminishes to the extent that its author is concerned with my credence.

I mention that only to elaborate on the inherent ludicrousness of somebody sitting down after such an experience and trying to write it out.

You know, whatever it is, this experience, supernatural or not, it's just something that you're using as literary fodder. That's it. Literature is a diversion like any other. It's not going to save your soul or your sanity. It's not going to illuminate some ultimate reality. The most a writer can do is sort of allude to some personal concern, however dire and intense it may be, in the course of amusing a reader. Even if your intention is to lay bare your soul and expose the most awful truths of creation, you end up at best producing the literary equivalent of some sporting spectacle. In fact, watching a horse race, for example, can be a spiritually, emotionally and intellectually richer experience than reading.

I find it interesting that you mentioned that one of your first ambitions as a horror writer was to write a Cthulhu Mythos tale, because you are one of the few people dealing with Lovecraft's cosmic metaphysics who hasn't dipped into the cosmogony he created.

Well, that was his territory.

But when you read Tales of the Cthulhu Mythos, *you saw other people do it. Was your reticence simply that you didn't want to poach on another writer's territory, or did you sense that using another writer's references wouldn't allow you to express yourself freely?*

Oh no, at the time I didn't even approach that level of self-consciousness. I was glad to be able to have an idea for a story and be able to write it to the last sentence. I don't know that my horror tales have anything to do with Lovecraft's cosmic metaphysics. I know that I lack two crucial elements of Lovecraft's sensibility-a sense of history and a scientific perspective on life.

For the most part, you seem to also avoid writing about traditional horror figures; such figures don't seem very "Ligottiesque." In your work, we don't see vampires, werewolves, the usual creatures that have become clichés in the field. But we do see some of the standard scenarios: the person who comes across the book of forbidden knowledge, the person who pries into corners he shouldn't pry into. Do you feel that traditional creatures have no value for you or in some way would limit your vision?

Not necessarily. I did write a story with a vampire in it, **"The Lost Art of Twilight."** Of course, any traditional figure can be used to a writer's purpose. I don't condescend to folklore or the history of cinema.

I can only assume that most such creatures haven't lent themselves to your ideas for fiction.

Right. Also, you have to believe that a lot of vampire, werewolf and ghost fiction is written just for the sake of writing a vampire, werewolf or ghost story, simply because vampire stories are hot at a particular time. There are so many ghost stories because there was a time when that was the most natural form if you wanted to write a supernatural story. The traditional supernatural figures are by definition the most familiar and accessible, therefore lending themselves most readily to fiction written for a popular audience.

On the other hand, M. R. James wrote ghost stories that weren't necessarily ghost stories—

For instance, "Oh Whistle and I'll Come to You My Lad"—

Right, his ghosts were very idiosyncratic, as was the manner in which he presented them. James' specters are so atrocious and bizarre, and their intentions are so malicious, that the famous "restraint" of his stories seems like the tentative restraining of a maniac. That's not the feeling that you get from a lot of ghost stories written at that time, for example the psychic investigation tales of Blackwood. In M. R. James, you get the feeling that someone is trying to transcribe a nightmare. There's so much that is off-kilter even in the realistic sections of his stories. Not to mention that James's personality comes through. James is somebody who found a natural medium for expressing a very grim and morbid temperament. He's sort of the A. E. Housman of supernatural horror.

Are you saying that essentially supernatural creatures are not in themselves objects of horror, but are tools for getting at more conceptual horrors?

Sure. Well, most of the time they are used for their own sake, and it's rather silly. I wrote a letter once to a writer I very much admire—I should say, rather, a poet, Joseph Payne Brennan. And I told him how much I appreciated his poetry, and took him to task for his fiction, in which I thought he used the supernatural for its own sake, to write mere adventure stories, and he wrote back a very nice letter saying that he wrote poetry for himself and fiction for the marketplace. Not that a supernatural story ought to serve as an allegory, though it has done exactly that for much of its history. But a really good supernatural tale should have a symbolic force in the way certain objects and events in dreams have a power to affect us, far beyond their literal significance. This is fairly basic.

One gets the idea that you have read works by many classic horror writers. Your work has a sense of the tradition of supernatural horror. As you have noted in other interviews, you can see the influence of other authors in your writing.

Yes, but there's more involved than just the horror tradition. There are other authors whom I admire and either have outright attempted to imitate or unwittingly have imitated who are not directly related to supernatural fiction, though they may be to some extent coherent with it. Some of these authors are Vladimir Nabokov, Bruno Schulz, various authors related to the symbolist movement in Europe, the philosopher E. M. Cioran, and Jorge Luis Borges.

I guess we could go story by story, and I could give you an author who comes to mind.

I thought that might be asking too much of you.

Well, I feel maybe I should take the fifth at this point. But if I'm going to do this properly I might as well come clean. Name a story.

"Dream of a Mannikin."

That was one of a number of stories that was written while I was reading Vladimir Nabokov, and it very much reflects, however grotesquely, the manic, hyperbolic, lyrical tone of Nabokov's fiction.

"The Greater Festival of Masks."

That's a real mishmash: German expressionism, Samuel Beckett, Ramsey Campbell, and other stuff.

"Masquerade of a Dead Sword."

Poe's "Masque of the Red Death" as rewritten by a sword 'n' sorcery hack.

"The Troubles of Dr. Thoss."

M. R. James, and the artwork of Harry Morris, whom I admire greatly.

"Drink to Me Only with Labyrinthine Eyes."

Stanley Elkin and the English metaphysical poets. Let's give 'em a hand, folks.

How about "Vastarien"?

Let's see. Maybe I can claim that as an original—or relatively original, since it was a half-hearted resurrection of a literary ambition I had before I became the assiduous epigone I am today. A long time ago, I used to daydream, as many have, about an ideal horror story. This was before I had ever written words down. I didn't know exactly what this story would be like, what the setting or characters would be, just some abstract notions like: "a story dreaming itself" and "absolute strangeness." I wrote a few stories in an attempt to approximate that ideal, but they weren't very good. So eventually I abandoned the whole idea.

One of your earliest stories, "The Last Feast of Harlequin," was published in the April 1990 Fantasy & Science Fiction. *It's much more naturalistic than one expects of a Tom Ligotti story. Although one can see affinities between that story and a more abstract, recent one, like "The Voice in the Bones" in* Crypt of Cthulhu #66, *there's a sharp contrast between the two in style and approach. Could you characterize the evolution in style between those two stories?*

This actually gets back to my notion of the ideal horror story. **"Voice in the Bones"** was one of the stories I wanted to set in the world of **"Vastarien,"** but it didn't turn out quite to be my ideal horror story. The reasons for this failure are kind of hard to explain.

Well, I'm glad you're addressing it, because somewhere I have written down the question "If Tom Ligotti could write the ideal horror story, what would it be?"

The ideal horror story, as I see it, is something that would be almost total nonsense to read but would have all the impact of that total nonsense that goes on while you're asleep, and that causes you to wake up screaming with no explanation why.

Do you think it is possible to write a completely abstract supernatural horror story, one with no definite setting or characters?

This is sort of like Flaubert's idea of writing a book without a subject. And of course Lovecraft described in his letters the dream of writing a story that would be a kind of play of cosmic forces.

This reminds of Ionesco's idea of a play that no audience would ever see, which brings us back to what you were saying about the artifice of writing horror fiction. No matter how you try to avoid it, you're going to bump into a paradox.

Exactly. I have some notes about the "forbidden book," in the Lovecraftian sense, that is, a kind of metaphysical obscenity, an offense against all conception of order. I think my conclusion was that the forbidden book would require the forbidden author to write it, though it might be a work of imagination and not, like the *Necronomicon*, a book of genuine revelation. Somebody probably could write such a book, but he would have to be so twisted and still capable of composing a text. Possibly, such a book might be written inadvertently, as an automatic composition. Of course, if you did write it, it would disturb you so much that you would no doubt destroy it. I think that there are probably a lot of horror writers who have had ideas that are too sick to think about very long, let alone develop into a story.

That reminds me of the Monty Python routine about the guy who develops the joke that's so funny that it kills him when he tells it.

Right. That's where the hypocrisy of horror writing really comes in—and a lot of the fun of it. If horror stories really had the effect of a nightmare on you, then no one would pick them up. The purpose of . . . not all horror stories, but at least a certain kind of horror story, could be actually to block horror or transform it into something that it isn't. I'm not talking about making it into entertainment, but more of using it as a form of self-hypnosis to escape the human predicament. In a story I wrote called **"The Medusa,"** the main character writes, "We may hide from horror only in the heart of horror." This goes completely against yourself as a functioning person who doesn't want to die or suffer some extraordinarily terrible experience. Nobody does. You're lying if you say you would. Or you lack imagination.

I wanted to get into the absence of definitively good and evil people in your fiction. The context of your stories seems quite different from the mundane world in which we judge what's good and what's evil. In your essay, "The Consolations of Horror," you talk about "booting non-supernatural horror right off the train." Do you see limitations in non-supernatural horror, most of which is rooted in questions of good and evil?

Well, so is most supernatural horror fiction.

It's a pretty easy template to work from.

It's also what most people care about. It's something that you're encouraged to write about, and seems to lend a work instant significance and weight. But good and evil, in the traditional moral sense, simply isn't an issue for a lot of writers, particularly modern writers. Beckett, for example. You would be hard pressed to write even the briefest paper on good and evil in Beckett. With Beckett, you've got nothing, and you've got . . . something. And not much of the latter.

For mortals like myself, it's very difficult not to think in terms of good and evil, moral or otherwise. Being something of a pessimist, I tend to think, in those rare moments when I really think, that existence is by its nature evil. And nothing is good.

I'd like to talk about the recurring motifs and metaphors you have evolved. I'm thinking specifically of puppet and mannequin figures, masks, the harlequin; one of my favorites is the image of reality on the "other side" as untidy, cluttered, junk-ridden. What sort of power do these things have for you, and how did they come to figure so prominently in your work?

I couldn't tell you, but they've haunted me since childhood. They're also stock characters and paraphernalia in literature, even in horror literature. A lot of it derives from nineteenth century literature: Hoffmann and the German Romantics, the French Decadents, Poe.

In many of your stories there comes a point where a character is grasping for the meaning of what is happening to him or her, but finds that meaning is simply not forthcoming. Characters are dragged off to their fates without the slightest consolation of knowing at least what is happening to them or why. I see this as a contrast to the predicament of Lovecraft's characters, who know why, or at least understand what has happened, and must live with the horror, knowing that they can't change it. Do you find the concept of something incomprehensible happening to you particularly terrifying?

I think everybody does. That's the foundation of the type of horror that interests me. Implicit in a weird tale is the inquiry, "Why me?" or simply, "Why?" Characters shout the question, or mutter it quietly. Much of the time, the reader must ask it on behalf of the doomed. But there never is any answer. And that's a situation we all ultimately find ourselves in.

Certainly that's part of the structure of dreams. After we wake up, we can rationalize why we dreamed something or felt that way, but in the dream, such answers aren't available. One thing just spills over into the next.

Exactly, we're left with an abstract panic. The Lovecraft stories I admire most are not the ones that have a lot of surface explanation, stories like "The Festival," "The Music of Erich Zann," "The Colour out of Space," and so on. Poe is a real master of this method, of course. In "The Masque of the Red Death," the surface horror is merely death, which appears as a symbol for something that is truly more terrible.

*One aspect of your work that I appreciate is its irony. In stories like **"Dream of a Mannikin"** or even **"Conversations in a Dead Language,"** there's an irreverent tone. It strikes me that such irony would have been almost impossible in the works of some of the classic writers, say Lovecraft or Blackwood. How is your work able to accommodate it and what does it achieve?*

I'm not sure my work is all that ironic. In **"Conversations in a Dead Language,"** perhaps you mean an unsympathetic perspective on the character.

I'm also thinking of the tone which seems to be—

—uncaring? Cruel?

Yeah, almost like you're poking fun at the character. There's something comical about it. Perhaps we need a better definition of irony.

I'm not sure it's irony that you're talking about. I don't see irony at all. I've never been real irony-conscious. The comic and the cruel are masterfully mixed in the work of a number of authors I admire, preeminently Roland Topor and Nikolai Gogol. Gogol's "comic" stories are all quite grim, and Topor's are as sick as underground comics.

Shifting gears a bit, why do you believe it is difficult to write a good or convincing supernatural horror novel? Would you care to comment on the few novels you do like and why they succeed or on ones that come close but don't succeed?

To give a simple answer to a complex issue: supernatural literature traffics in characters and incidents of an extravagant type which properly should turn up only in poetry, a genre whose stylistic and structural artificiality best accommodates the artificial, unreal subjects of the supernatural. Fiction, on the other hand, is a genre more suited to depicting the ordinary and the natural, being closely related to journalism, history, biography and other forms of prose documentation. So when you take subjects fitted to poetry and attempt to express them in fiction, you end up with something that's a bit ludicrous, like a grizzly bear in a tuxedo. I think this explains why most enduring and successful works of supernatural literature are the ones that most resemble poetry in their highly artificial approach to storytelling.

Obviously, the best stories of Poe, Machen and Lovecraft are evidence of this, but so are those of M. R. James, who created a wonderfully artificial manner for depicting an artificial world.

*In **"The Consolations of Horror,"** you skewer many hypotheses that have been offered for why we read horror. Why do you think critics need to analyze why we like horror fiction? Why did you add to critical speculation on the topic?*

I don't exactly think there's a need to analyze the motives for reading horror fiction, though a lot of people obviously would like to prove that there's something justifiable in social or psychological or even spiritual terms about this indulgence in what seems to be a morbid vice. Myself, I'm content to view a taste for supernatural literature as precisely what it appears to be: a means for damaged psyches to express their experience in a damaged universe, or to find reflection of this experience in the writings of others.

Finally, why do you think horror is looked down on as the bastard spawn of genres? Is this attitude generated by the quality of the fiction produced, or the nature of the literary form?

Horror fiction represents neither the worst nor the best of what has been achieved in literature. Since it focuses on a very narrow range of experience, it's understandably dismissed by those who believe that a comprehensive reflection of life in all its aspects is the hallmark of literary excellence. On the other hand, there are those who believe that only the essence, not the multifaceted elaborations, of existence should form the subject of artistic expression. And a few of us find in supernatural horror the closest thing to an expression of that essence.

Robert M. Price   (essay date 1991)

SOURCE: "Thomas Ligotti's Gnostic Quest," in *Studies in Weird Fiction,* No. 9, Spring, 1991, pp. 27-31.

[*Price is an American critic whose writings are principally devoted to the fields of Christian theology and the works of H. P. Lovecraft. He is the editor of* Crypt of Cthulhu: A Pulp Thriller and Theological Journal, *which published essays on Lovecraft and other writers of supernatural horror literature. In the following excerpt, Price examines the "distinct and disturbing worldview" that informs Ligotti's fiction.*]

Thomas Ligotti has made quite an impact on today's weird fiction field. There are many practitioners of "Dark Fantasy", a subgenre characterized by "mature", i.e. mainstream novelistic, writing. And many of these are storytellers well worth the reading. But in Ligotti the true aficionado of the weird finds this generation's Poe, today's Clark Ashton Smith. Lin Carter's judgment was right on target: "This Ligotti chap astonishes me. Seems like he came out of nowhere just recently and is already an accomplished master, as far as I'm concerned. His subtlety of effect, control of mood and atmosphere, and sheer power of eerie suggestiveness would have delighted Lovecraft himself."

Virtually all of Ligotti's fiction enshrines and presupposes a distinctive and disturbing worldview (whether held personally by the author himself, or fabricated for literary effect as I suspect and hope!). As Ligotti's character Professor Nobody explains to us, his eager students, the "logic of supernatural horror . . . is a logic that is founded on fear; it is a logic whose sole principle states: 'Existence equals Nightmare.' Unless life is a dream, nothing makes sense." In **"The Sect of the Idiot"**, this mad worldview is identified with H. P. Lovecraft's: all is idiot chaos. It is possible in Ligotti's universe to attain to a revelatory glimpse of this final truth of insanity, a "terrible enlightenment . . . revealing an intolerable knowledge, some ultimate disclosure concerning the order of things." And those who have shared this vision, unhappy prophets, seem always in Ligotti's tales to find themselves incarcerated in the microcosm of the madhouse, as do Victor Keirion (**"Vastarien"**) and John Doe (**"The Frolic"**). Dr. Locrian's Asylum actually functions as an occult research laboratory because the voices of the inmates "speak the supreme delirium of the planets . . . dancing in the blackness. In the wandering words of those lunatics . . . the ancient mysteries are restored." The author here sounds almost like psychologist R. D. Laing.

If it is the so-called madmen who perceive the truth of the Ligottian cosmos, what does this bode for the legions of the conventionally sane? Just that: we proclaim ourselves sane by mere shared convention, shared delusion. The monologue of Klaus Klingman in **"The Mystics of Muelenburg"** reveals that without the constant effort of us all to "stick to the common story", the world as we "know" it would rapidly begin to blur and dissolve, and in the rare moment of weariness we may be caught off guard and "let down our burden" of what sociologists of knowledge Berger and Luckmann have called "cognitive

world-maintenance". All this a Ligotti character calls "a hallucinatory view of creation" (**"The Mystics of Muelenburg"**). What is envisioned here might be called a version of George Berkeley's epistemology of Immaterialism without its lynchpin, God. To the old question whether a tree falling in a deserted forest makes noise, Berkeley answered Yes, because the omniscient God perceives it even if no one else does. Reality is perception and nothing more. But perceived reality is objectified, at least relative to us, because God sees all. In Ligotti's world, there is no such guarantee, so we have to keep careful watch or we will disabuse ourselves of "the myth of a natural universe—that is, one that adheres to certain continuities whether we wish them or not" (**"The Mystics of Muelenburg"**).

A related image is that of group hypnosis. In **"The Sect of the Idiot"** the insect-like Norns of Azathoth (My nomenclature for Ligotti's characters) keep the "world in a trance; a hypnotized parade of beings sleep-walking to the odious manipulations of their whispering masters, those hooded freaks *who were themselves among the hypnotized.*" Among their ranks we might also number the golem-creating wizard of **"Mad Night of Atonement"**, who himself turns out to be a vivified puppet.

A smaller-scale example of the same phenomenon, a microcosmic example if you will, is provided by the hypnotist of **"Drink to Me Only with Labyrinthine Eyes"**, whose spell keeps the whole crowd under the illusion of beauty until they are rudely awakened to what has all the while been the true horror of the situation. In this tale, which recalls at once "The Emperor's New Clothes" and Lovecraft's "The Outsider", we are tempted to see depicted Ligotti himself and his literary mission: to spin a web of enchantment carrying his audience to the final realization of the horror of all existence.

Closely related to the hypnosis theme is that of puppetry. Ligotti frequently compares characters to mere puppets, especially in **"Dream of a Mannikin"** and **"Dr. Voke and Mr. Veech"**. We should not overlook the many powerful puppet images of **"Mad Night of Atonement"**, with its puppet-making puppet-wizard, symbolizing the Creator himself, whose earthly guise is revealed to be that of a mannikin, and who created the world itself to be "a third-rate sideshow of beatific puppetry". We ourselves are destined to become no more than the "ghosts of puppets".

Ligotti's work, and his picture of reality, must be seen against the background of the Decadent movement. The finally desirable, beautiful, and true is "that summit or abyss of the unreal, that paradise of exhaustion, confusion, and debris where reality ends and where one may dwell among its ruins" (**"Vastarien"**). Mad Dr. Haxhausen extends the Creator's invitation to join him in his "paradise of ruins" (**"Mad Night of Atonement"**). Strictly speaking, the glory of decadence in view here is not the decay of reality on its own perceived level, but rather the decay, collapse, or ruination of that very level of perception.

Ligotti's most powerful statement of the decadent quest is surely the striking tale **"Order of Illusion"**. Here a member of a secret sect of decadents quits their ceremony, rather like Gautama spurning his ascetic brotherhood, in search of greater depths of enlightenment elsewhere. The protagonist wishes to sink ever deeper and so resolves to organize his own private rituals of defilement and debasement. Excrement is his sacrament, aborted foetuses are his altar boys, blasted trees his groined arches. For a moment he is satisfied—until these props of profanation start to take on, in his appreciative eyes, a numinous glow. They have become vehicles for the Holy in the strange form in which the decadent seeks it. But then all is lost! For how can one go further to profane the Holiness seen in such a form as this? Ligotti's hierophant of the hideous has discovered a veritable dialectic of decadence. One comes to see beauty and mystic wonder in the degraded, but then degradation itself comes, *ipso facto,* to be transfigured! And then the final degradation is the despair the decadent feels at ever finally being able to savor degradation—since the very savoring causes the dreaded transfiguration! Yet only one who has reached this stage of jaded frustration and disillusionment is fit to assume the pontificate of the bacchantes of desolation, which the protagonist does at the end of the story.

The hypnotized herd of the conventionally sane (Lovecraft's "self-blinded earth-gazers") may, in their uneasy fear, seek to fortify the illusion, as has the unnamed former owner of the strange house now occupied by Raymond Spare (**"In the Shadow of Another World"**). The peculiar structure had been built with certain safeguards in order to shield it from the incursions of the battering waves of extra-dimensional realities without. The result was a "spiritual wasteland . . . Sterile but . . . safe". Hence, of course, the name of the character Spare.

For those few seekers both beguiled and tormented by hints of a deeper truth, "the only value of this world lay in its power—at certain times—to suggest another world" (**"Vastarien"**). "It does indeed seem that the strict order of the visible world is only a semblance, one providing certain gross materials which become the basis for subtle *improvisations* of invisible forces. Hence, it may appear to some that a leafless tree is not a tree but a signpost to another realm" (**"The Journal of J. P. Drapeau"**).

Those tormented knights of nihilistic faith, like poor Faliol (**"Masquerade of a Dead Sword",**) who have eyes to see beyond this world may set off in quest of those "zones of fractured numinosity" (**"Alice's Last Adventure"**), "otherworlds", "little zones", "ultra-mental hinterlands of metaphysics" (**"Dream of a Mannikin"**), "places which concealed or suggested unknown orders of existences" (**"The Prodigy of Dreams"**). "We feel a sense of divinity in ruined places, abandoned places—shattered temples on mountaintops, crumbling catacombs, islands where a stone idol stands almost faceless" (**"Mad Night of Atonement"**).

Nathan Jeremy Stein is one such quester, "a haunter of spectral marketplaces, a visitant of discount houses of unreality, a bargain hunter in the deepest basement of the unknown" (**"Notes on the Writing of Horror: A Story"**). These are "persons interested in pursuing the existence of utter chaos and mayhem: that is, one of complete liberation at all conceivable levels" ("Selections from Lo-

vecraft"). Like Victor Keirion and the narrator of **"Les Fleurs"**, the Ligottian quester seeks "keys to an impossible kingdom". This is the Gnostic quest.

Historically, Gnosticism refers to a collection of Christian heresies beginning in the first or second century A.D. These were schools and systems of mysticism, some with cosmological speculations scarcely less fantastical than Ligotti's, in which adherents sought to escape this world and flee to another to which they felt they belonged. This feat would be accomplished in an experience of enlightenment. Ligotti's quest for esoteric knowledge, with its negation of the familiar, mundane world, recalls Gnosticism in a general way, but there are certain more specific references to it as well. For instance, the strange sect in **"The Last Feast of Harlequin"** claims roots in the ancient Gnosis of Saturninus. The contact point is that these Gnostics imagined the evil angels creating soulless humans who crawled the earth like worms. It develops that the sectarians in Ligotti's story are mere larvae in their human form, but evolve into loathsome wormlike entities. Thus the reference to Saturnian Gnosticism is exactly equivalent to the *Necronomicon* passage quoted in Lovecraft's "The Festival", in that that ancient reference, too, foreshadows the transmogrification of the sectarians of Kingsport into maggot-men.

One of the fundamental doctrines of Gnosticism was that of the imbecilic demiurge, a distant relation of the true divinity and the ill-advised creator of the dreadful material world despised by the superspiritual Gnostic Christians. Ligotti fancies the idea of a bungling creator who, like the Gnostic demiurge Saklas, is brought up short with the unwelcome knowledge that he is not after all the ultimate God. This notion underlines **"The Strange Design of Master Rignolo"**, in which a painter boasts of his queer canvases into which one may enter and dwell. He is mortified to discover that he himself is but a self-portrait of the *real* Rignolo! He is merely the demiurge. And recall once more the Creator who is himself a puppet in **"Mad Night of Atonement"**.

Gnostics believed that all souls had once existed in a heavenly preincarnational bliss, and that their eventual descent into the flesh was a degrading imprisonment. We can find this notion in at least two Ligotti tales. **"Charnelhouse of the Moon"** may be understood as a depiction of the idea that for the spirit to enter into organic life is at the same time to enter into the trap of endless and ever-repeated death. And in **"The Last Feast of Harlequin"** we hear chanted the ritual praises of "the unborn in paradise, . . . the pure, unlived lives".

Magister Ligotti warns of two false paths to be shunned in one's pursuit of forbidden knowledge. First, one may be too easily satisfied with the cheap trinkets that pass themselves off as bejeweled treasure. Most occult seekers, it is safe to say, founder here. But Victor Keirion has successfully overpassed this hurdle. He remains firm in

> his belief that there existed some arcana, of a different kind altogether from that proffered by the books before him, all of which were absorbed in the real, falsely hermetic ventures which consisted of circling the same absurd landscape. The

other worlds portrayed in these books inevitably served as annexes or reflections of this one; they were imposters of the authentic unreality which was the only realm of redemption . . . (**"Vastarien"**)

Similarly, Klaus Klingman must make his pupil first doubt facile claims of the arcane before he can penetrate beyond doubt to the amazing truth.

The second temptation also involves a premature halt, only here the danger is to become prematurely jaded, as the narrator of **"The Spectacles in the Drawer"** does. He reasons that all experiences, marvelous and mundane, finally boil down to mere experience so that it is hardly worth striking out from Samsara to reach Nirvana. He dismisses a bit of "Sacred Writ" as a "stupid book" despite the fact that its "mysteries . . . were among the most genuine of their kind", because all such grimoires are judged by him mere will-o'-the-wisps. Each repository of cryptical secrets unlocks deeper levels—of further secrets, which once divined will lead only to a new set of riddles! Each revelation is thus relativized and made anticlimactically mundane in its turn (**"The Spectacles in the Drawer"**). The chances are slim that the final goal can be attained in the short years of a human life. Thus the bored narrator has given up the Gnostic quest and hopes to dissuade Plomb, his self-appointed disciple, too. In the same way, the narrator of **"The Mystics of Muelenburg"** has at length abandoned the quest: "This was in the days when esoteric wisdom seemed to count for something in my mind".

Ligotti uses the figure of the mystagogue, the initiator into a forbidden knowledge, in many of his stories (and again we may suspect we see reflected his own role as a writer). Some characters fit this role in a fairly straightforward way: the "crow-man" in **"Vastarien"**, Klaus Klingman in **"The Mystics of Muelenburg"**, Dr. Voke, perhaps even Dr. Raymond Thoss in **"The Last Feast of Harlequin"**, Father Sevich in **"The Library of Byzantium"**, the shabby custodian of Cynothoglys in **"Prodigy of Dreams"**, the wise man Vinge in **"The Masquerade of a Dead Sword"**. Others play the role implicitly, including the hypnotist in **"Drink to Me Only with Labyrinthine Eyes"**, Dr. Thoss in **"The Troubles of Dr. Thoss"**, the tale-telling, soul-stealing Aunt Elise in **"The Christmas Eves of Aunt Elise"**, the sectarians of Azathoth, and the strange quartet in **"The Music of the Moon"**, and certainly Alice's father (**"Alice's Last Adventure"**), who gleefully teases, "We know what *that* means, don't we?"

Still closer examination might suggest that in all these cases Ligotti is depicting the mystagogue and her/his disciple as alter egos, with the result that the revelation at story's end is a self-revelation like that of the Muelenburgers who, if only temporarily, are brought to face the truth that some hidden part of their souls already knows. This master-disciple identity is made quite explicit in **"Dream of a Mannikin"** and **"Notes on the Writing of Horror: A Story"**, where the revealer and the receiver of the revelation are finally shown to be two aspects of the same psyche. The same link is implicit in stories in which the disciple repeats the experience of the master and suddenly discovers that the mystagogue has disappeared (e. g. **"The Music of the Moon"**, **"Dr. Locrian's Asylum"**, **"The Mystics of Muelenburg"**). In such cases the disciple replaces the master; the two are one. It is as if Klingman is the master in the past and the narrator is the same master at a later point in time. In **"The Sect of the Idiot"** no sooner does the narrator find the inhuman sectarians' chairs empty than he begins to change physically into one of them.

One striking example meets us in **"The Spectacles in the Drawer"**, in which the gullible buffoon Plomb seems to represent the rejected quester-persona of the cynical narrator himself. He scorns his disciple because, unlike himself, the poor "fool" still possesses the zeal to "plumb" the depths from which the narrator has turned away. The mystagogue and the disciples exchange roles, and Plomb finally forces on his former master "mysteries and marvels beyond anything I had ever suspected".

In **"In the Shadow of Another World"**, we have no less than three characters who represent different stages of the same life. The house on the borderland of realities was first the property of a mystic "whose name Spare never disclosed to me, though I knew it all the same". But we know what that means, *don't* we? He knows it because it is his own name! Spare eventually goes the way of his predecessor, vanishing amid the raging realities that beat about the house. The narrator goes from room to room in search of Spare, examining "the unprotected rooms of my mind".

Harry O. Morris illustration for "Dr. Voke and Mr. Veech."

Thus he is the house itself, too! He suspects he will one day recapitulate Spare's awful revelations, having escaped them only "on this occasion". Thus Spare is his own future self.

It is absolutely clear that the narrator of **"The Last Feast of Harlequin"** *is* his mentor Raymond Thoss at a later time, simply a recurrence of the same not in a later movement of the same symphony. Likewise, the psychic link between the narrator of **"The Library of Byzantium"** and Father Sevich symbolizes that they, too, are successive selves.

Finally we may consider Ligotti's use of that classic device of horror fiction, the secret or forbidden book. Among the tomes in the *"Librairie de Grimoires"* (**"Vastarien"**) are the *Necronomicon* of Lovecraft, the *Noctuary of Tine* (thus in **"Vastarien"**, but called "the lost grimoire of the Abbot of Tine" in **"The Spectacles in the Drawer"**), *Cynothoglys* (apparently the scripture of the dark divinity glimpsed in **"The Prodigy of Dreams"**), *Vastarien,* and "the forbidden *Psalms of the Silent*". The last two are especially interesting because of a modicum of explanation Ligotti supplies.

Of *Vastarien* we are told, marvelously, that it is "an extremely special book, that is not . . . yes, that is not about something, but actually *is* that something". "Vastarien" is the name of the realm into which the book transports the reader, but the tome cannot be called *"The Book of* Vastarien" for the reason Ligotti gives. It isn't about Vastarien; it is Vastarien. The book is even more scarce than the *Necronomicon,* since there is but one copy, and always has been, and it has patiently waited for its single destined reader to arrive. When he comes, Victor Keirion finds in it the portal to a veritable Nirvana of Naught.

Psalms of the Silent is the book "without a living author" (**"The Spectacles in the Drawer"**). Wisely, Ligotti never dispels the evocative quality of this title by explaining it, but perhaps we may be permitted a moment or two of exegetical pedantry. The title might imply that these psalms were learned from the dead, who presumably sing them in silence. They would have been transcribed by the living through the expedient of necromancy, just as Dr. Locrian interrogated the dead. Thus no living author. And in this case the title is exactly equivalent to the title *Songs of a Dead Dreamer!*

Or perhaps these psalms are simply to be chanted silently, as Faliol does, recalling how the sectarians of Azathoth seemed to communicate not by their buzzing but by their intermediate silences. In the same way, Father Sevich silently mouths the prayers in his nameless missal of masochism. (Here the secrecy of the book is double: it is written in an unknown language, but it is to be read silently anyway!)

Or it may be that these psalms are "a liturgy of shadows, a catechism of phantoms" (**"Vastarien"**) used by a secret sect, silent, as all true Gnostics must be as far as the outside world is concerned, because they possess "a knowledge that was unspoken and unspeakable" (**"Dr. Locrian's Asylum"**). Surely such psalmody punctuated the ceremony called "the Night of the Night" performed by the esoteric Order of Illusion.

These tantalizing texts would seem to be only a few that line the hidden shelves of the Library of Byzantium.

Ligotti on the novel form:

Carl T. Ford: *All the fiction you've written so far has been in the short story format. Have any plans to write a novel?*

Thomas Ligotti: No. For the most part I don't enjoy reading novels, and I'm sure I would not enjoy writing one. My interest as a reader is pretty much restricted to poetry, short stories, and essays. I'm defining "novel" in this case as an extended prose narrative featuring plenty of naturalistic dialogue and sympathetic contemporary characters. The few works of this type that I've been motivated to read were those that served as the basis for some movie I enjoyed and wanted to re-experience to the extent that the book would allow. These days I can simply rent the video.

Thomas Ligotti with Carl T. Ford, in an interview in Dagon, *September-December, 1988.*

Douglas E. Winter (essay date 1992)

SOURCE: "Scream de la Scream," in *Book World—The Washington Post,* February, 16, 1992, p. 9.

[*Winter is an American literary and film critic best known for his studies of Stephen King and Dario Argento. In the following excerpt, he praises Ligotti's ability to convey* "vague discomfort, a lingering doubt" *in his fiction.*]

Thomas Ligotti is the best-kept secret in contemporary horror fiction. For nearly a decade, while lesser talents have stocked the bookracks with a relentless supply of carbon-copy chills, Ligotti has labored, unheralded and virtually unknown, to create a canon of short stories so idiosyncratic as to defy almost any description save demented. Most of this writing has appeared in obscure magazines with such appetizing names as *Grue, Crypt of Cthulhu* and *Nyctalops,* known only to aficionados of dark alternative fiction. His first book, **Songs of a Dead Dreamer,** was published in an edition of some 350 copies. When, almost five years after its initial appearance, this collection of stories was bravely brought to the mass market by Carroll & Graf, the critical reception was overwhelming-with the delight of discovery, and for good reason: Thomas Ligotti is the best new American writer of weird fiction to appear in years.

Ligotti's long-awaited second book, **Grimscribe: His Lives and Works**, presents 13 new stories in the guise of a novel. Its eponymous narrator, like Ray Bradbury's *Illustrated Man* and Clive Barker's *Book of Blood,* is a living library of voices—the damned, the demonic, the dreamer, among others—all interwoven in a compelling celebration of the first-person. It is a hypnotic narration; each story is a singular experience, yet each turns on the other, creating what Ligotti rightly calls a "wheel of terror." These are whirlpools of words, drawing the reader ever inward to that place "where the mysteries are always new and dreams never end"—a melding of Jorge Luis Borges and Tommaso Landolfi with the pulp sensibilities of the legendary *Weird Tales* magazine.

The opening story, **"The Last Feast of Harlequin,"** is archetypal Ligotti. Its unnamed narrator, a dour and deadpan academic, travels to a remote rural village to study its quaint winter festival. That these revels disguise a perverse, primeval ritual should come as no surprise. Upon entering the warped wonderlands of Thomas Ligotti, the reader realizes very quickly that this is not a fiction of escape, but of the search for a grim epiphany, the revelation of something so vital (and, more often than not, vile) that it should have been known, yet that has escaped the narrator in his pride or hope or sloth.

The story is a reinvention of H.P. Lovecraft's "The Festival," and it is that much-mythologized (and maligned) writer of weird fiction with whom Ligotti inevitably must be compared. Like Lovecraft, Ligotti weaves an oppressive web of words, working his narrator, and his readers, toward the edge of an unknowable mystery—one of such ominous power that the mere hint of it is fatal: "This is only how it seems," Ligotti tells us, "and seeming is everything." Yet he avoids Lovecraft's excesses—the pseudoscience and adjectival addiction that marred even the Lovecraftian classics—and embraces a decadent undercurrent in a manner that would no doubt have caused the gentleman from Providence to blush.

The result is a rare kind of horror fiction, one that draws its power not from violence or shock, monsters or mayhem, but from the pursuit of a vague discomfort, a lingering doubt. Ligotti's prose is eerily genteel, written in utter defiance (or ignorance) of the filmic influences that have rendered most contemporary horror fiction into splatter-prose. Vital to his aesthetic is an insistently oneiric imagery—not simply a landscape, but a language, of nightmare. For once it is the telling, and not the showing, that is key, the stories themselves forming baroque ruins of dread and decay:

> They could show themselves anywhere, if always briefly. Upon a cellar wall there might appear an ill-formed visage among the damp and fractured stones, a hideous impersonation of a face infiltrating the dark corners of our homes. Other faces, leprous masks, would arise within the grain of panelled walls or wooden floors, spying for a moment before sinking back into the knotty shadows, withdrawing below the surface. And there were so many nameless patterns that might spread themselves across the boards of an old fence or the side of a shed, engravings all tangled and wizened like a subterranean craze of roots and tendrils, an underworld riot of branching convolutions, gnarled ornamentations.

At his best moments, Ligotti succeeds with morbid brilliance; at others, like Lovecraft, he simply over-whelms the reader with words. Reading *Grimscribe* is at times daunting, at others annoying, yet always a vindication of the literate tale of terror—a proposition that grows increasingly unthinkable in a decade that has come to think of "horror" as the realm of vampires and violence.

Stefan Dziemianowicz: Do you have personal favorites among your stories—assuming that one can express fondness for stories that deal with the things you write about? Or are there particular stories in which you feel you were more successful than others?

Thomas Ligotti: Okay, here are the stories that, let's say, I would most like other people to like: **"Dr. Locrian's Asylum," "The Greater Festival of Masks," "Vastarien," "The Night School," "The Glamour," "The Library of Byzantium," "Miss Plarr," "Mrs. Rinaldi's Angel," "The Voice in the Bones,"** and **"The Shadow at the Bottom of the World."** These stories seem to me to have a minimum of non-weird qualities. All the others, most of them, are "tainted" in some way, either stylistically or thematically.

Thomas Ligotti with Stefan Dziemianowicz, in an interview in Tekeli-Li!, *Winter-Spring, 1992.*

Harry O. Morris   (essay date 1992)

SOURCE: "Electro-Dynamics for the Beginner: An Appreciation of Thomas Ligotti," in *Tekeli-Li! Journal of Terror,* No. 4, Winter-Spring, 1992, pp. 40-1.

[*Morris is an American artist and illustrator whose seminal horror magazine* Nyctalops *was highly influential in the revival of the study of H. P. Lovecraft and other weird fiction writers. Morris's Silver Scarab Press published the first edition of Ligotti's Songs of a Dead Dreamer. The following is a personal appreciation of Ligotti's work.*]

Sutton Breiding had been visiting me in the house on Elm Street for three days. On the third night, after returning from a midnight showing of *Eraserhead,* we were edging toward the infernal zone—aided by the slow drizzle outside the moonlit windows, static on the TV, and a few glasses of gin. I was explaining why I had recently moved all my books of overtly horrific fiction, along with the texts of schizophrenia and suicidal tendencies, to the back of the shelves, when the single bare light bulb which had illuminated our conversation from above fritzed and exploded, sending a great shower of sparks into the room. This was followed by an utter darkness and silence. The event took place roughly in between the publication of *Nyctalops* #15 and #16 and prior to the first appearance of *The Punk Surrealist Cafe*—or, to date it somewhat more accurately, somewhere in the middle of 1980. That unexpected shock in the middle of the night was (I see now) a portent of the arrival of Thomas Ligotti a few weeks later via a neatly typed letter and manuscript. **"The Chymist."**

Up until that point, *Nyctalops* had stumblingly followed its own path and was knocking at the door of the unknown. Within the opening paragraphs of **"The Chymist,"** Ligotti threw open that door from inside and I went tumbling headfirst into the darkness. The door clanged shut with iron bars when the word "END" was reached, and *Nyctalops* had found its place. Of course, this wasn't "The End" of either the story or the relationship. **"The Chym-**

ist" does have a perfect ending ("Now, Rose of madness—Bloom!"), as a self-contained unit, bringing to climax the sly hints and implications of the Narrator's obsessive mission.

Like a moment's shower of sparks in the darkness, certain things are illuminated instantaneously in ways no normal light can hope to reveal. The sparks ignited by **"The Chymist"** flew off the page and lodged in my brain, and nothing can be the same again. As Simon ("Smirk," the Narrator) observes, looking down from that 22nd floor apartment:

> Look at those lights outlining the different venues and avenues below, look at their lines and interconnections. They're like a skeleton of something . . . of a dream. A skeleton ready at any moment to shift its structure to support a new shape, conforming to the demands of the dream.

What "got-like powers of proteation" does *sub-rosa* experience as the experiment moves on? (We already know that her evolution of the flesh will "knock the eyes out of whoever finds you when I leave here.") What are the "Great Chymists" who are dreaming through Simon "Smirk"? Where does his/her/their dream begin, let alone end? Maybe this is just one nightmare of Lucian Dregler's turning to stone in a small room under the stairs while courting the Medusa. Perhaps Rosetta will find herself in a small town festival—sitting in a basement room with other mask wearers, listening to their new faces grow in the dark. There is no beginning or ending, only the illusion. One may enter any one of Ligotti's stories and emerge in another—like crawling under your bed and coming out of a tumor growing on the wall in the next room.

By disallowing logic and psychological time, and by creating twisting cardboard sets with puppet characters, Ligotti has created an interconnected landscape of dread. We don't need to know what brand of underwear characters prefer or if they shop at the mall—the biggest joke in advice given to aspiring writers of horror by critics who often opine that HPL should have spent more time on "character development" in his fiction.

The core of Lovecraft's mythology is of similar orientation though more weighted down with symbolically functioning entities (Cthulhu, Azathoth, etc.) toward the end of his life. Thomas Ligotti is the only writer I can think of to continue at will the nihilistic nightmare vision of " . . . the dark universe yawning/Where the black planets roll without aim,/Where they roll in their horror unheeded, without/knowledge or lustre or name . . ." without tripping up on reusing the already overworked "known quantities" in the Mythos. In short, Tom searches throughout crooked avenues for those mad notes of Erich Zann lost to the wind and the Dark so long ago, while others have been content to quote from *The Necronomicon* available at the local library.

An awareness of the gulf is buried deep within all our psyches though obviously most inhabitants of this planet find various ways of suppressing or numbing it. A few have made this awareness central to their lives ("hiding from horror within the heart of horror"), and Ligotti is one of these. There is a perverse and admirable desire to open the window into hell for others to momentarily view, and Ligotti excels at this, being a master storyteller in the classical tradition of Meyrink, Schulz, Kier Cross, etc. He "sweet-talks" us (as in "The Statement of Randolph Carter") through a tube running up from the depths of a "crummy" sepulcher. He won't offer you a beer, but I'd think twice before partaking of the glowing liquid light powder which pours forth from the holes in his palms.

[Harry O. Morris]: Thomas Ligotti is . . . a mystery figure to me. I think he wants to remain that way; maybe it's best that he does. All the weird, horrible, wondrous things, all that creepy stuff that goes on, and here comes Ligotti. It's like you're sleepwalking down the street or tied down to a bed on an LSD trip or something, all these visions are flying out of our heads. And there's Ligotti writing that stuff down so I can understand it and other people can, too. I don't want to throw out a bunch of obscure names, but there are a few authors who in my mind really stand out who have that nightmare, sleepwalking quality about them and Ligotti to my mind is definitely one of those. He can see in the darkness.

[Tekeli-Li!]: *He's profoundly disturbing.*

For those who can appreciate it.

Do you think he's one of the finest horror writers around?

I'm a little bit biased because I know him, but I honestly do. His stories are timeless. The first story of his I read, **"The Chymist,"** just knocked me out and everything since is so deep and disturbing.

Harry O. Morris, in an interview in Tekeli-Li!, *Winter-Spring, 1992.*

Thomas Wiloch   (essay date 1992)

SOURCE: Review of *Grimscribe: His Lives and Works*, by Thomas Ligotti, in *The Bloomsbury Review*, Vol. 12, No. 4, June, 1992, pp. 16-17.

[*Wiloch is an American critic and author of several well-received collections of prose poems, including* Paper Mask *(1988),* Tales of Lord Shantih *(1990), and* Narcotic Signature *(1992). He also edited the "surrealist and horror" magazine* Grimoire *from 1982 through 1985. In the following review of* Grimscribe: His Lives and Works, *Wiloch commends the personal, nightmarish vision embodied in Ligotti's fiction.*]

Most horror writers are content to scare their readers with whatever cliché is close at hand: a possessed child, a haunted house, a sexy vampire. But Thomas Ligotti is different. He is a dark visionary sharing a private, surreal nightmare with his readers. His stories, featuring quirky characters and mysterious mayhem, take place in the deserted back streets of a netherland where it is always an autumn night, where the shadows are alive and trembling, and where enigmatic words are spoken by eccentric doctors or possessed mannequins. Ligotti is among the most compelling horror writers of today, his lush, hallucinatory work both lyrical and truly *disturbing.*

His second collection, **Grimscribe: His Lives and Works,** contains thirteen stories, including **"The Last Feast of Harlequin,"** a World Fantasy Award nominee. It is a long, Lovecraftian tale of a scholar investigating a deadly festival of clowns. Perhaps because of its strong debt to Lovecraft, it is more conventional than the usual Ligotti tale. More typical is **"Flowers of the Abyss,"** which is narrated by a character whose whispered words, we are informed, are carried to the reader by the wind, while **"The Cocoons"** tells a madly comic tale of a crazed psychiatrist and his two patients, one of whom is breeding monsters in an abandoned house.

Devotees of horror fiction will find Ligotti a welcome and exotic addition to the field, while mainstream readers may well judge him to be an entertaining writer of dark, surrealistic power.

Steven J. Mariconda (essay date 1992)

SOURCE: "The Ligotti Phenomenon," in *Necrofile: The Review of Horror Fiction,* No. 4, Spring, 1992, pp. 1-3.

[*Mariconda is an American critic specializing in the works of H. P. Lovecraft. In the following review of* Songs of a Dead Dreamer *and* Grimscribe: His Lives and Works, *he assesses Ligotti's achievement as a short story writer.*]

Until recently Thomas Ligotti was the most elusive of weird fictionists. His first collection, **Songs of a Dead Dreamer,** originally appeared in a 300-copy edition from Silver Scarab Press in 1986. Since then his reputation has flourished largely by word of mouth, spurred by feature issues of *Crypt of Cthulhu, Dagon,* and *Weird Tales.* It is with gratitude, and perhaps a sense of relief, that those of us who have attempted to keep up with the Ligotti phenomenon will greet these two volumes from Carroll & Graf. Having a significant amount of his work in one place is certainly better than trying to scout out appearances in small press magazines of varying obscurity. It also makes it much easier to assess Ligotti's achievement to date.

The accolades that precede Ligotti have, unfortunately, put him in the awkward position of having to live up to his advance notice. He has been lauded by some overeager supporters—even prior to the publication of these volumes—as one of the greatest living horror writers. The *Washington Post* tagged him "the most unexpected literary discovery since Clive Barker". Since Ligotti's approach is the antithesis of Barker's, this comparison is a little absurd. (When we recall that Barker was in turn the successor to Stephen King, it becomes even more comical: the realm in which Ligotti works bears no resemblance to King's commonplace world.) Ligotti has even been compared to Lovecraft (not unusual, perhaps, among horror writers) and Poe (which is far less common).

What separates Ligotti from Barker and King and puts him far ahead of most other horror writers, simply put, is his deeply felt sense of the unreal. This sense makes his stories compelling in a way that no amount of sentimentality, violence, and sex—those pillars of modern horror bestsellerism—can. His work speaks instead of an intimate familiarity with "a world that both surpasses and menaces this one", the knowledge of which evokes "a bizarre elation tainted with nausea" (**"The Sect of the Idiot"**).

The question of Lovecraft's influence is worthy of comment. Katherine Ramsland, writing in the *New York Times Book Review,* disingenuously condemned Ligotti's "apparent attempt to emulate H. P. Lovecraft". This is comparable to saying that the early Lovecraft should be censured for having been influenced by Poe. Each author, however, follows his respective mentor only while adding his own unique perspective. Ramsland apparently has never read a Cthulhu Mythos pastiche, for if she had she could easily distinguish between emulation and influence. Somebody, please, send her a copy of *The Watchers out of Time* . . .

Ligotti, Ramsland goes on, "fails to convey the threat of inescapable contamination that empowers Lovecraft's work". Again I must disagree with this assessment. In fact, I am not sure I even understand it. At his best Ligotti is resoundingly successful in convincing us that everywhere behind the common façade of life are other, sinister realms of entity more "real" than that through which we so blithely move.

What Lovecraft and Ligotti share most of all is a transcendent outlook. Ligotti reveres Lovecraft for his attempt "to convey with the greatest possible intensity a vision of the universe as a kind of enchanted nightmare". This vision is what the two writers have most in common, although, as Ramsey Campbell points out in his introduction to **Songs of a Dead Dreamer,** their respective terrors are of a quite different kind.

Vision alone, however, is not enough to create a fully realized weird tale. Skill in handling is critical. T. E. D. Klein, former editor of *Twilight Zone* magazine, once noted that 90% of all submissions fell into only a dozen or so plot categories. Given that the plot will be familiar, the approach will largely dictate a story's effectiveness. One false note and we become aware of the author's attempted manipulation.

Because the creation of atmosphere is key to the weird tale's success, the genre is largely a phenomenon of language. The objective is not to relate a series of causal events—to get from point A to point B—but to create a mood. Lovecraft enumerated some alternatives in his *Commonplace Book:* "intense, clutching, delirious horror; delicate dreamlike fantasy; realistic, scientific horror; very subtle adumbration."

Ligotti takes what might be considered the purest approach to the weird tale. It is also the riskiest. Realistic description is minimally important, and the style almost wholly carries the burden of drawing in the reader and creating atmosphere. The latter is largely a function of rhythm and imagery, which makes Ligotti's brand of weird fiction closely akin to the prose poem. This approach requires far more finesse than that needed to create a background of workaday verisimilitude, such as we might find in King's thousand-page litanies of brand names.

Ligotti intermittently falls short of the challenge, primarily in his earliest work. **"The Frolic"**, about a prison psychologist stalked by an unearthly patient, falls flat because of its stilted "domestic" dialogue. Other early stories use second-person narration (e.g. **"The Chymist"**, **"Alice's Last Adventure"**, and **"The Dream of a Mannikin"**, an awkward attempt to use the present tense) and wind up spectacular failures. In these instances Ligotti is unable to control his narrative voice, allowing his tendency toward irony to run wild. As a result the narratives seem contrived, the style affected.

Even these stories, however, hold hints of what is to come in the excellent tales that make up the bulk of the collections. The psychotic of **"The Frolic"**, we are told, has a "poetic geography to his interior dreamland" as determined by "his repeated mentioning of 'the jolly river of refuse' and 'the jagged heaps in shadows'. . . [of] a moonlit corridor where mirrors scream and laugh, dark peaks of some kind that won't remain still, [and] a stairway that's 'broken' in a very strange way". Thus Ligotti begins to cultivate his own poetic geography, the bizarre imagery that threads through his entire body of work.

In his recent study, *The Weird Tale*, S. T. Joshi argues that the work of the exceptional weird writer must be pervaded by a distinctive world view. This criterion Ligotti easily meets; his outlook is consistently manifest in these stories. They reflect a belief (as expressed in **"Vastarien"**) that "the only value of this world lay in its power—at certain times—to suggest another world". "There is an order of existence which is entirely strange" to human beings, he writes in **"The Journal of J. P. Drapeau"**: "the strict order of the world is only a semblance."

Ligotti's "hallucinatory view of creation" puts his work as much in the tradition of Gogol, Kafka, and Borges as in that of Machen, Blackwood, and Klein. His stories hardly seem set in any historical time period, and he is blatantly uninterested in creating the suspension of disbelief. We are welcomed into his fictional dominion only upon tacit agreement that "things are not what they seem . . . we are forever reminded of this . . . [and] enough of us ignore this truth to keep the world from collapsing" (**"The Mystics of Muelenburg"**).

Songs of a Dead Dreamer really hits its stride in **"The Christmas Eves of Aunt Elise: A Tale of Possession in Old Grosse Pointe"**, whose fine descriptions make Yuletide seem a malignant thing. The evil matriarch of the title annexes the narrator's memories of the family's Christmas Eves, even as she dispatches him to the limbo of "ragged creatures" and "weeping demons" from which he relates the tale. Even better is **"The Troubles of Dr. Thoss"**, in which an unimaginative and slovenly artist has a Campbellian encounter with the spectral local legend of a seacoast town.

The final six stories of *Dreamer* make us forget the book's weaker material. **"Dr. Locrian's Asylum"** tells of a sanitarium building "visible from every corner of town", and how the townspeople were eventually compelled to raze it. After doing so, however, the specters of the inmates—whose eyes "reflected the lifeless beauty of the silent, staring universe itself"—appear in the upper windows of the town buildings. The insane, it is hinted, possess "a strange alliance with other orders of existence" enhanced by the process undertaken by Dr. Locrian "to project them further into the absolute".

In **"The Sect of the Idiot"** life is described as "the nightmare that leaves its mark upon you in order to prove that it is, in fact, real". In dreams the narrator perceives the existence of a conclave of hooded insectlike priests. These beings rule the world by mesmerism but are themselves the hypnotic subjects of some higher, indeterminate power. Variants of the strange urban landscape described here occur to great effect in **"Vastarien"** (which opens with several paragraphs of Ligotti's most poetic prose) and **"The Journal of J. P. Drapeau"** in *Dreamer* and **"The Mystics of Muelenburg"** and **"The Cocoons"** in *Grimscribe*.

"Drapeau" again reveals how tenuous appearances are superseded by a far stranger reality. A visionary writer living in 1890s Bruges comes to realize that "an entirely different creature [is] hiding behind my face . . . behind those features [are] a being strange beyond all description". A related tale is **"The Greater Festival of Masks"**, one of several that concern themselves with masquerade—in the sense both of a gathering involving fantastic costumes and of surfaces that are mere disguise. A surreal atmosphere permeates this brief story of a man shopping for a mask to wear "during the declining days of the festival, when the old and the new, the real and the imaginary, truth and deception, all join". Forced to mind the shop when the proprietor slips away, he observes figures in a vacant lot throwing their masks on a pyre to reveal their "smooth and faceless faces". Finally he himself joins a congregation of those individuals, silent but for "that soft creaking of new faces breaking through old flesh". Ligotti's writing, fluent throughout the story, lends a sense of Poesque unease that culminates in the final paragraph:

> For the old festival of masks has ended, so that a greater festival may begin. And of the old time nothing will be said, for nothing will be known. But the old masks, false souls, will find something to remember, and perhaps they will speak of those days when they are alone behind doors that do not open, or in the darkness at the summit of stairs leading nowhere.

"The Greater Festival of Masks" forms the pendant to Ligotti's earlier and more conventional **"Last Feast of Harlequin"**. Ligotti weaves a complex tale of an anthropologist studying "the significance of the clown figure in diverse cultural contexts" who visits a small Midwest town to observe a "Fool's Feast". A skillful paragraph about the geographical "disharmonies" of the town (called Mirocaw) immediately creates a strong sense of disquietude. The narrator finds that one of his professors, who had written a dissertation on the town, now seems to be surreptitiously involved with the festival. Disguising himself as a member of the sectlike harlequins, the narrator witnesses a weird ritual of dissolution. In this story, which is dedicated to H. P. Lovecraft, Ligotti uses elements of "The Shadow over Innsmouth" and "The Festival" but adds a characteristic overlay of ambiguity and symbolic depth.

This story is contained in *Grimscribe,* which is the stronger of the two volumes. **"Nethescurial"**, another tale in the collection, shows Ligotti at his finest. Using some fairly conventional elements—a strange manuscript, a horrible idol, and an evil, worldwide cult—he creates something new and compelling. Once again it develops that "all of creation [is] a mere mask for . . . an absolute evil whose reality is mitigated only by our blindness to it". Though the ancient horror predictably reaches out to engulf the narrator, it does so in a manner that both startles and terrifies.

The well-modulated prose of this story is accompanied by a conception of equal strength. In other stories Ligotti is unable to strike the best balance of style and substance. As a result, **"The Flowers in the Abyss"**, the rambling **"Dreaming in Nortown"**, the bold but disastrous ventures into metafiction, **"Notes on the Writing of Horror: A Story"** and **"Professor Nobody's Little Lectures on Supernatural Horror"**, and some others in these volumes are quite forgettable.

But this problem largely besets the early tales. Ligotti ordinarily comes up with distinctive concepts and treatments that make his material seem fresh. **"In the Shadow of Another World"** reworks the haunted house theme with cosmic overtones: the mysterious old dwelling acts as a prism that resolves "a multi-faceted mural portraying the marriage of insanity and metaphysics". The idea behind **"The Spectacles in the Drawer"**, too, will be familiar: a pair of magic glasses allows one to see other realms of being (cf. M. R. James' "A View from a Hill"). Here, the narrator tricks his friend into believing he can see "an imaginary universe in a rivulet of his own blood" with the glasses. But the plan backfires in a most singular and horrifying way.

In this story and others, matter itself acquires a startling plasticity, one of "instantaneous evolutions, constant transformations of both appearance and essence". In **"The Mystics of Muelenburg"**, a medieval town experiences a "catastrophe of dreams":

> . . . precisely sculptured stone began to loosen and lump, an abandoned cart melded with the sucking mud of the street, and objects in desolate rooms lost themselves in the surfaces they pressed upon, making metal tongs mix with brick hearth, prismatic jewels with lavish velvet, a corpse with the wood of its coffin.

In **"Dr. Voke and Mr. Veech"**, too, we read of "wood waking up" within a disorienting narrative of a maker of mannequins that become animate.

In keeping with his presentation of people as bewildered beings in an incomprehensible universe, the author's horrors are often leavened with the absurd. Sometimes the cosmic is even complemented by a hint of the comic. **"The Cocoons"**, for example, opens this way:

> Early one morning, hours before sunrise, I was awakened by Dr. Dublanc. He was standing at the foot of my bed, lightly tugging on the covers. For a moment I was convinced, in my quasi-somnolent state, that a small animal was prancing about on the mattress, performing some nocturnal ritual unknown to higher forms of life.

Later we find out that perhaps this surmise was not so far-fetched after all. Drapeau's journal contains some similarly irrational musings: "I used to believe that during the night, while I slept, witches and monkeys removed parts of my body and played games with them, hiding my arms and legs, rolling my head across the floor. Of course I abandoned this belief as soon as I entered school, but not until much later did I discover the truth about it."

In all, Ligotti shows tremendous promise, and gives us much to look forward to as his work matures. He can only be lauded, even if uneven technique occasionally confounds his intentions. His unparalleled sensitivity to the weird makes him worth more to contemporary horror than any number of Stephen Kings, Anne Rices, or Dean R. Koontzes. Of the two collections, *Grimscribe* achieves near-classic status and is recommended to all. Those who find Ligotti to their taste will require *Songs of a Dead Dreamer* for the half-dozen outstanding tales it offers.

S. T. Joshi   (essay date 1993)

SOURCE: "Thomas Ligotti: The Escape from Life," in *Studies in Weird Fiction,* No. 12, Spring, 1993, pp. 30-6.

[*An American critic, Joshi is an important contemporary commentator on supernatural fiction, particularly the works of H. P. Lovecraft. In the following essay, he explores the theme of "escaping . . . from the mundane, the actual, the real" in Ligotti's fiction.*]

"There is no field other than the weird in which I have any aptitude or inclination for fictional composition. Life has never interested me so much as the escape from life." Ironically, this utterance by H. P. Lovecraft made when he was well into what he himself called his "quasi-realistic" phase, in which the weird is introduced subtly and gradually through the painstaking accumulation of realistic details in every aspect of the tale *except* that pertaining to the weird manifestation. And that Lovecraft was far from truly wishing for an "escape from life" is evident in his earnest concern for economic justice and political reform as the depression of the 1930s grinded on. *At the Mountains of Madness* could only have been written by one for whom the real world manifestly exists.

The whole notion of escaping from life—escaping, that is, from the mundane, the actual, the real—can apply much more pertinently to a very recent writer, Thomas Ligotti (b. 1953). Ligotti's interest is focussed more intensely on the weird, and only on the weird, than any author in the history of weird fiction. I do not think it would be possible to study, for example, the sociopolitical aspects of Ligotti's fiction—there do not seem to be any. His portrayal of human relationships, when it occurs at all, is either perfunctory or sardonic. Human characters, indeed, are virtually insignificant in themselves in his work, serving only as embodiments of or conduits to the unreal.

Ligotti is, indeed, one of the strangest phenomena in weird fiction, not only for the utter bizarrerie of his own work but for the curious way in which he has emerged as a leading writer in the field. Having published a certain number of stories in fan magazines (*Nyctalops*) or what might at best be called "semi-pro" magazines (*Fantasy Tales, Eldritch Tales*) in the early 1980s, Ligotti issued a collection of short stories, ***Songs of a Dead Dreamer*** from the specialty firm of Silver Scarab Press, operated by Harry O. Morris, Jr. When this volume emerged in 1986, Ligotti was still almost entirely unknown: I myself received a review copy of it and rather hastily and ignorantly dismissed it as mere "fan fiction". But Morris had, as it were, backed the right horse, for very shortly thereafter Ligotti was embraced by many of the leading writers and critics of the field (Ramsey Campbell had written an introduction to ***Songs of a Dead Dreamer***) and his reputation began to grow, although still in a sort of subterranean fashion. A British trade paperback of his collection, augmented with new stories (and, it must be admitted, with some of the more embarrassingly poor ones removed), emerged in 1989; this was reprinted in hardcover in this country in 1990 and in paperback the next year. A second collection, ***Grimscribe,*** appeared in late 1991. Ligotti is, however, still content to publish the majority of his work in the small press, although he has made occasional forays into full-fledged professional journals (*Magazine of Fantasy and Science Fiction*) and anthologies (Douglas E. Winter's *Prime Evil*, 1988). Perhaps this is just as well, for his work is certainly not best-seller material in the manner of Stephen King's or Clive Barker's.

If Ligotti's refreshing lack of self-promotion is virtually unique in what has become the big-business world of weird fiction, then his actual work is also entirely original and unclassifiable. His is the most distinctive voice in the field. This is not to say that he is necessarily the best weird fictionist now writing—Ramsey Campbell and T. E. D. Klein, at least, are still his superiors—but his work is perhaps the most easily recognisable of any current writer's because of its sheer difference from that of his contemporaries. Ligotti is one of the few modern weird writers to draw extensively from the older masters of the weird tale—Poe, Lovecraft, Blackwood, Machen—but his work is so far from being pastiche that it is difficult in all but a few cases to pinpoint actual literary influences.

The focus of all Ligotti's work is a systematic assault on the real world and the replacement of it with the unreal, the dreamlike, and the hallucinatory. Reality is, for Ligotti, a "grossly overrated affair" (**"Alice's Last Adventure"**). It is simply too prosy and dull, lacking in intrinsic value or dramatic interest. "It would be difficult to conceive of a creature for whom *this* world—its bare form seen with open eyes—represented a coveted paradise" (**"Vastarien"**). Accordingly, Ligotti's literary goal is to suggest that other realm which we glimpse either through dreams or, worse, stumble upon by accident in obscure corners of

this world. Ligotti has neatly summed up his aesthetic of the weird in **"The Consolations of Horror"**, a magnificent essay that ranks among his finest works:

> The horror story does the work of a certain kind of dream we all know. Sometimes it does this so well that even the most irrational and unlikely subject matter can infect the reader with a sense of realism beyond the realistic, a trick usually not seen outside the vaudeville of sleep. When is the last time you failed to be fooled by a nightmare, didn't suspend disbelief because its incidents weren't sufficiently true-to-life? The horror story is only true to dreams, especially those which involve us in mysterious ordeals, the passing of secrets, the passages of forbidden knowledge, and in more ways than one, the spilling of guts.

This tells us many things: the importance and prevalence of dream-imagery in Ligotti's work; the scorn of the "true-to-life"; and the notion of the quest—the quest for "secrets" and "knowledge" of the realm of the unreal. I shall examine all these points more detailedly later, but what I wish to consider now is the difficulty of classifying Ligotti's work within the standard distinctions existing within the weird tale. Many of his tales do not conform to the conventions of supernatural horror, which Maurice Lévy has compactly defined as work in which "the irrational makes an irruption into the real world". The "real world" exists so fragmentarily for Ligotti that the contrast between the "natural" and the "supernatural" is never sufficiently established. This is not (or not yet) meant as a criticism, but simply as a defining characteristic of Ligotti's writing. Nor can his tales be classified as "fantasy" (by which I mean the otherworldly fantasy of a Dunsany or Tolkien) because they are set in what is more or less recognisable as the "real world", but a real world depicted so sketchily—and, perhaps, with such a lack of enthusiasm—that its sole function seems to be as a springboard for the beyond. "Victor Keirion belonged to that wretched sect of souls who believe that the only value of this world lies in its power—at certain times—to suggest another world" (**"Vastarien"**). Ligotti in fact rejects such divisions in weird fiction as ontological or psychological horror.

> What seems important to me is not whether the spectre is within or outside of a character . . . but the power of the language and images of a story and the ultimate vision that they help to convey. For all that, everything that happens in every story ever written is merely an event in someone's imagination—exactly as are dreams, which take place on their own little plane of unreality, a realm of nowhere in which outside and inside are of equivalent ontological status, where within *is* within and both are phantasmal in essence.

And yet, does Ligotti flee from the real world simply because it is boring or "overrated"? In **"Professor Nobody's Little Lectures on Supernatural Horror"** he speaks of the "logic of supernatural horror" as "a logic that is founded on fear; it is a logic whose sole principle states: 'Existence equals Nightmare.' Unless life is a dream, nothing makes sense. For as a reality, it is a rank failure." Compare this with the character in **"The Mystics of Muelenburg"** who has found "a greater truth: that all is unreal", or of the narrator of **"Allan and Adelaide: An Arabesque"**: "I have seen the soul of the universe . . . and it is insane," or of the narrator of **"The Sect of the Idiot"**: "Life is the nightmare that leaves its mark upon you in order to prove that it is, in fact, real." What remarks like this suggest is that what we all take to be the real world is actually unreal and also mad. Consider **"The Journal of J. P. Drapeau"**:

> From the earliest days of man there has endured the conviction that there is an order of existence which is entirely strange to him. It does indeed seem that the strict order of the visible world is only a semblance, one providing certain gross materials which become the basis for subtle improvisations of invisible powers. Hence, it may appear to some that a leafless tree is not a tree but a signpost to another realm; that an old house is not a house but a thing possessing a will of its own; that the dead may throw off that heavy blanket of earth to walk in their sleep, and in ours. And these are merely a few of the infinite variations on the themes of the natural order as it is usually conceived.
>
> But is there really a strange world? Of course. Are there, then, two worlds? Not at all. There is only our own world and it alone is alien to us, intrinsically so by virtue of its lack of mysteries.

This utterance conveys perhaps as succinctly as any Ligotti's own quest: it is not, in the end, a replacement of the real world by the unreal, but a sort of turning the real world inside out to show that it was unreal all along.

The vehicle for this transformation is language. Ligotti has evolved a highly distinctive and idiosyncratic style that, with seeming effortlessness, metamorphoses existence into nightmare. Its closet analogy, on purely stylistic grounds, is the eccentric idiom of M. P. Shiel, although he is not a writer whom Ligotti acknowledges as an influence or model. And yet, the analogy is apt in more than one way. Lovecraft referred to Shiel's "Xélucha" as a "noxiously hideous fragment", and much of Ligotti's work could be so labelled: it stylistically echoes Shiel's tortuous, metaphor-laden prose poetry while at the same time seeking to capture that atmosphere of nightmarish or hallucinatory strangeness that typifies Shiel's best short work. Plot is almost everywhere negligible, and everything is subordinate to mood. There is in Ligotti also a considerable dose of Blackwood's searching exploration of the precise psychological effect of the weird upon human consciousness.

Ligotti, indeed, in essays, interviews, and stories, talks much of style and language, and every one of his stories, successful or otherwise, is written with impeccable meticulousness. In speaking of the need for subtlety in relating a weird tale, Ligotti has remarked that "extraordinary subjects require a certain deviousness in the telling, that a twisted or obscure technique is needed to realize the maximum power of the strange." This rather reminds me of T. S. Eliot's celebrated justification for the obscurity of Modernist poetry, and in fact the resemblance may not be entirely adventitious: the absence of any vivid or realistic

description of the contemporary world gives Ligotti's tales a curiously archaic cast, but in their allusiveness and disregard for the mechanics of plot they are strikingly modern. However much Ligotti draws upon the weird masters of the early part of the century, his work could only have been written by one sensitive to the ambiguities of this *fin de siècle*. If he errs rather more frequently than I would like on the side of excessive obscurity and excessive plotlessness, and if his style remains just on this side (and sometimes on the other side) of bombast and fustian, then it is perhaps an occupational hazard in the sort of highly intellectualised and self-conscious weird fiction Ligotti has chosen to write.

One of Ligotti's many distinctive attributes is the frequency with which he can metafictionally enunciate his own literary agenda in his tales. Many of his stories are just as much about the writing of horror tales as they are horror tales. In **"The Frolic"**, a psychiatrist's report of a madman's visions are uncannily like Ligotti's own aesthetic quest for the unreal:

> "There's actually quite a poetic geography to his interior dreamland as he describes it. He talked about a place that sounded like the back alleys of some cosmic slum, an inner-dimensional dead end. . . . Less fathomable are his memories of a moonlit corridor where mirrors scream and laugh, dark peaks of some kind that won't remain still, a stairway that's 'broken' in a very strange way . . . "

The book Victor Keirion finds in **"Vastarien"** is similar:

> It seemed to be a chronicle of strange dreams. Yet somehow the passages he examined were less a recollection of unruled visions than a tangible incarnation of them, not mere rhetoric but the thing itself. The use of language in the book was arrantly unnatural and the book's author unknown. Indeed, the text conveyed the impression of speaking for itself and speaking only to itself, the words flowing together like shadows that were cast by no forms outside the book. But although this volume appeared to be composed in a vernacular of mysteries, its words did inspire a sure understanding and created in their reader a visceral apprehension of the world they described, existing inseparable from it.

It is not surprising, therefore, that Ligotti has written, in addition to the actual essay **"The Consolations of Horror"**, several pseudo-essays on the writing of weird fiction. The most interesting of these is **"Notes on the Writing of Horror: A Story"**. This work proposes to narrate a tale in three distinct styles—the realistic, the traditional Gothic, and the experimental. In the course of this disquisition it becomes clear where Ligotti's own sympathies lie. He dispenses with the realistic technique, viciously parodying the Stephen King style of mundane realism ("Nathan is a normal and real character, sure. . . . And to make him a bit more real, one could supply his coat, his car, and grandfather's wristwatch with specific brand names, perhaps autobiographically borrowed from one's own closet, garage, and wrist"). The traditional Gothic style is a little more to Ligotti's liking, but only because "isolated supernatural incidents don't look as silly in a Gothic tale as they do in a realistic one." One would imagine that the experimental technique is in fact Ligotti's own, but his lukewarm account of it makes this doubtful. Then we find a fourth technique, and it gains Ligotti's resounding vote of approval: " . . . the proper style of horror is really that of the *personal confession*." This connects with a sentiment in **"The Consolations of Horror"**: "Nothing is worse than that which happens personally to a person." This may be nothing more than the old adage that you can't frighten anyone else unless you yourself are frightened, but in some fashion or other it leads to the curious notion that "the tale teller, ideally, should himself be a writer of horror fiction by trade." The number of writers in Ligotti's fiction is unusually high.

There are, of course, certain drawbacks to this extreme self-consciousness and awareness of the heritage of horror on Ligotti's part. I have already cited, in connexion with Peter Straub, Peter Penzoldt's comment that Lovecraft "was too well read", and I fear that criticism may apply even more aptly to Ligotti. The original edition of ***Songs of a Dead Dreamer*** contained some disastrous attempts at comic rewritings of classic horror tales—*The Island of Dr. Moreau, Dr. Jekyll and and Mr. Hyde, Frankenstein*—which Ligotti wisely removed in the later edition. Elsewhere he has perpetrated still more arid and jejune rewritings of Poe (**"Selections of Poe"**) and Lovecraft (**"Selections of Lovecraft"**). I am utterly at a loss to understand the purpose of these writings. Even a work such as **"Studies in Horror"**—a series of prose poems or vignettes each narrated in a different style (**"Transcendent Horror"**, **"Gothic Horror"**, **"Spectral Horror"**, etc.) —is certainly a *tour de force* of sorts and reveals Ligotti's mastery of these varied idioms, but the whole seems dry and academic. And a story like **"The Mystics of Muelenburg"** suffers from an attention to the niceties of language so excessive as to rob the words of their imagistic power. They don't add up to anything beyond themselves.

At this point I wish to make a brief digression to consider Ligotti's attitude to Lovecraft, since I believe it will enlighten us on his precise place in weird fiction. Ligotti has remarked: "I hope my stories are in the Lovecraftian tradition in that they may evoke a sense of terror whose source is something nightmarishly unreal, the implications of which are disturbingly weird and, in the magical sense, charming." But in explaining why he does not use the framework and nomenclature of Lovecraft's myth-cycle, Ligotti adds that "Lovecraft's universe . . . is a very specific model of reality, one whose portrayal demands a more realistic approach to fiction writing than mine is." The relatively tactful reference to realism is to be noted, since it contrasts violently with the snide attack on supernatural realism in **"Notes on the Writing of Horror"**. And yet, Lovecraft *was* a supernatural realist, and the difference between him and the brand-name realism of Stephen King is a difference of methodology and not, fundamentally, one of approach. Ligotti has flatly declared that he is most attracted to Lovecraft's early tales in which the dream element is more prevalent and the supernatural elements not always satisfactorily accounted for; he has remarked of the later work that "I find Lovecraft's fastidious attempts at creating a documentary style 'reality' an

obstacle to appreciating his work." Two stories by Ligotti are markedly Lovecraftian: **"The Sect of the Idiot"** appears to be influenced most by "The Music of Erich Zann" and "The Festival"; **"The Last Feast of Harlequin"** (dedicated "To the memory of H. P. Lovecraft") does indeed draw upon Lovecraft's late tale "The Shadow over Innsmouth" (but more perhaps upon "The Festival", Lovecraft's earlier working out of the same idea), but we shall see that this story is an extreme anomaly in Ligotti's fiction. In any event, a very crude distinction between Lovecraft and Ligotti might be enunciated as follows: whereas Lovecraft tries to make the unreal (i. e., the supernatural) real, Ligotti tries to make the real unreal (i. e., everything is "supernatural", or at any rate unnatural and monstrous).

Ligotti's emphasis on language has led him, like Lovecraft, to be very prodigal in the inventing of mythical books. *Vastarien, Cynothoglys, The Noctuary of Tine*—these are only a few of the cryptic volumes in the Ligottian library. The author has remarked:

> I have some notes about the "forbidden book," in the Lovecraftian sense, that is, a kind of metaphysical obscenity, an offense against all conception of order. I think my conclusion was that the forbidden book would require the forbidden author to write it, though it might be a work of imagination and not, like the *Necronomicon*, a book of genuine revelation.

Imagination as opposed to revelation: here again is a critical distinction between the Ligottian and the Lovecraftian universe. Lovecraft's tomes reveal loathsome truths about the real world, Ligotti's transport one to the unreal.

"Vastarien" is Ligotti's most searching exploration of the forbidden book theme. The plot of this richly atmospheric tale—which stands with **"The Last Feast of Harlequin"** at the pinnacle of Ligotti's achievement—is deceptively simple: a man finds a book and it drives him mad. But what a wealth of dense imagery is created by means of this seemingly hackneyed device! Victor Keirion searches for a book to transport him out of this world, but most of the "forbidden" books he finds are insufficient for the task: they are all

> sodden with an obscene reality, falsely hermetic ventures which consisted of circling the same absurd landscape. The other worlds portrayed in these books inevitably served as annexes of this one; they were impostors of the authentic unreality which was the only realm of redemption, however gruesome it might appear.

But *Vastarien* is different: it is " 'not *about* something, but actually is that something' ". This is a piquant conception, and a very neat resolution of the inveterate problem of the relation between the signifier and the signified—here they are one! But what sort of book is *Vastarien*? "To all appearances it seemed he had discovered the summit or abyss of the unreal, that paradise of exhaustion, confusion, and debris where reality ends and where one may dwell among its ruins." I shall return to this conception later.

It is already evident that one vehicle by which the unreal is reached is dream. I have no doubt that many of Ligotti's tales incorporate fragments of his own dreams; but there is certainly more to it than that. Consider another comment on Lovecraft: "Lovecraft dreamed the great dream of supernatural literature—to convey with the greatest possible intensity a vision of the universe as a kind of enchanting nightmare." This, too, is clearly Ligotti's dream. It is suggestive that, in answering a query as to why he took to writing horror fiction, he noted: "I've never been tempted to write anything that was not essentially nightmarish"—as if horror and nightmare are fundamentally synonymous.

Ligotti's treatment of the dream theme is complex and multifarious. On occasion it can be very simple, as in **"Oneiric Horror"**, an exquisite prose poem that does nothing but paint a dream. I wonder whether, as with Dunsany's *Book of Wonder,* Ligotti wrote this vignette as a sort of elaboration or commentary on the illustration by Harry O. Morris, Jr, that accompanies it. In any event, the details and objects of this dream are described with all the meticulous realism that other writers would bestow upon the real world. A very suggestive phrase in **"The Dream of a Mannikin"**—"the divinity of the dream"—is capable of two meanings: in the surface plot of the story it refers to the sense of irrefutable reality a dream conveys to its dreamer for the duration of its existence; but it also suggests—again metafictionally—the dominance of dream over reality.

"The Voice in the Bones" is pure nightmare—in every sense of the word it is a noxiously hideous fragment. I have no idea what the plot of this tale is or whether it coheres as a unity; but it contains some of the most potent dream-imagery I have ever read. Curiously, Ligotti seems dissatisfied with the tale, but it certainly comes close to one of his own desiderata: ". . . my ultimate aspiration as a horror writer would be to compose tales that on the surface would seem to be utter phantasmagoric nonsense, yet would convey all those incredible sensations and meanings that overwhelm us in our dreams".

This dream-world or other realm (although recall that it is not an "other" realm but merely an aspect—perhaps the "true" aspect—of this realm) takes a peculiar form in Ligotti. We have already cited some characteristics of it: the "back alleys of some cosmic slum" in **"The Frolic"**, the "paradise of exhaustion, confusion, and debris" in **"Vastarien"**. This notion of the world-as-junkheap is obsessively pervasive in Ligotti, and—although he himself merely states that this sort of imagery has "haunted me since childhood"—I wonder whether it has to do with Ligotti's general world view: "Being something of a pessimist, I tend to think, in those rare moments when I really think, that existence is by nature evil. And nothing is good". **"Mad Night of Atonement"**, a rather tiresome and long-winded story, enunciates this idea. Dr Francis Haxhausen, a sort of itinerant showman very much like Lovecraft's Nyarlathotep, has discovered the "law and the truth of the Creator": "what delight His heart" are "ruins and the ghosts of puppets":

> "All the lonesome pathetic things, all the desolate dusty things, all the misbegotten things, ruined things, failed things, all the imperfect sem-

blances and deteriorating remnants of what we arrogantly deign to call the real, to call . . . Life. In brief, the entire realm of the unreal—wherein He abides—is what He loves like nothing in this world."

This is, I take it, what Robert M. Price has termed Ligotti's Gnostic vision—the notion of the "imbecilic demiurge, a distant relation of the true divinity and the ill-advised creator of the dreadful material world". I wonder, too, whether the mannikin or puppet theme, which also recurs with great frequency in Ligotti's work, can be related to this idea. On the most elementary level the mannikin theme simply suggests a mockery of the human: Dr Haxhausen can momentarily turn human beings into puppets, and perhaps vice versa, and at the end of the tale it appears that Haxhausen's audience—and perhaps the entire world—has been so transformed (or perhaps was so all along). On another level the notion relates to Ligotti's conception of characterisation in weird fiction, as enunciated in **"The Consolations of Horror"**. In discussing "The Fall of the House of Usher" Ligotti notes that we do not genuinely care about the fates of the human characters in the tale—our perspective as readers is more godlike:

> This is a world created with built-in obsolescence, and to appreciate fully this downrunning cosmos one must take the perspective of its creator, which is all perspectives without getting sidetracked into a single one. . . . And the consolation in this is that we are supremely removed from the maddeningly tragic viewpoint of the human.

I cannot help feeling that there is a strain of misanthropy running through Ligotti's work (I hardly need add that this is not meant pejoratively): the protagonist of **"Alice's Last Adventure"** remarks acidly, "Thank goodness there's only one of everybody". The clinical detachment of Ligotti's narrative voice, the sardonic (or, in his poorer work, cheaply sarcastic) tone he adopts in reference to his human puppets, and the number of characters who reveal themselves by their own words to be pompous buffoons certainly underscore a basic scorn for human life.

Some of Ligotti's tales allow a little more of the observably real world than others, and a few of these are among his great successes. **"The Frolic"**, an early and relatively conventional story, is still powerful for the visions of a lunatic that so hideously defy the inept rationalisations of a psychiatrist to account for them naturalistically. **"Alice's Last Adventure"** recounts a rather old idea—fictional characters coming to life—but does so with great adeptness and cumulative power. I could have done without the trite ending—the author, overtaken by her creations, scribbles away to the bitter end—and I also think that this tale is remarkably similar in conception to Jonathan Carroll's *The Land of Laughs* (1980), although perhaps the idea was probably not derived directly from that work.

"Les Fleurs" is emblematic of the "twisted or obscure technique" that Ligotti employs in his work. Here again the plot seems simple—a man evidently lures and kills a series of women—but a profound unease is engendered in the reader because of the many features of the story that are left tantalisingly unexplained. The protagonist has apparently already killed one woman, Clare (it is never explained how), and is now pursuing another one, Daisy. At his apartment he shows her an odd object that looks something like a cactus or perhaps a furry animal (the function of this object is never clarified). He attends meetings of some sort (their nature and purpose are never elucidated). Finally he shows her a painting, but her reaction is not what he was expecting: she is nonplussed and perhaps a little disturbed. And when we read that Daisy now "truly possesse[s] a sure knowledge of my secrets" and that her fate is accordingly sealed, we realise the truth (or, at least, a fragment of the truth): the man is not a mere homicidal maniac but one who wishes to indoctrinate a woman of the proper sensitivity into his mysterious sect, but who must kill any who are not suitable.

Incredibly, **"The Last Feast of Harlequin"** is a relatively early tale of Ligotti's, and yet it is leagues away from the nightmarish unreality of the rest of his work. I trust it is not simply my bias toward supernatural realism that makes me rank this tale as Ligotti's best. If nothing else, it may perhaps be the very best homage to Lovecraft ever written. To call it a mere pastiche would be to do it an injustice.

The story follows traditional Lovecraftian lines: an anthropologist interested in exploring the "significance of the clown figure in diverse cultural contexts" reads an article by a former professor of his, Dr Raymond Thoss (who, I take it, is not the same as the Dr Thoss of **"The Troubles of Dr Thoss"**), about a festival that takes place every year in December in the Midwestern town of Mirocaw. He visits the town in the summer and thinks he sees Dr Thoss there, although he appears transformed into a sort of inarticulate derelict. This compels him actually to go to the town during the festival. He insinuates himself into the goings-on, dresses up as one of the many derelicts who seem to serve some sort of cryptic ritual function, is led by them into an underground chamber where horrors of various sorts transpire. This superficial and incomplete synopsis cannot even begin to suggest the tale's richness of texture, density of atmosphere, psychological and topographical realism, and—the most Lovecraftian feature of all—the notion of ancient and loathsome rituals surviving into the present day, related to and perhaps the origin of the most ancient human myth-cycles. If there is any complaint to be made of this story, it is that it appears to lack the cosmicism of Lovecraft's most representative work. The bulk of the story is very likely derived from Lovecraft's "The Festival" (1923), with a brief nod to "The Shadow over Innsmouth" at the end. The horror of the story seems to affect only random individuals rather than, as in the later Lovecraft, the entire race or the entire cosmos. Nevertheless, **"The Last Feast of Harlequin"** clearly demonstrates that Ligotti can write the sort of documentary realism he appears to scorn without losing the individuality of his own voice.

Thomas Ligotti has been writing for perhaps just over a decade, and it is certainly too early to predict what directions his development will take. That he will develop—or, more pertinently, that he will have to develop—is very clear. I think, frankly, that he has already said about all

that he has to say in his current idiom. My respect for Ligotti is considerable: he has literary gifts beyond what most other writers in this field could even dream of; he has a uniqueness of vision that sets his work radically apart from all others; he is a highly articulate spokesman for his brand of weird fiction; and he has read exhaustively in the best work in the field and has profited enormously thereby. But I am troubled by a number of things: his writing is so self-conscious and self-referential that it utterly lacks spontaneity and emotional vigour; its appeal seems directed almost wholly to the intellect; he seems, apparently by design, not to care about the complete reconciliation of the various supernatural features in a given tale; and a number of his stories—like **"The Shadow at the Bottom of the World"**, one of the most exquisitely modulated pieces of prose I have ever read—are flawlessly written by the sentence but do not in the end convey a very powerful impression. I fervently hope that Ligotti is not in danger—especially in light of the recent championing of his work by leading critics in the field—of becoming self-indulgent, overly obscure, and (worst of all) content to remain at the level he has attained. He will, I believe, have to start writing more *stories*—as opposed to the vignettes, prose poems, sketches, and fragments that so far constitute the bulk of his output—if he is to gain preeminence in the field. Ligotti's own tastes notwithstanding, few will doubt that Lovecraft initiated the most representative phase of his career when he adopted the realism of "The Call of Cthulhu" in 1926; if he had stopped writing before that point, I am not sure we would remember him. This is not to say that Ligotti's current work is somehow qualitatively equal to Lovecraft's pre-1926 work (it is, in some ways, rather better); nor, of course, is it possible to say that **"The Last Feast of Harlequin"** is a harbinger for a realistic phase on Ligotti's part, since it is an early work. But I think that Ligotti will have to write more tales like **"The Last Feast of Harlequin"** or **"Vastarien"** if he is to join the ranks of Lovecraft, Blackwood, Dunsany, Jackson, Campbell, and Klein. . . .

Thomas Ligotti (essay date 1994)

SOURCE: *Noctuary*, Robinson Publishing Ltd., 1994, 194 p.

[In the following essay, Ligotti defines what he perceives are the principal qualities of weird fiction.]

No one needs to be told about what is weird. It is something that becomes known in the early stages of every life. With the very first nightmare or a childhood bout of fever, an initiation takes place into a universal, and at the same time very secret society. Membership in this society is renewed by a lifelong series of encounters with the weird, which may assume a variety of forms and wears many faces. Some of these forms and faces are familiar only to oneself, while others are recognized by practically everybody, whether they will admit it or not.

Weird experience is in fact so prevalent that it is taken profoundly for granted, lying unnoticed in the back rooms of a person's life and even further removed in the life of the world at large. But it is always there, waiting to be recalled in those special moments that are all its own. These moments are for the most part rather brief and relatively rare: the intense weirdness of a dream fades upon waking and is often utterly forgotten; the twisted thoughts of a delirium soon uncoil themselves upon recovery from illness; even a first-hand, wide-awake confrontation with the extraordinary may lose the shocking strangeness it initially possessed and ultimately consign itself to one of those back rooms, those waiting rooms of the weird.

So the point is clear: experience of the weird is a fundamental and inescapable fact of life. And, like all such facts, it eventually finds its way into forms of artistic expression. One of those forms has been termed, of all things, weird fiction. The stories that constitute this literary genre are repositories of the weird; they are something like those remote rooms where the dreams and deliriums and spectral encounters are kept, except that they may be visited at any time and thus make up a vast museum where the weird is on permanent display.

But does anyone need to be told what weird fiction is all about, anymore than an introduction is required to the weird itself? It is strongly possible that the answer to this question is yes. The reason for this answer is that weird fiction is not something experienced in the same way by everyone: it is not a nightmare or a fit of fever; certainly it is not a meeting in the mist with something that is not supposed to be. It is only a type of story, and a story is an echo or a transmutation of experience, while also an experience in its own right, different from any other in the way it *happens* to someone and in the way it is felt. It seems probable, then, that the experience of weird stories can be enhanced and illuminated by focusing on their special qualities, their various forms and many faces.

For example, there is a well-known story that goes as follows: *A man awakes in the darkness and reaches over for his eyeglasses on the nightstand. The eyeglasses are placed in his hand.*

This is the bare bones of so many tales that have caused readers to shiver with a sense of the weird. You might simply accept this shiver and pass on to other things; you might even try to suppress the full power of this episode if it be too vividly conceived. On the other hand, it is possible, and considered by some to be desirable, to achieve the optimal receptiveness to the incident in question, to open up to it in order to allow its complete effect and suggestiveness to take hold.

This is not a matter of deliberate effort; on the contrary, how much more difficult it is to put this scene out of one's mind, especially if such a story is read at the proper time and under proper circumstances. Then it happens that a reader's own mind is filled with the darkness of that room in which someone, anyone, awakes. Then it happens that the inside of a reader's skull becomes the shadow-draped walls of that room and the whole drama is contained in a place from which there is no escape.

Stripped-down as this tale is, it nonetheless does not look for plot. There is the most natural of beginnings, the perfect action of the middle, and a curtain-closer of an end that drops down darkness upon darkness. There is a protagonist and an antagonist and a meeting between them which, abrupt as it is, remains crystalline in its fateful nature. No epilogue is required to settle the issue that the man has awakened to something that has been waiting for him, and for no one else, in that dark room. And the weirdness of it, looked full in the face, can be quite affecting.

Once again: A man awakes in the darkness and reaches over for his eyeglasses on the nightstand. The eyeglasses are placed in his hand.

At this point it should be recalled that there is an old identity between the words "weird" and "fate" (of which one notable modern instance is Clark Ashton Smith's "The Weird of Avoosl Wuthoqquan," the fate of the title character being one that is prophesied by a beggar and consummated by a famished monstrosity). And this old pair of synonyms insists on the resurrection of an old philosophy, even the oldest—that of fatalism.

To perceive, even if mistakenly, that all one's steps have been heading toward a prearranged appointment, to realize one has come face to face with what seems to have been waiting all along—this is the necessary framework, the supporting skeleton of the weird. Of course, fatalism, as a philosophical slant on human existence, has long since been out of fashion, eclipsed by a taste for indeterminacy and a mock-up of an "open-ended" universe. It nevertheless happens that certain ordeals in the lives of actual people may reinstate an ancient, irrational view of things. Such ordeals always strike one with their strangeness, their digression from the normal flow of events, and often provoke a universal protest: "Why me?" Be sure that this is not a question but an outcry. The person who screams it has been instilled with an astonishing suspicion that he, in fact, has been the perfect subject for a very specific "weird," a tailor-made fate, and that a prior engagement, in all its weirdness, was fulfilled at the appointed time and place.

No doubt this queer sense of destiny is an illusion. And the illusion is created by the same stuff that fleshes out the skeletal framework of the weird. This is the stuff of dreams, of fever, of unheard-of encounters; it clings to the bones of the weird and fills out its various forms and fills in its many faces. Because in order for the illusion of fate to be most deeply established, it must be connected to some matter that is out of the ordinary, something that was not considered part of the existential plan, though in retrospect cannot be seen otherwise.

After all, no weird revelation is involved when someone sees a dime on the sidewalk, picks up the coin, and pockets it. Even if this is not an everyday occurrence for a given individual, it remains without any overtones or implications of the fateful, the extraordinary. But suppose this coin has some unusual feature that, upon investigation, makes it a token of considerable wealth. Suddenly a great change, or at least the potential for change, enters into someone's life; suddenly the expected course of things threatens to veer off toward wholly unforeseen destinations.

It could seem that the coin might have been overlooked

as it lay on the pavement, that its finder might easily have passed it by as others surely had done. But whoever has found this unusual object and discovers its significance soon realizes something: he has been lured into a trap and is finding it difficult to imagine that things might have been different. The former prospects of his life become distant and can now be seen to have been tentative in any case: what did he ever really know about the path his life was on before he came upon that coin? Obviously very little. But what does he know about such things now that they have taken a rather melodramatic turn? No more than he ever did, which becomes even more apparent when he eventually falls victim to a spectral numismatist who wants his rare coin returned. Then our finder-keeper comes into a terrible knowledge about the unknowable, the mysterious, the truly weird aspect of his existence—the extraordinary fact of the universe and of one's being in it. Paradoxically, it is the uncommon event that may best demonstrate the common predicament.

At the same time the weird is, to repeat, a relatively elusive, unwonted phenomenon making its appearance in the moments that upset the routine and that are most willingly forgotten. As it happens in real life, the nightmare serves primarily to impart an awareness of what it means to be awake; the unfavorable diagnosis most often merely offers a lesson in the definition of health; and the supernatural itself cannot exist without the predominant norms of nature.

In fiction, however, those periods may be prolonged in which someone is trapped in an extraordinary fate. The entrapments presented in weird fiction may go so far as to be absolute, a full illustration of what was always in the works and only awaited discovery. Because the end of any weird story is also quite often a definitive end for the characters involved. Thus, it only remains for the reader to appreciate a foregone conclusion, a fate that is presented, in a manner of speaking, at arm's length.

The principal effect of weird fiction is a sense of what might be called *macabre unreality:* "macabre" because of that skeleton of fate, which points its exposed finger in the direction of doom; "unreal" because of the extraordinary habiliments of that fate, a flapping garb of mystery which will never uncover its secret. The double sense of macabre unreality attains its most piercing intensity in the enigma that is at the center of every great weird story. And it is this quality that forms the focus of one's appreciation of the weird in fiction.

By definition the weird story is based on an enigma that can never be dispelled if it be true to the weird experience—which may occur entirely in an author's imagination—that serves as its only justifiable provenance. While this enigma will definitely exude an ambiance of the graveyard, it menaces as much by its unreal nature, its disorienting strangeness, as by its connections with the great world of death. Such a narrative scheme is usefully contrasted with that of the realistic "suspense" story, in which a character is threatened with a familiar, often purely physical doom. Whatever identifiable manifestations and phenomena are presented in a weird story—from traditional ghosts to the scientific nightmares of the modern

age—there remains at the heart of the tale a kind of abyss from which the weird emerges and into which it cannot be pursued for purposes of analysis or resolution. Some enigmatic quality is thereby preserved in these tales of nameless and terrible unknowns. Like the finder of that "valuable" coin, the man who awakes in the night and reaches out for his eyeglasses is brought into proximity with an unknown, on this occasion in the form of a thing without a name. This is an extreme instance, perhaps the purest example, of a plot that recurs throughout the history of weird fiction.

Another, more distinguished, example of the enigmatic plot of a weird tale is that paradigm of weirdness—H. P. Lovecraft's "The Colour out of Space." In this story a complex of phenomena and events is set off by an intruding force of unknown origin and nature that comes to settle itself in a dark well at the center of the narrative and from there proceeds to rule like a faceless tyrant over every mechanism of the plot. When it finally makes its exit toward the end of the story, neither the characters involved nor the reader knows anything more about this visitor than they did at the beginning. This last statement is not entirely factual: what everyone quite certainly learns about the "colour" is that contact with this apparition from the stars is an introduction to that macabre unreality that is both a commonplace of the weird and yet also an experience to which one never grows accustomed—and with which one is *never* at ease.

Still other examples of the all-important enigma on which the great weird stories are founded could be proffered, from E. T. A. Hoffmann's "The Sandman" to Ramsey Campbell's "The Scar," but the point is evident by now: what is truly weird in both literature and life only carries a minimum of flesh on its bones—enough to allow certain issues to be raised and evoke the properly gruesome response but never so much that the shredded fingers stretched out to us turn into the customary gladhand of everyday affairs.

Admittedly, the extraordinary as a shaper of one's fate—that is, one's inevitable death—is a rather ostentatious

---

On Ligotti's versatility:

The strongest testament to Ligotti's versatility is the collection of very short pieces in the final section [of *Noctuary*], "Notebook of the Night." These sketched stories, extended images and ghostly snatches seem to burst from Ligotti's pen faster than he can get them down. Some of the ideas: seemingly solid flesh is actually quite mutable; you can fall into your dreams; a necropolis of dust and bones may be our truest reality; death itches. This last barrage of images leaves one in awe of Ligotti's artistry and—just for a second, confusing him with one of his characters—quietly wondering if it is due to genius or madness.

Linda Marotta in a review of Noctuary, Fangoria,
May, 1994.

and, more often than not, vulgar device for representing human existence. However, weird fiction seeks not to place before us the routine procedures most of our kind follow on the way to the grave but to recover some of the amazement we sometimes feel, and should probably feel more often, at existence in its essential aspect. To reclaim this sense of amazement at the monumentally macabre unreality of life is to awaken to the weird—just as the man in the room awakens in the perpetual hell of his brief story, shakes off his sleep-dulled sensibility, and reaches out to that unknown thing in the darkness. Now, even without his eyeglasses, he can truly see. And perhaps, if only for that moment of artificial terror that weird fiction affords, so can the rest of us.

Edward Bryant   (essay date 1994)

SOURCE: A review of *Noctuary* in *Locus,* Vol. 32, No. 3, March, 1994, pp. 31-2.

[*Bryant is an American science fiction and fantasy writer and critic. In the following review, he praises Ligotti's originality and his dense and complex literary style.*]

The horror of Detroit used to be its reputation as the murder capital of the United States. But before that unfortunate circumstance could be commemorated more permanently with granite markers, statues, and theme parks, the mantle of fatal greatness was passed on to such civilized garden spots as Washington, D.C. and Gary, Indiana. Fortunately for its terrifying image, however, Detroit has spawned at least two of modern horror's most distinctive practitioners: Kathe Koja and Thomas Ligotti. Each is *sui generis*. Neither can be mistaken for those generic writers whose covers stereotypically display a capering embossed skeleton or an evilly smirking moppet. Ligotti and Koja do not craft fiction that is all that simple-minded. It's not bubblegum prose. Neither writer's work is terribly warm and cuddly. But while Koja's work is considered by most to be innovative, cutting-edge, and stylishly hip, Ligotti's prose takes another tack.

Ligotti suggests something of a sharper H.P. Lovecraft (with perhaps a strong dash of Clark Ashton Smith and a real undercurrent of Mr. Poe) retooled for the last half of this twentieth century. I frankly feel that Ligotti is a far more exacting stylist than HPL, even when his dense style flirts with the prolix and embraces the darkly adjectival. At least Ligotti doesn't publicly disdain the swarthier races, and he does display both occasional close encounters with humor and unexpected brushes with contemporary idiom.

All this is by way of saying that Ligotti's prose is not exactly something light and frothy that the casual reader sucks down with a mental soda straw. This author's verbal obliquity can sometimes be so sufficiently frustrating as to challenge a reasonable degree of patience.

But it's also by way of saying that Ligotti's new collection, *Noctuary,* is a challenging and rewarding experience for the adventurous and eclectic reader. *Noctuary* is indeed a refuge of the night and all the disquieting terrors that inhabit the universe's shadowed corners. This is a perfect book to take along as reading material on long, thoughtful walks through old graveyards. And if those bone orchards anachronistically happen to be located in the midst of the crumbling cities, so much the better. The sensibility Ligotti's writing voice whispers in your ear may madden a reader reared on MTV—or even quick-cutting of a more traditional nature—but certainly is not dustily archaic.

The text of *Noctuary* neatly divides into four parts: an introductory essay in which the author eloquently discourses on his esthetic of weird fiction; two quartets of mostly new short fiction; and "Notebook of the Night", something of a commonplace book of 19 vignettes, effectively a mini-collection of prose poems. In Ligotti's "Foreword", he reminds us not only that experience of the weird is something we all encounter and define for ourselves, individually and early on, but also we should recall the ancient equivalency of "weird" and fate. He also makes the esthetic point, citing stories from Lovecraft, Campbell, and E.T.A. Hoffmann, that "/ what is truly weird in both literature and life only carries a minimum of flesh on its bones—enough to allow certain issues to be raised and evoke the properly gruesome response, but never so much that the shredded fingers stretched out to us turn into the customary gladhand of everyday affairs." In terms of graphic horrific content, Ligotti *does* carry only the minimum of flesh on the bones. And no, the grip extended to us as readers is certainly not a customary gladhand.

Case in point where the medium is the metaphor. There is a story called **"The Strange Design of Master Rignolo"**, in which two disjointedly odd gentlemen, perhaps late of an Ionesco play, pay a visit to the unusual landscape painter of the title. Here is what Grissul and Nolon discover as they contemplate the works of Master Rignolo: "They were all very similar to one another. Given such titles as 'Glistening Marsh', 'The Tract of Three Shadows', and 'The Stars, the Hills', they were not intended to resemble as much as *suggest* the promised scenes. A vague hint of material forms might emerge here and there, some familiar effect of color or outline, but for the most part they could be described as extremely remote in their perspective on tangible reality." Indeed, I am quoting out of context, but I do think that the lines do give some taste of how Ligotti's tales are told. The sinister, the ominous, but most of all, the apprehension of dread plays icy virtuoso fingers on the pipe organ of our nerves. In **"Master Rignolo"**, the two art patrons are far more than they first appear, and the hapless painter finds himself in even direr straits than, say, the poor artist in HPL's "Pickman's Model".

So it goes, throughout. In the longish account of **"The Tsalal"**, a "skeleton" town meets its long-time-in-coming weird. **"Mrs. Rinaldi's Angel"** shows us a child in the care of an old woman who specializes in dealing with "spectral afflictions." **"Conversations in a Dead Language"** is a wonderful Hallowe'en story showing us a man in a perpetual state of psychic trick-or-treat-dom. The initial scene of a pumpkin being carved is worth the price of admission.

As with most collections, not every story is as successful as every other. **"Mad Night of Atonement"**, for example, is a frustrating tale of science twined with metaphysics. We see a genuinely mad scientist running up against his fate. Penetrating this account several times left a number of glazed layers equally over my eyes and brain. Now I say this realizing that all horror fiction—indeed fiction of *any* variety—does not equally affect every reader. Universality of effect can be nice, but it's not easily achievable. And probably not all of Ligotti's dreads are mine as well. But I still do not think he knows science and scientists very well.

I particularly enjoyed the "Notebook of the Night" section, possibly because my brain was in a state more agreeably to digest the author's shorter, more discretely bundled weirds. So much here is especially dream-like, particularly reminiscent of some of my childhood feverdream recollections.

It is, in one of the vignettes, **"The Career of Nightmares"**, that Thomas Ligotti crafts a line that finally defines the reaction the sympathetic reader will take away from this collection: "Everyone recalls this final flight from the nightmare; everyone knows how to scream."

Everyone knows how to scream. I think there is no way to articulate it better.

Shawn Ramsey: *What is your greatest goal as an author of horror?*

Thomas Ligotti: I suppose my ultimate aspiration as a horror writer would be to compose tales that on the surface would seem to be utter phantasmagoric nonsense, yet would convey all those incredible sensations and meanings that overwhelm us in our dreams.

. . . . .

What do you consider your best work?

I really have to give the stock answer—that my best work is the one lying half-written underneath my bed.

Thomas Ligotti with Shawn Ramsey, in an interview in Deathrealm, *No. 8, Spring, 1989.*

Stefan R. Dziemianowicz (essay date 1994)

SOURCE: A review of *Noctuary* in *The New York Review of Science Fiction*, April, 1994, pp. 4-6.

[*In the following review, Dziemianowicz commends Ligotti's devotion to "an intense evocation of the weird" in his fiction.*]

Thomas Ligotti's first two story collections, **Songs of a Dead Dreamer** (1989) and **Grimscribe** (1991), revealed him to be a truly original writer whose approach to the weird tale is both innovative and virtually inimitable. There was every reason to expect his third collection would yield reading experiences unlike those found in any other book of weird fiction, and surprisingly they begin with his introduction. In lieu of the customary "how they got here" foreword or backslapping appreciation by a colleague that preface most story collections, Ligotti devotes nearly seven pages to defining weird fiction. It's not the

first time that he's probed the weird tale to see what makes it tick—the tongue-in-cheek **"Professor Nobody's Little Lectures on Supernatural Horror"** and the devious meld of critique and fiction **"Notes on the Writing of Horror"** were among the highlights of **Songs,** while the metafictional speculations of **"Nethescurial"** in **Grimscribe** extended his reputation as one of the weird tale's few living critical theorists. But "In the Night, In the Dark: A Note on the Appreciation of Weird Fiction" is Ligotti's most direct exploration of the ocean in which he swims. As such, it can be read as a roadmap not only to the stories that follow it, but to his work in general.

The distinguishing trademark of the weird tale, in Ligotti's estimation, is the element of fate.

> To perceive, even if mistakenly, that all one's steps have been heading toward a prearranged appointment, to realize one has come face to face with what seems to have been waiting all along—this is the necessary framework, the supporting skeleton of the weird Fate, in this context, is the power of a weird experience to give the illusion (usually discernible only in retrospect) that it is the culmination of a series of seemingly random everyday events.
> The pattern that manifests does not lead to illumination but, paradoxically, "into a terrible knowledge about the unknowable, the mysterious, the truly weird aspect of . . . existence—the extraordinary fact of the universe and of one's being in it." Perhaps most important, this enigma is "a kind of abyss from which the weird emerges and into which it cannot be pursued for purposes of analysis or resolution."

Fate, paradox, "a flapping garb of mystery which will never uncover its secret" and "an enigma that can never be dispelled if it be true to the weird experience"—it would be unfair to say that these elements are absent from most modern weird tales, but certainly they are diluted greatly when they are rendered through soothing scenarios that reinforce a sense of moral order, or suggest that the supernatural is at worst an unsightly blemish whose removal restores the cosmetic appearance of the cosmic scheme.

What makes Ligotti's fiction seem so openly in revolt against most modern weird fiction—and for that matter helps distinguish it from the work of Poe, Hoffmann, Lovecraft, and other classic writers from whose work his introductory insights are distilled—is his willingness to confront the grim implications of the weird tale head-on, and acknowledge that once the weird element is introduced into a story there is no going back to the comforting worldviews that have hitherto sustained the characters, and by proxy the reader. In this regard Ligotti is probably the genre's most committed purist, a writer who subordinates plot, character, and virtually every other narrative element that this kind of tale shares with other types of fiction to an intense evocation of the weird. Even the language that most writers use as a tool for crafting a weird effect becomes in Ligotti's hands an integral part of that effect, its ambiguous nuances reflecting the incomprehensibility of the thing it describes. The result of this all-or-nothing approach is stories that occasionally skirt obscurity, but much more often perfectly express the "disorient-ing strangeness" that is the hallmark of the weird.

Because Ligotti's tales depend as much on how they are told as what they tell, it is difficult to summarize them out of context. What's more, the stories in *Noctuary* seem or-dered even more consciously than those in *Grimscribe* (which was marketed as a sort of "fix-up" novel) to de-scribe an arc that moves the reader progressively deeper into Ligotti's "abyss" of the weird.

"The Medusa," the story that opens both the book and the section subtitled "Studies in Shadow," is on the surface one of Ligotti's more benign efforts. The enigma at its cen-ter is the titular monster, an object of perverse fascination for writer Lucian Dregler. Ligotti does not make it clear whether the Medusa Dregler seeks is the literal Gorgon of Greek mythology or simply a malign spirit that has per-sisted through the ages. However, there is no question that we are meant to think of it as indescribably foul, for it in-spires Dregler to jot notes interspersed throughout the text such as "The worshipants of the Medusa . . . are the most hideous citizens of this earth," and the cryptic epi-gram "We may hide from horror only in the heart of hor-ror."

The story follows a paradoxical progression typical of Li-gotti's tales, in which narrative events gradually withdraw from the external world to the psychological landscape of the protagonist, even as the horrors they evoke attain a scope that transcend the protagonist's solitary experience. Enticed by a colleague who promises to further his pursuit of the Medusa, Dregler agrees to keep an assignation at a used bookstore. This initiates a sequence of mysterious yet seemingly innocuous events which, colored by Dregler's expectations, set him irreversibly on the path to his weird fate. In the claustrophobic recesses of the book-store's basement Dregler encounters a mute woman who presses pieces of paper into his hand with prewritten an-swers to his questions on them. One bears a nearby ad-dress. Upon visiting that address, he is conducted into a seemingly ordinary room from where he experiences something which causes him to flee in panic.

Later, Dregler's colleague explains that the meeting with the woman in the bookstore was nothing but "a recondite practical joke" perpetrated by a mutual friend. This plot twist recalls Ligotti's earlier story **"The Spectacles in the Drawer,"** in which a curio collector tricks an annoying ac-quaintance into believing that a pair of plain eyeglasses is a gateway to "a far-off realm of secret truth," only to find the man destroyed by what he "sees" with them. Similar-ly, Dregler's anticipation of the outcome of his meeting with the Medusa appears to have afforded him a glimpse of another side of reality, one where she is a petrifying presence whose existence transforms hideously everything he sees. Though clouded in ambiguity, Dregler's final sur-render to his horrifying vision suggests a disturbing expla-nation for the story's epigram: we *all* "hide in the heart of horror" through our obliviousness to the dark possibili-ties of existence, and it is this merciful oblivion from which Dregler has been rudely awakened.

"The Medusa" is one of a handful of Ligotti stories

(among them **"The spectacles in the Drawer,"** **"Alice's Last Adventure"** and **"Vastarien"**) that leaves room for the explanation that its protagonist is simply a madman who has succumbed to his delusions. But as the opening hand dealt in *Noctuary,* it announces the high stakes Li-gotti plays for. In his literary universe, the occurrence of the inexplicable forces a harsh reassessment of the criteria by which the natural and supernatural, the real and the unreal, the normal and the uncanny are distinguished from one another.

If there is a "moral" to Ligotti's stories—although I can think of no other body of weird fiction outside of Lo-vecraft's where terms like "moral," "good" and "evil" have so little significance—it is the observation made by the narrator of his 1982 story **"Drink to Me Only with Labyrinthine Eyes"** that "nothing is what it seems to be." Eschewing familiar renderings of the supernatural as phe-nomena that stand out in sharp relief against a backdrop of "normalcy," Ligotti evokes the weird by showing how his characters' assumption of what is normal are based on narrow understandings of what can and cannot be. In the second and fourth stories in *Noctuary,* **"Conversations in a Dead Language"** and **"Mrs. Rinaldi's Angel,"** he wreaks intriguing variations on the child molester and vampire story, undermining the expectations for the predator-prey relationship common to both story types.

The events in **"Conversations"** take place over three suc-cessive Halloweens, and are seen from the point of view of a reclusive mailman decorating his house for the holi-day. Ligotti's sardonic description of pumpkin carving in overtones more appropriate for a ritual sacrifice is the first clue that this is no ordinary suburbanite preparing for trick-or-treaters:

> First he carved out an eye, spearing the triangle with the point of his knife and neatly drawing the pulpy thing from its socket. Pinching the blade, he slid his two fingers along the blunt edge, pushing the eye onto the newspaper he'd carefully placed next to the sink. Another eye, a nose, a howling oval mouth. Done. Except for manually scooping out the seedy and stringy en-trails and supplanting them with a squat little candle of the vigil type. Guide them, holy lan-tern, through darkness and disaster. To me. To meezy-weezy.

The mailman's avuncular repartee with his visitors is no more reassuring:

> Trick or treat: midget vampire, couldn't be more than six years old. Wave to Mom waiting on the sidewalk. "*Very* scary. Your parents must be proud. Did you do all that make-up work your-self," he whispered. The little thing mutely gazed up, its eyes underlidded with kohl-dark smudges. It then used a tiny finger, pointy nail painted black, to indicate the guardian figure near the street. "Mom, huh? Does she like sour-balls? Sure she does. Here's some for Mom and some more for yourself, nice red ones to suck on. That's what you scary vampires like, eh?"

Suspicions we're inside the head of a sort of Uncle Creepy in mufti are clinched by his obsession with a snickering brother-and-sister team who visit two years in a row. He is that familiar figure of horror fiction, the unassuming "monster in our midst," and Ligotti drives this theme home by rendering it against a background of increasing cold and darkness that reflect the character's worsening mood. When only the subdued sister shows up the third year, it's not hard to guess what has happened to the boy or who is responsible. Such characters inevitably meet with a gruesome and poetically just fate and Ligotti does not disappoint. However, he drops enough hints throughout the story to suggest that the apparent act of supernatural vengeance with which it ends really shows how grossly the mailman underestimated the peculiar nature of his child victim.

A similar unexpected role reversal underlies the horrors of **"Mrs. Rinaldi's Angel,"** which proffers dreams as parasitical "maggots of the mind and soul" that feed vampirically on our personalities and experiences. Here, a young boy plagued by nightmares seeks the aid of Mrs. Rinaldi, who has developed a homeopathic method for suppressing them and their corruption of the angelic soul. Beguiled by the seeming innocence of her patient, Mrs. Rinaldi forgets that some parasitic relationships are actually beneficial to the host. Relieved of the psychological debilitation brought on by his dreams, the boy finds he has an "appetite . . . for banqueting on the absurd and horrible, even the perfectly evil," which expands to fill the newly-created void in his nights.

Virtually nothing happens in **"The Prodigy of Dreams,"** the third story in the book's first section, yet it leaves one with the impression of a vast sweep of cosmic events rushing to an inevitable conclusion. Arthur Emerson is a scholar whose interests have been conditioned by an early sensitivity to "strange expanses not subject to common view" which he perceives as "a certain . . . confusion, a swirling, fluttering motion that was belied by the relative order of the seen." In a world where the most unremarkable sights are capable of suggesting chaos, those with even a hint of the unusual compound this sense simply by ordering several into a pattern of increasing inscrutability—the peculiar behavior of swans on a pond, a housecat turning nasty, the discovery in the cellar of the remains of several animals ordered "Like a trail of dominos winding round and round"—Ligotti sets the stage for Emerson's preordained rendezvous with Cynothoglys, "the god of changes and confusion" who serves as the demiurge behind perceived reality.

These three stories in the "Studies in Shadow" section certainly convey the "disorienting strangeness" that Ligotti strives for. However, the selections that most fully embody his introductory remarks on the role of fate in the weird tale are those set farther from the genre's usual byways, in the unique shadow world that is Ligotti's most distinctive contribution to weird fiction. Here, Ligotti integrates characters with obscure identities and motives into landscapes that seem to teeter perilously on the verge of chaos, and somehow manages to reveal a design in the bizarre events that unfold.

With its view of a world in which "the incredible sprawl of human history was no more than a pathetically partial record of universal metamorphoses," **"The Prodigy of Dreams"** anticipates the quarter of stories in the "Discourse on Blackness" section, each of which is driven by a vision of encroaching chaos. Chief among these is **"The Tsalal,"** the one story written originally for this volume. Set in the town of Moxton, a "place where the illusion of a reality was worn quite thin and where the gods of order and design could barely breathe," it presents a literal incursion of chaos in the person of Andrew Maness, a child born from the union of a mortal woman with the entity of the title, which represents the "absolute disorder" of the unreal. The unholy consummation was effected by Andrew's father, a man who once embraced "this great blackness, this shadow" when he realized it was "the very nucleus of our universe," something that formed the "dark background" against which the gods worshiped by men "forever carried on their escapades as best they could."

Centered around the pilgrimage of the elect of the Tsalal back to Moxton to prevent further penetration of their namesake into the world, the story recalls Ligotti's earlier work, **"The Mystics of Muelenburg,"** which tells of a village's horrifying discovery that reality is only a consensual illusion that falls apart when people cease to believe consciously in it. Indeed, the story encompasses many themes in Ligotti's fiction, including the idea of an everlengthening succession of deities controlling other deities, and the interface between the real and unreal in environments whose decay and squalor opens a window on the cosmic disorder to which all things entropically tend.

Thoughts from Ligotti's nonfiction (in particular his uncollected essay **"The Consolations of Horror"**) can be found here as well: Andrew's father collects Gothic horror stories, the abundance of which "were written for a world which had begun to slight the gods of order and design, to question their very existence and to exalt in the disorders of the grotesque." Add its nods to Poe (from whose "Narrative of A. Gordon Pym" the name Tsalal is taken) and Lovecraft (especially "The Dunwich Horror"), the two writers who have most noticeably influenced Ligotti's work, as well to the religious mythology that informs so much supernatural fiction (the story's events begin with a travesty of the virgin birth and end with an equally grotesque variation on the Holy Eucharist) and you have what I suspect Ligotti means to be another of his metafictional ruminations on how the weird tale—particularly his type of weird tale—works. It's not as inventive an experiment as his **"Notes on the Writing of Horror Fiction,"** which masterfully seduces the reader into believing he is reading an essay on the craft of horror before mutating unexpectedly into a tale of madness and murder, but it could serve as a fine introduction to Ligotti for readers unfamiliar with his work.

Despite the vagueness of its subject, **"The Tsalal"** shows a symmetry in structure lacking in the book's remaining stories. This is not to say that these stories are in any way unfinished, but rather that they maintain a level of abstractness appropriate for their concerns. The centerpiece of **"Mad Night of Atonement,"** for example, is a dramatic monologue delivered by Dr. Haxhausen, a renegade scientist cut from the same cloth as the eponymous character of **"Dr. Locrian's Asylum"** (1987), who apprehended the underlying truth of existence only after he embraced madness. Although Haxhausen once believed in the perfectability of life, his arcane studies have led him to accept our "true destiny of . . . disintegration." To promulgate his new philosophy, he tours the country with his "puppet machine," a kaleidoscopic contraption whose shafts of colored light reveal inorganic objects and the "cumbersome structures of biology" to be indistinguishable components in his *"tableau mort"* of life. Pursuing this idea of the homogenization of the inanimate and animate in **"The Strange Design of Master Rignolo,"** Ligotti introduces a painter whose surreal interpretations of familiar landscapes permit "a *living* communion with the void" that compels observers to literally "grow into" the substance of his paintings as they view them.

Ligotti's preoccupation with the breakdown of forms and shapes that confer meaning extends even to his narrative style. In an 1989 interview in *Deathrealm,* he remarked how his "ultimate aspiration as a horror writer would be to compose tales that on the surface would seem to be utter phantasmagoric nonsense, yet would convey all those incredible sensations and meanings that overwhelm us in our dreams." With its reproduction of not only powerful nightmare imagery, but the non-linear continuity of dreams and the rhythm with which their events oscillate between subjective and objective perception, **"The Voice in the Bones"** is the proper culmination of *Noctuary's* "Discourse on Blackness" section, rounding out the apparent organizational scheme of the book's contents and showing the direction in which all of the stories preceding it have been heading.

"The Voice in the Bones" also prepares the reader for the concluding "Notebook of the Night" section, which is comprised of some nineteen fragments and prose poems that develop a theme or idea through a single vivid image. Read out of context (as many of them undoubtedly were when they first appeared in *Fantasy Macabre* and other small press magazines), they might seem interesting sports of weird fiction. As the coda to *Noctuary,* though, they read like the raw material from which these stories are fashioned, and thus are as integral to the book as the introduction where Ligotti describes how such fashioning takes place. Regardless of whether one reads them as completed works in their own right or works in progress, they are just additional examples of the remarkable consistency of vision that ties together all of Ligotti's fiction and distinguishes his collections from the odd-lot gatherings typical of even our best short fiction writers. So far, Ligotti has managed to avoid the pitfall of his singular vision devolving into monotony and tedium. *Noctuary,* like *Songs of a Dead Dreamer* and *Grimscribe,* reads with the intense conviction of an author who writes what he does because he has little choice.

S. T. Joshi (essay date 1994)

SOURCE: "Reservations for Three," in *Necrofile: The Review of Horror Fiction,* No. 12, Spring 1994, pp. 11-13.

[*In the following essay, Joshi addresses the shortcomings in Ligotti's fiction, particularly the short stories collected in* Noctuary.]

Thomas Ligotti is no longer a secret. Although the first edition of his first book, *Songs of a Dead Dreamer* (1986), was released almost surreptitiously by a small-press publisher, it was picked up three years later by major firms in both America and England and very properly received enthusiastic reviews ("Put this volume on the shelf between Lovecraft and Poe, where it belongs"). His second volume, *Grimscribe: His Lives and Works* (1991), seems to have been reviewed even more favourably, as was only right for a collection that continued its author's unique and quite twisted vision of the world in tales that were still more deft in style, theme, and substance than those of its predecessor. Now we have *Noctuary* which gathers much of Ligotti's hitherto uncollected work and adds one lengthy new story.

What I have found refreshing about Ligotti up to this point is not merely his very distinctive contributions to the literature of the weird but his remarkable aloofness from the cliquishness that currently dominates commercial horror writing. He has flatly claimed his inability (perhaps a humble euphemism for unwillingness) to write a "horror novel"; he avoids the mutual backpatting (I'll blurb your book if you blurb mine) that has made such a mockery of critical standards in the field; he appears content to appear in the small press, largely because he is one of those "professional" writers who actually has a real job (he is an editor at Gale Research Co. in Detroit) and therefore does not need to churn out fiction by the yard to put food on the table. What all this boils down to is that Ligotti has so far demonstrated a high level of *artistic sincerity* that keeps him rigidly fixed on his own aesthetic goals as a writer and allows him to scorn the siren's song of quick profits that leads so often and so deservedly to quick oblivion.

And yet, what are we to make of a writer who has issued two collections in less than five years? This may not perhaps seem excessive, especially as his last two collections are quite slim and as there is only one original work in this newest volume. Certainly, the example of Ramsey Campbell is always there to remind us that quality and quantity need not be mutually exclusive. And yet, if I am less than enthusiastic about *Noctuary,* it is only because I do not wish to see Ligotti being pressured by his publishers or his readers into producing more than he comfortably can or assembling what frankly comes dangerously close to barrel-scrapings. That Ligotti's barrel-scrapings are generally superior to most other writers' best offerings is beside the point.

Noctuary is, for no especially compelling reason, divided into three sections, preceded by an introduction that reprints his **"Dark Chamber"** essay from *Necrofile* #1. That introduction is a discussion on the notion of "weird", both as a word and as a conception; but its title, "In the Night, in the Dark", points to the essence of Ligotti's work—the incursion of dream-elements into "ordinary" life. But, as I have said elsewhere, this is a misconstrual of Ligotti's method: it is not that he simply inserts the dreamlike into the "real", but that he shows that what we take to be "real" is itself a sort of mad dream. Although in his introduction Ligotti declares that "the supernatural itself cannot exist without the predominant norms of nature", those "norms"—if meant as a realistic portrayal of mundane life-are so lacking in his work that no genuine contrast with the unreal is established. This is by no means a flaw-it is meant merely as a characterisation of Ligotti's work. On the whole he seems so devoid of interest in the "real" world that he cannot take the trouble to describe it. The occasionally vivid tableau or sharp insight into human character that we stumble upon in his tales may make us aware that he does not lack the ability at either topographical or psychological realism; but Ligotti finds the real world in itself so prosy and wearying that he prefers merely to plunge the reader directly into the unreal. This method has both its virtues and its drawbacks. Its virtues are an extraordinarily distinctive texture that sets his work apart from all others in the field; its drawbacks are occasional lapses into obscurity, insubstantiality, and seeming pointlessness. I fear that *Noctuary* seems to me to present more of the drawbacks than the virtues.

Ligotti makes a great error in opening the volume with **"The Medusa"**, which displays him at his worst in a long-winded tale full of self-indulgent, smart-alecky, high-sounding sentences that in the end mean nothing. The problem with Ligotti is that much of the horror in his work is engendered purely by language, and is also of a sort that cannot be perceived directly by the emotions but must be filtered first through the intellect. He is as disdainful of the conventional "rules" of fiction-writing as Lovecraft or Dunsany was; one of the cardinal "errors" he commits is *talking about* an event or scenario instead of merely displaying it. In his best work this is not an error at all, for what Ligotti is attempting to do is to worry out all the weird overtones and atmospheric bizarreries of a given scenario, something that can only be accomplished by a sort of intellectualised rumination, not by a straightforward account of events. It is true that Ligotti's prose, even in fiction, has an uncannily nonfictional feel (so do Lovecraft's and Poe's); but in his poorer work, as in **"The Medusa"**, it lapses into a sophomoric pretentiousness that ill conceals the fact that he is writing very elegantly about absolutely nothing.

The other items in this first section—**"Conversations in a Dead Language"**, a subtle tale of supernatural revenge; **"The Prodigy of Dreams"**, which comes very close to realising Ligotti's goal of presenting the real world as the quintessence of nightmare; and **"Mrs Rinaldi's Angel"**, a less successful disquisition on dreams—range from the successful to the undistinguished; but I see no thematic links between them and no rationale in grouping them together.

The one original work in this volume, **"The Tsalal"**, is almost worth all the other stories combined. This tale concerns an individual, Andrew Maness, who is the incarnation of the Tsalal (a term taken consciously from Poe's *Narrative of Arthur Gordon Pym*), or "a *perfect blackness*". Maness' father, a reverend, has written a book called *Tsalal,* and Andrew ponders its significance:

" 'There is no nature to things,' you wrote in the book. 'There are no faces except masks held tight against the pitching chaos behind them.' You wrote that there is not true growth or evolution in the life of this world but only transformations of appearance, an incessant melting and molding of surfaces without underlying essence. Above all you pronounced that there is no salvation of any being because no beings exist as such, nothing exists to be saved—everything, everyone exists only to be drawn into the slow and endless swirling of mutations that we may see every second of our lives if we simply gaze through the eyes of the Tsalal."

I do not know if this accurately represents Ligotti's philosophy, but it is an ideal instance of that *intellectualised horror* of which he is such a master. Somehow Andrew Maness is the embodiment of this nihilistic existentialism, and only Ligotti could have written so compellingly hypnotic a tale around such a dryly philosophical conception.

"The Tsalal" opens the second section of the book, which presents other such memorable tales as **"Mad Night of Atonement"** (which utilises Ligotti's frequent humans-as-mannikins metaphor) and **"The Voice in the Bones"**, a pure nightmare with no realism of setting or coherence of plot to speak of but with as potent an atmosphere of the strange as I have ever encountered. These stories, in their various ways, are an encapsulation of what makes Ligotti so distinctive a voice in modern weird fiction.

The third section is a series of nineteen prose-poems, many under 500 words in length. It might be thought—given Ligotti's general scorn for the mechanics of plot and his emphasis on mood—that this would be an ideal form for him, but it is exactly here that his single-minded emphasis on pure verbal witchery presents its greatest drawbacks. Ligotti has failed to note that even the most delicate prose-poems—whether by Baudelaire or Clark Ashton Smith or Dunsany (*Fifty-one Tales*)—must present some unified or coherent narrative if they are to have any effect. Most of these items are simply too insubstantial, fragmentary, and directionless to amount to much. A passage from **"The Spectral Estate"** typifies their essence:

> Long exasperated by questions without answers, by answers without consequences, by truths which change nothing, we learn to become intoxicated by the mood of mystery itself, by the odor of the unknown. We are entranced by the subtle scents and wavering reflections of the unimaginable.

This is an ideal that Ligotti does not always fulfil; and most of these items, written with undeniable panache as they are, simply leave no impression upon the reader and are forgotten the moment they are finished.

I cannot sufficiently emphasise that my reservations about *Noctuary* stem only from the very high regard with which I regard Ligotti's work as a whole: he has set so high a standard for himself that anything that doesn't measure up to it seems a disappointment. Ligotti still remains the most refreshing voice in weird fiction, the one writer who can never be mistaken for someone else. I do confess, though, that I am a little concerned at the seeming lack of development in his work. He has been writing for about fifteen years—the same length of time that separates Lovecraft's "From Beyond" from "The Shadow out of Time". Where exactly is Ligotti going? Has he said all he has to say in his present mode? What further goals has he set for himself? It is, thankfully, inconceivable that Ligotti could ever write a novel unless he reverted to the idiom of his early **"Last Feast of Harlequin"** or some other nominally realistic style; but he has surely written enough "noxiously hideous fragments" (as Lovecraft characerised Shiel's "Xélucha") that one would like to see him do something different. And one does not want to see him resurrect, merely to fill a volume, old failures that are better left buried in the small-press journals where they first appeared. Ligotti is in the most enviable position a writer can be—the position of not having to write unless he wants to. He does not need to slap together a collection every two or three years if he cannot produce a sufficient crop of good work in that period. No one wants to see him become merely a high-grade Stephen King.

FURTHER READING

Bibliography

Ligotti, Thomas. "Thomas Ligotti Bibliography." *Tekeli-Li! Journal of Terror,* No. 4 (Winter-Spring 1992): 36-7.
Primary and secondary bibliography supplying original publication information and special issues of magazines devoted to Ligotti fiction and scholarship.

Criticism

Anderson, Douglas A. Review of *Songs of a Dead Dreamer,* by Thomas Ligotti. *Studies in Weird Fiction,* No. 7 (Spring 1990): 37-9.
Favorable review of the revised and expanded edition of Ligotti's first collection of short stories. Anderson examines the "specific set of attitudes and beliefs . . . underlying these stories and in many ways connecting them," and commends the collection as the most original in the horror genre in many years.

Cupp, Scott. "Penny Dreadfuls." *Mystery Scene,* No. 26 (June 1990): 115.
Review of the revised and expanded edition of *Songs of a Dead Dreamer.* Cupp assesses Ligotti's fiction as stylistically complex: "difficult to describe and often difficult to read." He identifies several stories, including "Dr. Locrian's Asylum," "The Christmas Eves of Aunt Elise," "The Lost Art of Twilight," and "Masquerade of a Dead Sword" as "classic pieces that will be read and remembered for ages."

Dagon: Thomas Ligotti Special Double Issue, Nos. 22-23 (September-December 1988): 3-82.
Includes critical essays by Mike Ashley, Stefan R.

Dziemianowicz, Simon MacCulloch, Christine Morris, and Robert M. Price, as well as an interview with Ligotti by Carl T. Ford, fiction by Ligotti, and a primary and secondary bibliography.

Review of *Grimscribe: His Lives and Works,* by Thomas Ligotti. *Kirkus Reviews* LIX, No. 20 (15 October 1991): 1306.
Approbatory review characterizing the collection as "high-style horror stories in a classic literary mode, in expressiveness not far from the American masters, Poe and H. P. Lovecraft."

LaFaille, Gene. "Science Fiction Universe: Science Fiction, Fantasy, and Horror." *Wilson Library Bulletin* (March 1994): 102-03.
Includes a review of *Noctuary* that cites the influence of nineteenth-century metaphysical fiction and of Edgar Allan Poe and H. P. Lovecraft on works that nonetheless exhibit great originality. LaFaille asserts that this collection helps "redefine the contemporary meaning of the term 'weird tale' within the genre of supernatural fiction."

Latham, Robert. Review of *Songs of a Dead Dreamer,* by Thomas Ligotti, in *Science Fiction & Fantasy Book Review Annual 1990,* edited by Robert A. Collins and Robert Latham, pp. 351-53. New York: Greenwood Press, 1991.
Pronounces Ligotti "clearly one of the most important horror writers of the 80s," commending his "carefully worked, lapidary fever-visions which clearly emerge from the stuff of dreams and personal obsession."

Review of *Songs of a Dead Dreamer,* by Thomas Ligotti. *Publisher's Weekly* (11 May 1990): 249.
Finds some of the pieces in the collection clever, but cites numerous stories for "combinations of murky prose, meaningless events, and lack of focus."

Robertson, Andy. "The Grim Scribe." *Interzone* (January 1992): 64.
Mixed review of Ligotti's second volume of short stories, applauding his originality and dark vision but maintaining that *Songs of a Dead Dreamer* was the superior collection. Robertson compares Ligotti's horrors to those of Lovecraft and Poe, finding that Ligotti's tales are "very subtle, very beautiful, but [lacking] bearing on the *real,* and that is their whole point and essence. And in the end, I think this leaves him the lesser writer . . . ."

"Special Thomas Ligotti Section." *Tekeli-Li! Journal of Terror,* No. 4 (Winter-Spring 1992): 18-41.
Includes essays by Stefan R. Dziemianowicz and Harry O. Morris, illustrations by Morris, and a short story and essay by Ligotti.

Weird Tales: Special Thomas Ligotti Issue. (Winter 1991-92): 3-130.
Includes three stories by Ligotti and an interview with Ligotti conducted by Darrell Schweitzer.

Additional coverage of Ligotti's life and career is contained in the following sources published by Gale Research: *Contemporary Literary Criticism,* Vol. 44; and *Contemporary Authors,* Vol. 123.

Leonard Michaels

1933-

American short story writer, novelist, and critic.

INTRODUCTION

Michaels is recognized as an innovative short story writer who considers the particular nature of postwar urban life. He is primarily noted for his dense, minimalist prose style and his detached, unsympathetic depictions of the violence of modern life. His first two story collections were set in New York and featured reoccurring characters in bizarre and chaotic situations. By avoiding overintellectualizing these predicaments and by retaining accurate self-perceptions, Michaels's characters are able to navigate the violence and emptiness of their lives. Michaels's later works deal with similar themes but are increasingly autobiographical.

Biographical Information

Michaels was born in New York to Leon and Anna Czeskies, Polish-Jewish immigrants. He spent his youth in Lower Manhattan where his father was a barber and both his parents were actively involved in community issues. Michaels writes in a particularly autobiographical style and his early experiences and impressions of life in New York City emerge often in his short stories. He received a B.A. from New York University in 1953, an M.A. from University of Michigan in 1956, and briefly pursued a Ph.D. at the University of California, Berkeley before returning in 1960 to Manhattan, where he devoted himself full time to writing short stories. There he met and married Sylvia Bloch, about whom he wrote in his novella *Sylvia*. During this period he taught English courses at Paterson State College in New Jersey and continued to write. However, Michaels's marriage was stormy and after he separated from Sylvia and reentered graduate school at the University of Michigan, she committed suicide. In 1966 Michaels earned a Ph.D. in English Romantic Language and married Priscilla Older, with whom he had two sons. Michaels wrote his dissertation on Lord Byron, whose writing Michaels has incorporated into and built upon in his short stories. For instance, a phrase in Byron's writing supplied the title for Michaels's second short story collection, *I Would Have Saved Them If I Could*. In 1969 while teaching English at University of California at Davis, Michaels published his first collection of short stories, *Going Places*. The collection was nominated for the National Book Award and earned Michaels a more prestigious teaching position at University of California at Berkeley, where he has remained. In 1975 he published his second collection *I Would Have Saved Them If I Could*. In 1977 he divorced his second wife and married poet Brenda Lynn Hillman with whom he had a daughter. However, this marriage also ended in divorce. In 1981 he

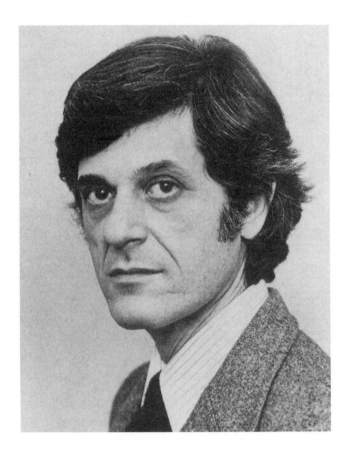

published his first novel, *The Mens Club*, which was adapted into a film. Michaels's most recent works, *Shuffle* and *Sylvia: A Fictional Memoir*, show a greater tendency to blend fiction with autobiography. He continues to live and write in California.

Major Works of Short Fiction

Michaels's works of short fiction share a common setting, New York City, and often address themes of graphic violence and sexuality. Many of his works are also linked by the reappearance of various characters. The most prominent recurring figure is Phillip Liebowitz, a young Jewish man coming of age in New York City, who believes that he embodies the city's essence. Although Liebowitz matures physically and undergoes other changes to his life from one story to another, his personality and general outlook on life remain constant. However, despite the many similarities of his short works, the way in which Michaels depicts his common themes and situations varies widely, employing realistic, absurd, and autobiographical modes. "Murderers," for instance, is about a group of teenage boys who watch a rabbi dance and make love to his wife. The boys are on a steep rooftop and one falls to his death;

the others are discovered and sent to a camp in New Jersey run by World War II veterans. While the topic and plot are unusual, Michaels tells the story in a realistic style. In contrast, Michaels's absurd stories feature fantastic events and often have a humorous tone. "Mildred," for example, concerns a woman who removes her womb and passes it amongst her guests so they can eat it. Michaels's principal autobiographical work is the collection *Shuffle,* which he has labeled a fictional autobiography. The account is clearly based on his youth and first marriage, but the extent to which it is fictional is unclear. One section is comprised of journal entries which span several years. There is no clear form; many of the entries are short annotations and thoughts apparently jotted down at random. Nevertheless, critics argue that the section appears to have been constructed with an overarching theme in mind. The second section is comprised of four short stories, one dealing with his father, another with his mother, and two others with Michaels himself. The final section, entitled "Sylvia," describes Michaels's relationship with his first wife, particularly its destructive dynamics and collapse. Michaels has expanded this section and reprinted it as a novella, also titled *Sylvia.*

Critical Reception

Michaels writes in a minimalist style that many critics, and Michaels himself, have compared with poetry. In interviews, Michaels has stated that he is more concerned with the sound of words and their rhythm than with developing plot or fleshing out characters. In comparing his first and second short story collections, critics have argued that the writing in *I Would Have Saved Them if I Could* is denser and that the style is highly effective when Michaels achieves the right tempo. However, other critics charge that the stark, reductive style alienates readers by failing to give them access to the characters' thoughts and rationales. They claim that readers who have no personal experience with the lifestyles of young Jews in New York City cannot relate to the ordeals and adventures of Michaels's characters and lose interest. Other critics contend that Michaels fails to resolve the conflicts he creates. For instance, in *Sylvia,* Michaels effectively describes the turmoil of the relationship and the sorrow of his loss at his wife's suicide, but he never reveals that he has gained an understanding of the event's significance over time.

PRINCIPAL WORKS

SHORT FICTION

Going Places   1969
I Would Have Saved Them If I Could   1975
Shuffle   1990
Sylvia: A Fictional Memoir   1992

OTHER MAJOR WORKS

The Mens Club   (novel)   1981
To Feel These Things   (autobiography)   1993

CRITICISM

Christopher Lehmann-Haupt   (essay date 1969)

SOURCE: "Short Stories—To Be Taken as Prescribed," in *The New York Times,* April 14, 1969, p. 43.

[*In the following excerpt, Lehmann-Haupt comments on Michaels's fictional technique in* Going Places.]

Leonard Michaels is a 35-year-old New Yorker, and the setting of most of the 13 stories in *Going Places* is the city. Mr. Michaels creates a hostile, violent, and absurd world in which people grope for each other longingly, yet can only touch one another by inflicting damage. In **"Manikin,"** a college girl hangs herself after being raped by a Turkish student and abandoned by her scholarly boyfriend because "as far as he was concerned the ceremony of innocence was drowned." In **"The Deal"** a young woman offers a kiss to a member of a Puerto Rican gang in exchange for the return of a lost glove. The boy, outwardly cool, is frightened, and provokes his gang to beat up the woman. Sex is like that in the stories—a transaction, tough and cruel.

Mr. Michaels's fictional technique is to propel coherent language and familiar situations to the boundaries of realism and then crash out into surrealistic dream territory. ("Groans issued from my mouth. They flew after her like a flock of bats.") When the machinery is working, the effects are powerful and original.

In **"City Boy"** a young man is convincingly trapped in that old nightmare of finding oneself naked in public streets. We sweat it out with him while the author fiddles. In **"Making Changes"** Mr. Michaels successfully evokes the pun of a New York cocktail party as a sexual orgy. Phillip takes a girl home from the party/orgy. "I . . . lifted her dress, and scribbled across her belly: PHILLIP'S. On her thighs, PHILLIP'S, PHILLIP'S." The girl goes out and returns later. "Before the room became dark I turned on my side to examine her belly and things. The PHILLIP'S were in each of the places. All about them like angry birds were: MAX'S, FRANK'S, HUGO'S, SIMON'S" "I kissed her. She kissed me. We had Henry Miller."

But something goes wrong in *Going Places.* I'm not certain whether it happens because the emotional impact of the stories is so similar or because the second half of the book simply isn't as good as the first. But the effects flatten out and become repetitive. The verbal jazz and hallucinogenic gigs get tiresome and seem only to be calling attention to themselves. When one gets to the last tale, the title story, it appears as an afterthought rather than as the thematic key.

Denis Donoghue   (essay date 1969)

SOURCE: "Couples," in *The New York Review of Books,* Vol. XIII, No. 1, July 10, 1969, pp. 17-20.

[*Donoghue is an Irish critic and educator whose works in-*

clude Jonathan Swift: An Introduction *(1967) and* The Arts without Mystery *(1984). In the following excerpt, Donoghue remarks on the theme of violence and Michaels's use of language in the stories from* Going Places.]

Leonard Michaels is a gut-writer. The paradigm of his fiction is simple: two people, locked in violence. The stories are set in "the city's dark going places," New York for instance, but the setting is not crucial, any city will answer. The people themselves hardly matter, except as conductors of violence; they are good for intensity and shock, nothing else. We are not required to care for them, but rather to be afflicted by the venom they secrete. The characters come in pairs, couples, Phillip and Veronica, Sarah Nilsin and Myron Bronsky, Melanie and Harry, Phillip and Cecily, Miller and Mildred. Their violence is the kind that couples engender: birth and copulation and then death. Sometimes the hero has a twin, as Phillip has his secret sharer, Henry; and then the girl, the stuttering Marjorie, provides the occasion, the incitement. Of Henry, Phillip says:

> A nose, eyes, a curious mouth, a face, my own
> felt face behind my eyes, an aspect of my mind,
> a habit of my thought—my friend, Henry.

But when the two people remain two, the reader feels that if the violence were to be stilled, as by divine intervention, the characters would cease to exist. Beyond the violence, they are nothing. So they tend to collapse, at any moment, into an undifferentiated medium, a vortex of feeling. The words on the page barely differentiate one mode of violence from another. Mechanically, the stories might be reduced to anecdotes, if the exacerbation were omitted, but the anecdotes count for less than the exacerbation, the grip of claw. In **"Going Places"** the story concerns Beckman, a taxi-driver, mugged. Out of hospital, he finds a job as assistant to a paint contractor. So much for the facts; but plot does not define the events within, the grinding of moment upon moment, until the last terror. In **"Crossbones"** Myron and Sarah dance various figures in their apartment until, finally, with the bones crossed, the bodies are consumed.

To do so much with words, Mr. Michaels drives his language hard. He writes in a high rush, the sentences tormenting each other, like the couples, as if nothing short of annihilation could suffice, the feeling being what it is. In several stories I was reminded of John Hawkes's *The Lime Twig*, an essay in modern Gothic which perhaps marked for Mr. Michaels the possibilities of the genre. But he is more than a promising pupil. *Going Places* contains thirteen short stories; four or five of them are impeccable. The title story, then **"Sticks and Stones," "The Deal," "Intimations,"** and **"Finn"** are the high places, but Mr. Michaels is a powerful writer even when his story wavers. When the balance fails and the story goes awry, there is an impression of inserted horror: the rhetoric strains beyond itself, and the story, self-regarding in its violence, becomes a Gothic conceit. The weaker stories die of their own excess: often because nothing is allowed to rebuke the fiction, no sense of fact is allowed to intervene. In **"Making Changes"** the Gothic excess is predictable and the story merely proves that, in such fiction, nearly anything

is possible while nothing is necessary. The composition is arbitrary, a matter of will. **"Fingers and Toes"** is decadent in this way, a grotesque translation of **"Sticks and Stones"**; it bears about the same relation to Mr. Michaels's best work as, say, in Nathanael West, *The Dream Life of Balso Snell* bears to *The Day of the Locust* and *Miss Lonelyhearts.* The proof is that the passages beyond the coupling violence are pastiche, dead matter, the fiction has congealed into stereotype.

But the best work is superb, and *Going Places,* one story with another, is a brilliant book. For me, the most powerful thing in the book is **"The Deal."** A girl, Abbe Carlyle, drops her glove: one of twenty boys, jammed together on the stoop, picks it up. Abbe asks for its return. The story proceeds, disclosing all the violence concealed in its first appearances. Mr. Michaels's special context is "the abuse of a thousand streets," and as he sends Abbe walking across this street to the grocery to buy cigarettes, the ordinary detail gradually admits the monster, the dog beneath the skin. Forty monstrous eyes tear Abbe to pieces: "the monster, watching, saw the glove fall away."

What is remarkable in the story, and unusual in Mr. Michaels's fiction, is the allowance given to common things. Usually, they do not count, but here in the form of pigeons whirling between buildings, a ten-wheel truck, and water running against the curb, they are allowed to press against the barbaric rush, one common force against another only less common, until at last the monster breaks loose. The story earns its extreme reach by allowing for everything in life which, extreme at the end, is ordinary till then. The characters are not, to begin with, sinister. Nor is Abbe. But in the sunshine Abbe, teasing herself, plays with the twenty-headed thing, and soon the play loses all form and ritual to become pure spirit, and pure will, pure violence. Normally, Mr. Michaels is content with the official possibilities of his genre; content, too, with its limitations. But in this story, as in **"Going Places,"** he forces the genre to accommodate itself to more stringent demands than those traditionally acknowledged in Gothic fiction. The turbulence of the story is not, then, arbitrary or wanton; it is certified, tested against the corresponding force of order in the form itself.

Lore Segal   (essay date 1969)

SOURCE: "Captivating Horrors," in *The New Republic,* Vol. 161, No. 3, July 19, 1969, pp. 31-3.

[*Segal is an Austrian-born American critic, novelist, and short story writer. In the following excerpt, Segal remarks on the themes of the stories from* Going Places.]

Leonard Michaels' first book [*Going Places*] affords a kind of pleasure that is different from what is usually felt in reading merely a good new writer; this is writing of a different order.

The themes in these stories are our modern familiars. Young love, brave or gentle deaths, though they persist in nature along with flowers and gardens, make us itchy when we meet up with them in books, but we sit back and keep a steady eye on orgies, rape, mayhem and suicide in city scenes and subwayscapes. Leonard Michaels makes these horrors horrible again and funny. Here is his New York: Phillip, of **"City Boy,"** having sinned, goofed, and in a state of nakedness, arrives "at the spit-mottled steps of the subway. I had hoped for vomit. Spit is no challenge for bare feet."

Some things are horrible we had not thought so before. This is Michaels on femininity, brutal, and ravenous for the attention on which it feeds: Mildred, "I'm not pretty." Miller, "Yes, you are." Mildred, "I know I'm attractive in a way . . . basically I hate my type. Do you like my hair?" "Your hair is very nice." Mildred, "You are stupid-looking. . . . You're the only stupid-looking boyfriend I ever had." Male visitors arrive and Mildred "now shining awake . . . curled tight in her chair . . . making knees, shins, ankles to look at," and here Michaels takes one of his fantastical leaps into what it is he is talking about: "Mildred sat up, showed us her womb. Max took it, squeezed it, passed it to Sleek. I had a bite. Max munched. . . ." Left alone with her man and the purpose for which femininity is intended, Mildred begins to cry. " 'Stop it,' I said. She cried . . . I pummeled my head . . . She stopped crying. I mashed my mouth with my knee. She smiled a little. 'Do it again.' " (It seems so much the thing of a lesser writer to tell us that "Rain drilled the window. Thunder burdened the air," that I choose to think Michaels must be burlesquing these same lesser writers.)

The other love object of *Going Places* is Marjory. Students to whom I read the story called **"Sticks and Stones"** deduced that the setting must be a small town on the theory that in New York no Marjory would get so much as a tumble. She has a tick and stutters. I can't tell if I invented her lame leg or if it's in the text. She is a city love object. Phillip comes to call. "It was a blind date. She met me at the door and smiled nicely. I could tell she was disappointed."

Men and women exacerbate each other's malaise. In **"Finn,"** Jews uncover each other's bitter Jewishness. In **"Manikin,"** the two foreigners, a Turk and Wanda Chung, are brutalized by their separation from people and language; one turns helplessly bestial, the other goes to earth with her hoard of sweets. And the well-to-do American young fare worst of all.

Critics like compassion in their writers but Leonard Michaels' pity is not the kind that taps those pleasurably painful tears for which we like ourselves; in stories like **"A Green Thought"** he piles disgust upon disgust, like a man scratching himself bloody to distract himself from the true seat of pain.

If *Going Places* has an upbeat note it is in the title piece which is a story of rebirth: Beckman, who seemed doomed to the cabdriver's hellish life "cramped, chilled, in a damp sweater and mucky underwear . . . debauched by the night's long, winding, resonant passages and the abuse of a thousand streets," finds salvation by means of a beating that nearly kills and does disfigure him. He wakes to a new life and a new job as a painter's assistant. Here is joy: "[there] burned thirty feet of hot brilliant color. Beckman yearned to participate, confront unpainted steel, paint it, see it become a fresh, different thing as he dissolved into

the ritual strokes." **"Going Places"** is, finally, the journey across a pipe suspended high over a factory floor, the destination is the painter's hand stretched out for a fresh paint can. The final pages of story and book comprise Beckman's long moment of vertigo. "He heard men shout from the platform. 'Don't let go, Beckman.' He did not let go." Beckman is not going anywhere.

Men working together care to call out to one another; a man keeps holding on. That is Michaels' upbeat note. When we read such matter with delight, the writer has done something extraordinary.

Leonard Michaels' writing at its best can be demonstrated not in comparison with another writer but with himself at his worst which is never bad. Such stories as **"Isaac,"** despite wonderful passages, and especially **"Intimations"** are in a state of raw hysteria. Conversely, the extreme horror of Beckman's cabdriver existence seems falsely whipped up. Lapses strike us because elsewhere the vision is so truly furious and so finely controlled. Again **"The Deal"** in any other collection would be an admirable tale: A girl bargains for the return of a lost glove in the possession of "a raggedy monster of boys . . . jammed together on the stoop." She is the best possible girl, friendly and gutsy, but the confrontation is too complex—girl versus boys, white vis-à-vis Puerto Rican, adult vis-à-vis a mix of children and young adults, the individual against a crowd. The "raggedy monster" acts *en masse* but unpredictably even to itself, and what might have been a decent, even a charming rapprochement turns ugly—a harbinger of confrontations in store for us all. Michaels cannot do less than see and write with precision. If these sentences seem self-conscious, earthbound with labor, it is because of his spectacular capacity, elsewhere, to get off the ground. He goes to the heart of his matter in a way that makes other writing seem circumstantial. There was Mildred's womb, and here is Max and Sleek in social conversation: "Max said, Sleek said." There are passages where the reader seems almost—never quite—to see how this is done, to watch the writer chase himself from thought to thought, sometimes playfully:

The City Boy has mounted his girl on the living-room carpet with her parents asleep on the other side of the door. ("Phillip, this is crazy," she says from time to time.) Father, in mother's service, comes in and throws Phillip out, "naked as a wolf. I needed poise. . . . I'd walk on my hands. Beards are fashionable. I kicked up my feet, kicked the elevator button, faced the door and waited. I bent one elbow like, a knee. The posture of a clothes model easy poised. . . ."

We watch him perform a miracle: The second part of **"Sticks and Stones"** juxtaposes the notion of loyalty in the grand manner with the shabby reality of what we actually feel. Phillip and Henry are friends. They have had each other's girl, that is to say the same girl—Marjory of the tick and stammer, and each considers himself deserving of death at the hands of the other while neither has the slightest wish of inflicting it, and so they run away from, of maybe after, one another, but certainly together. "Whirling suddenly I was out the door. Henry gasped and followed, tearing for a grip on the back of my head. We went down the night. . . . My hair was soon gone from the back of my head. When it grew in he ripped it out again. . . . Occasionally I heard him scream 'I have a gun. Shoot me. . . .' I ran on powerful legs. Over the years, they grew more powerful. . . . At last my arms disappeared and I was a head on legs. Running." Michaels has created a new object under the sun: The Running.

If Leonard Michaels' book poses that old chestnut of a question, How is it possible to read about what is bleak and hideous and be reading something hilarious and beautiful and pleasurable, the answer is the old one: It is at the miraculous point where this transformation happens that literature has occurred.

Barry Gross   (essay date 1969)

SOURCE: A review of *Going Places,* in *The Saturday Review,* New York, Vol. LII, No. 31, August 2, 1969, p. 27.

[*In the following excerpt, Gross finds Michaels's stories in* Going Places *disturbing yet unconvincing.*]

Leonard Michaels is indisputably an original talent. His stories vividly convey life as a bad dream, an inarguable but unaccountable horror, a sickening taste in the mouth that cannot be analyzed. Michaels's prose is perfectly suited to his subject, jittery and jarring. His rhythms are unpredictable: certain words seem to come at the wrong times but also seem inexplicably right, others appear to be missing but it is impossible to guess what they might be. Mr. Michaels skillfully disturbs. But where is the root of the disturbance? Mark Schorer reports that it is "the contemporary urban experience of helplessness, fumbling loss, grasping unrelatedness, absurdity, and sometimes horror." Maybe so. But more often than not the source seems to be Mr. Michaels himself, his own unique sensibility, rather than any generalized experience, urban or otherwise. Things happen because Mr. Michaels would have it so. Things happen arbitrarily, not, given a context, inevitably.

Mr. Michaels accords no deference to logic, not even to the internal logic of a dream. Which means that either the reader must be on Mr. Michaels's wave length or he must expend extraordinary efforts to get there. I am not unwilling to make whatever efforts are necessary to bridge the great gulf that separates me from Mr. Michaels's stories; but ultimately I am unable to.

Is the fault mine or Mr. Michaels's? My own experience and my own imagination are not his, and his are too peculiarly his own for me to share them. Perhaps if these were characters in a novel, perhaps if there were more time, perhaps, indeed, if that contemporary urban experience were established rather than merely assumed . . . As it is, however, I remain outside, very far outside. Maybe that is where Mr. Michaels intends me to be, but I don't relish being there.

The distance puts me on the defensive, speaks too insistently to me of my inadequacies *vis-à-vis* these stories. Which also might be Mr. Michaels's intention. But if it is, then he has made a mistake in putting his stories in a single volume. Because, after a point, I don't care. I turn from

an interested into a disinterested observer. If I had read these stories over a period of time as they were published, my interest might have been renewed. But I grow weary of watching and of being frustrated.

And yet, even if I had read Mr. Michaels's stories as they came out, the result might have been the same. If Frederick Crews is right that "the perpetual casualty" in Mr. Michaels's fiction "is the will toward rationality, purposeful action, any simple emotion," then I was bound to be disappointed. There is little I can do at this point about my own will toward rationality or my own insistence on purposeful action. Mr. Michaels does not convince me I am wrong in holding to them because he does not convince me we live in the same world. He has his vision and I have mine and so we stand at a fruitless stalemate. . . .

I am willing to grant that life is absurd, at least for argument's sake, but only as a starting point. Then I want to wonder if it *really* is or how it got that way or in what terms the absurdity might be measured or what it might be measured against.

There is my will toward rationality again. Am I asking too much? Of course I am. But Mr. Michaels gives me too little. However brilliant the techniques in his arsenal, I cannot help but wonder if the emotion that produces the same story over and over again might not be one of those "simple" ones Mr. Crews insists Mr. Michaels is arguing against.

Paul Zweig   (essay date 1975)

SOURCE: "Delicate Intentions," in *Harper's Magazine,* Vol. 251, No. 1504, September, 1975, pp. 68-9.

[*Zweig was an American critic, poet, and translator who is best known for his critical biography* Walt Whitman: The Making of the Poet *(1984). In the following excerpt, Zweig presents a highly favorable assessment of* I Would Have Saved Them If I Could.*]

Leonard Michaels's second collection of stories begins hot and doesn't cool down. In story after story, he wields his prose like a weapon: part bludgeon, part scalpel, it flickers, dense and resilient. With insane precision, he drops stink bombs. With a poet's twist of language, he decomposes civility into its not-so-secret elements of sex, perverse daydreams, inventive resentment. Every normal act is pitted with an abyss from which comes laughter, ridicule, murder. The brute is not the guest in the basement any more, he is not the secret (Freudian) of our "delicate intentions." The brute is in the streets, and "delicate intentions" are dead. That could be the subtitle of Michaels's book: The Death of Delicate Intentions.

In Michaels's urban madhouse, love is a hand job in the subway; community a surreal orgy on Sutton Place. Culture becomes a pornographer's view of the Holocaust: Nietzsche, Hegel, and Borges facing the world from the position of an exquisite mouth in a blue movie, kneeling before a row of male organs, the universal face to face with the particular. All of this is embodied in excruciatingly precise, almost sculptural, prose. The brute may be a maze of sexual kinks, but he never abdicates his gift of statement. Flaubert is in hell, but he is Flaubert nonetheless.

Here are the opening lines of a fine long story, **"The Captain,"** which climaxes the book:

> He smiled at her. She smiled at him and ate dessert, her pinky so nicely hooked it tore my heart. Dessert was pear under chocolate and flaming brandy. It slipped from spoon to blubbery dissolution. When I tried to taste, I swallowed. Then came a flickering city of liqueurs. Then marijuana, a language of green and gold popping around the table from mouth to mouth. Nothing went by me unlipped, nothing tasted. From course to course I'd swallowed textures, not tastes, like a cat gobbling kill. I'd eaten; I wanted to eat. Other guests flashed marvels achieved, readiness to die . . . I'd never been to such a dinner party, but I could tell it was first-rate. Teeth stabbed out of my ass to eat the chair.

The sentences stab and accumulate. Feelings solidify into images; they become part of the furniture; they crowd each other. Michaels shifts from parable to hallucination, from black humor to orchestrated perceptions. His story builds and, against all probability, doesn't clutter to a halt, but keeps on building, like Chinese boxes piling out of each other in quick succession. The party becomes an Orphic mystery overlooking the East River: the triumph of corrosive humor, giggles, penises, plush; a stand-up comic's complete fantasy.

I Would Have Saved Them If I Could is a medley of stories, some no more than a few lines long. In many of the short pieces, the narrative deflects into parable and illumination, resembling prose poems more than stories. There is a theatrical quality in many of these pieces, as of people talking to themselves. In Michaels's view, the mind in its natural state is not a surrealist but a gossip and a playwright mixed together. . . .

Michaels's themes are not new, nor, in a way, is his tone. His hero is the schlemiel of Jewish fiction. His madcap sex is how sons, after Portnoy, indulge the memory of Jewish mothers. The mother herself is present in a series of shrapnel-like fragments:

> "Everything is fine," I said. My mother said, "I hope so." "It is, it is." My mother said, "I hope so." I said, "Everything is wonderful. Couldn't be better. How do you feel?" My mother said, "Like a knife is pulling out of my liver."

The Freudian paradigm of sex to the rescue and biology as salvation isn't exactly original material these days, nor is the anticultural mania which has supplied the animus of so much recent literature. But Michaels doesn't care about new ideas—or old ones, for that matter. Ideas, themes, and tones are digested by his extraordinary stylistic gift and emerge transformed, hardened into an extreme. Liebowitz—his schlemiel—isn't only inept and defeated; he is predatory. He is a schlemiel with teeth, and a Charlie Chaplin toe of the shoe in the rear. He cancels the genre.

Michaels's characters drift between "small personal miseries and fantastic sex," but the fantasy debunks the sex,

and also debunks the debunking, leaving orgasm to perform by itself as an orgy of the particular, a weird flower of language. The unidentified hand in the subway is "a soft inquisitive spider pinching the tongue of his zipper, dragging it toward the iron floor that boomed in the bones of his rooted feet." The Hassidic rabbi and his wife:

> Twirling and individual, he stepped away snapping fingers, going high and light on his toes. A short bearded man, balls afling, cock shuddering like a springboard. . . . She, on the other hand, was somewhat reserved. A shift in one lush hip was total rumba.

At the thematic heart of the book is a sequence of essaylike fragments that form the strangest exercise in literary criticism I have ever read. It might be called literature read by the Holocaust. Borges, in love with paradox, according to Michaels, writes a story about a suspected Jew who experiences ecstasy while in jail awaiting his execution: the Gestapo, an organization of death, is responsible for the "secret miracle" of redemption through ecstasy. It turns out that Borges got this story not from any experience of "photographable reality" but from another story. Culture, for Michaels, is a daisy chain of such stories which recline high in the redemptive air, while, at a distance, visible if you look, "a suspected Jew of average height, with bad teeth, gray hair, nervous cough, tinted spectacles, delicate fingers, gentle musical voice—physically and exactly disintegrates . . . between a hard stone wall and the impact of specific bullets."

Borges's ennobling ecstasy is a paradox for onlookers. But the Holocaust, the trapped, crazed lives that people Michaels's stories, condemn the "onlookers" who prefer to lift experience into the perenity of cultural statement. For Michaels, perenity is obscenity. His characters, however ridiculous or defeated, live a dance of victory because, as one of them says, "I am not interested in being superior to my sensations."

As philosophies of culture go, this may be too simple. Yet, as a fictional theme, its very oversimplification becomes a strength, and a plea that reverberates in every story.

Although one senses the hovering of recent literary kin—Burroughs, Barthelme, perhaps Roth—these stories are more nearly poems, with a tightly reasoned quality that calls to mind more distant, stranger ancestors: Baudelaire's *Little Poems in Prose,* or Aloysius Bertrand's *Gaspard of the Night,* with an ingredient of Lenny Bruce diverting them into belly laughter.

I Would Have Saved Them If I Could must be read to be believed. It is surely one of the outstanding works of fiction of the year.

Irving Howe   (essay date 1975)

SOURCE: "Vectors," in *The New York Review of Books,* Vol. XXII, No. 18, November 13, 1975, p. 42.

[*A longtime editor of the leftist magazine* Dissent *and a regular contributor to* The New Republic, *Howe was one of America's most highly respected literary critics and social*

*historians. A socialist since the 1930s, his criticism is fre-
quently informed by a liberal social viewpoint. In the following excerpt, Howe remarks on the style of the stories in*
I Would Have Saved Them If I Could.]

A little culture can be a dangerous thing; more of it, still
more so. Reading this collection of stories [*I Would Have
Saved Them If I Could*] prompts one to wish that Leonard Michaels had never heard of alienation, sentiment of
being, nihilism; his fragile talent might then have flourished in comparative innocence. As it is, these stories are
crusted with the junk of fashionable culture, both the fashionable culture of today and the fashionable culture of yesterday. There is Bellovian swagger without Bellow's rich
complication; Rothian sexual assertiveness without
Roth's sense of fun; and there is Mailer, and Malamud,
and Borges, and Counter-Culture, all rendered "heavy" in
the sense that young people use that term. Behind the influences, references, knowingness, and bravado, one
glimpses a rather sweet sensibility with a small, damaged
gift for narrative and notation.

Mr. Michaels writes two kinds of stories: "American-
Jewish," flauntingly bold and inauthentic, and a Borges-
like stringing together of two or three paragraph sketches,
vignettes, and reflections, featuring Marx, Freud, Trotsky,
Nietzsche, Byron, Hegel, Dostoevsky, and other star players. This latter group of pieces I found impossible and
often incomprehensible; they strain, with painful eager-
ness, for gnomic profundity, fables encompassing the absurdity of existence, and philosophical gags. They are of
the sort likely to be described as "wild, man." The level
of wit is suggested by Mr. Michael's remark that Marx
was "an alienated Jew assuming the voice of Hegelienated
Jew." His profundity is suggested by an anecdote about a
woman who worries that people are starving while she
brushes her teeth and this upsets her morally. But "being
moral is a luxury, isn't it? No, it's asking the question.
That's why I spend my time stealing, fucking, and taking
dope." Wisdom literature is a risky genre.

The straight stories focus on urban trauma and blithe depravity. A gang of Jewish boys peeks into a rabbi's apartment as he makes love to his delectable wife, and then one
of the boys suffers the punishment of being shipped off to
summer camp. A man is stroked to ejaculation by a
stranger in the subway, whether male, female, or questionable is not clear and it hardly matters—it's just handiwork. A young married couple profit financially by submitting to sexual use at a corrupt publisher's party.

In delivering these sorry anecdotes Mr. Michaels affects
a minimal method—minimal narrative, minimal characterization, minimal detail. Bang, bang, hardly any emotional fuss, and we reach the end, like the man in the subway. What is absent from these stories—differentiated and
precise responses, say, among the boys peeking at the
rabbi, some firm if tacit valuation of what their conduct,
indeed, their whole story, signifies—is nothing less, as I
see it, than the traditional substance of literature.

That Mr. Michaels is, somewhere, sensitive to such a view
of his stories is indicated by the one about the young couple at the publisher's party, where he makes some effort

at complication, provides some detail regarding the flow
of confused feelings—and that makes it the one story in
the book which approaches the possibilities of serious
writing. But his work is mainly marked by a swaggering
reductionism, a naïve faith in the value of notation on the
fly. It may be said, by profound critics, that this is what
our life has been reduced to in the Age of Etc. Etc., but
I think it more likely that it's Mr. Michaels who is doing
the reduction, out of some modish idea that relieves him
of responsibility for regarding his characters as, perhaps,
human beings.

Charles Bazerman   (essay date 1975)

SOURCE: "Danger, Fear and Self-Revulsion," in *The
Nation,* New York, Vol. 221, No. 16, November 15, 1975,
pp. 502-04.

[*In the following excerpt, Bazerman remarks on Michaels's
concern with characterization in* I Would Have Saved
Them If I Could.]

Leonard Michaels's commitment to truth-in-fiction has
sharpened his stories to make this, his second collection,
surpass his earlier *Going Places.* The Michaels of the first
collection let philosophy and theatrics obscure his fictional impulse. The stories moved quickly from problems of
the soul to sexual adventure, mugging and suicide. The
troubled but smug attitudinizing never moved far from the
quasi-problems and quasi-solutions of fashionable psycho-
therapies. But the new collection, *I Would Have Saved
Them If I Could,* reveals the confused and scarred self behind the mask of fashionable attitudes. Persistently reaching for the feeling life of characters, Michaels no longer
needs to rely on the bizarre to gain startling effects; life's
intricacies are sufficiently eye-opening. What remains of
the bizarre is subordinated to the weightier emotional
freight of the stories.

On first reading, the opening story, **"Murderers,"** could
be mistaken for a comic routine overwhelmed by a pretentious metaphoric death. The scene in which four boys look
on from a neighboring roof while a young rabbi and his
wife begin to make love to the strains of Choo-Choo
Lopez's rendition of *The Miami Beach Rhumba* is in the
spirit of Lenny Bruce, but when Arnold Bloom in his excitement slips off the roof to his death, we wince at what
looks like strained symbolism. But there is more to the
story than that. Danger, fear and self-revulsion accompany the boys' discovery of the world. Arnold Bloom isn't
a sacrifice to the parental gods; he is just one who doesn't
survive the growing up. Those who do pay the price of
scars and involution. The other boys are shipped off to a
camp where the discipline of the world is enforced by
those who carry around life's lessons in their bodies. . . .

In **"Storytellers, Liars, and Bores"** the economic dilemma
of the beginning writer is defined by the two poles of Uncle
Zev and Tony Icona:

> My Uncle Zev told me about his years in a con-
> centration camp. "Write it," he said. "You'll
> make a million bucks." My friend Tony Icona
> gave me lessons in breaking and entering. Uncle

Zev's stories I couldn't use. Tony's lessons were as good as gold. Criminal life was intermittent and quick. It left me time to work at stories and learn about tearing them up.

It takes 6 pages for the writer to fall through all the degradations that art demands. Having shed all his friends—including the last and most boring memory—he is ready to meet Kafka in a dream. And Kafka, the master of the sublime, after shaking hands with the writer, wipes his fingers on his tie: the muse takes a lot out of you. The shifting tones of the narrative voice carry much of the meaning of the story, and suggest the attitudes of the writer toward himself and his art.

In *Going Places* the reader very rarely was given any indication of how lines were to be read, but in the present book the inflections are made clear. When Joyce Wolf's fiancé, Mandell, speaks, we know why he is to be despised. His repetitions that have no incremental effect, the adolescent use of "like" as an ineffective modifier, the self-important airs about ordinary lust, his casting of himself as the celebrant of love—all these are manifest in his speeches.

> Mandell asked if she had ever been celebrated.
>
> "Celebrated?"
>
> "I mean your body, has your body ever been celebrated?" Then, as if to refine the question: "I mean, like, has your body, like, been celebrated?"

The involutions of judgment and feeling that we find in these stories arise from the author's facing of himself and his life. Such a process rarely makes an attractive picture. The writer who wants to get at the truth of his own experience must admit how he has acted. And it won't do to work the self-glorifying vein of the picaresque novels of the 1960s nor the sentimentalizing vein of the more recent psychiatric sob and salvation stories. Nor does the confessional mode get at the truth of experience if it simply exploits a self-berating sensibility. Michaels's method is a good deal more serious than these. It tries to describe how people actually behave, how they respond to themselves and others and what their real limitations are.

The first-person stories of the collection, most of which appear to be narrated by a stand-in for the author, seem to me to be the better ones because they give Michaels's painful character analyses a center and a sympathy lacking in the third-person stories—like **"The Captain,"** which is unrelievedly cruel, and **"Trotsky's Garden,"** which is unrelievedly grandiose. In the first-person stories, Michaels shows his narrator coming to understand that the physical and spiritual deaths he sees happening to others are his own. . . .

Michaels's stories aim for the multi-layered intensity of Kafka's parables. That is shooting very high, but often enough he is right on target. Sometimes, as in the title story, **"I Would Have Saved Them If I Could,"** which is made up of meditative paragraphs, the philosophy outweighs the fiction. The central issue, suffering preserved as a presence through fiction, comes alive only enough for us to want to read the story in some future version.

Dust jacket for Michaels's first short story collection.

The issues Michaels writes about are difficult to capture. His writing is much denser than it seems to be at first. And his world is not attractive. So when he fails, we dislike what strike us as his pretensions. However, he succeeds often enough to make us take him seriously. He is in the process of becoming as good a writer as he thinks he is.

Eric Korn　(essay date 1977)

SOURCE: "Agony Column," in *The Times Literary Supplement,* No. 3911, February 25, 1977, p. 201.

[*In the following excerpt, Korn offers a negative review of* I Would Have Saved Them If I Could.]

> When my Uncle Moe dropped dead of a heart attack I became expert in the subway system. With a nickel I'd get to Queens, twist and zoom to Coney Island, twist again toward the George Washington Bridge—beyond which was darkness. I wanted proximity to darkness, strangeness. Who doesn't? The poor in spirit, the ignorant and frightened. My family came from Poland, then never went any place until they had heart attacks.

The opening sentence of the first story in [*I Would Have Saved Them If I Could*] contains the rest: the distinctive diction, the uncluttered style going straight to the self-pitying core, the manner at once cocky and ingratiating, the certainty that the agonies of middle-class New York Jews are somehow exemplary for the suffering world, which gives the author the right to answer his own rhetorical questions before anyone else can get a word in edgeways.

Unlike your average self-deprecating Manhattan schmuck, Phillip Liebowitz, narrator of most of these stories, "a New Yorker with an invulnerable core of sophistication", is competent. Expert with public transport, at basketball, at persuading girls to what he whimsically calls having sexual intercourse. Or rather at having them persuade him to have sexual intercourse. On the subway, in taxis, at parties. Well, we all have our cross to bear, and Phillip stylishly hefts his: "She'd been surprised, overwhelmed by his intensity. She'd never met a man so hungry. Now he was cool, like a hoodlum." Phillip's responses are unendearing: groped by a stranger on the downtown IRT, he thinks ecstatically: "people paid money for this". In **"The Captain"** he and his wife are on the make, screwing their separate ways into the same twenty-five grand job—Phillip sees himself aroused, as a "shark with blood in its nose and no appetite for analysis"; in **"Eating Out"**, a rosary of brief aperçus, not always in focus, sharkishness is universal, except with the linking figure, a familiar Jewish mother, with an agility in self-laceration beyond a shark's capabilities: " 'How are you, Ma?' She said: 'Me?' I said: 'Yes, how are you?' 'Me?' she said. 'Don't make me laugh'."

The view is always sidelong, a mirror glimpsed through a keyhole. In **"Murderers"** pubertal kids climb roofs to spy on the rabbi and his bride in erotic throes; one boy falls to his death:

> Nothing was discussed. The rabbi used his connections, arrangements were made. We were sent to a camp in New Jersey. . . . At night, lying in the bunkhouse, I listened to owls. I'd never before heard that sound, the sound of darkness, blooming, opening inside you like a mouth.

A sly knowingness evades what it assumes, allusiveness masquerades as precision. [**"I Would Have Saved Them If I Could"**] is an overloaded meditation on what history does to people like Dostoevsky, Jesus Christ, Jaromir Hladik (the protagonist of Borges's story—"The Secret Miracle"), and the narrator's uncle who kept a beauty parlour. One brief passage in the story is headed "Heraclitus, Hegel, Giacometti, Nietzsche, Wordsworth, Stevens". But the agonies described—the execution of three robbers observed by Byron, the Crucifixion, the death trains, ulcers—are not alike, or only trivially. He concludes:

> The earliest stories, then, already convey an exhilarating apprehension of the world as incessantly created of incessant death. Nothing changes. Stories, myths, ideologies, flowers, rivers, heavenly constellations are the phonemes of a mysterious logos. . . . Jaromir Hladik, among

substantial millions, is dead. From a certain point of view, none of this shit matters any more.

The implication (that the artist diminishes the reality of suffering) turns upon the author, in spades.

Larry Woiwode (essay date 1977)

SOURCE: "Out of the Fifties," in *Partisan Review,* Vol. XLIV, No. 1, 1977, pp. 125-30.

[*Woiwode is an American novelist, poet, and critic. In the following excerpt, he provides a favorable assessment of* I Would Have Saved Them If I Could.]

I Would Have Saved Them If I Could, Leonard Michaels's first work of fiction to appear since *Going Places,* which was nominated for the National Book Award in 1969, is a much denser, more mature, and more complex book. I say "work of fiction," because this new book is difficult to classify as a mere collection of short stories, as many reviewers are doing, or as pieces of a novel or fragmentary novel, such as Gogol gave up to let go into print, or a personal dialectic of the present world as seen through Michaels's eyes. There are thirteen separate sections altogether, some of them broken into smaller sections that are given separate titles within the encompassing title, as in **"Eating Out," "Downers,"** or in the remarkable title piece, **"I Would Have Saved Them If I Could,"** and together they form a sharply inscribed ideogram of some of our contemporary ambivalences.

The "I" or narrator of much of the book, Phillip Liebowitz, who is sometimes cast in the third person and appears in other guises, as he did in *Going Places,* but is a consistent character throughout, is a product of the peculiarities of the fifties, when he came of age. One of the most easily accessible and humorous sections of the book, **"In The Fifties,"** is a compounded litany of the attitudes and mores and meaningful stances and happenstances of that decade; done in wry pared-down sentences and compressed paragraphs. . . .

Dependent upon this period in American history, or decadence, and the narrator's upbringing, which began in Brooklyn and was generally among his family of recently emigrated Russian and Polish Jews, is the supposition that it is a dog-eat-dog world, or you are what you eat, to use a more seventyish phrase, or will become what you assimilate and consume. In **"Eating Out,"** this premise is developed in the most interrelated, logical, and frightening way—though much of the book is frightening; a kind of intellectual mind rape—and if relentlessness can be called a defect, I would say that Michaels's book, in nailing down its dialectic, suffers from its relentlessness, though sometimes I wish a few others would.

Babel is obviously Michaels's literary mentor, but it often seems that Hemingway is a favorite sounding board, the Americanized side of Michaels's fascination with violence, suicide, and death (which has "eat" at its center), and perhaps a bit of a patriarchal scourge, being anti-intellectual, a tyrant in most matters, and a fellow practitioner of the short sentence with the kick-back of a pistol shot; but then Hemingway was writing within his circumscribed limits, partly self-imposed, and place and time, and we have yet to define our own, if not some aspects of time itself. Some of the brilliant passages in this book help to do just that.

In **"Murderers,"** for instance, which calls to mind "The Killers," the narrator, Phillip, begins riding the subway after his uncle dies of a heart attack: "My family came from Poland, then never went anyplace until they had heart attacks," which is what Phillip, at least in a metaphorical sense, seems stricken with. He rides thousands of miles, mostly underground (this will later surface in a submarine image of Kafka in **"Storytellers, Liars, and Bores"**), on the New York City subway system, and one day some friends come up as he's scraping his heel on a curb (this troublesome foot—satyriasis? —reappears in **"Annabella's Hat,"** through the person of Lord Byron, in **"Hello Jack," "The Captain,"** and elsewhere in more subtle forms), and mention that the rabbi is headed for home, walking fast, which means to them that he's about to have intercourse with his wife.

The boys go up to a rooftop, and on up to the roof of a water tank, from which they have an excellent view of the Rabbi's apartment through an open window. They watch the rabbi and his wife dance naked to a rumba, and then see the two adults, prototypes of their upbringing—she bald and wigged in blond, he bearded and with his penis slapping in time—begin to have sex standing up. And here, partly, is the difference between Hemingway's twenties and Michaels's fifties. This voyeurism of the primal scene is in contrast to Nick Adams's many direct confrontations with different aspects of reality.

As the boys observe the rabbi and his wife engaged, one of them is masturbating in a "cocktail-mixer motion," one is watching that, all are aroused in different ways from their communal experience, and then one of them slips on the water tank roof; his "ring hooked on a nailhead and the ring and ring finger remained. The hand, the arm, the rest of him, were gone." And at that moment, in a "freak of ecstasy," the rabbi's wife sees the boys, and the rabbi, not yet aware of what's really happened, runs to the window and yells, "Murderers." The boys get sent to a camp in New Jersey, where, at night in the bunkhouse, Phillip listens to owls: "I'd never before heard that sound, the sound of darkness, blooming, opening inside you like a mouth." A city boy's vision of death in the natural world, which makes this reviewer wish that Michaels would mine more deeply the Orthodox heritage underlying his books and spoken of more openly in some of his casual published prose, a heritage as primitive and edifying as the Old Testament.

In **"Getting Lucky,"** which must have an eye of overview on Beckett's Godot, Liebowitz enters again, about fifteen years older, again riding the subway. He's now the employee of a scrofulous publisher, who will later reappear in the book, and as he rides dreamily to work he suddenly feels a hand, "a soft, inquisitive spider pinching the tongue of his zipper, dragging it toward the iron floor that boomed in the bones of his feet." He tries to figure out from the faces around him who's doing this, but doesn't want to make a scene. Was this perhaps a new fad, since fads in New York spread so rapidly? In the seventies, he

might be more aggressive and self-protective, perhaps like the woman who recently yelled at a subway exhibitionist, "That's the littlest one I've ever seen!" But now Liebowitz "didn't think 'filthy need.' He made a bland face. It felt good. Some might call this 'a beautiful experience.' "

He comes, but is unable to allow the experience to end there (for he's felt that this is the epitome of New York sophistication, and he's got for free something that many New Yorkers would pay for), and he's sure he recognizes his inamorata in a vacuous-looking, heavily made-up high school girl. She gets off at the next stop, and he follows her to the door of a Ladies Room, takes her arm, and is about to say, " 'You know me, don't you?' " At which point the "girl" whispers, " 'Get the claw off me, motherfucker, or I'll kick your balls!' " (Isn't this off? Wouldn't anybody who uses "motherfucker" say "kick you in the nuts," or are transvestites this peculiar even in speech?) Liebowitz goes out to the street, gets into a cab and hears its meter ticking—another detail that will occur at the book's end— as though toward the shortening of his life, and then the driver says, " '*Where,* mister.' " Liebowitz answers, " 'Nowhere.' "

Which echoes the reiterated refrain of Didi and Gogo and would be the end of a Hemingway piece, but Michaels, like Liebowitz, fortunately, perhaps, for our enlightenment, goes a bit further. The driver says to Liebowitz that this is costing him money; he can sit in the park for free. To which Liebowitz, recognizing in the "smug, annoyed superiority of the driver's tone" Manhattan's theme, replies, " 'I want to pay. Shut up.' " And, echoing the tone he's heard, brings the other side of himself full circle again.

This is indicative of the ambivalences that dreamers and moralists are strung upon, and part of the complex point that Michaels is trying to make in his nearly faultlessly organized second book. How does Trotsky, in **"Trotsky's Garden"** (apparently a parody of Barthelme's "Tolstoy's Museum," while at the same time functioning as a self-contained mantrap), for example, justify the number of deaths that have followed in his wake, largely due to his unshakable faith in his and Marx's and Engel's dialectical materialism? What has Trotsky learned of the soul of materialistic or merely common man? Trotsky, in Michaels's version, is in Mexico, in exile, staring out at his sunlit garden, which will be incorporated into his prose, as he writes of dialectical materialism. Meanwhile, "Dialectical materialism," Michaels writes, "in the heart of the day, draws a pickax from its raincoat." Trotsky is hit from behind in the head by the man in the raincoat, but manages, being who he is, to bite his assassin's hand and fling himself over his desk, to write, " 'On hot days in Mexico beware of raincoats.' "

Michaels has been compared by some reviewers to Barthelme, but has Barthelme, using the detritus of history or any of the absurd manifestations of contemporaneity he handles so well, ever made such a bloodily succinct point, except, possibly, in the "A Manual For Sons" section of his most recent *The Dead Father?* Michaels's and Barthelme's periodical publications, most of which are later gathered into their books, have appeared nearly concurrently over the years, and Michaels is, at this writing, for his illimitable exuberance, forty-three; Barthelme is forty-five. In many ways, in terms of influence, it seems surely possible that Michaels has touched on Barthelme as much as Barthelme on Michaels, especially since Barthelme didn't really delve deeply into anguish, Michaels's prime subject, until *The Dead Father*. Before Michaels was linked to such writers with the appearance of this book, he obviously had to conceive of and even compose many of its chapters, since they've been appearing in print since 1970. . . .

In his use of Trotsky, Byron, Dostoyevsky, Freud, Hegel, Kafka, Marx, Wordsworth, and other literary and cultural and philosophical figures from the past, usually not as mere entities from the past, but often as integrated characters and full-bodied spokesmen in his book, Michaels seems to be saying that our lives and histories pursue us, or that we are "chasing constructions," as Kafka wrote in one of his letters; and that men who attain prominence, whether during their lifetimes or through the hindsight of beatifying history, have been caught up in "the word." This is the same word that proceeded down to us out of the darkness and became light, and Michaels illuminates just how much, other than in the Scriptures, this history tends to gloss over, or simply lie.

Whether the above mentioned figures were savage, Christlike, malingering, conciliatory, emotional, cold, or whatever, they have always drawn to themselves forces equally opposed or apposite, or so Michaels seems to be saying, and these forces, seen from different perspectives, can make the man inside the figure seem entirely other than what he was, or is. Or, on the other hand, can help define his character with a more obvious congruity. The confined parameters of intellectuality have never been able to bring alive and deck out in flesh such a prescient point. Nor, perhaps, have Michaels's intellectual mentors been given such a healthy rap on their knuckles, which might be why so many of them have had their ire inflamed to near incoherence by this book, both in private conversation and in print—e. g., Irving Howe in his negative review in the November 13, 1975 issue of *The New York Review of Books*.

I Would Have Saved Them If I Could is a carefully constructed statement about our times, in our time, movingly developed, and each of its sections, interlocking and precise, progress to prepare us for the final one, **"The Captain,"** which could be the culmination of an elaborate novel. The levels of language, bargaining, usury, cannibalism, pseudo-moralism, moralism, fractured consciousness, and pertinent surrealism that permeate this piece, set at a publisher's party, as each character in the cast of minorities runs or shuffles or limps or fornicates around to find the ultimate big bang to blow away his or her grievance that the others present, opposed to him, mistrust (as well they might), is too complex to have the space here to begin to define. Michaels's book must be read as a whole.

As a whole, it is a luminous presentation of the density of an organized and assimilating mind, and though the relentlessness I've mentioned might be difficult for some to cope with, Michaels's short, strong, poetic sentences stand forth with a moral courage not to be found in the treacly, etiolated, and commercial prose of many of his contemporaries, not including, of course, Barthelme or Roth. His world, which fortunately isn't devoid of a resilient humor that can elicit bellylaughs and compassion, is both brutal and generously kind to the brutalized. He is the boy in **"Murderers"** who has fallen from the water tank, the Icarus of myths, the observer who's experienced secondhand the horror of the fall, and he is also the enraged rabbi and the enraged rabbi's wife being spied upon—all those whose relationships have been changed because of the complexity of the response, not to say the fall, which has been recorded by the moralist who perceives with emotion, the man with spectacles on his nose and autumn in his heart.

Anthony DeCurtis (essay date 1979)

SOURCE: "Self under Siege: The Stories of Leonard Michaels," in *Critique: Studies in Modern Fiction*, Vol. XXI, No. 2, 1979, pp. 101-11.

[In the following essay, DeCurtis surveys the style and themes of Michaels's short stories.]

In his two collections of stories, *Going Places* (1969) and *I Would Have Saved Them if I Could* (1975), Leonard Michaels depicts the contemporary struggle to shape a sensibility sufficiently intelligent, flexible, detached, and controlled to negotiate the contemporary world. The characteristic setting for his stories is New York City—the modern urban landscape, violent, unpredictable, energetic, taxing—challenging and meaningful enough to be a "vale of soul-making," dangerous and depersonalizing enough to be a hell. Michaels criticizes the modern tendency to perceive the problems of life in such an environment as intellectual puzzles, to be resolved by calling in reserves of greater and greater amounts of consciousness, but his criticism is not the silly, fashionable kind that derides all intellectual processes in the name of the emotional life betrayed. While some of his characters "suffer from too much consciousness . . . a sort of modern disease in which the operations of mind exceed the requirements of life," Michaels' positive characters are witty, smart individuals for whom thinking is an active, energetic process which culminates in actions in the world. By isolating the pitfall of being entrapped by mind to the point of emotional paralysis, of seeking in the mind for solutions which only action can bring, Michaels has defined a psychological dilemma central to contemporary American fiction.

The most pressing problem Michaels' characters face is maintaining their humanity in the brutalizing circumstances of contemporary life. Violence becomes the natural force in a world in which nothing is really natural. At once random and horrifyingly specific in its focus, violence represents a twofold threat. Its victims must resist turning themselves into unfeeling objects, able to cope because nothing can penetrate their guard, at the same time that they withstand the temptation to elevate themselves to the level of secular holy men, "seized" and purified by violence "as the spirit seizes the prophet." Similarly, the depersonalization of intimate relations poses a threat to anyone who wants to be more than another indistinct face in the mass: "it wasn't easy to think, to ignore the great pull of the worm bucket and pretend to individuation."

More generally, Michaels is concerned about the forces working in the twentieth century to annihilate any meaningful notion about the significance of the individual life.

Michaels' stories evoke a sense of how tenuous the props are which provide some semblance of continuity to modern lives. He describes an unnamed character in **"Storytellers, Liars and Bores"** as "A city girl, nine to five in an office. The days didn't return to her bound each to each by daisies. The weather report was her connection between Monday and Tuesday." Phillip Liebowitz, the most important recurring figure in Michaels' work, "makes his head out of cigarettes and coffee" in the morning before boarding the "screaming iron box" that is the subway. "Chewing gum, cigarettes, candy, drugs, alcohol, and taxicabs" carry the female character in **"Naked"** "from Monday to Friday." The kinds of relationships and work which provide more substantial links to one's days and weeks are difficult to locate and certainly to sustain. The tendency is to paste the fragments of one's life together and be like Beckman, the cabdriver in **"Going Places,"** described as "waiting for change to come into his life as if it might hail him from a corner like another fare."

The disruptiveness of modern life is a crucial theme in Michaels' stories, but too great an awareness of the problem debilitates some of his characters as much as no awareness of it at all dehumanizes others. Reading "avant-garde novels and philosophical commentaries on the modern predicament" does not help Melanie Green, the heroine of **"Manikin,"** deal with the rape which shatters the protected, unsatisfying life she had led. She ends up perceiving herself as being like an "armless, naked manikin" in a store window and eventually commits suicide. Discussions about "the keystone of modernity," "what's modern," the loss of "connection with the elemental life," occur with some frequency in Michael's stories and are symptoms of the very problem they assume as their topic. That these conversations typically take place at parties, the inevitable setting in contemporary literature of interactions which are artificial and contrived with the pretense of being intimate and communal, further emphasizes their shallowness. The female speaker in **"Being Moral"** states the situation most concisely: "Being moral is a luxury, isn't it? No, it's asking the question." To be self-conscious about consciousness, a part of our humanity, after all, is to paralyze oneself both emotionally and morally. No human action of any meaning is possible in such a state.

The question of moral knowledge itself is not abstract nor philosophical for Michaels, but rather intuitive, emotional, and affective. His characters often allow themselves to be confused by their intellect, using it to fabricate issues which help them avoid, not confront, external reality. In Michaels' own view, the real judgments, the real decisions, regardless of how his characters choose to act in the world, are made "in the pits of their minds where there were neither words nor ideas but only raging morality." Michaels posits a psychic landscape, obscured in daily life by the fog of obsessive ratiocination, where "life is true and bleak, where all things move in pure, deep knowledge of right and wrong or else they die." The farther his characters move from this environ, the more their actions be-

come parodic of actual life, the more they are living in bad faith. Again, one should not confuse this notion with a shallow primitivism in which the problems of life dissolve if one merely has one's guts in the right place. In the "pits" of the *mind,* intellect and emotion can fuse, producing energetic, appropriate action. Morality in Michaels' stories is passionate, intelligent engagement with the world, not the measurement of one's doings against one or another internalized, external standard. The complexities of life in the twentieth century do not allow for the latter.

The images Michaels uses to evoke the psychic underworld which can give us "pure, deep knowledge of right and wrong" are those of darkness and blackness. The light of reason and logic does not provide the means by which the situations of life can be comprehended and seen as subject to our control. Genuine insight is the product of emotion and intellect, and itself produces movement. Attempting to come to grips with his relationship to his friend, Henry, in **"Fingers and Toes,"** Phillip hits on a course of action: "The idea just came to me. I didn't struggle to establish thesis and antithesis. It came BOOMBA. Real ideas strike like eagles. A man who loves premises and conclusions loves a whore." The source for these "real ideas" is the darkness and blackness within ourselves, spaces to which we must have access while we take care not to determine too neatly what those spaces contain.

As a stylist, Michaels is most interested in condensed, compact expression. His desire for compression, which obviously does not allow for very much standard description, places rhetorical responsibility for communicating a story's meaning on its verbs. The emphasis on action and movement suggested by Michaels' striking verbs is reflected also in the title of some of his stories: **"Making Changes"** and **"Going Places."** While stagnation is deadening, motion makes us tap the sources for self-knowledge within the self. **"Murderers,"** the first story in *I Would Have Saved Them if I Could,* begins with an illustration of the theme: "When my Uncle Moe dropped dead of a heart attack I became expert in the subway system. With a nickel I'd get to Queens, twist again toward the George Washington Bridge—beyond which was darkness. I wanted proximity to darkness, strangeness." Motion in Michaels' stories differs from the movement suggested by, for example, Maria Wyeth's aimless freeway driving in Didion's *Play It as It Lays* or the repetitive "yo-yoing" in Pynchon's *V.* The "proximity to darkness" which Phillip's subway riding entails provides him with a means of coming to terms with his Uncle Moe's death and the emotional constriction which is his immigrant family's legacy. In other contexts, Phillip runs "down the night" at the end of **"Sticks and Stones"** and swims the night like a fish, "from blackness to blackness to blackness to blackness," at the end of **"Fingers and Toes."** Both of these stories center on Phillip's relationship to his friend, Henry, and their mutual involvement with Marjorie, currently Henry's consort, formerly Phillip's lover. Phillip's plunging into the night is not a strategy of avoidance but a means of working out his problems physically as well as mentally, the two processes becoming one. As he remarks in **"Sticks and Stones,"** "Trying to think, I ran the streets at night. My lungs were thrilled by darkness."

In story after story in which he appears, Phillip Liebowitz is concerned with maintaining his identity and not succumbing to the temptation to create an untrue self or to assume roles others thrust upon him. In amusing, significant ways, he reminds himself who he is, re-introduces himself to himself, sometimes in a casual, matter-of-fact manner, more often by defining himself in his own terms or in opposition to some false conception of himself: "I was a city boy. No innocent shitkicker from Jersey," he states in **"City Boy"**; "I was the A train, the Fifth Avenue bus. I could be a cop. My name was Phillip, my style New York City." More philosophically, in **"Sticks and Stones"** he comments, "I was neither Nietzsche, Don Juan, nor Chateaubriand. My name was Phillip." His battle to hold on to a coherent notion of himself in an environment that works to frustrate such efforts is an especially prominent theme in **"Making Changes."** Phillip meets a girl named Cecily at a party "clogged with bodies," into which she disappears, "virtually torn out of my hands." He wanders through the apartment searching for her, encountering a variety of vapid people, conversations, and situations. The orgy going full-steam is described by Phillip as "the worm bucket," suggesting the level of sexual communication taking place, while this bit of conversation between two characters named Cosmo and Tulip captures the party's intellectual tone:

> "Sexual enlightenment, the keystone of modernity, I dare say, can hardly be considered an atavistic intellectual debauch, Cosmo."
>
> "But the perversions . . ."
>
> "To be sure, the perversions of which we are so richly conscious are the natural inclination, indeed the style, of civilized beings."

The mindlessness of the conversation and the sexual undifferentiation of the orgy are not the only threats to Phillip's desire for "individuation." Others at the party repeatedly address him either impersonally, metaphorically, or incorrectly. "Wait there, you. . . . What sort of pervert are you?" is Tulip's opening gambit when she first spots Phillip. As he enters a bathroom, "A naked man sitting pertly in the tub said, 'I'll bet you're Zeus. I'm Danae.' I shook my head, backed out muttering, 'I'm Phillip.' " Finally, as he attempts to leave the party, having located Cecily, Phillip encounters a "big man" at the door who says to him, " 'I'm glad you came tonight, Harold.' 'I'm glad you're glad,' I said. 'Name is Stanley.' " In the thickening "stew" of the party, personal definitions are in danger of becoming undone. Phillip must resist the false selves others project upon him and maintain a clear vision of himself.

Creating possibilities for personal relationships, making claims on another while recognizing that person's individuality and avoiding possessiveness, becomes the focal theme of **"Making Changes"** after Phillip and Cecily leave the party. Having spent the night with him, Cecily is preparing to leave his apartment in the morning. He wants her to stay, but even as he asks her to, he alludes wittily, defensively, to the modern cultural assumptions which tend to make intimacy a virtual impossibility: "What can I say? I'm aware the couple is a lousy idea. I read books.

I go to the flicks. I'm hip. I live in New York. But I want you to come back. Will you come back?" By the end of the day and the story, they are reintroducing themselves to each other, names again becoming emblems for the self. Phillip asks her name: " 'Cecily,' she said. 'I'm Phillip,' I said, 'but you knew that. Cecily? Of course, Cecily.' "

Beckman, the central character in **"Going Places,"** has more awesome threats than an orgiastic party posed to his identity. The story, perhaps Michaels' fiercest and best, dramatizes compellingly a number of his most crucial themes: impersonal violence working as a force against individuals in the modern world; the imperative to change one's life which unforeseen crisis brings; the chilling sense that, regardless of how one's life is changed, brute circumstance can destroy lives as readily as crazed human agents.

A New York cabdriver, Beckman is robbed and beaten nearly to death by "two figures," a man and a woman, who hail him "in misty dismal twilight." Beckman's assailants strike impersonally but specifically, like the Turkish student in **"Manikin"** who robs the University Hotel and bludgeons the night porter "so murderously he took it in a personal way." The crimes themselves recede into the background in both these instances, becoming merely occasions and excuses for the exercise of arbitrary violence against other human beings. While Beckman pleads, "shrieking, 'Take my money,' " the woman chants, " 'Hey, hey, Beckman' . . . with the flat exuberance and dull inertia of a work song, repeated without change in pitch or intensity while fists rocked his skull and Beckman thrashed in the darkness." The woman sings her "work song" because violence is her job, her function, from which she is as numbingly detached as Beckman is from his driving. Her direct address to Beckman during the assault underscores Michaels' belief that the random, brutalizing events of the modern world, which seem to strike us arbitrarily, contain messages to us about our lives. As a cabdriver, Beckman had been drifting, living "a life made wretched by rattling kidneys, the stench of gasoline, of cigarettes, of perfume, and alcohol and vomit." He was a chauffeur to

> surly toughs, drunken women, whoring soldiers, vagrant blacks and whites, all the streaming, fearsome, pathetic riffraff refuse of the city's dark going places, through places in hell, while he, Beckman, driver of the cab, went merely everyplace, stopped, parked, dropped his head against the seat and lay mindless, cramped, chilled in a damp sweater and mucky underwear, lay seized by the leather seat, debauched by the night's long, winding, resonant passage and the abuse of a thousand streets. Everyplace Beckman, anyplace Beckman, he went noplace.

His close brush with death brings him up against the corrosive facts of his life, and to this degree, "the punches and kicks were heralds, however brutal, bearing oracles of his genius, the bludgeoning shapers of himself if properly understood." His beating, "precisely what he deserved," provides him with the impetus to seize control of his life rather than continue "waiting for change to come into his life as if it might hail him from a corner like another fare," or like the "two figures" who hailed him "in misty dismal twilight." His ability to comprehend the implications of what happened puts him in a position where he can reconstruct his life and allow himself the satisfactions that a sane human situation can provide. Despite the elevated language and allusions which express the message communicated to him by his misfortune, Beckman understands that he is not a saint of some kind but is now at least able to locate a middle-ground in which human choice is possible. His is not "a shaman's face," and he is "no prophet, but neither a bag scrunched into leather, glass, and steel, commanded by anyone to stop, go, ache, count change out of nasty fingers, breathe gas and hear youth ticked away in nickels."

Michaels understands that the modern world is bleaker, crueler, less predictable than current apostles of self-discovery would have us believe. Our options are only rarely determined by the extent of our self-knowledge. Neither a "prophet" nor an inanimate object, his mind, as well as his motives, focused in ways "entirely unlike the vague motions it had been given to while drifting through the dark streets of the city," Beckman lands a job with a paint contractor. The solidity of his new prospects is suggested by their seeming to him as "real as the hard, substantial hand which had enveloped and strongly shaken his hand" at the end of his job interview. On his first day at the job, Beckman crawls down a pipe high above an enormous factory to deliver a can of paint to one of his fellow-workers. He loses his balance momentarily, glances down to feel what the narrator earlier had termed the "proximity of annihilation," "the thrill of imminent nothing," and clings desperately to the pipe, willing or able neither to "let go nor drag toward the painter." As Beckman clutches the pipe, his life only as secure as his grip, Michaels evokes through imagery ("sweat," "spit," "steel") and analogy not only Beckman hanging on for his life in the factory, but his earlier descriptions of Beckman driving, living, and finally under attack in his cab:

> Against his mouth he smelled, then tasted, steel as it turned rancid with sweat and spit. He felt water pour slowly, beyond his will, into his pants as it had when they hit him and hit him for no reason and he twisted and shrieked on the floor of his cab. He felt the impulse to move and did not want to look around into the vacuous air, nor to imagine the beating or the possibility that the tremor in his chin and lips would become a long, fine scream spinning out the thread of his life as he dropped toward the machines and the concrete floor. He felt the impulse to move and he could remember how motion felt gathering, droning in the motor of his cab, to move him through the dark avenues of the city.

This portrait of Beckman grasping the pipe, squeezing "life against his chest," while the other painters shout, "Don't let go, Beckman," closes the last story of Michaels' first collection: "He did not let go. The tremor passed into muscle as rigid as the steel it squeezed."

"Going Places," then, traces Beckman's movement from aimless drifting to near death to self-awareness to a new sense of life's possibilities and leaves him struggling for his life in the final "place" to which he goes, hanging high above a factory's concrete floor. Catastrophes survived (and even learned from) provide no certainty for the future. Michaels develops this theme throughout his work but its clearest expression occurs in "The Subject at the Vanishing Point," a vignette in **"I Would Have Saved Them if I Could."** The narrator's grandfather is prepared to leave Poland but is prevented from going when a pogrom begins. He is in danger outside his neighborhood but is saved because "Suddenly—for good or ill isn't known—somebody flung him into a cellar." He returns home; everyone celebrates his survival, "But it was too late to get a visa," and he is forced to stay in Poland. Then, Michaels writes, "The Nazis came with the meaning of history—what flings you into a cellar saves you for bullets." For the person caught up in the circumstances of history as well as for isolated individuals like Beckman, the imminence of one's death is all that can provide either historical or personal meaning to one's life. In a world "incessantly created of incessant death," the process of self-creation is linked to the "proximity of darkness," "the proximity of annihilation." If one can be saved only "for bullets," what modes of action are available in the modern world? Like Beckman, we can embrace life—cold, unyielding, and dangerous as it is—and "not let go." In the midst of our energetic but ultimate impotence, we can be compassionate: "I would have saved them if I could."

Michaels derived the title for his second collection of stories from a remark in a letter by Lord Byron describing the guillotining in Rome of three criminals. A portion of the letter, "Lord Byron's Letter," is presented as a vignette. Despite its author and date, the letter stands as a central document about the modern perception of and response to horror. In Michaels' excerpt, Byron's remarks begin as casual, observant, and informative:

> The day before I left Rome I saw three robbers guillotined. The ceremony—including the *masqued* priests; the half-naked executioners; the bandaged criminals; the black Christ and his banner; the scaffold; the soldiery; the slow procession, and the quick rattle and heavy fall of the axe; the splash of blood, and the ghastliness of the exposed heads—is altogether more impressive than the vulgar and ungentlemanly "new drop" and dog-like agony of infliction upon the sufferers of the English sentence.

Byron goes on to compare the various responses of the three men to their imminent beheading and speculates further about the relative merits of guillotining in contrast with other means of execution: "It is better than the oriental way, and (I should think) than the axe of our ancestors. The pain seems little, and yet the effect to the spectator, and the preparation to the criminal, is very striking and chilling."

Byron's rendering of his own reactions to the criminals' deaths thrusts home the full implications of his epistolary narrative, and Michaels' appropriation of it, for the reader of contemporary fiction or, indeed, for anyone who lives in the contemporary world. Commenting on the effects of the executions on himself, Byron states:

> The first turned me quite hot and thirsty, and

made me shake so that I could hardly hold the opera-glass (I was close, but was determined to see, as one should see every thing, once, with attention); the second and third (which shows how dreadfully soon things grow indifferent), I am ashamed to say, had no effect on me as a horror, though I would have saved them if I could.

In much contemporary fiction, characters participate in the emotions Lord Byron describes. They, too, are connoisseurs of the grotesque; they hunger for experience, to see and do it all and intensely, but are finally left jaded and unsatisfied; they are initially appalled by their violent, horrific world, but ultimately confused about how to come to terms with it. Does the notion of shock lose its currency when one is shocked at every moment and when shock is compromised by fascination? Indifference seems at times to be the necessary strategy of a survivor in an environment in which brutality is the stuff of everyday, but the lingering sense of guilt and shame it entails intimates that such indifference may be morally indistinguishable from cowardice. Finally, the combination of positive intentions and powerlessness is deadly, because the real presence of either raises suspicions about the authenticity of the other. The ungenuine life beckons like a desert mirage when reality is emotionally and morally undifferentiated. Leonard Michaels' stories effectively dramatize the ennobling power of resistance to that false appeal.

Nicholas Delbanco   (essay date 1990)

SOURCE: "Melancholy Musing on the Game of Love," in *Chicago Tribune—Books,* August 19, 1990, p. 6.

[*An English-born American novelist and critic, Delbanco is acclaimed for his novel trilogy that chronicles an upper-class family in Vermont. In the following review, he finds* Shuffle *predictable and lacking in introspection.*]

Leonard Michaels's new collection—all too accurately titled *Shuffle*—is easy to dislike, hard to admire. It's a weary, foot-dragging sort of book, full of anomie and cigarette smoke and literary referents and sex. Much of the ground is familiar and much of the motion predictable: guy gets girl, guy leaves girl or is left by girl, guy gets her back by writing it all down. The writer comes from a warmly supportive immigrant family but is left in cold cities to fend for himself; he has male friends and a succession of predatory lovers and a despairing humor to get him through the night.

This brief text has three parts. The first, a **"Journal,"** consists of aphorisms and encounters and story-snippets accumulated over time; the second contains four very short reminiscences; the third, **"Sylvia,"** is an extended reconstruction of his failed marriage and suicidal wife.

Told in the first person, these pages have the feel of autobiography throughout. Yet the question of fictive truth must be addressed with some care. The autobiographer may be inventive and the artist reportorial; we should take our confessional prose with more than a fistful of salt. Though *Shuffle* is recognizably by the author of *Going Places* (1969), *I Would Have Saved Them If I Could* (1975) and, most recently, *The Men's Club* (1981), it reads like a mem-

oir. And fiction itself is a series of lies tricked out to recreate truth.

Three problems seem central here. First, there's a startling lack of alteration in the voice. The journal entries of 1961, included in the **"Sylvia"** section, are almost wholly similar in tone and preoccupation to those of the much later **"Journal."** The latter, almost 30 years subsequent, contains a two-line entry characteristic of the former: "She screamed and broke objects. Nevertheless, I refused to kill her."

This sort of tough-guy tautness may seem sentimental: "I talk to Annette only on the phone. Afraid we might touch." Or, one entry later, "I felt we knew each other. At his funeral, I thought, I will cry." There's a coyness in the presentation of the self, as if an artist's musing must be epigrammatic. And not all quotations count:

> Ortega says men are public, women are private. Montaigne says, if you want to know all about me, read my book. . . . In the same spirit, a man writes a letter, then decides not to mail it. He thinks it's himself, a great letter, too good for just one person. It should be published. . . . Real intimacy is for the world, not a friend.

Which brings us to the major problem. Such unwinking honesty is most fruitfully self-addressed; confessional texts require some component of introspection: why did I say this or behave that way; what sort of creature, *hypocrite lecteur,* do you hold here in your hand? The narrator of these stories has a chill accuracy in his assessment of the way that other folks behave and a clinical acuity of observation throughout. He is misanthropic—not to say misogynistic—to a fault. But he seldom turns inward or tries to draw conclusions, so that the book's final lines are tellingly precise. "I saw emptiness. I left the hospital with nothing, nothing at all."

For those who think that "nothing at all" is what outlasts a marriage and a loved one's suicide, such an end will be persuasive. But the very telling of the tale belies finality, and Michaels at his best displays a vivid brilliance that fills his lines with life. There's much wit in his characters, a controlled and near-erotic impatience with the mere surface of things. And that is why, though easy to dislike, his work compels admiration: there's a brittle power here throughout.

Richard Locke   (essay date 1990)

SOURCE: "New Twists on the Familiar," in *The Wall Street Journal,* August 21, 1990, p. A12.

[*In the following review, Locke offers a positive assessment of* Shuffle.]

Over the past 25 years, in essays and reviews, two collections of stories, a novel and the remarkable autobiographical fictions—verbal snapshots, anecdotes, journal entries, full-scale memoirs and stories—collected in his new book, *Shuffle,* Leonard Michaels has perfected a literary style of uncommon lucidity, force and ease. These are classical virtues, to be sure, but Mr. Michaels's subjects, his voice and emotional range, his intelligence and wit, all are distinctly American, late 20th century, anything but antique.

Out of familiar material—Lower East Side Jewish family life during the war, Greenwich Village sex and friendship in the '50s, and early '60s, ever more desperate sex and careerism in Berkeley, Los Angeles and New York from the time of women's liberation to the present age of glitz—he constructs literary miniatures that are dense but go like lightning. They seem larger, more spacious and alive with precise facts and meanings than most gasping novels. But for all their artful compression and meticulous diction, they're never precious, never merely out to shock or elicit snobbish admiration. They always stay close to the way people actually talk and act when they're too driven by their ferocious, guilty needs to even think about good manners.

Mr. Michaels has always cared more about his stories than literary fashion. Twenty years ago, when cast-iron whimsy and slap-happy sprawling comedies of the absurd were in style, he built sharp little diamond structures that said much more than most about radical sex and politics a la mode. When gray videotaped minimalism became the rage, he kept infusing stories with operatic feeling and color and an almost 19th-century belief in character. When feminism threatened to dwindle into parlor games, he wrote a novel, *The Men's Club,* that portrayed the sexes as participants in chemical warfare.

Most unfashionably, he's neither a self-advertising moralist nor an aesthetic nihilist. He still believes, it seems, that a literary work has an intrinsic moral power. His characters seethe and erupt in all too modern ways (breaking down, betraying each other, spouting radical chicanery or psychobabble), and he implies that they can and must be seen as desperate moral, psychological and historical beings. But he never passes facile, moralistic judgments; he dramatizes and leaves the rest to us. He often writes in fragments, but he constructs an immediately recognizable picture of "contemporary reality." In this he's closer to modernist collages than to postmodern videos. He's always telling stories with palpable beginnings, middles and ends. He's deadly serious, witty and bursting with feeling.

His new book falls into three sections. The first is a highly fractured journal of California sex, marriage and divorce among academics, shrinks and literary and movie types. We careen from social satire to a quote from Lord Byron ("And, after all, what is a lie?" "'Tis but the truth in masquerade") to a glimpse of Lower East Side family life ("I phoned my mother. She said, 'You sound happy. What's the matter?' ") to garish sexual anecdotes and confessions to scenes of tormented, competitive friendships. The key word seems to be "ferocity."

The central section of the book is the most traditional: strong, highly condensed memoirs of Mr. Michaels's father and mother, of a high-school English teacher (a former ball-turret gunner who brings his trauma to the teaching of *The Winter's Tale*), and a grad-school anecdote.

But the last and longest section is the triumph of the book: a memoir of the author's first marriage that portrays with great intensity and conviction his grim transition from late

adolescence to young manhood and maturity and, simultaneously, the shift in American life (feeling, thought, fantasy) that took place between the late '50s and the early '60s. Mr. Michaels's fiction has always shown the continuity between personal and political or cultural history, and in this narrative the central figure of Sylvia, an exotic Jewish-American Greenwich Village student with "a figure and face like Egyptian statuary," embodies the tortured, torturing spirit of the age. Reader, he married her, and it was truly hell.

In June 1960 he dropped out of graduate school and returned to New York with the vague idea of writing stories. Walking through Greenwich Village he feels a "new apocalyptic atmosphere . . . Elvis Presley and Allen Ginsberg were the kings of feeling, and the word *love* was like a proclamation with the force of *kill.* I saw a blunt admonition chalked on the wall of the subway station: —Hate. Weird delirium was in the air and in the sluggish, sensual crowds as I pressed toward the sooty-faced tenement . . ."

There he meets Sylvia Bloch and, "like a couple doomed to a sacrificial assignation," they make love in her squalid apartment:

> Through the tall, open window of the living room we saw the night sky and heard people proceed along MacDougal Street, as in a lunatic carnival, screaming, breaking glass, wanting to hit, needing meanness. Someone played a guitar in another apartment. Someone was crying. Lights flew across the walls and ceiling. Radios were loud. The city made its statement in the living room. None of it had to do with us, lying naked on the couch, just wide enough for two, against the brick wall.

It's all there, even in the beginning: the violent city, the violent age, their violent sex, her madness, his obsession, their combat, their mutual destruction. Such a story brings us as close to tragedy as contemporary prose is likely to get.

Anatole Broyard   (essay date 1990)

SOURCE: "Adrift in Sex," in *The New York Times Book Review,* September 9, 1990, pp. 14-15.

[*Broyard was an American critic, essayist, short story writer, and former editor of the* New York Times Book Review. *In the following review, he comments favorably on Michaels's earlier short story collections but finds* Shuffle *disappointing.*]

Contrary to public opinion, a literary reputation is one of the hardest things in the world to lose. People are loyal to their mistakes. An author can write a first novel that shows promise and then follow it with six more that plainly fail to keep that promise—yet the public, ever slow to change, clings to its first assessment. J. P. Donleavy's *Ginger Man* is only one of many examples.

Going Places, Leonard Michaels's first collection of stories (1969), showed promise and was wildly overpraised. Why? Simply because the time had come for this particular syndrome to take its place in American literature. He wrote the kind of prose that caused Philip Roth to ask in an essay, "Why is everyone being so bouncy?" The stories were trendy, pretentious and overblown, but they had *flair,* and we are always starved for flair.

Mr. Michaels's second collection of stories, *I Would Have Saved Them if I Could,* came out in 1975 and, surprisingly, they were *more* promising than the earlier ones. In fact, they were good in his special way, if you forgave them their sins. These stories were leaner, more truly quirky, full of almost danceable rhythms. They were New York City stories in the best sense, proud of their sophistication. They were less strained. Mr. Michaels was putting more of his energy into persuading us that his characters exist in the world, or at least in some world. He had discovered that, if you intensify a fault, it may turn into a style.

One can feel, and share, Mr. Michaels's pleasure in turning his sentences. There's affection—for the world and for literature—in them. Here are a few examples from *I Would Have Saved Them if I Could*: dancing the rumba in the nude with his wife, who is wearing a blond wig over her shaved head, "the rabbi stepped away to delight in blond imagination." "He was Mr. Life." "The breeze smelled of reasons to live." "Intelligence springs through my mind like a monkey, seizing the bars, shaking them." Sometimes he gets cute: "I thrash in a murk of days." Here's a nice passage in a story called **"Murderers,"** in which the boys are on a roof, observing the rabbi and his wife through their open window: "For a while I watched them. Then I gazed beyond into shimmering nullity, gray, blue, and green murmuring over rooftops and towers. I had watched them before. I could tantalize myself with this brief ocular perversion, the general cleansing nihil of a view. This was the beginning of philosophy. I indulged in ambience, in space like eons."

Still, there are as many flaws as felicities. "To make her know it, I broke her nose." He broke her nose? It's not even clear what he's making her know. The stories are riddled with gratuitous violence. "I knew two girls who had brains, talent, health, good looks, plenty to eat, and hanged themselves." There's a lot of talk, all through Mr. Michaels's work, of guns. In *Going Places,* we find this: "He punched out three of her teeth and strangled her until she dissolved in his hands and she scratched his left eye blind."

Perhaps the 1990's will be the decade when we can say that there's too much sex in a writer's work. For all its horrors, AIDS may have restored some perspective to our sexual behavior, at least in making us *think* about it. Mr. Michaels seems to write about sex almost exclusively. And there's something disreputable about characters—or authors—who are no longer in their first youth investing so much time and energy in the pursuit of sex. It's not as if it were the pursuit of happiness, as in Erica Jong or Henry Miller, for sex doesn't often make Mr. Michaels's characters happy. Instead, it's like a depressed sport, like going to the race track without betting on the horses.

It's a failure of imagination, isn't it, to write about the same thing all the time? So many disconsolate couples, ob-

scurely angry men and exasperating women. Mr. Michaels is the uncrowned king of heterosexual exasperation. The sex Mr. Michaels writes about seems to be a mere civil right, a waste product of psychology and the drift of our culture. One longs for some sign of genuine enthusiasm. The way it's isolated here, sex is both too personal and not personal enough. The characters are adrift in it, like people in a flood who abandon their homes for rowboats.

In **"Getting Lucky,"** one of the stories in *I Would Have Saved Them if I Could,* a man in a crowded New York City subway finds himself being explicitly masturbated by an unseen hand. Because of the press of people, he cannot see who is doing this, but welcomes it nevertheless. And this seems to be Mr. Michaels's message: that sex is good, under any circumstances. The character doesn't feel invaded or trespassed upon, but "lucky." "He realized suddenly that he felt—beyond pleasure—hip . . . proud to be a New Yorker."

Shuffle, Mr. Michaels's new collection—one doesn't know what to call it—is a shockingly bad book for a man of Mr. Michaels's stature. All the wryness has dried up and left him with a bad taste in his mouth. The book is like a man combing his hair in a bathroom mirror, and then inspecting the comb, counting the hairs. Even the title of the book seems like a confession. It's divided into six sections, two of them short, occasional pieces—**"Literary Talk"** and **"The Abandoned House"**—that can have no other conceivable purpose but to fatten the book or even merely to separate the others. They're like the stars and garters, disguising the naked truth, that strippers used to wear.

The journal, the longest part, is much the worst. To begin with, it's not a journal—a man writing to himself—at all, but an utterly random collection of "thoughts," vignettes, vaporings, hypothetical sexual couplings. Here's an example: "We made love all afternoon. Sonny said, 'Was it good?' My speech was slurred: 'Never in my life . . .' She said, 'I should be compensated.' "

Jewish-American fiction has evolved a certain kind of father: small, quaint, mildly rebellious, permanently old-fashioned. *Shuffle* has one of those fathers, a fiction. The protagonist's—there seems to be a protagonist here—mother is no better. The author appears to be offering us these two as a kind of atonement for all the sex and highfalutin shenanigans. There's even a wife, and she, of course, is insane. There is one story here about each of these. What more could anyone ask? The circle is complete. As a character in *I Would Have Saved Them if I Could* says, this is not real writing, but "*like* writing."

Gordon Lubold   (essay date 1990)

SOURCE: A review of *Shuffle,* in *West Coast Review of Books,* Vol. 15, No. 6, November-December, 1990, p. 21.

[*In the following review, Lubold remarks favorably on* Shuffle.]

This unique collection of short stories and "journal" entries [*Shuffle*] careens in and out of a writer's need to tell of his experience, but also satisfies his need (and ours) to explore the inner workings of the mind. And while there is a certain sense of indulgence in his writings, the reader comes away with a satisfying experience, having read candid and sincere pieces by a writer who seems to have worked through an uneasy kind of restlessness.

For example, the first section, entitled **"Journal,"** pulls together many of his unconnected thoughts and experiences. Each entry reads as if it were originally written on a small piece of paper and then left forgotten under a flowerpot, in a bottom drawer, or hidden inside a half-read book. There is a randomness, and a kind of (intentional) disconnectedness to them but an effort to weave together such random (though nevertheless valid) thoughts would probably be awkward and unwieldy. Instead, Michaels unapologetically presents a smattering of different facets of his life to form a broad mosaic.

One entry berates the ugliness of a monastery, and possibly a faith, while another suggests that writers never attain the kind of marked distinction that a medical student does when he earns his degree. In another, the writer goes to the movies and feels compelled to yell out at the hero, knocking him off his pedestal. When Michaels (or some adaptation of the writer) decides that the love interest is so beautiful so as not to warrant a comment, the writer watches as the blonde on screen tells him that she wants his baby. The couple in the movie then falls to the waiting couch, fully clothed. Michaels then compares the glamor and the size of the on-screen encounter with the banality of his own experience.

In a section called **"Sylvia,"** referring to the writer's wife of four years, Michaels relates the painful and chaotic life he shared with her. Writing as he is many years after the fact, Michaels tells of his wife's chronic insecurity and looming depression, with warmth and humor, but at a distance. No particular attempt is made to compare his experiences with the decade, but the period of the sixties in which he lived with her provides a subtle suggestion.

As Michaels interprets facts using his imagination, a reader gets a somehow more truthful, more striking understanding of the events and thoughts he includes. Like poetry, which can speak in images and oddly juxtaposed feelings, *Shuffle* leaves us with an impression which soothes our confusion and calms our aches. An inability to express what it all *means* lends itself to reflection on our own experiences.

Roz Kaveney   (essay date 1991)

SOURCE: A review of *Shuffle,* in *The Times Literary Supplement,* No. 4613, August 30, 1991, p. 19.

[*In the following excerpt, Kaveney faults the long stories in* Shuffle *for lacking a sense of authenticity.*]

Confession has the authority of other nakednesses, with the advantage that it can be faked more easily. A man is not on oath in what claims to be his authentic journal, or in stories which purport to be a true record of the past. Leonard Michaels is fully entitled to write what he likes and call it what he will; no fiction can be trusted as autobiography, and few autobiographies can either. Yet there remain responsibilities.

The major problem in *Shuffle* is that Michaels is portraying relations between the sexes as being essentially war, a war in which the male-viewpoint character is the innocent victim of aggression; the long story **"Sylvia"** portrays a 1960s marriage which is rancid from the beginning and goes into a decline. The touchy narrator finds his virility questioned by his wife, and crockery is endlessly thrown; eventually he leaves her, and she kills herself. There is no attempt to understand this; the whole point, we are told, is that people like this are a mystery to the narrator—she just came apart in his hands.

Even if this were not described as autobiographical fiction in the blurb, one would like some other evidence before the inquest brings in a convenient verdict, or at least some cross-examination of the witness. As it is, all we are allowed to see of the inner condition of his soul is that he and Sylvia were caught up in a decade he now sees as having been in love with death. It is in the actual writing that this perception of the relationship and its times comes to look most false, in sentences like "A few blocks east, at the Five Spot, Ornette eviscerated jazz essence through a raucous plastic sax". The pain may be authentic, but the prose is tinny through and through; and if we cannot trust the author's ear, why should we believe his wife is so utterly self-destroyed?

Much the same is true of the carefully selected chunks of journal—the sort of observations about pain and experience over which the writer coos "How true, how true" even as he writes them down, but which crumble on the tongue. He talks of friends and their confidences, in short snatches, intended as epiphanies but reading more like overhearings; he indulges in aphorisms which patronize experience, particularly sexual experience, rather than illuminating it.

All of this is a pity, because the four short stories which make up the rest of the book have a finished purity and an artful authenticity that is missing in the two longer, more unbuttoned pieces. We are taken through childhood, school and college, through being poor, learning about death, being a son. These are simple, admirable stories notable for what the body of the book lacks, the ring of truth.

Tom Clark   (essay date 1992)

SOURCE: "Unstuck in the '60s," in *Los Angeles Times Book Review,* October 11, 1992, pp. 3, 7.

[*Clark is an American critic, poet, biographer, and novelist. In the following review, he comments favorably on* Sylvia, *suggesting that the novella has the qualities of a fable.*]

The current commercial vogue in '60s nostalgia is predictably paralleled by a reactionary backlash, to which Leonard Michael's *Sylvia* offers a sharp, laconic text.

In styling his "fictional memoir," Michaels seems to be trying to touch a fact-based, occasionally journalistic reminiscence with the novelist's magic wand—a curious stroke considering that Michaels makes no bones about the verisimilitude of his tale to an ill-starred personal relationship conducted in the turbid hipster depths of 1960s Greenwich Village. This brief, sad story (advertised in the publicity copy as a rewrite of an autobiographical memoir published in Michaels' 1990 collection *Shuffle*), delivered in a detached, dispassionate and spare first-person recounting, has a palpable ring of truth. Indeed, that's the best thing about it.

It is 1960 at the outset. The narrator, a 27-year-old grad-school dropout and would-be writer, son of New York Jewish middle-class parents, has just returned home from Berkeley. He is confused about things, doesn't know what he wants to do with his life. But he is a good observer, and through his eyes—that is, out of author Michaels' memory and out of his old journals—we get a good look at the two principal characters of this book.

The heroine is Sylvia, a bright, attractive, enigmatic, unpredictable, insecure and ominously violence-prone 19-year-old classics student with whom, after a quick tryst, the narrator moves in. She maintains, in typically sloppy beatnik fashion, a squalid, roach-overrun sixth-floor walk-up on MacDougal Street. There, amid clouds of burning incense, hash smoke and roach killer, they begin a painful love affair that drags them through the next four years. Michaels' coolly distant reportorial technique is at its best in following this duel of self-destructive drives and weaknesses through all its psychological nuances, tensions and dynamics on the road to eventual disintegration.

The psychopathology behind the personal disaster that resolves Michaels' story is inferentially attributed at least in part to the historical epoch. More than just period backdrop, the '60s counterculture landscape—with representative icons like Jack Kerouac, Lenny Bruce and Allen Ginsberg stepping forward for cameo appearances, and well-known landmarks like the Five Spot, Cafe Figaro and Village Vanguard frequently heaving into view—becomes a major element in the action. And not always a positive one. It is the moral chaos and social confusion of the '60s, Michaels implies, that is ultimately responsible for the individual pathos of a wasted life. In a time when popular psychologists like R. D. Laing "[sing] praises to the condition of being nuts," Diane Arbus photographs freaks, Kerouac and Bruce blow their minds and rave in public, and "people [exceed] themselves . . . or the self " as a regular way of life, small wonder that things come out badly for Sylvia. Too much sex, drugs and freedom, working on her vulnerable, sensitive, dislocated nature, lead, by an awful inevitability, to tragedy.

Sylvia does have an interesting quality of fable about it, oddly given away by the very impartiality of its tone. "My life, after all, wasn't a story," the narrator comments after an unsuccessful visit to a shrink. "It was just moments, what happens from day to day, and it didn't mean anything, and there was no moral." But the judgment his younger self eschewed is not abdicated by the more mature Michaels, whose sketching of the aimless but intense relationship of two young people adrift in a world in which "there were really no large meanings, only cries of the phenomena" shows such a world to be, above all else, dangerous.

Dust jacket for Michaels's 1990 collection of autobiographical sketches.

Clancy Sigal   (essay date 1992)

SOURCE: "Life and Times of a She-Devil," in *Book World—Washington Post*, December 20, 1992, p. 6.

[*Sigal is an American-born novelist and critic. In the following review, he offers a mixed assessment of* Sylvia.]

If you accept that all over America couples are tearing one another to pieces, Leonard Michaels's short novel-memoir is a particularly glum and gory dispatch from the sex war front. But it does have an impressive force in the way that true madness carries its own conviction. Anyone who has ever had an even remotely similar experience will shudder on closing his blood-drenched book and reach for a very stiff drink.

Another way of reading Michaels's terrifying little memento of his mainly '60s marriage is: Don't stay too long in graduate school.

In the late '50s, Michaels was a professional grad student profitlessly rocketing around Ann Arbor and Columbia University. He took five years of English literature classes without getting his Ph.D. One can only imagine the profound, if not always visible, depression that must have enveloped this bookish, unformed, would-be writer. In his state, he was sucker meat for the woman who awaits us all if the gods are feeling particularly dyspeptic.

Remember the times. "Around then, Elvis Presley and Allen Ginsberg were kings of feeling, and the word *love* was like a proclamation with the force of *kill,*" recalls Michaels, perhaps revealing more about himself than the decade. Sylvia was an Olympic-class self-hater who had plenty of energy and idle time left over to hate Michaels, too, just for existing. Their frenzied love-making, as far as one can see, was based on mutual loathing as well as a "drama of betrayal" because she was cheating on her lover. She got her hooks into Michaels because her madness recognized in his passivity and dumb egomania the perfect patsy. She hated his work, despised her own feeble attempts at academic study, literally walked on nails (in her disrepaired shoe) until she bled, skewered his apprentice short stories ("I still believe our child will be very intelligent"), and blamed him for her failures.

"Fighting every day, we'd become ferociously intimate." Sylvia, caught up in the sound of her own screaming, threw Michaels's typewriter at him, clawed his face, slept in her clothes and—of course—tried suicide. "She had sliced her wrists very superficially. Having done it before, she was good at it." Too good. One angry day she swallowed 47 Seconals and never made it back. After what they had done to each other, I am surprised Michaels had any grief left, but his book ends almost on a regretful note.

Now, then, let's leave aside why Michaels did not leave Sylvia as any sensible man would: We don't, and that's a fact. So, depending on the gender and marital experience of the reader, we are free to fill in the many spaces the author leaves tantalizingly blank—including questions that go to the heart of any sado-masochistic marriage. The first question is really a surmise. Sylvia was a woman caught between pre-feminism and the first explosion of women's liberation, not that you would get any hint of social analysis from Michaels's account. What pressures, what free options versus terror of new possibilities, might afflict somebody like Sylvia already predisposed to the joys of "low self esteem"? The second query is this: Although I accept that Sylvia was, at her worst, clinically mad, and would have been viciously loony almost with anybody, what special provocations did Leonard Michaels bring to their hellish love?

There is an airless, claustrophobic, solipsistic quality to Michaels's book that probably reflects his dark relationship with Sylvia. I believe his account. It rings with awful truth. But the she-monster has been dead a long time, and the '60s was another country, so why not love her enough from a distance to make her human again by doing in this book what Sylvia and he could not do in life, understand each other?

There are a lot of Sylvias and Leonards out there today. Feminism has brought in its wake vengeance as well as awareness. Guilt tends to paralyze men under Sylvia's hammer. Cobras, they wilt under the stare of women determined to correct some awful cosmic imbalance even at the cost of their own healthy minds and prospects. Just as

Sylvia was, in her way, prehistoric, so is Leonard Michaels's scary book.

Leonard Michaels with Bonnie Lyons and Bill Oliver (interview date 1993)

SOURCE: An interview in *New England Review,* Vol. 15, No. 3, Fall, 1993, pp. 129-40.

[*In the following excerpted interview, Michaels discusses his working habits, literary influences, and the themes in* Shuffle *and some of his short stories.*]

[Lyons and Oliver]: *Why is most of your fiction written in the first person?*

[Michaels]: I suppose I'd rather write or sing a song than tell a story in the conventional way. The lyric impulse finds natural expression in the first person. . . .

When an idea for a story comes to you, does a kind of music or a particular rhythm accompany it?

I'll be driving along with my daughter in the car and she'll say, "What? What did you say?" And I'll realize that I'm mumbling to myself, trying to work out the first sentence of a story, looking for the beat, the sound, not the words exactly. Something like a meaning is at stake, but it comes to me as a picture or a mood. Not easily nameable. I might be working on a paragraph in a story and can't get it right, and I'm on the verge of throwing it all away. Then I notice a word that I can delete and improve a sentence. If one sentence improves, the next one does, too, and then the beat is suddenly clear and the whole paragraph might come to life. The point is, I deleted a word for reasons of sound. I wasn't using my brain particularly, but then a whole paragraph seemed to make a necessary sense. I wasn't concerned with sense, only sound, the rhythm of one sentence against another. Sound is just sound, completely meaningless, and yet it delivers sense, makes it exist.

When you're working on a story, do you read it aloud to yourself?

I hear it in my head. I used to read aloud to friends, but reading aloud, if you're a good reader, can disguise bad writing. Suppose your reading is terrific. The friends look happy. You're happy. You're happy. Then the story is published. You read it, as if for the first time, in silence. To your horror, you realize the story stinks. You didn't know it before because the desire to believe you wrote something good overwhelms evidence to the contrary. Like falling in love with the wrong person.

Shuffle *identifies itself as autobiography, but one of its effects, certainly, is to blur the distinction between fiction and non-fiction, and more specifically, to obscure the differences between journal entry, essay, and short story. Some of the journal entries in the first section, for instance, read like short stories, though you call them non-fiction. What, for you, distinguishes them from your short fiction?*

Some of the entries *are* short stories and could stand alone. I call the book autobiographical fiction. Other journal entries are fragmentary, suggestive rather than complete—

like entries you find in a writer's notebook. The journal section of *Shuffle* is supposed to seem continuous with my life, which is also incomplete. The fragments thus suggest a large ongoing thing, a life from which they are drawn. They also suggest time passing and a subliminal plot. But plot, like a sentence, can't be understood until it ends. The journal section is largely metaphoric and much depends on the sound, which can be a big part of metaphor. The lyric impulse dominates the first section of *Shuffle*. Almost anything in that first section can be read aloud effectively. That's not true of the autobiographical essays in section two. Nor is it true of the long third section called **"Sylvia."** When I read those other sections aloud people seem to be interested, they have an impact, but they also carry the sound of my personal voice in a way the journal entries don't. Something stronger than the mere sound of my voice obtains in the journal, and it's a kind of music. I think, for the most part, when you begin to hear, in a piece of prose, only the writer's personal voice, his voice droning on, then the lyric impulse is gone and what remains is boring.

In one of the fragments from the journal section, you describe a woman recounting a dream she had. You say, "Her voice remains neutral, as if it mustn't interfere with what she sees. The secret of writing." Is that the sort of thing you're talking about?

Exactly.

How does the writer's voice remain neutral?

The writer vanishes personally. Only a voice remains. If the writer remains, the work might become oppressive, tediously sincere. It makes an irrelevant appeal to one's noble instincts, to human solidarity with some man or woman. You can always tell when this happens at a public reading. You listen to somebody read and as soon as you hear the author's peculiar, daily, non-imaginative voice beginning to interfere, you start to lose interest. You think, oh, here's so-and-so trying to make me understand something or feel something or feel something. Here's so-and-so insisting, being rhetorical, not musical, and deaf to himself. That's when fiction turns into a kind of lying, or a tedious, expository form.

Isn't escaping the author's voice the same as escaping his personality, and isn't that opposed to the very idea of autobiography?

I'm playing with the idea of autobiography in *Shuffle*, nodding in the direction of hard fact. I'm acknowledging what I never have before, that I'm using data from my life. I'm showing a certain respect for actual experience, giving it moral weight. Still, the narrator in *Shuffle* isn't me, not really. It's not the me who would exist, say, in a report to the police, if I witnessed a crime, or participated in one, and told all. It's not that me; it's not scientific or confessional. Nevertheless, it comes very close, at certain moments, to being who I really am, because this time material demands it. Anyhow, I'm not the kind of writer who tells all, and I almost never use the real matter of my life. Sometimes my work sounds terribly personal, but it's still not me talking. Never has been. I've considered those moments when I veer close to self-revelation as being failures,

a betrayal of my instincts as a writer. I've paid a certain price for remaining true to what I think writing has to be.

What price is that?

I never got rich. Also, I'm not in anybody's gang, and I probably have more enemies than most writers.

Why is that?

Judging from some reviews of my work, some folks are made very angry by the things I write. I can't somehow project a benevolent authorial persona or tell readers what they need or like to hear. I wish I could because more than anything, Americans like to like. It's a deplorable and boring sensation, but very commercial. We live so much in Disneyland I don't understand why anyone would pay to go there.

You tell the story, in **Shuffle,** *of your grandfather going to get emigration papers one day too late, on the very day of a pogrom. Do you regard this as the central story of your family history? In its terrible ironies and its timing, doesn't it have some of the same qualities as your fiction?*

That event had a tragic effect on my mother's life. It determined her view of the world, her idea of her fellow human beings. Also her relation to me. For a while, I was all she had left of her own blood. I never knew my grandfather, but his fate had a bearing on mine. I acquired my mother's fears.

What sort of fears?

Fear of the world, fear of becoming part of it, a piece of nature. Dehumanized. It's not an uncommon fear. It's everywhere in literature. Jonah, in the Bible, gets swallowed by a big fish. What do you think that means? A great story; maybe the only story. It happens to everyone.

In **Shuffle,** *you describe an incident from childhood, in which you were forced to defend yourself in a fight. At that moment, you say, you became "a piece of nature" as opposed to "pogrom-obsessed* Yiddishkeit."

There are two worlds. One is very largely in your head and the other is the world outside. The world outside includes trees, birds, concrete, and the reality of people behaving in sometimes awful ways. It also includes sex. Inside your head you do not believe you can be a part of that world. It's dangerous, it's sickening, it's cruel, it's full of pleasure, usually bad pleasure. It's a world of force and action. It's not where you live, which is in this little intellectual cocoon. But all of a sudden I got into this fight on the playground, and I suddenly moved from one world to the other for the first time. That's what that incident is about: I made a fist, I hit back. It changed my life. I ceased to be entirely Jewish. Borges, talking about Israel, seems to believe, sadly, when Jews gave up victimhood, they became less interesting. All right, very sad. It happened to me in a small way. In a neighborhood on the Lower East Side of Manhattan, at the age of nine, terrified, I smashed another kid in the face and became less interesting.

In one part of **Shuffle,** *you describe brutish men eating— just eating. At another point, you describe an anxious mother, whose voice vibrates with awareness. Are these the two* *choices: to be unconscious and animalistic or to be hyper-conscious and riddled with anxiety?*

That sounds correct. I also say Jews are obsessed with meaning, which is a way of escaping the allure of nature. Meaning limits pleasure, but this in itself is another pleasure.

In one of the journal entries, you say that "Every wildness plays with death. I wanted to do dull, ordinary chores all day and be like nice people only to forget death, only to feel how I'm alive." Isn't this the opposite of what Phillip Liebowitz [a recurring character in Michaels's fiction] says at the beginning of one of your best known stories, "Murderers"? Phillip wants to escape the everyday. He's courting darkness, wants to take risks.

Phillip's a kid in that story. He doesn't know from nothing. He wants new experiences. The journal entry is written by someone much older than Phillip. He's had experience and encountered a real fear of death. He sees that experiments with life are flirtations with death. He thinks it would be nice to sink into dailiness, a round of dull chores, because that allows him to feel, safely, how he lives, how it is that he is basically and merely alive. The new voice says, I want to go to the grocery, clean the house, pay my bills, and sit up late organizing my tax records. I want to do these things because that's life. I want to creep in this petty pace from day to day.

Judging from the essay "My Father" [In Shuffle], your father was a very dutiful, unassuming man, someone people liked and who had a lot of friends. Do you think your own life, in so far as it's mirrored in the persona of Phillip Liebowitz, is in part a rejection of patriarchal duty and self-effacement?

Partly so. Phillip wants to be wild. He doesn't want to live with the feelings of others or the claims they might have on him. He doesn't want his existence limited in any way.

Phillip does a lot of running, literally and figuratively. Is he only running away from things or is he also running toward something?

In a sense, he runs from what he sees in other people, what they themselves can't see. Such seeing makes him feel nervous and guilty. He doesn't want to know anything about you that you don't know yourself. This moral uneasiness turns up elsewhere in my writing. It can also affect me as a reader. Sometimes, I quit reading a novel or story because the author tells things about his characters that strike me as unfair, as if the characters were being reduced and betrayed, their freedom denied them. I despise certain kinds of gossipy knowingness. Many people hunger for it, can't get through the day without feeding on TV soap operas. The media loves the sex life of politicians and movie stars. There's a rage for the illicit, as if nothing else were real.

Are you talking about journalism or a certain kind of fiction or both?

Both. There's revelation and then there's revelation. Chekhov reveals his characters, certainly, but he's always magnanimous. His revelations enlarge the reader's intelligent sympathies instead of merely titillating. He never clutches your attention with brutal revelation. Never gossips. When a writer does that sort of thing, usually assuming an ironic superiority to his characters, it's murder. People like murder too much.

It's interesting you should use the word "murder." The Rabbi in "Murderers" screams that charge at Phillip and his friends, calls them "murderers" for spying on his wife and him.

Yes, they watch him and his wife having sex. They pry into his life. And that's exactly what I mean. There exists a terrifying lust for that sort of voyeurism. You see it every day.

In "City Boy," Phillips says, "My name was Phillip, my style New York City." Do you see Phillip as an embodiment of New York and especially of Jewish New York?

Yes, Phillip is a fast talker, sees himself as a kind of psychological and psychosexual adventurer. He comes on as if he knows this and that and can glibly summarize people and their lives. And yet at every moment he sees himself as walking the edge of absurdity. He can topple very easily into the condition of the perfect fool, as he does in "City Boy," finding himself literally naked in public. Even in the midst of such humiliation, he tries to save face, to project this New York character, which is savvy and aggressive. This story, in particular, plays with the experience of embarrassment that is New York. I was at a Knicks basketball game once. This was years ago. The Knicks were losing, but the people all around me were screaming with delight. I didn't know why. Then finally I realized they had bet the Knicks would lose by a certain number of points. To them, if the Knicks lost by less than five, say, it was better than winning by one or ten or fifteen. To lose was to win, if you lost the right way. I was embarrassed by my lack of sophistication. Anyway, that's the New York where I grew up. I still think of it as a more interesting, more exquisite time and place. Like a black and white movie rather than vulgar color.

In "Sticks and Stones," Phillip's friend Henry complains that "there were no frontiers left; nothing left for a man to do but explore his own mind and go to the movies." Doesn't Phillip see things similarly, and isn't this aimlessness, this lack of appropriate manly endeavor, part of his problem, the reason behind his compulsive womanizing?

In fact, he doesn't have many women in his life. Count them. Phillip is virtually a monk. But it's possible that he shares his friend's complaint. Henry is a kind of alter ego for him.

As Phillip is for you?

I can't compare myself to my characters. It's hard for people to believe you really aren't the people you invent, except in a limited way. I'm more normal than Phillip, I hope. Three kids, the same job for over twenty years, and never late with a mortgage payment. I think I'm a lot more various than Phillip, too, capable of all sorts of things he would never admit to. He would never tell you, for example, about the nice things he's done in his life. But if you ask me, I could go on and on.

At one point, Phillip describes himself as "the enemy of Freud."

Yeah, the jerk. He's such a jerk for saying that. There couldn't be a more appropriate patient. He wants to believe the answers to his problems are perfectly clear and available, but he's completely victimized by impulses he doesn't begin to comprehend. He doesn't want to see the depths of his own lust, his raging animality.

Were the Phillip stories that appeared in your first collection [Going Places] originally part of a novel?

Originally, I did intend to write a picaresque novel about the adventures of Phillip Liebowitz, but it didn't hold together for me, so I let it break up and be the thing it wanted to be, a story collection.

Paul Zweig has said your typical protagonist "is the traditional schlemiel of Jewish fiction." But Leibowitz, he says, "is a schlemiel with teeth . . . he cancels the genre." Do you see Phillip as falling into the tradition of the schlemiel? And was canceling the genre your intention?

It wasn't my intention, but it sounds to me as if Zweig gets things essentially right. I like the idea of me canceling a genre. . . .

In the last story in Going Places, the character Beckman is left clinging to a pipe, way up in the air, holding on for his life, and the narrator says, "The tremor passed into muscle as rigid as the steel it squeezed." Is that meant to suggest that rigidity or hardness is necessary to survive?

Well, it might. Beckman is frozen in his musculature and can't go forward or back, as if he were suspended without a past or a future.

So the idea that the suffering he's undergone can somehow be a way out, or a redemption of sorts, is wishful thinking on his part? He's wrong?

Yes. Life is infinitely resourceful and can always get worse.

Are life's surprises necessarily bad?

They're ordinarily bad, I would imagine. It's almost un-American to talk like this, isn't it? But I happen to believe the surprises life brings might get worse and worse. Do you remember that ad for Holiday Inn? It promised, "No Surprises." That was deep.

Your work has sometimes been likened to Kafka's. Like him, you mix the realistic and the fantastic. Do you think you've been influenced by him?

I can't imagine any contemporary writer who hasn't been. I have actually been surprised to discover that I've said things in my work that I later discovered, in different form, in Kafka's diaries. I don't know what to make of that, except perhaps these coincidences arise from similarities in the culture we share. But probably Isaac Babel has been more an influence on me than Kafka. Kafka comes out of the same world as my paternal grandparents, that part of Eastern Europe, while Babel comes out of the same world as my mother's parents, who were from Odessa. Babel's world seems more artistically congenial to me.

What is it about Babel's stories that appeals to you?

Again, it has to do with lyric impulse. I don't see too much of that in Kafka. He is less a singer than a religious visionary. In Babel's stories problems aren't resolved by a rational step from A to B but by beautiful flights from A to C. This is accomplished only in song. You don't usually find that in Kafka, though "The Country Doctor" is a magnificent exception. In Babel you find many flights of sound and dazzling imagery, which have the effect of plot resolutions or thrilling closures. In Kafka you find extraordinary motions of mind, vaguely like logic, or psycho-logic, or Talmudic commentary based on the text of life.

Whom do you read among contemporary writers?

I read Latin American writers. Machado de Assis, Luisa Bombal, Borges, Fuentes, Paz, Mutis, Marquez—*Chronicle of a Death Foretold* is an astonishing masterpiece. Among American writers, many are friends. I can't talk about one or two without mentioning ten others. I've devoured the crime novels of Elmore Leonard, who I met only once, briefly. His work is tight, smart, scary, touching, funny. As for new, young writers, Cristina Garcia and Edward P. Jones seem to me outstanding. Mary Ward Brown's story collection, *Tongues of Flame,* is first-rate. All in all, I read too much to say what I read. It's like discussing my breathing habits.

You've often been compared to Philip Roth. Do you see any similarities?

I think we're pretty different. Roth builds a plot, I don't. His structures are brilliant, powerfully rational, mine are not. I suppose we have some of the same obsessions.

Sex forms a large part of your subject matter, and it's often described in very unappealing terms, as manipulative, violent, ugly.

I've described it in many different ways, but I guess in my early stories I was rigorously unsentimental, very much against romanticizing experience. My subject was lust. The word sex has had a peculiar fate in America. When Lady Macbeth says, "Unsex me here," she uses it well. . . .

Isn't ["I Would Have Saved Them If I Could"] about the limits of art and about the suspicion of anything, including art, that might divert us from a difficult truth or reconcile us to it?

Yes. I try to suggest in that story that there's no way to deal with the experience of the Holocaust and that Jews are obliged to carry around with them a memory of horror to which they can never be reconciled. Things that may appeal to us in our distress, all that offers redemption from that experience, that horror, is specious, including traditional theological justifications for human suffering. The story is against any means of escaping the memory of horrors, even through art. Of course, there's a contradiction in this, since my story is itself, I hope, artful. It was written and rewritten. If you're going to write the language, you have to write it as well as you can.

So, in writing about the Holocaust, you feel the obligation to be artful even as you point out the limitations of art?

Yes, a dual obligation. There is, on the one hand, the obligation to speak the truth, which in this case amounts to a statement against making statements. There is, on the other hand, the obligation as a writer to make the statement the best way you can. I think of Primo Levi. One of the problems for me in reading him is that he handles, with superb elegance, experiences that are grotesquely inelegant; monstrous. There's an astonishing inconsistency in the writing, since the writing entertains. I have a relative who survived the concentration camps. He tells stories about his experiences, but if he tries to write them, he begins to have heart trouble. He survived the camps but wouldn't survive his typewriter. The subject of the Holocaust poisons the intention to make it into art. But Levi is a genius. One reads him with trust that he understands much more than oneself.

Are you willing to talk about what you're working on now? Is Phillip Liebowitz, for example, still a source of inspiration? Do you return to him sometimes?

He doesn't exist anymore. There's a new voice. It's Herman. I've been writing a series of stories and also the beginning of a novel about Herman who's a waiter. The working title for the novel is *Herman, the Waiter.* He has idealized relationships with women. He goes through a series of enormously intense love affairs. As I say, I've already written a few stories about him. They're all about love, love, love, love, love.

So this marks a new direction for you?

Herman allows another view, makes possible a kind of talk that wasn't there for me before. His interests are different. They're more psychological, even spiritual. Less sexual as such. Maybe I've got apprehensions of life and death I didn't have earlier. My attitudes have changed. I'm still in the process of working it out. I'm not a very deliberate writer, I don't think things out in advance. I don't ever really know what I'm talking about until I've written it. I'll see an image, I'll hear a sound, and I'm usually surprised to see what it is I'm saying.

FURTHER READING

Criticism

Edwards, Thomas R. Review of *I Would Have Saved Them If I Could*, by Leonard Michaels. *The New York Times Book Review* (3 August 1975): 1, 2.

>   Favorably reviews Michaels's second short story collection.

Halio, Jay L. "Violence and After." *The Southern Review* 15, No. 3 (July 1979): 702-10.

>   Remarks favorably on *I Would Have Saved Them If I Could.*

Howard, Maureen. "Seize the Day." *Partisan Review* XXVII, No. 1 (1970): 129-37.

>   Comments favorably on *Going Places.*

Larsen, Anne. Review of *I Would Have Saved Them If I Could*, by Leonard Michaels. *The Village Voice* XX, No. 42 (20 October 1975): 56.

>   Finds that although Michaels's stories are sometimes overwrought, they all delve "deep into the problems of the modern condition: alienation, indifference, isolation, failed emotions, silent terror."

Matthews, Peter. Review of *Shuffle*, by Leonard Michaels. *Observer*, No. 10,429 (1 September 1991): 54.

>   Considers *Shuffle* "a strange, neurotic book" steeped in ambiguities and anxieties.

Taylor, Stephan. Review of *Going Places*, by Leonard Michaels. *The Village Voice* XV, No. 8 (19 February 1970): 6, 28.

>   Notes the richness of Michaels's prose and the predominance of the urban setting. Taylor also gives a detailed plot summary for most of the stories.

Review of *I Would Have Saved Them If I Could*, by Leonard Michaels. *The Virginia Quarterly Review* 52, No. 1 (Winter 1976): 10.

>   Negative assessment of the collection under review.

Additional coverage of Michaels's life and career is contained in the following sources published by Gale Research: *Contemporary Authors*, Vols. 61-64, rev. ed.; *Contemporary Authors New Revision Series*, Vol. 21; *Contemporary Literary Criticism*, Vols. 6, 25; *Dictionary of Literary Biography*, Vol. 130; and *Major 20th-Century Writers*.

Jayne Anne Phillips

1952-

American short story writer, novelist, and poet.

INTRODUCTION

Phillips has earned critical acclaim for her concise, poetic style, colloquial language, and macabre themes in such collections as *Sweethearts* (1976), *Black Tickets* (1979), and *Fast Lanes* (1984). In her short fiction, which is mostly set in rural West Virginia during the 1970s, Phillips portrays the disillusionment and aimlessness which followed the socially conscious counterculture movement of the 1960s. Her sensitive rendering of period and place has incited several critics to classify her as a "regional writer," although she disputes this description.

Biographical Information

Phillips was born and raised in the small middle-class town of Buckhannon, West Virginia. As a child she began reading voraciously, discovering it to be an escape from small-town life. She began to write poetry at age 15 upon the encouragement of a teacher who recognized her talent. After high school she attended West Virginia University and earned a B.A. in 1974. While at the university she was introduced to the verse of Theodore Roethke and Elizabeth Bishop, and began to publish her poetry in various literary magazines. In 1976 she entered the prestigious creative writing program at the University of Iowa and that year published her first collection of short stories, *Sweethearts*, under a small independent press. In 1978, the year she completed her Master of Fine Arts degree at Iowa, Vehicle Editions published her second collection of short stories and prose poems, entitled *Counting*. After graduating she taught briefly at Humboldt State University in California and also produced another collection of stories, *Black Tickets*. In 1984 Phillips published her only novel, *Machine Dreams,* as well as another collection of stories, *Fast Lanes*. Phillips lives in Brookline, Massachusetts, where she continues to write and occasionally to teach.

Major Works of Short Fiction

In her short fiction, Phillips focuses on a panoply of lost and depraved characters: the insane and unloved, drug addicts, murderers, and the sexually obsessed. Her stories commonly explore the dynamics of family relationships, which she sees as critical due to the transient and dispersed nature of contemporary American family life. Her first collection, *Sweethearts*, consists of 24 brief prose pieces. One story in particular, "Slave," concerns a young woman's sexuality and control over her lover. Phillips's first collection to be published by a major commercial press, *Black Tickets,* presents two contrasting views of

American life—that of family relationships and that of a diverse array of outcasts. In "Snow" a blind couple in California cope with raising two children. In "1934" a mother and daughter try to deal with the insanity of a husband and father who is ultimately institutionalized. "How Mickey Made It," a rambling monologue by a young punk rocker to his older lover about his sad life, exhibits Phillips's creative use of language. In the title story of her most recent collection, *Fast Lanes*, a young woman returning home to visit her mother shares a ride with a former lover who is a carpenter, musician, and former Peace Corps worker. Their dialogue about fast lanes on a highway is a metaphor for the perils of drug abuse, rootlessness, and immediate gratification.

Critical Reception

Phillips's collections of short fiction have all been critically and commercially successful: *Black Tickets* has been translated into twelve languages; *Sweethearts* has undergone three reprintings; actress Jessica Lange purchased the rights to Phillips's novel *Machine Dreams* for a film; and Phillips is the recipient of numerous awards, including the Pushcart Prize for *Sweethearts* and a Bunting Institute Fellowship from Radcliffe College in 1981 for her body of work. While most critics have praised Phillips's brief story format and "poet's feeling for language," others have disagreed, claiming that her stories are richer when she develops her characters and plots more fully in lengthier works. Other commentators have written favorably about Phillips's portrayal of her generation and the "grotesqueries" of her characters' lives.

PRINCIPAL WORKS

SHORT FICTION

Sweethearts 1976
Counting 1978
Black Tickets 1979
How Mickey Made It 1981
Fast Lanes 1984

OTHER MAJOR WORKS

Machine Dreams (novel) 1984

CRITICISM

John Irving (essay date 1979)

SOURCE: "Stories with Voiceprints," in *The New York Times Book Review*, September 30, 1979, pp. 13, 28.

[*An American novelist, short story writer, and essayist, Irving is the author of the best-selling novel* The World According to Garp *(1978). In the following essay, Irving analyzes the poetic language and tone of* Black Tickets.]

Of the almost 30 short fictions collected here [in *Black Tickets*], there are about 10 beauties and 10 that are perfectly satisfying, and then there are 10 ditties—some of them, single paragraphs—that are so small, isolated and mere exercises in "good writing" that they detract from the way the best of this book glows. Jayne Anne Phillips is a wonderful young writer, concerned with every sentence and seemingly always operating out of instincts that are visceral and true-perceived and observed originally, not imitated or fashionably learned. Yet the occasional reminder of what total praise she must have received in any creative-writing class hurts her; this fine book is punctuated with tiny voiceprints, little oddities too precious to the author—or, perhaps, to her memory of their praise—to be thrown away. One called **"Strangers in the Night"** is short enough to quote in its entirety:

> Like everyone else, she thought a lot about eating and sleeping. When she was sleeping she felt like death floating free, a white seed over the water. Eating, she thought about sex and chewed pears as though they were conscious.
>
> When she was making love she felt she was dancing in a churning water, floating, but attached to something else. Once she almost died

and went so far she saw how free the planet floated, how it is only a shadow, and was frightened back to herself. Later, when she explained this to him, he put his arms around her. She thought she had come home and they were in a shadow, dancing.

Someone in a writing class would have liked the brilliant "tone"; someone certainly would have loved the strangeness; and the careful prose would have been picked over, lovingly. As an occasional teacher of creative writing, I no doubt would have joined in the praise. But too many of these miniatures, these showoff pieces, mar the rougher and more wholly rendered stories in this book. Like many writers with natural reflexes for an important scene and schooled in paying loving attention to prose, Jayne Anne Phillips is at her best when she tells the biggest story she can imagine, and **"Black Tickets"** tells at least a dozen big ones. When her characters and their stories matter most to us, and to Miss Phillips, she stops writing every sentence with quite such self-conscious verve; she trusts in her own good gift for words and doesn't permit her language to swamp the clarity of the tale she's telling; she doesn't obscure her characters with virtuoso displays of "voice" and other exercises of the craft.

In the opening story the narrator says of her mother: "Her heart makes a sound that no one hears. The sound says each fetus floats, an island in the womb"; the absolutely focused affection for the characters in this story (called **"Wedding Pictures"**) makes Miss Phillips's extraordinary language not call attention to itself but just exist, naturally, enhancing the lushness of the scene. (Similarly, of a girl on a swing, she writes: "Her breasts balloon; the sky opens inside them.")

She also shows us the good instinct to tell stories in which something that matters takes place. In a classic getting-caught story, called **"Home,"** a young woman's mother overhears her daughter's lovemaking: "Here, in my house. Please, how much can you expect me to take? I don't know what to do about anything." And in a piece called **"Lechery,"** the narrator is a young prostitute who tells us how she picks up little boys: "I get them before they get pimples, I get them the first few times the eyes flutter and get strange . . . I do things they've never seen, I could let them touch but no. I arrange their hands and feet, keep them here forever . . . Sometimes they get tears in their eyes." It is a story full of more than astonishing eroticism; it explores those early, innocent sensations of lust—a titillation that can turn into something awful. It is a marvelous, dark story, where the shock of something sordid sometimes lurks at the end of desire; although we already know that, or should, Miss Phillips catches us by surprise.

She is especially effective with sex and drugs—and with the madness that can blossom from sex and from drugs. The title story is a long eulogy to someone destroyed in a drug-dealing life: "The morning before I never saw you again, I opened my eyes and your shorn hair was all over my naked front. You had cut it to a jagged bowl around dawn, standing over me with scissors and scattering the pieces." And this story, **"The Powder of the Angels and I'm Yours,"** begins: "She remembered swerving, cocaine lane, snowy baby in her veins . . . Daddy a government stoolie with a crazy daughter, screaming since puberty about those voices under beds whose instructions aren't clear."

Occasionally, Miss Phillips seems too conscious of being gross, as if too much of her intent is to shock us into noticing her writing itself. For example, there is a story about a junior high school girl who gets pregnant ("It was my brother. He's went off to the mills.") and who has her baby in a field full of yelping dogs; next morning "the dogs come in with pieces in their mouths." But her stronger stories can contain the grotesqueries of life; in fact, her strongest writing makes the grotesque tragically real and necessary, and never purely eye-catching or sensational.

Even when she fails, Miss Phillips is admirably ambitious; most good writers are overwriters at heart, particularly when they're young. Miss Phillips also cares a lot about her characters. **"1934,"** about an insane father, who is lovable but finally has to be put away, and **"Souvenir,"** about a daughter returning home to care for her terminally-ill mother, are two rich and moving works that recall Flannery O'Connor. My favorite is a story of voices called **"El Paso"**—a combination of Woolfian monologue and the grittiness of unrequited love found in Country and Western music (the story has all the characters and sounds of an encyclopedic album called "Best of Nashville"). "Like I said," says a character named Bimp, "I had another dancer. She was blond, from the East, up North I think. She had the look of someone didn't sweat much, just burned a coal inside. Ran off finally with some slick Mex to Panama. Could tell easy she was one to leave home over and over till her feet wore down to a root that just planted where she ran out of steam."

Only 27 years old, Jayne Anne Phillips is going to give us some fine things to read. Counting two limited editions (Truck Press and Vehicle Editions), this is her third collection of stories. It may irritate her to hear that I hope she is working on a novel, because I know it does irritate many short-story writers to hear it implied (especially from a novelist) that short stories are merely steps a novelist takes while learning to walk. I don't mean to imply that. Recent collections of stories as fine as T. Coraghessan Boyle's *Descent of Man,* William Trevor's *Lovers in Their Time,* Gail Godwin's *Dream Children* and the wonderful works of John Cheever should convince even the convicted novelist that stories are simply a different form of the art, not a smaller step. What I mean is that I hope Miss Phillips is writing a novel because she seems at her deepest and broadest when she sustains a narrative, manipulates a plot, develops characters through more than one phase of their life or their behavior. I believe she would shine in a novel.

Miss Phillips shines brightly enough in this collection to interest me in whatever she might write next, and I don't want to suggest that all of her smaller pieces are "ditties." In one called "Slave" she offers men and women a vision of orgasm that is so sympathetic to the differences in our sexes that we should read the book for it alone. It might make us think less of conquering each other and more of caring for each other.

In one small story called **"Sweethearts,"** Miss Phillips conjures up an old manager at the Sunday matinee. "Mr. Penny stood jingling his keys by the office door while we asked to use the phone. Before he turned the key he bent over and pulled us close with his bony arms. Stained fingers kneading our chests, he wrapped us in old tobacco and called us his little girls. I felt his wrinkled heart wheeze like a dog on a leash. Sweethearts, he whispered." This is a sweetheart of a book.

Peter S. Prescott   (essay date 1979)

SOURCE: "A Debut to Celebrate," in *Newsweek,* Vol. XCIV, No. 17, October 22, 1979, p. 116.

[*An award-winning journalist and critic, Prescott is the author of* Surroundings: Encounters with Contemporary Books, *an examination of American books published in the 1960s and early 1970s. In the following essay, he offers a mixed appraisal of* Black Tickets.]

The surest way to start a rush for the exits is to announce the appearance of a young woman writer whose principal theme is love. Nevertheless, a new talent claims our attention most effectively when it treats old themes with fresh energy. I believe Jayne Anne Phillips is indeed a remarkable new talent and if she writes about love, or the absence of love, she does so in a way that suggests nothing much can be expected from it. For the women and occasional men in these stories and vignettes, love is not romantic: it is something they may have had once and then lost; it is an obligation, a vestigial link between child and parent; it is something they hadn't known before they got involved with sex; it is above all the unfulfilled promise of redemption.

Phillips's characters are invalids: a few are blind, or mad, or addicted to drugs; others are terminally ill or waiting out their empty lives unloved; others still—the young women whom the author most intimately understands— have reached a dead time in their lives and are uncertain how to proceed. When she is writing at her best, which in this book is about half the time, Phillips regards these people with a tenderness unblemished by so much as a trace of sentimentality. This is an attitude not easy to achieve.

Real writers serve their material. They allow it to pass through them and have the opportunity to move beyond the daily limitations of being inside themselves. It's like being led by a whisper.

—Jayne Anne Phillips, in an interview with James N. Baker in Newsweek, *1979.*

Typically, her protagonist is a woman in her middle 20s, temporarily parted from a lover, who returns home for a few days' disheartening encounter with a widowed or divorced parent. The parent, aging and lonely, is perhaps conscious of having become one of life's supernumeraries and is mildly disapproving of the daughter's muddled life. Conversation is strained; so are the lines of affection, the bonds that were once strong but have now become frayed and entangling. In **"Home,"** the mother, upset by the loss of her own femininity, is embarrassed by evidence of her daughter's sexuality. In **"The Heavenly Animal,"** a kind of mirror image of **"Home,"** the daughter confronts her father's deteriorating existence, his continuing affection for her and the loss of a simpler past. In **"Souvenir,"** perhaps the most affecting of these stories about families, the daughter returns to find her mother dying of a malignancy, yet able to provide her daughter with the comfort that should rightly be the mother's.

If Phillips is most consistently successful when dealing with domestic themes, many of the stories in this collection deal with darker matters. Of these, the most striking—indeed, it is the most striking story in the book—is **"Lechery,"** a horrendous, oddly compassionate narrative in which a 14-year-old girl tells how, since she was 12, she has used sex to exert her power over timid and innocent boys. "I do things they've never seen, I could let them touch but no. I arrange their hands and feet, keep them here forever. Sometimes they tell me stories, they keep talking of baseball games and vicious battles with their friends. Lips pouty and soft, eyes a hard glass glitter. They lose the words and mumble like babies; I hold them just so, just tight, I sing the oldest songs." Abandoned by her parents and corrupted by adults, this child remains somehow untouched: "I'm pure, driven snow," she says at the end. Her invulnerability is both touching and alarming.

Of the 27 stories in **"Black Tickets,"** eleven are of conventional length and sixteen are extremely brief: complete stories compressed into a couple of paragraphs or pages. The shorter tales are, I think, on the whole less impressive than the longer; too often they seem no more than showcases for their author's surprising imagination and for her experiments in overwrought prose. No matter. One of Phillips's purposes in this book is to endow the inarticulate with a convincing eloquence and in this she often succeeds, as with a topless dancer who says of her lobsterman father: "He died when I was so young all he is to me is a furred chest and smell of oiled rope. He died of lobster is what Mom said, and she killed hundreds of them." Like many writers, Phillips performs best when her prose is plainest. Most of the time she writes plainly and compellingly; hers is an authentic and original voice and her debut in this collection just cause for celebration.

Laurie Stone (essay date 1979)

SOURCE: "Extreme Cases," in *The Village Voice,* Vol. XXIV, No. 44, October 29, 1979, pp. 40-1.

[Below, Stone provides a stylistic analysis of Black Tickets, *concluding that although the short fiction collection is riddled with elliptical, self-conscious prose, Phillips manifests promising talent as a short story writer.]*

In her third story collection [**Black Tickets**]—the first by a commercial press—27-year-old Jayne Anne Phillips begins her pieces with unmistakable hooks: "Walter Cron-

kite has had it, says Mom." "When I was fifteen back in Charleston, my cousin Phoebe taught me to strip." "I'm fine until he coughs." "She wanted to have orgasms more and more often." These openings suggest some enjoyable deviance or quirkiness to follow. But they also carry a louder, distracting message: "Read me, I'm good."

She is, often. But too commonly, Phillips's self-consciously poetic prose blocks drama and obscures meaning—especially when she writes from the points of view of extreme cases and grotesques: a wealthy, dying homosexual and his attendants, a prostitute who digs little boys, people blown apart by drugs, blindness, insanity. Phillips is ambitious in trying to imagine consciousnesses different from her own, but also a little sentimental about the shock-value and "serious art" dividends of strangeness.

Nearly all of Phillips's down-and-out characters in **Black Tickets** speak or are described in the same highly mannered dialect. Of a woman in **"Country"** the narrator says: "Finally she whored out of Baltimore hotels," which is followed by such half-sentences as, "movie house janitors' nicotined fingers and doughy thighs of the satin-haired dago cops" and "high-cheeked opal face, thick-browed, her smell raw in rooms." In **"El Paso"** a truck-driving cowboy-type named Dude says: "The light rolling now, leaked into dark, ripples the skin of the dark and flies fly in loose knots; low slow buzz in corners yellowed and pulled out by the light that rolls across the surfaces of things in yellow blocks." This elliptical language, meant to suggest levels of meaning, instead makes holes in meaning. Phillips's intoxication with her own words is inadvertently sobering.

The real pleasurable shock of Phillips's writing is the discovery that she also has a completely unfettered voice, used (too seldom) mainly in stories about floating young women who visit their parents periodically and think about men. **"Home,"** **"The Heavenly Animal,"** and **"Souvenir"** don't have the jazzy bravado of Phillips's show-off pieces—**"Black Tickets"** and **"El Paso"**—and they start and flow with more assurance than they end. But they're the most direct and honest of the longer works in the collection, and the language in these stories serves character and plot rather than the other way around.

"I'll get a ride to the university a few hours away and look up an old lover," says the woman in **"Home."** "I'm lucky. They always want to sleep with me for old time's sake." And with similar compression, the narrator of **"The Heavenly Animal"** begins with this refreshingly understated description: "Jancy's father always wanted to fix her car. Every time she came home for a visit, he called her at her mother's house and asked about the car with a second sentence."

Of the 27 stories in **Black Tickets,** 16 are very short, some only a paragraph. One of these, **"Slave,"** a tense and fearless meditation on orgasms, is wonderful and nearly flawless: "She herself had a tiny orgasm of fear when she saw someone she loved after a long separation, who usually no longer loved her. Something turned over once in her."

During **"Slave,"** something turns in the reader, too—the recognition of a considerable talent feeling its way.

Joseph Brown (essay date 1979)

SOURCE: A review of *Black Tickets,* in *America,* Vol. 141, No. 18, December 8, 1979, p. 376.

[*Brown is an American critic, journalist, and author of several children's books. Below, he commends* Black Tickets *for its surrealistic tone that remains in the memory of its readers.*]

The short stories, prose poems and surreal vignettes that comprise **Black Tickets** read like comments on life from one who has stood graveside with Samuel Beckett and nodded mournful agreement as he intoned, "Astride of a grave and a difficult birth. Down in the hole lingeringly, the gravedigger puts on the forceps. We have time to grow old. The air is full of our cries."

The 27 "cries" recorded by Jayne Ann Phillips in this her first publication, especially those of young women and teen-age girls, are reproduced with perfect pitch.

"Wedding Pictures," more a succinct three-paragraph poetic description than a story, introduces us, fugue-like, to the themes of emptiness, estrangement and despair which resonate through each succeeding page. From the incipient misery of children in **"Blind Girls," "Lechery"** and **"Under the Boardwalk,"** to the drug-induced horrors of **"The Powder of the Angels and I'm Yours"** and **"Black Tickets,"** to the perversion and psychoses in **"Sweethearts," "Satisfaction"** and **"1934,"** most of the stories are tickets by which we gain admission to watch Phillips present her characters in the fashion of the killer in the concluding story **"Gemcrack,"** who wants to "crack . . . and expose their light in the dark Saturdays, the night."

Black Tickets presents a creative variety of prose forms ranging from impressionistic essays and terse, cathartic outbursts to intimidatingly articulated nightmares. One of the most effectively innovative works is **"El Paso."** The story is a series of monologues, each one as stark and searing as the Texas desert "glaring as a lidless eye." The five speakers, life's detritus, are presented as they exist—separate, fragmented creatures who speak directly to the reader as if life mattered, but who know on the gut level that "it's already over."

Phillips's most successfully orchestrated and viable work is three stories that are stories in the modern recognizable sense of the word: **"Home," "The Heavenly Animal"** and **"Souvenir."** Each story sensitively enacts the moribund relations between daughters and mothers.

"Home" verifies Thomas Wolfe's dictum, and whenever the daughter does return to visit her mother, an alien being glazed over with the monotonous routine of television and incessant knitting, each visit becomes less endurable and more oxymoronic. In the final scene, the mother washes and rewashes dishes, tormented by the sounds of her daughter's lovemaking during the previous night with one of her many lovers. The sounds (the "cries") have rendered her own life, as well as her daughter's, more unbear-

ably inexplicable. "I heard you, I heard it. Here in my own house. Please, how much can you expect me to take? I don't know what to do about anything. She looks into the water, keeps looking. And we stand here just like this." Standing there, endlessly peripheral to one another.

When the 25-year-old daughter in **"The Heavenly Animal"** returns for separate visits with her divorced parents, they all struggle awkwardly to prove that once they did exist as relevant family members in an irretrievable past. Neither whiskey nor dalmane will blot out the daughter's awareness of their pathetic sham, however, and she drives off fighting not to lose herself in remembrances of things past, when "her father was driving. Her brothers had shining play pistols with leather holsters. Her mother wore clip-on earrings of tiny wreaths. They were all dressed in new clothes, and they moved down the road through the trees."

In **"Souvenir,"** the mother, dying with a malignant brain tumor, whispers to her daughter that "except for when the pain comes, it's all a show that goes on without me." This statement could have been made by every character in **Black Tickets.** These are the people Jayne Ann Phillips wants us to see, creatures who could have been sketched by Hogarth or Brueghel in their most hideous portrayals of life, creatures for whom life is only a show that goes on without them. Except, of course, when there's pain.

Quite possibly, much of this book will be forgotten in the weeks or months after it's been read, but I believe most readers will carry the stubs of **Black Tickets** around in their minds for years to come.

Garrett Epps (essay date 1979)

SOURCE: "Real Short Stories and Static Prose," in *The Washington Post,* December 21, 1979, p. C10.

[*In the following excerpt, Epps challenges early, excessively laudatory reviews of Phillips's writings, contending that although Phillips is talented and ambitious, she lacks genius.*]

[The dust jacket of **Black Tickets**] bears, at precisely albatross height, the message that it is "the unmistakable work of early genius." Genius, of course, is not civilized but terrible; but perhaps even more terrible for a young writer is to be hailed as a genius before she has mastered the basics of her art. **Black Tickets** makes an ambitious attempt to live up to its blurb, and fails. Jayne Anne Phillips, a 26-year-old writer with two chapbooks of stories to her credit, tries to write in a high colloquial style, pushing the spoken language—and the internal monologue—to its limits and beyond. Very occasionally this works, as when a cocaine freak tells her psychiatrist that "Paranoia . . . sounds like an exotic liqueur. You drink it down hot and it makes you shake," or when a man, traveling for the first time into forgotten valleys of Appalachia, exclaims, "This ain't the South . . . This is the goddamn past." But more often it produces clinkers such as "She born and died in Maine, she dying there still I guess" or "His ashed face nearly shone with some power." Not seldom it descends into incomprehensibility, as when the narrator of the title story apostrophizes his beloved:

Who sees you now Jamaica, how many of them
ever did. I got close, inside, in the whirling. Or
maybe you kept me out, crouched in your fetal
hum, but I knew where you were and mapped
a tonal geography no ear could name; found you
with a sonar plugged into the music of dark feed-
back that shoves us.

Much of *Black Tickets* is concerned with the low life of
contemporary America—murderers, strippers, prostitutes, drug pushers and heroin addicts. But Phillips' version of this nightmare world is flat, unconvincing and even
cliched. For example, she portrays a junkie hitting a vein
in a room straight out of *Monkey on My Back* or any other
'50s movie, where a neon sign "throws a splattered word
across the floor. Rooms, it says, blue Rooms."

In fact, the most satisfying of the stories in *Black Tickets*
are fairly conventional views of middle-class life, of young
women struggling to understand their parents and their
own lives. **"Souvenir,"** in which a young academic comes
home to help her mother face death, is the most successful
story in the book. Many of the others—including the title
story—fail because they are not stories at all, but static
prose poems (more than half the book's 27 "stories" are
less than one page long)—verbal indulgences in which
nothing happens, no characters are revealed, and no time
passes.

Jayne Anne Phillips has talent and ambition to be sure,
but these are not the same as genius. Both must be gentled
and trained until they move and stop at the rider's command. *Black Tickets* is not so much a book as a series of
stampedes, with intervals of grazing.

Thomas R. Edwards   (essay date 1980)

SOURCE: "It's Love!" in *The New York Review of Books,*
Vol. XXVII, No. 3, March 6, 1980, pp. 43-5.

[*Below, Edwards examines the tone of the stories in* Black
Tickets, *concluding that Phillips is at her best when portraying ordinary family life.*]

When she cares to invoke it, Jayne Anne Phillips also has
a strong sense of place (Appalachia, in her case), and she
could never be accused of saying too much. More than
half the stories in *Black Tickets* run to a page or less, and
the longer ones have no fat on them. Compared with
[Scott] Spencer and [Alice] Munro, who work coolly, well
within the limits of their means, Phillips writes with no-
ticeable power, even violence, so that her brevity seems
more a matter of conscious self-discipline than of natural
sensibility.

Her usual fictional material, as it happens, calls for self-
discipline. Consider the remarkable **"Under the Board
walk,"** a sketch of only five paragraphs. "Her name is
Joyce Castro," it flatly begins, "and she rides our school
bus. The Castros all look alike. Skinny, freckled, straw-
haired." Her father is a fundamentalist preacher, and
Joyce is never seen without her transistor radio: "Music
is the work of a devil that licks at her legs. She stands,
radio pressed to her face, lips working. Undah the boardwalk, down by the sea ee ee ye eh eh. Ona blanket with

my baybeh's where I'll be." She is shy, stares at the floor,
doesn't talk to the other kids. She is also pregnant, by her
brother ("The Castros all look alike"), who's gone off to
work in the steel mills.

The words of the song "Under the Boardwalk" come hideously true in the story's next to last paragraph, with perhaps a touch of overcalculation that yet doesn't spoil a
brilliantly imagined moment:

> She disappears from school but comes back a
> month later, having had it in a bloody way. She
> rolled up a horse blanket and walked to the field.
> Daddy thundering I won't lay eyes on your sin
> and big brother in Youngstown, holding a thing
> that burns orange fire. She rolls yelping, dogs
> come close and sniff. They circle. The sky cir-
> cles. Points of light up there that sting. Finally
> she sees that they are stars. Washing herself in
> the creek she remembers the scythe against the
> grass, its whispering rip.

Phillips finds a kind of beauty in this horror—the phallic
suggestion in the red-hot steel the brother holds and its association with the stinging "points of light," her animal
yelping that seems almost to create the ominously circling
dogs, the suggestion, in her seeing the stars and remembering the sound of the scythe through the grass, that giving
birth has been, even for her, a brief participation in natural
order.

But the story's final sentences return bleakly to things as
they are in Joyce's world. When she is alone in the house
the next day, "The dogs come in with pieces in their
mouths. She stands in the kitchen shaking while the Drifters do some easy moanin." Their simulated commercial
moaning is indeed easy, and it seems appallingly possible
that her "shaking" may be only her habitual, mindless reaction to the music and not a recognition of what the dogs
have brought her. This is remarkably alert and resourceful
writing.

But Phillips pays a price for her interest in human beings
who are frozen into their worst possible cases. Most of the
stories in *Black Tickets* examine the lives of people who
are desperately poor, morally deadened, in some way denied comfort, beauty, and love. Girls tell each other dirty
stories in a shack, while small boys listen avidly outside;
a crazed black woman beats up drunken derelicts while
policemen laugh, drug drops are made in porn movie lavatories; a rich old homosexual is cared for by a calculating
male nurse who spends all his spare time in peep shows;
a fourteen-year-old mute orphan girl sells dirty pictures
and hustles her body for her drug-addict pimp; a Son of
Sam type describes his quest for murderable girls; the
sighted daughter of blind parents watches her nearly blind
brother die of (apparently) a cerebral hemorrhage; and so
on. None of these alone, is an unworthy subject for art,
and Phillips's interest is compassionate; but in such heavy
concentration, horror begins to seem predictable, and then
positively funny. So represented, the world in effect becomes a machine designed to do the worst things possible—sidewalks are for displaying dog-puke, delivery boys
are for screwing suburban housewives while the prissy
neighbors watch with binoculars through the curtains;

public lavatories are for drunks and juveniles to throw up in.

Happily, a small group of these stories—and the best ones. I think—deals not with the lower depths but with more or less ordinary people in families, who are trying to love each other across a gap. Their common situation is the more or less reluctant return home of a young woman, usually a student or a teacher, who finds herself challenged or threatened by her parent's concern about what she's doing with her life. The parent, usually the mother, is invariably divorced or widowed, not at all ill-willed or obtuse, not very demanding but anxious to understand better what has replaced the old closeness they once had. These stories are full of beautiful touches that stand without need of explanation—a mother who leaves the house when she hears her daughter making love with her boyfriend, not out of offended assumptions about decency but because she fears getting interested again in sex, a father who touchingly deflects his worry about his daughter into an obsessive and annoying worry about the condition of her car.

Phillips wonderfully catches the tones and gestures in which familial love unexpectedly persists even after altered circumstances have made it impossible to express directly, the ways in which grown children, while cherishing even an unrewarding freedom, can be caught, and hurt, and consoled by their vestigial yearning for dependency, safety, a human closeness that usually seems forever lost. I don't of course mean that Phillips should devote her very promising talent to writing more stories about such parents and children, but I do think that her remarkable powers work best in the realm of the ordinary and the domestic.

Joseph Epstein   (essay date 1980)

SOURCE: "Too Much Even of Kreplach," in *The Hudson Review,* Vol. XXXIII, No. 1, Spring, 1980, pp. 97-110.

[*Epstein is an American critic, essayist, and author of nonfiction works concerning various aspects of contemporary American culture. In the following excerpt, he praises Phillips's convincing depictions of the diverse characters in her stories and her unique prose style.*]

Jayne Anne Phillips' stories are firmly imagined, written in a prose style that is quite unlike any other, and for the most part altogether successful in keeping one interested. Although in some of her stories she works for lyrical effects—imagining, as in her story **"Snow,"** the content of the dreams of the blind—she is also very much the slice-of-life writer, interested in the underlife of strippers, prostitutes, heroin addicts, itinerant cowboys, and other down-and-outers. Miss Phillips' slices of life are real slices, stale many of them, hardened, ragged, bugs crawling round in them. If she takes up a subject, no matter how distant it may be from any experience she can have had—**"The Patron,"** for example, is about a male nurse tending a rich and almost completely paralyzed old homosexual—she handles it without, to my ear, any false notes. In **"El Paso,"** the owner of a bar with strippers says of one of them, "She had that hard crumbled look of a dame that's

been around but don't know why." In **"Solo Dance,"** a vignette of a page, a daughter visits her father, who, two years divorced from her mother and now alone in the world, gets cancer. It is almost too much like life.

If any criticism is to be made of the stories in **Black Tickets,** I should say that those that deal with the subject of drugs—as does the title story—are the least successful. My sense of it is that using drugs is perhaps the one literature-proof subject in the world—that is, I do not think that interesting literature can be made of it. One might say upon reading descriptions of drug use, that's nicely done, but I suspect that if one hasn't shot heroin or swallowed acid oneself one cannot really come along for the trip via literature.

The stories I cared most about in **Black Tickets** may, by today's literary critical accounting, be thought the least ambitious. These are the stories about family life. In them a grown daughter comes home to a widowed mother (**"Home"**), or learns that her mother has cancer (**"Souvenir"**), or goes to lunch on senior citizens day at the neighborhood Catholic church with her divorced father (**"Heavenly Animal"**). But here is a description of that father:

> He was sixty-seven. **Tiny** blood vessels in his cheeks had burst. **There** was that redness in his skin, and the blue of shadows, gauntness of the weight loss a year ago. His skin got softer, and his eyelids translucent as crepe. His eyelashes were very short and reddish. The flesh dropped under his heavy brows. As a young man, he'd been almost sloe-eyed. Bedroom eyes, her mother called them. Now his eyes receded in the mysterious colors of his face.

In a letter to the Brigantine Literary Club, printed at the end of *In Plain Russian,* Vladimir Voinovich prints his response to a high school literary club that wrote to condemn him when its members learned that he was dismissed from the Soviet Writers' Union. In his letter he remarked upon "the true reader," who is someone, according to Voinovich, who divides the books he reads "into the good and the bad, the true and the false. A reader who devours good books either cries or laughs with them and accumulates intelligence, goodness, and compassion for others." If Vladimir Voinovich lived in this country, I would have no hesitation in sending him my copy of **Black Tickets.** I believe he would think very well of it.

Keith Cushman   (essay date 1981)

SOURCE: A Review of *Black Tickets,* in *Studies in Short Fiction,* Vol. 18, No. 1, Winter, 1981, pp. 92-4.

[*Below, Cushman gives a positive assessment of* Black Tickets.]

Jayne Anne Phillips brings a new voice and talent to familiar literary terrain. **Black Tickets** will buy you admission to Flannery O'Connor and Eudora Welty country, where the people, mostly poor whites, are invalids and grotesques and where all are desperately lonely. Love is at best something that happened a long time ago.

Phillips tries her range with all sorts of characters, many of whom tell their own stories. She takes a virtuoso delight in trying to get under the skin of strippers, bar owners, delinquent teen-aged girls, even homicidal maniacs. She is most convincing though in the several stories which depict the homecoming of a woman in her middle twenties, at the end of an affair and uncertain where to turn. Home is the place where, when you have to go there, they have to take you in. But these young women discover that the parents are now just as adrift and emotionally needy as they are. Only memories of happier times remain, and the memories are not to be trusted.

Jayne Anne Phillips was a poet before she became a short story writer. The poet's feeling for language and habit of condensation are qualities that set this collection apart. Phillips captures her disturbed characters in prose that is disturbing. The writing is bright and bold and sometimes eliptical, stylized but authentic:

> We went to the movies every Friday and Sunday. On Friday nights the Colonial filled with an oily fragrance of teen-agers while we hid in the back row of the balcony. An aura of light from the projection booth curved across our shoulders, round under cotton sweaters. Sacred grunts rose in black corners. The screen was far away and spilling color—big men sweating on their horses and women with powdered breasts floating under satin. Near the end the film smelled hot and twisted as boys shuddered and girls sank down in their seats. We ran to the lobby before the lights came up to stand by the big ash can and watch them walk slowly downstairs. Mouths swollen and ripe, they drifted down like a sigh of steam. The boys held their arms tense and shuffled from one foot to the other while the girls sniffed and combed their hair in the big mirror. Outside the neon lights on Main Street flashed stripes across asphalt in the rain. They tossed their heads and shivered like ponies.

Sixteen of the twenty-seven stories are extremely brief, a paragraph or two in length, and these highly compressed pieces are less successful. The brief stories tend to be splashy and self-indulgent, but they display in concentrated form Phillips' heady delight in the sounds and rhythms of the American language.

Black Tickets reminds me of the work of Ann Beattie, a better-established young woman who also writes about lonely people coping, not very successfully, with their bleak lives. Like Beattie, Phillips knows that the chilliest scenes of winter are to be found inside us. At the same time the two authors relate to their damaged characters quite differently. Phillips treats hers not only with fascination but also with compassion. That compassion is to be preferred to Beattie's icy detachment.

Black Tickets won the 1980 Sue Kaufman Prize for First Fiction presented by the American Academy and Institute of Arts and Letters. These stories are the work of a young writer, still trying to find her legs, but they also add up to a notable debut. Though it seems heretical to say it in the pages of *Studies in Short Fiction,* I'm looking forward to the novel Phillips is inevitably writing now.

Jayne Anne Phillips with Celia Gilbert   (interview date 1984)

SOURCE: An interview with Jayne Anne Phillips, in *Publishers Weekly,* Vol. 225, No. 23, June 8, 1984, pp. 65-6.

[*Gilbert is an American poet, editor, and critic. Below, Phillips discusses her life and writing career.*]

Phillips, 31, slender and lovely with brown hair parted simply in the middle and huge, intelligent eyes, is also the author of ***Black Tickets,*** a collection of short stories published in 1979, which won her instant critical acclaim and a large readership when it was translated into 12 languages.

Many of those stories were set in fictional Bellington, a small town in West Virginia like the one Phillips herself grew up in. Readers of ***Black Tickets*** will find in [her novel] *Machine Dreams* themes and incidents they remember from the short stories. Phillips has always been obsessed by the rootlessness of her generation and the accommodations families have to make to changing times.

"I didn't start out to write a novel," she says. "I had been meditating, brooding over some of the characters in the family stories of ***Black Tickets,*** but I planned nothing until I got deeply into the book. I wanted to write a book that worked associatively, rather than a book that worked according to a story or that took place in three days. I wanted to give a sense of time going on and beyond for the characters. . . ."

Phillips would never define herself as a political writer, nor are her characters at all interested in politics, but, she says, "I think writing about so-called ordinary people is a political statement because it's talking about everyday life and why it's precious and why it's worth defending against whatever forces. It was only when politics filtered down to ordinary people like the people in the book [*Machine Dreams*] that anything changed. If you feel yourself or your family to be immediately imperiled, well—people will do anything to keep from losing their children. It really comes down to survival, and then people realize they have to survive, against their own governments in some cases."

Phillips values affection and family ties. She grew up in a small town (pop. 8000) in West Virginia, the middle child and only girl born to a father who was in the road construction business and a mother who was a schoolteacher.

"West Virginia is a strange state," says Phillips. "It's never belonged to the South or the North. The rural population is larger than the urban one. Family and tradition are what's important there. It's hemmed in by hills and valleys. People don't *leave* West Virginia."

Yet, as a child, Phillips dreamed of traveling. "I was never the kind of kid who said, I want to be a mommy when I grow up. I was a voracious reader; I'd sit indoors all day in the summer reading a book. Not particularly good ones, but somehow very early I got the idea that language was some kind of private, secretive means of travel, a way of living beyond your own life."

Her mother encouraged independence in her children. "She wanted all her kids to be somebody," says Phillips. "She wanted us to be proud, in the sense that we wouldn't be ground down by anybody, and she communicated that to me especially because I was the girl and I'd have to protect myself, not my physical self as much as my spiritual self."

Her drive for independence and adventure is reflected in the material Phillips used in her short stories. She had jobs in amusement parks, motels, taught reading in a rural school and helped put herself through the University of West Virginia by working for a home improvements company.

It was at the University that she first began publishing her work, then poetry, in very small magazines. She liked that, she says, because it gave her a sense of privacy which she needed. "It was like a guarantee that my identity as a writer and my identity as a person were entirely separate. Part of that need came from growing up in a small town where everyone knew everyone else. But part, too, came from my feeling that the writer in the family structure is the one who has been entrusted with the psyche of the family. Obsessed, that person will explore it, perhaps trying to save the family by making a new environment. The writer is caught by being charged with this responsibility and, at the same time, running great risk for herself and the others. Of course, in reality you are always writing about yourself, but when you start out, if you're writing about family members or characters based on them, it's good to have this guarantee of secrecy."

I never have considered the reader. Nor have I ever written with any kind of plan, because the whole point is to follow the story to its center, not to impose some point of view. I believe that you are led to discover what things mean and how things relate to each other through the process of doing the work.

—Jayne Anne Phillips.

Out of the school in 1974, she traveled across the country, lived in the black section of Oakland for a while, and then went on to Colorado, supporting herself by waitressing. Writing about drifters, stripteasers and addicts, people on the road and at loose ends, she reflected part of her generation's experience, the generation that was of college age in the '70s.

"Unlike the people of the '60s, we didn't have a strong sense of goals, nor the illusion we could make a difference. They were very organized and considered themselves a community. Their enemy was an obvious one. By the '70s, people began to experience a kind of massive ennui. People felt on their own. Kids dropping acid did it to obliterate themselves, not to have a religious experience. Only people with a strong sense of self came through.

"On the other hand," Phillips continues, "we still thought of ourselves as outside the political system. The undergraduates I see today certainly don't; that's the last thing they want."

Phillips has been teaching since 1982 in the Creative Writing Program at Boston University. "Some of the undergraduates don't know if we fought North or South Vietnam. They don't have a sense of recent history at all. They feel they have no control over their government, and they're trying to make their personal situation as strong and protected as possible. They're concerned about money, and they want structures very much. In the '70s there was still enough security so that people felt they could be floaters. Now things are too shaky for that."

In 1976 Phillips was accepted by the writing program at Iowa on the basis of poems and only two short stories. In the summer of that year, on her 24th birthday ("I'm superstitious, says Phillips), Truck Press, a small press, brought out an edition of 24 one-page prose pieces of hers in a collection called *Sweethearts.* The book has subsequently gone into three printings. Phillips, who had started out as a poet, was changing.

"I became more challenged by the difficulty of writing fiction; I was really attracted by the *subversive* look of the paragraph," she says. "In a poem you're always having to confront the identity of the writer. In fiction the reader becomes less defended against that identity and more open to the text."

Iowa was a new experience for Phillips. She had never had a writing course before. It was the first time she'd ever lived in a community of writers, and she enjoyed both that and her respite from waitressing jobs. Reflecting on creative writing programs in general, Phillips has very definite ideas. Writers shouldn't become involved in them until, in a personal sense at least, they have established their identities as writers and until they have lived on their own for a while.

She's very enthusiastic about the support of small presses. After *Sweethearts* appeared, she worked with Annabelle Levitt, who publishes Vehicles Editions, on a book called *Counting*; this year in September, Levitt will do a short story collection of hers, called *Fast Lanes.* "It's nice now that I can support the small presses because I think it's important for those who've been helped early on to continue to publish with them," she says.

In 1978 Phillips attended the St. Lawrence writer's conference. There, meeting Seymour Lawrence, then an editor at Delacorte, she asked him if he was interested in publishing short stories. The answer was a firm no. Nothing daunted, she gave him a copy of *Sweethearts.* He asked to see her manuscript and, later that summer, at home, just as she was about to get into her car and set out to California to a job at Humboldt State University, the phone rang. Her mother rushed out of the house; Lawrence was on the phone and he was taking *Black Tickets.*

"Working with Sam has been a great experience," says Phillips with a smile. "He's not an editor who edits your copy; he leaves you entirely alone on that, but once he decides to take on an author, he's really committed to that person's work. Since it's very hard to find long-range relationships in the publishing world today, it's great to know that you have someone to stand by you.

"It was also his brainstorm," she adds, "to do a simultaneous quality trade paperback of *Black Tickets* in addition to the 2500 hardcovers they were bringing out. They did 10 or 15 thousand; for a first collection, that's an ideal way to publish."

Today, Lawrence is reaping the benefits of his loyalty to his author, as foreign rights for *Machine Dreams* have been sold for record amounts in England and Germany, and at home Pocket Books outbid Dell for paperback rights. Both BOMC and its subsidiary, QPBC, have chosen the books as an alternate.

While she is pleased by all this, Phillips doesn't feel it puts pressure on her. She defines herself as a writer who is a seeker, "a seeking consciousness, not even a person," in her phrase. "I write for my own psychic survival," she explains, "and that's why I never have considered the reader. Nor have I ever written with any kind of plan, because the whole point is to follow the story to its center, not to impose some point of view. I believe that you are led to discover what things mean and how things relate to each other through the process of doing the work. The real risk is to be strong enough to understand and accept what you're going to find out so that you are not destroyed by what you find. If there's a sense of surprise in the work, it's coming to grips with that risk that makes the revelation. That's the reason to do it.

"I'm the type of writer for whom writing is more painful than anything else, the kind of writer without the personal exuberance or ego orientation of those who are more like public performers. We are like acolytes, or novices, people who have put themselves at the mercy of something they surrender to completely.

"If I've had a good day, I feel that I've stumbled onto some kind of knowledge and I'm sort of wiped clean. I'm a little shell-shocked and awed, not at anything about myself, but at how things have ended up making sense.

"Once the book is done, I don't relate to it very personally because I feel that a work of art is completely separate from the personality that created it. It's on its own. There's much that the writer isn't even aware is there. The writer can take the credit for having seen it through, but not everything that came together in it.

"Of course, I care very deeply about what is in the book, so I hope that it's understood and valued, but I don't necessarily expect that it's going to be understood.

"I work very slowly," says Phillips. "I don't write every day. Sometimes I go for months without writing. I work like a poet, really, one line at at time. . . . But the writers who've influenced me, not for their style but their subject matter, were Welty, Porter, Faulkner and Edgar Lee Masters, writers who wrote about materially disenfranchised people who had rich histories and myths, stories that were almost destinies in themselves."

Michiko Kakutani (essay date 1987)

SOURCE: "Escape and Memory," in *The New York Times,* April 11, 1987, p. 14.

[*Below, Kakutani provides a thematic analysis of* Fast Lanes, *and compares the stories in the collection with several of Phillips's other works.*]

"Don't drive in the fast lane unless you're passing," says a character in the title story of this collection [*Fast Lanes*].

"Why not?" the narrator asks. "I pass everything anyway, so I might as well stay in the fast lane. I like fast lanes."

Certainly, many of Jayne Anne Phillips's people share this sentiment. They like the sensation of moving—they want to leave the small towns of their youth, jettison the unhappy past, and escape the circumscribed world of their parents. "They stayed in one place and sank with whatever they had," says one character. "But us—look at us. Roads. Sensation, floating, maps into more of the same. It's a blur, a pattern, a view from an airplane."

Another declares, "I'm sixteen and Escaped: school, family, house, and got what I want after *all that time* of bad-boy guilt trips." And a third remembers wanting "to physically escape the fields of feed corn fanning out from the boundaries of the two-lane road, escape the valley and the worn hills."

"In my memory," she goes on, "the town stays moistly humid, green, stifled with the summer fragrance of flowering weeds. I was afraid I would watch my father and Billy speak to each other forever while the dense, mustard-bitter flowers tangled in roadside ditches. Always, my father would wear his summer hat and white, short-sleeved shirt, Billy his earnest, young face."

In most cases, physical escape proves easy enough, but Ms. Phillips's characters remain haunted by memories of their youth. Each is to become "the one" in the family "who would remember everything"; and with the slippage of time, each will come to regard his or her small-town childhood as a kind of touchstone, a still point in a world of random change. They will remember the empty fields that predated the ranch houses with backyards, and they will remember the rooms in their parents' homes that echoed with the voices of aunts and uncles and cousins, before everyone moved away.

Like Bobbie Ann Mason, Mona Simpson, Marsha Norman and the late Breece D'J Pancake, Ms. Phillips is concerned with people who grew up in isolated regions of the country where land and family and small town traditions have only recently given way to the homogenizing effects of mass-market, fast-food culture, where old-fashioned mores still cast vestigal shadows of guilt over the hectic imperatives of the new. Here, within the space of a genera-

An excerpt from *Fast Lanes*:

"Don't drive in the fast lane unless you're passing." Thurman, his voice gravelly with wakefulness.

"Why not? I pass everything anyway, so I might as well stay in the fast lane. I like fast lanes."

"Oh, you do. Well. Someone even faster is going to come roaring up and eat your ass. How will you like that?" He switched off the radio. "God dammit, will you listen to me for a minute?"

I looked at him once, and kept driving.

"Pull the truck off the road," he said.

"Are you going to beat me, Thurman?"

"Pull off, right now."

I pulled off on the berm and shifted into neutral. A cattle truck passed us doing eighty, rocking the cab. There was a bawl and a smell and it was gone. Thurman sat with his back to the passenger door. "Take your hands off the wheel," he said.

"Thurman, what is this?"

"I'll tell you what it is. You're in trouble, and no fast lane is going to help."

"I don't want help. I'll just keep going until I find a way to get off."

"Good for you, sweetheart."

"Screw you."

"Hey, don't worry. You'll get no help from me. Last time I quit fast lanes I made myself a promise—no more Samaritan crap."

"You're all heart."

"You'd better worry about your own heart. You're the one with the racing pulse and the shakes, sleeping on floors and getting picked up by three jokers in a disco."

"OK, Thurman."

"Not OK. I've been there, I know what you're doing. You spend half your time in a full-throttle heat and the other half holding on when you realize how fast you're going. You don't even come up for air. Your insides are blue because you're suffocating. Your guts shake because you scare yourself. You get close enough to see death doesn't give a shit about you."

I turned off the ignition and the truck was silent. Noises of the highway went by, loud vibrations that took on the quality of musical tones. I don't know how long we sat there, maybe only a few minutes.

"Death isn't supposed to give a shit," I said, "is it? Death is a zero. Blue like ice is blue. Perfect. Barnes is perfect. Your father will be perfect, my father. All of us, cold and perfect." Thurman moved close to me across the seat. We were both sweating. He pulled his damp T-shirt away from his body and touched the cloth to my face. I whispered, as if someone were listening to us, "I don't mind the heat. I guess I want the heat."

"I know, I know. And we got heat. We got plenty of heat for you here in the USA."

The cotton of his shirt was soft and worn. "Let's drive," I said. "Who's driving?"

"What the hell. You drive."

"Do you want me to stay in the slow lane?"

"I don't care. Drive on the berm, drive up the median, drive upside down."

I pulled onto the highway with a few jerks but no grinding of gears. Thurman turned the radio back on to a gospel broadcast. There was a choir singing strong and heavy about a land on high in the sunshine; their group vibrato wavered in the dashboard.

"You're something else," came Thurman's voice. "You never did take your fucking hands off the wheel."

"I guess I didn't."

"Jesus. I don't know why I should worry about you. You'll probably come out of this with a new refrigerator and a trip to Mexico."

"Sure I will. A trip to the Gringo Hotel in Juárez, where they eat dog and hand out diseases."

He lit a cigarette and gazed out the window.

Jayne Anne Phillips, in her Fast Lanes, *E. P. Dutton/Seymour Lawrence, 1987.*

tion, rootlessness has become the price of freedom, alienation the cost of self-fulfillment. The old certainties have drifted out of reach for many of these people, and they are no longer able to pay lip service to their dreams.

In an earlier collection, the highly acclaimed **Black Tickets** (1979), Ms. Phillips addressed these themes through two sorts of stories—edgy, almost hallucinatory portraits of disaffected, drugged-out survivors of the 60's and more conventional examinations of family life. The latter gave birth, in turn, to *Machine Dreams* (1984), a seamless, magical novel that chronicled four decades of American life through the story of the Hampsons—a story told from the perspectives of various family members, beginning in the Depression with the romance of the parents, Jean and Mitch, and ending during the Vietnam War with the departure of their children, Billy and Danner.

One of the extraordinary things about *Machine Dreams* was Ms. Phillips's ability to give voice to each of these characters' thoughts and actions and to express them with such sympathy and understanding of language that the reader actually *heard* them talking. This same interest in point of view lies at the heart of **Fast Lanes.** Each of the seven stories in this volume is a first-person narrative or monologue delivered by one of the central characters, among others, a high-strung drifter scared by the prospect of a visit home (**"Fast Lanes"**), an unmarried soon-to-be mother addressing her unborn child (**"Bluegill"**); a woman (actually a version of Danner in *Machine Dreams*) recalling a sequence of events in high school that would initiate her brother and herself into the sad complexities of the grown-up world (**"Blue Moon"**).

Ms. Phillips's ear is almost unerring in nailing down the cadences and idiomatic peculiarities of individuals' talk— it would be interesting to see what sort of play she might create—and as ever, she writes beautifully, capturing elusive moods with startling images and scenes (a glimpse of teen-age girls in a high school pageant moving a tinfoil moon between candles in a gym; a boy covering his sometime lover with a sheet that billows out "like the rectangular flag of some pure and empty country.")

The problem with this collection, however, is that half the stories—especially **"How Mickey Made It," "Bluegill"** and **"Something That Happened"**—feel like little more than virtuosic exercises meant to show off the author's ventriloquial talents. Yes, we agree, Ms. Phillips is good at impersonating a middle-aged woman troubled by ulcers, an anxious pregnant woman, even a cocky, would-be rock star; and yet these pieces remain shiny tributes to her skills—they rarely open out in ways that might move us or shed light on history the way that, say, *Machine Dreams* did.

Perhaps the achievement of that novel has spoiled us. From many young writers, **Fast Lanes** would stand as a glittering, if somewhat slight, testament to their talents; from Ms. Phillips, it seems like a somewhat half-hearted practice run for something larger and much finer—a sort of space-filler between projects, intended to remind us of her presence.

Richard Eder   (essay date 1987)

SOURCE: A review of *Fast Lanes,* in *Los Angeles Times Book Review,* April 19, 1987, pp. 3, 11.

[*Eder is an American educator and critic who has worked as a reporter and foreign correspondent. Summarizing the stories in the collection, Eder commends their poetic language and complex characters.*]

Even though her ear for numb and displaced American voices is as sharp as that of any of her fellow writers, Jayne Anne Phillips does not, like the cooler practitioners, turn her stories entirely over to them.

She has a middle distance. She doesn't rule her characters, as in older styles of short-story writing. But she doesn't leave them by themselves, either.

The reader senses a listener as well as a voice. It is a listener who seeks the voice out, one who is interested in the characters, feelings, fates and souls of a wide variety of lives operating at all manner of temperatures. The listener is silent, maybe only implicit; but, as Strindberg and Beck-

ett have shown, a speech to a silent listener is the opposite of a monologue.

The first of the seven stories in **Fast Lanes** is an example. Mickey talks, compulsively, nakedly. Mickey is a struggling waif, a sporadically working rock musician who lives off the gritty pavement among other waifs; who falls, picks himself up, and goes on.

He talks one night to a woman he is with. He tells of his time in and out of a foster home and a state asylum. He tells of a year or two he spent in England, living with a woman and child and playing music: briefly free, in this unfamiliar world, from the perpetual burden of his street smarts, and able for a little while simply to live.

Mickey, hip and knowledgeable, could be a wilder, underprivileged version of a Jay McInerney or a Bret Easton Ellis narrator, except for one thing: Those voices address no one; they are dead ends. Mickey seeks a way out; instead of hugging his pain, he delivers it to the silent woman he is with, and in this lies all the difference.

To say "I hurt" to someone else is a beginning of self-compassion and, after that, a beginning of compassion. Hipness becomes a form of humanity instead of a substitute for it. We are moved, morally as well as emotionally, when Mickey laments a spaced-out girl he used to live with. When she burst dementedly into his room and tried to kill him, the police put a straightjacket on her.

"Have you ever seen someone you know in one?" Mickey asks. "She looked amputated, lopped off and exploding, her arms gone when I'd felt them holding me all that time before."

In the title story, a young woman whose life has speeded up to the point of going out of control returns from the West to see her mother in West Virginia. She is brittle and burnt out; drugs, sex and a drifting communal life have lost the magic they once had, but they are all she knows.

The story, beautifully devised to fit image to emotion, is about her journey home. It is a gradual, painful slowing-down. She gets a ride from Thurman, a carpenter, musician and former Peace Corpsman, who owns a pickup truck. Sharing the driving, she has to learn for the first time how to use gears and regulate speeds. Life, Thurman begins to teach her, is something more complex than jamming the accelerator to the floor and staying in the fast lane.

There is no patness or condescension in the teaching or the story. It is told in hints, flashes and symptoms, on the level of the narrator's own throbbing chaos. She turns to Thurman, but he is no more than half a step ahead of her. They quarrel, pull apart, and come together as she approaches home, dreading it. Staying in the fast lane may be lethal; shifting off it can be almost as perilous.

"I'll tell you this about fast lanes," Thurman says the night before he drops her off. "Don't close your eyes. Keep watching every minute. Watch in your sleep. If you're careful you can make it: the fast shift, the one right move. Sooner or later you'll see your chance."

The story is the closing of the cycle that began over three

decades ago with Kerouac's *On the Road.* It is the return trip, and Phillips gives it a full measure of pain, laced with tenderness.

The author's sympathy, her ability to imagine herself into the feelings of very different kinds of people, in no way lessens a precision that we are more used to finding at cooler temperatures.

In **"Rayme,"** the story of another drifting waif, who finally drifts off into madness, she writes:

"Rayme was like a telephone to another world. Her messages were syllables from an investigative dream, and her every movement was precise, like those of a driver unerringly steering an automobile by watching the road through the rear view mirror."

In **"Blue Moon,"** a mother forbids her son to go out for football because she had a boyfriend who died of a heart attack playing it. The boy's father, though disagreeing, remains silent. In one phrase, Phillips captures the distance and the unhealed scars in a marriage.

"He allowed her this undisputed commandment as though he refused to validate her long-ago loss by arguing about it."

The stories in *Fast Lanes* frequently hover on the edge of poetry. One or two—**"Blue Moon"** and **"Bess"**—are more heavily plotted than the others and seem to me less successful. Phillips gets all the movement she needs from her characters in the resilient struggling of their hearts against the eroding evidence of their senses.

David Remnick   (essay date 1987)

SOURCE: "Driving on the Shoulder," in *Book World— The Washington Post,* April 26, 1987, p. 9.

[*In the following excerpt, Remnick notes the inconsistent quality of the stories in* Fast Lanes.]

Fast Lanes, a collection of seven stories, is unfortunately a kind of holding pattern. Maybe the reader is hungry for the sort of ambition that Phillips showed in her novel [Machine Dreams]. Maybe it's mere impatience. And yet, with two sterling exceptions, *Fast Lanes* is not on a par with *Machine Dreams* or the best of *Black Tickets.*

The book opens with **"How Mickey Made It,"** a monologue by a would-be rock'n roller who, in sharp bursts of fast-talk, tells a woman of his lousy childhood and his flailing attempts at adult life. "I don't know I just never got along with my family, I mean they're not my family really since I'm adopted but they are my family—and it was always weird man, I mean they told me I was adopted from the start but still, all those years it was like, uh, how come I got such dark skin and how come I don't really FEEL it for you. When I was fourteen they gave me the address of the adoption agency and I found out I'm half Comanche and half Spanish . . ."

When stories such as **"How Mickey Made It"** don't make it, the reader begins to feel trapped, listening to an endless whine. It is obviously a subjective thing; some voices just

have more interest for some than others. But for this reader there are speakers and stories in *Fast Lanes* that have a dull, slumming quality, talking down and dirty and desperate without anything special to offer.

In **"Rayme"** we hear about a woman who sleeps on the floor, sits in the middle of highways, drops chunks of linoleum in her soup and makes sphinx-like remarks. It is a mannered performance. In **"Bluegills"** we hear the interior talk of a pregnant woman to her unborn child: "Hello my little bluegill, little shark face. Fanged one, sucker, hermaphrodite. Rose, bloom in the fog of the body; see how the gulls arch over us, singing their raucous squalls. They bring you sweet meats, tiny mice, spiders with clasped legs . . ." It is an ambitious piece but one marred by a self-conscious literary language that has tints of purple.

> **Ms Phillips's use of language is richly sensuous. She takes street slang all the way to poetry and back, hovering on the edge of surrealism but—except in some of the miniature (130 to 600 words) stories, which suggest an advanced Creative Writing class doing stream-of-consciousness exercises—always sustaining a lucid narrative flow.**
>
> *Carol Rumens, in the* Times Literary Supplement, *November 14, 1980.*

The two triumphs of the collection are the ones that seem least like set pieces. They are (merely?) stories, in which the voices serve developed, deeply felt narratives.

In the title story, Phillips draws a first-person portrait of a young, weary woman who hooks up with an itinerant carpenter for a cross-country trip. Phillips hints at the woman's range of problems—sexual and otherwise—with incident rather than talk. In **"Bess"** Phillips moves once more to the technique of monologue, and here she succeeds. An old woman, intelligent and possessed of a writer's memory of detail, spins a dark, yet casually paced, tale of her childhood and her relationship with her brother. Notice how Bess speaks—not the way a real person might, but rather as a real person seems to talk:

"Finally Warwick let us off by the big porch that was heaped with snow, then drove the sledge to the barn where Pa met him. We sisters went in to the fire, all of us shining with cold, and the fire warmed us, turned us one by one to our winter selves, dim in the dim house, the windows all shuttered against the cold, the lamps throwing off small glows."

"Fast Lanes" and **"Bess"** are such strong stories that they erase any disappointment one might have felt in the other five. They are among the best works of one of our most fascinating and gritty writers, and there can be little disappointment in that.

Jay McInerney (essay date 1987)

SOURCE: "Lost on the Open Road," in *The New York Times Book Review,* May 3, 1987, p. 7.

[*McInerney is an American novelist and author of the bestseller* Bright Lights, Big City *(1984). Below, he offers a positive assessment of* Fast Lanes.]

The fiction of Jayne Anne Phillips oscillates between two subjects: the world of the open road, runaways and drifters, and the deeply rooted regional American family. These two worlds are not necessarily exclusive. The wanderer sometimes returns home after a broken love affair or to nurse a dying parent.

Ms. Phillips's **Black Tickets** (1979) was a collection of stories characterized by the voices of lost children, misfits and damaged waifs. "Men whose childhoods were slow and smooth want my straitjacket stories," one narrator says, and readers of **Black Tickets** found themselves in the position of these smoothly raised men, eavesdropping on hypnotic monologues full of sex and violence and battered innocence—like that of the wise orphan of **"Lechery"** who sells dirty postcards and sexual thrills to adolescent schoolboys, or Rita in **"El Paso"** a topless dancer-cum-painter and the daughter of a witch. But there were also stories, like **"1934,"** about family and place—a meticulously evoked West Virginia landscape. This territory would be more fully developed in the author's 1984 novel *Machine Dreams.*

Fast Lanes, Ms. Phillips's new collection of stories, shows a range of moods and modes, working the highways and youth ghettos of American cities, as well as the rich and familiar soil of West Virginia past and present. The book begins with stories of youthful drift and confusion and gradually moves, with increasing authority, into the past and what we might call home.

"How Mickey Made It" is relentlessly up-to-the-minute, the monologue of a 20-year-old aspiring punk rocker and delinquent who just wants to get his own humongous slice of the American pie. The eponymous heroine of **"Rayme"** is a mentally ill young woman who drifts through the student ghetto of a university town. "A group of us floated among several large ramshackle houses, houses arranged above and below each other on steep streets: a gritty version of terraced dwellings in some exotic Asia." While the actual location is deliberately vague, that metaphor seems subtly suggestive of a particular time, the mini-era during which Vietnam shadowed the experience of American youth.

The time is one in which someone like Rayme, who puts pieces of linoleum in the commune's soup, can almost fit in. Since everyone else is taking mescaline, she is not so conspicuous: "All of us were consulting a series of maps bearing no relation to any physical geography, and Rayme was like a telephone to another world." The story is elegiac in its evocation of those times and of a particular inertial moment in youth: "Our destinations appeared to be interchangeable pauses in some long, lyric transit. This time that was nearly over, these years, seemed as close to family as most of us would ever get."

Pauses do not necessarily make good narratives, however. "This story could be about any of those people," the narrator says, referring to various roommates, "but it is about Rayme and comes to no conclusions." The narrators of the best stories in **Black Tickets** were deftly portrayed and moved through gritty, textured landscapes. But in the title story of **Fast Lanes** and in **"Rayme"** character and action almost disappear in a generalized evocation of the mescaline generation, in a blur of communal houses and highway signs. Rayme's madness finally feels too emblematic.

"Fast Lanes" is a long story about a trip across country—about two *dharma* bums in a makeshift alliance. The narrator has been living in Colorado, scrupulously avoiding any attachment to either the landscape or its inhabitants. When she needs to get back home to West Virginia, she finds herself sharing a pickup with Thurman, an acquaintance she once slept with. "We pulled out of town at dawn," she says. "I had the feeling, the floater's only fix: I was free, it didn't matter if I never saw these streets again; even as we passed them they receded and entered a realm of placeless streets. Even the people were gone, the good ones and the bad ones; I owned whatever real had occurred, I took it all. I was vanished, invisible, another apartment left empty behind me, my possessions given away, thrown away, packed away in taped boxes fit into an available vehicle."

Wishing to gather no moss, the narrator remains something of a blur, a woman running from unspecified hurts, beset by vague furies. Her heart races, she can barely stand the weight of sheets on top of her at night, and ultimately she tries to scare herself into some new accommodation with the world by temporarily going off with three male strangers and a pile of cocaine into the New Orleans night. But this dark night of the soul is only obliquely referred to and seems not to result in much of an epiphany. She is still running at the story's end, when Thurman is about to drop her off at home.

The metaphor that gives the story and the book its title is a cliché by now and inevitably evokes a tune by the Eagles. The narrator likes to drive in the fast lane, literally and figuratively. As Thurman tells her, "I've been there, I know what you're doing. You spend half your time in a full-throttle heat and the other half holding on when you realize how fast you're going." This straightforward thematizing is far from the oblique, dreamy logic of the best stories in **Black Tickets,** and it makes **Fast Lanes** seem like an earlier or transitional one.

On the other hand, **"Bluegill,"** a monologue addressed by a young woman to the fetus growing inside her, has the poetic density and richness of language that characterize Ms. Phillips's best fiction. Her finest stories read like prose poems, and the monologue seems the form with which she is most comfortable. Her best prose is metaphor-laden and sensual, with a minimum of connective tissue.

Machine Dreams, while advancing the history of a family

and to some extent a town and a nation, was largely constructed of first-person monologues. The novel's major narrative events—the disappearance of Billy Hampson in combat, his parent's wedding—tended to happen in the interstices. As in **"Bluegill,"** the language was rich, slow and sensual: we were shown how things look and feel and smell, and the cumulative detail made it almost impossible not to believe in the reality of the Hampson family. Moss gathered, shadows grew, characters became people, and the things they did came to seem inevitable.

In the two final stories in *Fast Lanes,* Ms. Phillips returns to this fertile terrain. **"Blue Moon"** might be an outtake from *Machine Dreams* (although the fictional histories don't perfectly fit). It deals with the high school years of Danner and Billy Hampson and focuses on the romance between Billy and Kato Shinner, an intense and doomed love that Ms. Phillips convinces us is no less important than an adult affair. The story proposes that it is, in fact, more important.

Kato, the daughter of the local pool hall owner, is a wild loner who dramatically slices her arm open after she hears that Billy may be going away to school the following year. As her father later remarks to Danner, Billy's sister, "Everyone's so shocked . . . like kids don't know enough to be that serious. Hell, that's when it happens." Indeed, Danner's mother has never quite got over her romance with her high school boyfriend, a football star who died of a heart attack after a game, thus sealing his hold on her life forever. Billy, too, will be permanently enthralled by Kato, whether he ever sees her again or not. "Everything was different now, larger, enveloped by a shadow." (The Billy of *Machine Dreams* never goes to military school; he goes off to Vietnam where he disappears.)

"Blue Moon" is a beautiful story, one in which the characters grow and change in the rich context of family and community. In **"Blue Moon"** and **"Bess,"** events have a dreamlike inevitability.

Moving deeper into the past of the Hampson family—the events take place early in the century—**"Bess"** synthesizes many of Ms. Phillips's concerns and contains some of her finest writing. Bess grows up on a remote West Virginia farm with 11 brothers and sisters, sleeping in the same room with her brother Warwick, who will remain, long after his death in a coal mine, the great love of her life. When Bess is courted, Warwick tries to interfere; and when she elopes, it is with a man who resembles him. Her husband is a gambler who abandons her in St. Louis; the slow and steady Aunt Bess of *Machine Dreams* is revealed here as one of Ms. Phillips's runaways. Warwick goes out West to retrieve Bess and pretends that the offspring of her brief union, Mitchell, is his own child. (Mitch Hampson in *Machine Dreams* believes his mother, Bess, is his aunt.)

"Bess" is narrated in the first person by an old woman for whom the events of 70 years ago are more vivid than anything in the present, and it is indicative of Ms. Phillips's powers that she is nowhere more convincing than in imagining and evoking this vanished era. By comparison, the stories with contemporary settings are arid and overly self-conscious.

A heterogeneous collection, stronger in parts than as a whole, *Fast Lanes* moves backward in time and gains authority as it does so. The reader seems to be watching a gifted writer develop a sense of voice and subject over the course of these stories. Although Ms. Phillips made her debut as something of a feminized Kerouac, a bard of bad girls and the open road, she appears to be evolving into a regional writer and family chronicler, a cousin of Reynolds Price and Eudora Welty.

Irving Malin (essay date 1987)

SOURCE: A review of *Fast Lanes,* in *Studies in Short Fiction,* Vol. 24, No. 3, Summer, 1987, p. 319.

[*Below, Malin appraises the collection of stories in* Fast Lanes *as an effective evocation of an era.*]

Jayne Anne Phillips uses *Fast Lanes* as the title of her spinning, vibrant book of stories. These words suggest (as do the stories) that life is a dangerous series of movements, unknown exits, and entrances. Her protagonists, for the most part, don't really know where they are going. They live moment by moment, day by day.

Although Phillips characterizes the sixties and seventies as a madness—collective *and* private—she refuses to put the blame on "society." She recognized that even in calm ages violence erupts, irrationality commands our lanes (lives). True, she writes in an objective way; she accepts accidents.

Phillips gives us the "freaks," the "druggies." But her style is wonderfully wrought so that it catches the moments, the needs and wishes of her generation. We have, then, a kind of contrast between the *speed* of her characters—and their times—and the precise underlying desire for slowness and tranquillity.

Here is a part of a typical Phillips paragraph: "I had moments of panic in which I seemed to be falling, spread-eagled, far away from myself, my whole body growing rapidly smaller and smaller. I could feel the spinning, the sensation of dropping. I held tightly to the door handle and concentrated on the moving windshield wiper in front of me, carefully watching its metal rib and rubber blade." The paragraph gives us the *falling*; at the same time it alerts us to *concentration* upon details which, in effect, slow things down a bit.

Phillips is a dangerous, distinctive writer because she widens the aperture of *our* focus.

Ellen Lesser (essay date 1987)

SOURCE: "A Quartet of Storytellers," in *The Women's Review of Books,* Vol. IV, Nos. 10-11, July-August, 1987, p. 24.

[*In the following essay, Lesser declares that despite the inconsistent quality of the seven stories in* Fast Lanes, *the best "are beautiful and moving enough, perhaps, to redeem the less successful."*]

Short stories used to be considered the fiction writer's

warm-up, an exercise period, a prelude to the *real* career—which was, of course, writing novels. No longer. Today, in what critics have grown found of calling the short-story renaissance, it is possible to make and sustain a career exclusively writing short fiction. Even those writers we think of as primarily novelists now seem sooner or later to publish a volume of stories, as if the rigors of the shorter form were not a warm-up but a kind of ultimate test, a series of advanced hurdles. Sure, you can tell a story in 300 pages. But can you do it in fifteen or twenty? Can a writer—with a necessarily limited number of brush strokes—make a sketch that suggests a whole world? Can she shape a piece of experience so that, with her final words, we get that feeling of wonder that tells us we've learned something, and something we've needed to know? Can she, in those few pages, make the story really *deliver*? This summer [1987], four of our best-known writers are represented by new collections of stories, and they meet the demands of the form with mixed, though always interesting, results.

One of the things a short-story writer must do—especially now, when stories proliferate—is to capture and keep our attention. In the opening story of ***Fast Lanes,*** Jayne Anne Phillips (author of a previous collection, ***Black Tickets,*** and a novel, *Machine Dreams)* works too hard at doing just that. Twenty-year-old Mickey of **"How Mickey Made It"** is a street-smart, aspiring punk-rock star. In the guise of an address to his older lover, Mickey speaks to us, or rather, assaults us with speech: "I'm a SINGER I don't go for that commercial shit I'LL DO IT MYSELF THANK YOU, Thaaannk Yooooooo!!! Whoo! Jesus." The voice Phillips creates for him is full of bravado and slang and words in all-caps to force a jangling, would-be punk rhythm. The problem is that the voice jangles too much, and inconsistently. This guy who can slang us to death, who spews forth an empty, hip philosophy ("Holding is a trip, right?") suddenly turns around and goes straight, lyrical, almost elegant: "I did it with dedication, like something was boiling over a fire inside me." After several pages, Mickey's rap does begin to sound like an exercise, an apprentice experiment. That impression gets clinched when we look back on the story's overall trajectory. Phillips throws in a bunch of what Mickey calls "bad stuff "—the violent, finally straitjacketed girlfriend; the foster mother on chemotherapy—but the tale fails to build toward any kind of real revelation.

When Mickey tries to turn his lover on to some English punk imports, he tells her, "this shit is REAL this is REAL music and they don't have to pretend it's sex." He lambasts the fakers, "the sparkly lights on their jeans and how they hold their fuckin streamline chromeline guitars like giant cocks." When she's at her best, Phillips knows she has a "real" story, and doesn't try so hard to impress us with the language that is her instrument. Happily, there are some real stories in ***Fast Lanes.*** A few of them evoke the late sixties and early seventies, a world of drifting characters who can ask, with the narrator of **"Rayme,"**

"Where were we all really going, and when would we ever arrive? Our destinations appeared to be interchangeable pauses in a long, lyrical transit." A more literal "transit" is the subject of the title story, where a woman and man travel in a pickup cross-country—he "floating," she "floating home." As they leave Denver at dawn, she gets "the feeling, the floater's only fix":

> I was free, it didn't matter if I never saw these streets again; even as we passed them they receded and entered a realm of placeless streets. Even the people were gone, the good ones and the bad ones; I owned whatever real had occurred, I took it all. I was vanished, invisible, another apartment left empty behind me, my possessions given away, thrown away, packed away in taped boxes fit into an available vehicle. The vehicle was the light, the early light and later the darkness.

Phillips captures the life and times of these floaters in a way that gives their moment, so recent, a poignantly period quality. Her flair for evoking bygone eras works to superb advantage in the closing tale, **"Bess,"** a haunting story of an obsessive sister-brother relationship in turn-of-the-century, small-town West Virginia. Here, without any experimental flash or linguistic fireworks, she fashions a beautiful, moving evocations of a lost time, a love, and the quality of memory—beautiful and moving enough, perhaps, to redeem the less successful among these seven short stories.

FURTHER READING

Biography

Adams, Michael J. "Jayne Anne Phillips (1952-)." In *Postmodern Fiction, A Bio-Bibliographical Guide*, edited by Larry McCaffery, pp. 481-83. New York: Greenwood Press, 1986.
　　A biographical sketch, a brief summary of *Black Tickets,* and a bibliography that lists Phillips's works and two secondary sources.

Criticism

Edelstein, David. "The Short Story of Jayne Anne Phillips." *Esquire* 104, No. 6 (December 1985): 107-12.
　　Overview of Phillips's writing career.

Peterson, Mary. "Earned Praise." *North American Review* 264, No. 4 (Winter 1979): 77-9.
　　Review of *Black Tickets.*

Rumens, Carol. "Peeling Back the Senses." *Times Literary Supplement* (London), No. 4050 (14 November 1980): 1280.
　　Positive review of *Black Tickets.*

Additional coverage of Phillips's life and career is contained in the following sources published by Gale Research: *Contemporary Authors*, Vol. 101; *Contemporary Authors New Revision Series*, Vol. 24; *Contemporary Literary Criticism*, Vols. 15, 33; *Dictionary of Literary Biography Yearbook: 1980*; and *Major 20th-Century Writers*.

Nathanael West

1903-1940

(Born Nathan Weinstein) American short fiction writer, scriptwriter, playwright, and editor.

INTRODUCTION

West was a prominent American fiction writer whose works portray the despair and alienation that many writers and artists have found the prevalent characteristics of twentieth-century existence. Best known for his short novels *Miss Lonelyhearts* and *The Day of the Locust*, he is regarded as a stylistic innovator whose works fit no standard literary classification. In his fiction West introduced a distorted, grotesque kind of humor that has led critics to call his short novels the forerunners in modern American literature of Surrealism and black humor.

Biographical Information

West was born in New York City to fairly well-to-do Lithuanian-Jewish immigrants. An undistinguished student, he failed to graduate from high school and was later dismissed from Tufts College because of poor attendance. However, the illegally obtained transcript of an older student with a similar name—and better grades—enabled West to transfer to Brown University, where he earned an English degree. After graduation West briefly lived in Paris before dwindling finances compelled him to return to New York, where he worked managing hotels owned by relatives. In 1932 West ventured into publishing, joining poet William Carlos Williams in coediting the journal *Contact*, of which only three issues appeared. In the mid-1930s West was encouraged by his brother-in-law S. J. Perelman, who was a successful Hollywood screenwriter, to move to Hollywood and work in the film industry. His experiences provided the material for his last novella, *The Day of the Locust*. Shortly after this work was published, West met and married Eileen McKenney, who had served as the subject of Ruth McKenney's *New Yorker* sketches that were adapted as the play *My Sister Eileen*. Eight months after their marriage, both were killed in an automobile accident.

Major Works of Short Fiction

West wrote and published four short novels in his lifetime. His first, *The Dream Life of Balso Snell*, has not received the amount of critical attention given to his other works. This short novel is a satiric denunciation of literary and artistic poses and poseurs, each represented by a character encountered by Balso Snell as he journeys through the bowels of the Trojan Horse. The episodic nature of the narrative led many early reviewers to criticize the work as disjointed and essentially formless. West's second short novel, *Miss Lonelyhearts*, is generally considered his most

artistically accomplished work. It is the story of a male newspaper advice columnist obsessed with the suffering of his correspondents and his inability to help them. *A Cool Million; or, The Dismantling of Lemuel Pitkin* is most often interpreted as a parody of the classic American success story—the rags-to-riches motif—popularized in the late-nineteenth-century novels of Horatio Alger. West's last published work, *The Day of the Locust*, has often been called the finest novel about Hollywood to come out of Hollywood, and subsequent books about the film industry are often compared with it. Critics generally agree that this work demonstrates development in West's skills as a fiction writer. *The Day of the Locust* differed from other Hollywood novels of the same era, such as F. Scott Fitzgerald's *The Last Tycoon*; rather than focusing on the rich and famous, West wrote about common people whose dreams are manufactured and manipulated by the movie industry, and who, West believed, harbored a fierce hatred behind their ostensible adoration of movie stars.

Critical Reception

Until the renewal of interest in West in the late 1950s, most critics considered him a minor short fiction writer.

Many still insist on such a classification because of the narrow range of his themes and subjects. However, Randall Reid has asserted that, within the limits allowed by his pessimistic vision, West is a "complex, wide-ranging, and subtle" author. Because his works are both unclassifiable and stylistically innovative, West has been a difficult writer to place within a literary tradition. Similarly, the extent of his influence on later writers is not easily ascertainable. Although not generally found to have been a direct literary influence on subsequent writers, West is noted as one of the progenitors—perhaps the earliest—of black humor and the grotesque in modern American fiction. He has been described by Carter M. Cramer as second only to William Faulkner as "the most experimental American novelist of any importance to write his major works during the bleak decade of the Great Depression."

PRINCIPAL WORKS

SHORT FICTION

The Dream Life of Balso Snell   1931
Miss Lonelyhearts   1933
A Cool Million; or, The Dismantling of Lemuel Pitkin
   1934
The Day of the Locust   1934
The Complete Works of Nathanael West   1957

CRITICISM

W. H. Auden   (essay date 1948)

SOURCE: "Interlude: West's Disease," in his *The Dyer's Hand and Other Essays,* Random House, Inc., 1962, pp. 238-45.

[*Often considered the poetic successor of W. B. Yeats and T. S. Eliot, Auden is also highly regarded for his literary criticism. As a member of a generation of British writers strongly influenced by the ideas of Karl Marx and Sigmund Freud, Auden considered social and psychological commentary important functions of literary criticism. As a committed follower of Christianity, he considered it necessary to view art in the context of moral and theological absolutes. Thus, he regarded art as a "secondary world" which should serve a definite purpose within the "primary world" of human history. This purpose is the creation of aesthetic beauty and moral order, qualities that exist only in imperfect form in the primary world but are intrinsic to the secondary world of art. In the following essay, which was originally published in 1948, Auden describes the spiritual malaise emblematic of West's protagonists.*]

Nathanael West is not, strictly speaking, a novelist; that is to say, he does not attempt an accurate description either of the social scene or of the subjective life of the mind. For his first book, he adopted the dream convention, but neither the incidents nor the language are credible as a transcription of a real dream. For his other three, he adopted the convention of a social narrative; his characters need real food, drink and money, and live in recognizable places like New York or Hollywood, but, taken as feigned history, they are absurd. Newspapers do, certainly, have Miss Lonelyhearts columns; but in real life these are written by sensible, not very sensitive, people who conscientiously give the best advice they can, but do not take the woes of their correspondents home with them from the office, people, in fact, like Betty of whom Mr. West's hero says scornfully:

> Her world was not the world and could never include the readers of his column. Her sureness was based on the power to limit experience arbitrarily. Moreover, his confusion was significant, while her order was not.

On Mr. West's paper, the column is entrusted to a man the walls of whose room

> were bare except for an ivory Christ that hung opposite the foot of the bed. He had removed the figure from the cross to which it had been fastened and had nailed it to the walls with large spikes. . . . As a boy in his father's church, he had discovered that something stirred in him when he shouted the name of Christ, something secret and enormously powerful. He had played with this thing, but had never allowed it to come alive. He knew now what this thing was—hysteria, a snake whose scales were tiny mirrors in which the dead world takes on a semblance of life, and how dead the world is . . . a world of doorknobs.

It is impossible to believe that such a character would ever apply for a Miss Lonelyhearts job (in the hope, apparently, of using it as a stepping-stone to a gossip column), or that, if by freak chance he did, any editor would hire him.

Again, the occupational vice of the editors one meets is an overestimation of the social and moral value of what a newspaper does. Mr. West's editor, Shrike, is a Mephisto who spends all his time exposing to his employees the meaninglessness of journalism:

> Miss Lonelyhearts, my friend, I advise you to give your readers stones. When they ask for bread don't give them crackers as does the Church, and don't, like the State, tell them to eat cake. Explain that man cannot live by bread alone and give them stones. Teach them to pray each morning: 'Give us this day our daily stone.'

Such a man, surely, would not be a Feature Editor long.

A writer may concern himself with a very limited area of life and still convince us that he is describing the real world, but one becomes suspicious when, as in West's case, whatever world he claims to be describing, the dream life of a highbrow, lowbrow existence in Hollywood, or the American political scene, all these worlds share the same peculiar traits—no married couples have children, no child has more than one parent, a high percentage of the inhabitants are cripples, and the only kind of personal relation is the sadomasochistic.

There is, too, a curious resemblance among the endings of his four books.

> His body broke free of the bard. It took on a life of its own; a life that knew nothing of the poet Balso. Only to death can this release be likened—the mechanics of decay. After death the body takes command; it performs the manual of disintegration with a marvelous certainty. So now, his body performed the evolutions of love with a like sureness. In this activity, Home and Duty, Love and Art were forgotten. . . . His body screamed and shouted as it marched and uncoiled; then with one heaving shout of triumph, it fell back quiet.

> He was running to succor them with love. The cripple turned to escape, but he was too slow and Miss Lonelyhearts caught him. . . . The gun inside the package exploded and Miss Lonelyhearts fell, dragging the cripple with him. They both rolled part of the way down stairs.

> 'I am a clown,' he began, 'but there are times when even clowns must grow serious. This is such a time. I . . .' Lem got no further. A shot rang out and he fell dead, drilled through the heart by an assassin's bullet.

> He was carried through the exit to the back street and lifted into a police car. The siren began to scream and at first he thought he was making the noise himself. He felt his lips with his hands. They were clamped tight. He knew then it was the siren. For some reason this made him laugh and he began to imitate the siren as loud as he could.

An orgasm, two sudden deaths by violence, a surrender to madness, are presented by West as different means for securing the same and desirable end, escape from the conscious Ego and its make-believe. Consciousness, it would seem, does not mean freedom to choose, but freedom to play a fantastic role, an unreality from which a man can only be delivered by some physical or mental explosion outside his voluntary control.

There are many admirable and extremely funny satirical passages in his books, but West is not a satirist. Satire presupposes conscience and reason as the judges between the true and the false, the moral and the immoral, to which it appeals, but for West these faculties are themselves the creators of unreality.

His books should, I think, be classified as Cautionary Tales, parables about a Kingdom of Hell whose ruler is not so much the Father of Lies as the Father of Wishes. Shakespeare gives a glimpse of this hell in *Hamlet,* and Dostoevsky has a lengthy description in *Notes from the Underground,* but they were interested in many hells and heavens. Compared with them, West has the advantages and disadvantages of the specialist who knows everything about one disease and nothing about any other. He was a sophisticated and highly skilled literary craftsman, but what gives all his books such a powerful and disturbing fascination, even **A Cool Million,** which must, I think, be judged a failure, owes nothing to calculation. West's descriptions of Inferno have the authenticity of firsthand ex-

perience: he has certainly been there, and the reader has the uncomfortable feeling that his was not a short visit.

All his main characters suffer from the same spiritual disease which, in honor of the man who devoted his life to studying it, we may call West's Disease. This is a disease of consciousness which renders it incapable of converting wishes into desires. A lie is false; what it asserts is not the case. A wish is fantastic; it knows what is the case but refuses to accept it. All wishes, whatever their apparent content, have the same and unvarying meaning: "I refuse to be what I am." A wish, therefore, is either innocent and frivolous, a kind of play, or a serious expression of guilt and despair, a hatred of oneself and every being one holds responsible for oneself.

Our subconscious life is a world ruled by wish but, since it is not a world of action, this is harmless; even nightmare is playful, but it is the task of consciousness to translate wish into desire. If, for whatever reason, self-hatred or self-pity, it fails to do this, it dooms a human being to a peculiar and horrid fate. To begin with, he cannot desire anything, for the present state of the self is the ground of every desire, and that is precisely what the wisher rejects. Nor can he believe anything, for a wish is not a belief; whatever he wishes he cannot help knowing that he could have wished something else. At first he may be content with switching from one wish to another:

> She would get some music on the radio, then lie down on her bed and shut her eyes. She had a large assortment of stories to choose from. After getting herself in the right mood, she would go over them in her mind as though they were a pack of cards, discarding one after another until she found one that suited. On some days she would run through the whole pack without making a choice. When that happened, she would either go down to Fine Street for an ice-cream soda or, if she were broke, thumb over the pack again and force herself to choose.

> While she admitted that her method was too mechanical for the best results and that it was better to slip into a dream naturally, she said that any dream was better than none and beggars couldn't be choosers.

But in time, this ceases to amuse, and the wisher is left with the despair which is the cause of all of them:

> When not keeping house, he sat in the back yard, called the patio by the real estate agent, in a broken down deck chair. In one of the closets he had found a tattered book and he held it in his lap without looking at it. There was a much better view to be had in any direction other than the one he faced. By moving his chair in a quarter circle he could have seen a large part of the canyon twisting down to the city below. He never thought of making this shift. From where he sat, he saw the closed door of the garage and a patch of its shabby, tarpaper roof.

A sufferer from West's Disease is not selfish but absolutely self-centered. A selfish man is one who satisfies his desires at other people's expense; for this reason, he tries to see what others are really like and often sees them extremely accurately in order that he may make use of them. But, to the self-centered man, other people only exist as images either of what he is or of what he is not, his feelings towards them are projections of the pity or the hatred he feels for himself and anything he does to them is really done to himself. Hence the inconsistent and unpredictable behavior of a sufferer from West's Disease: he may kiss your feet one moment and kick you in the jaw the next and, if you were to ask him why, he could not tell you.

In its final stages, the disease reduces itself to a craving for violent physical pain—this craving, unfortunately, can be projected onto others—for only violent pain can put an end to wishing *for* something and produce the real wish of necessity, the cry "Stop!"

All West's books contain cripples. A cripple is unfortunate and his misfortune is both singular and incurable. Hunchbacks, girls without noses, dwarfs, etc., are not sufficiently common in real life to appear as members of an unfortunate class, like the very poor. Each one makes the impression of a unique case. Further, the nature of the misfortune, a physical deformity, makes the victim repellent to the senses of the typical and normal, and there is nothing the cripple or others can do to change his condition. What attitude towards his own body can he have then but hatred? As used by West, the cripple is, I believe, a symbolic projection of the state of wishful self-despair, the state of those who will not accept themselves in order to change themselves into what they would or should become, and justify their refusal by thinking that being what they are is uniquely horrible and uncurable. To look at, Faye Greener is a pretty but not remarkable girl; in the eyes of Faye Greener, she is an exceptionally hideous spirit.

In saying that cripples have this significance in West's writing, I do not mean to say that he was necessarily aware of it. Indeed, I am inclined to think he was not. I suspect that, consciously, he thought pity and compassion were the same thing, but what the behavior of his "tender" characters shows is that all pity is self-pity and that he who pities others is incapable of compassion. Ruthlessly as he exposes his dreamers, he seems to believe that the only alternative to despair is to become a crook. Wishes may be unreal, but at least they are not, like all desires, wicked:

> His friends would go on telling such stories until they were too drunk to talk. They were aware of their childishness, but did not know how else to revenge themselves. At college, and perhaps for a year afterwards, they had believed in Beauty and in personal expression as an absolute end. When they lost this belief, they lost everything. Money and fame meant nothing to them. They were not worldly men.

The use of the word *worldly* is significant. West comes very near to accepting the doctrine of the Marquis de Sade—there are many resemblances between *A Cool Million* and *Justine*—to believing, that is, that the creation is essentially evil and that goodness is contrary to its laws, but his moral sense revolted against Sade's logical conclusion that it was therefore a man's duty to be as evil as pos-

sible. All West's "worldly" characters are bad men, most of them grotesquely bad, but here again his artistic instinct seems at times to contradict his conscious intentions. I do not think, for example, that he meant to make Wu Fong, the brothel-keeper, more sympathetic and worthy of respect than, say, Miss Lonelyhearts or Homer Simpson, but that is what he does:

> Wu Fong was a very shrewd man and a student of fashion. He saw that the trend was in the direction of home industry and home talent and when the Hearst papers began their "Buy American" campaign, he decided to get rid of all the foreigners in his employ and turn his establishment into a hundred percentum American place. He engaged Mr. Asa Goldstein to redecorate the house and that worthy designed a Pennsylvania Dutch, Old South, Log Cabin Pioneer, Victorian New York, Western Cattle Days, Californian Monterey, Indian and Modern Girl series of interiors. . . .
>
> He was as painstaking as a great artist and in order to be consistent as one he did away with the French cuisine and wines traditional to his business. Instead, he substituted an American kitchen and cellar. When a client visited Lena Haubengruber, it was possible for him to eat roast groundhog and drink Sam Thompson rye. While with Alice Sweethorne, he was served sow belly with grits and bourbon. In Mary Judkins' rooms he received, if he so desired, fried squirrel and corn liquor. In the suite occupied by Patricia Van Riis, lobster and champagne were the rule. The patrons of Powder River Rose usually ordered mountain oysters and washed them down with forty rod. And so on down the list. . . .

After so many self-centered despairers who cry in their baths or bare their souls in barrooms, a selfish man like this, who takes pride in doing something really well, even if it is running a brothel, seems almost a good man.

There have, no doubt, always been cases of West's Disease, but the chances of infection in a democratic and mechanized society like our own are much greater than in the more static and poorer societies of earlier times.

When, for most people, their work, their company, even their marriages, were determined, not by personal choice or ability, but by the class into which they were born, the individual was less tempted to develop a personal grudge against Fate; his fate was not his own but that of everyone around him.

But the greater the equality of opportunity in a society becomes, the more obvious becomes the inequality of the talent and character among individuals, and the more bitter and personal it must be to fail, particularly for those who have some talent but not enough to win them second or third place.

In societies with fewer opportunities for amusement, it was also easier to tell a mere wish from a real desire. If, in order to hear some music, a man has to wait for six months and then walk twenty miles, it is easy to tell whether the words, "I should like to hear some music," mean what they appear to mean, or merely, "At this moment I should like to forget myself." When all he has to do is press a switch, it is more difficult. He may easily come to believe that wishes can come true. This is the first symptom of West's Disease; the later symptoms are less pleasant, but nobody who has read Nathanael West can say that he wasn't warned.

While most of our writers have emphasized the conflict of the individual and society that results from the pursuit of selfhood, West is more concerned with the internal division within the individual that results from it.

—M. A. Klug, in *College Literature*, Winter, 1987.

Alan Ross (essay date 1957)

SOURCE: An introduction to *The Complete Works of Nathanael West,* Farrar, Straus and Giroux, Inc., 1957, pp. vii-xxii.

[*In the following essay, Ross provides an overview of West's fiction.*]

Writers, like seismographs, record the emotional charts of societies; so in the end, as obviously must happen, a period of time, with its behaviorisms and characteristics, conveys to our mental retina an instinctive pattern. The artist brings to the surface those x qualities that, mid-way between germs and tremors, lurk anonymously feeding on individual frustration. Once a society has been characterized or caricatured (has, in fact, been given a poetic or non-poetic name), it is freed. This release, which is primarily given by the artist, acts as a standard for the duration of that social pattern—its people, like actors in a silent film suddenly given words, move through the norms and extremes of their lives with a new-found conviction. The artistic truth, the "right" way of behavior for their time has been established. So, looking at them through the wrong end of a telescope, events appear as extensions or absorptions of those larger personalities that formalized them.

Yet, even when our patterns of culture appear to have been established, new, sometimes uncomfortable, evidences can materialize. A myth in the light of revaluation is often destroyed. Similarly, and unspectacularly out of seeming neglect, a myth can establish itself on the sole basis of its truth. Our conception of periods of time naturally alters as our knowledge of them increases. What seemed obvious to the point almost of stylization appears curiously in a new key. It is like a gramophone record that, having always been played on one side, is found to have another that is equally acceptable.

The twenties and thirties in both England and America have been meticulously documented. More nearly perhaps than in any previous era, literature became socially representational. The mirror held up to humanity, its eccentricities and perversions, its social and political attitude, disgorged a reflection that, if anything, was too close. The heroic distaste for heroism, the intellectual's distaste for himself and his embracing of his opposite, the divesting of romance from illusions amongst those most in love with illusions, all formed part of the dismantling of the human personality that an age, out of love with itself, one moment riding the waves, the next disembowelled at their base, found necessary to save its face. One by one each writer presented his or her case, then proceeded to destroy it—*Eyeless in Gaza, The Woman Who Rode Away, To the Lighthouse, Ulysses, The Memorial,* and in America, *Fiesta, The Great Gatsby, U.S.A., Appointment in Samarra*—one by one these cancelled each other out. Each successive writer grew to know too much. Sophistication left the novelist dry.

Yet in general there remained a mixture of nostalgia and sadness, a residue of that good living which illumines prose, as it does a face, with a kind of dispassionate tenderness and which is the by-product of emotional prosperity, of a knowledge of good days. In England the class struggle of the thirties was reflected in literature by gestures of *avant-garde* idealism. The artistic truth in literary sympathies appeared also to be a political truth—but it was a conclusion English writers arrived at through a series of well-bred intellectual convictions, rather than a brute confronting with the facts of economic disaster. Their prototypes in the American slump—the inheritors of the Jazz Age débris, the sawn-off idealists who found themselves with not even an empty bomb in their pockets—had to learn the harder way. Their pessimism was not the reverse side of politico-literary idealism, it was a despair born from being witnesses of a suffering enormously outside their control. The wisecrack had frozen in their cynical mouths, the cocktail bravado of sexual indulgence gone flat like bad champagne. Somewhere hidden, Man was being anonymously pinned down with this weight of suffering on his back, this noisy civilized burden demanding a new martyrdom. It is this ruthless outline of collapse that Nathanael West created more savagely and poetically than any other contemporary writer in his two important novels **Miss Lonelyhearts** and **The Day of the Locust**—blueprints of the faithless Christ-symbols that in the end stood for the American common man, like bitter flowers, as he lay on the ground at the stockades of his own defeat.

Altogether, Nathanael West wrote four novels. Besides the two already mentioned, which were the second (1933) and fourth (1939) in point of time, there were **The Dream Life of Balso Snell,** printed in a limited edition in 1931, and **A Cool Million,** published in 1934. West was born in 1903 (his real name was Nathan Weinstein), educated at Brown University, and then consecutively was manager of a residential hotel in New York, and associate editor, with William Carlos Williams, of a magazine called *Contact.* His wife was Eileen McKenney, the original of the book *My Sister Eileen,* written by Ruth McKenney, and West's own sister married S. J. Perelman. So his links with the semi-fashionable, literary and stage world were fairly constant until, after the publication of *Miss Lonelyhearts,* West went to Hollywood. He and his wife remained there till their death in a car accident in 1940. The last five years of his life West spent working on film scripts, among which were *Advice to the Lovelorn* (the adaptation of *Miss Lonelyhearts*), *Five Came Back, I Stole a Million, Spirit of Culver,* and *Men Against the Sky.* He was only thirty-seven at the time of his death. Perhaps the most remarkable things about West's career are its unevenness and its development. West's early writings are bitter, extremist, near surrealist and aggressive. The criticism underlying them is based on a disgust that is not far from hysteria: the language is obscure, extravagant, privately allusive and contemptuously scatalogical.

Yet after this unrelated little essay in intellectual gaucherie, West could suddenly strip his writing of all pretence, of all arrogant obscurantism, and produce a novel of the direct and economic intensity of *Miss Lonelyhearts,* in which every word is used exactly and functionally—and then again, in *A Cool Million,* forsake a personal style for mock-heroics and parody. Only several years later, when he had emerged from his incubatory period in Hollywood, and had written *The Day of the Locust,* was it apparent that West was somewhere on the way to integrating his gifts, to merging his bitterness and savagery into a wider, more organic pattern without losing his edge. *The Day of the Locust* marked his most important advance, the step from a political to a human view of drama. Basically, West was always a sociological writer, moved by the horrible emptiness of mass lives; and in this sense all his books are indictments, not so much of economic systems, but of life itself. *Life is terrible,* that was the despairing conclusion that led nowhere and which was the motive spring for his novels. For West there was no religious redemption to be found in human weakness, no transfiguring sense of good-and-evil, no compensation in the physical life. Seediness, apathy remained just seediness and apathy. The joke was on civilization, and West's own attitude was inexpressible through the perversion of great tides of compassion into relentless observation. So just as *Miss Lonelyhearts* is West's greatest book, because it is conceived most purely as a formal work of art, and is flawless within its structure, *The Day of the Locust* is his most mature because in it his criticism of life is not intruding between the characters, nor his pity confronting them. They exist simply in their relation to one another; the hidden reformer in West has contented himself with being an artist.

The Dream Life of Balso Snell, in any analysis of West's novels must, if it be considered at all, be subjected to a different sort of criteria—for the other three books, in the sense that they document from social, political, and what one might call "grotesque" angles, recognize symptoms of a disintegrating society, more or less hang together. *Balso Snell* analyses only the disintegration of the Self, and its illusion of superiority at its most pathetic moment of neurotic isolation. The story, since it is a dream, dispenses completely with plausibility. From its opening, when Balso Snell enters into the Trojan Horse, through his meetings in its viscous landscape with various unrelated figures—an art-loving guide, a naked man in a derby who calls himself Maloney the Areopagite, and who is engaged on writing the life of Saint Puce (a flea who lived in the armpit of Christ), a psychotic twelve-year-old boy with a passion for his schoolmistress whom he hopes to win by writing pseudo-Russian journals, till the end, when the schoolmistress materializes and after two metamorphoses is had by Balso Snell himself, the book is a piece of extreme exhibitionism. *Balso Snell* is a sneer in the bathroom mirror at Art—cocksure, contemptuous, well-informed and rejecting openly the object of its search. There is a revealing passage in the middle of the book, where Balso is reading a pamphlet written by the young boy, in which West explains the necessity for the extravagant bitterness of the book:

> All my acting has but one purpose, the attraction of the female. If it had been possible for me to attract by exhibiting a series of physical charms, my hatred would have been less, but I found it necessary to substitute strange conceits, wise and witty sayings, peculiar conduct, Art, for the muscles, teeth, hair of my rivals.

> All this much exhibited intelligence is but a development of the instinct to please. My case is similar to that of a bird called the Amblyornis inornata. As his name indicates, the Inornata is a dull-colored, ugly bird. Yet the Inornata is cousin to the Bird of Paradise. Because he lacks his cousin's brilliant plumage, he has to exteriorize internal feathers. . . . Still more, the Bird of Paradise cannot be blamed for the quality of his tail—it just grew. The Inornata, however, is held personally responsible for his performance as an artist.

> There was a time when I felt that I was indeed a rare spirit. Then I had genuinely expressed my personality with a babe's delight in confessing the details of its inner life. Soon, however, in order to interest my listeners, I found it necessary to shorten my long outpourings; to make them, by straining my imagination, spectacular. Oh! how much work goes into the search for the odd, the escape from the same!

> Because of women like Saniette, I acquired the habit of extravagant thought. I now convert everything into fantastic entertainment and the extraordinary has become an obsession. . . .

West's natural reticence, the laughing at his own laugh rather than be laughed at, the savage defensive attack he employs as arguments against what he really wishes to believe in, are all explained in *Balso Snell.* It is the clue to all his later books; yet, despite its moments of brilliant writing, its poetic economy, it is the one book West wrote in which private despair is not related to a social condition.

Miss Lonelyhearts, which has been called a 'modernized, faithless, Pilgrim's Progress', is the formalizing and objectifying of the rebellious vision of *Balso Snell.* West has accepted the fact that an audience exists, and that art is communication. Preoccupation with the self has given way to an identification with society, and the stone that *Balso Snell* dropped into the middle of the pond has now reached the outer banks.

Ostensibly, *Miss Lonelyhearts* tells the story of a reporter, who, detailed to write an agony column and answer daily the letters desperate with human misery addressed to his paper, finds the panacea he has to offer turning sour in his hand.

> Although the deadline was less than a quarter of an hour away, he was still working on his leader. He had gone as far as: "Life is worth while, for it is full of dreams and peace, gentleness and ecstasy, and faith that burns like a clear white flame on a grim dark altar." But he found it impossible to continue. The letters were no longer funny. He could not go on finding the same joke funny thirty times a day for months on end. And on most days he received more than thirty letters, all of them alike, stamped from the dough of suffering with a heart-shaped cookie knife.

Throughout the book, which interweaves Miss Lonelyhearts' own life with the episodic relations he has with his editor's wife, involvements with his correspondents, and his gradual conviction that Christian love alone can adequately soften this mass hopelessness, there is a constant counterpointing of Miss Lonelyhearts' struggle for some sort of solution to the human equation and his editor, Shrike's, destruction of it. Miss Lonelyhearts comes to stand for Intention, Shrike for Reality. From the very beginning, when Shrike, looking over Miss Lonelyhearts' typewriter, says: "The same old stuff. Why don't you give them something new and hopeful? Tell them about art. Here, I'll dictate: *Art is a Way Out,*" it is apparent that there can be no serious attempt to grapple with the problem (for there is no answer), but merely an attempt to sugar the pill in as hard-boiled, efficient and calculated a way as possible. Later in the book, when Miss Lonelyhearts himself has reached a position where he is as much in need of salvation as his most desperate reader, Shrike elaborates and then punctures the various fantasy escapes with which men dupe themselves. Shrike takes over Miss Lonelyhearts' rôle in real life, but instead of feeling bound to offer a remedy, his own frustration compels him to make any solution—Christ, Art, the reclusive life—appear phony because he himself refuses to accept their premises; speaking as one who no longer has illusions, he cannot bear to allow others the benefits of self-deception. *Miss Lonelyhearts* is short and brilliantly authentic. The newspaper background, the alternation of self-pity, ineffectual love-making, clinical disgust, and the hopeless efforts at a normal life, are contrived and pointed with a bare passion that charges the whole book with a hallucinatory fever. Though the properties of the story are extremely commonplace, little different from a hundred filmscripts or stories with a journalist-martyr theme, West's succinct handling of them and his approach through a central character that is neither aggressive nor successful, raise the story to the intensive level of a poem. Every word is part of a pattern and rhythm whose water-tight structure is so exactly balanced that a phrase too much or out of key would destroy the breathless control of the whole book. West is writing no longer with brilliant intellectual exhibitionism, but out of bitter necessity. The curious religious strain in West's writing, a sort of pessimistic Messianism in whose aura America becomes a glorified Oxford

Street, dirty, haphazard, doped, reaches its fullest expression towards the end of *Miss Lonelyhearts.* The final scene, where the cripple husband of one of the column's correspondents (a beefy nymphomaniac who has seduced Miss Lonelyhearts) calls on him and Miss Lonelyhearts thinks in his delusion that he is now one with Christ and that the cripple is a test of his love, culminates in a tragedy of miscomprehension which symbolizes terrifyingly and finally the unreality of the Christian myth. Miss Lonelyhearts runs down the stairs with his arms open to receive the cripple, who, imagining he is being attacked, shouts out. But Miss Lonelyhearts, interpreting the shout as a "cry for help from Desperate, Harold S., Catholic Mother, Broken-hearted, Broad-shoulders, Sick-of-it-all, Disillusioned-with-tubercular-husband. He was running to succour them with love," falls on the cripple as he turns to get away. A gun in the cripple's hand goes off and they both roll part of the way down the stairs.

That is the end of the book. West says nothing more—there is in fact no more to be said. But already in this book certain Westisms that remain constant in all four books, begin to emerge. Perhaps most important is West's view of character and his treatment of it. For none of his people are seen "in the round," as individuals created for their own distinctiveness; nor yet are they exactly "types" or vehicles for ideas in the Aldous Huxley manner. West uses subsidiary characters as an architect uses windows—to let in light on a central character and to show, but not offer him, escape. They exemplify modes of living that are never developed beyond the point where they become absurd; and at one point or another they all become absurd. These are West's primary characters: Beagle Darwin in *Balso Snell,* Shrike, Miss Lonelyhearts in *Miss Lonelyhearts,* Shagpoke Whipple in *A Cool Million,* Homer, Faye Greener and Tod in *The Day of the Locust.* But around them, and though they are main characters they never "come off" in the sense that West makes them succeed in their lives, there are a host of abnormal minor figures, whose abnormality and pathos act as a series of reservoirs, almost in the form of a Greek chorus, for West's savagery and inverted violence. As in the freak shows in Oxford Street, their deformity is a mockery of normality rather than vice versa. In *Balso Snell* it is the beautiful hunchback with whom Balso falls in love ("The lobby was crowded with the many beautiful girl-cripples who congregate there because Art is their only solace, most men looking upon their strange forms with distaste. But it was otherwise with Balso Snell. He likened their disarranged hips, their short legs, their humps, their splay feet, their wall-eyes, to ornament. Their strange fore-shortenings, hanging heads, bulging spinesacks, were a delight. . . ."), in *Miss Lonelyhearts* the cripple, Doyle, in *A Cool Million* nearly everyone; in *The Day of the Locust* it is no more than an awful horror at the blind forces of ignorance—symbolized in the riot at the end—that make escape from their decontamination impossible. In the end one has to live and die with the mob. But West's political satire is concerned with the way in which the sheeplike dependence of the mob, their malleableness, is made use of for ulterior political ends.

A Cool Million tackles this problem overtly. Written as

a burlesquing, melodramatic parody of the Horatio Alger best-seller, it describes, in prose that is like a long heavy wink, the adventures of a country bumpkin called Lemuel Pitkin in search of success on the American pattern of free enterprise. By the time he has finished he has been in jail, lost his teeth, his eyes, a leg, his scalp, witnessed an infinite number of rapes, riots, and been the tool for both Communist and Fascist organizations. Finally, he is shot by a political assassin and made a martyr.

In its awareness of political technique, its devastatingly true analysis of unrestricted Capitalist method, its foreshadowing of Americanism turned into a possible Fascism, *A Cool Million* is brilliantly successful. Unfortunately, having decided on a mock-melodramatic style ("when our hero regained consciousness," "In the half-gloom of the cabin, Lem was horrified to see the Pike man busily tearing off Betty's sole remaining piece of underwear. She was struggling as best she could, but the ruffian from Missouri was too strong for her," etc.), West sacrificed the stylistic hallmark that makes a writer's work compact and homogeneous.

The villain of the story is "Shagpoke" Whipple, an ex-President of the United States, and a believer in American opportunism. Whipple now lives in retirement in Rat River, where he is President of the National Bank: here he is visited one day by Lemuel Pitkin in search of advice. Whipple, citing his own past as precedent, tells Pitkin to go out into the world and make his fortune. Pitkin meets with one misfortune after the other, is duped, robbed and wrongfully imprisoned. In jail he finds Whipple, convicted of fraud after the failure of his bank. "My boy," says Whipple, when Pitkin meets him in the prison carrying a bedpan, "there are two evils undermining this country which we must fight tooth and nail. These two arch-enemies of the American spirit, the spirit of fair play and open competition, are Wall Street and the Communists." The next time Pitkin meets Whipple, some weeks after he is out of jail, he finds him in the process of starting his new political party—the National Revolutionary movement, "because," as he tells Pitkin, "how could I, Shagpoke Whipple, ever bring myself to accept a program which promised to take from American citizens their inalienable birthright, the right to sell their labor and their children's labor without restrictions as to either price or hours?" Pitkin is enrolled in the movement, made a Commander, and then when the first party meeting is broken up by international Jewish bankers and Communists, beaten up.

In the course of the book, almost every popular American bogy is caricatured. Pitkin is victimized in a series of near-slapstick episodes which, despite their rather labored telling, are extremely funny. Beneath them lurk a very real horror and an acute feeling of sinister inevitability. The epilogue describes a future national holiday, with the youth of America parading up and down Fifth Avenue in Pitkin's honor and singing the Lemuel Pitkin song:

A million hearts for Pitkin, oh!

To do and die with Pitkin, oh!

Reviewing them from a special stand is Shagpoke Whipple. When the paraders have marched past him and gath-

ered round his reviewing stand, Whipple addresses them in a remarkable closing speech that ends the book.

"What," he says, "made Lemuel Pitkin great? Let us examine his life. First we see him as a small boy, light of foot, fishing for bullheads in the Rat River of Vermont. Later, he attends the Ottsville High School, where he is captain of the nine and an excellent outfielder. Then he leaves for the big city to make his fortune. All this is in the honorable tradition of his country and its people and he has the right to expect certain rewards. Jail is his first reward. Poverty his second. Violence is his third. Death is his last."

Whipple goes on to analyze Pitkin's greatness, and then winds up with: "But he did not live or die in vain. Through his martyrdom the National Revolutionary Party triumphed, and by that triumph this country was delivered from sophistication, Marxism and International Capitalism. Through the National Revolution its people were purged of alien diseases and America became again American. Hail, Lemuel Pitkin! All Hail, the American Boy!"

West's last book, *The Day of the Locust,* written after he had been in Hollywood for three years, is by far his most ambitious and mature. It is the most objective of his novels, and the one in which his own personal integration most nearly coincides with the form of his book. Its deficiencies, such as they are, come from a slight slowness in the narrative's momentum, and a series of sub-plots whose interrelation is never developed quite closely enough. Once the real theme emerges, West's confident astringency of language seems to return and the last two-thirds of the book contain some of his very best writing.

Primarily, *The Day of the Locust* is about middle-aged, middle-class discontent—a discontent that is dangerous because it has developed from illusions of security, from a sense of betrayal, and now waits to feed on the misfortunes of individuals. Reactions are so dulled that only abnormality has the power to stimulate: abnormality and the drug of mob action. The background is Hollywood—not the Hollywood of film stars, but the Hollywood exemplified by unimportant hangers-on fighting unsuccessfully for a little limelight: Faye Greener, a small-time blonde, and her father Harry, a faded music-hall star; an ex-undergraduate artist lured by a talent scout to learn scenery design (Tod Hackett, the *Miss Lonelyhearts* symbol of the book); a retired clerk ordered to Hollywood for his health (Homer Simpson), and around these the men whom Faye attracts on the different levels of their lust—a Mexican cockfighter, a cowboy tailor's dummy, and a bookmaking dwarf. Like a chorus around them, in a yet wider circle, are the unnamed crowd extras—people "whose clothing was sombre and badly cut, bought from mail-order houses. They loitered on the corners or stood with their backs to the shop windows and stared at everyone who passed. When their stare was returned, their eyes filled with hatred. At this time Tod knew very little about them except that they had come to California to die."

It is these people, an endless procession of loiterers, of grown-up embittered Pitkins and Doyles, whom West makes potentially capable of mass riot, blood-letting and lynching, such as, in fact, takes place in the last chapter, at a *première;* most of the crowd, if asked the reason for their frenzy, would not have been able to answer. It was enough that their frustration had found an outlet: the provoking incident was not of consequence.

The tension and atmosphere of the novel, its tortured pity and hatred, are summed up in West's description of the crowd:

> New groups, whole families, kept arriving. He could see a change come over them as soon as they had become part of the crowd. Until they reached the line, they looked diffident, almost furtive, but the moment they had become part of it, they turned arrogant and pugnacious. It was a mistake to think them harmless curiosity seekers. They were savage and bitter, especially the middle-aged and the old, and had been made so by boredom and disappointment.
>
> All their lives they had slaved at some kind of dull, heavy labor, behind desks and counters . . . dreaming of the leisure that would be theirs when they had enough. Where else should they go but California, the land of sunshine and oranges?
>
> Once there, they discover that sunshine isn't enough. They get tired of oranges, even of avocado pears and passion fruit. Nothing happens. . . . Did they slave so long just to go to an occasional Iowa picnic? What else is there? They watch the waves come in at Venice. There wasn't any ocean where most of them came from, but after you've seen one wave, you've seen them all. The same is true of the airplanes at Glendale. If only a plane would crash once in a while so that they could watch the passengers being consumed in a "holocaust of flame," as the newspapers put it. But the planes never crash.
>
> Their boredom becomes more and more terrible. They realize that they've been tricked and burn with resentment. Every day of their lives they read the newspapers and went to the movies. Both fed them on lynchings, murder, sex crimes, explosions, wrecks, love nests, fires, miracles, revolutions, wars. This daily diet made sophisticates of them. The sun is a joke. Oranges can't titillate their jaded palates. Nothing can ever be violent enough to make taut their slack minds and bodies.

West's Hollywood is made up of degeneracy and brothels, of failure and sexual desire, of cock-fighting and third-rate boarding houses. But more than anything it is made up of significant boredom, of an etiolated ennui: the whole canvas on which the motiveless actions take place acquires a Breughel-like stillness, as if all the monstrous things going on were part of a very ordinary pattern. And, indeed, the pattern of all West's books is ordinary; it is only the extraordinary stylized grotesques on the edge, the narrative logic that touches the rim of fantasy, that charge it with the nervous garishness, the disproportionate perspective that, like the beautiful hunchbacks in *Balso Snell,* mock normality with their own freakishness.

West's slightness of reputation is not easy to understand, for *Miss Lonelyhearts* and *The Day of the Locust* rank almost with any novels that came out of America in the thirties—more condensed, penetrating and poetic than many, that with much larger scope and subsequent recognition, purported to give the lie to the American scene.

Perhaps the ruthlessness of West's portrait, his making of the whole political and economic racket so undisguisedly repulsive and meaningless, was too near the bone for an American audience with a mass neurosis, and a guilty conscience. There were, of course, other factors; the fact that the publisher of *The Dream Life of Balso Snell* went bankrupt almost immediately after the book was issued, and the shadow of an imminent war that took American thought beyond its own frontiers. Perhaps it is only now, when West's books are again being made available, that he will reach the wider audience, with a different view on both him and his times, of which he was originally deprived.

Stanley Edgar Hyman   (essay date 1962)

SOURCE: "Nathanael West," in *Nathanael West,* edited by Harold Bloom, Chelsea House Publishers, 1986, pp. 11-40.

[*As a longtime literary critic for the* New Yorker, *Hyman rose to a prominent position in American letters during the middle decades of the twentieth century. He is noted for his belief that much of modern literary criticism should depend on knowledge received from disciplines outside the field of literature; consequently, many of his best reviews and critical essays rely on his application of theories gleaned from such disciplines as cultural anthropology, psychology, and comparative religion. In the following excerpt from his study originally published in 1962, Hyman discusses the defining characteristics of West's short novels.*]

Since his death West's reputation has risen continuously. *Miss Lonelyhearts* has sold 190,000 copies in paperback, and *The Day of the Locust* 250,000. Scholarly articles about West, here and abroad, multiply cancerously. *Miss Lonelyhearts* has been made into a play, a more faithful film than the Lee Tracy one, and an opera. In 1946 it was translated into French by Marcelle Sibon as *Mademoiselle Coeur-Brisé,* with an introduction by Philippe Soupault, and it has had a visible effect on later French fiction. Since 1949, all West's books but the first have been published in England. When the four novels were reissued in this country in one volume in 1957, all the reviews were favorable, and there was general agreement that West was one of the most important writers of the thirties, as American as apple pie. West's picture appeared on the cover of the *Saturday Review,* looking very Jewish.

The Dream Life of Balso Snell (1931) is almost impossible to synopsize. A poet named Balso Snell finds the wooden Trojan Horse and has a picaresque journey up its alimentary canal. In the course of his travels he encounters: a Jewish guide; Maloney the Areopagite, a Catholic mystic; John Gilson, a precocious schoolboy; and Miss McGeeney, John's eighth-grade teacher. Each has a story, sometimes several stories, to tell, and their stories merge with their dreams and with Balso's dreams in a thoroughly confusing, and deliberately confusing, fashion. The book ends with Balso's orgasm, still in the bowels of the horse, during a dream of rapturous sexual intercourse with Miss McGeeney. Balso is dreaming the schoolboy's dream, and may have become the schoolboy.

The overwhelming impression the reader gets is of the corruption and repulsiveness of the flesh. In one of John Gilson's fantasies of beating a mistress, he explains his action: "I have a sty on my eye, a cold sore on my lip, a pimple where the edge of my collar touches my neck, another pimple in the corner of my mouth, and a drop of salt on the end of my nose." Furthermore, "It seems to me as though all the materials of life—wood, glass, wool, skin—are rubbing against my sty, my cold sore and my pimples." When Balso encounters Miss McGeeney, a middle-aged tweedy woman disguised for the moment as a beautiful naked young girl, she offers him her poetic vision: "Houses that are protuberances on the skin of streets—warts, tumors, pimples, corns, nipples, sebaceous cysts, hard and soft chancres."

In a dream within his dream, Balso is attracted to girl cripples: "He likened their disarranged hips, their short legs, their humps, their splay feet, their wall-eyes, to ornament." He cries tenderly to one of them, Janey the hunchback: "For me, your sores are like flowers: the new, pink, budlike sores, the full, rose-ripe sores, the sweet, seed-bearing sores. I shall cherish them all." One of Balso's beautiful memories in the book is of a girl he once loved who did nothing all day but put bits of meat and gravy, butter and cheese, on the petals of roses so that they would attract flies instead of butterflies and bees.

As the human body is seen as a running sore, Christianity is seen entirely in terms of Christ's wounded and bleeding body. Maloney the Areopagite is writing a hagiography of Saint Puce, a flea who was born, lived, and died in the armpit of Jesus Christ. Maloney's blasphemous idea that Saint Puce was born of the Holy Ghost enables West to mock the mysteries of Incarnation, as the flea's feasting on the divine flesh and blood enables West to mock Eucharist. The Passion is burlesqued by Maloney, who is encountered naked except for a derby stuck full of thorns, trying to crucify himself with thumbtacks, and by Beagle Darwin, a fictional invention of Miss McGeeney's, who does a juggling act, keeping in the air "the Nails, the Scourge, the Thorns, and a piece of the True Cross."

Nor is West's bitterness in the book reserved for Christianity. Judaism comes in for its share. The song in praise of obscene roundness that Balso makes when he starts his journey concludes:

> Round and Ringing Full
> As the Mouth of a Brimming Goblet
> The Rust-Laden Holes
> In Our Lord's Feet
> Entertain the Jew-Driven Nails.

The guide turns out to be not only a Jew, but a Jew who at the mention of such melodious Jewish names as Hernia Hornstein and Paresis Pearlberg finds it necessary to affirm: "I am a Jew. I'm a Jew! A Jew!" Balso answers politely that some of his best friends are Jews, and adds

Doughty's epigram: "The semites are like to a man sitting in a cloaca to the eyes, and whose brows touch heaven."

The strength of *Balso Snell* lies in its garish comic imagination. Maloney's crucifixion with thumbtacks is not only a serious theme that West's later work develops, it is also funny, and as a parody of the stance of Roman Catholic mysticism, devastating. The account in John Gilson's journal of his Gidean and Dostoevskian murder of an idiot dishwasher is repulsive but genuinely imagined, and its unconscious sexual motivation is boldly dramatized: stripping for the crime, John notices his genitals tight and hard; afterwards he feels like a happy young girl, "kittenish, cuney-cutey, darlingey, springtimey"; when he sees sailors on the street, he flirts and camps and feels "as though I were melting—all silk and perfumed, pink lace." The hunchback Janey is a nightmarish vision of the female body as terrifying, transformed into comedy: she has a hundred and forty-four exquisite teeth, and is pregnant in the hump.

Some of West's language in the book foreshadows his later triumphs. Janey imagines death to be "like putting on a wet [bathing] suit—shivery." John describes his dual nature to his fantasy-mistress, Saniette: "Think of two men—myself and the chauffeur within me. This chauffeur is very large and dressed in ugly ready-made clothing. His shoes, soiled from walking about the streets of a great city, are covered with animal ordure and chewing gum. His hands are covered with coarse woollen gloves. On his head is a derby hat." Sometimes John speaks in a voice we can hear as the youthful West's. He tells Balso: "I need women and because I can't buy or force them, I have to make poems for them. God knows how tired I am of using the insanity of Van Gogh and the adventures of Gauguin as can-openers." John explains his position in a pamphlet, which he sells to Balso for a dollar. In it he confesses: "If it had been possible for me to attract by exhibiting a series of physical charms, my hatred would have been less. But I found it necessary to substitute strange conceits, wise and witty sayings, peculiar conduct, Art, for the muscles, teeth, hair, of my rivals."

The weaknesses of *Balso Snell* are all characteristically juvenile. The principal one is the obsessive scatology, which soon becomes boring. "O Anus Mirabilis!" Balso cries of his rectal entrance to the Trojan Horse, and his roundness song takes off from that anal image. "Art is a sublime excrement," he is told by the Jewish guide (who seems to justify only the first half of Doughty's aphorism). John sees journal-keepers in excremental imagery: "They come to the paper with a constipation of ideas—eager, impatient. The white paper acts as a laxative. A diarrhoea of words is the result." When the idiot dishwasher swallows, John compares it to "a miniature toilet being flushed." As John beats Saniette, he cries: "O constipation of desire! O diarrhoea of love!" He has visions of writing a play that will conclude when "the ceiling of the theatre will be made to open and cover the occupants with tons of loose excrement." Balso speaks "with lips torn angry in laying duck's eggs from a chicken's rectum." James F. Light reports that West was fond of quoting Odo of Cluny's reference to the female as *"saccus stercoris,"* but the book's scatological obsession is clearly not restricted to the female. It is no less than a vision of the whole world as one vast dungheap.

Balso Snell is complex and stratified, so much so that at one point we get Janey's thinking as Beagle imagines it in a letter actually written by Miss McGeeney and read by Balso in his dream within a dream. But the book has no form, and consists merely of a series of encounters and complications, terminated rather than resolved by the orgasm. We can sense West's dissatisfaction with it as not fully realized in his re-use of some of its material in later works. Some of ***Balso Snell*** is extremely schoolboyish, like the guide's aphorism, "A hand in the Bush is worth two in the pocket," or Balso's comment on Maloney's story of the martyrdom and death of Saint Puce: "I think you're morbid. . . . Take cold showers."

When ***Miss Lonelyhearts*** was published two years later, in 1933, West told A. J. Liebling that it was entirely unlike ***Balso Snell***, "of quite a different make, wholesome, clean, holy, slightly mystic and inane." He describes it in "Some Notes on Miss Lonelyhearts" as a "portrait of a priest of our time who has had a religious experience." In it, West explains, "violent images are used to illustrate commonplace events. Violent acts are left almost bald." He credits William James's *Varieties of Religious Experience* for its psychology. Some or all of this may be Westian leg-pull.

The plot of ***Miss Lonelyhearts*** is Sophoclean irony, as simple and inevitable as the plot of ***Balso Snell*** is random and whimsical. A young newspaperman who writes the agony column of his paper as "Miss Lonelyhearts" has reached the point where the joke has gone sour. He becomes obsessed with the real misery of his correspondents, illuminated for him by the cynicism of William Shrike, the feature editor. Miss Lonelyhearts pursues Shrike's wife Mary, unsuccessfully, and cannot content himself with the love and radiant goodness of Betty, his fiancée. Eventually he finds his fate in two of his correspondents, the crippled Peter Doyle and his wife Fay. Miss Lonelyhearts is not punished for his tumble with Fay, but when on his next encounter he fights her off, it leads to his being shot by Doyle.

The characters are allegorical figures who are at the same time convincing as people. Miss Lonelyhearts is a New England puritan, the son of a Baptist minister. He has a true religious vocation or calling, but no institutional church to embody it. When Betty suggests that he quit the column, he tells her: "I can't quit. And even if I were to quit, it wouldn't make any difference. I wouldn't be able to forget the letters, no matter what I did."

In one of the most brilliant strokes in the book, he is never named, always identified only by his role. (In an earlier draft, West had named him Thomas Matlock, which we could translate "Doubter Wrestler," but no name at all is infinitely more effective.) Even when he telephones Fay Doyle for an assignation, he identifies himself only as "Miss Lonelyhearts, the man who does the column." In his namelessness, in his vocation without a church, Miss Lonelyhearts is clearly the prophet in the reluctance stage, when he denies the call and tells God that he stammers,

but Miss Lonelyhearts, the prophet of *our* time, is stuck there until death.

Miss Lonelyhearts identifies Betty as the principle of order: "She had often made him feel that when she straightened his tie, she straightened much more." The order that she represents is the innocent order of Nature, as opposed to the disorder of sinful Man. When Miss Lonelyhearts is sick, Betty comes to nourish him with hot soup, impose order on his room, and redeem him with a pastoral vision: "She told him about her childhood on a farm and of her love for animals, about country sounds and country smells and of how fresh and clean everything in the country is. She said that he ought to live there and that if he did, he would find that all his troubles were city troubles." When Miss Lonelyhearts is back on his feet, Betty takes him for a walk in the zoo, and he is "amused by her evident belief in the curative power of animals." Then she takes him to live in the country for a few days, in the book's great idyllic scene. Miss Lonelyhearts is beyond such help, but it is Betty's patient innocence—she is as soft and helpless as a kitten—that makes the book so heartbreaking. She is an innocent Eve to his fallen Adam, and he alone is driven out of Eden.

The book's four other principal characters are savage caricatures, in the root sense of "caricature" as the overloading of one attribute. Shrike is a dissociated half of Miss Lonelyhearts, his cynical intelligence, and it is interesting to learn that Shrike's rhetorical masterpiece, the great speech on the varieties of escape, was spoken by Miss Lonelyhearts in an earlier draft. Shrike's name is marvelously apt. The shrike or butcherbird impales its prey on thorns, and the name is a form of the word "shriek." Shrike is of course the mocker who hands Miss Lonelyhearts his crown of thorns, and throughout the book he is a shrieking bird of prey; when not a butcherbird, "a screaming, clumsy gull."

Shrike's wife Mary is one vast teasing mammary image. As Miss Lonelyhearts decides to telephone Mary in Delehanty's speakeasy, he sees a White Rock poster and observes that "the artist had taken a great deal of care in drawing her breasts and their nipples stuck out like tiny red hats." He then thinks of "the play Mary made with her breasts. She used them as the coquettes of long ago had used their fans. One of her tricks was to wear a medal low down on her chest. Whenever he asked to see it, instead of drawing it out she leaned over for him to look. Although he had often asked to see the medal, he had not yet found out what it represented." Miss Lonelyhearts and Mary go out for a gay evening, and Mary flaunts her breasts while talking of her mother's terrible death from cancer of the breast. He finally gets to see the medal, which reads "Awarded by the Boston Latin School for first place in the 100 yd. dash." When he takes her home he kisses her breasts, for the first time briefly slowing down her dash.

The Doyles are presented in inhuman or subhuman imagery. When, in answer to Fay's letter of sexual invitation, Miss Lonelyhearts decides to telephone her, he pictures her as "a tent, hair-covered and veined," and himself as a skeleton: "When he made the skeleton enter the flesh tent, it flowered at every joint." Fay appears and is a giant: "legs like Indian clubs, breasts like balloons and a brow like a pigeon." When he takes her arm, "It felt like a thigh." Following her up the stairs to his apartment, "he watched the action of her massive hams; they were like two enormous grindstones." Undressing, "she made sea sounds; something flapped like a sail; there was the creak of ropes; then he heard the wave-against-a-wharf smack of rubber on flesh. Her call for him to hurry was a sea-moan, and when he lay beside her, she heaved, tidal, moon-driven." Eventually Miss Lonelyhearts "crawled out of bed like an exhausted swimmer leaving the surf," and she soon drags him back.

If Fay is an oceanic monster, Peter Doyle is only a sinister puppy. In bringing Miss Lonelyhearts back to the apartment at Fay's order, he half-jokes, "Ain't I the pimp, to bring home a guy for my wife?" Fay reacts by hitting him in the mouth with a rolled-up newspaper, and his comic response is to growl like a dog and catch the paper with his teeth. When she lets go of her end, he drops to his hands and knees and continues to imitate a dog on the floor. As Miss Lonelyhearts leans over to help him up, "Doyle tore open Miss Lonelyhearts' fly, then rolled over on his back, laughing wildly." Fay, more properly, accepts him as a dog and kicks him.

The obsessive theme of *Miss Lonelyhearts* is human pain and suffering, but it is represented almost entirely as female suffering. This is first spelled out in the letters addressed to Miss Lonelyhearts: Sick-of-it-all is a Roman Catholic wife who has had seven children in twelve years, is pregnant again, and has kidney pains so excruciating that she cries all the time. Desperate is a sixteen-year-old born with a hole in her face instead of a nose, who wants to have dates like other girls. Harold S. writes about his thirteen-year-old deaf-and-dumb sister Gracie, who was raped by a man when she was playing on the roof, and who will be brutally punished if her parents find out about it. Broad Shoulders was hit by a car when she was first pregnant, and is alternately persecuted and deserted by an unbalanced husband, in five pages of ghastly detail. Miss Lonelyhearts gets only two letters about male suffering, one from a paralyzed boy who wants to play the violin, the other from Peter Doyle, who complains of the pain from his crippled leg and the general meaninglessness of life.

The theme of indignities committed on women comes up in another form in the stories Miss Lonelyhearts' friends tell in Delehanty's. They seem to be exclusively anecdotes of group rape, of one woman gang-raped by eight neighbors, of another kept in the back room of a speakeasy for three days, until "on the last day they sold tickets to niggers." Miss Lonelyhearts identifies himself with "wife-torturers, rapers of small children." At one point he tries giving his readers the traditional Christian justification for suffering, that it is Christ's gift to mankind to bring them to Him, but he tears up the column.

Ultimately the novel cannot justify or even explain suffering, only proclaim its omnipresence. Lying sick in bed, Miss Lonelyhearts gets a vision of human life: "He found himself in the window of a pawnship full of fur coats, diamond rings, watches, shotguns, fishing tackle, mandolins.

All these things were the paraphernalia of suffering. A tortured high light twisted on the blade of a gift knife, a battered horn grunted with pain." Finally his mind forms everything into a gigantic cross, and he falls asleep exhausted.

The book's desperate cry of pain and suffering comes to a focus in what Miss Lonelyhearts calls his "Christ complex." He recognizes that Christ is the only answer to his readers' letters, but that "if he did not want to get sick, he had to stay away from the Christ business. Besides, Christ was Shrike's particular joke." As Miss Lonelyhearts leaves the office and walks through a little park, the shadow of a lamppost pierces his side like a spear. Since nothing grows in the park's battered earth, he decides to ask his correspondents to come and water the soil with their tears. He imagines Shrike telling him to teach them to pray each morning, "Give us this day our daily stone," and thinks: "He had given his reader many stones; so many, in fact, that he had only one left—the stone that had formed in his gut."

Jesus Christ, Shrike says, is "the Miss Lonelyhearts of Miss Lonelyhearts." Miss Lonelyhearts has nailed an ivory Christ to the wall of his room with great spikes, but it disappoints him: "Instead of writhing, the Christ remained calmly decorative." Miss Lonelyhearts recalls: "As a boy in his father's church, he had discovered that something stirred in him when he shouted the name of Christ, something secret and enormously powerful." Unfortunately, he recognizes, it is not faith but hysteria: "For him, Christ was the most natural of excitements."

Miss Lonelyhearts tells Betty he is "a humanity lover," but Shrike more aptly identifies him a "leper licker." "If he could only believe in Christ," Miss Lonelyhearts thinks, "then everything would be simple and the letters extremely easy to answer." Later he recognizes that "Shrike had accelerated his sickness by teaching him to handle his one escape, Christ, with a thick glove of words." He decides that he has had a part in the general betrayal of suffering mankind: "The thing that made his share in it particularly bad was that he was capable of dreaming the Christ dream. He felt that he had failed at it, not so much because of Shrike's jokes or his own self-doubt, but because of his lack of humility." Miss Lonelyhearts concludes that "with him, even the word Christ was a vanity." When he gets drunk with Doyle, he calls on Christ joyously, and goes home with Doyle to bring the glad tidings to both Doyles, to heal their marriage. He preaches "love" to them and realizes that he is only writing another column, switches to preaching Christ Jesus, "the black fruit that hangs on the crosstree . . . the bidden fruit," and realizes that he is only echoing Shrike's poisoned rhetoric.

What Miss Lonelyhearts eventually achieves, since he cannot believe in the real Christ, and refuses to become a spurious Christ, is Peter's condition. He becomes the rock on which the new church will be founded, but it is the church of catatonic withdrawal. After three days in bed Miss Lonelyhearts attains a state of perfect calm, and the stone in his gut expands until he becomes "an ancient rock, smooth with experience." The Shrikes come to take him to a party at their apartment, and against this rock the waves of Shrike dash in vain. When Mary wriggles on Miss Lonelyhearts' lap in the cab, "the rock remained perfect." At the party he withstands Shrike's newest mockery, the Miss Lonelyhearts Game, with indifference: "What goes on in the sea is of no interest to the rock." Miss Lonelyhearts leaves the party with Betty: "She too should see the rock he had become." He shamelessly promises her marriage and domesticity: "The rock was a solidification of his feeling, his conscience, his sense of reality, his self-knowledge." He then goes back to his sickbed content: "The rock had been thoroughly tested and had been found perfect."

The next day Miss Lonelyhearts is burning with fever, and "the rock became a furnace." The room fills with grace, the illusory grace of madness, and as Doyle comes up the stairs with a pistol Miss Lonelyhearts rushes downstairs to embrace him and heal his crippled leg, a miracle that will embody his succoring all suffering mankind with love. Unable to escape Miss Lonelyhearts' mad embrace, terrified by Betty coming up the stairs, Doyle tries to toss away the gun, and Miss Lonelyhearts is accidentally shot. He falls dragging Doyle down the stairs in his arms.

It is of course a homosexual tableau—the men locked in embrace while the woman stands helplessly by—and behind his other miseries Miss Lonelyhearts has a powerful latent homosexuality. It is this that is ultimately the joke of his name and the book's title. It explains his acceptance of teasing dates with Mary and his coldness with Mary; he thinks of her excitement and notes: "No similar change ever took place in his own body, however. Like a dead man, only friction could make him warm or violence make him mobile." It explains his discontent with Betty. Most of all it explains his joy at being seduced by Fay—"He had always been the pursuer, but now found a strange pleasure in have the roles reversed"—and how quickly the pleasure turns to disgust.

The communion Miss Lonelyhearts achieves with Doyle in Delehanty's consists in their sitting silently holding hands, Miss Lonelyhearts pressing "with all the love he could manage" to overcome the revulsion he feels at Doyle's touch. Back at the Doyles, after Doyle has ripped open Miss Lonelyhearts' fly and been kicked by his wife, they hold hands again, and when Fay comes back in the room she says "What a sweet pair of fairies you guys are." It is West's ultimate irony that the symbolic embrace they manage at the end is one penetrating the body of the other with a bullet.

We could, if we so chose, write Miss Lonelyhearts' case history before the novel begins. Terrified of his stern religious father, identifying with his soft loving mother, the boy renounces his phallicism out of castration anxiety—a classic Oedipus complex. In these terms the Shrikes are Miss Lonelyhearts' Oedipal parents, abstracted as the father's loud voice and the mother's tantalizing breast. The scene at the end of Miss Lonelyhearts' date with Mary Shrike is horrifying and superb. Standing outside her apartment door, suddenly overcome with passion, he strips her naked under her fur coat while she keeps talking mindlessly of her mother's death, mumbling and repeating

herself, so that Shrike will not hear their sudden silence and come out. Finally Mary agrees to let Miss Lonelyhearts in if Shrike is not home, goes inside, and soon Shrike peers out the door, wearing only the top of his pajamas. It is the child's Oedipal vision perfectly dramatized: he can clutch at his mother's body but loses her each time to his more potent rival.

It should be noted that if this is the pattern of Miss Lonelyhearts' Oedipus complex, it is not that of West, nor are the Shrikes the pattern of West's parents. How conscious was West of all or any of this? I would guess, from the book's title, that he was entirely conscious of at least Miss Lonelyhearts' latent homosexuality. As for the Oedipus complex, all one can do is note West's remarks in "Some Notes on Miss Lonelyhearts": "Psychology has nothing to do with reality nor should it be used as motivation. The novelist is no longer a psychologist. Psychology can become much more important. The great body of case histories can be used in the way the ancient writers use their myths. Freud is your Bulfinch; you can not learn from him."

The techniques West uses to express his themes are perfectly suited to them. The most important is a pervasive desperate and savage tone, not only in the imagery of violence and suffering, but everywhere. It is the tone of a world where unreason is triumphant. Telling Miss Lonelyhearts that he is awaiting a girl "of great intelligence," Shrike "illustrated the word *intelligence* by carving two enormous breasts in the air with his hands." When Miss Lonelyhearts is in the country with Betty, a gas station attendant tells him amiably that "it wasn't the hunters who drove out the deer, but the yids." When Miss Lonelyhearts accidentally collides with a man in Delehanty's and turns to apologize, he is punched in the mouth.

The flowering cactus that blooms in this wasteland is Shrike's rhetoric. The book begins with a mock prayer he has composed for Miss Lonelyhearts, and every time Shrike appears he makes a masterly speech: on religion, on escapes, on the gospel of Miss Lonelyhearts according to Shrike. He composes a mock letter to God, in which Miss Lonelyhearts confesses shyly: "I read your column and like it very much." He is a cruel and relentless punster and wit. In his sadistic game at the party, Shrike reads aloud letters to Miss Lonelyhearts. He reads one from a pathetic old woman who sells pencils for a living, and concludes: "She has rheum in her eyes. Have you room in your heart for her?" He reads another, from the paralyzed boy who wants to play the violin, and concludes: "How pathetic! However, one can learn much from this parable. Label the boy Labor, the violin Capital, and so on . . ." Shrike's masterpiece, the brilliant evocation of the ultimate inadequacy of such escapes as the soil, the South Seas, Hedonism, and art, is a classic of modern rhetoric, as is his shorter speech on religion. Here are a few sentences from the latter: "Under the skin of man is a wondrous jungle where viens like lush tropical growths hang along overripe organs and weed-like entrails writhe in squirming tangles of red and yellow. In this jungle, flitting from rock-gray lungs to golden intestines, from liver to lights and back to liver again, lives a bird called the soul.

The Catholic hunts this bird with bread and wine, the Hebrew with a golden ruler, the Protestant on leaden feet with leaden words, the Buddhist with gestures, the Negro with blood."

The other cactus that flowers in the wasteland is sadistic violence. The book's most harrowing chapter, "Miss Lonelyhearts and the Lamb," is a dream or recollection of a college escapade, in which Miss Lonelyhearts and two other boys, after drinking all night, buy a lamb to barbecue in the woods. Miss Lonelyhearts persuades his companions to sacrifice it to God before barbecuing it. They lay the lamb on a flower-covered altar and Miss Lonelyhearts tries to cut its throat, but succeeds only in maiming it and breaking the knife. The lamb escapes and crawls off into the underbrush, and the boys flee. Later Miss Lonelyhearts goes back and crushes the lamb's head with a stone. This nightmarish scene, with its unholy suggestions of the sacrifices of Isaac and Christ, embodies the book's bitter paradox: that sadism is the perversion of love.

Visiting Betty early in the novel, aware "that only violence could make him supple," Miss Lonelyhearts reaches inside her robe and tugs at her nipple unpleasantly. "Let me pluck this rose," he says, "I want to wear it in my buttonhole." In "Miss Lonelyhearts and the Clean Old Man," he and a drunken friend find an old gentleman in a washroom, drag him to a speakeasy, and torment him with questions about his "homosexualistic tendencies." As they get nastier and nastier, Miss Lonelyhearts feels "as he had felt years before, when he had accidentally stepped on a small frog. Its spilled guts had filled him with pity, but when its suffering had become real to his senses, his pity had turned to rage and he had beaten it frantically until it was dead." He ends by twisting the old man's arm until the old man screams and someone hits Miss Lonelyhearts with a chair.

The book's only interval of decency, beauty, and peace is the pastoral idyll of the few days Miss Lonelyhearts spends with Betty in the country. They drive in a borrowed car to the deserted farmhouse in Connecticut where she was born. It is spring, and Miss Lonelyhearts "had to admit, even to himself, that the pale new leaves, shaped and colored like candle flames, were beautiful and that the air smelt clean and alive." They work at cleaning up the place, Betty cooks simple meals, and they go down to the pond to the pond to watch the deer. After they eat an apple that has ominous Biblical overtones, Betty reveals that she is a virgin and they go fraternally to bed. The next day they go for a naked swim; then, with "no wind to disturb the pull of the earth," Betty is ceremonially deflowered on the new grass. The reader is repeatedly warned that natural innocence cannot save Miss Lonelyhearts: the noise of birds and crickets is "a horrible racket" in his ears; in the woods, "in the deep shade there was nothing but death—rotten leaves, gray and white fungi, and over everything a funereal hush." When they get back to New York, "Miss Lonelyhearts knew that Betty had failed to cure him and that he had been right when he had said that he could never forget the letters." Later, when Miss Lonelyhearts is a rock and leaves Shrike's party with Betty, he tries to create a miniature idyll of innocence by taking her

out for a strawberry soda, but it fails. Pregnant by him and intending to have an abortion, Betty remains nevertheless in Edenic innocence; Miss Lonelyhearts is irretrievably fallen, and there is no savior who can redeem.

The book's pace is frantic and its imagery is garish, ugly, and compelling. The letters to Miss Lonelyhearts are "stamped from the dough of suffering with a heart-shaped cookie knife." The sky looks "as if it had been rubbed with a soiled eraser." A bloodshot eye in the peephole of Delehanty's glows "like a ruby in an antique iron ring." Finishing his sermon to the "intelligent" girl, Shrike "buried his triangular face like the blade of a hatchet in her neck." Miss Lonelyhearts' tongue is "a fat thumb," his heart "a congealed lump of icy fat," and his only feeling "icy fatness." Goldsmith, a colleague at the paper, has cheeks "like twin rolls of smooth pink toilet paper." Only the imagery of the Connecticut interlude temporarily thaws the iciness and erases the unpleasant associations with fatness and thumb. As Miss Lonelyhearts watches Betty naked, "She looked a little fat, but when she lifted something to the line, all the fat disappeared. Her raised arms pulled her breasts up until they were like pink-tipped thumbs."

The unique greatness of *Miss Lonelyhearts* seems to have come into the world with hardly a predecessor, but it has itself influenced a great many American novelists since. *Miss Lonelyhearts* seems to me one of the three finest American novels of our century. The other two are F. Scott Fitzgerald's *The Great Gatsby* and Ernest Hemingway's *The Sun Also Rises*. It shares with them a lost and victimized hero, a bitter sense of our civilization's falsity, a pervasive melancholy atmosphere of failure and defeat. If the tone of *Miss Lonelyhearts* is more strident, its images more garish, its pace more rapid and hysterical, it is as fitting an epitome of the thirties as they are the twenties. If nothing in the forties and fifties has similarly gone beyond *Miss Lonelyhearts* in violence and shock, it may be because it stands at the end of the line.

A Cool Million, subtitled "The Dismantling of Lemuel Pitkin," is a comic, even a parody, novel, to some extent a reversion to the world of *Balso Snell.* It tells the story of Lemuel Pitkin, a poor but honest Vermont boy, as he attempts to make his way in the world. As he confronts each experience with the old-fashioned virtues of honesty, sobriety, good sportsmanship, thrift, bravery, chivalry, and kindness, he is robbed, beaten up, mutilated, cheated, and victimized. In an interwoven subplot, Elizabeth Prail, a neighbor who similarly represents decent American girlhood, is sexually mistreated: raped, beaten by a sadist, kidnapped by white slavers and sold into prostitution, turned out to walk the streets, and so forth. Meanwhile their town banker, "Shagpoke" Whipple, a former President of the United States, creates an American fascist movement and takes over the country.

The total effect is that of a prolonged, perhaps overprolonged, jape. The stages of the action are the stages of Lem's dismantling: thrown into jail in a frame-up, he loses all his teeth because the warden believes teeth to be the source of moral infection; rescuing a banker and his daughter from a runaway horse, Lem loses an eye; kidnapped by agents of the Communist International, he is involved in an automobile collision and loses a thumb; trying to save Betty from rape, he is caught in a bear trap that the villain has planted, which costs him a leg, and while unconscious in the trap he is scalped by a Harvard-educated Indian. He is eventually hired as stooge for a vaudeville act and demolished during each performance; when he is hit with a mallet, "His toupee flew off, his eye and teeth popped out, and his wooden leg was knocked into the audience." Eventually Lem is shot down onstage while making a speech for American fascism. As a result of his martyrdom Whipple's Leather Shirts triumph, and Pitkin's Birthday becomes a national holiday, on which the youth of America parade singing "The Lemuel Pitkin Song."

What form the book has comes from these ritual stages of dismemberment, but in a truer sense *A Cool Million* is formless, an inorganic stringing together of comic set-pieces, with the preposterous incidents serving merely to raise the various topics West chooses to satirize. Thus Betty's residence in Wu Fong's brothel sets off pages of comic description, first of the brothel as a House of All Nations, then, when Wu Fong is converted by the "Buy American" campaign of the Hearst newspapers, into an all-American establishment. West joyously describes the regional costumes and decor of each girl at considerable length, concluding with the cuisine: "When a client visited Lena Haubengrauber, it was possible for him to eat roast groundhog and drink Sam Thompson rye. While with Alice Sweethorne, he was served sow belly with grits and bourbon. In Mary Judkin's room he received, if he so desired, fried squirrel and corn liquor. In the suite occupied by Patricia Van Riis, lobster and champagne wine were the rule. The patrons of Powder River Rose usually ordered mountain oysters and washed them down with forty-rod. And so on down the list: while with Dolores O'Riely, tortillas and prune brandy from the Imperial Valley; while with Princess Roan Fawn, baked dog and firewater; while with Betty Prail, fish chowder and Jamaica rum. Finally, those who sought the favors of the 'Modern Girl,' Miss Cobina Wiggs, were regaled with tomato and lettuce sandwiches and gin."

The introduction of a Pike County "ring-tail squealer" and "rip-tail roarer" gives West an opportunity to improvise tall talk and anecdotes concluding: "His bones are bleachin' in the canyon where he fell." The Indian chief who scalps Lem is a Spenglerian philosopher and critic of our gadget civilization, and his speech to the tribe to rouse them for the warpath is a long comic diatribe, culminating in: "But now all the secret places of the earth are full. Now even the Grand Canyon will no longer hold razor blades." Later Lem and Whipple join up with a traveling show exhibiting a Chamber of American Horrors, and West gives himself a chance to describe some of the horrors of American life. In one exhibit, all the materials are disguised: "Paper had been made to look like wood, wood like rubber, rubber like steel, steel like cheese, cheese like glass, and, finally, glass like paper." In another, function is disguised: "The visitor saw flower pots that were really victrolas, revolvers that held candy, candy that held collar buttons and so forth." West here is entirely indiscriminate. The accompanying pageant of American history

consists of sketches "in which Quakers were shown being branded, Indians brutalized and cheated, Negroes sold, children sweated to death," as though these acts were on the order of disguising paper to look like wood.

It is at once comic and depressing, the fitting work of a man Robert M. Coates has called "the most thoroughly pessimistic person I have ever known." If its indictment of American material civilization does not go very deep, its awareness of the precariousness of American freedom does, and the book is perhaps strongest as a political warning. Writing just after the accession of Hitler, West felt the vulnerability of America to totalitarianism disguised as superpatriotism, and he makes it disturbingly convincing. Whipple's bands of the mindless and disaffected, got up in fringed deerskin shirts, coonskin caps, and squirrel rifles, are the same joke as Lena Haubengrauber's clients washing down roast groundhog with Sam Thompson rye, but here it images our nightmare. Recruiting on street corners, Whipple alternates appeals to destroy the Jewish international bankers and the Bolshevik labor unions with shouts of "Remember the Alamo! Remember the Maine!" and "Back to the principles of Andy Jackson and Abe Lincoln!"

In his final tribute to the martyred Lemuel Pitkin at the end of the book, as his storm troops parade down Fifth Avenue, Whipple makes it clear that the true enemy from which his National Revolutionary party has delivered the country is "sophistication." Lem's life represented the expectations of American innocence, frustrated by "sophisticated aliens," and the revolution has been made by those who share Lem's expectations. As such it is the revolt of the frustrated and tormented lower middle class, a fantasy foreshadowing of the riot at the end of *The Day of the Locust.* To become the Horst Wessel of American fascism, in West's ugliest joke, Lem has stepped out of a Norman Rockwell cover for the *Saturday Evening Post.*

What makes this cautionary tale convincing in *A Cool Million* is West's sense of the pervasiveness of American violence. It is like the savagery of Russian life in Leskov or Gorki. We see Betty Prail at twelve, the night her family's house burns down and her parents are killed in the fire. When the firemen finally arrive, drunk, they do nothing to put out the fire. Instead they loot the house while the chief rapes Betty, leaving her naked and unconscious on the ground. She is then sent to an orphan asylum, and put out at fourteen to be a maid in the household of Deacon Slemp, where in addition to her other duties she is enthusiastically beaten twice a week on the bare behind by the Deacon, who gives her a quarter after each beating.

In this world where firemen are looters and rapists and church elders perverts and hypocrites, policemen appear only to beat up the victims of crimes. When Lem is first seized by the police, on his way to the big city to make his fortune, a patrolman clubs him on the head, one detective kicks him in the stomach, and a second kicks him behind the ear; all three actions unrelated to any of the remarks they make to Lem, but rather, natural reflexes. When Lem faints from the wound he received from stopping the runaway horse, he is found by a policeman, who establishes communication by kicking him in the groin. The brutal image of the police in the book is always the raised truncheon, the doubled fist, the foot drawn back.

The weaknesses of the book are perhaps the inevitable weaknesses of the form, jokes that do not come off and failures of tone. Sometimes the book is almost unbelievably corny and heavy-handed. When he is in this mood, West will even have someone address a Chinese in pidgin and be answered in flawless English.

The uncertainty of tone is mainly in regard to sex. When West is openly vulgar, he is fine, but on occasion he seems to smirk, and then he is less fine. A scene between Lem, captured by Wu Fong's men, dressed in a tight-fitting sailor suit, and set up as a homosexual prostitute in the brothel, and his client, a lisping Indian maharajah, is perhaps the most extreme failure. The first rape of Betty by the drunken fire chief is disturbing and effective, but her thousandth rape is boring and meaningless, as comedy, social comment, or even titillation. Betty is almost invariably unconscious when raped, an oddly necrophiliac touch, and sometimes the details lead us to expect a salacious illustration on the next page.

The world West shows us is for the most part repulsive and terrifying. It is his genius to have found objective correlatives for our sickness and fears: our maimed and ambivalent sexuality, our terror of the idiot mass, our helpless empathy with suffering, our love perverted into sadism and masochism.

—*Stanley Edgar Hyman*

West's last book, *The Day of the Locust* (1939), is a novel about a young painter named Tod Hackett, working at a Hollywood movie studio as a set and costume designer, and some people he encounters. These are principally Faye Greener, a beautiful young girl whom he loves; her father Harry, an old vaudeville comic; Earle Shoop, Faye's cowboy beau; Miguel, Earle's Mexican friend who breeds fighting cocks; Abe Kusich, a dwarf racetrack tout; and Homer Simpson, an innocent from the Midwest also in love with Faye. In the course of the novel Harry dies, and Faye and her friends go to live with Homer. The action is climaxed by a wild party at Homer's, after which Faye and Miguel end up in bed. This results, the next day, in Homer's demented murder of a boy, which in turn precipitates a riot in the streets, on which the book ends. The title comes from the plague of locusts visited on Pharaoh in the Book of Exodus.

Like the characters in *Miss Lonelyhearts,* the characters in *The Day of the Locust* tend to be symbolic abstractions, but here with some loss of human reality. Tod, who never quite comes to life (mainly, I think, because of West's efforts to keep him from being autobiographical), represents The Painter's Eye. All through the book he is planning a

great canvas, "The Burning of Los Angeles," which will sum up the whole violent and demented civilization. It is to show the city burning at high noon, set on fire by a gay holiday crowd, who appear carrying baseball bats and torches: "No longer bored, they sang and danced joyously in the red light of the flames." In the foreground, Tod and his friends flee the mob in various characteristic postures: Faye naked and running rather proudly, throwing her knees high; Homer half-asleep; Tod stopping to throw a stone at the crowd. Meanwhile the flames lick avidly "at a corinthian column that held up the palmleaf roof of a nutburger stand."

Faye is nothing like the Fay of *Miss Lonelyhearts* (as the Betty of *A Cool Million* is nothing like the Betty of *Miss Lonelyhearts*—West was overeconomical of names). Faye is seventeen, "a tall girl with wide, straight shoulders and long, swordlike legs." She has "a moon face, wide at the cheek bones and narrow at chin and brow," her hair is platinum-blonde, her breasts are "placed wide apart and their thrust" is "upward and outward," her buttocks look "like a heart upside down." She dresses like a child of twelve, eats an apple with her little finger curled, and has a brain the size of a walnut.

Like Betty in *Miss Lonelyhearts,* Faye represents Nature, but now Nature's appearance of innocence is seen as deceptive, and Faye is as far as can be from Betty. Tod looks at an inviting photograph of her, lying "with her arms and legs spread, as though welcoming a lover," and thinks: "Her invitation wasn't to pleasure, but to struggle, hard and sharp, closer to murder than to love. If you threw yourself on her, it would be like throwing yourself from the parapet of a skyscraper. You would do it with a scream. You couldn't expect to rise again. Your teeth would be driven into your skull like nails into a pine board and your back would be broken. You wouldn't even have time to sweat or close your eyes." What then is Tod's conclusion? "If she would only let him, he would be glad to throw himself, no matter what the cost." Luckily, she never lets him.

All experience rolls off Faye. She smells to Tod like "buckwheat in flower"; when she leans toward him, drooping slightly, "he had seen young birches droop like that at midday when they are over-heavy with sun." When she announces her intention of becoming a call girl, Tod decides that "her beauty was structural like a tree's, not a quality of her mind or heart. Perhaps even whoring wouldn't damage it for that reason." A spell of whoring does not in fact damage it, and when Tod sees her later: "She looked just born, everything moist and fresh, volatile and perfumed." In her natural acceptance of the world of sexuality, she is, as Homer tells Tod proudly, "a fine, wholesome child."

This vision of Nature emphasizes its infuriating invulnerability, and Tod not only wants to smash himself on it, but in other moods, to smash Faye. He thinks: "If he only had the courage to throw himself on her. Nothing less violent than rape would do. The sensation he felt was like that he got when holding an egg in his hand. Not that she was fragile or even seemed fragile. It wasn't that. It was her completeness, her egglike self-sufficiency, that made him want to crush her." Seeing her again, Tod feels: "Her self-sufficiency made him squirm and the desire to break its smooth surface with a blow, or at least a sudden obscene gesture, became irresistible." When Faye disappears at the end of the book, Tod cannot decide whether she has gone off with Miguel or gone back to being a call girl. "But either way she would come out all right," he thinks. "Nothing could hurt her. She was like a cork. No matter how rough the sea got, she would go dancing over the same waves that sank iron ships and tore away piers of reinforced concrete." Tod then produces an elaborate fantasy of waiting in a parking lot to knock Faye unconscious and rape her, and he steps from that into the riot of the book's last scene.

The men around Faye are in their different fashions as mindless as she. Her father, Harry Greener, after forty years in vaudeville and burlesque, no longer has any personality apart from his clowning role. "It was his sole method of defense," West explains. "Most people, he had discovered, won't go out of their way to punish a clown." West invents a superb clown act for him, presented in the form of an old clipping from the Sunday *Times,* but the clowning we see in the book is a more poignant sort, his comic act peddling home-made silver polish.

Faye's cowboy, Earle Shoop, is an image of virile idiocy. "He had a two-dimensional face that a talented child might have drawn with a ruler and a compass. His chin was perfectly round and his eyes, which were wide apart, were also round. His thin mouth ran at right angles to his straight, perpendicular nose. His reddish tan complexion was the same color from hairline to throat, as though washed in by an expert, and it completed his resemblance to a mechanical drawing." His conversation consists of "Lo, thar," "Nope," and "I was only funning."

The Mexican, Miguel, is an image of pure sensuality: "He was toffee-colored with large Armenian eyes and pouting black lips. His head was a mass of tight, ordered curls." When Faye responds to him, "his skin glowed and the oil in his black curls sparkled." Early in the book we see him rhumba with Faye, until jealousy drives Earle to smash him over the head with a stick. Later he tangos with her, a tango that ends in bed. "Mexicans are very good with women," Tod decides, as the moral of the episode.

Homer is the most completely abstracted character in the book. As Mary Shrike in *Miss Lonelyhearts* is entirely reduced to Breasts, so Homer is entirely reduced to an image of Hands, enormous hands independent of his body. We see him waking in the morning: "Every part was awake but his hands. They still slept. He was not surprised. They demanded special attention, had always demanded it. When he had been a child, he used to stick pins into them and once had even thrust them into a fire. Now he used only cold water." We see him plunge his hands into the washbasin: "They lay quietly on the bottom like a pair of strange aquatic animals. When they were thoroughly chilled and began to crawl about, he lifted them out and hid them in a towel." In the bath: "He kept his enormous hands folded quietly on his belly. Although absolutely still, they seemed curbed rather than resting." When Homer cuts his hand opening a can, "The wounded hand

writhed about on the kitchen table until it was carried to the sink by its mate and bathed tenderly in hot water."

When Faye cries at their first meeting, Homer makes "his big hands dance at the end of his arms," and "several times his hands moved forward to comfort her, but he succeeded in curbing them." As he and Faye sit and eat: "His hands began to bother him. He rubbed them against the edge of the table to relieve their itch, but it only stimulated them. When he clasped them behind his back, the strain became intolerable. They were hot and swollen. Using the dishes as an excuse, he held them under the cold water tap of the sink." When Faye leaves, Homer is too bashful to say anything affectionate, but: "His hands were braver. When Faye shook good-bye, they clutched and refused to let go." After she leaves, "His hands kept his thoughts busy. They trembled and jerked, as though troubled by dreams. To hold them still, he clasped them together. Their fingers twined like a tangle of thighs in miniature. He snatched them apart and sat on them."

This garish and remarkable image is built up throughout the book to embody all of Homer's repressed violence; the hands are strangler's hands, rapist's hands. For reasons impossible to imagine or justify, West let it all go to waste. When Homer's violence finally does break out, when Faye's leaving has driven him out of his mind, he kills a boy who has hit him in the face with a stone by stomping him to death, never touching him with his hands.

The most grotesque character in this gallery of grotesques is the dwarf, Abe Kusich. When Tod first meets him, he is wearing perfect dwarf headgear, a high green Tyrolean hat. Unfortunately, "the rest of his outfit didn't go well with the hat. Instead of shoes with long points and a leather apron, he wore a blue, double-breasted suit and a black shirt with a yellow tie. Instead of a crooked thorn stick, he carried a rolled copy of the *Daily Running Horse.*" His tiny size is made pathetic in an image of his catching Tod's attention by tugging at the bottom of his jacket, but it is accompanied by an unbelievable pugnacity, verbal and physical. He is a small murderous animal like Homer's hands, and he too finally erupts into violence, responding to a kick in the stomach from Earle by squeezing Earle's testicles until he collapses.

West's earlier title for **The Day of the Locust** was *The Cheated,* and the latent violence of the cheated, the mob that fires Los Angeles in Tod's picture, and riots in the flesh at the end of the book, is its major theme. The cheated are recognizable by sight in Hollywood: "Their clothing was somber and badly cut, bought from mail-order houses." They stand on the streets staring at passers-by, and "when their stare was returned, their eyes filled with hatred." They are the people who have "come to California to die." At one point Tod wonders "if he weren't exaggerating the importance of the people who come to California to die. Maybe they weren't really desperate enough to set a single city on fire, let alone the whole country." His ultimate discovery is that they are.

Some of the cheated come to Harry's funeral, "hoping for a dramatic incident of some sort, hoping at least for one of the mourners to be led weeping hysterically from the chapel." As he stares at them, "it seemed to Tod that they stared back at him with an expression of vicious, acrid boredom that trembled on the edge of violence." In the book's last scene, the cheated line up by the thousands outside Kahn's Persian Palace Theatre for the première of a new picture. The mob terrifies Tod, and he now recognizes it as a demonic collective entity, unstoppable once aroused except by machine guns. In one of West's rare Marxist slantings, the mob includes no workingmen, but is entirely "made up of the lower middle classes." Tod concludes:

> It was a mistake to think them harmless curiosity seekers. They were savage and bitter, especially the middle-aged and the old, and had been made so by boredom and disappointment.
>
> All their lives they had slaved at some kind of dull, heavy labor, behind desks and counters, in the fields and at tedious machines of all sorts, saving their pennies and dreaming of the leisure that would be theirs when they had enough. Finally that day came. They could draw a weekly income of ten or fifteen dollars. Where else should they go but California, the land of sunshine and oranges?
>
> Once there, they discovered that sunshine isn't enough. They get tired of oranges, even of avocado pears and passion fruit. Nothing happens. They don't know what to do with their time. They haven't the mental equipment for leisure, the money nor the physical equipment for pleasure. Did they slave so long just to go on an occasional Iowa picnic? What else is there? They watch the waves come in at Venice. There wasn't any ocean where most of them came from, but after you've seen one wave you've seen them all. The same is true of the airplanes at Glendale. If only a plane would crash once in a while so that they could watch the passengers being consumed in a 'holocaust of flame,' as the newspapers put it. But the planes never crash.
>
> Their boredom becomes more and more terrible. They realize that they've been tricked and burn with resentment. Every day of their lives they read the newspapers and went to the movies. Both fed them on lynchings, murder, sex crimes, explosions, wrecks, love nests, fires, miracles, revolutions, wars. This daily diet made sophisticates of them. The sun is a joke. Oranges can't titillate their jaded palates. Nothing can ever be violent enough to make taut their slack minds and bodies. They have been cheated and betrayed. They have slaved and saved for nothing.

As the marching Leather Shirts were West's fantasy of American fascism, the vicious mob of the cheated lower middle class is his fantasy of American democracy, and it is overpowering and terrifying. The rest of Hollywood, the cheaters, have no more cultural identity than the "cheated," but their plight is comic or pathetic rather than menacing. They inhabit the Chamber of American Horrors, come to life. They live in "Mexican ranch houses, Samoan huts, Mediterranean villas, Egyptian and Japanese temples, Swiss chalets, Tudor cottages, and every possible combination of these styles." Tod sees "a miniature Rhine

castle with tarpaper turrets pierced for archers. Next to it was a little highly colored shack with domes and minarets out of the *Arabian Nights.*" The house Homer rents is Irish peasant style: "It had an enormous and very crooked stone chimney, little dormer windows with big hoods and a thatched roof that came down very low on both sides of the front door. This door was of gumwood painted like fumed oak and it hung on enormous hinges. Although made by machine, the hinges had been carefully stamped to appear hand-forged. The same kind of care and skill had been used to make the roof thatching, which was not really straw but heavy fireproof paper colored and ribbed to look like straw." The living room is "Spanish," with red and gold silk armorial banners and a plaster galleon; the bedrooms "New England," with spool beds made of iron grained like wood.

The people are as spurious as the houses and things. An old Hollywood Indian called Chief Kiss-My-Towkus speaks a language of "Vas you dere, Sharley?" Human communication is impossible anywhere in Hollywood. At a party of movie people, the men go off to talk shop and at least one woman assumes that they are telling dirty jokes. Harry and Faye are unable to quarrel in words, but have bitter wordless battles in which he laughs insanely, she sings and dances. Even Faye's sensual gesture of wetting her lips with her tongue as she smiles is meaningless. At first Tod takes it to be an invitation, and dreams: "Her lips must taste of blood and salt." Eventually he discovers the truth: "It was one of her most characteristic gestures and very effective. It seemed to promise all sorts of undefined intimacies, yet it was really as simple and automatic as the word thanks. She used it to reward anyone for anything, no matter how unimportant."

One of the clues West gives to his conception of the nature and destiny of his characters is subtly dropped in a comic scene. Tod and Homer meet a neighbor of Homer's, Maybelle Loomis, and her eight-year-old son, Adore, whom she has trained as a performer. He is dressed as an adult, his eyebrows are plucked, and he sings a salacious song with a mechanical counterfeit of sexuality: "When he came to the final chorus, his buttocks writhed and his voice carried a top-heavy load of sexual pain." In a more personal display, Adore makes horrible faces at Homer, and Mrs. Loomis apologizes: "He thinks he's the Frankenstein monster." Adore *is* the Frankenstein monster, and it is he who is killed by Homer in the book's last scene. But Homer too is the Frankenstein monster, getting out of bed "in sections, like a poorly made automaton," and his hands are progeny monsters. Earle is a lesser monster, a wound-up cowboy toy, and Miguel is a phallic Jack-in-the-box. More than any of them, Faye is a Frankenstein monster, a mechanical woman self-created from bits of vanished film heroines, and her invulnerability is the invulnerability of the already dead. Here is the novel's deepest indictment of the American civilization it symbolizes in Hollywood: if the rubes are cheated by the image of an artificially colored orange, Tod is more deeply cheated by a zombie love; our dreams are fantasies of death.

In his article, "Some Notes on Violence," published in *Contact* in 1932, West writes: "What is melodramatic in

European writing is not necessarily so in American writing. For a European writer to make violence real, he has to do a great deal of careful psychology and sociology. He often needs three hundred pages to motivate one little murder. But not so the American writer. His audience has been prepared and is neither **sur**prised nor shocked if he omits artistic excuses for **familiar** events." The action of *The Day of the Locust* is the releasing of springs of violence that have been wound too tight: Abe's sexual maiming of Earle, Miguel smashing Abe against the wall in retaliation, Homer's brutal murder of Adore, the riot of the cheated. All of these are directly or indirectly inspired by Faye: Earle and Abe and Miguel are competing for Faye, Faye has made Homer insane, Homer's act triggers the mob's insanity.

The party scene consists of a progressive stripping of Faye. She receives her five male guests wearing a pair of green silk lounging pajamas with the top three buttons open. By the time she dances with Miguel all the buttons are open. In the succeeding fight her pajamas are badly torn, and she takes off the trousers, revealing tight black lace drawers. When Homer finds her in bed with Miguel, she is naked. It beautifully represents a metaphoric stripping of Faye in the course of the book. Darwin writes that we observe the face of Nature "bright with gladness," and forget the war to the death behind its innocent appearance. Faye is that bright glad face of Nature, and the stripping gradually reveals the violence and death her beauty conceals. The novel is a great unmasking of a death's head.

West's literary techniques in *The Day of the Locust* develop organically out of his themes. The imagery for Hollywood is wild and surrealist. Tod's friend Claude Estee, a successful screen writer, has a lifesize rubber dead horse, bloated and putrefying, in his swimming pool. The supermarket plays colored spotlights on the food: "The oranges were bathed in red, the lemons in yellow, the fish in pale green, the steaks in rose and the eggs in ivory." As Tod walks through the movie lot looking for Faye, it becomes the nightmare of history: stepping through the swinging door of a Western saloon, he finds himself in a Paris street; crossing a bridge marked "To Kamp Komfit," he finds himself in a Greek temple; he walks on, "skirting the skeleton of a Zeppelin, a bamboo stockade, an adobe fort, the wooden horse of Troy, a flight of baroque palace stairs that started in a bed of weeds and ended against the branches of an oak, part of the Fourteenth Street elevated station, a Dutch windmill, the bones of a dinosaur, the upper half of the Merrimac, a corner of a Mayan temple." "A dream dump," he concludes. "A Sargasso of the imagination!"

"Having known something of the Hollywood West saw at the time he was seeing it," Allan Seager has written, "I am of the opinion that *Locust* was not fantasy imagined but fantasy seen." Although West probably invented the specific details of the dead horse and the pale green supermarket fish, the fireproof paper thatch and his old favorite the Trojan Horse, there is a sense in which Seager's remark is true: these things are no more garish than what West actually did see in Hollywood. West's technique in the book is often, as Seager suggests, what the artists call *ob-*

jets trouvés: he finds in reality the symbol he needs, rather than creating it. When *The Day of the Locust* appeared, I recall thinking how masterfully West had invented the bloody sex-drenched details of the cockfight that leads up to the book's final party. Having since been to cockfights, I now know that every symbolic detail was realistically observed, and the object of my admiration in connection with the scene is no longer West's brilliance of invention but his brilliance of selection.

The humor of the book arises out of its themes, the incongruities of Hollywood and its lack of a cultural identity. Standing on the porch of his plantation mansion, Claude Estee cries, "Here, you black rascal! A mint julep," and a Chinese servant promptly brings a Scotch and soda. What do the Gingos, an Eskimo family brought to Hollywood to make retakes of an Arctic film, eat? Naturally, smoked salmon, white fish, and marinated herring, bought at Jewish delicatessens. The spoken language in the book is a tribute to the delicacy of West's ear. It includes Harry Greener's vaudeville jargon: "Joe was laying up with a whisker in the old Fifth Avenue when the stove exploded. It was the broad's husband who blew the whistle." Along with it there is the very different belligerent idiom of Abe Kusich, shouting "No quiff can give Abe Kusich the fingeroo and get away with it," calling Earle a "pee-hole bandit," or boasting after he has incapacitated him, "I fixed that buckeroo." At the same time there is the witty and epigrammatic conversation of Claude and Tod. Typically, Claude describes Mrs. Jenning's brothel as "a triumph of industrial design," Tod answers that he nevertheless finds it depressing, "like all places for deposit, banks, mail boxes, tombs, vending machines," and Claude then improvises on that set theme. Claude is clearly West's ideal vision of himself: "He was master of an involved comic rhetoric that permitted him to express his moral indignation and still keep his reputation for worldliness and wit."

Some of the images in the book are as powerful as any in *Miss Lonelyhearts.* One is bird blood. We see it first as Earle plucks some quail: "Their feathers fell to the ground, point first, weighted down by the tiny drop of blood that trembled on the tips of their quills." It reappears magnified and horrible as the losing cock's beak breaks: "A large bubble of blood rose where the beak had been." Another powerful image is of Homer crying, at first making a sound "like that of a dog lapping gruel," then in his madness sobbing "like an ax chopping pine, a heavy, hollow, chunking noise." A third image is the scene of male communion between Tod and Homer, resembling that between Miss Lonelyhearts and Doyle, and like it a prelude to violence. Tod and Homer leave the party to sit out on the curb, and Homer sits inarticulate, with a "sweet grin on his face," then takes Tod's hand and makes "trembling signals of affection."

The book's most vivid sustained image, perhaps more powerful than anything in *Miss Lonelyhearts,* is the riot, which is nightmarishly sexual as well as threatening. Swept along by the mob, Tod is thrown against a young girl whose clothes have been half torn off. With her thigh between his legs, she clings to him, and he discovers that she is being attacked from behind by an old man who has a hand inside her dress and is biting her neck. When Tod frees her from the old man, she is seized by another man, as Tod is swept impotently by. In another part of the crowd, they are talking with delight of a pervert who ripped up a girl with a pair of scissors, as they hug and pinch one another. Tod finally kicks off a woman trying to hang on to him, and escapes with no more than his leg broken, and a vision of the mob for his painting as "a great united front of screwballs and screwboxes."

Despite this and other very powerful scenes, I think that *The Day of the Locust* ultimately fails as a novel. Shifting from Tod to Homer and back to Tod, it has no dramatic unity, and in comparison with *Miss Lonelyhearts,* it has no moral core. Where Miss Lonelyhearts' inability to stay in Betty's Eden is heartbreaking, Tod's disillusion with Faye is only sobering, and where the end of the former is tragic, the end of this, Tod in the police car screaming along with the siren, is merely hysteric.

There is humor but little joy in West's novels, obsessive sexuality but few consummations (except for that sit-up-and-lie-down doll Betty Prail). The world West shows us is for the most part repulsive and terrifying. It is his genius to have found objective correlatives for our sickness and fears: our maimed and ambivalent sexuality, our terror of

the idiot mass, our helpless empathy with suffering, our love perverted into sadism and masochism. West did this in convincing present-day forms of the great myths: the Quest, the Scapegoat, the Holy Fool, the Dance of Death. His strength lay in his vulgarity and bad taste, his pessimism, his nastiness. West could never have been the affirmative political writer he sometimes imagined, or written the novels that he told his publisher, just before his death, he had planned: "simple, warm and kindly books." We must assume that if West had lived, he would have continued to write the sort of novels he had written before, perhaps even finer ones.

In his short tormented life, West achieved one authentically great novel, *Miss Lonelyhearts,* and three others less successful as wholes but full of brilliant and wonderful things. He was a true pioneer and culture hero, making it possible for the younger symbolists and fantasists who came after him, and who include our best writers, to do with relative ease what he did in defiance of the temper of his time, for so little reward, in isolation and in pain.

Victor Comerchero   (essay date 1964)

SOURCE: *Nathanael West: The Ironic Prophet,* Syracuse University Press, 1964, 189 p.

[*In the following essay, Comerchero discusses autobiographical aspects of West's fiction.*]

Flaubert, for whom West had great admiration, once declared, *"Madame Bovary, c'est moi,"* and *"Madame Bovary n'a rien de moi."* Such an apparent contradiction is resolved when one realizes Flaubert's close identification with his heroine and, at the same time, his tendency to paint character impersonally as if it were pure object.

Such subjectively derived inspiration and such clinical objectivity of execution are even more characteristic of West. Even less farfetched than Flaubert's declarations would have been West's that Balso Snell, John Gilson, Beagle Darwin, Claude Estee, Tod Hackett, Shrike, and Miss Lonelyhearts "are all me and yet none of myself," for there is an element of self-revelation in West's writing so striking that it cannot be ignored. It is so basic an aspect of his artistic method that one cannot completely understand his work without taking note of it, and it is so frequent that it permeates his work. Two passages serve as illustration:

> When a baby, I affected all the customary poses:
> I "laughed the icy laughter of the soul," I uttered "universal sighs"; I sang in "silver-fire verse"; I smiled the "enigmatic smile"; I sought "azure and elliptical routes." In everything I was completely the mad poet. I was one of those "great despisers," whom Nietzsche [sic] loved because "they are the great adorers; they are arrows of longing for the other shore." . . . You understand what I mean: like Rimbaud, I practiced having hallucinations.
>
> . . . . .
>
> Death is a very difficult thing for me to consider sincerely because I find certain precomposed

Dust jackets of the first editions of Nathanael West's works.

judgments awaiting my method of consideration to render it absurd. No matter how I form my comment I attach to it the criticisms sentimental, satirical, formal. With these judgments there goes a series of literary associations which remove me still further from genuine feeling. The very act of recognizing Death, Love, Beauty— all the major subjects—has become, from literature and exercise, impossible. (***Balso Snell***)

It would be easy to dismiss all such remarks as applicable solely to the characters portrayed if their pertinency to West were not so striking, and if there were not a peculiar consistency in the sum total of such remarks. Moreover, one discovers that these analytic passages dotting the portraits of various characters are insufficient in their respective settings to create a single person. Individually, each of West's characters remains a caricature; cumulatively, they create an engrossing picture of a "type," of a "collective man" who has been created in West's own image. What makes West's readers so painfully sensitive to the "Westian man" is an unconscious perception of the identification of author with character. The suggestive power of West's caricatures stems from their incomplete dissociation from real character. In lesser hands such psychoanalytic parallelism might be inartistic and offensive; more important, from a less sensitive intelligence incapable of experiencing and recreating complex, nuanced, and universal responses, such a method would fail to engage our emotions. That it succeeds in doing both is a tribute to West's talent and intelligence.

As one studies these analytic passages, one is struck by the nature of the self-revelation: West fails to use "real" incidents—that is to say, his self-revelation is rarely autobiographical. And when parallels exist between West and his characters, they are so muted as to be scarcely recognizable. Thus Homer's occupation as a hotel clerk vaguely recalls West's term at the Hotel Sutton; and Tod's position as a minor Hollywood designer or Claude Estee's as a successful screen writer is a slight switch on West, the minor Hollywood script writer. But even this highly transformed biographical self-revelation is extremely rare. The infrequency with which he used such experiences seems to be due not only to his antipathy toward pedestrian realism, to a surrealist belief that the subconscious offers a larger and more authentic clue to our being, but also to an innate shyness about dramatizing his objective existence. These factors largely shaped his art and made his creative world a half-world of impressions and mental states rather than one of substantial event. It is not strange, then, to find that West's characters reveal almost nothing about the author's life but a great deal about his psyche. Should this seem out of keeping with a shy temperament, one has only to note how muffled and ambiguous the revelation is to see West's complex attempt to disguise it. For all the exhibitionism of ***Balso Snell,*** West is basically secretive and retiring. Unlike Thomas Wolfe, he never pours forth his soul; and one never feels, with the possible exception, perhaps, in reading ***Balso Snell,*** that his self-revelation is cathartic: character development is neglected and analysis is so brief and pointed that the result is not nuanced character in all its multiplicity but personified attitudes and mental states simply and severely presented.

Intensely preoccupied by a few great problems, West created characters who not only crystallize such problems, but who, by a singular obsession, communicate his own intensity. Thus West uses his characters' grotesque obsessions—sometimes with something trivial, sometimes with something cosmic—to reveal his own. In this respect, one is again forced to use the Flaubertian analogy for purposes of clarification: to the extent that the characters are obsessed and, as a consequence, suffer, they are West; but because their obsession is literary—that is, exaggerated for dramatic purposes and so not exactly his own—they are nothing of him. In any event, it is clear that Westian man is essentially not a product of observation, but one of introspection. As a result of an enormous capacity for self-analysis, West was able to isolate the causes and manifestations of his mental states and to use them in his art. By dissecting his own personality, he was able to articulate psychological problems in sharp and concise terms. He did not, however, deal in generalities. His unique gift was his ability to create a semblance of character out of transfigured mental states. It is the ability to create personification, for in a significant sense West's characters are not created "in the round," with the human complexity which such a rounded portrait would entail; they are distillations. By means of this almost archetypal conception, West was able to recreate these transfigured mental states imagistically, without recourse to analysis. Had his world been more ordered, this ability would possibly have exhibited itself in allegory.

But allegory was impossible in West's disordered world. His characters do not arrange themselves into opposing camps of good and evil, or even of healthy and unhealthy—they are almost universally unhealthy; if there is any categorical division to be made in West's characters, it must be done in terms of their perceptions—those who are aware of "life" (the Westian personae: Balso Snell, Miss Lonelyhearts, Shrike, Tod Hackett, *et al.*) and those who are unaware (the Bettys, Fayes, and Lemuel Pitkins). Even this division is a trifle too neat, but nonetheless useful for purposes of illustration.

This disordered view of life is most evident in ***Balso Snell*** and ***The Day of the Locust,*** and these two works are the furthest from being allegory. That West's characters, once they become representative of an abstract "quality" or *idée fixe,* take on allegorical overtones is demonstrated by Miss Lonelyhearts.

West has described Miss Lonelyhearts as "the portrait of a priest of our time who has a religious experience. His case is classical . . ." and, one might almost add, an allegory of modern man's frustrating search for meaning before the inexplicable existence of evil in this world. Despite West's apparently facetious presentation of Miss Lonelyhearts' quest, it would be an error to believe that he was anything but deadly serious in his statement of such a problem. [In his *Nathanael West: An Interpretive Study,* 1961] James Light has suggested the prevalence of the quest motif in West's novels and has indicated his personal involvement in the theme:

. . . if there is any constant pattern in the novels

of West, it is the pilgrimage around which each novel centers. In each the hero is in search. . . .

> . . . more than likely . . . the reason West's novels are involved in the Quest is his rejection of a heritage, both familial and racial, that burdened West just as Joyce's heritage weighed on that great nay sayer. West's consciousness of his theme is evident from the beginning epigraph of *Balso* . . . and it is as a journey, dominated by a quest which ends in disillusionment, that West's novels should be read.

Tormented by a sense of alienation, his near total, Dadaistic rejection in *Balso Snell* of all possible objects of identification—culture, religion, art, heritage and family—made it inevitable that he would remain a seeker, a "wrestler with doubts." The questers who populate every one of West's novels are merely personae writhing under the same curse as their author. Their suffering troubles the reader not only because West analyzed and vividly recreated the intense neurotic anguish resulting from such a quest, but because he was able to transcend his personal involvement and render the quest in archetypal forms. In keeping with West's cul-de-sac pessimism, there is no Grail at the end of the quest. West had no answers and felt no need to do more than point to the seeker and to the nature of his suffering. "I believe there is a place for the fellow who yells fire and indicates where some of the smoke is coming from without actually dragging the hose to the spot. . . ."

West here is merely justifying a role which his personal vision of life forced upon him. He could never "put out the fire" raised by the problems he treated; the paralyzing despair resulting from awareness and shattered dreams, as well as the presence of cosmic injustice are, among others, for him insoluble problems. Even when his problems become more sociological, as they do in his last novels, West offers no solutions. The reader of *The Day of the Locust* has the terrifying feeling that he is watching the disintegration of a society; the ending with its apocalyptic overtones is part of the horrifying vision. The sense of helplessness he feels, resulting from West's ability to communicate the inevitability of the ending, may mirror West's own feeling. Perhaps some such "fatalism" may explain his willingness merely to point to the danger.

In a less sensitive individual, such a world view might become too insistent, might remain uncolored by subtle dependent attitudes; in West, however, it merely becomes a point of departure that led to the other attitudes and attributes which stamp his characters and his novels as uniquely his. In this respect, Robert M. Coates has pointed out [in his introduction to *Miss Lonelyhearts,* 1933] that "West was fundamentally a pessimist . . . but he carried his pessimism a little further than did most other writers, to the point indeed where it colored his whole outlook on life."

It is natural that West's pessimism should affect his entire world view when we recall that the pessimism is largely the result of discoveries made through introspection. Self-analysis, a method and seemingly a need in West, was also a source of pain: it made him extremely aware of his own

responses, of his helplessness to control them, and of his near total helplessness before the "laws of life." His attitude toward introspection is clear: the consequences of the resultant awareness it brings are anguish or destruction; but those who are without the awareness are ignobly simple-minded:

> With the return of self-consciousness, he knew that only violence could make him supple. It was Betty, however, that he criticized. Her world was not the world and could never include the readers of his column. Her sureness was based on the power to limit experience arbitrarily. Moreover, his confusion was significant, while her order was not.

West's desire and yet inability to solve the riddle of the world is mirrored here as clearly as is the importance and pain of self-consciousness. The partiality West reveals for his own state of mind does not offend; it is not only natural, but a direct consequence of his world view. In a meaningless world, nothing can have absolute meaning; however, a realization of such senseless disorder is more significant than a lack of it, and less dangerous, as West makes clear in *A Cool Million.* Neither alternative allows man to possess any great dignity, but somehow one feels that West gives whatever dignity is possible to those with awareness.

This theme of self-consciousness and its concomitant awareness rings like a bell throughout his work; and it is no accident that almost all his primary characters, with the deliberately striking offset exception of Lemuel Pitkin, are tortured by their introspective capacity. That it saves none of them and figuratively destroys them all is particularly revealing of West's own attitude.

Individually, each of West's characters remains a caricature; cumulatively, they create an engrossing picture of a "type," of a "collective man" who has been created in West's own image.

—*Victor Comerchero*

There is little doubt that the destruction of his protagonists increases the power of West's novels; it nevertheless fails to render their fate tragic. More important, however, the characters do not gain one's sympathy—at least no more of it than they already possessed—by being destroyed. More often than not, their fate fails to engage one, and sometimes it strikes one as comic.

The characters in *Balso Snell* are too ridiculous ever to trouble West's audience, but even in *Miss Lonelyhearts* and *The Day of the Locust* reader identification diminishes as the novels progress. Not only does the reader become less and less sympathetic to Miss Lonelyhearts' plight resulting from his increasing sensitivity to the letters, but his death itself in no way regains this lost sympathy. It does not increase his stature; if anything, it is so grotesquely comic that it almost disengages the reader. In like fashion, while Tod Hackett's consciously degrading fixation on Faye Greener both amuses and vaguely irritates, his breakdown at the end of the novel in no way engages the reader's emotions on the individual level; it merely adds to the general frenetic ending of the riot scene. Here again, one sees West's own ambivalent attitude toward introspection revealing itself. West did not like this "Hamletism" in himself; even though it was significant and necessary, it was too painful to be pleasant. There is an element of bitterness and of wistful regret, albeit carefully disguised, in the self-mockery of the following passage:

> An intelligent man finds it easy to laugh at himself, but his laughter is not sincere if it is thorough. If I could be Hamlet, or even a clown with a breaking heart 'neath his jester's motley, the role would be tolerable. But I always find it necessary to burlesque the mystery of feeling at its source; I must laugh at myself, and if the laugh is "bitter", I must laugh at the laugh. The ritual of feeling demands burlesque and, whether the burlesque is successful or not, a laugh. . . .
> (*Balso Snell*)

Even without Jack Sanford's remark [quoted in James Light's *Nathanael West: An Interpretive Study*] that West "hated . . . above all himself," such passages in West's novels would leave one with the uneasy feeling that West did not like himself. For him, such self-contempt is no crime; it is almost praise. It reflects the extreme idealist's usual dissatisfaction with himself for being less than perfect.

Seeing only the disparity between what he was and what he felt man should be, West tended to emphasize the ignoble aspects of his personality; he magnified their existence until minor flaws became great crimes. In a sense, he seems to have inherited that complex mixture of pride and metaphysical unworthiness that is a part of Jewish heritage. In West, this sense of unworthiness is magnified and generalized, for he was too realistic to fail to see that the bulk of mankind was considerably less perfect than himself. This realization did not, of course, make it easier for him to bear his own sexuality, artifice, self-deception, and a host of other real or imaginary faults. He had a certain prophetic Jewish idealism and intolerance that prevented him from extenuating man's frailty. He could have no sympathy for his faults and hence little for himself. In this respect, Beagle Darwin makes a comment which is especially revealing of West: "If I treated you savagely, I treated myself no gentler."

It is a deceptive remark when applied to West, for it glosses over his compassion. West's vision of man and of himself was a painful one, resulting in the seething indignation, in the savagely mocking laughter that marks his work. Yet he had a sense of sympathy for his characters—and for himself—which paradoxically seemed to forgive a great deal. James F. Light has attempted to explain the reader's ambivalent attitude toward West's characters by balancing West's sympathy toward his characters with his repulsion toward them:

> His [West's] attitude towards his characters shows sympathy, yet, at the same time, repulsion. Unlike his master Dostoevsky, West seldom seems able really to love the sordid people he depicts. Like Miss Lonelyhearts, West appears to be repelled by the primitive pathos he portrays, but unlike Miss Lonelyhearts, West seems unable to overcome the repugnance he feels for such sordid humanity. Sympathy, pity, he could give, but identification was beyond him. He could want to love, to lick lepers, but do it, he could not.

Light's remark is revealing; but suggesting as it does a West closer to Miss Lonelyhearts than to Tod Hackett, closer to Christ than to the Old Testament prophets, it fails to seize upon West's anger and violent indignation. Nothing so well explains the ruthlessness of West's portrait, the savagery of his indictment, or the "ascetic, saint-like aversion to the flesh that comes through on nearly every page" of his novels, as the contention that West felt compelled to assume a prophetic role. Yet, for all his prophetic idealism and intolerance, he lacked prophetic fervor or a prophet's sense of righteousness; he was too compassionate, too understanding, too humanitarian for either. It would not be stretching the matter unduly to apply the following comment, by Miss Lonelyhearts about himself, to West: "Humanity . . . I'm a humanity lover. All the broken bastards . . ."

This tension between abstract intolerance and concrete love of humanity is not a new phenomenon in human nature, but it is an important one in West. It explains a reader's mixed feelings about West's characters and novels—feelings, paralleling those of the author, of compassion in spite of oneself and in spite of "objective reality." Had West not had the ability to feel sympathy for basically unsympathetic characters, the reader would not care about his characters. Because of West's vision, unlovely as the characters are, the reader still cares about them; he cares because he feels that West's indignation is not aroused by his characters but by the system, whether socioeconomic or metaphysical, which creates such characters. With the exception of the already mentioned degree of personal distaste West had for himself and therefore for one of his personae, West did not create unsympathetic grotesques because of a personal animus; he created them because they were emblematic of a cancer in the body politic and, at the same time, of the absurdity of existence. As a result, the reader's revulsion remains generalized. Even when dealing with sordid abnormalities, West generally charged the portrait with a compassion that more than counterbalanced the revulsion.

[In the *New Yorker,* May 18, 1957] Norman Podhoretz has summed up West's ability to transcend both cynicism and sentimentality in order to arrive at a "strongminded, intelligent compassion":

> It [the comedy of West] is also the animating principle of true sympathy, which is why West's "particular kind of joking" has so deep a kinship with the particular kind of compassion that is allied to intelligence and is therefore proof against the assaults of both sentimentality and cynicism.

Any explanation for West's peculiar ambivalence is, of course, only partial, for it is difficult to isolate psychological reasons from esthetic ones. Certainly, as Light suggests, this tension between intolerance and love of humanity existed in West the man; but there is a hint that it was also a conscious intention. In an early essay on Euripides, West praised him for his fusion of feeling and satire, and he probably considered such a fusion worthy of imitation. The following remark from *Balso Snell* is revealing: "What more filled with the essentials of great art? —pity and irony." Whatever the explanation, this fusion of compassion and indignation is the trademark of West's novels. All other factors notwithstanding, it is the natural consequence of the author's complex self-concept and projective method of creating character.

To say that West "created character" is to overstate the matter. West created character by donning masks. This tendency to speak through personae may not be applicable to his minor characters, who are different in kind rather than degree, but it is applicable to most of his male characters: the guide, John Gilson, Beagle Hamlet Darwin, and Balso Snell; Shrike and Miss Lonelyhearts; and Tod Hackett and Claude Estee in *The Day of the Locust.* Only such an explanation, it seems, can account sufficiently for the consistency of these characters and for the parallels their attitudes have with those of the author.

While it is not the object here to determine the exact degree of correspondence between West and his characters, there is much evidence to indicate that West's self-revelatory attitudes had a way of cropping up in disguised form. For example, West's hatred of "three-name women writers (Thyra Samter Winslow, Viola Brothers Shore)" reached print in the form of a conversation in Delehanty's bar:

> One of them was complaining about the number of female writers.
>
> "And they've all got three names," he said. "Mary Roberts Wilcox, Ella Wheeler Catheter, Ford Mary Rinehart. . . ."
>
> Then some one started a train of stories by suggesting that what they all needed was a good rape. (*Miss Lonelyhearts*)

The most striking example of West's true voice unintentionally emerging is found in his treatment of Jewish characters. In every one of West's novels, even in his finished masterpiece, *Miss Lonelyhearts,* there is a Jew to be found who is unsympathetic. In fact, it would be more accurate to say that West has created only offensive Jewish portraits. This fact could be dismissed as a not too uncommon manifestation of Jewish anti-Semitism if it were merely that; but it is not. Nor is it merely a defensive device, although it certainly seems to be that in part. Rather, it seems to be the most startling example of West's need to treat personal problems in his work. What is so prominent about West's treatment of Jewish characters is his lack of detachment. His disguise is unsuccessful because it is strained.

Again one finds the peculiar tension in West's work between candor and secretiveness. In the revealing work

Balso Snell, with the author apparently conscious of what he is doing, there is a secretive passage which reflects West's sensitivity to the entire Jewish question, to the complex play of identification and alienation often felt by Jews who have lost their faith. West's self-consciousness at being Jewish was too personal and too painful for him to reveal; he must disguise it. But as always, West's disguises are weakest when there is greatest involvement. In this passage, his involvement is so great that his objectivity fails him. The result is an overly violent reaction, which by its extremity is only that much more revealing. In this respect, the extreme Jewish caricatures West created are an example of his attempt at detachment. By creating obnoxious Jewish characters, he perhaps felt that he was proving his lack of involvement in the complex Jewish problem. It is interesting to see how his Jewish self-consciousness reveals itself through the mask when, early in *Balso Snell,* West introduces the problem:

> "What a hernia! What a hernia!"
>
> The guide began to sputter with rage and Balso tried to pacify him by making believe he had not meant the scenery. "Hernia," he said, rolling the word on his tongue. "What a pity childish associations cling to beautiful words such as hernia, making their use as names impossible. Hernia! What a beautiful name for a girl! Hernia Hornstein! Paresis Pearlberg! Paranoia Puntz! How much more pleasing to the ear [and what other sense should a name please?] than Faith Rabinowitz or Hope Hilkowitz."
>
> But Balso had only blundered again. "Sirrah!" the guide cried in an enormous voice, "I am a Jew! and whenever anything Jewish is mentioned, I find it necessary to say that I am a Jew. I'm a Jew! A Jew!"
>
> "Oh, you mistake me," Balso said, "I have nothing against the Jews. I admire the Jews; they are a thrifty race. Some of my best friends are Jews." But his protests availed him little until he thought to quote C. M. Doughty's epigram. "The semites," Balso said with great firmness, "are like to a man sitting in a cloaca to the eyes, and whose brows touch heaven."

That West himself probably could never have uttered the remark, "I am a Jew! and whenever anything Jewish is mentioned, I find it necessary to say that I am a Jew. I'm a Jew! A Jew!" should not lead one to dismiss his identification with the guide. Certainly he was not that "type" of Jew, and he probably felt ashamed of and disgusted by such a person. However, this is beside the point, for writers are selective; they do not include in their works everything that they abhor. Nevertheless, by mocking an aspect of his existence, West had again dealt with a troublesome personal problem.

The subsequent remark by Balso Snell is arresting because Balso mouthes the usual non-Jewish line in an awkward situation. It is unnecessary to point out that West could never take such an approach; it is important, however, to make clear that Balso is the character with whom West is most closely identified throughout the novel. Furthermore, there is no reason to suppose that he has dropped his identification here. On the contrary, he seems to have increased it in order to show the impossibility of solving, and the ridiculousness of, the entire problem—of the guide's response, and of Balso's as well. He is merely using satiric irony and using two masks alternately in order to describe a real problem and to ridicule it out of existence by ironically pointing out the absurdity of both sides.

Such use of extreme masks is not unusual for West. He employs basically but two kinds of masks: the hopelessly unconscious and naïve, and the neurotically introspective. In both instances, the extremity of the posture is used to enhance the irony. West abruptly moves from the mask of naïveté to the mask of introspection—by far the more common one—in the person of John Gilson. Here West picks up a theme he is never to put down: self-consciousness and awareness. John Gilson's diary introduces the theme, and it never leaves the center of the journalistic stage thereafter. Two pages later, there comes the passage beginning "An intelligent man finds it easy to laugh at himself," a passage so tensely and mockingly self-conscious that one feels the author, in the manner of Rimbaud and the surrealists, must constantly have scrutinized himself as if he were another individual.

The consequences of the theme of self-consciousness seem so to have preoccupied West that he literally stops the movement of the novel to include "THE PAMPHLET," which is little more than a set of variations on the theme. He does not even bother to dramatize his self-revelation; his voice, for all its comic overtones, comes through the mask with disturbing clarity:

> While living with me, Saniette accepted my most desperate feats in somewhat the manner one watches the marvelous stunts of acrobats. Her casualness excited me so that I became more and more desperate in my performances. A tragedy with only one death is nothing in the theatre—why not two deaths? Why not a hundred? With some such idea as this in mind I exhibited my innermost organs: I wore my heart and genitals around my neck. At each exhibition I watched carefully to see how she received my performance—with a smile or with a tear. Though I exhibited myself as a clown, I wanted no mistakes to be made; I was a tragic clown.

> I have forgotten the time when I could look back at an affair with a woman and remember anything but a sequence of theatrical poses—poses that I assumed, no matter how aware I was of their ridiculousness, because they were amusing. All my acting has but one purpose, the attraction of the female.

> If it had been possible for me to attract by exhibiting a series of physical charms, my hatred would have been less. But I found it necessary to substitute strange conceits, wise and witty sayings, peculiar conduct. Art for the muscles, teeth, hair, of my rivals.

Though West has created an amusing passage, and one which introduces themes and characteristics recurrent in later works, his use of the mask here is rather pedestrian. One must turn to the Beagle Darwin passages of ***Balso***

Snell to see greater dexterity. Instead of using a mask to disguise a rather bare confession, as in "THE PAMPHLET," West employs two masks simultaneously, with one mask serving to analyze the other. Thus a close reading of the passage reveals that Janey Davenport, while holding the center of the stage, never actually speaks during the scene. Her words and thoughts are the figment of Beagle Darwin's imagination; it is he who, in the first letter, speaks for her and in the second, for himself. But West does not stop here. Characteristically, he pushes reality to an extreme that renders it absurd.

Introspection and imagined analysis of another person are not rare, but Beagle (whose middle name, significantly, is Hamlet), in an excess of self-conscious introspection, dons the mask of Janey Davenport not only to analyze her but to have her analyze him. For all the apparent sophistication of Beagle's approach, his naïve egoism is unusually prominent. But West seems to be trying to do more than reveal the naïveté of exaggerated sophistication. By filtering knowledge three times—through West to Beagle, who imagines Janey analyzing him—West has made the very concept of "projective" analysis, of refracted perceptions, idiotic; and, at the same time, he has revealed how futile and egocentric awareness really is. It would take someone of West's talent and pessimism to give the irony that final unpleasant twist. To compound the joke, this bit of introspective delicacy takes place in a dream within a dream.

In its over-all context, the opening line of the letter is a fine example of West's ironic power: "Darling Janey: You persist in misunderstanding me. Please understand. . . ." The substance of the self-revelatory mask, however, occurs a few paragraphs later:

> The ridiculous, the ridiculous, all day long he talks of nothing else but how ridiculous this, that, or the other thing is. And he means me. I am absurd. He is never satisfied with calling other people ridiculous, with him everything is ridiculous—himself, me. Of course I can laugh at Mother with him, or at the Hearth; but why must my own mother and home be ridiculous? I can laugh at Hobey, Joan, but I don't want to laugh at myself. I'm tired of laugh, laugh, laugh. I want to retain some portion of myself unlaughed at. There is something in me that I won't laugh at. I won't. I'll laugh at the outside world all he wants me to, but I won't, I don't want to laugh at my inner world.

One could continue to substantiate West's use of the mask to the point of tedium. Perhaps the most striking of numerous examples dealing with self-laughter is this glimpse of Harry Greener:

> He began to practice a variety of laughs, all of them theatrical, like a musician tuning up before a concert. He finally found the right one and let himself go. It was a victim's laugh.

West's mark is on Harry as it is on all his characters. It is his voice that is vaguely heard, and it is this voice that stamps the characters as uniquely his. One cannot understand "Westian man" without hearing the voice and the peculiar barking laugh. One is not offended by West's repeated projection of his own image: his relatively small output, his irony, his ability to assume intriguing poses—in essence, his complexity and the incompleteness of his revelation preclude this.

If one attempts to explain the dramatic intensity of West's work, it must be done not only in terms of his style but in terms of the complex and ironic personality behind it. West seems to have had a peculiar schism in his make-up which left his emotions and intellect at war with each other. Thus, for all his emotional involvement, his savagery and bitterness, one finds an intellectual detachment which gave him his great ability to mock emotions at their source. As early as *Balso Snell,* and perhaps there most prevalently, one finds this peculiar schism.

The split had a skeptical base: in such a senseless world, how could anyone take anything seriously? As a result, in his life as in his work, West's "particular kind of joking" was intended to show that the universe is always "rigged" against men and that their efforts against it are absurd. West's was the idealistic humanitarian's cynical laugh at himself and the world in an attempt to deny his own involvement in an agonizing perception. West mocked those aspects of existence that were most painful to him; as expected, the mockery became more violent as it became more personal. Thus, in *Balso Snell,* the most surrealistic of West's novels, and the product of his youth wherein one would expect the greatest emotional involvement, one finds him dissipating his intensity, as in the Saniette passages, through exuberant laughter.

The exaggerated expression characteristic of the entire novel is, to a large extent, defensive. West's adolescent identification with his characters was so strong, it was natural, West being the person he was, that it should reveal itself in such a manner. Moreover, as Fowlie has suggested, "There is a significant *rapprochement,* quite easy to make, between the adjectives *clowning* and *surrealist.* " But the pose of boisterous good humor was so unnatural to West that it could not be sustained. He felt too deeply the problems he was dealing with, and this confining pose so prevented him from treating the problems seriously that he employed it only once again in *A Cool Million.*

In *Miss Lonelyhearts* and *The Day of The Locust,* West assumed a pose more congenial to his basically serious nature. He was able to do so because he had moved away from surrealism (more so in the latter novel), because the works were the result of more mature conviction, and because these novels dealt with sociological as well as with generally insoluble psychological and philosophical problems—with the "human condition." The difficulties involved in a too boisterous expression of social criticism during the thirties are revealed in *A Cool Million.* Speculation as to the reasons for his growing "seriousness" aside, one clear impression emerges: West's examination of the human condition grew increasingly cool in his two major works. He was no longer suffering from the adolescent *Weltschmerz* he exhibited in *Balso Snell*; he no longer seemed to be the agonized young man who but recently discovered the presence of evil; he was, rather, in these works, a mature commentator who still remained involved in contemplation. In essence, he could treat the problems he dealt with seriously—within the limits of his proclivity

to mockery—and with greater intensity, because of his increased detachment. That he must continue to treat them is attested to by their recurrence.

Too realistic to shut his eyes, he was forced to express his particular world view; and whether accurate or not, his central message that life is empty and dreadful runs throughout all his works. The absoluteness of West's disillusionment paradoxically comforted him: prepared for the worst, he was hardly likely to be surprised. Defensive as his pessimism possibly was, it seems to have had as its wellspring his humanitarian idealism and his tender mentality. If, because of the depth of his pessimism, West seems to reveal a surrealistic sense of futility and nihilism—*Balso Snell* is thoroughly destructive, and Shrike is a confirmed philosophic nihilist—one must never forget that West was a reflector of nihilism, not a disciple of it—another way of saying that, like the Dadaists and early surrealists, he was a forerunner of later writers of the absurd. Life was futile and senseless; hope was the greatest delusion; and, as with all delusions, it inevitably led to despair or destruction.

But West could not dress his pessimistic world view in serious garb. A straightforward, conscientiously held and delivered pessimism is too obviously a sign of total engagement; it too patently reveals the holder's emotional state. In his work, as in his life, he was embarrassed by his emotions. He did not, however, try to hide his pessimism—he felt it much too deeply to be able to do so—he merely tried to disguise his involvement in it. This camouflage he accomplished by "escaping" into irony.

To explain this ironic response as the natural consequence of a basically retiring temperament is to force the explanation: some of it undoubtedly results from symbolist and surrealist elements in his art. Yet, there is an element of secretiveness in West so considerable that it is difficult to resolve its existence alongside an admirable candor without turning to his low self-esteem. In these terms, his reticence not only becomes almost admirable, it also reemphasizes his extreme sensitivity, a sensitivity so complex that the man would be more interesting than his work, were his work less the reflection of the man.

To classify this discussion of West's use of the mask as an example of the "intentional fallacy" appears to be too easy. The entire concept seems much more applicable to lyric poetry than to fiction. To insist on separating the author from his work in West's case is to insist on a fractional interpretation. One has great difficulty in understanding the subtle forces operating on West's apparently unsubtle characters unless one includes the author in any analysis of his work. In explaining the existence of one of the most powerful aspects of West's work—the suggestion of unspoken depths in his characters, or why his grotesques, while seeming to fail on the superficial level of reality, reveal a deeper one—it is necessary to turn to the subjective nature of his creation and to his ability to render such personal inspiration in enduring forms.

A. M. Tibbetts   (essay date 1965)

SOURCE: "Nathanael West's 'The Dream Life of Balso

Snell'," in *Studies in Short Fiction,* Vol. II, No. 2, Winter, 1965, pp. 105-12.

[*In the following essay, Tibbetts offers a thematic and stylistic analysis of West's novel.*]

The Dream Life of Balso Snell is usually called a novel, but it is actually no more than a long short story. It was Nathanael West's first major work, written before he was thirty, and it is important mainly for an understanding of West's later fiction, especially *Miss Lonelyhearts* and *The Day of the Locust.* The themes and techniques that West used in these novels are present in embryonic form in *The Dream Life of Balso Snell.* West is now a popular subject for criticism, and many critics believe that he was an excellent novelist and satirist. Most important among these critics is James Light, who has written the best extended evaluation of the *Works.* Light's belief is that *Balso Snell* is the story of a Quest, that Balso is "cynically" searching "for a central unity, an Over Soul, that will make the meaninglessness of multiplicity into the ultimate truth of some essential oneness." He also thinks that the story is "a rejection of the artistic, the rational, and the spiritual pretensions of man. In revealing man's ultimate phoniness, *Balso* emphasizes the illogic and confusion of man's dream life." Furthermore, Light believes that the story is a valid satire.

In this essay, I hope to prove, with two arguments, that Light has missed the mark in interpreting *Balso Snell.* First, I believe that West's main theme—in this story as in his novels—is centered on the *fractured personality,* a person who is cut off from humanity and whose world is without sanity or meaning. Such is the case with Miss Lonelyhearts, the hero of West's second novel, and also with most of the major characters in *The Day of the Locust.* Second, I wish to show that, owing to this disorientation of its characters, the satire of *Balso Snell* is rendered invalid.

The character of Balso Snell is himself unimportant, but he does serve to introduce the persons who help to create West's theme of the fractured personality. [In *Accent,* Autumn, 1957] Edward Schwartz claimed that the story seemed to him to be a "strangely detached self-study: it's as though West were two persons, one acting inside the dream, the other observing himself from the outside." Schwartz hit upon the fundamental pattern of the story, although he did not carry his analysis far enough. There are three persons instead of two, three representations of the same type of fractured personality. Each "person" (man) appears as the leading character of a small tale that is embedded in Snell's "dream life."

The first of these tales is told in diary form by John Raskolnikov Gilson, who meets Snell in the dream. Writes Gilson: "I am insane. I [the papers had it CULTURED FIEND SLAYS DISHWASHER] am insane." Gilson tells of buying a knife to kill an idiot, an ugly dishwasher who lives on the top floor of a theatrical rooming house. He catches the dishwasher in a drunken sleep and cuts his throat. Then, driven by panic, he runs out of the house and throws the knife into the river. When the knife is gone, he becomes happy.

Although Gilson's mind is wildly disordered, he yearns for order. He kills for several specific reasons. His imagination is a "wild beast" that cries for freedom: "I am continually tormented by the desire to indulge some strange thing, perceptible but indistinct, hidden in the swamps of my mind." He is obsessed by the psychological geometry of order: "Man spends a great deal of time making order out of chaos, yet insists that the emotions be disordered." The order-disorder of things, ideas, and emotions haunts him. He wants both to scatter and carefully to arrange the elements of his existence. He says: "Order is the test of sanity." He had killed to remain sane because the dishwasher "disturbed my sense of balance. I killed him thinking his death would permit me to regain my balance. My beloved balance!"

Gilson's life is dominated by the need to suffer. He lives in the theatrical rooming house, an unpleasant place, because he wants to be miserable. He describes himself before the murder: "I was a bundle of physical and mental tics. I climbed into myself like a bear into a hollow tree, and lay there long hours, overpowered by the heat, odor, and nastiness of I."

Laughter and sex also influence Gilson's life. He believes that it is terrible to hear a man laugh, worse than to hear him cry. For laughter can get out of hand, leading to hysteria. He tells of hearing a singer start laughing in the devil's serenade from *Faust.* The singer could not stop laughing. It was the hideous laughter of the dishwasher that first made Gilson want to kill him. Nor could Gilson control his sexual drive. He does the murder naked and notices his own sexual stimulation. At the end of his story, after he has thrown the knife into the river, he "turns" into a pretty young girl in sexual heat. He swings his hips for sailors passing by and postures like a prostitute. He sits on a bench alone, as a girl, "all silk and perfumed, pink lace."

There is no question but that John Raskolnikov Gilson is insane. He believes his mother is crazy because she rolls on the floor in grief at what he has done. Her kind of sanity, says Gilson coolly, means disordered thoughts and emotions; while his thoughts and emotions are "arranged, valued, placed."

All the forces of life—both civilized and "natural"—act uncontrollably upon Gilson, as they do upon the unidentified person (whom I shall call *X*) in the second tale within the novella. *X* is another fractured personality. Like Gilson, *X* has trouble with his emotions. More accurately, he cannot find them; he searches for them but comes away "empty-handed." His failure to find them he considers a sign of his intelligence. He feels no emotion at death; the death of his beloved does not move him.

As an exponent of head-over-heart, *X* finds it necessary to combat human feelings: "But I always find it necessary to burlesque the mystery of feeling at its source; I must laugh at myself, and if the laugh is 'bitter,' I must laugh at the laugh. The ritual of feeling demands burlesque. . . ." It is in this episode that we meet the first of West's women that torment his protagonists in the novels. Saniette is quiet, calm, resigned—she takes the beatings by *X* with "a slow, kind smile"—and, worst of all, she is optimistic. It is her optimism for which her lover cannot forgive her, and he is pleased when she dies and death proves her optimism false.

Saniette caused only part of the immense irritation that *X* feels. It is life itself that irritates him to hysteria and despair. He tells Saniette: "If I could only turn irritation into pain; could push the whole thing into insanity and so escape. . . . I can find no relief." Saniette does not understand, even though he beats her to assist her reasoning powers. He had explained to her how life maddened him, and later he explains how he is driven (like Gilson) by sex:

> "When you think of me, Saniette," I said, "think of two men—myself and the chauffeur within me. This chauffeur is very large and dressed in ugly ready-made clothing. His shoes, soiled from walking about the streets of a great city, are covered with animal ordure and chewing gum. His hands are covered with coarse woollen gloves. On his head is a derby hat.
>
> The name of this chauffeur is The Desire to Procreate.
>
> He sits within me like a man in an automobile. His heels are in my bowels, his knees on my heart, his face in my brain. His gloved hands hold me firmly by the tongue; his hands, covered with wool, refuse me speech for the emotions aroused by the face in my brain.
>
> From within, he governs the sensations I receive through my fingers, eyes, tongue and ears.
>
> Can you imagine how it feels to have this cloth-covered devil within one? While naked, were you ever embraced by a fully clothed man? Do you remember how his button-covered coat felt, how his heavy shoes felt against your skin? Imagine having this man inside of you, fumbling and fingering your heart and tongue with wool-covered hands, treading your tender organs with stumbling soiled feet."

The Desire to Procreate drives *X* to fantastic posings. He performs, acts, postures; and Saniette is his audience. He performs, he says, to attract the female. Women have caused him to do extravagant and extraordinary things, and the fantastic has become an obsession.

The story of *X,* which is mainly a flashback (Saniette is already dead as his story opens) closes with his beating her.

Beagle Darwin, a third fractured personality, appears in the life of Janey Davenport, another girl like Saniette, although probably prettier and younger. Janey came to Paris to get experiences and to learn French, but Darwin got her with child. She is an innocent. She loves her man and she wants very badly for him to love her fully and with tenderness. But he wants only her body, and instead of love he gives her satire and mockery. When she tells him she is pregnant, he laughs it off as a joke. Janey jumps from the fourth floor of her hotel and dies. A cab runs over her already dead body. Darwin comes upon the scene, recognizes Janey's pajamas, and retires confused. How shall he act? People will come to tell him of Janey's death. What can he say in the face of all these irritations?

He goes to a café and gets drunk. The whole affair becomes very funny to him and he begins, in his mind, to act and show off in preparation for the time when "they" come to tell him of Janey's death. It will be a great joke. Then he feels sorry for himself—life is a farce and he a compulsive clown. In his mind, he acts the clown before an applauding audience.

So far, I have ignored the plot of the story of which the three tales are a part. Perhaps *plot* is too strong a word, but there is a story line of sorts. It begins as Balso Snell (a poet) finds the ancient wooden horse of Troy and enters it by the anus. He finds himself in a real intestine and starts to meet strange people. First he meets a guide who is proudly a Jew. He and the guide insult each other for a time and then start travelling together up the intestine. They discuss art, the guide delivering a lecture on no-feet in nature. Balso, wearying of this, tears loose from the guide's clutch and flees.

As he runs up the intestine, he spies a strange figure, naked except for a derby stuck with thorns. This is Maloney the Areopagite, a self-styled catholic mystic, who is trying to crucify himself with thumbtacks. Maloney is busily teaching himself to suffer and to think on the lowliest of martyrs. He is writing a biography of Saint Puce, a martyred flea who began and ended his life under the arm of the Lord. He tells the story of Puce's martyrdom, breaking down at the end. Balso, not particularly affected, says that Maloney is morbid; he should stop thinking about such things and take cold showers.

Balso leaves the sobbing Maloney and continues up the intestine. Turning a bend, he sees a small boy hiding something in a hollow tree—it is the dairy of John Raskolnikov Gilson, presented as a theme for the boy's eighth grade English class, which is taught by Miss McGeeney. The diary blends into the Crime Journal, which is also called *The Making of a Fiend.*

After reading Gilson's story, Balso puts it back in the tree and wanders for a while. He is interrupted by Gilson himself, who is in short pants and looks less than twelve years old. The boy claims he wrote his "ridiculous story" as a Russian concoction because Miss McGeeney reads Russian novels and he wants to sleep with her. He has been quite successful with women; he wins them with art and poetry. To Balso he offers a pamphlet of his philosophical position for a dollar. The pamphlet is the story of *X.*

As Balso throws the pamphlet away, a naked girl calls to him. She is washing her charms in a public fountain and delivering a sexual speech to the poet. Balso runs to embrace her. Upon throwing his arms around her, he discovers that he has hold of the tweedy teacher, Miss McGeeney, middle-aged and homely. Balso would like to run away after discovering the naked girl's metamorphosis, but Miss McGeeney pins him down while she tells him about the biography she is writing: *Samuel Perkins: Smeller.* Perkins was a genius who was all nose—he could smell chords in D minor, isosceles triangles, and velvet. When Balso the poet has taken all of this he can stand, he hits Miss McGeeney "a terrific blow in the gut" and throws her into the fountain.

Balso is tired but he moves on. When he comes to a café built into the side of the intestine, he orders a beer, falls asleep, and dreams. His dream is of Janey Davenport, a tall cripple with a huge hump and "one hundred and forty-four exquisite teeth in rows of four." He takes this hunchback home and tries to seduce her. She says she will give herself to him if he kills Beagle Darwin, whose unborn child she carries in her hump. She gives him two letters from Beagle Darwin. They form the story of Darwin's rejection of Janey, who in the letters is a normal and pathetic girl.

The Beagle Darwin sequence is a part of the dream that Balso has had while sleeping over his beer in the café. When he wakes, he finds Miss McGeeney sitting at the table with him. She tells him that the letters are a part of a novel she is writing "in the manner of Richardson." After some conversation, Balso takes the school teacher behind some bushes and makes love to her, an action which ends the book.

The Dream Life of Balso Snell is presented surrealistically, but at the same time its episodes and comments on the world have an almost stony psychological solidity. West was apparently fascinated by the possible shards of the fractured personality. Each of the three tales within the novella presents a slightly different view of the same type of person. Gilson, *X,* and Darwin are emotionally pulled between sharply opposing forces that they cannot control. They want order in their lives, yet lust for disorder; they wish for whale-sized emotions, but distrust feeling of any kind; they wish to suffer, but cannot find tears; they need love, but hate; they must laugh at everything, but find nothing funny; they act, but loathe actors; they search frantically for reality, but find only the changing and dissolving films of imagination.

These psychic tensions in West's major characters create fractured personalities that are only lightly glued together. Their precisely-opposed desires keep them balanced on a knife-edge between sex-no sex, feeling-no feeling, mind-no mind, and art-no art. Then, instead of compromising or making a choice between opposites, they explode into violence—as Gilson murdered the dishwasher, as *X* beat up Saniette, and as Darwin drove Janey to suicide.

Most of the characters in *Miss Lonelyhearts* and *The Day of the Locust* are later versions of characters in *Balso Snell.* The girl Betty in *Miss Lonelyhearts* is another Janey Davenport. Betty is able to limit experience arbitrarily, which is what her sureness is based upon. Miss Lonelyhearts, like Gilson, *X,* and Darwin, cannot do this. He cannot choose between types of experience, and his only recourse is to violence. He can find nothing in life to focus on because he cannot deceive himself into believing in anything, not even in love. One can reasonably make similar judgements concerning the characters in *The Day of the Locust,* with the exception of the apparent protagonist, Tod Hackett, who is mainly a figure like Balso Snell, a "mirror" for the actions of the other characters.

West has often been called a satirist. Satire, however, requires above all a discernible point of view. The nearly total disorientation of *Balso Snell* moves it out of the

country of satire and into the country of surrealism and dadaism, although the story does have a number of brilliant, tiny burlesques. There is, for example, the Jewish guide's burlesque of exegetical criticism, which begins with a remark of Picasso's and ends with "there are no feet in nature." The best of the burlesques is the saint's legend of Saint Puce (a canonized flea), which is told by Maloney, the religious masochist:

> Saint Puce was born from an egg that was laid in the flesh of Christ while as a babe He played on the floor of the stable in Bethlehem. . . . In his prime, Saint Puce wandered far from his birthplace, that hairsilk pocketbook, the armpit of our Lord. He roamed the forest of God's chest and crossed the hill of His abdomen. He measured and sounded that fathomless well, the Navel of our Lord. He explored and charted every crevasse, ridge, and cavern of Christ's body. From notes taken during his travels he later wrote his great work, *A Geography of Our Lord.*
>
> After much wandering, tired, he returned at last to his home in the savoury forest. To spend, he thought, his remaining days in writing, worship, and contemplation. Happy in a church whose walls were the flesh of Christ, whose windows were rose with the blood of Christ, and on whose altars burned golden candles made of the sacred earwax.

The account of Saint Puce rises to razory satire; but most of West's burlesques seem pointless, irrelevant, and even unpleasant. While beating Saniette, for example, *X* thinks of "that strange man, John Raskolnikov Gilson, the Russian student. As I beat her, I shouted: 'O constipation of desire! O diarrhoea of love! O life within life! O mystery of being! O Young Women's Christian Association! Oh! Oh!' " Like Swift, West too often let his hatred for the human animal overrule his sense of artistic form and propriety; and also like Swift, his hatred was partly expressed by a fascination for man's lowest functions. At one point, Balso Snell plans to revenge himself on the sophisticates of the art world by luring them into the theatre, where in the middle of the play the ceiling will open and cover them with tons of excrement.

The Dream Life of Balso Snell shows the nervousness, discontent, and fear that tended to mar all of West's fiction. The quality of compulsiveness in West's fractured fictional personalities is the sign of a writer who has lost artistic control of his work. Owing to its kaleidoscope of conflicting psychological moods and artistic modes, and also owing to its self-conscious nihilism, West's story fails to make a consistent satiric point. In the last analysis, it is a "satire" without an object of attack except itself.

Alvin B. Kernan   (essay date 1965)

SOURCE: "The Mob Tendency: 'The Day of the Locust'," in his *The Plot of Satire,* Yale University Press, 1965, pp. 66-80.

[Kernan is an American educator and critic. In the follow-

ing essay, he examines the satiric qualities of West's short novel.]

> [The Profund Poet should] consider himself as a *Grotesque* painter, whose Works would be spoil'd by an Imitation of Nature, or Uniformity of Design. He is to mingle Bits of the most various, or discordant kinds, Landscape, History, Portraits, Animals, and connect them with a great deal of *Flourishing,* by *Heads* or *Tails,* as it shall please his Imagination, and contribute to his principal End, which is to glare by strong Oppositions of Colours, and surprize by Contrariety of Images . . . . His Design ought to be like a Labyrinth, out of which no body can get you clear but himself. (*Peri Bathous,* Ch. V)

The central character of Nathanael West's **The Day of the Locust** is a young painter, Tod Hackett, who has been brought to Hollywood to design costumes for one of the studios, and his problems as a painter of Hollywood parallel exactly the problems of West and other writers as satirists, who are driven to more and more bizarre styles to catch the disordering tendencies of dullness. When Tod leaves the Yale School of Fine Arts, his masters are the realists Winslow Homer and Thomas Ryder; he paints such solid, orderly, familiar subjects as "a fat red barn, old stone wall or sturdy Nantucket fisherman." But once in Hollywood he abandons realism and turns, "despite his race, training and heritage" to the caricaturists Goya and Daumier in search of an adequate style to portray the fantastic world of the Golden West. As he sees more of Hollywood, the fantastic turns to the nightmarish, and Tod begins.

> to think not only of Goya and Daumier but also of certain Italian artists of the seventeenth and eighteenth centuries, of Salvator Rosa, Francesco Guardi and Monsu Desiderio, the painters of Decay and Mystery. Looking downhill now, he could see compositions that might have actually been arranged from the Calabrian work of Rosa. There were partially demolished buildings and broken monuments, half-hidden by great, tortured trees, whose exposed roots writhed dramatically in the arid ground, and by shrubs that carried, not flowers or berries, but armories of spikes, hooks and swords.

> For Guardi and Desiderio there were bridges which bridged nothing, sculpture in trees, palaces that seemed of marble until a whole stone portico began to flap in the light breeze.

After a tour of such churches as the "Tabernacle of the Third Coming" where the "Crusade against Salt" is preached, Tod is forced to reject Goya and Daumier altogether because they treat their subjects with too much pity and without enough respect for their "awful anarchic power." Tod turns at last to Alessandro Magnasco and thinks how well he "would dramatize the contrast between . . . drained-out, feeble bodies and . . . wild, disordered minds."

Tod's master painting, "The Burning of Los Angeles," is a huge satiric canvas in which he uses the techniques of the painters of Decay and Mystery and creates those grotesque images which Pope sees as characteristic of the bathetic style:

> Across the top, parallel with the frame, he had drawn the burning city, a great bonfire of architectural styles, ranging from Egyptian to Cape Cod colonial. Through the center, winding from left to right, was a long hill street and down it, spilling into the middle foreground, came the mob carrying baseball bats and torches. For the faces of its members, he was using the innumerable sketches he had made of the people who come to California to die; the cultists of all sorts, economic as well as religious, the wave, airplane, funeral and preview watchers—all those poor devils who can only be stirred by the promise of miracles and then only to violence. A super "Dr. Know-All Pierce-All" had made the necessary promise and they were marching behind his banner in a great united front of screwballs and screwboxes to purify the land. No longer bored, they sang and danced joyously in the red light of the flames.

> In the lower foreground, men and women fled wildly before the vanguard of the crusading mob. Among them were Faye, Harry, Homer, Claude and himself. Faye ran proudly, throwing her knees high. Harry stumbled along behind her, holding on to his beloved derby hat with both hands. Homer seemed to be falling out of the canvas, his face half-asleep, his big hands clawing the air in anguished pantomime. Claude turned his head as he ran to thumb his nose at his pursuers. Tod himself picked up a small stone to throw before continuing his flight. . . . the tongues of fire . . . licked even more avidly at a corinthian column that held up the palmleaf roof of a nutburger stand.

Both Pope's advice to the Profund Poet and "The Burning of Los Angeles" serve as expanded glosses on the root meaning of the word "satire." The Latin root, the adjective *satura,* originally seems to have meant "filled or charged with a variety of things"—a hodgepodge, a farrago. In the course of time this adjective came to be used to form a noun which designated the type of poetry written by Lucilius, Horace, Persius, and Juvenal. Its meaning was then gradually extended to cover any piece of writing "which contains a sharp kind of irony or ridicule or even denunciation." Though largely forgotten, the root meaning of "satire" remains functional, for the world of satire is always a fantastic jumble of men and objects. Whatever particular form dullness may take in a given satire, it moves always toward the creation of messes, discordancies, mobs, on all levels and in all areas of life. Pope in *Peri Bathous* shows vulgarity creating disorder in poetry and language, and in *The Dunciad* he shows Dulness manufacturing confusion in grammar, literature, thought, the theater, education, religion, politics, and the human personality. Dulness' genius for disorder assumes the visible shape of the routs, straggling processions, and ever-growing mobs which her sons form throughout the poem, until at last, in Book IV, they achieve the ultimate mythic shape of the mob, Chaos and Uncreation, the primal mess from which the Cosmos was once constructed by the Creating Word.

As a moralist Nathanael West would seem to be about as far from Pope as it is possible to get. The neoclassical values of tradition, culture, common sense, and Nature are so diminished for West that he could once write, wryly but accurately, that "there is nothing to root for in my work and what is even worse, no rooters." But the particular form of dullness which is the disintegrating force in *The Day of the Locust* still seeks out and expresses itself in those jumbles and mobs which it finds so "naturally" in *The Dunciad,* or which new wealth and lack of taste create in Petronius' *Satyricon,* or which pedantry, ignorance, and the burning desire for fame discover so regularly in that greatest image of confusion, Swift's *Tale of a Tub.* A poet like Pope will often dramatize the mob tendency of dullness in a single line, using, or purposely misusing, some rhetorical device such as zeugma or antithesis: "Or lose her heart, or necklace, at a ball"—"Puffs, Powders, Patches, Bibles, Billet-doux." In a novelist like West the crowding effect is not so obviously rhetorical or so concentrated; it is built up in blocks of semirealistic description of scenes, characters, and actions. But the effect is still to show dullness' disorganization of all the fundamental patterns of sense.

The dynamics of *The Day of the Locust* are focused in Tod's painting, "The Burning of Los Angeles." In the background is the mob which exerts a downward and outward pressure on the people below and on the picture as a whole. The mob is made up of "the people who come to California to die." These are the retired farmers from the midwest, the "senior citizens" tired of ice and snow, the housewives and clerks and small merchants dissatisfied with their dull, dreary lives in some small town, who come to California for sunshine, orange juice, and excitement. But these people are already sophisticates in violence.

> Every day of their lives they read the newspapers and went to the movies. Both fed them on lynchings, murder, sex crimes, explosions, wrecks, love nests, fires, miracles, revolutions, war.

Only disappointment can follow, and they quickly discover that you can get enough orange juice and sunshine, that one wave in the ocean looks much like another, and that airplanes almost never crash and consume their passengers in a "holocaust of flame." As simpler entertainments fail, these people, dressed in their dark mail-order suits, begin to loiter on street corners staring with hard, bold gazes at the brighter passersby. Themselves empty of talent; lacking beauty, vitality, and intelligence; and completely without compassion, the people who come to California to die search more and more wildly for the life that is not in themselves. They attend funerals waiting for the collapse of a mourner or some other show of strong emotion, they follow movie stars hoping that their personalities will magically be changed by proximity to beauty and dynamism, they take up fad diets which promise health and vigor if they avoid meat and cooked vegetables, they learn "Brain-Breathing, The Secret of the Aztecs" in a search for contact with mysterious powers which will bring them to life. But nothing works, for "Nothing can ever be violent enough to make taut their slack minds and bodies. They have been cheated and betrayed. They have slaved and saved for nothing." As this realization comes home to them, their expressions change to "vicious, acrid boredom" that trembles on the "edge of violence," and their fury at being cheated becomes "an awful, anarchic power" that can "destroy civilization."

Before the destroying mob in "The Burning of Los Angeles" runs a group of fugitives made up of the principal characters of the novel. These men and women are imperfect, but each has some one virtue which the mob lacks. Faye Greener is completely emptyheaded, but she has a breathtaking beauty, "structural like a tree's, not a quality of her mind or heart"; her father Harry Greener is a clever vaudeville actor, a master of the art of staying alive in a world fraught with dangers; Claude Estee is a writer and a talented wit; Tod Hackett a painter; and Homer Simpson a simple man capable of and needing love and kindness. But they are not complete people. It seems as if some god with a wry sense of humor had decided to give them only one virtue apiece while withholding the auxiliary virtues needed to make the gift meaningful.

The relationship of these people to the mob in the background is not simple. They are in one way, as the picture suggests, the victims of the mob, pursued and destroyed because they are different and talented. In another sense they are the purveyors of excitement to the mob, the representatives of all those people in the "entertainment industries" who make a living manufacturing the fake "amour and glamor" needed by the tired barber in Purdue who has spent his day cutting hair. But these people with their single talents, while contemptuous of the mob which follows them, "run before" in another sense, for they too are people who have come to California to die. They too seek vicarious pleasure or strange experiences to compensate for lives which, despite their gifts, are still inadequate. Because they have money or are cleverer and more attractive, their escapes into fantasy are more expensive and glossed over with a show of indifference and sophistication. But they are still escapes. Claude Estee puts a dead horse made of inflated rubber at the bottom of his swimming pool, and he and his friends visit a fancy bawdy house to see pornographic films with such titles as "Le Prédicament de Marie, ou La Bonne Distraite." He lives in an exact reproduction of an old southern mansion where he stands on the porch trying to look like a Civil War colonel and calling "Here, you black rascal! A mint julep," to a Chinese servant who comes up with a scotch and soda. Faye Greener's beauty is so overwhelming that she can be described only as a Botticelli Venus, "smiling a subtle half smile uncontaminated by thought . . . just born, everything moist and fresh, volatile and perfumed." Yet because her beauty is joined with no other virtue, she cannot find her life in the world and seeks it instead in daydreams built on Hollywood plots. In her dream world she becomes a rich-young-girl cruising on her father's yacht in the South Seas. Engaged to a Russian count, she falls in love with a young sailor, and they alone are saved in the inevitable shipwreck. They swim to a desert island where she is attacked by a huge snake while bathing, etc., etc.

The major portion of *The Day of the Locust* is made up

of a panorama in which each of these talented people "dies" in some fashion. Harry Greener literally dies of a bad heart, exhausted and feeling cheated because he never became the great actor he thought he was. Homer Simpson's dreams of love sour into hate. He ends by killing a most unpleasant small boy and is in turn torn apart by an excitement-seeking mob. Claude and Faye survive physically, but their abilities, thwarted, lead only to sterility and emptiness. Tod Hackett ends as a wailing madman after being caught in the maelstrom of the mob.

This is West's image of Hollywood, but, as Richard Gehman says, "West used Hollywood as a microcosm . . . because . . . everything that is wrong with life in the United States is to be found there in rare purity, and because the unreality of the business of making pictures seemed a most proper setting for his 'halfworld'." The same point is made in *The Day of the Locust* where the people who come to California to die are described as the "cream of America's madmen" which is skimmed from a milk "just as rich as violence." West is not condemning all of American life but isolating and exposing in grotesque forms a peculiar danger or brand of dullness within it. This is, specifically, the peculiar emptiness of many people and lives, and the search for compensation in vicarious excitement and glamor. This appetite is always fed and sharpened by sensational newspapers, lurid writing, impossibly romantic movies, enthusiastic religions, health fads, and quackery of all kinds which trade on dullness, fear, and hatred. These substitutes for life, West shows, are necessarily illusions, and because they are such, they—like Jonson's alchemy or the contemporary half-world created by television and Madison Avenue—cannot but fail in the end to satisfy the impossible desires they have fed and fanned. When the inevitable drop to reality comes and it is discovered that sunshine, orange juice, and waves are not really very exciting, the cheated fools will turn to mobs and destroy civilizations to revenge themselves and "get a little fun out of life."

West offers no specific cure for these empty lives. In fact, like many satirists, he deliberately leaves any positive, reforming element out of his work in order to intensify the shrillness of the siren announcing disaster.

> If I put into *The Day of the Locust* any of the sincere, honest people who work . . . [in Hollywood] and are making such a great, progressive fight, those chapters couldn't be written satirically and the whole fabric of the peculiar half-world which I attempted to create would be badly torn by them . . . I believe there is a place for the fellow who yells fire and indicates where some of the smoke is coming from without actually dragging the hose to the spot.

I doubt if West really had any cure, except the dynamite blast of satire, for the deep-seated ills which he isolates, but he did diagnose the disease and predict its course with remarkable accuracy. Because he believed in no traditional value systems, he could only denote the disease in pragmatic and symbolic terms. He could not say, for example, that men were wrong to try to escape from unsatisfactory lives because each man is created by God as a part of a great plan; nor could he argue that every man has his allot-

ted work in society which, properly done, will be richly rewarding and serve the best interests of the society and the individual. But he could show again and again that while the phony may momentarily satisfy some desire for the impossible, that it can only disappoint more painfully, and dangerously, in the end. Eggs bathed in a rich cream-colored light in the supermarket can only turn out to be plain eggs when you get them home, and romantic dreams of passion and adventure lived in the darkness of the Bijou can only make more unsatisfactory the ordinary lives which inevitably begin again at the sidewalk.

The particular horror of West's satiric world is that in their search for romance the people who have come to California to die, and those who pander to their appetites, create such a grotesquely phony and pitifully illusionary world. Whatever they put their hand to is unreal, and unreality begins to build on unreality—furniture "painted to look like unpainted pine," or movie indians cracking jokes in fake German accents, "Vas you dere Sharley?" As the fake encrusts itself on the fake, obeying no law except the need for the novel, the result can only be fantastic disorder, combinations of things unrelated, great jumbles, and the division of those things which properly belong together. The search for glamor creates the strange dress of the Angelenos:

> Their sweaters, knickers, slacks, blue flannel jackets with brass buttons were fancy dress. The fat lady in the yachting cap was going shopping, not boating; the man in the Norfolk jacket and Tyrolean hat was returning, not from a mountain, but an insurance office; and the girl in slacks and sneaks with a bandanna around her head had just left a switchboard, not a tennis court.

A dwarf in a high green Tyrolean hat, black shirt, and yellow tie may be an amusing, harmless kind of disorder, but the disintegration of architecture and a city into a dream world sounds a more serious note:

> Only dynamite would be of any use against the Mexican ranch houses, Samoan huts, Mediterranean villas, Egyptian and Japanese temples, Swiss chalets, Tudor cottages, and every possible combination of these styles that lined the slopes of the canyon.

> When he noticed that they were all of plaster, lath and paper, he was charitable and blamed their shape on the materials used. Steel, stone and brick curb a builder's fancy a little, forcing him to distribute his stresses and weights and to keep his corners plumb, but plaster and paper know no law, not even that of gravity.

> On the corner of La Huerta Road was a miniature Rhine castle with traper turrets pierced for archers. Next to it was a little highly colored shack with domes and minarets out of the *Arabian Nights*.

The dreams that know no law, not even such impersonal laws as gravity and complementary colors, also ignore the simple laws of chronology and distance. The movies which feed this hunger for romance make cheap pretenses and a jumbled heap—"a Sargasso of the imagination"—

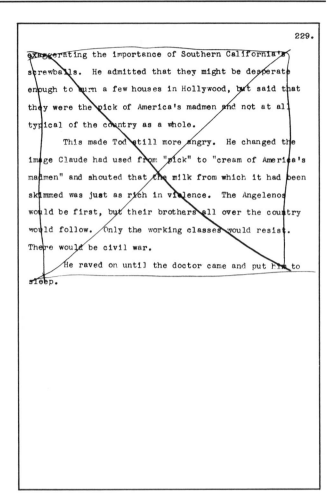

The last two pages of the manuscript of The Day of the Locust, *with a complete final chapter that West deleted.*

out of the long history of human efforts to achieve a civilization. Tod Hackett wanders through the "dream dump" of a studio lot, moving from a giant *papier mâché* sphinx across a manmade desert to the front of the Last Chance Saloon, from where he can see a conical grass hut in a jungle compound, a charging Arab on a white stallion, a truck loaded with snow and sled dogs, a Paris street, a Romanesque courtyard, and a group of people in riding costume eating cardboard food on a fiber lawn in front of a cellophane waterfall. Crossing a bridge, he comes to a "Greek temple dedicated to Eros. The god himself lay face downward in a pile of old newspapers and bottles." Tod moves on through a

> tangle of briars, old flats and iron junk, skirting the skeleton of a Zeppelin, a bamboo stockade, an adobe fort, the wooden horse of Troy, a flight of baroque palace stairs that started in a bed of weeds and ended against the branches of an oak, part of the Fourteenth Street elevated station, a Dutch windmill, the bones of a dinosaur, the upper half of the Merrimac, a corner of a Mayan temple, until he finally reached the road.

After this we can only ask, "What road?"

Not only does the search for dreams mangle history, making it impossible to believe in it or see in it such simple patterns even as enduring human courage or ingenuity; it fragments and jumbles the human character as well. *The Day of the Locust* is populated with strange inhuman mixtures and the broken wholes of men. A small child brought to Hollywood to win fame and fortune combines a childish innocence with phony adult manners, learned from the movies, such as bowing low and clicking his heels together when introduced. He moves his small body in a suggestive manner while dancing and singing sexy songs, which he does not understand. Men yearn to be women and croon lullabies to imaginary babies they pretend are real, and then they pretend to be men again. An incredibly beautiful young woman speaks always in the most vulgar tones and voices the most trivial of clichés. A "dried-up little man with the rubbed features and stooped shoulders of a postal clerk" pretends that he is a southern colonel and at the same time dresses in ivory shirts, black ties, red-checked trousers, and enormous rust-colored shoes.

This division of human nature becomes most apparent in Homer Simpson, the quiet hotel clerk who has wandered to Hollywood looking for health and for the love of which he is capable but can never find. He is described as large and muscular yet not looking strong or fertile. "He was like one of Picasso's great sterile athletes, who brood hopelessly on pink sand, staring at veined marble waves." He sleeps whenever he can, seeking in unconsciousness the peace he cannot find in the world. The disintegration of self which he has suffered is clearest in the disjunctive, awkward movements of his body, and particularly in his hands, which have become separated from the rest of his being:

> He got out of bed in sections, like a poorly made automaton, and carried his hands into the bathroom. He turned on the cold water. When the basin was full, he plunged his hands in up to the wrists. They lay quietly on the bottom like a pair of strange aquatic animals. When they were thoroughly chilled and began to crawl about, he lifted them out and hid them in a towel.

Beaten by a world where he cannot find or take what he needs, he retreats in on himself and coils back into the position of Uterine Flight. Then, in the final scene of the book, this kindly but ineffective man, frenzied by finding nothing but hatred and violence in people where he hoped for love and gentleness, turns into a savage murderer who stamps to death the small boy who throws a stone at him. Homer's simple dream of love and peace is more acceptable than the dreams of most of the people who come to California to die, but West's point would seem to be that Homer's is still a dream which, because it is not realistic and is therefore hopeless, leads to the same fragmentation and violence that grows from the more grotesque dreams of fame, passion, and adventure. The retreat into sleep to find peace is finally as fatal a dream as the visit to the movies to find love.

In *The Day of the Locust,* as in most satires, there is no consistent story and, therefore, by the usual standards, no plot. The narration does come back frequently to the life of a few major characters, and we are most often led on our tour of Hollywood by Tod Hackett. But the total effect is of phantasmagoria now thrusting forward a vaudeville act filled with brawny acrobats tossing a helpless clown about; then a shift to the charge of an army of extras up a plaster Mont St. Jean at Waterloo for the glory of Grotenstein Productions. We stop to watch a lizard emerge from a tin can and trap flies, pass on to a funeral, a scene on Hollywood Boulevard, and move in to look at the furnishings of a house. We attend the showing of a blue film in which all the members of a household attempt to seduce the maid, who is attempting to seduce the young daughter, and then move on to the Church of Christ Physical "where holiness was attained through the constant use of chestweights and spring grips." As disjunct as these scenes may seem to be, each shows the dream seekers searching for satisfaction and achieving only the flimsiest illusion, which in turn creates what is at first an amusing and then a terrifying disorder. This recurring movement from dream through illusion to disorder is the basic action of the novel. As these madmen search more and more feverishly for what is missing in their lives they turn all they touch to a mob. Clothing, furniture, architecture, history, the human personality are jumbled into monstrous collages, and under the pressure of the need for excitement and dreams every relationship, every ritual occasion,

every social meeting turns to bedlam, babel, riot. A funeral becomes a sideshow as an Eskimo family, the Four Gingos, grunts in time to a record of Bach's chorale, "Come Redeemer, Our Savior," and the sensation-seekers pour in from the street to look at the corpse. A church service turns to a scene in a madhouse as a man "from one of the colonies in the desert near Soboba Hot Springs where he had been conning over his soul on a diet of raw fruit and nuts" explodes in anger against the wicked world:

> The message he had brought to the city was one that an illiterate anchorite might have given decadent Rome. It was a crazy jumble of dietary rules, economics, and Biblical threats. He claimed to have seen the Tiger of Wrath stalking the walls of the citadel and the Jackal of Lust skulking in the shrubbery, and he connected these omens with "thirty dollars every Thursday" and meat eating.

The search for amusement creates cock-fights in which one bird cuts another to pieces and then eats its eyes. A typical "party" ends with a dwarf, frantic with lust for the cold Venus, Faye Greener, being kicked in the stomach when he tries to break in between two dancers.

> The dwarf struggled to his feet and stood with his head lowered like a tiny ram. . . . He charged between Earle's legs and dug upward with both hands. Earle screamed with pain . . . then groaned and started to sink to the floor, tearing Faye's silk pajamas on his way down.

> Miguel grabbed . . . [the dwarf] by the throat. . . . Lifting the little man free, Miguel shifted his grip to his ankles and dashed him against the wall, like a man killing a rabbit against a tree. He swung the dwarf back to slam him again.

The pressure toward disorder evident in each of these scenes is embodied in the episodic form of the novel, and it takes its final form in the great mob scene with which the book ends. Here, as in the scene of chaos and uncreation with which *The Dunciad* closes, all forms of dullness are gathered together to express their ultimate nature and to achieve the final shapelessness toward which they have been constantly moving. The crowd begins to gather to see the moving-picture stars arrive at a premiere at Khan's Persian Palace—"Mr. Khan a Pleasure Dome Decreed." As the people who came to California to die come up to the crowd they look "different, almost furtive," but once they enter it all their inhibitions are released and they become arrogant and pugnacious. The inevitable panders are present to stir the mixture more violently and amuse the folks at home who couldn't make it this year. Colored lights flash madly about, and a radio announcer stands above the crowd asking, in a high, hysterical voice broadcast over a national network and amplified for the benefit of those present, "can the police hold them? Can they? It doesn't look so, folks." The mob grows every moment, shoving, bulging, pushing, breaking out of any lines authority attempts to impose on it. Within, it mills about, stumbling and swirling and releasing the most primitive powers, hatred, lust, dislike for anyone different, and the desire to break and kill to avenge a life of emptiness.

Only a spark is needed to touch the mob off and release its full destructive power, and this comes when Homer Simpson, who has wandered into the crowd in a state of shock resulting from the loss of his own dream, kills the small boy who is tormenting him. One form of riot releases another: the rumor sweeps through the crowd that a pervert has attacked a child, and it explodes, surging and churning over all barriers. Homer is torn apart, Tod's leg is broken, an old man attacks a young girl pinned helpless by other bodies, men and women are crushed and trampled down. Here is "The Burning of Los Angeles," the great Vortex of Dulness sucking all down into nothingness, the final expression of the mob tendency.

Broken by the mob's awesome power, the satirist Tod Hackett goes mad. Taken to a police car, he begins to imitate the siren as loudly as he can. In the end the only style which the satirist can turn to is the wail sounding all the fires, bombings, accidents, and violences of a world which has tried to cure emptiness with illusion.

> **Intent on creating archetypal characters in an age of psychoanalysis, West probably felt that Freudian psychology was indispensable. But West is not interested in great subtlety; it is sufficient that the images convey the disorder.**
>
> **—Victor Comerchero, in his *Nathanael West: The Ironic Prophet*, 1964.**

Randall Reid (essay date 1967)

SOURCE: *The Fiction of Nathanael West: No Redeemer, No Promised Land,* The University of Chicago Press, 1967, 174 p.

[*Reid is an American educator, critic, and short story writer. In the following excerpt, he explores the major influences on* Miss Lonelyhearts.]

The general influence of Dostoevski on West's work is obvious. It was noted by Angel Flores in his 1933 review [in *Contempo*] of *Miss Lonelyhearts,* and it has been mentioned again in nearly every succeeding commentary on West. As these studies have pointed out, West was, like Dostoevski, fond of treating guilt-ridden, dualistic characters who live and act in a strangely hallucinatory world. But the influence is not limited to this general resemblance. [In James Light's *Nathanael West. An Interpretive Study,* 1961] John Sanford has recalled West's "little brag that he could rewrite Dostoevsky with a pair of shears," and in *Miss Lonelyhearts* that is very nearly what West did. He took his structure, and the psychology which underlies the structure, intact from *Crime and Punishment.* The case history of Raskolnikov was far more useful to him than any he found in James or Starbuck.

Both Raskolnikov and Miss Lonelyhearts are, when we meet them, already launched on an obsessive idea whose genesis is only hinted at. In both, the obsession ambiguously reflects a personal illness and a real external problem—it is simultaneously true that Miss Lonelyhearts is driven by "hysteria" and that he is driven by a clear perception of the misery of others, just as it is true that Raskolnikov is driven by a treacherous combination of pathological motives and real perceptions. In both cases, the external problem is the fact of apparently hopeless suffering. And in both cases, the resulting obsession focuses on the necessity of an heroic action—Raskolnikov imitates Napoleon; Miss Lonelyhearts imitates Christ. The heroic action raises a series of questions: Is the action desirable? Is the hero capable of it? Are his apparent motives real? Raskolnikov and Miss Lonelyhearts alternately doubt the action itself and their own worthiness to attempt it. Even their failures are ambiguous. Has the ideal failed, or has the hero failed his ideal?

Apart from their internal doubts, both Raskolnikov and Miss Lonelyhearts face two kinds of external opposition: cynical mockery and naïve orthodoxy. Porfiry Petrovitch and Svidrigailov mock Raskolnikov's attempt to play Superman; Shrike mocks Miss Lonelyhearts' attempt to play Christ. Sonia's orthodox Christianity is horrified by murder and godlessness; Betty's orthodox Americanism is repelled by misery and martyrdom. Both Raskolnikov and Miss Lonelyhearts are, in other words, poised between mocking antagonists and loving but incomprehending girls. Each attempts to resist the mockery and to destroy the simple faith: Raskolnikov invades Sonia's room to insist that all her sacrifice is futile, that only shame and suffering await her and the children she is trying to protect; Miss Lonelyhearts invades Betty's apartment to smash her Buddha-like serenity and insist on the reality of evil. Both resent a composure which seems to deny the heroic roles they have chosen. These parallels yield several satiric points. Sonia and Betty embody paradoxes: Sonia is the saintly whore whose spiritual purity contrasts with her physical degradation; Betty is the nice girl whose innocence is a form of corruption. When American orthodoxy replaces Russian orthodoxy, veneration of nature and success replaces veneration of love and sacrifice. Instead of "Take up your cross," Betty's advice is: Go into advertising.

Crime and Punishment also uses three narrative devices which West adopted: the set speech, the confession, and the dream. Both *Crime and Punishment* and *Miss Lonelyhearts* contain little true dialogue. Raskolnikov and Miss Lonelyhearts do not talk much, except to themselves. They are usually silent auditors for the extended and formal speech of others. Raskolnikov listens to Marmeladov, to Razumihin, to Porfiry Petrovitch, to Svidrigailov; Miss Lonelyhearts listens to Shrike, to Mary Shrike, to Mrs. Doyle. These extended speeches often seem, in both novels, simultaneously theatrical and natural. They sound rehearsed, but that is the way they ought to sound. The habitual confider (Marmeladov and Mary Shrike) is, after all, an actor. His tale of woe is a recital—the repetition of a story told so often that it is nearly memorized. And acting is the natural posture of seducers, detectives, and intellectuals. Svidrigailov, Porfiry Petrovitch, and Shrike are all self-conscious actors who deliberately exploit the artificiality of their roles; Shrike is the sort who fabricates his speeches in advance, hoarding every epigram which occurs to him. Both novels largely substitute the conventions of stage speech—soliloquy and monologue—for ordinary conversation, but both novels make this stage speech plausible by using self-conscious and self-dramatizing characters.

The confession—bogus and real—is also omnipresent in both novels. Raskolnikov hears the confessions of Marmeladov, Svidrigailov, and Porfiry Petrovitch; Miss Lonelyhearts receives endless confessional letters and hears the troubles of Mary Shrike and Mrs. Doyle. The confession is, of course, one form of the monologue or set speech. It also defines the auditor in curious ways. If confessing is a theatrical role, so is playing confessor, and both Raskolnikov and Miss Lonelyhearts are tormented in part by the implications of their roles. Further, the confessions of others define the protagonist. Both Miss Lonelyhearts and Raskolnikov are, as I have said, silent; they are only intermittently articulate and only intermittently conscious. Yet they are both complex. Neither speech nor introspection would, therefore, adequately reveal their preoccupations. The confessions they hear often do reveal them—or echo them, or extend them, or give them articulate form.

The spiritual progress of Raskolnikov and Miss Lonelyhearts is also revealed by a series of dreams. Each series culminates in a vision which signals conversion—Raskolnikov's microbe dream and Miss Lonelyhearts' communion with God. And each series begins with a memorable and prophetic vision whose significance lingers throughout the novel. Miss Lonelyhearts' dream of sacrificing the lamb functions—structurally and symbolically—exactly as does Raskolnikov's dream of the beating and slaughter of the mare. Both are flashback dreams, and both are literally plausible; each could be a real memory. In each dream, an idyllic scene shifts suddenly into a horrible spectacle. In each, the death of an animal is preceded by dreadfully prolonged suffering: the drunken peasants beat the mare with whips, clubs, and poles before finishing it off with an ax; Miss Lonelyhearts saws clumsily at the lamb's throat with a broken knife before smashing its head with a rock. Each dream reveals the hero's ambiguous role. Raskolnikov is simultaneously the murderous peasant with his ax, the tortured mare too weak to pull its load, and the anguished but helpless witness of cruelty (his "real" self in the dream); Miss Lonelyhearts is also simultaneously witness, executioner, and victim. And his dream contains, among other things, a synopsis of his destiny: he is "elected priest" in a blasphemous joke which, because of his inability to perform the priestly function, ends in grotesque terror.

In both *Crime and Punishment* and *Miss Lonelyhearts,* the rhythm of obsession dominates the narrative pattern. Miss Lonelyhearts and Raskolnikov alternate between frenzied, often directionless activity and near-catatonic withdrawal. They roam the world of streets, parks, and taverns, or they collapse into feverish stupor in their rooms. Neither action nor withdrawal works. Activity ends in violence or horror, and stupor is destroyed by the urgency of pain. This alternate frenzy and collapse makes very good psychological sense. It is the familiar and contradictory impulse of anyone whose condition is unbearable but unchangeable. It also becomes, in both novels, a metaphoric expression of the paradox which confronts each protagonist: something must be done, but nothing can be done.

And it becomes a good deal more. The psychology of obsession, as Dostoevski used it, involved a variety of technical devices which, when they appeared in *Miss Lonelyhearts,* were assumed to have come from the surrealists. We should remember, however, that the surrealists claimed Dostoevski as a spiritual father, and that Max Ernst's painting of the surrealist fraternity shows Dostoevski in the front row, holding Ernst himself on his lap. The "surrealist" elements in *Miss Lonelyhearts* were largely anticipated in *Crime and Punishment.* In both novels, the technique of distortion is basically realistic—it derives from the psychology of the hero. Obsession governs the experience of the hero, and the experience of the hero governs that reality the reader perceives. When the rhythm of obsession replaces the normal rhythm of time, external scenes and events become bizarre phenomena. The protagonist's consciousness is counterpointed against the normal rhythm; he awakens and rushes from his room, but it is not dawn which greets him. The streets may be sunny and crowded or black and empty. Or he may wander through the city so absorbed in his obsession that he loses all consciousness of his environment. Awareness suddenly returns with all the force of a mystic experience. Because in his last moment of consciousness the sun was high in the sky, the sudden perception that it is setting is a ghastly and unexplained miracle.

Both Raskolnikov and Miss Lonelyhearts respond to external reality as though it were an apparition or a revelation. They superstitiously read it for clues: Raskolnikov feels that some fate led him to overhear the tavern conversation about justified murder; Miss Lonelyhearts takes his cue from the phallic obelisk. They perceive reality as though it were a dream: Raskolnikov moves through a series of apparitional wagons, paint smells, fourth-floor rooms with yellow wallpaper and "chance" meetings; Miss Lonelyhearts is haunted by sea images, blood, nipples, phalli, flowers. In moments of preoccupation, they collide violently with external reality: Raskolnikov wanders in front of a wagon and is lashed by the coachman; Miss Lonelyhearts, dreaming of children dancing, steps back from the bar, collides with a man, and is punched in the mouth. At other moments, external reality seems only a mirror of the self's preoccupations: after learning of his sister's pursuit by Svidrigailov, Raskolnikov sees in the street a drunken girl pursued by a seducer; when Miss Lonelyhearts decides to call Mrs. Doyle, he finds the walls of the booth covered with obscene drawings. In both cases, the expressive use of external scene or incident is ambiguously meaningful. Raskolnikov's perception of the drunken girl and her pursuer reveals his own obsession, but it also reveals that the predatory evil which obsesses him actually exists. When Miss Lonelyhearts fixes "his eyes on two disembodied genitals." he reveals his own attempt to seize upon sexuality, but he also reveals that the world shares his obsession. And the crudely drawn, disembodied genitals further reveal that debasement of sexuality which makes it powerless to help.

Fantasy, hallucination, and dream are as natural to an obsessive character as theatrical speech is to a self-conscious character. The obsession projects itself outward, and expressionism is then a fact of perception, not just a literary technique. And there are, in the real world, obsessive environments as well as obsessive individuals. The worlds in which Raskolnikov and Miss Lonelyhearts live relentlessly confirm their obsessions. Misery and grotesque deformation are everywhere—outside the self as well as within. As James said, "The lunatic's visions of horror are all drawn from the material of daily fact." This union of personal obsession and universal reality creates the peculiar stifling atmosphere of both *Crime and Punishment* and *Miss Lonelyhearts.* Life seems to be an airless room or an oppressive dream from which one cannot wake. Appropriately, Svidrigailov remarks that what all men need is fresh air, and Shrike rehearses in parody the various forms of escape.

The psychology of obsession allows Dostoevski to treat his background symbolically without sacrificing the sense of reality. It also allows him to focus relentlessly upon his central themes. Obsession automatically produces unity of action—it perceives only that which is somehow relevant to the obsession. Life becomes, to the obsessive character, a drama in which everything—his surroundings, his actions, his dreams—are symbolic expressions of his own compulsion. When that compulsion derives from an accurate, if partial, vision of life, we have simultaneously the material for problem drama, realistic psychology, and symbolic tragedy. And all of these can be made to produce, as they do in *Crime and Punishment* and *Miss Lonelyhearts,* a unity of effect comparable to that of brilliantly staged drama.

Theatrical comparisons are inevitable. I have already mentioned the stage speech which both West and Dostoevski used, and it is also true that both were fond of stage entrances, exits, and curtain scenes. One could even find in *Hamlet*—or at least in some readings of *Hamlet*—a theatrical ancestor for the psychology and techniques I have described. In both West and Dostoevski, the basically "realistic" stage techniques frequently shade off into deliberate fantasy or contrivance. That Raskolnikov's aimless wanderings should lead him to the tavern where Svidrigailov waits is a psychologically plausible coincidence; that Svidrigailov should happen to take rooms next to Sonia or that Lebeziatnikoff should happen to room with the Marmeladovs is not. Nor is the erectile shadow of the obelisk in *Miss Lonelyhearts* literally plausible. Yet, instead of destroying the sense of reality, these artifices merely twist it. Both Raskolnikov and Miss Lonelyhearts are aware of the too appropriate incidents in their dramas. They struggle against the sense of being actors in a humiliating charade, of being trapped in a fantasy or a farce.

The number of parallels is nearly inexhaustible. The ambiguous sexuality of the "womanish" Porfiry Petrovitch is echoed by the Clean Old Man. Lizavetta "looks like a soldier," and Mrs. Doyle looks "like a police captain." Even the basic metaphors of *Miss Lonelyhearts* can be found in *Crime and Punishment.* Miss Lonelyhearts is "like a dead man" himself, and he broods upon the "dead world" and the necessity of "bringing it to life." Raskolnikov is fascinated by the story of Lazarus. That parable of resurrection becomes, in *Crime and Punishment,* an insistent analogue to Raskolnikov's own deadness and ultimate rebirth. The prevailing deadness in both novels is echoed by Shrike, with his "dead pan," and by Svidrigailov, with his irritable ennui and ultimate suicide. The metaphor of death and resurrection is, of course, fundamental to Christianity. Its use by two different authors is hardly startling. But neither, in this case, is it coincidental. West, I think, deliberately borrowed and inverted the terms of Dostoevski's contrast between life and death. Throughout *Crime and Punishment,* theory is opposed to life—life is organic, creative, concrete, infinite while theory is mechanical, dead, abstract, finite. Raskolnikov is reborn when he abandons his theory and submits to the diversity and uncertainty of life. But in *Miss Lonelyhearts,* the diversity of life is what destroys. The sea of life spawns nothing but junk—proliferating debris incapable of meaningful unity. Even in fantasy, Miss Lonelyhearts is overwhelmed by "marine refuse." His contacts with the nature-worshipping Betty and that embodiment of the life force, Mrs. Doyle, unite to destroy him—it is his affair with Mrs. Doyle that sends Doyle after him, and it is the pregnant Betty who cuts off Doyle's escape and makes the grotesque accident of Miss Lonelyhearts' death inevitable. In *Miss Lonelyhearts,* the life force is, like the sexuality of *Balso Snell,* governed by the "mechanics of decay."

It should be clear that West did not just prune away words with his pair of shears. He snipped off *Crime and Punishment*'s affirmative epilogue entirely, and he diminished more than the physical bulk of the rest of the novel. Scenes, speeches, characters have all drastically shrunk. Betty is a trivial Sonia, and Shrike is, compared to Svidrigailov, a stunted dwarf. Even the artificial conventions of *Crime and Punishment* have been made far more formal—the vast stage has become a puppet theater whose sets are obviously painted and abruptly changed, whose scenes move with the jerky animation of a cartoon, whose plot is as relentless as a syllogism. Obviously, there is a corresponding diminution of both dramatic power and psychological complexity. We need not argue that West was Dostoevski's equal. But we need not rank him among Dostoevski's imitators either. Miss Lonelyhearts' whole career implicitly repudiates the "solution" of *Crime and Punishment.* It takes Dostoveskian premises and makes them yield a conclusion which denies Dostoevskian answers, even parodying, in the person of Betty, Dostoevski's favorite instrument of salvation—the naïve representative of orthodox faith and instinctive love. And West did not just reproduce the techniques he took from Dostoevski. He exploited their possibilities in ways Dostoevski did not, and he deftly united them with apparently unrelated techniques borrowed from a variety of other writers and other arts. Though his borrowings from *Crime and Punishment* were in part respectful, they were hardly slavish. The case history of Raskolnikov merges, in West's hands, with other familiar histories to produce a truly classic case.

> [Man] has sought . . . in all climates and in all times, some means of escaping, were it only for a few hours, from his home in the mire. . . .
>
> —Baudelaire.

Or, as Miss Lonelyhearts says, "Men have always fought their misery with dreams." The influence of the symbolist poets upon West is as generally acknowledged as the influence of Dostoevski. It too was noted by Angel Flores in 1933, and it too has been expounded several times since, notably by Marc L. Ratner [in *American Literature,* January, 1960]. Flores quite properly expanded the symbolist influence into a tradition which runs from Coleridge to the surrealists, and he concluded that "West's most remarkable performance has been to bring Fyodor's dark angels into the Haunted Castle. . . ." This remark seems to me both astute and misleading. West certainly did fuse symbolist techniques with Dostoevskian themes, but that fusion was not as remarkable as Flores seems to suggest. For one thing, Fyodor's dark angels were first brought into the Haunted Castle by Dostoevski himself, not by West. As I have already argued, *Crime and Punishment* is an hallucinatory, symbolic novel. And Dostoevski touches Baudelaire at so many points that West's fusion of the two was more inevitable than remarkable. Both Baudelaire and Dostoevski repeatedly analyze the evils of egoism, the voluptuous pleasure of remorse, the stupidity of liberal utopianism, and the sin of ennui with its consequent spite and spiritual deadness. Like Dostoevski, Baudelaire is fond of treating the imprisoned self and its fantasies of escape. "Life is a hospital in which every patient is possessed by the desire to change his bed. . . ." The narrator of "Anywhere out of the World" considers going to Lisbon, Holland, Batavia, Tornio, the Baltic, the Pole, until: "At last my soul bursts into speech, and wisely cries to me: Anywhere, anywhere, as long as it be out of this world!" Ratner has suggested that this rehearsal of escapes was the model for Shrike's parodies on the South Seas, art, hedonism, and return to the soil. It may well have been. I would add, however, that Svidrigailov indulges in a similar rehearsal. He tells Raskolnikov that he may get married, or he may go to America, or he may go up in a balloon, or he may go on a journey where he will not need money. The last alternative, a disguised reference to suicide, is the one he adopts and the one which literally takes him out of this world.

Baudelare's description of the "artificial paradise" of hashish intoxication is directly relevant to *Miss Lonelyhearts.* It is, like Miss Lonelyhearts' career, a paradigm of the progress of delusion. To Baudelaire, the intoxication was evil not just because it was false but because it parodied religious experience. It carried the romantic egoist to damnation, not redemption. This is his description of the typical victim:

> A temperament half nervous and half splenetic seems to me to be the most favourable for the development of this particular intoxication; to this I shall add a cultivated mind, given to the study of form and colour; a tender heart, made weary by unhappiness, but still youthful; if you will

allow me, I shall go so far as to endow him with past faults, and, what must be the natural result in a nature easily aroused, if not positive remorse, at least a regret for time ill-spent and profaned. A taste for metaphysics, a knowledge of the different philosophical hypotheses regarding human destiny, are certainly not useless attributes, as are, no less, a love for virtue, for abstract, stoic, or mystical virtue, which is to be found in all books on which the modern child is fed, and which is declared to be the highest summit to which a distinguished spirit might attain. If I add to all this a delicate sensibility, that I omitted as a superogatory condition, I believe that I shall have gathered together the general elements commonly attributed to the modern man with a sensitive nature. . . . Let us now see what will become of this individual driven to distraction by Haschisch. Let us follow the development of his imagination to its ultimate and most splendid resting-place, to the man's belief in his own Divinity. . . . there develops that mysterious and temporary state of the spirit, when the full depth of life, beset with multiple problems, completely reveals itself in the spectacle before one's eyes, be that spectacle natural or merely trivial—when the first object seen becomes the perfect symbol. . . .

> A strange good-will manifested even toward strangers, a kind of philanthropy that owes more to pity than to love (here appears the first germ of that satanic spirit which will develop later in an extraordinary fashion) but which goes so far as to fear hurting anyone. . . . Cult, Adoration, Prayer, dreams of happiness surge and dart forth with the fierce energy and brilliance of fireworks. . . .

> He confounds completely dream with action, and his imagination becoming more and more enthusiastic before the enchanting spectacle of his corrected and idealized nature, substituting this fascinating picture of himself for his real individuality, so weak in will, so rich in vanity. . . .

> No one should be astonished at the final, the supreme thought born in the dreamer's mind: *I have become God!*

There are obvious differences, as well as similarities, between this hypothetical case history and Miss Lonelyhearts' experience. For one thing, Miss Lonelyhearts' delusion is achieved without drugs. Baudelaire, however, speaks of "each man's natural dose of opium" and consistently describes drugs as collaborators with, not just agents acting upon, an individual's natural tendencies. And the psychological stages through which the dreamer passes correspond closely to Miss Lonelyhearts' pattern.

More important, the symbolist techniques were perfectly suited to West's rewriting Dostoevski with a pair of shears. In *Crime and Punishment,* psychological states tend to be acted out, not just revealed. Symbolic background is often panoramic, not focused in a single detail. West reduced symbolic actions to isolated gestures and symbolic scenes to single images. Miss Lonelyhearts is repeatedly in that state "when the first object seen becomes the perfect symbol"—a phallic obelisk, a poster in a bar, a newspaper struggling in an empty sky. Further, the symbolist prose poem naturally fuses with the Dostoevskian set speech. Both are essentially essays, expositions of a psychological state or a meaningful experience or an abstract idea. By combining the two forms, West united the epigrammatic terseness and the suggestive imagery of the symbolists with the dramatic and narrative relevance of the set speech. Shrike's speeches, for example, are highly polished prose poems. They are also expressions of character, influences upon Miss Lonelyhearts' destiny, and significant comments within the philosophical context of the novel.

The difficulty with the Baudelairean prose poem is that it tends to be entirely too lucid and self-contained. When dropped into a narrative, it may be a lump which refuses to blend. West solved this difficulty in part by also borrowing the kaleidoscopic techniques of Rimbaud. His prose often echoes Rimbaudian rhythms.

> [*A Season in Hell*]: A villein, I must have made the journey to the Holy Land. . . . A leper, I am seated among potsherds and nettles, at the foot of a sun-eaten wall. —Later, a reiter, I must have bivouacked under German stars.

> [*Miss Lonelyhearts*]: Without dreaming he was aware of fireflies and the slop of oceans.

> Later a train rolled into a station where he was a reclining statue holding a stopped clock, a coach rumbled into the yard of an inn where he was sitting over a guitar, cap in hand, shedding the rain with his hump.

Rimbaud's shifting and dissolving images are as perfectly suited to transitional states of consciousness as the Baudelairean prose poem is to a single vision or idea.

Once again, West also borrowed from, and parodied, Huysmans. Shrike's description of the hedonist's last party is a radically compressed parody of a similar dinner in *Against the Grain*:

> [Huysmans]: The dining-room was hung with black and looked out on a strangely metamorphosed garden, the walks being strewn with charcoal, the little basin in the middle of the lawn bordered with a rim of black basalt and filled with ink; and the ordinary shrubs superseded by cypresses and pines. The dinner itself was served on a black cloth . . . illuminated by candelabra in which tall tapers flared.

> While a concealed orchestra played funeral marches, the guests were waited on by naked negresses. . . .

> The viands were served on black-bordered plates, —turtle soup, Russian black bread, ripe olives from Turkey, caviar . . . game dished up in sauces colored to resemble liquorice water and boot-blacking. . . .

> [Shrike]: "The guests are dressed in black, the waiters are coons, the table is a coffin carved for you by Eric Gill. You serve caviar and blackber-

ries and liquorice candy and coffee without cream."

Huysmans characteristically used a "surrealist" device—describing natural scenes as though they were artificial—which West borrowed, though he changed its flavor.

> [Huysmans]: The plain lay partly in the shadows cast by the hills, while the centre, where the moonlight fell, looked as if it were powdered with starch and smeared with cold-cream. . . .

> [West]: The gray sky looked as if it had been rubbed with a soiled eraser.

And Huysmans also used the corollary to this device—endowing inanimate objects with life. West's phallic obelisk with its rapidly lengthening shadow was anticipated by the various scenes in which Huysmans described church pillars and forests in deliberately phallic imagery.

Huysmans' literary theories are also pertinent to *Miss Lonelyhearts*. His hero, Des Esseintes, regarded the prose poem as the ideal form—with Baudelaire and Mallarmé as its masters—and worried about how to transfer it to the novel.

> Again and again Des Esseintes had pondered the distracting problem, how to write a novel concentrated in a few sentences, but which should yet contain the cohobated juice of the hundreds of pages always taken up in describing the setting, sketching the characters, gathering together the necessary incidental observations and minor details.

Huysmans himself never solved the problem. His novels are prolix, often dull, sometimes unintentionally ludicrous, and almost totally static. His novelistic prose poems sacrifice the compression of Baudelaire and Mallarmé without gaining dramatic unity or narrative continuity. And his prose is so flavored with artificial spices that "decadent" seems the only accurate critical term. He is, I think, convincing only when he describes the aberrations of lust and his own fascinated revulsion from everything female. Yet he was oddly useful to West. His style, in West's hands, undergoes a variety of parodies, from the direct ridicule of *Balso Snell* to the compressed borrowings of *Miss Lonelyhearts* to the curious new applications we shall examine in *A Cool Million* and *The Day of the Locust*. And of course West made the ideal of "a novel concentrated in a few sentences" his own.

> Lyric novels can be written according to Poe's definition of a lyric poem. . . .

> Leave slow growth to the book reviewers, you only have time to explode. Remember William Carlos William's description of the pioneer women who shot their children against the wilderness like cannonballs. Do the same with your novels.

West's reference to Poe merely cites, of course, the classic source for symbolist theories about the short poem and unity of effect. Baudelaire repeated Poe's theories and added the injunction: "Be always a poet, even in prose." Huysmans transferred the ideal from poems and tales to the novel, and West, in *Miss Lonelyhearts*, actually wrote a novel which meets the symbolist criteria.

But West took from the symbolists more than his reliance on hallucinatory images and the ideal of a poetic, highly compressed prose. The typical symbolist hero was perhaps as important to him as any symbolist techniques. From Poe to Huysmans, the dandy reigns supreme. He is always morbidly sensitive, exacerbated by vulgarity, tormented by dreams and fantasies, weak-willed but compulsive, fond of attenuated emotions and aesthetic eccentricities, perverse, disintegrating, withdrawn. This description would, I think, apply equally to Roderick Usher and to Des Esseintes. It would also apply in many ways to Miss Lonelyhearts, except that West's treatment of the symbolist character implicitly repudiates the symbolist values. [In his *Axel's Castel: A Study in the Imaginative Literature of 1870-1930*] Edmund Wilson has observed that the symbolist hero usually dwells in a state of neurotic isolation, "encouraging [his] private manias, ultimately preferring [his] absurdest chimeras to the most astonishing contemporary realities, ultimately mistaking [his] chimeras for realities." Even when dandyism is mixed with religion—as it is in Huysmans—the focus remains relentlessly on the self. The dramatic issue is the self's damnation or redemption, and the way of Grace leads not into the world but into further isolation from it—Axel's castle is simply exchanged for the cloister. The Christianity of the symbolists is, therefore, often as decadent as their dandyism. Neurotic isolation is a badge of superiority. The people, not the devil, symbolize all that is evil; and vulgarity, not pride or concupiscence, is the taint of the Beast. West, however, was not much interested in the superiorities of the sensitive soul. He took the common symbolist materials—a neurotic, exacerbated hero in a vulgarized world—and drew from them his own conclusion: in the vulgarization of modern life, it is the masses who are the real victims. "Men have always fought their misery with dreams. Although dreams were once powerful, they have been made puerile by the movies, radio and newspapers. Among many betrayals, this one is the worst." The fact of sordid misery compels Miss Lonelyhearts' quest. Though he is "sick" himself, there is no escape for him in personal salvation. He must redeem the suffering of others to fulfill his mission, and his final delusion and death are a failure, not a martyrdom—he becomes just another victim of a world he could not change and could not escape except by ceasing to exist.

The burden of *Miss Lonelyhearts* is finally, therefore, far more Dostoevskian than symbolist. Its hero attempts significant action in a context of other lives whose fate is entangled with his own—lives which may even be more important that his own. And the emphasis upon mass suffering was only one of West's departures from the symbolists. Where Baudelaire contrasted the "artificial paradise" of hashish intoxication with religious experience, West made them equivalent. In the world of *Miss Lonelyhearts,* all paradise is artificial. The religious faith which furnished Baudelaire and Huysmans a way out of this world becomes, in West, just another pipe dream, as fatal as it is false.

Robert I. Edenbaum   (essay date 1968)

SOURCE: "A Surfeit of Shoddy: Nathanael West's 'A Cool Million'," in *The Southern Humanities Review,* Vol. II, No. 4, Fall, 1968, pp. 427-39.

[*In the following essay, Edenbaum examines structural and thematic elements of West's novel.*]

Nathanael West's *A Cool Million* is a latter-day *Candide:* Lemuel Pitkin takes the place of Candide, though unlike Voltaire's innocent, he does not learn the virtue of tending his own garden. Betty Prail is Lemuel's Cunegunde—and undergoes nearly as many rapes as her predecessor. Nathan "Shagpoke" Whipple is the 20th century version of Pangloss, though the good doctor's "this is the best of all possible worlds" is changed to Whipple's "America is the best of all possible countries," or at least would be under his enlightened guidance. In *Candide,* furthermore, the hero escapes with random beatings and floggings, and Pangloss is mutilated; in *A Cool Millon,* all the mutilation befalls Lemuel Pitkin himself. Before his peregrinations end in death he loses his teeth, an eye, a thumb, a leg, and his scalp. Candide's experiences lead him to the good life, after a fashion; Lemuel's fail to teach him even the lesson learned by Miss Lonelyhearts' correspondents in West's earlier novel: "it dont pay to be innocent and is only a big disapointment." Lem dies as innocent as he was born.

As in *Candide,* the central trio of *A Cool Million* start out from the same place and cross one another's paths only to be separated again and again in the course of their wanderings. After the mortgage is foreclosed on Lem's mother's house, he leaves to make his fortune in New York, but before he gets out of New England, he is robbed of his money by a swindler, arrested for selling stolen property, beaten by the police, and sentenced to 15 years in jail (where he suffers his first mutilation when all his teeth are pulled in order to eliminate "a source of infection"). In jail he meets Whipple, who has been arrested after the failure of his bank. When Lem is released and at last gets to New York, he rescues a bank president and his daughter, losing an eye for his reward: West's twist on the standard incident in the Horatio Alger books. In New York he is again beaten by the police, then slugged with a lead pipe by a goon. Without knowing what his job really is, he becomes a confidence man. When he tries to rescue Betty Prail from a brothel, he is himself enrolled and only misses becoming a male prostitute when his false teeth and eye fall out at an opportune—or inopportune—moment; when he is thrown out of the brothel and tries to get help from the police, he is jailed yet again—only for 30 days, because he pleads guilty. And so go Lemuel Pitkin's adventures in the great world.

The central plot of *A Cool Million* gets under way when Lem meets Whipple in New York and the demagogue outlines his plan for the salvation of the country from the clutches of the Communists and the International Jewish Bankers through his proposed organization, the "Leather Shirts." The rest of the book is the story of Lem's encounters with the fat man in the Chesterfield overcoat, Operative 6385XM, also known as Comrade Z, agent for both the I.J.B. and the C.P. When Lem, Whipple, and Betty leave for California to work a goldmine which is to pay the expenses of the Leather Shirts, Lem is tricked and abducted by the man in the Chesterfield, and loses his thumb in the encounter. Later, when Whipple and Lem get jobs with a roadshow called "The Chamber of American Horrors, Animate and Inanimate Hideosities," it turns out to be an instrument for spreading subversive propaganda, under the control of the same secret agent. And it is Operative 6385XM (Comrade Z) who finally puts a bullet through Lem's heart and makes him the Horst Wessel of the Leather Shirts.

The humor of Lem's adventures is obviously very broad, perhaps too broad. So, too, is the stilted diction of the dialogue, and the running authorial commentary. But the method of *A Cool Million* is not as random as it seems to be at first reading. The novel projects the "world-view" of the lower-middle class as it is embodied in American yellow journalism, of the Hearst press in particular. The "ideological" framework of that press, on the one hand, and its actual content, on the other, are mutually exclusive. That is, to simplify the matter for the moment, in the Hearst ideology America is pure and uncorrupt, the best of all societies of the best of all possible people. But the destiny of that society, story by story, page by page, is worked out in terms of rapes, murders, sinister plots, sexual perversions, lynchings, fires, revolutions, wars—the popular idiom of violence. Raymond Gram Swing, in *Forerunners of American Fascism,* wrote that William Randolph Hearst was then (1935) the fullest expression of the American lower-middle class, that he was, in fact, a "portrait" of that class; his newspapers were "his own self-portrait." It is that portrait of America that West presents—and, of course, ridicules—in *A Cool Million.*

Swing suggests a list of Hearst's—and the lower-middle class's—basic attributes in 1935, a list which barely needs to be changed today. The Hearst press wages continual war on professors and intellectuals, and is contemptuous of academic freedom and free speech; it is hostile to the "alien" ideas of labor and apologetic for big business (except for the pretense of hatred for "big" bankers and Wall Street); it is admiring of the anti-communism of European fascism, and (in the thirties) was openly willing to substitute fascism for democracy. "Americanism" in a variety of meanings, Swing continues, is Hearst's key term; since World War I the credo of his patriotism, and that of his readers, includes isolationism (now read military internationalism) and antipathy to anything foreign, particularly radical people and ideas; strikes, for example, are "an import from Russia." I might add to this list the fact that sex is suspect, particularly among people of Non-Caucasian or foreign blood, who lust after the Anglo-Saxon purity of the American female.

After the San Francisco General Strike was broken ("by applying purely fascist methods, and by trampling on the most elementary of American liberties," in Swing's words), Hearst wrote in a signed editorial of July 23, 1934:

> As a matter of plain fact there never has been a "forgotten man" in this country.
>
> There never has been a class or a kind or a sect

or a section which has not been sympathetically considered and cared for by our government.

> There has never been in historical records of the world so much liberty and so much liberality, so much personal independence or so much individual and national prosperity so equally distributed . . .
>
> Let us follow faithfully the precepts of our Fathers, who led a little unconsidered nation to world supremacy.
>
> Let us reaffirm our loyalty to American traditions and American can institutions and fundamental American principles . . .
>
> Thank God the patriotic citizens of California have shown us the way.

That is an example of Hearst ideology and Hearst prose. The editorial, word for word, might be from the mouth of Shagpoke Whipple, for Hearst prose and ideology plus Hearst violence is the formula of *A Cool Million.*

From the title, which, according to the epigraph of the novel, stems from the "old saying" "John D. Rockefeller would give a cool million to have a stomach like yours," to the last words of the book—"All hail, the American boy"—*A Cool Million* presents a string of the most obvious and contradictory clichés. The world of the novel is as disordered and random as that of Miss Lonelyhearts; but if Miss Lonelyhearts superimposes his own order, order is imposed on Lemuel Pitkin's world. A contradiction is only a contradiction, disorder is only disorder, when you are on the outside looking in. If, like a reader of a Hearst newspaper, or of Miss Lonelyhearts' paper, or the people who accept the films made in the Hollywood dream-factory in *The Day of the Locust,* you are on the inside looking out, then all contradictions are resolved: disorder becomes order when you accept the stuff of dreams. And, in *A Cool Million,* the clichés of the American dream—racial, social, political, sexual, economic—are accepted and structured into a version of ordered insanity, if one quite different from that of *Miss Lonelyhearts.*

The world of *A Cool Million* is literally peopled with clichés—that is, with racial stereotypes. The major characters are, of course, of good New England stock. Mrs. Pitkin's mortgage is held by Squire Joshua Bird, whose agent is Lawyer Slemp. As long as the widow pays the 12 per cent interest which, with Yankee shrewdness, they demand, there is no talk of foreclosure. Things might go on thus forever, but the house, a colonial antique, attracts the attention of the villainous Jew, Asa Goldstein, an interior decorator from New York. The orphaned Betty Prail works as a maid at the house of Lawyer Slemp, a church deacon and a stern man who beats her regularly, twice a week, "on her bare behind with his bare hand"; but Lawyer Slemp always gives Betty a quarter when he has finished beating her, and she is not ungrateful for her lot. And so it might go on forever, until evil foreigners enter in the persons of greasy Italians, white-slavers who take Betty to New York and sell her to the wily Chinaman, the brothel-keeper Wu Fong.

When Lem is arrested on the train to New York, the police who beat him—like the police who beat him now and then throughout the novel—have heavy brogues. Officialdom is represented by such good American names as Ezekiel Purdy, the warden of the prison, and Elisha Barnes, the prosecuting attorney, and they, of course, quail at the very name of powerful forces like Wu Fong: "Take my advice and don't mention him around here" says Elisha Barnes when Lem seeks justice in attempting to rescue Betty from the evil Oriental. The court-appointed lawyer assigned to defend Lem when he is arrested for the second time is a Jew named Abromovitz. Foreigners are behind all ills of whatever nature; innocent American youth—and age—is up against their alien creeds and alien tastes.

The role of the big city, particularly New York where much of the action takes place, becomes clear when Shagpoke Whipple gets his Leather Shirt movement under way. New York is headquarters for both the C.P. and the I.J.B.—presumably because both center around Wall Street. Big cities in general are not really American; when Whipple realizes that the Chamber of American Horrors is un-American, the show is in Detroit, and Whipple tells Lem that they cannot make their move yet because there are too many Jews, Catholics, and union-members in Detroit. When they get to the "really American town" of Beulah, somewhere along the lower Mississippi, and Whipple wants to whip the populace into a frenzy over the subversive show, he is introduced to the town as "one of the few Yanks whom we of the South can trust and respect. He ain't no niggerlover, he don't give a damn for Jewish culture, and he knows the fine Italian hand of the Pope when he sees it." The crowd riots, crucifies a Jewish "drummer," lynches an Indian and several Negroes, and rapes the housekeeper of a Catholic priest. And, when Whipple's National Revolutionary Party is on the road to success throughout the country, New York, "because of its large foreign population," is one of the last holdouts against the Cause.

It is not only the politics of "foreigners" that is un-American, but their sexual propensities as well. The reason Betty is picked up by the white-slavers is that they have been sent to New England by Wu Fong to get a pure American girl. Wu Fong pays a high price for her because "many of his clients were from non-Aryan countries and would appreciate the services of a genuine American. Apropos of this, it is lamentable but a fact, nevertheless, that the inferior races greatly desire the women of their superiors. This is why the Negroes rape so many white women in our southern states." Betty's first client is "a pockmarked Armenian rug merchant from Malta"; his successors include "numbers of orientals, Slavs, Latins, Celts, and Semites." Lem himself nearly falls prey to the depraved taste of the darker races for the light: when he is captured by Wu Fong, the Oriental's men dress him in a sailor suit and force him to submit to the advances of the lisping, mincing Maharajah of Kanurani, "whose tastes were notorious." Only the dislocation of Lem's false teeth and eye saves him. In the ordered disorder of *A Cool Million* and the Hearst press, there is no distinction between sexual and political perversity: the communist is a rapist and vice versa. Thus, when Whipple harangues the mob

at Beulah, his argument shifts casually from politics to sex and back again.

From Whipple's point of view, Lemuel Pitkin is the American boy who did not have the freedom to prove himself without being "laughed at or conspired against by sophisticated aliens." Thus, the aim of his Leather Shirt movement is to purge America of "alien diseases," to make America once again American, to give back to the citizens of America "their inalienable birthright; the right to sell their labor and their children's labor without restrictions as to either prices or hours."

The economic and political clichés bandied about by Shagpoke Whipple include the conspiracy of the big bankers and the communists; the middle class nature of the true American public, a middle class crushed between Big Capital and Big Labor; the need for the opposition of the internationalism of capital and labor with the nationalism of the middle class. The pattern of clichés in *A Cool Million* is perhaps the most apparent element in West's satire on the values of the middle class. The obvious irony that Whipple himself and the people he addresses who accept his vision of America are in a state of economic and political collapse is emphasized and the irony redoubled in the shrewdness of that businessman to end all businessmen, Wu Fong.

Wu Fong's establishment is originally a "House of all Nations," with a girl "from every country in the known world" except America; hence his search for a Betty Prail. (The assumption, presumably, is that American girls don't go in for prostitution except by force.) There are some fifty girls in the brothel, each in a two-room suite "furnished and decorated in the style of the country from which she came." Thus, Conchita, the girl from Spain, had in her suite,

> a grand piano with a fancy shawl gracefully draped over it. Her arm-chair was upholstered in horsehide fastened by large buttons, and it had enormous steer horns for arms. On one of her walls a tiny balcony had been painted . . .

Each of the other suites is decorated with similar appropriateness, "with excellent taste and real historical knowledge . . ."

Wu Fong has all the resourcefulness and know-how of the American merchant-prince—perhaps more, for he survives the depression while others fail. West employs the vocabulary of business to indicate that Wu Fong works under accepted American principles: when the depression hits, he realizes that he is "over-stocked," and he decides to "specialize" in American goods. "He saw that the trend was in the direction of home industry and home talent, and when the Hearst papers began their 'Buy American' campaign he decided to get rid of all the foreigners in his employ and turn his establishment into an hundred per centum American place." He has no trouble getting new stock, for the depression has obliged respectable families to throw their children on the open market. He gets Asa Goldstein to design a series of strictly American interiors: Pennsylvania Dutch, Old South, Log Cabin Pioneer, Victorian New York, and others right up to Modern Girl. Wu

Fong is "as painstaking as a great artist," not only in decoration, which West details with relish, but in all details, in cuisine, for example: "When a client visited Lena Haubengrauber [Pennsylvania Dutch], it was possible for him to eat roast groundhog and drink Sam Thompson rye. While with Alice Sweethorne [Old South], he was served sow belly with grits and bourbon. In Mary Judkins' room [Log Cabin Pioneer] he received, if he so desired, fried squirrel and corn liquor." And so on.

W. H. Auden comments that West's "worldly men," like Wu Fong (as opposed to Miss Lonelyhearts' friends, who "were not worldly men"), are bad men, but that West's "artistic instinct seems at times to contradict his conscious intentions." Thus, according to Auden, Wu Fong is "more sympathetic and worthy of respect" than Miss Lonelyhearts and Homer Simpson (*The Day of the Locust*).

> After so many self-centered despaires who cry in their baths or bare their souls in bar-rooms, a selfish man like [Wu Fong], who takes a pride in doing something really well, even if it is running a brothel, seems almost a good man.

Auden is well aware that West did not intend Wu Fong to be more sympathetic than his other characters, but he bases his comment on his conviction of West's self-pity and despair, both of which made compassion for Homer or Miss Lonelyhearts impossible. But it is worth setting against the Auden passage another which says essentially the same thing from another bias. Isaac Rosenfeld wrote of *The Day of the Locust*, "There is so much gusto in [West's] satire, so much taste for the very thing he was destroying, that he achieved in this book a kind of serenity, as a man will when his love and hate work together."

Auden's attitude is less wrong than limited. He fails to see, in all West's work after *The Dream Life of Balso Snell*, the fierce hatred, not of people, but of the "shoddy" of industrial civilization, in art and artifact. Wu Fong's establishment is the archetype of all shoddy; nothing, least of all sex and love, is genuine in the hands of this "great artist" of America. Wu Fong's house is what C. S. Lewis says Spenser's Bower of Bliss is—a picture "of the whole sexual nature in disease." And it is typical of the entire civilization in disease of which West wrote.

There is a passage in *A Cool Million* which clearly indicates the consistent point of view behind this book and *Miss Lonelyhearts* and *The Day of the Locust.* That is the long speech with which the Indian Israel Satinpenny whips his tribe into action against the white man, action which wins, as its sole trophy, Lemuel Pitkin's scalp.

> In our father's memory this was a fair, sweet land, where a man could hear his heart beat without wondering if what he heard wasn't an alarm clock, where a man could fill his nose with pleasant flower odors without finding that they came from a bottle. Need I speak of streams that had never known the tyranny of iron pipes? Of deer that had never tasted hay? of wild ducks that had never been banded by the U. S. Department of Conservation?
>
> In return for the loss of these things, we accepted the white man's civilization, syphilis and the

radio, tuberculosis and the cinema. We accepted his civilization because he himself believed in it. But now that he has begun to doubt, why should we continue to accept? His final gift to us is doubt, a soul-corroding doubt. He rotted this land in the name of progress, and now it is he himself who is rotting. The stench of his fear stinks in the nostrils of the great god Manitou.

> . . . The paleface came and in his wisdom filled the sky with smoke and the rivers with refuse. What, in his wisdom, was he doing? I'll tell you. He was making clever cigarette lighters. He was making superb fountain pens. He was making paper bags, doorknobs, leatherette satchels. All the powers of water, air and earth he made to turn his wheels within wheels within wheels within wheels. They turned, sure enough, and the land was flooded with toilet paper, painted boxes to keep pins in, key rings, watch fobs, leatherette satchels.
>
> When the paleface controlled the things he manufactured, we red men could only wonder at and praise his ability to hide his vomit. But now all the secret places of the earth are filled. Now even the Grand Canyon will no longer hold razor blades. Now the dam, O Warriors, has broken and he is up to his neck in the articles of his manufacture.
>
> . . . I know that you can't put the clock back. But there is one thing you can do. You can stop that clock. You can smash that clock.
>
> The time is ripe. Riot and profaneness, poverty and violence are everywhere. The gates of pandemonium are open . . .
>
> O, brothers, this is the time to run upon his neck and the bosses of his armor. While he is sick and fainting, while he is dying of a surfeit of shoddy.

"Shoddy"—for it is not merely the corrupt and defiled that Satinpenny (and West) is talking about, but the pretence of worth or quality where none exists. The articles of the white man's manufacture, the "paraphernalia of suffering" of *Miss Lonelyhearts*, are the specious substitute for demanded dreams, whether that of Christ or of America. The only answer the white man can give, the only weapon with which he can offer to do battle with social entropy, is the clichés of Shagpoke Whipple. Whipple's answer, elsewhere in the novel, to Satinpenny's tirade against the white man's "wheels within wheels within wheels within wheels" is that "The wheel will turn, for that is the nature of wheels." But Whipple's wheels are not those Ezekiel sees in his vision: " . . . and their appearance and their work was as it were a wheel in the middle of a wheel . . . and they turned not when they went . . . Whithersoever the spirit was to go, they went, thither was their spirit to go; and the wheels were lifted over against them; for the spirit of the living creature was in the wheels." And so does Shagpoke Whipple agree, but his wheels are those of a two-dollar watch running down after the guarantee has expired.

When Whipple later in the book asks where Satinpenny obtained the guns and whiskey he needed for his revolt, it is a rhetorical question to which he knows the answer: Operative 6385XM, Comrade Z. For, of course, Chief Satinpenny's speech is no less subversive than his uprising, and the Chamber of American Horrors that Pitkin and Whipple join is "in reality a bureau for disseminating propaganda of the most subversive nature" run by the same agent. "Can this be a coincidence?" Whipple asks when he realizes that the inanimate part of the show "consisted of innumerable objects culled from the popular art of the country and of an equally large number of manufactured articles of the kind detested so heartily by Chief Satinpenny." Whether or not it is a coincidence the reader never discovers; but Whipple, like the Hearst press, has no trouble believing that criticisms of things as they are, are similar, not through coincidence of perception, but because they are all elements in a vast conspiracy. In any case the inanimate exhibit includes the manufactured objects which earn the Chief's wrath—the surreal objects which later constitute the entire world of Hollywood in *The Day of the Locust.* The exhibit includes "Paper . . . made to look like wood, wood like rubber, rubber like steel, steel like cheese, cheese like glass, and finally, glass like paper . . . instruments whose purposes were dual and sometimes triple or even sextuple . . . ." The violation of natural function holds here no less than at Wu Fong's.

The animate part of the show includes a series of sketches of "Quakers . . . being branded, Indians brutalized and cheated, Negroes sold, children sweated to death." Snodgrasse, the manager of the show, makes a speech in which he tries to relate the sketches and the objects, a speech "in which he claimed that the former had resulted in the latter. His arguments were not very convincing, however." For, of course, the narrative voice in *A Cool Million* is on the inside of Whipple's world, looking out.

Paul Valéry wrote of literature in the age of movies, radio, and television that it has become "an art which is based on the abuse of language—that is, it is based on language as a creator of illusions, and not on language as a means of transmitting realities." It is that illusory world that West satirized in *A Cool Million* as well as in the novels which are usually taken more seriously, *Miss Lonelyhearts* and *The Day of the Locust.* The book, in fact, is not an image of a world at all, but an image of an image—a portrait of William Randolph Hearst's "own self-portrait" of the lower-middle class. The result, instead of the insistence on absurd complexity of *The Dream Life of Balso Snell,* is insistence on equally absurd simplicity. *A Cool Million* can hardly be criticized for lacking depth, for it pretends to nothing more than flatness. Perhaps that is why the book fails to deal adequately with the Leather Shirts themselves; the dispossessed had to wait until *The Day of the Locust* to become a "transmitted reality" instead of a Hearstian image "based on the abuse of language."

Since the 'twenties American writers have produced enough satirical attacks on the national failings: on the racial and religious bigotry of North and South; on the political paranoia that is both a cause and an effect of the Cold War; on the manipulation of the great "classless" public by the mass media; on the violence that characterizes American life and entertainment; perhaps most important of all, since it may be a common denominator of all these, on the psychological affinity for totalitarianism that has led to repression in the past and may again in the future. *A Cool Million* is hardly unique and hardly the best of these books. West's comic vision of an American fascism is, in many respects, dated: the Leather Shirts are clearly an institution of the 'thirties (though, if the Khaki Shirts, Blue Shirts, Silver Shirts, *et al* are gone, the Minute Men have been resurrected in the 'sixties). Thoughts of a smooth, automated public relations fascism of the future do not bring to mind West's farce. But it is impossible to come across a passage like the following, from the second installment of Mary McCarthy's "Report from Vietnam" in the *New York Review of Books* for May 4, 1967, *without* thinking of West's "surfeit of shoddy": "Before the Americans came, there could have been no rusty coca-cola or beer cans or empty whiskey bottles. They had brought them. It was this indestructible mass production garbage . . . that made the country, which must once have been beautiful, hideous. In the past, the 'natural' garbage created by human beings and animals must have been reabsorbed by the landscape . . . The American way of life has donated this disfiguring industrial garbage to the Asian landscape, which is incapable of digesting it."

In a phrase Chief Satinpenny would have been pleased to incorporate into his war-speech, Miss McCarthy calls this "the fecal matter of our civilization." If West's book was prescient in 1934 it was so less in its presentation of the social ills which still plague this country or in its political prediction than in its identification of "industrial garbage" with the American way of life.

Max F. Schulz (essay date 1969)

SOURCE: "Nathanael West's 'Desperate Detachment'," in his *Radical Sophistication: Studies in Contemporary Jewish-American Novelists,* Ohio University Press, 1969, pp. 36-55.

[In the following excerpt, Schulz analyzes the complex nature of West's protagonists.]

Nathanael West is reputed to have remained detached from the grotesqueries of Hollywood during the many years he worked there and from the follies of the human world for the thirty-seven years he lived in it. Yet West's novels make it clear that in the deeper reaches of his mind he was obsessed with man's nightmarish dual nature: his neurotic isolation and his social impulse, his self-deception and his self-mockery. Unlike Singer, and so many of the current Jewish-American writers, West was unable to rest content in the human suspension between heavenly aspirations and earthly limitations, belief and skepticism, order and disorder. He portrays life in his novels as a conflict of inadequate imperatives offered to man by society and culture as guides to live by. Conflict supposes not equipoise between codeterminants but supremacy of one over another. In that sense each novel, despite its basic satirical intention, represents a search for absolutes. "Reality! Reality! If I could only discover the Real," John Gilson calls for in his "journal." "A Real that I could know with my senses." In the astringent disillusionment of West's hope of finding something real to believe in—"A Real that would wait for me to inspect it as a dog inspects a dead rabbit"—each novel ends as a mocking denunciation of a false dream: the bardic dream (*The Dream Life of Balso Snell*), the Christ dream (*Miss Lonelyhearts*), the Horatio Alger dream (*A Cool Million*), and the Hollywood dream (*The Day of the Locust*). West's bitter cognizance of betrayal is pervasive. The thoroughgoing nature of his sense of the fraudulence and destructiveness of life is brilliantly, almost excessively, portrayed by the Trojan Horse correlative in *The Dream Life of Balso Snell.* Synonymous in Western thought with falsity and the end of a civilization, the wooden horse—specifically its alimentary canal—becomes the hallucinatory terrain over which Balso Snell wanders. Thus West clearly identifies man's dream world with sham and *fin de siècle*. He uneasily describes its death rattle, while trying desperately to dissociate himself with a comic ploy from emotional involvement in its agony. Unfortunately for the complete success of his stories, he was unable to control his own sense of outrage and despair. His shriek of laughter, as Victor Comerchero notes, "keeps breaking into a sob."

The first work of a writer is more likely to rely on literary analogues than later works which draw directly on experience for their substance. Such is the case with the four novels of West. *The Dream Life of Balso Snell* satirizes the ineffectuality of the imagination by way of an inexhaustible stream of allusions to and parodies of English writers from Dryden to Joyce, and from Dostoevsky to the French Symbolists and Dadaists, as well as much miscellaneous Western thought. The novel is a book perversely bent on proclaiming the illusoriness of books. West is reported to have told Liebling "that he had written Balso as a protest against writing books." That is ostensibly its general satirical aim. In fact, the novel strikes out thematically in a variety of directions, foreshadowing most of the preoccupations of West in his subsequent novels. Of these I wish to look at one to demonstrate West's ambivalent involvement in the despairing world that he depicts.

An essential thematic antithesis in the story pits romantic love against the procreative instinct. Like the nympholeptic shepherd-king in Keats's *Endymion* (and like Samuel Perkins, the subject of a biography by Mary McGeeney), Balso Snell swoons in and out of a dream within his dream as he mentally pursues Miss McGeeney, his thoughts struggling "to make the circle of his sensory experience approach the infinite." The prevailing situation is one of incompatibility. Lust encounters conditions of courtly love, and sacred love the wiles of the seducer. "Oh, I loved a girl once," Balso Snell laments:

> All day she did nothing but place bits of meat on the petals of flowers. She choked the rose with butter and cake crumbs, soiling the crispness of its dainty petals with gravy and cheese. She wanted to attract flies, not butterflies or bees.

This perverse merger of the fleshly and the ethereal becomes inextricably ambiguous in the witty biography of Saint Puce, the flea "who was born, lived, and died, beneath the arm of our Lord." In his daily sensations of sup-

ping on Christ, whose body provided him with both meat and drink, Saint Puce enacted perpetual Holy Communion.

As the ironic tone of these two examples indicates, West will not allow the mystery of the "Two-become-One" to remain intact. For him the contraries reconciled are always coming undone. Like Fra Lippo Lippi he forever sees "the garden and God there / A-making man's wife"; and this lesson of "The value and significance of flesh" he "can't unlearn ten minutes afterward."

If the spiritual cannot exist without the incarnate, through substance then must we confirm our substancelessness. Thus West fashions his own infernal mystery. The ideal vanishes into solid flesh. "Who among us can boast that he was born three times, as was Dionysius?" B. Hamlet Darwin asks caustically.

> Or who can say, like Christ, that he was born of a virgin? . . . Alas! none of us. . . . You who were born from the womb, covered with slime and foul blood, 'midst cries of anguish and suffering.
>
> At your birth, instead of the Three Kings, the Dove, the Star of Bethlehem, there was only old Doctor Haasenschweitz who wore rubber gloves and carried a towel over his arm like a waiter.
>
> And how did the lover, your father, come to his beloved? . . . Did he come in the shape of a swan, a bull, or a shower of gold? No! But with his pants unsupported by braces, came he from the bathroom.

Unfortunately for West's peace of mind, as the savage despair of the passage suggests, he found no satisfaction in this reduction of the infinite into the corporeal either. In an acrid satire of fleshly desire the story (and dream) concludes with Balso having a nocturnal emission. (The entire story represents the strenuously intellectual efforts of Balso's body to have a wet dream.) Even sex, the urge to procreate, ends as a pointless solo exercise in release of tension, likened to "the mechanics of decay." At the instant of emission, West exultantly informs us that Balso's "body broke free of the bard" and "took on a life of its own" "that knew nothing of the poet Balso." Despite this freedom from the false constraints of the categorizing imagination, not life, not the organic, but death and the mechanical describe the evolutions of the body. The basic metaphor used is that of an army performing "the manual of disintegration," maneuvering automatically "with the confidence and training of chemicals acting under the stimulus of a catalytic agent." Release is described in terms of a mortally wounded soldier: "His body screamed and shouted as it marched . . . then with one heaving shout of triumph, it fell back quiet . . . victorious." Thus the "miracle was made manifest" in the One, West says sardonically.

> The One that is all things and yet no one of them: the priest and the god, the immolation, the sacrificial rite, the libation offered to ancestors, the incantation, the sacrificial egg, the altar, the ego and the alter ego, as well as the father, the child, and the grandfather of the universe, the

mystic doctrine, the purification, the syllable "Om," the path, the master, the witness, the receptacle, the Spirit of Public School 186, the last ferry that leaves for Weehawken at seven.

In the diminishing manner of the burlesque stanzas of Byron's *Don Juan,* this catalogue of the body's regality ("the Spirit of Public School 186"!) underscores the skepticism with which West assents to the enthronement of matter.

Worse, yet, mind returns in the form of false literary sentiment to adulterate further the autonomous reality of the body. In a brilliant analysis of its style [in *Nathanael West: the Ironic Prophet,* 1964], Victor Comerchero shows how Balso's imagined copulation with Mary McGeeney is a parody of the melting, swooning seduction of eighteenth-century sentimental literature, of the stereotype passion of pulp fiction, of the hard-boiled back-seat wrestle of the realistic school, of the decadent *fin de siècle* dreams of encounters with an oriental *femme fatale,* and of the Molly Bloom monologue at the conclusion of Joyce's *Ulysses.* Saturninely, if comically, West reveals that even Balso's "dreams have been corrupted by literature. When he dreams, even a wet dream, it is a literary one." Driven by sexual desire, Balso Snell in his dream exploration of the nature of mind and matter may have discovered complacently that the body reigns supreme; but West's interpretation of the same event is less optimistic. In acrid disillusionment he concludes (corroborated by the dream context of the narrative) that Balso's solution to the hopeless bifurcation of life is as chimerical as the empty constructs of the mind, which man fools himself into believing are a pledge of meaningful order in the world.

"If there is a vision of love" in West's fiction, Josephine Herbst has remarked [in the *Kenyon Review,* 1961], "it is etched in the acid of what love is not." **The Dream Life of Balso Snell** presents a satyr's conception of love, **Miss Lonelyhearts** that of the whorehouse madam turned church-choir mistress. From cynical exploiter of his correspondents' cries for help, Miss Lonelyhearts metamorphoses into a Christlike savior of these lost and lonely souls of modern civilization.

West's point of view, however, is more subtle and complex in **Miss Lonelyhearts** than in his other three novels. His virulent skepticism is forever testing the validity of a thought and seeking the motive behind an action. Thus, he constantly and ambivalently undercuts his effort to find a pattern in existence. The horrifying lives of Miss Lonelyhearts' readers unquestionably moves the columnist to sincere desire to succor them. But his conversion from hard-boiled columnist to soft-souled evangelist is compromised at every turn. The psychology of sex—the twentieth-century substitute for previous centuries' religious faith—is the instrument of his betrayal of others as well as of himself. More often than not he is depicted as selfishly demanding rather than selflessly giving of his love. His impulse toward the Divine Love of man and "all God's creation" advocated by Father Zossima in *The Brothers Karamazov,* which he has been reading, manifests itself in sexual cruelty, self-loathing seduction, latent homosexuality, and religious hysteria. Like infernal stations of the cross in his outrageous progress toward saintly love of humanity, he bloodily bungles (in a dream) the sacrifice of a lamb, viciously tugs at the nipples of his fiancée's breasts, brutally twists the arm of an old homosexual, calculatingly attempts to seduce his boss's wife, distastefully submits to the sexual advances of a correspondent, ardently holds hands with her crippled husband, eventually strikes the housewife seductress in the face again and again, and finally achieves union with Christ while in a fever.

Throughout this inverse way of the pilgrim, religious ardor is confused with sexual desire, love with lust, and lust with violence and destruction. Miss Lonelyhearts' addresses of love to Betty, Mary Shrike, and Mrs. Doyle are associated with a Mexican War obelisk that like a giant phallus "lengthening in rapid jerks," and "red and swollen in the dying sun," seems "about to spout a load of granite seed" of death. The arm of the "clean old man," who was pulled from the stall of a public restroom and accused by Miss Lonelyhearts of being a pervert, becomes "the arm of all the sick and miserable, broken and betrayed, inarticulate and impotent . . . of Desperate, Broken-hearted, Sick-of-it-all, Disillusioned-with-tubercular-husband." In its effort to create order out of the entropy about him, Miss Lonelyhearts' sensibility, ill from its encounter with Fay Doyle, nightmarishly grapples with the contents of a pawnshop window, "the paraphernalia of suffering." Out of this jumble of articles it attempts to construct a phallus. Failing in this, it works to form the paraphernalia into a gigantic cross on the shore of an ocean, but

> . . . every wave added to his stock faster than he could lengthen its arms. His labors were enormous. He staggered from the last wave line to his work, loaded down with marine refuse—bottles, shells, chunks of cork, fish heads, pieces of net.

The linkage of Christ with the sea has strong libidinous overtones (where Christ and a phallic snake and Christ and a fish are also joined). The prior encounter with Fay Doyle is described in marine terms. Her undressing in the dark is heard by Miss Lonelyhearts as "sea sounds":

> Something flapped like a sail; there was the creak of ropes; then he heard the wave-against-a-wharf smack of rubber on flesh. Her call to him to hurry was a sea-moan, and when he lay beside her, she heaved, tidal, moon-driven.

And in language that foreshadows his subsequent building of the cross, he staggers out of bed fifteen minutes later "like an exhausted swimmer leaving the surf." In short, moved by the inadequacy of sex to steady his nerves and allay his self-hatred, he sublimates his eroticism in Christian humility, as a complementary form of therapy.

West could not formulate the ambivalence of his hope for a religious solution to life more clearly. As if the condemnation of *agapé* is not vehement enough, Miss Lonelyhearts' religious conversion, as Victor Comerchero demonstrates conclusively [in his *Nathanael West,* 1964], has a homosexual origin, further underlining West's "mythic, mocking, agonizing" suspicion that "true compassion" is unendurable in this decaying world. In the plight of Miss Lonelyhearts West portrays a devastating debasement of the Ulysses and Sirens motif. And the blasphemously blind universe that he envisions, in which "the Miss Lonelyhearts are the priests of twentieth-century America," receives full confirmation when Miss Lonelyhearts interprets his fever as a religious experience and climbs out of bed to embrace the crippled Doyle, whom he believes "God had sent him so that Miss Lonelyhearts could perform a miracle and be certain of his conversion." But West in his heart of hearts knew that God was dead. Miss Lonelyhearts never quite qualifies for membership in Graham Greene's pantheon of tainted saints. West's faith is at once too strong of desire and too weak of belief. Miss Lonelyhearts' need for a confirmatory miracle italicizes this profound skepticism. And the consequences of his desire for certainty are ironically devastating on both the sacramental and psychological levels of the narrative. He rushes to embrace the cripple and heal his leg. Doyle, however, is terrified by Miss Lonelyhearts' mad charge and by Betty's sudden appearance at the bottom of the stairs. As they grapple, a pistol Doyle is carrying accidentally fires, killing Miss Lonelyhearts. Locked in each other's arms they roll down the stairs. The symbolic union of the two men at the end is no doubt on one level expressive of Miss Lonelyhearts' spiritual yearnings; but their embrace, as Stanley Edgar Hyman observes [in his *Nathanael West*, 1962], is also homosexual, the one ironically penetrating "the body of the other with a bullet," "while the woman stands helplessly by." The disparity in the novel between the simple narrative affirmation of religious faith and the underlying metaphoric insinuation of Oedipal obscenities adumbrates the tortured ambiguity of West's imagination—its attraction to a Christ dream that it could not believe in.

In *A Cool Million* and *The Day of the Locust,* West explores the *Zeitgeist* of the cheaters and the cheated on native grounds. The dreams are now distinctly the homegrown variety found sprouting in the land of opportunity. "America takes care of the honest and industrious and never fails them as long as they are both," Nathan "Shagpoke" Whipple expounds from his perch on a cracker barrel. "The story of Rockefeller and of Ford is the story of every great American," he tells Lemuel Pitkin, "and you should strive to make it your story. Like them, you were born poor and on a farm. Like them, by honesty and industry, you cannot fail to succeed." The rest of *A Cool Million* is West's saturnine retort. Not from rags to riches but to the same old shirtsleeves, not from log cabin to White House but to the same old mortgaged farm house—this is the just reward of the barefoot, but honest and industrious, American boy. With acrid irony West equates business enterprise with the imagination, foresight, and aggressiveness of Wu Fong's white slavery emporium; and economic success with unapprehended chicanery and thievery. The American capitalistic system is posited on the productive ideal that the building of a better mousetrap is always good for the community. West's answer is to demonstrate that the folklore of Horatio Alger is more likely to be destructive of the individual than to be beneficial to society. And so he gives us the allegory of Lemuel's inexorable dismemberment on the barricades of capitalism: *sans* teeth, eye, thumb, scalp, and leg. To the memory of this derelict of the American way of life, the fascistic "Leather Shirt" followers of Shagpoke Whipple shout at

the conclusion in a national holiday celebration of Lemuel's birthday, "All hail, the American Boy!"

Victor Comerchero contends that because of the broadly comic tone of *A Cool Million,* a reversion to the tone of *The Dream Life of Balso Snell,* it fails to engage the reader. Consequently one tends to miss the serious point of the novel; "one is so amused by America as West presents it that one is neither frightened nor angered by it." In his effort to set up a critical issue, a straw man, so to speak, Comerchero exaggerates the difficulty posed by the blurred focus of the book's tone. The plain fact is that few readers (critical commentators, that is) have missed the central warning of the novel. Comerchero's observation, however, about the strange refusal of the story to take itself seriously is penetrating. The "personal involvement" that he suggests as an explanation has more than a grain of truth in it, as this essay, I hope, makes clear. But Comerchero does not, unfortunately, make anything more of this insight.

With what in the story is West involved? One cannot see the temperament and agony of West in either Lemuel Pitkin or Shagpoke Whipple, as one can in Balso Snell, Miss Lonelyhearts, and Tod Hackett. Hence the disturbing reserve of the story, by way of its excessiveness, does not derive from West's effort to dissociate himself from the central characters. Closer to the simple truth, probably, is that West, like his great predecessor Swift, is engaged in a lover's quarrel with a world that does not live up to his expectations. The broadly vulgar style in which he tells the story is, of course, on one level a parody of the crass, didactic prose of the Horatio Alger tale. Not so much the economic system, however, as the noisome aura of sanctity which enshrouds it is the object of his attack. After all, in writing his books, West himself hoped to turn an honest dollar. That hope was appropriately enough strongest with *A Cool Million.* The pious cant of a Shagpoke Whipple celebrates the manufacturing process and the pursuit of gain as the golden ends of human activity. The result is that the manufactured article deteriorates into a by-product and man is lost sight of altogether, transformed into a helpless ministrant to his own inexorable dehumanization. In the "Chamber of American Horrors, Animate and Inanimate Hideosities," West brilliantly pictures the debasement of taste and of sensibility produced by this carnival atmosphere. Here the flotsam of an industrial civilization buttressed by a false ethic is accorded the revered permanence of museum exhibits. Man's Hippocratic ideal is enshrined in the patent medicine offerings of the drugstore: in a "Hercules wearing a small, compact truss" and in "a copy of Power's 'Greek Slave' with elastic bandages on all her joints." Technical know-how is displayed in the cheap imitative tricks of paper "made to look like wood, wood like rubber, rubber like steel, steel like cheese, cheese like glass, and, finally, glass like paper." So the inconstant and the deceptive are memorialized with sneaking admiration as a tribute to American technological genius.

In Greenfield Village, Henry Ford's monument to Americana, there is an ash heap meticulously encased and labeled as having come from behind Thomas Edison's Menlo Park laboratory. Gazing at this dump pile, one can never be quite sure of the degree of fetish worship and, contrariwise, of sly humor that it represents. Nor can one categorically isolate West's attitude in *A Cool Million.* Shagpoke Whipple, the homespun American philosopher, wins our sufferance; but Shagpoke the politician, the America-firster, terrifies us. Lemuel, the innocent pawn, evokes our pity; but Lemuel the fool, the classic rube, equally arouses our derision. The names that West chooses for his characters are invariably witty wordplays, adding an extra dimension to our understanding of that person. Lemuel Pitkin's last name is close in sound to pipkin. Whether we are right to associate pipkin with Lemuel, we cannot avoid the scathing sense of the diminutive in his name; hence in comparison to his namesake Lemuel Gulliver, his misfortunes are seen as a diminuendo echo of the Brobdingnag gulling suffered by Gulliver on *his* Whittingtonian travels in search of fame and fortune.

The big lie is certain. Less evident is the source of the lie: the ideals of the American Way of Life? the naïveté of such simpletons as Lemuel? the "sophisticated aliens" decried by Whipple? or the ingrained evil of an economic system? The tone of *A Cool Million* reflects West's own uncertainty of what to finger. For all his pessimism he was not a little bitten with the American dream of a new Eden in the wilderness, as Betty's and Miss Lonelyhearts' nostalgic interlude on the farm in Connecticut hints—a surprising performance for seemingly so confirmed an urban novelist. There is also his love of the Bucks County countryside and of hunting and fishing. And there is the prophet's fervent need to believe in something, which in West is strung taut by the contrary pull of the cynical side of his nature. It is no wonder in his daily life that he strove to divorce himself from the furious indignation which drove his artistic vision.

With *The Day of the Locust,* West's view of life approaches Swift's in the fourth book of *Gulliver's Travels.* Spectators and performers alike feel the lash of his derision. Attracted by its semblance of life, Midwesterners come to Hollywood only to be tricked into death by a diet of sophisticate sex. They gyrate from movie premiere to movie premiere, as much automatons as the celluloid celebrities they push and shove to glimpse. The cinematic promise of ripe love and of a richer, fuller life never materializes. Faye Greener is a pathetic imitation of the Hollywood sex goddess, her thoughts and mannerisms a pastiche of Grade B movies. Both Homer Simpson and Tod Hackett (note the puns on death and havoc in the latter's name) discover in her ever fresh lure of sexuality a fey, receding will-o'-the-wisp. Her appearance promises love, but it proves no more rewarding than the suggestive accents and movements of a screenland heroine. Each one's desire for renewal of person is eventually betrayed by her beauty, "whose invitation wasn't to pleasure, but to struggle, hard and sharp, closer to murder than to love." The mechanically destructive recoil of the mob at the end of the novel reflects West's view of what happens to man when his hopes end as tattered scarecrows of reality. The adulatory pursuit of celebrities blurs sinisterly into the sexual violence that underlies emotional hunger. Spasms surge periodically through the crowd. Smutty remarks pass freely from stranger to stranger. Men hug passing complacent women. With such senseless eroticism, the mob apes the dark underside of the lives of its screen heroes and heroines. Death is inextricably linked to love. Human energy is easily diverted from a life instinct to a death impulse. Thus the adoration of the premiere mob is manifested as the blight of locusts, just as the alteration of the primordial hills of southern California into travesties of exotic architecture is another manifestation of the locust's presence.

The Westian novel is concerned at its center with the instability of existence, which derives basically from a metaphysical reaction to the modern world picture of everything being in flux. What more frighteningly askew world of metamorphosis can one imagine than the one of architecture, aesthetics, music, and mathematics Miss McGeeney tells us that Samuel Perkins discovered "in the odors of a woman's body." In these terms the Hollywood setting of *The Day of the Locust* provides West with the most perfect of the correlatives he has used to set forth his vision of life. As is proper in the city dedicated to the making of movies—to the creation of shapes that alter before one's eyes—the guises and gestures of the celluloid world of shadowy change, of make-believe, become the status quo. A fat lady in yachting cap converts into a housewife going shopping; a man in Norfolk jacket and Tyrolean hat, an insurance agent returning from his office; and a girl in slacks and sneakers with a bandanna around her head, a receptionist leaving a switchboard. The painted canvas, plaster, and lath sets on the back lots of the film studios reappear as the Mexican ranch houses, Samoan huts, Mediterranean villas, Egyptian and Japanese temples, Swiss chalets, and Tudor cottages that line Pinyon Canyon at the end of Vine Street. Repeatedly the Westian man transmutes into a woman. John Gilson as Raskolnikov, after murdering a dishwasher, caresses his breasts "like a young girl who has suddenly become conscious of her body on a hot afternoon." He imitates "the mannered walk of a girl showing off before a group of boys," flirts with some sailors, going "through all the postures of a desperate prostitute," and "camping" for all it is worth. Lemuel is transformed momently into a male prostitute in Wu Fong's establishment. And Miss Lonelyhearts exhibits more than one symptom of the homosexual. The many periods in history endlessly shift their outlines. Searching for Faye, who has a bit part in the movie "Waterloo," Tod Hackett wanders through a kaleidoscope of time and place and of the artifices of civilization:

> The only bit of shade he could find was under an ocean liner made of painted canvas with real life-boats hanging from its davits. He stood in its narrow shadow for a while, then went on toward a great forty-foot papier mâché sphinx that loomed up in the distance. He had to cross a desert to reach it, a desert that was continually being made larger by a fleet of trucks dumping white sand. . . .
>
> He skirted the desert, making a wide turn to the right, and came to a western street with a plank sidewalk. On the porch of the "Last Chance Saloon" was a rocking chair. He sat down on it and lit a cigarette.
>
> From there he could see a jungle compound with

a water buffalo tethered to the side of a conical grass hut. Every few seconds the animal groaned musically. Suddenly an Arab charged by on a white stallion. He shouted at the man, but got no answer. A little while later he saw a truck with a load of snow and several malamute dogs. He shouted again. The driver shouted something back, but didn't stop.

Throwing away his cigarette, he went through the swinging doors of the saloon. There was no back to the building and he found himself in a Paris street. He followed it to its end, coming out in a Romanesque courtyard. He heard voices a short distance away and went toward them. On a lawn of fiber, a group of men and women in riding costume were picnicking. They were eating cardboard food in front of a cellophane waterfall.

Faye Greener and her father, Harry, have maintained their theatrical poses of movie siren and vaudeville clown so long that, in the words of Comerchero, each "has been dispossessed of his personality—of his identity—through disuse."

West's obsession with flux is a central controlling force in *The Dream Life of Balso Snell.* In keeping with the protean nature of a dream, shapes are forever altering before Balso's eyes. His first sight of Miss McGeeney is of a slim young girl "standing naked before him . . . washing her hidden charms in a public fountain." She calls to him in the erotically charged language of the Romance.

Throwing his arms around her, Balso interrupted her recitation sticking his tongue into her mouth. But when he closed his eyes to heighten the fun, he felt that he was embracing tweed. He opened them and saw that what he held in his arms was a middle aged woman dressed in a mannish suit and wearing hornrimmed glasses.

Balso's orgasm at the end of the book, while dreaming of having sexual intercourse with Miss McGeeney changed again, "alas! but with much of the old Mary left, particularly about the eyes", enacts not only the completion of his own desire but also the wish fulfillment of John Gilson's schoolboy dream of sleeping with her. Dreams figure in all the novels except *A Cool Million*—where the dream is conceived of as a nationwide and patriotic preoccupation with the getting and keeping of money. Critics have made much of the Freudian and Surrealistic impulse in West's frequent resort to dreams, and rightly so; but their significance for West is not restricted to the psychological and aesthetic. In their reflection of a volatile universe, they also have a strong metaphysical import.

Another instance of West's preoccupation with the metamorphosis of things is the recurrence in his novels of performers and of the blurring of distinction between performer and spectator. In one way or another almost all his characters pursue an occupation, usually as writer or actor or painter, which transforms one kind of reality into another kind. The poet Balso discovers to his dismay that the wooden horse "was inhabited solely by writers in search of an audience." Instead of writing he finds himself involuntarily reading the work of others. *Miss Lonely-*

hearts is a story about a nameless man writing the daily "agony column" for a newspaper, answering letters, written under pseudonyms by the afflicted, for the entertainment of the majority of its readers. Here columnist and correspondent blur together in their dual categories of writer and reader. Even Lemuel Pitkin ends as a human prop at the Bijou Theater, dismantled nightly of his toupee, false teeth, glass eye, and wooden leg by the comedy team of Riley and Robbins. The complete symbiosis of performer and spectator occurs in *The Day of the Locust,* when the surrealistic actions of the mob become confused in Tod's mind with his painting of "The Burning of Los Angeles," which depicts such a mob savagely chasing the objects of their adulation. Here participant and observer (not to mention the actual and the fanciful) fuse indistinguishably into a macabre dance of death, celebrating the impermanence of all things.

The despair implicit in this obsession with change cannot be exaggerated. West's Jeremiahlike search for permanent values was forever overturning proof of the transiency of things. "West's brilliance" as a novelist, Comerchero observes, "proceeds from his ability to generalize frustration." West's vision of frustration stems from his metaphysical sense of the helplessness of man trapped in an unstable universe.

"If I could be Hamlet, or even a clown with a breaking heart 'neath this jester's motley," the writer of The Pamphlet exclaims, "the role [of being man] would be tolerable. But I must always find it necessary to burlesque the mystery of feeling at its source; I must laugh at myself, and if the laugh is 'bitter,' I must laugh at the laugh." These lines are often quoted as expressive of the strenuous effort of West to dissociate himself from the horrors of his age. In his novels he tried to realize distance by treating his fictional characters with extreme objectivity. But the cold malice with which he analyzes their faults, like the excessive scatology or sexual and bodily nausea found in all his writing, reveals the radical nature of his revulsion, and the extremity of his reaction, to the frustrated aspirations of his protagonists—which were also (with the exception of homosexuality) his own frustrations. The Westian man is an early species on the evolutionary scale of *genus victima.* Like the Neanderthal man, as compared to present-day *Homo sapiens,* he excites our morbid interest and disgust more than our sympathy or love. West's involvement with him is that of the prophet. He has the reformer's instinct. He wishes reality to be different from what it is and people from what they are. He hates what will not heed his jeremiads, unlike a Malamud or a Bellow, who can love their fictional *schlemiels* without feeling a strong urge to reform them. In this fact lies one of the fundamental differences between the idealistic naïveté of West and his generation and the radical sophistication of the Jewish-American writers of the fifties and sixties.

Strong overtones of antifascism and anticapitalism characterize West's novels as sincere expressions of their time. As Josephine Herbst remembers him, "The horror of this age was in West's nerves, in his blood." In his passionate search for something to believe in, West exhibits the desperate commitment of the thirties; but in his bitter sense

> West's novels make it clear that in the deeper reaches of his mind he was obsessed with man's nightmarish dual nature: his neurotic isolation and his social impulse, his self-deception and his self-mockery.
>
> —*Max F. Schulz*

of betrayal by ideas, he suffers the anguished disillusionment of the liberal of the thirties in the decades that followed. His need for detachment was intense; but the age and his background made that well nigh impossible for him to realize. At a time when most of his Jewish contemporaries were still writing realistically of the Jewish experience in America, West was attempting to define symbolistically the larger American experience. His vocabulary necessarily relied heavily on literary fashion. His vision of American life was inevitably narrow and limited. His insecure control of his material, despite his inventiveness and his expenditure of incredible labor on his stories, foredoomed the results to shakiness of form, uncertainty of tone, inconstancy and occasional vulgarity of language, and finickiness of output. His passionate involvement in ideas led to his quasi-identification with the search for values of his central characters. Unfortunately, such identification with his fictional creations also inhibited his judgment of their quest. His stories are more heated and polemical than is good for them. He too often lost what a later generation would call his cool. Yet in his exploration of the meaning of Hollywood and in his probe of the psychic blows suffered by being American, he courageously homesteaded forty acres on which Mailer, Bellow, Fiedler, and the other contemporary Jewish-American novelists are currently building a Levittown.

T. R. Steiner   (essay date 1971)

SOURCE: "West's Lemuel and the American Dream," in *The Southern Review,* Louisiana State University, Vol. VII, No. 4, Autumn, 1971, pp. 994-1006.

[*Steiner is an Hungarian-born educator and critic. In the essay below, he compares the protagonist of* A Cool Million *to the rags-to-riches heroes of Horatio Alger's novels.*]

Nathanael West's *A Cool Million* remains the least appreciated of his works, to a large extent because it has not been read properly. Its mode of operation is only partially understood at best; hence readers' responses are at the same time not serious enough and too serious. Like the Horatio Alger novels, on which it is based (and in a way like *Gulliver's Travels,* from which it draws the name of its hero, Lemuel Pitkin), *A Cool Million* frequently purports to be a children's book. As such, although its literary mode may be parody or mock-heroic, West's novel is also fantasy, myth, dream-wish identification, imaginative "redemption," and pure play. Because of this important "la-

tent content," the book much more resembles *The Dream Life of Balso Snell* and *Miss Lonelyhearts* (called a modern myth by Victor Comerchero) than one might first have suspected. Its great difference from these earlier works is that they are more arty—a quality toward which West manifested much ambivalence.

I do not deny that the book has "serious" social and political content, and clearly shows West's anxiety that a Hitlerian dictatorship might come to Depression-fragmented America. But this content is trite: demagoguery and the blind force of mass-man had been staples of cultural and political analysis since de Tocqueville, Burckhardt, and Nietzsche had outlined them as particular dangers of democracy. West seems not so much interested in the fact of these monstrosities as in the popular imagination which makes it easier for them to thrive. That, rather than Nathan "Shagpoke" Whipple, is the arch-villain of his book. As overt pulp-magazine fiction, *A Cool Million* is a mirror of the popular imagination—an early piece of pop art, like Rauschenberg or Lichtenstein, using American cultural materials to comment on them, chanting American themes in a skewed, that is to say, "true," fashion. Here, it insinuates, is the landscape of the American psyche, which needs and creates Horatio Alger, racial stereotypes, pulp pornography. If we required yet another foil to make the mode of *A Cool Million* clear, it would be the many commentators on mass culture from Freud to Robert Warshow and Susan Sontag, but most notably George Orwell in his examination of boys' weekly papers and lewd postcards to get at the common Englishman. For a comparable reason, West consciously wrote a pornographic penny dreadful.

It is, therefore, meaningless to talk of West's style in the book since his effort must have been to divest himself of style, to become a scarcely literate and dirty-minded adolescent. West "supplies" only the invisible frame—the skewing of speeches, the introduction of super-grotesqueries, the revelation of what happens after the jump-cut—in short, the consciousness which the reader perceives above and controlling the naïve materials, the consciousness revealed by the mere fact of West's recognizable name on the book. So, the Alger material becomes very sophisticated and the skeleton for, as well as merging with, a whole series of American motifs, fictions, and myths; American Dreams certainly, but also American Nightmares. The American Boy wants to succeed and honorably have the boss's daughter (or at least a clean "white" girl like Fiedler's Blonde Maiden) but he also wants to destroy (in fantasy roles like the gangster) and to brutally deflower. He wouldn't mind being Tom Baxter piggishly taking frail Betty; he lusts after the international, dark sex of Wung's House of All Nations, and like the American Girl, desires exotic experience (but preferably with fabricated authenticity). Alger's hero becomes the picaro (the myth tends readily toward this metamorphosis because of American cultural and geographic mobility), touching North and South, mine and corral, farm and frontier. Here are Davy Crockett, Abe Lincoln, and the martyr Patrick Henry; here, introduced in one of Whipple's speeches, the great military landmarks—"Remember the Alamo! Remember the Maine!" Here Chingachgook and the comity of American bloods like that in Cooper and Melville. In outline, sketchy, fragmented, jocose form, then, *A Cool Million* is the encyclopedia of mythic "America." And West realizes that the Dreams mask horrors and coexist with nightmares—American xenophobia, anxiety, fear of the culturally exotic. Hence the racial stereotypes: cops are always Irish and revel in brutality; Chinese are inscrutable "celestials"; Indians retain the redness of their savagery; Jews, in their craft and cunning, deceive and steal. American populism hates, fears, but also identifies with the foreign, which enables it to have its darker fantasies. It is like Hitler, who (according to Alan Ross and Norman Cohn) turned the Jew into both the dark father whom he strove to destroy and the dark actor who fulfilled his erotic wishes. Although the Deep South riot which West describes could happen, West is least concerned with describing present reality, or predicting the future; the riot is a "sign of the times," a symbolic probability (very much in the Aristotelian sense) given the real nature of the native American psyche. It is a pleasing fiction to that psyche, the inverse corollary to the "constructive" egoism of the Alger myth. West sees, indeed, that whatever their outward manifestation, however much self-control or sacrifice even our good myths demand, they are power-myths either in essence or application, violent by nature as is every page of *A Cool Million.*

The dreams of power are analyzed as to their archetypes; so is the dream of martyrdom. For the essential structure of the book is not the successful life of an Alger protagonist but the creation of a martyr-hero for Whipple's National Revolutionary Party—the life not of J. P. Morgan but a mock-Christ. Strangely, those critics who see West as a symbolist, his central fictions as quest and sacrifice, and Lonelyhearts as a modern Christ, have not recognized the underlying fable of *A Cool Million.* Like Christ but without His consciousness, Pitkin bears a Revealed New Life, suffers, and dies for his Dream, leaving his "message" to American youth. Lemuel (the name means, literally, "belonging to God") has no earthly father; we are asked to see him (through the name of his widowed mother Sarah) as Isaac, Christ's type as sacrificial victim in the Old Testament. Whipple is his spiritual father, sending him into the world with a blessing (and, ironically, like Judas "selling" him to that world with the loan of thirty dollars). Before the quest—an attempt quite literally to "save his house"—begins, Lem kills the "furious animal" which assails the innocent Betty, conquers the bestial, pig-eyed Tom Baxter, but is tricked by that fraudulent "butcher boy," in an incident prefiguring his future defeats. Still, Lem tries to live the destined life, is kind, charitable, self-sacrificing; experiences degradation and poverty for Whippleism (the avatar of the Dream); and is slowly destroyed by the world his message is trying to "save." (Modern America here is Sodom, the Cities of the Plain, Roman Judaea—or their modern manifestation, Eliot's Waste Land, which West clearly seems to call on.) At least once, Pitkin is explicitly likened to Christ. Having been arrested for trying to accuse the powerful brother-keeper Wu Fong, he protests: " 'But I'm innocent . . . I'm innocent,' repeated Lem, a little desperately. 'So was Christ,' said Mr. Barnes with a sigh, 'and they nailed him'." And they nail Pitkin, in the mock crucifixion of the music-hall

scene. Standing between the two comics, Riley and Robbins (is it far-fetched to see this name as deliberately evoking the two thieves?), who use his destroyed body as a comic prop, Pitkin begins the revolutionary speech prepared for him by Whipple: " 'I am a clown . . . but there are times when even clowns must grow serious. This is such a time. I . . .' Lem got no further. A shot rang out and he fell dead, drilled through the heart by an assassin's bullet." Brilliantly, West prevents Lem from stepping out of his role. He must be interpreted by Whipple on the national holiday, Pitkin's birthday, which combines in a socio-religious ceremony elements of Washington's and Lincoln's Birthdays, Armistice Day, and Christmas: "Simple was his pilgrimage and brief, yet a thousand years hence, no story, no tragedy, no epic poem will be filled with greater wonder, or be followed by mankind with deeper feeling, than that which tells of the life and death of Lemuel Pitkin. . . . Although dead, yet he speaks. . . . He did not live or die in vain. Through his martyrdom the National Revolutionary Party triumphed, and by that triumph this country was delivered. . . . America became again American." Pitkin the redeemer: although "dismantled," his mantle has fallen on other shoulders. The book ends with a striking triptych: on the reviewing stand, as thousands of American youth "March for Pitkin," are Pitkin's mother (his Mary), Betty Prail (surely in her prostitution the Magdalene) and Whipple, at once the God, Judas, and Pope of Pitkinism.

So, joco-seriously, West sees Christ the hero in Horatio Alger, and a large degree of the Alger quality in Christ. The Greatest Story Ever Told has become in this book pulp-magazine uplift, and West realizes that for the popular imagination, Christ (or the archetypal questing hero) can function either as victor or victim. The risen "Christ" is an identificatory model; the fallen, a defenseless recipient of our yearning aggression. We worship the powerful, successful "Christ"; we prey on the meek, submissive, idealistic. Indeed, what West seems most responsive to in the Alger myth, and in some of the other American myths he parodies, is that they are exploitative. In the fallen world of modern America, the promises of the American Dream are used to harness the idealism, energy, and altruism of the young. The culture myth, in this novel transmitted by Whipple to Pitkin, implicitly says to the child, "The world is your oyster. Go out and succeed." But it does not prepare him for social and political realities; indeed, by its lie it disables him in the inevitable competition with knowing adults and boys who have wised up. Yet, the cultural ideal endures, virtually through the destruction of the idealistic child, betrayed promiscuously to sharper, con man, Indian, Southerner, WASP, Jew. However sympathetic Whipple may be at times, however consciously idealistic, he is the exploiter (already in the first scene bilking the innocent Lem). And however much of a looby Pitkin is, he functions—like Candide or Parson Adams—as the ingenue in satire, establishing (obviously without force or validity) an unshakeable blind belief in the right, the good, the committed.

Through his belief in the Dream, Pitkin is not only like the shoddy, sentimental Alger, but also like Clyde Griffiths, Gatsby, and the host of ingenue martyr-heroes of American twentieth-century fiction. But in one very significant way, *A Cool Million* differs from the novels of West's later friend, Fitzgerald, and "Swedes" like Dreiser. Its difference lies in the fact that *A Cool Million* was written by a Jew, and West's Jewishness deepens as well as personalizes this seemingly abstract, shallow book. Although the two-dimensionality may be attributed to aesthetic distancing, I think that it resulted mainly from West's conscious attempt to use a "witty" symbolic mode and his desire, conscious or not, to mythicize his own cultural experience. By the "Jewish" element I do not mean something as simple as West's often cited "anti-Semitism," which we are told led to the unsympathetic portraits of Jews in this book and the others (where are there sympathetic portraits here of any ethnic type?), because I think that West was no more anti-Semitic than many assimilated Jews. (To call the low self-esteem or self-hatred of these people—often resulting from their acceptance of the American Dream—anti-Semitism is ludicrously inaccurate.) In *A Cool Million,* West's Jewishness begins to be seen in the intertwining of native American and Christian (and New Testament) with Jewish (and Old Testament) strains. The hero, his mother, his spiritual father, indeed almost every character in the book, has at least one Jewish (or Hebrew) name: Yankees like Nathan Whipple, Levi Underdown, Ephraim Pierce; Indians like Jake Raven and Israel Satinpenny; an Irish Moe Riley; and Jewish Patriarchs like Asa Goldstein, Ezra Silverblatt, Seth Abromovitz. There is a lot of incidental fooling with these names—Jake Raven is violent ("raving," "ravin"); Satinpenny's first name reminds us of the commonplace equation of Red Indians with the Lost Tribe; two characters "pierce" and "rile," two Jews, are associated with pelf—but I think that their main point is to posit modern America as a kind of conglomerate, ironic Chosen People, sharing not only names but characteristics and cultural "artifacts." Thus, Asa Goldstein sells "Colonial Exteriors and Interiors" and Ezra Silverblatt supplies coonskin caps and other accessories to Whipple's Party. (For their trading in Americana, even at their own expense, Jews are indeed satirized heavily.) But the Yankees and Indians also are characterized by their greed and financial rapacity, while the two lawyers who "get" Pitkin are Seth Abromovitz and Elisha Barnes. The characteristic which all share is their violence, whether overt like that of Irish cops, Southern lynch mobs, or Indians, or disguised like that of Warden Purdy, who has all of Pitkin's teeth knocked out "to prevent infection." By taking the melting-pot metaphor seriously, making it one constructive principle of his book, West suggests that the Hebrew, Christian, and American myths are interpenetrable, indeed, interchangeable for "explaining" life in these eclectic United States. All of them talk about one life, which is man's.

But I think that the cultural interpenetration points to an experience and a problem more personal for West. Where could young Nathan Weinstein (or his Jewish contemporaries) find identificatory cultural myths in a nation whose early heroes are Anglo-Saxon or Nordic, who bear "American" names like George Washington, Abe Lincoln, Ethan Allen, Nathanael Greene, Patrick Henry, Nathan Hale? If Jews had come to the United States in great numbers around the mid-nineteenth century, this might

have proved a lesser problem because of the high esteem of Hebraism within the Boston-Concord circle. For two centuries Puritan and Quaker proper names had been consciously and happily chosen from Old Testament figures, and Melville's great diabolic hero is named after a King of Israel while the weaker—albeit less dangerous—men around him are called Starbuck, Stubb, and Flask. By the 1920s, with the anti-Semitism that attended mass immigration, there was little if any esteem: our culture heroes, "Black Jack" Pershing, George Herman "Babe" Ruth, Charles Lindbergh "the American Eagle" (Horatio Alger may well stand for all of these), were not Jews, and if they accidentally had Hebrew or "Jewish" names this stood in ironic counterpoint (as it does in *A Cool Million*) to their frequent anti-Semitism. Thus, in confronting American folk-heroes and culture myths, Jewish youth were at a farther remove than Hoosier farm-boys: the fictive distance of myth was there for everyone, but Horatio Alger did not even seem to be *about* Jews (this was also a problem for Poles, Italians, and Negroes, but West was none of these). Fiction after fiction said to them: "We're not about you." I am reminded of a fairly recent one, the Gillette Blade comic strip of the 1940s. Its obviously Anglo-Saxon heroes lived adventurous lives, saved archetypal American Beauties from horrible fates, and thus met their industrialist daddies. Then, metamorphosed by an obligatory shower and shave (the point of the ad), each hero would win both the Girl and the Job. But hath not the Jew a beard since it can be pulled? Mordecai Richler has spoken similarly of the dearth of Jewish identificatory models in sports, and thus can explain the almost hysterical ethnic responses to Sandy Koufax and Hank Greenberg (*Commentary,* Nov. 1966). (I remember a different tactic: in the early forties identifying with football players whose first name was the same as mine; hence, sharp in memory is not only Tom Harmon but the forgotten Tom Kuzma.) *A Cool Million* is implicitly about this problem, and West, again joco-seriously, says that the American mythic landscape is about and for Jews if they attend to it closely enough. Another, a more decisive, way to get into "America" was to change one's name, and West also did that.

We must not forget that West, for all the protestations of his non-Jewishness, lived a life so typical culturally that as I read James Light's brief account of it I frequently lived over remembered scenes. The son of immigrant parents, he began early to drift away from what little ethnic heritage he had—I would guess, from Light's version, because of the religious indifference of his father and the nominalist conception of Judaism by his mother. After an undistinguished high school career, he divested all the trappings at Brown, becoming an aesthete and Brooks Brothers dandy, writing for the rather avant-garde college literary magazine and making many non-Jewish friends. Still, despite his friendship with members of elite Christian fraternities, he was never pledged by one because of their exclusion clauses; and, later, despite his winning the Christian girl, he never wed her—perhaps in part, as Light suggests, because of "the religious difference." He changed his name in 1926, before leaving for France; moreover, he had been playing around with the persona "Nathan von Wallenstein Weinstein" for a long time. I would not do justice to the complexity of West's life, to his two-year Parisian sojourn and all of the other experiences which made him other than some pasteboard "fallen Jew," but the skeleton of that life is almost ludicrously exemplary, down to the pragmatic and possessive Jewish mother who moved in to serve "lavish meals" at his farm when he was a thirty-year-old practicing writer, and to his happy marriage of seven months—ended by double tragedy—to "My Sister Eileen," surely an archetypal American Girl.

So, *A Cool Million* is also symbolic spiritual autobiography—or for those who are wary of "biographical fallacy," an interplay of fictive positions which might have gone on in the head of West or some other second-generation "alien" boy. The novel records confrontation with the American myth. It certainly does not seem coincidental that Alice, the daughter of Levi Underdown, whom Lem saves by a bit of derring-do, echoes in name his sweetheart Alice Shephard; nor that this fictional "romantic" young lady, having "misunderstood the incident," at the same time protects and rejects Pitkin: "She smiled kindly at our hero, and led her irate parent from the scene." But this is at best windowdressing, an insider's joke, resembling others which seem directed at friends like S. J. Perelman. More importantly, much in the novel suggests that West identified with both his major characters. One, like Proust's Marcel and Kafka's "K," carries the name of his creator—Nathan Whipple, Nathan Weinstein, Nathanael West. The other is the young hero, the Christ, the American quester. He belongs to God, and he is the Lamb of God, like Christ, like the symbolic "Isaac" sacrificed by Abraham, like the *lemmele* his name suggests. But like Christ, and as his role demonstrates, Lemuel is also the holy fool (in Yiddish, the *lemech*). His last name also provides a range of associations: "kin" of the everlasting "pit" as Comerchero suggests? A relative of the mass audience which sits in the pit? Like the flea Saint Puce of *Balso* who lives in the armpit of Our Lord? A little bit of damnation himself? Pitkin Avenue, the Fifth Avenue and Champs Elysees of Jewish Brownsville? The relationship of Whipple and Pitkin is complex: Whipple is adult, practical, experienced, platitudinous, but ultimately successful; Pitkin is child, innocent, without language, a failure, but idealistic. I have already shown Whipple to be the God-Judas-Pope of Pitkinism. The relationship of the two also resembles that between Abraham and Isaac—Whipple "silently communes" with the picture of Abe Lincoln, obviously his model—but this mythic relation is ironically skewed like all the others as Abraham sacrifices his "son," not a symbol. All of the myths show division and ambivalence in West's imagination: an "adult" cultural voice presents images of success—known to be evil—to the aspiring adolescent, who is destroyed in their pursuit. And the adult self, Nathan, still strangely tied to West's former life, scourges the "American Boy" idealist, figuratively "whipping" him for temerity. It is the same kind of near-hysterical punishment of the questing innocent which underlies some of Swift's best satires: "Fool, how dare you aspire to a lot which is not man's? How dare you be other than a vile human." The author seems to be pointing to the probable cost of his having "gone West," in this book very nearly equated with having gone "Whipple," since that worthy allies himself with such American clichés and at one point

leads a gold-mining expedition West. "Going West"—opting for a life that mirrors the national dream—may beckon to the adolescent as ideal personal fulfillment; for the adult it means taking the national lie with full comprehension, with little real to compensate for lost innocence, altruism, and the particulars of an individual past. The book ends with no resolution of its underlying conflict, no synthesis of impossible innocence and vile experience, no celebration of heroic loss in the face of insuperable odds. Nathan Whipple has only venal success; but Lem Pitkin has died meaninglessly, in fact, in support of Whipple's Know-Nothing Americanism. One cannot live either as Child or Adult. *A Cool Million* also seems to examine the author's artistic decisions and the meaning of going West as a novelist. Near the end of the book both Pitkin and Whipple are constantly before audiences and show two presentational styles: Pitkin is the straight man, boffoing audiences by his deformities (are there echoes of *Balso Snell* here?), witlessly feeding their destructive lust, but never in control of his own act; Whipple is in control, lulling or inciting them with flatulent pieties, but totally wrapped in an inhuman rhetoric. Lem is killed just as he is about to speak seriously in his own person; and Whipple gets the girl, Lem's proud mother (West's wanted him to go into a more successful line than writing), and power. To command the audience of a hundred thousand, however, he debases the materials of Lem's passion into the heroic inanities of Americanism. Might this not have seemed the danger if Nathanael were to go all the way West?

The reader may be sympathetic to my analysis of the book so far, but I could never convince him—nor would I try—that he was reading anything but a low burlesque, a piece of slapstick. The tone is little like that of other "serious" books, unlike that of *Balso,* which is self-consciously artistic and derivatively literary, unlike *Gulliver* or the learned wit of *Gargantua;* most, I suppose, like the black comedies of our time. How do we explain this crude tone? What is West saying by it? Apparently, that if our Dreams derive from the popular imagination, they inevitably embody and reflect the quality of that imagination. American life may be verifiably grotesque, incredibly destructive in its effects, but in the average mind it registers in a form banal, slightly titillating, clichéd, impossible to take seriously. The mass—for whatever reasons, not the least of which is the seduction of fantasy—is uncaring of, anesthetized to, real experience. In popular apprehension, rape, for example, is not the brutal and painful forcing of a real woman, but something histrionic, played out in an "ideal" world of fancy, somehow detached from rapist and rapee—therefore, potentially ludicrous: "In the half gloom of the cabin . . . the Pike man [was] busily tearing off Betty's sole remaining piece of underwear. She was struggling as best she could, but the ruffian from Missouri was too strong for her. . . . At the sight of poor Lem weltering in his own blood, Betty fainted. In no way disturbed, the Missourian went coolly about his nefarious business and soon accomplished his purpose." On the one hand, this event is made meaningless; on the other, it shows West can write better soft-core pornography than the professionals. The rape of Betty exemplifies two key effects of *A Cool Million*: while deliberately pandering to the American predilection for lust and violence, it drains, through the even-tempered mechanicalness of its language, all human significance from its events. West forces the reader to see the artificiality of this language, but seems in no way to comment on it. That is, he does not posit—even by indirection—a more humane or moral use of language, certainly not an "art" use. (Indeed, the pretension of art is one of the balloons he pricks repeatedly from *Balso Snell* on.) And once again, West uses the medium to comment pessimistically on his own writing. He seems to be saying, "Look how well I write in these trashy American forms." Another in the line of American apocalyptists, closer to loving pornography and violence than hating them, West seems to point to the degree to which American Dreams and the mass psyche have penetrated his own imagination.

A Cool Million, then, is about the American power-success-violence ethic and how much it has corrupted even its satirist. Surely West, with his knowledge of Spengler, recognized that by taking his new name he was identifying himself with the decline of a doomed civilization. In *Day of the Locust* he comes to the farthest American Abendland, California, where the refugees from the nation's great heart have come to die. "Going West" becomes synonymous with the death wish, and we have been told that of all humanity which West hated, he hated himself most. In this context, the epigraph of the book, "John D. Rockefeller would give a cool million to have a stomach like yours," is ambiguous and frightening. Clearly it points to the psychosomatic danger of following the American Dream in its real nature, since Rockefeller and Henry Ford are for Whipple and the book types of Horatio Alger. But who is the "you" to whom the epigraph is addressed? Is it the reader (the "cool million," the "hypocrite lecteur," West's *semblable* and *frère*) who can live in that world and read the fantasy-record of its degradation without flinching? Or is it the author himself, in one of his persons so inured to horror and filth that he can treat it lightly, so much of—or aloofly above—degraded mankind that he does not retch as he records?

It may be late in the day to speak of any important American writer, much less Nathanael West, as a Jewish writer, and to involve one's own experience of Jewishness in a discussion of him. To do so invites scorn and misunderstanding. To do so, now that the Jews have made it very nearly to the center of the White Establishment, and other groups are suffering even more intensely their traditional fate of exclusion, runs the risk of seeming dated. Yet Leslie Fiedler in a *Partisan* essay (Summer, 1967) called West, for *Balso Snell,* the first of the modern American Jewish writers, and he is right—at least as far as *Balso* and *A Cool Million* are concerned. It is valuable, even necessary, to approach West with some understanding of the Jewish cultural milieu, if only to counteract the effect of his near-convert's fascination with Christ in *Miss Lonelyhearts* and to open up the body of Jewish-Hebrew reference in his books. It may be helpful, although certainly not necessary, for the critic to be personally familiar with the particular cultural shocks which West seems to have been an heir to, however much he tried to avoid or deny them. For whatever degree of universality there is in West's fictions about the American scene, I am convinced that he was an intensely personal writer, with a Freudian's heightened awareness that an author by indirections talks of his own wishes and fears and that his symbols plot his own inner landscape.

West's first short novel:

The job at the Kenmore Hall Hotel provided for West precisely what he had not had in New York before: a certain removal from his family and yet a fixed place—in short, the conditions for meditation. Infrequently in his room, more often sitting in the glassed-in hotel office—insulated from the people in the lobby, but still in visual contact with them—he was able to work on *The Dream Life of Balso Snell.* In the hotel, he developed his natural attitude of preoccupation into genuine meditation and night after night between 1927 and the last part of 1929 wrote and rewrote his book, first in pencil on yellow ruled paper, and eventually on typed sheets, correcting and retyping repeatedly. As late as 1930 he was calling it *The Journal of Balso Snell.* In some ways it was a journal of his own daily response to certain problems of attitude and definition, in art and life, then engaging him intensely. Only in minor details could *Balso Snell* be called directly autobiographical; but it is a book which does set down, boldly and directly, the character of West's imaginative life during the late twenties.

Jay Martin, in his Nathanael West: the Art of His Life, *Farrar, Straus and Giroux, 1970.*

Jonathan Raban   (essay date 1971)

SOURCE: "A Surfeit of Commodities: The Novels of Nathanael West," in *The American Novel and the Nineteen Twenties,* Edward Arnold, 1971, pp. 215-31.

[*In the following essay, Raban offers a stylistic and thematic analysis of West's short novels.*]

If Nathanael West did not exist, then Leslie Fiedler would probably have had to invent him. For West, after a couple of decades of critical *purdah,* has become a necessary figment of American literary mythology. Indeed, flicking over the pages of the *PMLA* bibliographies of the last ten years, one might reasonably assume that West's bones had long ago been picked clean by the assistant professors and their assiduous graduate students. The arrival, in the mid fifties, of what is now confidently termed 'the comic apocalyptic novel', occasioned an evangelical wave of ancestor baptism. In the search to legitimize recent writers like Joseph Heller, Terry Southern, Thomas Pynchon, Thomas Berger and the young novelist Edward Stewart (whose *Heads* strikes me as a very clever pastiche of the Westian style), West has been posthumously credited with a wonderfully virile and promiscuous talent for parenthood. Like most mythical figures, his powers have been variously, and exaggeratedly labelled: First American Surrealist, Sick Comedian, Dreamdumper, Nightmarist, Social Critic (of all things), Laughing Mortician. And for the mythmakers, West had an almost embarrassing abundance of convenient attributes: he was a Jew who renounced his religion; he was briefly expatriated during the twenties; he went the right distance out to the political left in the thirties; he worked in, and wrote about, Hollywood; he died young in a violent accident at the end of the decade. His four short, wildly uneven novels are a beachcomber's paradise; a junkshop of part-worn, part-used symbols and literary references. He is the indispensable minor modern novelist: once neglected, but now fully restored; use him anywhere, handy for your book or thesis. Especially suitable for Despair, Comedy and Violence.

Leslie Fiedler, who, along with Alan Ross in Britain, was among the first to open a West stall in the literary bazaar, puts the basic ingredients of the myth beautifully in *Waiting for the End:*

> He is the inventor for America of a peculiarly modern kind of book, whose claims are perfectly ambiguous. Reading his fiction, we do not know whether we are being presented with a nightmare endowed with the lineaments of reality, or with reality blurred to the uncertainty of nightmare. In either case, he must be read as a comic novelist, and his anti-heroes understood as comic characters, still as much shlemiels as any imagined by Fuchs, though they are presented as sacrificial victims, the only Christs possible in our skeptical world. In West, however, humor is expressed almost entirely in terms of the grotesque, which is to say, on the borderline between jest and horror; for violence is to him technique as well as subject matter, tone as well as theme.

Reading Fiedler, like reading most recent critics of West who tend slavishly to echo him, we hardly know whether we are being presented with a novelist and his actual work, or with a plausible diagram of a certain kind of writer, and a certain kind of literary technique, which arguably *ought* to exist somewhere in the labyrinth of recent American fiction. In the literary histories and the books on the modern novel, West most frequently exists as a cipher for a style which is far more readily identifiable with, say, Thomas Pynchon's *V* than with his own ***Miss Lonelyhearts.*** And in the earnest exegetical articles, symbolist explication of West's novels has gone into a wonderland of its own, full of failed Christs, illusions masquerading as realities, phallic guns and hatchets, ritual deaths and *shlemiels* galore. But all that is a long way away from the spikey, spoiled surface of the novels, themselves, with their short sentences facetiously pursuing their own metaphors into absurdity; their desperate patter of gags working their way through the prose like a nervous tic; characters like cartoons in livid crayon; everywhere an atmosphere of the kind of surrealism which might have been rigged up by an enterprising handyman in his back garden. Nowhere can the jitterbugging craze have worked itself into the texture of literature so successfully as in the frantic phrasing of West's style.

It's a profoundly maimed style; as unambiguous as a shriek. West's work is pathetically incomplete: re-reading his novels one watches again and again as the shrill personality of the author extrudes from behind the papery mask of his assumed style. With most novelists of a com-

parable public stature, the work is larger, more rounded, than the biography which produced it; with West, one needs biography in order to understand the peculiar hiatuses, the grammatical breaks, the awkwardnesses and the often uncontrolled hysteria of a fictional *oeuvre* that has been fractured, even ruined, by its own history.

West seemed destined to miss every available boat. He was six years younger than Hemingway, eight years younger than Fitzgerald; and by the time he graduated from college and joined the colony of expatriates in Paris, his near-contemporaries were already established writers. He was an awkward, gangling figure with an acned face, who aspired to Brooks Brothers suits and the latest dance steps. He had neither the glamour of Hemingway's war service and apprenticeship as a newspaperman, nor the polish of Fitzgerald's Ivy Leaguery. Brown University in the early twenties sounds like a dull, coltishly provincial establishment, where the sons of the small-professional and commercial middle class acted out a hammed pastiche of the Harvard-and-Princeton style. Worst, West was a Jew; he was born Nathan Wallenstein Weinstein, and grew up in a period when to be Jewish was to be stigmatized as a Robert Cohn, or one of Pound's Usurers, or Eliot's 'The jew squats on the windowsill, the owner,/ Spawned in some estaminet of Antwerp . . .' No Weinstein could join any of the fraternity clubs at Brown, or participate easily in the confident protestantism of the literary tone of the twenties. And West had an agonising sense of social propriety. He seems to have spent his time at Brown developing an edgy, imitative style that would hide his Jewishness under his Coca-Cola nickname of 'Pep'. John Sanford, who knew West in New York, wrote of him:

> More than anyone I ever knew Pep writhed under the accidental curse of his religion. . . . He changed his name, he changed his clothes, he changed his manners (we all did), in short he did everything possible to create the impression in his own mind—remember that, in his own mind—that he was just like Al Vanderbilt. It never quite came off. [Quoted in James F. Light, *Nathanael West: An Interpretative Study,* 1961]

Part of the Al Vanderbilt act consisted of West playing the country squire, surrounded by gun-dogs and toting a twelve-bore with which he was a spectacularly careless and inaccurate shot. He was an urban Jew who tried to storm WASP America with endless frantic mimicry; it's hard to miss the obsessive, yearning inadequacy which characterized his life style—a desperation channelled into the relentless acquisition of social masks. Dance floor lizard, home-town Raskolnikov, Paris bohemian (on a parental allowance), hotel clerk, hunter, movie writer . . . Whatever West did seemed to take on the characteristics of a theatrical role; a part to be learned and played out with slightly over-large gestures. Deeply embedded in his novels is the notion of life as a kind of vulgar, snobbish vaudeville show. Certainly West himself was adept at the painful clowning in which the touring performer gets up in rouge and worn white slicker suit, to go through a travesty of the high-life style.

He was, prototypically, a marginal man, perched uneasily on the edge of his society. His acute sense of social conformity led him into an infatuation with the values of the twenties which was so overdone that it turned insidiously into conscious parody. At the same time he inflected his own contortions with shrill, self-destructive irony; he was simultaneously inside and out, passionately involved in his own activity, yet able to mock it with a ribald series of Bronx cheers. In West's early work, the social style that one recognizes from the anecdotes of his classmates at Brown is readily turned into a literary trick—indeed becomes, at first, his sole piece of literary equipment.

In an unpublished, semi-autobiographical story called 'L'Affaire Beano', he treated the experience of expatriation in a tone of such bland condescension that the writing itself becomes merely a crude mode of exorcism:

> 'In order to be an artist one has to live like one.' We know now that this is nonsense, but in Paris in '25 and '26 we didn't know it. 'Artists are crazy' is another statement from the same credo. Of course all these ideas were foisted on us by the non-artists, but we didn't realize it then. We came to the business of being an artist with the definitions of the non-artists and took libels for the truth. In order to be recognized as artists, we were everything our enemies said we were.
>
> By the time I got to Paris, the business of being an artist had grown quite difficult. . . . When I got to Montparnasse, all the obvious roles had either been dropped or were being played by experts. But I made a lucky hit. Instead of trying for strangeness, I formalized and exaggerated the costume of a bond salesman. I wore carefully pressed Brooks Brothers clothing, sober but rich ties, and carried gloves and a tightly rolled umbrella. My manners were elaborate and I professed great horror at the slightest breach of the conventional. It was a success. I was asked to all the parties.

The confident air is too exaggerated; the inclusive use of 'we' too strident. West adopts a strategy of unearned absurdity: by reducing everything to short, slangy sentences, phrased in glib generalities, he achieves a thin horse-laugh at the expense of the narrator, of Paris, of the whole generation embodied in that sweeping 'we'. The passage exhibits a barely-veiled hysteria; it is *about* authorial distance; one feels West frantically disengaging himself from his subject, reaching for a language that is cool, urbane, above all, knowing. But West doesn't know when to stop, and the effect is blatantly unconvincing.

When West stepped off the boat from France, he had the manuscript of *The Dream Life of Balso Snell* in his valise. Talking to A. J. Liebling, he said that he had written his first novel as 'a protest against writing books'. Both the remark and the book itself are of a piece with West's nervously brash social style. *The Dream Life of Balso Snell* filters the figureheads of modernism—Dostievsky, Huysmans, Dada, Joyce—through the vulgarity of undergraduate revue. It is an impertinent satire, remarkably devoid of cunning, and maintains a consistent, irritating air of cocking a snook at the teachers, as West flails inaccurately around his pond of fashionable names. The core material of the novel was apparently in existence by 1924, when

West lent an *ur-Balso* manuscript to Quentin Reynolds, to use as a crib for a Spring Day speech. The surprise is that West could continue living with his skittish ephemerid until 1931, when the book was finally published.

Its optimistic target was to demolish western culture with a snigger; its effect is to set in motion the lineaments of a style of contrived bogusness—a style which, in *Miss Lonelyhearts* and *The Day of the Locust*, was to be sharpened into a literary weapon of considerable force and subtlety. For the intestines of the wooden horse, where *Balso Snell* takes place, contain the remains of a stew of partially digested rhetorics. The characters—John Raskolnikov Gilson, Miss McGeeney, Maloney the Areopagite—are ciphers enclosed by the platitudes of their own languages. Together they compose a kind of Bartholomew Fair of social and cultural clichés.

It is quite clear that West had little intention of satirizing his modern humours in any detail. The parodies of *Balso Snell* are parodies of parodies; they work on schoolboy notions of 'literary English', 'avant garde writing', 'religious rhetoric' and so on. When West turns on specific authors, he assimilates them into a childish convention; as in the garbled pastiche of Molly Bloom's soliloquy at the book's end:

> Hard-bitten. Casual. Smart. Been there before. I've had policemen. No trace of a feminine whimper. Decidedly revisiting well-known, well-ploughed ground. No new trees, wells, or even fences.
>
> Desperate for life. Live! Experience! Live one's own. Your body is an instrument, an organ or a drum. Harmony. Order. Breasts. The apple of my eye, the pear of my abdomen. What is life without love? I burn! I ache! Hurrah!
>
> Moooompitcher yaaaah. Oh I never hoped to know the passion, the sensuality hidden within you—yes yes. Drag me down into the mire, drag. Yes! And with your hair the lust from my eyes brush. Yes.. . Yes . . . Ooh! Ah!

Its badness is at least partially deliberate. For West's writing, by its very lack of satiric specificity, forces us to attend, not to the thing parodied (in this case *Ulysses*), but to the chaotic detritus of a consciousness brutally assaulted by this mess of styles, names, lists of objects. The random breaks, the structurelessness, the noisy nonsense, the constant posing of *Balso Snell* go to make up the actual subject of the book. And West is very good at recreating the stimuli of physical nausea as he lets his language cascade into a trough of absurdities. Again and again we are deluged by a style of gratuitous enumeration, as sentences reduplicate themselves in a runaway rhetoric, as repetitive as the flow of identical articles off an assembly line:

> 'And Death? —bah! What, then, is there still detaining you in this vale of tears?' Can it be that the only thing that bothers me in a statement of this sort is the wording? Or is it because there is something arty about Suicide? Suicide: Werther, the Cosmic Urge, the Soul, the Quest, and Otto Greenbaum, Phil Beta Kappa, Age seventeen— Life is unworthy of him; and Haldington Knape,

West in 1931, the year The Dream Life of Balso Snell *was published.*

Oxford, author, man-about-town, big game hunter—Life is too tiresome; and Terry Kornflower, poet, no hat, shirt open to the navel—Life is too crude; and Janey Davenport, pregnant, unmarried, jumps from a studio window in Paris—Life is too difficult . . .

Here is a style of writing which sets out to prove its own sogginess, its own inadequacy under the pressure of the objects which it is forced to catalogue platitudinously. The failed surface of *Balso Snell* represents West's attempt to exhibit language and a sensibility which have been raped to a point of retching exhaustion.

As a satire, *Balso Snell* is a pretentious flop. But as the inauguration of a style, it is an auspicious technical essay, marred by grandiose overreaching and by the intrusive uncertainty of the author. For West himself shows up anxiously every few pages, nudging the reader in the ribs, all too ready to explain just what he's trying to do. The book is full of passages with the ring of deadly earnestness about them:

> An intelligent man finds it easy to laugh at himself, but his laughter is not sincere if it is not thorough. If I could be Hamlet, or even a clown with a breaking heart 'neath his jester's motley, the role would be tolerable. But I always find it necessary to burlesque the mystery of feeling at its source; I must laugh at myself, and if the laugh is 'bitter', I must laugh at the laugh. The ritual of feeling demands burlesque and, whether the burlesque is successful or not, a laugh. . . .

This poses real problems. On the one hand, West cursorily tries to incorporate the passage itself with the other exhausted rhetorics of the book, by quoting 'bitter' and slipping in the phrase about the broken hearted clown (then overdoing it with the archaism "neath'); on the other, he allows it to stand as a *propria persona* statement. For a book as bland in its general approach as *Balso Snell*, such lapses act as remarkable confessions of insecurity. They work like distress signals, shouts for help from the centre of a muddle he clearly doesn't fully understand. He becomes the victim of his own lucidity; his language runs away with him, as if the mask had commandeered the face behind.

For West's novels, though they aspire to burlesque and laughter, rarely manage to climb out of that state of anxious self-scrutiny. His second book, *Miss Lonelyhearts* (1933), is frequently credited with being West's most assured and controlled piece of fiction; if that is true, it is only because he had learned to incorporate his uncertainty into the design and texture of his writing. Originally he was going to subtitle *Miss Lonelyhearts: A novel in the form of a comic strip*—and the tautness of that initial idea has stayed with the book, in its use of short illustrative chapters, stylized language and primary-coloured locations. The comic strip gives the novel its extraordinarily rapid tempo; working on West like a harness, so that his tendencies towards diversive extravaganza are kept firmly in check. But the apparent single-mindedness of *Miss Lonelyhearts* is deceptive: an uneasy tension throbs away in the novel, just under its carefully polished surface. (It is indicative of West's painstaking care with the book that he rewrote it more than six times: and, when working on it full-time, produced only 700-1,000 words a week.)

Like *Balso Snell, Miss Lonelyhearts* presents us with a menagerie of rhetorics; between them they make up a splintered portrait of a society that has become consumed by its own clichés. At the same time it is a novel which explores the possibility that the conventions of the Novel—its machinery of 'plot' and 'character' and psychological tensions and development—have been made unworkable by the urban industrial world of pulp media and cheapjack commodities. West does not merely crete 'two-dimensional' characters; he attempts to obliterate the notion of character altogether. For the people in *Miss Lonelyhearts*—Desperate, Broken-hearted, Sick-of-it-all, Mr. and Mrs. Doyle, Shrike, Betty and the rest—act simply as labels on which to stick a jaded, received language of sickening platitudes. The book basically belongs to them; it is their confusing and contradictory *noise* which assaults both the reader and Miss Lonelyhearts.

What then of Miss Lonelyhearts himself? The first phrase of the novel is 'The Miss Lonelyhearts of the New York *Post-Dispatch*...' and West never fully allows him to disambiguate himself from that definite, but inanimate, article. He is a function; a vibrating diaphragm set in the centre of the communications business, as stereotyped in his available roles as the voices which beset him. He is described once in the book, and the description is made in such generic terms that it almost becomes a parodic satire on the convention of bodying-out the central 'character' in all his particularities:

> Although his cheap clothes had too much style, he still looked like the son of a Baptist minister. A beard would become him, would accent his Old-Testament look. But even without a beard no one could fail to recognize the New England puritan. His forehead was high and narrow. His nose was long and fleshless. His bony chin was shaped and cleft like a hoof.

Compare this with the other descriptions in the book: of Shrike, 'Under the shining white globe of his brow, his features huddled together in a dead, gray triangle'; of Mr. Doyle, 'He looked like one of those composite photographs used by screen magazines in guessing contests'; of Mrs. Doyle, 'Legs like Indian clubs, breasts like balloons and a brow like a pigeon.' In all cases, the similes are there, not to illuminate, but to deaden the character. West robs each of them of any recognizably human attributes, and turns them into things. The language they speak is the mass-produced grammar and vocabulary of the newspaper, the magazine, the movie. Not only are they likened to objects, but on occasions become confused with objects. Thus in the chapter, 'Miss Lonelyhearts and the Party Dress', Miss Lonelyhearts begins by encountering Betty (a splendid talking doll out of a woman's weekly) person-to-person, then slides rapidly, through a dialogue of resounding banality, into an object-to-object relationship:

> He begged the party dress to marry him, saying all the things it expected to hear, all the things that went with strawberry sodas and farms in Connecticut. He was just what the party dress

expected him to be: simple and sweet, whimsical and poetic, a trifle collegiate yet very masculine.

This technique of synecdoche turns Shrike into a talking newspaperman's eyeshade, with his glibly cynical spiels; Doyle becomes merely an extension of his enormous cripple's shoe; and Miss Lonelyhearts himself grows into a walking evangelist's soapbox. By reducing his characters to these formulae West deadens our expectations of human sympathy or change: deeply rooted in the novel is the suggestion that the only way in which we can be surprised or moved is by the introduction of things so shocking or grotesque that they transcend all normal social categories. And this is the function of the letters—

> I sit and look at myself all day and cry. I have a big hole in the middle of my face that scares people even myself so I cant blame the boys for not wanting to take me out. My mother loves me, but she crys terrible when she looks at me.

The only alternative to cliché is illiteracy; the only alternative to the conditioned social responses of the Shrikes and the Mrs. Doyles is gross deformity. But we should, I think, be honest enough to admit that the letters rise to such a level of crude extremity that they are merely funny. The predicaments to which they refer are so unimaginably awful that one takes refuge in the comic-proletarian humour of bad spelling and impossible grammar. If we are shocked by, say, the first or second letter in the book, they soon become a convention as predictable as Betty's homely flutings. The girl with the hole in the middle of her face turns, along with all the other characters in the book, into just another cliché. What is truly shocking is our own incapacity to respond to, or to make sense of, the human confusion which the novel appears to enact.

I say 'appears to' because *Miss Lonelyhearts* works like a baited trap; it assaults the reader with extremities, then leaves him wondering, embarrassedly, about his own emotional inadequacy in the face of this battering. But West effectively prevents us from responding by deliberately deadening his characters and by turning even the most bizarre rhetorics in the book into cliché. What is real in the novel is the procession of images which focus, not on any fictional predicament inhabited by the characters, but on the dilemma of West the writer, the unwilling creator of this perverse menagerie.

For the central tone of the narrative is one of jokey circumspection; it pries, investigates, works in beautifully sharp visual flashes, constantly counterpointing the violent hysteria of the novel's social world. In the second chapter, for instance, Miss Lonelyhearts crosses a park on his way to the speakeasy:

> He entered the park at the North Gate and swallowed mouthfuls of the heavy shade that curtained its arch. He walked into the shadow of a lamp-post that lay on the path like a spear. It pierced him like a spear.

One is brought up sharp by that last sentence; it looks like a facetious indulgence, a piece of verbal by-play for which there shouldn't be room in a passage supposedly centering on Miss Lonelyhearts' agony over the desperation of his correspondents' lives. But in *Miss Lonelyhearts* there always is room; the narrative continually steps back and films in sardonic slow motion. In the middle of a violent row with Betty—

> He began to shout at her, accompanying his shouts with gestures that were too appropriate, like those of an old-fashioned actor.

The narrative is positively garrulous in its readiness to stop by the way and chat, throwing in eloquent, but static, similes. Its effect is to make the social situation both trivial and unreal; it offers an alternative world of objects and exact descriptions—a world of concretes: bottles ranged above a bar, the colour of tobacco smoke, a flapping newspaper, flagstones, clothes, domestic implements. Throughout the novel, West constantly shifts from his object-like people to objects themselves, which he treats with relish. His imagery is invariably more alive than the characters who occasion it, as if the ordering process of writing were of far greater importance than the people and events out of which novels are usually, if unfortunately, made.

The reader of *Miss Lonelyhearts* becomes its proto-author; his central problem is to shape the hectic and confused voices of the book into the stylized patterns offered him by West. The subject of the novel becomes the desperate play of sensibility as it attempts to reconcile the noisy, heterogeneous fragments of a mass-media world. The images become more contorted, to the point of growing surreal; the noises get louder; the paper characters dance frenziedly on the spot. But our attention remains fixed on the jugglery of West, the most psychologically convincing character in the novel, as he tries to keep all those multiple, crude voices and objects in balance. The trouble is that West seems to be in love with his own failure. The grotesquerie of the letters, of Miss Lonelyhearts' eventual death at the hands of Doyle, of the snatched sex and casual speakeasy brutality in the book, is carried out with a kind of sadistic delight. West's tone, as he transforms his people into mechanical devices or exhibits their pathetically stereotyped rhetorics, is never less than gay. He, not Miss Lonelyhearts, is the failed hero of the novel; he subsides under its pressures like an old-style tragedian, waving his arms and bellowing with obvious enjoyment.

As a novelist, West establishes himself by destroying his own creations with the easily-won indifference of a god. He grossly indulged himself in *A Cool Million* (1934), accurately subtitled, 'The Dismantling of Lemuel Pitkin'; an extended act of writer's vengeance on the notions of 'character' and 'society'. By reducing his hero to an innocent who is even flatter and more simple-minded than Alger's Ragged Dick, and by turning American fascism into a society more lurid than that of most horror comics, West gives himself the opportunity to write in a vein of extraordinary nastiness:

> He also made an unsuccessful attempt to find Mr. Whipple. At the Salvation Army post they told him that they had observed Mr. Whipple lying quietly in the gutter after the meeting of the 'Leather Shirts', but that when they looked the next day to see if he were still there they found only a large blood stain. Lem looked him-

self but failed even to find this stain, there being many cats in the neighbourhood.

One would surely have to be very insensitive indeed to find this humorous; it goes considerably further than the letters in *Miss Lonelyhearts* in its direct exploitation of a literary trick, enabled only by the complete unreality of the fictional characters and situations involved. There is a totalitarian streak in West's writing; a tendency to turn his novels into Charentons, where he can victimize his witless characters at his pleasure. For a novelist, it seems an odd revenge.

And West appears to have realized this in the five years that followed before the publication of *The Day of the Locust* (1939). In Tod Hackett, the Tiresias-like artist through whose eyes we see the waste land of Hollywood, West partially embodied his own predicament as a writer. When he first encounters Homer Simpson, the retired hotel clerk from Iowa, on the landing of the San Bernadino Arms, he behaves remarkably like West's authorial persona:

> Tod examined him eagerly. He didn't mean to be rude but at first glance this man seemed an exact model for the kind of person who comes to California to die, perfect in every detail down to fever eyes and unruly hands.

Through Tod, West is able to inflect his own aesthetic sadism with a degree of irony. But West and Tod jockey for position in the novel, and it's often difficult to determine who is in control where. So, after the marvelous description of Hollywood as a landscape of pure artifice and simulation, the last paragraph of chapter one reads:

> It is hard to laugh at the need for beauty and romance, no matter how tasteless, even horrible, the results of that need are. But it is easy to sigh. Few things are sadder than the truly monstrous.

Its tone is both apologetic and sententious. Does it belong to Tod or West? It reads like most professions of sentiment in West's fiction, as if it ought to go into quotation marks, yet its positioning in the chapter suggests that it is an authentic narrative voice which we must accept if we are to continue to collaborate with the novel. In combination with the passage describing Tod's specimen-hunting approach to Homer Simpson, it is a strong indicator of West's unease. In *The Day of the Locust*, he covers himself both ways by creating a promiscuous irony with which to ambiguate almost everything in the book.

The structure of *The Day of the Locust* is that of an exactly timed series of improvizations. It is built round its set-pieces: two celluloid battles, a Hollywood party, a cheap rooming house inhabited by the dreamers, a funeral, a cockfight and a gala première. Each of these major scenes are 'long shots'; they display the characters at a distance and treat them through a filter of imagery that rubs out their individual details and emphasizes their generic characteristics. They are balanced by interlinking flashback-biographies and close-ups which continually test the individual characters against the large thematic patterns proposed by Tod as he assembles the material for his painting, 'The Burning of Los Angeles', and tacitly underwritten by

West. This dialectical structure works smoothly and eloquently; for the first time, West is able to use the Novel as mode of exploration rather than flat statement.

More powerfully than ever before, the destruction of character grows organically out of the texture of the fiction. The magnificently realized location of Hollywood—the luric illusions of the studio lot and the Cape Cod colonial house in paper and plaster, the antiseptic smelling corridors of the San Berdadino Arms, the sickly, pervasive heat in which Harry Greener peddles his cans of home-made polish, the mawkish kitsch of the Californian way of love and death—provides a backdrop of epic dimensions, against which the characters scuttle pitifully, reduced to twitching puppets by the overpowering articulacy of their environment. And West manages his structural devices with a new cunning. In the fourth chapter, for instance, he alternates between brief, cruel portraits of the guests at Claude Estee's party and their tinny dialogues; then, just when the rhythm of the section demands a new portrait of a partygoer, West introduces the black mass at the bottom of the darkened swimming pool:

> A row of submerged floodlights illuminated the green water. The thing was a dead horse, or, rather, a life-size, realistic reproduction of one. Its legs stuck up stiff and straight and it had an enormous, distended belly. Its hammerhead lay twisted to one side and from its mouth, which was set in an agonized grin, hung a heavy, black tongue.

It is perfectly timed, and the party never recovers from the insidious suggestion of that passage: the twisted penis and the hanging tongue carry, like sustained bass notes, into the next chapter, where the party migrates to a brothel to watch blue movies.

In *The Day of the Locust*, the shifts of tone are rapid and unexpected; West darts in and out of his characters like a skilled saboteur. Describing Homer Simpson's move into his cottage, he spends four paragraphs of neutral narrative, in which the reader is allowed temporarily to inhabit Homer as a character, before shifting, through an intermediary paragraph, into a passage of brilliantly managed detachment:

> He got out of bed in sections, like a poorly made automation, and carried his hands into the bathroom. He turned on the cold water. When the basin was full, he plunged his hands in up to the wrists. They lay quietly on the bottom like a pair of strange aquatic animals. When they were thoroughly chilled and began to crawl about, he lifted them out and hid them in a towel.

This is far more fully developed, and less flashy, than the comparable images of *Miss Lonelyhearts.* Almost every character in the novel—Abe Kusich, the dwarf who is initially mistaken for a pile of soiled laundry; the cowboy, Earle Shoop, who has 'a two-dimensional face that a talented child might have drawn with a ruler and compass'; Harry Greener who behaves like an overwound mechanical toy when he had his first heart attack—is transmuted into the kind of object that can be found on the garbage dumps of an industrial society. But West does not simply

leave it at that; he gathers the threads of his images together to project them into a large and complete metaphor of estrangement. In Hollywood, the dreams are faked in the studios; the houses are faked on the hillsides; emotions are faked (consciously and with style) in Harry Greener's music hall routines; religion, and even death, are faked by the funeral industry (where Harry's shaved and rouged corpse is made to look 'like the interlocutor in a minstrel show'); and people are faked in a relentless process of image-making. The novel itself works like a production line; it takes the scattered ingredients of a recognizably real Hollywood and turns them into the hard, bright patterns of cheap industrial design.

For West never allows us to lose sight of the artifice of his own novel; his carefully managed structure is often deliberately obtrusive. One watches the novelist keep Harry Greener alive until the time is ripe for the funeral; then West, without warning, snuffs him out. And Tod's insistent interior monologues, as he collects characters and bits and pieces for his painting, are a way of reminding us that it is the process of the novel that is at stake; the characters and their situations are merely the bundles of hair and leaves and mud out of which the glittering structure may be composed. The final effect is of a lunatic baroque edifice which stuns the onlooker with its sheer brazenness, its air of suffocating overpopulation. *The Day of the Locust* obsessively accumulates its details; characters are switched into objects and added to the pile; objects themselves take on a bizarrely vivid life of their own; the landscape of Los Angeles is broken down into a heap of brightly painted junk. The apocalyptic finale, when the rioting mob lynch Homer Simpson, is both a description and an encapsulation of the process of the novel: the heat, stench, frustration and noise of a packed crowd is expanded to breaking point. Then one is left only with a quietened shuffle of people round an ambulance, while the artist goes into an hysterical imitation of the sound of its klaxon.

West never got beyond that point. His unease is taken to the edge of hysteria and left there. On the one hand there is the shrill confidence of his imagery, the harshly didactic rhythm of his sentences. He strains all the time for a literary voice that will carry the ring of the stern authoritarian, and rules his novels like a dictator. On the other, there is a strain of excruciatingly evident insecurity. His irony teeters between the gross (as in *A Cool Million*) and the nervously diffuse. His style of masquerade slips frequently into lapses of embarrassing earnestness. He is, preeminently, the novelist as victim.

West's fictional world is essentially one of objects, of commodities. When people enter it they become transfixed and assimilated into the dime-store jumble of parti-coloured rubbish. On this account, West is often called a surrealist (a title which he himself vehemently rejected). And, clearly, there are deliberate echoes of Huysmans's *A Rebours* in all of West's novels; the glutted consciousness, fed to the point of nausea with sensations, images, people, things, which forms the centre of each narrative often seems exactly like a coarsened and vulgarized version of Des Esseintes. It is almost as if Huysmans's hero had lived into the post-war boom of industrial manufacturing, and found his dreams on sale at every Woolworths'. But this is why West's work is a far cry from European surrealism; his wildly juxtaposed objects always belong to an explicitly commercial context. The passage most frequently quoted as evidence for his 'surrealism' is that section from *Miss Lonelyhearts* in which Betty and Shrike compete for the fevered columnist's soul. Lying ill in bed—

> He found himself in the window of a pawnshop full of fur coats, diamond rings, watches, shotguns, fishing tackle, mandolins. All these things were the paraphernalia of suffering. A tortured high light twisted on the blade of a gift knife, a battered horn grunted with pain . . .
>
> A trumpet, marked to sell for $2.49, gave the call to battle and Miss Lonelyhearts plunged into the fray. First he formed a phallus of old watches and rubber boots, then a heart of umbrellas and trout flies, then a diamond of musical instruments and derby hats, after these a circle, triangle, square, swastika. But nothing proved definitive and he began to make a gigantic cross. When the cross became too large for the pawnshop, he moved it to the shore of the ocean. There every wave added to his stock faster than he could lengthen its arms. His labours were enormous. He staggered from the last wave line to his work, loaded down with marine refuse—bottles, shells, chunks of cork, fish heads, pieces of net.

It is too easy merely to see that here are the lineaments of a painting by Ernst or Dali. We shouldn't miss the fact that the vision starts in a pawnshop; that the objects over which Miss Lonelyhearts exercises his sickened imagination are either pieces of rubbish or things in hock. West turns his hero into a crazed consumer, haphazardly patterning the goods on display; his revulsion is focussed on a peculiarly American style of mass commercial wastage. If it is surrealism, it is the home-town surrealism of the neighbourhood supermarket. One can echo this with passages from any of West's books; for instance, when Homer Simpson goes shopping in *The Day of the Locust*:

> The SunGold Market into which he turned was a large, brilliantly lit place. All the fixtures were chromium and the floors and walls were lined with white tile. Coloured spotlights played on the showcases and counters, heightening the natural hues of the different foods. The oranges were bathed in red, the lemons in yellow, the fish in pale green, the steaks in rose and the eggs in ivory . . .

Behind West's chilling, cartoonlike treatment of people and objects (and people-as-objects) there always lies the chink of money and the grinding of the industrial machine. He is a surfeited realist. The surface strangeness and 'violence' of his novels never rises far above the simple level of being sickened by the excess of an overstocked refrigerator or a sweaty crowd on a Christmas-shopping spree.

It seems helpful to remember Fitzgerald's thorny transition from the twenties to the thirties. In *The Great Gatsby* he was able to allow Daisy to weep over the beauty of Gatsby's opulent shirts; to catalogue with open-eyed wonder the magnificence of that machine for gutting oranges and the brilliant yellow of Gatsby's car. But in *Tender Is The Night,* his tone hardens. Nicole, the child of American success, is discovered in a psychiatric clinic which is explicitly described by Fitzgerald as a kind of spunging-house for a society that is going sour on its own affluence. Nicole, the consumer heroine—for whose sake

> trains began their run at Chicago and traversed the round belly of the continent to California; chicle factories fumed and link belts grew link by link in factories; men mixed toothpaste in vats and drew mouthwash out of copper hogsheads; girls canned tomatoes quickly in August or worked rudely at the Five-and-Tens on Christmas Eve; half-breed Indians toiled on Brazilian coffee plantations and dreamers were muscled out of patent rights on new tractors—these were some of the people who gave a tithe to Nicole and, as the whole system swayed and thundered onward, it lent a feverish bloom to such processes of hers as wholesale buying, like the flush of a fireman's face holding his post before a spreading blaze. She illustrated very simple principles, containing in herself her own doom, but illustrated them so accurately that there was grace in the procedure, and presently Rosemary would try to imitate it.

—shakes hysterically in the bathroom, immersed in some obscure schizophrenic fit. Surrounded by the *embarras de richesse* which he acquires with Nicole (and which prominently includes another pneumatic rubber horse), Dick subsides into broken alcoholism. The wealth of possibilities which seemed once to extend, like the green light over Daisy's dock, has narrowed down to the rank aftertaste of used commodities. Fitzgerald accommodates these opposites in his fiction with a wonderful doubleness of vision; West works obsessively around only the seamy underside of that flowed dream.

For West had a more parochial, mean and hysterical talent than the best of his contemporaries. Like Nicole, he vividly expressed the ruin that came in the wake of the spree; but unlike her, and unlike Fitzgerald too, he never participated in the style which the spree temporarily enabled. Perhaps his novels have been overvalued because American literary history has needed a scapegoat—a novelist so violated that he stands as a symbol for the violent estrangement with which the thirties looked back on the hopes and excesses of the previous decade. He created a voice of shrill, high-pitched nausea; and his mutilated novels are as much symptoms as they are diagnoses of the disease.

James F. Light   (essay date 1975)

SOURCE: "Varieties of Satire in the Art of Nathanael West," in *Studies in American Humor,* Vol. II, No. 1, April, 1975, pp. 46-60.

Since the death of Nathanael West in 1939 his work has gone from relative obscurity to ever increasing interpretation and evaluation. Various of his works, under the impetus of increasing enthusiasm, have been praised as "su-

Not a do-gooder, not given to social or political dogmas, West evidently believed that his work had some social value, some special insight not to be found in proletarian novels or religious tracts. West thought it important for man to know his own nature; within us the real dangers lurk.

—Edward Greenfield Schwartz, in Accent: A Quarterly of New Literature, *Autumn, 1957.*

perbly written," as "a minor classic [*Miss Lonelyhearts*]," as works [*Miss Lonelyhearts* and *The Day of the Locust*] "that deserve a place among the best twentieth century novels," and as "four novels" which are "permanent and true explorations into the Siberia of the human spirit." The major sources for West's art, such as James Joyce and the French surrealists, have been analyzed in detail, and even the most minute influences, such as Lynd Ward and Gilbert Seldes, have been tracked down with sedulous care. Victor Comerchero, in *Nathanael West: The Ironic Prophet,* has theorized that West used a "mythic lens through which to view his age," so that *Miss Lonelyhearts* "is a moving modernization of the Grail legend," and the totality of West's work is one vast, oblique revelation of West—or "Westian man"—himself: "Individually, each of West's characters remains a caricature; cumulatively, they create an engrossing picture of a 'type,' of a 'collective man' who has been created in West's own image." Stanley Hyman, in his monograph *Nathanael West,* finds *Miss Lonelyhearts* one of the three greatest novels of the twentieth century and claims that West converted the "sickness and fears" of modern existence into "convincing present-day forms of the great myths: The Quest, The Scapegoat, The Holy Fool, The Dance of Death." [In *Nathanael West: The Art of His Life*] Jay Martin, in his enthusiasm, finds that West, in his work as a whole, completed "a series of anti-novels in which is summarized the history of the twentieth century poetic imagination, from symbolism through surrealism and super-realism."

Nathanael West is obviously well on the way to becoming canonized—even the literary autholgies are now including his work—and as if to place the ultimate seal of approval upon his art, the movies *Lonelyhearts* (1959) and *The Day of the Locust* (1957) have insisted even more reverently than have the academic critics upon the fact that West's art is both profound and prophetic. The movie *The Day of the Locust,* for instance, captures, with considerable fidelity, a number of the more memorable images of the novel, and then depicts, with lengthy and pretentious fire, thunder, and brimstone, the apocalyptic vision on which the novel ends. In an epilogue, the movie adds another scene and another image, neither of which West had the foresight to include in the novel, in which Faye Greener returns to Tod Hackett's apartment to gaze senti-

mentally upon a rose which she had earlier seen blooming from a crack in one of the apartment walls. The pretentiousness of that symbolic rose, with its implications of beauty, fertility, and religion so totally in contrast to West's vision, suggests another falsification. That is that West's art itself is being distorted by the pretentiousness with which it is being treated by some of his admirers. Before it is too late, perhaps it is justifiable to suggest that even though West is both a serious and profound artist, he is first and foremost a satirist who felt in his bones "the necessity for laughing at everything—love, death, ambition, etc." What West thought of as "my particular kind of joking"—in which "there is nothing to root for . . . and what is even worse, no rooters"—is the joking with which West had the greatest success, but it should not be forgotten that West attempted a variety of satire in his work. That diversity expressed itself in individual works, as well as in the body of West's work, and it ranged from folk humor, most especially in the tall tale tradition, to the dominant surrealistic humor in *The Dream Life of Balso Snell,* to the prevailing black humor in *Miss Lonelyhearts,* to the essential parody and burlesque in *A Cool Million,* to the dominant apocalyptic humor in The *Day of the Locust,* to the allusive humor which runs as a recurring strain throughout West's work.

West's interest in folk humor is apparent in his first published work. Called **"A Barefaced Lie,"** it appeared in 1929 in *Overland Monthly* and was obviously indebted to such tall tales as Mark Twain's "Jim Baker's Bluejay Yarn" and T. B. Thorpe's "The Big Bear of Arkansas." In West's tale, the narrator seeks out a stagecoach driver named Boulder Bill because, as he notes in a passage reminiscent of the opening of Twain's "The Celebrated Jumping Frog of Calaveras County," "I had been advised by my friend, Red Patterson, the gum booter, to ride only with Boulder Bill—and to listen politely to all he had to say." When the narrator finds Boulder Bill, he turns out to be a huge man with a voice that even in a "whisper . . . was audible a block away." Boulder Bill invites the narrator to sit in front with him on the stagecoach ride, but insists that another passenger ride in the rear. The reason for this, Boulder Bill explains, is that the second passenger is a "low-down ornery skunk . . . the most bare-faced, mean, siwash liar that ever hit the country, and I can prove it to you." To make his point, Boulder Bill tells of how, a few days earlier, he had been visiting with his friends in a saloon and had told them of an experience he had had while putting packsaddles in the dark on a number of mules. Among the mules, according to Boulder Bill, was a bear, and Bill had cinched a packsaddle on him without knowing that he was a bear. Boulder Bill's friends "listened decently" to the story and "then talked it over," but in the midst of the discussion a "big-mouthed Yahoo"—the passenger whom Boulder Bill had earlier insisted sit in the rear of the stagecoach—"started on a regular hyena laugh" and said "That explains it." When invited to elaborate, the "Yahoo" tells of how, on the same day that Boulder Bill had cinched the bear and only a few hours later, he had seen

> an old bear standing on a stump grunting and jabbering away like he was the boss of things,

and there was two more bears down on the bar a-packing a load of salmon on another bear what had a packsaddle on, and two more bears still was catching salmon and carrying them up to the packyard. . . .

This tale sets everyone in the saloon to laughing, pounding each other on the back, and then to looking at Boulder Bill and snickering. For that reason Boulder Bill no longer feels free to show his face in the saloon, all because of that "Yahoo" who had told nothing but "bare-faced bear lies, partner—bare-faced bear lies. . . ."

Hardly a masterpiece, **"A Barefaced Lie"** proclaims the theme with which West's entire art is obsessed—lies and their exposure—and is a progenitor of the use of tall talk and tall tales in West's later work. An example of West's later use of tall talk occurs in *A Cool Million* in the character of the "rip-tail roarer" from Pike County who claims, "I kin whip my weight in wildcats, am a match for a dozen Injins to oncet, and can tackle a lion without flinchin'." Typical of West's exotic variations of the tall tale is the howler told by Miss McGeeney in *The Dream Life of Balso Snell.* Miss McGeeney is writing a biography, entitled *Samuel Perkins: Smeller,* of the man who wrote the biography of E. F. Fitzgerald, who wrote the biography of D. H. Hobson, who wrote the biography of James Boswell, who wrote the biography of Samuel Johnson; and it is Miss McGeeney's fond hope that in time someone "must surely take the hint" and write her own biography, so that "we will all go rattling down the halls of time . . . a tin can on the tail of Dr. Johnson." In her research, Miss McGeeney has been most especially impressed with the fact that all the veins and wrinkles of Perkins' body flowed directly toward his nose, and that fact implied the marvelous quality of his nose. Almost blind, totally deaf, and practically devoid of other sensory apparatus, Perkins had compensated for these defects by developing the capacities of his nose until he "could smell a chord in D Minor. . . . It has been said of him that he could smell an isosceles triangle. . . ." As an artist, dedicated to fullness of experience, Perkins had married, and from the variety of the odors of his wife's body "he had built . . . an architecture and an aesthetic, a music and a mathematic. . . . He had even discovered a politic, a hierarchy of odors: self-government direct. . . ." In Miss McGeeney's tale, West is undeniably satirizing the preciousness of some artists and the folly of some academic critics, but it is clear that the method of his satire is exaggeration, and the inspiration, at least in part, is the tall tale.

A second artistic form which West used for satiric effects is surrealism. Like satire itself, surrealism depends for its effects upon distortion (though the aim of surrealism—as, for instance, in Kafka's *The Metamorphosis*—is not necessarily humorous), and the purpose of the sincere surrealist is, through multiple kinds of distortion, to mock "rational" perceptions and to intimate the higher reality—the *surréel*—of the subconscious, illogical inward world of man. What West did in *The Dream Life of Balso Snell* was to use the forms of surrealism to satirize the spiritual pretensions of the surrealist—a fact which helps to explain West's irritation at Clifton Fadiman's claim that he was "The ablest of our surrealist authors." In fulfilling this

aim, West constructed a novel which dramatizes the chaotic ramblings of a wet dream. The dream-like illogic of the novel, less eerie than absurd, begins when the dream-hero, Balso Snell, while wandering around the ancient city of Troy, comes upon the famous Trojan Horse and enters it through the "Anus Mirabilis." The removal from reality is intensified in such episodes as that in which the hero, Balso Snell, reads a pair of letters within a dream within a dream, while the letters themselves narrate the speculations of a character named Beagle Hamlet Darwin over what might have happened if he had taken his mistress, Janey Davenport, to Paris with him. Throughout the novel West also uses shocking conceits to mock "rational" ideas and attitudes. The artistic creations of the male artist become comparable to the house of flowers built by the Amblyornis Inornata, a homely bird, in an effort to compare with the brilliant feathers of the Bird of Paradise, and the attempt "to exteriorize internal feathers" for both the Inornato and the human artist is the same: to attract the female. In another conceit the sexual urge becomes a chauffeur, dressed in ugly clothing and wearing a derby hat, that drives the automobile called man. In yet another conceit, man's dreams of eternal life become comparable to a race of men, the Phoenix Excrementi, who "eat themselves, digest themselves, and give birth to themselves by evacuating their bowels."

The characters of the novel, united only in the fact that they are all frustrated writers in search of an audience, are absurdly distorted creatures who force their opinions and their manuscripts upon Balso. Among them are a naked man, wearing only a derby hat with thorns protruding from it, who is "Attempting to crucify himself with thumbtacks" and who tells the tale of the martyrdom of a flea, St. Puce, upon the body of Christ; a boy in short pants who writes a Dostoevskyan journal about the murder of an idiot; a nude girl bathing her charms in an outdoor fountain who miraculously is transformed, when Balso kisses her, into a middle-aged woman in mannish tweeds; and a beautiful hunchback with one-hundred and forty-four teeth in rows of four who asks Balso to prove his love for her by murdering Beagle Hamlet Darwin, the man who has seduced and then abandoned her.

The narrative, the conceits, and the characters of *The Dream Life* are obviously inspired by the distortions of surrealism, but the implications of the pretentiousness of each of the tales that Balso hears is that art is not the "divine excrement" romanticized by George Moore but is instead closer to the balls, the physical reality, of Snell. When he enters the "Anus Mirabilis" of the Trojan Horse, Balso does so by reciting an invocation inspired by James Joyce, and seeking, like Joyce's Stephen Dedalus at the conclusion of *The Portrait of the Artist,* "To encounter for the millionth time the reality of experience," Balso finds that reality in sex. For West, however, the reality which is the animal sexual instinct must be preceded in man by the falsity which is the romantic sexual game. In the last chapter of *The Dream Life,* therefore, Balso Snell argues the case for sexual intercourse to his indifferent beloved. In hilarious parody, Balso asserts the political argument (intercourse is an expression of freedom), the philosophical argument (pleasure is desirable), the argument from art (the artist "must know what all the shooting is about,") and the argument from time ("The seconds, how they fly"). On her back, with her knees spread invitingly apart, Miss McGeeney listens patiently until Balso throws himself down beside her, at which point she coyly resists and then ultimately yields: "Moooompitcher yaaaah. . . . Drag me down into the mire, drag. Yes! And with your hair the lust from my eyes brush. Yes . . . Yes . . . Oph! Ah!" In such intercourse is the real "Yes" to the universe, the "Yes" that Joyce's Molly Blum recognized in her soliloquy at the end of *Ulysses* and which West parodies through Miss McGeeney's "Yes." In this union comes the release of the little death, and in it is "the mystic doctrine, the purification, the syllable 'Om. . . .'" This is the truth revealed by the climax of Balso's wet dream, and the surrealistic conception that through dreams and fantasies one might transcend the physical and find some supreme union with the universe is nonsense. West's advice to surrealists who believe such foolishness—or to anyone deluded by the pretensions of art, religion, or thought—is implied in his creature John Raskolnikov Gilson, who tries to retain his hold on reality by writing in his *Journal "while smelling the moistened forefinger of my left hand."* For fakers who would not heed such advice, West, like his creator Gilson, would have "the ceiling of the theatre . . . open and cover the occupants with tons of loose excrement."

A third kind of humor in West's work is the prevailing black humor of *Miss Lonelyhearts.* Such humor, or at least "grotesque black humor" rather than "absurd black humor," is rooted in total despair, sees the universe as absurd, and often uses violent and shocking images or surrealistic images yoking disparate concepts to destroy the complacency of its audience. Of such humor [Mathew Winston, in *Veins of Humor,* edited by Harry Levin] writes:

> Black humor often reveals life's shabbiness and criticizes in the manner of satire. But unlike satire, it does not assume a set of norms, implicit or explicit, against which one may contrast the mad world depicted by the author. It relies neither on "common sense" as a guide to proposition and decorum, nor on social, religious, or moral convention. This is not to say that the reader of black humor is without norms. He has them, and the writer of black humor exploits them. The reader's sense of decency allows the writer to shock, the reader's humanity allows him to horrify, the reader's sense of verisimilitude enables him to outrage, and the reader's familiarity with dramatic and fictional conventions allows him to parody. . . . Moreover, black humor challenges not only the standards of judgment on which the satirist relies, but also the very faculties of judgment.

The plot structure of *Miss Lonelyhearts,* yoking the concept of the martyrdom of Christ to the agony of an advice-to-the-lovelorn columnist, and implying a parallel between the myth of Christ's journey to the cross and the pilgrimage of Miss Lonelyhearts to his death, is not only a far fetched conceit but also a narrative calculated to shock conventionally religious minds. In an earlier time this kind of humor, or humour, would have been attributed to the black bile produced by the brain and responsible for human melancholy, but the ironic contrast implied in the central conceit of the novel brings, or is intended to bring, a thin and bitter smile to the modern reader. That vein of humor is apparent on the first page of the novel when the feature editor of the newspaper on which Miss Lonelyhearts works parodies the "Anima Christi":

> Soul of Miss L, glorify me
> Body of Miss L, nourish me
> Blood of Miss L, intoxicate me.

And it is evident in the countless letters of the helpless of the universe—Sick-of-it-all, Desperate, Broad Shoulders—that recount what life is like if one has, for instance, been born without a nose and must "sit and look at myself all day and cry. . . . My mother loves me but she crys terrible when she looks at me." The humor of the letters, however, turns inward upon Miss Lonelyhearts and, as he explains to his fiancé, "shows him that he is the victim of the joke and not its perpetrator." The consequent examination of the values on which his life is based leads to an even blacker joke: Miss Lonelyhearts desires to succor with love the helpless cripples of the universe, and his attempt to do so leads to his sickness, his hallucinations, and ultimately his death at the hands of one of those whom he would save. His "martyrdom" parodies that of Christ and by implication mocks the meaningfulness of either.

The universe in which West's indictment of Christian mythology takes place is typical of the creations of the writers of black humor. Violence is everywhere, especially exemplified in the sexual violence so common in the letters Miss Lonelyhearts receives, and order is non-existent. At one time in his quest for order in an irrational world, Miss Lonelyhearts remembers his sister dancing gravely and precisely to the patterned music of Mozart. So musing, he turns from the bar, accidentally jostles another man, and before he can beg pardon, receives a punch in the mouth. In this disordered wasteland, water, love, and fertility are missing; none of the flowers of spring are in the park, and even the year before, as Miss Lonelyhearts remembers it, "It had taken all the brutality of July to torture a few green spikes through the exhausted earth."

One character especially embodies the tone of black literary humor in *Miss Lonelyhearts.* He is the feature editor of the newspaper for which Miss Lonelyhearts works, and is named Shrike, after the bird which impales its prey upon a cross of thorns. A complete nihilist, he is a joke machine capable of such blasphemy as "I am a great saint. . . . I can walk on my own water. Haven't you heard of Shrike's passion in the luncheonette, or the Agony in the Soda Fountain?" Like all black humorists, Shrike is the foe of sentimentality, so that he can parody the most moving of the letters to Miss Lonelyhearts, as, for instance, when he creates a situation in which a young boy wants a violin but unfortunately is paralyzed and must be doomed only to clutch a toy violin to his chest while he makes the sounds of his music with his mouth. But, ends Shrike, "one can learn much from this parable. Label the boy Labor, the violin Capital, and so on. . . . " For Shrike, the dreams of man, in all their infinite variety, are material for ridicule. In the chapter "Miss Lonely-hearts in the Dismal Swamp," a perfect example of the fusion of wit and despair in black humor, Shrike parodies such escapes as the sail, the South seas, hedonism, and religion. The escape to Art he ridicules to Miss Lonely-hearts:

> "When you are cold, warm yourself before the flaming tints of Titian, when you are hungry, nourish yourself with great spiritual food . . . smoke a 3 B pipe, and remember these immortal lines: *When to the suddenness of melody the echo parting falls the failing day.* What a rhythm! Tell them to keep their society whores and pressed duck with oranges. For you *l'art vivant,* the living art, as you call it. Tell them that you know that your shoes are broken and that there are pimples on your face, yes, and that you have buck teeth and a club foot, but that you don't care, for tomorrow they are playing Beethoven's last quartets . . . and at home you have Shakespeare's plays in one volume."

Of all the dreams, the one that for Shrike is most absurd is the myth of Christ, the Miss Lonelyhearts of Miss Lonelyhearts, and Shrike's sharpest gibes are directed at that Fantasy. Mocking the aspirations of Miss Lonelyhearts, Shrike composes a biography—"The gospel according to Shrike"—in which Miss Lonelyhearts "wends his weary way" from the "University of Hard Knocks" to the "bed of his first whore," always "struggling valiantly to realize a high ideal," always climbing ever upward, "rung by weary rung . . . breathless with hallowed fire." What Shrike omits is the most bitter joke of all: Miss Lonelyhearts' accidental, meaningless death.

Yet another form of satire that West used in his art is the dominant parody and farce of *A Cool Million.* Indebted to the exaggerations of the tall tale and anticipating the pursuit of logic to insane conclusions exemplified in such novelists of the absurd as Joseph Heller, *A Cool Million* or *The Dismantling of Lemuel Pitkin* takes its narrative inspiration primarily from Voltaire—West thought of his novel as a twentieth-century *Candide*—so that the innocent hero of West's novel, like Voltaire's hero, sets out from home to seek his fortune. The adventures of both Lemuel Pitkin and Candide reveal a world of violence and greed—all of its dramatized farcically—and in it Lemuel loses his teeth, his eye, a thumb, a leg, his scalp, and ultimately his life. Where Candide ultimately learns something—and thus rejects the optimism of his tutor, Dr. Pangloss, that all is for the best in this best of all possible worlds—the ever gullible Lemuel remains faithful to the simplicities of the American dream preached by Lemuel's tutor Nathan "Shagpoke" Whipple. Like Abe Lincoln, whose life exemplifies for "Shagpoke" Whipple the fulfilment of the American dream, Lemuel dies in a theatre by an assassin's bullet, and his birthday is commemorated as a national holiday. Both holidays, West implies, have identical purposes: to preach the virtues of the American dream, by which every American boy can go into the world and by hard work, honesty, and probity make his fortune and win The Girl, and in so doing to delude and exploit the gullibles of America. Through the manipulation of such fools, dictators come to power, and Lincoln's

faith that you can't fool all of the people all of the time is irrelevant, for West, to that truth.

In his mockery of optimistic faith in both the American dream and the American people, West's most obvious parody is that of such novels of Horatio Alger as *Onward and Upward, Bound to Rise,* and *Sink or Swim.* Such Alger novels as these told, in plodding prose directed to the "dear reader," the story of "our hero" as he rose from low estate, most often as a newsboy or shoeshine boy, to wealth and fame. West not only parodied the language of Alger, but at times lifted phrases and sentences directly, so that *A Cool Million,* most especially in the first half of the novel, is laden with such clichés as "a veil of tears"; such archaisms as "our hero was loth to lie"; such heavy or unnaturally colloquial dialogue as "In these effete times, it is rare indeed for one to witness a hero in action," or "Me lad, the jig is up"; such moral asides as "justice will out"; and such authorial intrusions as, "As it will only delay my narrative . . . I will skip to his last sentence." Like Alger, West ends numerous chapters with melodramatic cliffhangers, and then shifts to another thread of his narrative; at the end of chapter three, for instance, Tom Baxter is left admiring the prostrate form of Lemuel's girl friend Betty Prail—"His little pig-like eyes shone with bestiality"—while the author begins the ensuing chapter, in Algerian prudery, with, "It is with reluctance that I leave Miss Prail . . . but I cannot with propriety continue my narrative beyond the point at which the bully undressed this unfortunate young lady."

In addition to the parody of Alger's prose, West mocks the rise of Alger's heroes by the dismantling of his own, and he does so in the typical coincidences and situations of the Algerian Novel. Such a coincidence occurs when Lemuel visits New York's Chinatown, and Betty Prail, who is being held by Chinese White-slavers, throws a bottle with a note at his feet; but instead of rescuing Betty, Lemuel himself is captured by the white slavers and dressed in a sailor suit to appease the sexual appetite of the Maharajah of Kanurani. Such an Algerian situation arises when Lemuel rescues a rich man and his pretty daughter from the path of frightened, onrushing horses; but West's world is not Alger's, so that Lemuel, instead of receiving the just rewards he deserves in an equitable world, loses his false teeth, is reprimanded as a careless groom by the rich man he has saved, cannot respond because his teeth are gone, and is injured by a flying stone so that ultimately he loses his eye.

A second object of parody is the leader, the beliefs, the forms, and the human materials of German fascism. The clown named Adolf Hitler, who was in the mid-thirties often conceived of as a ridiculous house painter with an absurd mustache, West molded into the native American type that West felt was embodied in the former American President Calvin Coolidge. To that dangerous clown, West gave the name Nathan "Shagpoke" Whipple. Out of his nationalist beliefs, his faith in the supremacy of white, Protestant Americans, and his memories of the German National Socialist Party, Whipple creates the platform for the National Revolutionary Party, popularly known as the Leather Shirts, and from his soapbox he preaches: "We must drive the Jewish international bankers out of Wall Street! We must destroy the Bolshevik labor unions! We must purge our country of all the alien elements and ideas that now interest her!" For his "storm troops" Whipple creates a native uniform—a coonskin cap, a deerskin shirt, and moccasins—and in the Southern heartland of America, where Whipple's rhetoric functions most effectively, he so arouses his supporters that

> They ran up the Confederate flag on the courthouse pole, and prepared to die in its defense.
>
> Other, more practical-minded citizens proceeded to rob the bank and loot the principal stores, and to free all their relatives who had the misfortune to be in jail.
>
> As time went on, the riot grew more general in character. . . . The heads of Negroes were paraded on poles. A Jewish drummer was nailed to the door of his hotel room. The housekeeper of the local Catholic priest was raped.

Beyond these major stylistic and thematic parodies, two others deserve mention. One is West's derision of radical writers and the propagandistic art they create. The author of such nonsense in *A Cool Million* is the poet Sylvanus Snodgrasse, who turns to communism because the American public does not buy his work. The same lack of talent that impedes his popular success, however, pervades his propaganda, so that his playlet about a "sleek salesman" who deceives widows and orphans into buying worthless bonds is filled with the sentiment and images—three children who cry "Goo, goo," two millionaires who laugh as they step over the dead bodies of those they've defrauded—reminiscent of such proletarian literature of the thirties as Clifford Odet's *Waiting for Lefty*. Finally, one must note West's parody of the "Buy American" campaign inspired by the Hearst chain of newspapers and for a while in the thirties a significant force in the market place. In *A Cool Million* a Chinese businessman whose trade is white slavery adopts, for commercial reasons, the Hearst credo, and transforms his bordello from a "House of All Nations" to a hundred percent American establishment. In his enthusiasm Wu Fong insists on artistic consistency, so that the food, the furnishings, and the costumes of his establishment are appropriate to the milieu of each of the girls. For instance, the room of Princess Roan Fawn is "papered with birch bark to make it look like a wigwam"; she does her "business on the floor"; her native costume is total nudity save for a wolf's tooth necklace and a bull's eye blanket; and her customers are served "baked dog and firewater" for dinner. This artistic attention to detail is so great that West observes, in a moral, Algerian parenthesis, that Wu Fong might have used his talents honestly, and "made even more money without having to carry the stigma of being a brothel-keeper. Alas!".

Yet another aspect of the humor of *A Cool Million* seems less inspired by Voltaire, Alger, and German fascism than it does by the pure farce of Punch and Judy and the Keystone Cops. One example of this kind of burlesque occurs when Lemuel is duped into participating in a confidence game by pretending to lose his glass eye in a jewelry store and then to offer a thousand dollar reward for its return.

Even more of a travesty is the job he takes in which, as a member of a comedy team, he is beaten violently so that his teeth, eye, wig, and leg are clubbed from his body. The extremes of this kind of humor, and of the humor of *A Cool Million,* generally are more appropriate to the talent of S. J. Perelman, to whom *A Cool Million,* is dedicated, than to the genius of Nathanael West, and perhaps for this reason *A Cool Million* is less successful artistically than any of West's other novels.

Nathanael West's last novel, *The Day of the Locust,* is not very funny, and West knew it well. Thinking of *The Day,* and apparently forgetting such works as *The Dream Life* and *A Cool Million,* West could write, "I do consider myself a comic writer, perhaps in an older and a much different tradition than Benchley or Sullivan. Humor is another thing. I am not a humorous writer I must admit and have no desire to be one." Even the reason for the lack of laughter in *The Day,* West expressed in his comment in the novel, "It is hard to laugh at the need for beauty and romance, no matter how tasteless, even horrible, the results of that need are. But it is easy to sigh. Few things are sadder than the truly monstrous."

In dramatizing *The Day,* West emphasized the experiences of two newcomers, Tod Hackett and Homer Simpson, in the promised land—one character claims "it's a paradise on earth"—of the Angelenos. Los Angeles, however, is an ironic paradise, and its citizens are more grotesque than angelic. Violence, corruption, and perversity infest the city, from bloody and illegal cockfights, to pornographic movies in brothels which are triumphs "of industrial design," where the refined madame "makes vice attractive by skillful packaging," to children singing blues songs with sexual groans and suggestive gestures. Eros, the God of love, lies face downward on a forgotten movie set overrun with bottles and newspapers, and love itself is mocked by comic rhetoric: "Love is like a vending machine, eh? . . . You insert a coin and press down the lever. There's some mechanical activity inside the bowels of the device. You receive a small sweet . . . and walk away, trying to look as though nothing had happened. It's good, but it's not for pictures." Dissolution and death are omnipresent, from the concern of one character with the formal arrangements of funerals to the obsession of Tod Hackett with such painters of decay as Salvator Rosa and Francesco Guardi. The meaning of death is continually mocked by such images as that of the clown, Harry Greener, in his coffin ("He looked like the interlocutor in a minstrel show"), to the conversation piece that one couple puts in their swimming pool (a rubber imitation of a dead horse, with an "enormous distended belly" and a mouth, from which a black tongue hangs, set in an "agonized grin"), to a movie scene of the Battle of Waterloo (which diminishes the heroism and the agony of the actual battle to the trivial farce of a movie set that collapses and leaves the producer with the problem of resolving the insurance claims of the wounded). In this angelic world, deceit, more than anything else, is the fundamental reality: houses are made of "plaster, lath, and paper" and have no architectural stability or human dignity; the natural colors of food are intensified by artificial lighting that makes oranges red, lemons yellow, and steaks rose; the dress of people bears no relation to their occupation or their nature; and above all, the movies made in the land of the angels bear no more relation to reality than do the props—picknickers on a fibre lawn, for instance, eat "cardboard food in front of a cellophane waterfall"—that are created to give the illusion of truth.

Save for Tod Hackett, the artist-observer, the people that inhabit this city are grotesques, some of them deceivers who are, for the most part, peripherally associated with the world of dreams called Hollywood, others of them the deceived who have slaved all their lives and then, in search of Paradise, have come to Los Angeles to die. In the latter there exists an inarticulate frustration and rage, stemming from their inward sterility of spirit, that nothing, not even violence, can permanently appease. It is these pathetic and frightening creatures, whom Homer Simpson embodies, that attend the services of such bizarre churches as the "Tabernacle of the Third Coming," where Tod hears one angry parishioner bring the message that he had "seen the Tiger of Wrath stalking the walls of the citadel and the Jackal of Lust skulking in the shrubbery," and it is out of the rage of these that there arises the inspiration for Tod Hackett's painting "The Burning of Los Angeles" and the apocalyptic violence on which the novel ends.

The central, bitter apocalyptic humor of the novel lies in the contrast between the Biblical revelation of St. John the divine and the revelation of Tod Hackett expressed in his painting of "The Burning of Los Angeles." Where St. John foresaw God's destruction of Rome, the Whore of Babylon, because of the materialism of the city and its violations of God's laws, Tod sees only a meaningless destruction of the city of the angels by a mass of human locusts. Possibly inspired by a messiah similar to the "super Dr. Know-All Pierce-All" who had come to power in Germany, these creatures must soon become uncontrollable because they have found, in their search for the promised land, that "the sun is a joke. Oranges can't titillate their jaded palates. Nothing can ever be violent enough to make taut their slack minds and bodies. They have been cheated and betrayed." For such as these, life itself is a small-minded joke played by an ignorant child like the monster Adore, who tries to lure Homer Simpson to pick up a purse tied to a string and then, when Homer won't play, flings a stone in his face. For such as these, life itself is a stone in the face, full only of boredom and bitterness that can never be resolved, just as Homer's sobs have neither accent nor progress and "would never reach a climax." For such as these, the only solution to their lives is death. It is that which they seek in the darkened churches where they worship the celluloid stars of the silver screen. It is that which Homer subconsciously seeks in his pursuit of the movie extra, Faye Greener, a creature whose invitation, even in the movies in which she appears as a seductive temptress, is "closer to murder than to love. If you threw yourself on her, it would be like throwing yourself from the parapet of a skyscraper." In his rampaging violence at the end of the novel, Homer invites his own death, and in it he achieves the only victory of his life. In the same way, the violence of the mob at the movie premiere has as its aim not only the conscious destruction of those who have cheated and betrayed them but also the subconscious destruction of self. In violence is momentary joy and in death is final victory—that assertion is West's answer to St. John's vision of the New Jerusalem and his invitation (Revelation 22,17) to "Come, let him who desires take the water of life without price." In the irony of that answer lies the essence of West's apocalpytic humor in *The Day.*

In his first novel, West conceived a character named Beagle Hamlet Darwin who commented in a letter to his mistress: "You once said to me that I talk like a man in a book. I not only talk but think and feel like one. I have spent my life in books; literature has deeply dyed my brain its own color." What Darwin says about himself is true also of Darwin's creator, and the evidence of this is in the innumerable allusions in West's novels. These range from the purely private, such as West's veiled allusion in *A Cool Million* to Alice Shepard, a former girl friend, as the Southern whore, Alice Sweethorne; to the very obvious, such as the Algerian language and situations in *A Cool Million*; to the extremely complicated, such as the echoes of Eliot's *Waste Land* and Christian mythology in *Miss Lonelyhearts,* which inspired Victor Comerchero to assert that "The world of *Miss Lonelyhearts* is the fallen world of myth"; to the allusive pastiches, such as the parodies on the philosophic and poetic arguments justifying sexual intercourse on which *The Dream Life of Balso Snell* ends. Perhaps no allusion in West's work, however, is more meaningful to his art as a whole, more frightening in its implications, or more witty in its expression than Beagle Hamlet Darwin's references in *The Dream Life* to Christ, Dionysius, and Gargantua. Calling on Dionysius to assist him in explaining "The tragedy of all of us," Darwin asserts the concept of spiritual Darwinism. Beagle Hamlet Darwin's theory states that each of us, from birth onward, is doomed to dream of being more than animal and thus to compete with the likes of Dionysius, born three times, or Christ, born of a virgin. The conception of common men, however, is more humorous than remarkable, for the human lover does not approach his beloved "in the shape of a swan, a bull, or a shower of gold" but rather he comes "with his pants unsupported by braces . . . from the bath-room." Similar is the reality of normal birth, where there are no kings, no doves, no stars of Bethlehem, but "only old Doctor Haasenchweitz who wore rubber gloves and carried a towel over his arm like a waiter." Thinking of this contrast, Darwin realizes the tragedy of the competition in which men must spend their lives, "a competition that demanded their being more than animals." Because of this inward need, men must forever dream, and to support their dreams they pathetically juggle the paraphernalia that they have created to justify their foolishness: "an Ivory Tower, a Still White Bird, The Holy Grail, The Nails, The Scourge, The Thorns, and a piece of The True Cross." Throughout his art West mocked this folly by satirizing, in a variety of forms, the dreams of man, but since he also comprehended that to live without dreams was worse than to exist with no dreams at all, he had no answer to this dilemma, and his art expresses none. Because of this lack of any ultimate answer, West's satire seems most successful when it is most irreverent, most scatological, most despairing, and most complex, but these qualities should never obscure the fact that it is laughter that is at the center of West's art.

West's Hollywood experience:

When West returned to Los Angeles, he was already thinking of writing a novel about Hollywood; and while there, he became an observer and explorer of Hollywood's offbeat life. He knew the bars and the people who frequented them along Hollywood Boulevard, and was often at Stanley Rose's Hollywood Boulevard bookstore. Rose was a colorful character who had never gone beyond the fourth grade; he had once been in prison, yet had later become a Hollywood agent. In the rear of his bookshop he opened a room where art exhibitions were held and writers gathered in its club-like atmosphere. In addition to West these writers included, at various times, Horace McCoy, William Saroyan, Erskine Caldwell, Dashiell Hammett, F. Scott Fitzgerald, and John O'Hara. Through Rose, West was also introduced to what Lillian Hellman called the "whorish, drunk, dope-taking world" of North Hollywood. With Rose, he met small-time gangsters, went to boxing matches, and to illegal cockfights in the Hollywood hills. He also explored the Mexican-American enclave of the city and seems to have known smugglers who operated back and forth between Mexico and Southern California. It was in this way that he acquired the insider's knowledge of the anomic underside of Hollywood that informs *The Day of the Locust.*

Robert Emmet Long, in his Nathanael West, *Frederick Ungar Publishing Co., 1985.*

Deborah Wyrick   (essay date 1979)

SOURCE: "Dadaist Collage Structure and Nathanael West's 'Dream Life of Balso Snell'," in *Nathanael West,* edited by Harold Bloom, Chelsea House Publishers, 1986, pp. 157-64.

[This essay was originally published in 1979.]

Most critics admire the structural mastery of Nathanael West's short novels, and many of them base their analyses upon the works' relationships with the visual arts. *Miss Lonelyhearts,* for instance, has been found to have a comic strip structure; *The Day of the Locust* can be seen as a combination of Eisensteinian film technique, ritual drama, and verbal "quotations" from old master paintings. Even the imploded Horatio Alger narrative of *A Cool Million* has been scripted into a Grade B double feature filler. Surprisingly, the question of structure in West's first novel, *The Dream Life of Balso Snell,* has been largely ignored. Instead, critics agree that it is formless, chaotic, a juvenile pastiche of bathroom jokes, college magazine parody, and borrowings from contemporary avant-garde authors. This consensus is not difficult to understand, for the sixty-two-page novella—which chronicles the journey of an everyman artist through the entrails of the Trojan horse, records his encounters with crazed representatives of West-

ern culture, and climaxes with an unsatisfying nocturnal emission—twists and turns like the intestines which serve as its setting. If one remembers, however, that architectural principles of West's other novels are drawn from the visual arts, one perhaps is justified in looking for a similar structural matrix for *Balso Snell.*

West's interest in the visual arts dates back at least as far as his high school years, when he drew cartoons for his summer camp newspaper. In college, he not only enrolled in art history courses, he also illustrated the Brown literary magazine, began a lifelong friendship with artist and author S. J. Perelman, and planned a series of books on great artists—a project on which he worked desultorily during his postgraduate trip to Paris in 1926. In Paris, he met Max Ernst, Louis Aragon, and Philippe Soupault, and he attached himself to the Dada/Surrealist bohemian circle. Although *Balso Snell* was not published until 1931, it was written between 1922 and 1929, the years West spent at Brown and in Paris, a time in which West was preoccupied with modern art. Consequently, one would not be surprised to find evidence of this interest in *Balso Snell.*

The evidentiary key lies in West's original epigraph for the book, a pronouncement by the German Dadaist artist Kurt Schwitters: "Everything that the artist expectorates is art." This sentiment was retained in the final version of the book through the statement of George Moore, "art is a sublime excrement." (*The Dream Life of Balso Snell,* in *The Complete Works of Nathanael West.* All further references to this novella will be to this edition.) In one sense, the Schwitters motto is a commentary on the philosophy behind the novella—that art is literally a wasteland, that Western culture is composed of the excretions and eliminations of humanity. In another sense, the motto and its companion epigram by Moore give a gloss on the controlling excremental joke which provides design for the novella. People buried in cloaca, throats which sound like flushing toilets, actions occurring in bathrooms, and ceilings which release fecal matter upon playgoers are just a few of West's scatological variations. Finally, however, the Schwitters reference implies not only an aesthetic but also a technique. Schwitters, an influential practicing artist as well as a Dadaist spokesman, was known for his *Merzbilder* (junk constructions), collages composed of contents of his wastebasket or of detritus discovered on the streets. Inheriting the art of collage from Picasso and Braque who, in the years after 1912, began pasting paper and material on to canvas rather than imitating their textures in paint, Schwitters radicalized this technique by building it from junk in order to express the Dadaist view of art as refuse. In *Balso Snell,* West translates visual collage into literary collage. Like Schwitters, his choice and arrangement of materials make a strong Dadaist statement.

The most striking features of visual collage are the use of borrowed or found materials rejuvenated by their placement in an unexpected context, the technique of superimposition, and the aesthetically pleasurable surprise afforded by the exercise of artistic control on an assemblage of seemingly unrelated items. *The Dream Life of Balso Snell* exhibits all three features. First, West filches freely from a plethora of other authors. His literary borrowings can be garbled into burlesque, like his mangling of Stephen Dedalus's invocation into, " 'O Beer! O Meyerbeer! O Bach! O Offenbach! Stand me now as ever in good stead.' " They can be exact, like the Euripidean prayer which becomes ludicrous when it is used as an expatriate cad's acknowledgement of the death of his mistress. They can be imitations, like the serious-toned Dostoevskian murder which dislocates surrealistically when West makes a twelve-year-old boy, John Gilson, the perpetrator. Usually, these snippets of other authors are close enough to the originals to give the impression that West is, like visual collagists, creating out of preexisting substances. When West warps them humorously, the effect is rather like Picasso's dissected bicycle antelope or Max Ernst's placement of anatomy manual cut-outs upon painted tightropes and trapezes; the pleasure arises from the mental comparison of the original object and its function to the transformed object and its new function.

The second structural collage technique is superimposition. In a Schwitters construction, for example, a paint-mixing stick can traverse a scrap of chicken wire which, in turn, is affixed to a torn newspaper glued to the canvas. This technique explodes the rigid two-dimensionality of traditional painting. Similarly, *The Dream Life of Balso Snell* breaks through the temporal confines of the novella by layering different literary units within single episodes, units stacked like upended nesting boxes shuttling back and forth in time in order to give a collagelike spatial texture and a Jungian temporal simultaneity.

For example, the sixth of the seven divisions which make up *Balso Snell* contains at least eight discrete formal entities piled one atop the other. The first level finds Balso Snell drinking in a café built into the horse's intestinal wall. He falls asleep and proceeds to the second level, in which he meets a gorgeous hunchback named Janey Davenport. In order to send Balso on a mock-chivalric quest, she presents him with a letter which becomes the third level of the section. At first, the letter to Janey from her lover, Beagle Darwin, explains his refusal to take her with him to Paris; but the letter also contains the fourth formal level of this episode—a fictionalized scenario about Janey's reactions to pregnancy which ends in her suicide. Returning to the second level, Janey shows Balso another letter, this one becoming the fifth separate element of the section. The new letter, also from Beagle to Janey, contains a sixth element—a third-person account of Beagle's projected reaction to Janey's projected death. Within this account resides the seventh level, a first-person soliloquy in which Beagle, now a hybrid Hamlet/Pagliacci, fulminates upon the tragedy of man. From this platform, he jumps onto the eighth level of the section, a play within a play complete with characters, dialogue, a chorus, and its own superimpositional flourishes of allusions to Greek playwrights, the Bible, Alexander Pope, and François Villon. This portion of *Balso Snell* ends as Beagle goes into his juggling act. Through the device of superimposition, man the actor—like Picasso's tragic clowns—can be painted from a cubistic perspective which changes sequential observation into simultaneous perception. Abruptly, the next section begins when the protagonist wakes up in

the café, the elaborate multistoried Janey Davenport episode having collapsed like Alice's house of cards. West uses this superimpositional structure with varying degrees of complexity throughout the book.

The third aspect of collage, the exercise of artistic control to unite apparently disparate elements, is at once the most elusive and the most fascinating as it applies to *The Dream Life of Balso Snell*. Just as the creator of a visual collage amalgamates his materials with repeated motifs of line, color, and spatial harmonies, West consolidates his literary collage with repeated motifs of style, symbol, and theme. West has packed his novella so densely that it would be impractical to unravel all these strands in a short analysis; nevertheless, an examination of some of his unifying threads can reveal the intricate texture of his work.

Allied to the stylistic technique of literary parody which laces the book from start to finish is West's habit of cultural name-dropping. For instance, his characters sprinkle their dialogue with roll calls of the famous, ranging from artists to religious figures to mythological personages. West also uses other stylistic unifying devices. Balso Snell, nominally a poet, can be counted upon to speak in clichés, emblems of bourgeois obtuseness and Dadaist ciphers of the modern breakdown in communication. Reassuring a Semitic guide, he states, " 'I admire the Jews; they are a thrifty race. Some of my best friends are Jews.' " He advises a morbid ascetic to " '[p]lay games. Don't read so many books. Take cold showers. Eat more meat' " and suggests that the psychotic Gilson ought to " 'run about more. Read less and play baseball.' " Here the protagonist responds to a series of confessions, another device which knits together the novella. Just as the grotesques of *Winesburg, Ohio*, reveal their secrets to George Willard, the grotesques of the Trojan horse confess their hidden natures to Balso Snell. The guide confesses his Jewishness, the ascetic his religio-erotic obsession; John Gilson's Journal forms a criminal and moral confession as do the dream letters of Beagle Darwin. A confession is an emptying out of unwanted aspects of self; as such, it is parallel to the Schwitters and Moore conceptions of art as expectoration and excrement. Akin to the confession is the ejaculatory lament. Most of the characters at one time or another erupt into Othelloesque series of "O! O! O! s," interjections which, as will be shown, also have thematic significance.

Other recurring stylistic devices are literalization and mock dialectic. For example, Maloney the Areopagite's account of St. Puce, the flea who lived in Christ's armpit, presents a literalization of Christ as the eucharistic meal and the temple of believers. Later, John Gilson literalizes his vulnerability by saying, "I wore my heart and genitals around my neck"; he literalizes his driving sexual desire as "the chauffeur within me." These sorts of literalizations create absurd images with a visual power similar to paintings by Ernst and Magritte. In addition, mock dialectic is set up throughout the book. However, when Christianity confronts Judaism, when actors confront their audiences, when—in general—the illusions of the mind confront the realities of the body, the result is not a synthesis. It may be nihilistic denial of both alternating poles of reference, or it may be a call similar to the one which rises from Jonathan Swift—whose ridiculously rational Houyhnhnms and filthily libidinous Yahoos must be among Balso Snell's dark muses—for readers to find the positive ground between the negative poles of reference. One cannot be sure whether West is urging readers to plunge into the gulf with Baudelaire or to bridge it with Swift.

Finally, throughout the book, West manipulates the symbolist technique of synaesthesia. St. Puce revels in sensual ecstasy with " '[t]he music of Our Lord's skin sliding over his flesh. . . . The odors of His Body—more fragrant than the Temple of Solomon. . . .' " John Gilson describes a reader's communion at a library in which books which "smelt like the breaths of their authors" seemed "to turn into flesh." The most extended instance of synaesthesia attaches to Gilson's teacher, Miss McGeeney's, biographical subject Samuel Perkins—the ultimate synaesthetic man who could " 'smell a chord in D minor . . . [or] the caress of velvet.' " Synaesthesia not only blends the individual senses, it also magnifies sensual perception as a whole into a guiding force of existence, a force propelled by Freudian physical compulsion and by Swiftian physical revulsion.

In *The Dream Life of Balso Snell,* one cannot separate symbol from theme, for West repeats and embellishes symbols throughout the book in order to create thematic unity. His symbol clusters and their resulting thematic patterns are circular rather than linear; in fact, they resemble interlocking radial webs of meaning. As has been noted earlier, the most memorable symbols are excremental and anal. Like Père Ubu's constantly reiterated scatological interjections, the fecal and rectal references in *Balso Snell* provide both shock value and thematic amplification. Not only is art excrement, so are love and sex. Balso's "Phoenix Excrementi," who devour themselves and give themselves rebirth through evacuation, show an "infantile cloacal conception of birth." As Gilson beats his mistress, he screams, " 'O constipation of desire! O diarrhoea of love.' " Beagle Darwin defines the tragedy of life as when "[c]oming from the bathroom, you discover that you have gonorrhoea, or you get a telegram that your mother is dead. . . ." Balso's passion for Miss McGeeney is recorded as " 'Oh!' His mouth formed an O with lips torn angry in laying duck's eggs from a chicken's rectum." These examples illustrate a constellation of images of sex and the life cycle, waste material, and death or violence. Actually, all sex is violent in *Balso Snell.* Gilson's murder of the idiot dishwasher is a ritual castration ending in a mock-Elizabethan "little death"; seduction becomes the breaking down of the walls of womanhood; Balso is driven to hit Miss McGeeney "in the gut"—a blow against the feminine principle; Janey's love for Beagle will end in suicide for her and artistic death for him; Balso's final wet dream is couched in violent military metaphors.

Again using the collage technique of superimposition, West erects smaller symbolic superstructures upon this larger thematic framework. There are images of impotence and autoeroticism: Gilson "climbed into [himself] like a bear into a hollow tree"; Perkins's penile nose reminds Miss McGeeney of the Brobdingnagian phallus of a self-abuser she had known. These images couple with fears of androgynous sexual identity. For example, after

the murder, Gilson—rather like Eliot's Tiresias—feels "like a happy girl" and trolls for sailors, subsequently inducing orgasm and vomiting; Balso's sexual assault on Miss McGeeney transforms her into "a middle aged woman dressed in a mannish suit." Animal symbolism of horses, birds, and dogs reinforces the theme of violence, excrement, and the physical self.

Similarly, the theme of violence, excrement, and the mental self is conveyed through West's use of theatrical symbolism. The novella begins with a reference to the "actor-emperor" Nero; it contains, as mentioned earlier, parodies of Shakespeare, of opera, and of Greek tragedies. At the book's midpoint, Gilson plans an art theater production at the end of which "the ceiling of the theater will be made to open and cover the occupants with tons of loose excrement," thereby creating a *deus ex entrailia* which condemns art, artists, and patrons alike. The characters in *Balso Snell,* frequently criticized as flat, are in fact a series of tragic and comic masks for the disintegrated psyche, a function clarified by the description of the idiot dishwasher. "[A] fat, pink and grey pig of a man . . . [h]is neck . . . smooth, white, fat, and covered all over with tiny blue veins like a piece of cheap marble," he symbolizes man in his grossest physicality, the supremacy of body over mind; consequently, "[h]e did not have a skull on the top of his neck, only a face . . . a face without side, back or top, like a mask." The ultimate reduction of art to a manifestation of sexual instinct is made by Gilson, when he states that "[a]ll my acting has but one purpose, the attraction of the female," and is echoed by Beagle Darwin's " '[l]ife is but the span from womb to tomb . . . a spasm of volupty: then . . . the comedy is over . . . ring down the curtain. . . .' " Other arts are subjected to the same sort of physical reduction: Balso calls " 'a beautiful Doric prostate gland' " a piece of " 'exposed plumbing' "; he learns that " 'the virtue of some sixteen year old maiden was the price paid for Ingres' *La Source*' "; he promises to " 'replace music in your affections' " when he tries to seduce Janey; he drags Miss McGeeney off to the bushes with *carpe diem* poetry.

Acting both as nucleus and circumference to this thematic and imagistic web is West's most subtle symbol—the circle. As noted above, characters in *Balso Snell* expel circles as the caterpillar did in *Alice in Wonderland*. These "O's" not only express bafflement or longing, they visually represent a problem central to individual creative existence. Although life is circular and finally hollow, its final scene may involve a surrender to romantic monism. Balso's guide explains the situation at the beginning of the book: " 'If the world is one (everything part of the same thing—called by Picasso nature) then nothing either begins or ends . . . nature is a circle.' " This philosophy frightens Balso so much that he tears loose and flees from the agglutinant Singular. Nevertheless, he cannot escape. The paean to roundness with which he initiates his quest for individuality foreshadows his defeat. Each episode brings Balso in contact with characters who reaffirm the relentless circularity of life and the plurality-annihilating monism which it generates. In the middle of the book, Miss McGeeney calls " 'the senses a circle' " which moves from birth to romance to excremental decay and back to birth, rather like the life processes of the "Phoenix Excrementi" and of Janey Davenport. At last, Balso capitulates to his sexual urges and is swallowed by a physical union which metamorphoses into a facetious philosophical reconciliation of opposites. "The Two become One. The One that is all things . . . the sacrificial egg, the altar, the ego and the alter ego . . . the syllable 'Om'. . . ." This absorption into universal unity produces the death of the individual—certainly the death of the artist. "His body broke free of the bard. It took on a life of its own; a life that knew nothing of the poet Balso. Only to death can this . . . be likened."

No more profoundly antimonistic or antitraditional statement could be made. The artist's quest for individuality ends in a black hole which sucks him into oblivion and sends art, sex, love, culture, and religion rushing in after him. This nihilistic message, then, helps identify *The Dream Life of Balso Snell* as a Dadaist work in intent as well as in structure. Acts of negative creation characterized by self-destruction, despair, shock value, spoof, nonsense, theatricality, spontaneity, and anticlassicism, Dadaist artworks—by their strident outrageousness—both exalt the personality of their creators and eulogize the "negative gesture which was to be the opposite of art, the violent language which was to be the execution of existing poetry." Like all varieties of Expressionist art, they appear in times of tension as revolts against the tyranny of mathematical thought, technical progress, and cultural dehumanization. Nevertheless, an attack on art through art, no matter how self-denigrating the artistic vehicle, always leads to a reaffirmation of art itself. Just as Balso could not escape the enclosing circles of being, the artist cannot escape his own creations. As the Dadaist author Tristan Tzara wrote in 1917, "DADA remains in the European framework of weaknesses; still it is a bunch of excrement, but we want to shit in different colors to ornament the zoo of art. . . ." Similarly, the intricate Dada collage structure employed by Nathanael West brands *The Dream Life of Balso Snell* as a genuine, if off-color, artistic creation. Like Schwitters—and, perhaps, in spite of his own intentions—West's aesthetic sensibilities transform ugly material into a beautiful composition. He ends up with a Dadaist collage that, by its very artistry, celebrates that which it wishes to destroy.

John Keyes   (essay date 1979)

SOURCE: "Personality in the Land of Wish: Popular Motifs in Nathanael West's 'The Day of the Locust'," in *The University of Windsor Review*, Vol. XV, No. 1, Fall-Winter, 1979, pp. 38-50.

It is by now a critical commonplace that the fiction of Nathanael West is rooted in and a comment on, the popular culture of his time: the newspaper, the comic strip, and detective fiction in *Miss Lonelyhearts*; the Horatio Alger myth in *A Cool Million*; the cinema in *The Day of the Locust*. But there is another species of the popular, integral to the structure and substance of his final novel, that has never been acknowledged or perceived, much less examined in detail. The subject of *The Day of the Locust* is fulfillment, the prerogative not only of cinema, but, in its dif-

ferent ways, of fairy tale as well; it is an ironic fulfillment, however, one exposing the limitations of wish, for behind the assumed role or mask of the Hollywood character we find neither a self nor a void but another and complementary role, perhaps identity, with its roots in this very different sort of popular culture. Hence, it is somewhat astonishing that the novel has not been typified before through that most elementary of critical devices, the simple cataloguing of its cast: platinum-haired heroine; moralizing hero; two "ruling" figures of socio-economic substance; helpful dwarf; servant giant; cowboy "earl"; primitive (a surrogate for the beast); sinister or defunct parental figures (wicked mother and derelict father who is also a professional clown)—all set in a silvery never-never land whose business is to make dreams come true. A trifle motley perhaps, but certainly a generic blend: one species of traditional folktale, the fairy tale or Märchen, with the folklore of industrial man.

The novel is West's *Blonde Beauty,* the quest of the girl with the golden hair, who is several Märchen heroines in one: Cinderella, Snow White, Beauty, Goldilocks. Faye Greener's handling of the Cinderella theme, the chorus girl's big chance, gave a realistic turn to miraculous events; she, like the artists of the Middle Ages, "seemed to think that fantasy could be made plausible by a humdrum technique." Since West's plausibility factor depends upon inversion, Faye, as we shall see, becomes Blonde Beauty as angel child as well as castrating bitch. Hence, the evident childlike references in her description: although seventeen, she is "as shiny as a new spoon. . . . dressed like a child of twelve in a white cotton dress with a blue sailor collar"; she is associated with children's food, with candy, ice cream, sodas, gingersnaps; and she eats like a child—she puts butter on her bread, covers it with sugar and takes a "big bite." Hence, too, her relation to children's literature, to fairy tale or nursery motifs.

Cinderella, as the others, is a type of the rejected child, in flux from the extreme of gratuitous deprivation or persecution to that of somewhat gratuitous reward. The motherless Faye, later orphaned, is also an outcast waif, a Hollywood extra as fervently imbued with the clichés of the business which rejects her, as her prototypes were with their own simple faiths. Perrault's Cinderella, however cloying to the adult, with a sweet-nurtured child with good taste; West's rude, quick-tempered Faye seems more appreciative of the Tarzan archetype. The relationship between the two can be examined in the "Cinderella Bar" episode, a parody of the royal ball where the transformed hearth-child enraptures the king's son. The bar is "a little stucco building in the shape of a lady's slipper," an echo of Grimm's golden slipper stuck on the staircase. Its "floor show consisted of female impersonators." The transformation motif thus becomes a sexual transvestism so extreme it is what it would imitate; it is the imitation of the man which is obscene. Perhaps the peasant as princess, whether Cinderella or Faye, should be first that which she is, before she aspires to be more. As Perrault's young prince was taken, so enchanted with Cinderella he could eat nothing, so Homer will not drink (it makes him sick). Faye, however, "in a nasty mood," forces champagne cocktails and brandy down her provider's throat, because his superiority is driving her crazy. The persecuted heroine thus turns persecutive—a response to boredom, at first unconscious, later malicious. But there is more: West realizes, as Perrault and Grimm do not, that perfection irritates, that the unrelieved example of constant virtue is a psychological as well as a moral affront to those of us, who, like the stepsisters, have no hope of maintaining the standard. Hence, Homer's "generosity was still more irritating. It was so helpless and unselfish that it made her feel mean and cruel, no matter how hard she tried to be kind." There are further reductions at the child's expense; the prince would dance with no one but Cinderella; "This is my partner," said Grimm's, permitting no cut-ins. Faye is really less in demand, dancing with an unidentified pickup and with Tod, who begs her to sleep with him. Even the compliment on her beauty—"I said you were the most beautiful girl in the place"—is reductive, a trade-last. And Homer's identification of fairies as "Momo," reflects more than the homosexual's mother-centred propensities; it reminds us, remotely, of the absent Fairy Godmother. It is understandable, then, that Faye, as anti-Cinderella, should hate them: what have they ever done for her?

The motif of supernatural assistance is, of course, fulfilled in the novel, although it is undercut. It need not be a Fairy Godmother; friendly, domesticated beasts and maternal old women are also found. As Grimm's Cinderella is aided by pigeons and turtle-doves, his Two-Eyes by a "wise woman," so Faye, destitute upon the death of Harry, is aided by a Dove called Mary; both the appelative and the behaviour—she takes Faye into her arms—suggest she fulfills both human and animal functions. She is only ironically successful. In the Grimm variant, "One Eye, Two-Eyes, and Three-Eyes," the destitute Two-Eyes, upon the helpful wise woman's advice, buries the entrails of an enchanted goat, slaughtered by her envious mother, which had been her sole source of provision; up comes a tree with silver leaves and golden apples. Mary Dove tries too, in a series of unconscious puns: "Show some guts, kid. Come on now, show some guts." But no enchanted apples appear; instead, there is merely an attempt to escape: as Grimm's Cinderella escaped into a pigeon-house, so Faye escapes into a coo. It is the officious Mrs. Johnson, the janitress, more hearth-linked, with a "face like a baked apple, soft and blotched"—she has no doubt been too near the fire—who sets the scene straight with an authoritative and businesslike manner, appropriate responses for this business landscape; but she offers only short-term assistance. For the longer period, Mary suffices, providing the requisite solution, although she forfeits the maternal pose to do it; both girls become very tough: "They laughed shrilly and went into the bathroom with their arms around each other." The standard of socio-economic gratification for prior deprivation—the royal marriage—is thus represented by the Dove's employer, Audrey Jenning, the woman embodying those traits our society esteems: culture and refinement, sound business sense, skillful packaging of the industrial product—and who has Mrs. Prince to tea. Will Cinderella, call girl in her chauffeured coach, someday call on Mr. Prince? The magic city's rewards are ironic; the hearth-child is back "on the turf."

But only, she claims, to pay for the funeral of her father. For Faye, true fulfillment is found in stardom, cinematic success, failing that, in being successfully cinematic with her public, her collection of men. If not in this episode, at least in others, she is, like Cinderella, a creature of entrances; perhaps the royal ball is the cock fight as well, where she peacocks for them all. She also acquires her rich garments and coach, although she momentarily steps out of the Cinderella mold to do it, moving, like Goldilocks, the nursery set freeloader, into the bear-like Homer's thatch-roofed "Irish" cottage; she exploits him for a "coat of summer ermine and a light blue Buick runabout." She gets her six attendants too: they are more likely lizards from the water-butt transformed to liveried footmen (West's Hollywood is a cactus garden), than mice transformed to horses (the horses can in any case be found, transformed again, under the hood of her Buick). Certainly Faye treats them as her footmen: she pats Abe, the dwarf, on his head and tweaks his nose; Miguel calls her "mum" and both he and Earle are welcomed with "stilted condescension"; "Mamma spank" she has told both Tod and Homer; even Claude has a "begging note in his voice." This American child-heroine instinctively understands the sexual power latent in the mother. Finally, like Cinderella, she disappears into the night, not in rags and a pumpkin, but, we must assume, with all she can, including both Buick and ermine, leaving behind, as clue to identity if not whereabouts, not a glass slipper, but a broken flask of gardenia perfume, a reminder, in the shattered receptacle, both of the anti-virginal capacity and the synthetic nature of this garden princess. The only compensation for the male, it seems, is the transvestite's lullaby: "Little man, you're crying, / I know why you're blue, / Someone took your kiddycar away." Better to go to sleep now: which, at the end of this children's matinee, is just what Homer does.

The other roles receive lesser stress. If, in some versions, though not in all, Goldilocks takes from the bears out of necessity, with Faye it is sheer aggrandizement masquerading as a business deal; if Goldilocks represents a sort of selfless socialism, Faye, then, is aggressive capitalism. In Grimm's "Little Snow White," moreover, the outcast child, in dire hunger, takes food from the absent dwarfs, but only a little from each "for she did not wish to take all from one only." Allowed to stay as a domestic, to cook, sew, wash, knit, she is treated as a sister; West's dwarf is more appreciative: "What a quiff! What a quiff!" he cries, "as though hypnotized"; and it is Homer who does the housework so his Goldilocks-Snow White will stay. Tod, however, fulfills the magic mirror motif of the Snow White analogue, unable to take his eyes from the fairest one of all, the photograph in the upper corner of his mirror frame: a still from a two reel farce with Faye in harem costume, occasion less of envy than of masochistic fantasy. Nor do enchanted objects pose a threat for the anti-Snow-White type; she understands too well the economics of survival. Faye may gulp her food, but poisoned apples could never lodge in her throat; she "gobbled up" Homer's salad, but ate the "large red apple . . . more slowly, nibbling daintily, her smallest finger curled away from the rest of her hand." The poisoned comb West handles with a pun: the bloody comb of the "dirty black hen" which Faye does not mind because "it's only natural." Nor is lace a danger; does she not dance on the crest (the comb) of the waves, only caught for the moment in its net of lace?

As Beauty, her preference for the primitive, the "gorilla", Miguel, to the earl, Shoop, is evident; the motif echoes both fairy tale and cinema as the heroine willingly seeks the embraces of the "monster" to those of the figure, however, ludicrous, signifying rescue. Beauty, of course, was rewarded for learning to discount appearance; accepting the Beast for what he is, not for what he seems to be, she sees him become a Prince, both figures in one, a literal dream come true, an apotheosis which is also sublimation. Miguel's gorilla nature only seems apparent (he merely wears a sweater called a "gorilla"); but in actual fact he is the novel's primitive, Faye's Tarzan: he sat "full in the light of the fire. His skin glowed and the oil in his black curls sparkled." Faye's unsublimated desire for him stands in ironic counterpoint to her cinematic aspirations which are forms of sublimation. The net effect is complicated: the reader reacts not only to West's text, but to his own conceptions of, and prior reactions to, the function and intrinsic worth of both cinema and fairy tale. Thus cynicism toward either can render Faye's response more genuine: an expression of uncomplicated id. But both, especially the simplicity of fairy tale, can comment upon our cynicism.

Since so many figures circle around Faye or what she represents, the novel seems a redaction of the type, the *Quest of the Princess with the Golden Hair*. Motifs common to this type are: a hero in quest of the princess; assistance of a magic horse, or, less commonly, a ship; loathesome animals which defile a prince's food (often represented as Harpies, winged female creatures); tasks imposed upon the hero (taming fierce animals or ploughing a field); happy ending with marriage of hero and princess. The princess may have solar connections: "in at least two fairy stories [she] is . . . named the Virgin of the Sun." Faye, too, is near to this: she seems linked to vegetation or Creation Myth. In her "new flower print dress . . . she was much more than pretty. . . . She looked just born, everything moist and fresh, volatile and perfumed"; not a Culture Hero, but an anti-Culture Heroine for a microcosmic society of male effetism, she stimulates not birth but the events which terminate the novel. In West, at least, the quest seems an ironic wasteland variant: parodic heroes seeking a mock sun or vegetative goddess in what is really a cultural desert. The winged loathesome animal motif is fulfilled by the titular and symbolic "Locust," which destroys not vegetation but the princely city itself.

My concerns, however, are with the hero. One obvious nominee is the rejected cowboy, Earle Shoop, linked to both horse and ship: "Let him ride a horse," says Mary Dove to Faye, "he's a cowboy, ain't he?"; and Earle Shoop=earlship (plus an echo of sloop from G. "Schlup"?). But even if in parodic form he fulfills the "tasks," taming fierce animals by caging and beheading quail, ploughing fields with his "crude hoedown," he is too obviously mechanical and cartoon-like to be of much concern. The real hero is Tod, related not only to the tasks of quest

encapsulated on the studio back lot, but also to those of watch or wooing adventures. Deprived by nature and circumstance, he cannot fulfill the tests of woo: "He had nothing to offer [Faye], neither money nor looks, and she could only love a handsome man and would only let a wealthy man love her." Nor, despite his observations and moral commentary, does he fulfill the functions of watch: like Prufrock, he is too much a part of the society he judges to presume to watch or warn; his Jeremiah instinct is a response to frustration, sublimated lust; and his art is less restorative than corrosive. Of course, he needs assistance, and he gets it, from another fairy-tale type, the helpful dwarf, Abe Kusich. But helpfulness becomes pugnacious interference, the magic horse a tip on the fifth at Caliente, Tragopan, the pheasant (etemologically, Gk. trágo(s), goat + Pän, Pan), an introduction to the phallic principle, which may, as well, be a reference to the cuckold; the tragopan has two fleshy, erectile horns on its head, and Tod is really the stuff of which cuckolds are made. "You could learn from him" (from Abe), Tod tells Homer. Indeed, both dwarf and giant are linked and counterpoised through head imagery, the latter's "small," the former's "slightly hydrocephalic." But the large, sloppy, "almost doltish" Tod, might learn from him too. Is Abe's tip, then, a "bum steer"? Perhaps for Tod it is, since it leads him indirectly to the castrating Faye, the mock sun goddess. We remember the bum steers of Hemingway, where the potentialities of sunrise were linked to the metaphor of phallicism. Better, I suppose, in a world as harsh as this one, to do your own horse riding, or to be the bull, not the hack or jade. Abe may be smashed on the wall like a rabbit, but he gleefully feels he "fixed that buckeroo." He at least can drive away, consigning them all to hell: Tod Hackett is driven.

Homer embodies all the archetypal traits of the giants of folklore. Despite his automatonic nature, he is human; he is also ironically related to the dragon concept: his "feelings were so intense that his head bobbed stiffly on his neck like that of a toy Chinese dragon." He is productive of changes in the landscape; he initiates the apocalyptic riot. He participates in the double nature of the archetype; at once benevolent, kindly, stupid and servile, he is metamorphosed finally, by provocation, into the ogre, a type of the man- or child-eating giant. His relationships throughout are with children; the Romola Martin episode, despite its metallic and homosexual associations, contains precise childlike references, and is the type of the other two, those with Faye and Adore Loomis. Homer's sexual contacts are basically childlike; those with children are basically sexual. Thus Adore's purse-on-a-string routine (recalling his sailboat on a string, which recalls Faye's blue sailor collar) is a sexual lure, both umbilical and uterine, which the sleepwalking giant, already in Uterine Flight, ignores. It is the stone hurled by Adore which brings him to life, a motif echoing and inverting David's struggle with the Biblical Goliath. Homer, the philistine giant from a philistine midwest, through murder of the "beloved" David figure, Adore, symbolically destroys Hollywood's quasi-culture. He is last seen, appropriately, in a harsh Goya image, the giant slaying episode at the hands of the mob; he is shoved against the sky, his jaw hanging open to scream: "A hand reached up and caught him by his open mouth and pulled him forward and down."

The remaining figures fall into the appropriate slots. Thus, Claude Estee, American aristocrat as Civil War colonel, represents the male side of the Hollywood reward, the embodiment of the questing hero's aspirations, not the heroine's (ostensibly, you should get the golden-haired figure if you can become the prince). Despite his marriage to Alice (Gmc.: of noble rank), it is the Claude-Audrey Jenning association which completes the royal marriage motif: the connecting link is prostitution, whether metaphoric or literal. This structural alignment is paralleled by another system of value, the family unit, perverted through continuance of the business ethic and weakened through the absence of a necessary member. West counterpoints the fatherless son with the motherless daughter, showing both mother-son and father-daughter relationships to be exploitative and rejecting. Maybelle Loomis is an ironic inversion of the wicked mother figure; rejecting her child through over- not under-attention, she exploits him for economic gain. Parental wish is here imposed upon the child. Harry Greener, though his prime function is as clown, is the masculine complement to Maybelle: less concerned with his daughter's professional or personal aspirations than with the bitter memories of the rejections of his past. The child's wish is here ignored by the parent. Both relationships deteriorate to mechanistic reflexes, to the artifices and mannerisms of the acting profession, to spurious forms of playing a role rather than the authenticity of Being. Not just the individual then, but the family, the microcosmic social unit supposed to substructure a meaningful community, is also fragmented. Synthesis of these fragments to one unit, to family completion, seems no more rewarding than their separation; metaphorically speaking, new fragments could splinter off, father-son and mother-daughter, Maybelle-Faye and Harry-Adore, all of which may be reflected in the opposed consequences of the fate of the children. Tod fears Faye would break his back; Homer, Tod's alter ego, frustrated by Faye, breaks the back of Adore, the child who stands in counterpoint to her. Thus, by the novel's end, both Harry and Adore are gone, while Maybelle and Faye remain, a new synthesis reflecting the greater resilience of the aggressive female principle. But it is hardly a reproductive synthesis.

The Day of the Locust, then, is a novel rooted in the popular in a double sense: in what has developed from, or been created by, the people (the fairy tale); and in what is created for the people, i. e., for popular consumption (the Hollywood culture, the cinema). Only the latter has been recorded in the prior criticism. But the novel is only partially comprehensible if we fail to perceive the relationship between its two species of the popular, a relationship with numerous artistic functions and effects. Certainly it tempers allegations of West's grotesquerie. And psychologically, West's treatment of the literature of wish should at least have been a therapeutic exercise, an attempt to free his projected or implied self from one symptom of that "Disease" from which, according to W. H. Auden, not only his characters but his historical self reputedly suffered. More significantly, it is also an instrument in the analysis of that disease, especially in its initial symptom,

the incapacity to convert wish into desire. West's attitude to the fairy tale is not ironic; the objective relationship of fairy tale to Hollywood is. The wish, the refusal to be oneself, as Auden puts it, may be "innocent and frivolous . . . or a serious expression of guilt and despair"; the former condition applies to the Märchen (where wishes are fulfilled in the subconscious and there is no need of desire), the latter to the cinematic landscape (where wishes are frustrated in the conscious world of action and there is no ability to form a true desire); and it is, of course, this negative sort of private wish which is the true species of the national. The novel is thus a form of reciprocal comment, of each side upon the other, fairy tale upon Hollywood cinema, and West can make his points without recourse to propaganda. This being so, it becomes successful proletarian literature in the wider sense of the term, a working class literature which can afford to obviate the propagandistic and the revolutionary; as William Empson says:

> The wider sense of the term includes such folk-literature as is by the people, for the people, and about the people. But most fairy stories and ballads, though "by" and "for," are not "about"; whereas pastoral though "about" is not "by" or "for."

Since pastoral, to Empson, is exemplified today by a more narrow view of proletarian, by a literature of workers, West's ironic variant is an attempt to be all three: its background fairy tale, with its roots in folk tradition, is essentially by the people (and for them as well), the foreground

---

On the critical rediscovery of West:

At the time of his death, West was so little known to the general public that he was identified in newspaper announcements of the crash as a Hollywood screenwriter, with greater prominence given to Eileen McKenney. Summing up, after the accident, Edmund Wilson wrote that West "left two books more finished and complete as works of art than almost anything else produced by his generation," yet West continued to be an esteemed but largely unread writer. In 1946, *Miss Lonelyhearts* was translated into French by Marcelle Sibon as *Mademoiselle Coeur-Brisé,* with an introduction by the surrealist writer Philippe Soupault, and it created a wave of interest in Nathanael West in France; and in the US, *Miss Lonelyhearts* and *The Day of the Locust* were reprinted by New Directions in the late forties and early fifties. It was not until *The Collected Works of Nathanael West* was published in 1957, however, that the West revival began. West today has been the subject of many scholarly studies and dissertations, and of a full-scale biography. His influence on a later generation of American writers—including not only many younger Jewish novelists but also the Black Humorists of the sixties and such "grotesque" novelists as Flannery O'Connor and John Hawkes—has been remarkable.

Robert Emmet Long, in his Nathanael West, *Frederick Ungar Publishing Co., 1985.*

narrative, with its source in Hollywood, is about them, and the reciprocal dialogue between the two offers a corrective, especially upon the foreground. His proletarian book thus becomes an incisive political and humanistic instrument, constituting through its form, a successful and convincing argument for a more organic and natural, far less mechanistic society.

Harold Bloom   (essay date 1986)

SOURCE: An introduction to *Nathanael West,* edited by Harold Bloom, Chelsea House Publishers, 1986, pp. 1-9.

[*Bloom is a prominent American critic and literary theorist. In the following introduction, he examines* Miss Lonelyhearts *as a Jewish-American novel.*]

Nathanael West, who died in an automobile accident in 1940 at the age of thirty-seven, wrote one remorseless masterpiece, *Miss Lonelyhearts* (1933). Despite some astonishing sequences, *The Day of the Locust* (1939) is an overpraised work, a waste of West's genius. Of the two lesser fictions, *The Dream Life of Balso Snell* (1931) is squalid and dreadful, with occasional passages of a rancid power, while *A Cool Million* (1934), though an outrageous parody of American picaresque, is a permanent work of American satire and seems to me underpraised. To call West uneven is therefore a litotes; he is a wild medley of magnificent writing and inadequate writing, except in *Miss Lonelyhearts* which excels *The Sun Also Rises, The Great Gatsby* and even *Sanctuary* as the perfected instance of a negative vision in modern American fiction. The greatest Faulkner, of *The Sound and the Fury, As I Lay Dying, Absalom, Absalom!* and *Light in August,* is the only American writer of prose fiction in this century who can be said to have surpassed *Miss Lonelyhearts.* West's spirit lives again in *The Crying of Lot 49* and some sequences in *Gravity's Rainbow,* but the negative sublimity of *Miss Lonelyhearts* proves to be beyond Pynchon's reach, or perhaps his ambition.

West, born Nathan Weinstein, is a significant episode in the long and tormented history of Jewish Gnosticism. The late Gershom Scholem's superb essay, "Redemption Through Sin," in his *The Messianic Idea in Judaism,* is the best commentary I know upon *Miss Lonelyhearts.* I once attempted to convey this to Scholem, who shrugged West off, quite properly from Scholem's viewpoint, when I remarked to him that West was manifestly a Jewish anti-Semite, and admitted that there were no allusions to Jewish esotericism or Kabbalah in his works. Nevertheless, for the stance of literary criticism, Jewish Gnosticism, as defined by Scholem, is the most illuminating context in which to study West's novels. It is a melancholy paradox that West, who did not wish to be Jewish in any way at all, remains the most indisputably Jewish writer yet to appear in America, a judgment at once aesthetic and moral. Nothing by Bellow, Malamud, Philip Roth, Mailer, or Ozick can compare to *Miss Lonelyhearts* as an achievement. West's Jewish heir, if he has one, may be Harold Brodkey, whose recent *Women and Angels,* excerpted from his immense novel-in-progress, can be regarded as another powerful instance of Jewish Gnosis, free of West's hatred of his own Jewishness.

Stanley Edgar Hyman, in his pamphlet on West (1962), concluded that, "His strength lay in his vulgarity and bad taste, his pessimism, his nastiness." Hyman remains West's most useful critic, but I would amend this by observing that these qualities in West's writing emanate from a negative theology, spiritually authentic, and given aesthetic dignity by the force of West's eloquent negations. West, like his grandest creation, Shrike, is a rhetorician of the abyss, in the tradition of Sabbatian nihilism that Scholem has expounded so masterfully. One thinks of ideas such as "the violation of the Torah has become its fulfillment, just as a grain of wheat must rot in the earth" or such as Jacob Frank's; "We are all now under the obligation to enter the abyss." The messianic intensity of the Sabbatians and Frankists results in a desperately hysterical and savage tonality which prophesies West's authentically religious book, *Miss Lonelyhearts,* a work profoundly Jewish but only in its negations, particularly the negation of the normative Judaic assumption of total sense in everything, life and text alike. *Miss Lonelyhearts* takes place in the world of Freud, where the fundamental assumption is that everything already has happened, and that nothing can be made new because total sense has been achieved, but then repressed or negated. Negatively Jewish, the book is also negatively American. Miss Lonelyhearts is a failed Walt Whitman (hence the naming of the cripple as Peter Doyle, Whitman's pathetic friend) and a fallen American Adam to Shrike's very American Satan. Despite the opinions of later critics, I continue to find Hyman's argument persuasive, and agree with him that the book's psychosexuality is marked by a repressed homosexual relation between Shrike and Miss Lonelyhearts. Hyman's Freudian observation that all the suffering in the book is essentially female seems valid, reminding us that Freud's "feminine masochism" is mostly encountered among men, according to Freud himself. Shrike, the butcherbird impaling his victim, Miss Lonelyhearts, upon the thorns of Christ, is himself as much an instance of "feminine masochism" as his victim. If Miss Lonelyhearts is close to pathological frenzy, Shrike is also consumed by religious hysteria, by a terrible nostalgia for God.

The book's bitter stylistic negation results in a spectacular verbal economy, in which literally every sentence is made to count, in more than one sense of "count." Freud's "negation" involves a cognitive return of the repressed, here through West's self-projection as Shrike, spit out but not disavowed. The same Freudian process depends upon an affective continuance of repression, here by West's self-introjection as Miss Lonelyhearts, at once West's inability to believe and his disavowed failure to love. Poor Miss Lonelyhearts, who receives no other name throughout the book, has been destroyed by Shrike's power of Satanic rhetoric before the book even opens. But then Shrike has destroyed himself first, for no one could withstand the sustained horror of Shrike's impaling rhetoric, which truly can be called West's horror:

> "I am a great saint," Shrike cried, "I can walk on my own water. Haven't you ever heard of Shrike's Passion in the Luncheonette, or the Agony in the Soda Fountain? Then I compared the wounds in Christ's body to the mouths of a

miraculous purse in which we deposit the small change of our sins. It is indeed an excellent conceit. But now let us consider the holes in our own bodies and into what these congenital wounds open. Under the skin of man is a wondrous jungle where veins like lush tropical growths hang along over-ripe organs and weed-like entrails writhe in squirming tangles of red and yellow. In this jungle, flitting from rock-gray lungs to golden intestines, from liver to lights and back to liver again, lives a bird called the soul. The Catholic hunts this bird with bread and wine, the Hebrew with a golden ruler, the Protestant on leaden feet with leaden words, the Buddhist with gestures, the Negro with blood. I spit on them all. Phooh! And I call upon you to spit. Phooh! Do you stuff birds? No, my dears, taxidermy is not religion. No! A thousand times no. Better, I say unto you, better a live bird in the jungle of the body than two stuffed birds on the library table."

I have always associated this great passage with what is central to West: the messianic longing for redemption, through sin if necessary. West's humor is almost always apocalyptic, in a mode quite original with him, though so influential since his death that we have difficulty seeing how strong the originality was. Originality, even in comic writing, becomes a difficulty. How are we to read the most outrageous of the letters sent to Miss Lonelyhearts, the one written by the sixteen-year-old girl without a nose?

I sit and look at myself all day and cry. I have a big hole in the middle of my face that scares people even myself so I cant blame the boys for not wanting to take me out. My mother loves me, but she crys terrible when she looks at me.

What did I do to deserve such a terrible bad fate? Even if I did do some bad things I didnt do any before I was a year old and I was born this way. I asked Papa and he says he doesnt know, but that maybe I did something in the other world before I was born or that maybe I was being punished for his sins. I dont believe that because he is a very nice man. Ought I commit suicide?

Sincerely yours,

Desperate

Defensive laughter is a complex reaction to grotesque suffering. In his 1928 essay on humor, Freud concluded that the above-the-I, the superego, speaks kindly words of comfort to the intimidated ego, and this speaking is humor, which Freud calls "the triumph of narcissism, the ego's victorious assertion of its own invulnerability." Clearly, Freud's "humor" does not include the Westian mode. Reading Desperate's "What did I do to deserve such a terrible bad fate?," our ego knows that it is defeated all the time, or at least is vulnerable to undeserved horror. West's humor has *no* liberating element whatsover, but is the humor of a vertigo ill-balanced on the edge of what ancient Gnosticism called the *kenoma,* the cosmological emptiness.

Shrike, West's superb Satanic tempter, achieves his apotheosis at the novel's midpoint, the eighth of its fifteen tab-

leaux, accurately titled "Miss Lonelyhearts in the Dismal Swamp." As Miss Lonelyhearts, sick with despair, lies in bed, the drunken Shrike bursts in, shouting his greatest rhetorical setpiece, certainly the finest tirade in modern American fiction. Cataloging the methods that Miss Lonelyhearts might employ to escape out of the Dismal Swamp, Shrike begins with a grand parody of the later D. H. Lawrence, in which the vitalism of *The Plumed Serpent* and *The Man Who Died* is carried into a gorgeous absurdity, a heavy sexuality that masks Shrike's Satanic fears of impotence:

You are fed up with the city and its teeming millions. The ways and means of men, as getting and leading and spending, you lay waste your inner world, are too much with you. The bus takes too long, while the subway is always crowded. So what do you do? So you buy a farm and walk behind your horse's moist behind, no collar or tie, plowing your broad swift acres. As you turn up the rich black soil, the wind carries the smell of pine and dung across the fields and the rhythm of an old, old work enters your soul. To this rhythm, you sow and weep and chivy your kine, not kin or kind, between the pregnant rows of corn and taters. Your step becomes the heavy sexual step of a dance-drunk Indian and you tread the seed down into the female earth. You plant, not dragon's teeth, but beans and greens. . . .

Confronting only silence, Shrike proceeds to parody the Melville of *Typee* and *Omoo,* and also Somerset Maugham's version of Gauguin in *The Moon and Sixpence:*

You live in a thatch hut with the daughter of a king, a slim young maiden in whose eyes is an ancient wisdom. Her breasts are golden speckled pears, her belly a melon, and her odor is like nothing so much as a jungle fern. In the evening, on the blue lagoon, under the silvery moon, to your love you croon in the soft sylabelew and vocabelew of her langorour tongorour. Your body is golden brown like hers, and tourists have need of the indignant finger of the missionary to point you out. They envy you your breech clout and carefree laugh and little brown bride and fingers instead of forks. But you don't return their envy, and when a beautiful society girl comes to your hut in the night, seeking to learn the secret of your happiness, you send her back to her yacht that hangs on the horizon like a nervous racehorse. And so you dream away the days, fishing, hunting, dancing, kissing, and picking flowers to twine in your hair. . . .

As Shrike says, this is a played-out mode, but his savage gusto in rendering it betrays his hatred of the religion of art, of the vision that sought a salvation in imaginative literature. What Shrike goes on to chant is an even more effective parody of the literary stances West rejected. Though Shrike calls it "Hedonism," the curious amalgam here of Hemingway and Ronald Firbank, with touches of Fitzgerald and the earlier Aldous Huxley, might better be named an aesthetic stoicism:

"You dedicate your life to the pursuit of pleasure. No overindulgence, mind you, but knowing that your body is a pleasure machine, you treat it carefully in order to get the most out of it. Golf as well as booze, Philadelphia Jack O'Brien and his chestweights as well as Spanish dancers. Nor do you neglect the pleasures of the mind. You fornicate under pictures by Matisse and Picasso, you drink from Renaissance glassware, and often you spend an evening beside the fireplace with Proust and an apple. Alas, after much good fun, the day comes when you realize that soon you must die. You keep a stiff upper lip and decide to give a last party. You invite all your old mistresses, trainers, artists and boon companions. The guests are dressed in black, the waiters are coons, the table is a coffin carved for you by Eric Gill. You serve caviar and blackberries and licorice candy and coffee without cream. After the dancing girls have finished, you get to your feet and call for silence in order to explain your philosophy of life. 'Life,' you say, 'is a club where they won't stand for squawks, where they deal you only one hand and you must sit in. So even if the cards are cold and marked by the hand of fate, play up, play up like a gentleman and a sport. Get tanked, grab what's on the buffet, use the girls upstairs, but remember, when you throw box cars, take the curtain like a dead game sport, don't squawk.' " . . .

Even this is only preparatory to Shrike's bitterest phase in his tirade, an extraordinary send-up of High Aestheticism proper, of Pater, George Moore, Wilde and the earlier W. B. Yeats:

> Art! Be an artist or a writer. When you are cold, warm yourself before the flaming tints of Titian, when you are hungry, nourish yourself with great spiritual foods by listening to the noble periods of Bach, the harmonies of Brahms and the thunder of Beethoven. Do you think there is anything in the fact that their names all begin with a B? But don't take a chance, smoke a 3 B pipe, and remember these immortal lines: *When to the suddenness of melody the echo parting falls the failing day.* What a rhythm! Tell them to keep their society whores and pressed duck with oranges. For you *l'art vivant,* the living art, as you call it. Tell them that you know that your shoes are broken and that there are pimples on your face, yes, and that you have buck teeth and a club foot, but that you don't care, for tomorrow they are playing Beethoven's last quartets in Carnegie Hall and at home you have Shakespeare's plays in one volume.

That last sentence, truly and deliciously Satanic, is one of West's greatest triumphs, but he surpasses it in the ultimate Shrikean rhapsody, after Shrike's candid avowal: "God alone is our escape." With marvelous appropriateness, West makes this at once the ultimate Miss Lonelyhearts letter, and also Shrike's most Satanic self-identification, in the form of a letter to Christ dictated for Miss Lonelyhearts by Shrike, who speaks absolutely for both of them:

> Dear Miss Lonelyhearts of Miss Lonelyhearts—
>
> I am twenty-six years old and in the newspaper

game. Life for me is a desert empty of comfort. I cannot find pleasure in food, drink, or women—nor do the arts give me joy any longer. The Leopard of Discontent walks the streets of my city; the Lion of Discouragement crouches outside the walls of my citadel. All is desolation and a vexation of spirit. I feel like hell. How can I believe, how can I have faith in this day and age? Is it true that the greatest scientists believe again in you?

> I read your column and like it very much. There you once wrote: 'When the salt has lost its savour, who shall savour it again?' Is the answer: 'None but the Saviour?'

> Thanking you very much for a quick reply, I remain yours truly,

> > A Regular Subscriber

"I feel like hell," the Miltonic "Myself am Hell," is Shrike's credo, and West's.

What is the relation of Shrike to West's rejected Jewishness? The question may seem illegitimate to many admirers of West, but it acquires considerable force in the context of the novel's sophisticated yet unhistorical Gnosticism. The way of nihilism means, according to Scholem, "to free oneself of all laws, conventions, and religions, to adopt every conceivable attitude and to reject it, and to follow one's leader step for step into the abyss." Scholem is paraphrasing the demonic Jacob Frank, an eighteenth century Jewish Shrike who brought the Sabbatian messianic movement to its final degradation. Frank would have recognized something of his own negations and nihilistic fervor in the closing passages that form a pattern in West's four novels:

> His body screamed and shouted as it marched and uncoiled; then, with one heaving shout of triumph, it fell back quiet.

> The army that a moment before had been thundering in his body retreated slowly—victorious, relieved.

> > (*The Dream Life of Balso Snell*)

> While they were struggling, Betty came in through the street door. She called to them to stop and started up the stairs. The cripple saw her cutting off his escape and tried to get rid of the package. He pulled his hand out. The gun inside the package exploded and Miss Lonelyhearts fell, dragging the cripple with him. They both rolled part of the way down the stairs.

> > (*Miss Lonelyhearts*)

> "Alas, Lemuel Pitkin himself did not have this chance, but instead was dismantled by the enemy. His teeth were pulled out. His eye was gouged from his head. His thumb was removed. His scalp was torn away. His leg was cut off. And, finally, he was shot through the heart.

> "But he did not live or die in vain. Through his martyrdom the National Revolutionary Party triumphed, and by that triumph this country was delivered from sophistication, Marxism and

International Capitalism. Through the National Revolution its people were purged of alien diseases and America became again American."

"Hail the martyrdom in the Bijou Theater!" roar Shagpoke's youthful hearers when he is finished.

"Hail, Lemuel Pitkin!"

"All hail, the American Boy!"

(*A Cool Million*)

He was carried through the exit to the back street and lifted into a police car. The siren began to scream and at first he thought he was making the noise himself. He felt his lips with his hands. They were clamped tight. He knew then it was the siren. For some reason this made him laugh and he began to imitate the siren as loud as he could.

(*The Day of the Locust*)

All four passages mutilate the human image, the image of God that normative Jewish tradition associates with our origins. "Our forefathers were always talking, only what good did it do them and what did they accomplish? But we are under the burden of silence," Jacob Frank said. What Frank's and West's forefathers always talked about was the ultimate forefather, Adam, who would have enjoyed the era of the Messiah, had he not sinned. West retains of tradition only the emptiness of the fallen image, the scattered spark of creation. The screaming and falling body, torn apart and maddened into a siren-like laughter, belongs at once to the American Surrealist poet, Balso Snell; the American Horst Wessel, poor Lemuel Pitkin; to Miss Lonelyhearts, the Whitmanian American Christ; and to Tod Hackett, painter of the American apocalypse. All are nihilistic versions of the mutilated image of God, or of what the Jewish Gnostic visionary, Nathan of Gaza, called the "thought-less" or nihilizing light.

West was a prophet of American violence, which he saw as augmenting progressively throughout our history. His satirical genius, for all its authentic and desperate range, has been defeated by American reality. Shagpoke Whipple, the Calvin Coolidge-like ex-President who becomes the American Hitler in *A Cool Million,* talks in terms that West intended as extravagant, but that now can be read all but daily in our newspapers. Here is Shagpoke at his best, urging us to hear what the dead Lemuel Pitkin has to tell us:

Of what is it that he speaks? Of the right of every American boy to go into the world and there receive fair play and a chance to make his fortune by industry and probity without being laughed at or conspired against by sophisticated aliens.

I turn to today's *New York Times* (March 29, 1985) and find there the text of a speech given by our President:

But may I just pause here for a second and tell you about a couple of fellows who came to see me the other day, young men. In 1981, just four years ago, they started a business with only a thousand dollars between them and everyone told them they were crazy. Last year their busi-

ness did a million and a half dollars and they expect to do two and a half million this year. And part of it was because they had the wit to use their names productively. Their business is using their names, the Cain and Abell electric business.

Reality may have triumphed over poor West, but only because he, doubtless as a ghost, inspired or wrote these Presidential remarks. The *Times* reports, sounding as dead-pan as Shrike, on the same page (B4), that the young entrepreneurs brought a present to Mr. Reagan. " 'We gave him a company jacket with Cain and Abell, Inc. on it,' Mr. Cain said." Perhaps West's ghost now writes not only Shagpokian speeches, but the very text of reality in our America.

FURTHER READING

Bibliography

White, William. *Nathanael West: A Comprehensive Bibliography*. Kent, Ohio: Kent State University Press, 1975, 209 p.
    Contains both primary and secondary bibliographic material. An appendix lists West's uncollected writings.

Biography

Martin, Jay. *Nathanael West: The Art of His Life*. New York: Farrar, Straus, and Giroux, 1970, 435 p.
    Provides a broad social and cultural history of West's era, drawing on interviews with West's friends and family members as well as letters and other unpublished private papers.

Criticism

Andreach, Robert J. "Nathanael West's *Miss Lonelyhearts*: Between the Dead Pan and the Unborn Christ." *Modern Fiction Studies* XII, No. 2 (Summer 1966): 251-60.
    Cites antagonism between paganism and Christianity as the unifying principle of *Miss Lonelyhearts*.

Baxter, Charles. "Nathanael West: Dead Letters and the Martyred Novelist." *West Coast Review* 9, No. 2 (October 1974): 3-11.
    Identifies the inability of language to alleviate suffering as the central theme of *Miss Lonelyhearts* and suggests that the protagonist's self-sacrifice is necessary because he is unable to help the letter-writers through written replies.

Betsky-Zweig, S. "The Cannonballed of Popular Culture: Nathanael West's *Miss Lonelyhearts* and *The Day of the Locust*." *Dutch Quarterly Review* 4, No. 4 (1974): 145-56.
    Describes West's novels as "cannonballs" shot in anger and sadness against American culture of the 1930s.

Comerchero, Victor. *Nathanael West: The Ironic Prophet*. Syracuse, N.Y.: Syracuse University Press, 1964, 189 p.
    Critical study of West's short fiction.

Fiedler, Leslie A. "Master of Dreams." *Partisan Review* XXXIV, No. 3 (Summer 1967): 339-56.
    Asserts that West's *The Dream Life of Balso Snell* should be viewed as a "fractured and dissolving parable

of the very process by which the emancipated Jew enters into the world of Western culture."

Frank, Mike. "The Passion of Miss Lonelyhearts according to Nathanael West." *Studies in Short Fiction* X, No. 1 (Winter 1973): 67-73.
    Rejects the interpretation that the characters of Betty and Miss Lonelyhearts represent two polarized attitudes toward life—innocence and experience—arguing that Betty is identified with the natural world, which in the novel is presented as cruel, random, and violent.

Fuchs, Miriam. "Nathanael West's *Miss Lonelyhearts*: The *Waste Land* Rescripted." *Studies in Short Fiction* 29, No. 1 (Winter 1992): 43-55.
    Traces the influence of T. S. Eliot's *The Waste Land* on West's short novel.

Gorak, Jan. "The Art of Significant Disorder: The Fiction of Nathanael West." In his *God the Artist: American Novelists in a Post-Realist Age*, pp. 37-58. Urbana: University of Illinois Press, 1987.
    Characterizes West's central theme as an example of the diminishing power of religious values in American lives in which the mass media has supplanted organized religion.

Hanlon, Robert M. "The Parody of the Sacred in Nathanael West's *Miss Lonelyhearts*." *The International Fiction Review* 4, No. 2 (July 1977): 190-93.
    Examines West's parody of Christian myth and ritual in *Miss Lonelyhearts*.

Hollis, C. Carroll. "Nathanael West and the 'Lonely Crowd'." *Thought* XXXIII, No. 130 (Autumn 1958): 398-416.
    Discusses the role of loneliness in West's life and his fiction.

Jones, Beverly. "Shrike as the Modernist Anti-Hero in Nathanael West's *Miss Lonelyhearts*." *Modern Fiction Studies* 36, No. 2 (Summer 1990): 218-24.
    Maintains that in his relentless exposure of the hypocrisy and irrationality of Miss Lonelyhearts's impulses toward religion, the editor Shrike functions not as an Antichrist or demon figure but as a nihilistic Modernist anti-hero.

Keyes, John. " 'Inarticulate Expressions of Genuine Suffering?': A Reply to the Correspondence in *Miss Lonelyhearts*." *University of Windsor Review* 20, No. 1 (Fall-Winter 1987): 11-25.
    Offers sustained analysis of the letters to Miss Lonelyhearts, maintaining that they have been consistently misinterpreted as expressions of authentic suffering when in fact they convey the irony and even humor of the human condition.

Klug, M. A. "Nathanael West: Prophet of Failure." *College Literature* XIV, No. 1 (Winter 1987): 17-31.
    Describes the role of the "failed artist" in West's short novels.

Long, Robert Emmet. *Nathanael West*. New York: Frederick Ungar, 1985, 202 p.
    Critical study of West's short novels.

Lorch, Thomas M. "West's *Miss Lonelyhearts*: Skepticism Mitigated?" *Renascence* XVIII, No. 2 (Winter 1966): 99-109.

Discusses the influence of William James's *Varieties of Religious Experience* and Edwin Diller Starbuck's *Psychology of Religion* on *Miss Lonelyhearts*, and the nature of Miss Lonelyhearts's religious experiences.

———. "The Inverted Structure of *Balso Snell*." *Studies in Short Fiction* IV, No. 1 (Fall 1986): 33-41.
    Examines the structure of West's novella, as well as its treatment of spiritual and literary matters.

Madden, David, ed. *Nathanael West: The Cheaters and the Cheated*. Deland, Fla.: Everett/Edwards, 1973, 346 p.
    Collection of biographical and critical essays.

Merrill, Catherine. "West's *The Dream Life of Balso Snell*." *The Explicator* 50, No. 3 (Spring 1992): 170-72.
    Brief summary and critical study of West's novella.

Michaels, I. Lloyd. "A Particular Kind of Joking: Burlesque, Vaudeville, and Nathanael West." *Studies in American Humor* 1, No. 3 (January 1975): 149-60.
    Analyzes the humor found in West's short fiction, concluding that West "discovered in burlesque a perspective which could express his indignation as it simultaneously concealed his despair."

Olsen, Bruce. "Nathanael West: The Use of Cynicism." In *Minor American Novelists*, edited by Charles Alva Hoyt, pp. 81-94. Carbondale: Southern Illinois University Press, 1970.
    Enumerates the major themes of West's fiction, focusing on the role of cynicism in his work.

Orvell, Miles D. "The Messianic Sexuality of Miss Lonelyhearts." *Studies in Short Fiction* X, No. 2 (Spring 1973): 159-67.
    Contends that *Miss Lonelyhearts* exemplifies one kind of response to modern life—the urge to transcend the human and attain the divine.

Podhoretz, Norman. "Nathanael West: A Particular Kind of Joking." In his *Doings and Undoings: The Fifties and After in American Writing*, pp. 66-75. New York: Noonday Press, 1953.
    Discusses West's use of humor in his short novels, maintaining that West's "sort of laughter . . . is rarely heard in American literature, for it is not only anti-'radical' but almost un-American in its refusal to admit the possibility of improvement, amelioration, or cure."

Poznar, Walter. "The Apocalyptic Vision in Nathanael West's *Miss Lonelyhearts*." In *Apocalyptic Visions Past and Present*, edited by JoAnn James and William J. Cloonan, pp. 111-19. Tallahassee: Florida State University Press, 1988.
    Claims that West's "apocalyptic vision" moves beyond repudiation of the spiritual barrenness of the American Dream to a relentless assessment of human nature itself as sterile, empty, and apathetic. Poznar suggests that West's bleak vision is somewhat ameliorated by his avoidance of facile, sardonic cynicism and the depth of his concern for the human condition.

Richardson, Robert D., Jr. "*Miss Lonelyhearts*." *The University Review* XXXIII, No. 2 (December 1966): 151-57.
    Terms *Miss Lonelyhearts* a novel about the disintegration of sanity in American life and discusses the book's imagery, plot, and prose style, contending that its chief interest lies in its brilliant communication of a story that is about the absence of meaningful communication.

Scharnhorst, Gary. "From Rags to Patches, or *A Cool Million* as Alter-Alger." *Ball State University Forum* XXI, No. 4 (Autumn 1980): 58-65.
Address West's satiric use of the Horatio Alger myth in *A Cool Million*, contending that he "mocked the facile optimism of Americans in their collective epic-dream."

Schwartz, Edward Greenfield. "The Novels of Nathanael West." *Accent* XVII, No. 4 (Autumn 1957): 251-62.
Traces the development of West's fiction.

Scott, Nathan A., Jr. *Nathanael West: A Critical Essay.* Grand Rapids, Mich.: William E. Eerdmans, 1971, 47 p.
Biographical and critical study of West.

Tropp, Martin. "Nathanael West and the Persistence of Hope." *Renascence* XXXI, No. 4 (Summer 1979): 205-14.
Contends that in *Miss Lonelyhearts* particularly, and to a lesser extent in his last two novels, West suggested that alternatives to suffering exist.

Wexelblatt, Robert. "*Miss Lonelyhearts* and the Rhetoric of Disintegration." *College Literature* XVI, No. 3 (Fall 1989): 219-31.
Examines West's formal strategies for presenting a novel about disorder and disintegration in a rigorously ordered and integrated manner.

Wisker, Alistair. "Rooting for West: The Cautionary Tales of Nathanael West." *Antigonish Review* 73 (Spring 1988): 129-43.
Brief overview of West's life and career, asserting West's relevance for contemporary readers.

Additional coverage of West's life and career is contained in the following sources published by Gale Research: *Contemporary Authors*, Vols. 104, 125; *Concise Dictionary of Literary Biography, 1929-1941*; *Dictionary of Literary Biography*, Vols. 4, 9, 28; *Major 20th-Century Authors*; and *Twentieth-Century Literary Criticism*, Vols. 1, 14, 44.

Appendix:

Select Bibliography of General Sources on Short Fiction

BOOKS OF CRITICISM

Allen, Walter. *The Short Story in English*. New York: Oxford University Press, 1981, 413 p.

Aycock, Wendell M., ed. *The Teller and the Tale: Aspects of the Short Story* (Proceedings of the Comparative Literature Symposium, Texas Tech University, Volume XIII). Lubbock: Texas Tech Press, 1982, 156 p.

Averill, Deborah. *The Irish Short Story from George Moore to Frank O'Connor*. Washington, D.C.: University Press of America, 1982, 329 p.

Bates, H. E. *The Modern Short Story: A Critical Survey*. Boston: Writer, 1941, 231 p.

Bayley, John. *The Short Story: Henry James to Elizabeth Bowen*. Great Britain: The Harvester Press Limited, 1988, 197 p.

Bennett, E. K. *A History of the German Novelle: From Goethe to Thomas Mann*. Cambridge: At the University Press, 1934, 296 p.

Bone, Robert. *Down Home: A History of Afro-American Short Fiction from Its Beginning to the End of the Harlem Renaissance*. Rev. ed. New York: Columbia University Press, 1988, 350 p.

Bruck, Peter. *The Black American Short Story in the Twentieth Century: A Collection of Critical Essays*. Amsterdam: B. R. Grüner Publishing Co., 1977, 209 p.

Burnett, Whit, and Burnett, Hallie. *The Modern Short Story in the Making*. New York: Hawthorn Books, 1964, 405 p.

Canby, Henry Seidel. *The Short Story in English*. New York: Henry Holt and Co., 1909, 386 p.

Current-García, Eugene. *The American Short Story before 1850: A Critical History*. Twayne's Critical History of the Short Story, edited by William Peden. Boston: Twayne Publishers, 1985, 168 p.

Flora, Joseph M., ed. *The English Short Story, 1880-1945: A Critical History*. Twayne's Critical History of the Short Story, edited by William Peden. Boston: Twayne Publishers, 1985, 215 p.

Foster, David William. *Studies in the Contemporary Spanish-American Short Story*. Columbia, Mo.: University of Missouri Press, 1979, 126 p.

George, Albert J. *Short Fiction in France, 1800-1850*. Syracuse, N.Y.: Syracuse University Press, 1964, 245 p.

Gerlach, John. *Toward an End: Closure and Structure in the American Short Story*. University, Ala.: The University of Alabama Press, 1985, 193 p.

Hankin, Cherry, ed. *Critical Essays on the New Zealand Short Story*. Auckland: Heinemann Publishers, 1982, 186 p.

Hanson, Clare, ed. *Re-Reading the Short Story*. London: MacMilian Press, 1989, 137 p.

Harris, Wendell V. *British Short Fiction in the Nineteenth Century*. Detroit: Wayne State University Press, 1979, 209 p.

Huntington, John. *Rationalizing Genius: Ideological Strategies in the Classic American Science Fiction Short Story.* New Brunswick: Rutgers University Press, 1989, 216 p.

Kilroy, James F., ed. *The Irish Short Story: A Critical History.* Twayne's Critical History of the Short Story, edited by William Peden. Boston: Twayne Publishers, 1984, 251 p.

Lee, A. Robert. *The Nineteenth-Century American Short Story.* Totowa, N. J.: Vision / Barnes & Noble, 1986, 196 p.

Leibowitz, Judith. *Narrative Purpose in the Novella.* The Hague: Mouton, 1974, 137 p.

Lohafer, Susan. *Coming to Terms with the Short Story.* Baton Rouge: Louisiana State University Press, 1983, 171 p.

Lohafer, Susan, and Clarey, Jo Ellyn. *Short Story Theory at a Crossroads.* Baton Rouge: Louisiana State University Press, 1989, 352 p.

Mann, Susan Garland. *The Short Story Cycle: A Genre Companion and Reference Guide.* New York: Greenwood Press, 1989, 228 p.

Matthews, Brander. *The Philosophy of the Short Story.* New York: Longmans, Green and Co., 1901, 83 p.

May, Charles E., ed. *Short Story Theories.* Athens, Oh.: Ohio University Press, 1976, 251 p.

McClave, Heather, ed. *Women Writers of the Short Story: A Collection of Critical Essays.* Englewood Cliffs, N. J.: Prentice-Hall, 1980, 171 p.

Moser, Charles, ed. *The Russian Short Story: A Critical History.* Twayne's Critical History of the Short Story, edited by William Peden. Boston: Twayne Publishers, 1986, 232 p.

New, W. H. *Dreams of Speech and Violence: The Art of the Short Story in Canada and New Zealand.* Toronto: The University of Toronto Press, 1987, 302 p.

Newman, Frances. *The Short Story's Mutations: From Petronius to Paul Morand.* New York: B. W. Huebsch, 1925, 332 p.

O'Connor, Frank. *The Lonely Voice: A Study of the Short Story.* Cleveland: World Publishing Co., 1963, 220 p.

O'Faolain, Sean. *The Short Story.* New York: Devin-Adair Co., 1951, 370 p.

Orel, Harold. *The Victorian Short Story: Development and Triumph of a Literary Genre.* Cambridge: Cambridge University Press, 1986, 213 p.

O'Toole, L. Michael. *Structure, Style and Interpretation in the Russian Short Story.* New Haven: Yale University Press, 1982, 272 p.

Pattee, Fred Lewis. *The Development of the American Short Story: An Historical Survey.* New York: Harper and Brothers Publishers, 1923, 388 p.

Peden, Margaret Sayers, ed. *The Latin American Short Story: A Critical History.* Twayne's Critical History of the Short Story, edited by William Peden. Boston: Twayne Publishers, 1983, 160 p.

Peden, William. *The American Short Story: Continuity and Change, 1940-1975.* Rev. ed. Boston: Houghton Mifflin Co., 1975, 215 p.

Reid, Ian. *The Short Story.* The Critical Idiom, edited by John D. Jump. London: Methuen and Co., 1977, 76 p.

Rhode, Robert D. *Setting in the American Short Story of Local Color, 1865-1900.* The Hague: Mouton, 1975, 189 p.

Rohrberger, Mary. *Hawthorne and the Modern Short Story: A Study in Genre.* The Hague: Mouton and Co., 1966, 148 p.

Shaw, Valerie, *The Short Story: A Critical Introduction.* London: Longman, 1983, 294 p.

Stephens, Michael. *The Dramaturgy of Style: Voice in Short Fiction.* Carbondale, Ill.: Southern Illinois University Press, 1986, 281 p.

Stevick, Philip, ed. *The American Short Story, 1900-1945: A Critical History.* Twayne's Critical History of the Short Story, edited by William Peden, Boston: Twayne Publishers, 1984, 209 p.

Summers, Hollis, ed. *Discussion of the Short Story.* Boston: D. C. Heath and Co., 1963, 118 p.

Vannatta, Dennis, ed. *The English Short Story, 1945-1980: A Critical History.* Twayne's Critical History of the Short Story, edited by William Peden. Boston: Twayne Publishers, 1985, 206 p.

Voss, Arthur. *The American Short Story: A Critical Survey.* Norman, Okla.: University of Oklahoma Press, 1973, 399 p.

Walker, Warren S. *Twentieth-Century Short Story Explication: New Series, Vol. 1: 1989-1990.* Hamden, Conn.: Shoe String, 1993, 366 p.

Ward, Alfred C. *Aspects of the Modern Short Story: English and American.* London: University of London Press, 1924, 307 p.

Weaver, Gordon, ed. *The American Short Story, 1945-1980: A Critical History.* Twayne's Critical History of the Short Story, edited by William Peden. Boston: Twayne Publishers, 1983, 150 p.

West, Ray B., Jr. *The Short Story in America, 1900-1950.* Chicago: Henry Regnery Co., 1952, 147 p.

Williams, Blanche Colton. *Our Short Story Writers.* New York: Moffat, Yard and Co., 1920, 357 p.

Wright, Austin McGiffert. *The American Short Story in the Twenties.* Chicago: University of Chicago Press, 1961, 425 p.

CRITICAL ANTHOLOGIES

Atkinson, W. Patterson, ed. *The Short-Story.* Boston: Allyn and Bacon, 1923, 317 p.

Baldwin, Charles Sears, ed. *American Short Stories.* New York: Longmans, Green and Co., 1904, 333 p.

Charters, Ann, ed. *The Story and Its Writer: An Introduction to Short Fiction.* New York: St. Martin's Press, 1983, 1239 p.

Current-García, Eugene, and Patrick, Walton R., eds. *American Short Stories: 1820 to the Present.* Key Editions, edited by John C. Gerber. Chicago: Scott, Foresman and Co., 1952, 633 p.

Fagin, N. Bryllion, ed. *America through the Short Story.* Boston: Little, Brown, and Co., 1936, 508 p.

Frakes, James R., and Traschen, Isadore, eds. *Short Fiction: A Critical Collection.* Prentice-Hall English Literature Series, edited by Maynard Mack. Englewood Cliffs, N.J.: Prentice-Hall, 1959, 459 p.

Gifford, Douglas, ed. *Scottish Short Stories, 1800-1900.* The Scottish Library, edited by Alexander Scott. London: Calder and Boyars, 1971, 350 p.

Gordon, Caroline, and Tate, Allen, eds. *The House of Fiction: An Anthology of the Short Story with Commentary.* Rev. ed. New York: Charles Scribner's Sons, 1960, 469 p.

Greet, T. Y., et. al. *The Worlds of Fiction: Stories in Context.* Boston: Houghton Mifflin Co., 1964, 429 p.

Gullason, Thomas A., and Caspar, Leonard, eds. *The World of Short Fiction: An International Collection.* New York: Harper and Row, 1962, 548 p.

Havighurst, Walter, ed. *Masters of the Modern Short Story.* New York: Harcourt, Brace and Co., 1945, 538 p.

Litz, A. Walton, ed. *Major American Short Stories.* New York: Oxford University Press, 1975, 823 p.

Matthews, Brander, ed. *The Short-Story: Specimens Illustrating Its Development.* New York: American Book Co., 1907, 399 p.

Menton, Seymour, ed. *The Spanish American Short Story: A Critical Anthology.* Berkeley and Los Angeles: University of California Press, 1980, 496 p.

Mzamane, Mbulelo Vizikhungo, ed. *Hungry Flames, and Other Black South African Short Stories.* Longman African Classics. Essex: Longman, 1986, 162 p.

Schorer, Mark, ed. *The Short Story: A Critical Anthology.* Rev. ed. Prentice-Hall English Literature Series, edited by Maynard Mack. Englewood Cliffs, N. J.: Prentice-Hall, 1967, 459 p.

Simpson, Claude M., ed. *The Local Colorists: American Short Stories, 1857-1900.* New York: Harper and Brothers Publishers, 1960, 340 p.

Stanton, Robert, ed. *The Short Story and the Reader.* New York: Henry Holt and Co., 1960, 557 p.

West, Ray B., Jr., ed. *American Short Stories.* New York: Thomas Y. Crowell Co., 1959, 267 p.

Short Story Criticism Indexes

Literary Criticism Series
Cumulative Author Index

SSC Cumulative Nationality Index
SSC Cumulative Title Index

How to Use This Index

The main references

Calvino, Italo
  1923-1985.....CLC **5, 8, 11, 22, 33, 39,**
                                    73; SSC 3

---

list all author entries in the following Gale Literary Criticism series:

BLC = *Black Literature Criticism*
CLC = *Contemporary Literary Criticism*
CLR = *Children's Literature Review*
CMLC = *Classical and Medieval Literature Criticism*
DA = *DISCovering Authors*
DC = *Drama Criticism*
HLC = *Hispanic Literature Criticism*
LC = *Literature Criticism from 1400 to 1800*
NCLC = *Nineteenth-Century Literature Criticism*
PC = *Poetry Criticism*
SSC = *Short Story Criticism*
TCLC = *Twentieth-Century Literary Criticism*
WLC = *World Literature Criticism, 1500 to the Present*

The cross-references

See also CANR 23; CA 85-88;
  obituary CA 116

---

list all author entries in the following Gale biographical and literary sources:

AAYA = *Authors & Artists for Young Adults*
AITN = *Authors in the News*
BEST = *Bestsellers*
BW = *Black Writers*
CA = *Contemporary Authors*
CAAS = *Contemporary Authors Autobiography Series*
CABS = *Contemporary Authors Bibliographical Series*
CANR = *Contemporary Authors New Revision Series*
CAP = *Contemporary Authors Permanent Series*
CDALB = *Concise Dictionary of American Literary Biography*
CDBLB = *Concise Dictionary of British Literary Biography*
DLB = *Dictionary of Literary Biography*
DLBD = *Dictionary of Literary Biography Documentary Series*
DLBY = *Dictionary of Literary Biography Yearbook*
HW = *Hispanic Writers*
JRDA = *Junior DISCovering Authors*
MAICYA = *Major Authors and Illustrators for Children and Young Adults*
MTCW = *Major 20th-Century Writers*
SAAS = *Something about the Author Autobiography Series*
SATA = *Something about the Author*
YABC = *Yesterday's Authors of Books for Children*

Literary Criticism Series
Cumulative Author Index

A.
See Arnold, Matthew

A. E. . . . . TCLC 3, 10
See also Russell, George William
See also DLB 19

A. M.
See Megged, Aharon

A. R. P-C
See Galsworthy, John

Abasiyanik, Sait Faik 1906-1954
See Sait Faik
See also CA 123

Abbey, Edward 1927-1989 . . . . . . CLC 36, 59
See also CA 45-48; 128; CANR 2, 41

Abbott, Lee K(ittredge) 1947- . . . . . . CLC 48
See also CA 124; DLB 130

Abe, Kobo 1924-1993 . . . . . CLC 8, 22, 53, 81
See also CA 65-68; 140; CANR 24; MTCW

Abelard, Peter c. 1079-c. 1142 . . . CMLC 11
See also DLB 115

Abell, Kjeld 1901-1961 . . . . CLC 15
See also CA 111

Abish, Walter 1931- . . . . CLC 22
See also CA 101; CANR 37; DLB 130

Abrahams, Peter (Henry) 1919- . . . . . CLC 4
See also BW 1; CA 57-60; CANR 26;
DLB 117; MTCW

Abrams, M(eyer) H(oward) 1912-. . . CLC 24
See also CA 57-60; CANR 13, 33; DLB 67

Abse, Dannie 1923- . . . . CLC 7, 29
See also CA 53-56; CAAS 1; CANR 4;
DLB 27

Achebe, (Albert) Chinua(lumogu)
1930- . . . . . CLC 1, 3, 5, 7, 11, 26, 51, 75;
BLC; DA; WLC
See also BW 2; CA 1-4R; CANR 6, 26;
CLR 20; DLB 117; MAICYA; MTCW;
SATA 38, 40

Acker, Kathy 1948- . . . . CLC 45
See also CA 117; 122

Ackroyd, Peter 1949- . . . . CLC 34, 52
See also CA 123; 127

Acorn, Milton 1923- . . . . CLC 15
See also CA 103; DLB 53

Adamov, Arthur 1908-1970 . . . . . . CLC 4, 25
See also CA 17-18; 25-28R; CAP 2; MTCW

Adams, Alice (Boyd) 1926- . . . CLC 6, 13, 46
See also CA 81-84; CANR 26; DLBY 86;
MTCW

Adams, Andy 1859-1935 . . . . TCLC 56
See also YABC 1

Adams, Douglas (Noel) 1952- . . . CLC 27, 60
See also AAYA 4; BEST 89:3; CA 106;
CANR 34; DLBY 83; JRDA

Adams, Francis 1862-1893 . . . . NCLC 33

Adams, Henry (Brooks)
1838-1918 . . . . TCLC 4, 52; DA
See also CA 104; 133; DLB 12, 47

Adams, Richard (George)
1920- . . . . CLC 4, 5, 18
See also AITN 1, 2; CA 49-52; CANR 3,
35; CLR 20; JRDA; MAICYA; MTCW;
SATA 7, 69

Adamson, Joy(-Friederike Victoria)
1910-1980 . . . . CLC 17
See also CA 69-72; 93-96; CANR 22;
MTCW; SATA 11, 22

Adcock, Fleur 1934- . . . . CLC 41
See also CA 25-28R; CANR 11, 34;
DLB 40

Addams, Charles (Samuel)
1912-1988 . . . . CLC 30
See also CA 61-64; 126; CANR 12

Addison, Joseph 1672-1719 . . . . LC 18
See also CDBLB 1660-1789; DLB 101

Adler, C(arole) S(chwerdtfeger)
1932- . . . . CLC 35
See also AAYA 4; CA 89-92; CANR 19,
40; JRDA; MAICYA; SAAS 15;
SATA 26, 63

Adler, Renata 1938- . . . . CLC 8, 31
See also CA 49-52; CANR 5, 22; MTCW

Ady, Endre 1877-1919 . . . . TCLC 11
See also CA 107

Aeschylus
525B.C.-456B.C. . . . . CMLC 11; DA

Afton, Effie
See Harper, Frances Ellen Watkins

Agapida, Fray Antonio
See Irving, Washington

Agee, James (Rufus)
1909-1955 . . . . TCLC 1, 19
See also AITN 1; CA 108;
CDALB 1941-1968; DLB 2, 26

Aghill, Gordon
See Silverberg, Robert

Agnon, S(hmuel) Y(osef Halevi)
1888-1970 . . . . CLC 4, 8, 14
See also CA 17-18; 25-28R; CAP 2; MTCW

Aherne, Owen
See Cassill, R(onald) V(erlin)

Ai 1947- . . . . CLC 4, 14, 69
See also CA 85-88; CAAS 13; DLB 120

Aickman, Robert (Fordyce)
1914-1981 . . . . CLC 57
See also CA 5-8R; CANR 3

Aiken, Conrad (Potter)
1889-1973 . . . CLC 1, 3, 5, 10, 52; SSC 9
See also CA 5-8R; 45-48; CANR 4;
CDALB 1929-1941; DLB 9, 45, 102;
MTCW; SATA 3, 30

Aiken, Joan (Delano) 1924- . . . . CLC 35
See also AAYA 1; CA 9-12R; CANR 4, 23,
34; CLR 1, 19; JRDA; MAICYA;
MTCW; SAAS 1; SATA 2, 30, 73

Ainsworth, William Harrison
1805-1882 . . . . NCLC 13
See also DLB 21; SATA 24

Aitmatov, Chingiz (Torekulovich)
1928- . . . . CLC 71
See also CA 103; CANR 38; MTCW;
SATA 56

Akers, Floyd
See Baum, L(yman) Frank

Akhmadulina, Bella Akhatovna
1937- . . . . CLC 53
See also CA 65-68

Akhmatova, Anna
1888-1966 . . . . CLC 11, 25, 64; PC 2
See also CA 19-20; 25-28R; CANR 35;
CAP 1; MTCW

Aksakov, Sergei Timofeyvich
1791-1859 . . . . NCLC 2

Aksenov, Vassily . . . . CLC 22
See also Aksyonov, Vassily (Pavlovich)

Aksyonov, Vassily (Pavlovich)
1932- . . . . CLC 37
See also Aksenov, Vassily
See also CA 53-56; CANR 12

Akutagawa Ryunosuke
1892-1927 . . . . TCLC 16
See also CA 117

Alain 1868-1951 . . . . TCLC 41

Alain-Fournier . . . . TCLC 6
See also Fournier, Henri Alban
See also DLB 65

Alarcon, Pedro Antonio de
1833-1891 . . . . NCLC 1

Alas (y Urena), Leopoldo (Enrique Garcia)
1852-1901 . . . . TCLC 29
See also CA 113; 131; HW

Albee, Edward (Franklin III)
1928- . . . . . . CLC 1, 2, 3, 5, 9, 11, 13, 25,
53; DA; WLC
See also AITN 1; CA 5-8R; CABS 3;
CANR 8; CDALB 1941-1968; DLB 7;
MTCW

Alberti, Rafael 1902- . . . . CLC 7
See also CA 85-88; DLB 108

Alcala-Galiano, Juan Valera y
See Valera y Alcala-Galiano, Juan

Alcott, Amos Bronson 1799-1888 . . NCLC 1
See also DLB 1

Alcott, Louisa May
1832-1888 . . . . NCLC 6; DA; WLC
See also CDALB 1865-1917; CLR 1;
DLB 1, 42, 79; JRDA; MAICYA;
YABC 1

Aldanov, M. A.
See Aldanov, Mark (Alexandrovich)

Aldanov, Mark (Alexandrovich)
1886(?)-1957 . . . . **TCLC 23**
See also CA 118

Aldington, Richard 1892-1962 . . . . . . **CLC 49**
See also CA 85-88; CANR 45; DLB 20, 36,
100

Aldiss, Brian W(ilson)
1925- . . . . **CLC 5, 14, 40**
See also CA 5-8R; CAAS 2; CANR 5, 28;
DLB 14; MTCW; SATA 34

Alegria, Claribel 1924- . . . . **CLC 75**
See also CA 131; CAAS 15; HW

Alegria, Fernando 1918- . . . . **CLC 57**
See also CA 9-12R; CANR 5, 32; HW

Aleichem, Sholom . . . . **TCLC 1, 35**
See also Rabinovitch, Sholem

Aleixandre, Vicente 1898-1984 . . . **CLC 9, 36**
See also CA 85-88; 114; CANR 26;
DLB 108; HW; MTCW

Alepoudelis, Odysseus
See Elytis, Odysseus

Aleshkovsky, Joseph 1929-
See Aleshkovsky, Yuz
See also CA 121; 128

Aleshkovsky, Yuz . . . . **CLC 44**
See also Aleshkovsky, Joseph

Alexander, Lloyd (Chudley) 1924- . . **CLC 35**
See also AAYA 1; CA 1-4R; CANR 1, 24,
38; CLR 1, 5; DLB 52; JRDA; MAICYA;
MTCW; SATA 3, 49

Alfau, Felipe 1902- . . . . **CLC 66**
See also CA 137

Alger, Horatio, Jr. 1832-1899 . . . . . **NCLC 8**
See also DLB 42; SATA 16

Algren, Nelson 1909-1981 . . . . **CLC 4, 10, 33**
See also CA 13-16R; 103; CANR 20;
CDALB 1941-1968; DLB 9; DLBY 81,
82; MTCW

Ali, Ahmed 1910- . . . . **CLC 69**
See also CA 25-28R; CANR 15, 34

Alighieri, Dante 1265-1321 . . . . **CMLC 3**

Allan, John B.
See Westlake, Donald E(dwin)

Allen, Edward 1948- . . . . **CLC 59**

Allen, Paula Gunn 1939- . . . . **CLC 84**
See also CA 112; 143; NNAL

Allen, Roland
See Ayckbourn, Alan

Allen, Sarah A.
See Hopkins, Pauline Elizabeth

Allen, Woody 1935- . . . . **CLC 16, 52**
See also AAYA 10; CA 33-36R; CANR 27,
38; DLB 44; MTCW

Allende, Isabel 1942- . . . . **CLC 39, 57; HLC**
See also CA 125; 130; HW; MTCW

Alleyn, Ellen
See Rossetti, Christina (Georgina)

Allingham, Margery (Louise)
1904-1966 . . . . **CLC 19**
See also CA 5-8R; 25-28R; CANR 4;
DLB 77; MTCW

Allingham, William 1824-1889 . . . **NCLC 25**
See also DLB 35

Allison, Dorothy E. 1949- . . . . **CLC 78**
See also CA 140

Allston, Washington 1779-1843 . . . . **NCLC 2**
See also DLB 1

Almedingen, E. M. . . . . **CLC 12**
See also Almedingen, Martha Edith von
See also SATA 3

Almedingen, Martha Edith von 1898-1971
See Almedingen, E. M.
See also CA 1-4R; CANR 1

Almqvist, Carl Jonas Love
1793-1866 . . . . **NCLC 42**

Alonso, Damaso 1898-1990 . . . . **CLC 14**
See also CA 110; 131; 130; DLB 108; HW

Alov
See Gogol, Nikolai (Vasilyevich)

Alta 1942- . . . . **CLC 19**
See also CA 57-60

Alter, Robert B(ernard) 1935- . . . . . . **CLC 34**
See also CA 49-52; CANR 1

Alther, Lisa 1944- . . . . **CLC 7, 41**
See also CA 65-68; CANR 12, 30; MTCW

Altman, Robert 1925- . . . . **CLC 16**
See also CA 73-76; CANR 43

Alvarez, A(lfred) 1929- . . . . **CLC 5, 13**
See also CA 1-4R; CANR 3, 33; DLB 14,
40

Alvarez, Alejandro Rodriguez 1903-1965
See Casona, Alejandro
See also CA 131; 93-96; HW

Amado, Jorge 1912- . . . . **CLC 13, 40; HLC**
See also CA 77-80; CANR 35; DLB 113;
MTCW

Ambler, Eric 1909- . . . . **CLC 4, 6, 9**
See also CA 9-12R; CANR 7, 38; DLB 77;
MTCW

Amichai, Yehuda 1924- . . . . . . **CLC 9, 22, 57**
See also CA 85-88; MTCW

Amiel, Henri Frederic 1821-1881 . . **NCLC 4**

Amis, Kingsley (William)
1922- . . **CLC 1, 2, 3, 5, 8, 13, 40, 44; DA**
See also AITN 2; CA 9-12R; CANR 8, 28;
CDBLB 1945-1960; DLB 15, 27, 100, 139;
MTCW

Amis, Martin (Louis)
1949- . . . . **CLC 4, 9, 38, 62**
See also BEST 90:3; CA 65-68; CANR 8,
27; DLB 14

Ammons, A(rchie) R(andolph)
1926- . . . . **CLC 2, 3, 5, 8, 9, 25, 57**
See also AITN 1; CA 9-12R; CANR 6, 36;
DLB 5; MTCW

Amo, Tauraatua i
See Adams, Henry (Brooks)

Anand, Mulk Raj 1905- . . . . **CLC 23**
See also CA 65-68; CANR 32; MTCW

Anatol
See Schnitzler, Arthur

Anaya, Rudolfo A(lfonso)
1937- . . . . **CLC 23; HLC**
See also CA 45-48; CAAS 4; CANR 1, 32;
DLB 82; HW 1; MTCW

Andersen, Hans Christian
1805-1875 . . **NCLC 7; DA; SSC 6; WLC**
See also CLR 6; MAICYA; YABC 1

Anderson, C. Farley
See Mencken, H(enry) L(ouis); Nathan,
George Jean

Anderson, Jessica (Margaret) Queale
. . . . **CLC 37**
See also CA 9-12R; CANR 4

Anderson, Jon (Victor) 1940- . . . . **CLC 9**
See also CA 25-28R; CANR 20

Anderson, Lindsay (Gordon)
1923- . . . . **CLC 20**
See also CA 125; 128

Anderson, Maxwell 1888-1959 . . . . . **TCLC 2**
See also CA 105; DLB 7

Anderson, Poul (William) 1926- . . . . **CLC 15**
See also AAYA 5; CA 1-4R; CAAS 2;
CANR 2, 15, 34; DLB 8; MTCW;
SATA 39

Anderson, Robert (Woodruff)
1917- . . . . **CLC 23**
See also AITN 1; CA 21-24R; CANR 32;
DLB 7

Anderson, Sherwood
1876-1941 . . . . **TCLC 1, 10, 24; DA;
SSC 1; WLC**
See also CA 104; 121; CDALB 1917-1929;
DLB 4, 9, 86; DLBD 1; MTCW

Andouard
See Giraudoux, (Hippolyte) Jean

Andrade, Carlos Drummond de . . . . . . **CLC 18**
See also Drummond de Andrade, Carlos

Andrade, Mario de 1893-1945 . . . . . **TCLC 43**

Andreas-Salome, Lou 1861-1937 . . . **TCLC 56**
See also DLB 66

Andrewes, Lancelot 1555-1626 . . . . **LC 5**

Andrews, Cicily Fairfield
See West, Rebecca

Andrews, Elton V.
See Pohl, Frederik

Andreyev, Leonid (Nikolaevich)
1871-1919 . . . . **TCLC 3**
See also CA 104

Andric, Ivo 1892-1975 . . . . **CLC 8**
See also CA 81-84; 57-60; CANR 43;
MTCW

Angelique, Pierre
See Bataille, Georges

Angell, Roger 1920- . . . . **CLC 26**
See also CA 57-60; CANR 13, 44

Angelou, Maya
1928- . . . . **CLC 12, 35, 64, 77; BLC; DA**
See also AAYA 7; BW 2; CA 65-68;
CANR 19, 42; DLB 38; MTCW;
SATA 49

Annensky, Innokenty Fyodorovich
1856-1909 . . . . **TCLC 14**
See also CA 110

Anon, Charles Robert
See Pessoa, Fernando (Antonio Nogueira)

Anouilh, Jean (Marie Lucien Pierre)
1910-1987 . . . . . . **CLC 1, 3, 8, 13, 40, 50**
See also CA 17-20R; 123; CANR 32;
MTCW

Anthony, Florence
See Ai

Anthony, John
See Ciardi, John (Anthony)

Anthony, Peter
See Shaffer, Anthony (Joshua); Shaffer, Peter (Levin)

Anthony, Piers 1934- .... **CLC 35**
See also AAYA 11; CA 21-24R; CANR 28; DLB 8; MTCW

Antoine, Marc
See Proust, (Valentin-Louis-George-Eugene-) Marcel

Antoninus, Brother
See Everson, William (Oliver)

Antonioni, Michelangelo 1912- ..... **CLC 20**
See also CA 73-76; CANR 45

Antschel, Paul 1920-1970...... **CLC 10, 19**
See also Celan, Paul
See also CA 85-88; CANR 33; MTCW

Anwar, Chairil 1922-1949 .... **TCLC 22**
See also CA 121

Apollinaire, Guillaume .. **TCLC 3, 8, 51; PC 7**
See also Kostrowitzki, Wilhelm Apollinaris de

Appelfeld, Aharon 1932- .... **CLC 23, 47**
See also CA 112; 133

Apple, Max (Isaac) 1941-........ **CLC 9, 33**
See also CA 81-84; CANR 19; DLB 130

Appleman, Philip (Dean) 1926- ..... **CLC 51**
See also CA 13-16R; CAAS 18; CANR 6, 29

Appleton, Lawrence
See Lovecraft, H(oward) P(hillips)

Apteryx
See Eliot, T(homas) S(tearns)

Apuleius, (Lucius Madaurensis)
125(?)-175(?) .... **CMLC 1**

Aquin, Hubert 1929-1977.......... **CLC 15**
See also CA 105; DLB 53

Aragon, Louis 1897-1982 ...... **CLC 3, 22**
See also CA 69-72; 108; CANR 28; DLB 72; MTCW

Arany, Janos 1817-1882........ **NCLC 34**

Arbuthnot, John 1667-1735 .... **LC 1**
See also DLB 101

Archer, Herbert Winslow
See Mencken, H(enry) L(ouis)

Archer, Jeffrey (Howard) 1940- .... **CLC 28**
See also BEST 89:3; CA 77-80; CANR 22

Archer, Jules 1915- .... **CLC 12**
See also CA 9-12R; CANR 6; SAAS 5; SATA 4

Archer, Lee
See Ellison, Harlan

Arden, John 1930- .... **CLC 6, 13, 15**
See also CA 13-16R; CAAS 4; CANR 31; DLB 13; MTCW

Arenas, Reinaldo
1943-1990 .... **CLC 41; HLC**
See also CA 124; 128; 133; HW

Arendt, Hannah 1906-1975 .... **CLC 66**
See also CA 17-20R; 61-64; CANR 26; MTCW

Aretino, Pietro 1492-1556 .... **LC 12**

Arghezi, Tudor.................... **CLC 80**
See also Theodorescu, Ion N.

Arguedas, Jose Maria
1911-1969 .... **CLC 10, 18**
See also CA 89-92; DLB 113; HW

Argueta, Manlio 1936-........... **CLC 31**
See also CA 131; HW

Ariosto, Ludovico 1474-1533........ **LC 6**

Aristides
See Epstein, Joseph

Aristophanes
450B.C.-385B.C.... **CMLC 4; DA; DC 2**

Arlt, Roberto (Godofredo Christophersen)
1900-1942 .... **TCLC 29; HLC**
See also CA 123; 131; HW

Armah, Ayi Kwei 1939- .... **CLC 5, 33; BLC**
See also BW 1; CA 61-64; CANR 21; DLB 117; MTCW

Armatrading, Joan 1950-......... **CLC 17**
See also CA 114

Arnette, Robert
See Silverberg, Robert

Arnim, Achim von (Ludwig Joachim von Arnim) 1781-1831 .... **NCLC 5**
See also DLB 90

Arnim, Bettina von 1785-1859.... **NCLC 38**
See also DLB 90

Arnold, Matthew
1822-1888 ..... **NCLC 6, 29; DA; PC 5; WLC**
See also CDBLB 1832-1890; DLB 32, 57

Arnold, Thomas 1795-1842 ...... **NCLC 18**
See also DLB 55

Arnow, Harriette (Louisa) Simpson
1908-1986 .... **CLC 2, 7, 18**
See also CA 9-12R; 118; CANR 14; DLB 6; MTCW; SATA 42, 47

Arp, Hans
See Arp, Jean

Arp, Jean 1887-1966.............. **CLC 5**
See also CA 81-84; 25-28R; CANR 42

Arrabal
See Arrabal, Fernando

Arrabal, Fernando 1932- ... **CLC 2, 9, 18, 58**
See also CA 9-12R; CANR 15

Arrick, Fran..................... **CLC 30**

Artaud, Antonin 1896-1948 ..... **TCLC 3, 36**
See also CA 104

Arthur, Ruth M(abel) 1905-1979.... **CLC 12**
See also CA 9-12R; 85-88; CANR 4; SATA 7, 26

Artsybashev, Mikhail (Petrovich)
1878-1927 .... **TCLC 31**

Arundel, Honor (Morfydd)
1919-1973 .... **CLC 17**
See also CA 21-22; 41-44R; CAP 2; SATA 4, 24

Asch, Sholem 1880-1957 .... **TCLC 3**
See also CA 105

Ash, Shalom
See Asch, Sholem

Ashbery, John (Lawrence)
1927- ...... **CLC 2, 3, 4, 6, 9, 13, 15, 25, 41, 77**
See also CA 5-8R; CANR 9, 37; DLB 5; DLBY 81; MTCW

Ashdown, Clifford
See Freeman, R(ichard) Austin

Ashe, Gordon
See Creasey, John

Ashton-Warner, Sylvia (Constance)
1908-1984 .... **CLC 19**
See also CA 69-72; 112; CANR 29; MTCW

Asimov, Isaac
1920-1992 ...... **CLC 1, 3, 9, 19, 26, 76**
See also BEST 90:2; CA 1-4R; 137; CANR 2, 19, 36; CLR 12; DLB 8; DLBY 92; JRDA; MAICYA; MTCW; SATA 1, 26, 74

Astley, Thea (Beatrice May)
1925- .... **CLC 41**
See also CA 65-68; CANR 11, 43

Aston, James
See White, T(erence) H(anbury)

Asturias, Miguel Angel
1899-1974 .... **CLC 3, 8, 13; HLC**
See also CA 25-28; 49-52; CANR 32; CAP 2; DLB 113; HW; MTCW

Atares, Carlos Saura
See Saura (Atares), Carlos

Atheling, William
See Pound, Ezra (Weston Loomis)

Atheling, William, Jr.
See Blish, James (Benjamin)

Atherton, Gertrude (Franklin Horn)
1857-1948 .... **TCLC 2**
See also CA 104; DLB 9, 78

Atherton, Lucius
See Masters, Edgar Lee

Atkins, Jack
See Harris, Mark

Atticus
See Fleming, Ian (Lancaster)

Atwood, Margaret (Eleanor)
1939- ..... **CLC 2, 3, 4, 8, 13, 15, 25, 44, 84; DA; PC 8; SSC 2; WLC**
See also AAYA 12; BEST 89:2; CA 49-52; CANR 3, 24, 33; DLB 53; MTCW; SATA 50

Aubigny, Pierre d'
See Mencken, H(enry) L(ouis)

Aubin, Penelope 1685-1731(?)........ **LC 9**
See also DLB 39

Auchincloss, Louis (Stanton)
1917- .... **CLC 4, 6, 9, 18, 45**
See also CA 1-4R; CANR 6, 29; DLB 2; DLBY 80; MTCW

Auden, W(ystan) H(ugh)
1907-1973 ...... **CLC 1, 2, 3, 4, 6, 9, 11, 14, 43; DA; PC 1; WLC**
See also CA 9-12R; 45-48; CANR 5; CDBLB 1914-1945; DLB 10, 20; MTCW

Audiberti, Jacques 1900-1965 ...... **CLC 38**
See also CA 25-28R

Barker, Harley Granville
See Granville-Barker, Harley
See also DLB 10

Barker, Howard 1946- . . . . CLC 37
See also CA 102; DLB 13

Barker, Pat 1943- . . . . CLC 32
See also CA 117; 122

Barlow, Joel 1754-1812 . . . . NCLC 23
See also DLB 37

Barnard, Mary (Ethel) 1909- . . . . CLC 48
See also CA 21-22; CAP 2

Barnes, Djuna
1892-1982 . . . CLC 3, 4, 8, 11, 29; SSC 3
See also CA 9-12R; 107; CANR 16; DLB 4,
9, 45; MTCW

Barnes, Julian 1946- . . . . CLC 42
See also CA 102; CANR 19; DLBY 93

Barnes, Peter 1931- . . . . CLC 5, 56
See also CA 65-68; CAAS 12; CANR 33,
34; DLB 13; MTCW

Baroja (y Nessi), Pio
1872-1956 . . . . TCLC 8; HLC
See also CA 104

Baron, David
See Pinter, Harold

Baron Corvo
See Rolfe, Frederick (William Serafino
Austin Lewis Mary)

Barondess, Sue K(aufman)
1926-1977 . . . . CLC 8
See also Kaufman, Sue
See also CA 1-4R; 69-72; CANR 1

Baron de Teive
See Pessoa, Fernando (Antonio Nogueira)

Barres, Maurice 1862-1923 . . . . TCLC 47
See also DLB 123

Barreto, Afonso Henrique de Lima
See Lima Barreto, Afonso Henrique de

Barrett, (Roger) Syd 1946- . . . . CLC 35
See also Pink Floyd

Barrett, William (Christopher)
1913-1992 . . . . CLC 27
See also CA 13-16R; 139; CANR 11

Barrie, J(ames) M(atthew)
1860-1937 . . . . TCLC 2
See also CA 104; 136; CDBLB 1890-1914;
CLR 16; DLB 10, 141; MAICYA;
YABC 1

Barrington, Michael
See Moorcock, Michael (John)

Barrol, Grady
See Bograd, Larry

Barry, Mike
See Malzberg, Barry N(athaniel)

Barry, Philip 1896-1949 . . . . TCLC 11
See also CA 109; DLB 7

Bart, Andre Schwarz
See Schwarz-Bart, Andre

Barth, John (Simmons)
1930- . . . . . . CLC 1, 2, 3, 5, 7, 9, 10, 14,
27, 51; SSC 10
See also AITN 1, 2; CA 1-4R; CABS 1;
CANR 5, 23; DLB 2; MTCW

Barthelme, Donald
1931-1989 . . . . . . CLC 1, 2, 3, 5, 6, 8, 13,
23, 46, 59; SSC 2
See also CA 21-24R; 129; CANR 20;
DLB 2; DLBY 80, 89; MTCW; SATA 7,
62

Barthelme, Frederick 1943- . . . . CLC 36
See also CA 114; 122; DLBY 85

Barthes, Roland (Gerard)
1915-1980 . . . . CLC 24, 83
See also CA 130; 97-100; MTCW

Barzun, Jacques (Martin) 1907- . . . . CLC 51
See also CA 61-64; CANR 22

Bashevis, Isaac
See Singer, Isaac Bashevis

Bashkirtseff, Marie 1859-1884 . . . NCLC 27

Basho
See Matsuo Basho

Bass, Kingsley B., Jr.
See Bullins, Ed

Bass, Rick 1958- . . . . CLC 79
See also CA 126

Bassani, Giorgio 1916- . . . . CLC 9
See also CA 65-68; CANR 33; DLB 128;
MTCW

Bastos, Augusto (Antonio) Roa
See Roa Bastos, Augusto (Antonio)

Bataille, Georges 1897-1962 . . . . CLC 29
See also CA 101; 89-92

Bates, H(erbert) E(rnest)
1905-1974 . . . . CLC 46; SSC 10
See also CA 93-96; 45-48; CANR 34;
MTCW

Bauchart
See Camus, Albert

Baudelaire, Charles
1821-1867 . . . . . NCLC 6, 29; DA; PC 1;
WLC

Baudrillard, Jean 1929- . . . . CLC 60

Baum, L(yman) Frank 1856-1919 . . . TCLC 7
See also CA 108; 133; CLR 15; DLB 22;
JRDA; MAICYA; MTCW; SATA 18

Baum, Louis F.
See Baum, L(yman) Frank

Baumbach, Jonathan 1933- . . . . . . CLC 6, 23
See also CA 13-16R; CAAS 5; CANR 12;
DLBY 80; MTCW

Bausch, Richard (Carl) 1945- . . . . . . CLC 51
See also CA 101; CAAS 14; CANR 43;
DLB 130

Baxter, Charles 1947- . . . . CLC 45, 78
See also CA 57-60; CANR 40; DLB 130

Baxter, George Owen
See Faust, Frederick (Schiller)

Baxter, James K(eir) 1926-1972 . . . . CLC 14
See also CA 77-80

Baxter, John
See Hunt, E(verette) Howard, Jr.

Bayer, Sylvia
See Glassco, John

Beagle, Peter S(oyer) 1939- . . . . CLC 7
See also CA 9-12R; CANR 4; DLBY 80;
SATA 60

Bean, Normal
See Burroughs, Edgar Rice

Beard, Charles A(ustin)
1874-1948 . . . . TCLC 15
See also CA 115; DLB 17; SATA 18

Beardsley, Aubrey 1872-1898 . . . . . NCLC 6

Beattie, Ann
1947- . . . . CLC 8, 13, 18, 40, 63; SSC 11
See also BEST 90:2; CA 81-84; DLBY 82;
MTCW

Beattie, James 1735-1803 . . . . NCLC 25
See also DLB 109

Beauchamp, Kathleen Mansfield 1888-1923
See Mansfield, Katherine
See also CA 104; 134; DA

Beaumarchais, Pierre-Augustin Caron de
1732-1799 . . . . DC 4

**Beauvoir, Simone (Lucie Ernestine Marie
Bertrand) de**
1908-1986 . . . . CLC 1, 2, 4, 8, 14, 31, 44,
50, 71; DA; WLC
See also CA 9-12R; 118; CANR 28;
DLB 72; DLBY 86; MTCW

Becker, Jurek 1937- . . . . CLC 7, 19
See also CA 85-88; DLB 75

Becker, Walter 1950- . . . . CLC 26

Beckett, Samuel (Barclay)
1906-1989 . . . . . . CLC 1, 2, 3, 4, 6, 9, 10,
11, 14, 18, 29, 57, 59, 83; DA; SSC 16;
WLC
See also CA 5-8R; 130; CANR 33;
CDBLB 1945-1960; DLB 13, 15;
DLBY 90; MTCW

Beckford, William 1760-1844 . . . . NCLC 16
See also DLB 39

Beckman, Gunnel 1910- . . . . CLC 26
See also CA 33-36R; CANR 15; CLR 25;
MAICYA; SAAS 9; SATA 6

Becque, Henri 1837-1899 . . . . NCLC 3

Beddoes, Thomas Lovell
1803-1849 . . . . NCLC 3
See also DLB 96

Bedford, Donald F.
See Fearing, Kenneth (Flexner)

Beecher, Catharine Esther
1800-1878 . . . . NCLC 30
See also DLB 1

Beecher, John 1904-1980 . . . . CLC 6
See also AITN 1; CA 5-8R; 105; CANR 8

Beer, Johann 1655-1700 . . . . LC 5

Beer, Patricia 1924- . . . . CLC 58
See also CA 61-64; CANR 13; DLB 40

Beerbohm, Henry Maximilian
1872-1956 . . . . TCLC 1, 24
See also CA 104; DLB 34, 100

Begiebing, Robert J(ohn) 1946- . . . . . CLC 70
See also CA 122; CANR 40

Behan, Brendan
1923-1964 . . . . CLC 1, 8, 11, 15, 79
See also CA 73-76; CANR 33;
CDBLB 1945-1960; DLB 13; MTCW

Behn, Aphra
1640(?)-1689 . . . . LC 1; DA; DC 4; WLC
See also DLB 39, 80, 131

Behrman, S(amuel) N(athaniel)
1893-1973 . . . . **CLC 40**
See also CA 13-16; 45-48; CAP 1; DLB 7,
44

Belasco, David 1853-1931 . . . . **TCLC 3**
See also CA 104; DLB 7

Belcheva, Elisaveta 1893- . . . . **CLC 10**

Beldone, Phil "Cheech"
See Ellison, Harlan

Beleno
See Azuela, Mariano

Belinski, Vissarion Grigoryevich
1811-1848 . . . . **NCLC 5**

Belitt, Ben 1911- . . . . **CLC 22**
See also CA 13-16R; CAAS 4; CANR 7;
DLB 5

Bell, James Madison
1826-1902 . . . . **TCLC 43; BLC**
See also BW 1; CA 122; 124; DLB 50

Bell, Madison (Smartt) 1957- . . . . . . **CLC 41**
See also CA 111; CANR 28

Bell, Marvin (Hartley) 1937- . . . . . **CLC 8, 31**
See also CA 21-24R; CAAS 14; DLB 5;
MTCW

Bell, W. L. D.
See Mencken, H(enry) L(ouis)

Bellamy, Atwood C.
See Mencken, H(enry) L(ouis)

Bellamy, Edward 1850-1898 . . . . . . **NCLC 4**
See also DLB 12

Bellin, Edward J.
See Kuttner, Henry

Belloc, (Joseph) Hilaire (Pierre)
1870-1953 . . . . **TCLC 7, 18**
See also CA 106; DLB 19, 100, 141;
YABC 1

Belloc, Joseph Peter Rene Hilaire
See Belloc, (Joseph) Hilaire (Pierre)

Belloc, Joseph Pierre Hilaire
See Belloc, (Joseph) Hilaire (Pierre)

Belloc, M. A.
See Lowndes, Marie Adelaide (Belloc)

Bellow, Saul
1915- . . . . . . **CLC 1, 2, 3, 6, 8, 10, 13, 15,
25, 33, 34, 63, 79; DA; SSC 14; WLC**
See also AITN 2; BEST 89:3; CA 5-8R;
CABS 1; CANR 29; CDALB 1941-1968;
DLB 2, 28; DLBD 3; DLBY 82; MTCW

Belser, Reimond Karel Maria de
1929- . . . . **CLC 14**

Bely, Andrey . . . . **TCLC 7**
See also Bugayev, Boris Nikolayevich

Benary, Margot
See Benary-Isbert, Margot

Benary-Isbert, Margot 1889-1979 . . . **CLC 12**
See also CA 5-8R; 89-92; CANR 4;
CLR 12; MAICYA; SATA 2, 21

Benavente (y Martinez), Jacinto
1866-1954 . . . . **TCLC 3**
See also CA 106; 131; HW; MTCW

Benchley, Peter (Bradford)
1940- . . . . **CLC 4, 8**
See also AITN 2; CA 17-20R; CANR 12,
35; MTCW; SATA 3

Benchley, Robert (Charles)
1889-1945 . . . . **TCLC 1, 55**
See also CA 105; DLB 11

Benedikt, Michael 1935- . . . . **CLC 4, 14**
See also CA 13-16R; CANR 7; DLB 5

Benet, Juan 1927- . . . . **CLC 28**
See also CA 143

Benet, Stephen Vincent
1898-1943 . . . . **TCLC 7; SSC 10**
See also CA 104; DLB 4, 48, 102; YABC 1

Benet, William Rose 1886-1950 . . . **TCLC 28**
See also CA 118; DLB 45

Benford, Gregory (Albert) 1941- . . . . **CLC 52**
See also CA 69-72; CANR 12, 24;
DLBY 82

Bengtsson, Frans (Gunnar)
1894-1954 . . . . **TCLC 48**

Benjamin, David
See Slavitt, David R(ytman)

Benjamin, Lois
See Gould, Lois

Benjamin, Walter 1892-1940 . . . . . . **TCLC 39**

Benn, Gottfried 1886-1956 . . . . **TCLC 3**
See also CA 106; DLB 56

Bennett, Alan 1934- . . . . **CLC 45, 77**
See also CA 103; CANR 35; MTCW

Bennett, (Enoch) Arnold
1867-1931 . . . . **TCLC 5, 20**
See also CA 106; CDBLB 1890-1914;
DLB 10, 34, 98

Bennett, Elizabeth
See Mitchell, Margaret (Munnerlyn)

Bennett, George Harold 1930-
See Bennett, Hal
See also BW 1; CA 97-100

Bennett, Hal . . . . **CLC 5**
See also Bennett, George Harold
See also DLB 33

Bennett, Jay 1912- . . . . **CLC 35**
See also AAYA 10; CA 69-72; CANR 11,
42; JRDA; SAAS 4; SATA 27, 41

Bennett, Louise (Simone)
1919- . . . . **CLC 28; BLC**
See also BW 2; DLB 117

Benson, E(dward) F(rederic)
1867-1940 . . . . **TCLC 27**
See also CA 114; DLB 135

Benson, Jackson J. 1930- . . . . **CLC 34**
See also CA 25-28R; DLB 111

Benson, Sally 1900-1972 . . . . **CLC 17**
See also CA 19-20; 37-40R; CAP 1;
SATA 1, 27, 35

Benson, Stella 1892-1933 . . . . **TCLC 17**
See also CA 117; DLB 36

Bentham, Jeremy 1748-1832 . . . . . **NCLC 38**
See also DLB 107

Bentley, E(dmund) C(lerihew)
1875-1956 . . . . **TCLC 12**
See also CA 108; DLB 70

Bentley, Eric (Russell) 1916- . . . . **CLC 24**
See also CA 5-8R; CANR 6

Beranger, Pierre Jean de
1780-1857 . . . . **NCLC 34**

Berger, Colonel
See Malraux, (Georges-)Andre

Berger, John (Peter) 1926- . . . . . . **CLC 2, 19**
See also CA 81-84; DLB 14

Berger, Melvin H. 1927- . . . . **CLC 12**
See also CA 5-8R; CANR 4; CLR 32;
SAAS 2; SATA 5

Berger, Thomas (Louis)
1924- . . . . **CLC 3, 5, 8, 11, 18, 38**
See also CA 1-4R; CANR 5, 28; DLB 2;
DLBY 80; MTCW

Bergman, (Ernst) Ingmar
1918- . . . . **CLC 16, 72**
See also CA 81-84; CANR 33

Bergson, Henri 1859-1941 . . . . **TCLC 32**

Bergstein, Eleanor 1938- . . . . **CLC 4**
See also CA 53-56; CANR 5

Berkoff, Steven 1937- . . . . **CLC 56**
See also CA 104

Bermant, Chaim (Icyk) 1929- . . . . . . **CLC 40**
See also CA 57-60; CANR 6, 31

Bern, Victoria
See Fisher, M(ary) F(rances) K(ennedy)

Bernanos, (Paul Louis) Georges
1888-1948 . . . . **TCLC 3**
See also CA 104; 130; DLB 72

Bernard, April 1956- . . . . **CLC 59**
See also CA 131

Berne, Victoria
See Fisher, M(ary) F(rances) K(ennedy)

Bernhard, Thomas
1931-1989 . . . . **CLC 3, 32, 61**
See also CA 85-88; 127; CANR 32;
DLB 85, 124; MTCW

Berrigan, Daniel 1921- . . . . **CLC 4**
See also CA 33-36R; CAAS 1; CANR 11,
43; DLB 5

Berrigan, Edmund Joseph Michael, Jr.
1934-1983
See Berrigan, Ted
See also CA 61-64; 110; CANR 14

Berrigan, Ted . . . . **CLC 37**
See also Berrigan, Edmund Joseph Michael,
Jr.
See also DLB 5

Berry, Charles Edward Anderson 1931-
See Berry, Chuck
See also CA 115

Berry, Chuck . . . . **CLC 17**
See also Berry, Charles Edward Anderson

Berry, Jonas
See Ashbery, John (Lawrence)

Berry, Wendell (Erdman)
1934- . . . . **CLC 4, 6, 8, 27, 46**
See also AITN 1; CA 73-76; DLB 5, 6

Berryman, John
1914-1972 . . . . . . **CLC 1, 2, 3, 4, 6, 8, 10,
13, 25, 62**
See also CA 13-16; 33-36R; CABS 2;
CANR 35; CAP 1; CDALB 1941-1968;
DLB 48; MTCW

Bertolucci, Bernardo 1940- . . . . **CLC 16**
See also CA 106

Bertrand, Aloysius 1807-1841 . . . . **NCLC 31**

Bertran de Born   c. 1140-1215 . . . . . **CMLC 5**

Besant, Annie (Wood)   1847-1933 . . . **TCLC 9**
See also CA 105

Bessie, Alvah   1904-1985 . . . . **CLC 23**
See also CA 5-8R; 116; CANR 2; DLB 26

Bethlen, T. D.
See Silverberg, Robert

Beti, Mongo . . . . **CLC 27; BLC**
See also Biyidi, Alexandre

Betjeman, John
1906-1984 . . . . **CLC 2, 6, 10, 34, 43**
See also CA 9-12R; 112; CANR 33;
CDBLB 1945-1960; DLB 20; DLBY 84;
MTCW

Bettelheim, Bruno   1903-1990 . . . . . . **CLC 79**
See also CA 81-84; 131; CANR 23; MTCW

Betti, Ugo   1892-1953 . . . . **TCLC 5**
See also CA 104

Betts, Doris (Waugh)   1932- . . . . **CLC 3, 6, 28**
See also CA 13-16R; CANR 9; DLBY 82

Bevan, Alistair
See Roberts, Keith (John Kingston)

Beynon, John
See Harris, John (Wyndham Parkes Lucas)
Beynon

Bialik, Chaim Nachman
1873-1934 . . . . **TCLC 25**

Bickerstaff, Isaac
See Swift, Jonathan

Bidart, Frank   1939- . . . . **CLC 33**
See also CA 140

Bienek, Horst   1930- . . . . **CLC 7, 11**
See also CA 73-76; DLB 75

Bierce, Ambrose (Gwinett)
1842-1914(?) . . . . **TCLC 1, 7, 44; DA;**
　　　　　　　　　　　　　　　　　　SSC 9; WLC
See also CA 104; 139; CDALB 1865-1917;
DLB 11, 12, 23, 71, 74

Billings, Josh
See Shaw, Henry Wheeler

Billington, (Lady) Rachel (Mary)
1942- . . . . **CLC 43**
See also AITN 2; CA 33-36R; CANR 44

Binyon, T(imothy) J(ohn)   1936- . . . . **CLC 34**
See also CA 111; CANR 28

Bioy Casares, Adolfo
1914- . . . . **CLC 4, 8, 13; HLC**
See also CA 29-32R; CANR 19, 43;
DLB 113; HW; MTCW

Bird, C.
See Ellison, Harlan

Bird, Cordwainer
See Ellison, Harlan

Bird, Robert Montgomery
1806-1854 . . . . **NCLC 1**

Birney, (Alfred) Earle
1904- . . . . **CLC 1, 4, 6, 11**
See also CA 1-4R; CANR 5, 20; DLB 88;
MTCW

Bishop, Elizabeth
1911-1979 . . . . . . **CLC 1, 4, 9, 13, 15, 32;**
　　　　　　　　　　　　　　　　　　　DA; PC 3
See also CA 5-8R; 89-92; CABS 2;
CANR 26; CDALB 1968-1988; DLB 5;
MTCW; SATA 24

Bishop, John   1935- . . . . **CLC 10**
See also CA 105

Bissett, Bill   1939- . . . . **CLC 18**
See also CA 69-72; CAAS 19; CANR 15;
DLB 53; MTCW

Bitov, Andrei (Georgievich)   1937- . . . **CLC 57**
See also CA 142

Biyidi, Alexandre   1932-
See Beti, Mongo
See also BW 1; CA 114; 124; MTCW

Bjarme, Brynjolf
See Ibsen, Henrik (Johan)

Bjornson, Bjornstjerne (Martinius)
1832-1910 . . . . **TCLC 7, 37**
See also CA 104

Black, Robert
See Holdstock, Robert P.

Blackburn, Paul   1926-1971 . . . . . . **CLC 9, 43**
See also CA 81-84; 33-36R; CANR 34;
DLB 16; DLBY 81

Black Elk   1863-1950 . . . . **TCLC 33**
See also CA 144

Black Hobart
See Sanders, (James) Ed(ward)

Blacklin, Malcolm
See Chambers, Aidan

Blackmore, R(ichard) D(oddridge)
1825-1900 . . . . **TCLC 27**
See also CA 120; DLB 18

Blackmur, R(ichard) P(almer)
1904-1965 . . . . **CLC 2, 24**
See also CA 11-12; 25-28R; CAP 1; DLB 63

Black Tarantula, The
See Acker, Kathy

Blackwood, Algernon (Henry)
1869-1951 . . . . **TCLC 5**
See also CA 105

Blackwood, Caroline   1931- . . . . **CLC 6, 9**
See also CA 85-88; CANR 32; DLB 14;
MTCW

Blade, Alexander
See Hamilton, Edmond; Silverberg, Robert

Blaga, Lucian   1895-1961 . . . . **CLC 75**

Blair, Eric (Arthur)   1903-1950
See Orwell, George
See also CA 104; 132; DA; MTCW;
SATA 29

Blais, Marie-Claire
1939- . . . . **CLC 2, 4, 6, 13, 22**
See also CA 21-24R; CAAS 4; CANR 38;
DLB 53; MTCW

Blaise, Clark   1940- . . . . **CLC 29**
See also AITN 2; CA 53-56; CAAS 3;
CANR 5; DLB 53

Blake, Nicholas
See Day Lewis, C(ecil)
See also DLB 77

Blake, William
1757-1827 . . . . . **NCLC 13, 37; DA; WLC**
See also CDBLB 1789-1832; DLB 93;
MAICYA; SATA 30

Blasco Ibanez, Vicente
1867-1928 . . . . **TCLC 12**
See also CA 110; 131; HW; MTCW

Blatty, William Peter   1928- . . . . **CLC 2**
See also CA 5-8R; CANR 9

Bleeck, Oliver
See Thomas, Ross (Elmore)

Blessing, Lee   1949- . . . . **CLC 54**

Blish, James (Benjamin)
1921-1975 . . . . **CLC 14**
See also CA 1-4R; 57-60; CANR 3; DLB 8;
MTCW; SATA 66

Bliss, Reginald
See Wells, H(erbert) G(eorge)

Blixen, Karen (Christentze Dinesen)
1885-1962
See Dinesen, Isak
See also CA 25-28; CANR 22; CAP 2;
MTCW; SATA 44

Bloch, Robert (Albert)   1917- . . . . . . **CLC 33**
See also CA 5-8R; CANR 5; DLB 44;
SATA 12

Blok, Alexander (Alexandrovich)
1880-1921 . . . . **TCLC 5**
See also CA 104

Blom, Jan
See Breytenbach, Breyten

Bloom, Harold   1930- . . . . **CLC 24**
See also CA 13-16R; CANR 39; DLB 67

Bloomfield, Aurelius
See Bourne, Randolph S(illiman)

Blount, Roy (Alton), Jr.   1941- . . . . . **CLC 38**
See also CA 53-56; CANR 10, 28; MTCW

Bloy, Leon   1846-1917 . . . . **TCLC 22**
See also CA 121; DLB 123

Blume, Judy (Sussman)   1938- . . . **CLC 12, 30**
See also AAYA 3; CA 29-32R; CANR 13,
37; CLR 2, 15; DLB 52; JRDA;
MAICYA; MTCW; SATA 2, 31

Blunden, Edmund (Charles)
1896-1974 . . . . **CLC 2, 56**
See also CA 17-18; 45-48; CAP 2; DLB 20,
100; MTCW

Bly, Robert (Elwood)
1926- . . . . **CLC 1, 2, 5, 10, 15, 38**
See also CA 5-8R; CANR 41; DLB 5;
MTCW

Boas, Franz   1858-1942 . . . . **TCLC 56**
See also CA 115

Bobette
See Simenon, Georges (Jacques Christian)

Boccaccio, Giovanni
1313-1375 . . . . **CMLC 13; SSC 10**

Bochco, Steven   1943- . . . . **CLC 35**
See also AAYA 11; CA 124; 138

Bodenheim, Maxwell   1892-1954 . . . **TCLC 44**
See also CA 110; DLB 9, 45

Bodker, Cecil   1927- . . . . **CLC 21**
See also CA 73-76; CANR 13, 44; CLR 23;
MAICYA; SATA 14

Brand, Millen 1906-1980 . . . . **CLC 7**
See also CA 21-24R; 97-100

Branden, Barbara . . . . **CLC 44**

Brandes, Georg (Morris Cohen)
1842-1927 . . . . **TCLC 10**
See also CA 105

Brandys, Kazimierz 1916- . . . . **CLC 62**

Branley, Franklyn M(ansfield)
1915- . . . . **CLC 21**
See also CA 33-36R; CANR 14, 39;
CLR 13; MAICYA; SAAS 16; SATA 4,
68

Brathwaite, Edward (Kamau)
1930- . . . . **CLC 11**
See also BW 2; CA 25-28R; CANR 11, 26;
DLB 125

Brautigan, Richard (Gary)
1935-1984 . . . . **CLC 1, 3, 5, 9, 12, 34, 42**
See also CA 53-56; 113; CANR 34; DLB 2,
5; DLBY 80, 84; MTCW; SATA 56

Braverman, Kate 1950- . . . . **CLC 67**
See also CA 89-92

Brecht, Bertolt
1898-1956 . . . . . . **TCLC 1, 6, 13, 35; DA;**
DC 3; WLC
See also CA 104; 133; DLB 56, 124; MTCW

Brecht, Eugen Berthold Friedrich
See Brecht, Bertolt

Bremer, Fredrika 1801-1865 . . . . . **NCLC 11**

Brennan, Christopher John
1870-1932 . . . . **TCLC 17**
See also CA 117

Brennan, Maeve 1917- . . . . **CLC 5**
See also CA 81-84

Brentano, Clemens (Maria)
1778-1842 . . . . **NCLC 1**

Brent of Bin Bin
See Franklin, (Stella Maraia Sarah) Miles

Brenton, Howard 1942- . . . . **CLC 31**
See also CA 69-72; CANR 33; DLB 13;
MTCW

Breslin, James 1930-
See Breslin, Jimmy
See also CA 73-76; CANR 31; MTCW

Breslin, Jimmy . . . . **CLC 4, 43**
See also Breslin, James
See also AITN 1

Bresson, Robert 1907- . . . . **CLC 16**
See also CA 110

Breton, Andre 1896-1966 . . . **CLC 2, 9, 15, 54**
See also CA 19-20; 25-28R; CANR 40;
CAP 2; DLB 65; MTCW

Breytenbach, Breyten 1939(?)- . . **CLC 23, 37**
See also CA 113; 129

Bridgers, Sue Ellen 1942- . . . . **CLC 26**
See also AAYA 8; CA 65-68; CANR 11,
36; CLR 18; DLB 52; JRDA; MAICYA;
SAAS 1; SATA 22

Bridges, Robert (Seymour)
1844-1930 . . . . **TCLC 1**
See also CA 104; CDBLB 1890-1914;
DLB 19, 98

Bridie, James . . . . **TCLC 3**
See also Mavor, Osborne Henry
See also DLB 10

Brin, David 1950- . . . . **CLC 34**
See also CA 102; CANR 24; SATA 65

Brink, Andre (Philippus)
1935- . . . . **CLC 18, 36**
See also CA 104; CANR 39; MTCW

Brinsmead, H(esba) F(ay) 1922- . . . . **CLC 21**
See also CA 21-24R; CANR 10; MAICYA;
SAAS 5; SATA 18, 78

Brittain, Vera (Mary)
1893(?)-1970 . . . . **CLC 23**
See also CA 13-16; 25-28R; CAP 1; MTCW

Broch, Hermann 1886-1951 . . . . . . **TCLC 20**
See also CA 117; DLB 85, 124

Brock, Rose
See Hansen, Joseph

Brodkey, Harold 1930- . . . . **CLC 56**
See also CA 111; DLB 130

Brodsky, Iosif Alexandrovich 1940-
See Brodsky, Joseph
See also AITN 1; CA 41-44R; CANR 37;
MTCW

Brodsky, Joseph . . **CLC 4, 6, 13, 36, 50; PC 9**
See also Brodsky, Iosif Alexandrovich

Brodsky, Michael Mark 1948- . . . . . **CLC 19**
See also CA 102; CANR 18, 41

Bromell, Henry 1947- . . . . **CLC 5**
See also CA 53-56; CANR 9

Bromfield, Louis (Brucker)
1896-1956 . . . . **TCLC 11**
See also CA 107; DLB 4, 9, 86

Broner, E(sther) M(asserman)
1930- . . . . **CLC 19**
See also CA 17-20R; CANR 8, 25; DLB 28

Bronk, William 1918- . . . . **CLC 10**
See also CA 89-92; CANR 23

Bronstein, Lev Davidovich
See Trotsky, Leon

Bronte, Anne 1820-1849 . . . . **NCLC 4**
See also DLB 21

Bronte, Charlotte
1816-1855 . . . **NCLC 3, 8, 33; DA; WLC**
See also CDBLB 1832-1890; DLB 21

Bronte, (Jane) Emily
1818-1848 . . . . **NCLC 16, 35; DA; PC 8;**
WLC
See also CDBLB 1832-1890; DLB 21, 32

Brooke, Frances 1724-1789 . . . . **LC 6**
See also DLB 39, 99

Brooke, Henry 1703(?)-1783 . . . . **LC 1**
See also DLB 39

Brooke, Rupert (Chawner)
1887-1915 . . . . **TCLC 2, 7; DA; WLC**
See also CA 104; 132; CDBLB 1914-1945;
DLB 19; MTCW

Brooke-Haven, P.
See Wodehouse, P(elham) G(renville)

Brooke-Rose, Christine 1926- . . . . . . **CLC 40**
See also CA 13-16R; DLB 14

Brookner, Anita 1928- . . . . . . **CLC 32, 34, 51**
See also CA 114; 120; CANR 37; DLBY 87;
MTCW

Brooks, Cleanth 1906- . . . . **CLC 24**
See also CA 17-20R; CANR 33, 35;
DLB 63; MTCW

Brooks, George
See Baum, L(yman) Frank

Brooks, Gwendolyn
1917- . . . . . . **CLC 1, 2, 4, 5, 15, 49; BLC;**
DA; PC 7; WLC
See also AITN 1; BW 2; CA 1-4R;
CANR 1, 27; CDALB 1941-1968;
CLR 27; DLB 5, 76; MTCW; SATA 6

Brooks, Mel . . . . **CLC 12**
See also Kaminsky, Melvin
See also DLB 26

Brooks, Peter 1938- . . . . **CLC 34**
See also CA 45-48; CANR 1

Brooks, Van Wyck 1886-1963 . . . . . . **CLC 29**
See also CA 1-4R; CANR 6; DLB 45, 63,
103

Brophy, Brigid (Antonia)
1929- . . . . **CLC 6, 11, 29**
See also CA 5-8R; CAAS 4; CANR 25;
DLB 14; MTCW

Brosman, Catharine Savage 1934- . . . . **CLC 9**
See also CA 61-64; CANR 21

Brother Antoninus
See Everson, William (Oliver)

Broughton, T(homas) Alan 1936- . . . **CLC 19**
See also CA 45-48; CANR 2, 23

Broumas, Olga 1949- . . . . **CLC 10, 73**
See also CA 85-88; CANR 20

Brown, Charles Brockden
1771-1810 . . . . **NCLC 22**
See also CDALB 1640-1865; DLB 37, 59,
73

Brown, Christy 1932-1981 . . . . **CLC 63**
See also CA 105; 104; DLB 14

Brown, Claude 1937- . . . . **CLC 30; BLC**
See also AAYA 7; BW 1; CA 73-76

Brown, Dee (Alexander) 1908- . . **CLC 18, 47**
See also CA 13-16R; CAAS 6; CANR 11,
45; DLBY 80; MTCW; SATA 5

Brown, George
See Wertmueller, Lina

Brown, George Douglas
1869-1902 . . . . **TCLC 28**

Brown, George Mackay 1921- . . . . **CLC 5, 48**
See also CA 21-24R; CAAS 6; CANR 12,
37; DLB 14, 27, 139; MTCW; SATA 35

Brown, (William) Larry 1951- . . . . . . **CLC 73**
See also CA 130; 134

Brown, Moses
See Barrett, William (Christopher)

Brown, Rita Mae 1944- . . . . . . **CLC 18, 43, 79**
See also CA 45-48; CANR 2, 11, 35;
MTCW

Brown, Roderick (Langmere) Haig-
See Haig-Brown, Roderick (Langmere)

Brown, Rosellen 1939- . . . . **CLC 32**
See also CA 77-80; CAAS 10; CANR 14, 44

Brown, Sterling Allen
1901-1989 . . . . **CLC 1, 23, 59; BLC**
See also BW 1; CA 85-88; 127; CANR 26;
DLB 48, 51, 63; MTCW

Brown, Will
See Ainsworth, William Harrison

Byron, George Gordon (Noel)
1788-1824 . . . . . . **NCLC 2, 12; DA; WLC**
See also CDBLB 1789-1832; DLB 96, 110

C.3.3.
See Wilde, Oscar (Fingal O'Flahertie Wills)

Caballero, Fernan 1796-1877. . . . . **NCLC 10**

Cabell, James Branch 1879-1958 . . . **TCLC 6**
See also CA 105; DLB 9, 78

Cable, George Washington
1844-1925 . . . . **TCLC 4; SSC 4**
See also CA 104; DLB 12, 74

Cabral de Melo Neto, Joao 1920-. . . **CLC 76**

Cabrera Infante, G(uillermo)
1929- . . . . **CLC 5, 25, 45; HLC**
See also CA 85-88; CANR 29; DLB 113;
HW; MTCW

Cade, Toni
See Bambara, Toni Cade

Cadmus
See Buchan, John

Caedmon fl. 658-680. . . . . **CMLC 7**

Caeiro, Alberto
See Pessoa, Fernando (Antonio Nogueira)

Cage, John (Milton, Jr.) 1912- . . . . . **CLC 41**
See also CA 13-16R; CANR 9

Cain, G.
See Cabrera Infante, G(uillermo)

Cain, Guillermo
See Cabrera Infante, G(uillermo)

Cain, James M(allahan)
1892-1977 . . . . **CLC 3, 11, 28**
See also AITN 1; CA 17-20R; 73-76;
CANR 8, 34; MTCW

Caine, Mark
See Raphael, Frederic (Michael)

Calasso, Roberto 1941- . . . . **CLC 81**
See also CA 143

Calderon de la Barca, Pedro
1600-1681 . . . . **LC 23; DC 3**

Caldwell, Erskine (Preston)
1903-1987 . . . . **CLC 1, 8, 14, 50, 60**
See also AITN 1; CA 1-4R; 121; CAAS 1;
CANR 2, 33; DLB 9, 86; MTCW

Caldwell, (Janet Miriam) Taylor (Holland)
1900-1985 . . . . **CLC 2, 28, 39**
See also CA 5-8R; 116; CANR 5

Calhoun, John Caldwell
1782-1850 . . . . **NCLC 15**
See also DLB 3

Calisher, Hortense
1911- . . . . **CLC 2, 4, 8, 38; SSC 15**
See also CA 1-4R; CANR 1, 22; DLB 2;
MTCW

Callaghan, Morley Edward
1903-1990 . . . . **CLC 3, 14, 41, 65**
See also CA 9-12R; 132; CANR 33;
DLB 68; MTCW

Calvino, Italo
1923-1985 . . . . . **CLC 5, 8, 11, 22, 33, 39,
73; SSC 3**
See also CA 85-88; 116; CANR 23; MTCW

Cameron, Carey 1952- . . . . **CLC 59**
See also CA 135

Cameron, Peter 1959-. . . . . **CLC 44**
See also CA 125

Campana, Dino 1885-1932. . . . . . . **TCLC 20**
See also CA 117; DLB 114

Campbell, John W(ood, Jr.)
1910-1971 . . . . **CLC 32**
See also CA 21-22; 29-32R; CANR 34;
CAP 2; DLB 8; MTCW

Campbell, Joseph 1904-1987 . . . . **CLC 69**
See also AAYA 3; BEST 89:2; CA 1-4R;
124; CANR 3, 28; MTCW

Campbell, (John) Ramsey 1946- . . . . **CLC 42**
See also CA 57-60; CANR 7

Campbell, (Ignatius) Roy (Dunnachie)
1901-1957 . . . . **TCLC 5**
See also CA 104; DLB 20

Campbell, Thomas 1777-1844 . . . . **NCLC 19**
See also DLB 93; 144

Campbell, Wilfred. . . . . **TCLC 9**
See also Campbell, William

Campbell, William 1858(?)-1918
See Campbell, Wilfred
See also CA 106; DLB 92

Campos, Alvaro de
See Pessoa, Fernando (Antonio Nogueira)

Camus, Albert
1913-1960 . . . . **CLC 1, 2, 4, 9, 11, 14, 32,
63, 69; DA; DC 2; SSC 9; WLC**
See also CA 89-92; DLB 72; MTCW

Canby, Vincent 1924-. . . . . **CLC 13**
See also CA 81-84

Cancale
See Desnos, Robert

Canetti, Elias 1905- . . . . . . **CLC 3, 14, 25, 75**
See also CA 21-24R; CANR 23; DLB 85,
124; MTCW

Canin, Ethan 1960-. . . . . **CLC 55**
See also CA 131; 135

Cannon, Curt
See Hunter, Evan

Cape, Judith
See Page, P(atricia) K(athleen)

Capek, Karel
1890-1938 . . . . . **TCLC 6, 37; DA; DC 1;
WLC**
See also CA 104; 140

Capote, Truman
1924-1984 . . . . . . **CLC 1, 3, 8, 13, 19, 34,
38, 58; DA; SSC 2; WLC**
See also CA 5-8R; 113; CANR 18;
CDALB 1941-1968; DLB 2; DLBY 80,
84; MTCW

Capra, Frank 1897-1991. . . . . **CLC 16**
See also CA 61-64; 135

Caputo, Philip 1941-. . . . . **CLC 32**
See also CA 73-76; CANR 40

Card, Orson Scott 1951- . . . . **CLC 44, 47, 50**
See also AAYA 11; CA 102; CANR 27;
MTCW

Cardenal (Martinez), Ernesto
1925- . . . . **CLC 31; HLC**
See also CA 49-52; CANR 2, 32; HW;
MTCW

Carducci, Giosue 1835-1907. . . . . . **TCLC 32**

Carew, Thomas 1595(?)-1640. . . . . . . **LC 13**
See also DLB 126

Carey, Ernestine Gilbreth 1908-. . . . **CLC 17**
See also CA 5-8R; SATA 2

Carey, Peter 1943-. . . . . **CLC 40, 55**
See also CA 123; 127; MTCW

Carleton, William 1794-1869. . . . . . **NCLC 3**

Carlisle, Henry (Coffin) 1926-. . . . . . **CLC 33**
See also CA 13-16R; CANR 15

Carlsen, Chris
See Holdstock, Robert P.

Carlson, Ron(ald F.) 1947-. . . . . **CLC 54**
See also CA 105; CANR 27

Carlyle, Thomas 1795-1881 . . **NCLC 22; DA**
See also CDBLB 1789-1832; DLB 55; 144

Carman, (William) Bliss
1861-1929 . . . . **TCLC 7**
See also CA 104; DLB 92

Carnegie, Dale 1888-1955 . . . . **TCLC 53**

Carossa, Hans 1878-1956. . . . . **TCLC 48**
See also DLB 66

Carpenter, Don(ald Richard)
1931- . . . . **CLC 41**
See also CA 45-48; CANR 1

Carpentier (y Valmont), Alejo
1904-1980 . . . . **CLC 8, 11, 38; HLC**
See also CA 65-68; 97-100; CANR 11;
DLB 113; HW

Carr, Emily 1871-1945. . . . . **TCLC 32**
See also DLB 68

Carr, John Dickson 1906-1977 . . . . . . **CLC 3**
See also CA 49-52; 69-72; CANR 3, 33;
MTCW

Carr, Philippa
See Hibbert, Eleanor Alice Burford

Carr, Virginia Spencer 1929-. . . . . . . **CLC 34**
See also CA 61-64; DLB 111

Carrier, Roch 1937-. . . . . **CLC 13, 78**
See also CA 130; DLB 53

Carroll, James P. 1943(?)-. . . . . **CLC 38**
See also CA 81-84

Carroll, Jim 1951-. . . . . **CLC 35**
See also CA 45-48; CANR 42

Carroll, Lewis. . . . . **NCLC 2; WLC**
See also Dodgson, Charles Lutwidge
See also CDBLB 1832-1890; CLR 2, 18;
DLB 18; JRDA

Carroll, Paul Vincent 1900-1968. . . . **CLC 10**
See also CA 9-12R; 25-28R; DLB 10

Carruth, Hayden
1921- . . . . . . **CLC 4, 7, 10, 18, 84; PC 10**
See also CA 9-12R; CANR 4, 38; DLB 5;
MTCW; SATA 47

Carson, Rachel Louise 1907-1964. . . **CLC 71**
See also CA 77-80; CANR 35; MTCW;
SATA 23

Carter, Angela (Olive)
1940-1992 . . . . . . **CLC 5, 41, 76; SSC 13**
See also CA 53-56; 136; CANR 12, 36;
DLB 14; MTCW; SATA 66;
SATA-Obit 70

Carter, Nick
See Smith, Martin Cruz

Carver, Raymond
    1938-1988 ... **CLC 22, 36, 53, 55; SSC 8**
    See also CA 33-36R; 126; CANR 17, 34;
    DLB 130; DLBY 84, 88; MTCW

Cary, (Arthur) Joyce (Lunel)
    1888-1957 .... **TCLC 1, 29**
    See also CA 104; CDBLB 1914-1945;
    DLB 15, 100

Casanova de Seingalt, Giovanni Jacopo
    1725-1798 .... **LC 13**

Casares, Adolfo Bioy
    See Bioy Casares, Adolfo

Casely-Hayford, J(oseph) E(phraim)
    1866-1930 .... **TCLC 24; BLC**
    See also BW 2; CA 123

Casey, John (Dudley) 1939-........ **CLC 59**
    See also BEST 90:2; CA 69-72; CANR 23

Casey, Michael 1947-............ **CLC 2**
    See also CA 65-68; DLB 5

Casey, Patrick
    See Thurman, Wallace (Henry)

Casey, Warren (Peter) 1935-1988 ... **CLC 12**
    See also CA 101; 127

Casona, Alejandro .... **CLC 49**
    See also Alvarez, Alejandro Rodriguez

Cassavetes, John 1929-1989........ **CLC 20**
    See also CA 85-88; 127

Cassill, R(onald) V(erlin) 1919-... **CLC 4, 23**
    See also CA 9-12R; CAAS 1; CANR 7, 45;
    DLB 6

Cassity, (Allen) Turner 1929- .... **CLC 6, 42**
    See also CA 17-20R; CAAS 8; CANR 11;
    DLB 105

Castaneda, Carlos 1931(?)-........ **CLC 12**
    See also CA 25-28R; CANR 32; HW;
    MTCW

Castedo, Elena 1937- .... **CLC 65**
    See also CA 132

Castedo-Ellerman, Elena
    See Castedo, Elena

Castellanos, Rosario
    1925-1974 .... **CLC 66; HLC**
    See also CA 131; 53-56; DLB 113; HW

Castelvetro, Lodovico 1505-1571..... **LC 12**

Castiglione, Baldassare 1478-1529 ... **LC 12**

Castle, Robert
    See Hamilton, Edmond

Castro, Guillen de 1569-1631........ **LC 19**

Castro, Rosalia de 1837-1885 ..... **NCLC 3**

Cather, Willa
    See Cather, Willa Sibert

Cather, Willa Sibert
    1873-1947 .... **TCLC 1, 11, 31; DA;
                                   SSC 2; WLC**
    See also CA 104; 128; CDALB 1865-1917;
    DLB 9, 54, 78; DLBD 1; MTCW;
    SATA 30

Catton, (Charles) Bruce
    1899-1978 .... **CLC 35**
    See also AITN 1; CA 5-8R; 81-84;
    CANR 7; DLB 17; SATA 2, 24

Cauldwell, Frank
    See King, Francis (Henry)

Caunitz, William J. 1933- .... **CLC 34**
    See also BEST 89:3; CA 125; 130

Causley, Charles (Stanley) 1917-..... **CLC 7**
    See also CA 9-12R; CANR 5, 35; CLR 30;
    DLB 27; MTCW; SATA 3, 66

Caute, David 1936-.............. **CLC 29**
    See also CA 1-4R; CAAS 4; CANR 1, 33;
    DLB 14

Cavafy, C(onstantine) P(eter)...... **TCLC 2, 7**
    See also Kavafis, Konstantinos Petrou

Cavallo, Evelyn
    See Spark, Muriel (Sarah)

Cavanna, Betty .... **CLC 12**
    See also Harrison, Elizabeth Cavanna
    See also JRDA; MAICYA; SAAS 4;
    SATA 1, 30

Caxton, William 1421(?)-1491(?)..... **LC 17**

Cayrol, Jean 1911-.............. **CLC 11**
    See also CA 89-92; DLB 83

Cela, Camilo Jose
    1916- .... **CLC 4, 13, 59; HLC**
    See also BEST 90:2; CA 21-24R; CAAS 10;
    CANR 21, 32; DLBY 89; HW; MTCW

Celan, Paul .... **CLC 53, 82; PC 10**
    See also Antschel, Paul
    See also DLB 69

Celine, Louis-Ferdinand
    .... **CLC 1, 3, 4, 7, 9, 15, 47**
    See also Destouches, Louis-Ferdinand
    See also DLB 72

Cellini, Benvenuto 1500-1571 .... **LC 7**

Cendrars, Blaise
    See Sauser-Hall, Frederic

Cernuda (y Bidon), Luis
    1902-1963 .... **CLC 54**
    See also CA 131; 89-92; DLB 134; HW

Cervantes (Saavedra), Miguel de
    1547-1616 ...... **LC 6, 23; DA; SSC 12;
                                              WLC**

Cesaire, Aime (Fernand)
    1913- .... **CLC 19, 32; BLC**
    See also BW 2; CA 65-68; CANR 24, 43;
    MTCW

Chabon, Michael 1965(?)- .... **CLC 55**
    See also CA 139

Chabrol, Claude 1930- .... **CLC 16**
    See also CA 110

Challans, Mary 1905-1983
    See Renault, Mary
    See also CA 81-84; 111; SATA 23, 36

Challis, George
    See Faust, Frederick (Schiller)

Chambers, Aidan 1934- .... **CLC 35**
    See also CA 25-28R; CANR 12, 31; JRDA;
    MAICYA; SAAS 12; SATA 1, 69

Chambers, James 1948-
    See Cliff, Jimmy
    See also CA 124

Chambers, Jessie
    See Lawrence, D(avid) H(erbert Richards)

Chambers, Robert W. 1865-1933... **TCLC 41**

Chandler, Raymond (Thornton)
    1888-1959 .... **TCLC 1, 7**
    See also CA 104; 129; CDALB 1929-1941;
    DLBD 6; MTCW

Chang, Jung 1952-.............. **CLC 71**
    See also CA 142

Channing, William Ellery
    1780-1842 .... **NCLC 17**
    See also DLB 1, 59

Chaplin, Charles Spencer
    1889-1977 .... **CLC 16**
    See also Chaplin, Charlie
    See also CA 81-84; 73-76

Chaplin, Charlie
    See Chaplin, Charles Spencer
    See also DLB 44

Chapman, George 1559(?)-1634...... **LC 22**
    See also DLB 62, 121

Chapman, Graham 1941-1989 ...... **CLC 21**
    See also Monty Python
    See also CA 116; 129; CANR 35

Chapman, John Jay 1862-1933 ..... **TCLC 7**
    See also CA 104

Chapman, Walker
    See Silverberg, Robert

Chappell, Fred (Davis) 1936-.... **CLC 40, 78**
    See also CA 5-8R; CAAS 4; CANR 8, 33;
    DLB 6, 105

Char, Rene(-Emile)
    1907-1988 .... **CLC 9, 11, 14, 55**
    See also CA 13-16R; 124; CANR 32;
    MTCW

Charby, Jay
    See Ellison, Harlan

Chardin, Pierre Teilhard de
    See Teilhard de Chardin, (Marie Joseph)
    Pierre

Charles I 1600-1649.............. **LC 13**

Charyn, Jerome 1937- .... **CLC 5, 8, 18**
    See also CA 5-8R; CAAS 1; CANR 7;
    DLBY 83; MTCW

Chase, Mary (Coyle) 1907-1981 ...... **DC 1**
    See also CA 77-80; 105; SATA 17, 29

Chase, Mary Ellen 1887-1973....... **CLC 2**
    See also CA 13-16; 41-44R; CAP 1;
    SATA 10

Chase, Nicholas
    See Hyde, Anthony

Chateaubriand, Francois Rene de
    1768-1848 .... **NCLC 3**
    See also DLB 119

Chatterje, Sarat Chandra 1876-1936(?)
    See Chatterji, Saratchandra
    See also CA 109

Chatterji, Bankim Chandra
    1838-1894 .... **NCLC 19**

Chatterji, Saratchandra .... **TCLC 13**
    See also Chatterje, Sarat Chandra

Chatterton, Thomas 1752-1770....... **LC 3**
    See also DLB 109

Chatwin, (Charles) Bruce
    1940-1989 .... **CLC 28, 57, 59**
    See also AAYA 4; BEST 90:1; CA 85-88;
    127

Day Lewis, C(ecil)
1904-1972 . . . . **CLC 1, 6, 10**
See also Blake, Nicholas
See also CA 13-16; 33-36R; CANR 34;
CAP 1; DLB 15, 20; MTCW

Dazai, Osamu . . . . **TCLC 11**
See also Tsushima, Shuji

de Andrade, Carlos Drummond
See Drummond de Andrade, Carlos

Deane, Norman
See Creasey, John

**de Beauvoir, Simone (Lucie Ernestine Marie
Bertrand)**
See Beauvoir, Simone (Lucie Ernestine
Marie Bertrand) de

de Brissac, Malcolm
See Dickinson, Peter (Malcolm)

de Chardin, Pierre Teilhard
See Teilhard de Chardin, (Marie Joseph)
Pierre

Dee, John 1527-1608 . . . . **LC 20**

Deer, Sandra 1940- . . . . **CLC 45**

De Ferrari, Gabriella . . . . **CLC 65**

Defoe, Daniel
1660(?)-1731 . . . . **LC 1; DA; WLC**
See also CDBLB 1660-1789; DLB 39, 95,
101; JRDA; MAICYA; SATA 22

de Gourmont, Remy
See Gourmont, Remy de

de Hartog, Jan 1914- . . . . **CLC 19**
See also CA 1-4R; CANR 1

de Hostos, E. M.
See Hostos (y Bonilla), Eugenio Maria de

de Hostos, Eugenio M.
See Hostos (y Bonilla), Eugenio Maria de

Deighton, Len . . . . **CLC 4, 7, 22, 46**
See also Deighton, Leonard Cyril
See also AAYA 6; BEST 89:2;
CDBLB 1960 to Present; DLB 87

Deighton, Leonard Cyril 1929-
See Deighton, Len
See also CA 9-12R; CANR 19, 33; MTCW

Dekker, Thomas 1572(?)-1632 . . . . . . **LC 22**
See also CDBLB Before 1660; DLB 62

de la Mare, Walter (John)
1873-1956 . . **TCLC 4, 53; SSC 14; WLC**
See also CDBLB 1914-1945; CLR 23;
DLB 19; SATA 16

Delaney, Franey
See O'Hara, John (Henry)

Delaney, Shelagh 1939- . . . . **CLC 29**
See also CA 17-20R; CANR 30;
CDBLB 1960 to Present; DLB 13;
MTCW

Delany, Mary (Granville Pendarves)
1700-1788 . . . . **LC 12**

Delany, Samuel R(ay, Jr.)
1942- . . . . **CLC 8, 14, 38; BLC**
See also BW 2; CA 81-84; CANR 27, 43;
DLB 8, 33; MTCW

De La Ramee, (Marie) Louise 1839-1908
See Ouida
See also SATA 20

de la Roche, Mazo 1879-1961 . . . . . . **CLC 14**
See also CA 85-88; CANR 30; DLB 68;
SATA 64

Delbanco, Nicholas (Franklin)
1942- . . . . **CLC 6, 13**
See also CA 17-20R; CAAS 2; CANR 29;
DLB 6

del Castillo, Michel 1933- . . . . **CLC 38**
See also CA 109

Deledda, Grazia (Cosima)
1875(?)-1936 . . . . **TCLC 23**
See also CA 123

Delibes, Miguel . . . . **CLC 8, 18**
See also Delibes Setien, Miguel

Delibes Setien, Miguel 1920-
See Delibes, Miguel
See also CA 45-48; CANR 1, 32; HW;
MTCW

DeLillo, Don
1936- . . . . . **CLC 8, 10, 13, 27, 39, 54, 76**
See also BEST 89:1; CA 81-84; CANR 21;
DLB 6; MTCW

de Lisser, H. G.
See De Lisser, Herbert George
See also DLB 117

De Lisser, Herbert George
1878-1944 . . . . **TCLC 12**
See also de Lisser, H. G.
See also BW 2; CA 109

Deloria, Vine (Victor), Jr. 1933- . . . . **CLC 21**
See also CA 53-56; CANR 5, 20; MTCW;
SATA 21

Del Vecchio, John M(ichael)
1947- . . . . **CLC 29**
See also CA 110; DLBD 9

de Man, Paul (Adolph Michel)
1919-1983 . . . . **CLC 55**
See also CA 128; 111; DLB 67; MTCW

De Marinis, Rick 1934- . . . . **CLC 54**
See also CA 57-60; CANR 9, 25

Demby, William 1922- . . . . **CLC 53; BLC**
See also BW 1; CA 81-84; DLB 33

Demijohn, Thom
See Disch, Thomas M(ichael)

de Montherlant, Henry (Milon)
See Montherlant, Henry (Milon) de

Demosthenes 384B.C.-322B.C. . . . **CMLC 13**

de Natale, Francine
See Malzberg, Barry N(athaniel)

Denby, Edwin (Orr) 1903-1983 . . . . . **CLC 48**
See also CA 138; 110

Denis, Julio
See Cortazar, Julio

Denmark, Harrison
See Zelazny, Roger (Joseph)

Dennis, John 1658-1734 . . . . **LC 11**
See also DLB 101

Dennis, Nigel (Forbes) 1912-1989 . . . . **CLC 8**
See also CA 25-28R; 129; DLB 13, 15;
MTCW

De Palma, Brian (Russell) 1940- . . . . **CLC 20**
See also CA 109

De Quincey, Thomas 1785-1859 . . . **NCLC 4**
See also CDBLB 1789-1832; DLB 110; 144

Deren, Eleanora 1908(?)-1961
See Deren, Maya
See also CA 111

Deren, Maya . . . . **CLC 16**
See also Deren, Eleanora

Derleth, August (William)
1909-1971 . . . . **CLC 31**
See also CA 1-4R; 29-32R; CANR 4;
DLB 9; SATA 5

de Routisie, Albert
See Aragon, Louis

Derrida, Jacques 1930- . . . . **CLC 24**
See also CA 124; 127

Derry Down Derry
See Lear, Edward

Dersonnes, Jacques
See Simenon, Georges (Jacques Christian)

Desai, Anita 1937- . . . . **CLC 19, 37**
See also CA 81-84; CANR 33; MTCW;
SATA 63

de Saint-Luc, Jean
See Glassco, John

de Saint Roman, Arnaud
See Aragon, Louis

Descartes, Rene 1596-1650 . . . . **LC 20**

De Sica, Vittorio 1901(?)-1974 . . . . . **CLC 20**
See also CA 117

Desnos, Robert 1900-1945 . . . . **TCLC 22**
See also CA 121

Destouches, Louis-Ferdinand
1894-1961 . . . . **CLC 9, 15**
See also Celine, Louis-Ferdinand
See also CA 85-88; CANR 28; MTCW

Deutsch, Babette 1895-1982 . . . . **CLC 18**
See also CA 1-4R; 108; CANR 4; DLB 45;
SATA 1, 33

Devenant, William 1606-1649 . . . . . . **LC 13**

Devkota, Laxmiprasad
1909-1959 . . . . **TCLC 23**
See also CA 123

De Voto, Bernard (Augustine)
1897-1955 . . . . **TCLC 29**
See also CA 113; DLB 9

De Vries, Peter
1910-1993 . . . . **CLC 1, 2, 3, 7, 10, 28, 46**
See also CA 17-20R; 142; CANR 41;
DLB 6; DLBY 82; MTCW

Dexter, Martin
See Faust, Frederick (Schiller)

Dexter, Pete 1943- . . . . **CLC 34, 55**
See also BEST 89:2; CA 127; 131; MTCW

Diamano, Silmang
See Senghor, Leopold Sedar

Diamond, Neil 1941- . . . . **CLC 30**
See also CA 108

di Bassetto, Corno
See Shaw, George Bernard

Dick, Philip K(indred)
1928-1982 . . . . **CLC 10, 30, 72**
See also CA 49-52; 106; CANR 2, 16;
DLB 8; MTCW

Dickens, Charles (John Huffam)
 1812-1870 ..... **NCLC 3, 8, 18, 26; DA;**
              WLC
 See also CDBLB 1832-1890; DLB 21, 55,
  70; JRDA; MAICYA; SATA 15

Dickey, James (Lafayette)
 1923- .... **CLC 1, 2, 4, 7, 10, 15, 47**
 See also AITN 1, 2; CA 9-12R; CABS 2;
  CANR 10; CDALB 1968-1988; DLB 5;
  DLBD 7; DLBY 82, 93; MTCW

Dickey, William 1928- .... **CLC 3, 28**
 See also CA 9-12R; CANR 24; DLB 5

Dickinson, Charles 1951- .... **CLC 49**
 See also CA 128

Dickinson, Emily (Elizabeth)
 1830-1886 .. **NCLC 21; DA; PC 1; WLC**
 See also CDALB 1865-1917; DLB 1;
  SATA 29

Dickinson, Peter (Malcolm)
 1927- .... **CLC 12, 35**
 See also AAYA 9; CA 41-44R; CANR 31;
  CLR 29; DLB 87; JRDA; MAICYA;
  SATA 5, 62

Dickson, Carr
 See Carr, John Dickson

Dickson, Carter
 See Carr, John Dickson

Didion, Joan 1934- ..... **CLC 1, 3, 8, 14, 32**
 See also AITN 1; CA 5-8R; CANR 14;
  CDALB 1968-1988; DLB 2; DLBY 81,
  86; MTCW

Dietrich, Robert
 See Hunt, E(verette) Howard, Jr.

Dillard, Annie 1945- .... **CLC 9, 60**
 See also AAYA 6; CA 49-52; CANR 3, 43;
  DLBY 80; MTCW; SATA 10

Dillard, R(ichard) H(enry) W(ilde)
 1937- .... **CLC 5**
 See also CA 21-24R; CAAS 7; CANR 10;
  DLB 5

Dillon, Eilis 1920- .... **CLC 17**
 See also CA 9-12R; CAAS 3; CANR 4, 38;
  CLR 26; MAICYA; SATA 2, 74

Dimont, Penelope
 See Mortimer, Penelope (Ruth)

Dinesen, Isak .... **CLC 10, 29; SSC 7**
 See also Blixen, Karen (Christentze
  Dinesen)

Ding Ling .... **CLC 68**
 See also Chiang Pin-chin

Disch, Thomas M(ichael) 1940- ... **CLC 7, 36**
 See also CA 21-24R; CAAS 4; CANR 17,
  36; CLR 18; DLB 8; MAICYA; MTCW;
  SAAS 15; SATA 54

Disch, Tom
 See Disch, Thomas M(ichael)

d'Isly, Georges
 See Simenon, Georges (Jacques Christian)

Disraeli, Benjamin 1804-1881 .. **NCLC 2, 39**
 See also DLB 21, 55

Ditcum, Steve
 See Crumb, R(obert)

Dixon, Paige
 See Corcoran, Barbara

Dixon, Stephen 1936- ..... **CLC 52; SSC 16**
 See also CA 89-92; CANR 17, 40; DLB 130

Dobell, Sydney Thompson
 1824-1874 .... **NCLC 43**
 See also DLB 32

Doblin, Alfred .... **TCLC 13**
 See also Doeblin, Alfred

Dobrolyubov, Nikolai Alexandrovich
 1836-1861 .... **NCLC 5**

Dobyns, Stephen 1941- .... **CLC 37**
 See also CA 45-48; CANR 2, 18

Doctorow, E(dgar) L(aurence)
 1931- ..... **CLC 6, 11, 15, 18, 37, 44, 65**
 See also AITN 2; BEST 89:3; CA 45-48;
  CANR 2, 33; CDALB 1968-1988; DLB 2,
  28; DLBY 80; MTCW

Dodgson, Charles Lutwidge 1832-1898
 See Carroll, Lewis
 See also CLR 2; DA; MAICYA; YABC 2

Dodson, Owen (Vincent)
 1914-1983 .... **CLC 79; BLC**
 See also BW 1; CA 65-68; 110; CANR 24;
  DLB 76

Doeblin, Alfred 1878-1957 .... **TCLC 13**
 See also Doblin, Alfred
 See also CA 110; 141; DLB 66

Doerr, Harriet 1910- .... **CLC 34**
 See also CA 117; 122

Domecq, H(onorio) Bustos
 See Bioy Casares, Adolfo; Borges, Jorge
  Luis

Domini, Rey
 See Lorde, Audre (Geraldine)

Dominique
 See Proust, (Valentin-Louis-George-Eugene-)
  Marcel

Don, A
 See Stephen, Leslie

Donaldson, Stephen R. 1947- .... **CLC 46**
 See also CA 89-92; CANR 13

Donleavy, J(ames) P(atrick)
 1926- .... **CLC 1, 4, 6, 10, 45**
 See also AITN 2; CA 9-12R; CANR 24;
  DLB 6; MTCW

Donne, John
 1572-1631 .... **LC 10, 24; DA; PC 1**
 See also CDBLB Before 1660; DLB 121

Donnell, David 1939(?)- .... **CLC 34**

Donoso (Yanez), Jose
 1924- .... **CLC 4, 8, 11, 32; HLC**
 See also CA 81-84; CANR 32; DLB 113;
  HW; MTCW

Donovan, John 1928-1992 .... **CLC 35**
 See also CA 97-100; 137; CLR 3;
  MAICYA; SATA 29

Don Roberto
 See Cunninghame Graham, R(obert)
  B(ontine)

Doolittle, Hilda
 1886-1961 ..... **CLC 3, 8, 14, 31, 34, 73;**
          DA; PC 5; WLC
 See also H. D.
 See also CA 97-100; CANR 35; DLB 4, 45;
  MTCW

Dorfman, Ariel 1942- ..... **CLC 48, 77; HLC**
 See also CA 124; 130; HW

Dorn, Edward (Merton) 1929- ... **CLC 10, 18**
 See also CA 93-96; CANR 42; DLB 5

Dorsan, Luc
 See Simenon, Georges (Jacques Christian)

Dorsange, Jean
 See Simenon, Georges (Jacques Christian)

Dos Passos, John (Roderigo)
 1896-1970 ...... **CLC 1, 4, 8, 11, 15, 25,**
         34, 82; DA; WLC
 See also CA 1-4R; 29-32R; CANR 3;
  CDALB 1929-1941; DLB 4, 9; DLBD 1;
  MTCW

Dossage, Jean
 See Simenon, Georges (Jacques Christian)

Dostoevsky, Fedor Mikhailovich
 1821-1881 ...... **NCLC 2, 7, 21, 33, 43;**
         DA; SSC 2; WLC

Doughty, Charles M(ontagu)
 1843-1926 .... **TCLC 27**
 See also CA 115; DLB 19, 57

Douglas, Ellen
 See Haxton, Josephine Ayres

Douglas, Gavin 1475(?)-1522 .... **LC 20**

Douglas, Keith 1920-1944 .... **TCLC 40**
 See also DLB 27

Douglas, Leonard
 See Bradbury, Ray (Douglas)

Douglas, Michael
 See Crichton, (John) Michael

Douglass, Frederick
 1817(?)-1895 .... **NCLC 7; BLC; DA;**
            WLC
 See also CDALB 1640-1865; DLB 1, 43, 50,
  79; SATA 29

Dourado, (Waldomiro Freitas) Autran
 1926- .... **CLC 23, 60**
 See also CA 25-28R; CANR 34

Dourado, Waldomiro Autran
 See Dourado, (Waldomiro Freitas) Autran

Dove, Rita (Frances)
 1952- .... **CLC 50, 81; PC 6**
 See also BW 2; CA 109; CAAS 19;
  CANR 27, 42; DLB 120

Dowell, Coleman 1925-1985 .... **CLC 60**
 See also CA 25-28R; 117; CANR 10;
  DLB 130

Dowson, Ernest Christopher
 1867-1900 .... **TCLC 4**
 See also CA 105; DLB 19, 135

Doyle, A. Conan
 See Doyle, Arthur Conan

Doyle, Arthur Conan
 1859-1930 .... **TCLC 7; DA; SSC 12;**
            WLC
 See also CA 104; 122; CDBLB 1890-1914;
  DLB 18, 70; MTCW; SATA 24

Doyle, Conan 1859-1930
 See Doyle, Arthur Conan

Doyle, John
 See Graves, Robert (von Ranke)

Doyle, Roddy 1958(?)- .... **CLC 81**
 See also CA 143

Doyle, Sir A. Conan
  See Doyle, Arthur Conan

Doyle, Sir Arthur Conan
  See Doyle, Arthur Conan

Dr. A
  See Asimov, Isaac; Silverstein, Alvin

Drabble, Margaret
  1939- . . . . **CLC 2, 3, 5, 8, 10, 22, 53**
  See also CA 13-16R; CANR 18, 35;
  CDBLB 1960 to Present; DLB 14;
  MTCW; SATA 48

Drapier, M. B.
  See Swift, Jonathan

Drayham, James
  See Mencken, H(enry) L(ouis)

Drayton, Michael 1563-1631 . . . . **LC 8**

Dreadstone, Carl
  See Campbell, (John) Ramsey

Dreiser, Theodore (Herman Albert)
  1871-1945 . . . . . . **TCLC 10, 18, 35; DA;**
                                              WLC
  See also CA 106; 132; CDALB 1865-1917;
  DLB 9, 12, 102, 137; DLBD 1; MTCW

Drexler, Rosalyn 1926- . . . . **CLC 2, 6**
  See also CA 81-84

Dreyer, Carl Theodor 1889-1968 . . . . **CLC 16**
  See also CA 116

Drieu la Rochelle, Pierre(-Eugene)
  1893-1945 . . . . **TCLC 21**
  See also CA 117; DLB 72

Drop Shot
  See Cable, George Washington

Droste-Hulshoff, Annette Freiin von
  1797-1848 . . . . **NCLC 3**
  See also DLB 133

Drummond, Walter
  See Silverberg, Robert

Drummond, William Henry
  1854-1907 . . . . **TCLC 25**
  See also DLB 92

Drummond de Andrade, Carlos
  1902-1987 . . . . **CLC 18**
  See also Andrade, Carlos Drummond de
  See also CA 132; 123

Drury, Allen (Stuart) 1918- . . . . **CLC 37**
  See also CA 57-60; CANR 18

Dryden, John
  1631-1700 . . . **LC 3, 21; DA; DC 3; WLC**
  See also CDBLB 1660-1789; DLB 80, 101,
  131

Duberman, Martin 1930- . . . . **CLC 8**
  See also CA 1-4R; CANR 2

Dubie, Norman (Evans) 1945- . . . . . . **CLC 36**
  See also CA 69-72; CANR 12; DLB 120

Du Bois, W(illiam) E(dward) B(urghardt)
  1868-1963 . . . . . . **CLC 1, 2, 13, 64; BLC;**
                                              DA; WLC
  See also BW 1; CA 85-88; CANR 34;
  CDALB 1865-1917; DLB 47, 50, 91;
  MTCW; SATA 42

Dubus, Andre 1936- . . . **CLC 13, 36; SSC 15**
  See also CA 21-24R; CANR 17; DLB 130

Duca Minimo
  See D'Annunzio, Gabriele

Ducharme, Rejean 1941- . . . . **CLC 74**
  See also DLB 60

Duclos, Charles Pinot 1704-1772 . . . . . **LC 1**

Dudek, Louis 1918- . . . . **CLC 11, 19**
  See also CA 45-48; CAAS 14; CANR 1;
  DLB 88

Duerrenmatt, Friedrich
  . . . . **CLC 1, 4, 8, 11, 15, 43**
  See also Duerrenmatt, Friedrich
  See also DLB 69, 124

Duerrenmatt, Friedrich
  1921-1990 . . . . . **CLC 1, 4, 8, 11, 15, 43**
  See also Duerrenmatt, Friedrich
  See also CA 17-20R; CANR 33; DLB 69,
  124; MTCW

Duffy, Bruce (?)- . . . . **CLC 50**

Duffy, Maureen 1933- . . . . **CLC 37**
  See also CA 25-28R; CANR 33; DLB 14;
  MTCW

Dugan, Alan 1923- . . . . **CLC 2, 6**
  See also CA 81-84; DLB 5

du Gard, Roger Martin
  See Martin du Gard, Roger

Duhamel, Georges 1884-1966 . . . . **CLC 8**
  See also CA 81-84; 25-28R; CANR 35;
  DLB 65; MTCW

Dujardin, Edouard (Emile Louis)
  1861-1949 . . . . **TCLC 13**
  See also CA 109; DLB 123

Dumas, Alexandre (Davy de la Pailleterie)
  1802-1870 . . . . **NCLC 11; DA; WLC**
  See also DLB 119; SATA 18

Dumas, Alexandre
  1824-1895 . . . . **NCLC 9; DC 1**

Dumas, Claudine
  See Malzberg, Barry N(athaniel)

Dumas, Henry L. 1934-1968 . . . . . **CLC 6, 62**
  See also BW 1; CA 85-88; DLB 41

du Maurier, Daphne
  1907-1989 . . . . **CLC 6, 11, 59**
  See also CA 5-8R; 128; CANR 6; MTCW;
  SATA 27, 60

Dunbar, Paul Laurence
  1872-1906 . . . . . . **TCLC 2, 12; BLC; DA;**
                                  PC 5; SSC 8; WLC
  See also BW 1; CA 104; 124;
  CDALB 1865-1917; DLB 50, 54, 78;
  SATA 34

Dunbar, William 1460(?)-1530(?) . . . . **LC 20**

Duncan, Lois 1934- . . . . **CLC 26**
  See also AAYA 4; CA 1-4R; CANR 2, 23,
  36; CLR 29; JRDA; MAICYA; SAAS 2;
  SATA 1, 36, 75

Duncan, Robert (Edward)
  1919-1988 . . . . **CLC 1, 2, 4, 7, 15, 41, 55;**
                                              PC 2
  See also CA 9-12R; 124; CANR 28; DLB 5,
  16; MTCW

Dunlap, William 1766-1839 . . . . **NCLC 2**
  See also DLB 30, 37, 59

Dunn, Douglas (Eaglesham)
  1942- . . . . **CLC 6, 40**
  See also CA 45-48; CANR 2, 33; DLB 40;
  MTCW

Dunn, Katherine (Karen) 1945- . . . . . **CLC 71**
  See also CA 33-36R

Dunn, Stephen 1939- . . . . **CLC 36**
  See also CA 33-36R; CANR 12; DLB 105

Dunne, Finley Peter 1867-1936 . . . . **TCLC 28**
  See also CA 108; DLB 11, 23

Dunne, John Gregory 1932- . . . . **CLC 28**
  See also CA 25-28R; CANR 14; DLBY 80

Dunsany, Edward John Moreton Drax
  Plunkett 1878-1957
  See Dunsany, Lord
  See also CA 104; DLB 10

Dunsany, Lord . . . . **TCLC 2**
  See also Dunsany, Edward John Moreton
  Drax Plunkett
  See also DLB 77

du Perry, Jean
  See Simenon, Georges (Jacques Christian)

Durang, Christopher (Ferdinand)
  1949- . . . . **CLC 27, 38**
  See also CA 105

Duras, Marguerite
  1914- . . . . . . **CLC 3, 6, 11, 20, 34, 40, 68**
  See also CA 25-28R; DLB 83; MTCW

Durban, (Rosa) Pam 1947- . . . . **CLC 39**
  See also CA 123

Durcan, Paul 1944- . . . . **CLC 43, 70**
  See also CA 134

Durkheim, Emile 1858-1917 . . . . . . **TCLC 55**

Durrell, Lawrence (George)
  1912-1990 . . . . **CLC 1, 4, 6, 8, 13, 27, 41**
  See also CA 9-12R; 132; CANR 40;
  CDBLB 1945-1960; DLB 15, 27;
  DLBY 90; MTCW

Dutt, Toru 1856-1877 . . . . **NCLC 29**

Dwight, Timothy 1752-1817 . . . . . . **NCLC 13**
  See also DLB 37

Dworkin, Andrea 1946- . . . . **CLC 43**
  See also CA 77-80; CANR 16, 39; MTCW

Dwyer, Deanna
  See Koontz, Dean R(ay)

Dwyer, K. R.
  See Koontz, Dean R(ay)

Dylan, Bob 1941- . . . . . . **CLC 3, 4, 6, 12, 77**
  See also CA 41-44R; DLB 16

Eagleton, Terence (Francis) 1943-
  See Eagleton, Terry
  See also CA 57-60; CANR 7, 23; MTCW

Eagleton, Terry . . . . **CLC 63**
  See also Eagleton, Terence (Francis)

Early, Jack
  See Scoppettone, Sandra

East, Michael
  See West, Morris L(anglo)

Eastaway, Edward
  See Thomas, (Philip) Edward

Eastlake, William (Derry) 1917- . . . . . **CLC 8**
  See also CA 5-8R; CAAS 1; CANR 5;
  DLB 6

Eastman, Charles A(lexander)
  1858-1939 . . . . **TCLC 55**
  See also YABC 1

Eberhart, Richard (Ghormley)
1904- .... **CLC 3, 11, 19, 56**
See also CA 1-4R; CANR 2;
CDALB 1941-1968; DLB 48; MTCW

Eberstadt, Fernanda 1960-........ **CLC 39**
See also CA 136

Echegaray (y Eizaguirre), Jose (Maria Waldo)
1832-1916 .... **TCLC 4**
See also CA 104; CANR 32; HW; MTCW

Echeverria, (Jose) Esteban (Antonino)
1805-1851 .... **NCLC 18**

Echo
See Proust, (Valentin-Louis-George-Eugene-)
Marcel

Eckert, Allan W. 1931- .... **CLC 17**
See also CA 13-16R; CANR 14, 45;
SATA 27, 29

Eckhart, Meister 1260(?)-1328(?) .. **CMLC 9**
See also DLB 115

Eckmar, F. R.
See de Hartog, Jan

Eco, Umberto 1932-......... **CLC 28, 60**
See also BEST 90:1; CA 77-80; CANR 12,
33; MTCW

Eddison, E(ric) R(ucker)
1882-1945 .... **TCLC 15**
See also CA 109

Edel, (Joseph) Leon 1907-...... **CLC 29, 34**
See also CA 1-4R; CANR 1, 22; DLB 103

Eden, Emily 1797-1869 .... **NCLC 10**

Edgar, David 1948-.............. **CLC 42**
See also CA 57-60; CANR 12; DLB 13;
MTCW

Edgerton, Clyde (Carlyle) 1944- .... **CLC 39**
See also CA 118; 134

Edgeworth, Maria 1767-1849...... **NCLC 1**
See also DLB 116; SATA 21

Edmonds, Paul
See Kuttner, Henry

Edmonds, Walter D(umaux) 1903- .. **CLC 35**
See also CA 5-8R; CANR 2; DLB 9;
MAICYA; SAAS 4; SATA 1, 27

Edmondson, Wallace
See Ellison, Harlan

Edson, Russell .... **CLC 13**
See also CA 33-36R

Edwards, G(erald) B(asil)
1899-1976 .... **CLC 25**
See also CA 110

Edwards, Gus 1939-.............. **CLC 43**
See also CA 108

Edwards, Jonathan 1703-1758.... **LC 7; DA**
See also DLB 24

Efron, Marina Ivanovna Tsvetaeva
See Tsvetaeva (Efron), Marina (Ivanovna)

Ehle, John (Marsden, Jr.) 1925-.... **CLC 27**
See also CA 9-12R

Ehrenbourg, Ilya (Grigoryevich)
See Ehrenburg, Ilya (Grigoryevich)

Ehrenburg, Ilya (Grigoryevich)
1891-1967 .... **CLC 18, 34, 62**
See also CA 102; 25-28R

Ehrenburg, Ilyo (Grigoryevich)
See Ehrenburg, Ilya (Grigoryevich)

Eich, Guenter 1907-1972 .... **CLC 15**
See also CA 111; 93-96; DLB 69, 124

Eichendorff, Joseph Freiherr von
1788-1857 .... **NCLC 8**
See also DLB 90

Eigner, Larry .... **CLC 9**
See also Eigner, Laurence (Joel)
See also DLB 5

Eigner, Laurence (Joel) 1927-
See Eigner, Larry
See also CA 9-12R; CANR 6

Eiseley, Loren Corey 1907-1977..... **CLC 7**
See also AAYA 5; CA 1-4R; 73-76;
CANR 6

Eisenstadt, Jill 1963-............. **CLC 50**
See also CA 140

Eisner, Simon
See Kornbluth, C(yril) M.

Ekeloef, (Bengt) Gunnar
1907-1968 .... **CLC 27**
See also Ekelof, (Bengt) Gunnar
See also CA 123; 25-28R

Ekelof, (Bengt) Gunnar............. **CLC 27**
See also Ekeloef, (Bengt) Gunnar

Ekwensi, C. O. D.
See Ekwensi, Cyprian (Odiatu Duaka)

Ekwensi, Cyprian (Odiatu Duaka)
1921- .... **CLC 4; BLC**
See also BW 2; CA 29-32R; CANR 18, 42;
DLB 117; MTCW; SATA 66

Elaine....................... **TCLC 18**
See also Leverson, Ada

El Crummo
See Crumb, R(obert)

Elia
See Lamb, Charles

Eliade, Mircea 1907-1986 .... **CLC 19**
See also CA 65-68; 119; CANR 30; MTCW

Eliot, A. D.
See Jewett, (Theodora) Sarah Orne

Eliot, Alice
See Jewett, (Theodora) Sarah Orne

Eliot, Dan
See Silverberg, Robert

Eliot, George
1819-1880 .... **NCLC 4, 13, 23, 41; DA;
WLC**
See also CDBLB 1832-1890; DLB 21, 35, 55

Eliot, John 1604-1690 .... **LC 5**
See also DLB 24

Eliot, T(homas) S(tearns)
1888-1965 ..... **CLC 1, 2, 3, 6, 9, 10, 13,
15, 24, 34, 41, 55, 57; DA; PC 5; WLC 2**
See also CA 5-8R; 25-28R; CANR 41;
CDALB 1929-1941; DLB 7, 10, 45, 63;
DLBY 88; MTCW

Elizabeth 1866-1941............. **TCLC 41**

Elkin, Stanley L(awrence)
1930- ... **CLC 4, 6, 9, 14, 27, 51; SSC 12**
See also CA 9-12R; CANR 8; DLB 2, 28;
DLBY 80; MTCW

Elledge, Scott.................... **CLC 34**

Elliott, Don
See Silverberg, Robert

Elliott, George P(aul) 1918-1980..... **CLC 2**
See also CA 1-4R; 97-100; CANR 2

Elliott, Janice 1931-.............. **CLC 47**
See also CA 13-16R; CANR 8, 29; DLB 14

Elliott, Sumner Locke 1917-1991 ... **CLC 38**
See also CA 5-8R; 134; CANR 2, 21

Elliott, William
See Bradbury, Ray (Douglas)

Ellis, A. E....................... **CLC 7**

Ellis, Alice Thomas............... **CLC 40**
See also Haycraft, Anna

Ellis, Bret Easton 1964-........ **CLC 39, 71**
See also AAYA 2; CA 118; 123

Ellis, (Henry) Havelock
1859-1939 .... **TCLC 14**
See also CA 109

Ellis, Landon
See Ellison, Harlan

Ellis, Trey 1962-................. **CLC 55**

Ellison, Harlan
1934- .... **CLC 1, 13, 42; SSC 14**
See also CA 5-8R; CANR 5; DLB 8;
MTCW

Ellison, Ralph (Waldo)
1914- ...... **CLC 1, 3, 11, 54; BLC; DA;
WLC**
See also BW 1; CA 9-12R; CANR 24;
CDALB 1941-1968; DLB 2, 76; MTCW

Ellmann, Lucy (Elizabeth) 1956-.... **CLC 61**
See also CA 128

Ellmann, Richard (David)
1918-1987 .... **CLC 50**
See also BEST 89:2; CA 1-4R; 122;
CANR 2, 28; DLB 103; DLBY 87;
MTCW

Elman, Richard 1934-............. **CLC 19**
See also CA 17-20R; CAAS 3

Elron
See Hubbard, L(afayette) Ron(ald)

Eluard, Paul..................... **TCLC 7, 41**
See also Grindel, Eugene

Elyot, Sir Thomas 1490(?)-1546..... **LC 11**

Elytis, Odysseus 1911-......... **CLC 15, 49**
See also CA 102; MTCW

Emecheta, (Florence Onye) Buchi
1944- .... **CLC 14, 48; BLC**
See also BW 2; CA 81-84; CANR 27;
DLB 117; MTCW; SATA 66

Emerson, Ralph Waldo
1803-1882 ......**NCLC 1, 38; DA; WLC**
See also CDALB 1640-1865; DLB 1, 59, 73

Eminescu, Mihail 1850-1889 ..... **NCLC 33**

Empson, William
1906-1984 .... **CLC 3, 8, 19, 33, 34**
See also CA 17-20R; 112; CANR 31;
DLB 20; MTCW

Enchi Fumiko (Ueda) 1905-1986.... **CLC 31**
See also CA 129; 121

Ende, Michael (Andreas Helmuth)
1929- .... **CLC 31**
See also CA 118; 124; CANR 36; CLR 14;
DLB 75; MAICYA; SATA 42, 61

Endo, Shusaku 1923-..... **CLC 7, 14, 19, 54**
See also CA 29-32R; CANR 21; MTCW

Engel, Marian 1933-1985......... **CLC 36**
See also CA 25-28R; CANR 12; DLB 53

Engelhardt, Frederick
See Hubbard, L(afayette) Ron(ald)

Enright, D(ennis) J(oseph)
1920-................... **CLC 4, 8, 31**
See also CA 1-4R; CANR 1, 42; DLB 27;
SATA 25

Enzensberger, Hans Magnus
1929-..................... **CLC 43**
See also CA 116; 119

Ephron, Nora 1941-.......... **CLC 17, 31**
See also AITN 2; CA 65-68; CANR 12, 39

Epsilon
See Betjeman, John

Epstein, Daniel Mark 1948-........ **CLC 7**
See also CA 49-52; CANR 2

Epstein, Jacob 1956-............ **CLC 19**
See also CA 114

Epstein, Joseph 1937-............ **CLC 39**
See also CA 112; 119

Epstein, Leslie 1938-............ **CLC 27**
See also CA 73-76; CAAS 12; CANR 23

Equiano, Olaudah
1745(?)-1797............ **LC 16; BLC**
See also DLB 37, 50

Erasmus, Desiderius 1469(?)-1536.... **LC 16**

Erdman, Paul E(mil) 1932-........ **CLC 25**
See also AITN 1; CA 61-64; CANR 13, 43

Erdrich, Louise 1954-......... **CLC 39, 54**
See also AAYA 10; BEST 89:1; CA 114;
CANR 41; MTCW

Erenburg, Ilya (Grigoryevich)
See Ehrenburg, Ilya (Grigoryevich)

Erickson, Stephen Michael 1950-
See Erickson, Steve
See also CA 129

Erickson, Steve................... **CLC 64**
See also Erickson, Stephen Michael

Ericson, Walter
See Fast, Howard (Melvin)

Eriksson, Buntel
See Bergman, (Ernst) Ingmar

Eschenbach, Wolfram von
See Wolfram von Eschenbach

Eseki, Bruno
See Mphahlele, Ezekiel

Esenin, Sergei (Alexandrovich)
1895-1925 .... **TCLC 4**
See also CA 104

Eshleman, Clayton 1935-........... **CLC 7**
See also CA 33-36R; CAAS 6; DLB 5

Espriella, Don Manuel Alvarez
See Southey, Robert

Espriu, Salvador 1913-1985......... **CLC 9**
See also CA 115; DLB 134

Espronceda, Jose de 1808-1842... **NCLC 39**

Esse, James
See Stephens, James

Esterbrook, Tom
See Hubbard, L(afayette) Ron(ald)

Estleman, Loren D. 1952-........ **CLC 48**
See also CA 85-88; CANR 27; MTCW

Eugenides, Jeffrey 1960(?)-........ **CLC 81**
See also CA 144

Euripides c. 485B.C.-406B.C. .... **DC 4**
See also DA

Evan, Evin
See Faust, Frederick (Schiller)

Evans, Evan
See Faust, Frederick (Schiller)

Evans, Marian
See Eliot, George

Evans, Mary Ann
See Eliot, George

Evarts, Esther
See Benson, Sally

Everett, Percival L. 1956-......... **CLC 57**
See also BW 2; CA 129

Everson, R(onald) G(ilmour)
1903-..................... **CLC 27**
See also CA 17-20R; DLB 88

Everson, William (Oliver)
1912-................... **CLC 1, 5, 14**
See also CA 9-12R; CANR 20; DLB 5, 16;
MTCW

Evtushenko, Evgenii Aleksandrovich
See Yevtushenko, Yevgeny (Alexandrovich)

Ewart, Gavin (Buchanan)
1916-................... **CLC 13, 46**
See also CA 89-92; CANR 17; DLB 40;
MTCW

Ewers, Hanns Heinz 1871-1943 ... **TCLC 12**
See also CA 109

Ewing, Frederick R.
See Sturgeon, Theodore (Hamilton)

Exley, Frederick (Earl)
1929-1992 .... **CLC 6, 11**
See also AITN 2; CA 81-84; 138; DLB 143;
DLBY 81

Eynhardt, Guillermo
See Quiroga, Horacio (Sylvestre)

Ezekiel, Nissim 1924-............. **CLC 61**
See also CA 61-64

Ezekiel, Tish O'Dowd 1943-....... **CLC 34**
See also CA 129

Fadeyev, A.
See Bulgya, Alexander Alexandrovich

Fadeyev, Alexander.............. **TCLC 53**
See also Bulgya, Alexander Alexandrovich

Fagen, Donald 1948-............. **CLC 26**

Fainzilberg, Ilya Arnoldovich 1897-1937
See Ilf, Ilya
See also CA 120

Fair, Ronald L. 1932-............. **CLC 18**
See also BW 1; CA 69-72; CANR 25;
DLB 33

Fairbairns, Zoe (Ann) 1948-....... **CLC 32**
See also CA 103; CANR 21

Falco, Gian
See Papini, Giovanni

Falconer, James
See Kirkup, James

Falconer, Kenneth
See Kornbluth, C(yril) M.

Falkland, Samuel
See Heijermans, Herman

Fallaci, Oriana 1930-............. **CLC 11**
See also CA 77-80; CANR 15; MTCW

Faludy, George 1913-............. **CLC 42**
See also CA 21-24R

Faludy, Gyoergy
See Faludy, George

Fanon, Frantz 1925-1961..... **CLC 74; BLC**
See also BW 1; CA 116; 89-92

Fanshawe, Ann .... **LC 11**

Fante, John (Thomas) 1911-1983 ... **CLC 60**
See also CA 69-72; 109; CANR 23;
DLB 130; DLBY 83

Farah, Nuruddin 1945-....... **CLC 53; BLC**
See also BW 2; CA 106; DLB 125

Fargue, Leon-Paul 1876(?)-1947 ... **TCLC 11**
See also CA 109

Farigoule, Louis
See Romains, Jules

Farina, Richard 1936(?)-1966 .... **CLC 9**
See also CA 81-84; 25-28R

Farley, Walter (Lorimer)
1915-1989 .... **CLC 17**
See also CA 17-20R; CANR 8, 29; DLB 22;
JRDA; MAICYA; SATA 2, 43

Farmer, Philip Jose 1918-....... **CLC 1, 19**
See also CA 1-4R; CANR 4, 35; DLB 8;
MTCW

Farquhar, George 1677-1707........ **LC 21**
See also DLB 84

Farrell, J(ames) G(ordon)
1935-1979 .... **CLC 6**
See also CA 73-76; 89-92; CANR 36;
DLB 14; MTCW

Farrell, James T(homas)
1904-1979 .... **CLC 1, 4, 8, 11, 66**
See also CA 5-8R; 89-92; CANR 9; DLB 4,
9, 86; DLBD 2; MTCW

Farren, Richard J.
See Betjeman, John

Farren, Richard M.
See Betjeman, John

Fassbinder, Rainer Werner
1946-1982 .... **CLC 20**
See also CA 93-96; 106; CANR 31

Fast, Howard (Melvin) 1914- ...... **CLC 23**
See also CA 1-4R; CAAS 18; CANR 1, 33;
DLB 9; SATA 7

Faulcon, Robert
See Holdstock, Robert P.

Faulkner, William (Cuthbert)
1897-1962 ..... **CLC 1, 3, 6, 8, 9, 11, 14,
18, 28, 52, 68; DA; SSC 1; WLC**
See also AAYA 7; CA 81-84; CANR 33;
CDALB 1929-1941; DLB 9, 11, 44, 102;
DLBD 2; DLBY 86; MTCW

Fauset, Jessie Redmon
1884(?)-1961 .... **CLC 19, 54; BLC**
See also BW 1; CA 109; DLB 51

Faust, Frederick (Schiller)
1892-1944(?) .... **TCLC 49**
See also CA 108

Author Index

Frye, (Herman) Northrop
1912-1991 . . . . **CLC 24, 70**
See also CA 5-8R; 133; CANR 8, 37;
DLB 67, 68; MTCW

Fuchs, Daniel 1909-1993 . . . . **CLC 8, 22**
See also CA 81-84; 142; CAAS 5;
CANR 40; DLB 9, 26, 28; DLBY 93

Fuchs, Daniel 1934- . . . . **CLC 34**
See also CA 37-40R; CANR 14

Fuentes, Carlos
1928- . . . . . . **CLC 3, 8, 10, 13, 22, 41, 60;**
DA; HLC; WLC
See also AAYA 4; AITN 2; CA 69-72;
CANR 10, 32; DLB 113; HW; MTCW

Fuentes, Gregorio Lopez y
See Lopez y Fuentes, Gregorio

Fugard, (Harold) Athol
1932- . . . . **CLC 5, 9, 14, 25, 40, 80; DC 3**
See also CA 85-88; CANR 32; MTCW

Fugard, Sheila 1932- . . . . **CLC 48**
See also CA 125

Fuller, Charles (H., Jr.)
1939- . . . . **CLC 25; BLC; DC 1**
See also BW 2; CA 108; 112; DLB 38;
MTCW

Fuller, John (Leopold) 1937- . . . . **CLC 62**
See also CA 21-24R; CANR 9, 44; DLB 40

Fuller, Margaret . . . . **NCLC 5**
See also Ossoli, Sarah Margaret (Fuller
marchesa d')

Fuller, Roy (Broadbent)
1912-1991 . . . . **CLC 4, 28**
See also CA 5-8R; 135; CAAS 10; DLB 15,
20

Fulton, Alice 1952- . . . . **CLC 52**
See also CA 116

Furphy, Joseph 1843-1912 . . . . **TCLC 25**

Fussell, Paul 1924- . . . . **CLC 74**
See also BEST 90:1; CA 17-20R; CANR 8,
21, 35; MTCW

Futabatei, Shimei 1864-1909 . . . . . . **TCLC 44**

Futrelle, Jacques 1875-1912 . . . . . . **TCLC 19**
See also CA 113

G. B. S.
See Shaw, George Bernard

Gaboriau, Emile 1835-1873 . . . . . . **NCLC 14**

Gadda, Carlo Emilio 1893-1973 . . . . **CLC 11**
See also CA 89-92

Gaddis, William
1922- . . . . **CLC 1, 3, 6, 8, 10, 19, 43**
See also CA 17-20R; CANR 21; DLB 2;
MTCW

Gaines, Ernest J(ames)
1933- . . . . **CLC 3, 11, 18; BLC**
See also AITN 1; BW 2; CA 9-12R;
CANR 6, 24, 42; CDALB 1968-1988;
DLB 2, 33; DLBY 80; MTCW

Gaitskill, Mary 1954- . . . . **CLC 69**
See also CA 128

Galdos, Benito Perez
See Perez Galdos, Benito

Gale, Zona 1874-1938 . . . . **TCLC 7**
See also CA 105; DLB 9, 78

Galeano, Eduardo (Hughes) 1940- . . . **CLC 72**
See also CA 29-32R; CANR 13, 32; HW

Galiano, Juan Valera y Alcala
See Valera y Alcala-Galiano, Juan

Gallagher, Tess 1943- . . . . **CLC 18, 63; PC 9**
See also CA 106; DLB 120

Gallant, Mavis
1922- . . . . **CLC 7, 18, 38; SSC 5**
See also CA 69-72; CANR 29; DLB 53;
MTCW

Gallant, Roy A(rthur) 1924- . . . . **CLC 17**
See also CA 5-8R; CANR 4, 29; CLR 30;
MAICYA; SATA 4, 68

Gallico, Paul (William) 1897-1976 . . . **CLC 2**
See also AITN 1; CA 5-8R; 69-72;
CANR 23; DLB 9; MAICYA; SATA 13

Gallup, Ralph
See Whitemore, Hugh (John)

Galsworthy, John
1867-1933 . . . . **TCLC 1, 45; DA; WLC 2**
See also CA 104; 141; CDBLB 1890-1914;
DLB 10, 34, 98

Galt, John 1779-1839 . . . . **NCLC 1**
See also DLB 99, 116

Galvin, James 1951- . . . . **CLC 38**
See also CA 108; CANR 26

Gamboa, Federico 1864-1939 . . . . . . **TCLC 36**

Gann, Ernest Kellogg 1910-1991 . . . . **CLC 23**
See also AITN 1; CA 1-4R; 136; CANR 1

Garcia, Cristina 1958- . . . . **CLC 76**
See also CA 141

Garcia Lorca, Federico
1898-1936 . . . . **TCLC 1, 7, 49; DA;**
DC 2; HLC; PC 3; WLC
See also CA 104; 131; DLB 108; HW;
MTCW

Garcia Marquez, Gabriel (Jose)
1928- . . . . **CLC 2, 3, 8, 10, 15, 27, 47, 55;**
DA; HLC; SSC 8; WLC
See also Marquez, Gabriel (Jose) Garcia
See also AAYA 3; BEST 89:1, 90:4;
CA 33-36R; CANR 10, 28; DLB 113;
HW; MTCW

Gard, Janice
See Latham, Jean Lee

Gard, Roger Martin du
See Martin du Gard, Roger

Gardam, Jane 1928- . . . . **CLC 43**
See also CA 49-52; CANR 2, 18, 33;
CLR 12; DLB 14; MAICYA; MTCW;
SAAS 9; SATA 28, 39, 76

Gardner, Herb . . . . **CLC 44**

Gardner, John (Champlin), Jr.
1933-1982 . . . . . **CLC 2, 3, 5, 7, 8, 10, 18,**
28, 34; SSC 7
See also AITN 1; CA 65-68; 107;
CANR 33; DLB 2; DLBY 82; MTCW;
SATA 31, 40

Gardner, John (Edmund) 1926- . . . . . **CLC 30**
See also CA 103; CANR 15; MTCW

Gardner, Noel
See Kuttner, Henry

Gardons, S. S.
See Snodgrass, W(illiam) D(e Witt)

Garfield, Leon 1921- . . . . **CLC 12**
See also AAYA 8; CA 17-20R; CANR 38,
41; CLR 21; JRDA; MAICYA; SATA 1,
32, 76

Garland, (Hannibal) Hamlin
1860-1940 . . . . **TCLC 3**
See also CA 104; DLB 12, 71, 78

Garneau, (Hector de) Saint-Denys
1912-1943 . . . . **TCLC 13**
See also CA 111; DLB 88

Garner, Alan 1934- . . . . **CLC 17**
See also CA 73-76; CANR 15; CLR 20;
MAICYA; MTCW; SATA 18, 69

Garner, Hugh 1913-1979 . . . . **CLC 13**
See also CA 69-72; CANR 31; DLB 68

Garnett, David 1892-1981 . . . . **CLC 3**
See also CA 5-8R; 103; CANR 17; DLB 34

Garos, Stephanie
See Katz, Steve

Garrett, George (Palmer)
1929- . . . . **CLC 3, 11, 51**
See also CA 1-4R; CAAS 5; CANR 1, 42;
DLB 2, 5, 130; DLBY 83

Garrick, David 1717-1779 . . . . **LC 15**
See also DLB 84

Garrigue, Jean 1914-1972 . . . . **CLC 2, 8**
See also CA 5-8R; 37-40R; CANR 20

Garrison, Frederick
See Sinclair, Upton (Beall)

Garth, Will
See Hamilton, Edmond; Kuttner, Henry

Garvey, Marcus (Moziah, Jr.)
1887-1940 . . . . **TCLC 41; BLC**
See also BW 1; CA 120; 124

Gary, Romain . . . . **CLC 25**
See also Kacew, Romain
See also DLB 83

Gascar, Pierre . . . . **CLC 11**
See also Fournier, Pierre

Gascoyne, David (Emery) 1916- . . . . **CLC 45**
See also CA 65-68; CANR 10, 28; DLB 20;
MTCW

Gaskell, Elizabeth Cleghorn
1810-1865 . . . . **NCLC 5**
See also CDBLB 1832-1890; DLB 21, 144

Gass, William H(oward)
1924- . . . **CLC 1, 2, 8, 11, 15, 39; SSC 12**
See also CA 17-20R; CANR 30; DLB 2;
MTCW

Gasset, Jose Ortega y
See Ortega y Gasset, Jose

Gautier, Theophile 1811-1872 . . . . . **NCLC 1**
See also DLB 119

Gawsworth, John
See Bates, H(erbert) E(rnest)

Gaye, Marvin (Penze) 1939-1984 . . . **CLC 26**
See also CA 112

Gebler, Carlo (Ernest) 1954- . . . . **CLC 39**
See also CA 119; 133

Gee, Maggie (Mary) 1948- . . . . **CLC 57**
See also CA 130

Gee, Maurice (Gough) 1931- . . . . **CLC 29**
See also CA 97-100; SATA 46

Gelbart, Larry (Simon)   1923- ...   **CLC 21, 61**
See also CA 73-76; CANR 45

Gelber, Jack   1932- ....   **CLC 1, 6, 14, 79**
See also CA 1-4R; CANR 2; DLB 7

Gellhorn, Martha (Ellis)   1908- ..   **CLC 14, 60**
See also CA 77-80; CANR 44; DLBY 82

Genet, Jean
1910-1986 ...   **CLC 1, 2, 5, 10, 14, 44, 46**
See also CA 13-16R; CANR 18; DLB 72;
DLBY 86; MTCW

Gent, Peter   1942- ....   **CLC 29**
See also AITN 1; CA 89-92; DLBY 82

Gentlewoman in New England, A
See Bradstreet, Anne

Gentlewoman in Those Parts, A
See Bradstreet, Anne

George, Jean Craighead   1919- .....   **CLC 35**
See also AAYA 8; CA 5-8R; CANR 25;
CLR 1; DLB 52; JRDA; MAICYA;
SATA 2, 68

George, Stefan (Anton)
1868-1933 ....   **TCLC 2, 14**
See also CA 104

Georges, Georges Martin
See Simenon, Georges (Jacques Christian)

Gerhardi, William Alexander
See Gerhardie, William Alexander

Gerhardie, William Alexander
1895-1977 ....   **CLC 5**
See also CA 25-28R; 73-76; CANR 18;
DLB 36

Gerstler, Amy   1956- ....   **CLC 70**

Gertler, T. ....   **CLC 34**
See also CA 116; 121

Ghalib   1797-1869 ....   **NCLC 39**

Ghelderode, Michel de
1898-1962 ....   **CLC 6, 11**
See also CA 85-88; CANR 40

Ghiselin, Brewster   1903- ....   **CLC 23**
See also CA 13-16R; CAAS 10; CANR 13

Ghose, Zulfikar   1935- ....   **CLC 42**
See also CA 65-68

Ghosh, Amitav   1956- ....   **CLC 44**

Giacosa, Giuseppe   1847-1906 ......   **TCLC 7**
See also CA 104

Gibb, Lee
See Waterhouse, Keith (Spencer)

Gibbon, Lewis Grassic ....   **TCLC 4**
See also Mitchell, James Leslie

Gibbons, Kaye   1960- ....   **CLC 50**

Gibran, Kahlil
1883-1931 ....   **TCLC 1, 9; PC 9**
See also CA 104

Gibson, William   1914- ....   **CLC 23; DA**
See also CA 9-12R; CANR 9, 42; DLB 7;
SATA 66

Gibson, William (Ford)   1948- ...   **CLC 39, 63**
See also AAYA 12; CA 126; 133

Gide, Andre (Paul Guillaume)
1869-1951 ....   **TCLC 5, 12, 36; DA;**
SSC 13; WLC
See also CA 104; 124; DLB 65; MTCW

Gifford, Barry (Colby)   1946- ....   **CLC 34**
See also CA 65-68; CANR 9, 30, 40

Gilbert, W(illiam) S(chwenck)
1836-1911 ....   **TCLC 3**
See also CA 104; SATA 36

Gilbreth, Frank B., Jr.   1911- ....   **CLC 17**
See also CA 9-12R; SATA 2

Gilchrist, Ellen   1935- ..   **CLC 34, 48; SSC 14**
See also CA 113; 116; CANR 41; DLB 130;
MTCW

Giles, Molly   1942- ....   **CLC 39**
See also CA 126

Gill, Patrick
See Creasey, John

Gilliam, Terry (Vance)   1940- ....   **CLC 21**
See also Monty Python
See also CA 108; 113; CANR 35

Gillian, Jerry
See Gilliam, Terry (Vance)

Gilliatt, Penelope (Ann Douglass)
1932-1993 ....   **CLC 2, 10, 13, 53**
See also AITN 2; CA 13-16R; 141; DLB 14

Gilman, Charlotte (Anna) Perkins (Stetson)
1860-1935 ....   **TCLC 9, 37; SSC 13**
See also CA 106

Gilmour, David   1949- ....   **CLC 35**
See also Pink Floyd
See also CA 138

Gilpin, William   1724-1804 ......   **NCLC 30**

Gilray, J. D.
See Mencken, H(enry) L(ouis)

Gilroy, Frank D(aniel)   1925- ....   **CLC 2**
See also CA 81-84; CANR 32; DLB 7

Ginsberg, Allen
1926- ....   **CLC 1, 2, 3, 4, 6, 13, 36, 69;**
DA; PC 4; WLC 3
See also AITN 1; CA 1-4R; CANR 2, 41;
CDALB 1941-1968; DLB 5, 16; MTCW

Ginzburg, Natalia
1916-1991 ....   **CLC 5, 11, 54, 70**
See also CA 85-88; 135; CANR 33; MTCW

Giono, Jean   1895-1970 ....   **CLC 4, 11**
See also CA 45-48; 29-32R; CANR 2, 35;
DLB 72; MTCW

Giovanni, Nikki
1943- ....   **CLC 2, 4, 19, 64; BLC; DA**
See also AITN 1; BW 2; CA 29-32R;
CAAS 6; CANR 18, 41; CLR 6; DLB 5,
41; MAICYA; MTCW; SATA 24

Giovene, Andrea   1904- ....   **CLC 7**
See also CA 85-88

Gippius, Zinaida (Nikolayevna)   1869-1945
See Hippius, Zinaida
See also CA 106

Giraudoux, (Hippolyte) Jean
1882-1944 ....   **TCLC 2, 7**
See also CA 104; DLB 65

Gironella, Jose Maria   1917- ....   **CLC 11**
See also CA 101

Gissing, George (Robert)
1857-1903 ....   **TCLC 3, 24, 47**
See also CA 105; DLB 18, 135

Giurlani, Aldo
See Palazzeschi, Aldo

Gladkov, Fyodor (Vasilyevich)
1883-1958 ....   **TCLC 27**

Glanville, Brian (Lester)   1931- ......   **CLC 6**
See also CA 5-8R; CAAS 9; CANR 3;
DLB 15, 139; SATA 42

Glasgow, Ellen (Anderson Gholson)
1873(?)-1945 ....   **TCLC 2, 7**
See also CA 104; DLB 9, 12

Glaspell, Susan (Keating)
1882(?)-1948 ....   **TCLC 55**
See also CA 110; DLB 7, 9, 78; YABC 2

Glassco, John   1909-1981 ....   **CLC 9**
See also CA 13-16R; 102; CANR 15;
DLB 68

Glasscock, Amnesia
See Steinbeck, John (Ernst)

Glasser, Ronald J.   1940(?)- ....   **CLC 37**

Glassman, Joyce
See Johnson, Joyce

Glendinning, Victoria   1937- ....   **CLC 50**
See also CA 120; 127

Glissant, Edouard   1928- ....   **CLC 10, 68**

Gloag, Julian   1930- ....   **CLC 40**
See also AITN 1; CA 65-68; CANR 10

Glowacki, Aleksander   1845-1912
See Prus, Boleslaw

Gluck, Louise (Elisabeth)
1943- ....   **CLC 7, 22, 44, 81**
See also Glueck, Louise
See also CA 33-36R; CANR 40; DLB 5

Glueck, Louise.................   **CLC 7, 22**
See also Gluck, Louise (Elisabeth)
See also DLB 5

Gobineau, Joseph Arthur (Comte) de
1816-1882 ....   **NCLC 17**
See also DLB 123

Godard, Jean-Luc   1930- ....   **CLC 20**
See also CA 93-96

Godden, (Margaret) Rumer   1907- ...   **CLC 53**
See also AAYA 6; CA 5-8R; CANR 4, 27,
36; CLR 20; MAICYA; SAAS 12;
SATA 3, 36

Godoy Alcayaga, Lucila   1889-1957
See Mistral, Gabriela
See also BW 2; CA 104; 131; HW; MTCW

Godwin, Gail (Kathleen)
1937- ....   **CLC 5, 8, 22, 31, 69**
See also CA 29-32R; CANR 15, 43; DLB 6;
MTCW

Godwin, William   1756-1836 ......   **NCLC 14**
See also CDBLB 1789-1832; DLB 39, 104,
142

Goethe, Johann Wolfgang von
1749-1832 ....   **NCLC 4, 22, 34; DA;**
PC 5; WLC 3
See also DLB 94

Gogarty, Oliver St. John
1878-1957 ....   **TCLC 15**
See also CA 109; DLB 15, 19

Gogol, Nikolai (Vasilyevich)
1809-1852 ....   **NCLC 5, 15, 31; DA;**
DC 1; SSC 4; WLC

Goines, Donald
1937(?)-1974 . . . . CLC 80; BLC
See also AITN 1; BW 1; CA 124; 114;
DLB 33

Gold, Herbert   1924- . . . . CLC 4, 7, 14, 42
See also CA 9-12R; CANR 17, 45; DLB 2;
DLBY 81

Goldbarth, Albert   1948- . . . . CLC 5, 38
See also CA 53-56; CANR 6, 40; DLB 120

Goldberg, Anatol   1910-1982 . . . . CLC 34
See also CA 131; 117

Goldemberg, Isaac   1945- . . . . CLC 52
See also CA 69-72; CAAS 12; CANR 11,
32; HW

Golding, William (Gerald)
1911-1993 . . . . CLC 1, 2, 3, 8, 10, 17, 27,
58, 81; DA; WLC
See also AAYA 5; CA 5-8R; 141;
CANR 13, 33; CDBLB 1945-1960;
DLB 15, 100; MTCW

Goldman, Emma   1869-1940 . . . . . . TCLC 13
See also CA 110

Goldman, Francisco   1955- . . . . CLC 76

Goldman, William (W.)   1931- . . . . CLC 1, 48
See also CA 9-12R; CANR 29; DLB 44

Goldmann, Lucien   1913-1970 . . . . . . CLC 24
See also CA 25-28; CAP 2

Goldoni, Carlo   1707-1793 . . . . LC 4

Goldsberry, Steven   1949- . . . . CLC 34
See also CA 131

Goldsmith, Oliver
1728-1774 . . . . LC 2; DA; WLC
See also CDBLB 1660-1789; DLB 39, 89,
104, 109, 142; SATA 26

Goldsmith, Peter
See Priestley, J(ohn) B(oynton)

Gombrowicz, Witold
1904-1969 . . . . CLC 4, 7, 11, 49
See also CA 19-20; 25-28R; CAP 2

Gomez de la Serna, Ramon
1888-1963 . . . . CLC 9
See also CA 116; HW

Goncharov, Ivan Alexandrovich
1812-1891 . . . . NCLC 1

Goncourt, Edmond (Louis Antoine Huot) de
1822-1896 . . . . NCLC 7
See also DLB 123

Goncourt, Jules (Alfred Huot) de
1830-1870 . . . . NCLC 7
See also DLB 123

Gontier, Fernande   19(?)- . . . . CLC 50

Goodman, Paul   1911-1972 . . . . CLC 1, 2, 4, 7
See also CA 19-20; 37-40R; CANR 34;
CAP 2; DLB 130; MTCW

Gordimer, Nadine
1923- . . . . CLC 3, 5, 7, 10, 18, 33, 51, 70;
DA
See also CA 5-8R; CANR 3, 28; MTCW

Gordon, Adam Lindsay
1833-1870 . . . . NCLC 21

Gordon, Caroline
1895-1981 . . . CLC 6, 13, 29, 83; SSC 15
See also CA 11-12; 103; CANR 36; CAP 1;
DLB 4, 9, 102; DLBY 81; MTCW

Gordon, Charles William   1860-1937
See Connor, Ralph
See also CA 109

Gordon, Mary (Catherine)
1949- . . . . CLC 13, 22
See also CA 102; CANR 44; DLB 6;
DLBY 81; MTCW

Gordon, Sol   1923- . . . . CLC 26
See also CA 53-56; CANR 4; SATA 11

Gordone, Charles   1925- . . . . CLC 1, 4
See also BW 1; CA 93-96; DLB 7; MTCW

Gorenko, Anna Andreevna
See Akhmatova, Anna

Gorky, Maxim . . . . TCLC 8; WLC
See also Peshkov, Alexei Maximovich

Goryan, Sirak
See Saroyan, William

Gosse, Edmund (William)
1849-1928 . . . . TCLC 28
See also CA 117; DLB 57, 144

Gotlieb, Phyllis Fay (Bloom)
1926- . . . . CLC 18
See also CA 13-16R; CANR 7; DLB 88

Gottesman, S. D.
See Kornbluth, C(yril) M.; Pohl, Frederik

Gottfried von Strassburg
fl. c. 1210- . . . . CMLC 10
See also DLB 138

Gould, Lois . . . . CLC 4, 10
See also CA 77-80; CANR 29; MTCW

Gourmont, Remy de   1858-1915 . . . . TCLC 17
See also CA 109

Govier, Katherine   1948- . . . . CLC 51
See also CA 101; CANR 18, 40

Goyen, (Charles) William
1915-1983 . . . . CLC 5, 8, 14, 40
See also AITN 2; CA 5-8R; 110; CANR 6;
DLB 2; DLBY 83

Goytisolo, Juan
1931- . . . . CLC 5, 10, 23; HLC
See also CA 85-88; CANR 32; HW; MTCW

Gozzano, Guido   1883-1916 . . . . PC 10
See also DLB 114

Gozzi, (Conte) Carlo   1720-1806 . . NCLC 23

Grabbe, Christian Dietrich
1801-1836 . . . . NCLC 2
See also DLB 133

Grace, Patricia   1937- . . . . CLC 56

Gracian y Morales, Baltasar
1601-1658 . . . . LC 15

Gracq, Julien . . . . CLC 11, 48
See also Poirier, Louis
See also DLB 83

Grade, Chaim   1910-1982 . . . . CLC 10
See also CA 93-96; 107

Graduate of Oxford, A
See Ruskin, John

Graham, John
See Phillips, David Graham

Graham, Jorie   1951- . . . . CLC 48
See also CA 111; DLB 120

Graham, R(obert) B(ontine) Cunninghame
See Cunninghame Graham, R(obert)
B(ontine)
See also DLB 98, 135

Graham, Robert
See Haldeman, Joe (William)

Graham, Tom
See Lewis, (Harry) Sinclair

Graham, W(illiam) S(ydney)
1918-1986 . . . . CLC 29
See also CA 73-76; 118; DLB 20

Graham, Winston (Mawdsley)
1910- . . . . CLC 23
See also CA 49-52; CANR 2, 22, 45;
DLB 77

Grant, Skeeter
See Spiegelman, Art

Granville-Barker, Harley
1877-1946 . . . . TCLC 2
See also Barker, Harley Granville
See also CA 104

Grass, Guenter (Wilhelm)
1927- . . . . . CLC 1, 2, 4, 6, 11, 15, 22, 32,
49; DA; WLC
See also CA 13-16R; CANR 20; DLB 75,
124; MTCW

Gratton, Thomas
See Hulme, T(homas) E(rnest)

Grau, Shirley Ann
1929- . . . . CLC 4, 9; SSC 15
See also CA 89-92; CANR 22; DLB 2;
MTCW

Gravel, Fern
See Hall, James Norman

Graver, Elizabeth   1964- . . . . CLC 70
See also CA 135

Graves, Richard Perceval   1945- . . . . CLC 44
See also CA 65-68; CANR 9, 26

Graves, Robert (von Ranke)
1895-1985 . . . . . . CLC 1, 2, 6, 11, 39, 44,
45; PC 6
See also CA 5-8R; 117; CANR 5, 36;
CDBLB 1914-1945; DLB 20, 100;
DLBY 85; MTCW; SATA 45

Gray, Alasdair   1934- . . . . CLC 41
See also CA 126; MTCW

Gray, Amlin   1946- . . . . CLC 29
See also CA 138

Gray, Francine du Plessix   1930- . . . . CLC 22
See also BEST 90:3; CA 61-64; CAAS 2;
CANR 11, 33; MTCW

Gray, John (Henry)   1866-1934 . . . . TCLC 19
See also CA 119

Gray, Simon (James Holliday)
1936- . . . . CLC 9, 14, 36
See also AITN 1; CA 21-24R; CAAS 3;
CANR 32; DLB 13; MTCW

Gray, Spalding   1941- . . . . CLC 49
See also CA 128

Gray, Thomas
1716-1771 . . . . . . LC 4; DA; PC 2; WLC
See also CDBLB 1660-1789; DLB 109

Grayson, David
See Baker, Ray Stannard

Grayson, Richard (A.) 1951- . . . . **CLC 38**
See also CA 85-88; CANR 14, 31

Greeley, Andrew M(oran) 1928- . . . . **CLC 28**
See also CA 5-8R; CAAS 7; CANR 7, 43;
MTCW

Green, Brian
See Card, Orson Scott

Green, Hannah
See Greenberg, Joanne (Goldenberg)

Green, Hannah . . . . **CLC 3**
See also CA 73-76

Green, Henry . . . . **CLC 2, 13**
See also Yorke, Henry Vincent
See also DLB 15

Green, Julian (Hartridge) 1900-
See Green, Julien
See also CA 21-24R; CANR 33; DLB 4, 72;
MTCW

Green, Julien . . . . **CLC 3, 11, 77**
See also Green, Julian (Hartridge)

Green, Paul (Eliot) 1894-1981 . . . . . . **CLC 25**
See also AITN 1; CA 5-8R; 103; CANR 3;
DLB 7, 9; DLBY 81

Greenberg, Ivan 1908-1973
See Rahv, Philip
See also CA 85-88

Greenberg, Joanne (Goldenberg)
1932- . . . . **CLC 7, 30**
See also AAYA 12; CA 5-8R; CANR 14,
32; SATA 25

Greenberg, Richard 1959(?)- . . . . **CLC 57**
See also CA 138

Greene, Bette 1934- . . . . **CLC 30**
See also AAYA 7; CA 53-56; CANR 4;
CLR 2; JRDA; MAICYA; SAAS 16;
SATA 8

Greene, Gael . . . . **CLC 8**
See also CA 13-16R; CANR 10

Greene, Graham
1904-1991 . . . . **CLC 1, 3, 6, 9, 14, 18, 27,
37, 70, 72; DA; WLC**
See also AITN 2; CA 13-16R; 133;
CANR 35; CDBLB 1945-1960; DLB 13,
15, 77, 100; DLBY 91; MTCW; SATA 20

Greer, Richard
See Silverberg, Robert

Greer, Richard
See Silverberg, Robert

Gregor, Arthur 1923- . . . . **CLC 9**
See also CA 25-28R; CAAS 10; CANR 11;
SATA 36

Gregor, Lee
See Pohl, Frederik

Gregory, Isabella Augusta (Persse)
1852-1932 . . . . **TCLC 1**
See also CA 104; DLB 10

Gregory, J. Dennis
See Williams, John A(lfred)

Grendon, Stephen
See Derleth, August (William)

Grenville, Kate 1950- . . . . **CLC 61**
See also CA 118

Grenville, Pelham
See Wodehouse, P(elham) G(renville)

Greve, Felix Paul (Berthold Friedrich)
1879-1948
See Grove, Frederick Philip
See also CA 104; 141

Grey, Zane 1872-1939 . . . . **TCLC 6**
See also CA 104; 132; DLB 9; MTCW

Grieg, (Johan) Nordahl (Brun)
1902-1943 . . . . **TCLC 10**
See also CA 107

Grieve, C(hristopher) M(urray)
1892-1978 . . . . **CLC 11, 19**
See also MacDiarmid, Hugh
See also CA 5-8R; 85-88; CANR 33;
MTCW

Griffin, Gerald 1803-1840 . . . . **NCLC 7**

Griffin, John Howard 1920-1980 . . . . **CLC 68**
See also AITN 1; CA 1-4R; 101; CANR 2

Griffin, Peter . . . . **CLC 39**

Griffiths, Trevor 1935- . . . . **CLC 13, 52**
See also CA 97-100; CANR 45; DLB 13

Grigson, Geoffrey (Edward Harvey)
1905-1985 . . . . **CLC 7, 39**
See also CA 25-28R; 118; CANR 20, 33;
DLB 27; MTCW

Grillparzer, Franz 1791-1872 . . . . . . **NCLC 1**
See also DLB 133

Grimble, Reverend Charles James
See Eliot, T(homas) S(tearns)

Grimke, Charlotte L(ottie) Forten
1837(?)-1914
See Forten, Charlotte L.
See also BW 1; CA 117; 124

Grimm, Jacob Ludwig Karl
1785-1863 . . . . **NCLC 3**
See also DLB 90; MAICYA; SATA 22

Grimm, Wilhelm Karl 1786-1859 . . **NCLC 3**
See also DLB 90; MAICYA; SATA 22

**Grimmelshausen, Johann Jakob Christoffel
von** 1621-1676 . . . . **LC 6**

Grindel, Eugene 1895-1952
See Eluard, Paul
See also CA 104

Grisham, John 1955(?)- . . . . **CLC 84**
See also CA 138

Grossman, David 1954- . . . . **CLC 67**
See also CA 138

Grossman, Vasily (Semenovich)
1905-1964 . . . . **CLC 41**
See also CA 124; 130; MTCW

Grove, Frederick Philip . . . . **TCLC 4**
See also Greve, Felix Paul (Berthold
Friedrich)
See also DLB 92

Grubb
See Crumb, R(obert)

Grumbach, Doris (Isaac)
1918- . . . . **CLC 13, 22, 64**
See also CA 5-8R; CAAS 2; CANR 9, 42

Grundtvig, Nicolai Frederik Severin
1783-1872 . . . . **NCLC 1**

Grunge
See Crumb, R(obert)

Grunwald, Lisa 1959- . . . . **CLC 44**
See also CA 120

Guare, John 1938- . . . . **CLC 8, 14, 29, 67**
See also CA 73-76; CANR 21; DLB 7;
MTCW

Gudjonsson, Halldor Kiljan 1902-
See Laxness, Halldor
See also CA 103

Guenter, Erich
See Eich, Guenter

Guest, Barbara 1920- . . . . **CLC 34**
See also CA 25-28R; CANR 11, 44; DLB 5

Guest, Judith (Ann) 1936- . . . . **CLC 8, 30**
See also AAYA 7; CA 77-80; CANR 15;
MTCW

Guild, Nicholas M. 1944- . . . . **CLC 33**
See also CA 93-96

Guillemin, Jacques
See Sartre, Jean-Paul

Guillen, Jorge 1893-1984 . . . . **CLC 11**
See also CA 89-92; 112; DLB 108; HW

Guillen (y Batista), Nicolas (Cristobal)
1902-1989 . . . . . **CLC 48, 79; BLC; HLC**
See also BW 2; CA 116; 125; 129; HW

Guillevic, (Eugene) 1907- . . . . **CLC 33**
See also CA 93-96

Guillois
See Desnos, Robert

Guiney, Louise Imogen
1861-1920 . . . . **TCLC 41**
See also DLB 54

Guiraldes, Ricardo (Guillermo)
1886-1927 . . . . **TCLC 39**
See also CA 131; HW; MTCW

Gunn, Bill . . . . **CLC 5**
See also Gunn, William Harrison
See also DLB 38

Gunn, Thom(son William)
1929- . . . . **CLC 3, 6, 18, 32, 81**
See also CA 17-20R; CANR 9, 33;
CDBLB 1960 to Present; DLB 27;
MTCW

Gunn, William Harrison 1934(?)-1989
See Gunn, Bill
See also AITN 1; BW 1; CA 13-16R; 128;
CANR 12, 25

Gunnars, Kristjana 1948- . . . . **CLC 69**
See also CA 113; DLB 60

Gurganus, Allan 1947- . . . . **CLC 70**
See also BEST 90:1; CA 135

Gurney, A(lbert) R(amsdell), Jr.
1930- . . . . **CLC 32, 50, 54**
See also CA 77-80; CANR 32

Gurney, Ivor (Bertie) 1890-1937 . . . **TCLC 33**

Gurney, Peter
See Gurney, A(lbert) R(amsdell), Jr.

Gustafson, Ralph (Barker) 1909- . . . . **CLC 36**
See also CA 21-24R; CANR 8, 45; DLB 88

Gut, Gom
See Simenon, Georges (Jacques Christian)

Guthrie, A(lfred) B(ertram), Jr.
1901-1991 . . . . **CLC 23**
See also CA 57-60; 134; CANR 24; DLB 6;
SATA 62; SATA-Obit 67

Guthrie, Isobel
See Grieve, C(hristopher) M(urray)

Henderson, Sylvia
See Ashton-Warner, Sylvia (Constance)

Henley, Beth . . . . **CLC 23**
See also Henley, Elizabeth Becker
See also CABS 3; DLBY 86

Henley, Elizabeth Becker 1952-
See Henley, Beth
See also CA 107; CANR 32; MTCW

Henley, William Ernest
1849-1903 . . . . **TCLC 8**
See also CA 105; DLB 19

Hennissart, Martha
See Lathen, Emma
See also CA 85-88

Henry, O. . . . . **TCLC 1, 19; SSC 5; WLC**
See also Porter, William Sydney

Henry, Patrick 1736-1799 . . . . **LC 25**

Henryson, Robert 1430(?)-1506(?). . . . **LC 20**

Henry VIII 1491-1547. . . . . **LC 10**

Henschke, Alfred
See Klabund

Hentoff, Nat(han Irving) 1925- . . . . . **CLC 26**
See also AAYA 4; CA 1-4R; CAAS 6;
CANR 5, 25; CLR 1; JRDA; MAICYA;
SATA 27, 42, 69

Heppenstall, (John) Rayner
1911-1981 . . . . **CLC 10**
See also CA 1-4R; 103; CANR 29

Herbert, Frank (Patrick)
1920-1986 . . . . **CLC 12, 23, 35, 44**
See also CA 53-56; 118; CANR 5, 43;
DLB 8; MTCW; SATA 9, 37, 47

Herbert, George 1593-1633 . . . . **LC 24; PC 4**
See also CDBLB Before 1660; DLB 126

Herbert, Zbigniew 1924- . . . . **CLC 9, 43**
See also CA 89-92; CANR 36; MTCW

Herbst, Josephine (Frey)
1897-1969 . . . . **CLC 34**
See also CA 5-8R; 25-28R; DLB 9

Hergesheimer, Joseph
1880-1954 . . . . **TCLC 11**
See also CA 109; DLB 102, 9

Herlihy, James Leo 1927-1993 . . . . . . **CLC 6**
See also CA 1-4R; 143; CANR 2

Hermogenes fl. c. 175- . . . . **CMLC 6**

Hernandez, Jose 1834-1886 . . . . . . **NCLC 17**

Herrick, Robert
1591-1674 . . . . **LC 13; DA; PC 9**
See also DLB 126

Herring, Guilles
See Somerville, Edith

Herriot, James 1916- . . . . **CLC 12**
See also Wight, James Alfred
See also AAYA 1; CANR 40

Herrmann, Dorothy 1941- . . . . **CLC 44**
See also CA 107

Herrmann, Taffy
See Herrmann, Dorothy

Hersey, John (Richard)
1914-1993 . . . . **CLC 1, 2, 7, 9, 40, 81**
See also CA 17-20R; 140; CANR 33;
DLB 6; MTCW; SATA 25;
SATA-Obit 76

Herzen, Aleksandr Ivanovich
1812-1870 . . . . **NCLC 10**

Herzl, Theodor 1860-1904 . . . . **TCLC 36**

Herzog, Werner 1942- . . . . **CLC 16**
See also CA 89-92

Hesiod c. 8th cent. B.C.- . . . . **CMLC 5**

Hesse, Hermann
1877-1962 . . . . **CLC 1, 2, 3, 6, 11, 17, 25,
69; DA; SSC 9; WLC**
See also CA 17-18; CAP 2; DLB 66;
MTCW; SATA 50

Hewes, Cady
See De Voto, Bernard (Augustine)

Heyen, William 1940- . . . . **CLC 13, 18**
See also CA 33-36R; CAAS 9; DLB 5

Heyerdahl, Thor 1914- . . . . **CLC 26**
See also CA 5-8R; CANR 5, 22; MTCW;
SATA 2, 52

Heym, Georg (Theodor Franz Arthur)
1887-1912 . . . . **TCLC 9**
See also CA 106

Heym, Stefan 1913- . . . . **CLC 41**
See also CA 9-12R; CANR 4; DLB 69

Heyse, Paul (Johann Ludwig von)
1830-1914 . . . . **TCLC 8**
See also CA 104; DLB 129

Hibbert, Eleanor Alice Burford
1906-1993 . . . . **CLC 7**
See also BEST 90:4; CA 17-20R; 140;
CANR 9, 28; SATA 2; SATA-Obit 74

Higgins, George V(incent)
1939- . . . . **CLC 4, 7, 10, 18**
See also CA 77-80; CAAS 5; CANR 17;
DLB 2; DLBY 81; MTCW

Higginson, Thomas Wentworth
1823-1911 . . . . **TCLC 36**
See also DLB 1, 64

Highet, Helen
See MacInnes, Helen (Clark)

Highsmith, (Mary) Patricia
1921- . . . . **CLC 2, 4, 14, 42**
See also CA 1-4R; CANR 1, 20; MTCW

Highwater, Jamake (Mamake)
1942(?)- . . . . **CLC 12**
See also AAYA 7; CA 65-68; CAAS 7;
CANR 10, 34; CLR 17; DLB 52;
DLBY 85; JRDA; MAICYA; SATA 30,
32, 69

Hijuelos, Oscar 1951- . . . . . . **CLC 65; HLC**
See also BEST 90:1; CA 123; HW

Hikmet, Nazim 1902(?)-1963 . . . . **CLC 40**
See also CA 141; 93-96

Hildesheimer, Wolfgang
1916-1991 . . . . **CLC 49**
See also CA 101; 135; DLB 69, 124

Hill, Geoffrey (William)
1932- . . . . **CLC 5, 8, 18, 45**
See also CA 81-84; CANR 21;
CDBLB 1960 to Present; DLB 40;
MTCW

Hill, George Roy 1921- . . . . **CLC 26**
See also CA 110; 122

Hill, John
See Koontz, Dean R(ay)

Hill, Susan (Elizabeth) 1942- . . . . **CLC 4**
See also CA 33-36R; CANR 29; DLB 14,
139; MTCW

Hillerman, Tony 1925- . . . . **CLC 62**
See also AAYA 6; BEST 89:1; CA 29-32R;
CANR 21, 42; SATA 6

Hillesum, Etty 1914-1943 . . . . **TCLC 49**
See also CA 137

Hilliard, Noel (Harvey) 1929- . . . . . . **CLC 15**
See also CA 9-12R; CANR 7

Hillis, Rick 1956- . . . . **CLC 66**
See also CA 134

Hilton, James 1900-1954 . . . . **TCLC 21**
See also CA 108; DLB 34, 77; SATA 34

Himes, Chester (Bomar)
1909-1984 . . . . **CLC 2, 4, 7, 18, 58; BLC**
See also BW 2; CA 25-28R; 114; CANR 22;
DLB 2, 76, 143; MTCW

Hinde, Thomas . . . . **CLC 6, 11**
See also Chitty, Thomas Willes

Hindin, Nathan
See Bloch, Robert (Albert)

Hine, (William) Daryl 1936- . . . . **CLC 15**
See also CA 1-4R; CAAS 15; CANR 1, 20;
DLB 60

Hinkson, Katharine Tynan
See Tynan, Katharine

Hinton, S(usan) E(loise)
1950- . . . . **CLC 30; DA**
See also AAYA 2; CA 81-84; CANR 32;
CLR 3, 23; JRDA; MAICYA; MTCW;
SATA 19, 58

Hippius, Zinaida . . . . **TCLC 9**
See also Gippius, Zinaida (Nikolayevna)

Hiraoka, Kimitake 1925-1970
See Mishima, Yukio
See also CA 97-100; 29-32R; MTCW

Hirsch, E(ric) D(onald), Jr. 1928- . . . **CLC 79**
See also CA 25-28R; CANR 27; DLB 67;
MTCW

Hirsch, Edward 1950- . . . . **CLC 31, 50**
See also CA 104; CANR 20, 42; DLB 120

Hitchcock, Alfred (Joseph)
1899-1980 . . . . **CLC 16**
See also CA 97-100; SATA 24, 27

Hitler, Adolf 1889-1945 . . . . **TCLC 53**
See also CA 117

Hoagland, Edward 1932- . . . . **CLC 28**
See also CA 1-4R; CANR 2, 31; DLB 6;
SATA 51

Hoban, Russell (Conwell) 1925- . . **CLC 7, 25**
See also CA 5-8R; CANR 23, 37; CLR 3;
DLB 52; MAICYA; MTCW; SATA 1,
40, 78

Hobbs, Perry
See Blackmur, R(ichard) P(almer)

Hobson, Laura Z(ametkin)
1900-1986 . . . . **CLC 7, 25**
See also CA 17-20R; 118; DLB 28;
SATA 52

Hochhuth, Rolf 1931- . . . . **CLC 4, 11, 18**
See also CA 5-8R; CANR 33; DLB 124;
MTCW

Hochman, Sandra 1936- . . . . **CLC 3, 8**
See also CA 5-8R; DLB 5

Hochwaelder, Fritz 1911-1986...... **CLC 36**
See also CA 29-32R; 120; CANR 42;
MTCW

Hochwalder, Fritz
See Hochwaelder, Fritz

Hocking, Mary (Eunice) 1921-..... **CLC 13**
See also CA 101; CANR 18, 40

Hodgins, Jack 1938-............ **CLC 23**
See also CA 93-96; DLB 60

Hodgson, William Hope
1877(?)-1918............... **TCLC 13**
See also CA 111; DLB 70

Hoffman, Alice 1952-............ **CLC 51**
See also CA 77-80; CANR 34; MTCW

Hoffman, Daniel (Gerard)
1923-.................. **CLC 6, 13, 23**
See also CA 1-4R; CANR 4; DLB 5

Hoffman, Stanley 1944-........... **CLC 5**
See also CA 77-80

Hoffman, William M(oses) 1939-... **CLC 40**
See also CA 57-60; CANR 11

Hoffmann, E(rnst) T(heodor) A(madeus)
1776-1822........... **NCLC 2; SSC 13**
See also DLB 90; SATA 27

Hofmann, Gert 1931-............ **CLC 54**
See also CA 128

Hofmannsthal, Hugo von
1874-1929........... **TCLC 11; DC 4**
See also CA 106; DLB 81, 118

Hogan, Linda 1947-............. **CLC 73**
See also CA 120; CANR 45

Hogarth, Charles
See Creasey, John

Hogg, James 1770-1835......... **NCLC 4**
See also DLB 93, 116

Holbach, Paul Henri Thiry Baron
1723-1789.................... **LC 14**

Holberg, Ludvig 1684-1754......... **LC 6**

Holden, Ursula 1921-............. **CLC 18**
See also CA 101; CAAS 8; CANR 22

Holderlin, (Johann Christian) Friedrich
1770-1843........... **NCLC 16; PC 4**

Holdstock, Robert
See Holdstock, Robert P.

Holdstock, Robert P. 1948-........ **CLC 39**
See also CA 131

Holland, Isabelle 1920-........... **CLC 21**
See also AAYA 11; CA 21-24R; CANR 10,
25; JRDA; MAICYA; SATA 8, 70

Holland, Marcus
See Caldwell, (Janet Miriam) Taylor
(Holland)

Hollander, John 1929-...... **CLC 2, 5, 8, 14**
See also CA 1-4R; CANR 1; DLB 5;
SATA 13

Hollander, Paul
See Silverberg, Robert

Holleran, Andrew 1943(?)-........ **CLC 38**
See also CA 144

Hollinghurst, Alan 1954-......... **CLC 55**
See also CA 114

Hollis, Jim
See Summers, Hollis (Spurgeon, Jr.)

Holmes, John
See Souster, (Holmes) Raymond

Holmes, John Clellon 1926-1988.... **CLC 56**
See also CA 9-12R; 125; CANR 4; DLB 16

Holmes, Oliver Wendell
1809-1894................. **NCLC 14**
See also CDALB 1640-1865; DLB 1;
SATA 34

Holmes, Raymond
See Souster, (Holmes) Raymond

Holt, Victoria
See Hibbert, Eleanor Alice Burford

Holub, Miroslav 1923-............. **CLC 4**
See also CA 21-24R; CANR 10

Homer c. 8th cent. B.C.-..... **CMLC 1; DA**

Honig, Edwin 1919-............ **CLC 33**
See also CA 5-8R; CAAS 8; CANR 4, 45;
DLB 5

Hood, Hugh (John Blagdon)
1928-.................. **CLC 15, 28**
See also CA 49-52; CAAS 17; CANR 1, 33;
DLB 53

Hood, Thomas 1799-1845....... **NCLC 16**
See also DLB 96

Hooker, (Peter) Jeremy 1941-...... **CLC 43**
See also CA 77-80; CANR 22; DLB 40

Hope, A(lec) D(erwent) 1907-.... **CLC 3, 51**
See also CA 21-24R; CANR 33; MTCW

Hope, Brian
See Creasey, John

Hope, Christopher (David Tully)
1944-...................... **CLC 52**
See also CA 106; SATA 62

Hopkins, Gerard Manley
1844-1889........ **NCLC 17; DA; WLC**
See also CDBLB 1890-1914; DLB 35, 57

Hopkins, John (Richard) 1931-...... **CLC 4**
See also CA 85-88

Hopkins, Pauline Elizabeth
1859-1930............ **TCLC 28; BLC**
See also BW 2; CA 141; DLB 50

Hopkinson, Francis 1737-1791...... **LC 25**
See also DLB 31

Hopley-Woolrich, Cornell George 1903-1968
See Woolrich, Cornell
See also CA 13-14; CAP 1

Horatio
See Proust, (Valentin-Louis-George-Eugene-)
Marcel

Horgan, Paul 1903-............ **CLC 9, 53**
See also CA 13-16R; CANR 9, 35;
DLB 102; DLBY 85; MTCW; SATA 13

Horn, Peter
See Kuttner, Henry

Hornem, Horace Esq.
See Byron, George Gordon (Noel)

Horovitz, Israel 1939-............ **CLC 56**
See also CA 33-36R; DLB 7

Horvath, Odon von
See Horvath, Oedoen von
See also DLB 85, 124

Horvath, Oedoen von 1901-1938... **TCLC 45**
See also Horvath, Odon von
See also CA 118

Horwitz, Julius 1920-1986......... **CLC 14**
See also CA 9-12R; 119; CANR 12

Hospital, Janette Turner 1942-..... **CLC 42**
See also CA 108

Hostos, E. M. de
See Hostos (y Bonilla), Eugenio Maria de

Hostos, Eugenio M. de
See Hostos (y Bonilla), Eugenio Maria de

Hostos, Eugenio Maria
See Hostos (y Bonilla), Eugenio Maria de

Hostos (y Bonilla), Eugenio Maria de
1839-1903................. **TCLC 24**
See also CA 123; 131; HW

Houdini
See Lovecraft, H(oward) P(hillips)

Hougan, Carolyn 1943-........... **CLC 34**
See also CA 139

Household, Geoffrey (Edward West)
1900-1988................... **CLC 11**
See also CA 77-80; 126; DLB 87; SATA 14,
59

Housman, A(lfred) E(dward)
1859-1936...... **TCLC 1, 10; DA; PC 2**
See also CA 104; 125; DLB 19; MTCW

Housman, Laurence 1865-1959..... **TCLC 7**
See also CA 106; DLB 10; SATA 25

Howard, Elizabeth Jane 1923-... **CLC 7, 29**
See also CA 5-8R; CANR 8

Howard, Maureen 1930-..... **CLC 5, 14, 46**
See also CA 53-56; CANR 31; DLBY 83;
MTCW

Howard, Richard 1929-...... **CLC 7, 10, 47**
See also AITN 1; CA 85-88; CANR 25;
DLB 5

Howard, Robert Ervin 1906-1936... **TCLC 8**
See also CA 105

Howard, Warren F.
See Pohl, Frederik

Howe, Fanny 1940-.............. **CLC 47**
See also CA 117; SATA 52

Howe, Julia Ward 1819-1910..... **TCLC 21**
See also CA 117; DLB 1

Howe, Susan 1937-............... **CLC 72**
See also DLB 120

Howe, Tina 1937-................ **CLC 48**
See also CA 109

Howell, James 1594(?)-1666........ **LC 13**

Howells, W. D.
See Howells, William Dean

Howells, William D.
See Howells, William Dean

Howells, William Dean
1837-1920............ **TCLC 7, 17, 41**
See also CA 104; 134; CDALB 1865-1917;
DLB 12, 64, 74, 79

Howes, Barbara 1914-............ **CLC 15**
See also CA 9-12R; CAAS 3; SATA 5

Hrabal, Bohumil 1914-........ **CLC 13, 67**
See also CA 106; CAAS 12

Hsun, Lu........................ **TCLC 3**
See also Shu-Jen, Chou

Hubbard, L(afayette) Ron(ald)
1911-1986 . . . . **CLC 43**
See also CA 77-80; 118; CANR 22

Huch, Ricarda (Octavia)
1864-1947 . . . . **TCLC 13**
See also CA 111; DLB 66

Huddle, David 1942- . . . . **CLC 49**
See also CA 57-60; DLB 130

Hudson, Jeffrey
See Crichton, (John) Michael

Hudson, W(illiam) H(enry)
1841-1922 . . . . **TCLC 29**
See also CA 115; DLB 98; SATA 35

Hueffer, Ford Madox
See Ford, Ford Madox

Hughart, Barry 1934- . . . . **CLC 39**
See also CA 137

Hughes, Colin
See Creasey, John

Hughes, David (John) 1930- . . . . **CLC 48**
See also CA 116; 129; DLB 14

Hughes, (James) Langston
1902-1967 . . . . . **CLC 1, 5, 10, 15, 35, 44;**
BLC; DA; DC 3; PC 1; SSC 6; WLC
See also AAYA 12; BW 1; CA 1-4R;
25-28R; CANR 1, 34; CDALB 1929-1941;
CLR 17; DLB 4, 7, 48, 51, 86; JRDA;
MAICYA; MTCW; SATA 4, 33

Hughes, Richard (Arthur Warren)
1900-1976 . . . . **CLC 1, 11**
See also CA 5-8R; 65-68; CANR 4;
DLB 15; MTCW; SATA 8, 25

Hughes, Ted
1930- . . . . **CLC 2, 4, 9, 14, 37; PC 7**
See also CA 1-4R; CANR 1, 33; CLR 3;
DLB 40; MAICYA; MTCW; SATA 27,
49

Hugo, Richard F(ranklin)
1923-1982 . . . . **CLC 6, 18, 32**
See also CA 49-52; 108; CANR 3; DLB 5

Hugo, Victor (Marie)
1802-1885 . . **NCLC 3, 10, 21; DA; WLC**
See also DLB 119; SATA 47

Huidobro, Vicente
See Huidobro Fernandez, Vicente Garcia

Huidobro Fernandez, Vicente Garcia
1893-1948 . . . . **TCLC 31**
See also CA 131; HW

Hulme, Keri 1947- . . . . **CLC 39**
See also CA 125

Hulme, T(homas) E(rnest)
1883-1917 . . . . **TCLC 21**
See also CA 117; DLB 19

Hume, David 1711-1776 . . . . **LC 7**
See also DLB 104

Humphrey, William 1924- . . . . **CLC 45**
See also CA 77-80; DLB 6

Humphreys, Emyr Owen 1919- . . . . . **CLC 47**
See also CA 5-8R; CANR 3, 24; DLB 15

Humphreys, Josephine 1945- . . . . **CLC 34, 57**
See also CA 121; 127

Hungerford, Pixie
See Brinsmead, H(esba) F(ay)

Hunt, E(verette) Howard, Jr.
1918- . . . . **CLC 3**
See also AITN 1; CA 45-48; CANR 2

Hunt, Kyle
See Creasey, John

Hunt, (James Henry) Leigh
1784-1859 . . . . **NCLC 1**

Hunt, Marsha 1946- . . . . **CLC 70**
See also BW 2; CA 143

Hunt, Violet 1866-1942 . . . . **TCLC 53**

Hunter, E. Waldo
See Sturgeon, Theodore (Hamilton)

Hunter, Evan 1926- . . . . **CLC 11, 31**
See also CA 5-8R; CANR 5, 38; DLBY 82;
MTCW; SATA 25

Hunter, Kristin (Eggleston) 1931- . . . **CLC 35**
See also AITN 1; BW 1; CA 13-16R;
CANR 13; CLR 3; DLB 33; MAICYA;
SAAS 10; SATA 12

Hunter, Mollie 1922- . . . . **CLC 21**
See also McIlwraith, Maureen Mollie
Hunter
See also CANR 37; CLR 25; JRDA;
MAICYA; SAAS 7; SATA 54

Hunter, Robert (?)-1734 . . . . **LC 7**

Hurston, Zora Neale
1903-1960 . . . . **CLC 7, 30, 61; BLC; DA;**
SSC 4
See also BW 1; CA 85-88; DLB 51, 86;
MTCW

Huston, John (Marcellus)
1906-1987 . . . . **CLC 20**
See also CA 73-76; 123; CANR 34; DLB 26

Hustvedt, Siri 1955- . . . . **CLC 76**
See also CA 137

Hutten, Ulrich von 1488-1523 . . . . . . **LC 16**

Huxley, Aldous (Leonard)
1894-1963 . . . . . **CLC 1, 3, 4, 5, 8, 11, 18,**
35, 79; DA; WLC
See also AAYA 11; CA 85-88; CANR 44;
CDBLB 1914-1945; DLB 36, 100;
MTCW; SATA 63

Huysmans, Charles Marie Georges
1848-1907
See Huysmans, Joris-Karl
See also CA 104

Huysmans, Joris-Karl . . . . **TCLC 7**
See also Huysmans, Charles Marie Georges
See also DLB 123

Hwang, David Henry
1957- . . . . **CLC 55; DC 4**
See also CA 127; 132

Hyde, Anthony 1946- . . . . **CLC 42**
See also CA 136

Hyde, Margaret O(ldroyd) 1917- . . . **CLC 21**
See also CA 1-4R; CANR 1, 36; CLR 23;
JRDA; MAICYA; SAAS 8; SATA 1, 42,
76

Hynes, James 1956(?)- . . . . **CLC 65**

Ian, Janis 1951- . . . . **CLC 21**
See also CA 105

Ibanez, Vicente Blasco
See Blasco Ibanez, Vicente

Ibarguengoitia, Jorge 1928-1983 . . . . **CLC 37**
See also CA 124; 113; HW

Ibsen, Henrik (Johan)
1828-1906 . . . . **TCLC 2, 8, 16, 37, 52;**
DA; DC 2; WLC
See also CA 104; 141

Ibuse Masuji 1898-1993 . . . . **CLC 22**
See also CA 127; 141

Ichikawa, Kon 1915- . . . . **CLC 20**
See also CA 121

Idle, Eric 1943- . . . . **CLC 21**
See also Monty Python
See also CA 116; CANR 35

Ignatow, David 1914- . . . . . . **CLC 4, 7, 14, 40**
See also CA 9-12R; CAAS 3; CANR 31;
DLB 5

Ihimaera, Witi 1944- . . . . **CLC 46**
See also CA 77-80

Ilf, Ilya . . . . **TCLC 21**
See also Fainzilberg, Ilya Arnoldovich

Immermann, Karl (Lebrecht)
1796-1840 . . . . **NCLC 4**
See also DLB 133

Inclan, Ramon (Maria) del Valle
See Valle-Inclan, Ramon (Maria) del

Infante, G(uillermo) Cabrera
See Cabrera Infante, G(uillermo)

Ingalls, Rachel (Holmes) 1940- . . . . . **CLC 42**
See also CA 123; 127

Ingamells, Rex 1913-1955 . . . . **TCLC 35**

Inge, William Motter
1913-1973 . . . . **CLC 1, 8, 19**
See also CA 9-12R; CDALB 1941-1968;
DLB 7; MTCW

Ingelow, Jean 1820-1897 . . . . **NCLC 39**
See also DLB 35; SATA 33

Ingram, Willis J.
See Harris, Mark

Innaurato, Albert (F.) 1948(?)- . . **CLC 21, 60**
See also CA 115; 122

Innes, Michael
See Stewart, J(ohn) I(nnes) M(ackintosh)

Ionesco, Eugene
1912-1994 . . . . **CLC 1, 4, 6, 9, 11, 15, 41;**
DA; WLC
See also CA 9-12R; 144; MTCW; SATA 7

Iqbal, Muhammad 1873-1938 . . . . . **TCLC 28**

Ireland, Patrick
See O'Doherty, Brian

Iron, Ralph
See Schreiner, Olive (Emilie Albertina)

Irving, John (Winslow)
1942- . . . . **CLC 13, 23, 38**
See also AAYA 8; BEST 89:3; CA 25-28R;
CANR 28; DLB 6; DLBY 82; MTCW

Irving, Washington
1783-1859 . . . . **NCLC 2, 19; DA; SSC 2;**
WLC
See also CDALB 1640-1865; DLB 3, 11, 30,
59, 73, 74; YABC 2

Irwin, P. K.
See Page, P(atricia) K(athleen)

Isaacs, Susan 1943- . . . . **CLC 32**
See also BEST 89:1; CA 89-92; CANR 20,
41; MTCW

Kaufman, Bob (Garnell)
1925-1986 . . . . **CLC 49**
See also BW 1; CA 41-44R; 118; CANR 22;
DLB 16, 41

Kaufman, George S. 1889-1961 . . . . . **CLC 38**
See also CA 108; 93-96; DLB 7

Kaufman, Sue . . . . **CLC 3, 8**
See also Barondess, Sue K(aufman)

Kavafis, Konstantinos Petrou 1863-1933
See Cavafy, C(onstantine) P(eter)
See also CA 104

Kavan, Anna 1901-1968 . . . . . . **CLC 5, 13, 82**
See also CA 5-8R; CANR 6; MTCW

Kavanagh, Dan
See Barnes, Julian

Kavanagh, Patrick (Joseph)
1904-1967 . . . . **CLC 22**
See also CA 123; 25-28R; DLB 15, 20;
MTCW

Kawabata, Yasunari
1899-1972 . . . . **CLC 2, 5, 9, 18**
See also CA 93-96; 33-36R

Kaye, M(ary) M(argaret) 1909- . . . . . **CLC 28**
See also CA 89-92; CANR 24; MTCW;
SATA 62

Kaye, Mollie
See Kaye, M(ary) M(argaret)

Kaye-Smith, Sheila 1887-1956 . . . . . **TCLC 20**
See also CA 118; DLB 36

Kaymor, Patrice Maguilene
See Senghor, Leopold Sedar

Kazan, Elia 1909- . . . . **CLC 6, 16, 63**
See also CA 21-24R; CANR 32

Kazantzakis, Nikos
1883(?)-1957 . . . . **TCLC 2, 5, 33**
See also CA 105; 132; MTCW

Kazin, Alfred 1915- . . . . **CLC 34, 38**
See also CA 1-4R; CAAS 7; CANR 1, 45;
DLB 67

Keane, Mary Nesta (Skrine) 1904-
See Keane, Molly
See also CA 108; 114

Keane, Molly . . . . **CLC 31**
See also Keane, Mary Nesta (Skrine)

Keates, Jonathan 19(?)- . . . . **CLC 34**

Keaton, Buster 1895-1966 . . . . **CLC 20**

Keats, John
1795-1821 . . . **NCLC 8; DA; PC 1; WLC**
See also CDBLB 1789-1832; DLB 96, 110

Keene, Donald 1922- . . . . **CLC 34**
See also CA 1-4R; CANR 5

Keillor, Garrison . . . . **CLC 40**
See also Keillor, Gary (Edward)
See also AAYA 2; BEST 89:3; DLBY 87;
SATA 58

Keillor, Gary (Edward) 1942-
See Keillor, Garrison
See also CA 111; 117; CANR 36; MTCW

Keith, Michael
See Hubbard, L(afayette) Ron(ald)

Keller, Gottfried 1819-1890 . . . . **NCLC 2**
See also DLB 129

Kellerman, Jonathan 1949- . . . . **CLC 44**
See also BEST 90:1; CA 106; CANR 29

Kelley, William Melvin 1937- . . . . . . **CLC 22**
See also BW 1; CA 77-80; CANR 27;
DLB 33

Kellogg, Marjorie 1922- . . . . **CLC 2**
See also CA 81-84

Kellow, Kathleen
See Hibbert, Eleanor Alice Burford

Kelly, M(ilton) T(erry) 1947- . . . . . . **CLC 55**
See also CA 97-100; CANR 19, 43

Kelman, James 1946- . . . . **CLC 58**

Kemal, Yashar 1923- . . . . **CLC 14, 29**
See also CA 89-92; CANR 44

Kemble, Fanny 1809-1893 . . . . **NCLC 18**
See also DLB 32

Kemelman, Harry 1908- . . . . **CLC 2**
See also AITN 1; CA 9-12R; CANR 6;
DLB 28

Kempe, Margery 1373(?)-1440(?) . . . . . **LC 6**

Kempis, Thomas a 1380-1471 . . . . **LC 11**

Kendall, Henry 1839-1882 . . . . **NCLC 12**

Keneally, Thomas (Michael)
1935- . . . . . . **CLC 5, 8, 10, 14, 19, 27, 43**
See also CA 85-88; CANR 10; MTCW

Kennedy, Adrienne (Lita)
1931- . . . . **CLC 66; BLC**
See also BW 2; CA 103; CABS 3;
CANR 26; DLB 38

Kennedy, John Pendleton
1795-1870 . . . . **NCLC 2**
See also DLB 3

Kennedy, Joseph Charles 1929- . . . . . . **CLC 8**
See also Kennedy, X. J.
See also CA 1-4R; CANR 4, 30, 40;
SATA 14

Kennedy, William 1928- . . . **CLC 6, 28, 34, 53**
See also AAYA 1; CA 85-88; CANR 14,
31; DLB 143; DLBY 85; MTCW;
SATA 57

Kennedy, X. J. . . . . **CLC 42**
See also Kennedy, Joseph Charles
See also CAAS 9; CLR 27; DLB 5

Kent, Kelvin
See Kuttner, Henry

Kenton, Maxwell
See Southern, Terry

Kenyon, Robert O.
See Kuttner, Henry

Kerouac, Jack . . . . . **CLC 1, 2, 3, 5, 14, 29, 61**
See also Kerouac, Jean-Louis Lebris de
See also CDALB 1941-1968; DLB 2, 16;
DLBD 3

Kerouac, Jean-Louis Lebris de 1922-1969
See Kerouac, Jack
See also AITN 1; CA 5-8R; 25-28R;
CANR 26; DA; MTCW; WLC

Kerr, Jean 1923- . . . . **CLC 22**
See also CA 5-8R; CANR 7

Kerr, M. E. . . . . **CLC 12, 35**
See also Meaker, Marijane (Agnes)
See also AAYA 2; CLR 29; SAAS 1

Kerr, Robert . . . . **CLC 55**

Kerrigan, (Thomas) Anthony
1918- . . . . **CLC 4, 6**
See also CA 49-52; CAAS 11; CANR 4

Kerry, Lois
See Duncan, Lois

Kesey, Ken (Elton)
1935- . . . . . . **CLC 1, 3, 6, 11, 46, 64; DA;
WLC**
See also CA 1-4R; CANR 22, 38;
CDALB 1968-1988; DLB 2, 16; MTCW;
SATA 66

Kesselring, Joseph (Otto)
1902-1967 . . . . **CLC 45**

Kessler, Jascha (Frederick) 1929- . . . . **CLC 4**
See also CA 17-20R; CANR 8

Kettelkamp, Larry (Dale) 1933- . . . . **CLC 12**
See also CA 29-32R; CANR 16; SAAS 3;
SATA 2

Keyber, Conny
See Fielding, Henry

Keyes, Daniel 1927- . . . . **CLC 80; DA**
See also CA 17-20R; CANR 10, 26;
SATA 37

Khayyam, Omar
1048-1131 . . . . **CMLC 11; PC 8**

Kherdian, David 1931- . . . . **CLC 6, 9**
See also CA 21-24R; CAAS 2; CANR 39;
CLR 24; JRDA; MAICYA; SATA 16, 74

Khlebnikov, Velimir . . . . **TCLC 20**
See also Khlebnikov, Viktor Vladimirovich

Khlebnikov, Viktor Vladimirovich 1885-1922
See Khlebnikov, Velimir
See also CA 117

Khodasevich, Vladislav (Felitsianovich)
1886-1939 . . . . **TCLC 15**
See also CA 115

Kielland, Alexander Lange
1849-1906 . . . . **TCLC 5**
See also CA 104

Kiely, Benedict 1919- . . . . **CLC 23, 43**
See also CA 1-4R; CANR 2; DLB 15

Kienzle, William X(avier) 1928- . . . . **CLC 25**
See also CA 93-96; CAAS 1; CANR 9, 31;
MTCW

Kierkegaard, Soren 1813-1855 . . . . **NCLC 34**

Killens, John Oliver 1916-1987 . . . . . **CLC 10**
See also BW 2; CA 77-80; 123; CAAS 2;
CANR 26; DLB 33

Killigrew, Anne 1660-1685 . . . . **LC 4**
See also DLB 131

Kim
See Simenon, Georges (Jacques Christian)

Kincaid, Jamaica 1949- . . . **CLC 43, 68; BLC**
See also BW 2; CA 125

King, Francis (Henry) 1923- . . . . . **CLC 8, 53**
See also CA 1-4R; CANR 1, 33; DLB 15,
139; MTCW

King, Martin Luther, Jr.
1929-1968 . . . . **CLC 83; BLC; DA**
See also BW 2; CA 25-28; CANR 27, 44;
CAP 2; MTCW; SATA 14

King, Stephen (Edwin)
1947- . . . . **CLC 12, 26, 37, 61**
See also AAYA 1; BEST 90:1; CA 61-64;
CANR 1, 30; DLB 143; DLBY 80;
JRDA; MTCW; SATA 9, 55

King, Steve
See King, Stephen (Edwin)

Kingman, Lee.................... CLC 17
  See also Natti, (Mary) Lee
  See also SAAS 3; SATA 1, 67

Kingsley, Charles 1819-1875..... NCLC 35
  See also DLB 21, 32; YABC 2

Kingsley, Sidney 1906-........... CLC 44
  See also CA 85-88; DLB 7

Kingsolver, Barbara 1955-...... CLC 55, 81
  See also CA 129; 134

Kingston, Maxine (Ting Ting) Hong
  1940-................ CLC 12, 19, 58
  See also AAYA 8; CA 69-72; CANR 13,
  38; DLBY 80; MTCW; SATA 53

Kinnell, Galway
  1927-........... CLC 1, 2, 3, 5, 13, 29
  See also CA 9-12R; CANR 10, 34; DLB 5;
  DLBY 87; MTCW

Kinsella, Thomas 1928-......... CLC 4, 19
  See also CA 17-20R; CANR 15; DLB 27;
  MTCW

Kinsella, W(illiam) P(atrick)
  1935-..................... CLC 27, 43
  See also AAYA 7; CA 97-100; CAAS 7;
  CANR 21, 35; MTCW

Kipling, (Joseph) Rudyard
  1865-1936...... TCLC 8, 17; DA; PC 3;
                        SSC 5; WLC
  See also CA 105; 120; CANR 33;
  CDBLB 1890-1914; DLB 19, 34, 141;
  MAICYA; MTCW; YABC 2

Kirkup, James 1918-.............. CLC 1
  See also CA 1-4R; CAAS 4; CANR 2;
  DLB 27; SATA 12

Kirkwood, James 1930(?)-1989...... CLC 9
  See also AITN 2; CA 1-4R; 128; CANR 6,
  40

Kis, Danilo 1935-1989........... CLC 57
  See also CA 109; 118; 129; MTCW

Kivi, Aleksis 1834-1872......... NCLC 30

Kizer, Carolyn (Ashley)
  1925-................ CLC 15, 39, 80
  See also CA 65-68; CAAS 5; CANR 24;
  DLB 5

Klabund 1890-1928.............. TCLC 44
  See also DLB 66

Klappert, Peter 1942-........... CLC 57
  See also CA 33-36R; DLB 5

Klein, A(braham) M(oses)
  1909-1972.................. CLC 19
  See also CA 101; 37-40R; DLB 68

Klein, Norma 1938-1989......... CLC 30
  See also AAYA 2; CA 41-44R; 128;
  CANR 15, 37; CLR 2, 19; JRDA;
  MAICYA; SAAS 1; SATA 7, 57

Klein, T(heodore) E(ibon) D(onald)
  1947-...................... CLC 34
  See also CA 119; CANR 44

Kleist, Heinrich von
  1777-1811............... NCLC 2, 37
  See also DLB 90

Klima, Ivan 1931-.............. CLC 56
  See also CA 25-28R; CANR 17

Klimentov, Andrei Platonovich 1899-1951
  See Platonov, Andrei
  See also CA 108

Klinger, Friedrich Maximilian von
  1752-1831................. NCLC 1
  See also DLB 94

Klopstock, Friedrich Gottlieb
  1724-1803................ NCLC 11
  See also DLB 97

Knebel, Fletcher 1911-1993........ CLC 14
  See also AITN 1; CA 1-4R; 140; CAAS 3;
  CANR 1, 36; SATA 36; SATA-Obit 75

Knickerbocker, Diedrich
  See Irving, Washington

Knight, Etheridge
  1931-1991.............. CLC 40; BLC
  See also BW 1; CA 21-24R; 133; CANR 23;
  DLB 41

Knight, Sarah Kemble 1666-1727..... LC 7
  See also DLB 24

Knister, Raymond 1899-1932..... TCLC 56
  See also DLB 68

Knowles, John
  1926-........... CLC 1, 4, 10, 26; DA
  See also AAYA 10; CA 17-20R; CANR 40;
  CDALB 1968-1988; DLB 6; MTCW;
  SATA 8

Knox, Calvin M.
  See Silverberg, Robert

Knye, Cassandra
  See Disch, Thomas M(ichael)

Koch, C(hristopher) J(ohn) 1932-... CLC 42
  See also CA 127

Koch, Christopher
  See Koch, C(hristopher) J(ohn)

Koch, Kenneth 1925-......... CLC 5, 8, 44
  See also CA 1-4R; CANR 6, 36; DLB 5;
  SATA 65

Kochanowski, Jan 1530-1584....... LC 10

Kock, Charles Paul de
  1794-1871................ NCLC 16

Koda Shigeyuki 1867-1947
  See Rohan, Koda
  See also CA 121

Koestler, Arthur
  1905-1983....... CLC 1, 3, 6, 8, 15, 33
  See also CA 1-4R; 109; CANR 1, 33;
  CDBLB 1945-1960; DLBY 83; MTCW

Kogawa, Joy Nozomi 1935-........ CLC 78
  See also CA 101; CANR 19

Kohout, Pavel 1928-.............. CLC 13
  See also CA 45-48; CANR 3

Koizumi, Yakumo
  See Hearn, (Patricio) Lafcadio (Tessima
  Carlos)

Kolmar, Gertrud 1894-1943...... TCLC 40

Konrad, George
  See Konrad, Gyoergy

Konrad, Gyoergy 1933-...... CLC 4, 10, 73
  See also CA 85-88

Konwicki, Tadeusz 1926-..... CLC 8, 28, 54
  See also CA 101; CAAS 9; CANR 39;
  MTCW

Koontz, Dean R(ay) 1945-........ CLC 78
  See also AAYA 9; BEST 89:3, 90:2;
  CA 108; CANR 19, 36; MTCW

Kopit, Arthur (Lee) 1937-.... CLC 1, 18, 33
  See also AITN 1; CA 81-84; CABS 3;
  DLB 7; MTCW

Kops, Bernard 1926-.............. CLC 4
  See also CA 5-8R; DLB 13

Kornbluth, C(yril) M. 1923-1958.... TCLC 8
  See also CA 105; DLB 8

Korolenko, V. G.
  See Korolenko, Vladimir Galaktionovich

Korolenko, Vladimir
  See Korolenko, Vladimir Galaktionovich

Korolenko, Vladimir G.
  See Korolenko, Vladimir Galaktionovich

Korolenko, Vladimir Galaktionovich
  1853-1921................. TCLC 22
  See also CA 121

Kosinski, Jerzy (Nikodem)
  1933-1991.... CLC 1, 2, 3, 6, 10, 15, 53,
                             70
  See also CA 17-20R; 134; CANR 9; DLB 2;
  DLBY 82; MTCW

Kostelanetz, Richard (Cory) 1940-.. CLC 28
  See also CA 13-16R; CAAS 8; CANR 38

Kostrowitzki, Wilhelm Apollinaris de
  1880-1918
  See Apollinaire, Guillaume
  See also CA 104

Kotlowitz, Robert 1924-........... CLC 4
  See also CA 33-36R; CANR 36

Kotzebue, August (Friedrich Ferdinand) von
  1761-1819................ NCLC 25
  See also DLB 94

Kotzwinkle, William 1938-... CLC 5, 14, 35
  See also CA 45-48; CANR 3, 44; CLR 6;
  MAICYA; SATA 24, 70

Kozol, Jonathan 1936-............ CLC 17
  See also CA 61-64; CANR 16, 45

Kozoll, Michael 1940(?)-.......... CLC 35

Kramer, Kathryn 19(?)-........... CLC 34

Kramer, Larry 1935-............. CLC 42
  See also CA 124; 126

Krasicki, Ignacy 1735-1801....... NCLC 8

Krasinski, Zygmunt 1812-1859.... NCLC 4

Kraus, Karl 1874-1936........... TCLC 5
  See also CA 104; DLB 118

Kreve (Mickevicius), Vincas
  1882-1954................. TCLC 27

Kristeva, Julia 1941-............ CLC 77

Kristofferson, Kris 1936-......... CLC 26
  See also CA 104

Krizanc, John 1956-.............. CLC 57

Krleza, Miroslav 1893-1981........ CLC 8
  See also CA 97-100; 105

Kroetsch, Robert 1927-...... CLC 5, 23, 57
  See also CA 17-20R; CANR 8, 38; DLB 53;
  MTCW

Kroetz, Franz
  See Kroetz, Franz Xaver

Kroetz, Franz Xaver 1946-........ CLC 41
  See also CA 130

Kroker, Arthur 1945-............ CLC 77

Kropotkin, Peter (Aleksieevich)
1842-1921 . . . . **TCLC 36**
See also CA 119

Krotkov, Yuri 1917- . . . . **CLC 19**
See also CA 102

Krumb
See Crumb, R(obert)

Krumgold, Joseph (Quincy)
1908-1980 . . . . **CLC 12**
See also CA 9-12R; 101; CANR 7;
MAICYA; SATA 1, 23, 48

Krumwitz
See Crumb, R(obert)

Krutch, Joseph Wood 1893-1970. . . . **CLC 24**
See also CA 1-4R; 25-28R; CANR 4;
DLB 63

Krutzch, Gus
See Eliot, T(homas) S(tearns)

Krylov, Ivan Andreevich
1768(?)-1844 . . . . **NCLC 1**

Kubin, Alfred 1877-1959 . . . . **TCLC 23**
See also CA 112; DLB 81

Kubrick, Stanley 1928- . . . . **CLC 16**
See also CA 81-84; CANR 33; DLB 26

Kumin, Maxine (Winokur)
1925- . . . . **CLC 5, 13, 28**
See also AITN 2; CA 1-4R; CAAS 8;
CANR 1, 21; DLB 5; MTCW; SATA 12

Kundera, Milan
1929- . . . . **CLC 4, 9, 19, 32, 68**
See also AAYA 2; CA 85-88; CANR 19;
MTCW

Kunitz, Stanley (Jasspon)
1905- . . . . **CLC 6, 11, 14**
See also CA 41-44R; CANR 26; DLB 48;
MTCW

Kunze, Reiner 1933- . . . . **CLC 10**
See also CA 93-96; DLB 75

Kuprin, Aleksandr Ivanovich
1870-1938 . . . . **TCLC 5**
See also CA 104

Kureishi, Hanif 1954(?)- . . . . **CLC 64**
See also CA 139

Kurosawa, Akira 1910- . . . . **CLC 16**
See also AAYA 11; CA 101

Kushner, Tony 1957(?)- . . . . **CLC 81**
See also CA 144

Kuttner, Henry 1915-1958 . . . . **TCLC 10**
See also CA 107; DLB 8

Kuzma, Greg 1944- . . . . **CLC 7**
See also CA 33-36R

Kuzmin, Mikhail 1872(?)-1936 . . . . **TCLC 40**

Kyd, Thomas 1558-1594 . . . . . . **LC 22; DC 3**
See also DLB 62

Kyprianos, Iossif
See Samarakis, Antonis

La Bruyere, Jean de 1645-1696 . . . . . . **LC 17**

Lacan, Jacques (Marie Emile)
1901-1981 . . . . **CLC 75**
See also CA 121; 104

Laclos, Pierre Ambroise Francois Choderlos
de 1741-1803 . . . . **NCLC 4**

La Colere, Francois
See Aragon, Louis

Lacolere, Francois
See Aragon, Louis

La Deshabilleuse
See Simenon, Georges (Jacques Christian)

Lady Gregory
See Gregory, Isabella Augusta (Persse)

Lady of Quality, A
See Bagnold, Enid

La Fayette, Marie (Madelaine Pioche de la
Vergne Comtes 1634-1693 . . . . . . **LC 2**

Lafayette, Rene
See Hubbard, L(afayette) Ron(ald)

Laforgue, Jules 1860-1887 . . . . **NCLC 5**

Lagerkvist, Paer (Fabian)
1891-1974 . . . . **CLC 7, 10, 13, 54**
See also Lagerkvist, Par
See also CA 85-88; 49-52; MTCW

Lagerkvist, Par
See Lagerkvist, Paer (Fabian)
See also SSC 12

Lagerloef, Selma (Ottiliana Lovisa)
1858-1940 . . . . **TCLC 4, 36**
See also Lagerlof, Selma (Ottiliana Lovisa)
See also CA 108; CLR 7; SATA 15

Lagerlof, Selma (Ottiliana Lovisa)
See Lagerloef, Selma (Ottiliana Lovisa)
See also CLR 7; SATA 15

La Guma, (Justin) Alex(ander)
1925-1985 . . . . **CLC 19**
See also BW 1; CA 49-52; 118; CANR 25;
DLB 117; MTCW

Laidlaw, A. K.
See Grieve, C(hristopher) M(urray)

Lainez, Manuel Mujica
See Mujica Lainez, Manuel
See also HW

Lamartine, Alphonse (Marie Louis Prat) de
1790-1869 . . . . **NCLC 11**

Lamb, Charles
1775-1834 . . . . **NCLC 10; DA; WLC**
See also CDBLB 1789-1832; DLB 93, 107;
SATA 17

Lamb, Lady Caroline 1785-1828 . . **NCLC 38**
See also DLB 116

Lamming, George (William)
1927- . . . . **CLC 2, 4, 66; BLC**
See also BW 2; CA 85-88; CANR 26;
DLB 125; MTCW

L'Amour, Louis (Dearborn)
1908-1988 . . . . **CLC 25, 55**
See also AITN 2; BEST 89:2; CA 1-4R;
125; CANR 3, 25, 40; DLBY 80; MTCW

Lampedusa, Giuseppe (Tomasi) di . . . **TCLC 13**
See also Tomasi di Lampedusa, Giuseppe

Lampman, Archibald 1861-1899 . . **NCLC 25**
See also DLB 92

Lancaster, Bruce 1896-1963 . . . . **CLC 36**
See also CA 9-10; CAP 1; SATA 9

Landau, Mark Alexandrovich
See Aldanov, Mark (Alexandrovich)

Landau-Aldanov, Mark Alexandrovich
See Aldanov, Mark (Alexandrovich)

Landis, John 1950- . . . . **CLC 26**
See also CA 112; 122

Landolfi, Tommaso 1908-1979 . . . **CLC 11, 49**
See also CA 127; 117

Landon, Letitia Elizabeth
1802-1838 . . . . **NCLC 15**
See also DLB 96

Landor, Walter Savage
1775-1864 . . . . **NCLC 14**
See also DLB 93, 107

Landwirth, Heinz 1927-
See Lind, Jakov
See also CA 9-12R; CANR 7

Lane, Patrick 1939- . . . . **CLC 25**
See also CA 97-100; DLB 53

Lang, Andrew 1844-1912 . . . . **TCLC 16**
See also CA 114; 137; DLB 98, 141;
MAICYA; SATA 16

Lang, Fritz 1890-1976 . . . . **CLC 20**
See also CA 77-80; 69-72; CANR 30

Lange, John
See Crichton, (John) Michael

Langer, Elinor 1939- . . . . **CLC 34**
See also CA 121

Langland, William
1330(?)-1400(?) . . . . **LC 19; DA**

Langstaff, Launcelot
See Irving, Washington

Lanier, Sidney 1842-1881 . . . . **NCLC 6**
See also DLB 64; MAICYA; SATA 18

Lanyer, Aemilia 1569-1645 . . . . **LC 10**

Lao Tzu . . . . **CMLC 7**

Lapine, James (Elliot) 1949- . . . . **CLC 39**
See also CA 123; 130

Larbaud, Valery (Nicolas)
1881-1957 . . . . **TCLC 9**
See also CA 106

Lardner, Ring
See Lardner, Ring(gold) W(ilmer)

Lardner, Ring W., Jr.
See Lardner, Ring(gold) W(ilmer)

Lardner, Ring(gold) W(ilmer)
1885-1933 . . . . **TCLC 2, 14**
See also CA 104; 131; CDALB 1917-1929;
DLB 11, 25, 86; MTCW

Laredo, Betty
See Codrescu, Andrei

Larkin, Maia
See Wojciechowska, Maia (Teresa)

Larkin, Philip (Arthur)
1922-1985 . . . . **CLC 3, 5, 8, 9, 13, 18, 33,**
39, 64
See also CA 5-8R; 117; CANR 24;
CDBLB 1960 to Present; DLB 27;
MTCW

Larra (y Sanchez de Castro), Mariano Jose de
1809-1837 . . . . **NCLC 17**

Larsen, Eric 1941- . . . . **CLC 55**
See also CA 132

Larsen, Nella 1891-1964 . . . . . **CLC 37; BLC**
See also BW 1; CA 125; DLB 51

Larson, Charles R(aymond) 1938- . . . **CLC 31**
See also CA 53-56; CANR 4

Latham, Jean Lee 1902- . . . . **CLC 12**
See also AITN 1; CA 5-8R; CANR 7;
MAICYA; SATA 2, 68

Latham, Mavis
See Clark, Mavis Thorpe

Lathen, Emma . . . . **CLC 2**
See also Hennissart, Martha; Latsis, Mary
J(ane)

Lathrop, Francis
See Leiber, Fritz (Reuter, Jr.)

Latsis, Mary J(ane)
See Lathen, Emma
See also CA 85-88

Lattimore, Richmond (Alexander)
1906-1984 . . . . **CLC 3**
See also CA 1-4R; 112; CANR 1

Laughlin, James 1914- . . . . **CLC 49**
See also CA 21-24R; CANR 9; DLB 48

Laurence, (Jean) Margaret (Wemyss)
1926-1987 . . **CLC 3, 6, 13, 50, 62; SSC 7**
See also CA 5-8R; 121; CANR 33; DLB 53;
MTCW; SATA 50

Laurent, Antoine 1952- . . . . **CLC 50**

Lauscher, Hermann
See Hesse, Hermann

Lautreamont, Comte de
1846-1870 . . . . **NCLC 12; SSC 14**

Laverty, Donald
See Blish, James (Benjamin)

Lavin, Mary 1912- . . . . . . **CLC 4, 18; SSC 4**
See also CA 9-12R; CANR 33; DLB 15;
MTCW

Lavond, Paul Dennis
See Kornbluth, C(yril) M.; Pohl, Frederik

Lawler, Raymond Evenor 1922- . . . . **CLC 58**
See also CA 103

Lawrence, D(avid) H(erbert Richards)
1885-1930 . . . . . . **TCLC 2, 9, 16, 33, 48;**
DA; SSC 4; WLC
See also CA 104; 121; CDBLB 1914-1945;
DLB 10, 19, 36, 98; MTCW

Lawrence, T(homas) E(dward)
1888-1935 . . . . **TCLC 18**
See also Dale, Colin
See also CA 115

Lawrence of Arabia
See Lawrence, T(homas) E(dward)

Lawson, Henry (Archibald Hertzberg)
1867-1922 . . . . **TCLC 27**
See also CA 120

Lawton, Dennis
See Faust, Frederick (Schiller)

Laxness, Halldor . . . . **CLC 25**
See also Gudjonsson, Halldor Kiljan

Layamon fl. c. 1200- . . . . **CMLC 10**

Laye, Camara 1928-1980 . . . **CLC 4, 38; BLC**
See also BW 1; CA 85-88; 97-100;
CANR 25; MTCW

Layton, Irving (Peter) 1912- . . . . . **CLC 2, 15**
See also CA 1-4R; CANR 2, 33, 43;
DLB 88; MTCW

Lazarus, Emma 1849-1887 . . . . **NCLC 8**

Lazarus, Felix
See Cable, George Washington

Lazarus, Henry
See Slavitt, David R(ytman)

Lea, Joan
See Neufeld, John (Arthur)

Leacock, Stephen (Butler)
1869-1944 . . . . **TCLC 2**
See also CA 104; 141; DLB 92

Lear, Edward 1812-1888 . . . . **NCLC 3**
See also CLR 1; DLB 32; MAICYA;
SATA 18

Lear, Norman (Milton) 1922- . . . . . . **CLC 12**
See also CA 73-76

Leavis, F(rank) R(aymond)
1895-1978 . . . . **CLC 24**
See also CA 21-24R; 77-80; CANR 44;
MTCW

Leavitt, David 1961- . . . . **CLC 34**
See also CA 116; 122; DLB 130

Leblanc, Maurice (Marie Emile)
1864-1941 . . . . **TCLC 49**
See also CA 110

Lebowitz, Fran(ces Ann)
1951(?)- . . . . **CLC 11, 36**
See also CA 81-84; CANR 14; MTCW

le Carre, John . . . . **CLC 3, 5, 9, 15, 28**
See also Cornwell, David (John Moore)
See also BEST 89:4; CDBLB 1960 to
Present; DLB 87

Le Clezio, J(ean) M(arie) G(ustave)
1940- . . . . **CLC 31**
See also CA 116; 128; DLB 83

Leconte de Lisle, Charles-Marie-Rene
1818-1894 . . . . **NCLC 29**

Le Coq, Monsieur
See Simenon, Georges (Jacques Christian)

Leduc, Violette 1907-1972 . . . . **CLC 22**
See also CA 13-14; 33-36R; CAP 1

Ledwidge, Francis 1887(?)-1917 . . . **TCLC 23**
See also CA 123; DLB 20

Lee, Andrea 1953- . . . . **CLC 36; BLC**
See also BW 1; CA 125

Lee, Andrew
See Auchincloss, Louis (Stanton)

Lee, Don L. . . . . **CLC 2**
See also Madhubuti, Haki R.

Lee, George W(ashington)
1894-1976 . . . . **CLC 52; BLC**
See also BW 1; CA 125; DLB 51

Lee, (Nelle) Harper
1926- . . . . **CLC 12, 60; DA; WLC**
See also CA 13-16R; CDALB 1941-1968;
DLB 6; MTCW; SATA 11

Lee, Julian
See Latham, Jean Lee

Lee, Larry
See Lee, Lawrence

Lee, Lawrence 1941-1990 . . . . **CLC 34**
See also CA 131; CANR 43

Lee, Manfred B(ennington)
1905-1971 . . . . **CLC 11**
See also Queen, Ellery
See also CA 1-4R; 29-32R; CANR 2;
DLB 137

Lee, Stan 1922- . . . . **CLC 17**
See also AAYA 5; CA 108; 111

Lee, Tanith 1947- . . . . **CLC 46**
See also CA 37-40R; SATA 8

Lee, Vernon . . . . **TCLC 5**
See also Paget, Violet
See also DLB 57

Lee, William
See Burroughs, William S(eward)

Lee, Willy
See Burroughs, William S(eward)

Lee-Hamilton, Eugene (Jacob)
1845-1907 . . . . **TCLC 22**
See also CA 117

Leet, Judith 1935- . . . . **CLC 11**

Le Fanu, Joseph Sheridan
1814-1873 . . . . **NCLC 9; SSC 14**
See also DLB 21, 70

Leffland, Ella 1931- . . . . **CLC 19**
See also CA 29-32R; CANR 35; DLBY 84;
SATA 65

Leger, Alexis
See Leger, (Marie-Rene Auguste) Alexis
Saint-Leger

Leger, (Marie-Rene Auguste) Alexis
Saint-Leger 1887-1975 . . . . **CLC 11**
See also Perse, St.-John
See also CA 13-16R; 61-64; CANR 43;
MTCW

Leger, Saintleger
See Leger, (Marie-Rene Auguste) Alexis
Saint-Leger

Le Guin, Ursula K(roeber)
1929- . . . . . **CLC 8, 13, 22, 45, 71; SSC 12**
See also AAYA 9; AITN 1; CA 21-24R;
CANR 9, 32; CDALB 1968-1988; CLR 3,
28; DLB 8, 52; JRDA; MAICYA;
MTCW; SATA 4, 52

Lehmann, Rosamond (Nina)
1901-1990 . . . . **CLC 5**
See also CA 77-80; 131; CANR 8; DLB 15

Leiber, Fritz (Reuter, Jr.)
1910-1992 . . . . **CLC 25**
See also CA 45-48; 139; CANR 2, 40;
DLB 8; MTCW; SATA 45;
SATA-Obit 73

Leimbach, Martha 1963-
See Leimbach, Marti
See also CA 130

Leimbach, Marti . . . . **CLC 65**
See also Leimbach, Martha

Leino, Eino . . . . **TCLC 24**
See also Loennbohm, Armas Eino Leopold

Leiris, Michel (Julien) 1901-1990 . . . **CLC 61**
See also CA 119; 128; 132

Leithauser, Brad 1953- . . . . **CLC 27**
See also CA 107; CANR 27; DLB 120

Lelchuk, Alan 1938- . . . . **CLC 5**
See also CA 45-48; CANR 1

Lem, Stanislaw 1921- . . . . **CLC 8, 15, 40**
See also CA 105; CAAS 1; CANR 32;
MTCW

Lemann, Nancy 1956- . . . . **CLC 39**
See also CA 118; 136

Lemonnier, (Antoine Louis) Camille
1844-1913 . . . . **TCLC 22**
See also CA 121

Lustig, Arnost 1926-............. **CLC 56**
See also AAYA 3; CA 69-72; SATA 56

Luther, Martin 1483-1546 .... **LC 9**

Luzi, Mario 1914-............... **CLC 13**
See also CA 61-64; CANR 9; DLB 128

Lynch, B. Suarez
See Bioy Casares, Adolfo; Borges, Jorge Luis

Lynch, David (K.) 1946-.......... **CLC 66**
See also CA 124; 129

Lynch, James
See Andreyev, Leonid (Nikolaevich)

Lynch Davis, B.
See Bioy Casares, Adolfo; Borges, Jorge Luis

Lyndsay, Sir David 1490-1555 ...... **LC 20**

Lynn, Kenneth S(chuyler) 1923-.... **CLC 50**
See also CA 1-4R; CANR 3, 27

Lynx
See West, Rebecca

Lyons, Marcus
See Blish, James (Benjamin)

Lyre, Pinchbeck
See Sassoon, Siegfried (Lorraine)

Lytle, Andrew (Nelson) 1902-...... **CLC 22**
See also CA 9-12R; DLB 6

Lyttelton, George 1709-1773 .... **LC 10**

Maas, Peter 1929-............... **CLC 29**
See also CA 93-96

Macaulay, Rose 1881-1958 ..... **TCLC 7, 44**
See also CA 104; DLB 36

Macaulay, Thomas Babington
1800-1859 .... **NCLC 42**
See also CDBLB 1832-1890; DLB 32, 55

MacBeth, George (Mann)
1932-1992 .... **CLC 2, 5, 9**
See also CA 25-28R; 136; DLB 40; MTCW;
SATA 4; SATA-Obit 70

MacCaig, Norman (Alexander)
1910- .... **CLC 36**
See also CA 9-12R; CANR 3, 34; DLB 27

MacCarthy, (Sir Charles Otto) Desmond
1877-1952 .... **TCLC 36**

MacDiarmid, Hugh
.... **CLC 2, 4, 11, 19, 63; PC 9**
See also Grieve, C(hristopher) M(urray)
See also CDBLB 1945-1960; DLB 20

MacDonald, Anson
See Heinlein, Robert A(nson)

Macdonald, Cynthia 1928-...... **CLC 13, 19**
See also CA 49-52; CANR 4, 44; DLB 105

MacDonald, George 1824-1905 ..... **TCLC 9**
See also CA 106; 137; DLB 18; MAICYA;
SATA 33

Macdonald, John
See Millar, Kenneth

MacDonald, John D(ann)
1916-1986 .... **CLC 3, 27, 44**
See also CA 1-4R; 121; CANR 1, 19;
DLB 8; DLBY 86; MTCW

Macdonald, John Ross
See Millar, Kenneth

Macdonald, Ross..... CLC 1, 2, 3, 14, 34, 41
See also Millar, Kenneth
See also DLBD 6

MacDougal, John
See Blish, James (Benjamin)

MacEwen, Gwendolyn (Margaret)
1941-1987 .... **CLC 13, 55**
See also CA 9-12R; 124; CANR 7, 22;
DLB 53; SATA 50, 55

Machado (y Ruiz), Antonio
1875-1939 .... **TCLC 3**
See also CA 104; DLB 108

Machado de Assis, Joaquim Maria
1839-1908 .... **TCLC 10; BLC**
See also CA 107

Machen, Arthur................... TCLC 4
See also Jones, Arthur Llewellyn
See also DLB 36

Machiavelli, Niccolo 1469-1527 .. **LC 8; DA**

MacInnes, Colin 1914-1976...... **CLC 4, 23**
See also CA 69-72; 65-68; CANR 21;
DLB 14; MTCW

MacInnes, Helen (Clark)
1907-1985 .... **CLC 27, 39**
See also CA 1-4R; 117; CANR 1, 28;
DLB 87; MTCW; SATA 22, 44

Mackay, Mary 1855-1924
See Corelli, Marie
See also CA 118

Mackenzie, Compton (Edward Montague)
1883-1972 .... **CLC 18**
See also CA 21-22; 37-40R; CAP 2;
DLB 34, 100

Mackenzie, Henry 1745-1831 .... **NCLC 41**
See also DLB 39

Mackintosh, Elizabeth 1896(?)-1952
See Tey, Josephine
See also CA 110

MacLaren, James
See Grieve, C(hristopher) M(urray)

Mac Laverty, Bernard 1942-....... **CLC 31**
See also CA 116; 118; CANR 43

MacLean, Alistair (Stuart)
1922-1987 .... **CLC 3, 13, 50, 63**
See also CA 57-60; 121; CANR 28; MTCW;
SATA 23, 50

Maclean, Norman (Fitzroy)
1902-1990 .... **CLC 78; SSC 13**
See also CA 102; 132

MacLeish, Archibald
1892-1982 .... **CLC 3, 8, 14, 68**
See also CA 9-12R; 106; CANR 33; DLB 4,
7, 45; DLBY 82; MTCW

MacLennan, (John) Hugh
1907-1990 .... **CLC 2, 14**
See also CA 5-8R; 142; CANR 33; DLB 68;
MTCW

MacLeod, Alistair 1936- .... **CLC 56**
See also CA 123; DLB 60

MacNeice, (Frederick) Louis
1907-1963 .... **CLC 1, 4, 10, 53**
See also CA 85-88; DLB 10, 20; MTCW

MacNeill, Dand
See Fraser, George MacDonald

Macpherson, (Jean) Jay 1931-...... **CLC 14**
See also CA 5-8R; DLB 53

MacShane, Frank 1927-.......... **CLC 39**
See also CA 9-12R; CANR 3, 33; DLB 111

Macumber, Mari
See Sandoz, Mari(e Susette)

Madach, Imre 1823-1864....... **NCLC 19**

Madden, (Jerry) David 1933- .... **CLC 5, 15**
See also CA 1-4R; CAAS 3; CANR 4, 45;
DLB 6; MTCW

Maddern, Al(an)
See Ellison, Harlan

Madhubuti, Haki R.
1942- .... **CLC 6, 73; BLC; PC 5**
See Lee, Don L.
See also BW 2; CA 73-76; CANR 24;
DLB 5, 41; DLBD 8

Madow, Pauline (Reichberg) .... **CLC 1**
See also CA 9-12R

Maepenn, Hugh
See Kuttner, Henry

Maepenn, K. H.
See Kuttner, Henry

Maeterlinck, Maurice 1862-1949 ... **TCLC 3**
See also CA 104; 136; SATA 66

Maginn, William 1794-1842...... **NCLC 8**
See also DLB 110

Mahapatra, Jayanta 1928-........ **CLC 33**
See also CA 73-76; CAAS 9; CANR 15, 33

Mahfouz, Naguib (Abdel Aziz Al-Sabilgi)
1911(?)-
See Mahfuz, Najib
See also BEST 89:2; CA 128; MTCW

Mahfuz, Najib................ CLC 52, 55
See also Mahfouz, Naguib (Abdel Aziz
Al-Sabilgi)
See also DLBY 88

Mahon, Derek 1941-.............. **CLC 27**
See also CA 113; 128; DLB 40

Mailer, Norman
1923- ...... **CLC 1, 2, 3, 4, 5, 8, 11, 14,**
28, 39, 74; DA
See also AITN 2; CA 9-12R; CABS 1;
CANR 28; CDALB 1968-1988; DLB 2,
16, 28; DLBD 3; DLBY 80, 83; MTCW

Maillet, Antonine 1929-.......... **CLC 54**
See also CA 115; 120; DLB 60

Mais, Roger 1905-1955 .... **TCLC 8**
See also BW 1; CA 105; 124; DLB 125;
MTCW

Maistre, Joseph de 1753-1821 .... **NCLC 37**

Maitland, Sara (Louise) 1950-...... **CLC 49**
See also CA 69-72; CANR 13

Major, Clarence
1936- .... **CLC 3, 19, 48; BLC**
See also BW 2; CA 21-24R; CAAS 6;
CANR 13, 25; DLB 33

Major, Kevin (Gerald) 1949-....... **CLC 26**
See also CA 97-100; CANR 21, 38;
CLR 11; DLB 60; JRDA; MAICYA;
SATA 32

Maki, James
See Ozu, Yasujiro

Malabaila, Damiano
See Levi, Primo

Malamud, Bernard
1914-1986 . . . . . . **CLC 1, 2, 3, 5, 8, 9, 11, 18, 27, 44, 78; DA; SSC 15; WLC**
See also CA 5-8R; 118; CABS 1; CANR 28; CDALB 1941-1968; DLB 2, 28; DLBY 80, 86; MTCW

Malaparte, Curzio 1898-1957 . . . . . **TCLC 52**

Malcolm, Dan
See Silverberg, Robert

Malcolm X . . . . **CLC 82; BLC**
See also Little, Malcolm

Malherbe, Francois de 1555-1628 . . . . . **LC 5**

Mallarme, Stephane
1842-1898 . . . . **NCLC 4, 41; PC 4**

Mallet-Joris, Francoise 1930- . . . . . . **CLC 11**
See also CA 65-68; CANR 17; DLB 83

Malley, Ern
See McAuley, James Phillip

Mallowan, Agatha Christie
See Christie, Agatha (Mary Clarissa)

Maloff, Saul 1922- . . . . **CLC 5**
See also CA 33-36R

Malone, Louis
See MacNeice, (Frederick) Louis

Malone, Michael (Christopher)
1942- . . . . **CLC 43**
See also CA 77-80; CANR 14, 32

Malory, (Sir) Thomas
1410(?)-1471(?) . . . . **LC 11; DA**
See also CDBLB Before 1660; SATA 33, 59

Malouf, (George Joseph) David
1934- . . . . **CLC 28**
See also CA 124

Malraux, (Georges-)Andre
1901-1976 . . . . . . **CLC 1, 4, 9, 13, 15, 57**
See also CA 21-22; 69-72; CANR 34; CAP 2; DLB 72; MTCW

Malzberg, Barry N(athaniel) 1939- . . . **CLC 7**
See also CA 61-64; CAAS 4; CANR 16; DLB 8

Mamet, David (Alan)
1947- . . . . **CLC 9, 15, 34, 46; DC 4**
See also AAYA 3; CA 81-84; CABS 3; CANR 15, 41; DLB 7; MTCW

Mamoulian, Rouben (Zachary)
1897-1987 . . . . **CLC 16**
See also CA 25-28R; 124

Mandelstam, Osip (Emilievich)
1891(?)-1938(?) . . . . **TCLC 2, 6**
See also CA 104

Mander, (Mary) Jane 1877-1949 . . . **TCLC 31**

Mandiargues, Andre Pieyre de . . . . . . **CLC 41**
See also Pieyre de Mandiargues, Andre
See also DLB 83

Mandrake, Ethel Belle
See Thurman, Wallace (Henry)

Mangan, James Clarence
1803-1849 . . . . **NCLC 27**

Maniere, J.-E.
See Giraudoux, (Hippolyte) Jean

Manley, (Mary) Delariviere
1672(?)-1724 . . . . **LC 1**
See also DLB 39, 80

Mann, Abel
See Creasey, John

Mann, (Luiz) Heinrich 1871-1950 . . . **TCLC 9**
See also CA 106; DLB 66

Mann, (Paul) Thomas
1875-1955 . . . . **TCLC 2, 8, 14, 21, 35, 44; DA; SSC 5; WLC**
See also CA 104; 128; DLB 66; MTCW

Manning, David
See Faust, Frederick (Schiller)

Manning, Frederic 1887(?)-1935 . . . **TCLC 25**
See also CA 124

Manning, Olivia 1915-1980 . . . . . . **CLC 5, 19**
See also CA 5-8R; 101; CANR 29; MTCW

Mano, D. Keith 1942- . . . . **CLC 2, 10**
See also CA 25-28R; CAAS 6; CANR 26; DLB 6

Mansfield, Katherine
. . . . **TCLC 2, 8, 39; SSC 9; WLC**
See also Beauchamp, Kathleen Mansfield

Manso, Peter 1940- . . . . **CLC 39**
See also CA 29-32R; CANR 44

Mantecon, Juan Jimenez
See Jimenez (Mantecon), Juan Ramon

Manton, Peter
See Creasey, John

Man Without a Spleen, A
See Chekhov, Anton (Pavlovich)

Manzoni, Alessandro 1785-1873 . . **NCLC 29**

Mapu, Abraham (ben Jekutiel)
1808-1867 . . . . **NCLC 18**

Mara, Sally
See Queneau, Raymond

Marat, Jean Paul 1743-1793 . . . . **LC 10**

Marcel, Gabriel Honore
1889-1973 . . . . **CLC 15**
See also CA 102; 45-48; MTCW

Marchbanks, Samuel
See Davies, (William) Robertson

Marchi, Giacomo
See Bassani, Giorgio

Margulies, Donald . . . . **CLC 76**

Marie de France c. 12th cent. - . . . . **CMLC 8**

Marie de l'Incarnation 1599-1672 . . . . **LC 10**

Mariner, Scott
See Pohl, Frederik

Marinetti, Filippo Tommaso
1876-1944 . . . . **TCLC 10**
See also CA 107; DLB 114

Marivaux, Pierre Carlet de Chamblain de
1688-1763 . . . . **LC 4**

Markandaya, Kamala . . . . **CLC 8, 38**
See also Taylor, Kamala (Purnaiya)

Markfield, Wallace 1926- . . . . **CLC 8**
See also CA 69-72; CAAS 3; DLB 2, 28

Markham, Edwin 1852-1940 . . . . . . **TCLC 47**
See also DLB 54

Markham, Robert
See Amis, Kingsley (William)

Marks, J
See Highwater, Jamake (Mamake)

Marks-Highwater, J
See Highwater, Jamake (Mamake)

Markson, David M(errill) 1927- . . . . **CLC 67**
See also CA 49-52; CANR 1

Marley, Bob . . . . **CLC 17**
See also Marley, Robert Nesta

Marley, Robert Nesta 1945-1981
See Marley, Bob
See also CA 107; 103

Marlowe, Christopher
1564-1593 . . . . . **LC 22; DA; DC 1; WLC**
See also CDBLB Before 1660; DLB 62

Marmontel, Jean-Francois
1723-1799 . . . . **LC 2**

Marquand, John P(hillips)
1893-1960 . . . . **CLC 2, 10**
See also CA 85-88; DLB 9, 102

Marquez, Gabriel (Jose) Garcia . . . . . . **CLC 68**
See also Garcia Marquez, Gabriel (Jose)

Marquis, Don(ald Robert Perry)
1878-1937 . . . . **TCLC 7**
See also CA 104; DLB 11, 25

Marric, J. J.
See Creasey, John

Marrow, Bernard
See Moore, Brian

Marryat, Frederick 1792-1848 . . . . **NCLC 3**
See also DLB 21

Marsden, James
See Creasey, John

Marsh, (Edith) Ngaio
1899-1982 . . . . **CLC 7, 53**
See also CA 9-12R; CANR 6; DLB 77; MTCW

Marshall, Garry 1934- . . . . **CLC 17**
See also AAYA 3; CA 111; SATA 60

Marshall, Paule
1929- . . . . . . **CLC 27, 72; BLC; SSC 3**
See also BW 2; CA 77-80; CANR 25; DLB 33; MTCW

Marsten, Richard
See Hunter, Evan

Martha, Henry
See Harris, Mark

Martin, Ken
See Hubbard, L(afayette) Ron(ald)

Martin, Richard
See Creasey, John

Martin, Steve 1945- . . . . **CLC 30**
See also CA 97-100; CANR 30; MTCW

Martin, Violet Florence
1862-1915 . . . . **TCLC 51**

Martin, Webber
See Silverberg, Robert

Martindale, Patrick Victor
See White, Patrick (Victor Martindale)

Martin du Gard, Roger
1881-1958 . . . . **TCLC 24**
See also CA 118; DLB 65

Martineau, Harriet 1802-1876 . . . . **NCLC 26**
See also DLB 21, 55; YABC 2

Martines, Julia
See O'Faolain, Julia

Martinez, Jacinto Benavente y
See Benavente (y Martinez), Jacinto

Martinez Ruiz, Jose 1873-1967
See Azorin; Ruiz, Jose Martinez
See also CA 93-96; HW

Martinez Sierra, Gregorio
1881-1947 .... TCLC 6
See also CA 115

Martinez Sierra, Maria (de la O'LeJarraga)
1874-1974 .... TCLC 6
See also CA 115

Martinsen, Martin
See Follett, Ken(neth Martin)

Martinson, Harry (Edmund)
1904-1978 .... CLC 14
See also CA 77-80; CANR 34

Marut, Ret
See Traven, B.

Marut, Robert
See Traven, B.

Marvell, Andrew
1621-1678 ..... LC 4; DA; PC 10; WLC
See also CDBLB 1660-1789; DLB 131

Marx, Karl (Heinrich)
1818-1883 .... NCLC 17
See also DLB 129

Masaoka Shiki.................. TCLC 18
See also Masaoka Tsunenori

Masaoka Tsunenori 1867-1902
See Masaoka Shiki
See also CA 117

Masefield, John (Edward)
1878-1967 .... CLC 11, 47
See also CA 19-20; 25-28R; CANR 33;
CAP 2; CDBLB 1890-1914; DLB 10;
MTCW; SATA 19

Maso, Carole 19(?)- .... CLC 44

Mason, Bobbie Ann
1940- .... CLC 28, 43, 82; SSC 4
See also AAYA 5; CA 53-56; CANR 11,
31; DLBY 87; MTCW

Mason, Ernst
See Pohl, Frederik

Mason, Lee W.
See Malzberg, Barry N(athaniel)

Mason, Nick 1945-............. CLC 35
See also Pink Floyd

Mason, Tally
See Derleth, August (William)

Mass, William
See Gibson, William

Masters, Edgar Lee
1868-1950 ..... TCLC 2, 25; DA; PC 1
See also CA 104; 133; CDALB 1865-1917;
DLB 54; MTCW

Masters, Hilary 1928- .... CLC 48
See also CA 25-28R; CANR 13

Mastrosimone, William 19(?)- ...... CLC 36

Mathe, Albert
See Camus, Albert

Matheson, Richard Burton 1926- ... CLC 37
See also CA 97-100; DLB 8, 44

Mathews, Harry 1930-.......... CLC 6, 52
See also CA 21-24R; CAAS 6; CANR 18,
40

Mathews, John Joseph 1894-1979... CLC 84
See also CA 19-20; 142; CANR 45; CAP 2

Mathias, Roland (Glyn) 1915-...... CLC 45
See also CA 97-100; CANR 19, 41; DLB 27

Matsuo Basho 1644-1694........... PC 3

Mattheson, Rodney
See Creasey, John

Matthews, Greg 1949- .... CLC 45
See also CA 135

Matthews, William 1942-......... CLC 40
See also CA 29-32R; CAAS 18; CANR 12;
DLB 5

Matthias, John (Edward) 1941-...... CLC 9
See also CA 33-36R

Matthiessen, Peter
1927- .... CLC 5, 7, 11, 32, 64
See also AAYA 6; BEST 90:4; CA 9-12R;
CANR 21; DLB 6; MTCW; SATA 27

Maturin, Charles Robert
1780(?)-1824 .... NCLC 6

Matute (Ausejo), Ana Maria
1925- .... CLC 11
See also CA 89-92; MTCW

Maugham, W. S.
See Maugham, W(illiam) Somerset

Maugham, W(illiam) Somerset
1874-1965 ...... CLC 1, 11, 15, 67; DA;
SSC 8; WLC
See also CA 5-8R; 25-28R; CANR 40;
CDBLB 1914-1945; DLB 10, 36, 77, 100;
MTCW; SATA 54

Maugham, William Somerset
See Maugham, W(illiam) Somerset

Maupassant, (Henri Rene Albert) Guy de
1850-1893 .... NCLC 1, 42; DA; SSC 1;
WLC
See also DLB 123

Maurhut, Richard
See Traven, B.

Mauriac, Claude 1914-............ CLC 9
See also CA 89-92; DLB 83

Mauriac, Francois (Charles)
1885-1970 .... CLC 4, 9, 56
See also CA 25-28; CAP 2; DLB 65;
MTCW

Mavor, Osborne Henry 1888-1951
See Bridie, James
See also CA 104

Maxwell, William (Keepers, Jr.)
1908- .... CLC 19
See also CA 93-96; DLBY 80

May, Elaine 1932- .... CLC 16
See also CA 124; 142; DLB 44

Mayakovski, Vladimir (Vladimirovich)
1893-1930 .... TCLC 4, 18
See also CA 104

Mayhew, Henry 1812-1887 ...... NCLC 31
See also DLB 18, 55

Maynard, Joyce 1953-............ CLC 23
See also CA 111; 129

Mayne, William (James Carter)
1928- .... CLC 12
See also CA 9-12R; CANR 37; CLR 25;
JRDA; MAICYA; SAAS 11; SATA 6, 68

Mayo, Jim
See L'Amour, Louis (Dearborn)

Maysles, Albert 1926- .... CLC 16
See also CA 29-32R

Maysles, David 1932-............ CLC 16

Mazer, Norma Fox 1931- .... CLC 26
See also AAYA 5; CA 69-72; CANR 12,
32; CLR 23; JRDA; MAICYA; SAAS 1;
SATA 24, 67

Mazzini, Guiseppe 1805-1872 .... NCLC 34

McAuley, James Phillip
1917-1976 .... CLC 45
See also CA 97-100

McBain, Ed
See Hunter, Evan

McBrien, William Augustine
1930- .... CLC 44
See also CA 107

McCaffrey, Anne (Inez) 1926-...... CLC 17
See also AAYA 6; AITN 2; BEST 89:2;
CA 25-28R; CANR 15, 35; DLB 8;
JRDA; MAICYA; MTCW; SAAS 11;
SATA 8, 70

McCann, Arthur
See Campbell, John W(ood, Jr.)

McCann, Edson
See Pohl, Frederik

McCarthy, Charles, Jr. 1933-
See McCarthy, Cormac
See also CANR 42

McCarthy, Cormac 1933-........ CLC 4, 57
See also McCarthy, Charles, Jr.
See also DLB 6, 143

McCarthy, Mary (Therese)
1912-1989 ... CLC 1, 3, 5, 14, 24, 39, 59
See also CA 5-8R; 129; CANR 16; DLB 2;
DLBY 81; MTCW

McCartney, (James) Paul
1942- .... CLC 12, 35

McCauley, Stephen (D.) 1955- ..... CLC 50
See also CA 141

McClure, Michael (Thomas)
1932- .... CLC 6, 10
See also CA 21-24R; CANR 17; DLB 16

McCorkle, Jill (Collins) 1958-...... CLC 51
See also CA 121; DLBY 87

McCourt, James 1941-............ CLC 5
See also CA 57-60

McCoy, Horace (Stanley)
1897-1955 .... TCLC 28
See also CA 108; DLB 9

McCrae, John 1872-1918........ TCLC 12
See also CA 109; DLB 92

McCreigh, James
See Pohl, Frederik

McCullers, (Lula) Carson (Smith)
1917-1967 .... CLC 1, 4, 10, 12, 48; DA;
SSC 9; WLC
See also CA 5-8R; 25-28R; CABS 1, 3;
CANR 18; CDALB 1941-1968; DLB 2, 7;
MTCW; SATA 27

McCulloch, John Tyler
See Burroughs, Edgar Rice

McCullough, Colleen 1938(?)- . . . . . . **CLC 27**
See also CA 81-84; CANR 17; MTCW

McElroy, Joseph 1930- . . . . **CLC 5, 47**
See also CA 17-20R

McEwan, Ian (Russell) 1948- . . . **CLC 13, 66**
See also BEST 90:4; CA 61-64; CANR 14,
41; DLB 14; MTCW

McFadden, David 1940- . . . . **CLC 48**
See also CA 104; DLB 60

McFarland, Dennis 1950- . . . . **CLC 65**

McGahern, John 1934- . . . . **CLC 5, 9, 48**
See also CA 17-20R; CANR 29; DLB 14;
MTCW

McGinley, Patrick (Anthony)
1937- . . . . **CLC 41**
See also CA 120; 127

McGinley, Phyllis 1905-1978 . . . . . . **CLC 14**
See also CA 9-12R; 77-80; CANR 19;
DLB 11, 48; SATA 2, 24, 44

McGinniss, Joe 1942- . . . . **CLC 32**
See also AITN 2; BEST 89:2; CA 25-28R;
CANR 26

McGivern, Maureen Daly
See Daly, Maureen

McGrath, Patrick 1950- . . . . **CLC 55**
See also CA 136

McGrath, Thomas (Matthew)
1916-1990 . . . . **CLC 28, 59**
See also CA 9-12R; 132; CANR 6, 33;
MTCW; SATA 41; SATA-Obit 66

McGuane, Thomas (Francis III)
1939- . . . . **CLC 3, 7, 18, 45**
See also AITN 2; CA 49-52; CANR 5, 24;
DLB 2; DLBY 80; MTCW

McGuckian, Medbh 1950- . . . . **CLC 48**
See also CA 143; DLB 40

McHale, Tom 1942(?)-1982 . . . . **CLC 3, 5**
See also AITN 1; CA 77-80; 106

McIlvanney, William 1936- . . . . **CLC 42**
See also CA 25-28R; DLB 14

McIlwraith, Maureen Mollie Hunter
See Hunter, Mollie
See also SATA 2

McInerney, Jay 1955- . . . . **CLC 34**
See also CA 116; 123

McIntyre, Vonda N(eel) 1948- . . . . . **CLC 18**
See also CA 81-84; CANR 17, 34; MTCW

McKay, Claude . . . . . **TCLC 7, 41; BLC; PC 2**
See also McKay, Festus Claudius
See also DLB 4, 45, 51, 117

McKay, Festus Claudius 1889-1948
See McKay, Claude
See also BW 1; CA 104; 124; DA; MTCW;
WLC

McKuen, Rod 1933- . . . . **CLC 1, 3**
See also AITN 1; CA 41-44R; CANR 40

McLoughlin, R. B.
See Mencken, H(enry) L(ouis)

McLuhan, (Herbert) Marshall
1911-1980 . . . . **CLC 37, 83**
See also CA 9-12R; 102; CANR 12, 34;
DLB 88; MTCW

McMillan, Terry (L.) 1951- . . . . . **CLC 50, 61**
See also BW 2; CA 140

McMurtry, Larry (Jeff)
1936- . . . . **CLC 2, 3, 7, 11, 27, 44**
See also AITN 2; BEST 89:2; CA 5-8R;
CANR 19, 43; CDALB 1968-1988;
DLB 2, 143; DLBY 80, 87; MTCW

McNally, T. M. 1961- . . . . **CLC 82**

McNally, Terrence 1939- . . . . . . **CLC 4, 7, 41**
See also CA 45-48; CANR 2; DLB 7

McNamer, Deirdre 1950- . . . . **CLC 70**

McNeile, Herman Cyril 1888-1937
See Sapper
See also DLB 77

McPhee, John (Angus) 1931- . . . . . . **CLC 36**
See also BEST 90:1; CA 65-68; CANR 20;
MTCW

McPherson, James Alan
1943- . . . . **CLC 19, 77**
See also BW 1; CA 25-28R; CAAS 17;
CANR 24; DLB 38; MTCW

McPherson, William (Alexander)
1933- . . . . **CLC 34**
See also CA 69-72; CANR 28

McSweeney, Kerry . . . . **CLC 34**

Mead, Margaret 1901-1978 . . . . **CLC 37**
See also AITN 1; CA 1-4R; 81-84;
CANR 4; MTCW; SATA 20

Meaker, Marijane (Agnes) 1927-
See Kerr, M. E.
See also CA 107; CANR 37; JRDA;
MAICYA; MTCW; SATA 20, 61

Medoff, Mark (Howard) 1940- . . . **CLC 6, 23**
See also AITN 1; CA 53-56; CANR 5;
DLB 7

Medvedev, P. N.
See Bakhtin, Mikhail Mikhailovich

Meged, Aharon
See Megged, Aharon

Meged, Aron
See Megged, Aharon

Megged, Aharon 1920- . . . . **CLC 9**
See also CA 49-52; CAAS 13; CANR 1

Mehta, Ved (Parkash) 1934- . . . . **CLC 37**
See also CA 1-4R; CANR 2, 23; MTCW

Melanter
See Blackmore, R(ichard) D(oddridge)

Melikow, Loris
See Hofmannsthal, Hugo von

Melmoth, Sebastian
See Wilde, Oscar (Fingal O'Flahertie Wills)

Meltzer, Milton 1915- . . . . **CLC 26**
See also AAYA 8; CA 13-16R; CANR 38;
CLR 13; DLB 61; JRDA; MAICYA;
SAAS 1; SATA 1, 50

Melville, Herman
1819-1891 . . . . **NCLC 3, 12, 29, 45; DA;**
SSC 1; WLC
See also CDALB 1640-1865; DLB 3, 74;
SATA 59

Menander
c. 342B.C.-c. 292B.C. . . . . **CMLC 9; DC 3**

Mencken, H(enry) L(ouis)
1880-1956 . . . . **TCLC 13**
See also CA 105; 125; CDALB 1917-1929;
DLB 11, 29, 63, 137; MTCW

Mercer, David 1928-1980 . . . . **CLC 5**
See also CA 9-12R; 102; CANR 23;
DLB 13; MTCW

Merchant, Paul
See Ellison, Harlan

Meredith, George 1828-1909 . . . **TCLC 17, 43**
See also CA 117; CDBLB 1832-1890;
DLB 18, 35, 57

Meredith, William (Morris)
1919- . . . . **CLC 4, 13, 22, 55**
See also CA 9-12R; CAAS 14; CANR 6, 40;
DLB 5

Merezhkovsky, Dmitry Sergeyevich
1865-1941 . . . . **TCLC 29**

Merimee, Prosper
1803-1870 . . . . **NCLC 6; SSC 7**
See also DLB 119

Merkin, Daphne 1954- . . . . **CLC 44**
See also CA 123

Merlin, Arthur
See Blish, James (Benjamin)

Merrill, James (Ingram)
1926- . . . . **CLC 2, 3, 6, 8, 13, 18, 34**
See also CA 13-16R; CANR 10; DLB 5;
DLBY 85; MTCW

Merriman, Alex
See Silverberg, Robert

Merritt, E. B.
See Waddington, Miriam

Merton, Thomas
1915-1968 . . **CLC 1, 3, 11, 34, 83; PC 10**
See also CA 5-8R; 25-28R; CANR 22;
DLB 48; DLBY 81; MTCW

Merwin, W(illiam) S(tanley)
1927- . . . . . . **CLC 1, 2, 3, 5, 8, 13, 18, 45**
See also CA 13-16R; CANR 15; DLB 5;
MTCW

Metcalf, John 1938- . . . . **CLC 37**
See also CA 113; DLB 60

Metcalf, Suzanne
See Baum, L(yman) Frank

Mew, Charlotte (Mary)
1870-1928 . . . . **TCLC 8**
See also CA 105; DLB 19, 135

Mewshaw, Michael 1943- . . . . **CLC 9**
See also CA 53-56; CANR 7; DLBY 80

Meyer, June
See Jordan, June

Meyer, Lynn
See Slavitt, David R(ytman)

Meyer-Meyrink, Gustav 1868-1932
See Meyrink, Gustav
See also CA 117

Meyers, Jeffrey 1939- . . . . **CLC 39**
See also CA 73-76; DLB 111

Meynell, Alice (Christina Gertrude Thompson)
1847-1922 . . . . **TCLC 6**
See also CA 104; DLB 19, 98

Meyrink, Gustav . . . . **TCLC 21**
See also Meyer-Meyrink, Gustav
See also DLB 81

Michaels, Leonard
  1933- . . . . **CLC 6, 25; SSC 16**
  See also CA 61-64; CANR 21; DLB 130;
  MTCW

Michaux, Henri 1899-1984 . . . . . **CLC 8, 19**
  See also CA 85-88; 114

Michelangelo 1475-1564 . . . . **LC 12**

Michelet, Jules 1798-1874 . . . . . . **NCLC 31**

Michener, James A(lbert)
  1907(?)- . . . . **CLC 1, 5, 11, 29, 60**
  See also AITN 1; BEST 90:1; CA 5-8R;
  CANR 21, 45; DLB 6; MTCW

Mickiewicz, Adam 1798-1855 . . . . . **NCLC 3**

Middleton, Christopher 1926- . . . . . . **CLC 13**
  See also CA 13-16R; CANR 29; DLB 40

Middleton, Stanley 1919- . . . . **CLC 7, 38**
  See also CA 25-28R; CANR 21; DLB 14

Migueis, Jose Rodrigues 1901- . . . . . **CLC 10**

Mikszath, Kalman 1847-1910 . . . . . **TCLC 31**

Miles, Josephine
  1911-1985 . . . . **CLC 1, 2, 14, 34, 39**
  See also CA 1-4R; 116; CANR 2; DLB 48

Militant
  See Sandburg, Carl (August)

Mill, John Stuart 1806-1873 . . . . . **NCLC 11**
  See also CDBLB 1832-1890; DLB 55

Millar, Kenneth 1915-1983 . . . . **CLC 14**
  See also Macdonald, Ross
  See also CA 9-12R; 110; CANR 16; DLB 2;
  DLBD 6; DLBY 83; MTCW

Millay, E. Vincent
  See Millay, Edna St. Vincent

Millay, Edna St. Vincent
  1892-1950 . . . . . . **TCLC 4, 49; DA; PC 6**
  See also CA 104; 130; CDALB 1917-1929;
  DLB 45; MTCW

Miller, Arthur
  1915- . . . . **CLC 1, 2, 6, 10, 15, 26, 47, 78;**
                                    DA; DC 1; WLC
  See also AITN 1; CA 1-4R; CABS 3;
  CANR 2, 30; CDALB 1941-1968; DLB 7;
  MTCW

Miller, Henry (Valentine)
  1891-1980 . . . . **CLC 1, 2, 4, 9, 14, 43, 84;**
                                         DA; WLC
  See also CA 9-12R; 97-100; CANR 33;
  CDALB 1929-1941; DLB 4, 9; DLBY 80;
  MTCW

Miller, Jason 1939(?)- . . . . **CLC 2**
  See also AITN 1; CA 73-76; DLB 7

Miller, Sue 1943- . . . . **CLC 44**
  See also BEST 90:3; CA 139; DLB 143

Miller, Walter M(ichael, Jr.)
  1923- . . . . **CLC 4, 30**
  See also CA 85-88; DLB 8

Millett, Kate 1934- . . . . **CLC 67**
  See also AITN 1; CA 73-76; CANR 32;
  MTCW

Millhauser, Steven 1943- . . . . **CLC 21, 54**
  See also CA 110; 111; DLB 2

Millin, Sarah Gertrude 1889-1968 . . **CLC 49**
  See also CA 102; 93-96

Milne, A(lan) A(lexander)
  1882-1956 . . . . **TCLC 6**
  See also CA 104; 133; CLR 1, 26; DLB 10,
  77, 100; MAICYA; MTCW; YABC 1

Milner, Ron(ald) 1938- . . . . **CLC 56; BLC**
  See also AITN 1; BW 1; CA 73-76;
  CANR 24; DLB 38; MTCW

Milosz, Czeslaw
  1911- . . . **CLC 5, 11, 22, 31, 56, 82; PC 8**
  See also CA 81-84; CANR 23; MTCW

Milton, John 1608-1674 . . . **LC 9; DA; WLC**
  See also CDBLB 1660-1789; DLB 131

Minehaha, Cornelius
  See Wedekind, (Benjamin) Frank(lin)

Miner, Valerie 1947- . . . . **CLC 40**
  See also CA 97-100

Minimo, Duca
  See D'Annunzio, Gabriele

Minot, Susan 1956- . . . . **CLC 44**
  See also CA 134

Minus, Ed 1938- . . . . **CLC 39**

Miranda, Javier
  See Bioy Casares, Adolfo

Mirbeau, Octave 1848-1917 . . . . . . **TCLC 55**
  See also DLB 123

Miro (Ferrer), Gabriel (Francisco Victor)
  1879-1930 . . . . **TCLC 5**
  See also CA 104

Mishima, Yukio
  . . . . . . **CLC 2, 4, 6, 9, 27; DC 1; SSC 4**
  See also Hiraoka, Kimitake

Mistral, Frederic 1830-1914 . . . . . . **TCLC 51**
  See also CA 122

Mistral, Gabriela . . . . **TCLC 2; HLC**
  See also Godoy Alcayaga, Lucila

Mistry, Rohinton 1952- . . . . **CLC 71**
  See also CA 141

Mitchell, Clyde
  See Ellison, Harlan; Silverberg, Robert

Mitchell, James Leslie 1901-1935
  See Gibbon, Lewis Grassic
  See also CA 104; DLB 15

Mitchell, Joni 1943- . . . . **CLC 12**
  See also CA 112

Mitchell, Margaret (Munnerlyn)
  1900-1949 . . . . **TCLC 11**
  See also CA 109; 125; DLB 9; MTCW

Mitchell, Peggy
  See Mitchell, Margaret (Munnerlyn)

Mitchell, S(ilas) Weir 1829-1914 . . **TCLC 36**

Mitchell, W(illiam) O(rmond)
  1914- . . . . **CLC 25**
  See also CA 77-80; CANR 15, 43; DLB 88

Mitford, Mary Russell 1787-1855 . . **NCLC 4**
  See also DLB 110, 116

Mitford, Nancy 1904-1973 . . . . **CLC 44**
  See also CA 9-12R

Miyamoto, Yuriko 1899-1951 . . . . . **TCLC 37**

Mo, Timothy (Peter) 1950(?)- . . . . . . **CLC 46**
  See also CA 117; MTCW

Modarressi, Taghi (M.) 1931- . . . . . . **CLC 44**
  See also CA 121; 134

Modiano, Patrick (Jean) 1945- . . . . . **CLC 18**
  See also CA 85-88; CANR 17, 40; DLB 83

Moerck, Paal
  See Roelvaag, O(le) E(dvart)

Mofolo, Thomas (Mokopu)
  1875(?)-1948 . . . . **TCLC 22; BLC**
  See also CA 121

Mohr, Nicholasa 1935- . . . . . . **CLC 12; HLC**
  See also AAYA 8; CA 49-52; CANR 1, 32;
  CLR 22; HW; JRDA; SAAS 8; SATA 8

Mojtabai, A(nn) G(race)
  1938- . . . . **CLC 5, 9, 15, 29**
  See also CA 85-88

Moliere 1622-1673 . . . . **LC 10; DA; WLC**

Molin, Charles
  See Mayne, William (James Carter)

Molnar, Ferenc 1878-1952 . . . . **TCLC 20**
  See also CA 109

Momaday, N(avarre) Scott
  1934- . . . . **CLC 2, 19; DA**
  See also AAYA 11; CA 25-28R; CANR 14,
  34; DLB 143; MTCW; NNAL; SATA 30,
  48

Monette, Paul 1945- . . . . **CLC 82**
  See also CA 139

Monroe, Harriet 1860-1936 . . . . **TCLC 12**
  See also CA 109; DLB 54, 91

Monroe, Lyle
  See Heinlein, Robert A(nson)

Montagu, Elizabeth 1917- . . . . **NCLC 7**
  See also CA 9-12R

Montagu, Mary (Pierrepont) Wortley
  1689-1762 . . . . **LC 9**
  See also DLB 95, 101

Montagu, W. H.
  See Coleridge, Samuel Taylor

Montague, John (Patrick)
  1929- . . . . **CLC 13, 46**
  See also CA 9-12R; CANR 9; DLB 40;
  MTCW

Montaigne, Michel (Eyquem) de
  1533-1592 . . . . **LC 8; DA; WLC**

Montale, Eugenio 1896-1981 . . . **CLC 7, 9, 18**
  See also CA 17-20R; 104; CANR 30;
  DLB 114; MTCW

Montesquieu, Charles-Louis de Secondat
  1689-1755 . . . . **LC 7**

Montgomery, (Robert) Bruce 1921-1978
  See Crispin, Edmund
  See also CA 104

Montgomery, L(ucy) M(aud)
  1874-1942 . . . . **TCLC 51**
  See also AAYA 12; CA 108; 137; CLR 8;
  DLB 92; JRDA; MAICYA; YABC 1

Montgomery, Marion H., Jr. 1925- . . **CLC 7**
  See also AITN 1; CA 1-4R; CANR 3;
  DLB 6

Montgomery, Max
  See Davenport, Guy (Mattison, Jr.)

Montherlant, Henry (Milon) de
  1896-1972 . . . . **CLC 8, 19**
  See also CA 85-88; 37-40R; DLB 72;
  MTCW

Munford, Robert 1737(?)-1783 .... **LC 5**
See also DLB 31

Mungo, Raymond 1946- .... **CLC 72**
See also CA 49-52; CANR 2

Munro, Alice
1931- .... **CLC 6, 10, 19, 50; SSC 3**
See also AITN 2; CA 33-36R; CANR 33;
DLB 53; MTCW; SATA 29

Munro, H(ector) H(ugh) 1870-1916
See Saki
See also CA 104; 130; CDBLB 1890-1914;
DA; DLB 34; MTCW; WLC

Murasaki, Lady .... **CMLC 1**

Murdoch, (Jean) Iris
1919- ...... **CLC 1, 2, 3, 4, 6, 8, 11, 15,**
22, 31, 51
See also CA 13-16R; CANR 8, 43;
CDBLB 1960 to Present; DLB 14;
MTCW

Murnau, Friedrich Wilhelm
See Plumpe, Friedrich Wilhelm

Murphy, Richard 1927- .... **CLC 41**
See also CA 29-32R; DLB 40

Murphy, Sylvia 1937- .... **CLC 34**
See also CA 121

Murphy, Thomas (Bernard) 1935- ... **CLC 51**
See also CA 101

Murray, Albert L. 1916- .... **CLC 73**
See also BW 2; CA 49-52; CANR 26;
DLB 38

Murray, Les(lie) A(llan) 1938- ..... **CLC 40**
See also CA 21-24R; CANR 11, 27

Murry, J. Middleton
See Murry, John Middleton

Murry, John Middleton
1889-1957 .... **TCLC 16**
See also CA 118

Musgrave, Susan 1951- .... **CLC 13, 54**
See also CA 69-72; CANR 45

Musil, Robert (Edler von)
1880-1942 .... **TCLC 12**
See also CA 109; DLB 81, 124

Musset, (Louis Charles) Alfred de
1810-1857 .... **NCLC 7**

My Brother's Brother
See Chekhov, Anton (Pavlovich)

Myers, Walter Dean 1937- ... **CLC 35; BLC**
See also AAYA 4; BW 2; CA 33-36R;
CANR 20, 42; CLR 4, 16; DLB 33;
JRDA; MAICYA; SAAS 2; SATA 27, 41,
71

Myers, Walter M.
See Myers, Walter Dean

Myles, Symon
See Follett, Ken(neth Martin)

Nabokov, Vladimir (Vladimirovich)
1899-1977 ..... **CLC 1, 2, 3, 6, 8, 11, 15,**
23, 44, 46, 64; DA; SSC 11; WLC
See also CA 5-8R; 69-72; CANR 20;
CDALB 1941-1968; DLB 2; DLBD 3;
DLBY 80, 91; MTCW

Nagai Kafu .... **TCLC 51**
See also Nagai Sokichi

Nagai Sokichi 1879-1959
See Nagai Kafu
See also CA 117

Nagy, Laszlo 1925-1978 .... **CLC 7**
See also CA 129; 112

Naipaul, Shiva(dhar Srinivasa)
1945-1985 .... **CLC 32, 39**
See also CA 110; 112; 116; CANR 33;
DLBY 85; MTCW

Naipaul, V(idiadhar) S(urajprasad)
1932- .... **CLC 4, 7, 9, 13, 18, 37**
See also CA 1-4R; CANR 1, 33;
CDBLB 1960 to Present; DLB 125;
DLBY 85; MTCW

Nakos, Lilika 1899(?)- .... **CLC 29**

Narayan, R(asipuram) K(rishnaswami)
1906- .... **CLC 7, 28, 47**
See also CA 81-84; CANR 33; MTCW;
SATA 62

Nash, (Frediric) Ogden 1902-1971 .. **CLC 23**
See also CA 13-14; 29-32R; CANR 34;
CAP 1; DLB 11; MAICYA; MTCW;
SATA 2, 46

Nathan, Daniel
See Dannay, Frederic

Nathan, George Jean 1882-1958 ... **TCLC 18**
See also Hatteras, Owen
See also CA 114; DLB 137

Natsume, Kinnosuke 1867-1916
See Natsume, Soseki
See also CA 104

Natsume, Soseki .... **TCLC 2, 10**
See also Natsume, Kinnosuke

Natti, (Mary) Lee 1919-
See Kingman, Lee
See also CA 5-8R; CANR 2

Naylor, Gloria
1950- .... **CLC 28, 52; BLC; DA**
See also AAYA 6; BW 2; CA 107;
CANR 27; MTCW

Neihardt, John Gneisenau
1881-1973 .... **CLC 32**
See also CA 13-14; CAP 1; DLB 9, 54

Nekrasov, Nikolai Alekseevich
1821-1878 .... **NCLC 11**

Nelligan, Emile 1879-1941 .... **TCLC 14**
See also CA 114; DLB 92

Nelson, Willie 1933- .... **CLC 17**
See also CA 107

Nemerov, Howard (Stanley)
1920-1991 .... **CLC 2, 6, 9, 36**
See also CA 1-4R; 134; CABS 2; CANR 1,
27; DLB 6; DLBY 83; MTCW

Neruda, Pablo
1904-1973 ..... **CLC 1, 2, 5, 7, 9, 28, 62;**
DA; HLC; PC 4; WLC
See also CA 19-20; 45-48; CAP 2; HW;
MTCW

Nerval, Gerard de 1808-1855 ...... **NCLC 1**

Nervo, (Jose) Amado (Ruiz de)
1870-1919 .... **TCLC 11**
See also CA 109; 131; HW

Nessi, Pio Baroja y
See Baroja (y Nessi), Pio

Nestroy, Johann 1801-1862 ...... **NCLC 42**
See also DLB 133

Neufeld, John (Arthur) 1938- ...... **CLC 17**
See also AAYA 11; CA 25-28R; CANR 11,
37; MAICYA; SAAS 3; SATA 6

Neville, Emily Cheney 1919- .... **CLC 12**
See also CA 5-8R; CANR 3, 37; JRDA;
MAICYA; SAAS 2; SATA 1

Newbound, Bernard Slade 1930-
See Slade, Bernard
See also CA 81-84

Newby, P(ercy) H(oward)
1918- .... **CLC 2, 13**
See also CA 5-8R; CANR 32; DLB 15;
MTCW

Newlove, Donald 1928- .... **CLC 6**
See also CA 29-32R; CANR 25

Newlove, John (Herbert) 1938- ..... **CLC 14**
See also CA 21-24R; CANR 9, 25

Newman, Charles 1938- .... **CLC 2, 8**
See also CA 21-24R

Newman, Edwin (Harold) 1919- .... **CLC 14**
See also AITN 1; CA 69-72; CANR 5

Newman, John Henry
1801-1890 .... **NCLC 38**
See also DLB 18, 32, 55

Newton, Suzanne 1936- .... **CLC 35**
See also CA 41-44R; CANR 14; JRDA;
SATA 5, 77

Nexo, Martin Andersen
1869-1954 .... **TCLC 43**

Nezval, Vitezslav 1900-1958 ...... **TCLC 44**
See also CA 123

Ng, Fae Myenne 1957(?)- .... **CLC 81**

Ngema, Mbongeni 1955- .... **CLC 57**
See also BW 2; CA 143

Ngugi, James T(hiong'o) .... **CLC 3, 7, 13**
See also Ngugi wa Thiong'o

Ngugi wa Thiong'o 1938- ..... **CLC 36; BLC**
See also Ngugi, James T(hiong'o)
See also BW 2; CA 81-84; CANR 27;
DLB 125; MTCW

Nichol, B(arrie) P(hillip)
1944-1988 .... **CLC 18**
See also CA 53-56; DLB 53; SATA 66

Nichols, John (Treadwell) 1940- .... **CLC 38**
See also CA 9-12R; CAAS 2; CANR 6;
DLBY 82

Nichols, Leigh
See Koontz, Dean R(ay)

Nichols, Peter (Richard)
1927- .... **CLC 5, 36, 65**
See also CA 104; CANR 33; DLB 13;
MTCW

Nicolas, F. R. E.
See Freeling, Nicolas

Niedecker, Lorine 1903-1970 .... **CLC 10, 42**
See also CA 25-28; CAP 2; DLB 48

Nietzsche, Friedrich (Wilhelm)
1844-1900 .... **TCLC 10, 18, 55**
See also CA 107; 121; DLB 129

Nievo, Ippolito 1831-1861 .... **NCLC 22**

Nightingale, Anne Redmon 1943-
See Redmon, Anne
See also CA 103

Nik.T.O.
See Annensky, Innokenty Fyodorovich

Nin, Anais
1903-1977 . . . . . . **CLC 1, 4, 8, 11, 14, 60;**
SSC 10
See also AITN 2; CA 13-16R; 69-72;
CANR 22; DLB 2, 4; MTCW

Nissenson, Hugh 1933- . . . . **CLC 4, 9**
See also CA 17-20R; CANR 27; DLB 28

Niven, Larry . . . . **CLC 8**
See also Niven, Laurence Van Cott
See also DLB 8

Niven, Laurence Van Cott 1938-
See Niven, Larry
See also CA 21-24R; CAAS 12; CANR 14,
44; MTCW

Nixon, Agnes Eckhardt 1927- . . . . . . **CLC 21**
See also CA 110

Nizan, Paul 1905-1940 . . . . **TCLC 40**
See also DLB 72

Nkosi, Lewis 1936- . . . . **CLC 45; BLC**
See also BW 1; CA 65-68; CANR 27

Nodier, (Jean) Charles (Emmanuel)
1780-1844 . . . . **NCLC 19**
See also DLB 119

Nolan, Christopher 1965- . . . . **CLC 58**
See also CA 111

Norden, Charles
See Durrell, Lawrence (George)

Nordhoff, Charles (Bernard)
1887-1947 . . . . **TCLC 23**
See also CA 108; DLB 9; SATA 23

Norfolk, Lawrence 1963- . . . . **CLC 76**
See also CA 144

Norman, Marsha 1947- . . . . **CLC 28**
See also CA 105; CABS 3; CANR 41;
DLBY 84

Norris, Benjamin Franklin, Jr.
1870-1902 . . . . **TCLC 24**
See also Norris, Frank
See also CA 110

Norris, Frank
See Norris, Benjamin Franklin, Jr.
See also CDALB 1865-1917; DLB 12, 71

Norris, Leslie 1921- . . . . **CLC 14**
See also CA 11-12; CANR 14; CAP 1;
DLB 27

North, Andrew
See Norton, Andre

North, Anthony
See Koontz, Dean R(ay)

North, Captain George
See Stevenson, Robert Louis (Balfour)

North, Milou
See Erdrich, Louise

Northrup, B. A.
See Hubbard, L(afayette) Ron(ald)

North Staffs
See Hulme, T(homas) E(rnest)

Norton, Alice Mary
See Norton, Andre
See also MAICYA; SATA 1, 43

Norton, Andre 1912- . . . . **CLC 12**
See also Norton, Alice Mary
See also CA 1-4R; CANR 2, 31; DLB 8, 52;
JRDA; MTCW

Norway, Nevil Shute 1899-1960
See Shute, Nevil
See also CA 102; 93-96

Norwid, Cyprian Kamil
1821-1883 . . . . **NCLC 17**

Nosille, Nabrah
See Ellison, Harlan

Nossack, Hans Erich 1901-1978 . . . . . **CLC 6**
See also CA 93-96; 85-88; DLB 69

Nosu, Chuji
See Ozu, Yasujiro

Nova, Craig 1945- . . . . **CLC 7, 31**
See also CA 45-48; CANR 2

Novak, Joseph
See Kosinski, Jerzy (Nikodem)

Novalis 1772-1801 . . . . **NCLC 13**
See also DLB 90

Nowlan, Alden (Albert) 1933-1983 . . **CLC 15**
See also CA 9-12R; CANR 5; DLB 53

Noyes, Alfred 1880-1958 . . . . **TCLC 7**
See also CA 104; DLB 20

Nunn, Kem 19(?)- . . . . **CLC 34**

Nye, Robert 1939- . . . . **CLC 13, 42**
See also CA 33-36R; CANR 29; DLB 14;
MTCW; SATA 6

Nyro, Laura 1947- . . . . **CLC 17**

Oates, Joyce Carol
1938- . . . . . . **CLC 1, 2, 3, 6, 9, 11, 15, 19,**
33, 52; DA; SSC 6; WLC
See also AITN 1; BEST 89:2; CA 5-8R;
CANR 25, 45; CDALB 1968-1988;
DLB 2, 5, 130; DLBY 81; MTCW

O'Brien, E. G.
See Clarke, Arthur C(harles)

O'Brien, Edna
1936- . . . **CLC 3, 5, 8, 13, 36, 65; SSC 10**
See also CA 1-4R; CANR 6, 41;
CDBLB 1960 to Present; DLB 14;
MTCW

O'Brien, Fitz-James 1828-1862 . . . **NCLC 21**
See also DLB 74

O'Brien, Flann . . . . **CLC 1, 4, 5, 7, 10, 47**
See also O Nuallain, Brian

O'Brien, Richard 1942- . . . . **CLC 17**
See also CA 124

O'Brien, Tim 1946- . . . . **CLC 7, 19, 40**
See also CA 85-88; CANR 40; DLBD 9;
DLBY 80

Obstfelder, Sigbjoern 1866-1900 . . . **TCLC 23**
See also CA 123

O'Casey, Sean
1880-1964 . . . . **CLC 1, 5, 9, 11, 15**
See also CA 89-92; CDBLB 1914-1945;
DLB 10; MTCW

O'Cathasaigh, Sean
See O'Casey, Sean

Ochs, Phil 1940-1976 . . . . **CLC 17**
See also CA 65-68

O'Connor, Edwin (Greene)
1918-1968 . . . . **CLC 14**
See also CA 93-96; 25-28R

O'Connor, (Mary) Flannery
1925-1964 . . . . **CLC 1, 2, 3, 6, 10, 13, 15,**
21, 66; DA; SSC 1; WLC
See also AAYA 7; CA 1-4R; CANR 3, 41;
CDALB 1941-1968; DLB 2; DLBY 80;
MTCW

O'Connor, Frank . . . . **CLC 23; SSC 5**
See also O'Donovan, Michael John

O'Dell, Scott 1898-1989 . . . . **CLC 30**
See also AAYA 3; CA 61-64; 129;
CANR 12, 30; CLR 1, 16; DLB 52;
JRDA; MAICYA; SATA 12, 60

Odets, Clifford 1906-1963 . . . . **CLC 2, 28**
See also CA 85-88; DLB 7, 26; MTCW

O'Doherty, Brian 1934- . . . . **CLC 76**
See also CA 105

O'Donnell, K. M.
See Malzberg, Barry N(athaniel)

O'Donnell, Lawrence
See Kuttner, Henry

O'Donovan, Michael John
1903-1966 . . . . **CLC 14**
See also O'Connor, Frank
See also CA 93-96

Oe, Kenzaburo 1935- . . . . **CLC 10, 36**
See also CA 97-100; CANR 36; MTCW

O'Faolain, Julia 1932- . . . . **CLC 6, 19, 47**
See also CA 81-84; CAAS 2; CANR 12;
DLB 14; MTCW

O'Faolain, Sean
1900-1991 . . . . **CLC 1, 7, 14, 32, 70;**
SSC 13
See also CA 61-64; 134; CANR 12;
DLB 15; MTCW

O'Flaherty, Liam
1896-1984 . . . . **CLC 5, 34; SSC 6**
See also CA 101; 113; CANR 35; DLB 36;
DLBY 84; MTCW

Ogilvy, Gavin
See Barrie, J(ames) M(atthew)

O'Grady, Standish James
1846-1928 . . . . **TCLC 5**
See also CA 104

O'Grady, Timothy 1951- . . . . **CLC 59**
See also CA 138

O'Hara, Frank
1926-1966 . . . . **CLC 2, 5, 13, 78**
See also CA 9-12R; 25-28R; CANR 33;
DLB 5, 16; MTCW

O'Hara, John (Henry)
1905-1970 . . . . **CLC 1, 2, 3, 6, 11, 42;**
SSC 15
See also CA 5-8R; 25-28R; CANR 31;
CDALB 1929-1941; DLB 9, 86; DLBD 2;
MTCW

O Hehir, Diana 1922- . . . . **CLC 41**
See also CA 93-96

Okigbo, Christopher (Ifenayichukwu)
1932-1967 . . . . . **CLC 25, 84; BLC; PC 7**
See also BW 1; CA 77-80; DLB 125;
MTCW

Olds, Sharon 1942-............ **CLC 32, 39**
See also CA 101; CANR 18, 41; DLB 120

Oldstyle, Jonathan
See Irving, Washington

Olesha, Yuri (Karlovich)
1899-1960 .... **CLC 8**
See also CA 85-88

Oliphant, Margaret (Oliphant Wilson)
1828-1897 .... **NCLC 11**
See also DLB 18

Oliver, Mary 1935-............ **CLC 19, 34**
See also CA 21-24R; CANR 9, 43; DLB 5

Olivier, Laurence (Kerr)
1907-1989 .... **CLC 20**
See also CA 111; 129

Olsen, Tillie
1913- .... **CLC 4, 13; DA; SSC 11**
See also CA 1-4R; CANR 1, 43; DLB 28;
DLBY 80; MTCW

Olson, Charles (John)
1910-1970 ..... **CLC 1, 2, 5, 6, 9, 11, 29**
See also CA 13-16; 25-28R; CABS 2;
CANR 35; CAP 1; DLB 5, 16; MTCW

Olson, Toby 1937- .... **CLC 28**
See also CA 65-68; CANR 9, 31

Olyesha, Yuri
See Olesha, Yuri (Karlovich)

Ondaatje, (Philip) Michael
1943- .... **CLC 14, 29, 51, 76**
See also CA 77-80; CANR 42; DLB 60

Oneal, Elizabeth 1934-
See Oneal, Zibby
See also CA 106; CANR 28; MAICYA;
SATA 30

Oneal, Zibby .... **CLC 30**
See also Oneal, Elizabeth
See also AAYA 5; CLR 13; JRDA

O'Neill, Eugene (Gladstone)
1888-1953 ...... **TCLC 1, 6, 27, 49; DA;
WLC**
See also AITN 1; CA 110; 132;
CDALB 1929-1941; DLB 7; MTCW

Onetti, Juan Carlos 1909- .... **CLC 7, 10**
See also CA 85-88; CANR 32; DLB 113;
HW; MTCW

O Nuallain, Brian 1911-1966
See O'Brien, Flann
See also CA 21-22; 25-28R; CAP 2

Oppen, George 1908-1984 .... **CLC 7, 13, 34**
See also CA 13-16R; 113; CANR 8; DLB 5

Oppenheim, E(dward) Phillips
1866-1946 .... **TCLC 45**
See also CA 111; DLB 70

Orlovitz, Gil 1918-1973 .... **CLC 22**
See also CA 77-80; 45-48; DLB 2, 5

Orris
See Ingelow, Jean

Ortega y Gasset, Jose
1883-1955 .... **TCLC 9; HLC**
See also CA 106; 130; HW; MTCW

Ortiz, Simon J(oseph) 1941- .... **CLC 45**
See also CA 134; DLB 120

Orton, Joe .... **CLC 4, 13, 43; DC 3**
See also Orton, John Kingsley
See also CDBLB 1960 to Present; DLB 13

Orton, John Kingsley 1933-1967
See Orton, Joe
See also CA 85-88; CANR 35; MTCW

Orwell, George
.... **TCLC 2, 6, 15, 31, 51; WLC**
See also Blair, Eric (Arthur)
See also CDBLB 1945-1960; DLB 15, 98

Osborne, David
See Silverberg, Robert

Osborne, George
See Silverberg, Robert

Osborne, John (James)
1929- .... **CLC 1, 2, 5, 11, 45; DA; WLC**
See also CA 13-16R; CANR 21;
CDBLB 1945-1960; DLB 13; MTCW

Osborne, Lawrence 1958- .... **CLC 50**

Oshima, Nagisa 1932- .... **CLC 20**
See also CA 116; 121

Oskison, John Milton
1874-1947 .... **TCLC 35**
See also CA 144

Ossoli, Sarah Margaret (Fuller marchesa d')
1810-1850
See Fuller, Margaret
See also SATA 25

Ostrovsky, Alexander
1823-1886 .... **NCLC 30**

Otero, Blas de 1916-1979.......... **CLC 11**
See also CA 89-92; DLB 134

Otto, Whitney 1955-.............. **CLC 70**
See also CA 140

Ouida .... **TCLC 43**
See also De La Ramee, (Marie) Louise
See also DLB 18

Ousmane, Sembene 1923- .... **CLC 66; BLC**
See also BW 1; CA 117; 125; MTCW

Ovid 43B.C.-18th cent. (?)... **CMLC 7; PC 2**

Owen, Hugh
See Faust, Frederick (Schiller)

Owen, Wilfred (Edward Salter)
1893-1918 ...... **TCLC 5, 27; DA; WLC**
See also CA 104; 141; CDBLB 1914-1945;
DLB 20

Owens, Rochelle 1936-............. **CLC 8**
See also CA 17-20R; CAAS 2; CANR 39

Oz, Amos 1939- ... **CLC 5, 8, 11, 27, 33, 54**
See also CA 53-56; CANR 27; MTCW

Ozick, Cynthia
1928- .... **CLC 3, 7, 28, 62; SSC 15**
See also BEST 90:1; CA 17-20R; CANR 23;
DLB 28; DLBY 82; MTCW

Ozu, Yasujiro 1903-1963.......... **CLC 16**
See also CA 112

Pacheco, C.
See Pessoa, Fernando (Antonio Nogueira)

Pa Chin
See Li Fei-kan

Pack, Robert 1929-.............. **CLC 13**
See also CA 1-4R; CANR 3, 44; DLB 5

Padgett, Lewis
See Kuttner, Henry

Padilla (Lorenzo), Heberto 1932-... **CLC 38**
See also AITN 1; CA 123; 131; HW

Page, Jimmy 1944-.............. **CLC 12**

Page, Louise 1955-.............. **CLC 40**
See also CA 140

Page, P(atricia) K(athleen)
1916-..................... **CLC 7, 18**
See also CA 53-56; CANR 4, 22; DLB 68;
MTCW

Paget, Violet 1856-1935
See Lee, Vernon
See also CA 104

Paget-Lowe, Henry
See Lovecraft, H(oward) P(hillips)

Paglia, Camille (Anna) 1947-....... **CLC 68**
See also CA 140

Paige, Richard
See Koontz, Dean R(ay)

Pakenham, Antonia
See Fraser, (Lady) Antonia (Pakenham)

Palamas, Kostes 1859-1943 .... **TCLC 5**
See also CA 105

Palazzeschi, Aldo 1885-1974...... **CLC 11**
See also CA 89-92; 53-56; DLB 114

Paley, Grace 1922-.... **CLC 4, 6, 37; SSC 8**
See also CA 25-28R; CANR 13; DLB 28;
MTCW

Palin, Michael (Edward) 1943-..... **CLC 21**
See also Monty Python
See also CA 107; CANR 35; SATA 67

Palliser, Charles 1947-............ **CLC 65**
See also CA 136

Palma, Ricardo 1833-1919........ **TCLC 29**

Pancake, Breece Dexter 1952-1979
See Pancake, Breece D'J
See also CA 123; 109

Pancake, Breece D'J.............. **CLC 29**
See also Pancake, Breece Dexter
See also DLB 130

Panko, Rudy
See Gogol, Nikolai (Vasilyevich)

Papadiamantis, Alexandros
1851-1911 .... **TCLC 29**

Papadiamantopoulos, Johannes 1856-1910
See Moreas, Jean
See also CA 117

Papini, Giovanni 1881-1956....... **TCLC 22**
See also CA 121

Paracelsus 1493-1541.............. **LC 14**

Parasol, Peter
See Stevens, Wallace

Parfenie, Maria
See Codrescu, Andrei

Parini, Jay (Lee) 1948- .... **CLC 54**
See also CA 97-100; CAAS 16; CANR 32

Park, Jordan
See Kornbluth, C(yril) M.; Pohl, Frederik

Parker, Bert
See Ellison, Harlan

Parker, Dorothy (Rothschild)
1893-1967 .... **CLC 15, 68; SSC 2**
See also CA 19-20; 25-28R; CAP 2;
DLB 11, 45, 86; MTCW

Parker, Robert B(rown) 1932-...... **CLC 27**
See also BEST 89:4; CA 49-52; CANR 1,
26; MTCW

Parkes, Lucas
See Harris, John (Wyndham Parkes Lucas)
Beynon

Parkin, Frank 1940-............. **CLC 43**

Parkman, Francis, Jr.
1823-1893 .... **NCLC 12**
See also DLB 1, 30

Parks, Gordon (Alexander Buchanan)
1912- .... **CLC 1, 16; BLC**
See also AITN 2; BW 2; CA 41-44R;
CANR 26; DLB 33; SATA 8

Parnell, Thomas 1679-1718 .... **LC 3**
See also DLB 94

Parra, Nicanor 1914-........ **CLC 2; HLC**
See also CA 85-88; CANR 32; HW; MTCW

Parrish, Mary Frances
See Fisher, M(ary) F(rances) K(ennedy)

Parson
See Coleridge, Samuel Taylor

Parson Lot
See Kingsley, Charles

Partridge, Anthony
See Oppenheim, E(dward) Phillips

Pascoli, Giovanni 1855-1912 ...... **TCLC 45**

Pasolini, Pier Paolo
1922-1975 .... **CLC 20, 37**
See also CA 93-96; 61-64; DLB 128;
MTCW

Pasquini
See Silone, Ignazio

Pastan, Linda (Olenik) 1932- ...... **CLC 27**
See also CA 61-64; CANR 18, 40; DLB 5

Pasternak, Boris (Leonidovich)
1890-1960 ...... **CLC 7, 10, 18, 63; DA;
PC 6; WLC**
See also CA 127; 116; MTCW

Patchen, Kenneth 1911-1972 ... **CLC 1, 2, 18**
See also CA 1-4R; 33-36R; CANR 3, 35;
DLB 16, 48; MTCW

Pater, Walter (Horatio)
1839-1894 .... **NCLC 7**
See also CDBLB 1832-1890; DLB 57

Paterson, A(ndrew) B(arton)
1864-1941 .... **TCLC 32**

Paterson, Katherine (Womeldorf)
1932- .... **CLC 12, 30**
See also AAYA 1; CA 21-24R; CANR 28;
CLR 7; DLB 52; JRDA; MAICYA;
MTCW; SATA 13, 53

Patmore, Coventry Kersey Dighton
1823-1896 .... **NCLC 9**
See also DLB 35, 98

Paton, Alan (Stewart)
1903-1988 ...... **CLC 4, 10, 25, 55; DA;
WLC**
See also CA 13-16; 125; CANR 22; CAP 1;
MTCW; SATA 11, 56

Paton Walsh, Gillian 1937-
See Walsh, Jill Paton
See also CANR 38; JRDA; MAICYA;
SAAS 3; SATA 4, 72

Paulding, James Kirke 1778-1860.. **NCLC 2**
See also DLB 3, 59, 74

Paulin, Thomas Neilson 1949-
See Paulin, Tom
See also CA 123; 128

Paulin, Tom .... **CLC 37**
See also Paulin, Thomas Neilson
See also DLB 40

Paustovsky, Konstantin (Georgievich)
1892-1968 .... **CLC 40**
See also CA 93-96; 25-28R

Pavese, Cesare 1908-1950 .... **TCLC 3**
See also CA 104; DLB 128

Pavic, Milorad 1929-............. **CLC 60**
See also CA 136

Payne, Alan
See Jakes, John (William)

Paz, Gil
See Lugones, Leopoldo

Paz, Octavio
1914- .... **CLC 3, 4, 6, 10, 19, 51, 65;
DA; HLC; PC 1; WLC**
See also CA 73-76; CANR 32; DLBY 90;
HW; MTCW

Peacock, Molly 1947-............. **CLC 60**
See also CA 103; DLB 120

Peacock, Thomas Love
1785-1866 .... **NCLC 22**
See also DLB 96, 116

Peake, Mervyn 1911-1968...... **CLC 7, 54**
See also CA 5-8R; 25-28R; CANR 3;
DLB 15; MTCW; SATA 23

Pearce, Philippa .... **CLC 21**
See also Christie, (Ann) Philippa
See also CLR 9; MAICYA; SATA 1, 67

Pearl, Eric
See Elman, Richard

Pearson, T(homas) R(eid) 1956- .... **CLC 39**
See also CA 120; 130

Peck, Dale 1968(?)- .... **CLC 81**

Peck, John 1941- .... **CLC 3**
See also CA 49-52; CANR 3

Peck, Richard (Wayne) 1934- ...... **CLC 21**
See also AAYA 1; CA 85-88; CANR 19,
38; JRDA; MAICYA; SAAS 2; SATA 18,
55

Peck, Robert Newton 1928-.... **CLC 17; DA**
See also AAYA 3; CA 81-84; CANR 31;
JRDA; MAICYA; SAAS 1; SATA 21, 62

Peckinpah, (David) Sam(uel)
1925-1984 .... **CLC 20**
See also CA 109; 114

Pedersen, Knut 1859-1952
See Hamsun, Knut
See also CA 104; 119; MTCW

Peeslake, Gaffer
See Durrell, Lawrence (George)

Peguy, Charles Pierre
1873-1914 .... **TCLC 10**
See also CA 107

Pena, Ramon del Valle y
See Valle-Inclan, Ramon (Maria) del

Pendennis, Arthur Esquir
See Thackeray, William Makepeace

Penn, William 1644-1718........... **LC 25**
See also DLB 24

Pepys, Samuel
1633-1703 .... **LC 11; DA; WLC**
See also CDBLB 1660-1789; DLB 101

Percy, Walker
1916-1990 .... **CLC 2, 3, 6, 8, 14, 18, 47,
65**
See also CA 1-4R; 131; CANR 1, 23;
DLB 2; DLBY 80, 90; MTCW

Perec, Georges 1936-1982 .... **CLC 56**
See also CA 141; DLB 83

Pereda (y Sanchez de Porrua), Jose Maria de
1833-1906 .... **TCLC 16**
See also CA 117

Pereda y Porrua, Jose Maria de
See Pereda (y Sanchez de Porrua), Jose
Maria de

Peregoy, George Weems
See Mencken, H(enry) L(ouis)

Perelman, S(idney) J(oseph)
1904-1979 ... **CLC 3, 5, 9, 15, 23, 44, 49**
See also AITN 1, 2; CA 73-76; 89-92;
CANR 18; DLB 11, 44; MTCW

Peret, Benjamin 1899-1959 .... **TCLC 20**
See also CA 117

Peretz, Isaac Loeb 1851(?)-1915... **TCLC 16**
See also CA 109

Peretz, Yitzhok Leibush
See Peretz, Isaac Loeb

Perez Galdos, Benito 1843-1920... **TCLC 27**
See also CA 125; HW

Perrault, Charles 1628-1703 .... **LC 2**
See also MAICYA; SATA 25

Perry, Brighton
See Sherwood, Robert E(mmet)

Perse, St.-John .... **CLC 4, 11, 46**
See also Leger, (Marie-Rene Auguste) Alexis
Saint-Leger

Peseenz, Tulio F.
See Lopez y Fuentes, Gregorio

Pesetsky, Bette 1932-............. **CLC 28**
See also CA 133; DLB 130

Peshkov, Alexei Maximovich 1868-1936
See Gorky, Maxim
See also CA 105; 141; DA

Pessoa, Fernando (Antonio Nogueira)
1888-1935 .... **TCLC 27; HLC**
See also CA 125

Peterkin, Julia Mood 1880-1961.... **CLC 31**
See also CA 102; DLB 9

Peters, Joan K. 1945-............. **CLC 39**

Peters, Robert L(ouis) 1924-........ **CLC 7**
See also CA 13-16R; CAAS 8; DLB 105

Petofi, Sandor 1823-1849......... **NCLC 21**

Petrakis, Harry Mark 1923-........ **CLC 3**
See also CA 9-12R; CANR 4, 30

Petrarch 1304-1374................. **PC 8**

Petrov, Evgeny .... **TCLC 21**
See also Kataev, Evgeny Petrovich

Petry, Ann (Lane) 1908- ...... **CLC 1, 7, 18**
See also BW 1; CA 5-8R; CAAS 6;
CANR 4; CLR 12; DLB 76; JRDA;
MAICYA; MTCW; SATA 5

Petursson, Halligrimur 1614-1674 .... **LC 8**

Philipson, Morris H. 1926- .... **CLC 53**
See also CA 1-4R; CANR 4

Phillips, David Graham
1867-1911 .... **TCLC 44**
See also CA 108; DLB 9, 12

Phillips, Jack
See Sandburg, Carl (August)

Phillips, Jayne Anne
1952- .... **CLC 15, 33; SSC 16**
See also CA 101; CANR 24; DLBY 80;
MTCW

Phillips, Richard
See Dick, Philip K(indred)

Phillips, Robert (Schaeffer) 1938-... **CLC 28**
See also CA 17-20R; CAAS 13; CANR 8;
DLB 105

Phillips, Ward
See Lovecraft, H(oward) P(hillips)

Piccolo, Lucio 1901-1969......... **CLC 13**
See also CA 97-100; DLB 114

Pickthall, Marjorie L(owry) C(hristie)
1883-1922 .... **TCLC 21**
See also CA 107; DLB 92

Pico della Mirandola, Giovanni
1463-1494 .... **LC 15**

Piercy, Marge
1936- .... **CLC 3, 6, 14, 18, 27, 62**
See also CA 21-24R; CAAS 1; CANR 13,
43; DLB 120; MTCW

Piers, Robert
See Anthony, Piers

Pieyre de Mandiargues, Andre 1909-1991
See Mandiargues, Andre Pieyre de
See also CA 103; 136; CANR 22

Pilnyak, Boris .... **TCLC 23**
See also Vogau, Boris Andreyevich

Pincherle, Alberto 1907-1990 ... **CLC 11, 18**
See also Moravia, Alberto
See also CA 25-28R; 132; CANR 33;
MTCW

Pinckney, Darryl 1953- .... **CLC 76**
See also BW 2; CA 143

Pindar 518B.C.-446B.C......... **CMLC 12**

Pineda, Cecile 1942-............. **CLC 39**
See also CA 118

Pinero, Arthur Wing 1855-1934 ... **TCLC 32**
See also CA 110; DLB 10

Pinero, Miguel (Antonio Gomez)
1946-1988 .... **CLC 4, 55**
See also CA 61-64; 125; CANR 29; HW

Pinget, Robert 1919- .... **CLC 7, 13, 37**
See also CA 85-88; DLB 83

Pink Floyd...................... **CLC 35**
See also Barrett, (Roger) Syd; Gilmour,
David; Mason, Nick; Waters, Roger;
Wright, Rick

Pinkney, Edward 1802-1828 ..... **NCLC 31**

Pinkwater, Daniel Manus 1941-.... **CLC 35**
See also Pinkwater, Manus
See also AAYA 1; CA 29-32R; CANR 12,
38; CLR 4; JRDA; MAICYA; SAAS 3;
SATA 46, 76

Pinkwater, Manus
See Pinkwater, Daniel Manus
See also SATA 8

Pinsky, Robert 1940-........ **CLC 9, 19, 38**
See also CA 29-32R; CAAS 4; DLBY 82

Pinta, Harold
See Pinter, Harold

Pinter, Harold
1930- ..... **CLC 1, 3, 6, 9, 11, 15, 27, 58,
73; DA; WLC**
See also CA 5-8R; CANR 33; CDBLB 1960
to Present; DLB 13; MTCW

Pirandello, Luigi
1867-1936 ...... **TCLC 4, 29; DA; WLC**
See also CA 104

Pirsig, Robert M(aynard)
1928-................... **CLC 4, 6, 73**
See also CA 53-56; CANR 42; MTCW;
SATA 39

Pisarev, Dmitry Ivanovich
1840-1868 .... **NCLC 25**

Pix, Mary (Griffith) 1666-1709....... **LC 8**
See also DLB 80

Pixerecourt, Guilbert de
1773-1844 .... **NCLC 39**

Plaidy, Jean
See Hibbert, Eleanor Alice Burford

Planche, James Robinson
1796-1880 .... **NCLC 42**

Plant, Robert 1948- .... **CLC 12**

Plante, David (Robert)
1940-................... **CLC 7, 23, 38**
See also CA 37-40R; CANR 12, 36;
DLBY 83; MTCW

Plath, Sylvia
1932-1963 ..... **CLC 1, 2, 3, 5, 9, 11, 14,
17, 50, 51, 62; DA; PC 1; WLC**
See also CA 19-20; CANR 34; CAP 2;
CDALB 1941-1968; DLB 5, 6; MTCW

Plato 428(?)B.C.-348(?)B.C.... **CMLC 8; DA**

Platonov, Andrei .... **TCLC 14**
See also Klimentov, Andrei Platonovich

Platt, Kin 1911- .... **CLC 26**
See also AAYA 11; CA 17-20R; CANR 11;
JRDA; SAAS 17; SATA 21

Plick et Plock
See Simenon, Georges (Jacques Christian)

Plimpton, George (Ames) 1927-..... **CLC 36**
See also AITN 1; CA 21-24R; CANR 32;
MTCW; SATA 10

Plomer, William Charles Franklin
1903-1973 .... **CLC 4, 8**
See also CA 21-22; CANR 34; CAP 2;
DLB 20; MTCW; SATA 24

Plowman, Piers
See Kavanagh, Patrick (Joseph)

Plum, J.
See Wodehouse, P(elham) G(renville)

Plumly, Stanley (Ross) 1939- ...... **CLC 33**
See also CA 108; 110; DLB 5

Plumpe, Friedrich Wilhelm
1888-1931 .... **TCLC 53**
See also CA 112

Poe, Edgar Allan
1809-1849 ..... **NCLC 1, 16; DA; PC 1;
SSC 1; WLC**
See also CDALB 1640-1865; DLB 3, 59, 73,
74; SATA 23

Poet of Titchfield Street, The
See Pound, Ezra (Weston Loomis)

Pohl, Frederik 1919- .... **CLC 18**
See also CA 61-64; CAAS 1; CANR 11, 37;
DLB 8; MTCW; SATA 24

Poirier, Louis 1910-
See Gracq, Julien
See also CA 122; 126

Poitier, Sidney 1927- .... **CLC 26**
See also BW 1; CA 117

Polanski, Roman 1933- .... **CLC 16**
See also CA 77-80

Poliakoff, Stephen 1952- .... **CLC 38**
See also CA 106; DLB 13

Police, The...................... **CLC 26**
See also Copeland, Stewart (Armstrong);
Summers, Andrew James; Sumner,
Gordon Matthew

Pollitt, Katha 1949- .... **CLC 28**
See also CA 120; 122; MTCW

Pollock, (Mary) Sharon 1936-...... **CLC 50**
See also CA 141; DLB 60

Pomerance, Bernard 1940-........ **CLC 13**
See also CA 101

Ponge, Francis (Jean Gaston Alfred)
1899-1988 .... **CLC 6, 18**
See also CA 85-88; 126; CANR 40

Pontoppidan, Henrik 1857-1943 ... **TCLC 29**

Poole, Josephine .... **CLC 17**
See also Helyar, Jane Penelope Josephine
See also SAAS 2; SATA 5

Popa, Vasko 1922-............... **CLC 19**
See also CA 112

Pope, Alexander
1688-1744 .... **LC 3; DA; WLC**
See also CDBLB 1660-1789; DLB 95, 101

Porter, Connie (Rose) 1959(?)- ..... **CLC 70**
See also BW 2; CA 142

Porter, Gene(va Grace) Stratton
1863(?)-1924 .... **TCLC 21**
See also CA 112

Porter, Katherine Anne
1890-1980 ...... **CLC 1, 3, 7, 10, 13, 15,
27; DA; SSC 4**
See also AITN 2; CA 1-4R; 101; CANR 1;
DLB 4, 9, 102; DLBY 80; MTCW;
SATA 23, 39

Porter, Peter (Neville Frederick)
1929-................. **CLC 5, 13, 33**
See also CA 85-88; DLB 40

Porter, William Sydney 1862-1910
See Henry, O.
See also CA 104; 131; CDALB 1865-1917;
DA; DLB 12, 78, 79; MTCW; YABC 2

Portillo (y Pacheco), Jose Lopez
See Lopez Portillo (y Pacheco), Jose

Post, Melville Davisson
1869-1930 .... **TCLC 39**
See also CA 110

Potok, Chaim 1929- . . . . **CLC 2, 7, 14, 26**
  See also AITN 1, 2; CA 17-20R; CANR 19,
  35; DLB 28; MTCW; SATA 33

Potter, Beatrice
  See Webb, (Martha) Beatrice (Potter)
  See also MAICYA

Potter, Dennis (Christopher George)
  1935- . . . . **CLC 58**
  See also CA 107; CANR 33; MTCW

Pound, Ezra (Weston Loomis)
  1885-1972 . . . . . . **CLC 1, 2, 3, 4, 5, 7, 10,**
             13, 18, 34, 48, 50; DA; PC 4; WLC
  See also CA 5-8R; 37-40R; CANR 40;
  CDALB 1917-1929; DLB 4, 45, 63;
  MTCW

Povod, Reinaldo 1959- . . . . **CLC 44**
  See also CA 136

Powell, Anthony (Dymoke)
  1905- . . . . **CLC 1, 3, 7, 9, 10, 31**
  See also CA 1-4R; CANR 1, 32;
  CDBLB 1945-1960; DLB 15; MTCW

Powell, Dawn 1897-1965 . . . . **CLC 66**
  See also CA 5-8R

Powell, Padgett 1952- . . . . **CLC 34**
  See also CA 126

Powers, J(ames) F(arl)
  1917- . . . . **CLC 1, 4, 8, 57; SSC 4**
  See also CA 1-4R; CANR 2; DLB 130;
  MTCW

Powers, John J(ames) 1945-
  See Powers, John R.
  See also CA 69-72

Powers, John R. . . . . **CLC 66**
  See also Powers, John J(ames)

Pownall, David 1938- . . . . **CLC 10**
  See also CA 89-92; CAAS 18; DLB 14

Powys, John Cowper
  1872-1963 . . . . **CLC 7, 9, 15, 46**
  See also CA 85-88; DLB 15; MTCW

Powys, T(heodore) F(rancis)
  1875-1953 . . . . **TCLC 9**
  See also CA 106; DLB 36

Prager, Emily 1952- . . . . **CLC 56**

Pratt, E(dwin) J(ohn)
  1883(?)-1964 . . . . **CLC 19**
  See also CA 141; 93-96; DLB 92

Premchand . . . . **TCLC 21**
  See also Srivastava, Dhanpat Rai

Preussler, Otfried 1923- . . . . **CLC 17**
  See also CA 77-80; SATA 24

Prevert, Jacques (Henri Marie)
  1900-1977 . . . . **CLC 15**
  See also CA 77-80; 69-72; CANR 29;
  MTCW; SATA 30

Prevost, Abbe (Antoine Francois)
  1697-1763 . . . . **LC 1**

Price, (Edward) Reynolds
  1933- . . . . **CLC 3, 6, 13, 43, 50, 63**
  See also CA 1-4R; CANR 1, 37; DLB 2

Price, Richard 1949- . . . . **CLC 6, 12**
  See also CA 49-52; CANR 3; DLBY 81

Prichard, Katharine Susannah
  1883-1969 . . . . **CLC 46**
  See also CA 11-12; CANR 33; CAP 1;
  MTCW; SATA 66

Priestley, J(ohn) B(oynton)
  1894-1984 . . . . **CLC 2, 5, 9, 34**
  See also CA 9-12R; 113; CANR 33;
  CDBLB 1914-1945; DLB 10, 34, 77, 100,
  139; DLBY 84; MTCW

Prince 1958(?)- . . . . **CLC 35**

Prince, F(rank) T(empleton) 1912- . . **CLC 22**
  See also CA 101; CANR 43; DLB 20

Prince Kropotkin
  See Kropotkin, Peter (Aleksieevich)

Prior, Matthew 1664-1721 . . . . **LC 4**
  See also DLB 95

Pritchard, William H(arrison)
  1932- . . . . **CLC 34**
  See also CA 65-68; CANR 23; DLB 111

Pritchett, V(ictor) S(awdon)
  1900- . . . . **CLC 5, 13, 15, 41; SSC 14**
  See also CA 61-64; CANR 31; DLB 15,
  139; MTCW

Private 19022
  See Manning, Frederic

Probst, Mark 1925- . . . . **CLC 59**
  See also CA 130

Prokosch, Frederic 1908-1989 . . . . **CLC 4, 48**
  See also CA 73-76; 128; DLB 48

Prophet, The
  See Dreiser, Theodore (Herman Albert)

Prose, Francine 1947- . . . . **CLC 45**
  See also CA 109; 112

Proudhon
  See Cunha, Euclides (Rodrigues Pimenta) da

Proulx, E. Annie 1935- . . . . **CLC 81**

Proust, (Valentin-Louis-George-Eugene-)
  Marcel
  1871-1922 . . . **TCLC 7, 13, 33; DA; WLC**
  See also CA 104; 120; DLB 65; MTCW

Prowler, Harley
  See Masters, Edgar Lee

Prus, Boleslaw . . . . **TCLC 48**
  See also Glowacki, Aleksander

Pryor, Richard (Franklin Lenox Thomas)
  1940- . . . . **CLC 26**
  See also CA 122

Przybyszewski, Stanislaw
  1868-1927 . . . . **TCLC 36**
  See also DLB 66

Pteleon
  See Grieve, C(hristopher) M(urray)

Puckett, Lute
  See Masters, Edgar Lee

Puig, Manuel
  1932-1990 . . . **CLC 3, 5, 10, 28, 65; HLC**
  See also CA 45-48; CANR 2, 32; DLB 113;
  HW; MTCW

Purdy, Al(fred Wellington)
  1918- . . . . **CLC 3, 6, 14, 50**
  See also CA 81-84; CAAS 17; CANR 42;
  DLB 88

Purdy, James (Amos)
  1923- . . . . **CLC 2, 4, 10, 28, 52**
  See also CA 33-36R; CAAS 1; CANR 19;
  DLB 2; MTCW

Pure, Simon
  See Swinnerton, Frank Arthur

Pushkin, Alexander (Sergeyevich)
  1799-1837 . . . . **NCLC 3, 27; DA; PC 10;**
                              WLC
  See also SATA 61

P'u Sung-ling 1640-1715 . . . . **LC 3**

Putnam, Arthur Lee
  See Alger, Horatio, Jr.

Puzo, Mario 1920- . . . . **CLC 1, 2, 6, 36**
  See also CA 65-68; CANR 4, 42; DLB 6;
  MTCW

Pym, Barbara (Mary Crampton)
  1913-1980 . . . . **CLC 13, 19, 37**
  See also CA 13-14; 97-100; CANR 13, 34;
  CAP 1; DLB 14; DLBY 87; MTCW

Pynchon, Thomas (Ruggles, Jr.)
  1937- . . . . . **CLC 2, 3, 6, 9, 11, 18, 33, 62,**
                 72; DA; SSC 14; WLC
  See also BEST 90:2; CA 17-20R; CANR 22;
  DLB 2; MTCW

Q
  See Quiller-Couch, Arthur Thomas

Qian Zhongshu
  See Ch'ien Chung-shu

Qroll
  See Dagerman, Stig (Halvard)

Quarrington, Paul (Lewis) 1953- . . . . **CLC 65**
  See also CA 129

Quasimodo, Salvatore 1901-1968 . . . **CLC 10**
  See also CA 13-16; 25-28R; CAP 1;
  DLB 114; MTCW

Queen, Ellery . . . . **CLC 3, 11**
  See also Dannay, Frederic; Davidson,
  Avram; Lee, Manfred B(ennington);
  Sturgeon, Theodore (Hamilton); Vance,
  John Holbrook

Queen, Ellery, Jr.
  See Dannay, Frederic; Lee, Manfred
  B(ennington)

Queneau, Raymond
  1903-1976 . . . . **CLC 2, 5, 10, 42**
  See also CA 77-80; 69-72; CANR 32;
  DLB 72; MTCW

Quevedo, Francisco de 1580-1645 . . . . **LC 23**

Quiller-Couch, Arthur Thomas
  1863-1944 . . . . **TCLC 53**
  See also CA 118; DLB 135

Quin, Ann (Marie) 1936-1973 . . . . **CLC 6**
  See also CA 9-12R; 45-48; DLB 14

Quinn, Martin
  See Smith, Martin Cruz

Quinn, Simon
  See Smith, Martin Cruz

Quiroga, Horacio (Sylvestre)
  1878-1937 . . . . **TCLC 20; HLC**
  See also CA 117; 131; HW; MTCW

Quoirez, Francoise 1935- . . . . **CLC 9**
  See also Sagan, Francoise
  See also CA 49-52; CANR 6, 39; MTCW

Raabe, Wilhelm 1831-1910 . . . . **TCLC 45**
  See also DLB 129

Rabe, David (William) 1940- . . . **CLC 4, 8, 33**
  See also CA 85-88; CABS 3; DLB 7

Rabelais, Francois
  1483-1553 . . . . **LC 5; DA; WLC**

Rabinovitch, Sholem 1859-1916
  See Aleichem, Sholom
  See also CA 104

Radcliffe, Ann (Ward) 1764-1823 .. **NCLC 6**
  See also DLB 39

Radiguet, Raymond 1903-1923 .... **TCLC 29**
  See also DLB 65

Radnoti, Miklos 1909-1944 .... **TCLC 16**
  See also CA 118

Rado, James 1939- .... **CLC 17**
  See also CA 105

Radvanyi, Netty 1900-1983
  See Seghers, Anna
  See also CA 85-88; 110

Rae, Ben
  See Griffiths, Trevor

Raeburn, John (Hay) 1941- .... **CLC 34**
  See also CA 57-60

Ragni, Gerome 1942-1991 .... **CLC 17**
  See also CA 105; 134

Rahv, Philip 1908-1973 .... **CLC 24**
  See also Greenberg, Ivan
  See also DLB 137

Raine, Craig 1944- .... **CLC 32**
  See also CA 108; CANR 29; DLB 40

Raine, Kathleen (Jessie) 1908- ... **CLC 7, 45**
  See also CA 85-88; DLB 20; MTCW

Rainis, Janis 1865-1929 .... **TCLC 29**

Rakosi, Carl .... **CLC 47**
  See also Rawley, Callman
  See also CAAS 5

Raleigh, Richard
  See Lovecraft, H(oward) P(hillips)

Rallentando, H. P.
  See Sayers, Dorothy L(eigh)

Ramal, Walter
  See de la Mare, Walter (John)

Ramon, Juan
  See Jimenez (Mantecon), Juan Ramon

Ramos, Graciliano 1892-1953 ..... **TCLC 32**

Rampersad, Arnold 1941- .... **CLC 44**
  See also BW 2; CA 127; 133; DLB 111

Rampling, Anne
  See Rice, Anne

Ramuz, Charles-Ferdinand
  1878-1947 .... **TCLC 33**

Rand, Ayn
  1905-1982 ...... **CLC 3, 30, 44, 79; DA;**
                              WLC
  See also AAYA 10; CA 13-16R; 105;
    CANR 27; MTCW

Randall, Dudley (Felker)
  1914- .... **CLC 1; BLC**
  See also BW 1; CA 25-28R; CANR 23;
    DLB 41

Randall, Robert
  See Silverberg, Robert

Ranger, Ken
  See Creasey, John

Ransom, John Crowe
  1888-1974 .... **CLC 2, 4, 5, 11, 24**
  See also CA 5-8R; 49-52; CANR 6, 34;
    DLB 45, 63; MTCW

Rao, Raja 1909- .... **CLC 25, 56**
  See also CA 73-76; MTCW

Raphael, Frederic (Michael)
  1931- .... **CLC 2, 14**
  See also CA 1-4R; CANR 1; DLB 14

Ratcliffe, James P.
  See Mencken, H(enry) L(ouis)

Rathbone, Julian 1935- .... **CLC 41**
  See also CA 101; CANR 34

Rattigan, Terence (Mervyn)
  1911-1977 .... **CLC 7**
  See also CA 85-88; 73-76;
    CDBLB 1945-1960; DLB 13; MTCW

Ratushinskaya, Irina 1954- .... **CLC 54**
  See also CA 129

Raven, Simon (Arthur Noel)
  1927- .... **CLC 14**
  See also CA 81-84

Rawley, Callman 1903-
  See Rakosi, Carl
  See also CA 21-24R; CANR 12, 32

Rawlings, Marjorie Kinnan
  1896-1953 .... **TCLC 4**
  See also CA 104; 137; DLB 9, 22, 102;
    JRDA; MAICYA; YABC 1

Ray, Satyajit 1921-1992 .... **CLC 16, 76**
  See also CA 114; 137

Read, Herbert Edward 1893-1968 .... **CLC 4**
  See also CA 85-88; 25-28R; DLB 20

Read, Piers Paul 1941- ...... **CLC 4, 10, 25**
  See also CA 21-24R; CANR 38; DLB 14;
    SATA 21

Reade, Charles 1814-1884 .... **NCLC 2**
  See also DLB 21

Reade, Hamish
  See Gray, Simon (James Holliday)

Reading, Peter 1946- .... **CLC 47**
  See also CA 103; DLB 40

Reaney, James 1926- .... **CLC 13**
  See also CA 41-44R; CAAS 15; CANR 42;
    DLB 68; SATA 43

Rebreanu, Liviu 1885-1944 .... **TCLC 28**

Rechy, John (Francisco)
  1934- .... **CLC 1, 7, 14, 18; HLC**
  See also CA 5-8R; CAAS 4; CANR 6, 32;
    DLB 122; DLBY 82; HW

Redcam, Tom 1870-1933 .... **TCLC 25**

Reddin, Keith .... **CLC 67**

Redgrove, Peter (William)
  1932- .... **CLC 6, 41**
  See also CA 1-4R; CANR 3, 39; DLB 40

Redmon, Anne .... **CLC 22**
  See also Nightingale, Anne Redmon
  See also DLBY 86

Reed, Eliot
  See Ambler, Eric

Reed, Ishmael
  1938- ... **CLC 2, 3, 5, 6, 13, 32, 60; BLC**
  See also BW 2; CA 21-24R; CANR 25;
    DLB 2, 5, 33; DLBD 8; MTCW

Reed, John (Silas) 1887-1920 ...... **TCLC 9**
  See also CA 106

Reed, Lou .... **CLC 21**
  See also Firbank, Louis

Reeve, Clara 1729-1807 .... **NCLC 19**
  See also DLB 39

Reid, Christopher (John) 1949- ..... **CLC 33**
  See also CA 140; DLB 40

Reid, Desmond
  See Moorcock, Michael (John)

Reid Banks, Lynne 1929-
  See Banks, Lynne Reid
  See also CA 1-4R; CANR 6, 22, 38;
    CLR 24; JRDA; MAICYA; SATA 22, 75

Reilly, William K.
  See Creasey, John

Reiner, Max
  See Caldwell, (Janet Miriam) Taylor
    (Holland)

Reis, Ricardo
  See Pessoa, Fernando (Antonio Nogueira)

Remarque, Erich Maria
  1898-1970 .... **CLC 21; DA**
  See also CA 77-80; 29-32R; DLB 56;
    MTCW

Remizov, A.
  See Remizov, Aleksei (Mikhailovich)

Remizov, A. M.
  See Remizov, Aleksei (Mikhailovich)

Remizov, Aleksei (Mikhailovich)
  1877-1957 .... **TCLC 27**
  See also CA 125; 133

Renan, Joseph Ernest
  1823-1892 .... **NCLC 26**

Renard, Jules 1864-1910 .... **TCLC 17**
  See also CA 117

Renault, Mary .... **CLC 3, 11, 17**
  See also Challans, Mary
  See also DLBY 83

Rendell, Ruth (Barbara) 1930- .. **CLC 28, 48**
  See also Vine, Barbara
  See also CA 109; CANR 32; DLB 87;
    MTCW

Renoir, Jean 1894-1979 .... **CLC 20**
  See also CA 129; 85-88

Resnais, Alain 1922- .... **CLC 16**

Reverdy, Pierre 1889-1960 .... **CLC 53**
  See also CA 97-100; 89-92

Rexroth, Kenneth
  1905-1982 ...... **CLC 1, 2, 6, 11, 22, 49**
  See also CA 5-8R; 107; CANR 14, 34;
    CDALB 1941-1968; DLB 16, 48;
    DLBY 82; MTCW

Reyes, Alfonso 1889-1959 .... **TCLC 33**
  See also CA 131; HW

Reyes y Basoalto, Ricardo Eliecer Neftali
  See Neruda, Pablo

Reymont, Wladyslaw (Stanislaw)
  1868(?)-1925 .... **TCLC 5**
  See also CA 104

Reynolds, Jonathan 1942- .... **CLC 6, 38**
  See also CA 65-68; CANR 28

Reynolds, Joshua 1723-1792 .... **LC 15**
  See also DLB 104

Reynolds, Michael Shane 1937- .... **CLC 44**
  See also CA 65-68; CANR 9

Rodman, Howard 1920(?)-1985..... **CLC 65**
See also CA 118

Rodman, Maia
See Wojciechowska, Maia (Teresa)

Rodriguez, Claudio 1934-.......... **CLC 10**
See also DLB 134

Roelvaag, O(le) E(dvart)
1876-1931 .... **TCLC 17**
See also CA 117; DLB 9

Roethke, Theodore (Huebner)
1908-1963 ...... **CLC 1, 3, 8, 11, 19, 46**
See also CA 81-84; CABS 2;
CDALB 1941-1968; DLB 5; MTCW

Rogers, Thomas Hunton 1927- ..... **CLC 57**
See also CA 89-92

Rogers, Will(iam Penn Adair)
1879-1935 .... **TCLC 8**
See also CA 105; 144; DLB 11

Rogin, Gilbert 1929-............. **CLC 18**
See also CA 65-68; CANR 15

Rohan, Koda .... **TCLC 22**
See also Koda Shigeyuki

Rohmer, Eric .... **CLC 16**
See also Scherer, Jean-Marie Maurice

Rohmer, Sax .... **TCLC 28**
See also Ward, Arthur Henry Sarsfield
See also DLB 70

Roiphe, Anne (Richardson)
1935-....................... **CLC 3, 9**
See also CA 89-92; CANR 45; DLBY 80

Rojas, Fernando de 1465-1541 ...... **LC 23**

**Rolfe, Frederick (William Serafino Austin
Lewis Mary)** 1860-1913..... **TCLC 12**
See also CA 107; DLB 34

Rolland, Romain 1866-1944....... **TCLC 23**
See also CA 118; DLB 65

Rolvaag, O(le) E(dvart)
See Roelvaag, O(le) E(dvart)

Romain Arnaud, Saint
See Aragon, Louis

Romains, Jules 1885-1972.......... **CLC 7**
See also CA 85-88; CANR 34; DLB 65;
MTCW

Romero, Jose Ruben 1890-1952 ... **TCLC 14**
See also CA 114; 131; HW

Ronsard, Pierre de 1524-1585....... **LC 6**

Rooke, Leon 1934-............ **CLC 25, 34**
See also CA 25-28R; CANR 23

Roper, William 1498-1578.......... **LC 10**

Roquelaure, A. N.
See Rice, Anne

Rosa, Joao Guimaraes 1908-1967 ... **CLC 23**
See also CA 89-92; DLB 113

Rosen, Richard (Dean) 1949-....... **CLC 39**
See also CA 77-80

Rosenberg, Isaac 1890-1918....... **TCLC 12**
See also CA 107; DLB 20

Rosenblatt, Joe .... **CLC 15**
See also Rosenblatt, Joseph

Rosenblatt, Joseph 1933-
See Rosenblatt, Joe
See also CA 89-92

Rosenfeld, Samuel 1896-1963
See Tzara, Tristan
See also CA 89-92

Rosenthal, M(acha) L(ouis) 1917-... **CLC 28**
See also CA 1-4R; CAAS 6; CANR 4;
DLB 5; SATA 59

Ross, Barnaby
See Dannay, Frederic

Ross, Bernard L.
See Follett, Ken(neth Martin)

Ross, J. H.
See Lawrence, T(homas) E(dward)

Ross, Martin
See Martin, Violet Florence
See also DLB 135

Ross, (James) Sinclair 1908-....... **CLC 13**
See also CA 73-76; DLB 88

Rossetti, Christina (Georgina)
1830-1894 ... **NCLC 2; DA; PC 7; WLC**
See also DLB 35; MAICYA; SATA 20

Rossetti, Dante Gabriel
1828-1882 .... **NCLC 4; DA; WLC**
See also CDBLB 1832-1890; DLB 35

Rossner, Judith (Perelman)
1935- .... **CLC 6, 9, 29**
See also AITN 2; BEST 90:3; CA 17-20R;
CANR 18; DLB 6; MTCW

Rostand, Edmond (Eugene Alexis)
1868-1918 .... **TCLC 6, 37; DA**
See also CA 104; 126; MTCW

Roth, Henry 1906-........... **CLC 2, 6, 11**
See also CA 11-12; CANR 38; CAP 1;
DLB 28; MTCW

Roth, Joseph 1894-1939.......... **TCLC 33**
See also DLB 85

Roth, Philip (Milton)
1933- ...... **CLC 1, 2, 3, 4, 6, 9, 15, 22,
31, 47, 66; DA; WLC**
See also BEST 90:3; CA 1-4R; CANR 1, 22,
36; CDALB 1968-1988; DLB 2, 28;
DLBY 82; MTCW

Rothenberg, Jerome 1931-....... **CLC 6, 57**
See also CA 45-48; CANR 1; DLB 5

Roumain, Jacques (Jean Baptiste)
1907-1944 .... **TCLC 19; BLC**
See also BW 1; CA 117; 125

Rourke, Constance (Mayfield)
1885-1941 .... **TCLC 12**
See also CA 107; YABC 1

Rousseau, Jean-Baptiste 1671-1741 ... **LC 9**

Rousseau, Jean-Jacques
1712-1778 .... **LC 14; DA; WLC**

Roussel, Raymond 1877-1933 ..... **TCLC 20**
See also CA 117

Rovit, Earl (Herbert) 1927-........ **CLC 7**
See also CA 5-8R; CANR 12

Rowe, Nicholas 1674-1718.......... **LC 8**
See also DLB 84

Rowley, Ames Dorrance
See Lovecraft, H(oward) P(hillips)

Rowson, Susanna Haswell
1762(?)-1824 .... **NCLC 5**
See also DLB 37

Roy, Gabrielle 1909-1983....... **CLC 10, 14**
See also CA 53-56; 110; CANR 5; DLB 68;
MTCW

Rozewicz, Tadeusz 1921-........ **CLC 9, 23**
See also CA 108; CANR 36; MTCW

Ruark, Gibbons 1941- .... **CLC 3**
See also CA 33-36R; CANR 14, 31;
DLB 120

Rubens, Bernice (Ruth) 1923-... **CLC 19, 31**
See also CA 25-28R; CANR 33; DLB 14;
MTCW

Rudkin, (James) David 1936- ...... **CLC 14**
See also CA 89-92; DLB 13

Rudnik, Raphael 1933-............ **CLC 7**
See also CA 29-32R

Ruffian, M.
See Hasek, Jaroslav (Matej Frantisek)

Ruiz, Jose Martinez .... **CLC 11**
See also Martinez Ruiz, Jose

Rukeyser, Muriel
1913-1980 .... **CLC 6, 10, 15, 27**
See also CA 5-8R; 93-96; CANR 26;
DLB 48; MTCW; SATA 22

Rule, Jane (Vance) 1931-.......... **CLC 27**
See also CA 25-28R; CAAS 18; CANR 12;
DLB 60

Rulfo, Juan 1918-1986.... **CLC 8, 80; HLC**
See also CA 85-88; 118; CANR 26;
DLB 113; HW; MTCW

Runeberg, Johan 1804-1877...... **NCLC 41**

Runyon, (Alfred) Damon
1884(?)-1946 .... **TCLC 10**
See also CA 107; DLB 11, 86

Rush, Norman 1933-............. **CLC 44**
See also CA 121; 126

Rushdie, (Ahmed) Salman
1947- .... **CLC 23, 31, 55**
See also BEST 89:3; CA 108; 111;
CANR 33; MTCW

Rushforth, Peter (Scott) 1945- ..... **CLC 19**
See also CA 101

Ruskin, John 1819-1900......... **TCLC 20**
See also CA 114; 129; CDBLB 1832-1890;
DLB 55; SATA 24

Russ, Joanna 1937-.............. **CLC 15**
See also CA 25-28R; CANR 11, 31; DLB 8;
MTCW

Russell, George William 1867-1935
See A. E.
See also CA 104; CDBLB 1890-1914

Russell, (Henry) Ken(neth Alfred)
1927-....................... **CLC 16**
See also CA 105

Russell, Willy 1947-.............. **CLC 60**

Rutherford, Mark .... **TCLC 25**
See also White, William Hale
See also DLB 18

Ruyslinck, Ward
See Belser, Reimond Karel Maria de

Ryan, Cornelius (John) 1920-1974 ... **CLC 7**
See also CA 69-72; 53-56; CANR 38

Ryan, Michael 1946- .... **CLC 65**
See also CA 49-52; DLBY 82

Sauser-Hall, Frederic 1887-1961.... **CLC 18**
See also CA 102; 93-96; CANR 36; MTCW

Saussure, Ferdinand de
1857-1913 .... **TCLC 49**

Savage, Catharine
See Brosman, Catharine Savage

Savage, Thomas 1915- .... **CLC 40**
See also CA 126; 132; CAAS 15

Savan, Glenn .... **CLC 50**

Saven, Glenn 19(?)- .... **CLC 50**

Sayers, Dorothy L(eigh)
1893-1957 .... **TCLC 2, 15**
See also CA 104; 119; CDBLB 1914-1945;
DLB 10, 36, 77, 100; MTCW

Sayers, Valerie 1952- .... **CLC 50**
See also CA 134

Sayles, John (Thomas)
1950- .... **CLC 7, 10, 14**
See also CA 57-60; CANR 41; DLB 44

Scammell, Michael .... **CLC 34**

Scannell, Vernon 1922- .... **CLC 49**
See also CA 5-8R; CANR 8, 24; DLB 27;
SATA 59

Scarlett, Susan
See Streatfeild, (Mary) Noel

Schaeffer, Susan Fromberg
1941- .... **CLC 6, 11, 22**
See also CA 49-52; CANR 18; DLB 28;
MTCW; SATA 22

Schary, Jill
See Robinson, Jill

Schell, Jonathan 1943- .... **CLC 35**
See also CA 73-76; CANR 12

Schelling, Friedrich Wilhelm Joseph von
1775-1854 .... **NCLC 30**
See also DLB 90

Scherer, Jean-Marie Maurice 1920-
See Rohmer, Eric
See also CA 110

Schevill, James (Erwin) 1920- .... **CLC 7**
See also CA 5-8R; CAAS 12

Schiller, Friedrich 1759-1805 .... **NCLC 39**
See also DLB 94

Schisgal, Murray (Joseph) 1926- ..... **CLC 6**
See also CA 21-24R

Schlee, Ann 1934- .... **CLC 35**
See also CA 101; CANR 29; SATA 36, 44

Schlegel, August Wilhelm von
1767-1845 .... **NCLC 15**
See also DLB 94

Schlegel, Friedrich 1772-1829 .... **NCLC 45**
See also DLB 90

Schlegel, Johann Elias (von)
1719(?)-1749 .... **LC 5**

Schlesinger, Arthur M(eier), Jr.
1917- .... **CLC 84**
See also AITN 1; CA 1-4R; CANR 1, 28;
DLB 17; MTCW; SATA 61

Schmidt, Arno (Otto) 1914-1979 .... **CLC 56**
See also CA 128; 109; DLB 69

Schmitz, Aron Hector 1861-1928
See Svevo, Italo
See also CA 104; 122; MTCW

Schnackenberg, Gjertrud 1953- ..... **CLC 40**
See also CA 116; DLB 120

Schneider, Leonard Alfred 1925-1966
See Bruce, Lenny
See also CA 89-92

Schnitzler, Arthur
1862-1931 .... **TCLC 4; SSC 15**
See also CA 104; DLB 81, 118

Schor, Sandra (M.) 1932(?)-1990 ... **CLC 65**
See also CA 132

Schorer, Mark 1908-1977 .... **CLC 9**
See also CA 5-8R; 73-76; CANR 7;
DLB 103

Schrader, Paul (Joseph) 1946- ...... **CLC 26**
See also CA 37-40R; CANR 41; DLB 44

Schreiner, Olive (Emilie Albertina)
1855-1920 .... **TCLC 9**
See also CA 105; DLB 18

Schulberg, Budd (Wilson)
1914- .... **CLC 7, 48**
See also CA 25-28R; CANR 19; DLB 6, 26,
28; DLBY 81

Schulz, Bruno
1892-1942 .... **TCLC 5, 51; SSC 13**
See also CA 115; 123

Schulz, Charles M(onroe) 1922- .... **CLC 12**
See also CA 9-12R; CANR 6; SATA 10

Schumacher, E(rnst) F(riedrich)
1911-1977 .... **CLC 80**
See also CA 81-84; 73-76; CANR 34

Schuyler, James Marcus
1923-1991 .... **CLC 5, 23**
See also CA 101; 134; DLB 5

Schwartz, Delmore (David)
1913-1966 ...... **CLC 2, 4, 10, 45; PC 8**
See also CA 17-18; 25-28R; CANR 35;
CAP 2; DLB 28, 48; MTCW

Schwartz, Ernst
See Ozu, Yasujiro

Schwartz, John Burnham 1965- .... **CLC 59**
See also CA 132

Schwartz, Lynne Sharon 1939- ..... **CLC 31**
See also CA 103; CANR 44

Schwartz, Muriel A.
See Eliot, T(homas) S(tearns)

Schwarz-Bart, Andre 1928- .... **CLC 2, 4**
See also CA 89-92

Schwarz-Bart, Simone 1938- .... **CLC 7**
See also BW 2; CA 97-100

Schwob, (Mayer Andre) Marcel
1867-1905 .... **TCLC 20**
See also CA 117; DLB 123

Sciascia, Leonardo
1921-1989 .... **CLC 8, 9, 41**
See also CA 85-88; 130; CANR 35; MTCW

Scoppettone, Sandra 1936- .... **CLC 26**
See also AAYA 11; CA 5-8R; CANR 41;
SATA 9

Scorsese, Martin 1942- .... **CLC 20**
See also CA 110; 114

Scotland, Jay
See Jakes, John (William)

Scott, Duncan Campbell
1862-1947 .... **TCLC 6**
See also CA 104; DLB 92

Scott, Evelyn 1893-1963.......... **CLC 43**
See also CA 104; 112; DLB 9, 48

Scott, F(rancis) R(eginald)
1899-1985 .... **CLC 22**
See also CA 101; 114; DLB 88

Scott, Frank
See Scott, F(rancis) R(eginald)

Scott, Joanna 1960- .... **CLC 50**
See also CA 126

Scott, Paul (Mark) 1920-1978.... **CLC 9, 60**
See also CA 81-84; 77-80; CANR 33;
DLB 14; MTCW

Scott, Walter
1771-1832 .... **NCLC 15; DA; WLC**
See also CDBLB 1789-1832; DLB 93, 107,
116, 144; YABC 2

Scribe, (Augustin) Eugene
1791-1861 .... **NCLC 16**

Scrum, R.
See Crumb, R(obert)

Scudery, Madeleine de 1607-1701..... **LC 2**

Scum
See Crumb, R(obert)

Scumbag, Little Bobby
See Crumb, R(obert)

Seabrook, John
See Hubbard, L(afayette) Ron(ald)

Sealy, I. Allan 1951- .... **CLC 55**

Search, Alexander
See Pessoa, Fernando (Antonio Nogueira)

Sebastian, Lee
See Silverberg, Robert

Sebastian Owl
See Thompson, Hunter S(tockton)

Sebestyen, Ouida 1924- .... **CLC 30**
See also AAYA 8; CA 107; CANR 40;
CLR 17; JRDA; MAICYA; SAAS 10;
SATA 39

Secundus, H. Scriblerus
See Fielding, Henry

Sedges, John
See Buck, Pearl S(ydenstricker)

Sedgwick, Catharine Maria
1789-1867 .... **NCLC 19**
See also DLB 1, 74

Seelye, John 1931- .... **CLC 7**

Seferiades, Giorgos Stylianou 1900-1971
See Seferis, George
See also CA 5-8R; 33-36R; CANR 5, 36;
MTCW

Seferis, George .... **CLC 5, 11**
See also Seferiades, Giorgos Stylianou

Segal, Erich (Wolf) 1937- .... **CLC 3, 10**
See also BEST 89:1; CA 25-28R; CANR 20,
36; DLBY 86; MTCW

Seger, Bob 1945-................. **CLC 35**

Seghers, Anna .... **CLC 7**
See also Radvanyi, Netty
See also DLB 69

Shu-Jen, Chou 1881-1936
See Hsun, Lu
See also CA 104

Shulman, Alix Kates 1932- ...... **CLC 2, 10**
See also CA 29-32R; CANR 43; SATA 7

Shuster, Joe 1914- .... **CLC 21**

Shute, Nevil .... **CLC 30**
See also Norway, Nevil Shute

Shuttle, Penelope (Diane) 1947- ..... **CLC 7**
See also CA 93-96; CANR 39; DLB 14, 40

Sidney, Mary 1561-1621 .... **LC 19**

Sidney, Sir Philip 1554-1586.... **LC 19; DA**
See also CDBLB Before 1660

Siegel, Jerome 1914- .... **CLC 21**
See also CA 116

Siegel, Jerry
See Siegel, Jerome

Sienkiewicz, Henryk (Adam Alexander Pius)
1846-1916 .... **TCLC 3**
See also CA 104; 134

Sierra, Gregorio Martinez
See Martinez Sierra, Gregorio

Sierra, Maria (de la O'LeJarraga) Martinez
See Martinez Sierra, Maria (de la O'LeJarraga)

Sigal, Clancy 1926- .... **CLC 7**
See also CA 1-4R

Sigourney, Lydia Howard (Huntley)
1791-1865 .... **NCLC 21**
See also DLB 1, 42, 73

Siguenza y Gongora, Carlos de
1645-1700 .... **LC 8**

Sigurjonsson, Johann 1880-1919... **TCLC 27**

Sikelianos, Angelos 1884-1951 .... **TCLC 39**

Silkin, Jon 1930- .... **CLC 2, 6, 43**
See also CA 5-8R; CAAS 5; DLB 27

Silko, Leslie (Marmon)
1948- .... **CLC 23, 74; DA**
See also CA 115; 122; CANR 45; DLB 143

Sillanpaa, Frans Eemil 1888-1964... **CLC 19**
See also CA 129; 93-96; MTCW

Sillitoe, Alan
1928- .... **CLC 1, 3, 6, 10, 19, 57**
See also AITN 1; CA 9-12R; CAAS 2;
CANR 8, 26; CDBLB 1960 to Present;
DLB 14, 139; MTCW; SATA 61

Silone, Ignazio 1900-1978 .... **CLC 4**
See also CA 25-28; 81-84; CANR 34;
CAP 2; MTCW

Silver, Joan Micklin 1935- .... **CLC 20**
See also CA 114; 121

Silver, Nicholas
See Faust, Frederick (Schiller)

Silverberg, Robert 1935- .... **CLC 7**
See also CA 1-4R; CAAS 3; CANR 1, 20,
36; DLB 8; MAICYA; MTCW; SATA 13

Silverstein, Alvin 1933- .... **CLC 17**
See also CA 49-52; CANR 2; CLR 25;
JRDA; MAICYA; SATA 8, 69

Silverstein, Virginia B(arbara Opshelor)
1937- .... **CLC 17**
See also CA 49-52; CANR 2; CLR 25;
JRDA; MAICYA; SATA 8, 69

Sim, Georges
See Simenon, Georges (Jacques Christian)

Simak, Clifford D(onald)
1904-1988 .... **CLC 1, 55**
See also CA 1-4R; 125; CANR 1, 35;
DLB 8; MTCW; SATA 56

Simenon, Georges (Jacques Christian)
1903-1989 .... **CLC 1, 2, 3, 8, 18, 47**
See also CA 85-88; 129; CANR 35;
DLB 72; DLBY 89; MTCW

Simic, Charles 1938-... **CLC 6, 9, 22, 49, 68**
See also CA 29-32R; CAAS 4; CANR 12,
33; DLB 105

Simmons, Charles (Paul) 1924- ..... **CLC 57**
See also CA 89-92

Simmons, Dan 1948- .... **CLC 44**
See also CA 138

Simmons, James (Stewart Alexander)
1933- .... **CLC 43**
See also CA 105; DLB 40

Simms, William Gilmore
1806-1870 .... **NCLC 3**
See also DLB 3, 30, 59, 73

Simon, Carly 1945-................ **CLC 26**
See also CA 105

Simon, Claude 1913-...... **CLC 4, 9, 15, 39**
See also CA 89-92; CANR 33; DLB 83;
MTCW

Simon, (Marvin) Neil
1927- .... **CLC 6, 11, 31, 39, 70**
See also AITN 1; CA 21-24R; CANR 26;
DLB 7; MTCW

Simon, Paul 1942(?)- .... **CLC 17**
See also CA 116

Simonon, Paul 1956(?)- .... **CLC 30**
See also Clash, The

Simpson, Harriette
See Arnow, Harriette (Louisa) Simpson

Simpson, Louis (Aston Marantz)
1923- .... **CLC 4, 7, 9, 32**
See also CA 1-4R; CAAS 4; CANR 1;
DLB 5; MTCW

Simpson, Mona (Elizabeth) 1957-... **CLC 44**
See also CA 122; 135

Simpson, N(orman) F(rederick)
1919- .... **CLC 29**
See also CA 13-16R; DLB 13

Sinclair, Andrew (Annandale)
1935- .... **CLC 2, 14**
See also CA 9-12R; CAAS 5; CANR 14, 38;
DLB 14; MTCW

Sinclair, Emil
See Hesse, Hermann

Sinclair, Iain 1943-.............. **CLC 76**
See also CA 132

Sinclair, Iain MacGregor
See Sinclair, Iain

Sinclair, Mary Amelia St. Clair 1865(?)-1946
See Sinclair, May
See also CA 104

Sinclair, May................. **TCLC 3, 11**
See also Sinclair, Mary Amelia St. Clair
See also DLB 36, 135

Sinclair, Upton (Beall)
1878-1968 ...... **CLC 1, 11, 15, 63; DA;
WLC**
See also CA 5-8R; 25-28R; CANR 7;
CDALB 1929-1941; DLB 9; MTCW;
SATA 9

Singer, Isaac
See Singer, Isaac Bashevis

Singer, Isaac Bashevis
1904-1991 .... **CLC 1, 3, 6, 9, 11, 15, 23,
38, 69; DA; SSC 3; WLC**
See also AITN 1, 2; CA 1-4R; 134;
CANR 1, 39; CDALB 1941-1968; CLR 1;
DLB 6, 28, 52; DLBY 91; JRDA;
MAICYA; MTCW; SATA 3, 27;
SATA-Obit 68

Singer, Israel Joshua 1893-1944 ... **TCLC 33**

Singh, Khushwant 1915-........... **CLC 11**
See also CA 9-12R; CAAS 9; CANR 6

Sinjohn, John
See Galsworthy, John

Sinyavsky, Andrei (Donatevich)
1925- .... **CLC 8**
See also CA 85-88

Sirin, V.
See Nabokov, Vladimir (Vladimirovich)

Sissman, L(ouis) E(dward)
1928-1976 .... **CLC 9, 18**
See also CA 21-24R; 65-68; CANR 13;
DLB 5

Sisson, C(harles) H(ubert) 1914-..... **CLC 8**
See also CA 1-4R; CAAS 3; CANR 3;
DLB 27

Sitwell, Dame Edith
1887-1964 .... **CLC 2, 9, 67; PC 3**
See also CA 9-12R; CANR 35;
CDBLB 1945-1960; DLB 20; MTCW

Sjoewall, Maj 1935-............... **CLC 7**
See also CA 65-68

Sjowall, Maj
See Sjoewall, Maj

Skelton, Robin 1925- .... **CLC 13**
See also AITN 2; CA 5-8R; CAAS 5;
CANR 28; DLB 27, 53

Skolimowski, Jerzy 1938- .... **CLC 20**
See also CA 128

Skram, Amalie (Bertha)
1847-1905 .... **TCLC 25**

Skvorecky, Josef (Vaclav)
1924- .... **CLC 15, 39, 69**
See also CA 61-64; CAAS 1; CANR 10, 34;
MTCW

Slade, Bernard................. **CLC 11, 46**
See also Newbound, Bernard Slade
See also CAAS 9; DLB 53

Slaughter, Carolyn 1946-.......... **CLC 56**
See also CA 85-88

Slaughter, Frank G(ill) 1908- ...... **CLC 29**
See also AITN 2; CA 5-8R; CANR 5

Slavitt, David R(ytman) 1935-.... **CLC 5, 14**
See also CA 21-24R; CAAS 3; CANR 41;
DLB 5, 6

Slesinger, Tess 1905-1945 .... **TCLC 10**
See also CA 107; DLB 102

Spenser, Edmund
1552(?)-1599 .... **LC 5; DA; PC 8; WLC**
See also CDBLB Before 1660

Spicer, Jack 1925-1965 ...... **CLC 8, 18, 72**
See also CA 85-88; DLB 5, 16

Spiegelman, Art 1948- .... **CLC 76**
See also AAYA 10; CA 125; **CANR 41**

Spielberg, Peter 1929- .... **CLC 6**
See also CA 5-8R; CANR 4; DLBY 81

Spielberg, Steven 1947- .... **CLC 20**
See also AAYA 8; CA 77-80; CANR 32;
SATA 32

Spillane, Frank Morrison 1918-
See Spillane, Mickey
See also CA 25-28R; CANR 28; MTCW;
SATA 66

Spillane, Mickey .... **CLC 3, 13**
See also Spillane, Frank Morrison

Spinoza, Benedictus de 1632-1677 .... **LC 9**

Spinrad, Norman (Richard) 1940- ... **CLC 46**
See also CA 37-40R; CAAS 19; CANR 20;
DLB 8

Spitteler, Carl (Friedrich Georg)
1845-1924 .... **TCLC 12**
See also CA 109; DLB 129

Spivack, Kathleen (Romola Drucker)
1938- .... **CLC 6**
See also CA 49-52

Spoto, Donald 1941- .... **CLC 39**
See also CA 65-68; CANR 11

Springsteen, Bruce (F.) 1949- ...... **CLC 17**
See also CA 111

Spurling, Hilary 1940- .... **CLC 34**
See also CA 104; CANR 25

Squires, (James) Radcliffe
1917-1993 .... **CLC 51**
See also CA 1-4R; 140; CANR 6, 21

Srivastava, Dhanpat Rai 1880(?)-1936
See Premchand
See also CA 118

Stacy, Donald
See Pohl, Frederik

Stael, Germaine de
See Stael-Holstein, Anne Louise Germaine
Necker Baronn
See also DLB 119

Stael-Holstein, Anne Louise Germaine Necker
Baronn 1766-1817 .... **NCLC 3**
See also Stael, Germaine de

Stafford, Jean 1915-1979 ... **CLC 4, 7, 19, 68**
See also CA 1-4R; 85-88; CANR 3; DLB 2;
MTCW; SATA 22

Stafford, William (Edgar)
1914-1993 .... **CLC 4, 7, 29**
See also CA 5-8R; 142; CAAS 3; CANR 5,
22; DLB 5

Staines, Trevor
See Brunner, John (Kilian Houston)

Stairs, Gordon
See Austin, Mary (Hunter)

Stannard, Martin 1947- .... **CLC 44**
See also CA 142

Stanton, Maura 1946- .... **CLC 9**
See also CA 89-92; CANR 15; DLB 120

Stanton, Schuyler
See Baum, L(yman) Frank

Stapledon, (William) Olaf
1886-1950 .... **TCLC 22**
See also CA 111; DLB 15

Starbuck, George (Edwin) 1931- .... **CLC 53**
See also CA 21-24R; CANR 23

Stark, Richard
See Westlake, Donald E(dwin)

Staunton, Schuyler
See Baum, L(yman) Frank

Stead, Christina (Ellen)
1902-1983 .... **CLC 2, 5, 8, 32, 80**
See also CA 13-16R; 109; CANR 33, 40;
MTCW

Stead, William Thomas
1849-1912 .... **TCLC 48**

Steele, Richard 1672-1729 .... **LC 18**
See also CDBLB 1660-1789; DLB 84, 101

Steele, Timothy (Reid) 1948- .... **CLC 45**
See also CA 93-96; CANR 16; DLB 120

Steffens, (Joseph) Lincoln
1866-1936 .... **TCLC 20**
See also CA 117

Stegner, Wallace (Earle)
1909-1993 .... **CLC 9, 49, 81**
See also AITN 1; BEST 90:3; CA 1-4R;
141; CAAS 9; CANR 1, 21; DLB 9;
DLBY 93; MTCW

Stein, Gertrude
1874-1946 ...... **TCLC 1, 6, 28, 48; DA;**
WLC
See also CA 104; 132; CDALB 1917-1929;
DLB 4, 54, 86; MTCW

Steinbeck, John (Ernst)
1902-1968 ...... **CLC 1, 5, 9, 13, 21, 34,**
45, 75; DA; SSC 11; WLC
See also AAYA 12; CA 1-4R; 25-28R;
CANR 1, 35; CDALB 1929-1941; DLB 7,
9; DLBD 2; MTCW; SATA 9

Steinem, Gloria 1934- .... **CLC 63**
See also CA 53-56; CANR 28; MTCW

Steiner, George 1929- .... **CLC 24**
See also CA 73-76; CANR 31; DLB 67;
MTCW; SATA 62

Steiner, K. Leslie
See Delany, Samuel R(ay, Jr.)

Steiner, Rudolf 1861-1925 .... **TCLC 13**
See also CA 107

Stendhal
1783-1842 ..... **NCLC 23, 46; DA; WLC**
See also DLB 119

Stephen, Leslie 1832-1904 .... **TCLC 23**
See also CA 123; DLB 57, 144

Stephen, Sir Leslie
See Stephen, Leslie

Stephen, Virginia
See Woolf, (Adeline) Virginia

Stephens, James 1882(?)-1950 ...... **TCLC 4**
See also CA 104; DLB 19

Stephens, Reed
See Donaldson, Stephen R.

Steptoe, Lydia
See Barnes, Djuna

Sterchi, Beat 1949- .... **CLC 65**

Sterling, Brett
See Bradbury, Ray (Douglas); Hamilton,
Edmond

Sterling, Bruce 1954- .... **CLC 72**
See also CA 119; CANR 44

Sterling, George 1869-1926 .... **TCLC 20**
See also CA 117; DLB 54

Stern, Gerald 1925- .... **CLC 40**
See also CA 81-84; CANR 28; DLB 105

Stern, Richard (Gustave) 1928-... **CLC 4, 39**
See also CA 1-4R; CANR 1, 25; DLBY 87

Sternberg, Josef von 1894-1969..... **CLC 20**
See also CA 81-84

Sterne, Laurence
1713-1768 .... **LC 2; DA; WLC**
See also CDBLB 1660-1789; DLB 39

Sternheim, (William Adolf) Carl
1878-1942 .... **TCLC 8**
See also CA 105; DLB 56, 118

Stevens, Mark 1951- .... **CLC 34**
See also CA 122

Stevens, Wallace
1879-1955 .... **TCLC 3, 12, 45; DA;**
PC 6; WLC
See also CA 104; 124; CDALB 1929-1941;
DLB 54; MTCW

Stevenson, Anne (Katharine)
1933- .... **CLC 7, 33**
See also CA 17-20R; CAAS 9; CANR 9, 33;
DLB 40; MTCW

Stevenson, Robert Louis (Balfour)
1850-1894 .... **NCLC 5, 14; DA;**
SSC 11; WLC
See also CDBLB 1890-1914; CLR 10, 11;
DLB 18, 57, 141; JRDA; MAICYA;
YABC 2

Stewart, J(ohn) I(nnes) M(ackintosh)
1906- .... **CLC 7, 14, 32**
See also CA 85-88; CAAS 3; MTCW

Stewart, Mary (Florence Elinor)
1916- .... **CLC 7, 35**
See also CA 1-4R; CANR 1; SATA 12

Stewart, Mary Rainbow
See Stewart, Mary (Florence Elinor)

Stifter, Adalbert 1805-1868 ...... **NCLC 41**
See also DLB 133

Still, James 1906- .... **CLC 49**
See also CA 65-68; CAAS 17; CANR 10,
26; DLB 9; SATA 29

Sting
See Sumner, Gordon Matthew

Stirling, Arthur
See Sinclair, Upton (Beall)

Stitt, Milan 1941- .... **CLC 29**
See also CA 69-72

Stockton, Francis Richard 1834-1902
See Stockton, Frank R.
See also CA 108; 137; MAICYA; SATA 44

Stockton, Frank R. .... **TCLC 47**
See also Stockton, Francis Richard
See also DLB 42, 74; SATA 32

Stoddard, Charles
See Kuttner, Henry

Stoker, Abraham 1847-1912
See Stoker, Bram
See also CA 105; DA; SATA 29

Stoker, Bram . . . . **TCLC 8; WLC**
See also Stoker, Abraham
See also CDBLB 1890-1914; DLB 36, 70

Stolz, Mary (Slattery) 1920- . . . . **CLC 12**
See also AAYA 8; AITN 1; CA 5-8R;
CANR 13, 41; JRDA; MAICYA;
SAAS 3; SATA 10, 71

Stone, Irving 1903-1989 . . . . **CLC 7**
See also AITN 1; CA 1-4R; 129; CAAS 3;
CANR 1, 23; MTCW; SATA 3;
SATA-Obit 64

Stone, Oliver 1946- . . . . **CLC 73**
See also CA 110

Stone, Robert (Anthony)
1937- . . . . **CLC 5, 23, 42**
See also CA 85-88; CANR 23; MTCW

Stone, Zachary
See Follett, Ken(neth Martin)

Stoppard, Tom
1937- . . . . . . **CLC 1, 3, 4, 5, 8, 15, 29, 34,
63; DA; WLC**
See also CA 81-84; CANR 39;
CDBLB 1960 to Present; DLB 13;
DLBY 85; MTCW

Storey, David (Malcolm)
1933- . . . . **CLC 2, 4, 5, 8**
See also CA 81-84; CANR 36; DLB 13, 14;
MTCW

Storm, Hyemeyohsts 1935- . . . . **CLC 3**
See also CA 81-84; CANR 45

Storm, (Hans) Theodor (Woldsen)
1817-1888 . . . . **NCLC 1**

Storni, Alfonsina
1892-1938 . . . . **TCLC 5; HLC**
See also CA 104; 131; HW

Stout, Rex (Todhunter) 1886-1975 . . . **CLC 3**
See also AITN 2; CA 61-64

Stow, (Julian) Randolph 1935- . . **CLC 23, 48**
See also CA 13-16R; CANR 33; MTCW

Stowe, Harriet (Elizabeth) Beecher
1811-1896 . . . . **NCLC 3; DA; WLC**
See also CDALB 1865-1917; DLB 1, 12, 42,
74; JRDA; MAICYA; YABC 1

Strachey, (Giles) Lytton
1880-1932 . . . . **TCLC 12**
See also CA 110; DLBD 10

Strand, Mark 1934- . . . . . . **CLC 6, 18, 41, 71**
See also CA 21-24R; CANR 40; DLB 5;
SATA 41

Straub, Peter (Francis) 1943- . . . . . . **CLC 28**
See also BEST 89:1; CA 85-88; CANR 28;
DLBY 84; MTCW

Strauss, Botho 1944- . . . . **CLC 22**
See also DLB 124

Streatfeild, (Mary) Noel
1895(?)-1986 . . . . **CLC 21**
See also CA 81-84; 120; CANR 31;
CLR 17; MAICYA; SATA 20, 48

Stribling, T(homas) S(igismund)
1881-1965 . . . . **CLC 23**
See also CA 107; DLB 9

Strindberg, (Johan) August
1849-1912 . . . . . . **TCLC 1, 8, 21, 47; DA;
WLC**
See also CA 104; 135

Stringer, Arthur 1874-1950 . . . . **TCLC 37**
See also DLB 92

Stringer, David
See Roberts, Keith (John Kingston)

Strugatskii, Arkadii (Natanovich)
1925-1991 . . . . **CLC 27**
See also CA 106; 135

Strugatskii, Boris (Natanovich)
1933- . . . . **CLC 27**
See also CA 106

Strummer, Joe 1953(?)- . . . . **CLC 30**
See also Clash, The

Stuart, Don A.
See Campbell, John W(ood, Jr.)

Stuart, Ian
See MacLean, Alistair (Stuart)

Stuart, Jesse (Hilton)
1906-1984 . . . . **CLC 1, 8, 11, 14, 34**
See also CA 5-8R; 112; CANR 31; DLB 9,
48, 102; DLBY 84; SATA 2, 36

Sturgeon, Theodore (Hamilton)
1918-1985 . . . . **CLC 22, 39**
See also Queen, Ellery
See also CA 81-84; 116; CANR 32; DLB 8;
DLBY 85; MTCW

Sturges, Preston 1898-1959 . . . . . . **TCLC 48**
See also CA 114; DLB 26

Styron, William
1925- . . . . **CLC 1, 3, 5, 11, 15, 60**
See also BEST 90:4; CA 5-8R; CANR 6, 33;
CDALB 1968-1988; DLB 2, 143;
DLBY 80; MTCW

Suarez Lynch, B.
See Bioy Casares, Adolfo; Borges, Jorge
Luis

Su Chien 1884-1918
See Su Man-shu
See also CA 123

Sudermann, Hermann 1857-1928 . . **TCLC 15**
See also CA 107; DLB 118

Sue, Eugene 1804-1857 . . . . **NCLC 1**
See also DLB 119

Sueskind, Patrick 1949- . . . . **CLC 44**

Sukenick, Ronald 1932- . . . . . **CLC 3, 4, 6, 48**
See also CA 25-28R; CAAS 8; CANR 32;
DLBY 81

Suknaski, Andrew 1942- . . . . **CLC 19**
See also CA 101; DLB 53

Sullivan, Vernon
See Vian, Boris

Sully Prudhomme 1839-1907 . . . . . . **TCLC 31**

Su Man-shu . . . . **TCLC 24**
See also Su Chien

Summerforest, Ivy B.
See Kirkup, James

Summers, Andrew James 1942- . . . . . **CLC 26**
See also Police, The

Summers, Andy
See Summers, Andrew James

Summers, Hollis (Spurgeon, Jr.)
1916- . . . . **CLC 10**
See also CA 5-8R; CANR 3; DLB 6

Summers, (Alphonsus Joseph-Mary Augustus)
Montague 1880-1948 . . . . **TCLC 16**
See also CA 118

Sumner, Gordon Matthew 1951- . . . . **CLC 26**
See also Police, The

Surtees, Robert Smith
1803-1864 . . . . **NCLC 14**
See also DLB 21

Susann, Jacqueline 1921-1974 . . . . . . **CLC 3**
See also AITN 1; CA 65-68; 53-56; MTCW

Suskind, Patrick
See Sueskind, Patrick

Sutcliff, Rosemary 1920-1992 . . . . . . **CLC 26**
See also AAYA 10; CA 5-8R; 139;
CANR 37; CLR 1; JRDA; MAICYA;
SATA 6, 44, 78; SATA-Obit 73

Sutro, Alfred 1863-1933 . . . . **TCLC 6**
See also CA 105; DLB 10

Sutton, Henry
See Slavitt, David R(ytman)

Svevo, Italo . . . . **TCLC 2, 35**
See also Schmitz, Aron Hector

Swados, Elizabeth 1951- . . . . **CLC 12**
See also CA 97-100

Swados, Harvey 1920-1972 . . . . **CLC 5**
See also CA 5-8R; 37-40R; CANR 6;
DLB 2

Swan, Gladys 1934- . . . . **CLC 69**
See also CA 101; CANR 17, 39

Swarthout, Glendon (Fred)
1918-1992 . . . . **CLC 35**
See also CA 1-4R; 139; CANR 1; SATA 26

Sweet, Sarah C.
See Jewett, (Theodora) Sarah Orne

Swenson, May
1919-1989 . . . . **CLC 4, 14, 61; DA**
See also CA 5-8R; 130; CANR 36; DLB 5;
MTCW; SATA 15

Swift, Augustus
See Lovecraft, H(oward) P(hillips)

Swift, Graham 1949- . . . . **CLC 41**
See also CA 117; 122

Swift, Jonathan
1667-1745 . . . . . . **LC 1; DA; PC 9; WLC**
See also CDBLB 1660-1789; DLB 39, 95,
101; SATA 19

Swinburne, Algernon Charles
1837-1909 . . . . . . **TCLC 8, 36; DA; WLC**
See also CA 105; 140; CDBLB 1832-1890;
DLB 35, 57

Swinfen, Ann . . . . **CLC 34**

Swinnerton, Frank Arthur
1884-1982 . . . . **CLC 31**
See also CA 108; DLB 34

Swithen, John
See King, Stephen (Edwin)

Sylvia
See Ashton-Warner, Sylvia (Constance)

Symmes, Robert Edward
See Duncan, Robert (Edward)

Symonds, John Addington
1840-1893 . . . . NCLC 34
See also DLB 57, 144

Symons, Arthur 1865-1945 . . . . TCLC 11
See also CA 107; DLB 19, 57

Symons, Julian (Gustave)
1912- . . . . CLC 2, 14, 32
See also CA 49-52; CAAS 3; CANR 3, 33;
DLB 87; DLBY 92; MTCW

Synge, (Edmund) J(ohn) M(illington)
1871-1909 . . . . TCLC 6, 37; DC 2
See also CA 104; 141; CDBLB 1890-1914;
DLB 10, 19

Syruc, J.
See Milosz, Czeslaw

Szirtes, George 1948- . . . . CLC 46
See also CA 109; CANR 27

Tabori, George 1914- . . . . CLC 19
See also CA 49-52; CANR 4

Tagore, Rabindranath
1861-1941 . . . . TCLC 3, 53; PC 8
See also CA 104; 120; MTCW

Taine, Hippolyte Adolphe
1828-1893 . . . . NCLC 15

Talese, Gay 1932- . . . . CLC 37
See also AITN 1; CA 1-4R; CANR 9;
MTCW

Tallent, Elizabeth (Ann) 1954- . . . . . CLC 45
See also CA 117; DLB 130

Tally, Ted 1952- . . . . CLC 42
See also CA 120; 124

Tamayo y Baus, Manuel
1829-1898 . . . . NCLC 1

Tammsaare, A(nton) H(ansen)
1878-1940 . . . . TCLC 27

Tan, Amy 1952- . . . . CLC 59
See also AAYA 9; BEST 89:3; CA 136;
SATA 75

Tandem, Felix
See Spitteler, Carl (Friedrich Georg)

Tanizaki, Jun'ichiro
1886-1965 . . . . CLC 8, 14, 28
See also CA 93-96; 25-28R

Tanner, William
See Amis, Kingsley (William)

Tao Lao
See Storni, Alfonsina

Tarassoff, Lev
See Troyat, Henri

Tarbell, Ida M(inerva)
1857-1944 . . . . TCLC 40
See also CA 122; DLB 47

Tarkington, (Newton) Booth
1869-1946 . . . . TCLC 9
See also CA 110; 143; DLB 9, 102;
SATA 17

Tarkovsky, Andrei (Arsenyevich)
1932-1986 . . . . CLC 75
See also CA 127

Tartt, Donna 1964(?)- . . . . CLC 76
See also CA 142

Tasso, Torquato 1544-1595 . . . . LC 5

Tate, (John Orley) Allen
1899-1979 . . . . CLC 2, 4, 6, 9, 11, 14, 24
See also CA 5-8R; 85-88; CANR 32;
DLB 4, 45, 63; MTCW

Tate, Ellalice
See Hibbert, Eleanor Alice Burford

Tate, James (Vincent) 1943- . . . CLC 2, 6, 25
See also CA 21-24R; CANR 29; DLB 5

Tavel, Ronald 1940- . . . . CLC 6
See also CA 21-24R; CANR 33

Taylor, Cecil Philip 1929-1981 . . . . . CLC 27
See also CA 25-28R; 105

Taylor, Edward 1642(?)-1729. . . . LC 11; DA
See also DLB 24

Taylor, Eleanor Ross 1920- . . . . CLC 5
See also CA 81-84

Taylor, Elizabeth 1912-1975 . . . CLC 2, 4, 29
See also CA 13-16R; CANR 9; DLB 139;
MTCW; SATA 13

Taylor, Henry (Splawn) 1942- . . . . . . CLC 44
See also CA 33-36R; CAAS 7; CANR 31;
DLB 5

Taylor, Kamala (Purnaiya) 1924-
See Markandaya, Kamala
See also CA 77-80

Taylor, Mildred D. . . . . CLC 21
See also AAYA 10; BW 1; CA 85-88;
CANR 25; CLR 9; DLB 52; JRDA;
MAICYA; SAAS 5; SATA 15, 70

Taylor, Peter (Hillsman)
1917- . . . . . . CLC 1, 4, 18, 37, 44, 50, 71;
SSC 10
See also CA 13-16R; CANR 9; DLBY 81;
MTCW

Taylor, Robert Lewis 1912- . . . . CLC 14
See also CA 1-4R; CANR 3; SATA 10

Tchekhov, Anton
See Chekhov, Anton (Pavlovich)

Teasdale, Sara 1884-1933. . . . . TCLC 4
See also CA 104; DLB 45; SATA 32

Tegner, Esaias 1782-1846. . . . . NCLC 2

Teilhard de Chardin, (Marie Joseph) Pierre
1881-1955 . . . . TCLC 9
See also CA 105

Temple, Ann
See Mortimer, Penelope (Ruth)

Tennant, Emma (Christina)
1937- . . . . CLC 13, 52
See also CA 65-68; CAAS 9; CANR 10, 38;
DLB 14

Tenneshaw, S. M.
See Silverberg, Robert

Tennyson, Alfred
1809-1892 . . NCLC 30; DA; PC 6; WLC
See also CDBLB 1832-1890; DLB 32

Teran, Lisa St. Aubin de . . . . CLC 36
See also St. Aubin de Teran, Lisa

Teresa de Jesus, St. 1515-1582 . . . . . . LC 18

Terkel, Louis 1912-
See Terkel, Studs
See also CA 57-60; CANR 18, 45; MTCW

Terkel, Studs . . . . CLC 38
See also Terkel, Louis
See also AITN 1

Terry, C. V.
See Slaughter, Frank G(ill)

Terry, Megan 1932- . . . . CLC 19
See also CA 77-80; CABS 3; CANR 43;
DLB 7

Tertz, Abram
See Sinyavsky, Andrei (Donatevich)

Tesich, Steve 1943(?)-. . . . . CLC 40, 69
See also CA 105; DLBY 83

Teternikov, Fyodor Kuzmich 1863-1927
See Sologub, Fyodor
See also CA 104

Tevis, Walter 1928-1984 . . . . CLC 42
See also CA 113

Tey, Josephine. . . . . TCLC 14
See also Mackintosh, Elizabeth
See also DLB 77

Thackeray, William Makepeace
1811-1863 . . . . NCLC 5, 14, 22, 43; DA;
WLC
See also CDBLB 1832-1890; DLB 21, 55;
SATA 23

Thakura, Ravindranatha
See Tagore, Rabindranath

Tharoor, Shashi 1956- . . . . CLC 70
See also CA 141

Thelwell, Michael Miles 1939- . . . . . CLC 22
See also BW 2; CA 101

Theobald, Lewis, Jr.
See Lovecraft, H(oward) P(hillips)

Theodorescu, Ion N. 1880-1967
See Arghezi, Tudor
See also CA 116

Theriault, Yves 1915-1983. . . . . CLC 79
See also CA 102; DLB 88

Theroux, Alexander (Louis)
1939- . . . . CLC 2, 25
See also CA 85-88; CANR 20

Theroux, Paul (Edward)
1941- . . . . CLC 5, 8, 11, 15, 28, 46
See also BEST 89:4; CA 33-36R; CANR 20,
45; DLB 2; MTCW; SATA 44

Thesen, Sharon 1946- . . . . CLC 56

Thevenin, Denis
See Duhamel, Georges

Thibault, Jacques Anatole Francois
1844-1924
See France, Anatole
See also CA 106; 127; MTCW

Thiele, Colin (Milton) 1920- . . . . CLC 17
See also CA 29-32R; CANR 12, 28;
CLR 27; MAICYA; SAAS 2; SATA 14,
72

Thomas, Audrey (Callahan)
1935- . . . . CLC 7, 13, 37
See also AITN 2; CA 21-24R; CAAS 19;
CANR 36; DLB 60; MTCW

Thomas, D(onald) M(ichael)
1935- . . . . CLC 13, 22, 31
See also CA 61-64; CAAS 11; CANR 17,
45; CDBLB 1960 to Present; DLB 40;
MTCW

Thomas, Dylan (Marlais)
1914-1953 ... **TCLC 1, 8, 45; DA; PC 2; SSC 3; WLC**
See also CA 104; 120; CDBLB 1945-1960; DLB 13, 20, 139; MTCW; SATA 60

Thomas, (Philip) Edward
1878-1917 .... **TCLC 10**
See also CA 106; DLB 19

Thomas, Joyce Carol 1938-........ **CLC 35**
See also AAYA 12; BW 2; CA 113; 116; CLR 19; DLB 33; JRDA; MAICYA; MTCW; SAAS 7; SATA 40, 78

Thomas, Lewis 1913-1993 .... **CLC 35**
See also CA 85-88; 143; CANR 38; MTCW

Thomas, Paul
See Mann, (Paul) Thomas

Thomas, Piri 1928-.............. **CLC 17**
See also CA 73-76; HW

Thomas, R(onald) S(tuart)
1913- .... **CLC 6, 13, 48**
See also CA 89-92; CAAS 4; CANR 30; CDBLB 1960 to Present; DLB 27; MTCW

Thomas, Ross (Elmore) 1926-...... **CLC 39**
See also CA 33-36R; CANR 22

Thompson, Francis Clegg
See Mencken, H(enry) L(ouis)

Thompson, Francis Joseph
1859-1907 .... **TCLC 4**
See also CA 104; CDBLB 1890-1914; DLB 19

Thompson, Hunter S(tockton)
1939- .... **CLC 9, 17, 40**
See also BEST 89:1; CA 17-20R; CANR 23; MTCW

Thompson, James Myers
See Thompson, Jim (Myers)

Thompson, Jim (Myers)
1906-1977(?) .... **CLC 69**
See also CA 140

Thompson, Judith .... **CLC 39**

Thomson, James 1700-1748........ **LC 16**

Thomson, James 1834-1882...... **NCLC 18**

Thoreau, Henry David
1817-1862 ...... **NCLC 7, 21; DA; WLC**
See also CDALB 1640-1865; DLB 1

Thornton, Hall
See Silverberg, Robert

Thurber, James (Grover)
1894-1961 ... **CLC 5, 11, 25; DA; SSC 1**
See also CA 73-76; CANR 17, 39; CDALB 1929-1941; DLB 4, 11, 22, 102; MAICYA; MTCW; SATA 13

Thurman, Wallace (Henry)
1902-1934 .... **TCLC 6; BLC**
See also BW 1; CA 104; 124; DLB 51

Ticheburn, Cheviot
See Ainsworth, William Harrison

Tieck, (Johann) Ludwig
1773-1853 .... **NCLC 5, 46**
See also DLB 90

Tiger, Derry
See Ellison, Harlan

Tilghman, Christopher 1948(?)-..... **CLC 65**

Tillinghast, Richard (Williford)
1940- .... **CLC 29**
See also CA 29-32R; CANR 26

Timrod, Henry 1828-1867 .... **NCLC 25**
See also DLB 3

Tindall, Gillian 1938-.............. **CLC 7**
See also CA 21-24R; CANR 11

Tiptree, James, Jr. .... **CLC 48, 50**
See also Sheldon, Alice Hastings Bradley
See also DLB 8

Titmarsh, Michael Angelo
See Thackeray, William Makepeace

Tocqueville, Alexis (Charles Henri Maurice
Clerel Comte) 1805-1859..... **NCLC 7**

Tolkien, J(ohn) R(onald) R(euel)
1892-1973 ...... **CLC 1, 2, 3, 8, 12, 38; DA; WLC**
See also AAYA 10; AITN 1; CA 17-18; 45-48; CANR 36; CAP 2; CDBLB 1914-1945; DLB 15; JRDA; MAICYA; MTCW; SATA 2, 24, 32

Toller, Ernst 1893-1939 .... **TCLC 10**
See also CA 107; DLB 124

Tolson, M. B.
See Tolson, Melvin B(eaunorus)

Tolson, Melvin B(eaunorus)
1898(?)-1966 .... **CLC 36; BLC**
See also BW 1; CA 124; 89-92; DLB 48, 76

Tolstoi, Aleksei Nikolaevich
See Tolstoy, Alexey Nikolaevich

Tolstoy, Alexey Nikolaevich
1882-1945 .... **TCLC 18**
See also CA 107

Tolstoy, Count Leo
See Tolstoy, Leo (Nikolaevich)

Tolstoy, Leo (Nikolaevich)
1828-1910 ..... **TCLC 4, 11, 17, 28, 44; DA; SSC 9; WLC**
See also CA 104; 123; SATA 26

Tomasi di Lampedusa, Giuseppe 1896-1957
See Lampedusa, Giuseppe (Tomasi) di
See also CA 111

Tomlin, Lily...................... **CLC 17**
See also Tomlin, Mary Jean

Tomlin, Mary Jean 1939(?)-
See Tomlin, Lily
See also CA 117

Tomlinson, (Alfred) Charles
1927- .... **CLC 2, 4, 6, 13, 45**
See also CA 5-8R; CANR 33; DLB 40

Tonson, Jacob
See Bennett, (Enoch) Arnold

Toole, John Kennedy
1937-1969 .... **CLC 19, 64**
See also CA 104; DLBY 81

Toomer, Jean
1894-1967 ...... **CLC 1, 4, 13, 22; BLC; PC 7; SSC 1**
See also BW 1; CA 85-88; CDALB 1917-1929; DLB 45, 51; MTCW

Torley, Luke
See Blish, James (Benjamin)

Tornimparte, Alessandra
See Ginzburg, Natalia

Torre, Raoul della
See Mencken, H(enry) L(ouis)

Torrey, E(dwin) Fuller 1937-....... **CLC 34**
See also CA 119

Torsvan, Ben Traven
See Traven, B.

Torsvan, Benno Traven
See Traven, B.

Torsvan, Berick Traven
See Traven, B.

Torsvan, Berwick Traven
See Traven, B.

Torsvan, Bruno Traven
See Traven, B.

Torsvan, Traven
See Traven, B.

Tournier, Michel (Edouard)
1924- .... **CLC 6, 23, 36**
See also CA 49-52; CANR 3, 36; DLB 83; MTCW; SATA 23

Tournimparte, Alessandra
See Ginzburg, Natalia

Towers, Ivar
See Kornbluth, C(yril) M.

Townsend, Sue 1946-.............. **CLC 61**
See also CA 119; 127; MTCW; SATA 48, 55

Townshend, Peter (Dennis Blandford)
1945- .... **CLC 17, 42**
See also CA 107

Tozzi, Federigo 1883-1920........ **TCLC 31**

Traill, Catharine Parr
1802-1899 .... **NCLC 31**
See also DLB 99

Trakl, Georg 1887-1914........... **TCLC 5**
See also CA 104

Transtroemer, Tomas (Goesta)
1931- .... **CLC 52, 65**
See also CA 117; 129; CAAS 17

Transtromer, Tomas Gosta
See Transtroemer, Tomas (Goesta)

Traven, B. (?)-1969............. **CLC 8, 11**
See also CA 19-20; 25-28R; CAP 2; DLB 9, 56; MTCW

Treitel, Jonathan 1959- .... **CLC 70**

Tremain, Rose 1943-.............. **CLC 42**
See also CA 97-100; CANR 44; DLB 14

Tremblay, Michel 1942-........... **CLC 29**
See also CA 116; 128; DLB 60; MTCW

Trevor, Glen
See Hilton, James

Trevor, William
1928- .... **CLC 7, 9, 14, 25, 71**
See also Cox, William Trevor
See also DLB 14, 139

Trifonov, Yuri (Valentinovich)
1925-1981 .... **CLC 45**
See also CA 126; 103; MTCW

Trilling, Lionel 1905-1975 .... **CLC 9, 11, 24**
See also CA 9-12R; 61-64; CANR 10; DLB 28, 63; MTCW

Trimball, W. H.
See Mencken, H(enry) L(ouis)

Tristan
   See Gomez de la Serna, Ramon

Tristram
   See Housman, A(lfred) E(dward)

Trogdon, William (Lewis)   1939-
   See Heat-Moon, William Least
   See also CA 115; 119

Trollope, Anthony
   1815-1882 ...... **NCLC 6, 33; DA; WLC**
   See also CDBLB 1832-1890; DLB 21, 57;
   SATA 22

Trollope, Frances   1779-1863 ..... **NCLC 30**
   See also DLB 21

Trotsky, Leon   1879-1940........ **TCLC 22**
   See also CA 118

Trotter (Cockburn), Catharine
   1679-1749 .... **LC 8**
   See also DLB 84

Trout, Kilgore
   See Farmer, Philip Jose

Trow, George W. S.   1943-......... **CLC 52**
   See also CA 126

Troyat, Henri   1911-............. **CLC 23**
   See also CA 45-48; CANR 2, 33; MTCW

Trudeau, G(arretson) B(eekman)   1948-
   See Trudeau, Garry B.
   See also CA 81-84; CANR 31; SATA 35

Trudeau, Garry B................ **CLC 12**
   See also Trudeau, G(arretson) B(eekman)
   See also AAYA 10; AITN 2

Truffaut, Francois   1932-1984....... **CLC 20**
   See also CA 81-84; 113; CANR 34

Trumbo, Dalton   1905-1976 .... **CLC 19**
   See also CA 21-24R; 69-72; CANR 10;
   DLB 26

Trumbull, John   1750-1831 ...... **NCLC 30**
   See also DLB 31

Trundlett, Helen B.
   See Eliot, T(homas) S(tearns)

Tryon, Thomas   1926-1991 .... **CLC 3, 11**
   See also AITN 1; CA 29-32R; 135;
   CANR 32; MTCW

Tryon, Tom
   See Tryon, Thomas

Ts'ao Hsueh-ch'in   1715(?)-1763....... **LC 1**

Tsushima, Shuji   1909-1948
   See Dazai, Osamu
   See also CA 107

Tsvetaeva (Efron), Marina (Ivanovna)
   1892-1941 .... **TCLC 7, 35**
   See also CA 104; 128; MTCW

Tuck, Lily   1938-................. **CLC 70**
   See also CA 139

Tu Fu   712-770..................... **PC 9**

Tunis, John R(oberts)   1889-1975 ... **CLC 12**
   See also CA 61-64; DLB 22; JRDA;
   MAICYA; SATA 30, 37

Tuohy, Frank..................... **CLC 37**
   See also Tuohy, John Francis
   See also DLB 14, 139

Tuohy, John Francis   1925-
   See Tuohy, Frank
   See also CA 5-8R; CANR 3

Turco, Lewis (Putnam)   1934- ... **CLC 11, 63**
   See also CA 13-16R; CANR 24; DLBY 84

Turgenev, Ivan
   1818-1883 ...... **NCLC 21; DA; SSC 7;**
   WLC

Turner, Frederick   1943-.......... **CLC 48**
   See also CA 73-76; CAAS 10; CANR 12,
   30; DLB 40

Tusan, Stan   1936-................ **CLC 22**
   See also CA 105

Tutu, Desmond M(pilo)
   1931-................. **CLC 80; BLC**
   See also BW 1; CA 125

Tutuola, Amos   1920- ... **CLC 5, 14, 29; BLC**
   See also BW 2; CA 9-12R; CANR 27;
   DLB 125; MTCW

Twain, Mark
   ... **TCLC 6, 12, 19, 36, 48; SSC 6; WLC**
   See also Clemens, Samuel Langhorne
   See also DLB 11, 12, 23, 64, 74

Tyler, Anne
   1941-........ **CLC 7, 11, 18, 28, 44, 59**
   See also BEST 89:1; CA 9-12R; CANR 11,
   33; DLB 6, 143; DLBY 82; MTCW;
   SATA 7

Tyler, Royall   1757-1826.......... **NCLC 3**
   See also DLB 37

Tynan, Katharine   1861-1931 .... **TCLC 3**
   See also CA 104

Tytell, John   1939- .... **CLC 50**
   See also CA 29-32R

Tyutchev, Fyodor   1803-1873 ..... **NCLC 34**

Tzara, Tristan .... **CLC 47**
   See also Rosenfeld, Samuel

Uhry, Alfred   1936-.............. **CLC 55**
   See also CA 127; 133

Ulf, Haerved
   See Strindberg, (Johan) August

Ulf, Harved
   See Strindberg, (Johan) August

Ulibarri, Sabine R(eyes)   1919- ..... **CLC 83**
   See also CA 131; DLB 82; HW

Unamuno (y Jugo), Miguel de
   1864-1936 .... **TCLC 2, 9; HLC; SSC 11**
   See also CA 104; 131; DLB 108; HW;
   MTCW

Undercliffe, Errol
   See Campbell, (John) Ramsey

Underwood, Miles
   See Glassco, John

Undset, Sigrid
   1882-1949 .... **TCLC 3; DA; WLC**
   See also CA 104; 129; MTCW

Ungaretti, Giuseppe
   1888-1970 .... **CLC 7, 11, 15**
   See also CA 19-20; 25-28R; CAP 2;
   DLB 114

Unger, Douglas   1952-............. **CLC 34**
   See also CA 130

Unsworth, Barry (Forster)   1930-.... **CLC 76**
   See also CA 25-28R; CANR 30

Updike, John (Hoyer)
   1932-...... **CLC 1, 2, 3, 5, 7, 9, 13, 15,**
   23, 34, 43, 70; DA; SSC 13; WLC
   See also CA 1-4R; CABS 1; CANR 4, 33;
   CDALB 1968-1988; DLB 2, 5, 143;
   DLBD 3; DLBY 80, 82; MTCW

Upshaw, Margaret Mitchell
   See Mitchell, Margaret (Munnerlyn)

Upton, Mark
   See Sanders, Lawrence

Urdang, Constance (Henriette)
   1922-...................... **CLC 47**
   See also CA 21-24R; CANR 9, 24

Uriel, Henry
   See Faust, Frederick (Schiller)

Uris, Leon (Marcus)   1924-...... **CLC 7, 32**
   See also AITN 1, 2; BEST 89:2; CA 1-4R;
   CANR 1, 40; MTCW; SATA 49

Urmuz
   See Codrescu, Andrei

Ustinov, Peter (Alexander)   1921- .... **CLC 1**
   See also AITN 1; CA 13-16R; CANR 25;
   DLB 13

V
   See Chekhov, Anton (Pavlovich)

Vaculik, Ludvik   1926- .... **CLC 7**
   See also CA 53-56

Valdez, Luis (Miguel)
   1940-................. **CLC 84; HLC**
   See also CA 101; CANR 32; DLB 122; HW

Valenzuela, Luisa   1938-... **CLC 31; SSC 14**
   See also CA 101; CANR 32; DLB 113; HW

Valera y Alcala-Galiano, Juan
   1824-1905 .... **TCLC 10**
   See also CA 106

Valery, (Ambroise) Paul (Toussaint Jules)
   1871-1945 .... **TCLC 4, 15; PC 9**
   See also CA 104; 122; MTCW

Valle-Inclan, Ramon (Maria) del
   1866-1936 .... **TCLC 5; HLC**
   See also CA 106; DLB 134

Vallejo, Antonio Buero
   See Buero Vallejo, Antonio

Vallejo, Cesar (Abraham)
   1892-1938 .... **TCLC 3, 56; HLC**
   See also CA 105; HW

Valle Y Pena, Ramon del
   See Valle-Inclan, Ramon (Maria) del

Van Ash, Cay   1918-............. **CLC 34**

Vanbrugh, Sir John   1664-1726 ...... **LC 21**
   See also DLB 80

Van Campen, Karl
   See Campbell, John W(ood, Jr.)

Vance, Gerald
   See Silverberg, Robert

Vance, Jack .... **CLC 35**
   See also Vance, John Holbrook
   See also DLB 8

Vance, John Holbrook   1916-
   See Queen, Ellery; Vance, Jack
   See also CA 29-32R; CANR 17; MTCW

Waddington, Miriam 1917- .... **CLC 28**
See also CA 21-24R; CANR 12, 30;
DLB 68

Wagman, Fredrica 1937- .... **CLC 7**
See also CA 97-100

Wagner, Richard 1813-1883....... **NCLC 9**
See also DLB 129

Wagner-Martin, Linda 1936-...... **CLC 50**

Wagoner, David (Russell)
1926- .... **CLC 3, 5, 15**
See also CA 1-4R; CAAS 3; CANR 2;
DLB 5; SATA 14

Wah, Fred(erick James) 1939-...... **CLC 44**
See also CA 107; 141; DLB 60

Wahloo, Per 1926-1975 .... **CLC 7**
See also CA 61-64

Wahloo, Peter
See Wahloo, Per

Wain, John (Barrington)
1925- .... **CLC 2, 11, 15, 46**
See also CA 5-8R; CAAS 4; CANR 23;
CDBLB 1960 to Present; DLB 15, 27,
139; MTCW

Wajda, Andrzej 1926-............. **CLC 16**
See also CA 102

Wakefield, Dan 1932-.............. **CLC 7**
See also CA 21-24R; CAAS 7

Wakoski, Diane
1937- .... **CLC 2, 4, 7, 9, 11, 40**
See also CA 13-16R; CAAS 1; CANR 9;
DLB 5

Wakoski-Sherbell, Diane
See Wakoski, Diane

Walcott, Derek (Alton)
1930- .... **CLC 2, 4, 9, 14, 25, 42, 67, 76;**
BLC
See also BW 2; CA 89-92; CANR 26;
DLB 117; DLBY 81; MTCW

Waldman, Anne 1945- .... **CLC 7**
See also CA 37-40R; CAAS 17; CANR 34;
DLB 16

Waldo, E. Hunter
See Sturgeon, Theodore (Hamilton)

Waldo, Edward Hamilton
See Sturgeon, Theodore (Hamilton)

Walker, Alice (Malsenior)
1944- .... **CLC 5, 6, 9, 19, 27, 46, 58;**
BLC; DA; SSC 5
See also AAYA 3; BEST 89:4; BW 2;
CA 37-40R; CANR 9, 27;
CDALB 1968-1988; DLB 6, 33, 143;
MTCW; SATA 31

Walker, David Harry 1911-1992.... **CLC 14**
See also CA 1-4R; 137; CANR 1; SATA 8;
SATA-Obit 71

Walker, Edward Joseph 1934-
See Walker, Ted
See also CA 21-24R; CANR 12, 28

Walker, George F. 1947-....... **CLC 44, 61**
See also CA 103; CANR 21, 43; DLB 60

Walker, Joseph A. 1935-.......... **CLC 19**
See also BW 1; CA 89-92; CANR 26;
DLB 38

Walker, Margaret (Abigail)
1915- .... **CLC 1, 6; BLC**
See also BW 2; CA 73-76; CANR 26;
DLB 76; MTCW

Walker, Ted.................... **CLC 13**
See also Walker, Edward Joseph
See also DLB 40

Wallace, David Foster 1962-....... **CLC 50**
See also CA 132

Wallace, Dexter
See Masters, Edgar Lee

Wallace, Irving 1916-1990....... **CLC 7, 13**
See also AITN 1; CA 1-4R; 132; CAAS 1;
CANR 1, 27; MTCW

Wallant, Edward Lewis
1926-1962 .... **CLC 5, 10**
See also CA 1-4R; CANR 22; DLB 2, 28,
143; MTCW

Walpole, Horace 1717-1797......... **LC 2**
See also DLB 39, 104

Walpole, Hugh (Seymour)
1884-1941 .... **TCLC 5**
See also CA 104; DLB 34

Walser, Martin 1927-............. **CLC 27**
See also CA 57-60; CANR 8; DLB 75, 124

Walser, Robert 1878-1956........ **TCLC 18**
See also CA 118; DLB 66

Walsh, Jill Paton................. **CLC 35**
See also Paton Walsh, Gillian
See also AAYA 11; CLR 2; SAAS 3

Walter, Villiam Christian
See Andersen, Hans Christian

Wambaugh, Joseph (Aloysius, Jr.)
1937- .... **CLC 3, 18**
See also AITN 1; BEST 89:3; CA 33-36R;
CANR 42; DLB 6; DLBY 83; MTCW

Ward, Arthur Henry Sarsfield 1883-1959
See Rohmer, Sax
See also CA 108

Ward, Douglas Turner 1930-....... **CLC 19**
See also BW 1; CA 81-84; CANR 27;
DLB 7, 38

Ward, Mary Augusta
See Ward, Mrs. Humphry

Ward, Mrs. Humphry
1851-1920 .... **TCLC 55**
See also DLB 18

Ward, Peter
See Faust, Frederick (Schiller)

Warhol, Andy 1928(?)-1987........ **CLC 20**
See also AAYA 12; BEST 89:4; CA 89-92;
121; CANR 34

Warner, Francis (Robert le Plastrier)
1937-...................... **CLC 14**
See also CA 53-56; CANR 11

Warner, Marina 1946-............ **CLC 59**
See also CA 65-68; CANR 21

Warner, Rex (Ernest) 1905-1986.... **CLC 45**
See also CA 89-92; 119; DLB 15

Warner, Susan (Bogert)
1819-1885 .... **NCLC 31**
See also DLB 3, 42

Warner, Sylvia (Constance) Ashton
See Ashton-Warner, Sylvia (Constance)

Warner, Sylvia Townsend
1893-1978 .... **CLC 7, 19**
See also CA 61-64; 77-80; CANR 16;
DLB 34, 139; MTCW

Warren, Mercy Otis 1728-1814... **NCLC 13**
See also DLB 31

Warren, Robert Penn
1905-1989 .... **CLC 1, 4, 6, 8, 10, 13, 18,**
39, 53, 59; DA; SSC 4; WLC
See also AITN 1; CA 13-16R; 129;
CANR 10; CDALB 1968-1988; DLB 2,
48; DLBY 80, 89; MTCW; SATA 46, 63

Warshofsky, Isaac
See Singer, Isaac Bashevis

Warton, Thomas 1728-1790........ **LC 15**
See also DLB 104, 109

Waruk, Kona
See Harris, (Theodore) Wilson

Warung, Price 1855-1911........ **TCLC 45**

Warwick, Jarvis
See Garner, Hugh

Washington, Alex
See Harris, Mark

Washington, Booker T(aliaferro)
1856-1915 .... **TCLC 10; BLC**
See also BW 1; CA 114; 125; SATA 28

Washington, George 1732-1799...... **LC 25**
See also DLB 31

Wassermann, (Karl) Jakob
1873-1934 .... **TCLC 6**
See also CA 104; DLB 66

Wasserstein, Wendy
1950- .... **CLC 32, 59; DC 4**
See also CA 121; 129; CABS 3

Waterhouse, Keith (Spencer)
1929-...................... **CLC 47**
See also CA 5-8R; CANR 38; DLB 13, 15;
MTCW

Waters, Roger 1944-.............. **CLC 35**
See also Pink Floyd

Watkins, Frances Ellen
See Harper, Frances Ellen Watkins

Watkins, Gerrold
See Malzberg, Barry N(athaniel)

Watkins, Paul 1964-.............. **CLC 55**
See also CA 132

Watkins, Vernon Phillips
1906-1967 .... **CLC 43**
See also CA 9-10; 25-28R; CAP 1; DLB 20

Watson, Irving S.
See Mencken, H(enry) L(ouis)

Watson, John H.
See Farmer, Philip Jose

Watson, Richard F.
See Silverberg, Robert

Waugh, Auberon (Alexander) 1939-... **CLC 7**
See also CA 45-48; CANR 6, 22; DLB 14

Waugh, Evelyn (Arthur St. John)
1903-1966 ...... **CLC 1, 3, 8, 13, 19, 27,**
44; DA; WLC
See also CA 85-88; 25-28R; CANR 22;
CDBLB 1914-1945; DLB 15; MTCW

Waugh, Harriet 1944- .... **CLC 6**
See also CA 85-88; CANR 22

Ways, C. R.
See Blount, Roy (Alton), Jr.

Waystaff, Simon
See Swift, Jonathan

Webb, (Martha) Beatrice (Potter)
1858-1943 .... TCLC 22
See also Potter, Beatrice
See also CA 117

Webb, Charles (Richard) 1939-...... CLC 7
See also CA 25-28R

Webb, James H(enry), Jr. 1946-.... CLC 22
See also CA 81-84

Webb, Mary (Gladys Meredith)
1881-1927 .... TCLC 24
See also CA 123; DLB 34

Webb, Mrs. Sidney
See Webb, (Martha) Beatrice (Potter)

Webb, Phyllis 1927-.............. CLC 18
See also CA 104; CANR 23; DLB 53

Webb, Sidney (James)
1859-1947 .... TCLC 22
See also CA 117

Webber, Andrew Lloyd............. CLC 21
See also Lloyd Webber, Andrew

Weber, Lenora Mattingly
1895-1971 .... CLC 12
See also CA 19-20; 29-32R; CAP 1;
SATA 2, 26

Webster, John 1579(?)-1634(?) .... DC 2
See also CDBLB Before 1660; DA; DLB 58;
WLC

Webster, Noah 1758-1843 .... NCLC 30

Wedekind, (Benjamin) Frank(lin)
1864-1918 .... TCLC 7
See also CA 104; DLB 118

Weidman, Jerome 1913-............ CLC 7
See also AITN 2; CA 1-4R; CANR 1;
DLB 28

Weil, Simone (Adolphine)
1909-1943 .... TCLC 23
See also CA 117

Weinstein, Nathan
See West, Nathanael

Weinstein, Nathan von Wallenstein
See West, Nathanael

Weir, Peter (Lindsay) 1944- .... CLC 20
See also CA 113; 123

Weiss, Peter (Ulrich)
1916-1982 .... CLC 3, 15, 51
See also CA 45-48; 106; CANR 3; DLB 69,
124

Weiss, Theodore (Russell)
1916-.................... CLC 3, 8, 14
See also CA 9-12R; CAAS 2; DLB 5

Welch, (Maurice) Denton
1915-1948 .... TCLC 22
See also CA 121

Welch, James 1940-......... CLC 6, 14, 52
See also CA 85-88; CANR 42

Weldon, Fay
1933(?)-....... CLC 6, 9, 11, 19, 36, 59
See also CA 21-24R; CANR 16;
CDBLB 1960 to Present; DLB 14;
MTCW

Wellek, Rene 1903- .... CLC 28
See also CA 5-8R; CAAS 7; CANR 8;
DLB 63

Weller, Michael 1942- .... CLC 10, 53
See also CA 85-88

Weller, Paul 1958-.............. CLC 26

Wellershoff, Dieter 1925-......... CLC 46
See also CA 89-92; CANR 16, 37

Welles, (George) Orson
1915-1985 .... CLC 20, 80
See also CA 93-96; 117

Wellman, Mac 1945- .... CLC 65

Wellman, Manly Wade 1903-1986 .. CLC 49
See also CA 1-4R; 118; CANR 6, 16, 44;
SATA 6, 47

Wells, Carolyn 1869(?)-1942 ..... TCLC 35
See also CA 113; DLB 11

Wells, H(erbert) G(eorge)
1866-1946 .... TCLC 6, 12, 19; DA;
SSC 6; WLC
See also CA 110; 121; CDBLB 1914-1945;
DLB 34, 70; MTCW; SATA 20

Wells, Rosemary 1943-........... CLC 12
See also CA 85-88; CLR 16; MAICYA;
SAAS 1; SATA 18, 69

Welty, Eudora
1909- ...... CLC 1, 2, 5, 14, 22, 33; DA;
SSC 1; WLC
See also CA 9-12R; CABS 1; CANR 32;
CDALB 1941-1968; DLB 2, 102, 143;
DLBY 87; MTCW

Wen I-to 1899-1946 .... TCLC 28

Wentworth, Robert
See Hamilton, Edmond

Werfel, Franz (V.) 1890-1945 ...... TCLC 8
See also CA 104; DLB 81, 124

Wergeland, Henrik Arnold
1808-1845 .... NCLC 5

Wersba, Barbara 1932-............ CLC 30
See also AAYA 2; CA 29-32R; CANR 16,
38; CLR 3; DLB 52; JRDA; MAICYA;
SAAS 2; SATA 1, 58

Wertmueller, Lina 1928- .... CLC 16
See also CA 97-100; CANR 39

Wescott, Glenway 1901-1987....... CLC 13
See also CA 13-16R; 121; CANR 23;
DLB 4, 9, 102

Wesker, Arnold 1932- .... CLC 3, 5, 42
See also CA 1-4R; CAAS 7; CANR 1, 33;
CDBLB 1960 to Present; DLB 13;
MTCW

Wesley, Richard (Errol) 1945-...... CLC 7
See also BW 1; CA 57-60; CANR 27;
DLB 38

Wessel, Johan Herman 1742-1785 .... LC 7

West, Anthony (Panther)
1914-1987 .... CLC 50
See also CA 45-48; 124; CANR 3, 19;
DLB 15

West, C. P.
See Wodehouse, P(elham) G(renville)

West, (Mary) Jessamyn
1902-1984 .... CLC 7, 17
See also CA 9-12R; 112; CANR 27; DLB 6;
DLBY 84; MTCW; SATA 37

West, Morris L(anglo) 1916-..... CLC 6, 33
See also CA 5-8R; CANR 24; MTCW

West, Nathanael
1903-1940 ..... TCLC 1, 14, 44; SSC 16
See also CA 104; 125; CDALB 1929-1941;
DLB 4, 9, 28; MTCW

West, Owen
See Koontz, Dean R(ay)

West, Paul 1930-............... CLC 7, 14
See also CA 13-16R; CAAS 7; CANR 22;
DLB 14

West, Rebecca 1892-1983 .. CLC 7, 9, 31, 50
See also CA 5-8R; 109; CANR 19; DLB 36;
DLBY 83; MTCW

Westall, Robert (Atkinson)
1929-1993 .... CLC 17
See also AAYA 12; CA 69-72; 141;
CANR 18; CLR 13; JRDA; MAICYA;
SAAS 2; SATA 23, 69; SATA-Obit 75

Westlake, Donald E(dwin)
1933-.................... CLC 7, 33
See also CA 17-20R; CAAS 13; CANR 16,
44

Westmacott, Mary
See Christie, Agatha (Mary Clarissa)

Weston, Allen
See Norton, Andre

Wetcheek, J. L.
See Feuchtwanger, Lion

Wetering, Janwillem van de
See van de Wetering, Janwillem

Wetherell, Elizabeth
See Warner, Susan (Bogert)

Whalen, Philip 1923-........... CLC 6, 29
See also CA 9-12R; CANR 5, 39; DLB 16

Wharton, Edith (Newbold Jones)
1862-1937 ...... TCLC 3, 9, 27, 53; DA;
SSC 6; WLC
See also CA 104; 132; CDALB 1865-1917;
DLB 4, 9, 12, 78; MTCW

Wharton, James
See Mencken, H(enry) L(ouis)

Wharton, William (a pseudonym)
.... CLC 18, 37
See also CA 93-96; DLBY 80

Wheatley (Peters), Phillis
1754(?)-1784 .... LC 3; BLC; DA; PC 3;
WLC
See also CDALB 1640-1865; DLB 31, 50

Wheelock, John Hall 1886-1978 .... CLC 14
See also CA 13-16R; 77-80; CANR 14;
DLB 45

White, E(lwyn) B(rooks)
1899-1985 .... CLC 10, 34, 39
See also AITN 2; CA 13-16R; 116;
CANR 16, 37; CLR 1, 21; DLB 11, 22;
MAICYA; MTCW; SATA 2, 29, 44

White, Edmund (Valentine III)
1940-..................... CLC 27
See also AAYA 7; CA 45-48; CANR 3, 19,
36; MTCW

White, Patrick (Victor Martindale)
1912-1990 .. CLC 3, 4, 5, 7, 9, 18, 65, 69
See also CA 81-84; 132; CANR 43; MTCW

White, Phyllis Dorothy James   1920-
See James, P. D.
See also CA 21-24R; CANR 17, 43; MTCW

White, T(erence) H(anbury)
1906-1964 . . . . **CLC 30**
See also CA 73-76; CANR 37; JRDA;
MAICYA; SATA 12

White, Terence de Vere   1912-. . . . . . **CLC 49**
See also CA 49-52; CANR 3

White, Walter F(rancis)
1893-1955 . . . . **TCLC 15**
See also White, Walter
See also BW 1; CA 115; 124; DLB 51

White, William Hale   1831-1913
See Rutherford, Mark
See also CA 121

Whitehead, E(dward) A(nthony)
1933- . . . . **CLC 5**
See also CA 65-68

Whitemore, Hugh (John)   1936-. . . . . **CLC 37**
See also CA 132

Whitman, Sarah Helen (Power)
1803-1878 . . . . **NCLC 19**
See also DLB 1

Whitman, Walt(er)
1819-1892 . . . . . **NCLC 4, 31; DA; PC 3;
WLC**
See also CDALB 1640-1865; DLB 3, 64;
SATA 20

Whitney, Phyllis A(yame)   1903-. . . . **CLC 42**
See also AITN 2; BEST 90:3; CA 1-4R;
CANR 3, 25, 38; JRDA; MAICYA;
SATA 1, 30

Whittemore, (Edward) Reed (Jr.)
1919- . . . . **CLC 4**
See also CA 9-12R; CAAS 8; CANR 4;
DLB 5

Whittier, John Greenleaf
1807-1892 . . . . **NCLC 8**
See also CDALB 1640-1865; DLB 1

Whittlebot, Hernia
See Coward, Noel (Peirce)

Wicker, Thomas Grey   1926-
See Wicker, Tom
See also CA 65-68; CANR 21

Wicker, Tom . . . . **CLC 7**
See also Wicker, Thomas Grey

Wideman, John Edgar
1941- . . . . **CLC 5, 34, 36, 67; BLC**
See also BW 2; CA 85-88; CANR 14, 42;
DLB 33, 143

Wiebe, Rudy (Henry)   1934-. . . **CLC 6, 11, 14**
See also CA 37-40R; CANR 42; DLB 60

Wieland, Christoph Martin
1733-1813 . . . . **NCLC 17**
See also DLB 97

Wieners, John   1934-. . . . . **CLC 7**
See also CA 13-16R; DLB 16

Wiesel, Elie(zer)
1928- . . . . **CLC 3, 5, 11, 37; DA**
See also AAYA 7; AITN 1; CA 5-8R;
CAAS 4; CANR 8, 40; DLB 83;
DLBY 87; MTCW; SATA 56

Wiggins, Marianne   1947-. . . . . **CLC 57**
See also BEST 89:3; CA 130

Wight, James Alfred   1916-
See Herriot, James
See also CA 77-80; SATA 44, 55

Wilbur, Richard (Purdy)
1921- . . . . **CLC 3, 6, 9, 14, 53; DA**
See also CA 1-4R; CABS 2; CANR 2, 29;
DLB 5; MTCW; SATA 9

Wild, Peter   1940-. . . . . **CLC 14**
See also CA 37-40R; DLB 5

Wilde, Oscar (Fingal O'Flahertie Wills)
1854(?)-1900 . . . . **TCLC 1, 8, 23, 41; DA;
SSC 11; WLC**
See also CA 104; 119; CDBLB 1890-1914;
DLB 10, 19, 34, 57, 141; SATA 24

Wilder, Billy . . . . **CLC 20**
See also Wilder, Samuel
See also DLB 26

Wilder, Samuel   1906-
See Wilder, Billy
See also CA 89-92

Wilder, Thornton (Niven)
1897-1975 . . . . . . **CLC 1, 5, 6, 10, 15, 35,
82; DA; DC 1; WLC**
See also AITN 2; CA 13-16R; 61-64;
CANR 40; DLB 4, 7, 9; MTCW

Wilding, Michael   1942-. . . . . **CLC 73**
See also CA 104; CANR 24

Wiley, Richard   1944-. . . . . **CLC 44**
See also CA 121; 129

Wilhelm, Kate . . . . **CLC 7**
See also Wilhelm, Katie Gertrude
See also CAAS 5; DLB 8

Wilhelm, Katie Gertrude   1928-
See Wilhelm, Kate
See also CA 37-40R; CANR 17, 36; MTCW

Wilkins, Mary
See Freeman, Mary Eleanor Wilkins

Willard, Nancy   1936-. . . . . **CLC 7, 37**
See also CA 89-92; CANR 10, 39; CLR 5;
DLB 5, 52; MAICYA; MTCW;
SATA 30, 37, 71

Williams, C(harles) K(enneth)
1936- . . . . **CLC 33, 56**
See also CA 37-40R; DLB 5

Williams, Charles
See Collier, James L(incoln)

Williams, Charles (Walter Stansby)
1886-1945 . . . . **TCLC 1, 11**
See also CA 104; DLB 100

Williams, (George) Emlyn
1905-1987 . . . . **CLC 15**
See also CA 104; 123; CANR 36; DLB 10,
77; MTCW

Williams, Hugo   1942-. . . . . **CLC 42**
See also CA 17-20R; CANR 45; DLB 40

Williams, J. Walker
See Wodehouse, P(elham) G(renville)

Williams, John A(lfred)
1925- . . . . **CLC 5, 13; BLC**
See also BW 2; CA 53-56; CAAS 3;
CANR 6, 26; DLB 2, 33

Williams, Jonathan (Chamberlain)
1929- . . . . **CLC 13**
See also CA 9-12R; CAAS 12; CANR 8;
DLB 5

Williams, Joy   1944-. . . . . **CLC 31**
See also CA 41-44R; CANR 22

Williams, Norman   1952-. . . . . **CLC 39**
See also CA 118

Williams, Tennessee
1911-1983 . . . . . **CLC 1, 2, 5, 7, 8, 11, 15,
19, 30, 39, 45, 71; DA; DC 4; WLC**
See also AITN 1, 2; CA 5-8R; 108;
CABS 3; CANR 31; CDALB 1941-1968;
DLB 7; DLBD 4; DLBY 83; MTCW

Williams, Thomas (Alonzo)
1926-1990 . . . . **CLC 14**
See also CA 1-4R; 132; CANR 2

Williams, William C.
See Williams, William Carlos

Williams, William Carlos
1883-1963 . . . . **CLC 1, 2, 5, 9, 13, 22, 42,
67; DA; PC 7**
See also CA 89-92; CANR 34;
CDALB 1917-1929; DLB 4, 16, 54, 86;
MTCW

Williamson, David (Keith)   1942-. . . . **CLC 56**
See also CA 103; CANR 41

Williamson, Jack. . . . . **CLC 29**
See also Williamson, John Stewart
See also CAAS 8; DLB 8

Williamson, John Stewart   1908-
See Williamson, Jack
See also CA 17-20R; CANR 23

Willie, Frederick
See Lovecraft, H(oward) P(hillips)

Willingham, Calder (Baynard, Jr.)
1922- . . . . **CLC 5, 51**
See also CA 5-8R; CANR 3; DLB 2, 44;
MTCW

Willis, Charles
See Clarke, Arthur C(harles)

Willy
See Colette, (Sidonie-Gabrielle)

Willy, Colette
See Colette, (Sidonie-Gabrielle)

Wilson, A(ndrew) N(orman)   1950-. . **CLC 33**
See also CA 112; 122; DLB 14

Wilson, Angus (Frank Johnstone)
1913-1991 . . . . **CLC 2, 3, 5, 25, 34**
See also CA 5-8R; 134; CANR 21; DLB 15,
139; MTCW

Wilson, August
1945-. . **CLC 39, 50, 63; BLC; DA; DC 2**
See also BW 2; CA 115; 122; CANR 42;
MTCW

Wilson, Brian   1942-. . . . . **CLC 12**

Wilson, Colin   1931-. . . . . **CLC 3, 14**
See also CA 1-4R; CAAS 5; CANR 1, 22,
33; DLB 14; MTCW

Wilson, Dirk
See Pohl, Frederik

Wilson, Edmund
1895-1972 . . . . **CLC 1, 2, 3, 8, 24**
See also CA 1-4R; 37-40R; CANR 1;
DLB 63; MTCW

Wilson, Ethel Davis (Bryant)
1888(?)-1980 . . . . **CLC 13**
See also CA 102; DLB 68; MTCW

Wilson, John   1785-1854. . . . . **NCLC 5**

Wilson, John (Anthony) Burgess 1917-1993
See Burgess, Anthony
See also CA 1-4R; 143; CANR 2; MTCW

Wilson, Lanford 1937- ...... **CLC 7, 14, 36**
See also CA 17-20R; CABS 3; CANR 45;
DLB 7

Wilson, Robert M. 1944- .... **CLC 7, 9**
See also CA 49-52; CANR 2, 41; MTCW

Wilson, Robert McLiam 1964- ..... **CLC 59**
See also CA 132

Wilson, Sloan 1920- .... **CLC 32**
See also CA 1-4R; CANR 1, 44

Wilson, Snoo 1948- .... **CLC 33**
See also CA 69-72

Wilson, William S(mith) 1932- ..... **CLC 49**
See also CA 81-84

Winchilsea, Anne (Kingsmill) Finch Counte
1661-1720 .... **LC 3**

Windham, Basil
See Wodehouse, P(elham) G(renville)

Wingrove, David (John) 1954- ...... **CLC 68**
See also CA 133

Winters, Janet Lewis .... **CLC 41**
See also Lewis, Janet
See also DLBY 87

Winters, (Arthur) Yvor
1900-1968 .... **CLC 4, 8, 32**
See also CA 11-12; 25-28R; CAP 1;
DLB 48; MTCW

Winterson, Jeanette 1959- .... **CLC 64**
See also CA 136

Wiseman, Frederick 1930- .... **CLC 20**

Wister, Owen 1860-1938 .... **TCLC 21**
See also CA 108; DLB 9, 78; SATA 62

Witkacy
See Witkiewicz, Stanislaw Ignacy

Witkiewicz, Stanislaw Ignacy
1885-1939 .... **TCLC 8**
See also CA 105

Wittig, Monique 1935(?)- .... **CLC 22**
See also CA 116; 135; DLB 83

Wittlin, Jozef 1896-1976 .... **CLC 25**
See also CA 49-52; 65-68; CANR 3

Wodehouse, P(elham) G(renville)
1881-1975 ... **CLC 1, 2, 5, 10, 22; SSC 2**
See also AITN 2; CA 45-48; 57-60;
CANR 3, 33; CDBLB 1914-1945;
DLB 34; MTCW; SATA 22

Woiwode, L.
See Woiwode, Larry (Alfred)

Woiwode, Larry (Alfred) 1941- ... **CLC 6, 10**
See also CA 73-76; CANR 16; DLB 6

Wojciechowska, Maia (Teresa)
1927- .... **CLC 26**
See also AAYA 8; CA 9-12R; CANR 4, 41;
CLR 1; JRDA; MAICYA; SAAS 1;
SATA 1, 28

Wolf, Christa 1929- .... **CLC 14, 29, 58**
See also CA 85-88; CANR 45; DLB 75;
MTCW

Wolfe, Gene (Rodman) 1931- .... **CLC 25**
See also CA 57-60; CAAS 9; CANR 6, 32;
DLB 8

Wolfe, George C. 1954- .... **CLC 49**

Wolfe, Thomas (Clayton)
1900-1938 ... **TCLC 4, 13, 29; DA; WLC**
See also CA 104; 132; CDALB 1929-1941;
DLB 9, 102; DLBD 2; DLBY 85; MTCW

Wolfe, Thomas Kennerly, Jr. 1931-
See Wolfe, Tom
See also CA 13-16R; CANR 9, 33; MTCW

Wolfe, Tom .... **CLC 1, 2, 9, 15, 35, 51**
See also Wolfe, Thomas Kennerly, Jr.
See also AAYA 8; AITN 2; BEST 89:1

Wolff, Geoffrey (Ansell) 1937- ..... **CLC 41**
See also CA 29-32R; CANR 29, 43

Wolff, Sonia
See Levitin, Sonia (Wolff)

Wolff, Tobias (Jonathan Ansell)
1945- .... **CLC 39, 64**
See also BEST 90:2; CA 114; 117; DLB 130

Wolfram von Eschenbach
c. 1170-c. 1220 .... **CMLC 5**
See also DLB 138

Wolitzer, Hilma 1930- .... **CLC 17**
See also CA 65-68; CANR 18, 40; SATA 31

Wollstonecraft, Mary 1759-1797...... **LC 5**
See also CDBLB 1789-1832; DLB 39, 104

Wonder, Stevie .... **CLC 12**
See also Morris, Steveland Judkins

Wong, Jade Snow 1922- .... **CLC 17**
See also CA 109

Woodcott, Keith
See Brunner, John (Kilian Houston)

Woodruff, Robert W.
See Mencken, H(enry) L(ouis)

Woolf, (Adeline) Virginia
1882-1941 .... **TCLC 1, 5, 20, 43, 56;**
DA; SSC 7; WLC
See also CA 104; 130; CDBLB 1914-1945;
DLB 36, 100; DLBD 10; MTCW

Woollcott, Alexander (Humphreys)
1887-1943 .... **TCLC 5**
See also CA 105; DLB 29

Woolrich, Cornell 1903-1968....... **CLC 77**
See also Hopley-Woolrich, Cornell George

Wordsworth, Dorothy
1771-1855 .... **NCLC 25**
See also DLB 107

Wordsworth, William
1770-1850 .... **NCLC 12, 38; DA; PC 4;**
WLC
See also CDBLB 1789-1832; DLB 93, 107

Wouk, Herman 1915- .... **CLC 1, 9, 38**
See also CA 5-8R; CANR 6, 33; DLBY 82;
MTCW

Wright, Charles (Penzel, Jr.)
1935- .... **CLC 6, 13, 28**
See also CA 29-32R; CAAS 7; CANR 23,
36; DLBY 82; MTCW

Wright, Charles Stevenson
1932- .... **CLC 49; BLC 3**
See also BW 1; CA 9-12R; CANR 26;
DLB 33

Wright, Jack R.
See Harris, Mark

Wright, James (Arlington)
1927-1980 .... **CLC 3, 5, 10, 28**
See also AITN 2; CA 49-52; 97-100;
CANR 4, 34; DLB 5; MTCW

Wright, Judith (Arandell)
1915- .... **CLC 11, 53**
See also CA 13-16R; CANR 31; MTCW;
SATA 14

Wright, L(aurali) R. 1939- .... **CLC 44**
See also CA 138

Wright, Richard (Nathaniel)
1908-1960 .... **CLC 1, 3, 4, 9, 14, 21, 48,**
74; BLC; DA; SSC 2; WLC
See also AAYA 5; BW 1; CA 108;
CDALB 1929-1941; DLB 76, 102;
DLBD 2; MTCW

Wright, Richard B(ruce) 1937- ...... **CLC 6**
See also CA 85-88; DLB 53

Wright, Rick 1945- .... **CLC 35**
See also Pink Floyd

Wright, Rowland
See Wells, Carolyn

Wright, Stephen Caldwell 1946- .... **CLC 33**
See also BW 2

Wright, Willard Huntington 1888-1939
See Van Dine, S. S.
See also CA 115

Wright, William 1930- .... **CLC 44**
See also CA 53-56; CANR 7, 23

Wu Ch'eng-en 1500(?)-1582(?)........ **LC 7**

Wu Ching-tzu 1701-1754 .... **LC 2**

Wurlitzer, Rudolph 1938(?)- ... **CLC 2, 4, 15**
See also CA 85-88

Wycherley, William 1641-1715 .... **LC 8, 21**
See also CDBLB 1660-1789; DLB 80

Wylie, Elinor (Morton Hoyt)
1885-1928 .... **TCLC 8**
See also CA 105; DLB 9, 45

Wylie, Philip (Gordon) 1902-1971... **CLC 43**
See also CA 21-22; 33-36R; CAP 2; DLB 9

Wyndham, John
See Harris, John (Wyndham Parkes Lucas
Beynon

Wyss, Johann David Von
1743-1818 .... **NCLC 10**
See also JRDA; MAICYA; SATA 27, 29

Yakumo Koizumi
See Hearn, (Patricio) Lafcadio (Tessima
Carlos)

Yanez, Jose Donoso
See Donoso (Yanez), Jose

Yanovsky, Basile S.
See Yanovsky, V(assily) S(emenovich)

Yanovsky, V(assily) S(emenovich)
1906-1989 .... **CLC 2, 18**
See also CA 97-100; 129

Yates, Richard 1926-1992 ..... **CLC 7, 8, 23**
See also CA 5-8R; 139; CANR 10, 43;
DLB 2; DLBY 81, 92

Yeats, W. B.
See Yeats, William Butler

Yeats, William Butler
1865-1939 . . . . . **TCLC 1, 11, 18, 31; DA; WLC**
See also CA 104; 127; CANR 45;
CDBLB 1890-1914; DLB 10, 19, 98;
MTCW

Yehoshua, A(braham) B.
1936- . . . . **CLC 13, 31**
See also CA 33-36R; CANR 43

Yep, Laurence Michael 1948- . . . . . . **CLC 35**
See also AAYA 5; CA 49-52; CANR 1;
CLR 3, 17; DLB 52; JRDA; MAICYA;
SATA 7, 69

Yerby, Frank G(arvin)
1916-1991 . . . . **CLC 1, 7, 22; BLC**
See also BW 1; CA 9-12R; 136; CANR 16;
DLB 76; MTCW

Yesenin, Sergei Alexandrovich
See Esenin, Sergei (Alexandrovich)

Yevtushenko, Yevgeny (Alexandrovich)
1933- . . . . **CLC 1, 3, 13, 26, 51**
See also CA 81-84; CANR 33; MTCW

Yezierska, Anzia 1885(?)-1970 . . . . . **CLC 46**
See also CA 126; 89-92; DLB 28; MTCW

Yglesias, Helen 1915- . . . . **CLC 7, 22**
See also CA 37-40R; CANR 15; MTCW

Yokomitsu Riichi 1898-1947 . . . . . . **TCLC 47**

Yonge, Charlotte (Mary)
1823-1901 . . . . **TCLC 48**
See also CA 109; DLB 18; SATA 17

York, Jeremy
See Creasey, John

York, Simon
See Heinlein, Robert A(nson)

Yorke, Henry Vincent 1905-1974 . . . **CLC 13**
See also Green, Henry
See also CA 85-88; 49-52

Yoshimoto, Banana . . . . **CLC 84**
See also Yoshimoto, Mahoko

Yoshimoto, Mahoko 1964-
See Yoshimoto, Banana
See also CA 144

Young, Al(bert James)
1939- . . . . **CLC 19; BLC**
See also BW 2; CA 29-32R; CANR 26;
DLB 33

Young, Andrew (John) 1885-1971 . . . . **CLC 5**
See also CA 5-8R; CANR 7, 29

Young, Collier
See Bloch, Robert (Albert)

Young, Edward 1683-1765 . . . . **LC 3**
See also DLB 95

Young, Marguerite 1909- . . . . **CLC 82**
See also CA 13-16; CAP 1

Young, Neil 1945- . . . . **CLC 17**
See also CA 110

Yourcenar, Marguerite
1903-1987 . . . . **CLC 19, 38, 50**
See also CA 69-72; CANR 23; DLB 72;
DLBY 88; MTCW

Yurick, Sol 1925- . . . . **CLC 6**
See also CA 13-16R; CANR 25

Zabolotskii, Nikolai Alekseevich
1903-1958 . . . . **TCLC 52**
See also CA 116

Zamiatin, Yevgenii
See Zamyatin, Evgeny Ivanovich

Zamyatin, Evgeny Ivanovich
1884-1937 . . . . **TCLC 8, 37**
See also CA 105

Zangwill, Israel 1864-1926 . . . . **TCLC 16**
See also CA 109; DLB 10, 135

Zappa, Francis Vincent, Jr. 1940-1993
See Zappa, Frank
See also CA 108; 143

Zappa, Frank . . . . **CLC 17**
See also Zappa, Francis Vincent, Jr.

Zaturenska, Marya 1902-1982 . . . . **CLC 6, 11**
See also CA 13-16R; 105; CANR 22

Zelazny, Roger (Joseph) 1937- . . . . . **CLC 21**
See also AAYA 7; CA 21-24R; CANR 26;
DLB 8; MTCW; SATA 39, 57

Zhdanov, Andrei A(lexandrovich)
1896-1948 . . . . **TCLC 18**
See also CA 117

Zhukovsky, Vasily 1783-1852 . . . . **NCLC 35**

Ziegenhagen, Eric . . . . **CLC 55**

Zimmer, Jill Schary
See Robinson, Jill

Zimmerman, Robert
See Dylan, Bob

Zindel, Paul 1936- . . . . **CLC 6, 26; DA**
See also AAYA 2; CA 73-76; CANR 31;
CLR 3; DLB 7, 52; JRDA; MAICYA;
MTCW; SATA 16, 58

Zinov'Ev, A. A.
See Zinoviev, Alexander (Aleksandrovich)

Zinoviev, Alexander (Aleksandrovich)
1922- . . . . **CLC 19**
See also CA 116; 133; CAAS 10

Zoilus
See Lovecraft, H(oward) P(hillips)

Zola, Emile (Edouard Charles Antoine)
1840-1902 . . . . . . **TCLC 1, 6, 21, 41; DA; WLC**
See also CA 104; 138; DLB 123

Zoline, Pamela 1941- . . . . **CLC 62**

Zorrilla y Moral, Jose 1817-1893 . . **NCLC 6**

Zoshchenko, Mikhail (Mikhailovich)
1895-1958 . . . . **TCLC 15; SSC 15**
See also CA 115

Zuckmayer, Carl 1896-1977 . . . . **CLC 18**
See also CA 69-72; DLB 56, 124

Zuk, Georges
See Skelton, Robin

Zukofsky, Louis
1904-1978 . . . . **CLC 1, 2, 4, 7, 11, 18**
See also CA 9-12R; 77-80; CANR 39;
DLB 5; MTCW

Zweig, Paul 1935-1984 . . . . **CLC 34, 42**
See also CA 85-88; 113

Zweig, Stefan 1881-1942 . . . . **TCLC 17**
See also CA 112; DLB 81, 118

SSC Cumulative Nationality Index

ALGERIAN
Camus, Albert **9**

AMERICAN
Aiken, Conrad **9**
Anderson, Sherwood **1**
Baldwin, James **10**
Barnes, Djuna **3**
Barth, John **10**
Barthelme, Donald **2**
Beattie, Ann **11**
Bellow, Saul **14**
Benét, Stephen Vincent **10**
Bierce, Ambrose **9**
Bowles, Paul **3**
Boyle, Kay **5**
Boyle, T. Coraghessan **16**
Cable, George Washington **4**
Calisher, Hortense **15**
Capote, Truman **2**
Carver, Raymond **8**
Cather, Willa **2**
Cheever, John **1**
Chesnutt, Charles Wadell **7**
Chopin, Kate **8**
Coover, Robert **15**
Crane, Stephen **7**
Davenport, Guy **16**
Dixon, Stephen **16**
Dubus, Andre **15**
Dunbar, Paul Laurence **8**
Elkin, Stanley **12**
Ellison, Harlan **14**
Faulkner, William **1**
Fitzgerald, F. Scott **6**
Freeman, Mary Wilkins **1**
Gardner, John **7**
Gass, William H. **12**
Gilchrist, Ellen **14**

Gilman, Charlotte Perkins **13**
Gordon, Caroline **15**
Grau, Shirley Ann **15**
Harte, Bret **8**
Hawthorne, Nathaniel **3**
Hemingway, Ernest **1**
Henry, O. **5**
Hughes, Langston **6**
Hurston, Zora Neale **4**
Irving, Washington **2**
Jackson, Shirley **9**
James, Henry **8**
Jewett, Sarah Orne **6**
Le Guin, Ursula K. **12**
Ligotti, Thomas **16**
London, Jack **4**
Maclean, Norman **13**
Malamud, Bernard **15**
Marshall, Paule **3**
Mason, Bobbie Ann **4**
McCullers, Carson **9**
Melville, Herman **1**
Michaels, Leonard **16**
Nabokov, Vladimir **11**
Oates, Joyce Carol **6**
O'Connor, Flannery **1**
O'Hara, John **15**
Olsen, Tillie **11**
Ozick, Cynthia **15**
Paley, Grace **8**
Parker, Dorothy **2**
Phillips, Jayne Anne **16**
Poe, Edgar Allan **1**
Porter, Katherine Anne **4**
Powers, J. F. **4**
Pynchon, Thomas **14**
Salinger, J. D. **2**
Singer, Isaac Bashevis **3**
Steinbeck, John **11**

Taylor, Peter **10**
Thurber, James **1**
Toomer, Jean **1**
Twain, Mark **6**
Updike, John **13**
Vonnegut, Kurt, Jr. **8**
Walker, Alice **5**
Warren, Robert Penn **4**
Welty, Eudora **1**
West, Nathanael **16**
Wharton, Edith **6**
Wright, Richard **2**

ARGENTINIAN
Borges, Jorge Luis **4**
Cortazar, Julio **7**
Valenzuela, Luisa **14**

AUSTRIAN
Kafka, Franz **5**
Schnitzler, Arthur **15**

CANADIAN
Atwood, Margaret **2**
Gallant, Mavis **5**
Laurence, Margaret **7**
Munro, Alice **3**

COLUMBIAN
García Márquez, Gabriel **8**

CUBAN
Calvino, Italo **3**

CZECHOSLOVAKIAN
Kafka, Franz **5**

DANISH
Andersen, Hans Christian **6**

SSC Cumulative Title Index

Title Index

Title Index

Title Index

Title Index

Title Index

"Some Blue Hills at Sundown" (Gilchrist) **14**:161

"Some Effects of the Mimer" (Levi) **12**:278

"Some Facts for Understanding the Perkians" (Cortazar)
See "Datos para entender a los perqueos"

"Some Get Wasted" (Marshall) **3**:303

"Someone Has Disturbed the Roses" (Garcia Marquez)
See "Alguien desordena estas rosas"

"Someone to Trust" (O'Hara) **15**:255, 264

"Someone Walking Around" (Cortazar)
See "Alguien que anda por ahí"

Some People, Places, and Things That Will Not Appear in My Next Novel (Cheever) **1**:92, 100

"Some Strange Disturbances in an Old House on Augier Street" ("An Account of Some Strange Disturbances in an Old House on Aungier Street"; "Strange Disturbances on Aungier Street") (Le Fanu) **14**:223-24, 238, 251

Something Childish, and Other Stories (Mansfield)
See *The Little Girl, and Other Stories*

Something in Common, and Other Stories (Hughes) **6**:122-23, 127, 133

Something I've Been Meaning to Tell You (Munro) **3**:328, 331, 335, 339, 346

"Something Squishy" (Wodehouse) **2**:355-56

"Something That Happened" (Phillips) **16**:335

Something to Remember Me By (Bellow) **14**:60-1

"Something to Write About" (Andersen) **6**:36

"Sometimes It's OK to Eat Inkwells" (Zoshchenko) **15**:407

"Somewhere Else" (Paley) **8**:420

"Some Words with a Mummy" (Poe) **1**:402

"So Much Water So Close to Home" (Carver) **8**:5, 14-15, 19, 21, 29, 42, 53, 57-60

"The Son" (Bunin) **5**:81, 103-04, 106, 108-10

"Son" ("The Dream") (Turgenev) **7**:321, 325-28, 338, 361

"Son" (Updike) **13**:387

"The Son From America" (Singer) **3**:374

"The Song" (Babel) **16**:27, 31, 52, 54-8

"The Song in the Garden" (Nin) **10**:306

"The Song of Songs" (Gilchrist) **14**:162-63

"The Song of the Flying Fish" (Chesterton) **1**:129, 138

"Song of the Shirt, 1941" (Parker) **2**:277, 280-81, 285-86

"The Song of the Triumphant Love" (Turgenev)
See "Pesn' torzhestruyushchey lyubvi"

"The Song of the Wren" (Bates) **10**:139

"Songs My Father Sang Me" (Bowen) **3**:41

"Songs My Mother Taught Me" (Calisher) **15**:8

Songs of a Dead Dreamer (Ligotti) **16**:261, 269-70, 279, 282-85, 287, 293, 296

"The Songs of Distant Earth" (Clarke) **3**:135-36

"Song without Words" (O'Connor) **5**:365, 371, 383, 398

"Sonny's Blues" (Baldwin) **10**:2-3, 5-7, 9, 12, 14-17, 21-5

"The Son of God and His Sorrow" (Oates) **6**:237

"A Son of the Celestial" (Cather) **2**:100, 102

"A Son of the Gods" (Bierce) **9**:55-6, 60, 63-4

A Son of the Sun (London) **4**:265

"The Son of the Wolf" (London) **4**:267

The Son of the Wolf: Tales of the Far North (London) **4**:250-52, 258, 264, 278-79, 281-82, 284-87, 290

"The Son's Veto" (Hardy) **2**:215-16, 223

"Sophistication" (Anderson) **1**:30, 42, 44-5

"The Sorcerer's Apprentice" (O'Connor) **5**:371-72

"Sorcières espagnoles" (Merimee) **7**:283

"Sorghum" (Mason) **4**:25

"Soročinskaja jamarka" ("The Fair at Sorotchintsy") (Gogol) **4**:85, 118, 121

"Sorrow" (Chekhov) **2**:128

"Sorrow-Acre" (Dinesen) **7**:164, 167, 170-71, 174, 177, 185-86, 188-90, 196, 205-08

"Sorrowful Mysteries" (Dubus) **15**:83

"The Sorrows of Gin" (Cheever) **1**:100

"Sorry Fugh" (Boyle) **16**:146, 148-49, 155

"Sosny" (Bunin) **5**:98-9

Sotto il sole giaguro (*Under the Jaguar Sun*) (Calvino) **3**:119

Soul Clap Hands and Sing (Marshall) **3**:299-304, 307-08, 316-17

"A Soulless Corporation" (Chesnutt) **7**:14

"The Soul of Laploshka" (Saki) **12**:316

"Souls Belated" (Wharton) **6**:423-25

"The Souls in Purgatory" (Merimee)
See "Les âmes du purgatoire"

"The Sound of the Singing" (Laurence) **7**:254, 259-60, 268

"The Sound of Waiting" (Calisher) **15**:7, 15, 19

"Sound Sweep" (Ballard) **1**:68

"Sound Track" (Calisher) **15**:9

"Soup on a Sausage Peg" (Andersen) **6**:13-4

"The Source" (Porter) **4**:339, 352, 363

"Source of the World" (Bates) **10**:121

"The South" (Borges) **4**:31

"The Southern Thruway" (Cortazar)
See "La autopista del sur"

"South of the Slot" (London) **4**:254

South Sea Tales (London) **4**:266, 283

"Souvenir" (Phillips) **16**:326-30

"A Souvenir of Japan" (Carter) **13**:4

"Souvenirs occulte" ("Occult Memories") (Villiers de l'Isle Adam) **14**:381-82, 389, 393

"The Spanish Bed" (Pritchett) **14**:263

"Spanish Blood" (Hughes) **6**:118, 132

"The Spanish Lady" (Munro) **3**:339

"A Spanish Priest" (Maugham) **8**:380

The Spanish Virgin, and Other Stories (Pritchett) **14**:268-69, 271

Spanking the Maid (Coover) **15**:47, 52-3

"A Spark Neglected Burns the House" (Tolstoy) **9**:388

The Spark (The 'Sixties) (Wharton) **6**:439-40

"Speck's Idea" (Gallant) **5**:147

"The Spectacles" (Poe) **1**:407-08

"The Spectacles in the Drawer" (Ligotti) **16**:278-79, 284, 294

"The Spectral Estate" (Ligotti) **16**:297

"Spectral Horror" (Ligotti) **16**:287

"The Spectre Bridegroom" (Irving) **2**:240-41, 246, 251, 255-56

"The Speculation of the Building Constructors" (Calvino)
See "La speculazione edilizia"

"La speculazione edilizia" ("A Plunge into Real Estate"; "The Speculation of the Building Constructors") (Calvino) **3**:91, 111-12, 117-18

"The Speech" (Pritchett) **14**:296-98

"Spelling" (Munro) **3**:339

"The Sphinx without a Secret: An Etching" (Wilde) **11**:386, 399, 407

"The Sphynx Apple" (Henry) **5**:162

"Spider, Spider" (Aiken) **9**:5, 12, 14, 32-3, 42

"Spielerglück" ("Gambler's Luck") (Hoffmann) **13**:188

Spiel im Morgengrauen (Schnitzler) **15**:345, 367

"Spillway" ("Beyond the End") (Barnes) **3**:8-10, 24

Spillway (Barnes) **3**:4-5, 12-14, 16, 22

"The Spinoza of Market Street" (Singer) **3**:361, 368, 375, 384

The Spinoza of Market Street, and Other Stories (Singer) **3**:370

"A Spinster's Tale" (Taylor) **10**:374-75, 386, 390, 397-98, 406, 409, 412-15, 417

"The Spiral" (Calvino)
See "La spirale"

"La spirale" ("The Spiral") (Calvino) **3**:92, 103-04, 108-09

"Spiritus" (Beattie) **11**:25, 29

"Sportsmanship" (O'Hara) **15**:248, 264-65

"Sport: The Kill" (O'Flaherty) **6**:261

"Spotted Horses" (Faulkner) **1**:167, 177

"The Spree" (Pritchett) **14**:260, 273, 285

"Spring" (Schulz)
See "Wiosna"

"A Spring Evening" (Bunin) **5**:90, 92, 102

Spring Freshets (Turgenev)
See *Veshnie vody*

"The Spring Hat" (Bates) **10**:123

"Spring in Fialta" (Nabokov) **11**:112, 114, 128-29

"A Spring Morning" (Pritchett) **14**:270, 298

"Spring Rain" (Malamud) **15**:235

"The Spring Running" (Kipling) **5**:287

"Spring Song of the Frogs" (Atwood) **2**:22

"Spring Sowing" (O'Flaherty) **6**:260-62, 264, 269, 271, 273, 281, 283

Spring Sowing (O'Flaherty) **6**:261-65, 278, 281, 283

"A Spring Sunday" (Jewett) **6**:156-57

Spring-Torrents (Turgenev)
See *Veshnie vody*

"A Sprinkle of Comedy" (Barnes) **3**:18

"Spunk" (Hurston) **4**:135-37, 150, 152

Spunk: The Selected Stories of Zora Neale Hurston (Hurston) **4**:155

"SQ" (Le Guin) **12**:230-31, 241

"Squadron Commander Trunov" (Babel) **16**:24, 26, 28-30, 52, 57-8

The Square Egg, and Other Sketches, with Three Plays (Saki) **12**:322

"Squire Toby's Will" (Le Fanu) **14**:223-24

"Sredni Vashtar" (Saki) **12**:287, 293-94, 297, 316-17, 320, 331, 333

"La srta. Cora" (Cortazar) **7**:62

"The S.S. *Cow Wheat*" (Babel) **16**:22

"The Stage Coach" (Irving) **2**:245

"The Stage Tavern" (Jewett) **6**:159

"Stalking the Nightmare" (Ellison) **14**:126-27

Stalky and Co. (Kipling) **5**:277-78, 282

"The Stalled Ox" (Saki) **12**:296

"The Stalls of Barchester Cathedral" (James) **16**:228-30, 232, 237, 245, 253, 256-57

Title Index

Title Index

Title Index